# Nineteenth-Century Literature Criticism

# Guide to Gale Literary Criticism Series

**When you need to review criticism of literary works, these are the Gale series to use:**

| If the author's death date is: | You should turn to: |
|---|---|
| After Dec. 31, 1959 (or author is still living) | ***CONTEMPORARY LITERARY CRITICISM***<br>for example: Jorge Luis Borges, Anthony Burgess, William Faulkner, Mary Gordon, Ernest Hemingway, Iris Murdoch |
| 1900 through 1959 | ***TWENTIETH-CENTURY LITERARY CRITICISM***<br>for example: Willa Cather, F. Scott Fitzgerald, Henry James, Mark Twain, Virginia Woolf |
| 1800 through 1899 | ***NINETEENTH-CENTURY LITERATURE CRITICISM***<br>for example: Fyodor Dostoevsky, Nathaniel Hawthorne, George Sand, William Wordsworth |
| 1400 through 1799 | ***LITERATURE CRITICISM FROM 1400 TO 1800 (excluding Shakespeare)***<br>for example: Anne Bradstreet, Daniel Defoe, Alexander Pope, François Rabelais, Jonathan Swift, Phillis Wheatley<br><br>***SHAKESPEAREAN CRITICISM***<br>Shakespeare's plays and poetry |
| Antiquity through 1399 | ***CLASSICAL AND MEDIEVAL LITERATURE CRITICISM***<br>for example: Dante, Homer, Plato, Sophocles, Vergil, the Beowulf Poet |

## Gale also publishes related criticism series:

### CHILDREN'S LITERATURE REVIEW

This series covers authors of all eras who have written for the preschool through high school audience.

### SHORT STORY CRITICISM

This series covers the major short fiction writers of all nationalities and periods of literary history.

### POETRY CRITICISM

This series covers poets of all nationalities and periods of literary history.

### DRAMA CRITICISM

This series covers dramatists of all nationalities and periods of literary history.

ISSN 0732-1864

Volume 10

# Nineteenth-Century Literature Criticism

Excerpts from Criticism of the
Works of Novelists, Poets, Playwrights,
Short Story Writers, and Other Creative Writers
Who Died between 1800 and 1900,
from the First Published Critical
Appraisals to Current Evaluations

Laurie Lanzen Harris
Emily B. Tennyson
Editors

Cherie D. Abbey
Associate Editor

 **Gale Research Inc.** • *DETROIT* • *WASHINGTON, D.C.* • *LONDON*

# STAFF

Laurie Lanzen Harris, Emily B. Tennyson, *Editors*

Cherie D. Abbey, *Associate Editor*

Jelena Obradovic Kronick, Patricia Askie Mackmiller,
Janet S. Mullane, Gail Ann Schulte, *Senior Assistant Editors*

Jeanne M. Lesinski, Robert Thomas Wilson, *Assistant Editors*

Phyllis Carmel Mendelson, Anna C. Wallbillich, *Contributing Editors*

Lizbeth A. Purdy, *Production Supervisor*
Denise Michlewicz Broderick, *Production Coordinator*
Eric Berger, *Assistant Production Coordinator*
Robin Du Blanc, Kelly King Howes, Sheila J. Nasea, *Editorial Assistants*

Victoria B. Cariappa, *Research Coordinator*
Jeannine Schiffman Davidson, *Assistant Research Coordinator*
Vincenza G. DiNoto, Daniel Kurt Gilbert, Filomena Sgambati,
Valerie J. Webster, Mary D. Wise, *Research Assistants*

Linda Marcella Pugliese, *Manuscript Coordinator*
Donna Craft, *Assistant Manuscript Coordinator*
Colleen M. Crane, Maureen A. Puhl, Rosetta Irene Simms, *Manuscript Assistants*

Jeanne A. Gough, *Permissions Supervisor*
Janice M. Mach, *Permissions Coordinator, Text*
Patricia A. Seefelt, *Permissions Coordinator, Illustrations*
Susan D. Nobles, *Assistant Permissions Coordinator*
Margaret A. Chamberlain, Sandra C. Davis, Mary M. Matuz, *Senior Permissions Assistants*
Kathy Grell, Josephine M. Keene, *Permissions Assistants*
H. Diane Cooper, Dorothy J. Fowler, Yolanda Parker, Mabel C. Schoening, *Permissions Clerks*
Margaret Mary Missar, *Photo Research*

# Contents

Preface   7

Authors to Appear in Future Volumes   11

Appendix   475

# Preface

The nineteenth century was a time of tremendous growth in human endeavor: in science, in social history, and particularly in literature. The era saw the development of the novel, witnessed radical changes from classicism to romanticism to realism, and contained intellectual and artistic ideas that continue to inspire authors of our own century. The importance of the writers of the nineteenth century is twofold, for they provide insight into their own time as well as into the universal nature of human experience.

The literary criticism of an era can also give us insight into the moral and intellectual atmosphere of the past, for the criteria by which a work of art is judged reflect current philosophical and social attitudes. Literary criticism takes many forms: the traditional essay, the book or play review, even the parodic poem. Criticism can also be of several types: normative, descriptive, interpretive, textual, appreciative, generic. Collectively, the range of critical response helps us to understand a work of art, an author, an era.

## The Scope of the Work

The success of two of Gale's current literary series, *Contemporary Literary Criticism (CLC)* and *Twentieth-Century Literary Criticism (TCLC)*, which excerpt criticism of creative writing from the twentieth century, suggested an equivalent need among students and teachers of literature of the nineteenth century. Moreover, since the analysis of this literature spans almost two hundred years, a vast amount of critical material confronts the student.

*Nineteenth-Century Literature Criticism (NCLC)* presents significant passages from published criticism on authors who died between 1800 and 1900. The author list for each volume of *NCLC* is carefully compiled to represent a variety of genres and nationalities and to cover authors who are currently regarded as the most important writers of this era as well as those whose contribution to literature and literary history is significant. The truly great writers are rare, and in the intervals between them lesser but genuine artists, as well as writers who enjoyed immense popularity in their own time and in their own countries, are important to the study of nineteenth-century literature. The length of each author's entry is intended to reflect the amount of attention the author has received from critics writing in English and from foreign critics in translation. Articles and books that have not been translated into English are excluded. However, since many of the major foreign studies have been translated into English and are excerpted in *NCLC*, author entries reflect the viewpoints of many nationalities. Each author entry represents a historical overview of critical reaction to the author's work: early criticism is presented to indicate initial responses and later selections represent any rise or decline in the author's literary reputation. We have also attempted to identify and include excerpts from the seminal essays on each author and to include recent critical comment providing modern perspectives on the writer. Thus, *NCLC* is designed to serve as an introduction for the student of nineteenth-century literature to the authors of that period and to the most significant commentators on these authors.

*NCLC* entries are intended to be definitive overviews. In order to devote more attention to each writer, approximately fifteen authors are included in each 600-page volume compared with about sixty authors in a *CLC* volume of similar size. Because of the great quantity of critical material available on many authors, and because of the resurgence of criticism generated by such events as an author's centennial or anniversary celebration, the republication of an author's works, or publication of a newly translated work or volume of letters, an author may appear more than once. Usually, a few author entries in each volume of *NCLC* are devoted to single works by major authors who have appeared previously in the series. Only those individual works that have been the subject of extensive criticism and are widely studied in literature courses are selected for this in-depth treatment. Gustave Flaubert's *Madame Bovary*, Nathaniel Hawthorne's *The Scarlet Letter*, and Victor Hugo's *Les misérables* are the subjects of such entries in *NCLC*, Volume 10.

## The Organization of the Book

An author section consists of the following elements: author heading, biographical and critical introduction, principal works, excerpts of criticism (each followed by a bibliographical citation), and an additional bibliography for further reading.

- The *author heading* consists of the author's full name, followed by birth and death dates. The unbracketed portion of the name denotes the form under which the author most commonly wrote. If an author wrote consistently under a pseudonym, the pseudonym will be listed in the author heading and the real name given in parentheses on the first line of the biographical and critical introduction. Also located at the beginning of the introduction are any name variations under which an author wrote, including transliterated forms for authors whose languages use nonroman alphabets. Uncertainty as to a birth or death date is indicated by a question mark.

- A *portrait* of the author is included when available. Many entries also feature illustrations of materials pertinent to an author's career, including manuscript pages, letters, book illustrations, and representations of important people, places, and events in an author's life.

- The *biographical and critical introduction* contains background information that elucidates the author's creative output. When applicable, biographical and critical introductions are followed by references to additional entries on the author in past volumes of *NCLC* and in other literary reference series published by Gale Research Company. These include *Dictionary of Literary Biography, Children's Literature Review,* and *Something about the Author.*

- The list of *principal works* is chronological by date of first book publication and identifies genres. In those instances where the first publication was in other than the English language, the title and date of the first English-language edition are given in brackets. Unless otherwise indicated, dramas are dated by the first performance, rather than first publication.

- *Criticism* is arranged chronologically in each author section to provide a perspective on any changes in critical evaluation over the years. In the text of each author entry, titles by the author are printed in boldface type. This allows the reader to ascertain without difficulty the works being discussed. For purposes of easier identification, the critic's name and the publication date of the essay are given at the beginning of each piece of criticism. Unsigned criticism is preceded by the title of the journal in which it appeared. For an anonymous essay later attributed to a critic, the critic's name appears in brackets at the beginning of the excerpt and in the bibliographical citation.

- Most essays are prefaced with *explanatory notes* as an additional aid to students using *NCLC.* The explanatory notes provide several types of useful information, including the reputation of the critic, the importance of a work of criticism, a synopsis of the essay, the specific approach of the critic (biographical, psychoanalytic, structuralist, etc.), and the growth of critical controversy or changes in critical trends regarding an author's work. In many cases, these notes include cross-references to related criticism in the author's entry or in the additional bibliography. Dates in parentheses within the explanatory notes refer to other essays in the author entry.

- A complete *bibliographical citation* designed to facilitate the location of the original essay or book follows each piece of criticism. An asterisk (*) at the end of the citation indicates that the essay is on more than one author.

- The *additional bibliography* appearing at the end of each author entry suggests further reading on the author. In some cases it includes essays for which the editors could not obtain reprint rights. An asterisk (*) at the end of a citation indicates that the essay is on more than one author.

An appendix lists the sources from which material in the volume is reprinted. It does not, however, list every book or periodical consulted for the volume.

## Cumulative Indexes

Each volume of *NCLC* includes a cumulative index to authors listing all the authors who have appeared in *Contemporary Literary Criticism, Twentieth-Century Literary Criticism, Nineteenth-Century Literature Criticism,* and *Literature Criticism from 1400 to 1800,* along with cross-references to the Gale series *Children's Literature Review, Authors in the News, Contemporary Authors, Contemporary Authors Autobiography Series, Dictionary of Literary Biography, Something about the Author,* and *Yesterday's Authors of Books for Children.* Users will welcome this cumulated author index as a useful tool for locating an author within the various series. The index, which lists birth and death dates when available, will be particularly valuable for those authors who are identified with a certain period but whose death date causes them to be placed in another, or for those authors whose careers span two periods. For example, Fedor Dostoevski is found in *NCLC,* yet Leo Tolstoy, another major nineteenth-century Russian novelist, is found in *TCLC.*

*NCLC* also includes a cumulative nationality index to authors. Authors are listed alphabetically by nationality, followed by the volume numbers in which they appear.

A cumulative index to critics is another useful feature of *NCLC.* Under each critic's name are listed the authors on whom the critic has written and the volume and page where the criticism appears.

## Acknowledgments

No work of this scope can be accomplished without the cooperation of many people. The editors especially wish to thank the copyright holders of the excerpts included in this volume, the permissions managers of the book and magazine publishing companies for assisting us in securing reprint rights, and the staffs of the Detroit Public Library, University of Michigan Library, and Wayne State University Library for making their resources available to us. We are also grateful to Anthony Bogucki for his assistance with copyright research.

## Suggestions Are Welcome

The editors welcome the comments and suggestions of readers to expand the coverage and enhance the usefulness of the series.

# Authors to Appear in Future Volumes

About, Edmond Francois 1828-1885
Aguilo I. Fuster, Maria 1825-1897
Ainsworth, William Harrison 1805-1882
Aksakov, Konstantin 1817-1860
Aleardi, Aleadro 1812-1878
Alecsandri, Vasile 1821-1890
Alencar, Jose 1829-1877
Alfieri, Vittorio 1749-1803
Allingham, William 1824-1889
Almquist, Carl Jonas Love 1793-1866
Alorne, Leonor de Almeida 1750-1839
Alsop, Richard 1761-1815
Altimirano, Ignacio Manuel 1834-1893
Alvarenga, Manuel Inacio da Silva
    1749-1814
Alvares de Azevedo, Manuel Antonio
    1831-1852
Anzengruber, Ludwig 1839-1889
Arany, Janos 1817-1882
Arene, Paul 1843-1893
Aribau, Bonaventura Carlos 1798-1862
Arjona de Cubas, Manuel Maria de
    1771-1820
Arnault, Antoine Vincent 1766-1834
Arneth, Alfred von 1819-1897
Arnim, Bettina von 1785-1859
Arnold, Thomas 1795-1842
Arriaza y Superviela, Juan Bautista
    1770-1837
Asbjornsen, Peter Christian 1812-1885
Ascasubi, Hilario 1807-1875
Atterbom, Per Daniel Amadeus
    1790-1855
Aubanel, Theodore 1829-1886
Auerbach, Berthold 1812-1882
Augier, Guillaume V.E. 1820-1889
Azeglio, Massimo D' 1798-1866
Azevedo, Guilherme de 1839-1882
Bakin (pseud. of Takizawa Okikani)
    1767-1848
Bakunin, Mikhail Aleksandrovich
    1814-1876
Baratynski, Jewgenij Abramovich
    1800-1844
Barnes, William 1801-1886
Batyushkov, Konstantin 1778-1855
Beattie, James 1735-1803
Beckford, William 1760-1844
Becquer, Gustavo Adolfo 1836-1870
Bentham, Jeremy 1748-1832
Beranger, Jean-Pierre de 1780-1857
Berchet, Ciovanni 1783-1851
Berzsenyi, Daniel 1776-1836
Black, William 1841-1898
Blair, Hugh 1718-1800
Blake, William 1757-1827
Blicher, Steen Steensen 1782-1848
Bocage, Manuel Maria Barbosa du
    1765-1805

Boratynsky, Yevgeny 1800-1844
Borel, Petrus 1809-1859
Boreman, Yokutiel 1825-1890
Borne, Ludwig 1786-1837
Botev, Hristo 1778-1842
Bremer, Fredrika 1801-1865
Brinckman, John 1814-1870
Bronte, Emily 1812-1848
Brown, Charles Brockden 1777-1810
Browning, Robert 1812-1889
Buchner, Georg 1813-1837
Burney, Fanney 1752-1840
Campbell, James Edwin 1867-1895
Campbell, Thomas 1777-1844
Carlyle, Thomas 1795-1881
Castelo Branco, Camilo 1825-1890
Castro Alves, Antonio de 1847-1871
Channing, William Ellery 1780-1842
Chatterje, Bankin Chanda 1838-1894
Chivers, Thomas Holly 1807?-1858
Claudius, Matthais 1740-1815
Clough, Arthur Hugh 1819-1861
Cobbett, William 1762-1835
Colenso, John William 1814-1883
Coleridge, Hartley 1796-1849
Collett, Camilla 1813-1895
Comte, Auguste 1798-1857
Conrad, Robert T. 1810-1858
Conscience, Hendrik 1812-1883
Cooke, Philip Pendleton 1816-1850
Corbiere, Edouard 1845-1875
Crabbe, George 1754-1832
Crawford, Isabella Valancy 1850-1886
Cruz E Sousa, Joao da 1861-1898
Desbordes-Valmore, Marceline
    1786-1859
Deschamps, Emile 1791-1871
Deus, Joao de 1830-1896
Dickinson, Emily 1830-1886
Dinis, Julio 1839-1871
Dinsmoor, Robert 1757-1836
Dumas, Alexandre (pere) 1802-1870
Du Maurier, George 1834-1896
Dwight, Timothy 1752-1817
Echeverria, Esteban 1805-1851
Eminescy, Mihai 1850-1889
Engels, Friedrich 1820-1895
Espronceda, Jose 1808-1842
Ettinger, Solomon 1799-1855
Euchel, Issac 1756-1804
Ferguson, Samuel 1810-1886
Fernandez de Lizardi, Jose Joaquin
    1776-1827
Fernandez de Moratin, Leandro
    1760-1828
Fet, Afanasy 1820-1892
Feuillet, Octave 1821-1890
Fontane, Theodor 1819-1898
Forster, John 1812-1876

Freiligrath, Hermann Ferdinand
    1810-1876
Freytag, Gustav 1816-1895
Gaboriau, Emile 1835-1873
Ganivet, Angel 1865-1898
Garrett, Almeida 1799-1854
Garshin, Vsevolod Mikhaylovich
    1855-1888
Gezelle, Guido 1830-1899
Ghalib, Asadullah Khan 1797-1869
Godwin, William 1756-1836
Goldschmidt, Meir Aron 1819-1887
Goncalves Dias, Antonio 1823-1864
Griboyedov, Aleksander Sergeyevich
    1795-1829
Grigor'yev, Appolon Aleksandrovich
    1822-1864
Groth, Klaus 1819-1899
Grun, Anastasius (pseud. of Anton
    Alexander Graf von Auersperg)
    1806-1876
Guerrazzi, Francesco Domenico
    1804-1873
Gutierrez Najera, Manuel 1859-1895
Gutzkow, Karl Ferdinand 1811-1878
Ha-Kohen, Shalom 1772-1845
Halleck, Fitz-Greene 1790-1867
Harris, George Washington 1814-1869
Hayne, Paul Hamilton 1830-1886
Hazlitt, William 1778-1830
Hebbel, Christian Friedrich 1813-1863
Hebel, Johann Peter 1760-1826
Hegel, Georg Wilhelm Friedrich
    1770-1831
Heiberg, Johann Ludvig 1813-1863
Herculano, Alexandre 1810-1866
Hernandez, Jose 1834-1886
Hertz, Henrik 1798-1870
Herwegh, Georg 1817-1875
Hoffman, Charles Fenno 1806-1884
Holderlin, Friedrich 1770-1843
Holmes, Oliver Wendell 1809-1894
Hood, Thomas 1799-1845
Hooper, Johnson Jones 1815-1863
Hopkins, Gerard Manley 1844-1889
Horton, George Moses 1798-1880
Howitt, William 1792-1879
Hughes, Thomas 1822-1896
Imlay, Gilbert 1754?-1828?
Irwin, Thomas Caulfield 1823-1892
Issacs, Jorge 1837-1895
Jacobsen, Jens Peter 1847-1885
Jippensha, Ikku 1765-1831
Kant, Immanuel 1724-1804
Karr, Jean Baptiste Alphonse 1808-1890
Keble, John 1792-1866
Khomyakov, Alexey S. 1804-1860
Kierkegaard, Soren 1813-1855
Kinglake, Alexander W. 1809-1891

Kingsley, Charles 1819-1875
Kivi, Alexis 1834-1872
Klopstock, Friedrich Gottlieb 1724-1803
Koltsov, Alexey Vasilyevich 1809-1842
Kotzebue, August von 1761-1819
Kraszewski, Josef Ignacy 1812-1887
Kreutzwald, Friedrich Reinhold
    1803-1882
Krochmal, Nahman 1785-1840
Krudener, Valeria Barbara Julia de
    Wietinghoff 1766-1824
Lamartine, Alphonse 1790-1869
Lampman, Archibald 1861-1899
Landon, Letitia Elizabeth 1802-1838
Landor, Walter Savage 1775-1864
Larra y Sanchez de Castro, Mariano
    1809-1837
Lautreamont (pseud. of Isodore Ducasse)
    1846-1870
Lebensohn, Micah Joseph 1828-1852
Leconte de Lisle, Charles-Marie-Rene
    1818-1894
Lenau, Nikolaus 1802-1850
Leontyev, Konstantin 1831-1891
Leopardi, Giacoma 1798-1837
Leskov, Nikolai 1831-1895
Lever, Charles James 1806-1872
Levisohn, Solomon 1789-1822
Lewes, George Henry 1817-1878
Lewis, Matthew Gregory 1775-1817
Leyden, John 1775-1811
Lobensohn, Micah Gregory 1775-1810
Longstreet, Augustus Baldwin 1790-1870
Lopez de Ayola y Herrera, Adelardo
    1819-1871
Lover, Samuel 1797-1868
Luzzato, Samuel David 1800-1865
Macedo, Joaquim Manuel de 1820-1882
Macha, Karel Hynek 1810-1836
Mackenzie, Henry 1745-1831
Malmon, Solomon 1754-1800
Mangan, James Clarence 1803-1849
Manzoni, Alessandro 1785-1873
Mapu, Abraham 1808-1868
Marii, Jose 1853-1895
Markovic, Svetozar 1846-1875
Martinez de La Rosa, Francisco
    1787-1862
Mathews, Cornelius 1817-1889
McCulloch, Thomas 1776-1843
Merriman, Brian 1747-1805
Meyer, Conrad Ferdinand 1825-1898
Montgomery, James 1771-1854
Moodie, Susanna 1803-1885
Morton, Sarah Wentworth 1759-1846
Muller, Friedrich 1749-1825

Murger, Henri 1822-1861
Nekrasov, Nikolai 1821-1877
Neruda, Jan 1834-1891
Nestroy, Johann 1801-1862
Newman, John Henry 1801-1890
Niccolini, Giambattista 1782-1861
Nievo, Ippolito 1831-1861
Nodier, Charles 1780-1844
Novalis (pseud. of Friedrich von
    Hardenberg) 1772-1801
Obradovic, Dositej 1742-1811
Oehlenschlager, Adam 1779-1850
Oliphant, Margaret 1828-1897
O'Neddy, Philothee (pseud. of
    Theophile Dondey) 1811-1875
O'Shaughnessy, Arthur William
    Edgar 1844-1881
Ostrovsky, Alexander 1823-1886
Paine, Thomas 1737-1809
Parkman, Francis 1823-1893
Peacock, Thomas Love 1785-1866
Perk, Jacques 1859-1881
Pisemsky, Alexey F. 1820-1881
Pompeia, Raul D'Avila 1863-1895
Popovic, Jovan Sterija 1806-1856
Praed, Winthrop Mackworth 1802-1839
Prati, Giovanni 1814-1884
Preseren, France 1800-1849
Pringle, Thomas 1789-1834
Procter, Adelaide Ann 1825-1864
Procter, Bryan Waller 1787-1874
Pye, Henry James 1745-1813
Quental, Antero Tarquinio de 1842-1891
Quinet, Edgar 1803-1875
Quintana, Manuel Jose 1772-1857
Radishchev, Aleksander 1749-1802
Raftery, Anthony 1784-1835
Raimund, Ferdinand 1790-1836
Reid, Mayne 1818-1883
Renan, Ernest 1823-1892
Reuter, Fritz 1810-1874
Rogers, Samuel 1763-1855
Ruckert, Friedrich 1788-1866
Runeberg, Johan 1804-1877
Rydberg, Viktor 1828-1895
Saavedra y Ramirez de Boquedano,
    Angel de 1791-1865
Sacher-Mosoch, Leopold von 1836-1895
Saltykov-Shchedrin, Mikhail 1826-1892
Satanov, Isaac 1732-1805
Schiller, Johann Friedrich 1759-1805
Schlegel, August 1767-1845
Schlegel, Karl 1772-1829
Scott, Sir Walter 1771-1832
Scribe, Augustin Eugene 1791-1861

Sedgwick, Catherine Maria 1789-1867
Senoa, August 1838-1881
Shelley, Mary W. 1797-1851
Shelley, Percy Bysshe 1792-1822
Shulman, Kalman 1819-1899
Sigourney, Lydia Howard Huntley
    1791-1856
Silva, Jose Asuncion 1865-1896
Slaveykov, Petko 1828-1895
Slowacki, Juliusz 1809-1848
Smith, Richard Penn 1799-1854
Smolenskin, Peretz 1842-1885
Stagnelius, Erik Johan 1793-1823
Staring, Antonie Christiaan
    Wynand 1767-1840
Stendhal (pseud. of Henri Beyle)
    1783-1842
Stifter, Adalbert 1805-1868
Stone, John Augustus 1801-1834
Taine, Hippolyte 1828-1893
Taunay, Alfredo d'Ecragnole 1843-1899
Taylor, Bayard 1825-1878
Tennyson, Alfred, Lord 1809-1892
Terry, Lucy (Lucy Terry Prince)
    1730-1821
Thompson, Daniel Pierce 1795-1868
Thompson, Samuel 1766-1816
Thomson, James 1834-1882
Tiedge, Christoph August 1752-1841
Timrod, Henry 1828-1867
Tommaseo, Nicolo 1802-1874
Tompa, Mihaly 1817-1888
Topelius, Zachris 1818-1898
Turgenev, Ivan 1818-1883
Tyutchev, Fedor I. 1803-1873
Uhland, Ludvig 1787-1862
Valaoritis, Aristotelis 1824-1879
Valles, Jules 1832-1885
Verde, Cesario 1855-1886
Vigny, Alfred Victor de 1797-1863
Villaverde, Cirilio 1812-1894
Vinje, Aasmund Olavsson 1818-1870
Vorosmarty, Mihaly 1800-1855
Warren, Mercy Otis 1728-1814
Weisse, Christian Felix 1726-1804
Welhaven, Johan S. 1807-1873
Werner, Zacharius 1768-1823
Wescott, Edward Noyes 1846-1898
Wessely, Nattali Herz 1725-1805
Whitman, Sarah Helen 1803-1878
Wieland, Christoph Martin 1733-1813
Woolson, Constance Fenimore
    1840-1894
Wordsworth, William 1770-1850
Zhukovsky, Vasily 1783-1852

# Walter Bagehot

## 1826-1877

English essayist, critic, journalist, editor, and letter writer.

Bagehot is regarded as one of the most versatile and influential authors of mid-Victorian England. In addition to literary criticism, he wrote several pioneering works in the fields of politics, sociology, and economics, including *The English Constitution, Physics and Politics; or, Thoughts on the Application of the Principles of "Natural Selection" and "Inheritance" to Political Society,* and *Lombard Street: A Description of the Money Market.* As editor of the London *Economist,* he was instrumental in shaping the financial policy of his generation. Despite their diverse subject matter, which has earned for Bagehot the reputation of a gifted amateur, his works are unified by a common approach characterized by an emphasis on factual information and an interest in the minds and personalities of literary figures, politicians, and economists. Bagehot's prose style is also a unifying feature; critics point out that all of his works reflect his belief that "the knack in style is to write like a human being." Many modern commentators contend that it is partly because of their "readable" quality, their clarity and humor, that Bagehot's writings, which were primarily composed as journalistic pieces for his contemporaries, are still enjoyed today.

Bagehot was born in Langport, England, to a prominent banker and his wife who consistently encouraged their son's intellectual development. At the age of thirteen, after attending Langport Grammar School, Bagehot was sent to Bristol College. There he studied under the noted ethnologist Dr. James Cowles Prichard, who instilled in Bagehot an interest in anthropology and ethnology that later inspired him to write *Physics and Politics.* Upon graduation, Bagehot entered University College in London, where he completed a master's degree in economics and studied history, philosophy, and nineteenth-century poetry. At his father's urging, Bagehot next studied law. However, the legal profession did not appeal to him, and in 1851, anxious and uncertain about his future, he left London to vacation in Paris. There Bagehot witnessed Louis Napoléon's coup d'etat, which he described in a series of seven letters addressed to the editor of the British journal the *Inquirer* that were later reprinted in *Literary Studies.* Bagehot's "Letters on the French Coup D'etat of 1851" outraged readers by defending Louis Napoléon's use of force to promote order in France. In these letters, Bagehot proposed the thesis that underlies most of his political essays: "The most essential mental quality for a free people, whose liberty is to be progressive, permanent, and on a large scale . . . is much *stupidity.*" Bagehot defined "stupidity" as a combination of common sense, sound judgment, and willingness to fully discuss political controversies before acting on them. He attached great importance to this concept as a prerequisite for political stability and used the term to describe the national character of the English who, in contrast to the French, whom he considered rash and impetuous, were ideally suited to parliamentary government.

When Bagehot returned to England from his yearlong stay in France, he decided against a career in law and instead joined the staff of his father's bank in Langport. He continued to work in finance throughout his life and eventually became the man-

ager of one of London's leading banks. Bagehot was attracted to the profession of banking partly because it offered leisure time for writing, and he soon began contributing literary criticism to the *Prospective Review* and later to the *National Review,* a periodical that he founded in 1855 with his close friend Richard Holt Hutton. A collection of Bagehot's early literary essays, *Estimates of Some Englishmen and Scotchmen,* was virtually unnoticed by critics, and it was not until their posthumous publication in *Literary Studies* that they attracted much scholarly attention. While assessments of Bagehot's importance as a literary critic vary widely, commentators have achieved a consensus regarding his critical method. Noting that he was indifferent to both prevailing literary standards and to the technical aspects of works of art, critics observe that Bagehot focused instead on the relationship between an author and his or her writings. His approach is generally considered that of a "literary psychologist," and critics uniformly admire what Woodrow Wilson described as the ability to view writers "with a Chaucerian insight into them as men." In the essay "Shakespeare—the Man," which is considered one of the best examples of this approach, Bagehot attempts to reconstruct the various aspects of William Shakespeare's personality from a close reading of his plays, arguing that it is always possible to deduce information about an author from his or her works. As a critic, Bagehot has been judged most harshly for his failure to formulate a theory of literature that exerted any widespread influence over either his contemporaries or successors. However some twentieth-century commentators, most notably René Wellek, regard Bagehot's essay "Wordsworth, Tennyson, and Browning; or, Pure, Ornate, and Grotesque Art in English Poetry" as a valuable contribution to the poetic theory of "type," a doctrine stating that it is the poet's duty to identify and depict what is universally and characteristically human.

In 1858, Bagehot married the oldest daughter of Sir James Wilson, the owner and founder of the influential London financial weekly the *Economist*. Three years later, Bagehot assumed the editorship of the paper, a post he retained until his death. Though Bagehot combined his duties at the *Economist* with his responsibilities as bank manager, he continued to write prolifically. Increasingly, his interests shifted from literary to political and economic subjects. Some of the best-known essays from this period are the pieces on eighteenth- and nineteenth-century British statesmen that are contained in *Biographical Studies*. Such titles as "The Character of Sir Robert Peel" and "What Lord Lyndhurst Really Was" reflect Bagehot's preoccupation with politicians' lives rather than with their achievements. These studies, like his literary essays, are primarily valued for their insight into human nature.

In 1867, Bagehot published *The English Constitution,* which is considered the most memorable result of his increased interest in politics. Generally regarded as the first attempt to describe the empirical rather than the theoretical function of the English Constitution, the work was early recognized as an original and significant contribution to the study of parliamentary government. Unlike previous writers who relied on the traditional theory of a division of powers between the executive and legislative branches of government, Bagehot, in the words of the earl of Balfour, looked "*closely and for himself* at real political life.*" By doing so, he concluded that the guiding principle of British government was the fusion, rather than the separation, of the executive and legislative branches, which he termed the "efficient secret of the Constitution." For the traditional theory of a division of powers between the two branches, Bagehot substituted the doctrine of "double government." He argued that the institutions of British government could be divided into two parts: the "dignified" part, composed of the monarchy and the House of Lords, and the "efficient" part, made up of the cabinet and the House of Commons. According to Bagehot, the dignified part secured the reverence and obedience of the English people, while the efficient part formulated the rules and policies by which the people were actually governed. Though changes in the English political system have rendered the book obsolete as a guide to the workings of modern British government, *The English Constitution* is still considered a standard text on the spirit of British politics.

The publication of *Physics and Politics* in 1872 further enhanced Bagehot's reputation as one of England's most original political thinkers. In this work, he explored the sociological implications of Charles Darwin's theory of evolution by studying the development of political societies in relation to the doctrine of natural selection. To explain how societies progressed from a primitive to an advanced level of political organization and cooperation, Bagehot devised an evolutionary scheme of three stages: the "preliminary age," when the objective was to initiate any type of government; the "fighting age," when societies that lacked cohesion gave way to those that were closely bound together by inflexible customs and laws; and the "age of discussion," when certain societies progressed from a government by customary law to a government in which individuals were permitted greater personal freedom. While Bagehot is frequently criticized for his failure to indicate the circumstances under which the earliest governments originated, many scholars praise *Physics and Politics* as the first attempt to apply evolutionary concepts to the study of the development of politics and society. Today the work is judged an important contribution to modern sociological thought as well as a pioneering essay in political psychology.

After the publication of *Physics and Politics,* Bagehot turned his attention to banking and finance. Hoping to convince London financiers that the Bank of England should increase its gold reserves, he published *Lombard Street*. In this work, Bagehot successfully employed the factual approach used in *The English Constitution* to produce what is now considered a classic for its realistic description of the methods of British banking. With *Lombard Street* and his weekly essays on banking in the *Economist*, Bagehot became one of London's most influential financial writers; constantly consulted on economic matters by members of both the Liberal and Conservative parties, he was dubbed "a sort of supplementary Chancellor of the Exchequer" by Prime Minister William Gladstone. From 1875 to 1877, Bagehot devoted himself almost solely to the writing of a three-part analysis of political economy, but poor health prevented him from finishing it. At the time of his death, he had completed only the introduction to the first part, which was intended to be an elaborate definition of the scope of political economy, and portions of the second and third parts, which were to consist of portraits and studies of such economic theorists as Adam Smith, David Ricardo, and Thomas Malthus. These fragments, along with several earlier essays on political economy, were later collected as *Economic Studies*.

While Bagehot's fame rests primarily on *The English Constitution,* all of his works have received steady critical attention since the late 1800s. Commentators frequently focus on his realistic approach and admire his willingness to look behind the forms of social, political, and economic institutions to discover, in the words of Matthew Arnold, "the *simple truth*" lying underneath. This realistic approach is also evident in his attempt to explain both the psychology of individual politicians and economists and its influence on historical events. Commentators have also continued to appreciate Bagehot's witty, colloquial prose style, and many contend that the enduring appeal of his writings is often due to their clarity, vitality, and humor.

With his wide range of interests, Bagehot is considered by many twentieth-century critics to embody one of the most valuable characteristics of the Victorian heritage. To these critics, he was intelligent and informed, even though an amateur, and his diversity enhanced all his intellectual pursuits. Yet, as Alastair Buchan points out, the diversity of Bagehot's writings has also damaged his reputation: because he ventured into four separate branches of scholarship—literature, politics, sociology, and economics—without acquiring a specialist's knowledge in any of them, his works have invariably suffered when judged by the highest standards in their fields. Critics concur that Bagehot most betrayed his lack of scholarship in the theoretical aspects of his writings, which are often deemed superficial and illogical. In contrast, those portions of his works where he described and analyzed the political, social, and economic issues of his day are repeatedly praised. Woodrow Wilson's summation of Bagehot's strengths explains both his influence upon his contemporaries and his continuing appeal to modern readers: "Occasionally, a man is born into the world whose mission it evidently is to clarify the thought of his generation, and to vivify it; to give it speed where it is slow, vision where it is blind, balance where it is out of poise, saving humor where it is dry,—and such a man was Walter Bagehot. When he wrote of history, he made it seem human and probable; when he wrote of political economy, he made it seem credible, entertaining,—nay, engaging even; when he wrote criticism, he wrote sense.''

## *PRINCIPAL WORKS

*Estimates of Some Englishmen and Scotchmen*  (criticism and essays)  1858
*The English Constitution*  (essay)  1867
*Physics and Politics; or, Thoughts on the Application of the Principles of "Natural Selection" and "Inheritance" to Political Society*  (essay)  1872
*Lombard Street: A Description of the Money Market* (essay)  1873
*Literary Studies.* 2 vols.  (criticism, essays, and letters) 1879
*Economic Studies*  (essays)  1880
*Biographical Studies*  (essays)  1881
*The Works of Walter Bagehot.* 5 vols.  (essays, criticism, and letters)  1889
***The Works and Life of Walter Bagehot.* 10 vols.  (essays, criticism, and letters)  1915
*The Collected Works of Walter Bagehot*  (essays and criticism)  1965-

*Many of Bagehot's writings were originally published in periodicals.

**This work also includes *Life of Walter Bagehot,* written by Emilie Isabel Barrington.

---

## MATTHEW ARNOLD  (letter date 1856)

[*Arnold is considered one of the most influential authors of the later Victorian period in England. While he is well known today as a poet, in his own time he asserted his greatest influence through his prose writings. Arnold's forceful literary criticism, which is based on his humanistic belief in the value of balance and clarity in literature, significantly shaped modern theory. The following excerpt is drawn from a letter written by Arnold to R. H. Hutton, a long-standing friend of Bagehot who joined him in establishing the* National Review *and edited several of his posthumously published works. In the letter, Arnold refers to unsigned essays that Bagehot contributed to the* National Review*].*

It was only a day or two ago that I read the article on Shelley in the last number [of the *National Review*]; that article and one or two others (in which I imagine that I trace the same hand) seem to me to be of the very first quality, showing not talent only, but a concern for the *simple truth* which is rare in English literature as it is in English politics and English religion—whatever zeal, vanity and ability may be exhibited by the performers in each of these three spheres. (pp. 247-48)

> *Matthew Arnold, in a letter to R. H. Hutton on October 27, 1856, in* The Works and Life of Walter Bagehot: The Life, Vol.X, *edited by Mrs. Russell Barrington, Longmans, Green, and Co., 1915, pp. 247-48.*

*THE SATURDAY REVIEW,* LONDON   (essay date 1867)

[*This anonymous reviewer briefly summarizes the leading ideas of* The English Constitution *and praises the work for its originality.*]

[*The English Constitution*] is a volume of shrewd, sensible, and in a great degree original, observations on the present working of the English Constitution. It is the fruit of much acute reflection, and of a large acquaintance with the varied facts of public life. It is written in a style singularly lucid and brilliant; and if in any respect faulty, only faulty because it is too clever, and diverts the attention too much from the matter to the form. Such a volume on a subject so novel cannot fail to be interesting. . . . Mr. Bagehot may well begin his volume by saying that something yet remains to be written on the English Constitution, and although his volume is only a volume of desultory remarks on this novel subject, yet it is so full of true and sagacious thought that no one will ever again set himself to study the English Constitution without consulting it. Of course a volume of desultory remarks has its weak side. It is sometimes very hard to see what the author is driving at; the book leaves no strong or definite impression; each page seems better than the chapter of which it is a part; and each chapter seems better than the volume. But in spite of this drawback it is a living book coming in place of a dead literature; it suggests, if it does not explain; it makes us see old things in a new way; and how great a merit this is may be estimated by those who will consider how few are the books of which it can be said.

The central idea of Mr. Bagehot's book is that the House of Commons is in the main an elective assembly. Its chief work is to elect that small body of actual rulers known as the Cabinet. But to this body it stands in a peculiar relation. For although the Cabinet is created by the House of Commons, yet the Cabinet can dissolve Parliament and put an end to the existence of its creator. The ultimate power in the British Constitution is therefore a newly-elected House of Commons. It is to that that the Cabinet can appeal, and by its decision the Cabinet must abide. The House of Commons, through the Cabinet, governs the country, and it is because it has to choose the Cabinet that it differs from an ordinary club. . . . [The] House is a good elective body, for the very reason that it is not merely an elective body. It watches over those it has elected, and can proceed to make a fresh choice if it pleases. It also continuously exercises other functions, the exercise of which gives it occupation, influence, and self-respect. It carries out the national will, it teaches the nation, it brings special grievances and special wants to light, it makes new laws, it checks the Cabinet; because, as the machinery of Government is in a large measure carried on by new laws made from year to year, it supervises the conduct of those whom it has appointed, but who have constantly to appeal to it. (p. 632)

That a good Cabinet should be formed and govern, there must . . . be a good body of primary electors, or constituents; and a good body of secondary electors, or members of the House of Commons. If a good Cabinet is formed, the kind of government it gives a nation is, as Mr. Bagehot thinks, and as most Englishmen think, the best in the world. . . . In his defence of Cabinet government Mr. Bagehot appears to us very successful, so far as he has chosen to enter on the subject. There are objections to Cabinet government which he does not notice, and in a volume of desultory remarks this is unavoidable. If any one chooses to maintain that the Presidential government of the United States, in the form in which we every day witness it going through some new stage of collapse, is a better form of government than the English system, he will find his theory satisfactorily upset in Mr. Bagehot's volume. But there are other objections to Cabinet government—objections founded on its helplessness, its waste of time, its tendency to make a nation think of words rather than things—which Mr. Bagehot does not meet. Probably he could have met them if he had tried, for he could have shown that every system of government is only a choice of evils; but he has not done so, and we must not speak of a partial work as of a complete one. Mr. Bagehot in one passage gives an intimation that the purpose has crossed his mind of writing a much more serious, elaborate, and exhaustive treatise, and we can only hope that his purpose may not fade away.

With good constituencies and a good House of Commons a good Cabinet may be formed; but is there nothing else needed? Must there also be a House of Lords and a Sovereign? No part of this volume is better than that in which a description is given of the House of Lords as it exists at the present day, and of the causes which have made and make it inferior to the House of Commons. None of Mr. Bagehot's remarks seem to us to surpass in acuteness and justice that in which he ascribes this inferiority to the circumstance that, as the House of Lords is avowedly founded on the claims of wealth and aristocracy, it must measure its members by a standard apart from that of personal eminence in its own assembly. A great lord is a great lord, even if he is a silent fool, whereas in the Commons a member is great because he is personally qualified to lead, and because the nation supports him in position. That it would be quite possible to do without a second Chamber which is always subordinate, may be considered theoretically arguable, even although the House of Lords is practically so useful in many ways. But must there be a Sovereign in order that Cabinet government may exist? This is the really important question. . . . No one can doubt that the tendency of things everywhere is to democracy, and can a democracy be governed by a Cabinet? Mr. Bagehot only goes a short way into this abstruse speculation, but so far as he goes he leads us to suppose that he inclines to the view that a system of Cabinet government may subsist without a Sovereign. (pp. 632-33)

> *"Bagehot on the English Constitution," in* The Saturday Review, *London, Vol. 23, No. 603, May 18, 1867, pp. 632-33.*

**THE SATURDAY REVIEW, LONDON** (essay date 1873)

[*The author of the following review analyzes Bagehot's theory of social progress as outlined in* Physics and Politics. *The critic faults Bagehot's failure to explain the causes of social progress, but praises his commentary on the way in which changes, once initiated, become widespread.*]

We need not inform our readers that Mr. Bagehot writes in a graceful style, and has much to say upon political topics that is well worth their attention. . . . [*Physics and Politics*] will be read with interest, though perhaps it is scarcely equal to his comment on the British Constitution. It may be described as an attempt to apply scientific reasoning to political theory, and is included in the catalogue of the "International Scientific Series." We must say, however, that it is only by using the term "science" in an extremely loose fashion that it can be brought under that head. Mr. Bagehot himself would be the last person to describe it as a statement of recognized principles; and, indeed, fond as people are of using big words in such a

connexion, any phrase which couples science and politics must be considered premature. Mr. Bagehot, however, tries to indicate in what manner various scientific theories, and especially those of Mr. Darwin and Mr. Herbert Spencer, may be applied to political speculations. The question is itself interesting, and, in the hands of a very able writer, its treatment leads to a number of remarks well worthy of observation, if not sufficiently systematic or well-established to be dignified with the name of science. . . . We will endeavour briefly to show at what point his doctrines appear to us to require modification or further development.

The general theory is summed up in his last chapter. As Mr. Bagehot points out, in confirmation of a valuable remark of Sir Henry Maine, we are apt to regard progress—whatever progress may mean—as a universal law of human nature; whilst yet nothing can be plainer than that a very large majority of mankind is and has been stationary. Hence it would be of the highest possible interest to discover what are the necessary conditions of progress. Looking back upon our savage progenitors, and tracing the various developments of the great races of the world, Mr. Bagehot perceives . . . that there are two general principles which form nations or races, as they have, on the Darwinian theory, formed species of animals and plants. There is the principle of hereditary resemblance, which makes us like our ancestors, and there is the principle of variability, which works through natural selection to cause gradual modifications of type. Now in the earlier ages of mankind, when every tribe had to fight for its existence, the condition of primary importance was the creation of certain fixed customs. A nation could not co-operate unless bound closely together by the iron hoops of custom; and those nations which had the best customs gradually predominated over their competitors. Unluckily the result of this tendency was that many customs became stereotyped, and the nations in which they prevailed passed into a stationary state. Those which preserved a certain flexibility then had the best chance of further development. The expression of this power was the advent of an "age of discussion." Following out some of the lines of thought suggested by Mr. Mill's *Liberty,* and adding some suggestions of his own, Mr. Bagehot insists on the vast importance of this element in a civilized nation, and concludes (it is not a very original conclusion) that "liberty is the strengthening and developing power—the light and heat of political nature." A doctrine upon which he lays much stress is the vast importance of what he calls in italics "*animated moderation*"—or, in rougher language, the need that nations, like men, should have "plenty of go," and yet "know when to pull up."

In a rough statement, this is the substance of a good deal of Mr. Bagehot's writing; and the first thought that occurs to us is that if we strip it of its scientific dress it comes to little more than a familiar platitude. All improvement implies a union of order and progress. Both are essential at every stage of natural development. Order can only be obtained amongst savages by brute force; and therefore, at very early periods, such an institution as slavery, which soon becomes mischievous in the highest degree, may be really useful. It is a necessary step towards division of labour and the development of a class with leisure for intellectual improvement. As men grow more intelligent, it becomes possible to secure order by appealing more to men's reason and less to their fears. Arbitrary force is mischievous as soon as it is superfluous; and what Mr. Bagehot calls an age of discussion may then be originated. All this is substantially true; but we can hardly call it new, or even admit that the scientific basis on which it is placed does very much to strengthen our confidence in the results. However, it is well to restate old doctrines in terms adapted to the age, and we welcome the new light which Mr. Bagehot has so far thrown upon the subject.

We have, however, a certain objection to his theory, or perhaps we should rather say that we are conscious of a gap which requires to be filled up. It is often objected to Mr. Darwin's theories that they do not give a law in the full sense of the word, but merely state a condition of progress. A beast of prey, he says, develops claws, because the rudimentary claw which occurs in some individual is useful in the struggle for existence. That explains the process by which claws, when once started, came into general use; but it does not attempt to explain the first appearance of the claw. To say that accident produced claws is merely to say in a roundabout fashion that we do not know how they were produced. In other words, there are laws of whose operation we are left in complete ignorance. This. . . illustrates the limits within which [Mr. Darwin's theories] are necessarily confined. Now Mr. Bagehot's theories involve the same difficulty, which frequently makes his doctrines look like a mere verbal explanation.

We take his own account of this difficulty in a particular case. The problem being, ''Why do men progress?'' the answer is, that they have a certain amount of ''variability.'' This sounds, as he remarks, like the old explanation by occult qualities. It is like saying that opium sends men to sleep because it has a soporific quality. No, replies Mr. Bagehot, the explanation is more than verbal. It states that men make progress when the fixity of custom has been developed up to a certain point, and not developed beyond it. ''The point of the solution is not the invention of an imaginary agency, but an assignment of comparative magnitude to two known agencies.'' Let us, however, look a little closer. To say that progress involves variability is saying nothing more than that, in order to change, men must be capable of changing. There is perhaps a little more in the further statement that men must have fixed customs. This is true; and is perhaps not quite self-evident. The addition that, if they are to improve, the customs must not be too fixed, is, as before, mere tautology; and therefore Mr. Bagehot's statement scarcely seems to come to any more than this, that a certain fixity of custom is desirable. Surely that is a proposition which nobody would ever think of denying, whether he was or was not a Darwinian. A really valuable remark would be made if Mr. Bagehot were capable of giving us any sort of rule as to the degree in which customs should be fixed. But this is obviously beyond his power or that of any man. When he tells us that fixity is more desirable at an early than at a later age, he is really making a statement which may be discussed with interest, and which, whether sound or otherwise, has a certain historical value. We have already explained our view of its meaning. But the bare assertion that variability is a condition of improvement seems to us to be no more than verbal, in spite of Mr. Bagehot's efforts to make something of it.

Although we cannot profess to be much struck by this part of the theory, we fully admit that Mr. Bagehot incidentally makes many valuable remarks on the way in which changes are actually brought about. He is too apt, indeed, to mistake a confession of ignorance for a statement of positive knowledge, but his remarks are often ingenious. Thus, for example, he attributes great importance to the process of what he calls unconscious imitation. He says—and the remark is true and curious—that ''every one who has written in more than one newspaper

knows how invariably his style catches the tone of each paper while he is writing for it, and changes to the tone of another when he begins to write for that.'' He explains in this way the origin of different schools of literature, and extends the remark to national character. Steele, for example, to use his illustration, struck out the notion of essay-writing. Addison took it up and perfected the art. The public taste was impressed, and a whole group of inferior writers was infected by the same style; and thus we account for the change between the days of Shakspeare and Bacon and those of Pope and Locke. The New England type of character has, he thinks, been developed after the same way by the attraction exercised by the first Puritan emigrants. Now it is plain that this is no explanation at all of the first cause of the phenomenon. Why did Steele take to writing essays, and why did they strike the public taste? It does not account for the cholera to say that A. caught it from B., and B. from C., and so on to the end of the alphabet. Why, we must ask, did Z. catch it? and, moreover, what were the conditions that made it catching? These are the real problems, and an answer to them would lead to valuable results—such, for example, as the importance of drainage. The answer given by Mr. Bagehot tends to distract attention from the real difficulty. If Steele had died in his infancy, would not the same literary type have been produced by somebody else? Were there not hundreds of men partaking of the same general sources of inspiration, and labouring to find a convenient mode of expressing themselves? A philosophical observer would inquire into the contemporary state of theology and philosophy, the social conditions, the influence of foreign countries, and a hundred other causes of a general character; and, so far as he allowed himself to be put off with Mr. Bagehot's answer, he would be tempted to believe that a profound change in national modes of thought and expression was simply accidental; and perhaps, very unphilosphically, to call accident a cause. Mr. Bagehot's remarks are useful as illustrating the method in which a change, once begun, is propagated; but they are obviously irrelevant in considering the determining causes of the change. We do not imagine that he would dispute this; but he seems scarcely to give sufficient prominence to the profounder movements of thought, because his whole attention is devoted to the external apparatus.

The same theory occurs, in connexion with a more distinct logical error, in another part of his book. Mr. Bagehot attributes great importance to the savage belief in lucky omens, and he explains their occurence in this way. An expedition, he says, fails when a magpie crosses its path, and a magpie is then supposed to be unlucky. Surely this is an inversion of the real process; and an inversion which again leads him to attribute exaggerated importance to mere chance. The case may be illustrated from his own anecdotes. Somebody told Scott to cure a disease by sleeping for a night on twelve smooth stones collected from twelve brooks. Does Mr. Bagehot suppose that this superstition originated in the accident that somebody had slept on twelve stones collected from twelve brooks, and been cured accordingly? How did anybody come to think of collecting the stones and sleeping upon them? Could such an accident possibly occur? Obviously the superstition originated in a deductive, and not an inductive, process. It was not the result of experiment, but an *à priori* theory derived from some notions as to the magic influence of the number twelve, and of stones in brooks. . . . [Surely] nothing can be plainer than that the association preceded the experiment, and indeed was the only reason for making an experiment of so arbitrary a character. The confusion of ideas depends upon the well-known law of the incapacity of an uncultivated mind to distinguish between objective and subjective impression. Mr. Bagehot when he was a boy used to play loo; and his childish companions found that a particular "fish" which was prettier than the others brought luck with it. Why? Not because a boy who had that fish had won a particular occasion, but because the pleasure of having a pretty fish was naturally associated with the pleasure of winning the game. The boys thought, like Mr. Bagehot, that a mysterious power called "luck" had a good deal to do in the world, and that when it meant to favour a boy, it would give him a pretty fish as well as a good set of cards. Similarly, for some reason not now traceable, savages disliked magpies; perhaps they are bad to eat, or their cry suggests alarm; and the unpleasant sensation produced by the flight of the bird suggested the unpleasant sensation of being defeated, which again, they fancied, might precede as well as follow the actual occurrence of a defeat. Why indeed should they attend to magpies more than to a hundred other phenomena, except that they already had some associations with it? . . . Mr. Bagehot imagines that some "Nestor of a savage tribe" remarked a coincidence, and that his authority gave popularity to the superstition founded upon it. Therefore he infers that "luck" played a great part in the world. The true process we take to be entirely different. Some obvious associations of ideas are suggested to all savage tribes, and give birth to superstitions which bind the "Nestor" as well as his fellows. And the examination of this process leads to the discovery of a curious mental law, which is left unnoticed if we accept Mr. Bagehot's crude explanation.

In spite of these errors, as they seem to us, which lower our estimate of the value of Mr. Bagehot's book, the line of his inquiries suggests to him many interesting remarks the value of which is not diminished by the questionable nature of some of his theories; and on the whole we can recommend the book as well deserving to be read by thoughtful students of politics. (pp. 89-90)

*"Bagehot's 'Physics and Politics','' in* The Saturday Review, *London, Vol. 35, No. 899, January 18, 1873, pp. 89-90.*

## G. BARNETT SMITH (essay date 1879)

[*In the following review of* Literary Studies, *Smith applauds the work for both its originality and suggestiveness.*]

One great charm of Mr. Bagehot's [*Literary Studies* is that it is] not moulded upon the style of any other writer. What he gives us is his own, and we can always learn something from a man who is original, who throws a tone and colour of his own into the questions which he handles. In almost all these essays are to be discovered some new ideas, and many forcible resettings of old ones. The characteristics of an author are seized upon almost as by intuition, and the reader rises from the perusal of each essay knowing far more upon the subject than he did before. Nor do the essays (except, perhaps, in the case of Shakespeare) take a limited range, over which the writer exhausts himself. He not only brings out many excellent things from his treasury, but he has a great facility for suggesting others—one of the most invaluable qualities in an author. The first of these essays, on 'The First Edinburgh Reviewers,' is probably one of the best. Mr. Bagehot traces the origin of the new order of periodical literature with great skill, and then gives us striking portraits of the early reviewers, who 'cultivated literature on a little oatmeal.' . . . Mr. Bagehot pays a well-deserved tribute to the founders of the *Edinburgh Review,* who fearlessly attacked the abuses of the time, and in one well-

chosen sentence he thus hits off the character of the Whigs: 'The Whigs are constitutional by instinct, as the Cavaliers were monarchical by devotion.' (pp. 305-06)

Mr. Hutton considers the essay on '**Hartley Coleridge**' the most perfect in style of any of Mr. Bagehot's writings [see Additional Bibliography, 1889]; but here I, for one, cannot agree with him. It is quite as suggestive and as deep searching as any other, and furnishes us with an admirable portrait of a very remarkable man; but in point of literary style it is not carefully executed. For example, here is a very singularly constructed sentence: 'He soon, however, went down to the Lakes, and there he, with *a single exception,* lived and died.' The italics are, of course, ours, but the phraseology should belong to no one. (pp. 307-08)

The essay upon Shelley is well worth reading, even after all that has recently been written upon this distinguished poet. Much of the criticism is profound. . . . (p. 308)

There is some exaggeration . . . in the statement that Shelley has delineated in his works no character except his own, or characters most strictly allied to his own. His mythological beings, it is true, have a good deal of his own personality in them, but Julian and Maddalo [in his *Julian and Maddalo: A Conversation*] are distinct individualities, and *The Cenci* shows that he could go out of himself. The personification of passions and impulses was a favourite mode of writing with Shelley, but it is a mistake to suppose that he was incapable of reproducing actual human character, or that he would not have done so had his life been extended. . . .

The essay on Shakespeare is worthy of all the praise Mr. Hutton gives it. It takes only one side of the great dramatist—who can be exhaustive on this subject?—that of the man, but this is excellently set forth. (p. 309)

Our author does not write with the eloquence of a De Quincey, neither can he vie with the deep and quaint suggestiveness of Emerson. He touches upon some points which have been referred to by Carlyle—notably the comparison between Shakespeare and Sir Walter Scott—but the larger questions associated with the poet and the dramatist he purposely does not deal with. Those points which he handles, however, he elucidates and enforces with power and insight. (p. 310)

These volumes are a distinct and substantial addition to critical literature. No one can read the various essays without being struck by their thoughtfulness, their suggestiveness, and their healthfulness. . . . On every topic Mr. Bagehot handles he has something to say worth hearing, and this is a great recommendation in an age when so much is published which has no relevancy to things in heaven, things in earth, or things under the earth. Those who allege that nothing can be learnt from criticism would do well to take up these essays: a study of them must inevitably lead to the dethronement of such an opinion. (p. 313)

*G. Barnett Smith, "Walter Bagehot," in* Fraser's Magazine, *n.s. Vol. XIX, No. CXI, March, 1879, pp. 298-313.*

## [G. WALKER] (essay date 1879)

[*Walker selects passages from* Literary Studies *to illustrate Bagehot's exceptional intellect. According to Walker, Bagehot's mind was distinguished by originality and receptiveness to ideas. These qualities, the critic contends, account for the success of* The English Constitution, *which sheds fresh light on a familiar subject and ranks with Alexis de Tocqueville's works among nineteenth-century political treatises.*]

Mr. Bagehot's death leaves a void in English literature which will not easily be filled. He was possessed of rare and peculiar intellectual powers, and he applied his talents to subjects which at the present day do not often form the study of men gifted with anything like his genius. The last fifty years have been a period of political change. Curiously enough, they have not in the main been a period of political speculation. Two men of marked originality have, the one in France [De Tocqueville] and the other in England [Mr. Bagehot], thrown new light on the theory of politics. . . . Mr. Bagehot's achievements have scarcely as yet been fully recognized, though students know that he has thrown more light on the essential character of the English Government than can be gained from the works of any other writer who has dealt with that well-worn but little understood subject, the English Constitution, and it will ultimately be perceived that he is, within a limited field, by far the most original political theorist who has appeared, at any rate in England, during the last half century.

Our present object is not, however, to estimate the value of Mr. Bagehot's speculations, but to point out what were the qualities of a genius which may be termed ''singular'' in the strict sense of the term, and left its peculiar impress on every line of Mr. Bagehot's works. The first and most obvious quality of his mind was originality. By this term we do not mean necessarily either strength or wide grasp of intellect. What we do mean is the power to look at all matters from points of view which are peculiar to the thinker himself. Take, for instance, Mr. Bagehot's whole account of the Edinburgh Reviewers [in **'Literary Studies'**]. The subject is one which lends itself to truisms. One would be inclined to think that nothing could be said on the topic which was at once true and new. The moment that Mr. Bagehot takes the matter in hand the reader feels that a considerable subject is never really exhausted. Jeffrey, Horner, Sydney Smith, Lord Eldon, are each set before us in a new aspect. There is no attempt at overstrained paradox, but we feel that the true character of the Toryism which the reviewers overthrew, their own powers and their weaknesses, are made apparent by being subjected to the light of an original genius. The following sentence with reference to Lord Eldon tells, for example, more than can be learnt from half a hundred histories such as that with which the industry and good sense of Mr. Walpole have recently afflicted the world:

> We read occasionally in conservative literature (the remark is as true of religion as of politics) alternations of sentences, the first an appeal to the coarsest prejudice, the next a subtle hint to a craving and insatiable scepticism. You may trace this even in Vesey, junior. Lord Eldon never read Hume or Montaigne, but sometimes, in the interstices of cumbrous law, you may find sentences with their meaning, if not in their manner: 'Dumpor's case always struck me as extraordinary; but if you depart from Dumpor's case, what is there to prevent a departure in every direction?'

This sentence, which is only one in a thousand examples of Mr. Bagehot's power of suggesting a whole view by a few brilliant touches, is remarkable as showing the close connection between his literary and his political criticism. The essay on the Edinburgh Reviewers happens to unite his interest in literature and his interest in politics. In truth they never seem

far apart from each other. From **'Lombard Street,'** or **'Physics and Politics'** may be picked out profound remarks on style and the criticisms on Lord Eldon easily suggest the kind of view which Mr. Bagehot was likely to take of the Constitution. The English Constitution with its paradoxes, its anomalies, its basis of sound sense, and (with due reverence be it said) its absurdities, was exactly the topic which suited Mr. Bagehot's powers. And his **'English Constitution'** is a masterpiece.

Something, however, more than what is fairly meant by originality was needed for enabling any one to throw new light on a topic which is so well known that, like the character of an old acquaintance, it cannot be understood. This necessary something is freshness, or openness of mind, and this intellectual pliability and readiness to admit new facts and to receive new impressions was precisely the quality which next to originality was the most marked characteristic of Mr. Bagehot's mind. Any reader who wishes to see this particular trait displayed in the strongest light, though not from the most favorable point of view, should read the letters on the *Coup d'État* written in January and February, 1852 [and first published in the *Inquirer*]. They are appended to the first volume of **'Literary Studies,'** and form as remarkable a production as any young man of twenty-six ever published. (pp. 436-37)

There was, perhaps, in England but one man except Lord Palmerston who perceived that the triumph of the *Coup d'État* was based on causes lying deep in the state of France and the character of Frenchmen. This one man was the then unknown correspondent of the *Inquirer*. He went to Paris and studied the *Coup d'État* as a doctor might examine into the symptoms of a new disease, or a lawyer might study a strange case. Mr. Bagehot analyzed the condition of Paris with extreme interest and with impartial calmness. He perceived, what we now all know, that the shopkeepers were panic-struck with fear of socialism; that the workmen hated the middle classes; that the Conservatives were unpatriotic and the Republicans impracticable; and, to put the matter shortly, that the President had a hand full of good cards and the skill to play his own game. Mr. Bagehot, moreover, never lost sight of the fact that the object of government is to protect the lives and property of ordinary men, and that ordinary men, who are the vast majority of any country, will hate any party who menaces their lives and property, and rally round any despot who protects their interests. Hence in 1851 he perceived what was the strength of the President, and wrote of the *Coup d'État* just as ten years later the mass of political writers, taught by experience, wrote of the Empire. His whole theory is summed up in these sentences:

> Mazzini sneers at the selfishness of shopkeepers. I am for the shopkeepers against him. There are people who think because they are Republican there shall be no more 'cakes and ale.' Aye, verily, but there will though, or else stiffish ginger will be hot in the mouth. Legislative assemblies, leading articles, essay eloquence—such are good, very good—useful, very useful; yet they can be done without. We can want them. Not so with all things. The selling of figs, the cobbling of shoes, the manufacturing of nails—these are the essence of life. And let whoso frameth a constitution of his country think on these things.

Of ''these things''—that is, of the connection between the commonest facts and the most general principles of politics—

our author thought to good purpose, and therefore saw exactly those aspects of truth which generally escape theorists. His defect, to speak quite frankly, was that he ''thought of these things'' a good deal too much. Something must be allowed for the irony which runs through the attitude of a man who, being himself the cleverest of theorists, is never so happy as when he can show how great are the social benefits arising from commonplace stupidity. A good deal must also be allowed for the natural passion of a youthful author for the maintenance of ingenious paradoxes. But when every allowance is made, it must be conceded that Mr. Bagehot's attitude towards the *Coup d'État,* if it shows the strength also betrays the weakness of his genius. ''I have seen so many ghosts,'' it has been said by a celebrated author, ''that I cannot believe in ghosts.'' We might conceive Mr. Bagehot in like manner saying, ''I have formed so many theories that I cannot believe in theories.'' Certainly his belief in the ordinary facts of life was out of proportion to his belief in moral principles. . . . [If] it were still the practice to work out literary comparisons, no more interesting topic could be chosen than a comparison between [De Tocqueville and Mr. Bagehot]. . . . De Tocqueville, in beauty of style, in width of generalization, in a kind of moral dignity, certainly rises far above Mr. Bagehot. But the advantage is not all on the side of the French author. Mr. Bagehot was never a slave to his own generalizations. He was never afraid to bring his theories into contact with the commonest facts. He had a far greater knowledge of mankind than seems to have been possessed by a writer who, though he had been a Minister, has always something in his mode of thought which savors of the Professor. Whole sides of human experience which were open to Mr. Bagehot were unknown to De Tocqueville. . . . De Tocqueville was so engrossed in working out the result of two or three fertile political principles as hardly to realize what were the motives which guided ordinary men in the political transactions of every-day life. Mr. Bagehot looked so sharply at the actual course of human action that his speculative conclusions were somewhat warped by his excessive appreciation of the influence exerted on what seemed the great issues of politics, by the petty motives and mean interests which govern the acts of vulgar and commonplace human beings. Yet, when this defect is allowed for, he remains, together with the eminent Frenchman with whom we have compared him, one of the few thinkers who in modern times have thrown on the theories of politics the light of originality and genius. (p. 437)

[G. Walker], ''Walter Bagehot,'' in The Nation, *Vol. XXVIII, No. 730, June 26, 1879, pp. 436-37.*

### ROBERT GIFFEN  (essay date 1880)

[Giffen, who was assistant editor of the Economist during Bage-hot's tenure as editor, provides a generous assessment of Lombard Street and Economic Studies. He argues that a ''very exceptional place must be claimed for Bagehot as an economic writer'' largely because of his ability to describe in simple and direct language both contemporary business practices and general principles of economic science.]

[Bagehot] was deeply interested in the art of money-making, and he imagined vividly the entire mental state of business men. How profits were made in different trades. . . was a constant study to him, as were the shifts and devices of the struggling and unsuccessful traders in all trades. The result is seen in every page almost of his writing. He is the very antithesis of the literary economists whom he describes as ''like physiologists who have never dissected; like astronomers who have never seen the stars.'' But the eye brings to a subject what it has the power of seeing, and there have been literary economists conversant with business and immersed in it as Bagehot was, whose eyes were blinded that they could not see.

Another feature I should like to put forward as characteristic of Bagehot was his ''quantitative'' sense—his knowledge and feeling of the ''how much'' in dealing with the complex working of economic tendencies. Much economic writing is abstract, and necessarily so. You can say, for instance, that import duties tend to diminish trade between countries, and that import duties on articles imported from abroad, the same kind of articles being produced at home, are peculiarly mischievous; or that fluctuating exchanges are injurious to trade. But in the concrete world there is something more to be done. Here the ''how much'' is very often the only vital question. . . . In dealing with concrete things . . . and the applications of his science, the economist must know where to place his emphasis—to be able to measure one evil against another and one force against another. And the sense necessary for this was Bagehot's in an unusual degree. This is conspicuously manifest in one of the discussions he was most interested in—that of the Bank reserve, which occupies so large a space in his *Lombard Street.* . . . But everywhere and always this quantitative sense was present when the discussion made it necessary. And the value of this quality cannot, I believe, be over-estimated. (pp. 553-54)

Every writer has the defect of his qualities, and I should say that Bagehot, while possessing the inventive and imaginative mind, which enabled him to discover and to describe so clearly, did not excel either in that laboured ratiocination or minute analysis which are essential to the highest success in some branches of economic study. He could both sustain a long argument and analyse minutely. Whatever he had to do he did thoroughly, and took what pains were necessary—in some cases he had conspicuously that transcendent capacity for taking trouble which Carlyle describes as the quality of genius. Still it did not ''come natural'' to him to do either of these things, and he was not here conspicuously successful. If the reader will compare chapters 12 and 13 of his essays on Silver [in *Some Articles on the Depreciation of Silver and on Topics Connected with It*] with the *Lombard Street,* or even the essay on the **''Cost of Production''** in [*Economic Studies*] with the first essay on the **''Postulates of Political Economy,''** he will perceive what I mean. The argument in the first cases is laboured and difficult, and I am not sure that it is throughout altogether clear, while in the second cases there is an ease and power and a transparent clearness which impress the most careless reader. Perhaps the two qualities are incompatible, but at any rate Bagehot was pre-eminently an inventor and describer, and that in bold and broad outlines, and not a labouring reasoner or exhaustive analyst. (p. 555)

Let me add a word or two on his style, at least on his later style, less buoyant and elastic than his earlier. . . . [As] Bagehot was fond of talking about style I came to know various points of excellence at which he consciously aimed. His natural tendency was that way, but he also laboured to be conversational, to put things in the most direct and picturesque manner, as people would talk to each other in common speech, to remember and use expressive colloquialisms. Such Americanisms as the ''shrinkage'' of values he had a real liking for, and constantly applied them. . . . Besides this conversational tone, Bagehot aimed at an excessive simplicity formed in part by his habit of writing for the *City* [the London financial district].

In his essay on Adam Smith he ascribes the success of the latter, compared with Hume, who also wrote soundly enough on political economy, to the directness and convincingness of his style, which impressed the ordinary business man, whereas Hume and other literary writers seemed to be playing with their subject. And Bagehot seemed to have been guided by this belief in his own later writing generally, as he certainly was in the *Economist.* He had always some typical City man in his mind's eye—a man not skilled in literature or the turnings of phrases, with a limited vocabulary and knowledge of theory, but keen as to facts and reading for the sake of information and guidance respecting what vitally concerned him. To please this ideal City man Bagehot would use harsh and crude or redundant expressions, sometimes ungrammatical if tried by ordinary tests; anything to drive his meaning home. Thus in turning over the pages of **Lombard Street** at random I find such phrases as "money-market money," "borrowable money," "alleviative treatment," "one of these purposes is the meeting a demand for cash"; and sentences like this, "Continental bankers and others instantly send great sums here, as soon as the rate shows that it can be done profitably," where the "instantly" is grammatically superfluous though it helps to drive the meaning home. For such awkwardnesses Bagehot not only did not care but he was even eager to use them sometimes if he thought they would arrest attention. He was always most careful, too, to see that the drift of any passage, the impression a hasty reader of the kind described would get from it, was exactly what he intended. He was never content merely with having the meaning there provided the words were delicately and nicely weighed; the meaning must shine through the words; and he detested all writing which gave a false impression, however verbally exact. . . . [His later style] was rhetoric deliberately and skilfully used by a master after years of practice, and which so impresses his meaning as no other writing I know of on economic subjects, except Adam Smith's, impresses. This style was a weapon admirably fitted for the work he did and was peculiarly qualified to do, though the description of it also shows of itself that there are some topics of economic discussion for which it is unfit. (pp. 556-57)

[Bagehot's work as an economist] consisted in thinking original thoughts as to the whole scope and method of political economy, as well as some important topics in it, and expressing these thoughts in a striking and convincing manner, and also in describing broadly and clearly the leading outlines of the science as well as the features of the modern organization of business—the great commerce—which he understood to be practically the subject-matter of the science. The two kinds of work were closely interconnected, his new ideas being the result of his general powers of vision and description; and his characteristic achievement, I should say, is that he has described the science and its subject-matter in such a way as to put them in a wholly new light. . . . It was for description in the highest sense of the word that Bagehot was peculiarly prepared when he came to the consideration of economic questions, and in description his characteristic work consists. (pp. 557-58)

His main statement [in **Economic Studies**] is that notions of English political economy, which is an abstract science, instead of being universally applicable to all men in all ages, as the founders of the science in some confused manner assumed, are in fact only applicable to real life with qualifications, and are only applicable approximately to societies organized for business on a basis of free contract and with capital and labour freely transferable, as that of England very nearly is now and

is tending more and more to be. . . . Many later writers of course have insisted on this abstract character of economics, and there is an angry quarrel, as is well known, between them and the "historical school" in political economy, because the latter insists that the science pretends to be concrete, or is nothing if it is not concrete, while they maintain that in that light it is manifestly not true. But what Bagehot has done is not merely, like other writers, to point out the abstract character of the science, but to prove as against the historical school that there is an age and society—the whole business world of England at the present time, and a large part of other modern communities—in which the assumptions of English political economy are approximately true in the concrete as well as in the abstract. (p. 559)

The field he travels over is very large, and his remarks are so suggestive, both as to differences in the economic condition of different countries, which modify the application to them of the English doctrines, and as to the gradual extension of the area over which the English doctrines are true in the concrete, that it would be impossible within any brief limits to give a full notion of the value of the work. . . . [It is enough] for the present to mark how much the leading idea of this book shifts the landmarks of economic study over a wide field and alters the whole view of the science.

In two other ways these **Economic Studies,** imperfect as they are, seem to me most valuable. The personal sketches of Adam Smith, Malthus, and Ricardo, with the fragment on Mill, help in the directest way to the comprehension of their characteristic work in economic science as Bagehot understood it. I doubt if his estimate of Adam Smith, whom it is not so easy to see round, is adequate; but the sketches of Malthus and Ricardo, the description of the accidental way in which the former, "a mild pottering person," came to accomplish his great revolution in economic thought, and the way in which Ricardo, a Jew by race, and accustomed to work in a market where the articles dealt in are immaterial, and where the assumptions of political economy are true, was able to found the abstract science as it is now understood, seem to be almost perfect. . . . [One of the best services Bagehot] has rendered to the study is perhaps to restore Ricardo to his proper position as an authority. The other way in which the book excels is in the richness and vigour of the remarks on business, which is no doubt a feature of all Bagehot's writing, but here comes out most strongly, as he is dealing with the entire differences between an economic and an non-economic age. He says of [Smith's] *Wealth of Nations,* that there are scarcely five consecutive pages in it "which do not contain some sound and solid observation, important in practice and replete with common sense. The most experienced men of business would have been proud of such a fund of just maxims fresh from life." And much the same, it seems to me, may be said of these **Economic Studies.** . . . (pp. 560-61)

In all [Bagehot] says about business he is like a witness to the facts of which political economy has to treat, and hence, I believe, the peculiar value of his description of the economic age which we find in these **Economic Studies.** It must be a never-failing subject of regret that the book is incomplete—that the testimony is cut short just when we begin to understand it, and see what it would have been. . . .

[**Lombard Street**] is also, and even more strikingly than the **Economic Studies,** a book of description. Bagehot's own alternative title for it was "a description of the money market." Its scope is not so wide, as the money market is only a department of the great field of the science, though an important department, but it is wide enough to make the book a considerable one, especially as Bagehot treats the subject. The money market is not only described in a series of remarkable pictures of its chief objects—the Bank of England, the Joint Stock banks, the private banks, and the discount houses—but the description necessarily involves a frequent reference to the whole organization of the "great commerce." The sources of the loanable fund with which the monetary institutions of Lombard Street have to deal, the democratic structure of English commerce which has arisen through the facility which men with small capital have of borrowing, the transferability of capital in England, the reasons for quick fluctuations in the value of money by which the action of the different institutions is affected, and many other peculiarities of the whole business organization, all come in for their share of explanation, and are fully explained in and for themselves after Bagehot's usual manner, and not merely by way of allusion as they bear on the subject in hand. In some degree, therefore, *Lombard Street* even anticipates the *Economic Studies.* . . . The *Economic Studies* make a greater work, but *Lombard Street* explains in some degree how it grew, and why Bagehot's testimony is so valuable as to the organization of the great commerce. He was a witness and observer of the central part of the organization, and it was his merit to have started the idea of giving a description, as well as to have carried it into execution. The conception of the London money market as an organization does not seem to have occurred to any one before. (pp. 561-62)

I may say that [*Lombard Street*] appears to me the most finished in form of anything that Bagehot has done. He was full of the subject which had occupied much of his life for many years before he wrote, and his aim, in which he perfectly succeeded, was to impress both men of business, to whom, as I have said, he consciously adapted his later style, and the outside world of literary and public men. . . . The only other work to compare it with is the *English Constitution,* which is a description of the organization of English political life, in the same realistic method as Bagehot has pursued in describing the organization or constitution of the City; but *Lombard Street* seems even more careful, thorough, and realistic. It shows the high-water mark of what Bagehot could do in point of form and execution, and adds to the regret that time was not left him to finish the *Economic Studies* in the same fashion.

Apart from its special excellence as a descriptive book, *Lombard Street* likewise contains, I believe, Bagehot's most valuable contributions to economic science, irrespective of what he has done in the *Economic Studies* and elsewhere to exhibit the relation of the science to others and its modification by the new ideas of the age. He was really, if not the discoverer, at any rate the first writer who insisted upon and worked out as a cardinal principle of the money market—the maintenance of the bank reserve. One has only to look back into the old books of political economy to see how completely the topic was not only overlooked, but not even dreamt of. But Bagehot makes it one of the themes and practical objects of the *Lombard Street.* . . . It seems to me that this doctrine alone is a very large contribution to economics, and would have done much to make the reputation of an economist who was that and nothing more. So much turns on the management of bank reserves as an influence on the economic condition of modern industrial communities, and that influence is becoming daily so much greater, that what Bagehot has done in this way cannot but grow in importance as time goes by.

Another important contribution he has made in *Lombard Street* is in popularising the notion of a tendency in business to ebb and flow—to be all excited and prosperous with a high level of prices at one time, and languid and unprosperous with a low level of prices at another. This rhythmical or cyclical movement in trade, though not yet fully accepted by literary economists, is a familiar enough idea to the ordinary speculator in the City, and is embedded in a well-known book . . . , Tooke's *History of Prices,* while there is much other business writing in which the same idea is found; but Bagehot takes it up and makes it his own, besides giving a psychological explanation of it, which should go far to make it acceptable even to the merely literary economist, who is clamorous for proof. Bagehot's own testimony as a witness should count for a great deal, his chapter on **"Why Lombard Street is sometimes highly excited and sometimes very dull,"** being in fact valuable as a piece of evidence as much as any other part of the description in the book. What Bagehot has done on this head seems also the more valuable, because along with the general tone of the book it popularises and generalises the idea of aggregate effects arising from the working of economic tendencies, which tendencies can be traced, and their effects within certain limits predicted. When we come to concrete economy we have not only to deal with modifications of the abstract science, but a new class of phenomena is brought before us which may be the subject of scientific treatment, and of this class *Lombard Street* gives a sketch, besides preparing the way for studying them by the outline of the business organization to which the phenomena relate. (pp. 562-64)

If my account be correct, a very exceptional place must be claimed for Bagehot as an economic writer. He has not only gained rank amongst the economists in the ordinary plane of their work, but in connecting the science with the physical philosophy of the time, and showing how the new ideas modify it, in resolving conflicting views by a higher generalisation and thus clearing away prejudices which impeded the study, in describing the features of the economic age of the world and the special features of the English business organization, besides attracting people to the study by interesting writing,—but he has performed one of those leading services which entitle him to foremost rank as an economic writer—to a place, I should think, in the succession of leading authors along with those he has himself sketched. Looking at the science as it was before him, and as it appears through his spectacles, it certainly seems to me difficult to assign him too high a place. (pp. 565-66)

*Robert Giffen, "Bagehot As an Economist," in* The Fortnightly Review, *n.s. Vol. XXVII, No. CLX, April 1, 1880, pp. 549-67.*

### [A. V. DICEY]   (essay date 1881)

[*Dicey studies passages from* Biographical Studies *to illustrate the distinguishing characteristics of Bagehot's intellect. According to Dicey, these qualities are "capacity for abstract speculation," "relish for actual, concrete, every-day facts," and "openness to truth." Dicey concludes his essay with a comparison of Bagehot's and John Stuart Mill's intellectual capabilities.*]

Bagehot has brought more knowledge of life and originality of mind to the elucidation of the theory and practice of English politics than any man since Burke. He is the only Englishman of first-rate talents who, during the last half-century, has applied the whole force of his mind to the analysis of the mass of laws, maxims, and habits which go to make up the English

Constitution. In the course of a few years he will undoubtedly be recognized by all the world as the most eminent of constitutionalists. If this recognition has not been yet attained, the failure, such as it is, is due mainly to the versatility of Bagehot's interests, and to the consequent difficulty felt by ordinary students in believing that a writer who excelled in so many fields of speculation—in the sphere of criticism, of imaginative literature, and of political economy—could be pre-eminent in one field; and to the lucidity of Bagehot's explanations, which led even those who learnt most from his pages into the delusion that what their teacher explained so easily was in itself easy to explain and hardly needed explanation. Those, however, and we believe they are an increasing body, who are daily more and more aware that the death of Bagehot deprived England of one of her most original thinkers, will welcome with very special interest the **'Biographical Studies.'** . . . This series of reviews and fugitive criticisms does not, indeed, add much to our knowledge of the writer's views or conclusions. It would be ridiculous to expect from fragments of his work the merits of complete and careful workmanship which had received the workman's last touches. But the very fact that the **'Studies'** are merely studies makes them peculiarly valuable as a means of acquiring an insight into Bagehot's mode of thought and into the secrets of his power. They do not, we repeat, add much to our knowledge of his views, but they add, or may add, a good deal to our understanding of Bagehot's genius.

The peculiarity of his mind, which gives the peculiar tone to every word he wrote, is the combination in him of three qualities which are not very often found apart, and are very rarely indeed found to co-exist in the same individual. These characteristics are capacity for abstract speculation—the keenest relish for actual, concrete, every-day facts—intense, one might almost say excessive, openness to truth (which is a different thing from the love of truth). The **'Biographical Studies'** are from the very nature of their subject not the work in which one would at first sight seek for the most marked specimens of our author's capacity for abstract speculation. It is rather to his constitutional or economical theories that his admirers would at first sight point for proof of his speculative ability. But, though the assertion may sound a little paradoxical, it is to our minds the simple truth that Bagehot's passion for facts is nowhere so remarkable as when he is dealing with theoretical topics, whilst his speculative turn of mind is nowhere better seen than in his mode of dealing with the characters and lives of actual living men. Take, for instance, almost at a chance, the following sentence from his **'English Constitution'**: ''Most people, when they read that the Queen walked on the slopes at Windsor—that the Prince of Wales went to the Derby—have imagined that too much thought and prominence were given to little things. But they have been in error; and it is nice to trace how the actions of a retired widow and an unemployed youth become of such importance.'' These words show exactly the point in which Bagehot differed from most theorists—from such able men, for example, as Hallam or Mill: in the very midst of speculative analysis of the influence and position of the monarchy he turns to the every-day, known, palpable fact of the interest excited by the Queen's walking on the slopes at Windsor. In a precisely analogous manner he is always prone to pass immediately from the anecdotes and trivialities of biography to some principle which they suggest, or rather of which they are a concrete example. All through his essay on Lord Brougham or his essay on Gladstone there are scattered remarks which you scarcely know whether to group under the head of comments on individual character, or under the head of reflections on human nature. ''Lord Brougham's intellectual

powers,'' writes Bagehot, ''were as fitted for the functions of a miscellaneous agitator as his moral character. The first of these, perhaps, is a singular faculty of conspicuous labor. In general, the work of agitation proceeds in this way.'' Then follows what may be equally well described as an inimitable analysis of public agitation, or an unrivalled analysis of the character of the great agitator who, even as chancellor, could not give up the rôle for which he was created by nature. Take, again, Bagehot's mode of criticising Gladstone's oratory. He gets from Mr. Gladstone himself a description of an orator's functions, whose ''work from its very inception is inextricably mixed up with practice,'' and ''is cast in the mould offered to him by the mind of his hearers''; and having obtained from the great minister this curious piece of unconscious self-portraiture, proceeds to draw a picture which is at once a sketch of Gladstone and an analysis of Parliamentary oratory.

We have spoken of Bagehot's powers of speculation and grasp of concrete facts as, what they certainly are in themselves, two different qualities. But we should fail to convey a true view of his mind if we did not insist upon the consideration that in his genius these two characteristics are so intimately blended that they form only one mode of looking at the world either of thought or of actual life. It is in this mixture of different characteristics that half the special power of his intellect, and more than half the special charm of his writing, lie. The following critique on Lord Brougham's restless activity is a charming specimen of Bagehot's style and manner of thought. . . :

> Now, it seems to be a law of the imagination that it only works in a mind of stillness. The noise and crush of life jar it. 'No man,' it has been said, 'can say, I *will* compose poetry'; he must wait until—from a brooding, half-desultory inaction—poetry may arise, like a gentle mist, delicately and of itself.
>
> I waited for the train at Coventry;
> I hung with grooms and porters on the bridge
> To watch the three tall spires; and there I shaped
> The city's legend into this.
>
> Lord Brougham would not have waited so. He would have rushed up into the town; he would have suggested an improvement, talked the science of the bridge, explained its history to the natives. The quiet race would think twenty people had been there. And, of course, in some ways this is admirable; such life and force are rare; even the 'grooms and porters' would not be insensible to such an aggressive intelligence—so much *knocking* mind. But, in the meantime, no lightly-touched picture of an old story would have arisen on his imagination. The city's legend would have been thrust out; the fairy frost-work of the fancy would have been struck away; there would have been talk on the schooling of the porter's eldest son.

In this passage, if anywhere, we have the concentrated essence of our author's genius. The touch, ''the quiet race would have thought that twenty men had been there,'' and ''there would have been talk on the schooling of the porter's eldest son,'' is really perfect. Brougham's force and Brougham's foibles are hit off in a sentence and a half. The expression, ''*knocking* mind,'' strikes not only at Brougham but at a whole class of character. But there is more in the passage than this. Who can fail to see that in the description of the "brooding, half-desultory inaction" which Bagehot assigns as the condition of disposition under which alone poetry may arise, there is suggested not only a whole theory as to the difference between active and poetical intelligence, but also a picture of one-half of Bagehot's own character? Here at last one comes across his openness to truth. He not only pursued truth, which is a rare thing, but, what is rarer, he let her come freely to him. This intellectual accessibility is patent to intelligent readers in all his writings. It is very closely connected both with his grasp of fact and with his extraordinary insight into character. It tinges every part of his speculations, and is seen nowhere more strongly than in that portion of his political views which has, rightly enough, excited some unfavorable comment. His estimate of Louis Napoleon inevitably jars on the feeling of every one who remembers either the *Coup d'État* or Sedan. One must, however, in fairness to Bagehot, admit that on the particular point which he pressed upon the attention of Englishmen at a time when they were filled with indignation at the massacre of the 2d of December, he was in the main right. He contended not so much that Louis Napoleon was not a scoundrel, as that his power rested on much more permanent foundations than on a success in a street-fight. That the calmness with which Bagehot analyzed the Imperial policy is not wholly a subject of praise, even intellectually, we admit. A man who is never carried away by passion will never understand passion; but it is indisputable that the coolness with which a young man just fresh from college could let all the facts of French politics, even when they were facts which he disliked, have free access to his judgment, is a remarkable testimony to his openness towards truth of every description.

Bagehot's intellectual qualities can in no way be better illustrated than by a comparison with the powers of a man who at present as far surpasses Bagehot in general reputation as he undoubtedly fell short of Bagehot in intellectual freshness and ingenuity. Neither the author of the '**English Constitution**' nor the author of the essay on 'Representative Government' would, we suspect, complain of being compared one with the other. Bagehot and Mill have some strong points of resemblance. Both were thinkers who throughout life mixed more or less in practical affairs. They were both political economists; they were both occupied with political and constitutional problems; they were both free from all undue reverence for received opinions; they were both devoted followers after truth. Yet, despite all these points of similarity, and others which might easily be discovered, it would be difficult to find two writers belonging to the same age and country, and even in a certain degree to the same school, whose turn of mind was at bottom more different. Mill . . . had a clear intellect, which, owing to his paternal training, had early acquired an extraordinary command of all the instruments of logic. . . . By the age of nineteen he could express himself with a clearness and precision rarely attained by a man of twenty-nine. His information was extensive, and his knowledge of the elements of different sciences remarkable. He lacked, however, and lacked through life, all originality of conception or grasp of facts. It was not exactly knowledge which failed him, but the power to bring into one view the experience of every-day existence and the conclusions which he had drawn from books or from reflection. Mill wrote much and ably about the British Constitution. We may be certain he never reflected on the light which might be thrown on the constitution of his country by explaining to himself and his readers how it happens that the English public cares to learn that "the Queen walked on the slopes at Windsor." Mill, again,

had none of Bagehot's power of letting truth flow easily into his mind.

What limited his power of acquiring truth was partly . . . excessive reverence for philosophic dogmas impressed upon him in youth, and partly also an inability, very commonly found with thinkers of considerable power, to gaze calmly at phenomena which do not apparently square with their theories. The truths he saw he could sedulously and devotedly pursue, but his warmest admirers will probably admit that there were truths which he was incapable of seeing. Of such incapacity hardly a trace can be found in Bagehot. His defect, if so it may be called, lay rather in excessive readiness to give weight to considerations which seemed at least fatal to the general theories—for example, in political economy—in the soundness of which he on the whole believed. . . . One feels certainly at times as though the weight given by Bagehot to special experience prevented him from following out to their due length the conclusions which he was above most men capable of deducing from general principles.

It must, however, always be carefully remembered that a dread of empty abstractions, which reminds one sometimes of Burke, was in Bagehot's case nothing but one form of his intense desire to ascertain and welcome what was true. (pp. 426-28)

[*A. V. Dicey*], "*Bagehot's 'Biographical Studies'*," in *The Nation, Vol. XXXII, No. 833, June 16, 1881, pp. 426-28.*

**FORREST MORGAN**   (essay date 1889)

[*Morgan surveys Bagehot's writings in the following excerpt from the preface to the first collected edition of his works. As one of the earliest critical appraisals of Bagehot to be published in the United States, Morgan's essay is of particular interest for its commentary on Bagehot's description of American democratic government in* The English Constitution.]

It will seem absurd to compare Bagehot with Coleridge, and there certainly was little enough resemblance in life or writings; but the chief work of both was the same,—to uproot the stubborn idea that nothing except what one is used to has any "case." Bagehot harps upon the fact that everything has a case; that institutions and practices are tools to do certain work vital to a society, and cannot be passed upon till we know its needs; and that those needs may demand alternate acceptance and rejection of given institutions, according as discipline is paralyzing progress or progress weakening discipline. He carries this to the very root, evidently taking keen pleasure in making out an excellent case for isolation, for persecution, for slavery, for state regulation of everything from religion to prices, for even the most paralyzing politico-religious despotism,—in short, for everything most hateful to the modern spirit and most mischievous in modern society; he makes it an arguable point whether his own arguments for toleration should be tolerated; he leaves prejudice in favor of any institution in the abstract not a leg to stand on. . . . [As] a piece of analysis to clarify the minds of the intellectual class in the study of events and institutions, to sober sectarian zeal and infuse caution into the framers of political elysiums, [the value of this teaching] can hardly be overrated.

"**Physics and Politics**," of which the above is the vital essence, seems to me his masterpiece, and not even yet rated at its true value. Both its size and its style, though important merits, are drawbacks to its gaining reverence: men will not believe that so small a book can be a great reservoir of new truth, or that one so easy to understand can be a great work of science. Yet after subtracting all its heavy debt to Darwin and Wallace, Spencer and Maine, Tylor and Lubbock, and all the other scientific and institutional research of his time, it remains one of the few epoch-making books of the century: the perspective of time may perhaps leave this and [Darwin's] ''Origin of Species'' standing out as having given us clearest knowledge of the springs of change and progress in the world,—this doing for human society what that did for organic life. And in one respect Bagehot's work, though inspired by the other, is the more striking,—it is so short. It is hardly more than a pamphlet, one can read it in an evening: yet it contains a mass of ideas which could be instructively expanded into several large volumes; and I do not know of any work which is a master-key to so many locks, and supplies the formula for so many knotty historical problems. Most important is the terrible clearness with which he brings out the lack of any necessary connection between the interests of the individual and those of the society (that is, the individuals of the future), and their direct antagonism often for ages; this fact alone is the source of half the tragedy of the world. But it makes the book a profoundly saddening one, as anything must be which recalls the infinite helplessness of human endeavor against the mighty forces of whose orbits we can hardly see the curve in thousands of years; one must have little imagination not to be impressed by it as by a great melancholy epic. It shows also (though Bagehot evidently did not perceive it) that ''the fools being in the right'' and the intelligent thought of a society wrong half the time results from natural law,—from the fact that ultimate benefit through the strengthening of the society involves vast immediate evils, the popular instinct feeling only the former and the cultivated thought perceiving only the latter; and consequently disproves his own political creed that a democratic government cannot be as good as a ''deferential'' one. In fact, that theory dissolves into a tissue of fallacies and verbal quibbles as soon as one begins to analyze it. (pp. ix-xi)

The economic worth or novelty of ''**Economic Studies**'' I am not competent to estimate; but that feature is not to me its chief interest, and I doubt if it is its chief value, which is rather historic and social. The book is mainly a re-survey of the ground traversed in ''**Physics and Politics**,'' with which it is identical in aim in a more limited sphere,—to prove that modern advantages were ancient ruin, and modern axioms ancient untruths. It buttresses the same points with many new illustrations and expositions; and contains besides a mass of the nicest and shrewdest observations on modern trade and society, full of truth and suggestiveness. That it was left a fragment is a very great loss to the world. . . . (p. xii)

Regarding the ''**English Constitution**,'' appreciation of its immense merits must be taken for granted; praising it is as superfluous as praising Shakespeare. Every student knows that it has revolutionized the fashion of writing on its subject, that its classifications of governments are accepted commonplaces, that it is the leading authority in its own field and a valued store of general political thought. As an analysis of the English system and an essay on comparative constitutions, it will not lose its value; as a treatise on the best form of constitution and a manual of advice for foreigners, it is a monument of the futility of such work, for the course of events since his death seems sardonically designed for the express purpose of making a wreck of it. The last decade has done more than the previous four to compel a total recasting of much political speculation based at once on long experience and seemingly unassailable theory. In [America] some apparent axioms, further confirmed

by the test of ninety years, have been upset by that of a hundred; in France, recent history has justified Bagehot's theory as a philosopher by stultifying his conclusions as an Englishman, and proving his governmental prescription to be quackery as a panacea; in his own country some of the leaders of thought are looking wistfully toward the conservatism of our system as an improvement on the unfettered democracy of theirs,— an ironical commentary on his book. . . . [The] difference in the [political] situation from that of a few years ago is so great that the rather complacent tone of the book already grates on one as being decidedly out of place, and even gives it an unjust appearance of shallowness. (pp. xii-xiii)

[Bagehot's utterances on American subjects] were in general so fair, often so weighty and valuable, and always so different in kind from the ignorant ill-will toward anything foreign in which every national press is steeped, that we can feel no irritation even where his judgment is most severe. Besides, he confined his criticisms mainly to positive institutions, which can be modified at will; and did little carping at social facts, which is scarcely more than a waste of breath even from a native and quite that from a foreigner,—such facts not being conscious creations but instinctive embodiments of social necessities, which adjust themselves as needed and which their very creators are powerless to change. It would be silly, therefore, to resent the little streaks of complacent John-Bullism which lurked even in that least insular of minds; but I confess to a touch of malicious satisfaction in this proof that he was human and an Englishman. Of this sort is the remark, in the most permanently delicious passage he ever wrote (that on early reading in the essay on Gibbon [in ''**Literary Studies**'']), ''Catch an American of thirty; tell him about the battle of Marathon,'' etc. What he supposed the historical teaching in American colleges to consist of, it is impossible to say; apparently, analyses of the battle of New Orleans, and panegyrics on Sam Houston and Davy Crockett. But all literature may be challenged to furnish anything equal in absurdity to the grave deliverance in ''**Physics and Politics**,'' that ''A Shelley in New England could hardly have lived, *and a race of Shelleys would have been impossible.*'' Shelley would have been no whit more out of key with the community than were Alcott and Thoreau, and he could not well have received less sympathy here than he did at home; and in what quarter or epoch of the world since the Silurian age ''a race of Shelleys'' would have been possible, defies imagination,—it certainly was not England in 1800 + . It is hard to believe that Bagehot did not have some intelligible thought in writing this piece of sublimated nonsense, but I cannot form the least idea what.

These of course are trifles; but in both the great aspects of [the American] system, the political and the social, he omits or mistakes essential facts. To be sure, in the social aspect he bases a gloomy view of the future on a much too complimentary view of the present; but it must have struck so impartial a seeker after truth as a *very* remarkable and gratifying coincidence, that both the political and the social system of his own country should be the best in the world, not only for present happiness but for future elevation.

First, politically. The ''**English Constitution**'' is ostensibly not a brief for that system, but a judicial work on comparative constitutions; and from such a standpoint it is a serious flaw that he ignores wholly the factor of stability, to which everywhere else he attaches supreme value. All progress and even good government must be sacrificed if necessary to keep the political fabric together, is the entire *raison d'être* of the ''**Let-**

ters on the Coup d'État''; if a government cannot keep itself alive, it makes no difference how good it is. Much of ''**Physics and Politics**'' and ''**Economic Studies**'' rests on the same thesis: unity of action is of such prime importance to the world that a disciplined band of semibarbarians often crushes out an advanced but loose-knit society; the same idea recurs again and again in his other writings. Yet when he contrasts the English with the American system, national feeling triumphs over abstract philosophy, with the result of exactly reversing the relations of the two systems. . . . My contention is, that every point he makes in favor of the English system—and his arguments are of immense weight and often unanswerable— is an equal point in favor of pure democracy and against his own distrust of the people, by showing that the freer they are left to their own will the better they manage. Nothing can be truer than that a cabinet system keeps the political education of the masses at the highest pitch, and that one like ours injuriously stints it. But thoroughness of political education results from directness of political power; and while a champion of democracy is perfectly consistent in thinking this an advantage and favoring cabinet government, its advocacy by Bagehot on that express ground presents the grotesque spectacle of a great thinker employing his best powers in confuting his own creed. (pp. xiii-xvi)

His theory of the social effects of democracy is wildly imaginary, and very diverting to an American. He actually assumes that the theory of democratic social equality is realized as a fact, and that bootblacks and porters are the social equals (or at least think themselves so and act as if they were) of the rich and the ''old families''; and bases on this assumption a highly complacent thesis of the great superiority of English society, as one of ''removable inequalities,'' which is one of the most elaborately absurd pieces of social speculation ever published. In the first place, his facts are all wrong. Social equality is a chimera anyway, and in few sections of the earth is there less either of the practice or the theory than in the older cities of the United States. . . . [Society] is stratified by money, family connections, and occupation, here as everywhere, and England itself cannot surpass the minuteness of gradations and the subtlety of distinctions. (p. xvi)

The biographical papers vary much in merit; but the best of them are of the very first rank, among not only his writings but all writings of the kind. Like the literary essays, they are at once helped and harmed by his passion for making the facts support a theory; but the benefit is much greater than the injury. They have two special merits in great strength: they are wonderfully vivid in portrayal of character,—the subjects stand out like silhouettes, and one knows them almost like the hero of a novel; and they present the important political features of the times with stereoscopic and unforgetable clearness. In these respects he far surpassed the most famous master in this line, Lord Macaulay. . . . Bagehot, too, has an unequaled skill in so stating his facts and his deductions as to force one to remember them,—the highest triumph of a literary style. A careless person may read an essay of Macaulay's with great delight, carry away a wealth of glittering sentences, and be absolutely unable to remember the course or connection of events,—the uniform brilliancy destroying the perspective and leaving nothing salient for the mind to grasp; but nobody who reads one of Bagehot's historical papers can lose the clue to the politics of the time any more than he can forget his name. (p. xviii)

The literary essays are unfailingly charming, and exhibit Bagehot's wit and freshness of view and keenness of insight, and

the wide scope of his thought, more thoroughly than any other of his writings; and their criticism is often of the highest value. Yet I do not rate them his best. They have the merit and the defect of a consistent purpose,—a central theory which the details are marshaled to support. The merit is, that it makes them worth writing at all; the defect, that the theory may be wrong or incomplete, and the facts garbled to make out a case for it. For example, Macaulay's character and views are both distorted to round out Bagehot's theory of the literary temperament and its effects. The theory is only half true to begin with: the shrinking from life and preference for books which he attributes to an unsensitive disposition is often enough the result of the exact reverse,—an over-sensitive one, like a flayed man, which makes it hard to distinguish impressions because all hurt alike. . . . Macaulay could not have been the able administrator and effective parliamentary speaker he was, without much more capacity to see life and men with his own eyes than Bagehot allows him; and how any one can read the ''Notes on the Indian Penal Code'' and still maintain that Macaulay's residence in India taught him nothing, I cannot comprehend. . . . Bagehot more than atones for this, however, by a signal service to Macaulay's repute in pointing out that the vulgar cant which rates him as a mere windy rhetorician is the exact reverse of the truth, and that the source of his merits and defects alike was hard unspiritual common-sense.

The miscellaneous nature of the essays was a great advantage to a shrewd and humorous mind like his, by not exacting a petty surface consistency: he could utter all sorts of contradictory or complementary half-truths, shoot the shafts of his wit at friend and foe alike, and gibe at all classes of society as their ridiculous aspects came into view. (pp. xix-xx)

[In ''**Lombard Street,**'' Bagehot] devoted the highest literary talent to the theme of his daily business, and has produced a book as solid as a market report and more charming than a novel. It is one of the marvels of literature. There has rarely been such an example of the triumph of style over matter,— Macaulay himself never succeeded in giving more exhaustless charm to things which few can make readable at all; and it is a striking example of his great faculty of illuminating every question by illustrations from the unlikeliest sources. There is a fascination about it surpassing that of any other of his writings: its luminous, easy, half-playful ''business talk'' is irresistibly captivating, and after reading it a hundred times, I cannot pick it up without reading a good share of it again. . . . [Its] merits or defects as a banker's manual will have nothing to do with its immortality, for sooner or later its use in that capacity must pass away. It will live as a picture, not as a textbook; ages after the London of our time is as extinct as the Athens of Pericles, it will be read with delight as incomparably the best description of that London's business essence that anywhere exists.

Of the ''**Articles on the Depreciation of Silver,**'' it must be said that the course of events has not thus far supported their thesis. It seems most probable that the increased use of tools of credit—which is the same thing as the growth of mutual confidence, bred by civilization and commerce—has permanently lessened the needful stock of coin, and that consequently the use and value of the bulkier metal have started on a downward road which can never ascend. . . . But aside from their main purpose, the articles contain much admirable exposition of trade facts and principles, richly worth studying. (pp. xxi-xxii)

[The ''**Letters on the French Coup d'État''**] are perennially entertaining and wholesome reading, full of racy wit and capital argument; they contain the essence of all his political philosophy, and he swerved very little from their main lines; and with all their limitations and perversities, they would be an invaluable manual for our politicians and legislators,—their faults are too opposed to our rooted instincts to do the smallest harm, and they harp on those primary objects of all government which demagogues and buncombe representatives forget or never knew. They are still more remarkable as the only writings of so young a man on such a subject whose matter is of any permanent value, and as showing how early his capacity for reducing the confused details of life to an embracing principle gained its full stature. (pp. xxii-xxiii)

> *Forrest Morgan, in a preface to* The Works of Walter
> Bagehot, Vol. I *by Walter Bagehot, edited by Forrest
> Morgan, The Travelers Insurance Company, 1889,
> pp. i-xxiv.*

## WOODROW WILSON   (essay date 1895)

[*The twenty-eighth president of the United States and the author of several political treatises, Wilson was influential in popularizing Bagehot's works among American readers. In the essay excerpted below, which first appeared in the* Atlantic Monthly *in November, 1895, Wilson focuses on Bagehot's strengths and weaknesses as a political thinker. While criticizing his inability to devise principles of political action for future generations and his opposition to popular government, Wilson praises Bagehot's political writings for their clarity and, especially, their humor. In addition, Wilson emphasizes the catholicity of Bagehot's intellect, attributing his political wisdom partly to his knowledge of literature, economics, and human nature.*]

Walter Bagehot is a name known to not a few of those who have a zest for the juiciest things of literature, for the wit that illuminates and the knowledge that refreshes. But his fame is still singularly disproportioned to his charm; and one feels once and again like publishing him, at least to all spirits of his own kind. It would be a most agreeable good fortune to introduce Bagehot to men who have not read him! To ask your friend to know Bagehot is like inviting him to seek pleasure. Occasionally, a man is born into the world whose mission it evidently is to clarify the thought of his generation, and to vivify it; to give it speed where it is slow, vision where it is blind, balance where it is out of poise, saving humor where it is dry,—and such a man was Walter Bagehot. When he wrote of history, he made it seem human and probable; when he wrote of political economy, he made it seem credible, entertaining,—nay, engaging even; when he wrote criticism, he wrote sense. You have in him a man who can jest to your instruction, who will beguile you into being informed beyond your wont and wise beyond your birthright. Full of manly, straightforward meaning, earnest to find the facts that guide and strengthen conduct, a lover of good men and seers, full of knowledge and a consuming desire for it, he is yet genial withal, with the geniality of a man of wit, and alive in every fibre of him, with a life he can communicate to you. One is constrained to agree, almost, with the verdict of a witty countryman of his . . . that when Bagehot died he "carried away into the next world more originality of thought than is now to be found in the three Estates of the Realm." (pp. 74-5)

Those who know Bagehot only as the writer of some of the most delightful and suggestive literary criticisms in the language wonder that he should have been an authority on practical politics; those who used to regard the "London Economist" as omniscient, and who knew him only as the editor of it,

marvel that he dabbled in literary criticism, and incline to ask themselves, when they learn of his vagaries in that direction, whether he can have been so safe a guide as they deemed him, after all; those who know him through his political writings alone venture upon the perusal of his miscellaneous essays with not a little surprise and misgiving that their master should wander so far afield. And yet the whole Bagehot is the only Bagehot. Each part of the man is incomplete, not only, but a trifle incomprehensible, also, without the other parts. What delights us most in his literary essays is their broad practical sagacity, so uniquely married as it is with pure taste and the style of a rapid artist in words. What makes his financial and political writings whole and sound is the scope of his mind outside finance and politics, the validity of his observation all around the circle of thought and affairs. He was the better critic for being a competent man of business and a trusted financial authority. He was the more sure-footed in his political judgments because of his play of mind in other and supplementary spheres of human activity. (pp. 82-3)

It would be superficial criticism to put forward Bagehot's political opinions as themselves the proof of his extraordinary power as a student and analyst of institutions. His life, his broad range of study, his quick versatility, his shrewd appreciation of common men, his excursions through all the fields that men traverse in their thought of one another and in their contact with the world's business,—these are the soil out of which his political judgments spring, from which they get their sap and bloom. In order to know institutions, you must know men; you must be able to imagine histories, to appreciate characters radically unlike your own, to see into the heart of society and assess its notions, great and small. Your average critic, it must be acknowledged, would be the worst possible commentator on affairs. He has all the movements of intelligence without any of its reality. But a man who sees authors with a Chaucerian insight into them as men, who knows literature as a realm of vital thought conceived by real men, of actual motive felt by concrete persons, this is a man whose opinions you may confidently ask, if not on current politics, at any rate on all that concerns the permanent relations of men in society.

It is for such reasons that one must first make known the most masterly of the critics of English political institutions as a man of catholic tastes and attainments, shrewdly observant of many kinds of men and affairs. Know him once in this way, and his mastery in political thought is explained. If I were to make choice, therefore, of extracts from his works with a view to recommend him as a politician, I should choose those passages which show him a man of infinite capacity to see and understand men of all kinds, past and present. (pp. 87-9)

Examples may be taken almost at random. There is the passage on Sydney Smith, in the essay on the **"First Edinburgh Reviewers."** We have all laughed with that great-hearted clerical wit; but it is questionable whether we have all appreciated him as a man who wrote and wrought wisdom. Indeed, Sydney Smith may be made a very delicate test of sound judgment, the which to apply to friends of whom you are suspicious. There was a man beneath those excellent witticisms, a big, wholesome, thinking man; but none save men of like wholesome natures can see and value his manhood and his mind at their real worth.

> Sydney Smith was an after-dinner writer. His
> words have a flow, a vigor, an expression, which
> is not given to hungry mortals. . . . There is
> little trace of labor in his composition; it is

poured forth like an unceasing torrent, rejoicing daily to run its course. And what courage there is in it! There is as much variety of pluck in writing across a sheet as in riding across a country. Cautious men . . . go tremulously, like a timid rider; they turn hither and thither; they do not go straight across a subject, like a masterly mind. A few sentences are enough for a master of sentences. The writing of Sydney Smith is suited to the broader kind of important questions. For anything requiring fine nicety of speculation, long elaborateness of deduction, evanescent sharpness of distinction, neither his style nor his mind was fit. He had no patience for long argument, no acuteness for delicate precision, no fangs for recondite research. Writers, like teeth, are divided into incisors and grinders. Sydney Smith was a molar. He did not run a long, sharp argument into the interior of a question; he did not, in the common phrase, go deeply into it; but he kept it steadily under the contract of a strong, capable, jawlike understanding,—pressing its surface, effacing its intricacies, grinding it down. Yet this is done without toil. The play of the molar is instinctive and placid; he could not help it; it would seem that he had an enjoyment in it.

One reads this with a feeling that Bagehot both knows and likes Sydney Smith, and heartily appreciates him as an engine of Whig thought; and with the conviction that Bagehot himself, knowing thus and enjoying Smith's freehand method of writing, could have done the like himself,—could himself have made English ring to all the old Whig tunes, like an anvil under the hammer. (pp. 89-91)

What strikes one most, perhaps, in . . . [such] passages, is the realizing imagination which illuminates them. And it is an imagination with a practical character all its own. It is not a creating, but a conceiving imagination; not the imagination of the fancy, but the imagination of the understanding. Conceiving imaginations, however, are of two kinds. For the one kind the understanding serves as a lamp of guidance; upon the other the understanding acts as an electric excitant, a keen irritant. Bagehot's was evidently of the first kind; Carlyle's, conspicuously of the second. There is something in common between the minds of these two men as they conceive society. Both have a capital grip upon the actual; both can conceive without confusion the complex phenomena of society; both send humorous glances of searching insight into the hearts of men. But it is the difference between them that most arrests our attention. Bagehot has the scientific imagination, Carlyle the passionate. Bagehot is the embodiment of witty common sense; all the movements of his mind illustrate that vivacious sanity which he has himself called "animated moderation." Carlyle, on the other hand, conceives men and their motives too often with a hot intolerance. . . . The actual which you touch in Bagehot is the practical, operative actual of a world of workshops and parliaments,—a world of which workshops and parliaments are the natural and desirable products. Carlyle flouts at modern legislative assemblies as "talking shops," and yearns for action such as is commanded by masters of action. . . . Bagehot points out that prompt, crude action is the instinct and practice of the savage; that talk, the deliberation of assemblies, the slow concert of masses of men, is the cultivated fruit of civilization, nourishing to all the powers of right action in a society which

is not simple and primitive, but advanced and complex. He is no more imposed upon by parliamentary debates than Carlyle is. He knows that they are stupid, and, so far as wise utterance goes, in large part futile, too. But he is not irritated, as Carlyle is, for, to say the fact, he sees more than Carlyle sees. He sees the force and value of the stupidity. He is wise, along with Burke, in regarding prejudice as the cement of society. He knows that slow thought is the ballast of a self-governing state. Stanch, knitted timbers are as necessary to the ship as sails. Unless the hull is conservative in holding stubbornly together in the face of every argument of sea weather, there'll be lives and fortunes lost. Bagehot can laugh at unreasoning bias. It brings a merry twinkle into his eye to undertake the good sport of dissecting stolid stupidity. But he would not for the world abolish bias and stupidity. He would much rather have society hold together; much rather see it grow than undertake to reconstruct it. (pp. 96-8)

Bagehot's limitations, though they do not obtrude themselves upon your attention as his excellencies do, are in truth as sharp-cut and clear as his thought itself. It would not be just the truth to say that his power is that of critical analysis only, for he can and does construct thought concerning antique and obscure systems of political life and social action. But it is true that he does not construct for the future. You receive stimulation from him and a certain feeling of elation. There is a fresh air stirring in all his utterances that is unspeakably refreshing. You open your mind to the fine influence, and feel younger for having been in such an atmosphere. It is an atmosphere clarified and bracing almost beyond example elsewhere. But you know what you lack in Bagehot if you have read Burke. You miss the deep eloquence which awakens purpose. You are not in contact with systems of thought or with principles that dictate action, but only with a perfect explanation.

You would go to Burke, not to Bagehot, for inspiration in the infinite tasks of self-government; though you would, if you were wise, go to Bagehot rather than to Burke if you wished to realize just what were the practical daily conditions under which those tasks were to be worked out.

Moreover, there is a deeper lack in Bagehot. He has no sympathy with the voiceless body of the people, with the "mass of unknown men." He conceives the work of government to be a work which is possible only to the instructed few. He would have the mass served, and served with devotion, but he would trouble to see them attempt to serve themselves. He has not the stout fibre and the unquestioning faith in the right and capacity of inorganic majorities which make the democrat. He has none of the heroic boldness necessary for faith in wholesale political aptitude and capacity. He takes democracy in detail in his thought, and to take it in detail makes it look very awkward indeed.

And yet surely it would not occur to the veriest democrat that ever vociferated the "sovereignty of the people" to take umbrage at anything Bagehot might chance to say in dissection of democracy. What he says is seldom provokingly true. There is something in it all that is better than a "saving clause," and that is a saving humor. Humor ever keeps the whole of his matter sound; it is an excellent salt that keeps sweet the sharpest of his sayings. Indeed, Bagehot's wit is so prominent among his gifts that I am tempted here to enter a general plea for wit as fit company for high thoughts and weighty subjects. (pp. 98-100)

Had I command of the culture of men, I should wish to raise up for the instruction and stimulation of my nation more than one sane, sagacious, penetrative critic of men and affairs like Walter Bagehot. But that, of course. The proper thesis to draw from his singular genius is this: It is not the constitutional lawyer, nor the student of the mere machinery and legal structure of institutions, nor the politician, a mere handler of that machinery, who is competent to understand and expound government; but the man who finds the materials for his thought far and wide, in everything that reveals character and circumstance and motive. It is necessary to stand with the poets as well as with lawgivers; with the fathers of the race as well as with your neighbor of to-day; with those who toil and are sick at heart as well as with those who prosper and laugh and take their pleasure; with the merchant and the manufacturer as well as with the closeted student; with the schoolmaster and with those whose only school is life; with the orator and with the men who have wrought always in silence; in the midst of thought and also in the midst of affairs, if you would really comprehend those great wholes of history and of character which are the vital substance of politics. (pp. 102-03)

*Woodrow Wilson, "A Literary Politician," in his* Mere Literature and Other Essays, *Houghton Mifflin Company, 1896, pp. 69-103.*

## LESLIE STEPHEN   (essay date 1900)

*[Stephen is considered one of the most important literary critics of the late Victorian and early Edwardian eras. In his criticism, which is often moral in tone, Stephen argues that all literature is nothing more than an imaginative rendering, in concrete terms, of a writer's philosophy or beliefs. It is the role of criticism, he contends, to translate into intellectual terms what the writer has told the reader through character, symbol, and plot. Stephen's analyses often include biographical judgments of the writer as well as the work. As Stephen once observed: "The whole art of criticism consists in learning to know the human being who is partially revealed to us in his spoken or his written words." The following discussion of Bagehot's literary career, focuses on his critical writings. One of the first commentators to praise Bagehot for his psychological insight into the relationship between an author's works and personality, Stephen argues that Bagehot was "most interested in the man behind the books." Stephen also notes that Bagehot's admiration for writers and politicians who displayed a "prosaic type of intellect" was somewhat paradoxical considering his own propensity for abstract theorizing. Stephen resolves the paradox by pointing out that Bagehot believed abstract theories were valid only if based upon facts. This essay originally appeared in 1900 in the* National Review.]

[Bagehot] had far too much intellect to accept the thoroughly cynical conclusions that since we can know nothing we may believe anything, and since philosophy is delusive give up the attempt to theorise at all. On the contrary, his weakness is a rather excessive tendency to theorise. It appears in the literary criticisms. . . . They have, above all things, the essential merits of freshness and sincerity. If he has not the special knowledge, he is absolutely free from the pedantry, of the literary expert. He has none of the cant of criticism, and never bores us with 'romantic and classical' or 'objective and subjective.' When he wants a general theory—as he always does—he strikes one out in the heat of the moment. He has almost a trick . . . of dividing all writers into two classes: philosophers are either 'seers' or 'gropers'; novelists are 'miscellaneous' or 'sentimental'; genius is symmetrical or irregular, and so forth. Such classifications will not always bear reflection: they only give emphasis to a particular aspect; but they show how his mind is always swarming with theories, and how he looks upon literature as a man primarily interested in the wider problems

of the life and character which literature reflects. Critics, of course, might find fault with many of his dicta. He is sometimes commonplace because he tells us how things strike him, and not the less that they have struck every competent writer in much the same way. He writes of Shakespeare and Milton as if he had discovered them for the first time; he can at times utter a crude judgment, because he is too indifferent—if that be possible—to orthodox literary authority, and his literary criticism diverges into psychological or political speculations which are hardly relevant. That means that he is really most interested in the man behind the books. It is characteristic that he attacks the common statement about Shakespeare which declares the man to be unknowable. Matthew Arnold's phrase, 'Others abide our question, thou art free!' is used, rightly or wrongly, to justify a theory which Bagehot holds—and I confess that I agree with him—to involve a complete fallacy. It is this interest in character, the comparative indifference to the technical qualities of books, which he values as bringing us into relations with living human beings, that gives a special quality to Bagehot's work. It implies no want of enthusiasm. Bagehot admires some men who had a personal interest for him, Clough and Hartley Coleridge, even more warmly than most authorities would sanction. He shows at any rate—and that is the vital point—how they affected one of their ablest contemporaries.

Bagehot's strong point, indeed, is insight into character: what one of his critics has called his 'Shakespearean' power of perceiving the working of men's minds. To possess that power a man must be a bit of what is harshly called a cynic. He must be able to check the sentimentalist tendency to lose all characterisation in a blaze of light. His hero-worship must be restrained by humour and common-sense. Carlyle, the great prophet of that creed, could draw most admirable portraits because there was a Diogenes behind the enthusiast; and an underlying shrewdness was always asserting itself behind the didactic panegyric. In Bagehot's case, again, this quality appears in the curious attractiveness for him of the more prosaic type of intellect. His article, for example, upon Macaulay shows the struggle in his mind. He accepts the contemporary estimate of that 'marvellous' book—[*The History of England*]—as was natural to a man whose youth coincided with Macaulay's culmination. He especially esteems a writer who can describe a commercial panic as accurately as M'Culloch, the 'driest of political economists,' and yet make his account as picturesque as a Waverley Novel. He feels keenly the limitations of Macaulay's mind: the incapacity ever to develop his early opinions; the 'bookishness' which made him the slave of accepted Whig formulae; the 'chill nature' (perhaps the word is hardly fair) which made him prefer the prosaic and respectable to the 'passionate eras of our history'. Yet he also recognised what is perhaps too much overlooked, Macaulay's solid common-sense, obscured as it may be by the defects which give so antiquated and wooden an aspect to his political doctrine. Bagehot, on one side, had strong affinities with the old-fashioned Liberalism in which he had been educated. Macaulay showed its merits as well as its defects. He represents that kind of 'stupidity' which Bagehot so thoroughly appreciated—the stupidity which is a safeguard against abstract theories. . . . [He] analysed with singular acuteness the character of Sir Robert Peel, to illustrate the thesis that a 'constitutional statesman is a man of common opinions and uncommon abilities.' He has to represent public opinion—the opinion, that is, of the average man; and it will come naturally to such a man to be converted quite honestly and yet just at the right time; that is, just when other men of business are converted. Originality and Byronic force and fervour would make that impossible. Byron's mind was volcanic, and flung out thoughts which crystallised into indestructible forms like lava. Peel's was one in which opinions resembled the 'daily accumulating insensible deposits of a rich alluvial soil.'

Articles in this vein, full of brilliant flashes of insight, show Bagehot's peculiar power. It is quaint enough to observe the audacious, rapid theorist . . . becoming paradoxical in praise of the commonplace. He was quite in earnest. He admired no one more than Sir G. Cornewall Lewis, the very type of the thoroughly prosaic, solid, utilitarian mind; and not the less that he was himself imaginative and, if not a poet, had marked poetical sensibility. The explanation may be suggested by the doctrine which he applied in his most valuable works. A scientific inquirer must accumulate knowledge of facts, for the whole fabric of science is based upon experience. But he must also be always speculating, co-ordinating, and combining his experience; his mind must be incessantly suggesting the theories till he hits upon the one clue that leads through the chaotic labyrinth which experience presents to puzzle us. Bagehot denounced and ridiculed the theorists who asked for no base of experience and placidly assumed that the fact would conform to the theory. So long as such theories prevail, there can be no stability and therefore no progress. 'Stupidity' is invaluable just so far as it involves a tacit demand that theories should be checked by plain practical application. But stupidity absolute—sheer impenetrability to ideas—was so little to his taste that a main purpose of his writing is to consider how it can be effectually kept under. As a dumb instinctive force, it wants a guide, and he is terribly afraid that it will become refractory and end by being master. There is the problem which he has to solve.

First of all, we must see the facts before our eyes. Bagehot's greatest merit is that he perceives and complies with this necessary condition of useful inquiry. He illustrates a maxim which he is fond of quoting from Paley. It is much harder to make men see that there is a difficulty than to make them understand the explanation when once they see the difficulty. We build up elaborate screens of words and formulae which effectually hide the facts, and make us content with sham explanations. 'The reason,' he says, 'why so few good books are written is that so few people that can write know anything.' An author 'has always lived in a room'; he has read books and knows the best authors, but he does not learn the use of his own ears and eyes. That is terribly true, as every author must sorrowfully admit; and probably it is nowhere truer than of English political philosophers. . . . Bagehot's book upon the British Constitution came like a revelation; simply because he had opened his eyes and looked at the facts. They were known to everybody; they had been known to everybody for generations; and yet, somehow or other, nobody had put them together. Every cog and wheel in the machinery had been described to its minutest details, but the theory supposed to be embodied in its working was hopelessly unreal. (pp. 165-73)

When Bagehot pointed out that the Cabinet was virtually a Committee of the legislative body, and the real Executive elected by and responsible to the Legislature, he was simply putting together notorious facts. They had, no doubt, been more or less recognised. Yet he was not only clearing away a mass of useless formulae, but almost making a discovery, and the rarest kind of discovery, that of the already known. . . . To have disengaged the facts so clearly from the mass of conventional fictions was a remarkable achievement. Bagehot revealed a

plain fact hidden from more pretentious philosophers who had been blinded by traditional formulae. (p. 176)

I have only to remark, in conclusion, how well [Bagehot's clear insight into facts] served him in one other inquiry. Bagehot called himself the last of the old economists. He had a strong sympathy with Ricardo, as with all the leaders of the old-fashioned do-nothing Liberalism. And yet he showed most effectually one of their weaknesses. His *Lombard Street* owes its power to his imaginative vivacity. Instead of the abstract 'economic man'—an embodied formula—he sees the real concrete banker, full of hopes and fires and passions, and shows how they impel him in actual counting-houses. So his discussion of the **'Postulates of Political Economy'** is an exposition of the errors which arise when we apply mere abstract formulae, unless we carefully translate them in terms of the facts instead of forcing the facts into the formulae. When a dull man of business talks of the currency question, says Bagehot, he puts 'bills' and 'bullion' into a sentence, and does not care what comes between them. He illustrates Hobbes's famous principle that words are the money of fools and the counters of the wise. The word currency loses all interest if we do not constantly look beyond the sign to the thing signified. Bagehot never forgets that condition of giving interest to his writing. Few readers will quite accept the opinion of his editor, that he has made *Lombard Street* as entertaining as a novel [see excerpt above by Forrest Morgan, 1889]. But he has been wonderfully successful in tackling so arid a topic; and the statement gives the impression made by the book. It seems as though the ordinary treatises had left us in the dull leaden cloud of a London fog, which, in Bagehot's treatment, disperses, to let us see distinctly and vividly the human beings previously represented by vague, colourless phantoms. (pp. 186-87)

*Leslie Stephen, ''Walter Bagehot,'' in his* Studies of a Biographer, *second series, Vol. III, G. P. Putnam's Sons, 1902, pp. 155-87.*

### GEORGE SAINTSBURY   (essay date 1911)

[*Saintsbury was a prominent English literary historian and critic of the late nineteenth and early twentieth centuries. A prolific writer, he composed a number of histories of English and European literature as well as several critical works on individual authors, styles, and periods. Here, Saintsbury commends Bagehot's literary criticism for its "sanity," "sense," and "good-humour."*]

The evils of dissipation of energy have been lamented by the grave and precise in all ages: and some have held that they are specially discoverable in the most modern times. It is very probable that Criticism may charge to this account the comparatively faint and scanty service done her by one who displayed so much faculty for that service as Walter Bagehot. A man whose vocations and avocations extend . . . from hunting to banking, and from arranging Christmas festivities to editing the *Economist,* can have but odd moments for literature. Yet this man's odd moments were far from unprofitable. His essay on *Pure, Ornate, and Grotesque Art in Poetry* would deserve a place even in a not voluminous collection of the best and most notable of its kind. The title, of course, indicates Wordsworth, Tennyson, and Browning: and the paper itself may be said to have been one of the earliest frankly to estate and recognise Tennyson—the earliest of importance perhaps to estate and recognise Browning—among the leaders of mid-nineteenth century poetry. As such titles are wont to do, it somewhat overreaches itself, and certainly implies or suggests a confusion as to the meaning of "pure." If pure is to mean "unadorned," Wordsworth is most certainly not at his poetical best when he has most of the quality, but generally at his worst; if it means "sheer," "intense," "quintessential," his best of poetry has certainly no more of it than the best of either of the other two. The classification suggests, and the text confirms, a certain "popularity" in Bagehot's criticism. But it is popular criticism of the very best kind, and certainly not to be despised because it has something of mid-nineteenth century, and Macaulayan, materialism and lack of subtlety. This *derbheit* sometimes led [Bagehot] wrong. . . , but oftener it contributed sense and sanity to his criticism. And there are not many better things in criticism than sanity and sense, especially when, as in Bagehot's case, they are combined with humour and with good-humour. (pp. 495-96)

> George Saintsbury, "English Criticism from 1860-1900," in his A History of English Criticism, W. Blackwood and Sons, 1911, pp. 468-514.*

**J. M. KEYNES** (essay date 1915)

[*In the excerpt below, the noted English economist Keynes reviews* The Works and Life of Walter Bagehot. *He cites Bagehot's capabilities as a "psychological analyser" of the "business men, financiers, and politicians" of his day as his greatest strength as a writer.*]

Bagehot's position amongst English economists is unique. Some of his contributions to the subject are generally acknowledged to be of the highest degree of excellence. And yet in some respects it would be just to say that he was not an economist at all. . . . How is it that Bagehot was an economist and yet not an economist? How did he manage to write one of the classics of Political Economy, and yet appear to his relations no more than a brilliant amateur in a subject which he had chosen as a hobby, while really a man of letters and very warm-hearted?

The clue may escape the reader of this volume or that. But now that [the publication of *The Works and Life of Walter Bagehot* has given us an opportunity] of spending some hours over Bagehot's works as a whole, free to dip into *Hartley Coleridge, Cowper,* or *Pitt*, along with the *Postulates of English Political Economy*, and the *Memoirs of the Right Honourable James Wilson*, the answer leaps to the question. Bagehot was a psychologist—a psychological analyser, not of the great or of genius, but of those of middle position, and primarily of business men, financiers, and politicians. He also wrote very well, and had a fine taste, which readily rejected what was shoddy. All these qualities in combination are able to render his literary studies sufficiently pleasant reading. They were adequate, even in 1864, at the height of [Tennyson's] reputation, to reject the pretensions of *Enoch Arden*. But they were equal only to a superficial interpretation of Shakespeare, Milton, or Gibbon. And Bagehot never reaches the level of his reputation except when he is describing or analysing what he has himself observed—that is to say, men of business, and politicians, and the public characters of his time. Nor was it merely the chance of opportunity and neighbourhood which led Bagehot to devote most of his attention to this class of persons. To the analyst whose gifts lay in the observation of what was neither too high nor too low, and who was not specially equipped for the understanding of genius and violent feeling on the one hand, or of servitude, confinement, and distress upon the other, what, in the sixties of the last century,

could offer so absorbing a field as those superior members of British middle class who ruled in Lombard Street and in Westminister? The *Literary Studies* were almost all written before Bagehot was thirty-three. After that he began to find out that it was much more satisfying to his powers to leave Béranger and Milton on one side, and to examine *Mr. Lowe as Chancellor of the Exchequer, Politics as a Profession,* and *Why Mr. Disraeli has Succeeded.*

Little of the sort has ever been attempted in any way equal to Bagehot's psychological observations of English men of business. No other English economist has had either the gifts or the opportunity. They are scattered through his contributions to the *Economist,* but are specially to be sought in the *Memoir of the Right Honourable James Wilson,* and, of course, in *Lombard Street.* (pp. 369-70)

The fate of *Lombard Street* itself has been somewhat curious. In form and intention it is a piece of pamphleteering, levelled at the magnates of the City [the London financial district] and designed to knock into their heads, for the guidance of future policy, two or three fundamental truths. Incidentally, a great deal is described, and in terms which no reader, however little he understands it, can find dull. But never was a book written with less eye on examination candidates. The purpose was practical, and much of it has been attained. But for the last twenty years the book has achieved a secondary destiny. It has become the one book in the whole library of economic literature which every economic student, however humble, will have read, though he may have read nothing else. Re-reading *Lombard Street,* I find it strikes me as only very moderately suited for this position. Part of it deals with obsolete facts and part with obsolete controversies, and a large part more is extremely difficult. I had forgotten how difficult the book is—read, that is to say, with a view to understanding the sentences and not merely for the enjoyment of their sound and general aspect. I suppose teachers prescribe it, fearful of disclosing prematurely the real character of the subject to be studied, and in hope to persuade the young student that Political Economy is quite different from what it really is, and much more amusing. And I suppose students read it with so much pleasure on account of certain occasional striking passages, which must affect anyone pleasurably, and a sort of glamour of intense reality which is immediately apparent even to readers who may have little or no idea of what, in fact, this reality is. To understand *Lombard Street* brings added pleasure. But it is not necessary to understand it much in order to enjoy it a good deal.

Perhaps the most striking and fundamental doctrine in *Lombard Street*—to recur to my thesis—is, in a sense, psychological rather than economic. I man the doctrine of the Reserve, and that the right way to stop a crisis is to lend freely. And the analysis of the position and government of the Bank of England, which is all extraordinarily well done, is valuable because it is at once felt to be a result of close and direct observation. The theoretical parts of *Lombard Street,* on the other hand, are not very good. The analysis of depressions and the account of the process by which prices rise are rather confused and rather superficial. Bagehot is not in the first rank when he travels outside the field of his own acute observation and attempts a train of inference which is too long for him or for which, not truly caring, he has not a steady patience. His essays on the *Depreciation of Silver,* for example, are clearly secondrate, neither good theory nor good fact. The essay on *Universal Money* is not without good passages, but does not particularly deserve to live.

Yet it is not just to Bagehot to limit his first-rate contributions to Political Economy to his observations of the mind and quality and character of the acutal living individuals who perform the operations of business. He was also immensely interested in another class of individuals, namely, economists themselves, and he loved to conjecture what sort of people the leading English economists were, and how it was they came to write in the manner they did. Bagehot's brief examination of the character of English economists, and of the quality, bias, and origins of English Political Economy (in the introduction to the *Economic Studies*), deserves to be printed as a preface to all our leading text-books. That Bagehot should have projected a work in three volumes on Political Economy, of which the second was to be made up of biographies of celebrated economists, is characteristic of an interest which is apparent in a great many of his essays. Nothing, for example, interested him so much about Adam Smith and Ricardo as that the absent student should have been so full of practical sagacity, while the stockbroker, who made a large fortune, was the founder of a science of abstractions. The reflection is to be found in one of his earliest essays, and recurs unchanged in one of his latest. It is largely because he was so much interested in the relations to what they wrote of Adam Smith and Ricardo themselves, and in their own minds and situations, that what he has to say about them is valuable. Such a comment as that "Adam Smith evidently hurries over the abstract part of it, because he thinks his readers will not attend to it," is worth a dozen pages of criticism now too minute for the time of day. (pp. 371-72)

*J. M. Keynes, "The Works of Bagehot," in The Economic Journal, Vol. XXV, No. 99, September, 1915, pp. 369-75.*

## THE EARL OF BALFOUR  (essay date 1927)

[*In addition to describing Bagehot's method of analysis in* The English Constitution, *the earl of Balfour discusses the role of the House of Lords and monarchy in performing what Bagehot termed the "efficient" and "dignified" functions of government. While noting that Bagehot succeeded in uncovering the actual workings of English government through a first-hand examination of political life, the earl of Balfour points out that he failed to recognize the importance of the English temperament and character in the development of the country's political system. This essay was written in 1927.*]

Constitutional treatises are not usually regarded as light reading, yet surely he who thinks Bagehot's **'English Constitution'** dull must have brought a dull mind to its perusal. The theme no doubt is weighty. But the author has treated it with an easy originality of manner and method which should make it as attractive to readers of this generation as to us who first read it some sixty years ago. Critics of manner may perhaps allege that the style occasionally wants finish; but they must be hard to please if they deny that it is forcible, rapid, high spirited, and clear—that it is always spontaneous and never lacks point.

To my thinking the method is as characteristic as the manner, and not less excellent. It is possible to theorize about politics in many different ways and from many different points of view. Constitutions may be traced historically, described legally, compared critically. . . . The field therefore is large, and, unless I mistake him, Bagehot was not by temperament averse to far-reaching generalizations. But in the volume of 1867 he wisely narrowed his main theme to a single question—how in the years round about 1865-6 (years within his own personal experience) was the work of governing Great Britain actually

performed? He did not pedantically eschew illustrative material. But he never wholly lost sight of his main subject and was rarely faithless to his method.

What was that method? It can perhaps best be understood from a judgement which, in one of his essays, he passes on the author of an unsuccessful political biography, namely that he 'did not look *closely and for himself* at real political life'. Bagehot was not infallible. But he *did* practise his own precepts; he *did* look *closely and for himself* at real political life. Hence his ceaseless endeavours to discover how public business was in fact transacted, as distinguished from the way in which its transactions was officially described; hence the contempt with which this master of political writing regarded what he called the 'literary' view of constitutional procedure. (pp. v-vi)

[The historical setting in which Bagehot wrote the **'English Constitution'**] is of some importance. It not only explains the allusions to passing events in Britain with which he enlivens his pages, but explains why almost all his foreign illustrations were drawn from America and not from Europe. In 1866 the only great nation which had experience of free institutions outside Great Britain was America. . . . It was natural therefore that he should look across the Atlantic if he desired to find a parallel, and perhaps a contrast, to the constitution he had undertaken to discuss.

For purposes of illustration he could not, I suppose, have done better. For the part of the British constitution which most interested him, and on which, as I think, he did his best work, was the one most obscured by 'literary' treatment, and least like anything to be found in the United States. Its real character could best be understood not through a study of its origins, but by comparing and, if need be, contrasting it with its great contemporary across the sea. This he called the Presidential system; the British practice he described as the Cabinet system; and if his readers desire to understand his conceptions of the latter, they cannot do better than observe where and how the two most obviously differ. (pp. vii-viii)

It might perhaps be thought that after his brilliant analysis of Cabinet Government there was little for Bagehot to say about the British Constitution except by way of epilogue. He had made a resolute effort to penetrate the legal forms and ceremonial trappings which cluster round ancient institutions till he reached the core of our national administration. He had insistently inquired how we—a self-governing community— did in fact govern ourselves; and to all seeming he had found the answer. We govern ourselves through a Cabinet, selected from the legislature, presided over by a Prime Minister, and entirely dependent on a House of Commons which we ourselves have chosen. What more is there to be said? It is true that we have a Second Chamber; but it plays, and in modern times has always played, a secondary part. It is true that we have a Monarchy; but what, under the Cabinet system, can the Monarch have to do but act on the advice of his Ministers, take the supreme part on great ceremonial occasions, and assist works of general beneficence by his sympathy and patronage? Or (to translate these questions into Bagehot's peculiar terminology) since the 'efficient parts' of the constitution work so well, why trouble much about the parts which are predominantly 'dignified'?

To this question Bagehot would, I think, have replied *in the first place* that in the case both of the House of Lords and the Monarchy there are 'efficient' as well as 'dignified' elements to be taken into account. And no doubt he is right. During the last 140 years or so in which the making of constitutions has greatly occupied the Western World, the need for a Second Chamber has rarely been successfully disputed; and the House of Lords, though not the invention of constitution-makers, has long and honourably filled that position. . . . [It is] richer in eminent specialists than the other House, and it certainly provides them with much fuller opportunities for expressing their views in Parliamentary debate. (pp. xiii-xiv)

[In the British Monarchy Bagehot also] found elements which belonged to the 'efficient' rather than to the 'dignified' parts of our Constitution. He held (most rightly) that, quite apart from forms and ceremonies, a Monarch of experience and capacity, fully informed on public affairs, and in close personal touch with his Ministers, would always be a most valuable element in the body politic. He thought the post of 'Sovereign over an intelligent and political people was the post which a wise man would choose above any other'. . . . With some naïveté he has indicated the sort of speech that on fitting occasions such as a King might make to his Ministers. He would address them (it appears) somewhat as follows:

> The responsibility of these measures is upon you. Whatever you think best must be done. Whatever you think best shall have my full and effectual support. *But* you will observe that for this reason and that reason what you propose to do is bad; for this reason and that reason what you do not propose is better. I do not oppose, it is my duty not to oppose; but observe that I *warn*. . . .
>
> (pp. xv-xvi)

There is a certain unintended humour in this sketch of an imaginary address by an imaginary Monarch to imaginary Ministers on the problems raised by an imaginary crisis. Its object, however, is clear enough, and no one need criticize its substance. It is at any rate in perfect harmony with Bagehot's view that constitutional Kings, *if* they possess character, ability, and industry, may even in matters of pure policy do very valuable service to the State.

But he was haunted by the 'if'. He argued that no long hereditary line, be it of Kings or be it of peasants, can maintain a steady level of excellence through many generations. In a Royal line there would doubtless be Queen Victorias and Prince Alberts. But there would also be George the Thirds and George the Fourths;—in other words, there would be men of character and industry but little ability; there would also be men of some ability but no character and little industry. Both these varieties, and others that could easily be imagined, must, even at the best, make an occasional appearance. When that happened we should have a 'bad Monarch', and (says Bagehot) while 'the benefits of a good monarch are almost invaluable, the evils of a bad monarch are almost irreparable'. . . . (pp. xvi-xvii)

Presumably this (surely somewhat excessive) estimate of Royal influence refers rather to social than to political affairs, and is therefore scarcely within the compass of a discussion on the Constitution. Let us then turn to politics proper, and consider his views on the Monarchy regarded as representing the 'dignified' side of our institutions. They are easily summarized. He thought it a national necessity, but a necessity born of our national weaknesses. On both these points his opinions were expressed with all his usual vigour. As regards *necessity,* he tells us, for example, that the 'use of the Queen (Victoria) in a dignified capacity is incalculable'; that 'without her in En-

gland the English Government would fail and pass away' . . . , and that 'the "efficient" part (*i.e.* the Cabinet system) depends upon the "dignified" part for the power which the "efficient" part requires but cannot itself produce'. As regards the national weaknesses which produced the necessity, he is quite as uncompromising; but his theories here require a commentary which I cannot omit. . . . (p. xvii)

Bagehot, it appears, was profoundly impressed by the inequalities he observed in the mental equipment of different sections of the community. He tells us that 'the lower orders, the middle orders, are still, when tried by the standard of the educated "ten thousand", narrow-minded, unintelligent, incurious'. And, he adds a little farther on, 'a philosophy which does not ceaselessly remember, which does not continually obtrude, the palpable difference of the various parts (of the population) will be a theory radically false'. . . . This is certainly not a fault with which his own philosophy can be justly charged. But what was the moral he drew from these uncomfortable reflections? It was that since the population consists of educated thousands and unintelligent millions we must count ourselves fortunate in the possession of a Constitution which has two aspects, appealing respectively to the intelligence of the few and the emotions of the many. For the educated thousands there is the 'efficient' aspect, the whole system of Parliaments, Cabinets, Party Government, and the rest. For the unintelligent millions there is the 'dignified' aspect (described also as 'theatrical', 'mystical', 'religious', or 'semi-religious'), which delights the eye, stirs the imagination, supplies motive power to the whole political system, and yet never strains the intellectual resources of the most ignorant or the most stupid. It is, of course, bound up with the Monarchy; indeed to all intents and purposes it *is* the Monarchy. It provides the disguise which happily prevents the ordinary Englishman from discovering that he is not living under a Monarchy but under a Republic;—for (says Bagehot) 'it is only a disguised Republic which is suited to such a being as the Englishman in such a century as the nineteenth'.

Our author indeed does not attempt to conceal the friendly surprise (flavoured with a little contempt?) with which he regards those of his countrymen (unhappily the vast majority) who are taken in by this travesty. 'So well is our Government concealed,' he says, 'that if you tell a cabman to drive to Downing Street he will most likely never have heard of it.' But, except in the interest of his profession, why should the cabman have heard of it? The implied criticism, of course, is that while he would certainly know Buckingham Palace where Queen Victoria was performing her 'dignified' duties, he knew nothing of Downing Street where her Cabinet was 'efficiently' carrying on the real business of Government. But need such ignorance provoke either surprise or blame? (pp. xvii-xix)

[Why should Downing Street,] the meeting-place of an unconnected succession of administrations. . . , differing from each other in opinion and glorying in their differences, arouse patriotic feelings in the ordinary citizen? Patriotism involves conceptions of unity and continuity. The coldest patriot recognizes himself as part (by birth or adoption) of an enduring 'Whole'. He has feelings, however vague, about its past. He entertains, however faintly, hopes and fears about its future. How can the machinery of Cabinet Government either suggest or strengthen sentiments like these, even at their lowest level? It assumes their existence. It cannot perform its duties without them. But are they its natural product? Admittedly it works through Party at every stage—Party Cabinets in Downing Street,

Party majorities in the House of Commons, Party majorities in the constituencies. These cannot of themselves give us unity, because they are at once the product and the instrument of partisan separations. They cannot of themselves give us continuity, because partisan majorities have ever proved unstable. They do the Nation's work and on the whole do it well; but is it not at the cost of deepening and hardening national divisions? If therefore Bagehot's cabman sought a shrine symbolic of his country's unity and continuity rather than of its controversies and quarrels, evidently it was to Buckingham Palace that he should have looked rather than to Downing Street.

I am disposed therefore to think that while Bagehot showed admirable skill in penetrating through external forms to administrative realities, he was not equally successful in penetrating through administrative realities to the national qualities which underlie them and make them possible. Indeed he hardly tried. Though the many uncomplimentary things he says about our national incapacities suffice to show that there is a problem to be solved, he made little effort to solve it. He held (as we know) that the vast majority of his fellow countrymen were 'narrow-minded, incurious, unintelligent,' moved for the most part rather by the outward shows than the inner verities of their constitution. Yet he would never have denied that throughout their history they had shown themselves eminently fitted for self-government. He thought them individually incapable of comprehending its 'efficient' parts. Yet he would certainly have owned that, collectively, they have given to the world an example of ordered freedom and reasonable statesmanship which nations not of English race or speech have never found it easy to equal. He would have owned that the institutions under which we are now living have neither been copied from an alien model, nor invented by domestic theorists, but are to all appearance the unpremeditated product of our qualities helped by our good fortune. To complete the bundle of paradoxes, his own teaching seems to show that while this country as a whole yields to no other in its corporate sense of unity and continuity, the working parts of its political system are organized . . . on a Party basis,—in other words, on systematized differences and unresolved discords.

The lines on which a solution of these problems can best be sought has already been indicated, but Bagehot never followed them for any distance. If we would find the true basis of the long-drawn process which has gradually converted medieval monarchy into a modern democracy, the process by which so much has been changed and so little destroyed, we must study temperament and character rather than intellect and theory. (pp. xx-xxii)

> *The Earl of Balfour, in an introduction to* The English Constitution *by Walter Bagehot, Oxford University Press, London, 1928, pp. v-xxvi.*

**MAX LERNER** (essay date 1930)

[*A Russian-born American political scientist, educator, and social commentator, Lerner served as editor of the* Nation *from 1936 to 1939 and has worked as a columnist for the* New York Post *since 1949. His numerous writings include the popular* It Is Later Than You Think *(1938), a study of contemporary politics, and what he considers his most ambitious work,* America As a Civilization: Life and Thought in the United States Today *(1957). Of his political philosophy, Lerner states: "My political convictions are on the left, although I belong to no party. I feel that my energies must lie with the movement toward a democratic socialism."*

*Here, he praises* Lombard Street, Economic Studies, The English Constitution, *and* Physics and Politics *as pioneering works in their respective fields of study. Bagehot was essentially a conservative thinker who possessed no "genuine social vision," according to Lerner. Nevertheless, his works are of interest to modern readers because of their "clear-eyed unfooled realism." This essay was written in 1930.*]

Bagehot's economic writing ranks with the best in the English tradition. The most enduring result of his increasing interest in banking, ***Lombard Street*** . . . , has become classic for its realistic description of the English banking system and its analysis of the logic of its functioning. It shifted the emphasis in the literature of the subject from the discussion of banking legislation and mechanics to an examination of the body of working rules and their effect. It resulted in a new understanding of the function of the Bank of England in keeping the banking reserves of the community.

But Bagehot's mind was not content with pragmatic work of this sort. In his ***Economic Studies*** . . . several essays deal with an analysis of the two basic postulates of English economic theory—the transferability of labor and of capital—and an examination of their validity in the changed economic world that Bagehot knew. In these and in a series of essays on Smith, Ricardo, and Malthus he effectively refuted any notion of the eternal validity of the theory of the founders and showed its necessary context in the England of their own time. Coming at a time when criticism of classical economics was maturing in England, these essays were influential for the cogency with which they called for revision of the classical body of theory within the limits of its own logical premises.

Much the same approach had even more far-reaching results in political science. Bagehot's ***English Constitution*** . . . is probably his most widely read book. In it he abandoned the contemporary preoccupation with political forms, as he abandoned also most of the preconceptions derived from physics. He sought to substitute a discussion of the actual functioning of the political institutions of his day in their cultural and traditional setting. There is something of an anthropological note here, as there is also in ***Lombard Street:*** it is the actual working rules that interest him, and he strips away everything unimportant to get at them. His exposition of the theory of Cabinet government, of the survival value of such institutions as an English monarchy and the House of Lords, and of the function of the House of Commons as an organ of administrative control, has been formative for all subsequent discussions. When anyone sets out today to write a realistic analysis of the English Constitution, like as not he has Bagehot in mind as his archetype. In fact, the book has achieved so complete an acceptance as representing the reality of English government that it has doubtless influenced the shape that political institutions tended to take. Looking back at it now, it seems difficult to decide which was the reality and which the representation. Resting its ultimate explanations of British political institutions on the nature of the British mind it takes its place as a pioneer essay in national political psychology.

The most original and ambitious writing that Bagehot did in social science was his ***Physics and Politics*** . . . , in which "physics" is metonymy for natural science and "politics" for social science. It is the first important attempt to bring out whatever implications Victorian science, especially Darwinism and the new ethnographic writings of Tylor and Lubbock, possessed for the study of the political community. Although its principal premises are thus the premises of biology—evolution and natural selection—and its material largely anthropological, it is in essence a brilliant essay in social psychology, mapping the significance for human history of such forces as custom and revolt, innovation and imitation, conflict and discussion, law and force. Modern social psychology has to a great extent followed in the wake of these leads.

In the heyday of the democratic dogma, Bagehot was an aristocrat at heart—almost an aristagogue. He would have considered himself too hard-headed to feel except at high-wrought moments any real sympathy for the democratic mass. . . . [He] showed the myopic spots in his outlook mainly in underestimating the masses as a creative political force. The common man was to him, as to Carlyle, merely so much human material to be governed well.

On the whole he found little fault with the government that existed. The English Constitution was a creditable achievement; Commons and Cabinet were pleasingly responsive to the electorate; Lords and King served to check a possible mobocracy and heighten the tone of politics. Nor was he less satisfied with the economic fabric. Lombard Street in his book manages to get its work done somehow. Did the scratchings of Karl Marx's pen in the British Museum, and the noise of the discussions in his stuffy parlor, reach Bagehot in the offices of the *Economist?* It is doubtful. He was a banker, one of those who possess the earth. His table was full, he had a horse to ride, cultured men as friends, and a magazine to accept everything he wrote.

I have set down these shortcomings that I might seem to extenuate nothing. It would be folly to claim for Bagehot more than he can lay claim to. He was little concerned with exploring the realm of social possibility. He was a realistic conservative—in some ways a reactionary. But whatever he was, he was a first-rater. What recommends him is his infernal wisdom, and it is that which will make him for a long time modern. If he never attained to the height of inspiration, if he never had any genuine social vision, he was also very rarely fooled. He has opened up for us few areas for social construction, and there is little in him that is gleaming for the eager eye. But there is little in him also for time to corrode.

What a way this Bagehot had of avoiding the flurries and pitfalls of his generation! When everyone else was swallowing Ricardo whole, he saw that the "laws of economics" applied in Ricardian form only to industrialized communities like England, and even to them only approximately. When they were prating about checks and balances and all the pulleys and weights of a mechanistic concept of politics, he wrote his essays on the English Constitution to reveal a living organism. When they were talking about the principles of banking, he wrote a book about Lombard Street—about English bankers as people and the English banking system as a tradition and a going concern. While English dons were still discussing Aristotle's classification of constitutions, or arguing the ethical theory of the state, he mixed a strange concoction of physics and politics and talked about the survival-power of states. In each case his contemporaries have been outlived.

Many of his readers in this decade have been struck with wonder at his insistent psychological approach. He is always reducing his inquiries to terms of how men act and why. Yet this is only a facet of the characteristic that gives all his work some unity—a clear-eyed unfooled realism. He was a psychologist because it helped him to visualize the better what concepts were involved in the situation. A succession of unlike characters marches across his pages. He gave much thought to each of them—Gibbon, Macaulay, Hartley Coleridge, Shelley, Sydney Smith, Adam Smith, Disraeli, Gladstone, Peel, Clough, Napoleon III, Lord Brougham. He studied the man of letters, the banker on Lombard Street, the politician in Parliament. Like Emerson, he saw them as the realities; institutions were their shadows.

He had, in short, a quantity of that merciless sense that survives half-centuries and fails to evoke the most modern smile of derision. He represents what the modern spirit, whittling away the pompous and the sentimental from Victorian thought, can still retain as a credible core. (pp. 310-13)

> *Max Lerner, "Walter Bagehot: A Credible Victorian," in his* Ideas Are Weapons: The History and Uses of Ideas, *The Viking Press, 1939, pp. 305-13.*

**HERBERT READ** (essay date 1930)

*[Read was a distinguished English critic who championed "organic" artistic expression and who was deeply concerned with the role of art in furthering human development. In the following excerpt, he contends that Bagehot's importance as a literary critic has been overshadowed by the success of his writings on politics and economics, and he provides a discussion of the author's critical theories. To Read, Bagehot ranks with Matthew Arnold and Samuel Taylor Coleridge among nineteenth-century literary critics.]*

[*The English Constitution, Physics and Politics,* and *Lombard Street*] perhaps with most people constitute Bagehot's chief claim to fame. And indeed they are almost unparalleled classics, belonging to a small group of which Sir Henry Maine's *Ancient Law* is the prototype, in which scientific subjects are endowed with literary qualities by sheer perspicuity of style and sustained animation of interest. These works are secure in their own particular sphere; our only complaint is that they have in some measure detracted from the singular interest of Bagehot's literary criticism. This is almost the best of its time, and only the speculative figure of Matthew Arnold prevents us from pronouncing it quite the best. Arnold's criticism was more deliberate; in a sense it was more cultured. It was scarcely more decisive. . . . [Arnold] was well aware of Bagehot, and already in 1856 had "traced the same hand" in a series of [Bagehot's] articles in the *National Review,* which articles seemed to him "to be of the very first quality, showing not talent only, but a concern for the *simple truth* which is rare in English literature as it is in English politics and English religion" [see excerpt above, 1856]. . . . [This is] a just estimate of the essential quality of Bagehot's criticism, and there is really little else to say about it, except to show the manner of it. This is nowhere so admirably evident as in the estimates he gives of some of his contemporaries. This is always the severest test of a critic, and if we can still read this part of his criticism with interest, we need have no fear for the rest. There is no nineteenth-century critic, Coleridge and Arnold not excepted, who comes out of such a test so admirably as Bagehot. His essays on two such diverse subjects as Dickens and Clough are not only the first but also the last words on these themes. This is a large claim for such a subject as Dickens, who has been the recipient of so much criticism—but how much of it is really criticism? How much of it is not rather the acceptance of a popular estimate and a rationalization of this estimate? If Bagehot made a mistake, it was to imagine that the popularity was impermanent; but his mistake saved him from the inhibitions that have affected later critics, and he had no hesitation in exposing "the natural fate of an unequal mind employing itself on a vast and various subject".

At the base of all Bagehot's criticism was a certain theory of imagination. He held that "the materials for the creative faculty must be provided by the receptive faculty. Before a man can imagine what will seem to be realities, he must be familiar with what are the realities". But, as he wrote in his essay on Shakespeare, "To a great experience one thing is essential, an experiencing nature". In these two observations Bagehot came nearer to an understanding of the process of literary inspiration than any other critic, with the possible exception of Coleridge. He realized that an imagination which does not build on experience is a baseless fabric; and though this is not an original view, it is one that is often forgotten. His further corollary, that there is no real experience without an experiencing nature, embodies a profounder truth; but this he illustrates rather than explains. Goethe, for example, is contrasted with Shakespeare, and Macaulay with Scott. He does not accuse Goethe and Scott of a lack of imagination—who would?—but he points in the former case "to the tone of his character and habits of his mind. He moved hither and thither through life, but he was always a man apart. He mixed with unnumbered kinds of men, with Courts and academies, students and women, camps and artists, but everywhere he was with them yet not of them. In every scene he was there, and he made it clear that he was there with reserve and as a stranger. He went there *to experience*".

This unexperiencing nature perhaps amounts to no more than a lack of sympathy, but if it were always recognized that sympathy is a necessary component of experience, criticism would be a briefer and more illuminating science.

It is well to remember Bagehot's insistence on sympathy because, in advancing a further and very distinctive characteristic of his criticism, we are in danger of reverting to that false impression of mere hard intellectuality. "What is not possible", he once wrote, "is to combine the pursuit of pleasure and the enjoyment of comfort with the characteristic pleasures of a strong mind"; and this was his indictment of the eighteenth century—through which, however, he recognized there ran "a tonic of business", of political business. His description of the period as "that in which men ceased to write for students and had not yet begun to write for women" has hardly been bettered. It defines three centuries in a sentence. But what he did admire in the eighteenth century, and in Gibbon in particular, was "a masculine tone; a firm strong perspicuous narrative of matter of fact, a plain argument, a contempt for everything which distinct definite people cannot entirely and thoroughly comprehend". And this is the manner of his own writing and the basis of his conception of style: "The most perfect books have been written not by those who thought much of books but by those who thought little, by those who were under the restraint of a sensitive talking world, to which books had contributed something and a various eager life the rest." Bagehot himself came near to this ideal; he was not merely a critic and economist but also a banker and politician; not merely the author of a most penetrative essay on Bishop Butler but also a good horseman and the owner of a pack of beagles. If anything was lacking it was the "sensitive talking world".

These varied interests gave to his mind a universality which is rare in literature but of incomparable value. It may seem, on a superficial view, that Bagehot dissipated his energies over too wide a field; that if he had concentrated on criticism, on politics, or on economics, he might have attained the highest possible reputation in one of these narrower spheres. That would be to mistake the quality of the man and to misjudge the proper value of criticism. The opinion of such a man on one literary topic is worth the life-work of a solitary pedant. . . . [Bagehot possessed that] *centrality* of mind which, on a different scale, he had admired in Béranger: "He puts things together; he refers things to a principle; rather, they group themselves in his intelligence insensibly round a principle. There is nothing *distrait* in his genius; the man has attained to be himself; a cool oneness, a poised personality, pervades him."

Such was the character of Bagehot himself; it omits only his wit and his humour, and these may be left to take care of themselves. Had he lived longer his achievement would have been different: he was still developing. But his niche is enviable as it is. (pp. 197-202)

*Herbert Read, "Bagehot," in his* The Sense of Glory: Essays in Criticism, *Harcourt, Brace Jovanovich, 1930, pp. 179-204.*

## C. H. DRIVER   (lecture date 1931-32)

[*In the following explication of* Physics and Politics, *Driver underscores the significance of the work to the development of modern sociological thought. According to the critic, Bagehot was the first of his contemporaries to recognize the profound sociological implications of the doctrine of evolution. In addition, Driver contends that* Physics and Politics *marks the beginning of a new psychological approach to politics: for the first time evolutionary theory was applied to the study of the development of the human intellect to explain the emergence of organized political communities. Driver's essay was first presented as a lecture at King's College, University of London, during the 1931-32 academic year.*]

[*Physics and Politics*] is not in any sense a book of 'research'; it is essentially a work of speculation. The central idea—the application of the doctrine of the "survival of the fittest" to the development of man and the evolution of his society—was derived from Darwin and Spencer. Hitherto the doctrine had been applied primarily in regard to the formation of biological species. Now Bagehot gave it a new application; that is why he said of his work that "it only amounts to searching out and following up an analogy." And if the central idea was borrowed so were the facts adduced in proof and illustration of it. Besides Spencer, six other writers are mainly responsible for his material: Huxley and Maudsley for his physiological ideas; Maine for his idea of early law; and Lubbock, Tylor, and M'Clennan for his ideas about custom and the nature of primitive societies.

*Physics and Politics* is a book difficult to classify. Indeed, it fits nowhere into conventional academic categories, for it is unique. The nearest approach to it is perhaps to be found in a remarkable essay written forty years earlier by Thomas Rowe Edmonds. But Bagehot's work is not only the product of an older and more mature mind; it also makes use of the great development which had taken place in the biological sciences during those intervening years. Like *Practical, Moral, and Political Economy*, *Physics and Politics* is a brilliant and suggestive guess; but it is based on more firmly established data, and its limits of error are in consequence considerably narrowed. The former book quite obviously stands at the turn of an epoch between the rationalism of the eighteenth century and the positivism of the nineteenth; whereas the latter book is no less obviously within the modern period, and speaks in a language and a spirit akin to our own.

Certainly the title of the book is a misnomer, for "Physics and Politics" conveys, to the present generation at least, no idea of the scope of its subject. Professor Ernest Barker [see Additional Bibliography] has suggested that the title should be "Psychics and Politics," and this would certainly convey a more adequate indication of its contents. But even that would not be entirely appropriate, for the psychological element in the essay is consequent upon a biological and anthropological approach to the fundamental problems of politics. It was essentially a sociological footnote to the doctrine of evolution prevailing in the sixties: a tentative peering not only outward into the remote darkness of prehistory, but also inward into the irrational and subrational forces of human nature inherited from the uncounted ages of the evolutionary process. Bagehot had an extraordinarily clear sense of the vast issues and problems raised by the "new knowledge," and it is little short of marvellous that he should have presented them so vividly in such a short compass—for his essay is only a little over fifty thousand words in length. One might almost call it a prospectus for future research work in the social sciences. To the questions he put anthropologists, social psychologists, and biologists are still daily bringing materials for an answer; and Bagehot's successors are not to be sought in any single linear sequence, but in half a dozen different lines of research. This does not mean to imply, of course, that later workers are necessarily indebted to him, or that he alone was responsible for later developments. It simply means that his brilliant, synthetic mind achieved an *aperçu* of the implications of the evolutionary theory for the sociologist well in advance of his contemporaries, and that subsequent investigation has confirmed the reality of the problems which he envisaged. The clear statement of the issues was itself an important step in intellectual advance.

The problem for which Bagehot attempted to sketch a solution was this: Assuming the truth of the doctrine of natural selection, how are we to account for the momentous *transition* from the brute level of the struggle for existence to the human level of social organisation and co-operation? To Bagehot this *transition* problem was the essential one, and the key to all subsequent development of the human race. In reality, it was the sociological counterpart to the biological problem of the 'missing link.' In the new pentateuch which natural science was writing Bagehot essayed to provide the exodus into human society once the genesis of species was granted. This central issue naturally gave rise to certain subsidiary problems: on the thither side of organised polity was the question, What like was pre-political man? And on the hither side of established society were the questions, How is national character formed? and What are the main processes of social change? Both Darwin and Spencer some eight years previously had seen the vital importance of the issue; but Bagehot's was the first attempt to solve it, and he alone saw at which particular stage of the life-process the key to the riddle might be found. Thus did he prepare the way for Darwin's fuller statement of the question in *The Descent of Man.* . . . (pp. 200-02)

For his answer to the great question, How did *Homo sapiens* pass from the animal to the social level of existence? Bagehot drew upon the newly acquired knowledge already mentioned. To him it had a fourfold significance. First, by making man himself an "antiquity" it suggests the necessity of reading in man's physical structure the whole story of its past development and successive adaptations. Emphasis will thus be put, as never before, on the facts of heredity and transmission. . . . But if the first lesson of biology is the emphasis on continuity the second lesson is the emphasis on the central position of the

nervous system in that story, both as it concerns the individual and the race. Regarding the *individual,* the primary fact is that of reflex action. Bagehot here quotes Huxley in his support. He contends that the development of the individual is synonymous with the development of an integrated system of reflex actions, be those reflex actions natural—*i.e.,* arising from the structure of the spinal cord—or artificial—*i.e.,* coming *via* the brain through conscious effort. Upon these latter Bagehot places the very greatest emphasis, and thus brings us face to face with the whole of the present-day controversy concerning 'conditioned reflexes.' Following Lamarck and Huxley, he believes that conscious effort produces habit, which in its turn becomes 'fixed' as a reflex by the nervous system. Thus the body becomes "charged with stored virtue and acquired faculty." Hence the fact and possibility of education depends on this power of the nervous system to organise conscious effort into reflex acts. As regards the *race,* Bagehot merely extends the above thesis to cover the whole of time. . . . (pp. 202-03)

The third lesson of the new biology is the meaning and reality of progress. This transmitted nerve element becomes "the connective tissue of civilisation," for it enables each generation to transmit to its successor qualities with which it itself did not start. Thus each age is enabled to begin with an improvement on the preceding one, "making nicer music from finer chords," however slow that process may be. Hence the fourth lesson concerns the primacy of moral causes in the developmental process. For Bagehot this is of paramount importance, and the key to his whole argument. It is the 'moral' cause of conscious effort which has physical consequences through the nerves. These consequences get conserved in the body. Thus "it is the continual effort of the beginning that creates the hoarded energy of the end," and the whole of recorded history and the formation of national character is to be interpreted in the light of this theorem. No matter how "mind" be eventually explained, the three essential facts—Effort, Conservation, Transmission—will always remain. "Our mind in some strange way acts on our nerves, and our nerves in some equally strange way store up the consequences, and somehow the result, as a rule and commonly enough, goes down to our descendants."

That assertion is the starting-point for the new sociology, inasmuch as it shows why the toil of the first generation becomes the transmitted aptitude of the next. Moreover, it suggests a totally new approach to the problem of the origin of politics and social processes. The investigator must now undertake the difficult task—with the help of ethnology, anthropology, and the ancillary sciences—of thinking away the physical and moral accretions produced by some thousands of years of development, and of reconstructing the nature and life of man before he had built up for himself that heritage of acquired reactions and social traditions. This heritage, it must be repeated, is a double one: partly physical and partly psychological. Bagehot was one of the first to realise the importance of this fact, and not the least interesting feature of his work is his attempt to explain the relation between these two kinds of acquisition. (pp. 204-05)

In this process of the emergence of socialised man Bagehot sees three great stages: the stage of no-polity, the stage of fixed polity, and the stage of flexible polity; or, as he calls them, the preliminary age, the fighting age, and the age of discussion. These phases overlap, and there is no sharp demarcation between them. Moreover, they are not uniform throughout the world. Some groups have remained fixed at a remote point on the line, while in more fortunate areas progress has been continuous. During the eons of prehistory all the branches of *Homo sapiens* must have developed somewhat, otherwise there would have been no survival whatever. All men progressed from the brute level, through the stage of no-polity, into the stage of fixed polity. But there many of them have stopped. Various factors—particularly the geographical—determined the point at which interpenetration of cultures—and, with it, progress—ceased. Bagehot therefore sets himself to answer three main questions: What was the nature of pre-political man, and how did he come to form a community? What forces held man together in such a community? What social processes caused the improvement and increasing flexibility of the community, and how are they now operative? All these questions are answered in terms of the prevailing doctrine of the "survival of the fittest." (p. 206)

Bagehot draws some ingenious conclusions for the present and the future from his theory of discussion. He thinks discussion does, and will, modify human nature. Many of our great social problems arise from the fact that we have inherited a human nature victorious from a barbarous age. That age fostered action above all else, and man is still prone more to action than to reflection. His most conspicuous failing is his inability to stay quiet and to find out things. Science could only develop with ages of sedentary thought, and only the few are scientists. It is here, in the first instance, that discussion may possibly modify inherited characteristics. Its immediate effect is to stop action, and to foster "the plain position of inevitable doubt." It is precisely because, as Macaulay says, a campaign cannot be directed by a debating society that Bagehot favours discussion. It prevents many campaigns besides the military from being conducted, inasmuch as it ensures elaborate consideration and provides "the greatest hindrance to the inherited mistake of human nature, to the desire to act promptly." Thereby is the League of Nations provided with one of its main arguments of justification.

In another important respect, however, Bagehot looks to discussion to change mankind. He sees in it a possibility of transforming the sex instinct and diminishing its strength. That instinct is far too strong for present-day needs. During the early struggle for existence the maximum of procreation was necessary, and civilised man now inherits this excessive instinct just as he inherits an excessive impulse to action. Misery, vice, and over-population result. But even this can be modified by an extension of the principle of discussion. In support of his contention Bagehot quotes Spencer's theory to the effect that there is a constant struggle in the human organism between "individuation" and "genesis," and that as the nervous system and the brain develop they withdraw vital energy which would otherwise have been used for reproduction. So, as man continues to evolve, his powers of reproduction may be expected to decrease. Bagehot interprets this to mean that those who can be induced to lead an intellectual life will be less procreative, for the amount of energy in each individual is limited; and "nothing promotes intellect like intellectual discussion, and nothing promotes intellectual discussion so much as government by discussion." . . . Finally, it is claimed, government by discussion will alter human nature by strengthening the socially desirable type of character and eliminating the "strongly idiosyncratic mind, violently disposed to extremes." Then will the spirit of reserved scepticism and quickened originality be distributed throughout society.

This explanation of the main stages of social evolution, however, does not fully account for all the differences to be found between groups at the same level of development, since it ignores many psychological processes taking place within the group at the same time that the external forces are operative. One of Bagehot's most striking contributions to the thought of his day is his sketch of just these processes. They are at work throughout the whole course of human development, and are an integral part of that movement.

Bagehot had no clear theory of the unconscious mind; yet he came very near to developing one. And he fully appreciated the strength and significance of unconscious forces in shaping the social life of man. His central thought is to be found in his theorem that "the propensity of man to imitate what is before him is one of the strongest parts of his nature." This fact he used to account for much that was otherwise inexplicable in life. It was but another instance of his realisation of the non-rational forces determining human society. No attempt was made by the author to explain the genesis of this propensity; it was taken for granted. . . . Nor were all its implications developed into anything like a system, as was done a few years later by Tarde in his *Lois de l'imitation*. As in other matters, a few brilliant suggestions were thrown out for the reader's consideration and then left. Yet enough was said to show how far-reaching the theory might be.

Bagehot is quite clear that this capacity for imitation must not be thought of as either voluntary or conscious. "It has its seat mainly in very obscure parts of the mind, whose notions, so far from having been consciously produced, are hardly felt to exist." This "copying propensity" induces man to become more and more like his neighbours. Bagehot instances the case of literary fashions. The growth of these shows in a limited field the working of a general principle operative throughout society. Somehow, and in some unconscious way, a writer "gets a sort of start." He gives the public what it wants; and by supplying something congenial to the minds around him he sets a fashion. But it is an entirely fortuitous occurrence, a chance predominance. Nor is the man who hits upon it necessarily a great man capable of developing his accidental discovery to the full. Yet once the discovery has been made it is quickly taken up by others and amplified. Thus is the character of an 'age' established; thus does the Elizabethan differ from the Augustan age, and so forth. (pp. 210-12)

Precisely the same processes are at work forming the national character. Chance predominance creates a model or type: probably a type which 'works' better than a previous one. The "invincible attraction" ruling all but the strongest minds does the rest and causes them to imitate what is in front of them. . . . It is because of this automatically operative process that such a wide diversity of group tradition is found in similar climatic and geographical areas. Bagehot allows but a small share to these forces in the growth of social patterns and traditions.

This capacity for imitation explains minor social processes too; or, rather, these other processes are but varied applications of the same principle. It accounts for continuous traditions in subordinate groups within the nation—*e.g.,* the style and attitude to be found on the staffs of periodicals. It explains the way in which "the fashion of female dress" spreads from Paris outward. It suggests a main cause not only for passing phases, but for more permanent modifications of tradition. Men are influenced by types rather than by tenets. . . . So both in religion and in politics we may regard a great man as a great new causal factor whose influence radiates forth by the spontaneous working of the laws of imitation. Lastly, Bagehot adumbrates an outline of the psychology of opinion and belief in these terms. He was not an academic psychologist, and his view of the human mind is in places somewhat confusing. Yet he did catch a clear glimpse both of the problem of belief and of some of the factors involved—a problem on which amazingly few people have worked since his day. His main theme is not dissimilar to that of Graham Wallas in *Human Nature in Politics*—that is, the essentially irrational basis of belief in most men.

Imitation and belief are both closely related, and spring from ''the obscurest parts of our nature.'' Just as we imitate what is around us, so we believe what our immediate neighbours believe. We all tend to yield to current infatuations. It is not so much the overt teaching of our friends and our Press: it is the circumambient *assumptions* which we cannot resist—the taken-for-granted-ness which presses upon us on all sides, so that even the greatest sage comes to imbibe the folly of his party or group. The invariable tendency is for the mind to accept as true whatever idea comes clearly before it. Unless we are on our guard the mere presentation of an idea from all sides will itself become a certificate of truth. So do men get caught by the infection of imitation ''in their most inward and intellectual part—their creed.'' (pp. 212-14)

[Bagehot] realised the implications for sociology of the theory of evolution, and raised questions which are still living issues. But he marks the beginning of the psychological approach to politics in a special sense. A psychological approach of a kind had . . . existed since the eighteenth century. . . . Bagehot's chief importance lies in the fact that he renewed that approach afer a crisis in the history of thought. For the Darwinian theory had produced a great difficulty. The doctrine of natural selection was essentially an individualistic one, implying the struggle of each against all. When Darwin wrote *The Origin of Species* he had not applied the principle to human beings or human society. How, then, could society come into being and subsequently develop from such anti-social beginnings?

Bagehot attempts to solve the problem by first stating it in psychological rather than in biological terms. He projects the whole process, so to speak, on to the plane of *mind*. Development is for him the emergence of new mental characteristics. But they are characteristics which have physical consequences in a physical sruggle. It is necessary to emphasise this point, because some commentators have written as though Bagehot's doctrine of the transmission of acquired characteristics was an unimportant part of his theory which might almost be separated from the rest of his teaching. But such a contention would surely destroy the unity of the argument of *Physics and Politics*. It is true that the brevity of Bagehot's book did not allow him to develop all the implications of his thesis. But to the present-day reader the argument is entirely homogeneous, and only the stricter sect of the neo-Darwinians would want to truncate it. Whereas, in fact, one can hardly classify Bagehot as a Darwinian at all, for he is much more in line with the doctrine of creative evolution than with the doctrine of natural selection. (p. 215)

Bagehot does not attempt to explain how mind emerged in the evolutionary process; he takes it for granted. But he does state very clearly that in the struggle beween the mind-body units of that process the balance was constantly being tipped in favour of mind as against the mere physical fact of bodily strength. That is why he begins his essay with a dissertation on the mind-body relationship. It is that relationship which gives mental acquisitions a physical consequence; and it is this hypothesis which enables him to state the whole problem in terms of mind. Consequently it is essential to his purpose that acquired characteristics should be transmitted. In the evolutionary struggle it is the mental traits rather than the physical which have increasing survival value. Two results, therefore, follow. On the one hand is increasing gregariousness, on the other greater control over the process itself. This control concerns not simply the mastery of external nature. The fact that it is a mental event implies control over man's responses to that nature through the growing power of self-determination of the group, and that is the meaning of the ''age of discussion.'' By adopting such a psychological attitude Bagehot escapes the antinomies which the biological doctrine of evolution seemed to present to the social scientist, and so wrote the first chapter of the new book of social psychology. But this was achieved, it must be remembered, by interpreting evolution in Lamarckian terms (derived from Spencer's early writings) rather than in purely Darwinian terms. There is a Darwinian gloss on the essay, it is true. But it might have been essentially the same without *The Origin of Species*.

Bagehot's work was only a beginning, and much was left unexplained. In two respects in particular had an advance to be made before the brilliant suggestions he had thrown out could be developed. First, a new analysis of instinct in the light of the new biology had to be provided. It is a strange fact that Bagehot completely drops the whole of the previous teaching about instinct. . . . Where he uses the word he does so only in the old metaphysical sense, which he rightly realises is virtually meaningless in the new biological context. Hence he is led to say that man has no instincts whatever. Perhaps some of the Behaviourists may approve of this attitude to-day, though that is not the same as saying that Bagehot's analysis of man's endowments was adequate. It was the work of Lloyd Morgan, L. T. Hobhouse, and William McDougall to pursue this line of investigation after an interval of a quarter of a century.

The second respect in which *Physics and Politics* needed supplementing was by the provision of a fuller analysis of the nature of the group mind. Bagehot had grasped some of the basic facts. He understood tradition as the common content of the minds composing the group; and he saw in imitation and suggestion important processes for its growth and transmission. But he suggested no method for its further investigation. Nevertheless, he made a big advance on the two other writers in this field, Comte and Spencer. (pp. 216-17)

> *C. H. Driver, ''Walter Bagehot and the Social Psychologists,'' in* The Social & Political Ideas of Some Representative Thinkers of the Victorian Age, *edited by F. J. C. Hearnshaw, George G. Harrap & Company Ltd., 1933, pp. 194-221.*

## G. M. YOUNG (essay date 1937)

*[Young's description of Bagehot as ''the Greatest Victorian'' is one of the most frequently quoted appraisals of the author. Bagehot is entitled to this distinction, Young asserts, for two reasons. First, his ideas have been more influential than those of his contemporaries in familiarizing modern readers with the most valuable element of the Victorian heritage, which Young describes as ''its robust and masculine sanity.'' Secondly, Bagehot exhibited, in both his writings and personal life, what Young considers the dominant characteristics of the Victorian mind: ''capaciousness and energy.'' Young's essay was first published in two parts, respectively entitled ''The Greatest Victorian'' and ''The Case of Walter Bagehot,'' in the* Spectator *on June 18 and July 2, 1937.]*

I have been turning over in my mind the names of some who might be candidates for the title of the Greatest Victorian. One needs a man, or woman, who is typical of a large and important class: rich in the abilities which the age fostered: one who made a difference, and under whose influence or direction we are still living. These being the notes by which posterity, looking back, recognizes the really great men of a former time, in whom, among the remembered figures of the Victorian Age are they best exemplified? (p. 237)

We are looking for a man who was in and of his age, and who could have been of no other: a man with sympathy to share, and genius to judge, its sentiments and movements: a man not too illustrious or too consummate to be companionable, but one, nevertheless, whose ideas took root and are still bearing; whose influence, passing from one fit mind to another, could transmit, and can still impart, the most precious element in Victorian civilization, its robust and masculine sanity. Such a man there was: and I award the place to Walter Bagehot.

I do not assert that Bagehot was the greatest man alive and working between 1837 and 1901: I am not sure that the statement would mean anything: and I agree that the landscape of that age is a range of varied eminences with no dominating peak. Indeed, in a footnote to my *Portrait,* which somehow got lost in the proofs, I suggested that anyone who wished to understand the Victorian mind should turn away from the remembered names and survey the careers of three men: Whitwell Elwin, Alderman Thomasson of Bolton, and Charles Adderley, first Lord Norton: reflecting, as he went, on the breadth of their interests, from sound prose to sound religion, and from town planning to Imperial policy, and the quiet and substantial permanence of what they did. It is along this level that we must look, to find 'if not the greatest, at least the truest' Victorian. As I looked, my eye fell on Walter Bagehot and there it has stayed. (pp. 240-41)

Of the Victorian mind, by which I mean the kind of intelligence that one learns to look for and recognize in the years of his maturity, say, from 1846 when he was twenty to 1877 when he died, the characteristics that most impress me are capaciousness and energy. It had room for so many ideas, and it threw them about as lustily as a giant baby playing skittles. The breadth and vigour of Bagehot's mind appear on every page he has left, and they were, we know, not less conspicuous in his conversation and the conduct of affairs. But what was peculiarly his own was the perfect management of all this energy and all these resources. He was as well aware of his superiority in intelligence as Matthew Arnold of his superiority in culture. But he carried it with such genial and ironic delight, that his influence—and he was through the *Economist* and the Reviews a very influential man—encountered no resistance. His paradoxes became axioms: and there are thousands of people thinking and even speaking Bagehot to-day, who might be hard put to it to say when exactly he lived and what exactly he did. (p. 241)

Bagehot was no lonely thinker, anticipating the commonplaces of another age. He was as thoroughly immersed in the Victorian matter as the most pugnacious, self-satisfied, dogmatic business man of his day. In his profession as banker, economist and editor he was highly successful. . . . He could even write verses, beginning (or ending, I forget which)

Thou Church of Rome!

and it was his affectionate and humorous interest in all the doings of his time that furnished him with the material of his

philosophy. Of Macaulay he acutely says that he lacked 'the experiencing mind'. Bagehot's mind was always experiencing, and always working its observation into pattern, into system, but—and here we touch on his central excellence or virtue— into a system open towards the future. (p. 243)

*G. M. Young, "The Greatest Victorian," in his* To-day and Yesterday: Collected Essays and Addresses, *Rupert Hart-Davis, 1948, pp. 237-43.*

**WILLIAM IRVINE**  (essay date 1939)

[*Irvine's* Walter Bagehot, *from which the following excerpt is drawn, is primarily concerned with Bagehot's literary criticism, but it also includes a brief discussion of his writings on politics and economics and a comparison of Bagehot's religious and political thought to that of the eighteenth-century English statesman Edmund Burke. In the excerpt below, Irvine first outlines the leading ideas of Bagehot's critical doctrine, concentrating on his insistence that literature be both pleasing and instructive and his belief that the most fit subjects for literary treatment were those that reflected universal truth. Irvine also relates Bagehot's wide range of knowledge and practical experience as a banker, editor, and economist to his ability to present the authors he reviewed not as "literary abstractions" but as "total personalities."*]

Bagehot was a man of several professions and one avocation. That avocation was literary criticism. When the serious business of banking and editing was over, he retired to his study, read literature and wrote upon it. Writing was chiefly a means of relaxation, and his attitude was somewhat that of the "tired business man"—not that he thought of art merely as idle recreation or as an opportunity for "emotional release." His study jacket did not, with a characteristically twentieth-century magic, transform him from a captain of industry into a gushing aesthete. He brought to bear upon literature, as upon economics and political philosophy, the same keen, disciplined intellect, the same rich and many-sided experience. But his state of mind was that of a man who wished not merely to instruct his readers but to amuse himself, who wrote not anxiously and laboriously, but with exhilaration and easy abandon. The literary essays represent that part of his mind which found no adequate expression in a column of figures, the ephemeral pages of *The Economist,* or the grave and sedate tomes of **Lombard Street** and **The English Constitution.**

This point should not be pushed too far, nor the literary essays too sharply distinguished from the rest of Bagehot's writings. His view of all subjects was serious and responsible, as his manner of discussing them was often frivolous and audacious. A man so vitally concerned, in so many fields of inquiry, with the liberal and human aspects of truth would hardly treat with lightness the most liberal and human of all studies. Yet his literary work suggests unmistakably the attitude of mind in which it was written. Its virtues are those of fine conversation. The mood is easy and confident, the tone witty and vivacious, the thought free and lively. The author gives himself up to flights of eloquence and sallies of humour which, in a more guarded and anxious moment, he would scarcely have attempted. He allows his ideas to take their own direction, and turns literature into economics and history with a boldness which disgusts the studious critic and delights the ordinary reader. Unconsciously he is drawn to the thoughts closest to his heart and the things deepest in his experience. **"William Cowper"** bears the dark suggestion of his mother's insanity, **"Hartley Coleridge"** the trace of his own childhood. The literary essays have some of the excitement of confession and all the charm of intimacy. They are as the conversations of a great man recorded by himself.

But they have also the faults of good conversation. The industry, the keen self-vigilance of the more deliberate author are lacking. Bagehot retreats from tedious labour. He scorns exhaustive preliminary research, and having worked out the interesting parts of an argument, fails to tie them together with hard, solid logic. He elaborates airy metaphysical distinctions as readily as one might discuss the weather. In the exhilaration of thought he sometimes swallows large potations of theory pure, without any adulteration of truth. He is too much at the mercy of his talents, and in **"Hartley Coleridge,"** for example, esteems an author highly because he understands him vividly. His prejudices sit too complacently upon him. He is too patronizing toward French art and French genius. He is too little on his guard, for one naturally so cautious and detached, against the Victorian within him. He makes too great a virtue of Dickens's purity, too black a crime of Thackeray's "suggestiveness." He is a little too much struck with Browning's "nastiness." The literary essays have in them more vital personality and more careless thought—one is almost inclined to say—more truth and more error than any of Bagehot's other writings.

Perhaps the least impressive part of Bagehot's criticism is his literary theory. It is a curious mixture of solid conservatism and brilliant guesswork, of safe intuition and dangerous speculation. Seeking instinctively principles which have stood the test of time, he bases himself firmly on Aristotle. Upon fundamentals he is naturally, instinctively sensible, as upon particular and subsidiary questions he is frequently both reliable and profound. Altogether he is the broadest and most liberal Aristotelian of his age. Yet nearly everything he says is tinctured with fallacy. There is a carelessness in logic and definition, an eagerness to ascend to a paradise of speculation upon the backs of dazzling first thoughts. Indeed, he is not quite deeply enough in earnest always to resist an exciting inspiration. Consequently the mask is off. The vilifier of intellect, the eulogist of stupidity frequently gives himself up to a strong natural inclination—to the intoxicating pursuit of intoxicating ideas. In the literary essays Bagehot might be said to arrive at error by logic and at truth by instinct.

As an Aristotelian he was considerably influenced by some of the great modern exponents of classic tradition, notably by Coleridge and Matthew Arnold, and to a lesser extent by Goethe. A steady contempt for French genius seems to have blinded him to the depth and penetration of French criticism. (pp. 84-7)

Bagehot is not one of those who would hide literature in an ivory tower dedicated to the worship of beauty. Literature is indissolubly connected with life. Under favourable conditions it is a cultural and moral force of the first importance. "We need," he declares, "an intellectual possession analogous to our own life; which reflects, embodies, improves it; on which we can repose; which will recur to us in the placid moments—which will be a latent principle even in the acute crises of life." Literature should not be deliberately didactic in a narrow and immediate sense, but inevitably didactic in a larger sense. Poetry, at its best, "is a deep thing, a teaching thing, the most surely and wisely elevating of human things." Moreover, "though pleasure is not the end of poetry, pleasing is a condition of poetry." Bagehot does not of course maintain the theory of the sugar-coated pill. His interpretation of the words "teach" and "please" is both liberal and profound. Of Browning's "Caliban upon Setebos" he writes:

An exceptional monstrosity of horrid ugliness cannot be made pleasing, except it be made to suggest—to recall—the perfection, the beauty, from which it is a deviation. Perhaps in extreme cases no art is equal to this; but then such self-imposed problems should not be worked by the artist; these out-of-the-way and detestable subjects should be let alone by him.

But if ugliness is something which is out-of-the-way, exceptional, and monstrous, beauty must be something which is central, typical, and human. Such beauty is also truth. In its grace there is meaning, as in its meaning grace. Literature impregnated with such beauty instructs while it pleases and pleases while it instructs. Matthew Arnold observes in the same vein: "To the elementary part of our nature, to our passions, that which is great and passionate is always interesting"—and, he might have added, instructive.

Arnold has another saying which goes straight to the heart of Bagehot's literary philosophy. "What is really precious and inspiring," he asks, "in all that we get from literature, except this sense of an immediate contact with genius itself, and the stimulus toward what is true and excellent which we derive from it?" In all save the deep reverence implied, which for men, however great, so detached a critic could not feel, this sentence might have come from the pen of Bagehot. His instinct for the practical, the human, led him always to the author as the great reality behind every book. Created personalities interested him infinitely less. A natural aristocrat, he was naturally drawn to the great aristocrats of the mind who find in literature their fullest expression and development, and as he has a conception of highest beauty, so he has a conception of highest genius. As he gives the highest place to an art which is deeply and broadly founded in life, yet restrained and noble, so he esteems most an author who carries with him the discipline of a high and moral culture through the stress and excitement and rich experience of a worldly career. Shakespeare, the supreme artist and successful business man, he honours above all authors, yet deplores the wildness of his genius, even while admiring its breadth and magnitude. He writes with respect and approval of the versatile mind of Scott, with critical wit of the narrow and studious mind of Gibbon. He exalts the "symmetrical genius" of Plato above the "irregular genius" of Dickens. His preference is, as always, for the Greek virtues.

"Poetry," says Aristotle, ". . . is a more philosophical and a higher thing than history: for poetry tends to express the universal, history the particular. By the universal I mean how a person of a certain type will on occasion speak or act; according to the law of probability or necessity." Behind these observations lies the idea that the infinite variety of human nature groups itself into certain types, and that these types are themselves but aspects of a universal human truth. . . . Aristotle characteristically regards the universal from the point of view of human action. Bagehot approached it from the point of view of subject-matter. He emphasized not so much that the universal is probable, as that it is selective.

We have the word "picturesque," he says, to describe such a scene in nature as includes all the typical features of a landscape and is therefore a fit subject for painting. Why not have a word "literesque"?

> The word *"literesque"* would mean, if we possessed it, that perfect combination in *subject*

*matter* of literature, which suits the *art* of literature. We often meet people, and say of them, sometimes meaning well and sometimes ill: "How well so-and-so would do in a book!" Such people are by no means the best people; but they are the most effective people—the most remarkable people.

Such people are typical:

> When we see the *type* of the genus, at once we seem to comprehend its character; the inferior specimens are explained by the perfect embodiment; the approximations are definable when we know the ideal to which they draw near. There are an infinite number of classes of human beings, but in each of these classes there is a distinctive type which, if we could expand it in words, would define the class.

Such a type would form part of a purified reality, a reality freed from the accidental and extraneous, and "the poet must find in that reality, the *literesque* man, the *literesque* scene, which Nature intends for him, and which will live in his page."

But there are authors who do not see, or but imperfectly see, this typical reality. Some are too much fascinated by particular theories or systems of thought, and to these writers Bagehot would assign a lesser rank:

> A Schiller, a Euripides, a Ben Jonson, cares for *ideas*—for the parings of the intellect, and the distillation of the mind; a Shakespeare, a Homer, a Goethe, finds his mental occupation, the true home of his natural thoughts, in the real world.

Some authors again seek strange and exciting subjects. They depict not the typical, but the exceptional, the peculiar, the marvellous. To these also Bagehot assigns a lesser place, because he feels they treat subject-matter of lesser importance.

Again, the typical is much affected by the circumstances in which it is delineated. Characters may be represented as talented or untalented, as of high or low rank, and all are not equally suitable for the best art. Men of exalted station who are involved in great crises and who decide the affairs of nations are more striking to the imagination than other men, and if they are also men of great and varied abilities, including within themselves a large portion of human nature, they seem, when represented in a work of art, to stand as gigantic symbols for all humanity. Their thoughts and actions have about them the majesty of abstract truth, and even their crimes have an awfulness which prevents us from turning away in disgust. In short, the noblest art depicts the universal in circumstances of solemnity and grandeur. Such art is to be found in the second book of [Milton's] *Paradise Lost:*

> The debate in Pandaemonium is a debate among these typical characters at the greatest conceivable crisis, and with adjuncts of solemnity which no other situation could rival. It is the greatest classical triumph, the highest achievement of the pure style in English literature; it is the greatest description of the highest and most typical characters with the most choice circumstances and in the fewest words.

Yet Bagehot realized perfectly well that human nature is weak and high classic art neglected: "But little deep poetry is very popular, and *no* severe art." The ordinary reader much prefers familiar prose to high poetry, and the serial novel to the Homeric epic. Bagehot's attitude is charcteristically moderative. He judged all art critically, and that which pretended to be great, by the highest and most rigid standards, yet he excluded nothing that deserved the name, however trivial, from consideration. He was quick to point out the deficiencies of popular taste, but no less quick to reprehend the narrowness of an author who forgot that he wrote for human beings. (pp. 87-92)

In surveying as a whole Bagehot's theoretical ideas on literature and criticism, one is struck with their coherence. One is surprised that what are for the most part disjointed and occasional remarks, dropped in the course of a criticism, should, at least in broad outline, hang so well together. The basis of this consistency, as of all other consistency in Bagehot, lies ultimately in the concept of the moderate and many-sided man. . . . [This] lies at the very centre of Bagehot's thought, as the standard of all that is excellent and desirable. The best literature should be broad in its contact with life, moral and serious in its thought and tone, noble and restrained in its style, because the moderate and many-sided man, as a reader and critic, prefers such literature, and because, as an author, he produces it. This is the ultimate logic and meaning of Bagehot's literary theory. (pp. 140-41)

Bagehot brought to the study of literature almost every species of equipment but that of the literary historian. He had been educated for the Bar; he had acquired the specialized knowledge of an economist; he had gained practical experience as a banker, editor, and politician; and in the course of a studious life he had accumulated broad, heterogeneous information ranging all the way from biological science to Anglican theology. The result is that his essays seem to have an added dimension. The persons they describe appear not from the single aspect of their literary significance, but from the many aspects of their various interests and achievements. We hear of Jeffrey both as critic and as editor, of Crabb Robinson not only as a collector of literary lions, but as a successful member of the Bar. We become more definitely aware that there are sound politics in Shakespeare's plays and excellent political economy in Scott's novels. We are given the opinion of a politician upon the parliamentary career of Gibbon. In short, we feel that we are in the presence not of literary abstractions, but of total personalities. We see literature in its "connection with reality and affairs."

At no time does Bagehot's peculiar training stand him in such good stead as when he delineates the past. Nor have his descriptions merely the charm of a close familiarity with many phases of life. Some historians have the faculty of making a past age vivid through the accumulation of encyclopaedic detail. Bagehot had the faculty of talking about it like a contemporary. Intrinsically, his representations are not so circumstantial, and in some respects, not so vivid, as those of certain other first-class writers, yet his tone is more assured, more familiar. He creates the illusion of describing personal experience, and that illusion is worth a world of fact and rhetoric. What is the source of his peculiar power? He has himself observed that "the speciality of pursuits is attended with a timidity of mind." Bagehot had the intellectual courage of a broad and versatile training. He writes with the ready confidence and easy adaptability of one who is accustomed to assume many points of view, to be at home in a great variety of surroundings, and to find beneath all the strange and multifarious phenomena of society that strange, familiar thing—human nature. (pp. 164-66)

> *William Irvine, in his* Walter Bagehot, *1939. Reprint by Archon Books, 1970, 303 p.*

## V. S. PRITCHETT (essay date 1944)

[*Pritchett, a modern British writer, is respected for his mastery of the short story and for what critics describe as his judicious, reliable, and insightful literary criticism. He writes in the conversational tone of the familiar essay, approaching literature from the viewpoint of an informed but not overly scholarly reader. Pritchett's critical method is to stress his own experience, judgment, and sense of literary art, as opposed to following a codified critical doctrine derived from a school of psychological or philosophical theory. In this excerpt from a review of* Literary Studies *and* Biographical Studies, *Pritchett stresses that Bagehot's works are devoid of the moralizing that characterizes the writings of most of his contemporaries. He points to Bagehot's "analytical approach" to literature and politics in asserting that his thought is more representative of the twentieth century than of the Victorian age.*]

In literature every century produces its sports and throws out its new mutation. Stendhal was right in thinking he was born out of his time and was writing for readers a hundred years away. Clough comes more closely to us than he did to his contemporaries. It is not entirely a question of opinion or subject. It is rather a question of accent. These unrepresentative writers have a voice that is younger, more disengaged than the voices of their colleagues. Walter Bagehot is an even better example than Clough among the Victorians. We open him and at once we are at home. Well-established in his own time, by the cast of his imagination he nevertheless belongs to us. It is as if Nature had grown bored with the monotonous production of histrionic Victorians between 1800 and 1860 and was amusing herself with the blasphemous experiment of slipping in a man of the twentieth century.

I do not mean to convey that the opinions of Walter Bagehot on literature and politics are our opinions; his scorn of the masses and the extreme caution of his adventurous mind when it came to the brink of reform, are very far from the mood of our time. Bagehot's attraction is that he speaks in our accent; he has our drastic habit of mind, our analytical approach. Above all he has cut down the load of intellectual baggage the Victorians always travelled with, those unshapely moral portmanteaux, those handy Gladstone bags laden with causes and endeavours, those bursting holdalls, swollen with the impedimenta of bad conscience, those theatrical hampers filled with the costumes of social guilt. His arrivals and departures do not pile up the platforms and cloakrooms with the admonitory luggage his contemporaries could never do without. Bagehot travels light. And it is not mere week-end travel. The moral earnestness of his contemporaries was an encumbrance because moral earnestness is a diffusion. It spreads. It clouds. It blurs outlines and, in its beneficence, runs one thing into another. Like jealousy, it is a passion which seizes *every* particle of the air and is hungry for every available burden. Bagehot's mind, on the contrary, was occupied with the decisive, the definitive, with elimination not with multiplication. It was an adventurous mind that wanted to clear the ground and put the issue. It was an intellect not a worth; an imagination and not a missionary; a judgement and not a fulmination, a prophecy or a prayer.

Many writers betray themselves by their fondness for a single word. . . . [The] reader of Bagehot might guess he was in the company of a banker, as well as a politician and critic of literature, by Bagehot's amusing addiction to "sagacious" and "sagacity." Sagacity, I suppose, connotes the wisdom of experience, a natural percipience that is distinct from the wisdom we are taught by textbook, pulpit and platform; and as a man of affairs, a Lombard Street man and politician, Bagehot seems to have thought sagacity the most desirable, if not the highest, human quality. Scott was sagacious. Dickens was not. The sagacious man mistrusts great changes. He knows what the world is. Sagacity, in Bagehot, represents the Tory taste of a Liberal mind. It is the breath of life coming into the stuffiness of the study, an animal buoyancy and shrewdness driving the abstract out of the window and into the draughty universe, where it belongs. Bagehot brings life into literature, turns politics into men. Like Bacon, he has an immediate sense of "men's business and men's bosoms." . . .

The trouble about sagacity is that it almost assumes foregone conclusions; people who have an animated detachment about everything tend to assume that the ground they stand on never moves. Such a criticism can be made of Bagehot. But there was far more than sagacity to his mind. He speaks in a voice like ours, because he has detached himself from the manner of the Victorian conscience. He had no humanitarian sympathy for the poor but, looking at Dickens or more particularly at the imitators of Dickens, he seems to suggest that these writers haven't either. They felt guilty and they merely covet that sympathy. There is no cant in Bagehot. "There is a pale, whitey-brown substance," he wrote to his friend Richard Holt Hutton, "in so-and-so's books which people who don't think take for thought, but it isn't." It is typical of Bagehot that when he was in Paris in 1851 at the time of the *coup d'état,* he helped build barricades in the street for the people whom he opposed, and then frankly said he got away out of danger to watch. The point is that Bagehot was a kind of social naturalist. He is one of the Victorians whose intellect was enormously influenced by Darwin and the scientific attitude; and the moral controversies seemed to have marked him far less than the method did. It left him with an increased, and perhaps, too, agreeable and convenient sense of the infinite difficulties and distractions which lie between us and "discovering the truth." . . .

The freshness, the freedom, the wit and the clear epigrammatic style [of Bagehot's *Literary Studies* and *Biographical Studies*] are readable at once. His humour and his irony leap energetically out of a strong mind. On Milton's pamphlet on divorce he writes, with an eye on the feminist movement: "Milton had a sincere desire to preserve men from the society of unsocial and unsympathising women." Of Lady Mary Wortley Montagu: "she lived before the age in which people waste half their lives in washing the whole of their persons." He is fond of clearing the ground by cutting it in two and then contrasting the two parts. There are two kinds of novels: the regular and irregular, two kinds of men, the impulsive and the men of principle; there are two views of the world, that it is visible or invisible. There are two kinds of folly exemplified in the life of the eighteenth and nineteenth centuries:

> The London of the eighteenth century was an aristocratic world, which lived to itself, which displayed the virtues and developed the vices of an aristocracy which was under little fear of external control or check. . . . (In the nine-

teenth) Public opinion now rules, and it is an opinion which constrains the conduct, and narrows the experience, and dwarfs the violence, and minimises the frankness of the highest classes, while it diminishes their vices, supports their conscience, and precludes their grossness.

Again, our senses teach us what the world is; our intuitions where it is. We turn from the former to the latter:

> The immeasurable depth folds us in. "Eternity," as the original thinker said, "is everlasting." We breathe a deep breath. And perhaps we have higher moments. We comprehend the "unintelligible world," we see into "the life of things," we fancy we know whence we came and whither we go, words we have repeated for years have meaning for the first time; texts of old Scripture seem to apply to *us*. . . . And—and—Mr. Thackeray would say "You come back to town, and order dinner at a restaurant, and read Beranger once more." Yes—even Providence "works by a scheme of averages."

One expects this kind of mind to be sound on the sagacious Scott but to be insensitive to Shelley, yet this is not so. In Bagehot's essay on Shelley, his analysis of the sinlessness of impulse, his response to the archetypal, the abstract and the vision of the Universe in Shelley, are remarkable in a "sagacious" man of the world. Bagehot's judgment is not a judge's; it is imaginative. And his imagination led him, as a critic, first of all to define the type of mind he had to deal with and to describe its spiritual geography. He perceived that "a cold consciousness of the world" often intrudes after the rapture of Shelley's lyrics and that "in many of his poems the failing of the feeling is as beautiful as its short moment of hope and buoyancy"—a sentence which conveys how complete Bagehot's sympathetic imagination could be in its grasp of a temperament alien to his own and less well-seated. The truth is that Bagehot's genial and pragmatic nature did not quite close the door on the frightening and even exhilarating wildernesses which lie outside the office of the man of affairs; he, too, was disturbed by the sight of wastes which lay before Clough's shrinking figure, and by the cold, astronomic universe of eons and space which Shelley could call up and with which he would assault our moral vision.

Bagehot's essay on Scott is on more solid ground. Scott's Toryism "was a subtle compound of the natural instinct of the artist with the plain sagacity of the man of the world." In this essay Bagehot reveals both the strength and the weakness of his attitude to the poor. The poor are too mean to be a continuous subject for a work of art; that now reads oddly to us. But Bagehot was protesting also against the rosy-tinted sentimentalising of the poor in the Victorian novel which revolts the taste so often in Dickens; clear-headed as always, he revolted against the rationalising of guilt. And he perceived what I believe no other critic has perceived, that Scott's pictures of the poor were the only sound and honest ones in the English novel up to that time. Bagehot, of course, relied on the ancient truth that the poor are always with us, a truth which at any rate had some validity up to the eighteenth century. Where he was wrong was in not observing that the poor of the Industrial Revolution were not the old poor. They were a new race, something more terrible than had ever been seen in Europe

before. On Scott's religion Bagehot's discernment works well. He misses the political or historical impulse in that religion and relies on the obvious fact that Scott was satirising his own childhood creed; but there is one good sentence here: "The aspect of religion which Scott delineates best is that which appears in griefs, especially in the grief of strong characters. His strong *natural* nature felt the power of death."

It is the pleasure of Bagehot's criticism that its penetration is directed by a strong natural nature that felt the power of life.

> *V. S. Pritchett, in a review of "Literary Studies" and "Biographical Studies," in* The New Statesman & Nation, *Vol. XXVIII, No. 701, July 29, 1944, p. 74.*

## JACQUES BARZUN    (essay date 1948)

> [*Barzun is a French-born American educator and writer whose wide range of learning has produced distinguished works in several fields, including history, culture, musicology, literary criticism, and biography. His contributions to these various disciplines are contained in such modern classics of scholarship and critical insight as* Darwin, Marx, Wagner *(1941),* Berlioz and the Romantic Century *(1950),* The House of the Intellect *(1959), and the recent biography* A Stroll with William James *(1983). In his introduction to* Physics and Politics, *Barzun emphasizes that Bagehot was essentially a political thinker who, though not a practicing politician, possessed a statesmanlike sense of the paradoxical nature of government. Arguing that Bagehot's works can be properly interpreted only if they are read in light of his "double vision" of politics, Barzun outlines Bagehot's concept of the two fundamental paradoxes in government: "the* moral *paradox that the public good is not to be achieved by following the rules of private good" and "the* psychological *paradox that stability and change are equally necessary though diametrically opposed." Barzun concludes that Bagehot's examination of these contradictions constitutes his greatest contribution to political thought.*]

[*Physics and Politics* has long been "well-known"], yet it is seldom read, and Walter Bagehot, its author, has never become a familiar name. Not long ago he was identified in print as "banker and shipowner, joint editor of the *National Review* after 1855, and editor of the *Economist* from 1860 till his death." This is of the order of "Shakespeare—Realtor at Stratford-on-Avon"—not quite, perhaps, for Bagehot was indeed notable as banker and editor. But his achievements as a political thinker and a literary critic are so much greater and more lasting that his genius should be as unmistakable as his versatility.

It is good to have occasion to restate this conviction, though Bagehot's hold on the public will probably not be strengthened by the mere reissuing of his *Physics and Politics.* For with this, as with all his books, one needs special orientation toward his thought and character to understand, not what he is saying—since he is the clearest of prose writers—but what he intends. I remember first reading *Physics and Politics* some twenty years ago and being at once entertained, outraged, and not enlightened. The impression I carried away was the one produced by his answer to the question he raises in Chapter VI: in what respects is "a village of English colonists . . . superior to a tribe of Australian natives who roam about them"? "Indisputably," says Bagehot, the English are superior "in one, and that a main sense. . . . They can beat the Australians in war when they like; they can take from them anything they like, and kill any of them they choose."

Bagehot goes on to speak of other superiorities, in comfort, culture, and practical knowledge, but that "one and main sense" of the white man's eminence stuck in my throat and prevented for a time my swallowing anything else of Bagehot's. I classed him as an unrepentant social Darwinist: was not the book itself an inquiry into the law of progress by considering the light that Darwinism (physics) shed on human society (politics)? True, it was more concise and more perceptive than Darwin's own attempt in *The Descent of Man,* but I could not reconcile myself to the apparent complacency of a critic who put the slum civilization of London or Manchester above Australian culture, however primitive. All my admiration of boomerangs rose against it.

Today we have lost a good deal of the post-Darwinian passion to find out who is superior to whom; we have lost it, that is, as a speculative interest, but we have hardly escaped as yet from the consequences of its earlier form. We have in fact just emerged from a struggle with powers whose first principle was belief in their own supremacy, and who were making it good by ''taking what they liked and killing whom they chose.'' So we may be readier than I was in the twenties to judge with fairness Bagehot's chapter on **''The Use of Conflict.''** We can appreciate the exquisite accuracy of his remark that ''the progress of the military art is the most conspicuous, I was about to say the most *showy,* fact in human history.'' And when he proposes as a generality that ''in every particular state of the world, those nations which are strongest tend to prevail over the others; and in certain marked peculiarities the strongest tend to be the best,'' we must concede that he is at least dealing candidly with an inescapable problem. In modern jargon, he is dealing with power politics, and if he heard us he would point out that the phrase says the same thing twice over: politics is for power; that is its connection with physics, whether physics be symbolized by the tiger or by uranium 235.

If this is the simple unpalatable point of *Physics and Politics,* why must we read further and interpret it in the light of Bagehot's other works—*The English Constitution,* the wonderful fantasia on banking, *Lombard Street,* and the several dozen essays on historical, economic, and literary subjects? One answer is: we go to Bagehot for something that seems very difficult to convey accurately through mere definition or single examples—the true character of political man. This character, in turn is important to discover, because on it depends the possibility of leading a life above ''physics,'' a life better than that of the jungle.

Though not himself a practicing statesman, Bagehot lived and worked in the very center of nineteenth-century England's politics, finance, and social struggle. As lucid in exposition as he was gifted in observation, he had, moreover, that special temperament which marks off the potential ruler from the ordinary citizen. His strangeness therefore defines that temperament. Looking on such a scene as Bagehot saw, the ordinary citizen takes it for granted that a statesman is simply a man with a good head for details who is given enlarged powers and responsibilities. The comon man does not see—is not in a position to see—that these powers are as fluid as water, and these responsibilities as massive as mountains; and that consequently the ruler cannot act as if he were an honest motorman driving a streetcar. The workaday virtues, the black-and-white morality of good and evil, the easy personifying of groups, classes, and nations as if they were solid entities with one will and one mind—all this suddenly becomes childish and frivolous when applied to affairs of state. In that realm the practical and even the superior mind must undergo re-education as if called upon to cipher in an utterly foreign system of numbers or to survey a field of non-Euclidian dimensions.

Some men are born with the intuition that this is so, that the common analogy between a good man, a good ruler, and a good nation is false. Bagehot, from the age of fifteen—the time of his earliest essay—had this perception. He was born political, like Alexander Hamilton, Dr. Johnson, Rousseau, Burke, Machiavelli, Lincoln, Hobbes, Tocqueville, or Bernard Shaw; and like them of course he has been called hard and cynical. He is quoted, correctly as we have seen, on the side of power. When other words of his, equally characteristic, are quoted on the side of freedom, of public instruction, and of democratic diversity, he is put down (like Shaw) as a paradoxer, or worse, as an inconsistent trifler—for, again like Shaw, it is Bagehot's misfortune to be witty.

In short, the difficulty of the political man in making himself understood is that he tries to bring together what the common man has decided must be kept asunder. The good man of commerce will accept a saint and understand his concentration; will shudder at a cynic and grasp the point of *his* specialization; but how few—particularly if they are contemporary with the events—can fully share Bagehot's feelings when he says:

> Look back to the time . . . when the Socialists, not under speculative philosophers like Proudhon and Louis Blanc, but under practical rascals and energetic murderers like Sobrier and Caussidière, made their final stand; and when against them, on the other side, the National Guard (mostly solid shopkeepers, three-parts ruined by the events of February) fought, I will not say bravely or valiantly, but furiously, frantically, savagely, as one reads in old books that half starved burgesses in beleaguered towns have sometimes fought, for the food of their children; let any sceptic hear of the atrocities of the friends of order, and the atrocities of the advocates of disorder, and he will, I imagine, no longer be sceptical on two points: he will hope that if he ever have to fight it will not be with a fanatic Socialist, nor against a demi-bankrupt fighting for his shop; and he will admit that in a country subject to collisions . . . no earthly blessing is in any degree comparable to a power which will stave off, long delay, or permanently prevent . . . such bloodshed.

Reread this paragraph and notice at every turn what must be called the double vision of the man destined for statecraft—the cool awareness of everything at once—that rascals and murderers can be practical and energetic; that defenders of property fight for their children's food, like the others—he ''will *not* say'' bravely, but savagely—whence atrocities on both sides and the need of a power to quell or neutralize this fury of waste. There is the root idea of government itself in this account, which contrasts so completely with our familiar moral views. For ''we'' are partisans first; we have ''principles,'' loyalties—to socialism or to shopkeeping—and we ascribe virtues accordingly. The socialists, or any progressive group you like, are heroes dying for freedom; the property-owners are rational defenders of law and order; and the power that would stop civil war by an even greater show of force is tyranny incarnate.

The tragedy of man is that there is a sense in which these last statements are just as true as Bagehot's. The steps in past political progress which we most venerate were in actuality riotous, fanatical, marred by atrocities. But the political thinker or statesman cannot give in to this spectator's view of history. He must act for a greater interest than progress itself; he must perpetuate order, which he does by keeping the multitudinous aggressions of men in balance against one another. His task is paradoxical because, through order, he intends that moral force, which always does have the last word, shall not be a last word spoken from beyond the grave. This is why *immediate* morality is not his concern. Bagehot felt this so intimately that in his youth he performed what is perhaps the most symbolical act of statecraft on record.

Aged not quite twenty-six . . . , he was vacationing in Paris, and also reporting, as correspondent for a Liberal and Unitarian paper, the *coup d'état* of Napoleon III. To the dismay of his friends and his editor, his seven long letters were an elaborate defense of the approaching dictatorship. He explained—and the paragraph I have quoted was part of the explanation—the necessity of order in France at whatever cost. But by a singular yet characteristic turn of mind, he was at the same time risking his life to help the republicans build barricades against the usurper.

This conscious self-contradiction, akin to the maturest political wisdom, has many meanings. It can signify for us the states-man's conflict between his own ideal allegiance and what he deems the present public interest—the virtue of compromise. It can also symbolize the permanent need for checks and bal-ances—nothing must triumph absolutely lest absolutism result. It can finally typify Bagehot's own conviction that dictatorship has only a crude and temporary use. When fifteen years later he reviewed the state of France in his essay **"Caesareanism as It Now Exists,"** he did conclude to this effect. The Second Empire "is an admirable government for present and coarse purposes, but a detestable government for future and refined purposes . . . because it stops the *teaching apparatus;* it stops the effectual inculcation of important thought upon the mass of mankind . . ." and it will end by corrupting the nation.

This "teaching" and this important thought that Bagehot is worried about is not the formal instruction of the people and even less the activities of professed intellectuals. It is the busi-ness of keeping "the mass of mankind" alive to their own changing needs, so that statesmanship can devise and bring about changes in established institutions. The nineteenth cen-tury was not allowed to forget that the world does move, po-litically as well as cosmically. This historical fact confronts us with the second great paradox or contradiction that Bagehot explored and explained. The first was the *moral* paradox that the public good is not to be achieved by following the rules of private good. Now we face the *psychological* paradox that stability and change are equally necessary though diametrically opposed. But are men capable of being at once quiescent and active, habit-ridden and original?

Bagehot's answer cannot be given in digest; it must be read in nearly everything he wrote on "such a being as man, in such a world as the present one." Whether he discussed Shake-speare or Bishop Butler or the governors of the Bank of En-gland, Bagehot scrutinizes men as acting creatures, and he always starts from their concrete diversity: "Men are formed, indeed, on no ideal type. Human nature has tendencies too various and circumstances too complex. All men's characters have sides and aspects not to be comprehended in a single definition." Training and what he calls in [*Physics and Politics*] the "cake of custom" solidify this flexibility: "Take the soft mind of the boy and (strong and exceptional aptitudes excepted) you make him merchant, barrister, butcher, baker, surgeon,

or apothecary. But once make him an apothecary and he will never afterwards bake wholesome bread; make him a butcher, and he will kill too extensively even for a surgeon. . . ." From this pleasant exaggeration Bagehot argues that just as acquired habit makes the professional man, so it makes the sober citizen of a particular state. Upon this miracle rest the stability and the comfort of good government; gently drilled by habit, ev-erybody knows what to do and, as we say, "behaves."

This fact leads Bagehot to the enunciation of his unforgettable thesis that the true source of strength in the government of England is the stupidity of the population. British freedom has the same roots, though it flowers in the not quite so dense atmosphere of the people's elected House of Commons. There are in Parliament "the few invaluable members who sit and think," but the "'best' English people keep their mind in a state of decorous dullness. . . . Take Sir Robert Peel—our last great statesman, the greatest Member of Parliament that ever lived, an absolutely perfect transactor of public business. Was there ever such a dull man? Can anyone, without horror, foresee the reading of his memoirs?"

This stolid attention to business, however makes for astonishing steadiness and, once committed to a free government, keeps the nation (as Tocqueville hoped for the United States) in "a rut of freedom." The best maker of ruts is party organization, which is essential to majority rule. "If everybody does what he thinks is right," says Bagehot, "there will be 657 amend-ments to every motion, and none of them will be carried or the motion either." The irrelevant feelings of party interest must be aroused and used to push forward the real and complex enterprises of state. (pp. v-xvi)

Abstractly put, Bagehot's view of the psychological stuff of good government is that men in the mass are not, as is wrongly said, ruled by their imaginations, but rather "by the weakness of their imaginations. The nature of a constitution, the action of an assembly . . . are complex facts, difficult to know, and easy to mistake." Government therefore needs symbols "to impose on the common people—not necessarily to impose on them what is untrue, yet less what is hurtful; but still to impose on their quiescent imaginations what would otherwise not be there."

But do not be alarmed—or indignant. Plausible as this de-scription is, it tells only half the story—else there would be no paradox. The other half consists in the second great need of government after stability, the need of change; which in turn requires Bagehot's "teaching apparatus," defined by him in the single word "agitation." The stupid, steady, sensible, unimaginative people must be stirred up, made to think and to alter their ways, though not suddenly or spastically, for then they might jump out of the rut of freedom altogether and their acquired wisdom would be lost. "It is agitation, agitation alone, which teaches. . . . With our newspapers and our speeches—with our clamorous multitudes of indifferent tongues—we beat the ideas of the few into the minds of the many."

Though he wrote seventy-five years ago, Bagehot saw the dangers of the short cut, variously represented by the dictator with a doctrine, the single party with a doctrine, the palace revolution with a doctrine. There is little to choose among them, for although it might be thought that the effect of be-lieving in a new theory of government would be to strengthen the cause of government itself, the opposite is true. The doc-trinaire does not want to *govern* the country—*this* country—*now:* he wants to push his opponents into the sea and rule a docile remainder of fellow believers. It is all physics and no politics, the unconscious and naïve aim of even great reforms being to remove the difficulties of government. If the reader has an object at heart, let him test himself: whether it is to ''abolish'' war or the practice of tipping, does his mind fly at once to compulsion—''there ought to be a law''? Then let him multiply the objects and imagine the multitude to be compelled and he will find himself among those Bagehot describes:

> Having . . . ideas, they want to enforce them on mankind—to make them heard, and admitted, and obeyed before, in simple competition with other ideas, they would ever be so naturally. At this very moment there are the most rigid Comtists teaching that we ought to be governed by a hierarchy—a combination of savants orthodox in science. Yet who can doubt that Comte would have been hanged by his own hierarchy . . .?

For Comte substitute the name of any doctrinaire you prefer, and for his hypothetical hanging think of any purge, trial, or scapegoat sacrifice that comes to mind, and you have before you the dilemma of the twentieth century.

Bagehot's own system, in so far as he has any, comes to rest on the ever more instructed consent of the governed. One might contrast this instructed consent with the dogmatic *conceit* that he so much reproved in the French. Against them he quotes their own saying that there is somebody wiser than Napoleon and Talleyrand and that is Everybody. This ''many-sided sense,'' adds Bagehot, ''finds no microcosm in any single individual.'' Yet this common wisdom is made up, as mysteriously as the common will, of single individual convictions. ''Very few people are good judges of a good constitution; but everybody's eyes are excellent judges of good light; every man's feet are profound in the theory of agreeable stones.''

This is ''democratic'' enough, but it implies that statesmanship, political theory, literature, and ethics, though affecting the happiness of men, nearly always seem to them remote from their living concerns. Agitation may turn the eyes of the public toward new views and feelings or new problems to be settled, but the gap between the philosopher and the crowd cannot be permanently closed, because to them ideas are not facts. ''The selling of figs, the cobbling of shoes, the manufacturing of nails—these are the essence of life. And let whoso frameth a constitution for his country think on these things.''

Writing at the height of the Victorian epoch, when, in his own words, ''the middle classes were the despotic power in England'' and public opinion ruled (''the opinion of the bald-headed man at the back of the omnibus''), Bagehot could reasonably count on a certain acceleration of the teaching apparatus to keep pace with the steadily increasing demands on government. Teaching the new enfranchised masses after 1870 might in time make an isocratic (that is, equal-voting) community workable with the aid of ''diffused intelligence.'' Hence Bagehot remained, like Burke, a great respecter of Time—time for teaching, for change, for the solidifying of new habits and the preparation of new changes. (pp. xvi-xix)

From his influential position as banker and editor of the chief business journal in England—the *Economist*—Bagehot did all he could to humanize and instruct what he called ''these most tedious times.'' He constantly tempered the stiff laissez-faire doctrines of his associates, punctured the swollen ignorance of politicians, worked for a Concert of Europe, combated Na-

poleon III's transatlantic follies, foresaw and made palatable the slackening of British imperial controls. Some of his characteristic views—which he put forth as obvious means of intelligent conservation—would still have been called ''advanced'' after the first World War. This gives a measure of how tedious his own times were to him.

To keep himself enlivened, he cultivated the twin arts of conversation and criticism—specialties in which he naturally continued to be a philosopher-at-large. His sympathy for the quick and the dead, the luminous and the dense, was wholly magnanimous. When he warns us that ''the business of a critic is criticism'' and we brace ourselves to expect an attack, we are given instead a reconstruction—as, for example, of the motives which make Macaulay's history unlikely, too clear, overpowering for its subject. We may disagree, but we remain in Bagehot's debt for a lively lesson upon the nature of men, writers, historiography, politics, oratory, poetry, religion, and metaphysics.

In a word, Bagehot preserves his statesmanlike character wherever he goes. He writes of Dickens and Wordsworth, Bishop Butler and Gibbon, Shelley, Shakespeare, and Lady Mary Wortley Montagu, with unequal approval but equal generosity; and every life, every work, every mistake unfolds for him some hidden measure of worldly truth which he makes patent. To him, at any rate, no one can impute the limitation he gave as the reason why so few good books are written: it is because ''so few people that can write know anything . . . an author has always lived in a room, has read books . . . but he is out of the way of employing his own eyes and ears.''

Bagehot used his, unquestionably, and was inclined to praise Shakespeare most of all for his ''experiencing mind,'' in the same sense as he deplored Gibbon's incapacity to deal with the lower reaches of truth: ''He cannot mention Asia *Minor*.'' Yet even this preference for the empirical is not exclusive for Bagehot; he understood too well the contributory causes of significant defects: ''Those . . . who are set on what is high will be proportionately offended by the intrusion of what is low.'' He says this of Milton and thereby makes it clear that we are not going to be shown the poet in his deviations from some imagined paragon, but rather the poet *in situation,* times and temperament being accepted as given.

This power to recapture the feel—and the feeling—of the man in his past is again the work of a historical-minded statesman— the statesman as critic. And the double vision that makes a lifelike unity out of an apparent discrepancy (just like our physical sight) also dictates Bagehot's stylistic form: it amounts to a very special brand of irony. Ordinary irony states a thing and means its opposite. Bagehot's kind intends both the thing and its opposite, relishing the simultaneity. (pp. xxi-xxiv)

[What] Bagehot most treasured in life was the very thing he congratulated his compatriots on lacking: they have ''no notion of the *play* of mind; no conception that the charm of society depends upon it. They think cleverness an antic, and have a constant though needless horror of being thought to have any of it.'' In Bagehot's play of mind, clearly, words take a leading part, precisely because they can accumulate meanings, give off wave after wave of combined and conflicting connotations, as a vibrating string does harmonics. In his own reading he found that good prose is a sensation; indeed, some writers ''believe that their words are good to eat, as well as to read; they [enjoy] rolling them about the mouth like sugar-plums and gradually smoothing off any knots or excrescences.''

Gifted as he was in this very art, and enabled by circumstances to practice it in relative leisure and with modest honor, Bagehot could have reversed his aphorism that an aristocracy is the symbol of mind, and asserted that mind—"the viviparous, animating intellect"—was the sign of aristocracy. But the implications of this, as he knew, would threaten the moderate vivacity of spirits he desired. That mind is not an unmixed blessing was one of those truths which make men not so much free as sad. For the developed imagination re-creates a reality that is often unpleasant, just as the rational mind discovers that its groundwork is irrational. "People who have thought know that inquiring is suffering," and Bagehot concludes—with an adverb to soothe the rationalist whom he refutes: "Unfortunately, mysticism is true." Even the process of truth-seeking is not pure bliss: "Deduction is a game, but induction is a grievance."

Underneath it all, Bagehot had an inkling that democracy, despite its dependence on enlightenment, might increasingly dispossess intellect. "People are so deafened with the loud reiteration of half-truths that they have neither curiosity nor energy for elaborate investigation. The very word 'elaborate' is become a reproach." He comforted himself with the fact that great communities have scarcely ever been ruled by their highest thought, and that perhaps there might exist in future what he called "deferential nations"—nations that would acknowledge an educated minority as [their] surrogates in elections. With this suggestion, we are once again in politics, Fabian and Shavian politics, in a world that has presumably (but what a presumption!) mastered "physics" for worthy purposes.

In such a world as the present, Bagehot, though occasionally lapsing into gloom, did his best to make up for the spate of half-truths by giving us his double ones. This, long before Samuel Butler and Bernard Shaw, was his chosen function, and it remains his glory and perpetual challenge. He almost always graced it with high-spirited humor, conscious that to be great is to be difficult and misunderstood. He speaks and shocks us, then adds: "As St. Athanasius aptly observes, 'for the sake of the women who may be led astray, I will this very instant explain my sentiments.'" (pp. xxiv-xxvi)

> *Jacques Barzun, in an introduction to* Physics and Politics; or, Thoughts on the Application of the Principles of "Natural Selection" and "Inheritance" to Political Society *by Walter Bagehot, Alfred A. Knopf, 1948, pp. v-xxvi.*

## ALASTAIR BUCHAN (essay date 1959)

[*Buchan's* The Spare Chancellor: The Life of Walter Bagehot *is a biographical and critical study that provides a balanced overview of Bagehot's writings. Here, Buchan summarizes Bagehot's achievements, arguing that his greatest contributions "not only to English letters but to modern life itself" were twofold: he anticipated some of the intellectual preoccupations of the twentieth century and developed a widely imitated "new prose style for the transmission of serious ideas," which is characterized by simplicity, humor, clarity, and vitality.*]

[Bagehot is] one of the most difficult figures in English letters to treat with justice. Since he was bold enough to venture with so much dash into four separate fields of scholarship and controversy, literature, politics, sociology and economics, he has rightly been judged by the highest standards of each, and inevitably he has not held his place in the front rank of any. (p. 246)

He was not really a critic of literature in the accepted sense, for he brought no objective standard to bear upon either prose or poetry: he was a student of the minds of great writers, a different art. He did not aspire to be a political philosopher, and though *The English Constitution* has had as great an effect on the way in which those who must operate a parliamentary government look at the tool they have in their hands from Westminster via Canberra to Delhi and Ghana as ever *L'Esprit des Lois* had on the European and American governments of an earlier day, it is notes on how to cultivate a flourishing tree rather than on how to plant. *Physics and Politics* is a remarkable book—perhaps the most brilliant study of social psychology of the whole nineteenth century—. . . but it falls short of his own aim for its concluding definition of verifiable progress has no permanent meaning. *Lombard Street* is one of the ablest pieces of special pleading ever written—the more so for being in a good cause—and a wonderful description of business psychology as well. But he died before he could make any permanent contribution to economic thought. The indictment of Bagehot is that his books are neither fish nor fowl, that they contain neither the fieldwork and precise observation of the social and the political scientist, a Lyell, Maine or Darwin on the one hand, or the prophetic insights of the reflective thinker, a Mill, a Tocqueville or even an Arnold, on the other.

Before deciding where this leaves him, there is one question which the diversity of his work must make one ask. Would his achievement have been greater if he had narrowed and concentrated his interests? He said of Nassau Senior:

> that he scattered and wasted in a semi-abstract discussion of practical topics, powers which were fit to have produced a lasting and considerable work of philosophy.

Was it true of himself? The answer quite simply must be— No. If he had stuck to literary criticism, he would have been only a good, rather than a great, critic, for . . . the process of steeling himself to live in the real world had involved the atrophy of his sense of tragedy, and in consequence, as he said of Scott, he lacked "the consecrating power". If he had confined himself to political analysis, he could have achieved nothing finer than *The English Constitution* and his articles in *The Economist* taken together, because he wished only to modify and explain rather than recast the system which he found. If he had engrossed himself in social psychology, instead of moving on to *Lombard Street* and *Economic Studies,* he might have arrived at a more positive conclusion about the way and direction in which social progress is politically achieved, but the case-work on which a lasting hypothesis could be constructed was at that time very meagre. The promise of *Economic Studies* as a map of the new economic country of the last quarter of the nineteenth century was considerable, but Bagehot had few illusions that he possessed the powers of a great economic thinker. Indeed, one can regret that, rather than concentrating his talents, he did not diversify them even more and turn historian as well. For his mastery of character, the power of his studies of Bolingbroke, Pitt and Peel as well as of minor figures, the sense of historical proportion he displayed in his essay on Macaulay, his psychological realism, show that he had the makings of a great historian. Had he chosen, he could have reinterpreted the two centuries before his own, avoiding the historicism of Macaulay, with a balance and brilliance which would have left his reputation in no doubt. (pp. 246-48)

But such speculations can be misleading if they obscure the unity of his method or lead to any neglect of the two important and enduring contributions which he did make, not only to English letters but to modern life itself—in the desire to comprehend, and the ability to elucidate, the workings of a complex society.... My own reflections on Bagehot have led me to carry [G. M. Young's judgment (see excerpt above, 1937)] a stage further. His "robust and masculine sanity", though won at a certain price, relates him to his time: his opinions as contrasted with his doubts were for the most part those of his intelligent contemporaries.... But in the way in which he used his mind, his insights and his intuition, he was far ahead of his own day. There had been many excellent observers of the contemporary scene before him, from Chaucer down through Hazlitt. Bagehot was one of those rare men of real intellect who recognize that analysis is as worthy of a man's best powers as advocacy, that modern society has achieved a complexity which makes it as important to know where it stands and what its constituency is, as where it is going or where it should go. He is the true ancestor of our modern view that the knowledge of what a society is really like, what drives it, what checks it, what distorts its judgment, cannot be gleaned from statistics or mere facts alone, but is as much the province of the literary and imaginative arts as of the moral and metric sciences. If mid-twentieth-century England can be distinguished, at its best, from mid-Victorian England, at its best, by a certain toughness of mental fiber, by an enhanced ability to look reality in the eye, to distinguish between the formal and the effective, and to accept its own shortcomings without too much tragedy, then Bagehot has a claim to be called not only the perfect Victorian, but the first of our own contemporaries.

His other achievement, the formulation of a new prose style for the transmission of serious ideas, is easier to identify. There are thousands of people all over the world—not just in England, but in the United States, in India, wherever English is the language of ideas—who are, consciously or unconsciously, writing in Bagehot's style. What he did was to loosen and unmat the architectural form of serious prose which he had inherited by way of Macaulay from the Augustans, and to inject into the language of politics and economics some of the color and verve that Hazlitt and an earlier generation had developed for slighter themes.

At times his style seems so colloquial that it has the appearance of mere haste. Nevertheless he knew what he was doing, and he was ready to give this impression because he was in fact writing for his ordinary contemporaries. (pp. 248-50)

As he slowly and deliberately shed the old ornate forms throughout his literary essays, he did not acquire what has been called the "neutral" Victorian style which replaced the older formal and the older plain rhythms of English prose. He had no horror of slang: he was the inventor of the word "padding" to mean filling out a paper or book. He used American importations.... He was prepared to sacrifice euphony and form, to use phrases in an odd way, sometimes in an awkward way, in order to drive his meaning home, for he had learned from Adam Smith that to be convincing, especially to an unimaginative business man, it was essential to be graphic. (p. 250)

Bagehot was a less subtle ironist than Arnold, for his humor was more earthy, and at all costs it was essential to be clear. His writing became plainer as he grew older because he grappled more and more with subjects where flights of imagery or colorful language might confuse rather than enhance his meaning. Since he had an exceptionally clear mind, he had no respect for jargon or for the hubris of those writers, particularly in his

own field, who believe that their reputation is advanced by devising a private language. (p. 251)

Bagehot had in varying measures the qualities which F. L. Lucas has suggested as the elements of style: character, simplicity, humor, vitality, and above all the twin marks of courtesy towards the reader—clarity and brevity. Despite the trenchancy and originality of his books and longer essays, Bagehot was at his best in *The Economist,* when he was working under pressure, within a defined compass, writing, as he thought an editor should, "as a trustee for the subscribers". What Matthew Arnold called "his concern for the *simple truth*" [see excerpt above, 1856], with the accent as much on the first as on the second word, has been the test of great journalists—J. A. Spender and C. P. Scott, Walter Lippmann, Geoffrey Crowther—ever since. It is hardly surprising that the prose style he developed as a journalist, with its irony and restrained use of paradox, its proportion and simplicity, its slum clearance of irrelevant ideas, its fine balance between reverence and impudence, between humor and gravity, should have made him a model for three generations of journalists, teachers, officials, diplomats or any writer who must elucidate a complex subject and bring an inert idea to life. (pp. 251-52)

[Bagehot] stands in the true line of descent of one great Western tradition—no special possession of England but more apt to flower there—that of the amateur. It was characteristic of his mind that he should have pressed for abolishing the distinction between barristers and solicitors, for he had a conviction of the unity of experience, and he refused to be intimidated by the growing fragmentation of knowledge into hydra-headed forms of expertise, from framing and expressing his own opinions. His occasional slipshod judgments and his many inaccuracies were a personal weakness, for his haste and lack of precision would have made him a careless man even if he had [never] lifted a pen. But by treading as an intelligent and informed amateur in the land of the specialist, by having the courage of his insight, by using one form of experience to comprehend another, he not only threw new light on ancient questions of human behavior but helped lay the foundations of a bridge, that is in need of repair today, between the expert and the lay mind. (p. 254)

*Alastair Buchan, in his* The Spare Chancellor: The Life of Walter Bagehot, *1959. Reprint by Michigan State University Press, 1960, 278 p.*

## R.H.S. CROSSMAN (essay date 1963)

[*In his introduction to* The English Constitution, *Crossman discusses the work in relation to Jeremy Bentham's and John Stuart Mill's utilitarian analyses of English government and compares Bagehot's views on the role of class structure in British politics to those of Karl Marx. Crossman attributes the continuing appeal of* The English Constitution *to its "journalistic quality." He notes that while earlier writers on the British constitution had relied on the traditional theory of a division of powers between the executive and legislative branches of government, Bagehot, who had become accustomed as a journalist to describing the contemporary political scene "as he actually saw it," provided a more realistic look at the operation of English government. By doing so, the critic states, Bagehot discovered that "the efficient secret of the Constitution" rested in the fusion, not the separation, of the executive and legislative branches. Crossman disputes Norman St. John-Stevas's contention (see Additional Bibliography, 1959) that Bagehot misrepresented the function of the monarchy in* The English Constitution *and concludes that the work "can*] *still be read as the classical account of the classical period of parliamentary government.''*]

There can be very few studies of [the English] parliamentary system that were so rapidly overtaken by events as Walter Bagehot's *The English Constitution*. First composed as a series of essays for *The Fortnightly,* it was published in book form in 1867—the very year of Disraeli's Reform Act which abruptly and finally ended the period of classical parliamentary government it describes. As an account of contemporary fact, the book was out of date almost before it could be reviewed. Since then we have had countless studies by political scientists and constitutional lawyers, interspersed occasionally with the reflections of a retired politician. Yet for anyone who wants to understand the workings of British politics—be he university student, foreign observer or merely a curious elector—*The English Constitution* still remains the best introduction available.

What is the secret of this remarkable longevity—this timeless quality in a book dashed off as a serial? Why has this boisterous account of Westminster at the turn of the last century become a classic, whereas the learned works of Lowell and Anson, of Berriedale Keith and Jennings began to date and require revision as soon as they were published? One reason why Bagehot's political writings are still so fresh and relevant is the very journalistic quality which prevented their importance being fully appreciated by his contemporaries. . . . Bagehot, in fact, was one of the greatest political journalists of his—or indeed of any age—equally skilled in the crafts of reporter, leader writer or editor; and it was by eschewing 'literary' pretensions and sticking to his trade that he achieved immortality. For it was in the course of describing the contemporary political scene, as he actually saw it, that he hit upon the secret of British politics—the difference between myth and reality, and also between the dignified and the efficient exercise of power. (pp. 1-2)

Bagehot was never content to utter common thoughts. Even in his regular stint of weekly journalism he continued to dazzle his readers, and at the same time to reveal to them new and unexpected insights into British politics. Here his political essays have something in common with Trollope's political novels. Trollope described British politics exclusively in terms of individual and social behaviour, Bagehot in terms of the management of men and the exercise of power. In both cases, however, run of the mill work turned out to order is still read with profit because, while reflecting the surface glitter of Victorian politics, it also exposes the realities behind the façade, forcing us a hundred years later to face the problems we ourselves are seeking to evade, and providing a sharp and sometimes merciless critique of the compromises by which we still try–and fail—to resolve them.

Perhaps the best way of seeing why Bagehot's occasional journalism has outlasted works of far greater philosophic and literary pretensions is to compare *The English Constitution* with Mill's *Representative Government*—a treatise which covered much the same ground and was regarded with much more deference by his contemporaries. . . . Though he publicly always paid his respects to Mill, Bagehot's practical and sceptical mind could not but resent the ascendancy which this highminded intellectual exerted over his whole generation. To the author of *Lombard Street,* the influence on economic thinking of Mill's *Political Economy* seemed pernicious; taught to think in terms of its smooth abstractions, the student would find it more difficult to observe how the businessmen and bankers, who are the proper study of the political economist, really behave.

His attitude to *Representative Government* was very similar. He was irked by the uncritical acceptance which its analysis had received. This dislike is revealed in the very first sentence of *The English Constitution:*

> 'On all great subjects', says Mr. Mill, 'much remains to be said', and of none is this more true than of the English Constitution . . . an observer who looks at the living reality will wonder at the contrast to the paper description.

These opening words had always seemed to me obscure and pointless until I re-read *Representative Government* and realised that Bagehot was replying directly to Mill and challenging his uncritical acceptance of the traditional 'paper description' of the Constitution.

The suppressed vehemence of Bagehot's attack is all the more striking when we realise that the two men were very largely agreed about the aims and objects of representative government. Both were Liberals who welcomed unreservedly the transfer of power to the middle classes which had occurred since 1832. And they were in full agreement that the greatest threat to British freedom lay in an extension of the suffrage that would concede to the working class that 'despotic power' which was still securely in the hands of 'the bald-headed man at the back of the omnibus'.

In the preface to the second edition [of *The English Constitution*], Bagehot expressed the fear that both men felt, with brutal frankness:

> It must be remembered that a political combination of the lower classes, as such and for their own objects, is an evil of the first magnitude; that a permanent combination of them would make them (now that so many of them have the suffrage) supreme in the country; and that their supremacy, in the state they now are, means the supremacy of ignorance over instruction and of numbers over knowledge. So long as they are not taught to act together, there is a chance of this beng averted. . . .

Although Mill called himself a democrat he was just as inflexibly opposed to what he described as 'the tyranny of the majority'. Indeed, as they both saw it, the one great issue of British politics in the 1860's was how to prevent the party politicians, for purely opportunist reasons, making concessions to democracy which would substitute government by ignorance and brute numbers for government by discussion. (pp. 5-7)

What is it then that made Bagehot accuse Mill of mistaking 'a paper description' for the living reality? The answer of course is to be found in Bagehot's distinction between the dignified and the efficient parts of the Constitution, and in the central rôle he allots to the Cabinet.

Of this there had not been a word in *Representative Government*. Mill relied on the old-fashioned notion of a division of power between the executive and the legislature, re-defining it as a division between an elected Parliament and a bureaucracy selected by competitive examination and headed by Ministers responsible to Parliament. What he completely failed to see was that these Ministers banded together as the Cabinet formed the linch pin of the Constitution, a new central authority which could manage the state. In the whole of *Representative Government* I can find only the one mention of the Cabinet. . . . In Bagehot's eyes, this was Hamlet without the Prince.

Mill's failure to see 'the efficient secret of the Constitution' led him quite logically to rely on electoral reform as the main bulwark against the tyranny of the majority. Bagehot devotes nearly a third of his chapter on the House of Commons to a withering attack on what he describes as 'a ruinous innovation' which would strengthen the party machine outside Parliament, and so destroy both the independence of the individual Member and the moderation of the House of Commons—the two conditions he regarded as 'essential to the bare possiblity of parliamentry government'. Electoral devices for excluding the working class from political power were, in his view, either futile or positively dangerous to the rule of the middle class. This could only be maintained by ensuring that all effective power and all important decisions were reserved to the efficient part of the Constitution, and simultaneously providing the working class with a standard of life which would make them content to remain loyal subjects of the Crown, effectively excluded from the secret of power. (pp. 8-9)

Bagehot was as afraid as Mill of the effects of universal suffrage. But he saw—as Mill did not see—that the danger could not be averted by literary tests, plural voting, proportional representation, and all the other devices recommended in *Representative Government*. The wise man, he held, will resist large extensions of the suffrage. But if this delaying action fails, he will realise that 'the only effective security against the rule of an ignorant, miserable and vicious democracy, is to take care that the democracy shall be educated, and comfortable and moral'.

Bagehot's refutation of Mill, the liberal reformer, has stood the test of time. Wherever proportional representation has been tried, it has fulfilled his prediction that it would undermine the independence of the M.P. [Member of Parliament] and increase the powers of the party managers who control the electoral list. Nevertheless, one must add in fairness to Mill that on the central issue—whether it would be possible to combine government by discussion with universal suffrage, and to preserve British liberties in the 'face of a political combination of the lower class'—Bagehot's predictions of disaster were even shriller than Mill's; and on two particular issues—female suffrage and the reform of the civil service by entry through competitive examination—Mill showed more foresight than his sceptical young critic. (p. 10)

Like so many notable advances in human knowledge, [Bagehot's discovery of 'the efficient secret of the English Constitution'] seemed quite obvious once it had been stated and accepted as true. What was, when it was first published, a deeply shocking approach has long since become a standard technique of political science, and the secret which Bagehot dramatically revealed is now a commonplace of political discussion. (pp. 10-11)

In the 1860's, the standard accounts of the English Constitution were still the work of lawyers and historians who accepted the traditional division of powers—Queen, Lords and Commons—at its face value. And it was still believed that political philosophy should be concerned with 'first principles'. Conservative political theorists demonstrated how the Constitution derived from first principles; Liberal reformers showed what changes must be made in order to bring it into accord with first principles.

The first break in this traditional approach to the Constitution had been made long before, by Jeremy Bentham in his famous attack on Blackstone in 1776. When it was published, his *Fragment on Government* was as shocking a document as Bagehot's **The English Constitution** 90 years later. By assuming that human beings are moved only by self-love, and that the main rôle of moral and political principles is to cover up 'sinister interests', Bentham provided himself with an excellent instrument for smashing constitutional façades, and revealing the forces at work behind them. But this aggressive, critical phase of utilitarianism did not last very long. By the time that Bagehot came to London the utilitarian analysis that Bentham had first developed, as a technique for demolishing the religious and legal defences of aristocratic wealth and privilege, had been transformed by John Stuart Mill into a thoroughly respectable philosophy—complete with a fine new set of first principles. (p. 11)

Unfortunately, however, in the course of humanising Utilitarianism, [Mill] had introduced a whole string of contradictions and—even more serious—had blunted the cutting edge of its radical, social analysis. Under his hand it had become a defence of the new middle class establishment, nearly as hypocritical and unconvincing as the system that Bentham had assailed 90 years before. What was needed therefore was a new critique of the Constitution based on an analysis as fearless as Bentham's, but more sophisticated.

Walter Bagehot was ideally equipped for this task. He had none of J. S. Mill's philosophic pretensions, and he was a much more thorough-going sceptic than Bentham who could never rid himself of his belief that man would be perfectible once kings and aristocracies had disappeared. With an amused contempt for reformers, and a positive dislike for intellectuals and theorists, Bagehot set out to succeed where the Utilitarians had so conspicuously failed—to describe the English Constitution in terms, not of first principles but of the real behaviour of those who operate it.

In his New Model, Bagehot retained two basic assumptions of the old Utilitarians. Like them he held that there is nothing mysterious about government; it is simply a special kind of management—the management of those institutions which we call the State—and he also accepted the view that by and large the group which controls the State at any time will manage it in its own interests. But at this point his refinement of Bentham's analysis began. Unlike his precedessors he realised that, in all human activity, tradition and habit are at least as important motives as self-interest. (pp. 12-13)

Bagehot disposed not only of utilitarian psychology but of a fallacy which still survives in a great deal of so-called progressive thought—the idea that in a democracy the educated citizen will be able to free himself from habitual attitudes and traditional loyalties, so that he can think things out for himself, and, in each decision he takes, make up his own mind in terms of cool self-interest. Anyone who applies these precepts in his personal life runs the risk of a nervous breakdown; and the consequences for a nation which adopts this kind of atomised individualism as its pattern of political behaviour will be even more disastrous. In the nation, as in any other group, it is not the individual, thinking and acting for himself that normally settles an issue, but the force of habit and tradition, working through groups and associations. And this analysis remains equally true and relevant whether you are a Conservative trying to defend the *status quo* or a left-winger trying to change it.

It is class interest and group interest, not individual interest, that normally dominate the politics of a free people. (pp. 13-14)

By his distinction between the dignified and the efficient parts of the Constitution, and his assumption that the former are preserved in order to conceal and win allegiance to the latter, Bagehot had provided himself with just that precision-instrument of political analysis which Bentham and . . . [Mill] had lacked. With these two postulates as his working hypotheses, he found it possible to give a simple and rational description of how political power is actually distributed, and how decisions of state are really taken. . . . (p. 16)

Since [according to Bagehot] the Monarchy and the Lords are now merely dignified parts of the Constitution, and the Commons has mainly [the function of electing the Prime Minister], it is clear that effective power is normally concentrated in the hands of the Prime Minister and his colleagues. The text-books may tell us that the safeguards of British freedom lie in the separation of three co-ordinated powers, the Monarchy, the Lords and the Commons. But this theory of checks and balances . . . is now a fiction.

> The efficient secret of the English Constitution may be described as the close union, the nearly complete fusion, of the executive and legislative powers. . . .

This fusion takes place in the Cabinet:

> a board of control chosen by the legislature, out of persons whom it trusts and knows, to rule the nation. . . . A Cabinet is a combining committee—a *hyphen* which joins, a *buckle* which fastens, the legislative part of the State to the executive part of the State. In its origin it belongs to the one, in its functions it belongs to the other. . . .
>
> (p. 20)

Exactly how is this fusion of executive and legislative power achieved? The first answer to this question is to be found in the office of Prime Minister. Once elected by the Commons the Prime Minister exerts powers greater than those of any American President, since he it is who nominates the Ministry and selects the Cabinet over which he presides. In this new middle class régime, in fact, the nation is run by a board of control headed by a powerful managing director. In the second place, the Cabinet from the moment it is created exerts a special control over the Commons. Constitutionally it is only the chief committee of the Commons. But the right of dissolution which it possesses transforms it into 'an executive which can annihilate the legislature, as well as an executive which is the nominee of the legislature. It *was* made, but it *can* unmake; it was derivative in its origin, but it is destructive in its action'. . . .

The third factor which makes possible the fusion of executive and legislative power is the peculiar structure of the Cabinet itself. In *Representative Government*, Mill had loftily announced that committees are incapable of effective action or firm decisions: effective control of the modern state must be handed over to a tiny *élite* of well-qualified public servants, each with his own clearly defined field of responsiblity, and the right to take decisions under the general supervision of a departmental minister. By explaining for the first time the workings of the Cabinet, Bagehot was able to prove Mill wrong. What holds a British Cabinet together and makes it truly ef-

ficient, he tells us, is a combination of party loyalty, collective responsibility and secrecy. In departmental matters, ministers are individually responsible to Parliament, and play the rôle *vis-à-vis* their permanent civil servants that Mill had recommended. But on all the great decisions of state the Cabinet takes its decisions and acts collectively. In the secrecy of this committee, each member is free to express his views. But once the decision has been taken they are all automatically committed, by the doctrine of Cabinet responsibility, to support it in public. (p. 21)

[It] is necessary to draw attention to one important confusion which runs through all Bagehot's political writings, and flawed what otherwise seems to me a faultless piece of social analysis. This flaw is an ambiguity in his concept of 'the efficient secret'. Bagehot could never quite make up his mind whether he was a historian describing a process of development that had been going on since 1832, or whether it was his real purpose to recommend to the new middle class rulers of the country a Machiavellian piece of social engineering. Sometimes he is content to develop his thesis, about the rôle of tradition and habit in preserving ancient institutions after effective power has moved elsewhere, and to note how convenient this is to political stability. But there are a number of passages in which he seems to have quite a different purpose—one not so dissimilar from that of Plato when he wrote the *Republic*.

Plato's primary concern was philosophic. But because he was convinced that Greek civilisation was being destroyed by democracy, he was also passionately interested in teaching an *élite* of young aristocrats how to establish a city state immune to its debilitating effects. The *Republic* is a description of how the Guardians of civilisation should be educated. Plato wastes little time in discussing the schooling which the subject classes would require. Their main political characteristic, he tells us, will be a deferential willingness to accept the rule of their superiors. And in order to induce this deference he invents the myth of the 'Noble Lie', which tells the citizens that they were born either of golden, silver, iron or copper parents; and that if the state is not to perish these classes must remain fixed for ever, so that power remains securely in the hands of the golden class of Guardians. (pp. 26-7)

If anyone had ever asked Bagehot point-blank whether he accepted the doctrine of the Noble Lie, I am pretty sure that he would have brushed aside the notion that, when he wrote **The English Constitution,** he was trying to organise an open conspiracy and equip its members with a new technique of government. Nevertheless, the Platonic aim is there in the book. Of course the converts to Bagehot's doctrine would be called nothing as high-falutin' as Guardians. But he undoubtedly felt that the new middle-class—unsure of itself and ignorant of the art of politics—needed to be shocked out of its complacency and confronted with the problems of power.

But he did not *always* think in this way, and frequently reverted to the rôle of the amused and amusing spectator. Throughout *The English Constitution,* indeed, he wavers between two views of political science, treating it sometimes as a strictly descriptive discipline, and sometime as a practical study of the techniques of manipulating power.

Whenever he took this second view and began to peddle his ingenious contrivances for containing the masses, Bagehot relapsed into the fallacies which he had exposed and rejected in the Utilitarianism of Bentham and Mill. He had seen clearly enough that what invalidated their concept of society, as a mere collection of self-interested individuals and groups, was its disregard for habit and tradition. Yet there are passages of *The English Constitution* where he falls into the same trap.

It is in his treatment of Monarchy that this becomes most obvious. At the end of an admirable analysis of how and why the strength of the Monarchy had increased since 1832, he adds this paragraph:

> Lastly, constitutional royalty . . . acts as a *disguise*. It enables our real rulers to change without heedless people knowing it. The masses of Englishmen are not fit for an elective government; if they knew how near they were to it, they would be surprised, and almost tremble. . . .

Did he really mean that when Lord John Russell was replaced by Lord Palmerston as Premier, the mass of the people were unaware of the fact? Or was he suggesting that on hearing the news they came to the conclusion that the Queen had merely changed the servant through whom she gave her orders? It would be tempting to dismiss this passage as a temporary aberration. But there are many others. Here is one of them:

> The poorer and more ignorant classes—those who would most feel excitement, who would most be misled by excitement—*really believe that the Queen governs*. You could not explain to them the recondite difference between 'reigning' and 'governing'; . . . the ideas necessary to comprehend it do not exist in their minds. . . .

From such passages it is clear that in certain moods Bagehot did regard the Monarchy as a contrivance for exploiting the 'bovine stupidity' of the people and keeping them deferential. . . .

> England is the type of deferential countries, and the manner in which it is so, and has become so, is extremely curious. The middle classes— the ordinary majority of educated men—are in the present day the despotic power in England. . . .
>
> (pp. 27-9)

The 'despotic power' of the middle class has a familiar ring. It reminds us of Karl Marx's theory of class war. And the reminder is apt, since Marx and Bagehot agree that economic class is the determining factor in the structure of government. If we eliminate verbal differences, we can list the following principles to which they both adhere.

1. In a modern capitalistic state, effective power is concentrated in the hands of the bourgeois class.

2. Representative institutions are a form of government deliberately contrived to maintain the class dictatorship of the bourgeoisie.

3. The stability of this political superstructure requires that the people should be kept deferential. They must never be permitted to realise what power they could wield. They must be hoodwinked by rituals; their ideals harnessed to harmless cults and their patriotism twisted into allegiance to a Monarchy remodelled to serve the interests of the bourgeoisie.

In compiling this list of agreed principles, I have preferred to use Marxist clichés. But underneath the difference of language

and ideology, there is a very remarkable resemblance between Bagehot's theory of class politics, and Marx's theory of class war. Nor should we be unduly surprised that the Liberal reactionary and the Communist revolutionary were in such cynical agreement about the differences between appearance and reality in British politics, and the ingenious contrivances by which the real power of the business community is concealed from the public eye. After all, both had been trained by years of practical journalism to take nothing in politics at its face value. Both were political economists in a period when the social sciences were still in their infancy, and when there was no separation between politics and economics which could prevent them describing the whole structure of the new capitalist society arising before their eyes. And they were both studying exactly the same society in exactly the same epoch— Britain in the 1850's and 1860's. The first volume of *Das Kapital* was published in the same year as *The English Constitution*.

I myself am in no doubt that Marx and Bagehot together provide far the most original and perceptive investigation of classical free enterprise and classical parliamentary government. If their accounts read very differently, this is because Marx constricted his analysis within a Hegelian framework, whereas Bagehot dismissed speculative philosophy as pretentious nonsense.

Nevertheless, despite this difference in their intellectual backgrounds, they shared a fervent and rather uncritical belief in the powers of social science. Both were products of an age when it seemed certain that, within a few decades, all the problems of society could be resolved by the application to them of the methods of applied science and applied technology. And it is because they shared this belief that their analyses of the relationship between economics and politics, and between class and government, sometimes fall into the same fallacies. Both men were too ready to accept simple mechanistic accounts of how political and social institutions 'really work'; and too optimistic about the possibility of discovering the scientific laws which determined historical development.

As a result, both succumbed to the temptation to 'explain' politics in terms of class-struggle. Politicians, as Marx and Bagehot both realised, when they were criticising other writers, very rarely take decisions which settle anything, far less change the course of history. What happens in politics is far more often the result of impersonal forces than of the activity of individuals or groups working according to rational and previously articulated plans. Of course, human will and personality do have an important and sometimes a decisive effect—but always within limits set by forces outside their control. And it is the task of the journalist, social scientist and historian to separate these elements giving each its correct importance.

A hundred years ago, when history-writing and social science were both in their infancy, there was a natural temptation to accept no fact on trust, to dismiss conventional chronicles as legends, and to look for 'the real forces' whose operation these facts and legends concealed. The theory that politics could be explained in terms of a secret struggle of classes was the kind of hypothesis that was bound to attract the early social scientists. . . . Bagehot and Marx were fully justified when they shocked their contemporaries by exposing for the first time the importance of economic class in British politics. What vitiated both their accounts was their inclination to oversimplify class conflict, and to interpret the development of representative institutions and the working of the parliamentary system as a Machiavellian conspiracy of the bourgeoisie. (pp. 29-31)

In Britain, the influence of Marx—at least until the 1930's—was negligible, and the class analysis of society was employed not as an instrument of revolution but as part of the defence of the *status quo*. It was Bagehot, in fact, not Marx who set the pattern. And the main stereotype he left on the English mind was the contrast between the cleverness of our rulers, who really understand how to manage politics, and the stupidity of the common people who were not born or trained to rule.

Was there ever any truth in this stereotype? The first part of it has been controverted by no one more effectively than by Bagehot. In essay after essay he demonstrated what a disadvantage it is in British politics to be interested in ideas, or concerned with principles. In the person of Lord Althorp, he painted the picture of the ideal British statesman:

> A leader's mind 'ought to be like a reserve fund—not invested in showy securities, but sure to be come at when wanted, and always of staple value. And this Lord Althorp's mind was; there was not an epigram in the whole of it; everything was solid and ordinary. Men seemed to have trusted him much as they trust a faithful animal, entirely believing that he would not deceive if he could, and that he could not if he would.'

When he was not describing the Cabinet as an ingenious contrivance, Bagehot saw more clearly than anyone that the British ruling class would never tolerate a Machiavelli for long, and that its real strength was not cleverness or clarity of thought, but a sense of tradition which it shared with the common people, and its native ability to know the time for firmness and the time for concession. 'An acquiescent credulity' he remarked of Sir Robert Peel, 'is a quality of such men's nature. They cannot help being sure that what everyone says is true'.

So when Bagehot talked as though the Monarchy was a contrivance, and the Cabinet was a mechanism whose working had been deliberately concealed, he was being false to the understanding of the British ruling class which made him the outstanding political journalist of his time. If the Monarchy had ever been used—as Bagehot sometimes said it should be used—by men who saw through its rituals and only wanted to dupe the masses, its magic power would have been punctured at once. The myths and legends of a Monarchy are only credible to the masses so long as those who propagate them believe their own propaganda. What gives the British Monarchy its unique strength is the fact that the court, the aristocracy and the church—not to mention the middle classes—are just as credulous worshippers of it as the masses.

And the same applies to the 'efficient secret' of the Constitution. Years after Cabinet government had become an anachronism, its legend was being spread with utter sincerity by the Privy Councillors and permanent civil servants who, if Bagehot's Machiavellian theory of politics had been correct, should have been contriving the next secret mechanism, for denying to the mass of the people knowledge of where power resides. Indeed I am tempted to reverse Bagehot's stereotype and to assert that the secret of our political stability is the deferential attitude of our rulers, and the fact that the astringent scepticism which corrodes reverence for authority is only to be found among the masses on the sidelines of politics. (pp. 32-3)

[It has been suggested by Norman St. John-Stevas] that Bagehot's description of 'The Magic of Monarchy' was a brilliant anachronism—untrue when he wrote it but approximating very closely to 20th century realities. Queen Victoria's letters, we are told, show that she played a far more active rôle in politics—usually against reform—than Bagehot's theory suggested. . . . (p. 36)

Such criticism, it seems to me, is the result of reading into *The English Constitution* the stereotype of 'the retired widow and the unemployed youth' created by the famous first paragraph of the chapter on Monarchy. This does not, as is so often assumed, summarise the pages that follow. Unlike his liberal imitators, who did fall into the error of writing off the Monarchy as a mere symbol, Bagehot knew very well that the Prince Consort had played a most important rôle in politics; and he assumed that, after Albert's death, the Queen was almost certainly continuing to interfere. Among courtiers, he remarks, 'it is an accepted secret doctrine that the Crown does more than it seems. But there is a wide discrepancy in opinion as to the quality of that action . . . Now the best Liberal politicians say *"We* shall never know, but when history is written our children may know, what we owe to the Queen and Prince Albert"'. . . . Later on he hints very clearly that the Prince of Wales, when in due course he became Edward VII, was likely to be a dangerous busybody undoing the good work that Albert had done through the Queen.

The truth is that, in distinguishing between the dignified and the efficient parts of the Constitution, Bagehot was far too acute an observer of the deliberate confusion in which British government functions to suggest that the separation was absolute. The House of Commons, he was careful to observe, is dignified as well as efficient; and the Monarch, from his unique vantage-point above the party fray, has the power to do untold good and untold harm. Nothing in Queen Victoria's letters, therefore, invalidates Bagehot's account of the rôle that she was playing in the 1860's.

It seems to me, therefore, that *The English Constitution* can still be read as the classical account of the classical period of parliamentary government. The secret which Bagehot claimed to have discovered does indeed provide the correct explanation of the relationship between the Commons and the Cabinet as it emerged between 1832 and 1867. (pp. 36-7)

> *R.H.S. Crossman, in an introduction to* The English Constitution *by Walter Bagehot, Collins, 1963, pp. 1-57.*

## NORMAN St. JOHN-STEVAS  (essay date 1963)

[*The editor of the most recent collection of Bagehot's works, St. John-Stevas is considered one of the author's most perceptive twentieth-century critics. He is particularly admired for his detailed examination of* The English Constitution *in* Walter Bagehot: A Study of His Life and Thought Together with a Selection from His Political Writings (*see Additional Bibliography*). *St. John-Stevas's later work,* Walter Bagehot, *from which the following excerpt is drawn, is an appreciative overview of Bagehot's literary career that focuses on his critical writings. Here, St. John-Stevas discusses Bagehot's works in relation to his life, contending that he was a "no-nonsense, experienced man of the world" as well as a "mystic" whose "distinction as a writer can . . . be traced to [his] capacity to bridge the gulf between the practical and intellectual worlds." While St. John-Stevas dismisses Bagehot's critical theories, he praises his assessments of his contemporaries and concludes that he was a "great critic" because of the "insights which he continually gives into a writer's essential genius."*]

The appeal of Bagehot, both as a man and as a writer is irresistible. He combined a mind of extraordinary keenness and subtlety with a nature dominated by deep and passionate feeling. . . . Intellectual detachment stamps all his work, yet from his youth he was immersed in the world of affairs both as a banker and an editor. . . . He had little sympathy with the Victorian cult of ceaseless activity, but no thinker has been more convinced of the value of activity as a basis for the life of the mind. The theme of the educative efficacy of affairs recurs throughout his works. 'The exclusive devotion to books tires', he writes in his essay on Macaulay. 'We require to love and hate, to act and live.' He ridiculed Carlyle's dictum that the 'true University of this day is a collection of books' as being ridiculous 'if you wish to form a bookworm but not else'. The uniqueness of Bagehot as a man and his distinction as a writer can both be traced to this capacity to bridge the gulf between the practical and intellectual worlds, so that the opposing impulses in his character made for unity rather than for division. (pp. 8-9)

Bagehot brought to his writing every kind of equipment save that of a literary historian. By education a classicist and philosopher, he supplemented this formal training by voracious reading until the end of his life. Such a reader, as he himself points out in his essay on Bishop Butler 'is apt, when he comes to write, to exhibit his reading in casual references and careless innuendoes, which run out insensibly from the fullness of his literary memory'. This gives a richness to his style. As a banker and editor he knew men and the world of law, politics and commerce. He used this knowledge to illustrate and give body to his literary judgements. (pp. 10-11)

Bagehot has some quirks of style the principal of which is a passion for dividing subjects into two classes. . . . No reader of Bagehot can go very far without discovering examples of this tendency. In his essay on Bishop Butler he divides religion into two kinds, natural and supernatural, the one inspired by the God of imagination, the other by the God of conscience. One is based on beauty: the other on fear. There are, we learn, two kinds of genius, regular and irregular: two kinds of biography, exhaustive and selective: two kinds of goodness, sensuous and ascetic: two kinds of fiction, ubiquitous and sentimental, and these examples could be multiplied. (p. 12)

Perhaps his 'duomania' as Professor Irvine, an earlier critic, has described it, can be traced back to a fundamental division in his own character. Bagehot, as some of his contemporaries saw him, and as we see him through his political essays in particular, was a sardonic, no-nonsense, experienced man of the world. But there was Bagehot's other self, closer to the 'dark realities' of life, and which perhaps for that reason he sheered away from in later life, the passionate, mystical Bagehot . . . , who we know chiefly by tantalizing glimpses in his literary essays. (pp. 12-13)

[Enjoyment is] the essence of Bagehot's approach to literature. He read and wrote as a recreation. He was not an academic critic: he made no attempt to cover systematically any particular period: he was a journalist of genius who enjoyed reviewing books. . . . Bagehot's literary essays are accordingly a very personal collection. (p. 17)

The earliest author he tackled was Shakespeare. The essay is perhaps his finest and gives us not only a picture of Shakespeare but a very clear idea of Bagehot. His essay on Milton is not so successful. He does not seem really to like his subject and this is confirmed by external evidence. 'I am grinding away

at Milton', he writes to his wife in 1859. The reader catches the noise. Bagehot wrote a number of essays on the eighteenth century. Unlike Carlyle and Newman and many of his contemporaries, it was a period he appreciated. His essay on Gibbon is a comic masterpiece, but I do not rank the rest of his eighteenth century essays very high. That on Cowper is inadequate: his account of Sterne is inclined to be repetitive: his discussion of Bishop Butler is rather too abstract for general modern taste, as well as for Bagehot's distinctive genius. Lady Mary Wortley Montagu is too slight a figure for a major literary assessment but she gives Bagehot a good opportunity to paint a picture of eighteenth century life and manners. Most will prefer his nineteenth century essays. Those on the early nineteenth century writers, on Hartley Coleridge, the Edinburgh Reviewers, Shelley and Wordsworth, are particularly fine. **'Hartley Coleridge'** shows Bagehot's style at its perfection, although it was only the second literary essay he wrote. . . . Curiously, for one familiar with French literature, he wrote about only one French author, Béranger. Bagehot did not take a very high view of French literary genius and as he says in his essay on Cowper: 'For the English, after all, the best literature is the English. We understand the language; the manners are familiar to us; the scene at home; the associations our own. Of course, a man who has not read Homer is like a man who has not seen the ocean. There is a great object of which he has no idea. But we cannot be always seeing the ocean.'

Bagehot's criticism is practical rather than metaphysical. He says in his essay on Tennyson's *Idylls* that 'the English mind likes to work on stuff' and in this respect Bagehot's mind was very English. Apart from his essay on Tennyson, Wordsworth and Browning there is little speculative in his critical writings. Like Matthew Arnold, Bagehot was always aware that literature was connected with life, and was as much interested in the man who wrote the work as he was in the work itself. When Bagehot's friend Hutton edited his works for publication after his death he divided them into 'biographical' and 'literary' studies, but this dichotomy is distorting. All Bagehot's literary essays are up to a point biographical and a more satisfactory division is into literary and historical. Bagehot moves freely between the life of the writer and the writer's works, treating them as a unity and using points gleaned from one to illustrate the other. (pp. 17-19)

Had Bagehot written nothing other than his essay on Gibbon it would have entitled him to a place amongst the great English comic writers. The central thread of the essay is the comic contrast between the sedate figure of Gibbon sitting peacefully in his study and the stream of world-shaking events he is describing: 'You should do everything, said Lord Chesterfield, in minuet time. It was in that time that Gibbon wrote his history, and such was the manner of the age. You fancy him in a suit of flowered velvet, with a bag and sword, wisely smiling, composedly rounding his periods. . . . You seem to see the grave bows, the formal politeness, the finished deference.' Perhaps, says Bagehot mischievously, 'when a Visigoth broke a head, he thought that that was all. Not so; he was making history: Gibbon has written it down.' This comic element is found throughout his writings: he was a very clever writer but unlike Lytton Strachey he rarely yields to the temptation to distort. Bagehot was witty, sardonic and ironic; but you find less sophisticated forms of humour in his work. Sometimes he is carried away by a sheer sense of fun. (p. 28)

Was Bagehot a great critic? The contemporary literary establishment would probably deny it, and if judgement was to be based exclusively on [his literary theories] . . . one would be inclined to agree. They do not show Bagehot at his best, and they have not exercised any widespread influence. But if one looks at Bagehot's works as a whole, if one considers the insights which he continually gives into a writer's essential genius, one is bound to answer affirmatively. But precisely because his criticism is so highly idiosyncratic, so personal, he has founded no school. Yet . . . , his criticism has a philosophic and metaphysical as well as a personal foundation. It has a lucidity and penetration which entitle it to a high place in nineteenth century criticism. Only when he writes on Wordsworth is he tempted to descend to mere adulation. Sometimes he makes a bad error of judgement as when he assigns Byron to permanent oblivion. But these are small defects. . . . A stiff test of a critic is his assessment of contemporaries and Bagehot does well by this criterion. As Saintsbury noted: he was one of the first to recognize Browning and Tennyson as among the leaders of mid-nineteenth century poetry [see excerpt above, 1911]; his analysis of Clough is extraordinarily perceptive: his assessments of Dickens and Thackeray are astringent and incisive. One can only regret the gaps in his criticism: he has left us nothing on the Brontës or on Meredith and only one tantalizing sentence on George Eliot praising her as 'the greatest living writer of fiction'.

When all is said and done, the only sensible test of good criticism is whether people still read it. Bagehot's criticism has this undeniable merit: it has survived. His more academic contemporaries have been forgotten. (pp. 36-7)

*Norman St. John-Stevas, in his* Walter Bagehot, *Longmans, Green & Co., 1963, 42 p.*

## RENÉ WELLEK (essay date 1965)

[*Wellek's* A History of Modern Criticism, *from which the following excerpt is drawn, is a major, comprehensive study of the literary critics of the last three centuries. His critical method, as demonstrated in* A History, *is one of describing, analyzing, and evaluating a work solely in terms of the problems it poses for itself and how the writer solves them. Here, Wellek describes and assesses Bagehot's critical approach. He argues that the author's greatest contribution to literary criticism was his "Wordsworth, Tennyson, and Browning; or, Pure, Ornate, and Grotesque Art in English Poetry." This essay, Wellek contends, is most notable for its formulation of the poetic theory of "type," a doctrine which states that the poet's duty is to identify and depict what is universally and characteristically human.*]

Bagehot seems not very important today, though he is sane, representative, and symptomatic enough to deserve some attention. For him the center of literature is occupied by the great normal geniuses, the "painters of essential human nature" such as Shakespeare and Scott. Shakespeare is a universal man who conveys a "general impression of entire calmness and equability." Scott has a steady insight, "a peculiar healthiness," "a conservative imagination" whose principal object is "the structure—the undulation and diversified composition of human society." He has an accurate knowledge of political economy—high praise from an editor of *The Economist;* Scott knows that the world is neither a world of exact justice nor an "uncared-for world" deserted by God. Bagehot sees Scott's failings and limitations: his sentimental view of woman, his lack of a searching, abstract intellect, his indifference to the deeper reaches of the soul. But even these deficiencies are paradoxically virtues. In politics and theology Bagehot praised "stupidity," the prejudice of Burke or the ignorance of Bishop

Butler, who were his intellectual masters. Bagehot sees, for instance, the national appeal of the poetry of Cowper in "these exact delineations of what the English people really prefer," "torpid, in-door, tea-tabular felicity."

Compared to these "normal" authors most others seem to Bagehot eccentric, "unsymmetrical." Dickens "has been led by a sort of pre-Raphaelite *cultus* of reality" into error: he gives us caricatures instead of people. "You could no more fancy Sam Weller [in *The Pickwick Papers*], or Mark Tapley [in *Martin Chuzzlewit*], or the Artful Dodger [in *Oliver Twist*] really existing, than you can fancy a talking duck or a writing bear." His poor people "have taken to their poverty very thoroughly." "A tone of objection to the necessary constitution of human society" displeases the Tory critic. He prefers Thackeray for his "stern and humble realism," but also objects that Thackeray "thought too much of social inequalities" and distinctions but in his writings "was too severe on those who, in cruder and baser ways, showed that they also were thinking much." Bagehot classes Laurence Sterne with Thackeray for his pity and humanity, but is repelled by Sterne's oddity: his "antediluvian fun," his indecency, his utter lack of form and order. Since Bagehot pronounces that "an imperative law of the writing art is that a book should go straight on" and that "eccentricity is no fit subject for literary art," he must conclude that *Tristram Shandy* is an example of "barbarous, provincial art": "redolent of an inferior society."

Bagehot's toleration for deviations from his ideal, well-centered man varies in different essays. Hartley Coleridge is treated with sympathy as a charming dreamer who never "grasped the idea of fact and reality." Clough is admired for his struggles with an undefinable religion, and his poetry defended as "intellectual poetry" of limited appeal but genuine merit. On the other hand, Béranger is disparaged as a common, genial, skeptical, democratic man who appears to Bagehot particularly French in his limitations. He lacks "*back*" thought." He has no access to the "strong, noble imagination," "the solid stuff" in which the English excel.

Surprisingly, and possibly inconsistently, there comes a point at which Bagehot transcends this somewhat commonplace ideal of normal art. Off and on he adopts the romantic concepts of the imagination and nature: mainly, it would appear, from Hazlitt, whom he greatly admired and whose style and method must have influenced him. Imagination is "a living thing, a kind of growing plant" beyond the limits of consciousness, working unseen, in a state of "stealing calm." Imagination "detects the secrets of the universe, explains Nature, reveals what is above Nature." It is "a glancing faculty" which loves contrasts and opposites. Shakespeare's imagination, says Bagehot, dimly echoing Coleridge's formula, "seems to be floating between the contrasts of things." Bagehot sees no evidence for any difference between imagination and fancy, but assigns to fancy a subordinate role of amplification and ornamentation. Wordsworth and Shelley represent this realm of imagination, which is for Bagehot the realm of the highest and purest poetry. He chides Jeffrey for dismissing Wordsworth's mysticism. "The misfortune is that mysticism is true," that there is "a religion of Nature, or more exactly, the religion of the imagination." Wordsworth's "works are the Scriptures of the intellectual life," because of "this haunting, supernatural, mystical view of Nature." Though Bagehot disapproved of Shelley's politics and religion, he classes him with Wordsworth for his "classical," pure imagination: simple, abstract, aspiring to the unconditioned. He treats him sympathetically even as a person:

his impulsive temperament "passes through evil, but preserves its purity." Keats contrasts with Shelley as a fanciful, ornamental, romantic poet. Keats used to pepper his tongue, "to enjoy in all the grandeur the cool flavour of delicious claret," while Shelley was a "water-drinker." Surprisingly, and most unjustly, S. T. Coleridge is found lacking in the proper romantic nature worship: he was, after a brief Wordsworthian phase, "utterly destitute of any perception of beauty in landscape or nature." Equally unjustly Bagehot condemns Pope as the "poet of fashionable life" which has "no reference whatever to the beauties of the material universe." "The poetry (if such it is) of Pope would be just as true if all the trees were yellow and all the grass flesh-colour."

In Bagehot's most ambitious literary essay, **"Wordsworth, Tennyson, and Browning: or Pure, Ornate and Grotesque Art in English Poetry"** . . . , this typology is elaborated at length. The pure, imaginative, classical Wordsworth contrasts with the ornate, fanciful, romantic Tennyson and with the grotesque, realistic, medieval Browning. Keats would be grouped with Tennyson, Shelley with Wordsworth. Milton is brought into the scheme as combining a simple classical subject matter with ornate, profuse imagery. The details of the characterization seem often doubtful: the medievalism of Browning is overplayed for the sake of the thesis—it apparently means only something like the minute realism of the pre-Raphaelites—and obviously the term "classical" applies to Wordsworth and Shelley in too peculiar a meaning to find acceptance. The historical continuity from Wordsworth to Tennyson, from Shelley to Browning is ignored. But the game of contrasts among the three poets gives occasion for Bagehot's most interesting proposal: "We want a word *literatesque*, fit to be put into a book," on the analogy of *picturesque*, "fit to be put into a picture." "Literatesque" would mean "that perfect combination in *subject-matter* of literature, which suits the *art* of literature." It is the "typical form, the rememberable idea." "The business of the poet is with types; and those types are mirrored in reality." "The poet must find in that reality, the *literatesque* man, the *literatesque* scene, which nature intends for him, and which will live in his page." Bagehot is well aware of the ancestry of his notion: he appeals to the debate between Schiller and Goethe on the *Urpflanze*. The symbolic plant is the type and "Goethe was right in searching for this in reality and nature; Schiller was right in saying that it was an 'idea.' " In modern poetry this "type" is the poet himself. Of course the poet does "not describe himself *as* himself: autobiography is not his object; he takes himself as a specimen of human nature . . . He takes such of his moods as are most characteristic, as most typify certain moods of certain men, or certain moods of all men." Poets describe what is "generic, not what is special and individual."

In a different context Bagehot arrived at this personal but typical poetry by way of a history of genres. "Poetry begins in Impersonality. Homer is a voice." Dramatic art, Greek drama in particular, is a transition to the lyric, which expresses some one mood, some single sentiment, some isolated longing in human nature. It deals not with man as a whole, but with man piecemeal. Lyrical poets must not be judged literally from their lyrics, since these are "discourses." " . . . But the modern poet is neither epic, nor dramatic, nor lyric in the old sense. He is "self-delineative": he depicts his mind "viewed as a whole." Modern "egotistical" poetry, that of Wordsworth or Shelley or Byron, is actually "allied to the epic," since it is concerned with the delineation of one character, one hero, as Homer with Achilles or Vergil with Aeneas.

Bagehot returns to the portrait or character of the poet in all his essays but to the representative, universalized character—for "art can only deal with the universal," with the idea, the typical and representative. In practice this often means the average national type: Béranger or Cowper, neither of whom expresses the highest possibilities of his respective nation; or it means the universal man represented by Shakespeare. In an essay **"Shakespeare—the Man"** . . . Bagehot defends the view that personality must be discernible through writings even where we have no biographical evidence. "A person who knows nothing of an author he has read, will not know much of the author whom he has seen." He quotes the description of the fleeing hare from [Shakespeare's] *Venus and Adonis* . . . and comments: "It is absurd, by the way, to say that we know *nothing* about the man who wrote that; we know that he has been after a hare. It is idle to allege that mere imagination would tell him that a hare is apt to run among a flock of sheep, or that its so doing disconcerts the scent of hounds." Shakespeare is contrasted with Scott, who had a much more limited "organization," and with Goethe, who seems to Bagehot "always a man apart from life." Goethe went to every scene "with a reserve and as a stranger. He went there *to experience*." Shakespeare was not merely "with men, but of men," a universal man, but also a man of the people. Though Bagehot sees something of Shakespeare's latent melancholy, his "insight into the musing life of man," his general portrait is disconcertingly Victorian: a "substantial man," "a judge of dogs," "an outdoor sporting man," a patriot distrusting the mob, etc. Bagehot is too wary of the abnormal: he disparages even Falstaff as an artistic misconception and complains of Hamlet as a divided nature who seems to him an inferior subject for art.

Bagehot's central thesis about personality in writing may be right, but in practice he is unable to see in Shakespeare more than what he is looking for: the social and moral ideals of his time.

Bagehot's taste is limited, preoccupied with the normal, distrustful of everything eccentric, even Philistine in the Arnoldian sense. But in theory Bagehot hit upon an important theme: the "type," which almost simultaneously engaged the attention of Taine in France and Dobrolyubov in Russia. He gave it an original twist with the concept of "egotistical," "self-delineative," but representative poetry. (pp. 180-85)

> *René Wellek, "Arnold, Bagehot, and Stephen," in his* A History of Modern Criticism, 1750-1950: The Later Nineteenth Century, *Vol. 4, Yale University Press, 1965, pp. 155-90.\**

**HENRY FAIRLIE** (essay date 1971)

[*In the following review of the political essays collected in Volumes III and IV of* The Collected Works of Walter Bagehot, *Fairlie exposes the narrowness of Bagehot's description of the "model" constitutional statesman. Pointing out that Bagehot's ideal statesman was merely one who expressed the opinions of "the new commercial class for which [Bagehot] primarily wrote," Fairlie cautions against applying Bagehot's model to societies other than his own. According to Fairlie, Bagehot's "acquiescence in the industrial and commercial system" blinded him to the most important social and political issues of his time; his failure to recognize the full significance of such contemporary movements as the extension of voting privileges and the industrial revolution reveals that he lacked the "common sense for which he is so often praised." S.A.M. Westwater differs with Fairlie's interpretation of Bagehot's political thought (see excerpt below, 1977).*]

The immediate appeal which Bagehot makes is not hard to understand. "Papa and I," he wrote to his mother at the age of twelve, "have such nice chats about Sir R. Peel and the little Queen"; and it is as nice chats about public affairs and public men that the collected essays and articles remain so fresh, even at a third or fourth reading. There is, of course, more to Bagehot than this. (p. 30)

Bagehot, said G. M. Young, raised common sense to the power of genius. It is a comfortable and English thought. But if common sense is so raised, it ceases to be common sense; and this is exactly what happened with Bagehot. He raised common sense to a principle, almost to a system, by which men and nations should govern themselves and their affairs. But common sense cannot bear such a weight and, in the process, what is common-sensical becomes nonsensical. Reading these essays and articles again, one is still captured by the marvellously quotable individual judgments, in which common sense is, indeed raised to the power of epigram. But the total effect—the total scheme, if one may use so un-English an idea—is one of considerable contrariness.

Bagehot has been reviewed by succeeding generations of journalists and critics. . . . But no reviewer has ever pointed out that what Bagehot said of Peel as a constitutional statesman can just as well be said of him as a political journalist: "a man of common opinions and uncommon abilities . . . the powers of a first-rate man and the creed of a second-rate man." Such may be the condition of all political journalists; and, once one accepts this, one can accept Bagehot. But it is precisely this that neither he nor his eulogists will allow us to accept. He himself exalted the press. Daily newspapers, weekly journals, monthly reviews: to him, they were a high attribute of a high civilisation: specifically of that civilisation which the middle class had created in England in the nineteenth century. The *Economist* and the *National Review* really were, to him, powers for good in the land; and he was a power for good in the *Economist* and the *National Review*. The garland he thus wove for himself, posterity has amiably placed on his brow.

Bagehot is today enjoying something of a vogue, much as Trollope did twenty years ago. . . . The social and political order which [his essays] described has passed, yet we enjoy their celebrations of it. The reason is apparent enough. "Wherein," asked Michael Sadleir, "lies the strange potency" of the novels of Trollope? "It lies surely in his acceptance and his profound understanding of ordinary life. In the tale of English literature he is—to put the matter in a phrase—the supreme novelist of acquiescence." One is tempted to use the very same phrase about Bagehot: that he was a novelist of acquiescence. He likes to take a character and arrange a plot around him. This is the reason for the titles: **"Adam Smith as a Person"**; **"What Lord Lyndhurst Really Was"**; **"Why Mr Disraeli has Succeeded."** They are like the chapter headings of a Victorian novel, and one would not be in the least surprised if he had adapted Trollope's own title: "Harriet Martineau: Can We Forgive Her?" In fact—and no political journalist would criticise his good fortune—Bagehot had found a gimmick. By his title and his opening sentence, he stated his fictional problem. How could a man like Adam Smith write *The Wealth of Nations*? Actually, there is no problem. But he persuades us that there is, and his racy sketch follows.

Bagehot's primary concern, then, was with political character, and this is, of course, a particularly English obsession. No one in America is much interested in political character. . . . [The] difference in attitude between England and America is aptly illustrated by the difference between the titles of Bagehot's essays and the titles of Richard Hofstadter's equally brilliant (although so different in their execution) sketches of American statesmen: "Thomas Jefferson: the Aristocrat as Democrat?"; "Andrew Jackson: and the Rise of Liberal Capitalism"; "John C. Calhoun: the Marx of the Master Class." They are not presented to us as characters, and no American could ever have written, or could write, Bagehot's sustained delineation, in his essay on Brougham, of all that makes the character of an agitator.

This delight in political character is itself a form of the deference which Bagehot noticed in the English people. They enjoy a character at the head of their affairs, and they will enjoy even a failure if he has character enough. . . . No one has depicted political character with more facility than Bagehot, or has made it more apparent why the concern with it is a source of acquiescence, of deference, in a whole people. One should not, therefore, be surprised to find that Bagehot himself was acquiescent, indeed deferential. He knew the character of his subject: it was his own. (pp. 30-1)

[Bagehot] was intent on making his way in the world, and he was not much disposed to spoil his chances by martyrdom. "I think I am with the majority—a healthy habit for a young man to contract," he wrote to his mother from Paris, at the time of the *coup d'état* in 1851. He would strive to be with the majority for the rest of his life, and he would all too easily succeed. One can read nothing about Bagehot—his letters, the memories of his family and his friends, the haunting early intimacy with Clough—without wondering how much of his spirit—sensitive, romantic, passionate—he crushed, in order to write **Lombard Street**.

Even on the evidence of the political journalism in these recent volumes, one cannot help asking what he might have been. His earliest journalism took the form of the **"Letters on the French *Coup d'État* of 1851."** . . . They were audacious and provoking, not unlike the juvenilia by which new political journalists today announce their arrival in the columns of the *Spectator* or the *New Statesman*. But in the second of them, there is an authentic accent which was soon to be lost in his public writing, an accent of protest against the meaninglessness of the industrial civilisation which was being created in Europe. He is at the point of arguing that employment in France depends on the Parisian trade, "the jewellery, the baubles, the silks, the luxuries," when he exclaims:

> For this is the odd peculiarity of commercial civilisation. The life, the welfare, the existence, of thousands depends on their being paid for doing what seems nothing when done . . . people contrive to go out to their work, and to find work to employ them actually until the evening, body and soul are kept together, and this is what mankind have to show for their six thousand years of toil and trouble.

"To keep up this system," he adds, "we must sacrifice everything . . . ; at all hazards, and if we can, mankind must be kept alive." The protest is fierce . . . but the acquiescence is almost immediate. The system may be meaningless, but the system must be preserved, and it cannot be preserved without financial confidence. "No man liked to take a long bill; no one could imagine to himself what was coming. . . . Six weeks ago society was living from hand to mouth; now she feels sure of the next meal."

On these grounds, he acquiesced in the *coup d'état* of Louis Napoleon and (although with some later qualifications) in the Second Empire. So it was always to be: acquiescence in the industrial and commercial system which, ''at all hazards, and if we can,'' must be preserved, and acquiescence in the man and the class—the man characterising the class—which could most surely preserve it. He saw very clearly—as clearly on some points, Crossman suggests [see excerpt above, 1963], as Marx—but, seeing, he acquiesced. The end, given the class and the men to whom he deferred, could only be a wordly cynicism, in place of the vein of irony which lay within him. (pp. 31-2)

[Bagehot's primary interest] was the characters of those who rule. Since he was aware—and how could he not be aware, given the great clash between the landed and the commercial interests which dominated English politics in the middle of the nineteenth century?—of the importance of class as *a* determining factor in politics, he then made the connection which was to become his theme. The character of a politician—his political character, his character *as* a politician—is the expression of class: not of the class from which he comes, although that may happen to be true, but of the class which he aspires to lead. It may not seem a very profound insight, but Bagehot pursued it with both brilliance and perversity. At the beginning and end of the biographical essays stand Bolingbroke and Disraeli, both of whom found the country party ''in a state of dumb power'', and each of whom ''became at once important in Parliament, because he was the eloquent spokesman of many inaudible voices''. That is a moderate statement to which there can be no exception. But, in between, the main body of the essays covers the politicians in whom the new commercial interest found its voice, and at once the theme takes on a new importance: or, rather, it mutates into his most familiar, his most frequently repeated, assertion, that the constitutional statesman must express the creed of the average man. This assertion is so often quoted, and so often praised, that we must be clear what it meant to Bagehot. It is not nearly so innocent as it at first seems.

There is no questioning its importance to Bagehot. He says it of Pitt: ''the successful power to give in a more than ordinary manner the true feelings and sentiments of ordinary men.'' He says it of Peel . . . and pushes the point home: ''Public opinion . . . rules; and public opinion is the opinion of the average man.'' He manages to twist the point round, and say it even of Palmerston: ''He was not a common man, but a common man might have been made out of him. He had in him all that a common man has and something more.'' He says it when he speaks of Gladstone: ''In a free country, we must use the sort of argument which plain men understand.'' Moreover, this theme, so persistently reiterated, is closely connected to another: his praise of ''stupidity'' as a virtue in a free people. Why did a clever man so exalt the average man, and then go a step further, and exalt him for his stupidity?

Succeeding generations of clever men have found the argument seductive. But we must realise that all his talk of ''the average man'' obscures the fact that Bagehot was not talking of public opinion as we understand it at all. We do not imagine that public opinion is as uniform and as coherent as Bagehot suggests: even in public opinion polls, we attend to income groups, social groups, age groups, regional groups. Bagehot was able to talk readily of the common opinion of ordinary men because he was talking of a single class, which was then unusually uniform and coherent: the industrial and commercial and, to

some extent, the professional middle class of England: the class for which he wrote and which he gratified. When he talks of politicians who had a following outside this class, he no longer says that they represented the common creed of average men; he stipulates their class, and does not identify the class as the nation of average men: thus Derby is described as ''one who talks the political dialect of English country gentlemen.'' As for the working class, it is nowhere conceded that they had any opinion at all. By his criteria, he was right: they had no opinion which could find any political voice, either in Parliament or in the newspapers and reviews he revered.

It is fallacious, therefore, to take Bagehot's theme and say that it is valid as a generally applicable description of the character of a constitutional statesman. He was talking of the constitutional statesman required by a specific class at a particular moment: ''The middle classes—the ordinary majority of educated men [who] are in the present day the despotic power in England.'' Moreover, it was this which he could not maintain after the Reform Act of 1867. As his introduction to the second edition of *The English Constitution* and some of the later essays show, he understood what had happened as a result of the Act; but what had happened had also destroyed the picture of the constitutional statesman which he had carefully drawn in earlier years. He had never been able to take the measure of Disraeli, who flew in the face of the opinion of ''the ordinary majority of educated men'' of the mid-Victorian middle class. But, now, he saw that even Gladstone—especially Gladstone—was reaching to a new audience, and doing something quite other than expressing *their* common opinion. Gladstone's speech at Greenwich in 1871, he said ''marks the coming of the time when it will be one of the most important qualifications of a prime minister to exert a direct control over the masses.'' One should notice that word, *control:* it introduces a new concept which is a direct contradiction of the character of the constitutional statesman he depicted before 1867.

In short, Bagehot described the politics of a dominant class and the character of the politicians who suited it. The apparatus of the state, he said with abundant clarity, is in the hands of one economic class, and the men who managed that apparatus represented the character of that class. They are men of uncommon abilities, who give expression to *its* common opinions. His fault, partly the result of the brilliance of his prose, was that he was not satisfied with describing what he saw, but translated it into a model, and provided a model political character to fit into it. Bagehot has too often been praised for the acuteness of his observation, for putting things down as he saw them. He was no better at that than the rest of us, perhaps a little worse. The models which he had created possessed him and, because of their clarity as models, have possessed us.

The power of these models is evident in some of the more obvious tricks of his writing. His reiteration of his themes, over so many years, is itself suggestive. Did things really change so little, either during the century he wrote about, or during the quarter of a century when he wrote? When he says the same things about so many different people, as in the quotations given above, are we not justified in thinking that his models were exercising too strong a fascination over him? Moreover, can we not see how he uses these models in a further trick . . .? (pp. 33-5)

From time to time, while reading these volumes, one comes across an unattributed quotation. There it is, between quotation marks, and usually introduced with a salute. The thing, he says, has been put well and cannot be put better. They are, of course, quotations from himself. . . . Bagehot's unique method—offering a quotation as if it comes from another expert, wise and authoritative—seems to be more than a stylistic trick. It is part of the whole equipment with which he constructs his models: the impersonal criteria are established—this is what everyone of common sense knows to be true—and the personal judgments are then presented to the unwary reader.

If we look at the major biographical essays, and at some of the shorter biographical articles, we can see how the models distort, at the same time (no one, needless to say, would deny this) as they instruct and entertain. Two of his subjects—Bolingbroke and Pitt—lived and acted before Bagehot's own time; and it is generally agreed that these are the least satisfactory essays. Both men are judged—Bolingbroke, on the whole, unfavourably; Pitt, on the whole, favourably—as if they were acting within the model political system which Bagehot had constructed. He accuses Bolingbroke of failing to observe "how few and plain are the alternatives of common business," which may have been true of the middle years of the nineteenth century, and may even be true today, but was certainly not true of a period when the Whig settlement had not been firmly established; when the Hanoverian succession had not been accomplished and, when accomplished, had not been made safe; and when the first Stuart attempt to regain the throne had still to be met and defeated. The unsatisfactory essay on Pitt suffers from the same attempt to judge him as a model constitutional statesman within Bagehot's model political system: Pitt is, in some respects, admirable, and what is admirable belongs, not to his own times, but to Bagehot's; he was "the first English minister who discussed political questions with the cultivated thoughtfulness and considerate discretion which seem to characterise us now," a remark of such impudence and cocksureness that one would not believe it could have been made if one did not know already that it had been made by Bagehot. (p. 35)

Like many of his contemporaries in Britain, Bagehot feared the imperialism of the United States: its restless conviction that it had a "manifest destiny" to occupy an entire continent. . . . This was—and it remains—a wholly respectable attitude. But Bagehot, in following the course of the Civil War, allowed it to distort his judgment. Until very late, he assumed that the Union "will be, or already is dissolved." Until very late, he wholly misread the character of Lincoln, arguing that he must, "from his previous life and defective education, be wanting in the liberal acquirements and mental training which are the principal elements of an enlarged statesmanship": a perfect example of the inadequacy of his model of a constitutional statesman. From start to finish, he misunderstood the constitution of the United States—its extraordinary capacity for development—and he ignored the manner in which, by his interpretation of its "war power," Lincoln took all the authority he required. Few misjudgments of a political journalist can have been so great as his expressed opinion that "there is no *head* at Washington."

In his comments on both the Second Empire in France and the Civil War in America, Bagehot exposed the fallacy which lay in the models which he constructed. He had many insights into the nature of politics and into the character of politicians. But, out of these insights, he constructed models of efficient political institutions and of efficient constitutional statesmen which were relevant only to the Britain of his generation, but which he insularly insisted were relevant to other countries and to other times. As the result of the sedcuction of his writings, to which we cannot help falling victims, we too easily follow him in his fallacy.

Walter Bagehot is far too important in the history of British political journalism to leave it there. These . . . volumes of his collected works force even the most modest practitioner of the trade to consider in what it consists. His influence lies—one cannot say heavily: his lightness is both his strength and his weakness—across us all. If this was political journalism at its best, can we—and, more important, should we—in our age practise it? Has he misled us, by the iridescence of his writing, into a totally false view of British politics and our purpose in commenting on them? The political column in Britain today, which was recreated in the *Spectator* fifteen years ago, and whose revival has influenced all other forms of political journalism, owes much to him. It is highly personal; it is racy; it offers glimpses of politics from the inside; it is concerned with, and delights in, political character; it takes a sardonic but, on the whole, affectionate view of British political institutions; and it barely varies from journal to journal. The total effect . . . is much the same as the effect created by Bagehot which I described at the beginning: a weekly serial of "nice chats about Sir R. Peel and the little Queen"; and some of us are more to blame than others.

If we turn, then, to Bagehot, as the almost undisputed master of our trade, does his example offer any illumination? Unfortunately, it does. It is unfortunate, because a protracted reading of his political journalism leaves one, in the end, with an impression of levity; and one suspects that a protracted reading of all the political columns in Britain in the past fifteen years would have the same effect. What Bagehot says cannot be separated from how he says it. "His speeches," he wrote of Bright, "are very amusing reading, and, as a rule, those are best known to posterity who can amuse posterity." The sentence and the sentiment are characteristic: seductive but false. Walpole? Pitt? Peel? Russell? Gladstone? They are hardly men who amuse us, yet it is they whom we best know. As so often, Bagehot is describing himself under the pretence of describing his subject. With some justification, he looked forward to his fame in posterity more self-consciously than any political journalist today can think it pertinent to do; and he would make sure of it by entertaining.

We may excuse him that vanity. But was it not also his purpose *first* to entertain his contemporary audience: the new commercial class for which he primarily wrote and the *Economist* was primarily published? He teased it, but he never teased it unmercifully. He always left it with a leg, and sufficient firm ground, to stand on. Was his trick of adapting the language of practical business to describe the life of politics not intended to reassure it? Mr. Bagehot, one can even now hear them saying in Manchester or Leeds, would have his little flights of fancy . . . but, in the end, he returned to talking about public affairs in terms of *transaction*. Was this not part of his skill in writing *pour épater la bourgeoisie*? How he titillated them! How he would pull the leg of the Royal Family; but it should remain. How sardonically he observed the dignified, as well as efficient, aspects of the House of Commons; but they should be allowed to stay. Peel was narrow and shallow; but "you must be content with what you can obtain—the business gentleman." There was no reason why the merchants and the millowners should not sleep with easy consciences in their large houses, above the slums they had created, when the clever Mr Bagehot in London told them that there was no other way. (pp. 39-40)

If one relied on his writings alone, copious as they are, one would know next to nothing of the social and intellectual ferment of the time in which he lived. One comes away from them hardly believing that, when he was at the height of his powers, Matthew Arnold was publishing *Culture and Anarchy* and John Ruskin was blasting his contemporaries with *Time and Tide:* that he followed Carlyle. If his virtue, as his admirers claim, was that he set down what he saw, then one must say that he saw very little; and, in what he saw, he acquiesced with little more than a wry amusement.

This acquiescence was extended to the past. He had a lackadaisical attitude to the great issues which had mattered to it. "The Bill," he said, talking of the Reform Bill of 1832, "is to us hardly more than other bills." Again, in another essay, "Who now doubts on the Catholic question? It is no longer a 'question'." Issues and questions do not die in this manner; and, in the end, his own opposition to the Reform Bill of 1867 compelled him to reconsider the "characteristic defects" of the Reform Bill of 1832. "While these lingered in the books they were matters of dull teaching, and no one cared for them; but Mr Disraeli has embodied them, and they are living among us. The traditional sing-song of eulogy is broken by a sharp question." This is among the most revealing sentences he wrote. "The traditional sing-song of eulogy" to the Reform Bill of 1832 had never been universal. There were many who had foreseen at the time, and who had continued for a generation to foretell, its almost certain consequences. But Bagehot was not interested until it was too late, until the consequences had been embodied in another Reform Bill, and were "living among us." When political journalism is drained, to this extent, of intellectual commitment—of ideology, if one will—does it not become all sail and no anchor? Is this not the searching question which Bagehot compels us to ask? (p. 40)

The criticisms which I have made of Bagehot are substantial, and they may be starkly summarised by returning to the point which I made at the beginning: that the common sense for which he is so often praised turned too regularly into considerable nonsense. It was not common sense to ignore the evils of the industrial revolution. . . . It was not common sense to defend the "instructed" against the "uninstructed", and fail to see, as Arnold did, that the new class which he regarded as "instructed" was not such at all. (He darkly confronted the truth in 1867: hence his remark that the men of 1832 had been "without culture".) It was not common sense so to misunderstand the forces which were active in Ireland that he could write, "We confess that the temporary anger of the Irish Protestants—and it can only be temporary—seems to us insignificant," and that "Ireland will not gain the repeal of the Union." (Has any of us made a more lapidary misjudgment of a major issue?) It was not common sense so to misread the American constitution that he did not, until it was proved, understand the strength of the leadership which it could provide. It was not common sense so to misinterpret the character and system of Napoleon III that he did not, until it also was proved, understand the "Caesarism", and the weaknesses of "Caesarism", which must be their unavoidable consequences. If all this . . . is common sense raised to the power of genius, then all one can anxiously ask is to be rid of the genius or the common sense; one or the other.

One is not complaining that he was wrong—it is better within limits, to be wrong than to say nothing—but that he exalted a practical—a non-intellectual—approach to the politics of his day which excluded almost every great issue. He could no more grasp a great issue than he could grasp a great man. If one wishes to understand the politics of his age, one will learn

more from Arnold or Ruskin, from Mill or Maine, than from all his journalism. (p. 41)

*Henry Fairlie, "Walter Bagehot; or, The Political Journalist As Entertainer," in* Encounter, *Vol. XXXVI, No. 30, March, 1971, pp. 30-41.*

## C. H. SISSON  (essay date 1972)

[*Sisson's* The Case of Walter Bagehot, *from which the following excerpt is taken, is a sharply negative appraisal of the author. Labeling Bagehot a "banker from the skin inwards," Sisson attempts to show that he exalted the middle-class "man of affairs" in all his works in order to further his own interests. Here, Sisson ascribes defects in Bagehot's literary, economic, and political essays to Bagehot's preoccupation with finance. Sisson's interpretation of Bagehot's works is disputed by S.A.M. Westwater (1977).*]

Walter Bagehot's interest in literature was, as much as anything, an interest in people. His literary essays do not take one far into the methods or peculiar ends of literature: the manner of his own writing shows that he had not the sort of relationship with words which is necessary for entry into such subjects. This deficiency does not signify merely a lack of interest in literary fripperies; it is a limitation of his penetration. It is the superficial social man which interests him—an amusing, even instructive, subject but one which has its full depth only when backed by the sort of curiosity about *man,* the sort of apprehension of his further reaches, which the voice of literature represents. Two of Bagehot's early literary essays—that on Hartley Coleridge and that on Shakespeare—illustrate this point. Most of what he has to say about Hartley Coleridge is about what he considered to be his social peculiarities. . . . That Hartley did not do anything—of a kind Bagehot could recognise as being anything—was the subject of puzzled reproach more than once in the course of the essay. Hartley's 'outward life was a simple blank'. He walked around, talked to farmers in the Lake District; sometimes he talked to undergraduates or to women, but he did not do anything noticeable such as running a bank. 'There are undoubtedly persons', says Bagehot—and there is a wealth of experience behind his words—'who, though in general perfectly sane, and even with superior powers of thought or fancy, are as completely unable as the most helpless lunatic to manage any pecuniary transactions.' Hartley was one of these. No wonder there was nothing to tell of him in thirty years! The superior genius of Shakespeare, on the other hand, is proved by nothing so much as his extreme prudence. His success was not so much in writing the plays as in investing money into a successful playhouse and thus being able to return to Stratford and make the local citizens treat him with respect. There is a certain contempt for the mere poet, the mere intellectual, throughout Bagehot's literary essays. The 'tendency to, and the faculty for, self-delineation' which Bagehot not merely finds characteristic of Hartley Coleridge but of which he finds traces, for example, in Gray, is 'very closely connected with' 'dreaminess of disposition and impotence of character'. 'Persons very subject to these can grasp no external object, comprehend no external being; they can do no external thing, and therefore they are left to themselves.' Bagehot's insistence on these points is very marked. There can be no doubt that it represents the anxiety of a man who has to bustle to prove his worth.

A similar concern shows itself in the essay on Cowper. There is the same crying up of the man of the world, as if every man were not a man of *some* world, and a singular air of patronage towards a writer who was, after all, the source of a stream of limpid English which represents a very high development of the intelligence. . . . [Bagehot] introduces the subject with a hurrah for marriage and money, either of which 'breaks the lot of literary and refined inaction once and for ever'. He goes on to say how 'singularly fortunate' Cowper's position was, because he had the choice of several lucrative public offices, where the work required no ability, instead of having to meet 'the long labours of an open profession'. The tone is that of a meritocrat, though it was not only merit which gave Bagehot his entrée into the bank or into the *Economist*. 'It seemed at first scarcely possible that even the least strenuous of men should be found unequal to duties so little arduous or exciting.' It is a curiously unsympathetic way of talking, for anyone who has read Cowper's own account of his apprehensions. There is a falsifying lack of sympathy, too, in Bagehot's account of Cowper's life at Olney, as it is reflected in *The Task*, as if the meaning of the poet's haven entirely escaped him. It is not the house on the market-place, with its incessant screaming of children and barking of dogs and the miserably poor inhabitants of the adjoining lane, that Bagehot has in mind, but the Victorian comfort of [his] house at Herd's Hill, when he says: 'Have we not always hated this life? What can be worse than regular meals, clock-moving servants, a time for everything, and everthing then done. . . .' And there is something of Bagehot's rather nasty contempt for ordinary people in what follows about 'a common gardener, a slow parson, a heavy assortment of near relations'. A 'placid house flowing with milk and sugar— all that the fates can stuff together of substantial comfort, and fed and fatted monotony'; that surely reflects Bagehot's life rather than Cowper's. (pp. 37-9)

Throughout Bagehot's literary essays the same preoccupations recur. Literature is an avenue to subjects which interest him more. He might have said—in various forms did say—that the author interested him more than the book. There is a sense in which that is the proper end of all such studies. In the best critics the man is weighed through the book. This is the case, patently, in Johnson's *Lives of the Poets;* it is also the case, though less obviously, in the technical criticism of Ezra Pound. Bagehot's interest is of a different, and much more superficial kind. He does not seek out the idiosyncrasy, or the genius, the particular tone or cadence which gives an author his value, in order to understand what possibilities of the human mind are peculiarly represented by the author he is studying. He stops short, through sheer incapacity, of any such wide apprehension of his subject and sets up instead a commonplace figure with which he can amuse his public and demonstrate his own abilities. The essay on Shakespeare is a blatant example of this. No doubt Shakespeare was glad to make some money, and we hope he did, but the abilities of this kind which Shakespeare may have had in common with Bagehot are not what make him Shakespeare. A critic who helps us with an obscure point in the text, or who throws light on the structure of a sonnet, does more for our understanding of the poet than all Bagehot's dashing essay can do. Bagehot lacked patience and humility before his subjects as well as any technical grasp of what his poets were up to. (p. 40)

[It is] characteristic of Bagehot in his literary essays that he sets up, not man as the measure of all things but the mere man of affairs as the measure of his betters. In a sense he could not help this, for he was himself that mere man of affairs, only endowed with a certain facility of pen which is not to be taken for granted in such people. . . . It is not merely individual authors, but the collective achievements of the human mind,

that he looks at in this way. There is something supercilious about the way in which Bagehot talks of 'the simple *naïveté* of the old world' in his essay on *Béranger*. He thrusts forward comforts of middle-class Victorian life with a snigger, saying they 'may or may not be great benefits according to a recondite philosophy' and knowing that he will have the support of all decent mediocrities in putting at the centre of the intellectual stage what belongs to the periphery. It is of a piece with this that, while praising the admirable Béranger, he has by implication to take a swipe at Racine as not exhibiting 'the higher freedom of the impelling imagination'.

It is in the essay on *Wordsworth, Tennyson and Browning* . . . that Bagehot comes nearest to putting forward a theory of literature. . . . In this essay Bagehot propounds a literary theory which has all the characteristics of shoddiness and showiness which one comes to expect in his work. After a disquisition on the *picturesque,* in relation to painting—which is really a discourse on the mid-Victorian consumer's notion of what a picture should be like—he invents the rather tasteless word *literatesque* to describe the same quality in relation to writing. It stands for 'that perfect combination in *subject-matter* of literature, which suits the *art* of literature'. There are the people who would look well in a book and the people who would not. Those who would are not necessarily the best people, but they are 'the most effective'. This is virtually a recipe for the ordinary trade novel, in Bagehot's day or in our own. Bagehot's notions of literature, fundamentally, are those of Lord Jeffrey, about whom he had written some years before in his essay on *The First Edinburgh Reviewers.* . . . Jeffrey derided Wordsworth for having produced work which was not *literatesque,* by the standards of the ordinary educated taste of his day. By Bagehot's day Wordsworth has been taken into the system. The expectation of the ordinary educated reader had changed, but the system of recommending whatever is in accordance with his expectations, in a bright and knowing way which confirms the reader's confidence in his own ingenuity, is the same with Bagehot as with Jeffrey. . . . [Bagehot's] ideas are of an extraordinary vulgarity. He talks of the greatest artists as showing 'an enthusiam for reality'. One has only to think of Dr. Johnson to get the measure of that phrase, which combines a silly notion of enthusiasm with an ordinary busy-body's notion of reality. When one finds that Ben Jonson is classed as one who lacked the qualifying enthusiasm, lived on 'the parings of the intellect' and was unable to grasp the 'real world' of Vincent Stuckey [Bagehot's uncle, a successful banker], one has the measure of Bagehot as a literary critic.

In the biographical essays Bagehot undoubtedly shows his talent to better advantage, and more particularly when he was dealing with a mind well within his own scope. The various men of affairs he wrote about were the best subjects for him, not merely because it was in the affairs of money and bustle that his heart lay but because his condescending manner becomes him best when he is writing about someone who has intellect enough genuinely to condescend to. The study in which Bagehot shows us most of his own mind is perhaps that on *The Character of Sir Robert Peel.* He stood just far enough back from Peel, in intellectual perspectives as well as in time. He starts his study with a reflection on the pastness of the past which has the colour of his habitual thoughts. We look over old letters, he says, and are surprised to find that what seemed important then no longer is so, and that people believed then things we do not believe now and revolved questions which for us are no longer questions at all. The illustration he gives is the question of what was called 'Catholic emancipation', which agitated the world in Peel's day and on which Peel, like so many other slow-moving men, took first one side and then the other, ending, of course, on what was proving to be the popular side and became the course of history. 'Who now doubts on the Catholic Question?' asks Bagehot. 'It is no longer a "question".' It is as if Bagehot were saying, looking back over a series of old prints, 'What funny clothes they wore!' Yet Bagehot, it is to be remembered, is the advocate of the reality of the actual. He is the man who asserts repeatedly that what ordinary men, and above all men of business, are about day by day is of a seriousness which puts in the shade the frivolities of mere intellect or mere religion. With the passage of time—even of a little time—the reality of these great affairs fades to nothing, but we are invited to believe that what is currently held to be important—the new candidate for the attention of practical men—is very much *something*. The approach is the opposite of that of a Burke or a Swift, who are holding fast to something permanent and, without relaxing their hold on the business of the day, are able to see it as a manifestation of more permanent interests. Bagehot has the effrontery to speak elsewhere of 'a clever affectation of commonsense . . . in all Swift's political writings' and to contrast the Dean of St. Patrick's unfavourably with Sidney Smith, another buoyant character with a grip of iron on reality, according to Bagehot, while Swift perhaps 'had no heart' and was not sympathetic to bankers. No doubt the question of the civil rights of Roman Catholics in England is not one that could be tactfully broached again in Bagehot's day, any more than it could be in our own, but it is not a matter for astonishment that it was once thought important. . . . Bagehot's corrosive views on religion, which dismissed the claims of the Church of England and welcomed the Italian-Irish intervention not for its truth but as something which gave him another card to be played off against orthodoxy, naturally inclined him to see merely the question of political expediency. Once that was out of the way, there was no question at all, for him. One opinion was as good as another and reality was not implicated in the argument at all. Sensible men of business had long concluded that such matters should not stand in the way of the expansion of commerce.

'This world is given to those whom this world can trust,' Bagehot says, and his cleverness was to take the world's side of the argument, the side of the winners against that of the losers. It is a version of the cynicism of Machiavelli, adapted to less dangerous times. Bagehot, of course, had none of the profound reserves entertained by the Florentine secretary, and he did not see the evil as evil. For his mind there was not truth and falsehood, apprehended with varying degrees of clarity, but a stream of opinions from which the clever man fished out the ones most likely to be acceptable to the world of the moment. (pp. 41-4)

Bagehot's *début* as a political writer was with the **Letters on the French Coup d'État of 1851,** which are a remarkable performance for a young man of twenty-six. Bagehot as yet had no experience of affairs, but by hereditary instinct or domestic training he managed to exhibit all the prudence of a man whose common sense would always get the better of him. He was of course writing for a Unitarian journal, and there is an extravagance in his manner which suggests that he was giving himself the pleasure of causing astonishment among its grave readers. . . . (p. 56)

Bagehot devotes a whole letter to the subject of the morality of the *coup d'état.* The subject had a fascination for him. He

was, of course, a Utilitarian, and he applied his doctrine with little enough subtlety. 'Mankind must be kept alive': therefore, everything must be sacrificed to this end. There is a destructive frivolity about his lumping together of 'Parliaments, liberty, leading articles, essays, eloquence' as things that must go by the board to keep life going. It amounts to an assertion that, in comparison with the common comforts, all the rest is hot air. Bagehot so explains the need for Napoleon's *coup.* 'According to the common belief of common people, their common comforts were in considerable danger. The debasing torture of acute apprehension was eating into the crude pleasure of stupid lives.' There is something singularly unpleasant about the tone of this, from someone who had had less cause than most for apprehension as where his next meal—to say nothing of his next respectful attentions—were coming from. Nor is the facility with which Bagehot gives approval to the government's severities, very agreeable. 'The severity with which the riot was put down on the first Thursday in December', he writes, 'has, I observe, produced an extreme effect in England. . . . But better one *émeute* now than many in May.' He was presuming on his small experience. 'There are things more demoralising than death.' It is the death of other people he is speaking of. It was not thus that Swift spoke of the sufferings of the lower orders. 'And when Esau came fainting from the Field, at the Point to die, it is no wonder that he sold his Birth-Right for a Mess of Pottage.' There was no *saeva indignatio* about Bagehot; one might say there was, instead, an ugly frivolity. A few words of Swift sweep him away: 'When I am in Danger of bursting, I will go and whisper among the Reeds.' (pp. 59-60)

**The English Constitution** is the work by which Bagehot is best known; it is, so to speak, the reason for Bagehot. . . . The idea of his greatness—of his being, even, 'the greatest Victorian' [see excerpt above by G. M. Young, 1937], rests on this book, for such an idea must rest on something. It has had other than literary supports. Not only have a lot of people read **The English Constitution** but influential people have had cause to remember it. Most classics are put out of mind, by most men of affairs, but one that purports to explain their own activities will not be lost sight of. A book which insinuates, as this one continuously does, that these activities are incomparably important and to be criticised by no standards but those of the actors themselves, is sure to be dear to them. . . . Bagehot's book has also the advantage of being readable, which is unusual in this class of literature, once the flutter of contemporary interest has gone. It is at any rate unusual, as Balfour pointed out [see excerpt above, 1927], that a constitutional treatise can be regarded as light reading. Bagehot's book is certainly that. It is light, like so much of Bagehot's writing, with the style of man who is letting you into a secret, or revealing something perfectly obvious which you, poor fool, have missed. Bagehot is not a very well-bred writer, and the herd of knowing commentators we now suffer from have a real affinity with him. (pp. 61-2)

Bagehot was always preaching the merits of stupidity, but he meant that smart-alecry could not survive without it. If there is contempt, in Bagehot, for the 'inferior people', there is an equal if more uneasy contempt for all that was above him. That is why [The English Constitution] has so been taken up by the managerial classes; it teaches admiration of themselves. Bagehot himself points out that the two parts he describes in the constitution [the 'efficient' part, represented by the House of Commons and the Cabinet, and the 'dignified' part, represented by the monarchy and the House of Lords,] are not 'separable with microscopic accuracy'. The Queen *could* be useful, when she was helping the managers; a cabinet might even be dignified, though this could not happen very often. The respect for the higher powers was not respect *for* anything. Indeed the only thing worth the respect of an intelligent man was what went on inside the counting-house, but the vulgar would not understand that—better for them that they should not, perhaps. (p. 65)

[The] notion of separating the efficient and dignified parts of government is very corrosive. It is a way of discrediting part of the apparatus, and when people seek to discredit a bit of the machinery of government one should ask who they are and what they design to put in its place. There should be no doubt that, so far as the monarchy is concerned, Bagehot's book is intentionally subversive, and that, so far as his description of it is correct, he is describing a decayed polity. (p. 69)

Having misdirected his youth towards the study of literature, for which he had no talent, and then towards the study of politics, to which he made a destructive contribution, Bagehot turned in his later years to wholly serious matters. *Lombard Street* . . . is a paean in praise of money. (p. 85)

Bagehot was writing in the great bulge of Victorian prosperity, and was conscious of these advantages, if that is what they were. His tone is that of a man showing off his plush furniture for the benefit of less fortunate people. 'Everyone is aware,' he says, 'that England is the greatest moneyed country in the world; every one admits that it has much more immediately disposable and ready cash than any other country. But very few persons are aware *how much* greater the ready balance— the floating fund which can be lent to any one or for any purpose—is in England than it is anywhere else in the world.' Money was economic power, and Bagehot never asked the critical question as to whether this unprecedented concentration was a good thing, or whether it was a proper use of the dignified parts of government, about which he had written so cynically in *The English Constitution,* to act as a screen for the *sub-rosa* activities of bankers. (pp. 85-6)

Bagehot saw clearly that the government of the Bank of England was in fact a national function; he would have [its] Board of Directors turned from semi-trustees for the nation to real trustees, with a trust deed which made their responsibilities clear. The system he recommended was, really, that the country should be run by men of business looking towards a written republican constitution, in the trust deed of the bank, while the eyes of the common people were averted in the direction of the Crown, where there was no power but, for vulgar minds, much entertainment. The theory of *The English Constitution* is really the counterpart of the theory of *Lombard Street* and it is the latter which is at the centre of Bagehot's notions of government. (p. 90)

[Bagehot] is a banker from the skin inwards, and the attraction of his work on financial matters is that it is that of a man who can actually talk, with some facility, about the operations which his ordinary colleagues, the ordinary sensible men of business, merely perform. *Lombard Street,* Keynes says, 'is a piece of pamphleteering. . . . Perhaps [its] most striking and fundamental doctrine . . . is, in a sense, psychological rather than economic . . . the doctrine of the Reserve, and that the right way to stop a crisis is to lend freely' [see excerpt above, 1915]. Psychologically, it might be added, the appeal of the doctrine to Bagehot was that he was recommending *other people* to lend freely, in time of panic, as a way of saving Bagehot. He describes the panic of the Money Market rather as one might

have described the Fire of London, and indeed it must have been rather like that. The bad news would 'spread in an instant through all the Money Market at a moment of terror; no one can say exactly who carries it, but in half an hour it will be carried on all sides, and will intensify the terror everywhere'. This was perhaps the central horror of his life. . . . (p. 97)

*Lombard Street* is, in many ways, the most personal of Bagehot's books. . . . He saw that banking was changing, and, correctly, expected that private banking would come to an end. The paragraphs in which he celebrates the life of that *milieu*— his own—comes nearer to poetry than anything he ever wrote. . . . (p. 98)

Bagehot's distinction was to have carried this technique of affairs into the business of writing. He was a journalist. Nearly all his writing was done, in the first instance, for the periodical press. So was De Quincey's, but De Quincey was no mere success and all the time he was looking for a point of rest behind the confusions of the matters of the day. With Bagehot, the provisional became so far as is possible a principle. You had to move smartly to keep up with him. He used his observations not to define his position, for he had none, but to defend himself. His method was not to yield to reality but to be clever about it, and to ingratiate himself sufficiently to make sure that he was not left alone. There is an affable, matey tone about his work which has made thousands of mediocrities feel at home with him. He is not only clever himself, but gives a distinct impression that he is one of a band of like-minded conspirators, to which the reader is invited to attach himself. This accounts for the destructive element in much of his work.

It is a trick which has often passed for liberalism. Bagehot's account of *The English Constitution* is based on it. Everything which has claims to be objectively important is smilingly shown to be unimportant, or important in some arcane way intelligible only to the group of conspirators, who will never submit to any truth unless it is manifestly useable to their own advantage. The plausibility of this position lies in the fact that, precisely, it is advantageous to know the truth. The real question is as to the kind of advantage it gives, and as to the order of precedence between advantage and truth. To put the advantage first, and then to accept such truths as do not interfere with it, is a political proceeding which is favoured far beyond the bounds of what are ordinarily thought of as politics. It is Bagehot's method, and accounts for the relativism which allows him to re-arrange reality incessantly to suit situations, with a foremost eye always on his own. (p. 111)

What we get from Bagehot is not so much a theory as a position, and not so much a position as a form of tactics. It is Walter Bagehot whom the successive positions are intended to protect. . . . He was a gifted man who pushed around in the world, and he liked to think that there was only pushing and shoving, though he owed more to the discretion which keeps people on the winning side. No doubt a great deal of life is like this, and more than any other writer of talent Bagehot embodies the forces of successful action. But it is successful action in a particular *milieu,* that of the rising finance and journalism of nineteenth-century England. Bagehot operated in a field of natural selection from which the more desperate assaults, and the more desperate risks, had already been eliminated. (p. 121)

> *C. H. Sisson, in his* The Case of Walter Bagehot, *Faber and Faber, 1972, 143 p.*

**S.A.M. WESTWATER**   (essay date 1977)

[*Westwater refutes the charges of Henry Fairlie (1971) and C. H. Sisson (1972) that Bagehot acquiesced to a political philosophy.*

*Rather, the critic maintains that Bagehot's middle-of-the-road approach to nineteenth-century social, political, and religious issues reflects the prudent views of a man whose "liberal conscience" convinced him of the necessity for change but whose "conservative temperament," combined with his study of evolutionary theory, taught him that progress should be gradual.*]

[Henry Fairlie and C. H. Sisson] make of Bagehot's moderation a covert for cowardice and deceit. Fairlie cynically observes that there was no reason why merchants should not sleep with easy consciences above the slums they had created when clever Mr. Bagehot told them there was no other way. Sisson, too, accuses Bagehot of an "ugly frivolity" and contends that his writings on the French Coup amount to an assertion that in comparison with common comforts all is "hot air." It is not common comfort or acquiescence to a system that Bagehot exalts; rather, it is human life itself. Order, the fabric of civilization, is vastly more important than any political theory or uneasy freedom. What these critics seem to ignore is the rich humanistic vein in Bagehot, his strong religious faith, and his reliance on reason. In interpreting Bagehot to modern readers, recent critics concentrate too heavily on Bagehot's political writings and do not consider the total thinker as revealed in his literary studies or in *Physics and Politics* and *The English Constitution*. Perhaps if they had examined these works, they would have discovered the so-called "puzzle of his nature." Not common sense but balance is the key to the understanding of the man.

Bagehot's balance results from his having a conservative temperament abutting a liberal conscience. It should be noted that he recognizes the psychological as well as the political connotations of the terms. The liberal "turn of mind," he wrote, "denotes the willingness to admit new ideas . . . and the perfect impartiality with which these ideas . . . are canvassed and considered." On the other hand, the conservative turn of mind denotes "adhesiveness to the early and probably inherited ideas of childhood. . . ." The admixture of intellectual and emotional tendencies made Bagehot a conservative by temperament. His conscience, however, threw him into the ranks of the liberals. Thus, Bagehot's characteristic stance is midway between the main currents of nineteenth-century thought on religious, political, and scientific interests. His middle way is not the comfortable resort of the uncommitted traveller, but rather the protective shelter of the universal pilgrim, shunted off a known road by the violent momentum of change. (pp. 41-2)

Bagehot's healthy regard for change made him, intellectually at least, an avowed liberal believing, "What health is to the animal, Liberalism is to the polity." For him liberty was not only the foundation of growth; it was coextensive with life.

In his 1855 essay, **"The First Edinburgh Reviewers,"** Bagehot gloried in the clearance of all encrusted obstructions that prevented the free flow of spontaneous activity. He excoriated Lord Eldon because, as Prime Minister, he barred Catholic emancipation, refused to alter the Court of Chancery, and hindered the abolition of capital punishment for petty crimes. Elsewhere he contemptuously referred to George III as a "consecrated obstruction." Liberal in the early nineteenth-century sense of the word, Bagehot's conscience refused to accept the slightest tyranny repressing human growth.

He recognized that the problem with later liberalism rested not so much in the political sphere as it did in the social and moral areas. Bagehot accepted the fact that arbitrary control and harsh punishment might force a man and prevent him from becoming a nuisance to society. Was coercion, however, as a moral

discipline, doing anything for the character of the man himself? Mill had convincingly taught that you cannot compel humankind to be good. Liberalism aimed to instruct a man to discipline himself to develop his own will and to order his own life. Hobhouse summarized it thus: "Liberalism is the belief that society can safely be founded on this self-directing power of personality. . . ." Bagehot concurred. But what he emphasized more than other liberals of his age was the necessity for time to cultivate and bring the liberal ideal to fruition. "Poise of mind" to Bagehot involved "the power of true passiveness—the faculty of 'waiting' till the streams of impressions . . . have done all that they have to do, and cut their full type plainly upon the mind." The theory of evolution had sobered him into the realization that natural growth is always slow. A precipitous granting of liberal privileges might, in the long run, destroy liberalism's goal. He always distrusted swift, violent action fearing that it led to extinction. Only the tamed in nature and society were preserved. Both *The English Constitution* . . . and *Physics and Politics* . . . reveal the profound effect scientific evolution had on Bagehot's thinking, a fact that Fairlie and Sisson have ignored or overlooked. (pp. 42-3)

More than any other event the Reform Act of 1867 made Bagehot search for a brake on a liberalism that was too easily equated with democracy. He described a point at left of center from which position the men of the new polity would arise:

> The best Government for free states, both past history and present experience seem to me to prove, is a Government . . . of the Left Centre. The centre . . . is the representative of the great neutral mass, which is not violently in favour either of one side in politics or of the other; which inclines now more in one direction, and now more in the other; which is often nominally divided between Left and Right, between the movement and non-movement parties, and which then forms a certain "common element" of which both parties partake. . . . The Left Centre is that side of this steadying and balancing element which inclines to progress, which is alive to new ideas. . . . In short the Left Centre wants to introduce tested innovations when the average man begins to comprehend them. . . .

The "Left Centre" neither drives so slowly as to miss the train nor so fast as to meet with an accident. Obviously Bagehot recognized that as an individual and as a member of the body politic, the new evolutionary man would have the best chance for survival if he could reconcile his two-fold strain of liberalism and conservatism. This proclivity for the center, for a point of view balanced between opposing schools of thought, is not to be ascribed to mere caution or to pusillanimity (as Fairlie and Sisson ascribe it), but to prudence. The prudent man considers all the possibilities of a discussion, makes a choice, and then acts on that decisive choice. Believing that his highest endowment is reason and his lowest an impatient urge to act, the prudent man avoids the extremes of palsied thought and rash impetuosity.

Bagehot championed growth. But he wanted change approached from the left with a concomitant pressure from the right which would force a qualitative examination of progress itself, not so much an onward as an upward development. What had hitherto been regarded as progress frequently had insufficient regard for the stability that he believed essential for the genuine advancement of political man. He placed a great emphasis on change in terms of development from the past, rather than in terms of fresh starts on untested theories. . . . He advised his fellow Victorians to tread carefully up the mount of progress, in a rational manner, remembering the experiences of the past, understanding the present acquisition of new knowledge, and shrewdly alert to the dangers of the future. The rationality he endorsed emphasized not only the power of reasoning but also the power of hearing the reasons of others, of comparing them quietly with one's own reason and then being guided by the results. (pp. 43-4)

Bagehot might well be the *Homo Prudentissimus* of the Victorian era, but prudent in the best Latin sense, not in the modern prejorative connotation of "cautious" or "safe" as Bagehot is viewed by Sisson and Fairlie. He had a "meditative tact," and a "selective judgement" which made him sort out from the varied thoughts, discoveries, and speculations of his age those ideas which are universally, in the Tennysonian phrase, "true, healthy and valuable." His writings reveal the result— an eminently balanced point of view marked by a stern sense of practicality and a cautious optimism. In a sense he described his own success when he wrote: "Success in life . . . depends as we have seen, more than anything else on 'animated moderation,' on a certain combination of energy of mind and balance of mind, hard to attain and harder to keep."

Bagehot's "animated moderation" must be examined not only in the political writings as Sisson [and Fairlie] . . . have done, but also in his literary, scientific, and historical studies. To neglect any of these is to have an incomplete, if not erroneous view of his total thought. The earliest essays, published by Bagehot himself under the title *Estimates of Some Englishmen and Scotchmen,* . . . reveal a groping for answers to religious and moral questions. His analysis of literary figures essentially reduces all literature to discovering a man's relation to the moral universe. He insists on the solidly conservative principle that a divine moral order governs the world, and on the obstinately imperfect nature of man. (pp. 44-5)

Bagehot believed it imperative to recognize a divine plan infusing what was most valuable in the past with what, it could be hoped, would be more beneficial in the future. Religion gave man a "confidence in the universe" and guided him "to take the world as it comes." Without a divine principle evolution was merely a series of unintellgible ideas. By building on common sense and appealing to universal impulses, Bagehot would establish religion as a "fortifying element" in man's development. If ideals underwent a decline, widespread decadence would smother motives that had inspired the best in human civilization. Evolution, interpreted chiefly as a struggle for life, seemed to ignore such principles, and Bagehot pointed out both in *Physics and Politics* and *The English Constitution* that something in man's nature, if not in the animal's, demanded restraint and control. Moreover, the Darwinian revolution issued in new attitudes toward both past and future: it focussed on both origins and ends, vastly extending the time scale of history and at the same time reinforcing the idea of progress through ordered growth.

With its emphasis on variety, evolution convinced Bagehot that the extension of the franchise after 1832 prostituted the liberal ideal by equating liberty with equality. The great leveller, wealth, now became the molding force that tended to obliterate variety. In his view an arid materialism was hostile to the values of the past and unconcerned with the culture of the future. To Bagehot all men were plainly not equal: "The most strange fact, though the most certain in nature, is the

unequal development of the human race." Imitation of the favored few was a safer way of insuring individual liberty and privacy than allowing inexperienced, uneducated hordes to practice leadership. Bagehot had the true conservative's feeling for caste. Prejudice, rank, inequality kept alive man's progressive instincts. Agitation could be a means of instruction just as benign stupidity could induce the corrective process of discussion.

In his political and historical essays, Bagehot searched for, but never found, the ideal political leader. Neither did he construct the "model political system" as Fairlie has contended. Elements of goodness, intelligence, and imagination reside in all men, in all ages, and, when the exigencies of the polity demand, these human resources may be tapped and much of the mystery and complexity that shrouds human activity can be removed. But Bagehot never lost sight of conflicting human motives or of the power of passion to sway human affairs. His essays on Peel, Pitt, Brougham and Bolingbroke, Lyndhurst and Lewis show his absorption in the dualism of human nature. (pp. 45-6)

Again and again he is to be found midway between other leading thinkers of his time. In politics we find him equidistant between the anti-liberal paternalism expounded by Carlyle and Ruskin and the liberal doctrine of individual liberty associated most with the writings of Mill. In religion he rests approximately halfway between the growing ritualism of Newman's Oxford Anglicanism and the morality-oriented secularism of J. S. Mill and the Utilitarian School. He occupies another central point of contrast between Marx's outright rejection of religion and Arnold's equation of religion with culture. In science his chief interest lay in the new theories of evolution where, typically, he attempts to find a *via media* by combining the Darwinian hypothesis with a firm belief in teleology. Borrowing from both Spencer and Darwin, nonetheless, he refused to replace Providence with chance. He sided with neither the angels nor the apes; instead, he held to a humanistic belief in the powers of man (notwithstanding his newly discovered humble genesis) to progress slowly but surely in accordance with a design, the origin of which rested in a Supreme Being that had from the beginning supplied an inherent need. If man was an animal, he was for Bagehot an indisputably religious animal. (p. 47)

There is the steady insistence in all his writings that, in his pilgrimage through time, man's ultimate reliance is on reason. What else is Bagehot's "conservatism of reflection" but a highlighting of his contention that passion (under the guise of "correct bureaucracy," "all-involving democracy," and "quickly striking despotism") and not reason is the key characteristic of man? Reason becomes the crucial dimension of man's moral activity. Without reason the blind impulses of self-love and avarice will drive the noble aims of liberalism into a destructive abyss. Reason is the faculty of discrimination and judgment which gives meaning to man's morally circumscribed sphere of action.

For Bagehot, the liberal principle of health in a body politic is unity, based on the simultaneous operation of self-love and love for one's fellow man. Ideally, love is the medium that preserves the liberal society in a sort of colloidal stability, but Bagehot's works convincingly demonstrate the conservative attitude that all political man can do is to ensure that most of the conditions for the attainment of the liberal ideal are present. More importantly, the members of the polity must be watchful to bar the blackguard and the fool from attaining office, since they would make the approach to the good life impossible. Bagehot's works reveal his profound concern with the dangers and ills of his own period. For him it was more important in his age to stem evil than it was to extend the good. (pp. 47-8)

Sisson and Fairlie totally ignore the gently musing tone of Bagehot's writings which are underscored by currents of vivacious humor that save the essays from pessimism, although, by temperament, Walter Bagehot had an admittedly strong pessimistic vein.... A world weariness, which never moldered into a cloying self-pity, made him look upon ordinary living with dry disdain: "Take it as you will, human life is like the earth on which man dwells. There are exquisite beauties, grand imposing objects, scattered here and there; but the spaces between are wide; the mass of common clay is huge; the dead level of vacant life of common-place geography is immense." His "ticket-of-leave" attitude gave to his writings an amateur's extraordinary freedom. A gold medalist in philosophy, a lawyer who successfully passed the bar, a banker, broker, economist, and writer—who better could survey with the amateur's universal eye the vast sweep of the mid-Victorian era? He saw the whole of life, and, as a gifted journalist, he kept a sharp eye to the effects produced on the masses. John Stuart Mill appealed to the genius of society, the individual; Matthew Arnold, to the "Socrates in each man's breast," the "remnant"; Carlyle, to the "captains of industry"; but Walter Bagehot sought the man at the back of the bus:

> The middle class—the ordinary majority of educated men—are in the present day the despotic power in England. "Public opinion" nowadays "is the opinion of the bald-headed man at the back of the omnibus."

> (pp. 48-9)

Middle-class men, men from the wide "spaces between," emerged from a position of near obscurity to one of dominance in the Victorian era. Because he was not so much *Victorianorum Maximus* as he was *Victorianum Maxime*—most Victorian of the Victorians—G. M. Young chose Bagehot as the greatest man of the age [see excerpt above, 1937]. He was the dispassionate man at the center honestly testing the vast "mass of common clay" in Victorian life and its few "imposing objects." His trust lay, however, in the wide sweep of "shopkeeping humanity," and much of his "writing in hooks and eyes" was intended to acquaint his readers with the problems and loose ends that had to be tackled and fastened in a complicated time of change. In the last analysis the title most befitting Walter Bagehot is neither *Victorianorum Maximus* nor *Victorianum Maxime* but *Homo Prudentissimus*—a most prudent Everyman of any age—a man whom no age can ignore, least of all contemn. (p. 49)

> *S.A.M. Westwater, "Walter Bagehot: A Reassessment," in* The Antioch Review, *Vol. XXXV, No. 1, Winter, 1977, pp. 39-49.*

---

## ADDITIONAL BIBLIOGRAPHY

Barker, Sir Ernest. "The Scientific School—after Spencer." In his *Political Thought in England: 1848 to 1914*, 2d ed., pp. 113-39. London: Oxford University Press, 1950.*
  Contends that *Physics and Politics* marks the beginning of the psychological approach to political organization.

Barrington, Emilie Isabel. *The Works and Life of Walter Bagehot: Life of Walter Bagehot*, Vol. X. London: Longmans, Green, and Co., 1915, 478 p.
  The first and most exhaustive biography of Bagehot, written by his sister-in-law. Barrington's biography includes both personal recollections of Bagehot by his contemporaries and numerous extracts from his correspondence and diaries.

Barzun, Jacques. "Bagehot, or the Human Comedy." In his *The Energies of Art: Studies of Authors Classic and Modern*, pp. 195-225. New York: Harper & Brothers, Publishers, 1956.
  An expanded version of Barzun's 1948 introduction to *Physics and Politics* (see excerpt above) that includes biographical information and a more detailed discussion of Bagehot's concept of "agitation," or the necessity of educating the masses in order to promote gradual political change.

Baumann, Arthur A. "Walter Bagehot." In his *The Last Victorians*, pp. 167-83. Philadelphia: J. B. Lippincott Co., 1927.
  Examines Bagehot's influence upon the political philosophy of the mid-Victorian age. Baumann also contrasts Bagehot's observations on English government as recorded in *The English Constitution* with British government in the early-twentieth century.

Beer, Samuel. "Tradition and Nationality: A Classic Revisited." *The American Political Science Review* LXVIII, No. 3 (September 1974): 1292-95.
  Argues that Bagehot misrepresented the facts of nineteenth-century British politics in *The English Constitution* by insisting on the separation of the "dignified" and "efficient" functions of government.

Birrell, Augustine. "Walter Bagehot." In his *The Collected Essays & Addresses of the Rt. Hon. Augustine Birrell: 1880-1920*, Vol. 2, pp. 213-35. New York: Charles Scribner's Sons, 1923.
  An appreciative assessment of Bagehot's literary career. Birrell admires the author's lively, unpretentious style and praises his works for their originality, humor, and worldliness. While stressing that all of Bagehot's writings are informed by his interest in business and politics, Birrell notes that they also reflect his enthusiasm for the works of the poet William Wordsworth and the theologian John Henry Newman.

Briggs, Asa. "Trollope, Bagehot, and the English Constitution." In her *Victorian People: A Reassessment of Persons and Themes, 1851-67*, rev. ed., pp. 87-115. Chicago: University of Chicago Press, 1970.*
  Contends that the political climate of mid-nineteenth-century England is best described in *The English Constitution* and the novels of Anthony Trollope. Briggs notes similarities between Bagehot's and Trollope's presentations of the political issues of their day and provides a historical overview of English government during the ministry of John Henry Palmerston.

Brinton, Crane. "The Prosperous Victorians: Bagehot." In his *English Political Thought in the Nineteenth Century*, pp. 180-98. London: Ernest Benn, 1933.
  Examines Bagehot's liberal political views within the context of his attitude toward individual freedom.

Burgess, Anthony. "Bagehot on Books." *The Spectator* 216, No. 7176 (7 January 1966): 15.
  A discussion of Bagehot's literary criticism in which Burgess defends the author against charges of amateurism and lack of discrimination.

Cunliffe, John W. "Mid-Victorian Scientists, Publicists, Historians, and Essayists: Walter Bagehot (1826-1877)." In his *Leaders of the Victorian Revolution*, pp. 181-83. New York: D. Appleton-Century Co., 1934.
  A laudatory account of Bagehot's life and career that focuses on *The English Constitution* and *Lombard Street*.

Haley, Sir William. "Walter Bagehot: A Literary Appreciation." In *The Collected Works of Walter Bagehot*, Vol. I, by Walter Bagehot, edited by Norman St. John-Stevas, pp. 84-106. Cambridge: Harvard University Press, 1965.

A detailed examination of Bagehot's literary criticism. Stressing that these writings are informed by both "practical" judgment and "romantic" imagination, Haley demonstrates that in such essays as *"Festus"* and *"Tennyson's Idylls"* Bagehot expressed "equal regard for the worlds of practice and feeling."

Himmelfarb, Gertrude. "Walter Bagehot: A Common Man with Uncommon Ideas." In her *Victorian Minds*, pp. 220-35. New York: Alfred A. Knopf, 1968.

An analysis of Bagehot's literary and political essays in which Himmelfarb demonstrates that the author was endowed with a keen sense of the paradoxical nature of reality.

Hirst, Francis W. "Walter Bagehot." In *The Economist, 1843-1943: A Centenary Volume*, pp. 64-72. London: Oxford University Press, 1943.

A commendatory overview of Bagehot's economic writings. Hirst was editor of the *Economist* from 1907 to 1916.

Hofstadter, Richard. "Evolution, Ethics, and Society." In his *Social Darwinism in American Thought*, rev. ed., pp. 84-104. New York: George Braziller, 1959.*

Describes the leading ideas of *Physics and Politics*.

Hutchison, Keith. "Hero for the Right." *The Nation* 192, No. 1 (7 January 1961): 15-16.

A review of Alastair Buchan's *The Spare Chancellor: The Life of Walter Bagehot* (see excerpt above). Hutchison emphasizes Bagehot's political conservatism.

[Hutton, Richard Holt]. "Walter Bagehot." *The Living Age* XVIII, No. 1715 (28 April 1877): 245-48.

An obituary describing the effect of Bagehot's intellectual detachment on his writings and political sympathies. A long-standing friend of Bagehot, Hutton joined him in establishing the *National Review* and edited several of his posthumously published works.

———. "First Memoir" and "Second Memoir." In *The Works of Walter Bagehot*, Vol. I, by Walter Bagehot, edited by Forrest Morgan, pp. xxv-lxii, pp. lxii-lxviii. Hartford, Conn.: Travelers Insurance Co., 1889.

Two biographical essays. In the first, Hutton traces the development of Bagehot's ideas on religion, politics, and economics, while in the second, he provides a brief overview of his writing career. Early critics relied heavily on Hutton's memoirs for information concerning Bagehot's life.

Jackson, Holbrook. "Walter Bagehot: Writer and Banker." *The Living Age* 317, No. 4112 (28 April 1923): 230-34.

An analysis of Bagehot's literary criticism. Jackson briefly touches upon Bagehot's disregard for prevailing literary standards and his habit of analyzing works of literature as expressions of their authors' personalities.

Kohn, Hans. Introduction to *Physics and Politics*, by Walter Bagehot, pp. vii-xvii. Boston: Beacon Press, 1956.

A general overview of Bagehot's literary career that emphasizes *Physics and Politics*. Kohn discusses the leading idea of *Physics and Politics*—the desirability of "government by discussion"—in relation to British politics during the late nineteenth and early twentieth centuries.

Marriott, Sir J.A.R. "Walter Bagehot." *The Fortnightly Review* CXIX, No. DCCX (1 February 1923): 263-72.

Regards Bagehot's matter-of-fact approach to politics and economics as an outgrowth of his practical knowledge of business and finance.

McGovern, William Montgomery. "The Social Darwinists and Their Allies." In his *From Luther to Hitler: The History of Fascist-Nazi Political Philosophy*, pp. 453-527. Boston: Houghton Mifflin Co., 1941.*

Briefly outlines the political philosophy advanced in *Physics and Politics* and describes Bagehot's contribution to the "etatist," or state socialist, political tradition. McGovern contends that Bagehot, the English philosopher Herbert Spencer, and the Austrian sociologist Ludwig Gumplowicz were the most notable nine-

teenth-century thinkers to study social and political development in terms of Charles Darwin's theory of evolution.

Murray, Rev. Robert H. "Bagehot's Seminal Mind." In his *Studies in the English Social and Political Thinkers of the Nineteenth Century: Herbert Spencer to Ramsay MacDonald*, Vol. II, pp. 220-73. Cambridge, England: W. Heffer & Sons, 1929.

Combines biographical facts with an overview of the ideas expressed in *The English Constitution, Physics and Politics*, and *Literary Studies*. Murray, who considers Bagehot "one of the outstanding imaginative intellects of the nineteenth century," concludes his essay with a discussion of the wide-ranging influence of Bagehot's social, political, and economic thought.

Rostow, Walt W. "Bagehot and the Trade Cycle." In *The Economist, 1843-1943: A Centenary Volume*, pp. 155-74. London: Oxford University Press, 1943.

A detailed analysis of Bagehot's trade-cycle theory as outlined in *Lombard Street* and his essays in the *Economist*.

Sampson, George. "Walter Bagehot (1826-1926)." *The Bookman*, London LXIX, No. 413 (February 1926): 243-46.

A biographical and critical essay commemorating the centenary of Bagehot's birth. Sampson reserves his highest praise for *Physics and Politics*.

Stanford, Derek. "Bagehot and the Monarchy." *Modern Age: A Conservative Review* 3, No. 1 (Winter 1958-59): 33-9.

Uses Bagehot's analysis of the "dignified" functions of the English monarchy to support his contention that the British queen plays an invaluable role as a "symbolical individual" who inspires the English public with confidence in the government.

Stang, Richard. "The Sacred Office, the Critics: W. C. Roscoe, Walter Bagehot, and R. H. Hutton, the Search for Tragedy." In *The Theory of the Novel in England: 1850-1870*, pp. 51-60. New York: Columbia University Press; London: Routledge & Kegan Paul, 1959.*

Discusses Bagehot, W. C. Roscoe, and R. H. Hutton as three Victorian literary critics who valued the insight into human character displayed in the novels of George Eliot. Stang argues that Bagehot, Roscoe, and Hutton used Eliot's works as a standard by which to judge other novels.

St. John-Stevas, Norman. "Walter Bagehot: 1826-1877." In his *Walter Bagehot: A Study of His Life and Thought Together with a Selection from His Political Writings*, pp. 1-117. Bloomington: Indiana University Press, 1959.

A highly regarded examination of Bagehot's political, economic, and religious views. St. John-Stevas's essay is chiefly noted for its detailed discussion of *The English Constitution*. In addition to assessing the validity of Bagehot's conclusions in the work, St. John-Stevas uses specific historical examples to illustrate how the operation of British government has altered since the mid-Victorian era.

———. Introduction to *Bagehot's Historical Essays*, by Walter Bagehot, edited by Norman St. John-Stevas, pp. vii-xlii. Garden City, N.Y.: Doubleday & Co., Anchor Books, 1965.

A close study of Bagehot's essays on eighteenth- and nineteenth-century English statesmen. St. John-Stevas is primarily interested in these essays for the light they shed on Bagehot's political ideas, and his commentary focuses on the author's opposition to the Reform Act of 1867 and antipathy for democratic government as it existed in the United States.

Sullivan, Harry R. *Walter Bagehot*. Twayne's English Authors Series, edited by Sylvia E. Bowman, no. 182. Boston: Twayne Publishers, 1975, 171 p.

An appreciative biographical and critical study. Sullivan's expressed purpose is to present Bagehot as "one who in manner, expression, and thought represents the more excellent accomplishments of Victorianism at its apex." Sullivan quotes liberally from Bagehot's writings and provides a detailed account of the ideas presented in his literary and political essays, *The English Constitution*, and *Physics and Politics*.

Wain, John. "An Introduction to Bagehot." *Review of English Literature* 1, No. 4 (October 1960): 66-72.

> A consideration of Bagehot as an amateur literary critic.

Wheare, K. C. *Walter Bagehot: Lecture on a Master Mind.* Proceedings of the British Academy, vol. LX. London: Oxford University Press, 1974, 29 p.

> An introduction to Bagehot's political essays. Citing *The English Constitution* as Bagehot's "masterpiece," Wheare praises the work as both a source book on current constitutional questions and a classic description of English government during the ministry of John Henry Palmerston.

Wilson, Woodrow. "A Wit and a Seer." *The Atlantic Monthly* 82, No. 4579 (July 1898): 527-40.

> A laudatory biographical and critical sketch. Wilson singles out the lively, conversational style of Bagehot's writings for particular admiration and briefly summarizes the leading ideas of *The English Constitution, Physics and Politics, Lombard Street,* and "Letters on the French Coup D'etat of 1851."

Withers, Hartley. Introduction to *Lombard Street,* by Walter Bagehot, pp. vii-xix. London: John Murray, 1915.

> Describes changes in the British money market since the publication of *Lombard Street.* Withers notes that the two greatest modifications in the money market—the increase in the Bank of England's gold reserves and the rise of joint stock banking—were predicted by Bagehot.

# Fernán Caballero

## 1796-1877

(Pseudonym of Cecilia Böhl de Faber) Spanish novelist, essayist, and novella, short story, and sketch writer.

Caballero was one of Spain's most popular and influential novelists during the mid-nineteenth century. In her works, she combined a strong advocacy of traditional Hispanic values with realistic portraits of regional life and customs among the Spanish people. Her ability to capture the picturesque elements of a locale and reproduce the speech and mannerisms of Andalusian Spain is evident in such novels as *La gaviota: Novela de costumbres (The Sea Gull)*. This and other works made her a pivotal figure in the development of the ''costumbrismo'' genre whose practitioners sought to record with precise detail the entire range of characteristics peculiar to a given area. Today Caballero is known for her contribution to the growth of realism in the Spanish novel and for her sensitive attention to the problems faced by women within the confines of their traditional roles in Spanish society.

Born at Morges, Switzerland, of a German father and Spanish mother, Caballero attended a French boarding school run by nuns in Hamburg, Germany, and there was imbued with the strict Catholicism that characterized her later thought and writings. Her father, Nikolaus Böhl von Faber, was the head of a business firm near Cadiz, Spain, but for political and financial reasons the family resided in Hamburg from 1805 to 1813. An important Hispanist, Böhl von Faber published several scholarly works on Spanish folklore and drama. Caballero acquired his interests as well as her mother's concern with the place of women in society. After the family returned to Cadiz, Caballero, now nineteen, entered into an unfortunate marriage with an army captain with whom she was incompatible. The couple soon moved to Puerto Rico, but within a year the captain was dead of apoplexy, and Caballero returned to Spain. In 1822, she married Francisco Ruiz del Arco, the marqués de Arco-Hermoso, embarking upon what was to prove the happiest period of her life. During this time she was exposed to the folklore and scenery that provided the substance of her creative output. The marqués died in 1835, and two years later Caballero married Antonio Arrom de Ayala, a man seventeen years younger than she. In 1859, however, their marriage, too, ended in tragedy, when after prolonged financial difficulties, Arrom de Ayala commited suicide in London.

During her years as the marquesa de Arco-Hermoso, Caballero made notes for works of various types, drawing on the legends, folktales, and personalities she encountered in daily life. Because of her social status, she was exposed to both the sophistication of Spanish city life and the traditionally conservative villages of the countryside. She strongly identified with the provincial way of life and believed the future of Spain lay in avoiding the currents of liberalism stirring throughout Europe. Her rigidly orthodox, often xenophobic views on religion, politics, and society were to become a central feature of her writings.

It is not clear when Caballero first began to transform the materials she had collected into finished works. The years 1835-45 were her most prolific, but the novel *La familia de*

*Alvareda: Novela original de costumbres populares (The Alvareda Family)* was completed as early as 1828. By 1835 she had begun to publish short stories in periodicals, and in 1849, after taking the name ''Fernán Caballero'' from a small town in the region of La Mancha, she began to publish works she had previously written, including her most important novel, *The Sea Gull*, which appeared serially in the newspaper *El heraldo*.

*The Sea Gull* is often described as both the prototype of the modern Spanish novel and the first important novel produced by the ''costumbrismo'' school. Notable for its realistic approach to Spanish people and customs, the work appeared at a time when romantic settings and characters borrowed from foreign literature were the staple of Spanish fiction. The plot concerns a fisherman's daughter who marries a German doctor and achieves a brilliant singing career in Madrid. Later she falls in love with a bullfighter and returns in disgrace to her country village, her husband dead and her voice ruined. Caballero contrasts the simple and pious pattern of village life with the cosmopolitan beliefs and practices she thought threatened traditional Spanish values. The text is interspersed with descriptions of Andalusian personalities, scenery, and folklore, all vividly and precisely portrayed in a manner new to Spanish fiction. The novel also contains frequent didactic asides on the topic of religion, the proper place of the church in Spanish society, and the author's disillusionment over the eroding influence of the traditional Catholic faith in Spain.

*The Sea Gull* prompted one contemporary critic to refer to Caballero as "the Spanish Walter Scott," and its critical and popular success was followed by the serialized publication of eight more novels in 1849. Among these works, *The Alvareda Family* is considered one of the author's most noteworthy achievements. In this novel, Caballero focused on life in a small village, recording the "ideas, sentiments, and customs" of "Andalusian country people." The complex story chronicles the tragedy of a family torn apart by murder, jealousy, and hatred.

After the initial flood of Caballero's works in 1849, she continued to publish regularly until 1855; then her output diminished until her death. In her novel *Clemencia: Novela de costumbres,* published in 1852, the title character's experiences in marriage closely parallel the author's own. Admired for its sympathetic insight into the dilemmas of Spanish women in a patriarchal society, *Clemencia* displays the conflict between Caballero's conservative ideals and her desire that women achieve autonomy. Among her other significant works after 1849 is the collection of shorter pieces *Cuadros de costumbres populares andaluces (National Pictures),* which contains descriptive accounts of rural life designed to exemplify a moral or proverb.

In 1857, Caballero was provided a home in Seville by Queen Isabel II in appreciation for her contribution to Spanish literature, and she lived there until the Spanish revolution of 1868. In later years, she found herself in financial straits, with her reputation in decline and the prevailing direction of Spanish society wholly at odds with her ideals. She led a retired life in humble lodgings until her death.

Critics have generally agreed that the chief obstacle to an appreciation of Caballero's works is the presence of her conservative ideology throughout her writings. The didactic portions of her narratives have been called intrusive, irrelevant, and aesthetically inappropriate. Though the novelty of her nationalistic and realistic approach to Spanish materials won her early popularity, regard for her works diminished at the end of the nineteenth century as her conservative views fell into increasing disfavor. Modern commentators, however, for whom these ideological battles are largely a matter of history, have asserted that despite her retrogressive approach to thematic materials, she was a pioneer who introduced a new type of novel to Spain that is innovative in its realistic approach to description and in its attention to the problems of women in Spanish society. If her use of realistic materials for her own moral purposes differentiates her work from that of the Spanish realists whom she influenced, her successors adopted her descriptive methods—if not her reactionary aims—all the same. She remains, therefore, a seminal figure in the history of the Spanish novel.

## *PRINCIPAL WORKS

*Clemencia: Novela de costumbres*   (novel)   1852
*Cuadros de costumbres populares andaluces*   (sketches)   1852
   [*National Pictures,* 1882]
*Lágrimas: Novela de costumbres contemporáneas*   (novel)   1853
*Obras completas.* 19 vols.   (novels, novellas, sketches, short stories, and essays)   1855-59

**La familia de Alvareda: Novela original de costumbres populares*   (novel)   1856; published in *Obras completas*
   [*The Alvareda Family* published in *The Castle and the Cottage in Spain,* 1861]
*La gaviota: Novela de costumbres*   (novel)   1856; published in *Obras completas*
   [*La gaviota: A Spanish Novel,* 1864; also published as *The Sea Gull,* 1867]
*La farisea*   (novel)   1863
*Obras completas.* 17 vols.   (novels, novellas, sketches, short stories, essays, and letters)   1905-14
*Obras de Fernán Caballero.* 5 vols.   (novels, novellas, sketches, short stories, and essays)   1961

*Most of Caballero's works were first published serially in newspapers.

**This work was written in 1828.

---

### CHARLES DE MAZADE   (essay date 1858)

[*The following extract is from an article which originally appeared in the* Revue des deux mondes *in 1858.*]

Doubtless, Fernán Caballero has not . . . the virile strength and the patient skill in reproduction of the Scotch novelist; yet like Walter Scott, she has a keen and searching sense of the traditional and local life of the region of which she has made herself at once the historian and the poet. Fernán Caballero loves Spain, which is her first, her only inspiration; she loves Spain in its landscapes, in its manners, in its past, in its legends, and even in its miseries, which are not without their grandeur. . . . Her creations, her combinations, her personages have not a shade of imitation; they are taken from the heart of national life. They emanate from the observation of reality and from a feeling for the poetry of things, two qualities which, being united and balancing each other, constitute real and original invention. . . . But in her pages of a delicate psychology, boldness of analysis does not go far, and the interest of the particular narrative (for example, in the novels *Elia* and *Clemencia*) is not so much perhaps in the development of a passion, of an idea, or in the anatomical treatment of a moral situation, as in the variety of the scenes, in the contrast of characters, and in the ingenious novelty of a succession of pictures in which Spanish life is reflected. Each of the novels of Fernán Caballero is like a gallery of types, some sketched with a light and rapid touch, others traced out lovingly. . . .

The people of Andalusia—the people particularly—find in Fernán Caballero a sympathetic and indefatigable historian, and the most charming tales of the Spanish novelist are, so to speak, an intimate and varied epos of country-life. Now under the form of a dramatic fiction, again under the guise of simple pictures of manners, she combines all shades of this popular existence in which moral nature is in marvelous harmony with physical nature. She has made her domain of that part of Andalusia, as found on the coast, in the mountains, on the plains. (pp. 220-21)

*Charles de Mazade, in an extract, translated by J.D.M. Ford, in* Main Currents of Spanish Literature *by J.D.M. Ford, Henry Holt and Company, 1919, pp. 220-21.*

## [WILLIAM STIGAND]   (essay date 1861)

*[Stigand applauds the emergence of Caballero as a novelist of substance and originality within the context of contemporary Spanish literature. Dividing her works into three categories—Andalusian, Sevillian, and anecdotal—the critic deplores her reactionary views while offering high praise for her descriptive abilities. The article concludes: "No living writer has shed so bright a lustre on Spanish literature."]*

[The appearance] of an author like Fernan Caballero, a really original writer of fictions offering vivid delineations of the manners and characters of the living populations of the most poetic province of the Peninsula [Andalusia], is an event in the literary history of Spain, and we may even add, in that of Europe. (p. 100)

With the exception of a few indifferent historical romances, the country of Cervantes has in modern times produced no novelist who was not a wearisome imitator of foreign models, and the few novel readers of Spain found sufficient entertainment in the translations of Sue and Dumas in the *feuilletons* of the newspapers.

These novels of Fernan Caballero are a great step in advance, and their merit has been more than sufficiently recognised by the literary authorities of Madrid and Seville, and received a due share of recognition at Paris and Berlin. We trust they may inaugurate a new birth of Spanish literature; but the resuscitation of literary excellence in a country which has long been so dead to art and literature as Spain, will require a long period of time. Where there is no taste for literature, of course literature is unremunerative. That a country should be enabled to enjoy a few books in a year, it must be content some how or other to pay for a great many bad ones, and to be able to offer a fair reward to meritorious writers. This is very far from being the case in Spain, where for the most part nobody reads and therefore nobody buys. (pp. 100-01)

It needs a very slight acquaintance with the history of the literature of Europe, to know that such was not formerly the case. That the spirit of romance was, in the early ages of chivalry, as active in Spain as in any part of Europe, and that the prose romances of Spain exceeded in influence those of any other country, in forming the characters of the chevaliers of the fifteenth and sixteenth centuries. Hence it might have been foretold, that of the various kinds of novels the romantic and descriptive was the least repugnant to the old Spanish spirit; and that in order for a writer successfully to undertake such a novel, it would be necessary for him to have a passionate attachment to the national manners and characteristics, and a corresponding dislike to the foreign and the new—such are the qualities we find united in Fernan Caballero. Our surprise at the appearance of such a novelist in Spain, is lessened by the fact that the author is partly of German extraction, and that the writer shows abundant evidence of being deeply tinctured with the study of heretical romance; for quotations from Schiller and Goëthe, from Walter Scott and Bulwer, as well as Balzac, Lamartine, Dumas, Octave Feuillet and Leon Gozlan are of great frequency in her pages.

The whole collection of these tales may be divided into three classes: those which represent Andalusian life as it exists among the *labradores* and *campesinos* of the country, which are thoroughly rustic and natural in their character; those which give delineations of society as it exists in Seville, where the scenes for the most part pass in the *patios* and *tertulias* of the palaces of the Sevillian aristocracy; and those of a shorter kind, in which the interest lies not in the characters of the persons and the description of scenery or manners, but in the brief selection of incidents, which are intended to point a moral or adorn a proverb. There are one or two tales, such as 'La Gaviota' and 'Una en Otra,' which unite our first two classifications, but we class 'La Gaviota,' with the first for the sake of the heroine. The first class, then, comprising **'La Gaviota,' 'La Familia de Alvareda,'** and **'Simon Verde,'** are brilliant and fascinating pictures of Andalusian life, vivid with local colour, rapid in movement, and flavoured delightfully with that 'Sal Andaluz,' which is as proverbial in Spain as Attic wit was in the classic world; and these we intend to review somewhat fully.

Fernan Caballero's pictures of town life are by no means so attractive; although they will have much interest for those who wish to get a correct view of the present state of society among the upper and middle classes, drawn by a writer of the old Spanish school, whose prejudices Fernan Caballero shares to an amusing degree; but her digressions of continual recurrence against the spirit of the age intrude upon the current of the story, and her incessant laudations of the most intolerant abuses and childish superstitions of Spanish Catholicism are both wearisome and ridiculous. Personages are introduced to caricature modern ideas, like Don Narciso Delgado, the Spanish encyclopaedist and adorer of a *Ser Supremo,* and Sir George Percy, the representative of the *blasé* and heretic Englishman; these are weakly conceived, untrue to nature, and fit only to figure in a farce. The heroines are *fades* from extreme goodness and convent innocence of character; yet the novels are redeemed from insipidity by some good portraits of old Spanish characters, and by here and there the graceful figure of a young, natural, lively and high-spirited girl of true Spanish physiognomy.

Of the last order of stories, many are written with power and contain fine descriptive passages, but the nature of the subjects is such as rather to please an uncultivated taste: their interest is the interest of crime; they principally treat of murder, assassinations, miracles, changed and supposititious children, and those grosser sources of fiction which we now leave to our theatres of the East and the students of the Newgate Calendar; but the attraction of this class of subjects for Fernan Caballero may be explained by her ultra-catholic tendencies.

To pass to Fernan Caballero's best tales: it must be allowed that she has been fortunate in obtaining Andalusia for her province as a novelist; where the brilliancy of the skies, the transparency of the atmosphere, and the fertility of the soil are rivalled by the never-failing gaiety, the quick perceptions, the poetic vivacity, the graceful manners and gay costume of the inhabitants. (pp. 101-03)

Of the tales characteristic of this fortunate land in these volumes **'Simon Verde'** alone comes to a happy close. Strangely enough, for a writer who advocates so passionately the happy effects of Catholicism and the old Spanish spirit, nearly all Fernan Caballero's tales end in a tragic and sinister manner; perhaps, however, the author might reply to us with the proverb, *Cosa cumplida solo en la otra vida.* **'Simon Verde,'** however, though it is a touching picture of an honest, simple, and open-hearted *campesino* contending with adverse destiny, and finally being rewarded, is not so well adapted to display Fernan Caballero's peculiar powers as the **'Gaviota'** or **'La Familia de Alvareda.'** **'La Gaviota'** is perhaps the finest story in the volumes. An objection may indeed be made to the choice of the heroine, as her character cannot enlist deeply the sympathies of the reader; but the truth of the descriptions and of the personages of the novel are so vividly wrought out, that we forget the fault, if any, of the subject in that intense realism which is the real charm of the story. (p. 108)

[Although] we cannot help wishing that the authoress had abstained from disfiguring her works by incongruous assaults on modern ideas, which are out of place in a well-conceived work of the imagination, yet we do not fail to recognise the novels of Fernan Caballero as an important addition to the most valued products of modern fiction. Her descriptive powers are of the highest order, as our readers may infer from some of the extracts we have translated, which are far more striking in the picturesque and energetic language of Spain. Here and there we light upon those touches of human nature, in the prattle of childhood, the garrulity of age, or the associations of domestic life, which make the whole world kin. And although these tales are perhaps too essentially Spanish ever to attain a great popularity in foreign countries, they are well calculated to revive the interest of cultivated minds in that noble language and that romantic people. Fernan Caballero has been hailed, in the enthusiastic panegyrics of her countrymen, as the Walter Scott of Spain; and although that title may be the exaggeration of national partiality, it is certain that no living writer has shed so bright a lustre on Spanish literature. (p. 129)

> [*William Stigand*], "*The Novels of Fernan Caballero*," *in* The Edinburgh Review, *Vol. CXIV, No. CCXXXI, July, 1861, pp. 99-129.*

### FRASER'S MAGAZINE   (essay date 1867)

[*In the unsigned essay excerpted below, the critic focuses on* The Sea Gull *as a vivid portrayal of Spanish life and customs. Commending Caballero's description, the critic finds her narrative construction awkward.*]

Perhaps no novel has ever exhibited national characteristics more vividly [than the *Gaviota*]: the characteristics of men and women developed under a special order of circumstances, of religion, of government, and of climate, including their different influences upon the lower and the upper classes of society. The movement of the story takes the reader first into the peasant's home, in a small village on the Andalusian coast, and afterwards into the drawing-rooms of Seville, and leaves him desiring a more intimate acquaintance with the Spanish peasantry, and unwilling to form any with the Spanish aristocracy. The fashionable assemblies to which we are introduced, are full of such nothingness as generally belongs to the circles of fashion, of empty gossipings, of uninteresting scandal, and of that most tiresome of all forms of dialogue which consists of repartee without wit: a continual exhibition of damp damaged fireworks, which feebly fizz and will never go off. On the other hand the groups of peasantry gathering together in the village of Villamar are full of orginality, of imaginative simplicity, of fervent faith, of the belief in things unseen which lends the deepest interest to things seen, of warm affections, of keen perception and shrewd observation forcibly illustrated by racy proverbs; a proverbial philosophy. . . , with a picturesque fancy which finds abundant illustration in the constant presence of fertility and beauty, and in a rich store of romantic legends, such as naturally accumulate among a people passionate and demonstrative, who are given to much talking and no reading, and depend upon the priesthood for all their learning. The author of the *Gaviota* can, with a few strokes of the pen, bring a whole village into existence, can show its active life and its still life with equal power, can transport you to its

ardent atmosphere, to its glowing sky and hot blue sea. She can draw many varieties of human character without any apparent effort. She can represent the types of the brutal and the selfish, of the generous and the gentle, and the more mixed qualities of more ordinary people. She can do all this, but she cannot tell a story well. She cannot deal smoothly with the progress of events. She cannot easily unfold the consequence from the cause; her narration has a short uneasy motion, and it is at times confused where there is no necessary perplexity of plot.

The links are not joined together in her chain. She introduces every fresh incident with a start, with a 'once upon a time,' or 'one day it happened,' in the juvenile fairy tale style; like a driver who urges his horses with a series of jerks, never commanding an equal pace; or a singer who has not mastered the gliding transition from one passage to another, which is known among musicians as the *legato*. The plot of the *Gaviota* is not intricate, and would have a sufficient, if not a very powerful interest, supposing it were better handled. (pp. 193-94)

[An element of the disagreeable prevails in the story], for of the three principal characters, two are of a revolting brutality; the third is feeble to a point which entails a painful contempt, and they all come to a miserable end.

But they are set forth with an artistic skill and consistent purpose which justifies the author as an interpreter of nature, and the scenes in which they breathe and move are relieved by the brighter images of the peasant's home. It is in the sunny village of Villamar that we are disposed to linger. . . ; where strange and sometimes beautiful traditions stimulate the imagination; where a fervent piety is the moving principle of life; where friends are friendly; where kind words are true ones; where generosity sees no cause for boasting; and in short, where a true Christian spirit binds the community together. (p. 195)

> "*A Spanish and a Danish Novel*," *in* Fraser's Magazine, *Vol. LXXVI, No. CCCCLII, August, 1867, pp. 190-203.*

### M. BETHAM-EDWARDS   (essay date 1880)

[*Betham-Edwards suggests that Caballero's strengths as a writer derive from her conservatism and sincerity. While Betham-Edwards is critical of her haphazard handling of style and structure, she also asserts that it is precisely her disregard for literary conventions that gives her works their unique power.*]

It is not astonishing that, in spite of the power of this great writer [Caballero] and the fascination of the language in which she wrote, her name should be almost unknown in England. Spain, if indeed, as Schopenhauer describes it, "the subtlest of nations," is, at the same time, the least advanced as far as progress is concerned, and the farthest removed from actual tendencies of thought. When, therefore, we enter the region of modern Spanish fiction, we find ourselves in a wholly new world, and cannot without an effort extend our sympathies to phases of character and conditions of life wholly unlike our own. But the effort once made to make the acquaintance of Fernan Caballero we soon become sensible of a witchery that holds us fast; we feel, as we read her glowing pages, that the very singularity and remoteness of their subject have charm. We are grateful to the author for being as conservative as the nation she portrays, for indeed and in truth it is nothing less than the Spanish nation that this daughter of Spain has pictured for us. This is her title of honour, and had she been one shade more cosmopolitan, one whit less conservative, she could not have accomplished her task with anything like the same success. Would we learn then to know her country people—would we become acquainted with the sprightly Madrileño, the shrewd Andalusian, the Sevillan beauty, the rustic heroine, the stately Marquesa of "sangre azul," the homely son of the soil, as well as the dashing young officer, "what it is they say and do," we have but to turn to the little library of fiction bearing the pseudonym of Fernan Caballero. Possessed of extraordinary insight into character and passionate sympathy, ever limited to Spain and things Spanish, she has identified herself with its literature by a series of works, remarkable above all for their sincerity. So sincere is she, so bent on giving utterance to the thought uppermost in her mind, that she has damaged her novels, considered as works of art, by disregard of the great models. She will be true to herself at any cost. Familiar alike with French, German, English, and Italian literature, she has profited by none in matters of style and form. She seems to have wilfully abstained from profiting by them, and without quarrelling with her for not being a stylist, we should have been grateful for a little more respect shown to accepted canons of taste. Yet so naïve, picturesque, and forcible is her language, so true to life are her characters, so replete are these stories with poetry and passion, that we forgive technical imperfections and read each to the end.

Never was writer better able to rely on her own powers or to dispense with artificial literary aids! A world of charm lies in the language alone, that delicious Castilian of which she was so thoroughly mistress. Then, by way of background for her stories, she had certainly some of the most striking scenery in the world, as all travellers in Southern Spain can attest; whilst for plastic human nature, with which to vivify her pictures, she had the richly-endowed, deeply-poetic, witty and subtle Spanish character, no less familiar to her than native speech and country.

What true genius could do with such materials, unaided by anything in the shape of the critical faculty, Fernan Caballero's stories all show. There is not one perhaps that can be regarded as a work of art, and there is not one that the reader will lay down unfinished. Schiller somewhere characterises the true artist by his capacity for "knowing what to leave out." Fernan Caballero never seemed to suppose it necessary to leave anything out; snatches of song, anecdote, wise saws, and, worst of all, long digressions interrupt the progress of her narratives, making some of them a farrago rather than a consistent whole. Yet the strength and spirit animating every line, and the variety and force of her characters, make up for all artistic shortcomings. It might be, that had she begun to write earlier, or had she been a humble author dependent on her pen for bread, she would have taken pains to write better. (pp. 145-46)

[Fernan Caballero's real strength lies in the manner in which she] dips her bucket into the pure well of human affection, and with it waters the hard, unsympathetic world! Her peasant-folk, alike young and old, and of either sex, are inimitable. . . . Nor does our author excel alone when dealing with pathetic subjects. The rich humour of the Spanish character is rendered by her in a manner worthy of the countrywoman of Cervantes, and especially is the deep religious feeling of the people brought out in every one of these rural stories. Religion perhaps is more of a reality to the Catholic peasant of Andalusia than to any other class in the world, and we feel that there is no exaggeration in Fernan Caballero's presentments of priestly authority as an influence of first importance in daily life. (p. 147)

We cannot wonder at Fernan Caballero's glorification of the Catholic faith, in season and out of season, seeing the effect of it on the life of the people. Of free inquiry, of emancipation from superstitious beliefs, of winnowed theological dogmas, she has not the faintest notion. Catholicism as it is, as it has been, is her highest ideal of man's spiritual development; she will have no compromise, no secular education, no alliance of science with theology. The whole or nothing for her, and the same spirit of exclusiveness is seen in her views on social life. The least infiltration of foreign manners and customs, the most inoffensive reform in matters of social usage, fill her with disgust. Learned, cosmopolitan, as she was in her literary tastes, generous and sympathetic by nature, she is yet the narrowest, intellectually speaking, of all writers to be placed on her own level. (p. 148)

Foreign readers will without doubt attribute the charm of [her] novels to their truthfulness, sparkle, and animation, but the bulk of Fernan Caballero's country-people must naturally be drawn to them by the deep devotional feeling in which every page is steeped. Not one but a thousand touches might be cited illustrative of the ever-present reality of Catholicism to the writer's mind, and deeply poetic many of these touches are. (p. 151)

Would any readers fain know more of a richly-gifted and poetic people, and a subtle, if not "the subtlest of nations," they must then go to the pages of Fernan Caballero, the greatest woman writer of Spain, and certainly one of the most gifted novelists of our day. (p. 152)

> *M. Betham-Edwards, "The Novels of Fernan Caballero," in* Macmillan's Magazine, *Vol. XLIII, No. 254, December, 1880, pp. 145-52.*

**BENEDETTO CROCE** (essay date 1923)

[*Croce was an Italian philosopher, historian, editor, and literary critic whose writings span the first half of the twentieth century. He founded and edited the literary and political journal* La critica, *whose independence, objectivity, and strong stand against fascism earned him the respect of his contemporaries. According to Croce, the only proper form of literary history is the* caratteristica, *or critical characterization, of the poetic personality and work of a single artist: its goal is to demonstrate the unity of the author's intention, its expression in the creative work, and the reader's response. In his appreciative essay on Caballero, Croce explores the qualities of her works as a product of the "spring of poetry" which "was bubbling in her heart." Comparing her writings with those of the French novelist George Sand, Croce suggests that Caballero possessed "a truer vein of poetry" than her contemporary, one founded on the sincerity and depth of her religious convictions and social conservatism. Though he faults Caballero's uneven style of narration, he argues that her stylistic defects are transcended by the unaffected fervor of her sentiments and convictions. The work from which the following excerpt was taken was originally published in 1923 as* Poesia e non poesia: Note sulla letteratura europea del secolo decimonono.*]

I believe discoverable a truer vein of poetry, even of "idyllic poetry," in the modest Spanish authoress who concealed herself under the name of Fernán Caballero (Cecilia Böhl de Faber) than in the very celebrated Georges Sand. She too was a polemist and a propagandist as ardent as the lady of Nohant, but in a precisely opposite sense, that is to say Catholic, traditionalistic and almost reactionary; yet I find in her a solidity of mind, a simplicity of heart and a liveliness of imagination which the other did not possess, for all her superior facility and virtuosity. In the history of poetry one often verifies the saying that the first shall be last and the last first.

To tell the truth, the very polemic and apostolate of the Caballero seem to me far more securely founded and more seriously justified than the turbid feminism and the superficial socialism of Georges Sand. The old Spain, so great and glorious, so Catholic and so warlike, after having suddenly shaken herself free from the sleep into which she had fallen after having combated French and Napoleonic imperialism with her popular resources, instead of persisting in the character which she had re-asserted with such prowess, began to accept new social and political forms, as presented to her by many of her national writers, and, accepting their point of view and beginning to vacillate in her ancient faith and habits, seemingly accepting as just the criticisms and satires directed against her by foreign writers. This work of the innovators, liberals and free-thinkers was a defiance of her sacred past, which still formed the lively and actual present of so great a part of the Spanish people; Fernán Caballero took up the gauntlet. (pp. 230-31)

[Her] polemic, which took colour and character from its reference to Spanish life, was a particular aspect and instance of the polemic of historicism against intellectualistic radicalism, with which the nineteenth century opened. Not only had it political value at the time it appeared, but a true ideal value, so much so that we are ourselves constrained to have recourse to it, as coming generations will also certainly be obliged to do. What ideal value, on the other hand, is retained by the much-vaunted claim to follow the stimulus of the erotic imagination, or the desired fusion of the social classes by means of the marriage of ladies with workmen, advocated and maintained by Georges Sand? It will be said that the Caballero did not invent the idea of that polemic in support of tradition. Certainly, and it is difficult to determine who exactly did invent it, because it arose everywhere in Europe as the result of inevitable historical necessity. But she represented it very well, so far as it concerned her, and reproduced it anew in new conditions, by re-living it in herself.

With a view to secure this end, which is the first and most apparent of her work, the Caballero selected "the picture of customs," popular Spanish customs, more particularly Andalusian, and doing this with full spontaneity, she seemed also to conform to a literary example which had found in Scott its greatest protagonist; hence this authoress, whom we shall freely term the Catholic Sand, was hailed by preference as "the Spanish Walter Scott" by her contemporaries. So urgent to her seemed the duty she had assumed of defending the old religious and moral forms of the country, that she always protested against those who looked upon the stories she told as "romances" or "artistic works." More than once she declared, "I have not intended to write novels; I have tried to give a true, exact, genuine idea of Spain and of its society, to describe the internal life of our people, its beliefs, its feelings, its acute sayings; I have tried to rehabilitate things which the ignorant nineteenth century has trodden under its heavy and audacious foot, holy and religious things, religious practices and their lofty and tender significance, ancient and pure Spanish customs, the national character and mode of feeling, the bonds that unite society and the family, restraint in everything, and especially in those ridiculous passions which are affected without being really felt (because fortunately great passion is rare), modest virtues. The so-called romantic part of my work is intended only as the framework of the vast building that I have set myself to construct." She also confessed that her intention

not only went beyond art, but even led her to oppose herself to art, sacrificing the logic of what she described as the *donnée*, that is to say, the artistic motive, to the advantage of the moral lesson which she desired to teach.

She wished her stories to be edifying, such as should illustrate themes dear to her or give occasion to the development of such themes by means of examples of good and evil. She was an orator in the good cause, a preacher who did not indulge in artistic subtleties, and when necessary ill-treated art, provided she obtained the end in view. She experienced the greatest satisfaction when she was able to assure readers that the story she told was true, that is to say, had really happened, and that in it was to be found, not only a model, but also a document.

But the orator of the good, far more and far differently from him who aims only at encompassing and persuading his readers for his own utilitarian ends, must attain to his means from poetry, in order to penetrate to the bottom of his reader's souls and touch their deepest chords. And we have heard the Caballero talk of "poetry," when opposing the eye of the heart to that of cold reason, and she had been poetically moved prior to giving herself at a late age, about fifty, to her work of defence and apostolate. She had contemplated, dreamed and idealized much, yet she continued always to regard the world with the feeling of a poet, and as a poet lent an ear to the voices that murmured within her. Those who approached her say that after having spoken with her and breathed the perfume of her goodness, they saw the actions of men and the spectacles of nature in a new way, and felt their heart full of sweet tears and of a longing to accomplish good deeds.

She wished to make people love the country, plants, flowers, the earth rich with a thousand animals and insects, all of them curious to observe, humble life, villages with a narrow horizon; but she already loved these things and spoke of them in accents of trembling affection. (pp. 232-35)

The Caballero found . . . expressions of a poetic world of joy, of smiling, of vexation, of religion, already formed and included them in her narratives; but by thus finding, selecting, arranging them advantageously, her poetic spirit in a certain way makes them hers, encloses them in her world of dream, changing them into a part of her soul. (p. 242)

Certainly the stories of Fernán Caballero have evident defects, in part confessed by the authoress herself: they are edifying tales, frequently not so much simple as artless, laxly woven together, verbose, interrupted at every step with reflections, considerations and exhortations. She wrote what seemed to her to be useful for her work as an apostle, but certainly more than her real artistic inspiration warranted. In Spain itself there was no lack of folk who found her stories tiresome and frankly said so, or defined them like Juan Valera (I find this in one of Caballero's letters) *arroz con leche*, rice and milk; and now there are some who consider that she wrote badly, that she did not possess *el castizo estilo*, the purged style, that she was a "Balzac *debilitado*," and the like. But Fernán Caballero, spontaneity itself as she was, living intensely the lives that she had created, was able on occasion to tell a story with power and sobriety and to show herself to be a worthy heiress of the Spanish story-tellers, from the author of the *Lazarillo* to the great Cervantes and the authors of the picaresque romances. (p. 243)

[The] practical tendency predominated in the Caballero, rendering her careless or impatient of artistic elaboration and resulting in the defects noted by us, for the rest sufficiently evident in themselves. But Caballero's work is able to resist this practical tendency and the bad literary effects which result from it, because, differently from other women writers, she did not look with one eye at the paper and the other at the public (as Heine would have put it), she attempted no blandishments, she paid no attention to arranging herself in such a way as to excite or to seduce the imaginations of readers, she did not expand and falsify feelings and passions, nor raise them to the rank of theories, but was animated with a pure and serious conviction, and possessed sound judgment. And above all a spring of poetry was bubbling in her heart, which maintained itself fresh and lively even in the midst of the fervent apostolate which she exercised in the service of her faith as a Catholic of the old Church and as a Spaniard of the old Spain. (pp. 250-51)

> *Benedetto Croce, "Fernán Caballero," in his* European Literature in the Nineteenth Century, *translated by Douglas Ainslie, Alfred A. Knopf, 1924, pp. 230-51.*

### L. B. WALTON  (essay date 1927)

[*Walton summarizes Caballero's legacy to Spanish literature. He emphasizes the originality of her approach to Spanish materials in* The Sea Gull, *but is highly critical of the book's construction and didacticism. He contends that her chief merit as a writer lies in "the effort to express the hidden beauty and significance of ordinary life which is characteristic of the realistic novel at its best."*]

Until 1850 the Spanish novel had merely reflected the dominant tendencies of foreign literatures; but . . . in Fernán Caballero, we at last find a writer of independence and originality, an author who is not content with mere imitation. Avoiding the alluring net spread by Scott and Dumas, she attempts to create original works based upon personal observation of the life she knew so well: the varied, colourful existence of Andalusia. Temperamentally she was well equipped for her task, for she had, in addition to the fertile imagination of the Spaniard, the Teuton's love of accuracy and detail. Passionately attached to her adopted country, she saw great possibilities in the sketch of national and local customs. She determined to develop it beyond the stage of the *ébauche.* . . . Although it is not altogether free from the defects of the "romantic" tradition which had dominated Spain for half a century, *La Gaviota,* the firstfruits of her labours, is a creditable piece of work. The story is extremely simple; indeed its author admits in her Preface that it can scarcely be termed a "novel" in the accepted sense of the word. . . . Marisalada is the centre of interest throughout the story, and in her portrayal of this strange, wild creature, Fernán Caballero shows herself to be a psychologist of no mean order. Marisalada is a bizarre compound of the "noble savage" dear to Rousseau, and the modern "emancipated" woman of the Sandian tradition. A creature of instinct and passion, she is the complete antithesis of her lover who, we may imagine, is an expression of the Teutonic element in the author's character, as Marisalada is that of the Spanish. The minor figures in the first part—la tía María, Dolores, Manuel, Don Modesto Guerrero, "Rosa Mística," "Turris Davídica," Momo and Gabriel—are admirably drawn. In her portrayal of the two old "devotas" Fernán Caballero anticipates the delicious irony of Galdós, who delighted in rendering such types. The first part of the novel might aptly be likened to a portrait gallery, a series of *genre* studies to which we are introduced one by one. (pp. 20-1)

In the second part of the novel the scene is transferred to Seville, where we are introduced to various types representative of Andalusian society—General Santa María, the ardent patriot; Eloisa, the cosmopolitan; the Condesa de Algar; the Marquesa de Guadalcanal; Pepe Vera, the "torero"; and the incredible Englishman Sir John Burnwood. . . . This second part is, on the whole, unconvincing. It brings out clearly a cardinal defect in the literary equipment of the author, a defect which she is able to conceal when she deals with more primitive types. Fernán Caballero had no adequate experience of life. Her aristocrats, especially, smack of the novelette, and her Englishmen are fantastic. She moved in a restricted circle and lacked the gift, peculiar to great genius, of making a little experience go a very long way. It is, indeed, impossible to join unreservedly in the paean of unqualified praise with which *La Gaviota* was greeted by certain Spanish critics. Apart from the superficiality of its author's observation, revealed by many of the characters in it, *La Gaviota* is a badly constructed book. It is far too long. There is a notable insufficiency of plot and action to justify two volumes, the first of two hundred and three, the second of two hundred and thirty-six, pages. The author has not succeeded in emancipating herself completely from the evil traditions of the neo-chivalresque school, and deliberate imitations of the style and mannerisms of Scott appear in *La Gaviota,* and strike one as being utterly out of place. She indulges frequently in sentimental rhetoric and long, wearisome digressions; her description of Seville might have been taken straight from the pages of Baedeker; she allows herself to be led into a tiresome didacticism—these are but a few of the charges one might bring against this well-meaning pioneer of realism in the Spanish novel. Fernán Caballero lacked, in fine, the resources of heart and mind which are inseparable from genius. She had, however, none of that arrogance which so often characterises the mediocre artist. (pp. 21-3)

Her claims to "españolismo" are amply justified, for her work, in spite of certain affectations due to borrowing from Scott, has the authentic flavour of the soil, and in it we can discern the love of truth, the power of observation and the effort to express the hidden beauty and significance of ordinary life which is characteristic of the realistic novel at its best. When Fernán Caballero entered the literary arena, the Spanish public was weary of the dull and interminable pseudo-historical romance. It yearned for a truer presentation of life; and found what it required in *La Gaviota, Clemencia, Lágrimas* and *La Familia de Alvareda.* These works by Fernán Caballero renewed European interest in Spanish literature, an interest which had been steadily on the wane since its momentary revival by the Schlegels in the early years of the century. (pp. 23-4)

> *L. B. Walton, "A Brief Survey of Spanish Fiction Prior to the Appearance of 'La fontana de oro'," in his* Pérez Galdós and the Spanish Novel of the Nineteenth Century, *J. M. Dent & Sons Ltd., 1927, pp. 1-27.**

### CHARLES B. QUALIA  (essay date 1951)

[*Qualia surveys the influence of* The Sea Gull *on the modern Spanish novel, asserting that the Spanish realists who followed Caballero owed their methods to her example, despite their rejection of her conservative ideals. Qualia also suggests that Caballero's didactic intent was to further her literary theories as well as her view of morality. According to Qualia, the novelist's importance as a literary theorist has been overlooked.*]

*La Gaviota* holds a leading place in the development of the modern novel in Spain. Most of those who have had occasion to pronounce themselves upon the subject agree that modern realism in the novel of Spain began with *La Gaviota.*

If modern realism in the novel of Spain did stem from *La Gaviota,* it should be interesting from this vantage point of time to analyze and reappraise the contribution made. Let us recall first that justly famous Chapter IV of the Second Part of *La Gaviota* in which Fernán set down her ideas of the novel. Among the negative precepts, the author teaches that Spaniards should not try to write historical novels, because these require learned writers. They should not try the fantastic or sentimental novels, because they are contrary to Spanish genius, and novels of horror should be left to others, but Spaniards are urged to write the *novela de costumbres. . . .* (p. 63)

Fernán Caballero further taught that Spaniards should depict themselves as they are and that they should observe reality instead of dreaming up incidents. This spirit of observation which Fernán taught in theory and put into practice is the very core and essence of the realistic novel. . . . [The] spirit of didacticism of Fernán Caballero that is justly condemned by most critics in the subject matter of her novels becomes a virtue in the propagation of the theories of realism for the Spanish novel, and she embodied them in the very first example itself. In the development of Spanish letters practice has so often led the way, with little theoretical and intellectual discussion to direct the disciples of a movement. In Fernán Spanish realism had both a creative writer and a preceptor. She was a woman of exceptional intellectual attainments and she placed them at the service of her art. It is regrettable that Spanish critics and literary historians have never recognized her importance as a theorist.

She not only taught that Spaniards should write *novelas de costumbres* of Spain, but of a single region as well, and she gave the example. When Fernán Caballero wrote of *novelas de costumbres,* she did not mean merely the picturesque; she had in mind something much more profound. . . . [As] early as 1853 Fernán Caballero saw Spanish society as a whole *como materia novelable,* and she did not conceive superficial, picturesque manners and customs as the only part of realism. She included *el modo de opinar* of the people and their *indole,* or moral qualities. She gives to the novel here in theory all the scope that Galdós claims for it in his Academy speech and that he gave to it in practice. If Fernán does not portray the same struggles of the people of Spain that Galdós portrays, it is because her work reflects the ideas and ideals of a conservative of the Spain of Isabella II, whereas Galdós belongs to the generation that followed the September Revolution and he reflects the thinking and the struggles of that generation. How much of Galdós's method and technique is owed to Fernán's theories of the novel would be difficult to say, but her statements and her examples are there. Galdós and other post-revolution novelists can be presumed to have profited vastly by them. Fernán Caballero also saw that history could likewise serve the realist by recreating the Spain of a recent past and so she wrote *Elia o la España de treinta años ha.* . . . Likewise, in depicting social gatherings of the upper classes with which she was so familiar, she introduces an element of realism into *La Gaviota* that was to be used very effectively by her successors in the novel and by Benavente in his dramas of upper and middle class society, namely, the clash of ideas. Far from lacking the ability to represent the upper levels of society of her day, she does it with full knowledge and self-assurance,

for she had "observed" such scenes first in the home of her parents and later in the palace of Arco Hermoso. The discussions among the guests at those tertulias concerning art, literature, politics, religion, and social problems present the method. The difference between this and later realism lies in the changed conditions of Spanish society and in the bias of the author. This introduction of the study of ideas into the novel is the most advanced and profound feature of her realism, for it was the very element which was susceptible of the greatest development. This is the battle of ideas and idealogies that reflects the struggle of the people of Spain to adjust themselves to new and changing conditions, with which the second half of the century is so largely concerned. Fernán Caballero sensed the pressure for change and she urged Spaniards to hold to their old institutions, customs, and beliefs by depicting them in a favorable light. She fought to retain the *statu quo.* Galdós appeared in 1870, and turned the guns in the opposite direction. He advocated change and revolt against traditionalism, but he did not introduce the method, the technique. Galdós simply developed further the technique that he found ready made, just as the Generation of 1898 further evolved the technique of their predecessors in order to make it suit new situations, new conditions, and applied the study to new areas. (pp. 63-5)

While Asensio clearly indicates that the novel in the nineteenth century evolved, and he mentions specifically the changes brought in by Alarcón, Valera, Pérez Galdós, and Pereda, yet the novel in the hands of these writers evolved within the framework of realism, which Fernán put in vogue. Writing in 1897, Menéndez y Pelayo too credits Fernán Caballero with the reintroduction of true realism into the Spanish novel, based upon the spirit of observation. . . . Juan Valera also credits her with a "profunda facultad de observación." Perhaps no one will object to the suggestion that in the depiction of picturesque *cuadros de costumbres* in his novels, Don Juan could owe a debt to the teachings and examples of Doña Cecilia, but what most students of Juan Valera might object to is the suggestion that the method and technique of his novels of ideas might owe a greater debt to Fernán than had been supposed. From Fernán Caballero to Pío Baroja and Pérez de Ayala the content of the Spanish novel has vastly changed, but the vessel itself has retained the same general outline and the study of life still depends upon observation.

Critics have pointed out many times during the past hundred years that didacticism often mars the novelistic art of Fernán Caballero, and no one has more severely criticized her for this defect than Palacio Valdés, whose art of the novel, after that of Pereda and Trueba, is perhaps most heavily indebted to hers even in its own didacticism. No one could deny that didacticism mars Fernán's art. However, it should be pointed out here that her tendency to be theoretical and to teach led her not only to moralize on social questions but also to teach the art of the novel as well. She set down her theories of the novel within the novels themselves, in prefaces, in footnotes, and in her letters. For one who was breaking new ground, giving the novel a new direction, a new purpose, this is a fact that should be emphasized. Fernán Caballero was driven by her didactic bent to teach literary art far more than any of her successors and she was a conscious literary artist in a much higher degree than has been noted heretofore. Fernán's traditionalist ideology blurred somewhat the vision of her critics. Her reactionary ideas with regard to the social and political structure of Spain, her intense religious faith, and her strong propensity to didacticism have tended to reduce in the eyes of some Spanish critics and historians the true value and scope of her contribution to modern realism. (pp. 65-6)

To sum up, then, we find that *La Gaviota* and other works of Fernán Caballero have retained a remarkable visibility if measured by the number of editions made in the hundred years that have elapsed since the first publication of the novel. Measured by the amount of criticism devoted to it, *La Gaviota* was accorded a full measure of attention and importance by Spanish critics of the nineteenth century, but the importance of her theories of the novel has been overlooked. In the current century we find no reappraisal of Fernán Caballero. The critical ideas of the nineteenth century are more or less repeated. We hope that a reappraisal by Spanish critics will follow upon the hundredth anniversary of the publication of *La Gaviota*. (pp. 66-7)

*Charles B. Qualia, "'La Gaviota' One Hundred Years After," in* Hispania, *Vol. XXXIV, No. l, February, 1951, pp. 63-7.*

GERALD BRENAN    (essay date 1951)

[*Brenan briefly evaluates the importance of* The Sea Gull.]

The importance of the *costumbristas* is that they decided the main lines that the novel was to follow during the rest of the century. The novelists, with a few exceptions, sat down to write with the aim of describing the life and customs of the city or province in which they lived and only secondarily of telling a story of general human interest. Sometimes they wrote in praise of their *patria chica,* more often they drew a dark picture of it, but they always took care to describe its general pattern, even when this meant making considerable interruptions in the plot. If this approach had obvious disadvantages, it at least made certain that the Spanish novel should draw its strength from the observed social life of a community rather than from the personal experience of the novelist. Such a rule, in Spain at least, was salutary.

The first of these novels—for I omit those historical romances inspired by a misunderstanding of Scott—was *La Gaviota.* . . . (p. 379)

Caballero is a woman who deserves well of her adopted country. She was the first person to interest herself in the artistic talents of the peasants and working classes, collecting and publishing the stories they told and the *coplas* they sang. Since Lope de Vega no Spanish writer has thought any of these worth listening to. She also, as we have said, wrote the first novel of contemporary life. It is true that *La Gaviota,* which is the best of her works of fiction, is not, artistically speaking, a good book. The characters, though plausible, are types rather than living people and do not change or grow as the plot develops. There is also too much emphasis on *costumbrismo* and too much Germanic zest for instructing us. But she has a wide range of observation and sympathy: her crude, egoistic heroine and her bull-fighter are convincing in their static way and, even when we feel the weakness of the novelising, we go on reading. As an intelligent and widely travelled woman explaining to us the social pattern of Andalusian life, she contrives, I think, to hold the attention. (p. 380)

*Gerald Brenan, "Nineteenth-Century Prose," in his* The Literature of the Spanish People: From Roman Times to the Present Day, *Cambridge at the University Press, 1951, pp. 377-416.**

LAWRENCE H. KLIBBE    (essay date 1973)

[*In the following selections from his study of Caballero's life and works, Klibbe discusses* The Sea Gull, The Alvareda Family, *and* Clemencia. *His commentary on* The Sea Gull *focuses on Caballero's theoretical approach to the Spanish novel as reflected both in her prologue and in her characters' argument about Spanish literature. Klibbe suggests that the date and various elements of* The Alvareda Family *place it with other French and English works as an early example of the realistic novel that developed later in the century. Asserting that the structure of* The Alvareda Family *has much in common with classical Spanish drama, the critic makes an extended comparison of the theatrical elements in the novel with those of the* comedia *of the Golden Age of Spanish literature. The critic's approach to* Clemencia *centers on the novel's autobiographical elements and on Caballero's attempt to portray a viable alternative to the modernization of Spain in the values shared by Clemencia and Pablo.*]

Fernán Caballero advanced the theory as well as the practice of the modern Spanish novel by the prologue to [*The Sea Gull*], later added to the book version, but an accepted guide to her ideas at the time of composition and serial publication.

This brief, succinct prologue to *The Sea Gull* is also a direct, precise statement of Fernán Caballero's aims and is likewise an important manifesto of the definitive break between Romanticism and Realism. The terminology, however, is expressed as the distinction between a "novel" and a "novel of customs"; but the differences are clearly stated, revealing thereby a firm understanding of the new orientation for this genre. She is, in fact, wary about the use of the word "novel" to classify *The Sea Gull* because *la novela* is evidently associated too closely with Romanticism for her; and the novel is likewise synonymous with the imagination, in her view. The *novela de costumbres,* then, will not emphasize the prominent features of the Romantic novel so that imagination and the plot, or the intrigue, are relegated to minor roles in the construction of *The Sea Gull.*

Instead of utilizing the Romantic formulae of a complicated, exotic plot and giving free rein to imaginative treatment of the story, Fernán Caballero somewhat modestly claims that it is only necessary "to compile and to copy" in order to compose the new novel, such as *The Sea Gull.* Observation opposed to imagination, truth opposed to invention, led logically to the need of the novel being set in the present and in Spain where the two criteria were at first hand for the writer. Characters also existed in the rural and urban social strata although Fernán Caballero does not claim that all her characters are so directly sketched. For example, she moves forward in the direction of character studies when she writes that the actors in her drama of *The Sea Gull* are neither totally good or perfect, nor are they completely evil, as in melodramas, referring to the Romantic theater. Fernán Caballero, in her acceptance of the Balzacian idea, attempts to indicate the "characteristic trait" of the personages, creating of course types, but at the same time individual persons.

However, Fernán Caballero interrupted these thoughts on the art of *The Sea Gull* by analyzing her countrymen honestly and frankly, and also by defending the Spaniard against the criticism of foreigners. No contradiction exists in these apparently distinct treatments, and she is very perceptive about the national temperament, after the previous probes of Larra, before the extensive critiques of Galdós, and yet relevant for any understanding of the future problem for the Generation of 1898. Fernán Caballero places her countrymen in four classes: the vociferous defenders of the national tradition who refuse to admit adverse comments, except in the political sphere; the fawning imitators of foreign models, refusing to consider anything Spanish to be worthwhile; the irrational advocates of a Spain already enjoying the best of all possible worlds; and the fourth group, representing the majority of Spaniards (including Doña Cecilia, as she insists), who favor an eclectic approach by accepting slowly and gradually any foreign ideas. This last class first weighs change from abroad against a scrutiny of present conditions and only makes modifications if these new approaches are in accord with the Spanish or native character. In short, the analysis and understanding of *lo castizo,* the purely Spanish, must take place before European developments are admitted; but the Pyrenees certainly provides no ideological, philosophical, or social barrier to national progress. These views of Fernán Caballero, similar to Unamuno's ideas at the beginning of *En torno al casticismo (On the Problem of Spanishness),* are of course essentially moderate and conservative; but the tone is encouraging at this critical direction of Spanish life and literature in the second half of the nineteenth century.

These theories of the prologue are reinforced within **The Sea Gull** during the discussions in the second part at the social gatherings in Sevilla and Madrid, where Fernán Caballero also attempts "to give an exact, true and genuine idea of Spain" and where "the European public might have a correct idea of Spain and of Spaniards," as she states in the prologue. This defense of Spaniards against foreign misinterpretations and harsh criticisms is of course interesting in view of Fernán Caballero's parentage and her own extensive residence abroad, including the present problem of the original version of **The Sea Gull** in French as a language in which, apparently, she wrote more easily than in Spanish. She even seems a little strident in her opinion that foreigners have consistently misinterpreted the Spanish character and scene, and that her compatriots have not corrected the European image of Spain by their own explanations. Also, this desire for a truthful, accurate foreign opinion serves as some argument for the favorable picture of rural life, customs, and characters, especially in the first part of **The Sea Gull.** (pp. 46-8)

Fernán Caballero's aim to write a novel of customs is achieved through observation, a Realistic feature, but the selection of material is nonetheless subjected to her ideological beliefs: traditional, monarchical, Catholic, conformist. Her Realism is also placed at the service of her Romanticism about Spain so that the scenes are idealized, the favorable aspects of rural life are selected, and the characters are devoid of complex personalities, unaware or scornful of any worries in their daily lives. Her transitional Realism, consequently, can be judged only on the basis of these two cornerstones of her art, which, at the same time, lead to the novel of Regionalism, of local color or *Costumbrismo,* of a novel steeped in national, provincial descriptions. Fernán Caballero followed closely upon the successes of the *costumbristas,* and it is perhaps no coincidence that the *Los españoles pintados por sí mismos (The Spaniards Painted by Themselves),* the culmination of the *costumbrista* effort, coincides with the composition of **The Sea Gull.**

For Fernán Caballero, then, her *novela de costumbres* is based on local color sketches which contribute on many occasions nothing to the deemphasized plot and action, but provide, to a degree, an independent unit. Chapters can be read separately as descriptive essays or even as short stories. (p. 57)

When Fernán Caballero defined her intentions in a novel as "the poetization of reality," she was endeavoring to portray

a picture of nature and life, true and accurate in her observations, devoid of the fantastic, exotic descriptions of the Romantics. However, she was a product of the Romantic ambiance through influences of time, parents, and education so that the pictorial quality of Andalusian scenes reflects these sources. At times, her descriptions resemble paintings, similar to those of her friend, the Duque de Rivas, in his plays and poems; the canvases of the French Romantics, such as Delacroix; and the American examples, Cooper in his vision of the hinterland and the Hudson River school of painters. Her Romanticism in descriptive background, subtly conveying the love of nature and the advantages of the simple, harmonious ways of rural life, contributes to poetic, thoughtful frames for the plot; the effectiveness also depends on Fernán Caballero's desire to express openly, strongly, her ideological point of view.

In Chapter V, Stein's impressions of Villamar and the surrounding area form a Romantic mood, prepared of course by his own innate sentimentality:

> The end of October had been rainy, and November was appearing in her heavy, green cloak of winter.
>
> Stein was walking one day in front of the monastery from where an immense and uniform perspective was revealed: to the right, the limitless sea; to the left, the endless pasture land. In the middle, level with the horizon, the dark profile of the ruins of Fort St. Christopher was outlined, like the image of nothingness amidst the immensity. The sea, which the slightest gust did not disturb, was gently stirring, lifting effortlessly its waves, gilded by the sun's glare, like a queen allowing her golden cloak to flow. The monastery, with its large, severe, and angular contours, was in harmony with the solemn and monotonous landscape; its mass hid the only open point of the horizon in that uniform panorama.
>
> At that point was the village of Villamar, situated beside a river as flowing and turbulent in winter, as poor and stagnant in summer. The surrounding areas, well cultivated, presented from a distance the look of a chessboard, on whose squares the color green varied in a thousand ways; here the yellowish grapevine still covered with foliage; there the ashy green of an olive tree, or the emerald green of wheat, which the autumn rains had caused to shoot forth; or by the dark green of the fig trees; and all this divided by the bluish green of the plants by the fences. Some fishing boats were crossing along the mouth of the river; at the side of the monastery was seen a chapel on a hill; in front rose a large cross in the form of a pyramid of whitewashed rubblework; behind was an enclosure covered with crosses painted black. This was the cemetery. . . .

The grandeur of nature, overpowering and awesome, seems eternal while the works of man appear small and some buildings are in ruins—a Romantic concept, standing out sharply in this passage. The variations on the color green add depth and observation to the surroundings of Villamar; and the changing yet reliable seasons contribute the sentiment of hope and faith. Finally, the religious symbol of the cemetery reminds all, subtly and surely, that man, like the buildings and the seasons, must vanish; but the image, also a Romantic favorite, is skillfully placed at the end without a direct moralizing call to traditional religion.

Thus, when Fernán Caballero's ideology does not get in the way of her poetic observations and realistic descriptions, or at least, when her strongly-held views are kept in check by her artistry, the individual passages increase the aesthetic values of *The Sea Gull*. And the lesson or the author's philosophy need not be omitted, as they are not in the above illustration; but the tone should not be proselytizing, and the praise of her faith needs no aura of triumphancy, which Croce grasped as a defect of Fernán Caballero, to be effective [see excerpt above, 1923]. (pp. 60-2)

The contrast is clear between the local color sketches and stories of the chapters in Villamar, which still retain interest as well as historical value, and the polished, frivolous, and often hypocritical chatter of the drawing rooms. The action is halted, the motivation is lacking for audience reaction, no artistic revelations come forth; and, in short, these lengthy scenes represent the weakest element in the construction of *The Sea Gull*. The unimportance of high society, which may have been one of Fernán Caballero's aims, is lost in an unsuccessful literary treatment, remedied easily by the simple omission of so many pages of tedious conversations.

The redeeming feature, however, of the dialogues in the salons during the second part—and the valuable contribution for an understanding of *The Sea Gull* as a novel, the author's theories, and the novelistic art—is the debate about the Spanish novel. The discussions should, of course, reflect the viewpoints outlined in the prologue, and they do confirm and amplify that brief theory of the Realistic novel. . . . (pp. 66-7)

Rafael, perhaps the liveliest and most sympathetic guest at the various gatherings in the second part, proposes that all contribute to the composition of a novel; and the argument erupts immediately and with animated disagreement about the question: What is a novel? If the novel is written in French, published serially, and with seductions and adulteries, then it will be an imitation of the prevailing currents and nothing original. "It's not a good idea to make women interesting because of their faults," and "nothing is less interesting in the eyes of sensible people than to see a light-headed girl letting herself be seduced, or a lewd woman cheating on her husband," declares the Countess of Algar's mother, the Marchioness. . . . Ironically, of course, the three characteristics of the novel at that time, noted above, refer to *The Sea Gull*.

Suicide is banished from the novel, "frightful suicide, unknown here until now, and which has succeeded in weakening if not in destroying the Faith," . . . a dictum which Fernán Caballero obeyed in all her stories, but certainly a tragic statement in view of [her third husband's] later suicide. The pithy definition of Fernán Caballero's *novela de costumbres* is then stated, appropriately by the Countess of Algar: "We are not to paint the Spanish people as foreigners; we shall portray ourselves as we are." . . . Stein prophetically asks: "But with the restrictions imposed by the Marchioness, what kind of romantic outcome can a novel have which is generally based on an unfortunate passion?" . . . The clue to the final chapter of *The Sea Gull*, after the letter explaining Stein's romantic

fate, is then given as "Time makes an end to all, no matter what the novelists say who dream instead of observing; besides, can't there be any other theme but an unfortunate passion?" . . . (pp. 67-8)

The new novel should have no ostentation in the form of foreign words and phrases, but, instead, the language should be rooted firmly in the dictionary—accepted usage of the Spanish language, as defined by the Royal Spanish Academy. Euphuisms are to be avoided; "God" is preferable to the high-sounding expressions of the Enlightenment, these in order to avoid the question of a direct, firm faith. Fernán Caballero's worthwhile defense of simplicity of language is shrewdly blended with her advocacy of traditional, orthodox religious values. This imaginary exercise in the composition of a novel deals with the issue of the subjects, and the Countess suggests that "let us put aside any weaknesses, tears, crimes, and exaggerated expressions," and "let us make something good, elegant and cheerful." However, Rafael objects that virtue, or pure goodness, throughout a novel would result in an insipid, flat story; and, in short, that the warp and woof of the novel is the deviation from the path of noble and normal behavior.

How should this new novel be classified as to genre? Stein, reflecting his German background (as Rafael in opposition suggests), proposes "a fantastic novel," which is rejected on the complaint that "a Spanish fantastic novel would be an unbearable affectation." . . . This Gothic novel is then balanced by Stein with the other type of Romantic novel, the heroic, sad, or sentimental story; but Rafael finally ends any attempt to impose a current, Romantic mode: "There is no type which is less suited to the Spanish temper than the weeping type." . . . A division of the novelistic art is proposed as "the historical novel, which we shall leave to learned writers, and the novel of customs, which is exactly the right one for mediocre writers like us"; . . . and the Countess, accepting immediately this promising solution, is rewarded by Rafael with this advocacy of the new novel, the *novela de costumbres*:

> It is the very best novel . . . useful and agreeable. Each nation should write its own. Written with accuracy and with a true spirit of observation, they would help a great deal in the study of humanity, history, moral practice, and for the knowledge of times and places. If I were the queen, I would order a novel of customs to be written in every province, without omitting anything in references and analyses. . . .
>
> (pp. 68-9)

In short, Fernán Caballero, by 1845, during the writing of *The Sea Gull*, had evolved a theory of the modern novel and the role of the novelist, not necessarily intrusive, but certainly faithful to feelings and observations. Her terminology may be awkward, such as the classifications of the historical novel and the novel of customs; but her general understanding of the new novel, where, in the prologue to *The Sea Gull*, the same unsure manner of defining the two strands of the nineteenth-century novel is also apparent, is clear and sound: the Romantic novel is unsatisfactory in a rapidly changing age and is unsuited for a faithful portrait of Spain (and any other country in this period), and a new novel, rooted in observation and local color sketches, is the answer for the revival of the novelistic genre. (pp. 70-1)

No critic, sympathetic or unfavorable to Fernán Caballero's effort in *The Sea Gull* (and other works), denies that the personal, intrusive ideas and beliefs of the author lack an objective, positive quality in the novel when these views become a repeated, dogmatic aspect of this artistic creation. Of course, every literary work reflects the writer's philosophy, and a novelist is certainly within his domain to insert these ideological orientations—if the book in question is not converted into a proselytizing tract. There seems critically no disagreement that Fernán Caballero's defect in *The Sea Gull* is her undue emphasis upon her faith in the traditional values of Spain.

The Church is the mainstay, for Fernán Caballero, of a virtuous, individual morality and the source of charitable, chivalric ideals; and the physical features of Catholic power in Villamar and Sevilla add beauty, inspiration, and a sense of history to the landscape and for the benefit of the people. The neglect of the ecclesiastical properties provides a springboard for an attack on the Enlightenment and Liberalism as the causes for this decline of the Church. Fernán Caballero's simplistic interpretation of history revolves around the failure to remain in place: every motion forward since 1700 (when the Bourbons from France ascended the Spanish throne and brought with them foreign models) has really been a step backward. In the last chapter of *The Sea Gull*, "the novelties of the time" brought the use of contemporary, political names for roads, etc., instead of saints' names as in the past; and Mystical Rose suspiciously comments upon the Pope's mildly liberal reforms. In 1848, Pius IX had of course acquired the reputation since his election two years previously of a pontiff of the nineteenth century, unlike his immediate predecessors in Rome. Symbolically perhaps, Brother Gabriel's death, reported in the last paragraph of *The Sea Gull*, reads like the continuing decline of Catholicism, a decline accelerated by the seizure of church lands in the 1830's which Fernán Caballero—and her characters, Stein, Aunt María, and others—strongly criticized in the novel's first part. These fears, pessimism, and sadness coincide with the appearance of the Catholic traditionalists, Jaime Balmes and Juan Donoso Cortés, who in their writings espoused similar attitudes.

Santaló's death provides Fernán Caballero with the occasion for her most vehement defense of Catholicism. The scene, Romantic, melodramatic, and compellingly effective as a climactic moment of the plot, is marred by the scar of Catholic triumphalism. "Nothing could give splendor and life to this moral truth, as the way we have just described it," insists Fernán Caballero, "that in the midst of the tumult and tempests of evil passions, the voice of holy religion allows itself to be heard at intervals, grave and powerful, soft and firm even to those very ones who forget and deny it." . . . Indeed, Fernán Caballero, in these sincere, fervent, but artistically weak sermons, resembles a preacher more than a convincing novelist: "Catholics maintain for death all the solemn respect that God has given it by His adoption of it as a sacrifice in expiation. . . . All was repose and peace inside because God despoils death of its horrors and anxieties when the soul is raised to heaven with the cry for mercy, being surrounded by fervent hearts on earth repeating: mercy, mercy!" . . . (pp. 78-80)

The aristocracy and, concomitantly, the monarchy (although this institution is seldom mentioned in *The Sea Gull*), serve as the model and guide of good manners, moral leadership, and maintenance of political stability in Fernán Caballero's Spain; and the Duke of Almansa, from his introduction in the first chapter always behaves as an exemplary nobleman, despite his vague infatuation for Marisalada, which he humbly confesses to the duchess, an equivalent portrait of the noblewoman. All

the participants at the social gatherings in Sevilla and Madrid are, as members of the ruling class, directed by patriotic, national sentiments toward Spain—a spiritual pride in the homeland, closely associated with aristocratic and humble characters alike. There are differences of opinion about love of country and the defense of Spanish ways of life, but Fernán Caballero ardently espouses the cause of Spain. She is also optimistic about the values of the country, and the advantages far outweigh any vices, such as the bullfight.

Fernán Caballero is, then, essentially conservative, conformist, and traditionalist; and she dreads, for example, the word "progress" as a code term for the worst of possible worlds, a "progress" which is advancing for the erosion of the above-mentioned institutions, already in sad disarray. The world of Fernán Caballero may be summarized by the dates of *The Sea Gull*: in 1848, when the novel ends, the internal changes, the European revolutions, and even papal liberalism, have converted Villamar (and Spain) into a tragic caricature of the village of 1838, when Stein arrived in the second chapter, and where the old life is being swept away by the outside whirlwinds of change. If Fernán Caballero could have stopped at the present, at 1838, she would not have been overjoyed at this theoretical compromise because, in short, even the many local color sketches, extensively and lovingly described in the book's first part, would not have signified the realization of her ideology. For the impossible vision of Fernán Caballero, for her "exact, true, and genuine idea of Spain," as she declares in *The Sea Gull*'s prologue, ten years earlier—1828—characterized the ideal period when Spanish traditions and institutions held unchallenged sway over the national life and governance.

The observations, descriptions, and folklore of Andalucía—Fernán Caballero's art at its best in *The Sea Gull*—and the scenes, also, in Sevilla and Madrid emerge, not as the literary rendition of foreign influences and readings (although these aspects are not completely discounted), but as the author's interests and experiences as the Marquesa de Arco-Hermoso in the Andalusian village of Dos Hermanas, other picturesque vicinities, and the two cities mentioned above. Fernán Caballero recalled her own days, the happiest of her life, as she once admitted, and referred in *The Sea Gull* to this better world (a decade before the novel's beginning) when the future for her seemed destined to be a continuation of the present. This vision, of course, corresponded only in part to the historical, political realities of the reign of Fernando VII; but the personal promise around this year, 1828, when she met Washington Irving and was occupied in "compiling and copying" (as she defined the *novela de costumbres*) coincided with a felicitous if illusory ideology about Spain and Spanish life. Her backward rather than forward view, nevertheless, won audiences at that time and literary immortality, with autobiographical, impressionistic strands woven skillfully in a *costumbrista*, realistic, and photographic embroidery. (pp. 80-1)

Fernán Caballero, in "a word to the reader" to introduce [*The Family of Alvareda*,] her "original novel of popular customs," explains that:

> The plot of this novel, which we have announced as destined exclusively to paint the people, is a real fact, and the narration, faithful in the main, to the point of having kept the same expressions used by those who figure in it, without doing any more than omitting occasionally some crudeness. Also, the action has been transferred to a period prior to the one in

which it took place, and something has been added at the beginning and at the end.

We are not unaware that, with the elements lent by the case, one might have been able to derive more literary profit, treating it with the classical emphasis, the rich romantic coloring, or the romanesque aesthetics.

But as we do not aspire to cause an effect but to paint things of the people such as they are, we have not wished to separate ourselves in one iota from naturalness and from truth. The language, except for aspirating the h's and eliminating the d's, is that of the Andalusian country people, just as are here their ideas, sentiments, and customs.

Many years of a study, made with constancy and with love, permit us to assure everyone who might argue the contrary that he is not as versed in the details as we are. . . .

(pp. 82-3)

Fernán Caballero, then, at another earlier date in the nascent development of a Realistic novel, knows precisely what she wants to achieve: a truthful story, based securely on real facts in most instances and certainly in the essential parts, and a background of Andalusian scenery, characters, psychology, and speech, resulting from the author's observations. Again, her terminology is uncertain about the exact direction of this new novel—a new novel because the prior patterns of the eighteenth-century genre will be discarded, and the current vogues of Romantic and Gothic novels (a clear distinction exists for Fernán Caballero between these two phases of Romanticism) are too permeated with imagination and fantasy for the mid-nineteenth century. The surprising conclusion again is that Fernán Caballero with this short novel, well planned and well executed—and if the ideas in her few words to the readers correspond to the approximate date of composition of *The Family of Alvareda* . . .—belongs chronologically with more notable relatives in the English and French literary families of Realism. (p. 83)

The three parts of *The Family of Alvareda* correspond in several ways to the theory of the *comedia* of the Golden Age or, at least, as Lope de Vega attempted to define the dramatic genre in *Arte nuevo de hacer comedias (New Art of Writing Plays)* in 1609. Fernán Caballero, persistently endeavoring to escape the classification of novels for her books, certainly found in *The Family of Alvareda* a successful formula, despite the lack of any sure evidence that she definitely imitated the classical theater. The first two parts of the novel offer the widest appeal, while the third part shows Fernán Caballero too concerned with the moral and didactic lessons to be acquired from Perico's—and Rita's—tragedy. In the first part, all the main characters are introduced, the conflicts are established, the action is rapid, and the section ends on an exciting, unexpected turn, with the arrival of the French grenadier, his murder, and Ventura's flight. There are few digressive elements, a minimum of description, and the local color sketches, stories, and legends, short and narrative in conception and execution. (pp. 91-2)

The chapters of this first part are short, and each chapter is almost a contained unit with a scene, usually of conflict or confrontation. For example, the first chapter depicts Ventura and Perico, friends and intended in-laws, but with very distinct personalities; the second chapter introduces the women in the story with some hints of Rita's antipathetic nature; the third chapter presents the argument between Perico and his mother about the former's marriage to Rita; the fourth chapter offers a lesson in country wit and wisdom in the marriage contract terms, argued by Ana and Pedro; the fifth chapter is another light, semihumorous depiction of Ana and Pedro on a trip to Alcalá; and the seventh chapter, ending the first part, provides a scene of violence with the historical introduction of the French invasion. (pp. 92-3)

The second part follows equally a dramatic curve of rising action, conflicts erupting initially as psychological and finally as physical; and the section terminates with not only murder, but the flight of a main character. Indeed, the parallels between the first two parts of the novel reveal a well-structured organization by the author; she has effectively repeated the same patterns of an increasingly rising confrontation among her characters. The second part is better motivated and psychologically more realistic—and contemporary—than the first part. In the first part, Fernán Caballero is essentially looking backward to the patriotic, national pride in the War of Independence, certainly a favorite among Spanish authors and a legitimate source of literary endeavors, but the French grenadier's sudden appearance is somewhat of a *deus ex machina* despite Ventura's and Perico's earlier discussion in the first chapter about joining the army to fight the invaders in 1810. Both parts, building up then to high points of violence, bloodshed, murder, and flight, differ markedly, however: the Romantic aura, especially in the first chapter of the second part, supplies a Gothic setting with a raging storm as the opening physical feature, soon to be reflected in the tempestuous, personal relations of the families in Dos Hermanas. The *cuadros de costumbres* are almost absent in the middle division, but the use of dances and songs, woven ably into the plot progression, renders local color and reflects Andalusian folklore—those two additions of Fernán Caballero proudly present in her novels and stories. The first chapter, as in the introductory episode of the first part, serves as the presentation of all the characters once again united with Ventura's Romantic return; and, ironically, all seems placid and prosperous for the future. But in the second chapter, Ventura's adventures as a soldier have stirred Rita's imagination, and her interest in him slowly emerges. This mood of *tempo lento* vanishes in the third chapter when the first conflict takes place in the discovery of Ventura and Rita alone in the stable, and the die is cast for trouble. This trouble develops in the bitter dialogue between Ana and Rita about the latter's infidelity; and Fernán Caballero, briefly and forcefully, achieves a masterly use of dialogue in the vocal clashes. The three following chapters continue the mounting sense of disaster with Perico's ire aroused by Rita's absence and affair; with the argument between the two men, balanced skillfully by the succinct analyses of their individual motives, reactions, thoughts, and behavior; with Ventura's abandonment of emotion for reason and, unfortunately, Perico's change from a reasonable man to a person of irrational vengeance—a convincing demonstration of characterization and literary technique. Once more, *The Family of Alvareda* concludes in a manner very reminiscent of the *comedia* by the dramatic arrival of Ventura's body in the street of Dos Hermanas, the residents gathering in shocked witness of the tragedy, the traumatic effects upon the women in the story, and Pedro's melodramatic outburst against Rita at the moment, theatrically staged, of his uncovering of his son's blood-stained corpse—all accomplished with an economy of words, a general absence of description, and the emphasis upon the events speaking for themselves.

There is a general critical consensus that the third part of *The Family of Alvareda* is the weakest, artistically and thematically, of the three actions because Fernán Caballero succumbs to her cardinal sin as a writer by allowing ideology to supersede aesthetics. Also, the Romantic and Gothic traits, which she opposed in a novel and by which frequently classified the whole genre, predominate in the last part. Almost the entire argument revolves around Perico's fate as an outcast from society—a Romantic hero in many ways—and the first chapter, conveniently staged during another of Fernán Caballero's favorite storms, also introduces a darling of Romanticism, the good, noble bandit. Based apparently on an historical figure, Diego Corrientes, a "Robin Hood" of Spain like the Roque Guinart whom Don Quijote and Sancho meet on their journey to Barcelona, the Diego of Fernán Caballero's creation proves faithful to her stress upon realism and observation, as she interpreted these aspects, with the Romantic characterization an influence from the past and a help for her theses. The Romantic contrast appears in the figure of "El Presidiario," who serves as the antithesis of Diego. For example, Diego saves and protects Perico, while "El Presidiario" is openly opposed to the newcomer's entry into the ranks of the gang; and, Judas-like (if the Romantic analogy secularizing the New Testament is pursued), "El Presidiario" betrays Diego who accepts heroically and stoically his fate. If the third part of the novel seems to veer sharply in the direction of the Romantic drama, nevertheless the analogies with the *comedia* still invite a valid comparison because, as critics have recognized consistently, the resemblances between the Spanish theaters of Romanticism and the Golden Age are many and important. The abortive robbery of the church in the seventh chapter is highly melodramatic, and the heightening of emotion and fear by natural phenomena, such as the moonbeam suddenly appearing through a window and falling at the feet of a statue dedicated to the Virgin Mary, foreshadows happenings in several *leyendas* (legends) of Bécquer, a fellow Sevillian of Fernán Caballero, and whom she mentions offhandedly elsewhere in her works.

Structurally, also, this third part continues the winning formula of the two preceding parts by constructing slowly and evenly an approaching confrontation, necessarily violent and disastrous, this time by the fact that criminals are involved in robberies and ambushes, between the law and the gang, culminating in Perico's sentence of death. The pace of the rapidly changing scenes is sustained easily by the variety of Perico's adventures, the danger concomitant in each chapter, and characters themselves who reflect the atmosphere of desperate rogues in unsavory enterprises. Likewise, although Perico's fate is sealed by Fernán Caballero's emphasis upon his solitary, depressed condition and state of mind, the exact measures by which her tragic character will be punished follow logically and in an artistically mature form from each prior chapter. The outcome of the individual scene is uncertain, with the possibility in all instances that Diego's band may be successful or that the authorities may apprehend the outlaws. However, each successive step in Perico's decline and fall is never arrested by the chance of salvation. Still, his redemption is at hand at the moment he opposes the church desecration, when first proposed by the Celestina-like gypsy, is confirmed by his role in preventing the robbery by the shouts, and is finally triumphant by confession and absolution before execution. Of course, the heavy veneer of moralistic, religious, and theological redemption by Fernán Caballero predominates throughout the vignettes, but the psychological study of Perico is still well motivated, persuasive, and realistic. The epilogue, a final sermon on the tragedy of the Alvareda family, returns to a mode of realism, familiar in the first two parts; and Melampo (the word is theatrical in origin and symbolic in the novel, referring to a prompter's candle or light in the theater) contributes by his death a melodramatic, sentimental, and instructive note to this novel.

If the structure of *The Family of Alvareda* resembles significantly and skillfully a theatrical piece, and especially the *comedia* with Romantic devices, the background is nonetheless composed of the threefold interest of Fernán Caballero in observation, realism, and *costumbrismo*. The novel certainly offers a major advance in the Realistic movement with not only photographic reproduction—the novelist's main claim in her view—but another contribution in nineteenth-century Realism appears in characterization, the psychological distinctions of individuals, and the rudimentary comprehension glimpsed at times of the vagaries of human nature and actions.

Although the quantity of local color sketches as brief insertions in *The Family of Alvareda* is small (particularly with reference to *The Sea Gull*, as indicated previously), the novel is certainly a *costumbrista* work, explained concisely by Fernán Caballero in "a word to the reader." The main example, the history and legend about Dos Hermanas, is matched by the description of the village's background at the novel's beginning and Fernán Caballero, once again contrasting Romantic and Realistic concepts, defends her theory on the first page: "In order to make this village, which has the reputation of being very ugly, a picturesque and showy place, it would be necessary to have an imagination which might create, and the person who describes it here only paints." ... The setting is economically detailed, and Fernán Caballero loses no time in introducing her characters and her story so that the *costumbrista* values of *The Family of Alvareda* derive from the real-life plot and the Andalusian characters. In short, the author has not granted herself the pleasure, as will her regionalist successors, such as Pereda, of composing very long, poetically-phrased geographical descriptions. Her artistry in these aspects brings the book to the high level of the novelistic Realism of Galdós and Valera. (pp. 93-7)

Critical impartiality and justice call attention to adverse points of *The Family of Alvareda,* points which commentators have in fact regretted consistently for having lowered the reputation and importance of the work. But the merits of Fernán Caballero's Realism certainly stand out in this novel in two modern, major ways: the *costumbrismo* and the characterization. Some instances of the local color sketches have been indicated already, and these instances perhaps overshadow the less conspicuous qualities of the Andalusian background. (p. 100)

Fernán Caballero's characterization in *The Family of Alvareda,* while more limited to one class of people than to the broader areas of society in *The Sea Gull,* nevertheless presents some similarities with personages of the later novel. Rita and Marisalada, in particular, are molded from the same stamp; and Fernán Caballero in *The Family of Alvareda* first evolved the type of woman who will appear in a pattern in many works, reaching an apogee in *La farisea (The Woman of the Pharisees),* one of her last and most popular books. (p. 102)

Of course, most of the characters, as in *The Sea Gull,* represent Andalusian types rather than individual actors in the story. Fernán Caballero's women are depicted in general more sympathetically and praiseworthily than the men, and she is especially devoted to the concept of the mother, loyal, suffering, humble, and wise. As a grandmother, the female character holds together the family by serving as a link between the children, to whom she relates the folklore and tradition of Andalucía, and the mother, sometimes unconcerned about preservation of the past. Ana and María in *The Family of Alvareda* bear close resemblances, similar to the portrait of Aunt María in *The Sea Gull*. These examples have their origin in Fernán Caballero's idealization of life: the older generation symbolizes the past, and the conservative, traditional viewpoints stress that a younger generation looks to the elders for advice and follows closely, with few if any missteps (and any changes would be usually erroneous for the author) from the guidelines already established. Here seems the ideological concept for another pattern in Fernán Caballero's work; and again, ideology has superimposed itself upon the literary creation. Nonetheless, the types provide warm-hearted appeal and readily acceptable realism; and they are indeed representative of not only Andalusian country folk but of universal qualities. In this manner, by avoiding the extremes of Romantic, sentimental characters (such as Stein in *The Sea Gull*), Fernán Caballero has with success grafted local color portrayals to the body of her story.

In drawing her masculine characters, Fernán Caballero strove to render in Pedro a personage equivalent to the women, Ana and María. The two antagonists, Ventura and Perico, show another side to this coin of the Andalusian peasant: they are honorable, loyal, and courageous, of course; but they are quick-tempered, emotional, and compelled to live up to a code of honor, as in the *comedia*. Ironically, this defense of honor is exactly the precipitating cause of the tragedy; and the pride of both former friends also leads irrevocably to their mutual downfall and death. There are indeed in *The Family of Alvareda* no real villains (with the exception of the minor participant, "El Presidiario"), and Rita's contrition and suffering redeem her sufficiently from that classification as well as the previous forgiveness of the families after the preaching mission has aroused in them the spirit of charity. Diego, of course, is truly noble and honorable, especially at the time of his capture. In fact, Fernán Caballero, in the characterization of this earlier and first novel, has attained an equivalent level of literary psychology in her personages that she reached in *The Sea Gull*, about seventeen years later. Also, her characters are more in accord with regional, local color individuals; and she has interestingly avoided the pitfalls of Romanticism—against which she wrote so emphatically—in all the principal actors, although traces of the Romantic techniques exist in other aspects of the book, particularly the third part. Her success at such a date, around 1828, is remarkable. . . . (pp. 103-04)

*Clemencia,* of course, must be read critically . . . as a running autobiography on Fernán Caballero's life, an interpretation which apparently eluded her contemporaries and still contains room for further clarification. The novel, then, is more than one additional contribution to Fernán Caballero's Realism: *Clemencia* stands out as an example of the confessional literature, popularized by the Romantics in all countries, and as a frank, honest, psychological study of an individual woman. *Clemencia,* before any currents in the novel of introspective, unique, and fascinating characterizations, provides glimpses into the dilemmas posed to a woman by the rigidities (and mounting challenges) of the nineteenth-century Spanish social system. (p. 113)

[The whole setting of *Clemencia* is] very evidently Romantic, although of course the familiar drawing rooms (as in *The Sea Gull*) supply realistic, *costumbrista* surroundings, drawn again from Fernán Caballero's observations and memories as the Marquesa de Arco-Hermoso. And again, to solve the developing plot complications, so Romantic and moralistic, Fernán Caballero turns toward a realistic solution, in keeping with her ideological orientations, however. Clemencia's rejection of Percy is more profoundly the refusal to accept the nineteenth-century currents of positivism, irreverence, cynicism, and amorality (according to Fernán Caballero). Clemencia and Percy symbolize two worlds: she is the representative of the past, holding to the ideals and virtues disappearing quickly and sadly; he is the modern man—and the symbol of the victorious future, unfortunately for the author—who will also destroy all vestiges of the idealized, sentimentalized traditions. Nevertheless, in this novel Fernán Caballero does not admit defeat, ending her story with an exemplary thesis of the superiority of the past. Clemencia returns to the country estate, where she spent so many happy fruitful years (eight to be exact) in the second part; and she marries Pablo, whom she recognizes as the guardian of moral, religious, and traditional qualities, admitting to herself humbly that she was led by emotional factors rather than by logical analysis to reject him previously as a model husband. Together, they will care for the *mayorazgo* (preserving thereby the past), become the center of a small, influential society by dint of their good example as a happy, married couple; and, in short, become an island of virtue and tradition, lashed by the stormy seas of outside events, however, as Clemencia and Pablo are aware from visitors' remarks about the attacks of foreigners—and Spaniards—on their way of life. Of course, this conclusion is idealistic and sentimental; but Fernán Caballero has attempted to shift from a Romantic to a Realistic attitude in her heroine, from passion to love, from foreign lover to native husband, from the city to the country, and from the new to the old. These traits, while not limited to the novel of Realism, are found in some degree in later works of her successors, such as Pereda, Alarcón, and Palacio Valdés, that is to say, in the regional, local color novel. But Clemencia's choice between Percy and Pablo is certainly motivated logically and successfully, and perhaps the evident sources in her own life enabled Fernán Caballero to depict with this verisimilitude an advanced psychological portrait of a woman, trapped by very human and normal instincts.

The novel, nevertheless, lacks in the admittedly realistic and natural dialogue a contemporary interest for the present reader, which may be a compensatory explanation for the popularity of Fernán Caballero's novel in her own generation. For example, the discussions in the drawing rooms only once bring up one of the important topics of *The Sea Gull,* the modern novel. Clemencia, on this single occasion, insists that a moral aim or object is essential in the novel, more so in the spirit than in the words, "as the English generally practice it." Style, in fact, whether it be the individual expression of the writer or the correct usage of the language, may indeed be no more than a minor aspect of the novel; and Clemencia even states that an erudite, flowery vocabulary, without a corresponding naturalness and sincerity, detracts from the interest and acceptance of audiences. Although much, perhaps most, of *Clemencia* is authentic in terms of autobiography (as continuing criticism has confirmed), the literary biography still contains problems and is a mine for future raw materials about Fernán Caballero. (pp. 117-18)

*Lawrence H. Klibbe, in his* Fernán Caballero, *Twayne Publishers, Inc., 1973, 182 p.*

## LUCÍA FOX-LOCKERT (essay date 1979)

[*Fox-Lockert discusses Caballero's use of the three protagonists in* Clemencia *to portray her version of the ideal Spanish woman. Discerning symbolic significance in the names of the three characters, the critic asserts that each of the women represents a different path in life, with Clemencia standing for the "golden mean."*]

All of the names of the protagonists [in *Clemencia*] are symbolic. Constancia (Constance), in her love for Bruno as well as in her love for God, manifests a temperamental obstinacy which causes her to act in extremes. In the fulfillment of her family duties there is a certain masochism; she wants to be punished, she wants to pay for the sense of guilt she still has for hating her mother: "Blinded by love and pride, I did not love the mother who gave me life."... She goes from one type of renunciation (marriage with Bruno) to another type of renunciation (life). Her temperament causes her to act as if her reality was the only one and she ignores all that goes on around her. Alegría (Joy) is the extreme example of the search for egotistical pleasure. In comparison with Constancia she is frivolous, excitable and practical. It does not bother her to lie to her mother about her husband's urgent call to Madrid nor does she mind scandalizing society. Alegría is detested by the author because she represents the type of woman who breaks the traditional molds for the behavior of the good Spanish woman. Clemencia is the golden mean. Her name (Mercy) indicates a virtue: the moderation of justice. But more than the representation of a virtue, she becomes for the author the epitome of the Spanish Ideal.

Clemencia, in her several stages, represents the various alternatives for the women of this period. In her first years, she manifests a sense of obedience and submission. When her mother dies at her birth, her father sends her to a convent to be educated by nuns. When she leaves the convent, the contrast is great. The Marquesa Cortegana, whose name is appropriate (*corte* means "court" and *gana* means "win") for a woman who wins in all she does, provides a mundane and superficial atmosphere consisting of letters, gossip, and friends who, in order not to be bored, get together every night with other young people in order to flirt. The widow of Matamoros is loyal to her name (killer of Moors) as a dynamic, manipulative woman who never fails to take advantage of every opportunity to impose her will on the Marquesa. The two cousins who constantly make fun of Clemencia are, in a certain aspect, trials for her humility and her perseverance in her nunnish beliefs. Her first marriage is the greatest test of her obedience. But what else could a girl in her position do? She had no place to go if she disobeyed her aunt and besides, without a dowry, how could she refuse the proposal of a rich young man from a distinguished family? Clemencia is the typical girl who has only one path in life and who follows it. In her second period she is a widow living with her in-laws. Now her greatest virtue is conformity. She takes easily to the house's system and to the teachings of the priest, which are very similar to those of the convent. With one exception, she can there use her own judgment because she has already had some experience with human wretchedness. The moment of her true test, unencumbered by

family or social pressures, comes in her third period, when she has her own house, friends and lands. There she may choose her own spouse.

There are two different currents of influence at work in Spain at this time. One comes from France, for social upheaval and political chaos followed the Revolution. The other comes from England, a current much more open, free, flexible, thoughtful and protestant—both in terms of sexuality and of morals. Clemencia must use all of her religious, moral and spiritual preparation to counteract the constant attacks of Sir George. In her change from innocence to maturity she has to re-evaluate all that she has learned before of love, marriage, sexuality, kindness and mercy. The last test, corresponding to her name, comes with Sir George and the poor. Sir George is incapable of feeling compassion even though he is capable of giving money to charity. What he needs, in Clemencia's opinion, is a human feeling for Christian charity. She also has to re-examine the true values she looks for in matrimony. Her two cousins give two opposite views: a religious life or a profane life. She has confidence that, with a solid marriage, adherence to the teachings of the Church, and living near to the land, a married woman with children is the hope of Spain. But how can she accomplish this goal with men for whom love is an appearance and who have no concern for her most vital and profound desires? Her only recourse is the memory of those idyllic moments spent with Pablo when the priest taught them the fundamental doctrines of the church. She sincerely believes that Pablo will make her happy. The author is very much convinced that this is the correct solution, and since she has molded Clemencia somewhat according to her own biography, this is also probably what Cecilia Bohl de Faber needed in order to be happy. (pp. 45-7)

Clemencia is a completely traditional woman who has two qualities that are very much a part of today's world: she needs to be loved for herself and not as a doll, as something pleasing to the eye or as an amusing clown; and she wants to base her selection of a husband on thought and not on an emotional impulse. She comes to a knowledge of her own worth and of her mission in life. After having lived in the country and in the city, she can choose the country based on her own experience. After having a brilliant but cold man like Sir George and a mediocre but devoted man like Pablo, she chooses the latter. After having been loved only for her body by her first husband, she chooses from among those men who surround her the man who best seems to recognize her virtues.

Alegría is the anti-heroine of the novel and thus adds a different dimension to it. She rejects motherhood as the principal reason for marriage and she wants her freedom at any cost. She warns Clemencia not to remarry, since as a wife she will not be able to do the things she wishes. Clearly, Alegría is speaking of her own condition following her husband's abandonment. I am also sure that her friends rejected her and made her life miserable. Alegría is an admirable character for the courage she shows in throwing society's hypocrisy back in its face, especially with regards to men: her husband and her lover are both cowards who cannot face up to their obligations, both men rally around the system of honor and leave her to fend for herself. Perhaps Alegría is a premature version of the modern woman. Her warning to Clemencia is that all she may expect is many children and many years with the same man, who keeps a mistress somewhere. It is to be hoped that her fears may never come to pass, but they nevertheless serve as a warning to the young of the flaws of married life. (p. 48)

> *Lucía Fox-Lockert, "Fernán Caballero (Cecilia Bohl de Faber): 'Clemencia' (1852)," in her* Women Novelists in Spain and Spanish America, *The Scarecrow Press, Inc., 1979, pp. 36-48.*

---

## ADDITIONAL BIBLIOGRAPHY

Hespelt, E. Herman. "The Porto Rican Episode in the Life of Fernán Caballero." *Revista de estudios hispanicos* I, No. 2 (1928): 162-67.
> A brief biographical study of Caballero's life in Puerto Rico with her first husband.

Williams, Stanley T. "Washington Irving and Fernan Caballero." *The Journal of English and Germanic Philology* XXIX, No. 3 (July 1930): 352-66.*
> Explores the mutually influential friendship between Caballero and Washington Irving, including the part the latter may have played in encouraging Caballero to publish her works.

# John Wilson Croker

## 1780-1857

Irish essayist, editor, historian, and poet.

Croker was an influential Tory politician and a principal contributor to the conservative journal the *Quarterly Review*. Nicknamed the "slashing critic" for his vitriolic literary reviews, he was both admired and berated by his contemporaries. Croker's writings are now considered dated, yet they continue to attract the attention of some scholars and students of nineteenth-century literary history.

Croker was born and raised in Galway, Ireland. After graduating from Trinity College, Dublin, he studied for the bar at Lincoln's Inn, London, and began to practice law. However, Croker was equally interested in literature, and in 1804 he anonymously published his first work, a verse satire entitled *Familiar Epistles to Frederick E. Jones, Esq., on the Present State of the Irish Stage* that quickly became a popular success. Croker then composed a number of pamphlets on Irish affairs and several short poems, including his popular ballad, *The Battles of Talavera,* which depicted military campaigns in Spain led by Arthur Wellesley, the duke of Wellington. During this period, Croker also entered politics and rapidly established his reputation as a prominent Tory after his election to the British Parliament in 1807. In 1809, he was appointed secretary of the navy, a position he held for twenty-one years. Although Croker retired from politics in 1830, he continued to write throughout his life.

Croker contributed regularly to the *Quarterly Review,* a Tory periodical that had been founded to counter the Whig-influenced *Edinburgh Review.* Between 1809 and 1854, he published over two hundred articles on a variety of topics, including politics, history, and literature. His accusatory, biting style quickly brought him notoriety as a critic. He often allowed the author's political stance to color his response, focused on minor imperfections of a work, and, according to several critics, distorted the author's intent by interpreting words and phrases out of context. While some commentators praise Croker's knowledge of literature and critical acumen, others maintain that his political bias and vituperative commentary seriously undermine the quality and credibility of his work. A frequently cited example of his critical method is his essay "Keats's *Endymion,*" the harshness of which caused the English poet Percy Bysshe Shelley to accuse Croker of precipitating John Keats's death. Croker's criticism moved another of his contemporaries, the English statesman and novelist Benjamin Disraeli, to caricature him as the unjust and vindictive critic Rigby in his novel *Coningsby; or, The New Generation.*

In addition to his contributions to the *Quarterly Review,* Croker edited several biographies and collections of letters. The best known of these works, James Boswell's landmark biography, *The Life of Samuel Johnson, LL.D., Including a Journal of a Tour to the Hebrides, by James Boswell, Esq.,* elicited mixed reviews. Croker's principal detractor, the liberal statesman and essayist Thomas Babington Macaulay, labeled the work "ill compiled, ill arranged, ill expressed, and ill printed." Macaulay's scathing criticism is generally thought to reflect his opinion of Croker's politics rather than his editorial ability, for the

two passionately opposed each other in parliamentary matters. Despite reservations concerning Macaulay's political bias, several other nineteenth-century commentators agreed with his estimate of *The Life of Samuel Johnson.* Although the English statesman and critic Thomas Carlyle praised Croker's translations of Greek and Latin in *The Life of Samuel Johnson,* Carlyle also cited Croker's ignorance of Johnson's era and lack of insight into human nature as major flaws. Croker's supporters included John Gibson Lockhart, also a contributor to the *Quarterly Review,* and John Wilson, who wrote for the Tory periodical *Blackwood's Edinburgh Magazine.* Judging Macaulay's criticism politically motivated and inconsequential, they praised Croker's literary knowledge and editorial ability. Wilson lauded *The Life of Samuel Johnson* as "the best variorum edition since the revival of letters," and Lockhart stated that he considered it "the best *edition* of an English book that has appeared in our time." Though highly controversial in his time, Croker's edition of *The Life of Samuel Johnson* is largely overlooked today.

The posthumously published edition of Croker's letters and diaries, entitled *The Croker Papers,* contains journal entries about and correspondence with such prominent Tory leaders as Sir Robert Peel and the duke of Wellington. While some critics suggest that the work is valuable as a historical document, others contend that it offers no new insights into the era.

Like all of Croker's writings, *The Croker Papers* is topical and enjoyed only short-lived popularity. Although his works are considered dated and are seldom studied today, Croker is nevertheless recognized as an important contributor to nineteenth-century periodical literature.

## PRINCIPAL WORKS

*Familiar Epistles to Frederick E. Jones, Esq., on the
    Present State of the Irish Stage* (epistles) 1804
*The Battles of Talavera* (poetry) 1809
"Keats's *Endymion*" (essay) 1818; published in journal
    *Quarterly Review*
*The Life of Samuel Johnson, LL.D., Including a Journal of
    a Tour to the Hebrides, by James Boswell, Esq.* [editor]
    (biography and journal) 1831
*The Croker Papers*. 3 vols. (letters and diaries) 1884

---

**JOHN WILSON CROKER** (essay date 1804)

[*This excerpt was drawn from the preface to Croker's 1804 publication* Familiar Epistles to Frederick E. Jones, Esq., on the Present State of the Irish Stage.]

[The letters that comprise **Familiar Epistles to Frederick Jones, Esq., on the Present State of the Irish Stage**] are the hasty effusions of my holy-day leisure, and originally aspired to no higher rank in the literary world, than a place in the public papers; but after some trials, I found, that the Dublin Editors and Mr. Jones, had sworn an inviolable friendship, and that no essay in which his name was mentioned, would be inserted "sans son aveu" [without his authorization].

I really have no very exalted opinion of the merit of my verses, . . . yet I am vain enough to hope, that they may be worth a shilling or two, (were it only to laugh at) and therefore I present them to those, who have a shilling to throw away, in the only shape in which it is, in Ireland, possible to publish them.

To my *readers* . . . I can only promise, that tho' they may not be much amused by my rhymes, they shall at least be exercised in some of the moral virtues; for besides the generosity of giving the poor bookseller a shilling for what is perhaps not worth a farthing, they will also have to applaud themselves for much patience and long suffering. . . . (pp. v-vi)

Let me now say a few words on the style and matter of these epistles:

Were that an *easy style* which is easily written, I should have no paternal fears of the success of this little book. We, sub-alterns of poetry, should soon become the field officers, and no one who had the insolence to take any pains with his appearance, would be permitted to show himself on the parade of a bookseller's counter, but unhappily this regulation has not yet taken place, and an ill judging world still throws in our teeth

> You write with ease to show your breeding,
> But *easy* writing's damn'ed *hard* reading.

On this topic then, gentle reader, I have only to refer you to my title page, in which you will find my gracious permission to throw down my book when ever it shall tire you, and take it up again, when you have nothing else to do. (pp. xiii-xv)

*John Wilson Croker, in a preface to ''Familiar Epistles to Frederick J—s [Jones], Esq., on the Present State of the Irish Stage,'' in his* Familiar Epistles to Frederick Jones, Esq., on the Present State of the Irish Stage; The Amazoniad; or, Figure and Fashion; Histrionic Epistles; The Battles of Talavera, *Garland Publishing, Inc., 1979, pp. v-xix.*

**LE BEAU MONDE AND MONTHLY REGISTER** (essay date 1809)

[*In the following excerpt from a negative review of* The Battles of Talavera, *the anonymous critic accuses Croker of plagiarizing the imagery of Sir Walter Scott.*]

The style which the celebrity of Walter Scott's poems has rendered so prevalent, is . . . introduced as the vehicle of celebration [in **The Battles of Talavera**]. We, who consider the *manner* as injurious to the vivid figures and poetical descriptions which generally constitute the *matter* of [Walter Scott's] *Lay of the Last Minstrel*, and of *Marmion*, cannot be highly gratified with a continuation of that *manner*, without the recommendation of new and impressive imagery. There is, in the poems of the modern Border Minstrel, a continued display of that genuine characteristic of true poetry, "*a rich simplicity.*" Few recent authors seem to be aware that *simplicity* can be *rich*. Of that *simplicity* of *nature* which is abundant in beauties of idea and of expression they are wholly unconscious; and therefore when they would write with *naïveté*, they affect to throw aside every embellishment, as if vacancy of thought and nakedness of diction had any coincidence with the ever-varying and luxuriant language of sentiment, tenderness and vivacity. The author of **The Battles of Talavera** is indeed not one of this squeamish class of modern poetasters: he abounds with imagery—*not his own!* and we frequently meet two or three of Walter Scott's metaphors contending for a line, or jostling against each other at the fag-end of a stanza: thus—

> And rising on *the storms of fate,*
>     His rapid genius *soars,*
> *Sees* at a glance his whole resource,
> *Drains* from each stronger point *its force.*
>     And on the weaker *pours:*
> Present where'er his soldiers bleed,
>     He rushes through the fray;
> And, *so the dangerous chances need,*
> In high emprise and desperate deed.
>     *Squanders* himself away!

No man who pretends to *think*, could *write* in this manner: but there are writers who, having no faculty in their minds of drilling the ideas with which they are fain to recruit their own vacant imaginations from the works of other authors, suffer them to rush out of their feeble cantonments *helter-skelter, higgledy-piggledy, one a-top of t'other,* to the perversion of meaning, the confusion of metaphor, and the destruction of common-sense. Were it not for this crash of imagery which so repeatedly recurs, we should be inclined to commend many passages which, taken separately, have considerable merit. The 18th, 22d, and the commencement of the 23d stanza, possess much animated description; yet in these, the author seems to delight in destroying the strength and beauty of every figure, by some wretched conceit or broken metaphor. Thus where he has told us—

> And when the fresh'ning breezes broke
> A chasm in the *volumned* smoke,
> *Busy* and black was seen to wave
>     The iron harvest of the field—

in which passage, with the exception of the strange word *volumned*, and the low word *busy*, there is some degree of poetry, he conceitedly adds—

> That harvest which, *in slaughter till'd,*
> Is gather'd in the grave.

Now, this *harvest* in a field of battle, even with its epithet *iron*, we have met with in various authors, and have understood it as metaphorically applied to the warriors; but when we are told of warriors *till'd in slaughter,* we must either consent to admire every thing that is incomprehensible, or else condemn with those who honestly condemn whatever is ridiculously absurd. (pp. 97-8)

> *A review of "The Battles of Talavera: A Poem," in* Le Beau Monde and Monthly Register, *Vol. II, No. VIII, November, 1809, pp. 97-8.*

**[WALTER SCOTT]** (essay date 1809)

[*Scott was a Scottish novelist, poet, historian, biographer, and critic of the Romantic period who is best known for his historical novels, which were great popular successes. He was a friend of Croker and, like him, a frequent contributor to the* Quarterly Review. *In this excerpt, Scott discusses* The Battles of Talavera, *in which he detects both merits and defects.*]

[**The Battles of Talavera**] is written in that irregular Pindaric measure first appplied to serious composition by Mr. Walter Scott, and it is doing no injustice to the ingenious author to say, that in many passages, we were from the similarity of the stanza and of the subject, involuntarily reminded of the battle of Flodden, in the sixth book of *Marmion.* The feeling, however, went no farther than the perception of that kindred resemblance between those of the same family which is usually most striking at first sight, and becomes less remarkable, and at length invisible, as we increase in intimacy with those in whom it exists. In one respect, the choice of the measure is more judicious on the part of the nameless bard, than on that of Mr. Scott. (pp. 427-28)

[The opening of the battle] contains some passages of great merit. Realizing his narrative with an art, which has been thought almost irreconcilable with poetry, the author . . . undertakes to give us a distinct idea of those manoeuvres and movements upon which the success of the day depended; and by clothing them with the striking circumstances which hide the otherwise technical and somewhat familiar detail of the Gazette, he has succeeded at once in preserving the form and leading circumstances, and 'all the current of the heady fight;' and, generally speaking, in presenting them to the fancy in a manner as poetical as they are clear to the understanding. In treading however upon a line so very narrow, he has sometimes glided into bombast on the one hand, or into flat, bald and vulgar expression upon the other. Although, for instance, the word '*firelocks*' he used technically, and somewhat pedantically, to express the men who bear them, we cannot permit a poet to speak with impunity of

> Full fifty-thousand *muskets bright*
> Led by old warriors train'd to fight.

*Spears,* we know, is used for *spear-men;* but this is a license sanctioned by antiquity, and not to be extended to modern implements of war. In other places, the ardour of the poet is expressed in language too turgid and inflated. (pp. 430-31)

The miscarriage of [the British] cavalry amid the broken ground in which the French . . . formed their column, its causes and consequences, the main battle itself, and all its alternations of success, are described in the same glowing and vivid language; which we will venture to say is not that of one who writes with a view to his own distinction as a poet, but who feels that living fire glow within him which impels him to fling into verse his animated and enthusiastic feelings of exultation on contemplating such a subject as the battle of Talavera. (pp. 431-32)

We have shunned, in the present instance, the unpleasant task of pointing out, and dwelling upon individual inaccuracies. There are several hasty expressions, flat lines, and deficient rhymes, which prove to us little more than that the composition was a hurried one. (p. 432)

> [*Walter Scott*], *in a review of "The Battles of Talavera: A Poem," in* The Quarterly Review, *Vol. II, November, 1809, pp. 426-33.*

**THE ECLECTIC REVIEW** (essay date 1810)

[*The following excerpt was drawn from a mixed review of* The Battles of Talavera.]

If we consider [**The Battles of Talavera**] as a political pamphlet in the interest of an aspiring party, designed to bolster up the fame of Lord Wellington, and justify the expeditious partiality which adorned his head with a coronet at the moment when his withered laurels were falling off, we, who are of no party, cannot profess to be very anxious for its success. . . .

Considering the work, however, as a narrative poem, it certainly displays very superior talents; and if, instead of being a palpable imitation of Walter Scott, it had united to many other merits that of originality in the style of execution, we should have hailed it as one of the most extraordinary productions of the age. (p. 372)

> *A review of "The Battles of Talavera: A Poem," in* The Eclectic Review, *Vol. VI, April, 1810, pp. 372-73.*

**PERCY BYSSHE SHELLEY** (essay date 1821)

[*Regarded as a major English poet, Shelley was a leading figure in the English Romantic movement. His so-called "defense of poetry," in which he investigated poetry's relation to the history of civilization, was an important contribution to nineteenth-century aesthetics. Shelley knew John Keats, although the two were not close friends, and composed the poem* Adonais: An Elegy on the Death of the Poet John Keats *to express both his admiration of Keats's genius and his outrage at critics' injustice to him. In the following excerpt from the preface to the poem, dated 1821, Shelley charges that Croker's "savage criticism" of Keats's* Endymion *precipitated his fatal illness.*]

[The genius of Keats] was not less delicate and fragile than it was beautiful; and, where canker-worms abound, what wonder if its young flower was blighted in the bud? The savage criticism on his *Endymion* which appeared in the *Quarterly Review* produced the most violent effect on his susceptible mind. The agitation thus originated ended in the rupture of a blood-vessel in the lungs; a rapid consumption ensued; and the succeeding acknowledgments, from more candid critics, of the true greatness of his powers, were ineffectual to heal the wound thus wantonly inflicted.

It may be well said that these wretched men know not what they do. They scatter their insults and their slanders without heed as to whether the poisoned shaft lights on a heart made callous by many blows, or one, like Keats's, composed of more penetrable stuff. One of their associates is, to my knowledge, a most base and unprincipled calumniator. As to *Endymion*, was it a poem, whatever might be its defects, to be treated contemptuously by those who had celebrated with various degrees of complacency and panegyric . . . a long list of the illustrious obscure? . . . What gnat did they strain at here, after having swallowed all those camels? Against what woman taken in adultery dares the foremost of these literary prostitutes to cast his opprobrious stone? Miserable man! you, one of the meanest, have wantonly defaced one of the noblest, specimens of the workmanship of God. Nor shall it be your excuse that, murderer as you are, you have spoken daggers, but used none. (p. 70)

*Percy Bysshe Shelley, in a preface to "Adonais: An Elegy on the Death of John Keats," in his* Adonais, *edited by William Michael Rossetti, Oxford at the Clarendon Press, Oxford, 1891, pp. 69-71.*

**[THOMAS BABINGTON MACAULAY]**   (essay date 1831)

[*Macaulay was an English writer and statesman. As a member of the Whig party, he encountered the opposition of Croker, who was a staunch Tory. It is thought that Macaulay used his vituperative review of Croker's edition of* The Life of Samuel Johnson, *excerpted below, to vent his spleen against Croker's politics. In a letter to Macvey Napier, the editor of the* Edinburgh Review, *Macaulay called his article "an exposure of Croker's monstrous blunders," which included historical inaccuracies and structural defects.*]

[Croker's edition of Boswell's *The Life of Samuel Johnson*] has greatly disappointed us. Whatever faults we may have been prepared to find in it, we fully expected that it would be a valuable addition to English literature; that it would contain many curious facts, and many judicious remarks; that the style of the notes would be neat, clear, and precise; and that the typographical execution would be, as in new editions of classical works it ought to be, almost faultless. We are sorry to be obliged to say, that the merits of Mr Croker's performance are on a par with those of a certain leg of mutton on which Dr Johnson dined, while travelling from London to Oxford, and which he, with characteristic energy, pronounced to be 'as bad as bad could be; ill fed, ill killed, ill kept and ill dressed.' . . . [This edition] is ill compiled, ill arranged, ill expressed, and ill printed.

Nothing in the work has astonished us so much as the ignorance or carelessness of Mr Croker, with respect to facts and dates. Many of his blunders are such as we should be surprised to hear any well-educated gentleman commit, even in conversation. The notes absolutely swarm with mistatements, into which the editor never would have fallen, if he had taken the slightest pains to investigate the truth of his assertions, or if he had even been well acquainted with the very book on which he undertook to comment. (pp. 1-2)

We will not multiply instances of [his] scandalous inaccuracy. It is clear, that a writer who, even when warmed by the text on which he is commenting, falls into such mistakes as these, is entitled to no confidence whatever. . . . How can his readers take on trust his statements concerning the births, marriages, divorces, and deaths of a crowd of people, whose names are

scarcely known to this generation? It is not likely that a person who is ignorant of what almost every body knows, can know that of which almost every body is ignorant. We did not open this book with any wish to find blemishes in it. We have made no curious researches. The work itself, and a very common knowledge of literary and political history, have enabled us to detect the mistakes which we have pointed out, and many other mistakes of the same kind. We must say, and we say it with regret, that we do not consider the authority of Mr Croker, unsupported by other evidence, as sufficient to justify any writer who may follow him, in relating a single anecdote, or in assigning a date to a single event.

Mr Croker shows almost as much ignorance and heedlessness in his criticisms as in his statements concerning facts. Dr Johnson said, very reasonably as it appears to us, that some of the satires of Juvenal are too gross for imitation. Mr Croker . . . resents this aspersion on Juvenal, and indeed refuses to believe that the doctor can have said any thing so absurd. 'He probably said—some *passages* of them—for there are none of Juvenal's satires to which the same objection may be made as to one of Horace's, that it is *altogether* gross and licentious.' Surely Mr Croker can never have read the second and ninth satires of Juvenal.

Indeed, the decisions of this editor on points of classical learning, though pronounced in a very authoritative tone, are generally such, that if a schoolboy under our care were to utter them, our soul assuredly should not spare for his crying. It is no disgrace to a gentleman, who has been engaged during nearly thirty years in political life, that he has forgotten his Greek and Latin. But he becomes justly ridiculous, if, when no longer able to construe a plain sentence, he affects to sit in judgment on the most delicate questions of style and metre. (pp. 7-8)

A very large proportion of the two thousand five hundred notes which the editor boasts of having added to those of Boswell and Malone, consists of the flattest and poorest reflections—reflections such as the least intelligent reader is quite competent to make for himself, and such as no intelligent reader would think it worth while to utter aloud. They remind us of nothing so much as of those profound and interesting annotations which are penciled by sempstresses and apothecaries' boys on the dog-eared margins of novels borrowed from circulating libraries—'How beautiful!'—'cursed prosy'—'I don't like Sir Reginald Malcolm at all.'—'I think Pelham is a sad dandy.' Mr Croker is perpetually stopping us in our progress through the most delightful narrative in the language, to observe, that really Doctor Johnson was very rude. . . .

We cannot speak more favourably of the manner in which the notes are written, than of the matter of which they consist. We find in every page words used in wrong senses, and constructions which violate the plainest rules of grammar. We have the low vulgarism of 'mutual friend,' for 'common friend.' We have 'fallacy,' used as synonymous with 'falsehood,' or 'mistatement.' (p. 12)

We must add that the printer has done his best to fill both the text and notes with all sorts of blunders; and he and the editor have between them made the book so bad, that we do not well see how it could have been worse.

When we turn from the commentary of Mr Croker to the work of our old friend Boswell, we find it not only worse printed than in any other edition with which we are acquainted, but mangled in the most wanton manner. Much that Boswell inserted in his narrative is, without the shadow of a reason, degraded to the appendix. The editor has also taken upon himself to alter or omit passages which he considers as indecorous. This prudery is quite unintelligible to us. There is nothing immoral in Boswell's book—nothing which tends to inflame the passions. He sometimes used plain words. But if this be a taint which requires expurgation, it would be desirable to begin by expurgating the morning and evening lessons. Mr Croker has performed the delicate office which he has undertaken in the most capricious manner. A strong, old-fashioned, English word, familiar to all who read their Bibles, is exchanged for a softer synonyme in some passages, and suffered to stand unaltered in others. (p. 13)

[Mr Croker's insertions] are not chosen as Boswell would have chosen them. They are not introduced as Boswell would have introduced them. They differ from the quotations scattered through the original *Life of Johnson,* as a withered bough stuck in the ground differs from a tree skilfully transplanted, with all its life about it. (p. 14)

The course which Mr Croker ought to have taken is quite clear. He should have reprinted Boswell's narrative precisely as Boswell wrote it; and in the notes or the appendix he should have placed any anecdotes which he might have thought it advisable to quote from other writers. This would have been a much more convenient course for the reader. . . . We greatly doubt whether even the Tour to the Hebrides ought to have been inserted in the midst of the *Life.* There is one marked distinction between the two works. Most of the Tour was seen by Johnson in manuscript. It does not appear that he ever saw any part of the *Life.* (pp. 14-15)

[*Thomas Babington Macaulay*], *"Croker's 'Edition of Boswell's Life of Johnson',"* in The Edinburgh Review, *Vol. LIV, No. CVII, September, 1831, pp. 1-38.*

---

**[WILLIAM MAGINN]**   (essay date 1831)

[*One of the most prominent journalists in England during the first half of the nineteenth century, Maginn wrote prolifically for a variety of English periodicals. His articles range from burlesques in verse to literary criticism and contain a rich blend of farcical humor, classical allusions, and political commentary. The following excerpt was drawn from the popular* Gallery of Illustrious Literary Characters, *a series of brief biographical sketches on prominent literary figures that appeared in* Fraser's Magazine *between 1830 and 1838.*]

Born a wit, [Mr. Croker] has contented himself with laughing at the pretensions of others, without making any effort of his own. In his earlier days, the butts whom he selected were the most important which the idleness of a provincial city could afford—the players in the Dublin theatre. As he advanced in life, he found objects of ridicule and laughter in the more serious-looking mummers who fill, in this country, the offices of statesmen and senators. The same spirit that gave causticity to the *Familiar Epistles,* animated the pen which assailed Whigs and Whiggery in the satiric articles, grave and gay, of the *New Whig Guide,* the *John Bull,* the *Quarterly Review,* and fifty other vehicles of minor renown. But the glories of the profession from which he selected his original victims, the stage, are not more fugacious than those of the political wit. His gibes, his sarcasms, his bitter allusions, his graphic comicalities, his quizzes, his parodies—are all admirable at the moment, and objects of the highest applause with his party—in a few years

they are gone—as flat as uncorked soda-water, the bubbling gas fled for ever, and the vapid residue only left behind. Therefore it is that those who, like us, think highly of Mr. Croker's genius, are anxious that he should, yet, while his powers are as vigorous as ever, give the world something by which succeeding generations may appreciate him. His edition of *Boswell's Johnson* is an amusing and almost a necessary book; but the industry and the ingenuity wasted upon the *choses de néant,* which, after all, make up the staple of his additions, might have been better applied. Such works convey little more renown than those official treatises which it *was* lately his duty to superintend. He was once asked, at a large party, by the bluestocking Countess of B——, if he had brought out any new work. "Nothing," he replied, "since the last Mutiny Act." He silenced the intrusive lady; but now that he is free from *such* routine toil, ought we not to expect something else? We are much mistaken if he has not some concealed work, some treasured gem, which may yet, but perhaps not until after his death, burst suddenly upon the world. In many matters he is a professed admirer of Horace Walpole—in some respects an imitator. Do we hazard an unlucky guess, when we say that nothing is more probable than that "Memoirs to serve for the History of England in the first —— years of the nineteenth century," lurk in the escritoire of the ex-secretary, and that every day is adding to its store. If such a book do [*sic*] exist, what queer characters of certain persons, what shrewd remarks on party history, what thorough contempt for mouth-honoured leaders, what biting sarcasm and unsparing satire, may we not be prepared to find! But as we have anticipated that its publication will not take place until after the death of its author, we hope that its appearance will be long protracted.

[*William Maginn*], *"Right Hon. John Wilson Croker,"* in Fraser's Magazine, *Vol. IV, No. XX, September, 1831, p. 240.*

---

**[JOHN WILSON]**   (essay date 1831)

[*A Scottish critic, essayist, novelist, poet, and short story writer, Wilson is best known as Christopher North, the name he assumed when writing for* Blackwood's Edinburgh Magazine, *a Tory periodical to which he was a principal contributor for over twenty-five years. He is chiefly famous for his* Noctes Ambrosianae, *a series of witty dialogues originally published in* Blackwood's *between 1822 and 1835 in which contemporary issues and personalities are treated at once with levity, gravity, and pungent satire. Wilson is not recognized as a great critic. His criticism, which was frequently written in haste, is often deficient in sagacity, analysis, and finish. He could be severe and stinging, and he reserved his harshest words for gifted young writers whom he sincerely wanted to help by objectively analyzing their work. His other critical opinions are largely regarded as the projections of his varying moods. In this excerpt from the* Noctes Ambrosianae, *Wilson defends Croker's edition of* The Life of Samuel Johnson *against Thomas Babington Macaulay's harsh criticism in the* Edinburgh Review *(see excerpt above, 1831), popularly known as the "Blue and Yellow." The characters of the Ettrick Shepherd and Timothy Tickler were based on James Hogg and Robert Sym. Wilson incorporated details from Croker's rebuttal,* Answers to the Edinburgh Reviewer of Croker's "Boswell," *into the unexcerpted portion of the dialogue.*]

TICKLER.

. . . What is your opinion, North, of Croker's Edition of *Boswell's Johnson*?

NORTH.

The same—generally—as that of the *Westminster* Reviewer.

TICKLER.
Aye! And pray what is that?

NORTH.
That it is the best variorum edition since the revival of letters.

TICKLER.
Croker is certainly one of the cleverest and acutest of living men.

SHEPHERD.
No unlike yourself, sir, I jalouse.

NORTH.
He is—and much more. He is a man of great abilities, and an admirable scholar. But he is much more than that—he is a political writer of the highest order, as many of his essays in the *Quarterly Review* prove—which are full of the Philosophy of History.

TICKLER.
Pray, what have you got to say of the charges brought against him, in the last number of the Blue and Yellow, of pitiable imbecility and scandalous ignorance?

NORTH.
James, have the goodness to hand me over the seven volumes lying yonder on the small table.

SHEPHERD.
Yon in the east nyeuck? There. And here's the Blue and Yellow sittin' on the tap o' them like an Incubus.

NORTH.
Having paid some little attention to the literary history of the period to which they refer, perhaps I may be able to amuse you for half an hour by an exposure of some of the *betises* of this prick-ma-dainty Reviewer. (p. 829)

SHEPHERD.
[Has] the cretur failed in pintin' out ony inaccuracies ava in Mr Crocker?

NORTH.
[He] has charged Mr Croker, in some instances, ignorantly, and in others falsely, of ignorance and falsehood; and such being the Reviewer's own sins in the course of half a sheet of the Blue and Yellow, manifestly got up with much assiduity, for he quotes, I perceive, from all the five volumes, is it not contemptible to hear his chuckle over Mr Croker, who, in the course of between two and three thousand additions to Boswell, has been shewn to have fallen, perhaps, into some half dozen errors or inaccuracies, one of them evidently a misprint—one an expression apparently incorrect, because elliptical—and the others—

SHEPHERD.
Mere trifles if like the alledged lave o' them. . . .

NORTH.
Mr Croker has been convicted of the "gross and scandalous" inaccuracy of having assigned wrong dates to the deaths of Derrick, Sir Herbert Croft, and the amiable Sir William Forbes, biographer of Beattie.

SHEPHERD.
What'n enormities! He maun drie pennance by a pilgrimage to Loch Derg. What other crimes has Mr Croker committed?

NORTH.
He has, moreover, attributed to Henry Bate Dudley, the Fight-ing Parson, the Editorship of the old Morning Herald, instead of the old Morning Post.

SHEPHERD.
What a sinner!

NORTH.
And he has erroneously said, that Burgoyne's surrender at Saratoga took place in March 1778, instead of October 1777. He is mistaken, too, in saying that Lord Townshend was not Secretary of State till 1720.

SHEPHERD.
In short, the seven deadly sins!

NORTH.
The perpetration of which has so incensed the immaculate and infallible Reviewer, that he has not scrupled to assert that the whole of Mr Croker's part of the work is ill compiled, ill arranged, ill expressed, and ill printed. (p. 838)

[*John Wilson*], "Noctes Ambrosianae, No. LIX," in Blackwood's Edinburgh Magazine, *Vol. XXX, No. CLXXXVII, November, 1831, pp. 802-46.*

## [J. G. LOCKHART]   (essay date 1831)

[*Although Lockhart wrote several novels, his fame rests on his biography of Sir Walter Scott and his critical contributions to* Blackwood's Edinburgh Magazine *and the* Quarterly Review. *From 1817 to 1825, he was a principal contributor to* Blackwood's, *a Tory periodical that was founded to counter the influential Whig journal the* Edinburgh Review. *His trenchant wit contributed to the early success of the magazine and earned him the nickname of "The Scorpion." Later, as editor of the* Quarterly, *he was less acerbic. He is regarded as a versatile if somewhat severe critic whose opinions of his contemporaries, though lacking depth, are generally considered accurate when not distorted by political animosities. In his review of* The Life of Samuel Johnson, *Lockhart discusses the merits and defects of the work and calls it "the best edition of an English book that has appeared in our time."*]

Had the task [of annotating **'Boswell's Johnson'**] been much longer deferred, hardly a single individual that had ever moved in the society of Johnson and his worshipping biographer would have remained. Even the generation that had fed in youth upon the table-talk of the great doctor's surviving associates, were beginning to be thinned among us. Mr. Croker's character and position offered, of course, the readiest access to such living sources of information as could still be appealed to; and probably few would have questioned his sagacity in detecting the proper points of inquiry—his prompt and unwearied diligence in following out hints and suggestions; in short, his abundant qualifications for discharging, in regard to such a book, all the editorial functions. . . . But if Mr. Croker had only done in the most satisfactory manner what was thus looked for at his hands, we should have had a far different book before us, and his general reputation would have owed little, if anything, to the achievement. He has gone a long way, indeed, beyond the usual scope and purpose of anecdotical note-makers. Not sat-isfied with hunting out whatever facts could be explained as to detail, or added to the already enormous mass, from the dust of forgotten pamphlets, the scattered stores of manuscript correspondence, and the oral communications of persons of all ranks and conditions, from Lord Stowell, Sir Walter Scott, Sir James Mackintosh, Mr. D'Israeli, and Mr. Markland, down to the obscurest descendants of Johnson's connexions in early provincial life;—not satisfied with equalling, to all appearance, in this sort of diligence the utmost exertions of any commen-

*This portrait of Croker by Daniel Maclise formed part of the popular* Gallery of Illustrious Literary Characters. *The Bettmann Archive, Inc.*

tator that ever staked his glory on the rectification of a date, he has brought his own piercing, strong, and liberal understanding, enriched with most multifarious knowledge of books, more especially of literary and political biography, and expanded by as extensive observation of men and manners, as has fallen to the lot of any living person—he has brought, in a word, the whole vigour of his own mental resources to bear upon this, at first sight, sufficiently unostentatious field of labour—and produced, in consequence, a book which, were every correction of detail it contains, every *hiatus* it fills up as to mere matters of fact, every name, every date, even every new anecdote it gives, all obliterated at a stroke, would still keep its place and its worth;—nay, which, if it actually had omitted all and every one of these things, would, perhaps, have done more for Mr. Croker's estimation with the general mob of readers, than it has done, or must do, in its present more complete condition. (pp. 2-3)

[Many] who think, like ourselves, of the style in which Mr. Croker has acquitted himself of the higher part of his task, will perhaps wish that he may never in future undertake any such task at all, but exercise his talents in original works alone. Heartily concurring, however, in the hope that many purely original works may hereafter proceed from his pen, we cannot but express, nevertheless, our earnest desire that we may have him from time to time before us in the editorial capacity also. (p. 4)

Enlarged and illuminated, as we now have it, by the industrious researches and the sagacious running criticism of Mr. Croker, **'Boswell's Johnson'** is, without doubt,—excepting, yet hardly excepting, a few immortal monuments of creative genius,— that English book, which, were this island to be sunk tomorrow

with all that it inhabits, would be most prized in other days and countries, by the students 'of us and of our history.' . . .

Mr. Croker has handled throughout with exquisite skill the character of Boswell himself, especially as elicited in the turn and colouring of particular statements with regard to which we have the means of comparing him with other witnesses. (p. 11)

On the whole, in spite of a few trivial mistakes and inadvertencies, easy to be corrected hereafter, we may safely pronounce this **'Boswell'** the best *edition* of an English book that has appeared in our time. (p. 46)

> [*J. G. Lockhart*], *"Croker's 'Edition of Boswell',"* in The Quarterly Review, *Vol. XLVI, No. XCI, November, 1831, pp. 1-46.*

### [THOMAS CARLYLE]   (essay date 1832)

> [*A noted nineteenth-century essayist, historian, critic, and social commentator, Carlyle was a central figure of the Victorian age in England. In his writings, Carlyle advocated a Christian work ethic and stressed the importance of order, piety, and spiritual fulfillment. Known to his contemporaries as the "Sage of Chelsea," Carlyle exerted a powerful moral influence in an era of rapidly shifting values. In this excerpt from his review of* The Life of Samuel Johnson, *Carlyle assesses Croker's editorial skill, which he considers limited. He concludes that Croker's is the worst edition of James Boswell's biography of Johnson.*]

That Mr. Croker should undertake to edit *Boswell's Life of Johnson,* was a praiseworthy but no miraculous procedure: neither could the accomplishment of such undertaking be, in an epoch like ours, anywise regarded as an event in Universal

History; the right or the wrong accomplishment thereof was, in very truth, one of the most insignificant of things. (p. 379)

[For the task of editing this book] he had various qualifications: his own voluntary resolution to do it; his high place in society unlocking all manner of archives to him; not less, perhaps, a certain anecdotico-biographic turn of mind, natural or acquired; we mean, a love for the *minuter* events of History, and talent for investigating these. Let us admit, too, that he has been very diligent; seems to have made inquiries perseveringly, far and near; as well as drawn freely from his own ample stores; and so tells us, to appearance quite accurately, much that he has not found lying on the highways, but has had to seek and dig for. Numerous persons, chiefly of quality, rise to view in these Notes; when and also where they came into this world, received office or promotion, died, and were buried . . . is faithfully enough set down. Whereby all that their various and doubtless widely-scattered Tombstones could have taught us, is here presented, at once, in a bound Book. (pp. 379-80)

[The] spirit of Diligence, exhibited in this department, seems to attend the Editor honestly throughout: he keeps every where a watchful outlook on his Text; reconciling the distant with the present, or at least indicating and regretting their irreconcilability; elucidating, smoothing down; in all ways, exercising, according to ability, a strict editorial superintendence. Any little Latin or even Greek phrase is rendered into English, in general with perfect accuracy; citations are verified, or else corrected. On all hands, moreover, there is a certain spirit of Decency maintained and insisted on: if not good morals, yet good manners, are rigidly inculcated; if not Religion, and a devout Christian heart, yet Orthodoxy, and a cleanly, Shovel-hatted look,—which, as compared with flat Nothing, is something very considerable. Grant too, as no contemptible triumph of this latter spirit, that though the Editor is known as a decided Politician and Party-man, he has carefully subdued all temptations to transgress in that way: except by quite involuntary indications, and rather as it were the pervading temper of the whole, you could not discover on which side of the Political Warfare he is enlisted and fights. This, as we said, is a great triumph of the Decency-principle: for this, and for these other graces and performances, let the Editor have all praise.

Herewith, however, must the praise unfortunately terminate. Diligence, Fidelity, Decency, are good and indispensable: yet, without Faculty, without Light, they will not do the work. Along with that Tombstone-information, perhaps even without much of it, we could have liked to gain some answer, in one way or other, to this wide question: What and how was *English Life* in Johnson's time; wherein has ours grown to differ therefrom? . . . This was indeed specially the problem which a Commentator and Editor had to solve: a complete solution of it should have been filled and prepared with perfect insight into it; then, whether in the way of express Dissertation, of incidental Exposition and Indication, opportunities enough would have occurred of bringing out the same: what was dark in the figure of the Past had thereby been enlightened. . . . Of all which very little has been attempted here; accomplished, we should say, next to nothing, or altogether nothing.

Excuse, no doubt, is in readiness for such omission; and, indeed, for innumerable other failings;—as where, for example, the Editor will punctually explain what is already sun-clear; and then anon, not without frankness, declare frequently enough that "the Editor does not understand," that "the Editor cannot guess,"—while, for most part, the Reader cannot help both guessing and seeing. (pp. 380-81)

[It,] from a very early stage of the business, becomes afflictively apparent, how much the Editor, so well furnished with all external appliances and means, is from within unfurnished with means, for forming to himself any just notion of Johnson, or of Johnson's Life; and therefore of speaking on that subject with much hope of edifying. Too lightly is it from the first taken for granted that *Hunger,* the great basis of our life, is also its apex and ultimate perfection; that as "Neediness and Greediness and Vainglory" are the chief qualities of most men, so no man, not even a Johnson, acts or can think of acting on any other principle. Whatsoever, therefore, cannot be referred to the two former categories (Need and Greed), is without scruple ranged under the latter. It is here properly that our Editor becomes burdensome; and, to the weaker sort, even a nuisance. (p. 381)

[Another fundamental failing] is that our Editor has fatally, and almost surprisingly, mistaken the limits of an Editor's function; and so, instead of working on the margin with his Pen, to elucidate as best might be, strikes boldly into the body of the page with his Scissors, and there clips at discretion! Four Books Mr. C. had by him, wherefrom to gather light for the fifth, which was Boswell's. What does he do but now, in the placidest manner,—slit the whole five into slips, and sew these together . . . exactly at his own convenience; giving Boswell the credit of the whole! . . .

A situation almost original; not to be tried a second time! (pp. 381-82)

[There] is simply *no* Edition of *Boswell* to which this last would seem preferable. (p. 382)

*[Thomas Carlyle], in a review of "Boswell's Life of Johnson," in Fraser's Magazine, Vol. V. No. XXVIII, May, 1832, pp. 379-413.*

## BENTLEY'S MISCELLANY  (essay date 1856)

[*Commenting on Croker's criticism in the* Quarterly Review, *the reviewer labels him* "*par excellence the 'slashing' critic.*"]

Mr. Croker's innumerable articles [in the *Quarterly Review*] teem with examples of what is most microscopic in captious criticism. Some men, it has been remarked by Archbishop Whately, are so excessively acute at detecting imperfections, that they scarcely notice excellences: in looking at a peacock's train, they would fix on every spot where the feathers were worn or the colours faded, and see nothing else. Mr. Croker may see something else in the peacock, and with both eyes; but he has the trick of seeing, with half an eye, every spot or blemish or any such thing in the plunge *in pleno*. The exultation with which he lights on a slip of the pen, or shows up a misprint, or turns inside out a distorted fact, or turns upside down an inverted inference, is supreme. (p. 328)

Mr. Croker is commonly reputed to be *par excellence* the "slashing" critic. *MacGrawler,* in Sir Bulwer Lytton's romance, when imparting to his protégé, young Paul, the mysteries of the critical craft, thus explains the meaning of that term: "To slash is, speaking grammatically, to employ the accusative, or accusing case; you must cut up your book right and left, top and bottom, root and branch." (p. 329)

[There] is good stuff in Mr. Croker's compositions, with every allowance for the bad and the indifferent. And as it will take something more than a stinging article, a very "slasher" in its way, by Macaulay [see excerpt above, 1831], to upset the credit

of Croker's *Boswell;* so will it take something more than a Disraelitish caricature, *vraisemblant,* and salient-pointed as that may be, to extinguish the vitality of the (in a twofold sense) well-read veteran's contributions . . . to the *Quarterly Review.*
(p. 330)

"*Prosings by Monkshood about the Essayists and Reviewers: A Quartet of Quarterly Reviewers,*" in Bentley's Miscellany, *Vol. XL, 1856, pp. 316-30.\**

## LITTELL'S LIVING AGE   (essay date 1857)

[*In the following excerpt from an obituary notice, the critic comments briefly on Croker's criticism in the* Quarterly Review.]

The object of the *Quarterly* being not to criticize but to crush, its method necessarily consisted in "exposing" its antagonists; and Croker with his great command of facts, his knowledge of literature, his keenness as counsel, and his power of satire, was able to cut up a feeble subject with all the power of a dashing anatomical demonstrator. But the man who rests his case on a dogmatic appeal to details and literal points of accuracy inevitably lays himself open to retorts of the same kind, with an exaggerated appreciation of his blunders. It was so with Croker. Probably his criticism will be found to be frequently correct; his facts, as in the case of the Johnson annotations, valuable. But a mistake in that mouth of dogmatism is a hundredfold more glaring than in the mouth of modesty. Croker has been held up as a model of malignant virulence and reckless falsehood. He has played the part of the Devil in literature. The hackneyed saying has been applied to him and his position in the world, that nothing became him like his leaving it; and certainly, few acts have so injured a veteran as his reappearances in the world, even when he was in the right. In the memory of society he has been presumed to take no part in literary conflicts except for a malignant purpose, and the simple fact that the contest lay between a Croker and a Russell or a Macaulay was sufficient to tell people which was in the right: if Croker was not in the wrong, he ought to have been.
(p. 182)

"*John Wilson Croker,*" in Littell's Living Age, *Vol. LV, No. 699, October 17, 1857, pp. 182-83.*

## PERCY FITZGERALD   (essay date 1882)

[*Fitzgerald focuses on the highly subjective style of Croker's literary criticism in the* Quarterly Review.]

It is in [Croker's] connection with the 'Quarterly Review,' from its foundation in 1809, for over forty years, that his career is interesting. His devotion to the journal was extraordinary; and it is evident from the perusal of his always recognisable articles that his heart was in the business. The extraordinary number of these papers, the ardent eager style in which they were written, show that he was prompted by each subject to a deliverance; just as a popular speaker in the House of Commons is prompted to a sudden reply. But the angry, hostile, and too often malicious tone of these papers shows that his passion, rather than a calm judicial temper, was what imparted to them their spirit. It is impossible at the same time not to admire the amount of general knowledge acquired in the particular case, and the vigorously malignant fashion in which he exposed follies and contradictions; but, at the same time, there was often vast unfairness shown in straining the sense to make a point. (p. 223)

The person he hunted down and exposed with the most effective logic and rancour was 'Bonaparte,' together with the Wardens, O'Mearas, and other apologists. His profound knowledge of the incidents and literature of the French Revolution helped *bonnement* to this effective exposure. It is amusing to read the violence of his language to the 'Ogre,' who is dealt with as a sort of bravo. At one point, on alluding to an escape from assassination, he says plainly, that it was a pity the attempt had not been successful. His advocates were branded as liars and knaves, and certainly more amusing reading could not be found than his gibbeting of Bertram, Montholon, and others, who are shown up as a gang of unscrupulous adventurers— which no doubt they were. The various essays on the Duke of Wellington's campaigns, including Waterloo, all show the same abundant knowledge of details, and have been published as separate works by the author.

But in the case of a few persons—notably ladies—the reviewer's passion is shown in a way that will seem extraordinary compared with the courteous and temperate style we are accustomed to in our own time. Mr. Croker's morbid views as to ladies' ages, and the vast trouble he went to, searching registers for evidence to convict them of untruth, caused much amusement at the time. His ungenerous attacks on Lady Morgan are, perhaps, unexampled as a display of critical rancour. When the lady published her 'France' in the two great quartos then fashionable, he fell on her as some wild animal in the Zoological Gardens would on a piece of meat at feeding-time. (p. 224)

After some . . . preliminaries, calling her 'the elegant Lady Morgan, a mere bookseller's drudge,' he goes seriously to work:

> Our charges (to omit minor faults) fall readily under the heads of Bad Taste—Bombast and Nonsense—Blunders—Ignorance of the French Language and Manners—General Ignorance— Jacobinism—Falsehood—Licentiousness, and Impiety. We undertake, as we have said, to prove them from Lady Morgan's own mouth. BAD TASTE.—The work is composed in the most confused manner, and written in the worst style—if it be not an abuse of language to call that a *style* which is merely a jargon. There is neither order in the subjects nor connection between the parts. It is a huge aggregation of disjointed sentences, so jumbled together, that we seriously assert that no injury will be done to the volume by beginning with the last chapter and reading backwards to the first; and yet it has all the affectation of order: it is divided into *parts.*
>
> (p. 225)

What must have been the gall and blackness of the man's heart that could pen such abuse! And what could have been the cause of such hostility? In her Memoirs it is stated that he was a sort of devoted admirer of the lady's when he was in Dublin, and a rather obsequious letter of his is given. Yet in his article he declares that he did not know her!

This animosity was a sort of mania; or perhaps the subject so quickened and stimulated his peculiar style of writing, that he could not resist giving the unfortunate authoress 'a swashing blow,' *passim,* as it were, in other articles on other subjects. Even the persons who alluded to her with anything like favour were certain to receive about the same treatment. And relations came in for the same irate assaults. (p. 227)

Another lady as cruelly mauled by him was Miss Burney, whose work, indeed, offered but too tempting openings. Another was Lady Charlotte Bury, whose vivacious 'Diary of the Times of George IV.,' full of piquant incidents, traits of manners, and 'characteristical' letters, was dismissed as 'a catchpenny,' untruthful and worthless. Now, it is extraordinary to what an extent the innumerable books of Memoirs since published support all that is set out in it, though so fiercely impugned at the time. The same rehabilitation is being gradually extended to Sir N. Wraxall's curious volumes, now about being reprinted with new notes by Messrs. Bickers. Moore's 'Diary' was similarly assailed, blows being also aimed at Lord Russell, the editor; and when the latter retorted, it is characteristic to find the veteran reviewer, then eighty, indignant at the attack and addressing bitter remonstrances. All these lucubrations were set out and emphasised by a series of arts now fallen out of use and unknown to the present race of reviewers: a copious use of italics, in combination with capitals of various degrees and sizes, which lent a curious 'bill-poster' air, and certainly doubled the effect of his points. The last expiring effort of the veteran was his counter-thrust to Macaulay—a review of his history in return for the review of Croker's **'Boswell'** a dozen years before, and which was held to have been but a weak effort. (p. 228)

Altogether, a man of strange power and vigour, and unrestrained by scruples. With him the 'slashing reviewer' went out. (p. 229)

*Percy Fitzgerald, "A Slashing Reviewer," in Belgravia, Vol. XLVII, No. 186, April, 1882, pp. 223-29.*

**THE SPECTATOR** (essay date 1884)

[*The following excerpt was drawn from a mixed review of* The Croker Papers.]

[With Croker] charity had no place in politics or literature. He gave no quarter, and he expected none. Did a man differ from him in party? Did he write a book? Then every act of his life, every word he had ever uttered, would be ransacked to condemn him. He never spared an enemy; he would not even spare a friend. If once a disagreement took place, every claim of friendship was gone. He found that Moore's Diary contained some slighting references to his intellectual powers. The biographer was a Whig. This was enough; and the reviewer proceeded with relentless ingenuity to piece together from the Diary the proofs of Moore's faithlessness and neglect as a husband, and this while he professed to respect the feelings of the bereaved widow. Macaulay said of him, truly enough:—"Croker is a man who would go a hundred miles, through sleet and snow, on the top of a coach in a December night, to search a parish register for the sake of showing that a man was illegitimate, or a woman older than she says she is." Of real enthusiasm, of high-mindedness, of nobility of sentiment, he was incapable. His patriotism never rose beyond a strict devotion to party, or his loyalty beyond frigid eulogiums of the Crown, the Church of England, and the landed interest. . . .

That readers of [the **Croker Papers**] will find in them the character of Mr. Croker we have depicted substantiated, we do not expect. Indeed, they will find something very different, and far more pleasant. The reflection will not, however, be wanting, that a man must be either a very great knave or a very

great fool, if his own letters and the letters of his friends show him anything but great and good. The result of reading the book alone, and judging Mr. Croker solely by the evidence there afforded, is as unfair for him as it would be unfair against him to read nothing but the attacks of his opponents. But let any one, when he has read the book before us, next turn to some of Mr. Croker's own articles in the *Quarterly*,—say, the article on Moore, and with it the correspondence with Lord John Russell, or any other impartial sources of information. The result of such reading can hardly be but to dissipate the too favourable opinion that the **Croker Papers,** read alone, will produce. . . . The three large volumes of which the book consists are full of matter, and that of the most interesting kind. Few men who have lived intimately with those at the head of affairs have been possessed of the same diligence and literary skill as Croker. He knew everything that was going on round him, and he had the faculty to discriminate what was most worthy of note. For the history of the first fifty years of this century this book will always be consulted, not only for mere biographical details of great men, but because it contains the evidence of a peculiar school of English political principles. The Duke of Cumberland, Lord Eldon, and Mr. Croker represented, in the opinion of their contemporaries, a certain bitter, uncompromising, almost brutal, form of Toryism, which was something quite different from that associated with the names of Canning and Sir Robert Peel. When future historians wish to realise what this high Tory spirit was, they will turn to Mr. Croker's letters and diaries, and find it there embalmed. (p. 1484)

*"The Croker Papers," in* The Spectator, *Vol. 57, No. 2941, November 8, 1884, pp. 1483-85.*

**[G. R. GLEIG]** (essay date 1884)

[*Gleig suggests that Croker left a body of work incommensurate with his abilities.*]

[*The Correspondence and Diaries of the Right Hon.* **John Wilson Croker,** commonly known as **The Croker Papers**] will be eagerly sought for and read, not so much because, like the life of Pitt, or Nelson, or Wellington, it describes the career of a born leader of men, as because it throws a flood of light over one of the most important periods, political, social, and literary, in the history of England and of Europe. The part actually played in that complicated game by the hero of the tale was not, perhaps, very important. He may claim to have been the adviser of Cabinet Ministers, of personages, and of even royalty. He was undoubtedly much in their confidence, and his influence over the press, or a portion of it, was considerable. But his interference in great events was indirect rather than authoritative, and a foremost place among the men of letters of his day he can scarcely be said to have achieved. Still the volumes we are now about to introduce to the notice of our readers will, unless we greatly deceive ourselves, interest them to the full as much as the most outspoken of the many self-revelations of statesmen and authors with which the public has of late years been favoured. (p. 553)

It is unfortunate for Croker's reputation as an author that he never found time to devote his great powers to the elucidation of any one masterful object. Had he gone on with his history of the French Revolution, he might have taken his place as a historian beside Hume and Grote, and even beside Gibbon. For he was not the man to treat that great convulsion, as Macaulay has treated his romance of William III., from a mere party point of view, much less as an isolated fact in time's progress. We should have had, on the contrary, or we deceive ourselves, effects traced back to their causes—far enough to make us acquainted with every incident, small or great, which conduced to bring on the decline and fall of the French monarchy. Instead of this we have only two or three papers in the 'Quarterly Review,' each of them excellent to the extent to which it goes, but as a whole unsatisfactory, because without either system or continuity. Again, his edition of Boswell's **'Johnson,'** however creditable to him as an investigator into the manners and habits of thought which characterised a particular period in literary history, scarcely gives him his proper place in literature. We are doubtless indebted to him for the skill with which he has supplemented what was wanting in Boswell's story; yet, after all, it is not Croker's life of Johnson, but Boswell's, which we have been reading; and when we lay aside the book, it is much more of Johnson, and even of Boswell, that we think, than of Croker.

Besides editing Boswell, Croker meditated giving to the world a new edition of Pope. . . . But though he made considerable progress in collecting materials for his work, and had gone so far as to agree with Mr. Murray concerning the terms on which the copyright should be parted with, he by-and-by abandoned the project, and made over his notes—and very valuable notes they were—to the Rev. Mr. Elwin. It was as well, perhaps, that he did so; for while we cannot doubt that he might have ably performed a task for which his familiarity with the literature of our Augustan age peculiarly fitted him, it may be questioned whether, in his case, the game would have been worth the candle. We think of him, therefore, weighed in this scale, as of an author who might have done infinitely better than he did had not circumstances induced him to be content with the reputation of a painstaking English scholar and a very able and brilliant essayist. (pp. 814-15)

> [G. R. Gleig], "The Right Hon. John Wilson Croker—No. 1" and "The Right Hon. John Wilson Croker—Conclusion," in Blackwood's Edinburgh Magazine, Vol. CXXXVI, Nos. DCCCXXIX and DCCCXXX, November and December, 1884, pp. 553-78, 799-816.

### [SPENCER WALPOLE] (essay date 1885)

> [Walpole discusses Croker's critical method and editorial capabilities and concludes that his writings deserve little praise.]

Mr. Croker held so high and so peculiar a position in both the political and the literary world, and filled it so long, that we expected to derive both entertainment and information from the perusal of his *Diaries* and his *Correspondence* [also known as *The Croker Papers*]. Nor have we been wholly disappointed by the book itself. Mr. Croker, indeed, can hardly be said to have kept a journal; and, if his articles had not been brighter than his letters, the animosity which he provoked in his lifetime would have been less intense. The true interest, however, of the work before us arises from the light which it throws on the times in which Mr. Croker lived, and on the characters of the men whom he knew. If the historian will not be compelled by its publication to restate many of his facts, he may possibly be tempted to repaint some of his portraits. (p. 1)

The most serious of the charges made against [Mr. Croker] as a literary man is that his virulent and intemperate language imparted a deplorable tone and temper to literary criticism. This is what Lord John Russell meant when he wrote of Mr. Croker's 'malignity;' what Lord Macaulay meant when he wrote of his rancour [see excerpt above, 1831]; and what Miss Mar-

tineau meant when she declared that he had a 'malignant ulcer' in his mind [see Additional Bibliography]. (p. 3)

Mr. Croker occasionally preserved a good story; and some of the most entertaining pages of this book are devoted to the reproduction of these anecdotes. Some of them curiously illustrate the times. (p. 5)

[We] agree with Lord Macaulay's main criticism [of *The Life of Samuel Johnson*]. We think that Mr. Croker spoiled Boswell by incorporating Mrs. Thrale's anecdotes and much of Sir John Hawkins's lumbering book in the text. We think, too, that few authors would care to face the formidable assault which the reviewer made on Mr. Croker. Never before, and never since, to our knowledge at any rate, has [a] reviewer detected so long and so serious a category of errors in any considerable work. If Mr. Croker's book survived the attack, it was not because it was a perfect edition of Boswell but because many of its defects, when they were once pointed out, were capable of correction in later issues, and because, as Lord Macaulay himself admitted, 'there is much curious information in it.' (p. 32)

Mr. Croker was neither a great politician nor a great writer. He had much information, but little knowledge; much acuteness of vision, but no breadth of view. His articles were no doubt caustic enough, but his style was not good; he was as fond of italics as a school-girl; and the use of italics almost always implies an incapacity to emphasise argument by language. He occasionally struck hard, but his blows were the blows of a shillelagh rather than of a rapier. He could knock down his adversary and trample upon him, but he had not the fencer's skill in parry and attack. If he had no lightness of touch, he was also destitute of the keener humour. (p. 33)

Whatever merit may be due to a man who lives and dies obstinately fighting for a wrong cause was his. We can give him neither as a man of letters nor as a man of affairs other praise. (p. 37)

> [Spencer Walpole], "The Croker Papers," in The Edinburgh Review, Vol. CLXI, No. CCCXXIX, January, 1885, pp. 1-37.

### THE NATION (essay date 1885)

> [The following is a brief negative assessment of The Croker Papers.]

People have long looked forward with considerable expectations to the publication of the Croker Papers, and now that Croker's **'Correspondence and Diaries'** [commonly known as **'The Croker Papers'**] are before the world, readers who have anticipated either historical revelations or interesting anecdotes will find themselves bitterly disappointed. [This] book contains no information which may not be obtained from sources which have long been open to every student. His hero, it is true, was the acquaintance or friend of many eminent persons; but Croker had none of the Boswellian faculty for portraying the character and conversation of his associates, and it is also probable that Croker, who was constantly lecturing every one, great or small, with whom he came in contact, and whose own conversation became at last, to judge from his letters, no better than monotonous variations on the well-worn theme of "I told you so," did not contrive to elicit much either of brilliancy or of confidence from the companions who had the misfortune or the advantage of his acquaintance. (p. 121)

*"John Wilson Croker," in* The Nation, *Vol. XL, No. 1023, February 5, 1885, pp. 121-23.*

**HEDVA BEN-ISRAEL** (essay date 1968)

[*Ben-Israel asserts that Croker is underappreciated as a historian of the French Revolution, arguing that his method of historical analysis anticipated later historical approaches to study of the Revolution.*]

[Reading Croker's articles on the French Revolution that appeared in the *Quarterly Review*] for the first time, one is struck by the unexpected scholarship and the soundness of the ideas on how the history of the Revolution ought to be studied. Above all, in the problems presented by the vast and growing amount of material, Croker was far ahead of his times. His excellent historical qualities make it appear that the neglect of his work has been unjustified. With his collections, his methodical investigations, and special aptitudes, he could have produced an unusually well-documented and accurate history for the time. The fact remains, however, that he did not write it. The collection of essays shows that he covered the early period of the Revolution systematically. His sharp criticism of other historians' facts was a valuable contribution in a period preceding that of critical history; but such work kept him more busy disproving other historians' points and errors than making his own overall constructions. Criticism and analysis of other historians' writings would have characterized anything Croker might have written.

The personal element which was prominent in his writings did not represent a biographical interest in the Revolution, because it was chiefly the political man which interested Croker. His history would have been, as are his essays, purely political. If we take out of the essays the criticism of historians, and the discussion of sources, and look for the historical compositions, we find them centred on the political behaviour of the prominent figures and the criminal behaviour of the unnamed. Croker looked into the daily working of the Revolutionary machine. He examined the episodes and tried to put his finger, through the knowledge of details, on the points of contact between the policies of the men in power and the actual happenings in the streets. In all his investigations Croker did not see and did not look beyond the personalities, intentions and actions of men. He complained that historians treated the Revolution too much as a tale of blood and fire and neglected the problems of politics, of the personal rivalries and of the institutions.

Although it was Croker who used the new word 'phantasmagoria', to describe the Revolution, no idea could be further from his mind than that there was any unfathomable mystery about it. The only mysteries Croker admitted were those for which sources were not obtainable, as, for instance, the oral discussions that preceded important actions. He thought he could explain everything if only he could look into the hearts and minds of certain people. Croker was not mystified by anything which might appear fatalistic, nor by mass movements, nor by the strange phenomena of human behaviour. Human nature he believed was always the same. All a historian had to do was to apply the usual standard of motives and passions that he knew to exist. For such a task Croker was eminently fitted; he was a master detective with the useful tool of an over-suspicious and uncharitable mind. He was therefore at his best about people whom he disliked. His great shortcoming, even from the point of view of his own method, was his extraordinary limited view of human nature. (pp. 201-02)

*Hedva Ben-Israel, "John Wilson Croker," in her* English Historians on the French Revolution, *Cambridge at the University Press, 1968, pp. 175-202.*

**PETER F. MORGAN** (essay date 1977)

[*Morgan examines Croker's critical method as well as the moral and political attitudes that inform his essays on poetry, the novel, and history and memoir writing.*]

Croker's Toryism and puritanism have an old-fashioned quality, but at the same time they are aroused most strongly in his critical articles in defense of contemporary manners and institutions and against subversive contemporary developments. The moral severity which he expresses has a long tradition behind it, but he invokes it particularly in defense of two values very characteristic of the nineteenth century, the innocence of woman and the sanctity of private life. Moreover, in dealing with these subjects Croker betrays an ambivalence characteristic of the period, or which indeed we tend to associate rather with the Victorians.

At a more elemental level, Croker defends what he values in literature against Pope's foe, the stupid, as it manifests itself in the incomprehensible, the incoherent, the ignorant, the dull, and the insipid. Croker also attacks the presumptuous and the egotistic, like John Galt foolishly setting himself up against Shakespeare . . . , Leigh Hunt laying down new canons of poetry and criticism . . . , and Mme. D'Arblay showing "the most horse-leech egotism that literature or Bedlam has yet exhibited." . . . Croker, like Pope, also attacks the mannered, the pompous, the inflated, and the false.

Croker is afraid that the virtue of the reader, especially that of the feminine and the young reader, is in peril. In 1836 he declares emphatically: "she who *dares to read a single page* of the hundred thousand licentious pages with which the last five years have inundated society, is *lost for ever.*" . . . The danger is even greater and more grotesque in the confrontation of two people in real life, for the presentation of the Socialist Robert Owen at Court poses a threat "to the unsuspecting purity of a Virgin Queen." . . . (pp. 62-3)

Croker is equally fearful that the "security of private life" is threatened . . . , in particular by a tradition of intimate writing that goes back to Boswell's "Journey with Dr. Johnson to the Hebrides." On this ground Croker regrets the publication of the prayers of Johnson, as well as of the life of Benjamin Robert Haydon. . . . The threat to privacy must be diminished, as far as the severity of the written word can achieve this. Thus Croker, like Southey, his fellow Tory and *Quarterly Review*er advocates censorship, either direct or indirect. He deplores the obscenity of Pope, Swift, and "even Addison"; and he regrets the unbowdlerized publication of the works of Charles Hanbury Williams. . . .

Croker feels that he must defend the citadel of Tory England against demoralised Frenchmen abroad and subversive Whigs and Liberals at home. Thus his critical posture is a defensive one. He delivers heavy blows in order to protect the values which he holds dear. He also feels the need to justify such severity, particularly in later years. For example, he writes concerning Walpole's *Memoirs:* "If any reader should be inclined to think that we assign too much importance to this detection and exposure, we beg leave to remind him that . . . Walpole is likely at first sight to obtain a confidence which he in no degree merits, and that his pertinacious efforts to poison history require that at *each successive attempt* the antidote should be administered." . . .

Croker's Tory bias can be observed in most of his reviews. His animosity is aroused not only by the ultra-Liberal man of letters such as Hunt and Shelley, and, by association, Keats and later Tennyson, but also by his Parliamentary opponent, the Whig Macaulay. The threat posed by such men as Hunt is, of course, magnified in the light of contemporary events in France, but it is a political threat in only one of its aspects. It is even more dangerous morally and religiously. Such men, in Croker's view, are followers not of Christ, but of Lucretius and Epicurus. . . . (p. 63)

It is noteworthy that Croker's attack on Keats . . . is preceded by onslaughts on Leigh Hunt, with a note directed against Shelley . . . , though this last is probably not by the author of the article himself. Croker's attack on Keats is only incidental to a whole barrage directed about this time not merely by Croker, but also by other *Quarterly Review*ers, against the body of what he calls "ignorant scribblers and . . . exasperated jacobins." . . . Besides the writers already named, these include Hazlitt. Croker considers Keats merely as a "neophyte" in the faith of which Hunt is "hierophant." . . . Similarly, fifteen years later, Tennyson is presented as merely a follower of Keats. . . . (pp. 63-4)

In Croker's criticism moralism, jingoism and Toryism go together with literary values which are asserted less explosively. Thus, he is grateful that English good taste and sense have discovered the golden mean between the extremes of classical and romantic which so perplex the French. . . . This literary evaluation parallels Croker's idealistic view of England politically, at least until the Reform Bill of 1832. Negatively, he attacks Keats and Hunt not merely for their supposed religious and political views, but also, more tolerably, for their innovations in versification and poetic diction.

Croker's literary values can be seen most pleasantly in his early treatments of the novels, particularly the work of Maria Edgeworth and Scott. He admires Edgeworth's novels because they combine the general with the individual, and "the varieties of human character into one action." . . . He praises such a combination of values later in George Croly, the author of *Paris: A Poem,* since he exhibits "a union of piety and poetry, of what is right in politics, respectable in morals, correct in taste, and splendid in imagination." . . . Edgeworth's work is, moreover, probable, as well as moving and elevating. With his romantic contemporaries Croker stresses the importance of feeling, even though with him it is feeling that is delimited by considerations of religion and morality. He emphasises the importance of feeling even in wit, and he deplores its absence from the heartless, misanthropic writings of Voltaire, Swift, and Walpole. . . . The acceptable didactic element Croker admires in the fiction of Edgeworth, as he deplores its absence from Fielding and Smollett, not to mention Sterne with his "obscure and filthy sensualities." . . . On the other hand, Croker later is unable to tolerate the didacticism of Charles Kingsley and "the Socialist school." . . .

The speculative slant of [his] early reviews is perhaps less innate than an attempt to emulate a similar feature in Jeffrey's contributions to the *Edinburgh Review.* In 1814 Croker presents a pocket history of the novel which he sees as progressing from the level of the ideal to that of the general, represented by the admired LeSage and Fielding, and to that of the individual, represented by Edgeworth and Scott. In these last down-to-

earth writers there is less evidence of moral elevation, but the didactic element is happily still strong.

Croker admires realism in the novel, as in pictorial art, but this is realism tempered by the important considerations already noted. Unadulterated fidelity to fact is to be deplored as morally dangerous. Only a short step separates the "disgusting" accuracy of Godwin's *Mandeville* . . . from the fantastic insanity of his daughter's *Frankenstein*. . . . This is comparable to the later attitude of Abraham Hayward in the *Quarterly,* where he objects to the excessive realism of Dickens's prison scenes in *Pickwick* as being out of place in "books of this sort." Hayward generalizes: "When the object is merely to soften or agitate, the ideal should greatly preponderate over the actual." . . . (p. 64)

On anti-realistic grounds Croker regrets Scott's attempt to combine history with romance in *Waverly.* In reviewing *The Antiquary* in April, 1816, he declares the attempt to have been a failure. Moreover, the combination is undesirable, not only for the sake of achieving the appropriate fictional aura, but also from the standpoint of general morality. Further, the combination takes away from the dignity and truthfulness of history itself. Croker thinks of history very austerely, carefully distinguishing, for example, between the quality of Walpole's letters and that of his memoirs: "the gossip and scandal, which in a familiar letter are not merely tolerated, but, as it were, expected and welcomed, are grievous offences against good taste as well as good faith when it is attempted to array them in the grave and responsible character of history." . . . Thus, in dealing with memoirs the historian must work as carefully as a judge in a court of law: "Walpole is like any other prejudiced witness: though there may be a predominance of falsehood and a general discolouration, there will yet be, in a long and varied narration, a considerable portion of voluntary or involuntary truth. The art of using such a witness to advantage is a minute study of the admitted facts—a general balancing of the antagonist testimonies, and a conscientious sifting of the evidence in each minute portion of the case, so as finally to discriminate between the real colour of the transaction and the partial colour of the narrative." Croker's image of himself here as a judge is characteristic of the [*Quarterly Review*er], but he develops the image in an attractive and unusual aesthetic direction, as he continues: "It ought to be something like restoring an old picture which has been painted over: you must wash off the whole varnish, and then proceed with great care and caution to remove the suppositious touches from the original ground." . . . Similarly, Croker would examine such a work as Macaulay's in order "to discover, to analyze, to decompose the anecdotical colouring . . . and to separate the general course of events from the exceptive instances which the anecdotical historians build so much upon." From such an austere, craftsmanlike point of view Croker criticizes other historians as well. (pp. 64-5)

All these comments can be read as subordinate to his grand attack on Macaulay on account of his *literary* approach, following in the footsteps of Scott . . . , relying too heavily on flashy rhetoric and insubstantial anecdote. The critic's attitude, which possesses the aesthetic quality already remarked, is vividly summarized in a letter written before reading and reviewing Macaulay's work:

> I should like to distinguish History properly so called, from history moralized or dramatized as by Shakespeare and Scott, or made anecdotical like, as I presume from the extracts,

Macaulay's. History should be a statue, cold, colourless, if you will, but giving the limbs and features, the forms and the dimensions with unalterable, severe mechanical exactness; and not a picture to be coloured to the artist's eye, to be seen in a particular light, and to be helped out with accessories of detail selected not for truth but for effect. I admit that such pictorial history is more amusing; but does it really give you a truer view of the state of things? I doubt— and I can quite understand your eye being relieved in turning from the gaudy gaslight of Macaulay to the soberer taper of Mr. Grote. . . .

Though he aspires to be the judge of good history-writing, Croker is more at ease with the memoirs of the eighteenth century, particularly those of Horace Walpole. There is some ambivalence here. He lavishes eight articles on an author whom he declares to be cold, heartless, insincere, vain, selfish, misanthropic, sarcastic, unamiable, and irreligious. The explicit justification for the interest in Walpole is to be found not only in his historical importance, but also in the qualities of his letters. These, though cold and betraying a search for effect rather than the truth, are at their best when witty and full of gossip, and when gleams of good sense and feeling shine through. Above all, Croker praises Walpole's letters on stylistic grounds, admiring their epigrammatic and metaphoric cast. . . .

The problem of fascination and repulsion, latent and manageable where Walpole and the eighteenth century are concerned, comes to the fore in connection with modern, and particularly modern French, literature. Croker writes of Béranger: ''We confess that we feel some hesitation and difficulty in risking to offend the morals and the taste of our readers, by alluding to the indecency and impiety of the original passages . . . but such an exposure is, we think, necessary to an understanding of the state of the public mind in France.'' . . . (p. 65)

Croker is especially fascinated by modern French novels: ''We have upon our table before us upwards of one hundred novels of this class published within the last five years . . . and there is not in that number half a dozen . . . in which a lapse of female chastity is not the main incident; there are not ten in which that lapse is not adulterous;—in not a few it is accompanied by incest and other unnatural profligacies; and in a majority it is attended by suicide and murder.'' In these novels there are ''passages which swarm in every page, but which we trembled and shuddered to read, and which we dare not copy.'' . . . Croker is thus faced with the problem of justifying his interest in such immoral works, as well as the public discussion of them. He solves the difficulty in the following way:

> If . . . *ours* was the only channel by which the existence of such works could be known, no consideration would induce us to mention them; but when it is notorious that they are advertised in a thousand ways over the whole reading world—when we see them exhibited even in London in the windows of respectable shops— when they are to be had in circulating libraries—when we know, *as we do know*—that they find their way, under the specious title of *'the last new novel,'* into the hands of persons wholly or partially ignorant of their real character— nay, into *ladies' book clubs*—we feel that is our duty to *stigmatize* them with a BRAND which may awaken the attention of those who,

not condescending themselves to read what they may consider as mere harmless trash, might and *do* unconsciously permit these conductors of moral contagion to infect their dwellings. . . .

In the eyes of one nineteenth-century critic, at least, Croker's technique of suppression-revelation was unsuccessful. E. M. Thompson commented in his copy of the edition of the letters of Lady Suffolk that Croker had been ''too squeamish in suppressing indecent words—for his *stars* often suggest a worse word than really occurs.''

In his general defense of what he considers to be valuable, and when he is on quite safe ground, Croker employs a method the vigor of which quickly becomes severity and then brutality. He justifies such a transition in reviewing Maturin's *Melmoth the Wanderer:*

> On the occasion of Mr. Maturin's former novel, we veiled our disgust, and, out of respect for the clerical character, conveyed our censure under the appearance of irony; we endeavoured *castigare ridendo,* anxiously hoping by that lenient method of treatment to be spared the necessity of having recourse to the more violent remedies:—but we have been disappointed, and the new ravings of the unhappy patient exceed the old in folly and indelicacy. Indeed, Mr. Maturin has contrived, by a *'curiosa infelicitas'*, to unite in this work all the worst particularities of the worst modern novels. Compared with it, Lady Morgan is almost intelligible— The Monk, decent—The Vampire, amiable— and Frankenstein, natural. . . .

(pp. 65-6)

Croker is, of course, perfectly conscious of his art. He calls himself with some justice ''the old *flagellifer*.'' . . . An aspect of his vigorous method is a lack of chivalry towards women, such as Lady Morgan and Mme D'Arblay. This is in marked contrast to the Whig courtesy of Jeffrey and Macaulay in the *Edinburgh Review.*

The instruments of Croker's severity include a pseudo-scientific classificatory method, as used against Lady Morgan's *France:* ''Bad taste—Bombast and Nonsense—Blunders—Ignorance of the French Language and Manners—General Ignorance—Jacobinism—Falsehood—Licentiousness, and Impiety.'' . . . Another instrument is the use of fragments snatched out of context, for example, in reviewing Hunt's *Rimini*. . . . This was a technique perfected by Jeffrey. Croker also uses an unsubtle irony, as against Tennyson . . . , as well as hyperbole, ridicule, and downright abuse. As an example of the last, in an early review Croker calls George Colman ''a *poetical jack-pudding*'' . . . , but his favorite words of condemnation are ''trash'' and ''poison.'' This last is applied to both Moore and Macaulay. However, the most refined point of abuse stings with an esoteric gallicism. Croker writes of Macaulay as a ''*badigeonneur*'' . . . and of Moore's ''*polissonerie*.'' . . .

The underlying seriousness of Croker's attitudes has been stressed here, but it should be noted that both publisher and public welcomed his ''short, smart'' articles because they added ''zest'' to the *Quarterly Review.* Croker himself believed that the public appetite craved ''a great deal of the *piquant*.'' He wrote to Murray, quoting Touchstone: ''a fool 'is meat and drink to me' . . . Pray help me to a fool and I will return him to you roasted, boiled, fricassied or devilled, as you may please.'' . . .

One may note the combination of cannibalism and sensuality in the imagery here. It is unfortunate from the literary point of view that the fools thus cooked and eaten included Keats and Tennyson.

In conclusion, it must be acknowledged that Croker played an important role as an early participant in the influential periodical literature of the nineteenth century. He wrote from a conservative standpoint, and he showed a real appreciation of scholarship, both historical and literary. However, he was perhaps more concerned with defending the status quo than with vindicating a Burkeian tradition. He flashed out with savage satire against radical and innovative writers. He betrays as he does so the elements of rancor and of ambivalence in his age. His is one voice in the expression of a wide spectrum of critical opinion, on whose range the formidable culture of nineteenth-century England burgeoned. (p. 67)

> *Peter F. Morgan, "Croker As Literary Critic in the 'Quarterly Review'," in* The Wordsworth Circle, *Vol. VIII, No. 1, Winter, 1977, pp. 62-8.*

---

## ADDITIONAL BIBLIOGRAPHY

Brightfield, Myron F. *John Wilson Croker.* Berkeley: University of California Press, 1940, 464 p.

A book-length biography of Croker. Brightfield's study contains excerpts from Croker's correspondence and a bibliography of his works.

De Beer, E. S. "Macaulay and Croker: The Review of Croker's Boswell." *Review of English Studies* X, No. 40 (1959): 388-97.*

A discussion of the animosity between Thomas Babington Macaulay and Croker based on the former's harsh review of Croker's edition of *The Life of Samuel Johnson* by James Boswell (see excerpt above, 1831).

Feiling, Keith Grahame. "Croker." In his *Sketches in Nineteenth Century Biography*, pp. 55-67. 1930. Reprint. Freeport, N.Y.: Books for Libraries Press, 1970.

A biographical sketch that focuses on Croker's political career.

Kern, John D; Schneider, Elisabeth; and Griggs, Irwin. "Lockhart to Croker on the *Quarterly.*" *PMLA* LX, No. I, Part I (March 1945): 175-98.*

Reprints extracts from those of John Gibson Lockhart's letters to Croker that shed light on the authorship of articles published anonymously in the *Quarterly Review*.

[Kirvan, A. V.] "M. Montalembert and John Wilson Croker; or, *Traduttore Traditore.*" *Fraser's Magazine* LIII, No. CCCXVII (May 1856): 563-83.

A detailed critique of Croker's translation from French of *The Political Future of England* by Le Comte de Montalembert.

Lucas, F. L. "Croker and Tennyson." *The Times Literary Supplement*, No. 2339 (30 November 1946): 596.*

Suggests that Croker, rather than John Gibson Lockhart, was the author of the *Quarterly Review*'s 1833 attack on Alfred Lord Tennyson's *Poems*.

Martineau, Harriet. "John Wilson Croker." In her *Biographical Sketches*, pp. 60-9. New York: Leypoldt & Holt, 1869.

A frequently quoted biographical sketch that portrays Croker as vindictive and narrow-minded.

# Emily Eden

## 1797-1869

English novelist and letter writer.

Eden was a gently satirical novelist whose wit and manner in *The Semi-Attached Couple* and *The Semi-Detached House* are often compared with those of Jane Austen. Of secondary importance is her reputation as an observant and humorously ironic letter writer established by such collections as *Letters from India*. Living at the center of the most influential political and social circles of her age, Eden captured in her novels and letters much of the flavor of aristocratic Whig society in England during the first half of the nineteenth century.

Born into a large family in Westminster, Eden was schooled at home by her mother, a tutor, and a succession of governesses. Her father, the first Baron Auckland, had a distinguished diplomatic career and served in various capacities, including ambassador to Spain and Holland. As a result, Eden grew up in a politically and socially sophisticated environment, surrounded by prominent statesmen and future prime ministers. After the deaths of her father in 1814 and her mother four years later, she lived with her sister Fanny and brother George. She later accompanied them to India where George served as governor-general from 1836-1842. Following the deaths of George and Fanny in 1849, Eden's health declined, and though her house had become a popular meeting place for many notable politicians, she gradually retired from society until her death in 1869.

Eden's experiences in India provided the material for two collections of letters, *"Up the Country": Letters Written to Her Sister from the Upper Provinces of India* and *Letters from India*. Both works have elicited praise for their vivid and perceptive commentary. To many critics, Eden's correspondence exemplifies the finer qualities of letter writing as a literary form because she relates personal experiences and observations that translate for the reader into larger, more universal truths. Another collection, *Miss Eden's Letters,* bears testimony to the enduring interest of her correspondence. Critics have praised its cultured sensibility and humane insight into the people and politics that made up the society in which she lived.

Eden first turned to writing fiction in the early 1830s when she began the work later published as *The Semi-Attached Couple*. She pursued her writing as a hobby, sharing her work with a close friend who was also writing a book. The partially completed novel was set aside for almost thirty years, and only the success of *The Semi-Detached House* prompted Eden to resurrect her earlier work. The plot of *The Semi-Attached Couple* concerns a husband and wife whose upbringing makes them initially unsuited to one another, but who eventually understand the strength of their feelings after the husband suffers a serious illness. In style and subject matter the novel owes much to the works of Jane Austen. This influence is particularly evident in Eden's witty and satirical approach to the niceties of social intercourse, with its subtle shades of snobbery and rank. Her debt to Austen is still marked—though less so—in Eden's later novel.

*The Semi-Detached House* details the difficulties faced by Lady Chester, a young upper-class woman, when she is thrust into

close proximity with strangers after moving into a semi-detached house while her husband is abroad. Eden uses Lady Chester's situation to analyze the awkward relations between members of diverse social classes and the effects of wealth and financial speculation on the social aspirations of a growing middle class. When this work became a popular success, Eden's publisher requested another novel, and *The Semi-Attached Couple* was published the following year. Comparing the two novels, critics have focused on the vivacity and effortless comedy of *The Semi-Attached Couple* versus the economical structure and serious purpose of *The Semi-Detached House*.

Eden's works have received positive commentary whenever accorded critical attention. The republication of her novels in the 1920s and 1940s brought forth consistent praise from the small group of critics who reviewed them, and a recent single volume edition of the novels also elicited appreciative remarks. While John Gore has suggested Eden as a rival to Austen, most critics agree that though both authors are effective novelists of manners, the latter far surpasses the former in depth of characterization and moral insight. Other reviewers single out Eden's novels for their historically accurate renderings of a social class and for their polished—if limited—satire. Today Eden is considered a minor novelist, quietly celebrated by a limited audience for her humorous evocations of upper-class Whig society.

**PRINCIPAL WORKS**

*The Semi-Detached House*  (novel)  1859
*The Semi-Attached Couple*  (novel)  1860
*"Up the Country": Letters Written to Her Sister from the*
    *Upper Provinces of India*  (letters)  1866
*Letters from India*  (letters)  1872
*Miss Eden's Letters*  (letters)  1919

---

**WALTER BAGEHOT**  (essay date 1859)

[*Bagehot was a prominent nineteenth-century English economist, journalist, and critic. In the following essay, he compares Eden's portrayal of social snobbery in* The Semi-Detached House *with that of William Makepeace Thackeray. Bagehot describes Eden's treatment of snobbery as a "healthier" one than Thackeray's and declares the novel's chief merit to be its "cheerful and habitual good sense." This essay was first published in the* Saturday Review *on August 27, 1859.*]

Although [the *Semi-Detached House*] is not exactly a novel with a dogma, it is a novel with a notion. The notion is that we ought not to dislike to live in a semi-detached house. (p. 169)

The purpose of the book, in so far as it has a purpose, is to teach us that we should take life easily and frankly—associate with the people whom chance throws in our way, if they seem sensible and pleasant—that we should not be too much pleased at speaking to persons of superior rank, nor too anxious to avoid those who may be below us. Our readers will say that, after all, this is not very new, and it certainly is not. But it is a great achievement to teach an old lesson in an enlivening way, and this is a lesson which it is rather difficult to teach with perfect good taste. Mr. Thackeray, for example, has been teaching it with consummate ability for many years; but perhaps he makes too much of it. We fancy he considers it both more difficult and more important than it really is. He a little over-rates the intensity of the snobbish propensities—he dwells on them almost sympathizingly. . . . We can scarcely perhaps give the *Semi-Detached House* a higher sort of praise than that it teaches Mr. Thackeray's peculiar doctrine in a healthier and better way than he does. The two varieties of snobbishness—that of running from our inferiors and that of making up to our superiors—both occur pretty often in this book, and both are laughed at. They are allowed to be venial sins, but it is shown that they are ludicrous—that they interfere with the tranquillity of life and with the chances of enjoyment that turn up in it—that sensible persons, whatever their rank may be, laugh at them. Of course there is nothing new in the lesson; but there is a good-natured contempt in the way it is given that is telling. We can fancy it curing, or half-curing, the vice. Mr. Thackeray, we fear, only teaches people to hide the indications of it. (pp. 169-70)

One defect of the lesson not to object to a 'semi-detached house' is that it will not make a plot of itself. The authoress of the book, wishing to have a plot, like other novelists, has been obliged to annex one from other sources. She has not, however, thought it worth while to look out for a complicated one. The hero is a certain man named Willis, who has lost his wife, and trades on his disconsolateness ever after. He really makes a great deal of it in general society. Much attention is paid him by way of relief, and the minor comforts of life are constantly

offered to him by way of compensation. These, however, he resists, and perseveres in his unconquerable depression, naturally feeling that while it obtained him so many pleasant things it would be foolish to relinquish it. There is one pursuit in life in which a conspicuous grief for a deceased wife is likely to be rather an incumbrance than a help—and that is, the wooing of a second. In Mr. Willis's case the difficulty is increased by his having selected a matter-of-fact young lady who works out her ideas with unusual distinctness. (p. 172)

We do not know whether such a plot was intended to be anything; but it is nothing. No art could spin much out of so slight a material. Besides, the moment Mr. Willis ceases to be mournful, he ceases to be anything. He has, in other respects, no more character than the mute in a funeral. He displays all through the book one trait, and one only. The moment he loses that, he vanishes in our fancy entirely. As this is the case, we need not say that the merit of the book does not lie in the story, but in its sparkling dialogue, its good subsidiary characters, and its cheerful and habitual good sense. (p. 173)

> *Walter Bagehot, in his* The Collected Works of Walter Bagehot: Literary Essays, Vol. II, *edited by Norman St. John-Stevas, The Economist, 1965, 400 p.*

**EMILY EDEN**  (essay date 1860)

[*In her preface to* The Semi-Attached Couple, *Eden discusses some of the societal changes that had transpired since she began her novel three decades earlier. She asserts that its age has rendered it something of a historical curiosity, but hopes that as such it may still be of interest.*]

[*The Semi-Attached Couple*] was partly written nearly thirty years ago, before railroads were established, and travelling carriages-and-four superseded; before postage-stamps had extinguished the privilege of franking, and before the Reform Bill had limited the duration of the polling at borough elections to a single day. In re-writing it I might easily have introduced these and other modern innovations; but as I believe the manners of England to be as much changed as her customs, there would have been discrepancies between my scenes and characters: the background would not have harmonized with the figures.

When I wrote it, I thought it a tolerably faithful representation of modern society; but some young friends who are still living in the world, from which I have long retired, and who have read it with the indulgence of happy youth, condescendingly assure me that it is amusing, inasmuch as it is a curious picture of old-fashioned society. Therefore, in giving it to the world, I trust that to my own contemporaries it may have the charm of reminding them of their youth, and that to the young it may have the recommendation of being a strange Chronicle of the Olden Time.

> *Emily Eden, in a preface to her* The Semi-Attached Couple, *1860. Reprint by The Dial Press, 1979, p. ix.*

***THE SATURDAY REVIEW,*** LONDON  (essay date 1866)

[*In* Up the Country, *Miss Eden has performed an astonishing feat*], writing two volumes about life in India which are thoroughly amusing and readable from the first page to the last. It is a feat which only those can really appreciate who know from doleful experience how monotonous Indian life is. . . . Her journal about a dull country is infinitely more amusing than nineteen out of twenty journals about interesting countries. . . . (p. 209)

[We do homage to Miss Eden's] miraculous gift of weaving a charming story out of materials which are a proverb for their dryness, and we have no profane wish to inquire whether her book does or does not contain really valuable information. We pronounce her, without hesitation, one of the greatest bene-factors to India that have arisen in our day. She has rescued it from the imputation of being dull. . . .

Among the most humorous touches in the book are those de-scribing the sufferings which the Governor-General's rank sub-jects him to at the hands of merciless secretaries, who will not hear of his unbending one inch from the proper magnificent routine. . . .

[Though] the authoress is chiefly indebted for her descriptions to her native friends, she gets plenty of good-humoured fun out of Europeans. . . . [She] never seems to go anywhere with-out bringing back some comical trait of character or life, which is described in the happiest style. Everybody and everything is pressed into the service of good-natured caricature, or rather comes into it quite naturally, for the humour is rarely or never strained, although there is scarcely a page which is not enli-vened by some touch of it. (p. 210)

Nor, indeed, is it quite fair to treat her work as if its chief or only merit were that it is amusing. It is something so new to find a book about India thoroughly enjoyable from beginning to end, that this is naturally perhaps the first aspect that suggests itself. But, to say nothing of the really instructive, no less than pleasant, glimpses it affords of Eastern life, *Up the Country* has much more than mere humour to recommend it. We have already said that it is a work which one is more disposed gratefully to welcome than to analyse, but we may perhaps so far venture upon an analysis as to add that probably it owes one of its chief charms to the gentle touches which here and there remind us of the writer's yearning for her English home. On merely artistic grounds, the quiet English home, with its simple life and small circle of loving friends, makes an effective background to the noisy pomp and strange dusky faces which surround the wanderer in the distant East. But its introduction is due to a purer and more pleasing source of inspiration than conscious art—to a genuine kindliness and warmth of sentiment which lends so indescribable a charm to the writings of an English lady when it is combined with a genial sense of humour and a highly cultivated taste. (pp. 210-11)

> *A review of "Up the Country," in* The Saturday Review, *London, Vol. 22, No. 564, August 18, 1866, pp. 209-11.*

### THE TIMES LITERARY SUPPLEMENT   (essay date 1919)

How, in writing of Miss Eden's letters, is one to avoid the old commonplace about the penny post and the death of letter writing? From Miss Eden herself, . . . one would have expected witty letters. But [her correspondent] Pamela FitzGerald, in no way distinguished save as the daughter of Lord Edward and the mother of a very large family, in our opinion surpasses her. She is, perhaps, the more spontaneous and the richer natured of the two. Be this as it may, the memorable thing is that both ladies have the art of letter writing by nature. . . . You will not find them rashly confiding, or introspective; their sense of humour is their standby; they would rather laugh than cry; and whatever they think proper for a letter they know how

to put into words. . . . [Miss Eden's letters are] easy, witty, controlled, the young lady knowing how to turn a sentence as, presumably, she knew how to run her needle in and out of the pattern of her embroidery. . . . Neither Miss Eden nor Miss FitzGerald, one is refreshed to find, dwells in decencies for ever; they are surprisingly open in their speech. Both of them, too, have a passion for the country, even in its more horrid aspects. . . .

[These letters provide] a story, a drama; the characters marry and change and grow up, and we watch them changing beneath our eyes. . . . Miss Eden's letters bring so much of life into view, and hint at so much more than we can see, that far from falling asleep over her pages, as [the editor] predicts, we feel that we have been completely woken up and set gossiping.

> *"Real Letters," in* The Times Literary Supplement, *No. 929, November 6, 1919, p. 626.*

### THE SPECTATOR   (essay date 1920)

[Miss Eden's] abiding claim to the notice of posterity was her talent for friendly letter-writing. She had the true note of col-loquial case which few people ever achieve in their letters, and still fewer retain. She gossips charmingly; her observations on her friends and acquaintances are not the mere threadbare in-anities which can interest only those who know the persons concerned, but real characteristic illuminative things which are nearly as pleasant to read now as they were when they were written eighty or ninety years ago. Her most intimate friend, Pamela [FitzGerald] . . . , had an equally marked gift for talking with the pen, and perhaps greater vivacity and humour: and the correspondence between these two brilliant women, which is preserved in [*Miss Eden's Letters*], abounds in gay nonsense, vivid descriptions, shrewd reflections, and fine wholesome, lovable human nature. . . .

High spirits, wit, taste, insight, fine breeding, never go stale; the letters are as modern as Mme. de Sévigné's—more modern, probably, than those you got by the last post.

> *"The Gentlest Art," in* The Spectator, *Vol. 124, No. 4780, February 7, 1920, p. 179.*

### JOHN GORE   (essay date 1924)

*[In the following excerpt, Gore favorably compares Eden's work to the novels of Jane Austen.]*

Were I to-morrow condemned for my presumption to a life sentence, with the right to take with me to prison one novel from all the world, and one only, I should not hesitate over my choice, but should plump for *Pride and Prejudice*, but assuredly I would take with me [Emily Eden's] *The Semi-attached Couple* in preference to *Sense and Sensibility*. (p. 495)

In plot and characterisation [*The Semi-attached Couple*] is a curious parallel to *Pride and Prejudice*, and there can be no doubt that Miss Austen's masterpiece—then at the height of its popularity—was not absent from Miss Eden's consciousness when she wrote, and that the Douglas family had their origin in the Bennets. (p. 496)

There is, indeed, in the character of Teviot, more than a touch of Darcy; that selfishness "in practice but not in theory" is common to both the young men, and though Teviot had not, like Darcy, fallen in love "beneath him," a pride, bred of spoiling and flattery from childhood, led him remorselessly to learn the bitter lesson from a young and inexperienced girl. (p. 497)

That *The Semi-attached Couple* is a gold mine to the social historian is not in doubt. It gives an unrivalled picture of the family life of a great Whig family in the early part of the nineteenth century, and few who take it up will deny its charm and humour, or manage to resist the peculiar "atmosphere" with which Miss Eden has managed to invest her story.

Miss Austen laid her characters, for the most part, a degree lower in the social scale, and only seldom turned her attention to the aristocracy. Miss Eden, on the other hand, frankly despised the middle classes and the landed gentry, and depicted intimately the life of her own exclusive world, and could yet draw, a thing which, curiously, Miss Austen never once attempted, the characters of servants, with brilliance of touch and a knowledge of flunkeiana which Thackeray might have envied.

It has been said of Miss Austen that if, by her upbringing, she was shielded from the truth, very little of the truth was shielded from her. And it has been said that genius means nothing more than the power of guessing right. Miss Austen is acknowledged as a genius, and genius is not claimed for Miss Eden. The latter knew her world, and knew considerably more about life, men and women, than did Miss Austen.

The genius of Miss Austen made up for her inexperience by accurate guessing. It is claimed for Miss Eden that by a power of selecting judiciously from her own wide experience, she was often able to accomplish what the genius of Miss Austen accomplished.

It is best to be a good guesser—a genius. It is better to be a judicious and clever photographer than an indifferent guesser.

Miss Eden's description of Teviot's feelings in the height of his passion reveals the fact that she knew a good deal about men, and, like Miss Austen, little of the truth was shielded from her. . . . [Her style] is easy, and falls into a graceful and natural antithesis, and everywhere abounds in humour. (pp. 497-98)

With servants, Miss Eden could accomplish what Miss Austen never attempted, dared not even guess; and the letter from Lady Teviot's maid to Lady Eskdale's maid, written from St. Mary's, where the Teviots were honeymooning, should find a place in any collection of gems of the gentle art, and will stand for all time among the master pieces of below-stairs humour. (p. 499)

It is with the Douglas family that Miss Eden brings back most nearly the atmosphere of *Pride and Prejudice*. Indeed, in the characters and home life of Mr. and Mrs. Douglas, an almost unique literary parallel is produced.

The spite and vulgarity of Mrs. Douglas irresistibly brings to mind Mrs. Bennet, and the husbands, small squires, interested in their turnips, less vulgar than their wives, lazy-minded, tolerant, disliking spiteful criticism of their richer neighbours who gave such good dinners, fond of their daughters, bored with their wives, are parallels so close as to leave a doubt in the mind of anyone intimately familiar with both novels, as to which gentleman was squire of Longbourn, and which of Thornbank. (pp. 499-500)

[The book] teems with neat little thumb-nails, and reveals a charming wit. All the minor characters are clever miniatures, with the exception only of Lady Portmore, where Miss Eden

departed from the admirable standard she set herself, and laid on the colours with a trowel.

Lady Eskdale is triumphantly convincing as she sails through life, sheltered from the mildest winds. Fondly addressed as "dear" by her nephews, she inspired terror in the breasts of unfortunates not in the charmed circle. Eliza Douglas, resembling rather Catherine Morland than any other of Miss Austen's girls, has none of the wit of Elizabeth Bennet. She owes her settlement in life to a facility for hero-worship, and a gentle willingness to please, when, in a fit of loneliness, the prematurely bored Col. Beaufort (Ernest, aged 26!) surrenders to her promise to fetch and carry for him through life, and attend to his farm accounts, as she does for papa's, in the gloomy barrack of an estate which the Colonel has seldom visited. Lord Beaufort, Mary Forrester, Fisherwick, the unkempt secretary, with his blind devotion for his political chief, the foreigner more British than the Briton, all these characters walked in real life across the saloons of Bowood, Chatsworth, Panshanger, Brocket, Lansdowne and Devonshire Houses.

Miss Eden, proud, diffident, dreading publicity, hiding her talent, brings this extinct race before us with a sureness of touch which has not received, hitherto, the approbation which it is entitled to expect from posterity. (p. 500)

The country which Miss Eden opens out in *The Semi-attached Couple* belongs, indeed, to a civilisation far older, far stranger to us to-day than the land of the Pharoahs. It is on that account that to a generation which pines for something fresh, something new, Miss Eden should come as a Godsend, and obtain, at this late hour, that place in the Pantheon of Novelists which she merits; not perhaps in the Hall of Honour, not in the centre of the Bouquet, but near by, as befits one who, though not the Rose, has lived with the Rose. (p. 501)

*John Gore, "A Rival to Jane Austen," in* The London Mercury, *Vol. IX, No. 53, March, 1924, pp. 495-501.*

## THE TIMES LITERARY SUPPLEMENT   (essay date 1927)

"The Semi-attached Couple" has now had its appearance refurnished to suit modern tastes. . . . [It] has been benevolently and wisely rescued, though possibly to the surprise of those on whose tables it still lingers. One may hope that this rescue will be followed by that of "The Semi-detached House." But perhaps "The Semi-attached Couple" is the more interesting of the two; for it was written thirty years before the other, and Miss Eden, in her preface, when it was at last published, suggested that to the young it might have the interest of a "strange Chronicle of the Olden time" [see excerpt above, 1860]. In which case the older book is probably the better, and, as Miss Eden points out, things had changed by the time it was published and the later novel was written. Things had changed; and the Whig aristocracy was no longer so perfectly homogeneous and easily observable a world, a world so eminently suitable both for the chronicler of "olden time" and for those who like such chronicles, for the social historian in fact. But the world was also narrow enough for the novelist; and Miss Eden was a novelist who could scarcely have written novels at all if she had not had an easily charted world before her. She knew her world entirely by experience, and not by the imagination and intuition of the born novelist. The comparison between her and Jane Austen is natural and not to be avoided; and in his preface Mr. Gore does not avoid it, for he says that Jane Austen probably knew much less, from experience at any rate, about life than did Miss Eden. But Jane

Austen, he concedes, had genius, and by genius is meant the power of guessing right. Perhaps then it would have been better if Jane Austen had lived in an ampler world, though this seems a rash thing to say, and certainly the narrower the world she lived in and observed, the better it was for Miss Eden's novels. . . .

It is surely to the smallness of her cosmos that we must attribute that matured, and even magnificent, calm with which Miss Eden dealt with the complexities of life. Indeed she noticed very little complexity, but just enough to make her novel. . . . Such a novel could perhaps only have been written in an age of security and certainty, and by one who was typical of that age; for nowadays to attain that same calm it is necessary to write about innocent and rural pursuits. In Miss Eden's second novel the middle classes have arrived and they unsettle everything. Miss Eden tried to settle it; but she is not so convincing as when she had nothing to settle and everything to observe and experience.

> *"Miss Eden's Novels," in* The Times Literary Supplement, *No. 1350, December 15, 1927, p. 955.*

### ANTHONY EDEN   (essay date 1928)

[*Anthony Eden, a distant relation of the novelist, wrote a number of historical works and several volumes of political memoirs. He is chiefly remembered for his distinguished political career that spanned more than three decades and culminated in his tenure as prime minister of England from 1955-57. In his introduction to* The Semi-Detached House, *he focuses on the novel as a product of the author's unique personality, one formed by "all the gifts and prejudices of her birth and upbringing."*]

[Eden's novels] offer an interesting contrast; each had its champions at the time of its first publication, each will have them to-day. While *The Semi-Detached House* may lack something of the vivacity of its earlier rival, it can claim more of serious purpose in the narrative. *The Semi-Detached House* is the more carefully designed; it is written with a surer and a maturer pen.

There is naturally a tendency to compare Emily Eden with others among her contemporaries, and to trace the influence of her predecessors in her writing. But such exercises will not lead us very far, for the influences which Miss Eden underwent, and of which that of Miss Austen's novels was probably the most important, were but secondary in their action upon her. From first to last in every word she wrote Emily Eden was intensely herself, and too masterful a personality to follow in the wake of any influence, however strong. Throughout her writings her own personality is the dominant note.

Miss Eden wrote of those among whom she had been born, and with whom she was to spend all but a few years of her life. She was Emily Eden, with all the gifts and prejudices of her birth and upbringing, the daughter of "Haughty Nell," a Whig in the days of Government by Whig oligarchy. All her life was spent within that small circle which to her was England, and which indeed did represent England abroad and govern England at home. She knew that world and loved it; what more natural than that she should write about it with ease and charm, and with a rare gift of humour?

We may complain that the world which Miss Eden portrays for us in her two novels is small, but for her it was complete; and how well she knew it! We shall not regret the experience if we follow her into it. (pp. viii-ix)

*The Maharajah Ranjit Singh as drawn by Eden during her travels in India.*

*The Semi-Detached House* cannot be acclaimed as a work of genius. Its writing formed the pastime of a woman of fashion when fashion was the world. Emily Eden, clever, well-read, a good letter-writer and a witty conversationalist, found its writing a pleasant exercise. Those who read her books again may enjoy with her the leisured ease of the age of which she wrote, and may spend with her a passing hour among those whose lives were cast in pleasant places. If they lived in glasshouses, have we the right to cast a stone? (p. xii)

> *Anthony Eden, in an introduction to* The Semi-Detached House *by Emily Eden, Frederick A. Stokes Company Publishers, 1928, pp. v-xii.*

### THE NEW YORK TIMES BOOK REVIEW   (essay date 1928)

Lovers of Jane Austen will find much to please them in ["**The Semi-Attached Couple**"], . . . so frankly and obviously fashioned after the model of "Pride and Prejudice." Yet though the author of "**The Semi-Attached Couple**" was evidently a close student of the adorable Jane, her novel is no mere imitation, but a tale with much spirit and many merits of its own. The world in which the Hon. Emily Eden . . . moved, was necessarily very different from that of the Steventon parsonage where lived the peerless Miss Austen, so that, in a way, "**The**

Semi-Attached Couple" supplements and enlarges the view of eighteenth century society presented by "Emma" and the rest. For while Miss Eden's work has none of the genius of Jane Austen's, and little of her wit, while there is no character in "The Semi-Attached Couple" to be compared with any among Miss Austen's more notable creations, and Helen Beaufort is colorless indeed beside Elizabeth Bennett, Mrs. Douglas might well have played a secondary part in "Sense and Sensibility," or even in "Mansfield Park." . . .

[It] is on its characterization, its atmosphere and agreeable style that the importance of Miss Eden's novel depends, not on its plot. It is a lively, clearly drawn picture of the aristocratic English life of the time, its people are many of them likable and all of them real, and it is related with no small amount of humor. Mrs. Douglas, who firmly believed that: "Nothing is too bad to be true, and nothing is true that is not bad," and could with difficulty be persuaded to make any exception in her general policy of thinking the worst of every one, is a flesh-and-blood person, and though Lady Portmore is over-emphasized to the verge of caricature, it is a caricature of an entirely recognizable type, a female of a species we have all met, while Lord Beaufort and Mary Forrester, who began with more than the little averson recommended by Mrs. Malaprop, are a delightful couple. A lively, entertaining comedy of manners, full of shrewd observation, thoroughly readable and often very amusing. "The Semi-Attached Couple" was worth rescuing for the benefit of those in search of enjoyment, as well as for that of readers who wish to know something of the habits and ways of thought of a great English "country" family, one hundred years ago.

*"In Jane Austen's England," in* The New York Times Book Review, *April 29, 1928, p. 8.*

### MURIEL MASEFIELD   (essay date 1934)

Lovers of Jane Austen, who lay down *Persuasion* or *Sanditon* with a sigh, because there is no more for them to re-read until a lapse of time has made it possible to begin once more with *Sense and Sensibility,* may find a welcome balm in two novels by Emily Eden, which are in the same tradition and yet have their own individuality and period *bouquet*. It is not claimed that these two novels are works of genius, but they amply fulfil the promise of their titles—*The Semi-Attached Couple* and *The Semi-Detached House*—with an attractive blend of satire and scenes of particularly pleasing family life, and they were written by a woman of the world about the society which she knew as intimately as Jane Austen knew that of the country gentry of her day. (p. 90)

To modern readers, to whom both books are necessarily *period pieces, The Semi-Attached Couple* is the more attractive of the two, even if the other is a better constructed story. . . . (pp. 91-2)

[In *The Semi-Detached House*] minor characters are well developed, with play for Emily Eden's satirical vein. . . . The Baroness is rather too much exaggerated to be convincing, but the Hopkinson circle is very real.

These two novels are slight and short, but they leave a pleasant taste on the mental palate, and their blend of irony and good feeling saves them from insipidity: they are also free from tedious padding and over-strained morality. Once again, they are to be recommended to lovers of Jane Austen to bridge at

least one of the recurring gaps between re-readings of her novels. (p. 94)

*Muriel Masefield, "Emily Eden and Her Novels," in her* Women Novelists from Fanny Burney to George Eliot, *1934. Reprint by Books for Libraries Press, 1967; distributed by Arno Press, Inc., pp. 90-4.*

### ANTHONY EDEN   (essay date 1947)

Emily Eden had a humble opinion of her two novels. They are unpretentious. Only little more than a century separates us from the times of which Miss Eden wrote. Yet the sweep of the changes, both mechanical and political, has completely transformed her world. . . . In the pages of Miss Eden's novels, we can live again the world in which she lived. She knew it very well, for she was herself throughout her life a personality around whom much of it revolved. Her opportunities for observation were exceptional; she records the result for us here [in *The Semi-Attached Couple*] with wit, and charm, and humour.

In the days of which Miss Eden wrote, a few families may be said to have absorbed the political life and influence of England. From their places in the two Houses of Parliament and from their country houses, in which parties of them might stay together for a month or more at a time, they virtually ruled Britain during a challenging phase of her national existence. Miss Eden herself was born during the Napoleonic Wars, and was a member of, or related to, many of the families with whom this power lay. She knew the political scene intimately, and could portray it with a light but sure touch which was essentially her own. (pp. xv-xvi)

[Her] people and scenes and also, perhaps most of all, the vivid picture of the Election in the days before the secret ballot, are vivid and realistic—are, in fact, the England of that day.

To read *The Semi-Attached Couple* again is to get a glimpse of the social history of an England of which scarcely a vestige remains. Yet it is not necessarily to deplore the changes in order to enjoy this picture of a world remote from our own in its entire pattern of life and close to our own in the humanity of its characters. (p. xvi)

*Anthony Eden, in an introduction to* The Semi-Attached Couple *by Emily Eden, Houghton Mifflin Company, 1947, pp. vii-xvi.*

### ERNESTINE EVANS   (essay date 1947)

Everybody in [*The Semi-Attached Couple*] is definitely a character, and speaks and acts with individual style. The movement of the story through visits, weddings, elections, illnesses and more weddings is as if all the old prints of the period had pleasantly turned into cinema with no fell propaganda purpose, but robust zeal to entertain. . . .

For me the jewels in the book are the descriptions of the elections days, days not day, before the Reform bill. . . . Jane Austen, to whom the Hon. Emily is often compared, never saw politics with so sharp an eye. Bribery and persuasion, the beer, the heartlessness, the plums and pay-offs are described most fruitily. The Hon. Emily was a lady, but she missed very little, and she enjoyed it all—how cabinets are made, and marriages, weather and the seasons, the manners of high society, its servants and neighbors, its fools parasites, and above all, its landed freedom from a lot of modern pressures. No more entertaining conversation piece is likely to come to porch or library this summer. The Hon. Emily's little novel survives its long burial intact.

*Ernestine Evans, "Marvellous Married Pair," in* New York Herald Tribune Weekly Book Review, *June 15, 1947, p. 2.*

## CARLOS BAKER  (essay date 1948)

Shorter and slighter than its predecessor, **"The Semi-Detached House"** confronted its author with a severer test of her skill as story-teller: Could she make her characters sufficiently engaging so that a sympathetic reader would be continuously interested in their welfare throughout a tale in which almost nothing happens? Her success is clear. No scene-shaking antics distort her quiet and often witty prose. Will the debutante Hopkinson daughters achieve the happy status of matrons? Will their widower brother-in-law win the hand of the lonely heiress? In such inconsequential matters, the reader finds himself taking a surprising interest because it is possible to like the characters as simple people—a rare phenomenon in current fiction. When the two halves of the titular house have come pleasantly together and vanquished their problems and got what was coming to them, the little idyl is complete and the reader is satisfied.

One is sorry to observe in this connection a hint or two of anti-Semitism in the otherwise irreproachable authoress. Since the prejudice is neither pervasive nor unmixed with pity, sensitive readers may be willing to forgive this historic lady her historic fault.

*Carlos Baker, "Idyllic, Mid-Victorian," in* The New York Times Book Review, *October 17, 1948, p. 46.*

## VALERIE GROSVENOR MYER  (essay date 1979)

[*In her introduction to a single volume edition of* The Semi-Attached Couple *and* The Semi-Detached House, *Myer addresses Eden's strengths and weaknesses as a novelist of the upper-class society in which she lived. Stressing both the historical value of Eden's writing and its witty charm, Myer discusses the author's portrait of newlywed life in* The Semi-Attached Couple *and her treatment of the relations between members of different social classes in* The Semi-Detached House.]

[Emily Eden] was an aristocratic spinster, shrewd, well-read and observant, and above all witty. . . . Emily's letters are full of lively political commentary and gossip, yet the world of politics, so important in her daily life, is only lightly touched on in the novels. In her journal for June 14 1838, she wrote: "I am interested in Indian politics just now, but could not make them interesting on paper." She made documentary use of her Indian experience, but restricted her fiction to the world of London society, though her life extended far outside. It was richer, more varied and interesting than that of most women at any time.

Her eye was sharp; her books are comedies of manners and her dialogue is racy and amusing. Unlike greater, but less aristocratic novelists, she knew how the upper classes in the nineteenth century talked among themselves, and we believe her. Both novels are rich mines for the social historian. *Nouveaux-riches* characters pepper their talk with French phrases; the more secure laugh at them for it. The amiable, jolly (and perfectly *comme il faut*) Lord Chester in **The Semi-Detached House** speaks of a friend's "old woman" and his "kids." (p. iii)

**The Semi-Attached Couple** is about the early adjustments of marriage. . . . The quarrels of young Lord and Lady Teviot take place in settings of enormous luxury, and their problems may seem remote and trivial to us. But Emily Eden observed the isolation and grief that the "splendid" marriage must have brought to so many of her contemporaries. Girls married off from the schoolroom to men they hardly knew, required to adapt to new roles, suffered various forms of shock. The misunderstandings between Lady Helen and her husband arise convincingly from the socio-economic context. (p. iv)

Their expectations of marriage are different because of the differences in their formative experiences. Emily Eden is as aware as any post-Freudian of the importance of nurture. The dilemma of such marriages must have been real enough, but Emily was unable to find a true fictional solution. Lord Teviot falls seriously ill while travelling abroad and Helen flies to his side to nurse him. The convention that sickness ennobles both the sufferer and the nurse was to run tiresomely through Victorian fiction. As a means of reconciling Helen and her husband, it is a transparent plot-manipulation; in real life, such couples doubtless went their separate ways.

Dickens and George Eliot were later to show the disastrous consequences for the married relationship of the Victorian oppression which fashioned infantile women. There is nothing of this in Emily Eden; like Jane Austen's heroines, Emily's are restricted socially, but seem to notice it less than Jane's do, perhaps because they are grander and richer. Although Helen is unrestrained in her intimacy with her sisters, in her relationship with her husband she operates largely under the social code of discretion in which she has been strictly schooled by her mama. As Lady Eskdale is an idealised character, Emily Eden does not, I think, criticise the conventional upbringing Helen receives; but she does recognise and depict the problems caused by the separation of men's lives and women's in her society.

There are frequent affectionate references to Jane Austen, and her influence on both books is marked. Emily Eden's satire is sharp and convincing, though less savage than Jane Austen's; like Jane Austen's, Emily Eden's observation and pointed wit make us give sudden snorts of laughter. **The Semi-Attached Couple** refers explicitly to *Pride and Prejudice* and could be described as basically the same story with the equivalent of the Darcy family as the main characters. The story of the Douglases . . . is a framing device to open and close the plot.

Mrs. Douglas is a splendid bitch, drawn with truth and accuracy. Her theme-song is how her friends have aged since she saw them last. Mrs. Douglas

> had never had the slightest pretension to good looks; in fact, though it is wrong to say anything so ill-natured, she was excessively plain, always had been so, and had a soreness on the subject of beauty, that looked perhaps as like envy as any other quality. As she had no hope of raising herself to the rank of beauty, her only chance was bringing others down to her level; people may go on talking for ever of the jealousies of pretty women; but for real, genuine, hard-working envy, there is nothing like an ugly woman with a taste for admiration. Her mortified vanity curdles into malevolence; and she calumniates where she cannot rival.

*A drawing by Eden, showing cheetahs sent by the King of Oude to accompany her brother George's expedition through northern India.*

Emily Eden's quality is shown by the unexpected adjective "hard-working", normally a term of approbation; its application to envy is piquant, for we realise that Mrs. Douglas brings to her spiteful, self-absorbed malice all her vital energies, which might profitably have been used for more worthwhile things. Her husband's response (he has married her for her money, not her looks) is to "let her have a reasonable share of her own way, and spend a reasonable portion of her own money; he abstained from all vivid admiration of beauty within her hearing."

***The Semi-Detached House***, written later but published first, is a better book, more original, better plotted. (pp. iv-vi)

There are echoes of [Austen's] *Persuasion*; the bluff seafaring Captain Hopkinson remarks of the dubious Baron that he is unlikely to set the Thames on fire, a comment made in *Persuasion* by Admiral Croft about Sir Walter Elliott. But Sir Walter represents a dying rural squirearchy, while the Baron represents a new threat, the deplorable world of mushroom financial empires. Business is now king; landowners no longer live on rents, timber and other produce; they indulge in speculation. There are financial crashes. There is a thread of malicious anti-semitism in this part of the plot. There is some fun at the expense of those members of Parliament, "radical in politics and unpolished in manner, who had manfully voted for the removal of Jewish disabilities. Whether they knew what the disabilities were, or what would be the effect of their removal, is doubtful; but they somehow had an idea that they were voting against gentlemen and bishops, and church and state, and they felt proud of themselves." Emily expects her readers to respond by sharing the prejudices of her time and her class.

Emily Eden, in her position, could hardly be expected to take a radical line herself. She takes the standard aristocratic view that polished manners and intelligent conversation are desirable when they can be found, but, failing the cultivated arts, goodness of heart is the next best thing and is to be cherished. "It is really refreshing to hear conversation about facts, not about people," says Lady Chester. There are several literary allusions, and leading characters know Shakespeare, Wordsworth and Byron well enough to quote extensively. But there is sympathy for the uncultured but goodhearted Mrs. Hopkinson, who, faced with the prospect of meeting a cabinet minister, gets all flustered because she "cannot read *The Times* and should not know a reform bill from a budget."

"Tact, which is only another name for consideration of the feelings of others, is compatible with unpolished manner," writes Emily in the authorial voice. Mrs. Hopkinson's confusions delight us, but her unaffected goodness earns respect.

Mrs. Hopkinson is bewildered by the literary conversation of the clever, unhappy, detached Rachel (a modern character), niece to the odious Baroness. Rachel, in danger of being asked to make an inventory for a removal, responds,

> Ye household cares, vex not my mind
> With your inglorious strife,
> Nor seek in sordid chains to bind
> My free aesthetic life,

a poem she tells us she made up herself on the spur of the moment.

Mrs. Hopkinson is puzzled by the word "aesthetic," which was newly fashionable at the time. . . . Rachel wonders how it would be possible to manage without it. Rachel is alienated by her intelligence and the only use she can find for her analytical powers is to account for her own unhappiness. She recognises it is her loveless childhood that has made her "what I am—cold, distrustful, unloved and unloving."

She marries the gloomy widower Willis, who makes a great parade of being inconsolable for a wife he did not truly love. There is an element of macabre farce about the present he chooses for his little boy: the gift is a model tomb, with a skeleton on a spring which jumps out when the lid is opened.

But Willis is the necessary touch of shadow in a sunny picture. The gloomy puritanism of the nineteenth century does not weigh very heavily on these characters, who are in general cheerful, though it is sketched in on the periphery of their lives. (pp. vii-viii)

> *Valerie Grosvenor Myer, in an introduction to* The Semi-Attached Couple *by Emily Eden, The Dial Press, 1979, pp. iii-viii.*

## MARGHANITA LASKI  (essay date 1980)

[*Laski acknowledges that "nastiness and a sufficient relish of polished cynicism spice" Eden's novels, but concludes that the author was unsuccessful in creating "nasty" characters of consistency and credibility.*]

Emily Eden knew well that unadulterated decency is, at least to the novel-reader, dull. . . . So both in [*The Semi-detached House*] and in *The Semi-attached Couple* . . . nastiness and a sufficient relish of polished cynicism spice the stories.

There is no pretending that Emily Eden is an *excellent* novelist, and the comparisons with Jane Austen which are often made are not really relevant. But we have always enjoyed a wide range of good novelists of the second class, and such is she. There are some things she can manage very well, like silly young women and jealous young men, and loving family life. She has sometimes a memorably witty turn of the pen, as when she describes a woman as wearing "a mistaken bonnet". And she is coolly good on babies, whether in the one book, when the adoring women are convinced they have made the baby laugh, but "To impartial observers the face made by baby under this manipulation was one of unutterable disgust and annoyance"; or, in the other book, when the new baby has just been shown to its aristocratic grandfather and the young mother anxiously asks, "Was the baby good?"—"as if it has passed its six hours of life in deep study of the whole duty of man."

Where, to my mind, Miss Eden fails is with her nasty people, and this is odd, since most novelists find nasty people easier to make than nice ones. In *The Semi-attached Couple*, Miss Eden's main nasties are the mischief-making egotistical Lady

Portmore and the jealous malicious Mrs Douglas, mother of the amiable secondary heroine. Lady Portmore is never more than the sum of her attributes, shown so repeatedly in action as to bore; and the same is true of Mrs Douglas until the acquisition of an unexpected son-in-law converts her, not very probably, to something nearer gentleness. Again, in *The Semi-detached House* the resolutely mournful widower becomes boring in his resolute mournfulness, though he too has an improbable conversion, through his love for the good, though nearly marred Jewish heiress Rachel. But Rachel's flashy, social-climbing, and only apparently rich Jewish relations are relentlessly intolerable.

So long as Jane Austen is quite forgotten, much pleasure derives from reading Emily Eden's stories, and not least as novels of manners. (pp. 182-83)

> *Marghanita Laski, "Keep the Home Fires Burning,"* in Country Life, *Vol. CLXVII, No. 4306, January 17, 1980, pp. 182-83.**

## PHYLLIS ROSE   (essay date 1982)

[*Rose praises Eden's handling of emotion and characterization in* The Semi-Attached Couple.]

The only thing more gratifying to find than a good book is a good book which has been neglected. **"The Semi-Attached Couple,"** . . . popular for years, then largely forgotten, is a comic gem about how difficult it can be to get used to being married, even if you are young and beautiful and your husband is rich and titled. . . .

Emily Eden wrote in frank admiration of Jane Austen, so similarities between her work and Austen's should not be surprising. Eden picks up just after an Austen novel would end, with the splendid match—in this case between the lovely Helen Beaufort and that most eligible bachelor, Lord Teviot. It is a story of misunderstandings and cross-purposes intensified rather than dispelled by marriage, a tale of pride and reticence. Teviot, madly in love with his wife, resents her attachment to her family, and any sign of high spirits in her not directly caused by himself. She reads his furious jealousy as disapproval; unused to passion, an innocent, scared of him, she loses her vivacity. He is all the more convinced that she does not love him. It is a sophisticated psychological drama played out in pleasant country houses, at dinners, on visits, through letters, in witty dialogue and with clever commentary.

The first sentence of the book, which presents the ill-natured Mrs. Douglas speaking in a "tone of triumphant sourness," signals us that Eden writes in that epigrammatic tradition of wit and precision which stretches back through Austen to the 18th century and surfaces occasionally later in the work of such 20th-century writers as Nancy Mitford and E. F. Benson. . . .

Like Jane Austen, Emily Eden is particularly shrewd with emotional dynamics, pithy psychological characterization and the application of the general to the particular. . . .

The Edens were a powerful and well-connected family; Emily Eden observed a broader cut of life, at a higher social level, than Jane Austen. If you open her selected letters—and I recommend them to you . . .—you sense immediately her social authority. (p. 9)

The combination of public engagements and domestic satisfaction which distinguished Emily Eden's family life informs her fiction as well, giving it a genial worldliness quite different from the dominant spirit of Jane Austen's tenser depth charges. Eden's *semi*-novels result from that tradition of moral commentary, character assessment and sheer narrative that is embodied in gossip about other people's marriages; they have the pleasant accents of good conversation—and some of its unpleasant accents, too. . . .

Emily Eden is not Jane Austen but she is a fine writer whose life, letters and novels deserve attention and will delight those who give it. (p. 28)

> *Phyllis Rose, "Taking Up Where Jane Austen Left Off," in* The New York Times Book Review, *April 25, 1982, pp. 9, 28.*

**ADDITIONAL BIBLIOGRAPHY**

Courtney, Janet E. "Voyagers to India: Emily Eden." In her *The Adventurous Thirties: A Chapter in the Women's Movement*, pp. 113-26. London: Oxford University Press, Humphrey Milford, 1933.
> Describes Eden's life and travels with her brother and sister when the former served as governor-general of India. Courtney emphasizes Eden's intelligence, fortitude, and independence in coping with life on the subcontinent.

Dunbar, Janet. *Golden Interlude: The Edens in India, 1836-1842.* London: John Murray, 1955, 239 p.
> A chronological account of the Edens' life in India, including the military and political events that transpired under George Eden's leadership of the country.

Hannay, Prudence. "Emily Eden As a Letter-Writer." *History Today* 21 (July 1971): 491-501.
> A largely biographical article outlining the course of Eden's life as reflected in her letters.

# Gustave Flaubert

## 1821-1880

French novelist and short story writer.

The following entry presents criticism on Flaubert's novel *Madame Bovary: Moeurs de province* (1857; translated as *Madame Bovary: A Tale of Provincial Life,* 1881). For a complete discussion of Flaubert's career, see *NCLC,* Vol. 2.

*Madame Bovary* is considered Flaubert's masterpiece and the most influential French novel of the nineteenth century. Through painstaking attention to detail and constant revision, Flaubert created a dispassionate rendering of psychological detail and achieved an exquisite prose style that has served as a model for innumerable writers. The novel has also significantly influenced the art of criticism. Since its publication, *Madame Bovary* has become one of the most frequently discussed books in the history of world literature, and the quality of commentary leads many scholars to concur with Paul de Man's assertion that "contemporary criticism of fiction owes more to this novel than to any other nineteenth century work."

Flaubert was born in Rouen, where his father was chief surgeon at the city hospital, the Hôtel Dieu, and his mother was a well-known and respected woman from a provincial bourgeois family. Flaubert lived with his parents, brother Achille, and sister Caroline in an apartment at the hospital. Many commentators acknowledge the dual influence of the bourgeois and medical environments on the author; in fact, Charles Augustin Sainte-Beuve commented, "Son and brother of eminent doctors, M. Gustave Flaubert wields the pen as others wield the scalpel." As a youth, he attended school at the Collège Royal de Rouen, traveled with his family throughout France, and spent summer vacations at Trouville. There, Flaubert first met Elisa Schlesinger, a married woman for whom he harbored a lifelong infatuation. Although Flaubert was interested in literature and began to write at an early age, upon receiving his baccalaureate degree he honored his parents' wishes and reluctantly registered for law school in Paris. In 1844, he experienced the first attack of what is now believed to have been epilepsy; as a result, he abandoned his law studies and devoted himself to writing. Both his father and sister died in 1846, and the author, his mother, and his infant niece moved to the family home at Croisset, near Rouen. Except for several trips abroad and to Paris, Flaubert remained at Croisset until his death.

The genesis of *Madame Bovary* is well known. In 1849, Flaubert completed the first version of *La tentation de Saint Antoine (The Temptation of Saint Antony),* a novel inspired by a painting by the elder Brueghel. After reading the novel aloud to his friends Maxime Du Camp and Louis Bouilhet, Flaubert asked for their frank opinion. They declared the work a failure, saying, "We think you should throw it into the fire, and never speak of it again." According to Du Camp and Bouilhet, the subject of Saint Antony was an unfortunate choice because it encouraged Flaubert's tendency toward excessive lyricism and lack of precision, and they persuaded him to abandon historical subjects and begin a novel that would be contemporary in content and realistic in intent. In his *Souvenirs littéraires,* Du Camp contended that he then told Flaubert a true story about a local provincial couple whom sources refer to by various

names, including Delaunay, Delamare, Delamarre, and Deslauriers. The wife disgraced herself within the community by incurring large debts and taking a lover, and she subsequently committed suicide; her husband, a doctor, killed himself soon after. In addition to Du Camp's commentary, scholars note several other sources that may have provided the inspiration for *Madame Bovary.* After Flaubert's death, a manuscript entitled *Mémoires de Mme Ludovica* was found among his papers. This work is purportedly an autobiography of Louise Pradier, wife of the painter James Pradier and a friend of Flaubert, and some critics see a resemblance to the life of Emma Bovary. Others dispute that Flaubert modeled his story after any source, pointing to his declaration "Madame Bovary, c'est moi," or, Madame Bovary is myself. Because his letters demonstrate a fascination with stories of aspiring and frustrated women and because several early unpublished works include themes and prototypes of characters that appear in *Madame Bovary,* many conclude that Flaubert's imagination was in fact the primary source for the novel.

During the composition of *Madame Bovary,* which occupied him from 1851 to 1856, Flaubert corresponded with Louise Colet, his "Muse" and mistress until 1854. These letters are hailed by critics for their insight into his method of composition, artistic technique, and aesthetic doctrine. Flaubert closely documented his phenomenal effort and the novel's progress in his letters, and they bear witness to the slow and laborious development of *Madame Bovary*. Flaubert composed at most a few paragraphs each day, and these he would repeatedly revise; writing was for him an arduous process, made more difficult by his obsessive concern with stylistic perfection. His goal was to achieve a style "as rhythmical as verse and as precise as the language of science." He rejected the use of synonyms; instead, he searched for *le seul mot juste*, or the most precise word, to convey each thought. Yet he also sought rhythm and harmony in his prose, evaluating every word for its exact meaning as well as the sound it produced within the sentence.

An equally important goal for Flaubert in composing *Madame Bovary* was to achieve an objective, impartial, and impersonal work of art: "Nowhere in my book must the author express his emotions or opinions." Flaubert struggled throughout his career to overcome a natural romantic tendency toward lyricism, fantasy, and exoticism. While expressing this tendency in his other works, he purposely avoided it in *Madame Bovary:* "No lyricism, no comments, the author's personality absent." He believed that an objective work required documentation, or the impartial recording of every detail that could explain the psychology of the characters and their role in the story. Still, most critics do not believe that his work consists solely of observation; indeed, many credit him with combining insight from direct experience with his profound imagination.

Often described as a satire on romantic beliefs and the provincial bourgeoisie, *Madame Bovary* relates the story of Emma Bovary, a bored housewife whose dreams of romantic love, primarily gathered from popular novels, are unfulfilled through her marriage to a simple country doctor. She attempts to realize her fantasies through love affairs with a local landowner and a law clerk, and later through extravagant purchases. Unable to pay her debts and unwilling to bear her disgrace or to tolerate or conform to bourgeois values, she commits suicide.

The novel was first published in serial form from October 1 to December 15, 1856, in the French periodical *Revue de Paris*. The autocratic government of Napoléon III rigidly controlled the press, often censoring the republican views expressed in the journal. Thus, the *Revue* was already a government target, and some critics view the attack on *Madame Bovary* as politically motivated. The administration suspended publication of the *Revue* and charged its editors, printer, and Flaubert with offenses against public and religious morals. During the trial, the lawyer for the prosecution, Ernest Pinard, portrayed the novel as blasphemous and obscene, citing the lascivious details, Emma's revelry in her adulterous affairs, and the mixture of the sacred with the profane. The lawyer for the defense, Marie-Antoine-Jules Sénard, countered that the novel was indeed a moral work, describing Flaubert's intention as "the incitement to virtue through horror of vice." According to Sénard, Emma's adultery provides only the illusion of happiness—adultery soon loses its glamour and leads to disillusionment, torment, regret, and remorse. The ending of the novel, Sénard argued, underscores its moral nature. Following the uninspired prosecution and the brilliant defense (see *NCLC*, Vol. 2), Flaubert and his colleagues were acquitted on February 7, 1857. When published in book form two months after the trial, *Madame Bovary* enjoyed both widespread sales and significant serious commentary, much of which echoed the arguments presented in the obscenity trial.

Most critics concur that the two most perceptive essays on *Madame Bovary* in the nineteenth century were written by Sainte-Beuve and Charles Baudelaire (see *NCLC*, Vol. 2), and their comments are considered the foundation for subsequent criticism of the novel. According to Sainte-Beuve, the complete absence of goodness formed the principal defect of the novel, and he particularly faulted the unrelieved pessimistic view of provincial life: "Pettiness, squalor, pretentiousness, stupidity, routine, monotony, and boredom. The fields and villages, so natural and true, . . . will serve [Flaubert] only as a setting for portraying vulgar, banal, blindly ambitious creatures, totally ignorant or only semiliterate whose love affairs are devoid of delicacy." However, Sainte-Beuve commended the work's impersonal tone, contending that no character spoke for the author. Recognizing Flaubert's style as his distinguishing quality, Sainte-Beuve also praised his use of point of view, calling it "the keystone of his method, his poetics." Baudelaire's appreciative essay, which is said to demonstrate his complete understanding of the underpinnings of the novel, delineates Flaubert's thought processes as he created *Madame Bovary*. After summarizing criticism by Sainte-Beuve and others that the novel lacks characters "representing morality or expressing the conscience of the author," Baudelaire responded, "Absurdity! Eternal and incorrigible confusion of functions and genres! A true work of art needs no indictment." Baudelaire contended that Flaubert included no obvious moral, thus forcing his readers to draw their own conclusions. Baudelaire was one of the few critics to demonstrate any sympathy for Emma, finding her more deserving of pity than of approbation, blame, or scorn.

Nineteenth-century critical discussion of *Madame Bovary* focused on several different topics, and opinions varied widely on each. The novel was frequently discussed in relation to the romantic and realist literary movements: several critics noted such romantic qualities as lyricism and the influence of various romantic writers on Emma, while others pointed to its realistic characterizations and close description of scenery. Another concern was whether the novel was deliberately immoral, or, instead, a warning against immoral behavior. Closely tied to this topic was the debate over whether Flaubert's artistry, which many critics praised, could compensate for the offensive subject. In addition, the value of Flaubert's objectivity and analytical approach was hotly debated. Not until the end of the century, when there was greater recognition of the distinction between ethics and aesthetics, did critics begin to evaluate Flaubert and his novel on the basis of his artistry.

The most important modern evaluations of *Madame Bovary* date from the 1930s, as commentators adopted the approach of the developing New Criticism movement to provide close explications of imagery and language. The major topics in twentieth-century criticism of *Madame Bovary* reflect the qualities Flaubert highlighted in his letters. Many critics have examined his technical virtuosity in the novel, focusing on its style and structure, the narrative stance of the author, and the use of imagery and symbolism. Modern scholars have also studied the letters and early drafts of *Madame Bovary* for insight into Flaubert's creative process.

Various elements of Flaubert's literary technique have been singled out for praise, including the style and structure of the novel. Style was discussed by Albert Thibaudet and Marcel Proust in the French periodical *Nouvelle revue française*. In his important but untranslated essay, Thibaudet pointed to Flaubert's style and concluded that he was not a born writer. Proust demurred, arguing that despite Flaubert's inexpert handling of metaphor, he was a natural prose stylist by virtue of his grammatical innovations (see *NCLC*, Vol. 2). In particular, Proust commended his use of tenses, specifically the imperfect, to convey a sense of "time *passing*." W. von Wartburg studied sentence structure and diction in *Madame Bovary*, noting Flaubert's search for the exact word that would illuminate the "inner unity between word, thing, and concept." Several critics, notably Stephen Ullmann, have analyzed Flaubert's use of *le style indirect libre*, or free indirect speech, as a method of discourse. Vladimir Nabokov appraised Flaubert's "counterpoint method," which consists of "parallel interlinings and interruptions of two or more conversations or trains of thought." Both Martin Turnell and Victor Brombert have investigated the relationship between structure and symbolism.

Opinion of Flaubert's narrative stance in *Madame Bovary* has varied widely since the nineteenth century. His contemporaries considered Flaubert an impersonal writer because he did not make his views clearly known; today, his narrative technique is widely praised and is one of the most important issues in modern criticism of the novel. Percy Lubbock (see *NCLC*, Vol. 2) was the first to analyze this subject in depth. He contended that although Flaubert does not use direct interpolations, his presence is demonstrated by the selection of material, the description of detail, and, most importantly, the fluctuating narrative point of view. According to Lubbock, Flaubert both identifies with Emma, describing her environment from her perspective, and views her objectively. Subsequent critics have developed Lubbock's discovery of a dual narrative perspective: Erich Auerbach analyzed authorial stance in relation to the development of realism, lauding Flaubert's innovative objective and subjective method of presentation; Jean Rousset commented on Flaubert's use of varying narrative perspectives and specifically noted the smooth and imperceptible transitions between them; and Brombert praised the dual perspective as ambiguous for its combination of ironic mockery and sympathetic understanding.

Analyses of Flaubert's use of imagery and symbol figure prominently in criticism of *Madame Bovary*. Proust briefly discussed Flaubert's use of metaphors, which he dismissed as weak and lacking in beauty. Both D. L. Demorest and Jean Pierre Richard argued that Flaubert's water imagery symbolizes physical love, although Richard also contended that it represents dissolution or death. Georges Poulet uncovered in *Madame Bovary* a recurring "metaphor of the circle," linking it to the author's conception of reality. Rousset detailed the relationship between the novel's narrative structure and the symbolic importance of windows, which provide a panoramic perspective to the novel. Brombert discussed imagery in relation to structure, arguing that the novel is constructed around clusters of interrelated images that form cyclic themes.

Several critics have explored Flaubert's use of imagery in conjunction with his letters and early drafts of *Madame Bovary* to illuminate his creative process. This approach was first used by Charles Du Bos, who analyzed excerpts from the letters to uncover the "inner environment," or creative unconscious, in which the work originated. Similarly, Albert Béguin compared passages from the original draft of the novel with the published version, noting stylistic alterations that weaken the work. Richard's discussion focuses on imagery as a means of understanding Flaubert's psychological state and its manifestation in *Madame Bovary*. In examining the letters and early drafts, Richard attempted to identify specific experiences from Flaubert's life and trace their transformation into recurrent images and themes in the novel.

In analyzing the variety of critical approaches to *Madame Bovary*, Paul de Man has described a division among Flaubert scholars: many English and American critics have focused on objective technique, while many French critics preferred to explore Flaubert's subjective voice, which includes the rich metaphorical style that they consider Flaubert's natural idiom. De Man thus explained the concentration by French writers on the early drafts, with their profusion of metaphorical and figurative elements. The diversity of critical methods and the vast quantity of exegesis devoted to *Madame Bovary* attests to the validity of Lubbock's conclusion that this work "remains perpetually the novel of all novels which the criticism of fiction cannot overlook." Today, commentators consistently acknowledge Flaubert's contribution to the development of the novel, lauding *Madame Bovary* as one of the most important forces in creating the modern novel as a conscious art form. Recognized for its objective characterization, irony, narrative technique, and use of imagery and symbolism, *Madame Bovary* is universally hailed as Flaubert's masterpiece.

---

## GUSTAVE FLAUBERT  (letter dates 1851-54)

[*The following excerpt includes letters written by Flaubert to Louise Colet, his mistress during the composition of* Madame Bovary. *Critics often turn to Flaubert's correspondence for insight into his artistic technique, method of composition, and aesthetic doctrine. Flaubert closely documented his phenomenal effort and the novel's progress in these letters, so that by reading them one can witness the slow and laborious development of* Madame Bovary. *The dissolution of Flaubert's relationship with Colet in 1854 ended their correspondence before he completed the novel.*]

*[October 23, 1851]*

I am finding it very hard to get my novel started. I suffer from stylistic abscesses; and sentences keep itching without coming to a head. I am fretting, scratching. What a heavy oar the pen is, and what a strong current ideas are to row in! This makes me so desperate that I enjoy it considerably. In this state I spent a good day today, with the window open, the sun on the river, and the greatest serenity in the world. I wrote one page and sketched three more. A fortnight from now I hope to be in gear, but the colors I am working with are so new to me that I keep staring at them in astonishment. (p. 151)

• • • • •

*[March 20, 1852]*

I did nothing for two days—very bored, very idle, very drowsy. Then I gave my clock a mighty winding, and now my life has resumed the tic-tac of its pendulum. I have gone back to my eternal Greek, and will master it in a few months, because that is what I have sworn to do; and to my novel—which will be finished God knows when. There is nothing at once so frightening and so consoling as having a long task ahead. There are so many obstacles to overcome, the hours one devotes to it are so satisfying. For the moment, I am up to my neck in a young girl's dreams . . . The entire value of my book, if it has any, will consist of my having known how to walk straight ahead on a hair, balanced above the two abysses of lyricism and vulgarity (which I want to fuse in a narrative analysis). When I think of what it can be, I am dazzled. But then, when I reflect that so much beauty has been entrusted to me—to me—I am so terrified that I am seized with cramps and long to rush off and hide, no matter where. I have been working like a mule for fifteen long years. All my life I have lived in this maniacal stubbornness, keeping all my other passions locked up in cages and visiting them only now and then, for diversion. Oh, if I ever produce a good book I'll have earned it! Would to God that Buffon's blasphemous words were true ["genius is a matter of endless patience"]. I should certainly be among the foremost. (p. 157)

• • • • •

*[April 24, 1852]*

If I haven't written sooner in reply to your sad, discouraged letter, it's because I have been in a great fit of work. The day before yesterday I went to bed at five in the morning and yesterday at three. Since last Monday I have put everything else aside, and have done nothing all week but sweat over my **Bovary**, disgruntled at making such slow progress. I have now reached my ball, which I will begin Monday. I hope that may go better. Since you last saw me I have written 25 pages in all (25 pages in six weeks). They were rough going. Tomorrow I shall read them to Bouilhet. I have gone over them so much myself, copied them, changed them, shuffled them, that for the time being I see them very confusedly. But I think they will stand up. You speak of your discouragements: if you could see mine! Sometimes I don't understand why my arms don't drop from my body with fatigue, why my brain doesn't melt away. I am leading an austere life, stripped of all external pleasure, and am sustained only by a kind of permanent frenzy, which sometimes makes me weep tears of impotence but never abates. I love my work with a love that is frantic and perverted, as an ascetic loves the hair shirt that scratches his belly.

Sometimes, when I am empty, when words don't come, when I find I haven't written a single sentence after scribbling whole pages, I collapse on my couch and lie there dazed, bogged in a swamp of despair, hating myself and blaming myself for this demented pride that makes me pant after a chimera. A quarter of an hour later, everything has changed; my heart is pounding with joy. Last Wednesday I had to get up and fetch my handkerchief; tears were streaming down my face. I had been moved by my own writing: the emotion I had conceived, the phrase that rendered it, and the satisfaction of having found the phrase— all were causing me the most exquisite pleasure. At least I think that all those elements were present in this emotion, which after all was predominantly a matter of nerves. There exist even higher emotions of this same kind: those which are devoid of the sensory element. These are superior, in moral beauty, to virtue—so independent are they of any personal factor, of any human implication. Occasionally (at great moments of illumination) I have had glimpses, in the glow of an enthusiasm that made me thrill from head to foot, of such a state of mind, superior to life itself, a state in which fame counts for nothing and even happiness is superfluous. If everything around us, instead of permanently conspiring to drown us in a slough of mud, contributed rather to keep our spirits healthy, who can tell whether we might not be able to do for aesthetics what stoicism did for morals? (p. 158)

At times I have feelings of great despair and emptiness—doubts that taunt me in the midst of my simplest satisfactions. And yet I would not exchange all this for anything, because my conscience tells me that I am fulfilling my duty, obeying a decree of fate—that I am doing what is Good, that I am in the Right. . . .

I envision a style: a style that would be beautiful, that someone will invent some day, ten years or ten centuries from now, one that would be rhythmic as verse, precise as the language of the sciences, undulant, deep-voiced as a cello, tipped with flame: a style that would pierce your idea like a dagger, and on which your thought would sail easily ahead over a smooth surface, like a skiff before a good tail wind. Prose was born yesterday: you have to keep that in mind. Verse is the form par excellence of ancient literatures. All possible prosodic variations have been discovered; but that is far from being the case with prose. (p. 159)

• • • • •

*[June 13, 1852]*

I like clear, sharp sentences, sentences which stand erect, erect while running—almost an impossibility. The ideal of prose has reached an unheard-of degree of difficulty: there must be no more archaisms, clichés; contemporary ideas must be expressed using the appropriate crude terms; everything must be as clear as Voltaire, as abrim with substance as Montaigne, as vigorous as La Bruyère, and always streaming with color. (p. 160)

• • • • •

*[July 22, 1852]*

I am in the midst of copying and correcting (with much scratching out) all my first part of **Bovary**. My eyes are smarting. I should like to be able to read these one hundred and fifty-eight [manuscript] pages at a single glance and grasp them with all their details in a single thought. A week from Sunday I shall reread the whole thing to Bouilhet; and the next day, or the day after, you will see me. What a bitch of a thing prose is! It is never finished; there is always something to be done over. However, I think it can be given the consistency of verse. A good prose sentence should be like a good line of poetry— *unchangeable*, just as rhythmic, just as sonorous. Such, at least, is my ambition (one thing I am sure of: no one has ever conceived a more perfect type of prose than I; but as to the execution, how many weaknesses, how many weaknesses, oh God!) Nor does it seem to me impossible to give psychological analysis the swiftness, clarity, and impetus of a purely dramatic narrative. This has never been attempted, and it would be beautiful. Have I succeeded a little in this? I have no idea. As of this moment I have no clear opinion about my work. (p. 166)

• • • • •

*[September 1, 1852]*

You speak about women's sufferings: I am in the midst of them. You will see that I have had to descend deeply into the well of feelings. If my book is good, it will gently caress many a feminine wound: more than one woman will smile as she recognizes herself in it. Oh, I'll be well acquainted with what they go through, poor unsung souls! And with the secret sadness that oozes from them, like the moss on the walls of their provincial backyards . . . (pp. 167-68)

• • • • •

*[September 19, 1852]*

What trouble my **Bovary** is giving me! Still, I am beginning to see my way a little. Never in my life have I written anything more difficult than what I am doing now—trivial dialogue. This inn scene will perhaps take me three months, I can't tell. There are moments when I want to weep, I feel so powerless. But I'll die rather than botch it. I have to portray, simultaneously and in the same conversation, five or six characters (who speak), several others (who are spoken about), the setting itself, and the entire town, giving physical descriptions of people and objects; and in the midst of all that I have to show a man and a woman who are beginning (through a similarity in tastes) to be a little taken with each other. If only I had space! But the whole thing has to move quickly without being dry, and it requires a certain development without being spread thin; and many details which would be more striking here I have to keep in reserve for use later. I am going to put everything down quickly, proceeding by a series of sketches of the ensemble. By repeated revision I can perhaps pull it together. The language itself is a great stumbling-block. My characters are completely commonplace, but they have to speak in a literary style, and the politeness of the language takes away so much picturesqueness from their way of expressing themselves! (p. 170)

•  •  •  •  •

[*October 9, 1852*]

Things have been going well for two or three days. I am doing a conversation between a young man and a young woman about literature, the sea, the mountains, music—all the poetical subjects. It is something that could be taken seriously, and yet I fully intend it as grotesque. This will be the first time, I think, that a book makes fun of its leading lady and its leading man. The irony does not detract from the pathetic aspect, but rather intensifies it. In my third part, which will be full of farcical things, I want my readers to weep. (pp. 171-72)

•  •  •  •  •

[*November 22, 1852*]

I am working quite well, I mean with plenty of energy, but it is difficult to give adequate expression to something one has never felt: long preparations are necessary, and one must devilishly rack one's brains to achieve one's aim without going too far. The gradual development of my character's emotional life is giving me a lot of trouble; and everything in this novel depends on it: for in my opinion ideas can be as entertaining as actions, but in order to be so they must flow one from the other like a series of cascades, carrying the reader along amid the throbbing of sentences and the seething of metaphors. When we next see each other, I shall have made a great step ahead: I'll be plunged into love, the core of my subject, and the fate of my book will be decided; but I think that just now I'm in a dangerous pass. (p. 173)

•  •  •  •  •

[*January 12, 1853*]

I am hideously worried, mortally depressed. My accursed ***Bovary*** is torturing me and driving me mad. Last Sunday Bouilhet raised some objections to one of my characters and to the plan. I can do nothing about it: though there is some truth in what he says, I feel the opposite is true also. Ah, I am very tired and very discouraged! You call me Master. What a wretched Master!

No—perhaps the whole thing hasn't had enough spadework, for distinctions between thought and style are a sophism. Everything depends on the conception. So much the worse! I am going to push on, and as fast as I can, in order to have a complete picture. There are moments when all this makes me want to croak. Ah! I'll be well acquainted with them, the agonies of Art! (p. 179)

•  •  •  •  •

[*January 15, 1853*]

Last week I spent *five days writing one page*, and I dropped everything else for it—my Greek, my English; I gave myself up to it entirely. What worries me in my book is the element of *entertainment*. That side is weak; there is not enough action. I maintain, however, that *ideas* are action. It is more difficult to hold the reader's interest with them, I know, but if the style is right it can be done. I now have fifty pages in a row without a single event. It is an uninterrupted portrayal of a bourgeois existence and of a love that remains inactive—a love all the more difficult to depict because it is both timid and deep, but alas! lacking in inner turbulence, because my gentleman is of a sober temperament. I had something similar in the first part: the husband loves his wife somewhat after the same fashion as her lover. Here are two mediocrities in the same milieu, and I must differentiate between them. If I bring it off, it will be a great achievement, I think, for it will be like painting in monotone without contrasts—not easy. But I fear that all these subtleties will be wearisome, and that the reader will long for more movement. Still, one must be loyal to one's concept. If I tried to insert action, I would be following a rule, and would spoil everything. One must sing with one's own voice, and mine will never be dramatic or attractive. Besides, I am convinced that everything is a question of style, or rather of form, of presentation. (pp. 179-80)

•  •  •  •  •

[*March 27, 1853*]

[The] more I realize the difficulties of writing, the more daring I become; this is what keeps me from pedantry, into which I would otherwise doubtless fall. I have plans for writing that will keep me busy till the end of my life, and though I sometimes have bitter moments that make me almost scream with rage (so acutely do I feel my own impotence and weakness), I have others when I can scarcely contain myself for joy. Something deep and ultra-voluptuous gushes out of me, like an ejaculation of the soul. I feel transported, drunk with my own thought, as though a hot gust of perfume were being wafted to me through some inner conduit. I shall never go very far: I know my limitations. But the goal I have set for myself will be achieved by others: thanks to me, someone more talented, more instinctive, will be set on the right path. . . . Some day I may find a good motif, a melody completely suited to my voice, neither too high nor too low. In any case, I shall have lived nobly and often delightfully.

There is a saying by La Bruyère that serves me as a guide: ''A good author likes to think that he writes reasonably.'' That is what I ask—to write reasonably; and it's asking a good deal. Still, one thing is depressing, and that is to see how easily the great men achieve their effects by means extraneous to Art. What is more badly put together than much of Rabelais, Cervantes, Molière and Hugo? But such quick punches! Such power in a single word! We have to pile up a mass of little pebbles to build our pyramids; theirs, a hundred times greater, are hewn in monoliths. But to seek to imitate the methods of those geniuses would be fatal. They are great for the very reason that they have no methods. (pp. 181-82)

•  •  •  •  •

[*April 13, 1853*]

Finally I am beginning to see a little light in my accursed dialogue with the curé. But frankly, there are moments when I almost feel like vomiting *physically,* the whole thing is so low. I want to express the following situation: my little lady, in an access of religiosity, goes to church; at the door she finds the curé, who, in a dialogue (on no definite subject) shows himself to be so stupid, trivial, inept, sordid, that she goes away disgusted and undevout. And my curé is a very good man, indeed an excellent fellow, but he thinks only of the physical side (the sufferings of the poor, no bread, no firewood), and has no inkling of my lady's moral lapses or her vague mystical aspirations; he is very chaste, faithfully performs all his duties. This must have six or seven pages at the most, and must contain no comment, no analysis (it will all be in direct dialogue). Furthermore, since I consider it very cheap to write dialogue substituting dashes for ''he said'' and ''he answered,'' you can imagine it isn't easy to avoid repetitions of the same turns of phrase. So: you are thus initiated into the torture I have been undergoing for a fortnight. By the end of next week, however, I hope it will all be off my hands. Then, after ten more pages (two long passages), I'll have finished the first section of my Part Two. My lovers are ready for adultery: soon they will be committing it. (pp. 184-85)

・ ・ ・ ・ ・

[*June 25, 1853*]

Only now have I finished my first section of Part Two, the very section I had planned to have ready before our last meeting in Mantes. You see how slow I have been. I'll spend a few more days reading it over and recopying it, and a week from tomorrow will spill it all out to the Hon. Bouilhet. If it passes the test, that will be one great worry the less—and a good thing, too, believe me, for the substructure was very flimsy. Apart from that, I think the book will have a big defect, namely faulty proportions in regard to length. I already have two hundred sixty pages which are merely preliminary to the action, containing more or less disguised descriptions of character, . . . of landscapes, of places. My conclusion, which will be my little lady's death, her burial and her husband's subsequent grief, will be at least sixty pages. That leaves, for the body of the action itself, one hundred twenty to one hundred sixty pages at the most. Isn't that a great flaw? What reassures me (though only moderately) is that the book is a biography rather than a story with a complicated plot. The drama plays only a small part in it, and if this dramatic element is skillfully blended with the rest, so that a uniform, overall tonality is achieved, then perhaps the lack of harmonious development of the various phases will pass unnoticed. Besides, I think that this is rather characteristic of life itself. The sexual act may last only a minute, though it has been anticipated for months! Our passions are like volcanoes: they are always rumbling, but eruption is only intermittent. (pp. 188-89)

・ ・ ・ ・ ・

[*July 15, 1853*]

I have been in excellent form this week. I have written eight pages, all of which I think can stand pretty much as they are. Tonight I have just sketched my entire big scene of the Agricultural Show. It will be enormous—thirty pages at least. Against the background of this rustico-municipal celebration, with all its details (all my secondary characters will be shown talking and in action), there must be continuous dialogue between a gentleman and the lady he is ''warming up.'' Moreover, somewhere in the middle I have a solemn speech by a councillor from the Prefecture, and at the end (this I have already done) a newspaper article written by my pharmacist, who gives an account of the celebration in fine philosophical,

poetical, progressive style. You see it is no small chore. I am sure of my local color and of many of my effects; but it's a devilish job to keep it from getting too long. And yet this kind of thing must be full and ample. Once this is behind me, I shall soon reach my fornication in the autumn woods, with the lovers' horses cropping the leaves beside them; and then I think I'll have clear sailing—I'll have passed Charybdis, at least, even though Scylla may remain to be negotiated. (p. 194)

・ ・ ・ ・ ・

[*October 12, 1853*]

My head is on fire, as it used to be after a long day on horseback. Today it's my pen that I've been riding—and hard. I have been writing since half-past noon without stopping, except for an occasional five minutes to smoke my pipe, and just now an hour for dinner. My agricultural show was giving me such trouble that I decided to put aside Greek and Latin until it was finished, and beginning today I am devoting myself to it exclusively. It is taking too long! Sometimes I think it will be the death of me, and I want to come and see you.

Bouilhet says it will be the best scene in the book. What I am sure of is that it will be new, and that I am aiming at something good. If the effects of a symphony have ever been conveyed in a book, it will be in these pages. I want the reader to hear everything together, like one great roar—the bellowing of bulls, the sighing of lovers, the bombast of official oratory. The sun shines down on it all, and there are gusts of wind that threaten to blow off the women's big bonnets. The most arduous passages in **Saint Antoine** were child's play in comparison. I achieve dramatic effect simply by the interweaving of dialogue and by contrasts of character. I am in the midst of it now. In less than a week I'll have tied the knot on which all the rest depends. I keep feeling that my brain is too small to encompass this complex situation in a single glance. I write ten pages at a time, dashing from one sentence to another. (p. 199)

・ ・ ・ ・ ・

[*October 25, 1853*]

**Bovary** is marching ahead again. Bouilhet was pleased on Sunday. But he was in such high spirits, and so preoccupied with Eros (not that I was the object of his passion), that perhaps he judged too favorably. I am waiting for his second reading, to be sure I am on the right track. I can't be far off it, however. This agricultural show will take me another full six weeks (a good month after my return from Paris). But the difficulties that remain are mostly in the execution. Then I will have to go over the whole thing, as the style is a little choppy. Some passages will have to be rewritten, others eliminated. So it will have taken me from July to the end of November to write *one scene!* If at least I enjoyed doing it! But I will never like this book, no matter how successfully I may bring it off. Now that I have a clear view of it as a whole, it disgusts me. But at least it will have been good training. I'll have learned how to do dialogue and portraits. I will write other books! The pleasure of criticism surely has a charm of its own, and if a fault you find in your work leads you to conceive a greater beauty, isn't this conception alone a delight in itself, almost a promise? (p. 200)

・ ・ ・ ・ ・

[*December 23, 1853*]

I must love you to write you tonight, for I am *exhausted*. My skull feels encased in an iron helmet. Since two o'clock yesterday afternoon (except for about twenty-five minutes for dinner), I have been writing **Bovary**. I am in full fornication, in the very midst of it: my lovers are sweating and gasping. This has been one of the rare days of my life passed completely in illusion, from beginning to end. At six o'clock tonight, as I was writing the word ''hysterics,'' I was so swept away, was bellowing so loudly and feeling so deeply what my little Bovary was going through, that I was afraid of having hysterics myself. I got up from my table and opened the window to calm myself. My head was spinning. Now I have great pains in my knees, in my back, and in my head. I feel like a man who has been fucking too much (forgive the expression)—a kind of rapturous lassitude. And since I am in the midst of love it is only proper that I should not fall asleep before sending you a caress, a kiss, and whatever thoughts are left in me.

Will what I have written be good? I have no idea—I am hurrying a little, to be able to show Bouilhet a complete section when he comes. What is certain is that my book has been going at a lively rate for the past week. May it continue so, for I am weary of my usual snail's pace. But I fear the awakening, the disillusion that may come when the pages are copied. No matter: for better or worse, it is a delicious thing to write, to be no longer yourself but to move in an entire universe of your own creating. Today, for instance, as man and woman, both lover and mistress, I rode in a forest on an autumn afternoon under the yellow leaves, and I was also the horses, the leaves, the wind, the words my people uttered, even the red sun that made them almost close their love-drowned eyes.

Is this pride or piety? Is it a foolish overflow of exaggerated self-satisfaction, or is it really a vague and noble religious instinct? But when I brood over these marvelous pleasures I have enjoyed, I would be tempted to offer God a prayer of thanks if I knew he could hear me. Praised may he be for not creating me a cotton merchant, a vaudevillian, a wit, etc.! (p. 203)

•　•　•　•　•

[*January 2, 1854*]

[Bouilhet] was pleased with my fornication scene. However, before said passage I had one of transition, eight lines, which took me three days and doesn't contain a superfluous word—but which I have to do over again because it's too slow. It is direct dialogue, which I must change to indirect, and there isn't room to say what needs to be said. It must all be very fast and incidental, to be as though thrown away, almost unnoticeable in the book. Following which I still have three or four corrections to make—infinitely small, but they will take me all next week. How slow! How slow! No matter: I keep going. In fact I've taken a long step ahead, and feel a great inner relief, which makes me quite gay and cheerful, even though tonight I was literally sweating from the effort. It's so hard to undo what has been done, and done well, in order to insert something new in its place without revealing the joint.

Preoccupation with morality makes a work of imagination so false and boring! I am strongly attracted to criticism. The novel I am writing sharpens my ability in this respect, for it is above all a work of criticism, or rather of anatomy. The reader will be unaware, I hope, of all the psychological workings concealed beneath the form, but he will feel their effect. Another side of me longs to write great, sumptuous things—battles, sieges, descriptions of the fabulous ancient Orient. Thursday night I spent two lovely hours with my head in my hands, thinking of the bright multicolored walls of Ecbatana. Nothing has been written about all that. How many things still float in

the limbo of human thought! It isn't subjects that are lacking, but men. (p. 207)

*Gustave Flaubert, in extracts from nineteen letters to Louise Colet from October 23, 1851 to January 2, 1854, in his* The Letters of Gustave Flaubert: 1830-1857, *edited and translated by Francis Steegmuller, Cambridge, Mass.: Belknap Press, 1980, pp. 150-207.*

### EDMOND DE GONCOURT AND JULES DE GONCOURT (journal date 1860)

[*The Goncourt brothers were literary innovators who are noted for their diverse contributions to the world of letters. In their best-known work,* Journal des Goncourts, *a diary that contains a detailed record of Parisian literary society, the brothers proved themselves to be adept historians of their age. In the following passage from the* Journal, *the Goncourts praise Flaubert's scrupulous fidelity to reality in* Madame Bovary. *They imply, however, that because the novel relies so heavily on ''the material side of art and thought,'' it may not become immortal like more imaginative works.*]

Fundamentally and in fact, **Madame Bovary**—a masterpiece in its genre, the last word of truth in the novel—represents a very material side of art and thought. The accessories in it live as vividly and almost on the same level as the people. The physical setting is in such high relief around the feelings and passions that it almost stifles them. It is a work which paints for the

*A caricature of Flaubert by Giraud.*

eyes much more than it speaks to the soul. The noblest and strongest part of the book is much closer to painting than to literature. It is the stereopticon pushed to its furthest illusion.

The true is the basis of all art; it is its foundation and its conscience. But why are the mind and the soul not completely satisfied with it? Shouldn't there be an alloy of the false in order for a work to be regarded as a masterpiece by posterity? How does it happen that [Bernardin de Saint-Pierre's] *Paul et Virginie*—that romantic novel in which I do not feel the real, but always the imagined life of the characters, their dreamlike nature—will always be considered an immortal masterpiece, whereas **Madame Bovary**, a stronger book, having the force of maturity instead of youthfulness, of observation instead of imagination, of being composed from life instead of poetically imagined, will be looked on merely as a prodigious feat but never will achieve the standing of books like *Paul et Virginie*, a kind of Bible of the human imagination? Because it lacks that grain of falsehood which is, perhaps, the ideal of a work of art? (p. 55)

> *Edmond de Goncourt and Jules de Goncourt, in a journal entry of December 10, 1860, in their* Paris and the Arts, 1851-1896: From the Goncourt ''Journal,'' *edited and translated by George J. Becker and Edith Philips, Cornell University Press, 1971, pp. 54-5.*

## G[EORGE] SAND   (letter date 1876)

[*Sand was one of France's most celebrated and controversial writers. Writing effortlessly, yet maintaining an impressive richness of style and unity of construction, she produced nearly sixty novels, a lengthy autobiography, numerous essays, twenty-five plays, and approximately 20,000 letters during her lifetime. Sand's flamboyant lifestyle interfered with serious critical assessment of her works from the beginning of her career; however, she eventually won acceptance as an artist by her contemporaries and is now noted for her bold exploration of such issues as sexual freedom and independence for women. Sand and Flaubert enjoyed a close friendship, and they corresponded regularly during the last years of her life. The following excerpt from one of these letters illustrates their differences on the subject of emotion in art. She faults his impartiality in* Madame Bovary, *claiming that it would have been a stronger book if Flaubert had expressed his opinion of the characters.*]

One must write for all those who have a thirst to read and who can profit by good reading. Then one must go straight to the most elevated morality within oneself, and not make a mystery of the moral and profitable meaning of one's book. People found that with **Madame Bovary**. If one part of the public cried scandal, the healthiest and the broadest part saw in it a severe and striking lesson given to a woman without conscience and without faith, to vanity, to ambition, to irrationality. They pitied her; art required that, but the lesson was clear, and it would have been more so, it would have been so for *everybody*, if you had wished it, if you had shown more clearly the opinion that you had, and that the public ought to have had, about the heroine, her husband, and her lovers.

That desire to depict things as they are, the adventures of life as they present themselves to the eye, is not well thought out, in my opinion. Depict inert things as a realist, as a poet, it's all the same to me, but, when one touches on the emotions of the human heart, it is another thing. You cannot abstract yourself from this contemplation; for man, that is yourself, and men, that is the reader. Whatever you do, your tale is a con-

versation between you and the reader. If you show him the evil coldly, without ever showing him the good he is angry. He wonders if it is he that is bad, or if it is you. You work, however, to rouse him and to interest him; you will never succeed if you are not roused yourself, or if you hide it so well that he thinks you indifferent. He is right: supreme impartiality is an anti-human thing, and a novel ought to be human above everything. If it is not, the public is not pleased in its being well written, well composed and conscientious in every detail. The essential quality is not there: interest. The reader breaks away likewise from a book where all the characters are good without distinctions and without weaknesses; he sees clearly that that is not human either. I believe that art, this special art of narration, is only worth while through the opposition of characters; but, in their struggle, I prefer to see the right prevail. Let events overwhelm the honest men, I agree to that, but let him not be soiled or belittled by them, and let him go to the stake feeling that he is happier than his executioners. (pp. 355-56)

> *G[eorge] Sand, in a letter to Gustave Flaubert on January 12, 1876, in* The George Sand—Gustave Flaubert Letters *by George Sand and Gustave Flaubert, translated by Aimee L. McKenzie, Boni and Liveright Publishers, 1921, pp. 350-56.*

## ÉMILE ZOLA   (essay date 1880)

[*Zola was a nineteenth-century French novelist, short story writer, critic, essayist, dramatist, poet, and journalist. In Zola's writings, the realism that characterized the works of Flaubert, Honoré de Balzac, and the Goncourt brothers lost some of its artistic qualities, gained features of the scientific and sociological document, and was reborn as Naturalism. Although Zola's scientific conception of literature is no longer popular, he served as Naturalism's most devoted spokesman and his* Les Rougon-Macquart, *a twenty-novel series, is considered the masterpiece of the French Naturalist movement. Here, Zola commends Flaubert's temperate and judicious use of description of surroundings, which ''do not submerge the character.'' This essay was first published in French in 1880 in* Le roman expérimental.]

Gustave Flaubert is the novelist who, up to the present time, has employed description with the greatest moderation. The surroundings occupy a discreet equilibrium with him; they do not submerge the character, and nearly always content themselves with determining it. This is what gives **''Mme. Bovary''** and **''L'Education Sentimentale''** so much force. It can truthfully be said that Gustave Flaubert has reduced to strict necessity the long appraiser's enumerations with which Balzac lumbered up the beginning of his novels. He is temperate, which is a rare quality; he gives the salient trait, the main lines, the peculiarity which paints, and that is sufficient to make the picture a never to be forgotten one. I would counsel anyone to study Gustave Flaubert, for description or for the necessary painting of surroundings, each time that they complete or explain a character. (p. 235)

> *Émile Zola, ''The Novel: Description,'' in his* The Experimental Novel and Other Essays, *translated by Belle M. Sherman, The Cassell Publishing Co., 1894, pp. 231-37.**

## MATTHEW ARNOLD   (essay date 1887)

[*Arnold is considered one of the most influential authors of the later Victorian period in England. While he is well known today as a poet, in his own time he asserted his greatest influence through his prose writings. Arnold's forceful literary criticism, which is based on his humanistic belief in the value of balance and clarity in literature, significantly shaped modern theory. Here, Arnold compares* Madame Bovary *to* Anna Karenina *by Leo Tolstoi. Arnold's assessment of* Madame Bovary *is strongly negative. He describes Flaubert as "cruel" and* Madame Bovary *as "a work of petrified feeling" that contains "an atmosphere of bitterness, irony, impotence." This essay was first published in the* Fortnightly Review, *December, 1887.*]

[Tolstoi] deals abundantly with criminal passion and with adultery, but he does not seem to feel himself owing any service to the goddess Lubricity, or bound to put in touches at this goddess's dictation. Much in *Anna Karénine* is painful, much is unpleasant, but nothing is of a nature to trouble the senses, or to please those who wish their senses troubled. This taint is wholly absent. In the French novels where it is so abundantly present its baneful effects do not end with itself. Burns long ago remarked with deep truth that it *petrifies feeling*. . . . Undoubtedly the taint in question is present in *Madame Bovary*, although to a much less degree than in more recent French novels, which will be in every one's mind. But *Madame Bovary*, with this taint, is a work of *petrified feeling*; over it hangs an atmosphere of bitterness, irony, impotence; not a personage in the book to rejoice or console us; the springs of freshness and feeling are not there to create such personages. Emma Bovary follows a course in some respects like that of Anna, but where, in Emma Bovary, is Anna's charm? The treasures of compassion, tenderness, insight, which alone, amid such guilt and misery, can enable charm to subsist and to emerge, are wanting to Flaubert. He is cruel, with the cruelty of petrified feeling, to his poor heroine; he pursues her without pity or pause, as with malignity; he is harder upon her himself than any reader even, I think, will be inclined to be. (pp. 275-76)

> *Matthew Arnold, "Count Leo Tolstoi," in his* Essays in Criticism, second series, *The Macmillan Company, 1924, pp. 253-99.*

### [WALTER PATER]   (essay date 1889)

[*In the following review of Flaubert's letters, Pater discusses what they reveal about Flaubert's literary philosophy as well as the creation and intent of* Madame Bovary.]

Impersonality in art, the literary ideal of Gustave Flaubert, is perhaps no more possible than realism. The artist *will* be felt; his subjectivity must and will colour the incidents, as his very bodily eye *selects* the aspects of things. By force of an immense and continuous effort, however, the whole scope of which [his] letters enable us to measure, Flaubert did keep '**Madame Bovary**' at a great distance from himself; the author might be thought to have been completely hidden out of sight in his work. Yet even here he transpires, clearly enough, from time to time; and the morbid sense of life, everywhere impressed in the very atmosphere of that sombre history, came certainly of the writer himself. The cruelty of the ways of things—that is a conviction of which the development is partly traceable in these letters.

> Provided the brain remains! That is the chief thing. But how nothingness invades us! We are scarcely born ere decay begins for us, in such a way that the whole of life is but one long combat with it, more and more triumphant, on its part, to the consummation, namely, death; and then the reign of decay is exclusive. There

have been at most two or three years in which I was really entire—from seventeen to nineteen. I was splendid just then, though I scarce like to say so now; enough to attract the eyes of a whole assembly of spectators, as happened to me at Rouen, on the first presentation of 'Ruy Blas.' Ever since then I have deteriorated at a furious pace. There are mornings when I feel afraid to look at myself, so worn and used-up am I grown.

'**Madame Bovary**,' of course, was a tribute to science; and Flaubert had no dread, great hopes rather, of the service of science in imaginative literature, though the combat between scientific truth—mental physiology and the like—and that perfectly finished academic style he preferred, might prove a hard one. We might be all of us, since Sophocles—well, "tattooed savages!" but still, there was "something else in art besides rectitude of line and the well-polished surface." The difficulty lay in the limitations of language, which it would be the literary artist's true contention to enlarge. "We have too many things, too few words. 'Tis from that comes the torture of the fine literary conscience." But it was one's duty, none the less, to accept all, "imprint all, and, above all, fix one's *point d'appui* in the present." Literature, he held, would take more and more the modes of action which now seem to belong exclusively to science. It would be, above all, *exposante*—by way of exposition; by which, he was careful to point out, he by no means intended *didactic*. One must make pictures, by way of showing nature as she really is; only, the pictures must be complete ones. We must paint both sides, the upper and under. Style—what it might be, if writers faithfully cherished it—that was the subject of his perpetual consideration. (p. 155)

> [*Walter Pater*], *in a review of "Correspondance de Gustave Flaubert," in* The Athenaeum, *No. 3223, August 3, 1889, pp. 155-56.*

### HENRY JAMES   (essay date 1893)

[*James was an American-born English novelist, short story writer, critic, and essayist of the late nineteenth and early twentieth centuries. He is regarded as one of the greatest novelists of the English language and is also admired as a lucid and insightful critic. As a young man he travelled extensively throughout Great Britain and Europe and benefited from the friendship and influence of many of the leading figures of nineteenth-century art and literature, including Flaubert. James's essay on Flaubert, from which the following is drawn, discusses his correspondence and briefly touches on* Madame Bovary. *Here, James describes how Flaubert's patient planning resulted in a masterpiece. For additional commentary by James, see* NCLC, *Vol. 2, and excerpt below, 1902.*]

[Everything in Flaubert's literary life was] planned and plotted and prepared. One moves in it through an atmosphere of the darkest, though the most innocent, conspiracy. He was perpetually laying a train, a train of which the inflammable substance was "style." His great originality was that the long siege of his youth was successful. I can recall no second case in which poetic justice has interfered so gracefully. He began *Madame Bovary* from afar off, not as an amusement, or a profit, or a clever novel, or even a work of art, or a *morçeau de vie*, as his successors say to-day, not even, either, as the best thing he could make it; but as a premeditated classic, a masterpiece pure and simple, a thing of conscious perfection and a contribution of the first magnitude to the literature of his country.

There would have been every congruity in his encountering proportionate failure and the full face of that irony in things of which he was so inveterate a student. . . . The masterpiece at the end of years would inevitably fall very flat, and the overweening spirit be left somehow to its illusions. The solution in fact was very different, and as Flaubert had deliberately sown so exactly and magnificently did he reap. The perfection of **Madame Bovary** is one of the commonplaces of criticism, the position of it one of the highest a man of letters dare dream of, the possession of it one of the glories of France. No calculation was ever better fulfilled, nor any train more successfully laid. (p. 335)

> Henry James, *"Gustave Flaubert," in* Macmillan's Magazine, *Vol. LXVII, No. 401, March, 1893, pp. 332-43.*

## PAUL BOURGET   (lecture date 1897)

[*Bourget's lecture, from which the following excerpt is drawn, was originally delivered on June 23, 1897, at the Taylorian Institute, Oxford. Bourget outlines Flaubert's life, its influence on his work and artistic principles, and presents what is considered the first authoritative assessment to appear in England of the historical importance of* Madame Bovary. *For Bourget, the significance of the work resides in its successful blend of romanticism and "Science," or realism: "What made the appearance in print of* Madame Bovary *an event of the greatest importance, a date, in fact, in the history of the French novel, was the blending of both schools in one book, equal in plastic power to the finest pages of Victor Hugo or Gautier, and worthy of being compared for its analytic lucidity with the master-chapters of Balzac and Stendhal." For additional commentary on the novel's relationship to romanticism and realism, see excerpts by Émile Faguet (1899), Henry James (1902), Martin Turnell (1950), Leo Bersani (1974), Anthony Thorlby (see Additional Bibliography), and Charles Augustin Sainte-Beuve and Charles Baudelaire (see NCLC, Vol. 2).*]

[If] you now turn to the pages of **Madame Bovary**, what do you find in them? A minute and faithful copy of a life in utter contrast with the proud, unsullied existence of this young Faustus [Flaubert], imprisoned in his cell. All the scenes depicted in this relentless novel deal only with sordid hopes, base passions, abortive minds, and ignoble feelings—an assemblage of misshapen souls above which hovers the idiotic smile of Homais the apothecary, that typical *bourgeois,* a very marvel of stupidity! The effect of amazement sought by Flaubert is thus accomplished. His faultless prose, now rich in colour like a Flemish painting, now hewn in solid marble like a Greek statue, again rhythmical and pliant like a phrase of music, is applied to the description of beings so dwarfed and misshapen that the use made of this instrument of genius startles, confounds, almost produces a feeling of actual pain. How is the writer affected by these mental and physical infirmities which he scans with so keen a glance and records in such matchless style? We shall never know, any more than what he thinks of the depravity of his characters, of the social state that produced them, or the moral distempers from which they suffer. The book is there before us, a living reality, like an object in nature. It stands unsupported, as Flaubert wished it to stand, "by the sheer power of its style, just as the earth, independent of support, is balanced in the heavens." (pp. 159-60)

Take up once more his **Madame Bovary,** which he professed to have written in that uncompromisingly objective spirit. Let us consider wherein lies that which, in the opinion of even the most prejudiced judges, makes it a book of surpassing excellence. It is not the minute precision of his facts. The proceed-

ings recorded in the *Gazette des Tribunaux* afford just as precise information with respect to provincial manners. Neither does it reside in the difficulties the writer had to overcome in order to set forth in such masterly style so uninteresting and commonplace a story. The sharp outlining of the figures, after the manner of the Dutch masters, the bold relief of the style, causing every object to be seen as through a magnifying glass, a grammatical correctness which never allows itself a reiteration, an assonance, or a hiatus—all this technical skill, when carried to such a high degree of perfection, would rather be likely to produce an impression of artificiality, almost of sleight of hand, and, indeed, Sainte-Beuve had, from the first, cautioned the too facile writer against the danger of excessive strain. No; what raises this tale to the dignity of a symbol, what makes of this account of the errors of a petty, ill-mated *bourgeoise* a heartrending human elegy, is the fact that the writer, in spite of all his hard-and-fast theories, has not been able entirely to abstract his own personality. In vain did he choose a subject as far removed as possible from his own moral atmosphere, and tell his tale simply without a single comment, delineating each of his characters with the same impassive impartiality, without passing judgment, without pointing a moral. In spite of all, his vision of life betrays him. That evil from which he suffered all his life, that intemperance of thought which unfitted him for his time and place, he has involuntarily, instinctively ascribed to his prosaic heroes. Thought, ill-directed and led astray by a false ideal and worthless literature, but thought for all that, urged on Emma Bovary to her guilty adventures, and every page of the book is a violent and passionate protest against the havoc wrought by the discrepancy between imaginative dreams and the realities of life in the mind of one assuredly below the average, but yet too refined, too dainty for her surroundings. (pp. 161-62)

[Throughout] his writings this man, who aimed at being impassive, impersonal and unconcerned, proves to have chosen as the prime motive of all his books that evil from which he suffered himself—the being unable to fashion his life in accordance with his thought and dreams. Only, whereas in his own case that thought, those dreams, were carried to their highest degree of intensity, his artistic theories led him to depict in his novels lives in which thought and imagination were at a minimum, and this very circumstance heightens the truth of his writings. We perceive, underlying his subdued irony, his reserve, his self-constraint, a world of emotions which he does not reveal. It was Diderot, I believe, who, in the course of one of his rambling disquisitions on Art, gave utterance to that admirable saying: An artist is always greater by what he keeps back than by what he expresses. Flaubert, that master of expression, would certainly have protested against this sentiment, and yet no work proclaims its truth more strikingly than his own; so true it is that we are all, to use an old simile, the weavers of a piece of tapestry of which we see but the wrong side, while the design is hidden from us.

When we consider Gustave Flaubert in this light, as a Romantic oppressed by his surroundings, impelled by circumstances to adopt the most extreme theories of the Art for Art school, and yet induced by the natural impulse of his genius to imbue his writings with the sorrowful melancholy of his mind, we realise more clearly the reasons which made him the head of a school. . . . [He] had taken his place among French men of letters at the precise moment when that literature was divided between the two currents personified by the two greatest names of the middle of the century—Victor Hugo and Balzac.

With Hugo a new school of rhetoric had sprung into existence, one that was all colour and form; and the talent of painting with words had attained its highest degree of development. With Balzac a spirit of scientific investigation had invaded the novel, and almost from the first either school had exhibited its inherent defect: in the former school the poverty of thought, in the latter the poverty of style. What made the appearance in print of *Madame Bovary* an event of the greatest importance, a date, in fact, in the history of the French novel, was the blending of both schools in one book, equal in plastic power to the finest pages of Victor Hugo or Gautier, and worthy of being compared for its analytic lucidity with the master-chapters of Balzac and Stendhal. This combination of the two tendencies of the age, of Romanticism and Science, Flaubert had been at no pains to acquire. His theory of Art for Art's sake had led him to it by a play of logic which he himself wondered at all his life. It was his systematic striving to be impersonal which, by causing him to abstract himself in presence of the object, had brought him to that precision of minute analysis. Having deliberately chosen as the subject of his first novel a commonplace prosaic story, it chanced that he composed a study of life written in his highly-finished prose. (pp. 162-63)

To conceive a novel the subject of which is every-day, humble truth, as Maupassant says at the beginning of *Une Vie*, a novel sufficiently true to nature to be of use in writing a history of the manners of the age, like a police report, and to write that novel in a prose, highly coloured and plastic, precise and learned, in what the Goncourts used, barbarously enough, to call an "artist style," such was the ideal, derived from *Madame Bovary*, which, according to their temperaments, the emasculate miniature-painters of [the Goncourts'] *Renée Mauperin*, the powerful seer of [Zola's] *L'Assommoir*, the hyper-sensitive chronicler of [Daudet's] *Le Nabab*, and the genial storyteller of [Maupassant's] *Une Vie*, all strove to follow out. Flaubert, that lyrical poet, born of a physician, and brought up in a hospital, had found this synthesis of Romanticism and science ready-made in his brain. He had also been at hand to perceive and to express, as it could best be done by an ardent idealist, cooped up amid all the wretched meanness of a provincial town, the loathing of a man of letters for surrounding mediocrity, which is one shape of the revolt against democracy. Finally, and for this reason, he remains ever present among us, in spite of the new developments assumed by contemporary French literature, for he gave to all writers the most splendid example of passionate, exclusive love of literature. (pp. 163-64)

*Paul Bourget, "Gustave Flaubert," translated by C. Heywood, in* The Fortnightly Review, *Vol. LXII, No. CCCLXVII, July 1, 1897, pp. 152-64.*

**ÉMILE FAGUET** (essay date 1899)

[*Faguet, a French literary historian and critic, was influential during the late nineteenth and early twentieth centuries. His critical writings are recognized for their emphasis on the aesthetic qualities of a work as well as an understanding of the history and evolution of French poetry. Faguet's study* Flaubert *was first published in 1899 in French. In the excerpt below, he discusses the author in relation to the romantic and realistic movements. According to Faguet,* Madame Bovary *is a reaction to and a warning against romanticism as found in the works of Sir Walter Scott, Lord Byron, Alphonse de Lamartine, and, especially, George Sand. For additional commentary on the novel's relationship to romanticism and realism, see excerpts by Paul Bourget (1897), Henry James (1902), Martin Turnell (1950), Leo Bersani (1974),*

*Anthony Thorlby (see Additional Bibliography), and Charles Augustin Sainte-Beuve and Charles Baudelaire (see NCLC, Vol. 2).*]

[*Madame Bovary*] is an act of ardent reaction against romanticism. Again and again it reads like a pamphlet against romanticism and a warning against its influence. Who is responsible for Mme. Bovary's straying? Walter Scott, Byron, Lamartine, George Sand, poetical albums and love anthologies—all the literature of imagination and of sensibility. Another book of Flaubert's is entitled *Sentimental Education*; this might have been called *Romantic Education*. It is a curious thing, which does honour to them both, that Flaubert and George Sand should have become loving friends towards the end of their lives. At the beginning, Flaubert might have been looked upon by George Sand as a furious enemy. Emma is George Sand's heroine with all the poetry turned into ridicule. Flaubert seems to say in every page of his novel: 'Do you want to know what is the real Valentine, the real Indiana, the real Lelia? Here she is, it is Emma Rouault.' 'And do you want to know what becomes of a woman whose education has consisted in George Sand's books? Here she is, Emma Rouault.' So that the terrible mocker of the *bourgeois* has written a book which is directly inspired by the spirit of the 1840 *bourgeois*. Their recriminations against romanticism 'which rehabilitates and poetises the courtesan,' against George Sand, the Muse of Adultery, are to be found in acts and in facts in *Madame Bovary*.

This intention is not doubtful. We read in each line of the novel: '*Bourgeois* are fools; the woman who has aspirations towards an artistic life and who wants to escape from *bourgeois*-dom is the most foolish of all.' Flaubert's eternal dualism, at once his torment and his strength, here appears. . . . There was in him a Romanticist who looked upon reality as flat and a Realist who looked upon romance as empty, an artist who thought the *bourgeois* ridiculous and a *bourgeois* who thought artists affected; the whole was contained in a misanthrope who mocked at everybody. If *Madame Bovary* is so great a masterpiece, it is because Flaubert has thrown himself wholly into it, and the book has therefore been written by a Romanticist gloating over *bourgeois* types, and by a Realist analysing the brain of one of George Sand's heroines in order to show how nonsensical are her spiritual ambitions. And he took in both executions an extreme pleasure which went not without some ferocity. Such an opportunity of exhaling at the same time the Romanticists' hatred of the *bourgeois* and the *bourgeois'* rancour against Romanticism was indeed a feast.

As to the morality of the work, I will say nothing about it. *Madame Bovary* may be pernicious or it may be salutary. It is easy to take Emma as a model and to consider that nothing would be easier than to avoid the mistakes in domestic economy which have alone—and not her immoral conduct—led her to death; thus the book will be perverting. It is as easy to believe, as does the author, that material disorder always follows moral disorder, and that the one associated with the other must lead to ruin; thus will the book be highly moral. On the whole, it will be salutary or unwholesome according to the spirit in which it is read, which means that every reader will make of it what he already himself is, and that it is therefore neither one thing nor the other. We might repeat the celebrated though untrue saying, that the book is as moral as Experience is. Only, Experience is not moral. Neither is it immoral. It does not teach Vice, for Vice is not particularly successful; nor does it teach Virtue, for Virtue is not particularly successful either. It teaches a medium course which is made up of prudence and of the care to avoid excess in all things, in good as in evil. It teaches

*The Hôtel Dieu at Rouen, where Flaubert was born.*

order, regularity, honesty, punctuality and foresight, all of them average qualities, not virtues. Every Realistic novel, if it is well written, will teach these and nothing else.

*Madame Bovary* is a very well written Realistic novel. (pp. 130-33)

> *Émile Faguet, in his* Flaubert, *translated by Mrs. R. L. Devonshire, Houghton Mifflin Company, 1914, 238 p.*

**HENRY JAMES** (essay date 1902)

[*James discusses two topics in regard to* Madame Bovary: *the novel's relation to romanticism and realism, and its style. He responds to several points made by Émile Faguet (see* NCLC, *Vol. 2, and excerpt above, 1899). To James, the romantic element is to be found solely in Emma, and he notes the realistic background with which Flaubert surrounds his heroine. Like Faguet, James contends that by making the main character "an embodiment of helpless romanticism," Flaubert assured the success of the work. Yet James also challenges Faguet's praise of Emma, characterizing her as "ignorant, foolish, flimsy, unhappy," and "really too small an affair." Flaubert's greatest accomplishment, according to James, is his technical ability, which renders the work eternally suggestive and interesting despite the shallowness of Emma. For further criticism by James, see* NCLC, *Vol. 2, and excerpt above, 1893. For additional commentary on the novel's*

*relationship to romanticism and realism, see excerpts by Paul Bourget (1897), Martin Turnell (1950), Victor Brombert (1966), Leo Bersani (1974), Anthony Thorlby (see Additional Bibliography), and Charles Augustin Sainte-Beuve and Charles Baudelaire (see* NCLC, *Vol. 2). Discussions of Flaubert's style are also provided by Erich Auerbach (1942-45), W. von Wartburg (1946), Martin Turnell (1950), Stephen Ullmann (1957), Victor Brombert (1966), and Marcel Proust and Percy Lubbock (see* NCLC, *Vol. 2).*]

[Flaubert's] imagination was great and splendid; in spite of which, strangely enough, his masterpiece is not his most imaginative work. *Madame Bovary,* beyond question, holds that first place, and *Madame Bovary* is concerned with the career of a country doctor's wife in a petty Norman town. The elements of the picture are of the fewest, the situation of the heroine almost of the meanest, the material for interest—considering the interest yielded—of the most unpromising; but these facts only throw into relief one of those incalculable phenomena that attend the proceedings of genius. *Madame Bovary* was doomed, by circumstances and causes—the freshness of comparative youth and good faith on the author's part being perhaps the chief—definitely to take its position, even though its subject were fundamentally a negation of the remote, the magnificent and the strange, the stuff of his fondest and most characteristic dreams. It would have seemed very nearly to have excluded the play of the imagination, and the way this faculty of Flaubert's nevertheless comes in is one of those accidents, manoeuvres, inspirations—we hardly know what to call them—by which masterpieces are made. He, of course, knew more or less what he was doing for his book in making Emma Bovary a victim of the imaginative habit, but he must have been far from designing or measuring that total effect which renders the work so general, so complete, an expression of himself. His separate idiosyncrasies, his irritated sensibility to the life about him, with the power to catch it in the fact and hold it hard, and his hunger for style and history and poetry, for the rich and the rare, are here represented together as they are not in his later writings. . . . M. Faguet has, of course, excellently noted this—that the fortune and felicity of the book were assured by the stroke that made the central figure an embodiment of helpless romanticism. Flaubert himself but narrowly escaped, after all, being such an embodiment, and he is thus able to express the romantic mind with extraordinary truth. As to the rest of the matter, he had the luck of having been, from the first, in possession; having begun so early to nurse and elaborate his plan that, familiarity and the native air, the native soil, aiding, he had finally made out, to the last lurking shade, the small, sordid, sunny, dusty village-picture, with its emptiness constituted and peopled. It is in the background and the accessories that the real—the real of his theme—abides; and the romantic—the romantic of his theme—accordingly occupies the front. Emma Bovary's poor adventures are a tragedy for the very reason that, in a world unsuspecting, unassisting, unconsoling, she has herself to distil the rich and the rare. Ignorant, unguided, undiverted, ridden by the very nature of her consciousness, she makes of the business an inordinate failure, a failure which, in its turn, makes for Flaubert the most elaborate, the most *told* of anecdotes. (pp. xiii-xv)

And yet it is not, after all—and here comes in the curiosity of the matter—that the place the book has taken is so overwhelmingly explained by its inherent dignity. Here comes in especially its fund of admonition for alien readers. The dignity of its matter is the dignity of Mme. Bovary herself as a vessel of experience—a question as to which, unmistakably, I judge, we can only depart from the consensus of French critical opinion. M. Faguet, for example, praises the character of the heroine as one of the most seized and rendered figures of women in all literature, praises it as a field for the display of the romantic spirit that leaves nothing to be desired. Subject to an observation that I shall presently make and that bears heavily, in general, I think, on Flaubert as a painter of life—subject to this restriction he is right; which is a proof that a work of art may be markedly challengeable and yet be perfect, and that when it is perfect nothing else particularly matters. *Madame Bovary* has a perfection that not only stamps it, but that makes it stand almost alone; it holds itself with such a supreme, unapproachable assurance as both excites and defies judgment. For it deals not in the least—as to unapproachability—with things exalted or refined; it only confers on its sufficiently vulgar substance a final, unsurpassable form. The form is *in itself* as interesting, as active, as much of the essence of the subject as the idea, and yet so close is its fit and so inseparable its life that we catch it at no moment on any errand of its own. That, verily, is to be genuine and whole. The work is a classic because the thing, such as it is, is ideally *done,* and because it shows that in such doing eternal beauty may dwell. A pretty young woman who lives, socially and morally speaking, in a hole, and who is ignorant, foolish, flimsy, unhappy, takes a pair of lovers by whom she is successively deserted; in the midst of which, giving up her husband and her child, letting everything go, she sinks deeper into duplicity, debt, despair, and arrives on the spot, on the small scene itself of her poor

depravities, at a pitiful, tragic end. She does these things, above all, while remaining absorbed in the romantic vision, and she remains absorbed in the romantic vision while fairly rolling in the dust. That is the triumph of the book, as the triumph stands—that Emma interests us by the nature of her consciousness and the play of her mind, thanks to the reality and the beauty with which these things are invested. It is not only that they represent *her* state; they are so true, so observed, so felt, and especially so shown, that they represent the state, actual or potential, of all persons like her—persons romantically determined. Then her setting, the medium in which she struggles, becomes in its way as important, becomes eminent with the eminence of art; the tiny world in which she revolves, the contracted cage in which she flutters, is hung out in space for us, and her companions in captivity there are as true as herself.

I have said enough to show . . . [that Flaubert has], in this picture, expressed something of his intimate self, given his heroine something of his own imagination: a point, precisely, that brings me back to the restriction at which I just now hinted, in which M. Faguet fails to indulge and yet which is immediate for the alien reader. Emma Bovary, in spite of the nature of her consciousness and in spite of her reflecting so much of that of her creator, is really too small an affair. That, critically speaking, is, in view both of the value and the fortune of her history, the wonderful circumstance. She associates herself with Frédéric Moreau in *L'Education* to suggest for us a question that can be answered, I hold, only to Flaubert's detriment. Emma taken alone would possibly not so directly press it; but, in her company, the hero of our author's second study of the "real" drives it home. Why did Flaubert choose, as special conduits of the life he proposed to depict, such inferior, and in the case of Frédéric such abject, human specimens? I insist only in respect to the latter—the perfection of *Madame Bovary* scarce leaving one much warrant for wishing anything different; even here, however, the general scale and size of Emma, who is small even of her sort, should be a warning to hyperbole. If I say that in the matter of Frédéric, at all events, the answer is inevitably detrimental, I mean that it weighs heavily on our author's general credit. He wished in each case to make a picture of experience—middling experience, it is true—and of the world close to him; but if he imagined nothing better for his purpose than such a heroine and such a hero, we are forced to believe it to have been by a defect of his mind. And that sign of weakness remains even if it be objected that the images in question were addressed to his purpose better than others would have been: the purpose itself then shows as inferior. (pp. xvii-xx)

*Madame Bovary,* subject to whatever qualification, is absolutely the most literary of novels—so literary that it covers us with its mantle. It shows us, once for all, that there is no *intrinsic* need of a debasement of the type. The mantle I speak of is wrought with surpassing fineness, and we may always—under stress of whatever charge of illiteracy, frivolity, vulgarity—flaunt it as the flag of the guild. Let us therefore frankly concede that to surround Flaubert with our consideration is the least return we can make for such a privilege. The consideration, moreover, is idle unless it be real, unless it be intelligent enough to measure his effort and his success. Of the effort as mere effort I have already spoken—of the desperate difficulty involved for him in making his form square with his conception; and I by no means attach a general importance to these secrets of the workshop, which are but as the contortions of the fastidious muse, the servant of the oracle. They are really, rather, secrets of the kitchen and contortions of the priestess of *that* tripod—they are not an upstairs matter. It is of their specially distinctive importance I am now speaking, of the light shed on them by the results before us.

They all represent the pursuit of a style—of the right one, and they would still be interesting if the style had not been achieved. *Madame Bovary, Salammbô, Saint-Antoine, L'Education,* are so written and so composed—though the last-named in a minor degree—that the more we look at them the more we find in them, in this kind, a beauty of intention and of effect; the more they form, in the too often dreary desert of fictive prose, a class by themselves, a little living oasis. So far as that desert is our own English—by which I of course also mean our own American—province, it supplies with remarkable rarity this particular source of relief. So strikingly is that the case that a critic betrayed at artless moments into advocating the claims of composition is apt to find himself as blankly met as if he were advocating the claims of trigonometry.... For signal examples of what composition, distribution, arrangement can do, of how they can intensify the life of a work of art, we have to go elsewhere; and the value of Flaubert for us is that he admirably points the moral. This is the great explanation of the ''classic'' fortune of *Madame Bovary* in especial, as well as an aspect of that work endlessly suggestive. (pp. xxvi-xxvii)

I speak from the point of view of his interest to a reader of his own craft, the point of view of his extraordinary technical wealth—though, indeed, when I think of the general power of *Madame Bovary* I find myself desiring not to narrow the ground of the lesson, not to connect it, to its prejudice, with the idea of the ''technical,'' so abhorrent, in whatever art, to the Anglo-Saxon mind. Without proposing Flaubert as the type of the newspaper novelist, or as an easy alternative to golf or the bicycle, we should do him an injustice in failing to insist that a masterpiece like *Madame Bovary* may benefit by its roundness even with the simple-minded. It has that sign of all rare works that there is something in it for every one. It may be read ever so attentively, enjoyed ever so freely, without a suspicion of how it is written, to say nothing of put together; it may equally be read under the excitement of these perceptions alone. Both readers will have been transported—which is all any reader can ask. Leaving the former, however that may be, to state the case for himself, I state it yet again for the latter, if only on this final ground. The book and its companions represent for us a practical solution—Flaubert's own troubled yet settled one—of the eternal dilemma of the painter of life. From the moment the painter deals at all with life directly, his desire is not to deal with it stintedly. It at the same time remains true that from the moment he desires to produce forms in which it shall be preserved, he desires that these forms, things of *his* creation, shall not be ignoble. He must make them complete and beautiful, intrinsically interesting, under peril of disgrace.... The question, for the artist, can only be of doing the artistic utmost, and thereby of *seeing* the general task. When it is seen with the intensity with which it presented itself to Flaubert, a lifetime is none too much for fairly tackling it. It must either be left alone or be dealt with, and to leave it alone is a comparatively simple matter. (pp. xxxvi-xxxviii)

> *Henry James, ''Gustave Flaubert,'' in* Madame Bovary *by Gustave Flaubert, translated by W. Blaydes, P. F. Collier & Son, 1902, pp. v-xliii.*

## WILLIAM C. FRIERSON (essay date 1925)

[*Frierson examines Flaubert's manipulation of his source materials in* Madame Bovary. *He quotes from Maxime Du Camp's* Souvenirs littéraires, *which documents the story of the Delamarre family, who, according to Du Camp, provided the basis for* Madame Bovary. *Frierson examines Flaubert's artistic transformation of these individuals into the characters of his novel.*]

In a study of the development of fiction within the last hundred years it is difficult to find a single work of equal importance to *Madame Bovary.* The book established the type of the naturalistic or ''experimental'' novel, and is the basis of the principles according to which much of the fiction of the Goncourts, Zola, Maupassant, Turgenief, George Moore, Henry James, and Arnold Bennett was written. Those of the contemporary novelists who seek in fiction to give a conscious expression of actuality consider the reading of the work a necessary act of apprenticeship.... Before the publication of *Madame Bovary* no novelist had taken his story from a human event of a seriously significant nature, analyzed the motives which had been the directing forces, and expressed the result of his investigation without partiality or prejudice—changing it only insofar as to make it fit in with a rationalized scheme of human nature and a technical plan of dramatic effectiveness. With the publication of *Madame Bovary* fiction entered into a new phase of its development. The novel ceased to be merely a tale or a sermon and became a contemplative study of life.

There is a double tragedy in the story of Madame Bovary; it is the tragedy of Charles Bovary as well as that of Emma. And the tragedy is unalloyed by any consolation which the descent of the avenging hand of justice may give to those who hold to the principle of retribution. The readers of the account are far too implicated for that. They have connived with the principles, they have sanctioned the actions, and, when the result is confusion and tragedy, they cannot hold up hands to High Heaven demanding punishment for those responsible nor even sanction the punishment given to the unfortunates. For the readers realize that no one is responsible—unless it be High Heaven. So the double tragedy becomes a triple tragedy in that it is also the tragedy of the pathetic incompleteness of life.

And it is this last aspect of the tragedy which gives it poignancy. After all, the death of the Bovarys is not a matter of great import. They are endeared to us somewhat because we realize that they possess, generally speaking, the good intent and that they are human. They are acquaintances of ours who wish to live but who are forced to die. They are largely exempt from our blame and we pity them at their death. But even our pity does not give an air of serenity to the final resolution. It only forces the reader to contemplate the matter of a humanity which acts by nature, by habit, and by impulse in a short-sighted and pathetic fashion. (pp. 178-79)

[Flaubert's purpose] seems to have been very much the same as that credited to him by Zola. For it was Zola who said that Flaubert had, in *Madame Bovary,* reared a magnificent marble temple to human incapacity and folly. Flaubert was humanitarian only artistically; the human sympathy in his account is for his own creations, not for mankind. He had long ago despaired of his fellow-creatures. ''Humanity'', he says in a letter, ''represents nothing new. Its irremediable worthlessness filled my soul even in my early days with bitterness. And this is why I now experience no disappointment''. (pp. 179-80)

[Thus for] Flaubert to put his heart into a book it was necessary that the book be different from life. Life repelled Flaubert. Humanity's spirit was not his spirit, and its desires were not his desires. He would delve into life, but he was careful not to write down all that he found there. (p. 180)

Let us consider the story of *Madame Bovary* in its original crudity and see what part the art of Flaubert played in elevating it into the sphere of contemplation.

The story of the Bovarys is that of the Delamarre family, and the best account of its history is given in the *Souvenirs Littéraires* of Maxime Ducamp. . . .

[Delamarre] was a poor devil of a medical officer of health who had been brought up by père Flaubert and whom we had all known. He had settled as a doctor at Bon-Secours, near Rouen. After losing his first wife, a woman elder than himself, he had married a young girl without fortune, who had received some kind of education at a boarding school in Rouen. This second wife was not beautiful; she was small, had dull yellow hair, and a face covered with freckles. She was full of pretension, and despised her husband whom she considered a fool. Round and fair in person, her small bones were well-covered, and in her bearing and general carriage there were flexible, undulating movements like those of an eel. Her voice, vulgarized by its lower Normandy accents, full of caressing tones, and her eyes of uncertain color, green, grey, or blue, according to the light, had a pleading expression which never left them. [Delamarre] adored his wife who was perfectly indifferent to him, was fond of picking up adventures, and gave way to her passions unrestrainedly. She was victim to one of those phases of nervous illness which attack anaemic patients. She became scarcely responsible for her actions, and as good advice was the only form of treatment tried in her case, she did not improve in health. Loaded with debt, persecuted with creditors, and ill-treated by the lover she robbed her husband to satisfy, she finally poisoned herself in a fit of despair. She left a little girl, whom [Delamarre] resolved to bring up as best he could, but the poor man was ruined, had no means of paying his debts, and knew that he was pointed at with the finger of scorn . . . His courage also failed him; weary of life he prepared himself a portion of cyanide of potassium and followed his wife whose loss had left him inconsolable.

Not a very heart-rending tragedy, to be sure. Nemesis has functioned with due solemnity and equity. Delamarre is punished for being a fool and his wife is punished for being a sinner, and, what is more, an ugly and unintelligent sinner. It is a tale for the village mothers to tell their daughters and for the village fathers to tell their sons.

Flaubert could not put his heart into telling this story because he could not sympathize with the actions of the characters. Like Milton, to draw with feeling he must admire, and it was therefore necessary for him to eradicate evil from the natures of the principal personages in his story.

Evil to Flaubert had a strange meaning. It meant grossness; it meant what is artistically out of harmony or incongruous.

In *Madame Bovary* the author is striving for certain character reactions, and in the above account of Maxime Ducamp certain human factors are out of harmony with his design. It is out of

harmony, in the first place, for the central female figure to be small, ugly, have dull yellow hair and a face covered with freckles. It is out of harmony because she is to be represented as physically attractive, and it is an artistic evil for a physically attractive woman to have freckles. Accordingly Flaubert gives her a pale complexion. As dull yellow hair is not particularly pleasing to French taste, the author prescribes the authentic black, and even adds as a choice refinement a faint down on the upper lip. The green-grey-blue eyes are changed to suit the type, the author making them large brown ones which seem black on account of the lashes. It appears that Flaubert shares Byron's dislike for "dumpy" women, and accordingly he keeps Emma's size a dead secret, giving us to understand that her figure is most attractive. Rodolphe says so at first glance. And Rodolphe says, furthermore, that she is beautiful. When Charles makes this same statement we do not accept it, but to Rodolphe's ideas about women we listen eagerly. There is also to Emma's credit a small foot and a Parisian style. Thus equipped Emma commands respect; she is a personage. She may act as Mme Delamarre acted, but actions which brought censure on Mme Delamarre for being "full of pretension" are in Emma those of a woman of some bearing and dignity. Emma is still a "woman without fortune"—else the plot would be ruined. But Flaubert seeks to heighten her position by making her the daughter of an apparently wealthy farmer who is in financial difficulties.

But Emma does not depend upon her looks for her charm; she is rather intelligent and highly developed emotionally. She loves nature when in sentimental moods, loves music, loves poetry. She loves romantic novels, also, but begins to study history and philosophy. She had cultural aspirations and is appreciative of the refinements of life. In certain moods, furthermore, she has an attractive touch of quaint piety.

Already we see that if this person is substituted for the Mme [Delamarre] in Ducamp's *Souvenirs,* that rather uninteresting account would be greatly changed. In Flaubert's narrative the motivation is heightened with the introduction of a somewhat attractive character, and the sympathetic interest of the reader is secured. But this is only one step. (pp. 180-82)

[It] was considered by Flaubert as ill-advised from an artistic point of view for Emma to give herself without restraint to each chance lover. Not only would she lose the reader's sympathetic respect, but the element of conflict would not be sufficiently intensified. Accordingly Emma is made, in the reader's eyes, virtuous. She is virtuous before she commits adultery, and she is virtuous afterwards. She is virtuous in that she is free from our blame. Disappointment is felt by the reader when Emma and Léon part at first without confessing their love, and it is difficult to see how a reader could resist the temptation to urge Emma on in her adultery with Rodolphe. The motivation for the act is ten times strong enough. The thing is inevitable. (p. 183)

[We see in Emma's life] the struggle of a limited, finite soul for its birthright. The struggle is for happiness, but it is also for expansion. . . . We see limited intelligences groping for self-realization in their pathetic and individual fashions—for Rodolphe, amusement; for Emma, love; for Charles, comfort. (p. 184)

As for Emma's extravagance and short-sightedness which bring ruin upon her, Flaubert has nothing to change. Her actions are mere weaknesses—human failings to be pitied. The integrity of Emma is maintained by her refusal to sell herself to the one man who would have helped her, M. Guillaumin. (p. 185)

[In comparing Flaubert's characters with those] of Ducamp, the chief factors in Flaubert's art become evident. They are: rationalized and universal motivation, a bid for sympathetic complicity on the part of the reader with the action, and the eradication of abnormal and exceptional elements—a dispassionate account in a spirit of infinite compassion and "salted with the tang of the soil which is bitter".

There is pathos in the account and there is sorrow. It is very serious and very sad. It is sadder than it would have been had the story ended in the characteristically tragic manner which makes us feel that something valuable has been irretrievably lost. "Father forgive them", Flaubert would have cried had he been able, "they know not what they do".

Art to Flaubert was "higher than life" because he conceived it to represent life intensified, life with the rough edges smoothed off. As for life itself, "it is so hideous", wrote Flaubert, "that the only way of enduring it is to avoid it. And it may only be avoided by living in art, in ceaseless search for truth rendered by beauty". For it was the truths of human nature with which he was concerned, and it was in order to portray these truths artistically that he eradicated the abnormal elements. He was concious, however, of the limitations under which he worked.

*A photograph by Nadar of Flaubert's friend Maxime Du Camp, who many critics believe suggested the story of* Madame Bovary *to Flaubert.*

Of one scene in **Madame Bovary** he says, "Even perfectly succeeded in it will never be beautiful on account of the subject".

No wonder the author of **Madame Bovary** objected to being called a realist because to him the term bore the implication of copywork! (p. 186)

[Some] mention should be made of Flaubert's method of presentation. The rather evident distinguishing feature is that he brought the background up almost into the foreground. There are few landscapes and vistas in his account; there are houses, streets, a chemistry shop, an inn, and, above all, people. Just as in an impressionist picture we see the color of an object influenced by surrounding objects, so in Flaubert's writings are the immediate influences of surroundings reflected. Speech, ideas, emotions and customs—all have their interplay and effect. Figures are never isolated; there are no mere portraits; we are shown at close view a succession of scenes.

And Flaubert, moreover, like the impressionists, "looked with the eyes of a new made Adam" at the spectacle of life, and painted with strong yet delicate strokes "whatever he saw on the top of God's green earth". He was fully aware of his sensitiveness. "There is", we find him saying, "at present such a gulf fixed between myself and the rest of the world that I oftentimes experience a feeling of astonishment when I hear even the most ordinary and casual things . . . there are certain gestures, certain intonations of voice which fill me with surprise, and there are certain silly things which nearly make me giddy". It was these startling and significant gestures and phrases which were to Flaubert the essence of pictorial art; they could stand for pages of careless description. "The unexpected is in everything", is the essence of his advice to de Maupassant. "The least object contains an unknown element or aspect. Find that". (pp. 187-88)

> William C. Frierson, "The Naturalistic Technique of Flaubert from an Analytical Appreciation of 'Madame Bovary' and a Study of Flaubert's Letters," in The French Quarterly, Vol. VII, Nos. 3 & 4, September & December, 1925, pp. 178-88.

### D. L. DEMOREST  (essay date 1931)

> [*Demorest's study* L'expression figurée dans l'oeuvre de Flaubert *originally appeared in French in 1931. This work, of which only a small portion has been translated, contains a comprehensive statistical analysis of imagery in* Madame Bovary. *In the following excerpt, Demorest discusses Flaubert's use of water imagery as symbols for sensuous, physical love. For additional commentary on imagery and symbolism in* Madame Bovary, *see Martin Turnell (1950), Jean Pierre Richard (1954), Georges Poulet (1955), Jean Rousset (1962), and Victor Brombert (1966).*]

Flaubert's images are chosen to convey a precise impression of a character, a situation, a moment, or a mood. As the serpent is the symbol of Eve the lost woman, so, for Flaubert, water is the symbol of Venus the delectable. And these illustrate admirably Emma's soul as it evokes, at every instant, lakes, torrents and oceans, these same oceans whose waves evoke all that is disastrous in love. Therefore images of fluidity appear so frequently in the novel, interpreting both sensations and sentiments. (p. 280)

[Many] of the basic images associated with the psychological analyses of the characters are not original: days resemble one another like waves, love is unquenchable, happiness dries up, Emma's love diminishes beneath her "like the water of a river which is absorbed by its bed.'' Others are somewhat unpleasant, such as this one which nevertheless shows the subjective value which Flaubert attached to these images: when he looks at Emma, Léon feels that his soul "fleeing toward her, broke like a wave against the contours of her head, and was drawn irresistibly down into the whiteness of her breast."

Among the images of the objective world, we see Emma's glance drowned in lassitude; or again, as she goes toward her downfall in the forest: "through her veil . . . her face appeared in a bluish transparency as if she were swimming through azure waves." The author obviously gave particular attention to this image since the early drafts contain several versions where the veil falls "like black waves," where there are "bluish undulations," or "an ultramarine cloud," "the transparent water of a few azure waves." They include no less than four variants on the idea of "swimming." When she gives herself to Rodolphe she feels "her blood flow through her flesh like a river of milk" and "love so long pent up, erupted in joyous outbursts." As she rides toward the forest, her imagination transforms the mist in the valley into one of those Lamartinian lakes of which she dreams:

> From the height on which they were the whole valley seemed an immense pale lake sending off its vapor into the air. Clumps of trees here and there stood out like black rocks, and the tall lines of poplars that rose above the mist were like a beach stirred by the wind.

Emma's reactions to nature as seen in the last two examples appear in many other passages such as her panoramic view of Rouen on her way to and from her meetings with Léon, where she imagines herself surrounded by the "passions of one hundred and twenty thousand souls"; or again, when she perceives the shadows of the trees in the garden, that night when our romantic heroine asks Rodolphe whether he has brought his pistols to defend her against Charles should he appear:

> The city appeared . . . drowned in the fog . . . The islands looked like giant fishes lying motionless on the water . . . From time to time a gust of wind would drive off the clouds towards the slopes of Saint Catherine, like aerial waves breaking silently against a cliff.

> All the lights of the city . . . forming a luminous mist.

> Masses of deeper darkness stood out here and there in the night . . . and would sway like immense black waves pressing forward to engulf them.

This last passage represents, in images of the objective world, everything which threatens to engulf this precarious love, while many other passages carry out the theme of masses of water in movement. In his sketches for her promenade with Léon, Flaubert writes: "fields . . . furrows following one another, . . . white waves of a motionless ocean"; and in the scene of the horseback ride, just before she gives herself to Rodolphe, "the ground trembled beneath her feet as on the bridge of a ship." When Rodolphe abandons her, she thinks of throwing herself out of the attic window, and "the ground of the village Square seemed to tilt over and climb up the walls, the floor to pitch forward like in a tossing boat." Later after the first visit to the cathedral, Emma's liaison with Léon is sealed in a coach. And in one of those double images where the antithesis

contains the synthesis, and which are obviously symbolic, the idea of a ship of love is fused with that of death: "a cab with all blinds drawn that reappeared incessantly, more tightly sealed than a tomb and tossed around like a ship on the waves." The bed on which Emma and Léon drift unconsciously toward shipwreck is a "large mahogany bed shaped like a boat."

Shipwreck comes, and as Emma leaves Rouen for the last time she passes in front of the cathedral just as people are leaving after the Vespers service. The majestic verger, who had appeared to her at the beginning of her affair with Léon (among the statues and the tombs in the chapels) like a sort of life-preserver to which her honor should have clung, now appears to her again at the end of her career like a rock of retribution upon which all her hopes have shattered:

> People were coming out after vespers; the crowd flowed out through the three portals like a river through the three arches of a bridge, and in the middle, more immobile than a rock, stood the verger.

Desperate, and "swept away in her memories as in a raging tempest" she suddenly thinks of Rodolphe. She runs to him. "She was irresistible, with a tear trembling in her eye, like a raindrop in a blue flower-cup, after the storm." After her supreme effort with him fails, Emma, stunned, crosses the fields and "the earth seemed to her more yielding than the sea, and the furrows seemed to her immense brown waves breaking into foam." These lines bring to mind the image of the pitching ship with huge black waves cited above, and already prefigures the following image of her last terrestrial voyage: "The black cloth decorated with silver tears, flapped from time to time in the wind, revealing the coffin underneath. The tired bearers walked more slowly, and the bier advanced jerkily, like a boat that pitches with every wave."

We can see more clearly now why "her journey to Vaubyessard had made a gap in her life, like the huge crevasses that a thunderstorm will sometimes carve in the mountains, in the course of a single night," and why love is spoken of as overflowing in a raging torrent, or falling on life like a tempest from heaven. Peace is said to be more vague than the ocean, Emma's room becomes a dark ocean. Finally there is the passage describing Emma's life after Vaubyessard, ironically fusing the present and future in showing her scanning the solitude of her life with desperate eyes like a sailor in distress. (pp. 280-82)

[Since Flaubert] had trained himself in the art of seeing things as they are, without subjective distortions, it is not surprising that *Madame Bovary* contains several passages which aim only at precise description. Indeed we may rather wonder why there are so few in this book in which the descriptions are otherwise so admirably clear. This is because Flaubert's use of figurative language, while clearly defining a shape or movement, is aimed primarily at evoking the striking and suggestive image, though never at the expense of objective precision. Flaubert preferred not to divert the attention of the reader with purely descriptive metaphors in a work whose main objective was to attain that profound and complex reality which only the combined talents of a writer who was an artist as well as a physiologist, a psychologist as well as a historian of moral customs, could reveal. (pp. 291-92)

*D. L. Demorest, "Structures of Imagery in 'Madame Bovary',"* in *"Madame Bovary" by Gustave Flaubert: Backgrounds and Sources, Essays in Criticism, edited and translated by Paul de Man, W. W. Norton & Company, Inc., 1965, pp. 280-92.*

## ALBERT THIBAUDET (essay date 1935)

[*Thibaudet was an early twentieth-century French literary critic and follower of the French philosopher Henri Bergson. He is often described as versatile, well informed, and original, and critics cite his unfinished* Histoire de la littérature française de 1789 à nos jours, *first published in 1936, as his major critical treatise. In this work, Thibaudet classified authors by the generations of 1789, 1820, 1850, 1885, and 1914-1918, rather than by literary movements. In the excerpt below, Thibaudet investigates Flaubert's handling of the theme of fate in* Madame Bovary. *Focusing his attention on Emma, Thibaudet cites the debate in the untranslated French study* Le roman naturaliste. *There, Ferdinand Brunetière argued that Emma's determining characteristic is sensuality, while Émile Faguet posited that it is imagination; Thibaudet concludes that both play a prominent role. Yet the most important factor, according to Thibaudet, is fate: "Emma is a victim of circumstance." This essay originally appeared in his French study* Gustave Flaubert *in 1935.*]

In the years around 1850, so decisive in the history of the novel, an inner logic was developed within the novel, from Balzac to Flaubert, just as an inner logic took form in French tragedy from Corneille to Racine. The novels of Balzac are constructed novels, sometimes excessively so; his imagination always remained lit, like the fire in the Cyclops' smithies. Balzac was a novelist endowed with the same natural power that inspired Corneille as a dramatist. But Flaubert set out from the antipodes of the Balzacian novel when he wrote the following sentence, one which would certainly have been endorsed by [Racine,] the author of *Berenice*: "I would like to write books in which I have only to write sentences, if I may say so, just as I have only to breathe in order to remain alive; I am bored by the subtleties of composition, by combinations aimed at effect, by all the calculations involved in the design, but which, nevertheless, are art, for style depends on these and on these alone." Spontaneity of conception remains for him the highest value. This spontaneity, which is that of Racine, not that of Corneille or Balzac, does not prevent him from carrying out all the demands of his art with consummate skill. With cold detachment, he performs the technical machinations which bore him to tears; for Balzac, they would have been an inherent part of the work from its very beginning, a part of the original organic idea. The technique of *Madame Bovary* has become a model for all novels, as that of [Racine's] *Andromache* is considered the model for all tragedies. (p. 372)

And yet, Flaubert himself had serious misgivings about the organization of his novel. . . .

> I think that the book will have a serious weakness, namely the relative length of the parts. I already have 260 pages that contain only preparatory action . . . The conclusion, which will narrate the death of my heroine, her burial and the ensuing distress of the husband, will take at least 260 pages. This leaves only 120 to 160 pages for the action properly speaking.

In his own defense, he states that the book is

> a biography, rather than a developed dramatic situation. It contains little action: if the dramatic element remains thoroughly immersed in the general tone of the work, the lack of proportion between the different episodes and their

development is likely to remain unnoticed. Moreover, it seems to me that life itself is a little like that.

Flaubert's choice of vocabulary is quite revealing here. "Action" and "dramatic element" are used as closely synonymous with composition or organization; it seems that the novel can do without them precisely because it is unlike the theater. The theater abstracts and retains privileged moments, moments of crisis; as such, it is forced to compose and to organize: it must group the moments in such a way that a maximum of useful effort is contained in a minimum of time and space. The dramatist is governed by time, whereas the novelist controls it; he can cut an entire life out of the cloth of time, and do so at his own will. Flaubert's novel is not a "human comedy" like Balzac's, but a pure novel. (pp. 372-73)

[Like Charles Dickens's] *David Copperfield* or George Eliot's *The Mill on the Floss*, **Madame Bovary** can be called a biography. But rather than the biography of one individual, it is a sequence of interrelated life histories. From a certain point of view, the individual biography which delimits the novel's dimension in time, is that of Charles Bovary, not Emma's. The book opens with his entrance into college—and with his cap—and it ends with his death.

To be more accurate, **Madame Bovary** seems to be a biography of human life in general rather than of a particular person. . . . To be human is to feel oneself as a conglomeration of possibilities, a multiplicity of potential personalities; the artist is the one who makes this potential real. It would take some effort to apply so general a truth to all characters in Flaubert's novel—such as, for instance, Charles Bovary. The first pages of the novel consist of memories from school-life. They are a first introduction into this complex world. . . . [From] the school scene on, which is like a summary of existence, Charles's entire life is prefigured. Without realizing it, Charles had already been selected as a mate by the Emma Flaubert who was going to drag him into the light of notoriety and make him part of an inseparable couple. (pp. 373-74)

Flaubert's novel is entirely contained between Charles Bovary's cap and his profound statement at the end, the only one he will ever pronounce, after which nothing is left for him to do but drop to the ground like a ripe apple: "Fate willed it this way!" Such is Charles's beginning and his end. In a page of his early travel impressions entitled **Along Fields and Sea Shores** Flaubert had already revealed his intention of writing the chapter on hats that is still missing in literature; the passage on Breton hats is a prelude to Charles's famous cap. With its "dumb ugliness that had depths of expression like an imbecile's face," the whole of Yonville-l'Abbaye is already contained in the cap. A miserable life, but a life just the same; the novel of a miserable life, but nevertheless a life, is being prepared to crown the forehead of the same child, whose name is not Charles but Legion. (p. 374)

This type of lyricism or, rather, of counterlyricism is very typical of Flaubert. It demands some preparation to be appreciated and many a reader approves it with misgivings. The detail of the hat is as essential as it is gratuitous—a proper definition, be it said in passing, of pure lyricism and of spontaneous symbolism as well. (p. 375)

The development of the action, in **Madame Bovary**, does not occur by a simple succession of events but by the concentric expansion of a theme, first encountered in its simplest form, then gradually gaining in richness and complexity. The process reflects the very motion of fate. We call "fated" a development that was already contained in a previous situation but without being apparent. We have a feeling of fatality when we feel that life was not worth living, because we have come back to exactly the same point from which we started, and discovered that the road which was to be one of discovery turns out to be the circular path of our prison walls.

And yet, this novel of fate is a novel of life and of hope.

When we consider these creatures as completed and unified destinies, their lives are indeed heart-rending failures; but all of them have known the sacred moments after which there can only be decline and preparation for the grave. Charles experiences it when, hidden in a cartload, he sees the signal announcing from the window of Rouault's farmhouse that he has been accepted. Emma experiences it in the early phases of her love for Rodolphe. Seen as a whole, the novel is not one-sidedly pessimistic; dark and light are evenly marked. Flaubert has not reached the total desolation of *Bouvard and Pécuchet*. Tostes and Yonville are like two concentric circles. Tostes is a more empty and cursory image than Yonville. The transition from one town to another, from one form of existence in the Bovary household to another which is yet the same, is a masterpiece of subtle progression. Tostes resembles Yonville as a sketch resembles the final picture. Flaubert takes pains not to fill in the details of his earlier outline, yet all the earlier characteristics of Yonville are already there, albeit in the general and abstract outline, without proper names, like an architectural model. "Every day at the same time the schoolmaster in a black skullcap opened the shutters of his house, and the village policeman, wearing his sword over his blouse, passed by." The two nameless figures suffice here to express the routine of a small town. (pp. 375-76)

The end of the story at Tostes also ends the actual marital life of Madame Bovary. Since all the attention is concentrated on Emma and Charles's joint existence, no other characters are needed; Flaubert introduces none, except for the servant. Tostes is no stage on which things are happening; Flaubert uses it to show how Charles lives, sleeps, dresses, and eats, how he gets on his wife's nerves and depresses her. The first part closes when she throws her bridal bouquet in the fire. "She watched it burn . . . the little pasteboard berries burst. . . ."

This sketch is followed by the completed picture, the stage on which characters and events will appear. Tostes was the small town; Yonville too is the small town but it is Yonville as well. Tostes lost itself to become the typical small town, but now the small town mingles with the reality of Yonville and becomes this reality; it is the usual transubstantiation of art. This is why the second part begins with a detailed description of Yonville, in the manner of Balzac. The purpose is to create a genuine setting, to set the stage, not for a human comedy but for the comedy of human stupidity and suffering. Flaubert goes about this task with a quiet and merciless thoroughness: the notary's house, the church, the townhall, and facing the Golden Lion Hotel, M. Homais' pharmacy with its red and green bocals, which shine in the evening like Bengal fires. The dinner at the Golden Lion follows the typical, perhaps all too typical, technique of exposition, as in Racine's *Bajazet*: all the inhabitants of Yonville are successively described from the point of view that reveals them most clearly, and Homais is allowed to dominate the scene. This is the chosen setting in which all the characters, and especially Emma, will come to light and their destinies unfold.

Emma passes with good reason for one of the most masterful portraits of a woman in fiction; the most living and the truest to life. "A masterpiece," [the French prelate] Dupanloup told Dumas, "yes, a true masterpiece, for those who have been confessors in the provinces." Flaubert substituted his artistic intuition for the confessor's experience; he would not have created this masterpiece if he hadn't identified with his heroine and shared her existence. He created her, not only out of the recollections of his own soul, but out of the recollections of his own flesh. She is never seen from the same distant and ironic viewpoint as the other characters in the book. Women are well aware of this and recognize in her their inner beauty and their inner suffering, as a man endowed with a noble imagination is bound to recognize himself in Don Quixote. (pp. 376-77)

Emma is a true heroine—unlike Sancho and Homais, who are counterheroes—because she has senses. In trying to explain the superiority of *Madame Bovary* over the *Sentimental Education*, Brunetière said [in *Le roman naturaliste*] that Emma's character represents something "stronger and more refined than the commonplace" without which there can not be a truly great novel. "In the nature of this woman, commonplace as she is, there is something extreme and, for that reason, rare. It is the refinement of her senses." There is nothing extreme or rare in any of the characters in the *Education*. But Faguet writes [in the same work]: "Mme. Bovary is not exactly a sensuous person; she is above all a 'romantic,' a mental type, as the psychologists would call it; her first fault stems from an unbridled imagination rather than from a lack of control over the senses. The reason for the first downfall is her desire to know love; in her second downfall, she is moved by the desire to give herself to the man she loves."

Brunetière is right, not Faguet. Emma is first and foremost a person of sensuous nature; she is like the artist in that she is endowed with an unusual degree of sensuality. This is why, as an artist, Flaubert can identify with her and assert: I myself am Mme. Bovary. Whenever Emma is seen in purely sensuous terms, he speaks of her with a delicate, almost religious feeling, the way Milton speaks of Eve. He relinquishes his cold and detached tone and shifts to a lyrical voice, indicating that the author is using the character as a substitute for himself. So, for instance, when she has first given herself to Rodolphe:

> The shades of night were falling: the horizontal sun passing between the branches dazzled the eyes. Here and there around her in the leaves or on the ground, trembled luminous patches, as if humming-birds flying about had scattered their feathers. Silence was everywhere; something sweet seemed to come forth from the trees. She felt her heartbeat return, and the blood coursing through her flesh like a river of milk. Then far away, beyond the wood, on the other hills, she heard a vague prolonged cry, a voice which lingered, and in silence she heard it mingling like music with the last pulsations of her throbbing nerves. Rodolphe, a cigar between his lips, was mending with his penknife one of the two broken bridles.

If the novel itself is like a substance in motion, then Emma is the one who is being carried by the flow of this stream. She is the stream, whereas Rodolphe is only another pebble among the stones deposited on the riverbanks.

Flaubert was able to forestall his own critics, and he rightly showed that "intelligent readers want their characters all of a piece and consistent, as they only appear in books." For him, to the contrary, "Ulysses is, perhaps, the strongest character-type in all ancient literature, and Hamlet in modern literature," because of their complexity. Mme. Bovary is not simple. Her sensuality is combined with a vulgar imagination and a considerable degree of naïveté—or, in other words, of stupidity. Flaubert needed a character of this kind to satisfy his poetical as well as his critical instinct, his sense of beauty as well as his taste for a sad, grotesque incongruity.

Emma, like Don Quixote, doesn't place her desire and the things she desires on the same plane. Emma's sensuous desire, like Don Quixote's generous fantasies, are in themselves magnificent realities in which Flaubert and Cervantes project the best part of themselves. They admire desire and abandonment, but they have contempt for the things desired, the miserable bottle that comes out of a ridiculous pharmacy. Neither have any illusions about the value of the object desired by the imagination, and one half of their artistic nature—the realist half—mercilessly paints these mediocre and derisive objects.

Apart from her sensuous desire, everything else about Emma is mediocre. Flaubert marks her with this terrible trait: "She was incapable of understanding what she did not experience, or of believing anything that did not take on a conventional form." At heart, she is still the Norman peasant, "callous, not very responsive to the emotions of others, like most people of peasant stock whose souls always retain some of the coarseness of their father's hands."

She is more ardent that passionate. She loves life, pleasure, love itself much more than she loves a man; she is made to have lovers rather than a lover. It is true that she loves Rodolphe with all the fervor of her body, and with him she experiences the moment of her complete, perfect and brief fulfillment; her illness, however, after Rodolphe's desertion, is sufficient to cure her of this love. She does not die from love, but from weakness and a total inability to look ahead, a naïveté which makes her an easy prey to deceit in love as well as in business. She lives in the present and is unable to resist the slightest impulse.... The final stages of her life that will lead her to her death are strictly personal, limited to the injustice and the criminality of the solitary self. Flaubert's novel is as Jansenist in spirit as Racine's *Phèdre*, and he has treated Emma's death as a damnation. He has made the devil present in the figure of the blind man, the grimacing monster she glimpsed during her adulterous trips to Rouen, the beggar to whom she throws her last piece of silver, as a lost soul is cast to the devil by the act of suicide. She dies with an atrocious laugh of horror and despair, as she hears him singing under her window, "thinking she saw the hideous face of the poor wretch loom out of the eternal darkness like a menace." This symbol of damnation was certainly present in Flaubert's mind; he wrote to Bouilhet that the blind man had to be present at Emma's death and that, for that reason, he needed to invent the episode of Homais' ointment. Lamartine, who was greatly disturbed by *Madame Bovary,* told Flaubert that he found the end of the book revolting: the punishment greatly surpassed the crime. It is true that we are here in a very different mood than in *Jocelyn.*

The fact is that Lamartine, in *Jocelyn,* was delighting in himself, while Flaubert, in *Madame Bovary,* subjects himself to the most scathing self-criticism. Emma symbolizes the double illusion which he has only very recently overcome. First, the illusion that things change for the better in time, an illusion as necessary to life as water is to plants: "She did not believe that things could remain the same in different places, and since the portion of her life that lay behind her had been bad, no doubt that which remained to be lived would be better." Then, the same illusion in spatial terms: "The closer things were to her, the more her thoughts turned away from them. All her immediate surroundings, the boring countryside, the stupid petty bourgeois, the mediocrity of existence, seemed to her to be exceptions in the world, a particular fate of which she was the victim, while an immense domain of passion and happiness stretched out beyond, as far as the eye could reach." When she is in the convent, she dreams of the outside world; later, she will remember these schooldays as her only moments of true happiness, because at that time the entire world was still a blank page and her heart full of infinite possibilities. On returning home to her father, she can no longer cope with country life and she accepts Charles, the healthy doctor who rides around on horseback, merely because he represents the outside world. When she marries him, she dreams of other places. It is true then, after all, that she is Brunetière's sensuous woman as well as Faguet's woman of imagination. But she is still something else besides.

She is also the person without luck. From a certain point of view, *Madame Bovary* is the novel of failure and bad luck, of a particularly unfortunate concentration of circumstances. Is Emma really altogether ridiculous and wrong when she believes that, in another setting and surrounded by different people, she might have been relatively happy? Don Quixote was bound to be disappointed, for he lives in a time and place when it is much easier to find windmills than knights-errant. His misadventures are not a matter of good or bad fortune; but, to a very considerable extent, Emma is a victim of circumstance. Considering how easily and thoroughly she is seduced by her lovers, it would seem that a certain kind of husband would conceivably have satisfied her heart and her senses. But Charles, one could say, has been systematically invented to be her undoer. She "made efforts to love him and repented in tears for having given in to another." It took the incident of the clubfoot to make her realize once and forever the incurable stupidity of her husband. In his failure, Charles becomes the cause and the symbol for all the failures in Emma's life. She could have experienced the great revenge and pride of women, to give birth to a man. "She hoped for a son; he would be strong and dark; she would call him Georges, and this idea of having a male child was like a revenge for all her impotence in the past." But it is a girl. In looking for religious help, she might have had better luck than with the unusually inept Bournisien, another character worthy of her bad luck. Her only acquaintance at Yonville is Mme. Homais who, by a refined irony of fate, is the female equivalent of Bovary himself. And Lheureux! with Homais, the one who ends up on top, as fortunate in life as his name suggests. ["Heureux" means happy in French; Lheureux is "the happy one" or, ironically, the one associated with happiness.] The walls against which she will finally dash herself to pieces have been erected around her as by an evil artist. When Charles says: Fate willed it that way! the reader acquiesces, and feels he has been reading the story of an ill-starred woman. *Madame Bovary,* like [Abbé Prévost's] *Manon Lescaut,* is a novel of love; like *Don Quixote,* it is a novel of the fictional imagination—but, aside from this, it is also, like Voltaire's *Candide,* a novel of fate.

A novel of fate, of destiny, can only exist in the absence of a strong will power. This is true in Emma's case. She is sustained by no will power, either from within herself, or from her husband. She is surrounded by the will of others, the will to seduce her in the person of Rodolphe, and the will to despoil her in Lheureux. In the absence of will power, she has enough passion, enough spontaneous excitement and somber selfishness to drive a man to criminal deeds. In her question: "Have you got your gun?" We see her willingness to make Rodolphe into a murderer; in her "At your office," that she would make Léon a thief.... (pp. 377-81)

Though she is a creature of passion, she doesn't kill herself out of love but for money; she is not punished as an adulterous woman, but as an untidy housekeeper. This has surprised some, who consider that the two parts of the novel are not consistent with each other. But logical consistency, in fiction, is a certain road to disaster; there is no need for the two parts to be logically connected. In the flesh and the blood of a living creature, they are perfectly coherent. For women, beauty is first of all a matter of décor and, for the bourgeois daughter of a farmer, the substance of life is likely to consist of a rather showy kind of cheap silverware.... In the nineteenth century, [the love of money] was a fundamental theme of the realistic novel. In the bourgeois world (as well as the other), love and money go together just as closely as love goes together with ambition, pride, and the affairs of the king in classical tragedy. In the final part of the novel, Léon and Lheureux are the two extremities of the candle that Emma is burning at both ends.

*Louis Bouilhet, a friend of Flaubert's who contributed to the genesis of* Madame Bovary.

All this aspect of the novel is prefigured in the evening at Vaubeyssard. The soles of Emma's satin shoes "were yellowed with the slippery wax of the dancing floor. Her heart resembled them; in its contact with wealth, something had rubbed off on it that could not be removed." At first, in her schoolgirl dreams, she had dreamt of love as an almost otherworldly experience. The ball at the châtcau convinces her that the world of the keepsakes and the novels really exists, and she identifies it with the world of wealth. She is left with the empty cigar case which she has picked up and by means of which, as with an archeological document, she reconstructs a world of love and luxury, joined like body and soul in the dream of an ideal life. "In her desire, she would confuse the sensuous pleasures of wealth with the raptures of the heart, the refinement of manners with the delicacy of sentiments." Her life will follow a parallel course on the financial and on the sentimental plane. The disappointments of the one coincide with the troubles of the other. Rodolphe and Lheureux are placed on either side of her life to exploit and destroy her, not through malicious intent, but because they act in accordance with the law of nature and society. They act according to the "right" of the seducer, which in France is always backed by established custom, and by the "right" of the usurer which is mistaken for law. After Rodolphe's letter, Emma falls ill and almost dies; after Lheureux's distraint, she dies in fact. The two faces of her destiny are symmetrical. This destiny is all of a piece. "The desires, the longing for money, and the melancholy of passion all blended into one suffering, and instead of putting it out of her mind, she made her thoughts cling to it, urging herself to pain and seeking everywhere the opportunity to revive it. A poorly served dish, a half open door would aggravate her; she bewailed the clothes she did not have, the happiness she had missed, her overexalted dreams, her too cramped home."

Like Sancho Panza and Molière's Tartuffe, Mme. Bovary is so real that she transcends reality and has become a type. The victim of love and the victim of usury do not seem a harmonious combination in the eyes of certain critics.... It seems, however, that a creature of fiction can only become a type when it exhibits such apparent anomalies of character; it seems that in this field also, as in the law of binocular vision, a perspective of real depth can only be achieved by the juxtaposition of two images. When Flaubert embarked on the gigantic *Temptation of Saint Anthony*, he had meant to write his *Faust*. He must have realized his mistake. It is striking, however, that it is precisely after his trip to the Orient, when he has given up his *Temptation* and embarked, at Bouilhet's advice, on the story of Delamarre and Delamarre's wife, that he succeeds in creating something close to a French *Faust*. (pp. 382-83)

> *Albert Thibaudet, " 'Madame Bovary'," in* Madame Bovary by Gustave Flaubert: Backgrounds and Sources, Essays in Criticism, *edited and translated by Paul de Man, W. W. Norton & Company, Inc., 1965, pp. 371-83.*

**ERICH AUERBACH**   (essay date 1942-45)

*[Auerbach was a German-born American philologist and critic. He is best known for his* Mimesis: Dargestellte Wirklichkeit in der abendländischen Literatur (Mimesis: The Representation of Reality in Western Literature), *a landmark study in which the critic explores the interpretation of reality through literary representation. The breadth of Auerbach's learning is evident in the scope of the work: he begins with an examination of literary imitation in the Bible and Homer and progresses through literary history to an explication of the works of such modern writers as*

*Marcel Proust and Virginia Woolf. Auerbach's discussion of nine-teenth-century authors includes commentary on Flaubert, Sten-dhal, Johann Wolfgang von Goethe, Johann Christoph von Schiller, and Fedor Dostoevski. In the following essay, which was written between 1942 and 1945 and published in* Mimesis, *Auerbach discusses Flaubert's use of technique and point of view. To that end, Auerbach closely examines two brief passages from* Madame Bovary; *the passage that begins this excerpt occurs in Part I, Chapter 1. According to this critic, Flaubert had an original method of storytelling: "In a series of pure pictures . . . a gray and random human destiny moves toward its end." Thus, the story is advanced through pictorial representation. Auerbach also investigates Flaubert's narrative perspective and relates it to the development of realism. In contrast with such contemporary re-alistic writers as Stendhal and Honoré de Balzac, Flaubert neither comments on his characters nor identifies with them. Instead, as evidenced in the passages discussed below, he adopts a dual narrative stance that encompasses both the objective and subjec-tive: although Flaubert employs an external narrator who presents Emma as part of the scene, the narrator recounts the experience from her perspective. Yet the manner of description is that of the author, who explains Emma's confused emotional experience with an understanding that she lacks. An examination of the relation-ship between subjective experience and the objective world in* Madame Bovary *is presented by Georges Poulet (1955). For additional commentary on Flaubert's style, technique, and nar-rative perspective in the novel, see excerpts by Henry James (1902), W. von Wartburg (1946), Martin Turnell (1950), Stephen Ullmann (1957), Jean Rousset (1962), Victor Brombert (1966), Leo Bersani (see Additional Bibliography), and Marcel Proust and Percy Lubbock (see* NCLC, *Vol. 2). For further commentary on* Madame Bovary *by Auerbach, see* NCLC, *Vol. 2.]*

Mais c'était surtout aux heures des repas qu'elle n'en pouvait plus, dans cette petite salle au rez-de-chaussée, avec le poêle qui fumait, la porte qui criait, les murs qui suintaient, les pavés humides; toute l'amertume de l'existence lui semblait servie sur son assiette, et, à la fumée du bouilli, il montait du fond de son âme comme d'autres bouffées d'affadissement. Charles était long à manger; elle grignotait quelques noi-settes, ou bien, appuyée du coude, s'amusait, avec la pointe de son couteau, de faire des raies sur la toile cirée.

(But it was above all at mealtimes that she could bear it no longer, in that little room on the ground floor, with the smoking stove, the creaking door, the oozing walls, the damp floor-tiles; all the bitterness of life seemed to be served to her on her plate, and, with the steam from the boiled beef, there rose from the depths of her soul other exhalations as it were of disgust. Charles was a slow eater; she would nibble a few hazel-nuts, or else, leaning on her elbow, would amuse herself making marks on the oil-cloth with the point of her table-knife.)

The paragraph forms the climax of a presentation whose subject is Emma Bovary's dissatisfaction with her life in Tostes. She has long hoped for a sudden event which would give a new turn to it—to her life without elegance, adventure, and love, in the depths of the provinces, beside a mediocre and boring husband; she has even made preparations for such an event, has lavished care on herself and her house, as if to earn that turn of fate, to be worthy of it; when it does not come, she is seized with unrest and despair. All this Flaubert describes in several pictures which portray Emma's world as it now appears

to her; its cheerlessness, unvaryingness, grayness, staleness, airlessness, and inescapability now first become clearly ap-parent to her when she has no more hope of fleeing from it. Our paragraph is the climax of the portrayal of her despair. (pp. 482-83)

The paragraph itself presents a picture—man and wife together at mealtime. But the picture is not presented in and for itself; it is subordinated to the dominant subject, Emma's despair. Hence it is not put before the reader directly: here the two sit at table—there the reader stands watching them. Instead, the reader first sees Emma, who has been much in evidence in the preceeding pages, and he sees the picture first through her; directly, he sees only Emma's inner state; he sees what goes on at the meal indirectly, from within her state, in the light of her perception. The first words of the paragraph, *Mais c'était surtout aux heures des repas qu'elle n'en pouvait plus . . .* state the theme, and all that follows is but a development of it. Not only are the phrases dependent upon *dans* and *avec*, which define the physical scene, a commentary on *elle n'en pouvait plus* in their piling up of the individual elements of discomfort, but the following clause too, which tells of the distaste aroused in her by the food, accords with the principal purpose both in sense and rhythm. When we read further, *Charles était long à manger*, this, though gramatically a new sentence and rhythmically a new movement, is still only a resumption, a variation, of the principal theme; not until we come to the contrast between his leisurely eating and her disgust and to the nervous gestures of her despair, which are described imme-diately afterward, does the sentence acquire its true signifi-cance. The husband, unconcernedly eating, becomes ludicrous and almost ghastly; when Emma looks at him and sees him sitting there eating, he becomes the actual cause of the *elle n'en pouvait plus;* because everything else that arouses her desperation—the gloomy room, the commonplace food, the lack of a tablecloth, the hopelessness of it all—appears to her, and through her to the reader also, as something that is con-nected with him, that emanates from him, and that would be entirely different if he were different from what he is.

The situation, then, is not presented simply as a picture, but we are first given Emma and then the situation through her. It is not, however, a matter—as it is in many first-person novels and other later works of a similar type—of a simple represen-tation of the content of Emma's consciousness, of *what* she feels *as* she feels it. Though the light which illuminates the picture proceeds from her, she is yet herself part of the picture, she is situated within it. . . . Here it is not Emma who speaks, but the writer. *Le poêle qui fumait, la porte qui criait, les murs qui suintaient, les pavés humides*—all this, of course, Emma sees and feels, but she would not be able to sum it all up in this way. *Toute l'amertume de l'existence lui semblait servie sur son assiette*—she doubtless has such a feeling; but if she wanted to express it, it would not come out like that; she has neither the intelligence nor the cold candor of self-accounting necessary for such a formulation. To be sure, there is nothing of Flaubert's life in these words, but only Emma's; Flaubert does nothing but bestow the power of mature expression upon the material which she affords, in its complete subjectivity. If Emma could do this herself, she would no longer be what she is, she would have outgrown herself and thereby saved herself. So she does not simply see, but is herself seen as one seeing, and is thus judged, simply through a plain description of her subjective life, out of her own feelings. Reading in a later passage (part 2, chapter 12): *jamais Charles ne lui paraissait aussi désagréable, avoir les doigts aussi carrés, l'esprit aussi lourd, les façons si communes* . . . , the reader perhaps thinks for a moment that this strange series is an emotional piling up of the causes that time and again bring Emma's aversion to her husband to the boiling point, and that she herself is, as it were, inwardly speaking these words. . . . But this would be a mistake. We have here, to be sure, a number of paradigmatic causes of Emma's aversion, but they are put together deliberately by the writer, not emotionally by Emma. For Emma feels much more, and much more confusedly; she sees other things than these—in his body, his manners, his dress; memories mix in, meanwhile she perhaps hears him speak, perhaps feels his hand, his breath, sees him walk about, good-hearted, limited, unappetizing, and unaware; she has countless confused impressions. The only thing that is clearly defined is the result of all this, her aversion to him, which she must hide. Flaubert transfers the clearness to the impressions; he selects three, apparently quite at random, but which are paradigmatically taken from Bovary's physique, his mentality, and his behavior; and he arranges them as if they were three shocks which Emma felt one after the other. This is not at all a naturalistic representation of consciousness. Natural shocks occur quite differently. The ordering hand of the writer is present here, deliberately summing up the confusion of the psychological situation in the direction toward which it tends of itself—the direction of "aversion to Charles Bovary." This ordering of the psychological situation does not, to be sure, derive its standards from without, but from the material of the situation itself. It is the type of ordering which must be employed if the situation itself is to be translated into language without admixture.

In a comparison of this type of presentation with those of Stendhal and Balzac, it is to be observed . . . that here too the two distinguishing characteristics of modern realism are to be found; here too real everyday occurrences in a low social stratum, the provincial petty bourgeoisie, are taken very seriously . . . ; here too everyday occurrences are accurately and profoundly set in a definite period of contemporary history (the period of the bourgeois monarchy)—less obviously than in Stendhal or Balzac, but unmistakably. In these two basic characteristics the three writers are at one, in contradistinction to all earlier realism; but Flaubert's attitude toward his subject is entirely different. In Stendhal and Balzac we frequently and indeed almost constantly hear what the writer thinks of his characters and events; sometimes Balzac accompanies his narrative with a running commentary—emotional or ironic or ethical or historical or economic. We also very frequently hear what the characters themselves think and feel, and often in such a manner that, in the passage concerned, the writer identifies himself with the character. Both these things are almost wholly absent from Flaubert's work. (pp. 483-86)

[The passage above] shows man and wife at table, the most everyday situation imaginable. Before Flaubert, it would have been conceivable as literature only as part of a comic tale, an idyl, or a satire. Here it is a picture of discomfort, and not a momentary and passing one, but a chronic discomfort, which completely rules an entire life, Emma Bovary's. To be sure, various things come later, among them love episodes; but no one could see the scene at table as part of the exposition for a love episode, just as no one would call **Madame Bovary** a love story in general. The novel is the representation of an entire human existence which has no issue; and our passage is a part of it, which, however, contains the whole. Nothing particular happens in the scene, nothing particular has happened just before it. It is a random moment from the regularly recurring hours at which the husband and wife eat together. They

are not quarreling, there is no sort of tangible conflict. Emma is in complete despair, but her despair is not occasioned by any definite catastrophe; there is nothing purely concrete which she has lost or for which she has wished. Certainly she has many wishes, but they are entirely vague—elegance, love, a varied life; there must always have been such unconcrete despair, but no one ever thought of taking it seriously in literary works before; such formless tragedy, if it may be called tragedy, which is set in motion by the general situation itself, was first made conceivable as literature by romanticism; probably Flaubert was the first to have represented it in people of slight intellectual culture and fairly low social station; certainly he is the first who directly captures the chronic character of this psychological situation. Nothing happens, but that nothing has become a heavy, oppressive, threatening something. How he accomplishes this we have already seen; he organizes into compact and unequivocal discourse the confused impressions of discomfort which arise in Emma at sight of the room, the meal, her husband. Elsewhere too he seldom narrates events which carry the action quickly forward; in a series of pure pictures—pictures transforming the nothingness of listless and uniform days into an oppressive condition of repugnance, boredom, false hopes, paralyzing disappointments, and piteous fears—a gray and random human destiny moves toward its end. (pp. 488-89)

*Erich Auerbach, "In the Hôtel de la Mole," in his* Mimesis: The Representation of Reality in Western Literature, *translated by Willard R. Trask, Princeton University Press, 1953, pp. 454-92.**

### W. VON WARTBURG (essay date 1946)

[*Von Wartburg's essay was previously published in French as* Évolution et structure de la langue française *in 1946. Here, the critic studies Flaubert's use of language in relation to realism. Diction, for Flaubert, is never arbitrary or unreasoned. Instead, according to von Wartburg, Flaubert "is aware of an inner unity between word, thing, and concept, between sentence and thought." For additional commentary on Flaubert's style and technique in* Madame Bovary, *see excerpts by Henry James (1902), Erich Auerbach (1942-45), Martin Turnell (1950), Stephen Ullmann (1957), Victor Brombert (1966), and Marcel Proust and Percy Lubbock (see NCLC, Vol. 2).*]

In their vocabulary as well as in their style, the realists seem to be the direct successors of the romantics. Yet Flaubert's use of language is very different from Balzac's. It is true that the Norman master has the pharmacist Homais use a mixture of scientific and colloquial speech that fully reveals his shortcomings and the evil caused by an incomplete semi-education. The village priest Bournisien speaks in commonplaces whose presumably elevated tone clashes with his lowly character. But whereas in Balzac every sentence is like a spontaneous, uncontrolled outburst originating in the fire of composition, Flaubert's every expression, phrase, or sentence has been most carefully tested. Realism removed many social, moral, and puristic barriers that stood in the way of numberless words. While making considerable use of this new-gained freedom, Flaubert curtails it by a set of new restrictions. He doesn't want the freedom to become lawlessness; such a relaxation of rules would take language away from its spiritual origins. Flaubert cannot tolerate the distance which, as a result of the development of civilization and of language, now separates the inner feeling from its expression, the thing from the word. . . . His entire life-work was aimed at bridging this distance. Flaubert demands a new discipline, which he first of all forces upon himself. He wishes to create a style unlike any other known before.

The huge vocabulary now available will allow him to find the right expression for every shade of meaning; on the other hand, every sentence must make use of the full esthetic, rhythmical, descriptive, and auditive resources of the language. Flaubert's own definition of style has often been quoted: "I think of a style that would be beautiful . . . rhythmical like poetry, precise like the language of science, capable of the sustained melody of a violincello and scintillating like fire. A style that would enter the mind like a stiletto and on which our thought could travel as over smooth water, like a boat with a favorable breeze. We must realize that prose has only just begun to discover its possibilities." Other considered words merely as symbols pointing toward the objects they designate; they thought them adequate when they were able to perform this service. But Flaubert is aware of a mysterious unity between the word and the object. "Style," he writes, "is by itself an absolute way of perceiving things." . . . The realists among the scholastic philosophers had contested the assertion of the nominalists, who thought of names as universals: *Universalia sunt nomina.* The realists considered them to be mere *realia.* Without being aware of it, Flaubert renewed in his way the ancient debate, transferring it to the level of language. He is aware of an inner unity between word, thing, and concept, between sentence and thought. This intimate union between the word and the thing

it names finds its equivalence in the relationship between the sentence and its enunciatory function. The choice and the order of words reveal the state of mind of the characters.

In one of his letters, Flaubert himself stated: "Those fellows still stick to the old notion that form is like a garment. But no! form is the very flesh of thought, as thought is the soul of life." . . . Flaubert was to devote his life's work to the inner unity between words and things. Before him, the best authors had used some of the resources of language, but they had done so unconsciously. They worked by instinct, rather than with a full knowledge of the expressive power of words. Flaubert was able to cast the light of human consciousness on what had remained in darkness. He did for language what Descartes did for the Self when he made it the foundation of human consciousness. (pp. 357-59)

> W. von Wartburg, "Flaubert's Language," in "Madame Bovary" by Gustave Flaubert: Backgrounds and Sources, Essays in Criticism, *edited and translated by Paul de Man, W. W. Norton & Company, Inc., 1965, pp. 357-59.*

## ALBERT BÉGUIN (essay date 1950)

[*In the following essay, originally published as "En relisant* Madame Bovary" *in* La table ronde, *March 27, 1950, Béguin compares the original draft of the novel with the much-revised published version. Béguin notes that Flaubert made three kinds of alterations: he diluted descriptions of sensual experience, eliminated subtle psychological nuances of the characters, and omitted spontaneous metaphors that lend a poetic quality to the early drafts. Despite great admiration for the novel, Béguin contends that these alterations weaken the work and laments that Flaubert "never ceased wasting some of his most precious gifts in order to satisfy the tyrannical demands of an aesthetic prejudice." Other critics who probe Flaubert's letters and early drafts of* Madame Bovary *as a key to his creative expression include Jean Pierre Richard (1954) and Charles Du Bos (see Additional Bibliography).*]

There are certain books one can not reread without being seduced again by the effect they made upon us when we first read them. *Madame Bovary* is surrounded by just such a protective halo. Even after one has lost one's taste for Flaubert's rhetoric, or learned to prefer by far the bitter sadness of *The Sentimental Education* to the firm structure of *Madame Bovary,* the novel nevertheless retains its power; perhaps we should call it the power of an irresistible boredom. The book is closer to truth than to life; it is too tightly written, built on the obsessive continuity of successive paragraphs patterned on the same few rhythmical designs. Each new reading leaves one more disappointed. Something seems to be lacking that one hoped to find again. Certain suggestions, physical sensations, and inward states of being lingered on in one's memory, and one looks in vain for them in the text. One of Flaubert's main qualities is that he suggests more than he says; this talent is not without danger, when it turns out that the book, at a few years' distance, seems much less rich than one remembered.

It has long since been known that Flaubert's exhausting labor consisted mostly of cutting down and that, from his earliest version to the final text, he made a systematic effort to prune away anything that seemed superfluous. (p. 292)

[In reading the original draft of *Madame Bovary*], predating the version that took Flaubert so many years of patient labor, one has the real impression of meeting a different work. The style has not yet been polished; it is uneven and frequently

*A photograph of Flaubert by Nadar.*

faulty, though amazingly free in invention. The human content, however, is infinitely richer than in the printed version. And yet, Flaubert has made few changes in the organization of his narrative; the different scenes follow each other in the same order, no important episodes have been suppressed, the characters remain the same. If the book is almost twice as long, it is because Flaubert ruthlessly eliminated from every paragraph, from every sentence, whatever could not be fitted to the movement of language which he wanted to obtain. He succeeded in this at the expense of numerous psychological insights and of admirable beauties of expression, often of exceptional originality.

This is not the place to reopen the old debate between Proust and Thibaudet on whether Flaubert was a born writer, or a writer devoid of original talent. One might say that, while he was the first to perceive, with the perspicacity of a great innovator, certain undiscovered aspects of the human soul, he had to keep most of them hidden because their expression would have required a freedom in the handling of language for which he was not yet ready. Obsessed by the *idée fixe* of a perfect form (an idea which may very well not apply to the novel and to the expression of a temporal experience that is infinitely complex), Flaubert wrote by nature a shapeless language about which he had serious misgivings. This language was marvelously suited for experimentation and discovery; it could alternate sudden explorations in depth with the suggestive flights of an extraordinarily fertile lyricism of images. It reads with difficulty, because it has been awkwardly composed, but it leads from surprise to surprise.

The passages most affected by Flaubert's pruning are of three kinds. Flaubert first tones down the passages in which physical life is too boldly described. Then, he mercilessly sacrifices thousands of psychological shades in the description of the characters, of their daydreams, their moments of reminiscence which make of his entire work an early "remembrance of things past." Finally, he eliminates often very beautiful metaphors that occur spontaneously, and give to the first version a poetic quality entirely lacking in the edited text. A few examples are necessary at this point.

Flaubert was certainly not being prudish when he cut the passages that reveal his very keen interest in the movements of sensuous life. True, he is no doubt acting out of concern for general decorum when he erases the four-letter words that frequently occur in his first drafts. But these are emendations of the same order as the suppression of many terms that stem from Norman dialect. However, when he tones down certain erotic passages, he is not merely acting out of fear of being considered crude. "Emma, left by herself and unable to sleep, felt such a violent desire for Rodolphe that she fancied she had to see him at once, without delay" becomes "She fancied she had to see Rodolphe at once." Elsewhere, referring to the meetings between Emma and Léon, one reads: ". . . Then they faced each other; they looked at each other, touching with their hands, their faces, their breasts, as if they didn't have senses enough with which to savor the joys of love, burning with desire, stamping their feet while staring at each other with lascivious laughs, until they could no longer wait for the moment of possession." In the printed version, this becomes the colorless lines: ". . . they faced each other, with voluptuous laughs and tender words." A little further on, Flaubert eliminates a long passage on the pleasures of love which ended like this: ". . . the pleasures of the senses did not invalidate this ideal image; to the contrary, they made it stronger. Emma

reconquered happiness in this blonde-colored passion and, knowing how uncertain it was, tried to increase it by means of all the artifices of her tenderness, savoring it with the craving of the poor, the thirst of the sick, the avarice of the elderly." No prudery is involved in the elimination of such passages, nor is prudery the main consideration in the suppression of rather strange scenes, such as the moment in which the officiating priest anoints the feet of the dying Mme. Bovary and awakens in her husband the memory of their wedding night, or the macabre scene in which Charles presses his lips on the forehead of her dead body in a "horrible kiss, of which the sensation remains forever on his lips, as a foretaste of the final putrefaction." In all these emendations, Flaubert obviously defeats himself as a writer; the original sentence, because of its violence and truthfulness, does not lend itself to reorganization: it grows awkward and confused. In order to safeguard the uniformity of rhythm and in obedience to the accepted principle of style, sacrifices become necessary. One should add an obvious lack of boldness on Flaubert's behalf in the face of certain verbal inventions that seem too unusual—such as, for instance, the "blonde-colored passion" which would have delighted a contemporary writer but which Flaubert doesn't dare to keep.

The same scruples, in a man who is held captive by his conception of style, lead him to eschew the majority of the psychological observations which gave the first version its pre-Proustian character. Something of this undoubtedly subsists in the novel as we know it; part of its suggestive power stems precisely from the recurring theme of involuntary recollection. This resurrection of the past (coupled with a prefiguration of the future) occurs in all the characters without exception and at all times; it constitutes the main ingredient of what has been called "bovarysme." The examples in the first draft however are both more frequent and more striking. Instead of Emma Bovary, it is her clod of a husband who experiences "intermittences of the heart" upon returning to the Bertaux farm after the death of his first wife: "Interrupted for a moment by this forgotten episode, his distant feeling was recovered, the past became the present and his memory a renewed emotion." He sees Emma again, and "the poor branches of his heart, nailed down by his restricted existence as on a flat wall beyond which they were not allowed to spread, upon receiving the glow that emanated from the young girl, blossomed in thousands of buds, of little flowers." One could find innumerable instances of similar quotations, in which the reverie leads to a strange awareness of subjective time. After the evening at Vaubyessard castle, Emma loses the sense of passing time: "What was it that set so far asunder the morning of the day before yesterday and the evening of today, so that both now seemed like two different existences put end to end?" (Final version: "What was it that set thus far asunder the morning of the day before yesterday and the evening of today?"). Much later, after the sinister orgy with Léon and his friends, Emma wanders through Rouen at dawn "her head full of noise, colors and sadness"; it seems to her that she is reliving an earlier moment of her life, although she is unable to remember "the place, the cause, or the time" at which it took place. At last she realizes that she is remembering the dance that she has only just left: "It seemed way behind her in a distant past, and already so far gone that she regretted no longer being there." Nothing of this observation remains in the revised text, with an unquestionable loss of depth and originality. Much less intimately linked with such metamorphoses of time, Emma's ennui becomes much more banal as it loses its metaphysical component.

Still for the same reason, Flaubert dispenses with the images that arise spontaneously in his first writing. When the memory of Rodolphe, buried away in Emma's heart, begins to fade away, the first version alone has a lyrical passage: "She had sung over him the funeral dirge of her lost youth . . . Between him and herself now stretched a long gallery of unknown pains, full of darkness, dust, and gold." The musical and color metaphors that recur in the early drafts gave them a particularly intense poetic quality to which, again, Flaubert refuses to abandon himself. The tyrannical law of the verbal cadence once more stifles the deeper rhythm, the multiple rhythm of the flesh, the image and time, which Flaubert perceived better than anyone but to which he seems to have refused to listen when he prepared his final manuscript.

I know of no other equally pathetic case in which a literary success could be achieved only at the cost of a secret undoing. In the course of his labors, Flaubert goes through two very different stages. In the first stage, which is that of invention, he listens as to an inner dictation and tries to follow as closely as possible the hidden movements of the inner life—something of which he has an astoundingly subtle knowledge. He is particularly astute at exploring the confines where the psychological and the physiological merge; these mysterious border regions are first to claim his attention. Like a clairvoyant blind man, he seeks his way to the discovery of an almost inexpressible reality. One can recognize this stage in a passage from the earlier version, when he speaks of the long daily letters that Emma writes to Rodolphe: ". . . Her sensations were reawakened by her efforts to translate them. In this way, Emma drew out her passion by passing it through the laminating presses of style. Yet it lost nothing of its solidity since the satisfaction of her desires added each day something new."

However, in the next stage, when Flaubert reconsidered his text for an infinite number of further revisions, his writing ceased to be this magical and Proustian devicc to resurrect the past. The rescuing act of memory no longer occurs and the expression "Laminating presses of style" takes on an altogether different meaning. Detached henceforth from the deeper realities which he had begun to discover, the novelist's only concern is to perfect what he now merely considers as a mass of sound that demands to be ordered. He no longer needs to record, as he did before, thousands of sensations in order to re-create one imaginary instant and, by means of this artificial reconstruction, put himself exactly in the same situation as the character he is describing. At first he had to identify himself as closely as possible with his creation, reliving his emotions, sharing his dreams; but now the author has to create a distance between himself and the character. Hence Flaubert's constant complaints about his labors, which were apparently an endless ordeal. All the flights of the imagination have died down; what remains on the page is a heavy and shapeless mass that demands to be modeled into shape in order to represent, not life itself, but an ideal model, an aesthetic canon of perfection. (pp. 293-96)

If it were not a vain game, one would like to dream of a Flaubert born fifty or seventy years later, who could have accepted without further ado the gift of a style beyond rules and a way of writing capable of recapturing exactly the inner movement it was expressing. Writing at the time of Proust, he would perhaps have known a happiness that was refused to him as long as he worshipped the idol of Art, to which he sacrificed his soul and his blood. But, in that case, we would not now have that irreplaceable great book **Madame Bovary,** the book of the impossible escape, the heavy-hearted poem of eternal *ennui.* (p. 297)

*Albert Béguin, "On Rereading 'Madame Bovary'," in "Madame Bovary" by Gustave Flaubert: Backgrounds and Sources, Essays in Criticism, edited and translated by Paul de Man, W. W. Norton & Company, Inc., 1965, pp. 292-97.*

**MARTIN TURNELL**  (essay date 1950)

[*In the following excerpt, Turnell presents a negative assessment of* Madame Bovary. *He begins by discussing the novel in relation to romanticism. The work's strength, according to Turnell, rests on its union of a romantic outlook with a realistic setting, which prevented the excesses of other romantic works. The weakness of the novel results from Flaubert's attitude toward Emma. To examine this attitude, Turnell divides the novel into five parts and discusses the most significant passages from each. His analysis of the symbolism and structure of* Madame Bovary *reveals that "in spite of its superficial moral orthodoxy, it is an onslaught on the whole basis of human feelings and on all spiritual and moral values." Turnell concludes that in his negative portrayal of Emma and her society, Flaubert demonstrates an immature, cynical world view and thus ultimately fails as a novelist. For additional commentary by Turnell, see excerpt below, 1957. Other critics who examine the novel's relationship to romanticism and realism include Paul Bourget (1897), Émile Faguet (1899), Henry James (1902), Victor Brombert (1966), Leo Bersani (1974), Anthony Thorlby (see Additional Bibliography), and Charles Augustin Sainte-Beuve and Charles Baudelaire (see* NCLC, Vol. 2). *For additional remarks on Flaubert's technique, see excerpts by Henry James (1902), Erich Auerbach (1942-45), W. von Wartburg (1946), Stephen Ullmann (1957), Victor Brombert (1966), and Marcel Proust and Percy Lubbock (see* NCLC, Vol. 2). *Further discussions of symbolism in* Madame Bovary *are provided by D. L. Demorest*

*A depiction of Flaubert at age thirty, when he began writing* Madame Bovary.

*(1931), Jean Pierre Richard (1954), Georges Poulet (1955), Jean Rousset (1962), and Victor Brombert (1966).]*

**Madame Bovary** is a study of the Romantic outlook. Its principal theme is the Romantic longing for a happiness which the world of common experience can never satisfy, the disillusionment which springs from the clash between the inner dream and an empty, hostile universe. Emma's misfortunes are caused by her inability to adapt herself to the world of everyday life. Her hunt for a Romantic passion leads to adultery which undermines her character, involves her in a life of subterfuge and deceit, and in the dubious financial transactions which ultimately drive her to suicide. . . .

The strength of **Madame Bovary** lies largely in the fact that it is not merely a study of the Romantic outlook, but of the Romantic outlook in a realistic setting which effectively prevented it from degenerating into another extravaganza in the manner of [Chateaubriand's] **René** or from being no more than a superior version of **Novembre.** The setting was not only a discipline; it made the book into a novel. For Emma's disillusionment does not spring merely from her desire for an impossible happiness. It springs from the conflict between impulses and emotions which are often sound and the pervading middle-class *bêtise* which corrodes them. (p. 258)

Now day-dreaming is not the monopoly or the vice of any one class. Emma appeals to those 'stock responses' from which not even the most sensitive readers are completely free. This leads them to assume that she is a symbol of universal validity without considering the value of the emotions which she symbolizes, and it explains their somewhat exaggerated estimate of the novel.

**Madame Bovary** is a remarkable book because of the subtlety with which Flaubert explored his theme, but it is not the flawless masterpiece for which it is usually taken. Its weaknesses lie partly in its execution and partly in the novelist's attitude towards his principal character. When Stendhal used the story of Berthet as his starting-point in *Le Rouge et le noir,* it became an *opportunity* for the display of his magnificent gifts and he created something which far transcended his original. Although the story of the Delamare family provided Flaubert with a discipline, it was also a *temptation.* We may suspect that he attempted a dispassionate analysis of the Romantic malady in the unconscious hope of curing himself of its ravages, but he was not really successful. It became an excuse . . . for exploiting all sorts of private manias.

Flaubert's relation to the Romantic Movement was a curious and an interesting one. Its impress is apparent on almost every page he wrote, but though it accounts for some of his most serious weaknesses, it also enabled him to make some of his most important discoveries. . . . [The Romantic Movement] blurred the division between man and nature, dream and reality, creating a new kind of awareness which could not be expressed in classic French prose. Its writers had moments of insight, but their work reveals a progressive movement away from the psychological realism of the seventeenth and eighteenth centuries, and it tends to dissolve into a flood of unrelated words and images. Flaubert attempted, with varying success, to create a style which was capable of exact analysis and which would at the same time make use of the colour and suggestiveness discovered by the Romantics.

There is a striking passage in Part I, chapter 7, which throws some light on Flaubert's originality. . . . (pp. 259-60)

She thought, at times, that these days of what people called the honeymoon, were the most beautiful that she had ever known. To savour their sweetness to the full, she should, of course, have travelled to those lands with sounding names where newly wedded bliss is spent in exquisite languor. Seated in a post-chaise behind curtains of blue silk, she should have climbed, at a foot's pace, precipitous mountain roads, listening to the postillion's song echoing from the rocks to the accompaniment of goats' bells and the muted sound of falling water. She should have breathed at sunset, on the shores of sea bays in the South, the scent of lemon trees, and at night, alone with her husband on a villa terrace, have stood hand in hand, watching the stars and planning for the future. It seemed to her that happiness must flourish better in some special places than elsewhere, as some plants grow best in certain kinds of soil. Why was it not her fate to lean upon the balcony of a Swiss chalet or hide her melancholy in some Highland cottage, with a husband dressed in black, long-skirted velvet coat, soft leather boots, a pointed hat, and ruffles at his wrist?

At a first reading one might pardonably suppose that this is no more than an unusually well-written description of a Romantic day-dream, but in reality it is far more than that. It is not only one of the central passages in **Madame Bovary,** it is also a landmark in the development of the European novel. The feelings are not in the nature of the undertaking very profound or very original, but in analysing the content of the Romantic *rêverie* Flaubert comes closer, perhaps, than any of his predecessors to the intimate workings of consciousness and his method clearly points the way to the inner monologue.

The passage, so far from being a straightforward description, is a deliberate piece of stylization which anticipates the method that was later used with conspicuous success by the Symbolists. For Flaubert translates feelings into *visual* images, enabling him to control expression by building each image into the final picture—in this case an imaginary voyage—and to register the transitions from one set of feelings to another with greater fidelity than had been possible before. The result seems to me to be a complete success and the passage an artistic whole. It is not, strictly speaking, a description at all, but the dramatic presentation of a 'mental event'. There is complete identity between image and feeling. Every image is a particle of Emma's sensibility and a strand in the final pattern. The 'lune de miel' is the symbol of a vague feeling of happiness associated with Emma's childhood, but its function is complex. It is the first of a series of images—landscapes, sounds, perfumes—which lead naturally from one to the other, and it also marks the point at which Emma's contact with the actual world ends and the *rêverie* begins. Her feeling of happiness is the material out of which she constructs an adventure in an imaginary world which has the sharpness and heightened reality of an hallucination. The *noms sonores,* the *douceur* and the *suaves paresses* build up a general impression of softness and languor, a lazy voluptuous happiness. As they echo and answer one another, so too do the sounds—the song which reverberates in the mountains is answered by the tinkle of the goats' bells, mingles with the muffled sound of the cascade and finally dies away in the silence of a summer night. When we come to 'Il lui semblait que certains lieux . . .' we notice a change in the tone of the passage. The note of exaltation symbolized by 'lune de miel', with which it opens, changes to a wistfulness as she contemplates a *bonheur* which already belongs to the past, and this is followed by a sudden sinking as the *bonheur* is transformed into *tristesse*. The image which dominates the first part of the passage and gives the whole its particular flavour is the image of the blue silk blinds with their smooth vivid tactile suggestions. . . . The blinds are drawn and are supposed to conceal strange depths of passion at play within the coach. So we have the impression of a blue mist radiating over the whole scene and enveloping it. The most striking thing about the passage, however, is the absence of the Romantic lover. The drawn blinds do not conceal an exotic passion, but an empty coach or a coach in which there is only a lonely woman. (pp. 260-62)

The passage leaves us with a sense of absence and this is the crux of the book. The account of the *physical* absence of the lover here is completed by the account of his *psychological* absence in another place. . . . (p. 262)

> On the eve of each of their meetings she told herself that *this* time their happiness would be unclouded, only to confess, after the event, that she felt no emotions out of the ordinary. Such recurrent disappointments were always swept away by a renewed surge of hope, and when she next saw him, she was more on fire, more exigent, than ever. She flung off her clothes with a sort of brutal violence, tearing at her thin stay-lace so that it hissed about her hips like a slithering snake. She tiptoed across the room on her bare feet to make sure that the door was really locked, and then, with a single gesture, let her things fall to the floor. Pale, speechless, solemn, she threw herself into his arms with a prolonged shudder.

The first sentence describes with great insight the central experience of Flaubert's work. The sensation of 'falling out of love' is not, perhaps, an unusual one, but Flaubert invests it with immense significance. He is the great master of negation. Some of the most impressive pages in his books describe the sudden collapse of all feeling, the void which suddenly opens at the supreme moments of life and the realization that not simply one's emotional life, but one's whole world has fallen into ruin. There is no crash, no disaster—it is this that makes it so horrifying—life simply comes to an end. When you look into it, you find that there is nothing there.

What I have called physical and psychological absence is combined in the *long frisson*. Emma's tragedy is twofold. It lies in her inability to adapt herself to the normal world and in her failure to construct a durable inner life which would compensate for its drabness. The *long frisson* reflects the tendency of the human mind to escape from the disenchantment of awakening and from the pressure of thought by deliberately submerging itself in primitive animal contacts, as Emma does here. It is a mental blackout, a voluptuous swoon in which the intelligence is completely suspended. The placing of the closing words and the punctuation—'et pâle, sans parler, sérieuse, elle s'abattait . . .'—convey the sensation of someone losing consciousness, falling into nothingness. The words are interesting for another reason. They mark the limit of Flaubert's power of analysis. . . . It is his own starved sensibility, his own incapacity for deep feeling that he portrays in Emma. (pp. 262-63)

*Madame Bovary* purports to be a study of the romantic outlook, but it is only partly that and partly an expression of the nov-

elist's personal attitude which could not always be conveyed through the symbols that he chose and was sometimes in flagrant conflict with them. 'Madame Bovary, c'est moi,' he said on another occasion. She was, but she was also the narrator as well as the heroine of *Novembre*. The similarity of outlook between the autobiographical story written when he was twenty-one and *Madame Bovary* is striking, and it brings home forcibly how little Flaubert developed. (p. 263)

There was nothing new in Flaubert's preoccupation with sexual passion, but his approach differs sensibly from that of his predecessors. The great dramatists and novelists of the past had concentrated on it because it is one of the profoundest of human instincts and enabled them to make some of the most searching studies of human nature that we possess. In Flaubert it had the reverse effect, narrowing instead of widening the scope of his work. He was aware of its importance, but he was only interested in its destructive effect on personality, and he selected it because it was the most vulnerable point for his carefully planned attack on human nature. For when we look into the structure of *Madame Bovary*, we find that so far from being a detached study of sexual mania and in spite of its superficial moral orthodoxy, it is an onslaught on the whole basis of human feeling and on all spiritual and moral values.

The first fifty pages, where he keeps his personal preoccupations severely under control, are amongst the best that Flaubert ever wrote. The main characters are introduced and their significance sketched. The narrative moves swiftly and economically forward. There is no padding and none of those disastrous descriptions of external reality which contribute so much to the ruin of *L'Éducation sentimentale*.

The book opens with the arrival of the absurd Charles Bovary as a new boy at his school. It is a delightful piece of comedy, but Flaubert's intention was serious. The description of his peculiar hat is a characteristic example of his symbolism which enables him to prepare the setting for Emma. . . . (p. 264)

> It was a nondescript sort of object, combining a number of different features—part woollen comforter, part military headdress, part pillbox, part fur bonnet, part cotton nightcap; one of those shoddy affairs which, like the face of an idiot, seems to express a certain secretive significance. Its general shape was that of an egg, and the upper part, stiffened with whalebone, rose from a base consisting of three bulging, circular, sausage-like protuberances. Above these was a pattern of alternating lozenges of rabbit-fur and velvet separated from one another by strips of some scarlet material. Higher still was a species of sack ending in a polygon of cardboard covered with a complicated design in braid and finished off with a long, and excessively thin, cord from which depended a small cross of gold thread in place of a tassel. The whole contraption was brand new, and had a bright, shining peak.
>
> (pp. 264-65)

The catalogue, which begins with a busby and ends with a nightcap, is clearly arranged in descending order and points to the moral and material decline of father and son. The ironical *composite* is one of the operative words. Charles's hat may contain 'elements' of several different kinds of hat, but it does not belong completely to any recognizable category. It is a stupid, shapeless muddle like the wearer and the society in which he lives. The downward movement leads naturally to "une de ces pauvres choses. . .dont la laideur muette a des profondeurs d'expression comme le visage d'un imbécile."

The poor, silly good-natured Charles becomes the incarnation of *la bêtise*, and Flaubert emphasizes the depth of his stupidity. The second sentence develops not merely the idea of shapelessness, but its nature and extent. The downward movement is succeeded by an unwinding movement whose importance will shortly become apparent. The grotesque, egg-shaped hat, with its tiers of ridiculous ornaments, suggests a society constructed in layers where each layer exemplifies its particular kind of stupidity. Nor should we overlook the point of the 'trois boudins circulaires'. For the novel is in a sense a widening 'circle'. Flaubert is concerned to explore stupidity at one level— the middle-class level. The cord with the cross on the end is probably intended to suggest a clown's hat and looks forward to Charles's failure as a doctor. He thus becomes one of a 'circle' which includes Bournisien and Homais. In this circle he stands, as they do, for professional incompetence. When later on, his incompetence leads to the amputation of Hippolyte's leg, the unfortunate man becomes a projection of Bovary's stupidity, and the thud of his wooden leg on the paving drives homes remorselessly the idea of professional failure. I have spoken of the unwinding movement of the second sentence. The story which 'unfolds' in the novel appears to be no more than a development of something which is implicit in the image of Charles's hat. The wearer, you feel, is bound to come to grief. The stolid, unimaginative Charles is not merely a bad doctor; he stands for the ordinary man, for humdrum everyday reality, and the first phase closes with his diastrous alliance with the unbalanced over-imaginative Emma.

The rift between them begins shortly after their marriage. They are invited to stay with the Comte de Vaubyessard for the family ball. Emma finds herself for a moment in an aristocratic world, a world of luxury and romance which suddenly seems to offer everything for which she has unconsciously been longing. . . . (pp. 265-66)

> Their evening coats, better cut than those of their fellow guests, seemed to be made of a more elastic cloth; their hair, which they wore in clustered curls over their temples, and lustrous with pomade, of a silkier texture. They had the colouring which comes of wealth, that pallor which is enhanced by the white sheen of china, the iridescence of watered satin, the polish of fine furniture, and is maintained by a diet of exquisite food never indulged in to excess. Their necks moved freely above low cravats, their long whiskers fell over turned-down collars, and they wiped their lips with embroidered handkerchiefs marked with large monograms and diffusing a sweet perfume. Those on the threshold of middle age looked young, while the more youthful of their company had an air of maturity. Their indifferent glances told of passions dulled by daily satisfaction, and through their polished manners showed that peculiar aggressiveness which comes of easy conquests, the handling of thoroughbred horses and the society of loose women.

I think we must admit that Flaubert achieves something here which his predecessors had not attempted, something of which

classical French prose for all its merits was perhaps incapable. In a few lines, with a few deft touches, he *evokes* the life of a highly civilized society; the description of the cut of a coat, the turn of a head, is sufficient to reveal the essential gifts of the ruling class which had made France great. The final sentence, with its restrained irony, indicates both the strength and the weakness of this society. It would be difficult to improve on his description of its patrician dignity and pride: 'Dans leurs regards indifférents flottait la quiétude des passions journellement assouvies; et, à travers leurs maniéres douces, perçait cette brutalité particulière. . . .' Nor would it be easy to improve upon the way in which Flaubert hints at the weaknesses which had led to the ruin of the French nobility when he speaks of 'la domination de choses à demi faciles . . . le maniement des chevaux de race et la société des femmes perdues'. This sort of language—this combination of evocation and critical appraisal—is one of Flaubert's most effective and important innovations. (pp. 266-67)

The third phase opens with the Bovary's removal to Yonville-l'Abbaye and Emma's first encounter with Léon. The confused and excited feelings released by her visit to la Vaubyessard seek an outlet. She hovers on the verge of adultery and is only saved by Léon's departure for Paris. In her perplexity her mind turns to religion and Flaubert takes the opportunity of making a critique of religion. . . . (p. 268)

> One evening when she was sitting by the open window watching Lestiboudois, the sexton, trimming the box-hedge, she suddenly heard the sound of the Angelus bell.
>
> It was the beginning of April, when the primroses are in bloom. A warm wind was blowing over the dug flower-beds, and the gardens, like women, seemed to be furbishing their finery for the gaieties of summer. . . . The mist of evening was drifting between the leafless poplars, blurring their outline with a violet haze, paler and more transparent than a fine gauze hung upon their branches. Cattle were moving in the distance, but her ear could catch neither the noise of their hooves nor the sound of their lowing. The bell, continuously ringing, struck upon the air with its note of peaceful lamentation.
>
> The repeated tolling took the young woman's mind back to the memories of childhood and of her school. She remembered the branched candlesticks which used to stand upon the altar, overtopping the flower-filled vases and the tabernacle with its little columns. She would have liked, as then, to be an unnoticed unit in the long line of white veils in which, here and there, the stiff coils of the good sisters kneeling at their desks, showed as accents of black. At Mass, on Sundays, whenever she raised her head, she could see the sweet face of the Virgin in a blue cloud of eddying incense. At such moments she had been conscious of deep emotion, had felt alone and immaterial. . . . It was almost without knowing what she was doing, that she set out towards the church, ready to enter into any act of devotion provided only that her feelings might be wholly absorbed, and the outer world forgotten.

It is an admirable example of Flaubert's art at its finest. The insistent ringing of the church bell through a process of sensuous suggestion, which bears a striking resemblance to Proust's *mémoire involontaire,* sets the mechanism of memory in motion. The dying away of the sounds from the external world marks the beginning of the *rêverie,* so that the final stroke of the bell merges into the remembered sound of the bell at the convent. The images dovetail perfectly into one another. 'Les jardins, comme des femmes, semblent faire leur toilette pour les fêtes de l'été', suggests the flowers on the altar and the white veils of the schoolgirls on feast days. The 'vapeur du soir . . . d'une teinte violette' floats into the 'tourbillons bleuâtres de l'encens'. There is no direct comment, but Flaubert by employing the same method that he used in the account of the ball at la Vaubyessard shows that Emma's religion is of the same quality as her dreams of Romantic love. It is largely emotional, a desire to return to her childhood and be one of a row of little girls in white veils, or to plunge into 'n'importe quelle dévotion' provided that like the *long frisson* it brings oblivion, 'que l'existence entière y disparût'.

On her way to the church she meets the Abbé Bournisien to whom she turns for help, but he completely fails to understand her. The intention of this memorable scene is to show the inability of the Church to provide a solution. It reminds us to some extent of the Russian films with their hideous, bloated bourgeois; but while one is reading it, it is effective enough. This double criticism disposes of religion and Emma is now ripe for a fall.

The fourth phase is the liaison with Rodolphe. The outstanding scene, which from a technical point of view has had an immense influence, is the visit of Emma and Rodolphe to the Comices Agricoles. Flaubert was very proud of it, as he had every right to be, and compared it to a symphony. Thibaudet shrewdly suggested that it was arranged in three tiers like a mediæval mystery. The animals and peasants were at the bottom, the platform with the distinguished visitor and the local notabilities in the middle, and the lovers at the window above. He went on to point out that the animal noises, the speeches from the platform and the conversation between the lovers were all varieties of *la bêtise* which blended in the symphony. The *conseiller de préfecture's* speech certainly alternates with the dialogue between the lovers; the platitudes about religion, duty, progress and patriotism and Rodolphe's platitudes about enduring passion and the new morality answer one another mockingly, cancel one another out, leaving the reader with the impression that love and duty are mere shams, that nothing has value. The effect is intensified when the speech is followed by the distribution of prizes to deserving farmers. . . .

> He pounced upon her hand. She did not withdraw it.
>
> 'We must work together for the good of farming,' cried the President.
>
> 'Recently, for instance, when I came to your house . . .'
>
> '. . . To Monsieur Bizet of Quincampoix . . .'
>
> 'Did I know that we should be together in this place?'
>
> '. . . Seventy francs!'
>
> 'A hundred times I even strove to break from you, but ever followed, ever stayed . . .'

> '. . . Manures. . . .'
>
> 'As I should so dearly love to stay this evening, to-morrow, all the days of my life!'
>
> '. . . To Monsieur Caron of Argueil, a gold medal. . . .'
>
> 'For never have I found a charm so powerful in the companionship of anybody. . . .'
>
> '. . . To Monsieur Bain of Givry-Saint-Martin . . .'
>
> 'This memory of you will be with me always . . .'
>
> '. . . For a merino ram. . . .'
>
> 'But you will forget me: I shall be for you as a shadow that has passed. . . .'
>
> '. . . To Monsieur Belot of Notre-Dame . . .'
>
> 'But no! Tell me I shall count for something in your thoughts and in your life!'
>
> 'Pig class—a prize of sixty francs, divided between Monsieur Lehérissé and Monsieur Cullembourg. . . .'

The opening announcement is an ironic comment on Emma and Rodolphe, standing furtively hand in hand. For we know that at bottom they are anything but 'bonnes cultures'. When Rodolphe cries: 'Savais-je que je vous accompagnerais?' the mocking voice, which chimes in with 'Soixante et dix francs', becomes the voice of the courtesan announcing the price of her favours or of the hard-boiled man of the world making an offer for those favours. When Rodolphe whispers that he stayed because he could not tear himself away, the strident voice answers jeeringly: 'Fumiers.' The promise to remain 'this evening, to-morrow, all the days of my life' is greeted derisively by: 'Une médaille d'or!' 'J'emporterai votre souvenir' is answered by 'Un bélier de mérinos'. In the final announcement the irony grows savage. 'I shall count for something in your thoughts and in your life shan't I?' asks Rodolphe. The voice retorts, brutally: 'Race porcine *ex æquo*—Pigs, the pair of you.'

I think it will be agreed that this scene is a decidedly impressive performance, an ironical commentary not merely on Emma's assumed modesty and Rodolphe's vows of eternal fidelity, but on the whole basis of love. It ends by transforming the pair into a couple of pigs rolling over each other on the dung-heap. For the words which give it its particular tone are *fumiers* and *race porcine.* They sum up Rodolphe's views on love and there seems little doubt that Flaubert himself shared them, or that he used this slick, shallow adventurer as part of his general plan for bringing it into discredit. (pp. 268-72)

The final phase of the novel opens with Léon's return and Emma's liaison with him. The prelude is their meeting in Rouen Cathedral which is followed by the celebrated drive in the cab with its drawn blinds. It is interesting to recall that when the novel was originally published in serial form in the *Revue de Paris* this was one of the first scenes which the editors insisted on cutting. It may seem strange that the people who had apparently passed the ride with Rodolphe and the seduction in the forest should have felt any scruples over the second scene. I think we must assume that they sensed obscurely what to-day is plain. It is possible to argue that the symbolism is sometimes a little obvious, but on the whole it is an impressive display of literary craftsmanship with the pompous, boring guide pursuing the distracted lovers round the cathedral, the cab travelling at breakneck speed, the wretched perspiring *cocher* and the furious voice bellowing at him from inside the cab every time he slows down.

The cathedral and the cab both possess a moral significance, but there is a contrast between them. When Léon compares the cathedral mentally to 'un boudoir gigantesque [qui] se disposait autour d'elle', the significance is clearly sexual and anticipates the highly Freudian 'cab'. For Emma the cathedral provides a momentary and ineffectual moral support before she gives in. The drive 'sans parti pris ni direction, au hasard' stands for a loss of moral direction which can only have one end. . . . (p. 273)

The last fifty pages possess the same qualities as the first fifty. They are the traditional excellences of the finest European novels. In these pages, too, Flaubert displays all his technical mastery. Emma becomes a trapped animal trying desperately to escape from her enemies. All through the novel we are conscious of the dialogue which goes on ceaselessly—sometimes in an undertone, sometimes openly—between Bournisien and Homais, between the Ecclesiastic and the Progressive, between the religious and the secularist *bêtise*. In the final pages the other characters also become symbolic figures, and we see them crowding in on Emma with hostile faces. Lheureux is the Usurer demanding, insistently, his pound of flesh; the beggar, with his hideous deformity and his ghastly song, is Death or, possibly, as Thibaudet suggests, the Devil to whom she throws her last five-franc piece. Rodolphe and Léon are both variations of the Faithless Lover. The sense of her enemies closing in on Emma in a constantly narrowing circle gives the final chapters their dramatic force. The clandestine journeys to Rouen to see Léon when she is supposed to be having music lessons are replaced by a different sort of journey. Emma rushes to and fro between Rouen and Yonville in a frantic attempt to borrow money to keep her creditors at bay and avoid being sold up. She fails. Her main outlet has been blocked and she is confined to Yonville. She moves hither and thither at Yonville, seeks refuge with the old nurse where, by an ominous association of ideas, the sound of the spinning-wheel recalls the sound of Binet's lathe on the day she nearly committed suicide after Rodolphe's defection. She is on the point of selling herself to the local solicitor, pays a visit to the tax-gatherer. As so often happens in Flaubert, these scenes remind us of a film in which we watch the action from different angles and different heights. We go with her into Rodolphe's château and into the solicitor's breakfast-room, but we watch her visit to Binet from above and through the eyes of spiteful neighbours. . . . (pp. 275-76)

There is another important change in these closing pages. The novelist manages to forget himself and keep his eye on his principal figure. The morbid satisfaction with which he has recorded her misfortunes gives way to a pity which adds another dimension to the book. The scene is which she tries to obtain money from Rodolphe shows Flaubert at his best. . . . (p. 277)

> 'But a poor man like you doesn't lavish silver on the butt of a gun, or buy a clock inlaid with tortoiseshell'—she went on, pointing to a buhl timepiece—'or silver-gilt whistles for riding-crops'—she touched them as she spoke—'or trinkets for watch-chains. . . . Why, the smallest of these knick-knacks could be turned into

money. . . . Not that *I* want them . . . you can keep the lot for all I care!'

> She threw the links from her so violently that the gold chain broke against the wall.

> 'I would have given you everything, would have sold all I had. I would have worked with my hands, would have begged on the roads, just for a smile, a look, just to hear you say "thank you".'

This is a different Emma from the unbalanced romantic who is studied throughout the greater part of the book. Her voice, freed from the confusing undertones of her creator, has a different accent. There is no blur here. The simple, direct words contrast strangely with her muddled dreams. They come straight from the heart and appeal to something far deeper in us.

We cannot help noticing that Flaubert displayed a marked reluctance to give due weight to what was valid and genuine in Emma. She was not, as Henry James alleged, a woman who was 'naturally depraved'. She possessed a number of solid virtues which were deliberately played down by the novelist. It was after all to her credit that she possessed too much sensibility to fit comfortably into the appalling provincial society of Yonville l'Abbaye and it was her misfortune that she was not big enough to find a way out of the dilemma. We cannot withhold our approval from her attempts to improve her mind or from the pride that she took in her personal appearance and in the running of her house. The truth is that Flaubert sacrificed far too much to his *thèse*. These virtues express his instinctive appreciation of what was sane and well-balanced in the French middle classes. In sacrificing them to a doctrinaire pessimism, which was held intellectually instead of arising from his contemplation of his material, he destroyed the findings of his own sensibility and involved himself in a confusion of values. We may conclude, too, that it was this nihilism, this sense that nothing—neither religion, morals nor love—has value rather than a few lurid scenes which really upset French *mères de famille* in the year 1857 and led to Flaubert's prosecution for indecency. (pp. 277-78)

While *Madame Bovary* is admittedly only partly successful on account of conflicting attitudes, it still has to be decided what value should be attached to Flaubert's pessimism, whether it was a mature conception of life or an immature cynicism which is masquerading as mature vision.

Thibaudet was in no doubt about the answer:

> The world described in *Madame Bovary* [he said] is a world which is falling apart. . . . But in every society when something is destroyed, another thing takes its place. When the Bovarys' fortune collapses, Lheureux's rises. . . . The novel has two sides—the defeat of Emma and the triumph of Homais.
>
> (pp. 278-79)

There is no doubt that Thibaudet correctly described Flaubert's intentions. And if sheer technical power were insufficient, we should have to agree that *Madame Bovary* was one of the greatest of novels. Yet somehow we remain unconvinced by the irony as we are unconvinced by the pessimism. For Flaubert's figures will not bear the weight of the symbolism that he tried to attach to them. We cannot fail to notice that he was continually tipping the scales, trying to give these sordid provincials an importance which they were far from possessing.

*Flaubert's home at Croisset, where he wrote* Madame Bovary.

What he exhibits with superb accomplishment is in fact an immature cynicism masquerading as mature wisdom. (p. 279)

> Martin Turnell, "'Madame Bovary'," in his The Novel in France: Mme. de la Fayette, Laclos, Constant, Stendhal, Balzac, Flaubert, Proust, *Hamish Hamilton, 1950, pp. 258-79.*

### JEAN PIERRE RICHARD   (essay date 1954)

[*Richard's essay was first published in French in 1954 as* Littérature et sensation. *He examines the images in Flaubert's writing to explore his psychological state and its manifestation in* Madame Bovary. *To understand Flaubert's creative process, Richard examines the letters and various drafts of* Madame Bovary *to identify specific experiences from Flaubert's life and trace how those experiences are translated into recurrent themes in his work. Here, he discusses the image of water and its representation of love, sensuality, and dissolution, or death. For additional commentary on imagery and symbolism in* Madame Bovary, *see Martin Turnell (1950), Georges Poulet (1955), Jean Rousset (1962), and Victor Brombert (1966). Other critics who probe Flaubert's letters and early drafts of* Madame Bovary *as a key to his creative expression include Albert Béguin (1950) and Charles Du Bos (see Additional Bibliography).*]

Flaubert is not, by nature, a compartmentalized creature; in his world all things communicate with each other. This coherence, which links together the inner experience, the concrete experience, and the metaphorical expression, is perhaps the most attractive aspect of his genius. The statistical study of the imagery undertaken by M. Demorest [see excerpt above, 1931]

reveals that love is most often expressed, especially in the most spontaneous works and in the early versions of the big novels, by images of water and fluidity. And M. Demorest rightly concludes that this preference indicates a certain unrest, an awareness of the fact that passion causes instability, almost a condemnation of love. It seems to us that it expresses even more clearly the essential truth that, in its nature as well as in its structure, love is a dissolution of the human personality. (p. 426)

But we have even better evidence: In Flaubert's everyday existence, at the root of his most commonplace tastes and habits as well as in the most ordinary scenes of his novels, we find this same obsessive concern with water, experienced as a dissolving and diluting force. The Turkish bath atmosphere, for instance, so well described by Charles du Bos in his marvelous essay on Flaubert, should not merely be taken for a metaphor. Flaubert loved steam baths:

> The other day, I took a bath. I was alone at the bottom of the tub . . . Hot water was flowing all around me; stretched out like a calf, I let all kinds of thoughts go through my head; all my pores were quietly dilating. It was a highly voluptuous and gently melancholical experience to be thus taking a bath all by myself, lost among those large dark rooms in which the slightest noise echoed like a cannon shot, while the naked Kellaks called out to each other and handled me like embalmers preparing a body for the tomb.

The body dilates and grows numb. Consciousness loses itself in the dark. We abandon ourselves to a happy passivity. Half dispossessed of all awareness, we become mummified.

At other moments, the same pleasure can grow more active, and water becomes like a body against which one rubs oneself, until total interpenetration is achieved:

> I took a bath in the Red Sea. It was one of the most voluptuous pleasures in my life. I rolled myself in the water as on thousands of liquid teats that covered my entire body.

Woman attracts as if she were water, and water caresses like a woman. In his bath, Flaubert experiences the voluptuous pleasure of a complete fusion, while remaining just conscious enough not to lose himself entirely, just powerful enough to let his muscles dominate the liquid element; the swimmer enters the water to which he abandons himself, while remaining poised on the surface. The bath is a prelude to lovemaking.

The *boat* is an even more detached experience. The full thickness of the hull protects one against the invading waters. The boat defies and conquers the water, even while being carried by it. Consequently, the boat-rides—near the end of **Madame Bovary,** for instance—suit the moment when love checks itself rather than overflows. Lost in the happy emptiness of their sensations, the two lovers allow themselves to be carried together by the languid movement of the moment, rather than losing themselves into each other. The flow of the river gives direction to the amorous effusion and orients its slow languor. Water makes them live *with* each other, makes them realize that, carried by the universal flux, they nevertheless exist and travel together. (pp. 426-27)

Running waters occupy only a minor part in Flaubert's dreams. They tear apart before they absorb, and he responds primarily to the slow *oozing* of one element into another. The continuity that wraps all things into one single entity fascinates him, and the most fascinating of all continuities, the most mysterious and the least visible, is the movement of water as it originates, its apparition at the surface of a solid object. Certain solids perspire in Flaubert's writing. It is not by chance that **Madame Bovary** takes place in an atmosphere of saturated humidity in which all things, sensations, feelings, houses, and landscapes make up a world of oozing waters. For it was to be the novel of "lascivious dampness," of "poor hidden souls, damp with melancholy, closed in like the courtyards in the provinces whose walls are covered with moss." In Flaubert's own statement, he set out to reproduce "the musty color that surrounds the lives of lower insects." Charles Bovary, for instance, literally oozes with boredom and greyness: "the long thin hairs that covered his cheeks like a blonde moisture . . . covered his expressionless face with a pale fuzz"—a most effective image, showing stupidity grown visible, like a mushroom. Most of the time, this mildew does not coagulate enough to become moss or fungus. Instead, one sees the surface of things slowly swell and grow heavy, until a liquid *drop* comes into being and falls to the ground. This obscure operation awakens all kinds of dark responses in Flaubert's soul and he never ceases to meditate upon it.

The drop is indeed a particularly mysterious entity, first of all because of its origin: it originates out of nothing, or rather, it grows like a pearl on elements with which it has nothing in common. The imagination can quite easily reconcile itself to the notion of an underground current coming to the surface; such an event is at least founded on a continuity that may not be visible, but is easily imagined. On the other hand, it is very difficult to account for the apparition of a drop on the flat surface of a wall or a rock. Everything on this flat plane seems to prohibit its formation; and yet, there it is, alive, born elsewhere, sign of the fact that one has to penetrate either beyond the wall or into the drop itself to capture the obscure power that brought it into existence. . . . [The] drop is formed, not at the beginning, but at the climax of life. It appears when the inner self relaxes and lets go; it counteracts for a moment the excess of passivity by concentrating and objectifying it. It is like the avowal of weakness or the overflow of a saturation no longer able to keep itself in check. . . . Consequently, drops appear in all the scenes of desire, of ennui and of death, in all the moments in which someone, on the verge of disappearing, has to gather himself into a moment of unity, albeit liquid and ephemeral, before vanishing into nothingness. This suspended state of saturation before one abandons oneself to desire, is perfectly represented by the drop; and when it falls to the ground, it renders the heavy explosion of pleasure.

When he falls in love with Emma, Charles watches the drops of a springlike rain fall on the young woman's umbrella:

> One day, during a thaw, the bark of the trees in the yard was oozing, the snow melted on the roofs of the buildings . . . She stood on the threshold; went to fetch her sunshade . . . Beneath it, she smiled at the gentle warmth; drops of water fell one by one on the taut silk.

Elsewhere, in a scene of satisfied sensuality, Emma looks at the moonlight which is like "a monstrous candlestick, from which fell drops of melting diamond. . . ." These are the overflowings of a satisfied ripeness, echoing the manifestations of her tenderness; too, there is the fall, in the night, "of a ripe peach that fell all by itself from the espalier." The same movement of saturation followed by falling is present in the ripening fruit and the melting snow. . . . We can go one step further still: ripeness turns into its own excess, the person bursts open like a rotten fruit, losing himself among all things. The dead Emma does not quite disappear forever: it seemed to Charles that "she slowly expanded beyond her own limits and diffused into all surrounding things, into the silence, into the night . . . and into the liquid drops that oozed from the walls. . . ." Death and life come together in the same oozing drop.

But the symbolism of the drop goes even further: instead of imitating the mere movement of desire, it can recapture its very consciousness. Instead of concentrating on the origin and the end of desire, the imagination will focus on its renewal, its repetition. For any particular drop is only one element in a series of drops, and it necessarily lives within the continuity of this successive movement. It causes a moment of discontinuity, a momentary interruption that suspends the persistent flow of desire and thus awakens us from a state of torpor into a semiconsciousness. Letting oneself live, as it were, drop by drop, one feels satisfied; without losing touch altogether with the feeling of satisfaction, consciousness gains brief moments of relief while waiting for the next drop of desire to come into being, and this allows it to recover its strength and self-awareness. When Emma and Léon are frozen into mutual contemplation, they listen to the running water of a fountain:

> The water running in the courtyard, dripping from the pump into the watering can, kept time and created a palpitation.

The regularity of the successive drops gives a semblance of life to feelings numbed by the monotony of desire; they awaken at least the consciousness of an inward palpitation and create an obscure feeling of duration. The rhythmical pattern of desire, alternating between rise and fulfillment, gives shape to the continuously expanding movement of their love, as little shocks of self-awareness shake them, like the movements of the oars shake a boat on a river:

> The heavy boat advanced slowly, shaken by regular movements . . . The square oars tinkled against the irons and, with the breathing of the oarsman, this created an even, regular rhythm into the silence.

Desire has at last found its deeper rhythm, its proper beat. Water is not only the element that absorbs and slides; it can also suggest an inner balance within the human being. (pp. 428-31)

For Flaubert, fullness is, from beginning to end, like the movement of a rising sea. When Emma has been betrayed by Rodolphe and wants to throw herself out of the window of her attic, she feels physically attracted by the void; she is possessed as by a liquid form of dizziness: "the ground of the village square seemed to tilt over and climb up the walls. . . ." She was "right at the edge, almost hanging, surrounded by vast space . . . She had but to yield, to let herself be taken." Death is like a passive giving in to this liquid tide which has never ceased to be there, sustaining and absorbing life all along.

> What satisfaction she felt, when she leaned at last on something solid, something sturdier than love. . . .

Like Spendius and Mathô in **Salammbo**, Emma looks desperately for the rescuing pavement underneath that will stop her from drowning. "She tried naively to find support in something, in the love of her little girl, the cares of her household." But these efforts are in vain, and she knows it: how to find support outside, if one is unable to find it within oneself? All Emma finds in herself are floating masses of feeling, like the ceaseless motion of dark waters, nothing solid or pure. She has no feelings which she can take hold of, for feelings, by themselves, have no substantial existence; they merely represent the various affective tonalities through which she moves with gliding motion. It is impossible to isolate a definite part, to divide it by analysis. It is impossible to divide the even flow of feeling; it runs along like an opaque mass than yields nothing to the searching eye. (pp. 431-32)

The flow of inner duration draws together elements of the most diverse origin and gathers them into a heterogeneous mass. Feeling has no synthetic power in this case; it is the result of a group of impulses that keep living side by side, without assimilation, as long as the feeling lasts; they will resume their independent existence when the flow of feeling has subsided. When, at other moments, the driving force of an active passion is lacking, psychological changes occur by a kind of fermentation, due to the excessively stagnant state of each separate feeling as it remains caught within itself: "All was mixed together, all these frustrations, all these fermentations turned into bitterness. . . ." "Love *turned* into melancholy." This chemical transformation is not a change of state, but merely a change into another liquid state, a change in the consistency of the flow that keeps running incessantly within the self.

At such moments, one lives as if carried by the current. "I am driven from thought to thought, like a piece of dry grass on a river, carried down the stream wave by wave. . . ." This slow and heavy water is like the stirrings of boredom. It drags us down carried by the impulse of a weakened imagination, an easy prey to the most inauthentic, mechanical associations of ideas. Emma's imagination wanders among the pages of the keepsake albums. No strong tie links the images together; the present is nowhere enriched by the imagination of the future. Whatever future there is, is considered to be beyond our reach, and in the middle of the most attractive dreams, she abandons herself to a kind of degradation of her being, of which she is aware, and which spoils even the pleasures of the imagination.

At other moments however, especially when it is directed towards the past, this same coagulating power of dreams can lead to valid and stable combinations. Experiences of time and of place come together, carried by the stream of memory. I no longer know where I am, who I am; the numbness that gains my senses makes me lose all awareness of my concrete situation. A drowsy state follows in which time and space are blurred. At times, this may happen before falling asleep. Just before dropping off, Emma dreams that she falls asleep in some other place, in a luxurious house that quickly grows into a reality:

> For, in a double and simultaneous perception, her thoughts mixed with the things that surrounded her, the cotton curtains became silk, the candlesticks on the chimney became silver, etc. . . .

In this confusion of places and settings, the illusion, for an instant, is successful. More often, it is some exterior motion that causes the necessary drowsiness—for instance, the rocking motion of a carriage in which a traveller is being conveyed: Charles Bovary, seated in the cart that takes him, in the early hours of the morning, to the farm of old Rouault, Emma in the carriage taking her home after the dance at Vaubyessard or in the Yonville stagecoach after her days of lovemaking with Léon. . . . In the case of Charles Bovary, the sensations that are tightly fused together are even more specific:

> He would fall again into a tepid drowsiness, in which his most recent sensation came back to him. He saw himself *at the same time*, both husband and student, lying on his own bed beside his wife as he had just left it, and walking busily about in an operating room. He felt under his elbow the sensation of a desk in an amphitheater which was also his pillow at home . . . He smelled the odor of cataplasms and of his wife's hair . . . And it all mingled into one whole seeking for something with an uneasy longing, unable to lift its lead-weighted wings, while the confused memory turned round and round in place below.

From this admirable text, which is itself like a pathetic effort to express the obscure something that lies hidden underneath the heavy and clumsy opacity of words, two main indications can be derived. The first concerns the concrete unity of original and repeated experience. Sensation and memory are experienced simultaneously, as if they were one and the same: "they (memory and sensation) oscillate, then blend together," as a correction to the above text puts it, like two liquid masses intimately blending together. But it would be hard to believe that such a perfect blending together could be a product of mere chance: there must be an essential analogy between the present sensation and the past memory, an analogy which, with the assistance of the half-sleep, actually caused both impressions to fuse into one. The smell of the cataplasms, which is also at the same time the smell of the hair, locates the sensation—memory in an area where sensation and disgust are one: both sensations (the hair and the cataplasms) bathe, as it were, into the same reaction of repulsion, each enriched by the particular quality of disgust that characterizes it: medical disgust in the first case, sexual disgust in the latter. . . . Elsewhere, in a more awake state of consciousness, subterranean relationships of the same type will be expressed by metaphors. But here, we are in an area that precedes that of metaphor, on the level where all substance is experienced as identical.

Even more important is the emphasis, in this same passage, on the restless desire, the blurred memory that "turns round and round . . . below." Further corrections refer to it as a "loaded-down desire," "one with something persistent and obtuse . . . fighting in vain in the depths of consciousness . . . in order to come to the surface and find the light of day," in an effort akin to—and here is the clarifying metaphor—"that of his heavy eyelids that fell back by themselves." The struggle is that of a half-stifled being, reaching in vain towards light and air, but incessantly dragged down again by its own apathy. The memory, which is itself penetrated with anxiety—"Charles tried to call to mind all the fractures he had seen, and how they were treated"—tries to pierce the opacity of the drowsy mind; it tries to fight the double tendency towards osmosis and towards horizontality, an evening out, which is characteristic of all liquid matter. Consciousness acts to attract it to the surface, force it into expression; but its own weight throws it back into the dark and drowsy sleep, the depths of which language can not penetrate. This desperate struggle to rise above one's own state of being resembles that of someone caught in quicksand or of an acrobat whose limbs are sheathed in lead: "in writing this book, I am like a man trying to play the piano with balls of lead attached to every articulation in my fingers." Emerging from a bath, the body seems to have tripled in weight. Everything seemed to direct Flaubert towards the ease of a spontaneous fluidity, but he chooses instead to write the books "for which he is least gifted": writing is to him like an awakening of the mind, the emergence of consciousness.

And he will most effectively wake himself by taking his own drowsiness, his own experience, for the object of his description. Most of Flaubert's characters seem to exist in a state of drugged semi-awareness. They "stagger around like people suffering from exhaustion," overcome by some "irresistible torper like that of someone who has drunk a deadly beverage." They are bewitched, "with a kind of mist in their head," which "neither the priest nor the doctor are able to dispell." All these dazed characters end by devouring themselves out of sheer sloth. They collapse for good when they achieve their own deaths. Unlike Balzac's victims, [Emma] is not a victim of the mechanical power of money; she is defeated by weakness, by passivity, and most of all by lies, lies that are "like quicksand: one single step taken in that direction, and the heart itself is conquered . . ." Her death is like a pathological drowning in quicksand. . . . Death is the final dissolution, prefigured in sleep, sensation, and love. One says farewell, relinquishes all possessions. . . . Nothing, in fact, could be more familiar, more reassuring; ever since their birth, Flaubert's characters have been engaged in dying. . . . (pp. 432-36)

*Jean Pierre Richard, "Love and Memory in 'Madame Bovary'," in "Madame Bovary" by Gustave Flaubert: Backgrounds and Sources, Essays in Criticism, edited and translated by Paul de Man, W. W. Norton & Company, Inc., 1965, pp. 426-38.*

## GEORGES POULET   (essay date 1955)

[*Poulet has been described as an existentialist critic who in his most important work attempts to reconstruct an author's "consciousness," or relation to, and understanding of, time and space, nature and society. A key element of his early criticism was his belief that every author lives in an isolated world defined by individual consciousness and so cannot be understood in terms of generalizations about an era or period. The task of the critic is to enter this individual consciousness and define it. In his later work, however, Poulet has come to see individual consciousnesses as united in an all-embracing spirit of a time, and he often discusses writers in terms of the widespread characteristics of an age. Poulet takes as his point of departure the work of two earlier critics: Charles du Bos, who probed Flaubert's creative unconscious (see Additional Bibliography), and Erich Auerbach, who discussed his objective representation of reality in* Madame Bovary *(see excerpt above, 1942-45). Here, Poulet contends that "the metaphor of the circle" is integral and constant in Flaubert's works, and he examines passages from the author's letters to illuminate how this metaphor underscores Flaubert's conception of the circular nature of reality. For further commentary by Poulet, see NCLC, Vol. 2. For additional commentary on imagery and symbolism in* Madame Bovary, *see Martin Turnell (1950), Jean Pierre Richard (1954), Jean Rousset (1962), and Victor Brombert (1966).*]

In his book *Mimesis*, for almost a decade the standard study of the concept of reality in Western literature . . . , Professor Erich Auerbach quotes the following passage from **Madame Bovary**:

> But it was above all at mealtimes that she could bear it no longer, in that little room on the ground floor, with the smoking stove, the creaking door, the oozing walls, the damp floor-tiles; all the bitterness of life seemed to be served to her on her plate, and, with the steam from the boiled beef, there rose from the depths of her soul other exhalations as it were of disgust. Charles was a slow eater; she would nibble a few hazel-nuts, or else, leaning on her elbow, would amuse herself making marks on the oil-cloth with the point of her table-knife.

This passage, Auerbach declares, forms the climax of a presentation whose subject is Emma Bovary's dissatisfaction with her life at Tostes. In several cumulative pictures Flaubert describes the cheerlessness, drabness, unvaryingness, narrowness of Emma's world. This paragraph is therefore the climax of the portrayal of her despair. In itself it presents a picture: man and wife together at mealtime. But the picture is not represented in and for itself; it is subordinated to the dominant subject, Emma's despair. We are first given Emma, and then the situation through her. It is not, however, Mr. Auerbach continues, a matter of simple representation of the content of Emma's consciousness, of what she feels, as she feels it. Though the light which illuminates the picture proceeds from her, she is yet herself part of the picture, she is situated within it.

It may be useful to reflect upon these enlightening, yet not completely satisfying remarks. No doubt, Flaubert's method consists in presenting, as an object for our contemplation, a subjective being which, in its stead, has for its own object of contemplation the surrounding reality of things. Emma, as Mr. Auerbach points out, ''does not simply see, but is herself seen as one seeing.'' If Flaubert had simply decided to paint her from the outside, she would be merely an object among objects. With the room, the stove, the walls, the plate and the husband, she would be part and parcel of the plurality of things. If, on the other hand, Flaubert had wanted to make of her somebody like Bloom in [James Joyce's] *Ulysses,* or Clarissa Dalloway in [Virginia Woolf's] *Mrs. Dalloway,* i.e., a purely subjective being, then there would have been no husband, plate, walls, stone or room. Nothing would have been left, except the sensations and emotions caused in Emma by these objects; and there would have been no Emma, or at least in us no consciousness of her as a person standing against a background of things, since she would have been reduced to the status of a stream of thoughts and feelings. In both cases something essential in Flaubert's novel would have been lost, in one case the objective world, in the other the subjective mind, and in both, the extremely delicate relationship between objective and subjective, which is the very substance of the novel. It is this constant relation which not only links together the dual aspects of the novel, but which also keeps each of these two realities from fragmenting itself into a sheer multiplicity, here of thoughts and emotions, there of objects. There is in *Madame Bovary* an inner coherence, and this coherence is due to the fact that things, simultaneous or successive, are constantly fused together in the unity of a single perceptive mind, and that conversely this mind is kept from disappearing in the flux of its own unconsciousness by the objectivity of a world with which it is in constant touch. This essential interrelation is excellently commented upon by Mr. Auerbach in his examination of the paragraph of *Madame Bovary* quoted above. But it seems to me that there is still something to be done. For in this paragraph there is not only a theoretical representation of reality; there is also a concrete medium through which this representation has been achieved. It is the business of the critic to examine, within the text, by what action Flaubert accomplished his purpose, i.e., to show vividly the interrelation of a consciousness and its environment.

Let us therefore go back to the text. First we read: *Mais c'était surtout aux heures des repas . . .* What is given to us at first, is time. This time is not a continuity. It is a moment which repeats itself again and again, but which is also, when it happens, the present moment of Emma's life; the moment, above all moments, when actually she cannot bear her existence any more. Thus what we have at first, is something purely and intensely subjective, an awareness of time, an awareness of despair. But as soon as this awareness is revealed, it is immediately located within a place, *la petite salle,* and surrounded with a long enumeration of details, all objective in themselves, but all endowed with affective powers: a stove that smokes, a door that creaks, walls oozing, floor-tiles which are damp. To these details there must be added all the other particulars, which the author does not mention in this paragraph, but which were described at great length in the preceding pages, and which are present in the memory of the reader, as they are indeed in the memory of Emma herself. Thus what is given here is greatly swollen by what was given before. Details have an enormous cumulative power. This is the power of number, or, to use an Aristotelian distinction, this is a numbering and not a numbered number. The multiplicity—in itself meaningless—of all these details, takes force and meaning from the fact that they all affect in the same way the same person. Therefore, from their outside location around Emma, they combine their force and

their weight, in order to come down and bring pressure upon her. To express this coming down and in, of the outside reality, crowding on consciousness. Flaubert writes this sentence: All the bitterness of life seemed to be served to her on her plate, and with the steam from the boiled beef, there rose from the depths of her soul other exhalations as it were of disgust.

Let us consider successively the two balanced parts of this sentence. The first one is straight and to the point. One can feel in the directness with which it rushes toward its goal, the very motion by which the influx of despair, emanating from the surrounding objects, passes through a sort of tangible space, in order to reach the subject. To give this effect, Flaubert has purposely inverted the objective and the subjective. Instead of a room, a stove, a door, a tiled floor, there is now a ''bitterness of life.'' The multiple objects have been transformed into their subjective equivalents; just as, conversely, the soul of Emma, which is the goal of the combined offensive carried out by things, has been symbolically represented by the narrow objective circumference of her plate. Thus a deliberate confusion has been created between the subjective and the objective; as if, by penetrating into Emma's soul, the images of things had lost their objectivity and been transformed into feelings, or as if Emma, by becoming affective by material things, had become also somehow material.

But there are still more discoveries to be made in this wonderful sentence. Its beauty consists in rendering exactly by the physical notion of the words, the psychic motion of the meaning. First the general expression, all the bitterness of life, substitutes to the manifold of things a subjective totality encompassing the whole of existence. Then, through the rapid flow of the following words, ''seemed to be served to her on her plate,'' this peripheral reality shrinks down from all sides to lodge itself within the narrowest place, the plate of Emma. So the psychic motion, which in itself is invisible, has become a local and therefore a perceptible motion, through the figure of a space crossed over by the bitterness of existence finding its final home in the object on which is concentrated the attention of Emma. We are witnessing here an extraordinary narrowing of space, a rush of all causal forces, gathering from the depth of the past and from the three dimensions of external space, to converge on a central point, Emma's consciousness. But as soon as Flaubert has created this motion from the periphery to the center, he gives us a reverse motion from the center toward the periphery: and, with the steam from the boiled beef, there rose from the depths of her soul other exhalations as it were of disgust. After the contraction the dilation. We do not doubt but that these exhalations go upward and outward, to join the outer regions wherefrom the condensed bitterness of existence came downward into Emma's plate. Thus, crossed over in both directions, the Flaubertian *milieu* appears as a vast surrounding space which spreads from Emma to an indeterminate circumference, and from the circumference to the consciousness of Emma.

This circular character of Flaubert's representation of reality is not a mere metaphor; or, if it is one, it is not one invented for the sake of the argument. On the contrary this metaphor occurs so often, and, when it occurs, fits so well and plays such an important part in the context, that we must consider it as the essential image by which Flaubert expresses the interrelation of objective world and subjective being. My purpose is to examine the different aspects and meanings presented by this metaphor in the work of Flaubert.

Let us take another passage from **Madame Bovary**. It can be found in a first draft of the novel.... The moment of Emma's life here described belongs to a period slightly antecedent to the passage examined previously. Here she is shown during a walk she takes with her dog, a little Italian greyhound, in the country near Tostes:

> She began by *looking round her mechanically* to see if nothing had changed, since last she had been there. She found the same wall flowers on the stones, on the slabs of the wall the same patches of dried up lichen, the same pebbles in the beds of nettles, and the three windows, always closed, which were rotting away... Her thoughts, aimless at first, were wandering at random, like the handsome greyhound who, unleashed, was *running round and round in the field,* chasing a rat in a furrow, or bringing himself to a stop in order to nibble the poppies ... But when she had thus let her eyes roam over the horizon, whereas her *diffused* attention had barely skimmed a thousand ideas following each other, then, *as two concentric circles at once contracting their circumferences,* her thoughts retired within herself, her wavering glances became transfixed, and sitting on the ground under the beeches, prodding the grass with the ivory tip of her sunshade, she was always coming back to this question: Why, oh dear, why did I marry?

Here, beyond question, the metaphor of the circle cannot be overlooked. It plays a conspicuous part. At first everything tends to become peripheral. Emma's thoughts wander at random, her eyes roam over the horizon, her attention is spread on a thousand ideas. The things that she perceives, the thoughts that she thinks, get farther and farther in the distance, and finally they distribute themselves in such a way that they form two concentric circles whose central point is Emma's consciousness. To give the right emphasis to this general impression of circularity, Flaubert has taken care to prefigure it by another circle, the one physically described by the dog running round and round in the field. But this is not all. Let us read again the beginning of the long sentence which constitutes the second half of the paragraph: But when she had thus let her eyes roam over the horizon, whereas her diffused attention had barely skimmed a thousand ideas following each other.... No doubt, these long undulating clauses, progressively opening, are shaped in this particular form, so as to give a physical impression of the corresponding widening of Emma's thoughts and feelings. But if we read the second part of the sentence, we detect a striking difference of rhythm. The clauses are shorter, straighter and faster; her thoughts retired within herself, her wavering glances became transfixed.... She was always coming back to this question. Here, manifestly, diffusion has been replaced by contraction. The circles are shrinking, the thoughts from all sides are coming back, the words are running, as if impatient to reach their goal and to come to a full stop. This final fixation of all motions is represented in two, or even in three distinct ways. Just as the dog, who was running round in the field, comes to a full stop in order to nibble the poppies, so Emma's mind, which was wandering far away in circles among her memories and dreams, comes back to an idea on which it concentrates. And, in a way, this idea is different from all preceding ones, since it is not diffuse, remote and infinitely varied, but precise, intimate and abso-

lutely unique. It is not circumferential, it is central. However this one central thought is closely connected with the previous multiplicity. It is out of this multiplicity that it was issued. It was this very multiplicity which, by fusion, contraction and inward motion, produced finally the central thought, as the result and summing up. Thus the center contains the circumference. And this center is represented once more, symbolically, by a single dimensionless object, which has replaced in the picture the whole landscape: the pointed tip of a sunshade, digging the ground. The circular horizon has shrunk to a mere point.

This infinite contraction of the mental and external spaces is in no way mysterious, either in itself or in its occurrence. It is the most natural motion of the human mind. We know that it is because the diffused attention of Emma, wandering aimlessly, has touched many ideas, that these ideas have awakened, echoed in her mind, evoked the picture of her whole existence, and given expression finally to the question which was at the core of her consciousness. Nothing was more genuine than this moving inward from the circumference to the center. And, on the other hand, nothing was less instantaneous. From extreme excentricity to extreme concentricity, it is step by step, by a slow and repeated process, that the thought goes back to the self. From the circumference to the center of the psychic circle, we see a gradual progress, we feel the time, we measure the distance. (pp. 245-50)

Everywhere in the work of Flaubert there is the obsession of narrow endless circularity. But nowhere does it appear more strikingly than in the story of Emma Bovary. Emma is essentially a person who feels herself enclosed and stifled within the bounds of the place where she lives and of the moment in which she thinks. Her whole existence at Tostes or at Yonville seems to her a shutting up within walls, a groping around inside narrow limits; limits so narrow that sometimes they seem to join each other, to condense into a point, the point of time and space where she is constrained to live. She is here, here only, in the dimensionless *here;* she is forbidden forever to escape outside, into the infinite *elsewhere*. Nevertheless this *elsewhere* exists, it exists everywhere else, it is spreading on every side, and it is toward that *elsewhere* that her longing irradiates incessantly. The extraordinary constriction of Emma's existence, reduced to a mere punctum, is described by Flaubert in this passage, taken from the first version of **Madame Bovary:**

> Then the train of the same days started again. They were going to follow each other in the same manner, in Indian file, always similar, innumerable, bringing nothing. And they were before her, hundreds and thousands of them, enough for ten or twenty years! It will never finish, it will last until her death. The other lives, constricted, flat, cramped as they were, had at least some chance of an adventure, of a broadening *of their limits*. Sometimes there dropped an accident which shook their surface. An unexpected happening could *create peripeties ad infinitum* ... But, for her, nothing would happen.

First of all, the beauty of this passage is due to the intense feeling of duration which impregnates it: Then the train of the same days started again. Duration appears here as a mere prolongation of the past into the present. But it appears also as a prolongation of the present into the future: They were going to follow each other in the same manner, in Indian file. The three dimensions of time, past, present and future, identify themselves with one another, in such a way, that they become a uniform and continuous texture. As far as the eye can reach, duration extends, forward, backward, always the same, forming a homogeneous bulk of temporal matter. But by a process which, in his famous sonnet *Le Cygne,* Mallarmé will repeat, this vast extent of duration, spread uniformly on all sides, is also experienced by Emma as the narrowest possible span of time. The very uniformity of all past, present and future moments of existence, transforms and contracts all of them into a single moment; and this moment, incessantly rediscovered along the retrospective and prospective expanse of time, is never discovered but as the same narrow span infinitely repeated. So time is just an endless void of duration, in the middle of which life appears constricted, identical to itself, bringing nothing. However, this life is compared by Emma to others. These other lives, "constricted, flat, cramped as they were, had at least some chance of an adventure, of a broadening of their limits." Adventure considered as a widening of existence, is described by a symbol well-known since the Stoics: "Sometimes there dropped an accident which shook their surface. An unexpected happening could create peripeties ad infinitum." No doubt the image suggested here is the one of a stone dropped in a pool. From the point where it strikes the surface, concentric waves go out in all directions. The circles widen, multiply, get farther from the center. So an adventure, an accident, something unprovoked, uncalled for, may fall suddenly into the pool of life, burst into its stillness, produce circles of events going outward. The accident in itself is nothing; just a piece of gravel thrown in the water. But the small whirlpool it creates breaks the limits of the still narrow circle of existence, to replace them by an infinite circumference. The most insignificant event may be the starting point of an immense future.

Everything, therefore, depends on these occurrences. But, thinks Emma, they only happen to other people, they will never happen to me. Now, in spite of Emma's forebodings, it is precisely Flaubert's purpose to make things happen to her. Not many happenings, just three or four. Emma's life is a pool in which, occasionally, stones are thrown. Or, more exactly, it is a series of pools, each one a little bigger than the preceding one, first the father's farm, then Tostes, then Yonville, finally Yonville plus Rouen. In the stillness of each of these pools, at a particular time, a stone is thrown. This throwing of the stone is invariably the appearance of a new lover. From the moment he comes out, there start waves of emotion, which for a time broaden Emma's life; up to the moment when, the lover having gone, the emotion being spent, Emma is brought back by a retrogressive process to her starting point.

Let us examine this starting point in the first and most fugitive of Emma's love affairs.

Invited with her husband to a ball in an aristocratic country house, *le château de la Vaubyessard,* Emma has been deeply moved by this incidental excursion in a *milieu* so different from hers. She has danced in the arms of a Parisian Viscount, whose elegance has made on her a profound expression: "All things turning around them, the lamps, the furniture, the wainscoting, the floor like a disc on a pivot." Let us keep in mind these physical gyrations in which we must see a prefiguration of the mental gyrations which, later on, will proceed in Emma's mind. The day after, Emma leaves the château and the Viscount, to come back to the narrow circle of her ordinary life. The only keepsake she has brought back from that memorable event is a cigar case which may, or may not, have belonged to the

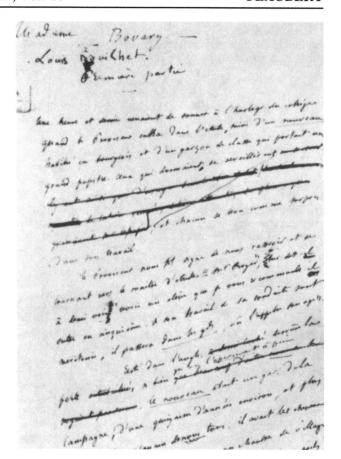

*The first page of the manuscript of* Madame Bovary.

Viscount. Now this fortuitous dancing partner, whom Emma will not see any more, is a very small pebble in her life. Nevertheless we will see, starting from the point of its falling, waves and waves of dreams irradiating in Emma's imagination. To follow this phenomenon, we have not only the final version of the novel, but also some preliminary drafts, and even in the primitive scenario referring to Emma's life after her return, we find this sentence: "The Viscount is a center, he disappears, but the surroundings stay and widen." Another version, more elaborated, gives the explanation of this cryptic statement. First we are informed that sometimes Emma looks at the cigar-case, which makes her dream of the Viscount. She wants to imagine his life in Paris, and she reads books about life in the capital. These books are mostly novels. Then comes the important passage:

> The memory of the Viscount was always passing, like a ghost, into what she was reading. She found his picture on every page. Examining the imaginary personages, she was always making parallels and comparisons with him. Thus he was enhanced by their poetry and he reflected his reality upon their fiction. Then *the circle of which he was the center, where all rays converged, gradually widened round him,* and, spreading equally in this expanse, the Viscount's personality became more and more diluted, like a drop of red wine that one lets fall in a glass of water.

The image of the drop of wine corresponds closely to the one of the pebble. In both instances a fallen object, by dilation or dilution, becomes the center and generating point of a circular motion. In the final version the image changes once again, but still represents the figure of a circle:

> The memory of the Viscount always returned as she read. Between him and the imaginary personages she made comparisons. But the circle of which he *was the center gradually widened round him,* and the *halo* that he bore, drawing away from his head, broadened out beyond, lighting up other dreams.

Here, instead of the pebble, or the drop of wine, we have the halo. The circle, narrow at first, becomes progressively so wide that it loses touch with the center, and, identifying itself with other dreams, irradiates confusedly in the distance toward a sort of peripheral happiness:

> *At the far end of life's vista, high above,* she thus saw happiness lying in a marvellous abode.

Here again we have a fundamental process of the Flaubertian mind, just the opposite of the one which makes the mind contract within narrow limits. It is the process of expansion, which generates innumerable reveries, leading from a central thought to a profusion of eddying images. (pp. 251-54)

The theme of the spiral is frequent in Flaubert. . . . Very likely, through the symbol of an ever-rising spiral, Flaubert wanted once more to illustrate the circular widening of horizons, that we found already in *Madame Bovary.* If we want further proof, let us recall this other sentence from the *Correspondance:* "The heart in its affections, like mankind in its ideas, *spreads endlessly in widening circles.*" Elsewhere Flaubert writes: "All feeling is an extension." But in the whole of the *Correspondance* there is nothing nearer *Madame Bovary* than the following passage: "My existence, like a stagnant swamp, is so still that *the least event dropping in it, causes innumerable circles. . . .*"

Yet in spreading outward the mind runs risks of which Flaubert was well aware. The first one, that we have already seen, is the risk of losing touch with the center of one's thoughts, and therefore with all order and precision. . . . [Out of the] multiplicity of directions and desegregation of all images in the void of space, a new danger appears, which is the danger of giddiness, madness, mental hemorrhage that nothing can stem. Flaubert writes: "I have often felt madness coming in for me. In my poor head there was a whirl of ideas and images, and it seemed to me that my consciousness, my very self, was sinking like a ship in the tempest." The ship sinks at the center of the whirl, while at the periphery there is a maddening circular motion. This is just such a psychic catastrophe as we witness in *Madame Bovary,* when Emma, rejected by Rodolphe, goes back through the fields. There is no center left in her, or, more exactly the mental center of her self is a bursting point, exploding and projecting itself in countless fragments in all directions:

> She remained lost in stupor, and having no more consciousness of herself than through the beating of her arteries, that she seemed to hear bursting forth like a deafening music filling all the fields. The earth beneath her feet was more yielding than the sea, and the furrows seemed to be immense brown waves breaking into foam. Everything in her head, of memories, ideas, went off at once like a thousand fireworks. . . .

> Suddenly it seemed to her that fiery *spheres* were exploding in the air like detonating balls when they strike, and were whirling, whirling to melt at last upon the snow between the branches of the trees. In the midst of each of them appeared the face of Rodolphe. They multiplied and drew near her, penetrating her. Then all disappeared.

But at the opposite extreme of this ultimate state of mind, where there is no longer any circle, or center, or any existential coherence whatsoever, there are in *Madame Bovary* all the passages where the eccentric and concentric motions balance each other, and the circumference does not lose its relation to the center. (pp. 255-57)

[What] Flaubert intended to show in *Madame Bovary* is a life which at one moment contracts and at another unfolds; a life which sometimes is reduced to a moment without duration and a point without dimension; and which sometimes, from that moment and from that point, extends to a circular consciousness of all its duration, of all the depths of its dreams, of all the spatiality of its environment:

> All these reminiscences were *widening her existence.* They seemed to form immensities of feelings, *to which she turned.*

The relation, here, is from a dimensionless present to the vastness of peripheral life. But it may also happen conversely that from the breadth of a present existence, now peripheral, all the activities of the soul converge on a single central object.

Thus in the *Correspondance:*

> It is to you that my thought flows back, when I have been through the circles of my reveries; *I cast myself on this thought at full length,* like a weary traveller on the grass alongside the road.

But, above all, this admirable passage of the first *Madame Bovary,* where we find the same image:

> She concentrated on this recollection; it became *the center* of her spleen; all her thoughts *converged upon it . . .* The humblest details, the past, the future, memories of simple words, fancies, comparisons, disgusts, she piled everything into this recollection, *her soul stretched at full length toward this center of heat.*

All these texts prove clearly that what Flaubert conceived and succeeded in devising, is a new way of presenting the relations between the mind and all surrounding reality, a more convincing way than the one used by his predecessors. While 18th century novelists, and Stendhal himself, were satisfied to go with the hero along the narrow track of successive time, and while Balzac constructed most of his plots as a line of force projected very straight in time and space, Flaubert is the first who builds his novels around a series of centers encompassed by their environments. For the first time in the history of the novel, human consciousness shows itself as it is, as a sort of core, around which sensations, thoughts and memories move in a perceptible space. Thus it becomes possible to discover and express the depth of the human mind; a depth which can be conceived as an expanse through which radiations diverge, or, conversely, as the convergence of all peripheral life upon the sentient being. (pp. 258-59)

[The] main purpose of Flaubert's novel is to create relation and order. This order is formal. From the center to the circumference, from the circumference to the center, there are constant relations. These are the relations set by the sentient subject between each moment of its consciousness and its total environment.... Sensible and emotive elements form a tangible circle, at the core of which there is, to quote the most perfect expression of Flaubert, *"A luminous center, toward which the entirety of things converge."* (p. 260)

> Georges Poulet, *"The Circle and the Center: Reality and 'Madame Bovary',"* in The Western Review, *Vol. 19, No. 4, Summer, 1955, pp. 245-60.*

## MARTIN TURNELL   (essay date 1957)

[*Turnell presents a retrospective on* Madame Bovary *on the centenary of its publication, examining the relationship between imagery, form, and allegory in the novel. The following excerpt presents his discussion of characterization. For further commentary by Turnell, see excerpt above, 1950.*]

Flaubert possessed many admirable qualities, but psychological insight was not among them. It was not so much a personal weakness as a failing which belonged to the age. The French novel produced no great psychologist between Stendhal and Proust. Flaubert's characters do not deepen our knowledge of human nature like those of the French classic novelists. The relations between them are not personal relations in the normal sense. They are figures in the pattern rather than people. The novelist manipulates them not merely with the same skill, but in the same way that he manipulates his images.

This is strikingly demonstrated as soon as we turn from the principal to the secondary characters. They not only have considerably less psychology than Emma; they are both simplified and stylized, and resemble the characters in primitive comedy or in allegory. They are sufficiently individualized for the novelist's purpose, but their individuality derives, as in primitive comedy, from repetition—from the constant repetition of the same foolish things in slightly different terms. The primitive-allegorical element is also apparent in Flaubert's choice of names. If Bovary fits Charles like a label, it is probably because it contains an allusion to the words *boeuf* or *bovin*. (This supposition is strengthened when we remember that after Emma's death Léon marries a Mlle Leboeuf.) The name of the Abbé Bournisien seems intended to suggest *borné*. Homais, as we know from Flaubert's notes, is a pejorative form of *homme*. Its owner is "the little man," the product of the brash enlightenment of the nineteenth century which was as abhorrent to Flaubert as to any *dévot*. Lheureux is the happy or fortunate man, and in this context the successful swindler.

It is not difficult to see how the characters fit into the allegorical framework. Charles is not merely the dumb ox; he is the stock figure of the dupe, the *cocu*, the *mari trompé*, who has been handed down from primitive comedy through the Molière of *George Dandin*. Bournisien is the Priest, Rodolphe and Léon the Faithless Swains, Lheureux the Usurer, Homais the Quack.

These are the people who form the society which is slowly choking Emma and into whose hands she plays. She is tricked by her enemies and let down by her friends. Her husband fails her because he cannot understand her Romantic *élans*; the priest because her emotional religion is beyond his comprehension. Her lovers take fright and walk out on her. She plays Homais' game by egging her husband on to make the experiment on

the club-foot because the quack can only rise if the qualified physician comes to grief. She plays into the hands of Lheureux by her extravagance; and her signature to his bills—that peculiarly nineteenth-century instrument of disaster which looms so large in Balzac—brings ruin to her husband and herself.

Although Emma's Romanticism is a species of *bêtise*, Flaubert felt a tenderness for her which he did not feel for any of his other characters. She may be foolish and deceitful, but she is more sympathetic and more sensitive than they, [and] is in the last resort superior to them all. There were personal reasons for Flaubert's preference. Her predicament was his own. It was the predicament of the Romantic individualist trapped in a hostile civilization which provided no outlet for his natural aspirations.... Emma is imprisoned in a double circle—a circle which is at once physical and psychological. It is the physical circle formed by the nondescript country, the "contrée bâtarde où le langage est sans accentuation comme le paysage sans caractère"; and the psychological circle formed by the people with their maddeningly stupid remarks. In addition to everything else the journeys are attempts to break out of the double circle. One can go further still. Emma is not only imprisoned in a double circle; she is imprisoned in a shrinking circle. What makes the climax so dramatic is the spectacle of her going round and round in an ever-narrowing circle as Lheureux with his pack of bankers, bailiffs and process-servers close in on her. The victim's death does not put an end to the chase; it swells the pack which turns on the husband, recalling in an odd way the opening scene of the book. Once again poor foolish Charles finds himself the centre of a jeering hostile throng. The music mistress demands payment for lessons that Emma never had; the lending library for books she never borrowed. The trusted maid elopes with a lover and steals the remainder of her dead mistress's wardrobe. We are even told that Emma "corrupted" the widower from beyond the grave. It is, indeed, the discovery of her correspondence with her lovers which puts the finishing touch on the handiwork of Lheureux and the rest: the husband is hounded to death as surely is the wife.

"The world described in **Madame Bovary**," said Thibaudet, "is a world which is falling apart ... But in every society when something is destroyed another thing takes its place." Homais and Lheureux do in fact triumph, and the novel closes with an ironical twist of the Quack receiving a medal for political services after getting rid of three more doctors, and having the unhappy Blindman shut up in the name of Progress because he cannot cure him with his dubious potions. We must, however, be clear about the meaning of these events. In Flaubert's Yonville, as surely as in Stendhal's Parma, we are watching a world in microcosm. However shabby its representatives, the world which is falling apart is the traditional world, the world of the liberal professions: the world which is taking its place, which is rising in the persons of Homais and Lheureux, is the world of "spivs." The exchanges between Bournisien and Homais are something more than comic relief, something more than the bickerings of the village priest and the village rationalist. They reflect the conflict between religion and science which rent France in the nineteenth century. There is, indeed, something prophetic about the pair Homais-Lheureux. It was the ascent of men like these which brought France to the brink of destruction. We cannot contemplate the activities of the small-time usurer without thinking of what was happening in Paris on a huge scale during the Second Empire, and was chronicled by Zola in a novel like *L'Argent*. We cannot forget that it was the triumph of the free-thinking lower-middle class, which emerged from the Revolution, that later produced the split between Right and Left in France—a split which completed in the moral sphere the damage done by speculation in the material sphere. (pp. 546-50)

Martin Turnell, "'Madame Bovary'," in *The Sewanee Review, Vol. LXV, No. 4, Autumn, 1957, pp. 531-50.*

**STEPHEN ULLMANN**  (essay date 1957)

[*Ullmann provides a detailed stylistic analysis of* le style indirect libre, *or free indirect speech, and explores its definition, historical development, and place in Flaubert's work. Although Flaubert was not the first to use this device, Ullmann considers him one of its greatest practitioners. For additional commentary on Flaubert's style and technique in* Madame Bovary, *see excerpts by Henry James (1902), Erich Auerbach (1942-45), W. von Wartburg (1946), Martin Turnell (1950), Victor Brombert (1966), and Marcel Proust and Percy Lubbock (see NCLC, Vol. 2).*]

With **Madame Bovary,** [Flaubert's use of free indirect speech] reaches full maturity as a device of style. . . . The new method has penetrated into the very fabric of Flaubert's style; the only element which remains largely impervious to it is description. Even there, natural phenomena are sometimes evoked through their impact on the mind:

> En face, au delà des toits, le grand ciel pur
> s'étendait, avec le soleil rouge se couchant.
> Qu'il devait faire bon là-bas! Quelle fraîcheur
> sous la hêtraie! Et il ouvrait les narines pour
> aspirer les bonnes odeurs de la campagne, qui
> ne venaient pas jusqu'à lui. . . .

But most of the descriptive details so dear to Flaubert could not be forced into this mould. This was one great obstacle to the attainment of that attitude of artistic impersonality which was the corner-stone of his programme.

Of the two basic types of free indirect style, it is the reproduction of *speech* which has made the most spectacular progress: it is now almost as frequent as the reporting of thoughts. Its range of application is very wide. It can be confined to a brief sentence, an incidental comment, prepared or completely isolated; by the time it is realized that somebody's words have been quoted, the narrative has moved on. . . . (p. 106)

The transcription of 'inner speech' presents an equally varied picture. It ranges from fleeting thoughts to fully developed internal monologues. Sometimes it is no more than a brief inner question or exclamation interrupting for a moment the flow of the narrative. . . . (p. 110)

Free indirect style also provides a natural vehicle for reveries, lyrical effusions and self-analysis. In Flaubert, these processes are still extensively rationalized; he does not attempt to record faithfully the raw material of mental experience. This is not yet the 'stream of consciousness' technique which was to be practised by Joyce and other writers, though it is undoubtedly a significant step in that direction. In another respect, too, the reporting is not entirely realistic: occasionally, the author is carried away by his own rhetoric and makes his characters think in a language which is obviously his, not theirs. . . . (p. 112)

The author's intrusion may become so marked that the free indirect form will be no more than a façade:

> N'importe! elle n'était pas heureuse, ne l'avait
> jamais été. D'où venait donc cette insuffisance

de la vie, cette pourriture instantanée des choses où elle s'appuyait? . . . Mais, s'il y avait quelque part un être fort et beau, une nature valeureuse, pleine à la fois d'exaltation et de raffinements, un coeur de poète sous une forme d'ange, lyre aux cordes d'airain, sonnant vers le ciel des épithalames élégiaques, pourquoi, par hasard, ne le trouverait-elle pas? Oh! quelle impossibilité! Rien, d'ailleurs, ne valait la peine d'une recherche; tout mentait! Chaque sourire cachait un bâillement d'ennui, chaque joie une malédiction, tout plaisir son dégoût, et les meilleurs baisers ne vous laissaient sur la lèvre qu'une irréalisable envie d'une volupté plus haute. . . .

The ideas are Emma Bovary's, but, with all her fondness for Romantic novels, she would never have thought of 'épithalames élégiaques', and the elaborate structure of the last sentence, the delicately balanced triple rhythm broadening into a more ample movement which leads up to the final climax, unmistakably bears Flaubert's own stamp. (pp. 112-13)

There were several reasons why Flaubert should have been the first writer to exploit the free indirect method. Some were connected with his personal preferences and idiosyncrasies. His hyper-sensitive ear shrank from the accumulation of *qui*-s and *que*-s to which even the best stylists of the Classical period had remained indifferent. 'Je répète encore une fois', he wrote in his correspondence, 'que jusqu'à nous, jusqu'aux très modernes, on n'avait pas l'idée de l'harmonie soutenue du style, les *qui*, les *que* enchevêtrés les uns dans les autres reviennent incessamment dans ces grands écrivains.' French lacks the ease with which subordinating conjunctions and pronouns can be omitted in English, but free indirect style goes a long way to remedy this weakness. On the positive side, Flaubert's well-known fondness for the Imperfect naturally prompted him to use a construction where this tense would play a prominent part and acquire delicate stylistic values.

But one must probe deeper into Flaubert's aesthetic to discover the real root of his preference for free indirect style. Much has been written on his doctrine of impassivity, on the objective and impersonal attitude which he adopted in his novels. He himself reverted time and again to the problem, most pregnantly perhaps in an often quoted passage of his correspondence:

> L'auteur, dans son oeuvre, doit être comme
> Dieu dans l'univers, présent partout et visible
> nulle part. L'Art étant une seconde nature, le
> créateur de cette nature-là doit agir par des
> procédés analogues. Que l'on sente dans tous
> les atomes, à tous les aspects, une impassibilité
> cachée et infinie. L'effet, pour le spectateur,
> doit être une espèce d'ébahissement. Comment
> tout cela s'est-il fait? doit-on dire, et qu'on se
> sente écrasé sans savoir pourquoi.

Free indirect style is the exact equivalent, on the linguistic plane, of this withdrawal of the author from his work. He prefers, as far as possible, not to intervene directly; he merely reports the words and thoughts of his characters, and even refrains from explicitly stating that he is doing so. Such discreet self-effacement will run the risk of being misunderstood: the half-formulated thoughts and day-dreams of the characters may be attributed to their maker. Indeed it has been suggested that, if the nature of internal monologue had been known at the time, this would have been a strong argument for the defence at the trial of **Madame Bovary:** some of the allegedly revolting passages imputed to the author were really Emma's thoughts expressed in free indirect style.

Yet impersonality did not mean aloofness for Flaubert; it had as its complement a capacity for sympathetic self-identification with the protagonists of the story. Flaubert himself has spoken of this 'faculté panthéiste', and while at work on **Madame Bovary,** he wrote to Louise Colet: 'C'est une délicieuse chose que d'écrire, que de n'être plus soi, mais de circuler dans toute la création dont on parle.' . . . Free indirect style provided a congenial expression for this attitude: it is an essentially mimetic device and supersedes the borderline between narrative and inner speech, so that the two imperceptibly merge into one another.

The free indirect technique was not the only syntactical innovation started by Flaubert. It takes its place among other experiments: novel uses of the Imperfect, of the Present Participle, of certain conjunctions and pronouns, of the indefinite article, and similar developments. By these changes, Flaubert initiated a large-scale reform of literary syntax which was followed up by other writers and is still in progress. These efforts to make syntax more flexible and more expressive were closely bound up with Flaubert's conception of style. The sentence, he proclaimed, must not only be perfectly orchestrated in itself; it must also be completely attuned to the idea which it expresses. Style is not something external, a mere garment of thought; in Flaubert's memorable simile, it must penetrate into the thought like a stiletto. This new vision of style has had a decisive influence on European literature, and a hundred years after **Madame Bovary,** its impact has scarcely weakened. (pp. 118-20)

*Stephen Ullmann, "Reported Speech and Internal Monologue in Flaubert," in his* Style in the French Novel, *1957. Reprint by Barnes & Noble, 1964, pp. 94-120.*

### JEAN-PAUL SARTRE   (essay date 1960)

*[Sartre was one of the chief contributors to the philosophical movement of Existentialism. Along with Martin Heidegger and Albert Camus, Sartre is the most prominent representative of the atheist branch of this movement, as distinguished from the Christian Existentialism of such writers as Karl Barth and Gabriel Marcel. Both groups, however, share the common assumptions that the individual is free to choose a course of action according to his or her will and is under a moral imperative to acknowledge a responsibility to society and act in accordance with this responsibility. In addition, Sartre's doctrine of Existentialism posits a universe with neither a God nor an absolute meaning. For Sartre, the human condition is best characterized as a state of anxiety in which individuals are "condemned to be free" to create what they will of their lives. Sartre's numerous literary and philosophical essays appear in the ten volumes of his* Situations. *These literary essays chronicle the development of Sartre's critical theories and are considered by many critics as outlines for his studies of Charles Baudelaire, Jean Genet, and Flaubert. He examines his subjects in light of the social conditions under which they wrote and the changes they underwent as a result of historical events. This method is described in part in* Qu'est-ce que la littérature? (What is Literature?). *In this work, Sartre denies the importance of stylistic analysis in literary criticism, favoring instead an examination of the social and political issues that make up the substance of a given work of literature. Sartre wrote: "[The] function of the writer is to act in such a way that nobody can be ignorant of the world and that nobody may say that he is innocent of what it's all about." Sartre's essay on Flaubert was originally published in French in 1960 as "Question de méthode," the prefatory essay to* Critique de la raison dialectique, Vol. 1. *In the following excerpt, Sartre views Flaubert's work as "a hypothesis and a research tool to clarify the biography." Using this approach, he combines a sociological and psychological study of Flaubert's life with a stylistic analysis of the work itself. He uses Flaubert and* Madame Bovary *to define a new method of looking at an author—an existential approach that he describes as "a regressive-progressive and analytic-synthetic method." By moving back and forth between the author's life and work, Sartre develops an understanding of the complex relationship between the two. Many critics consider this essay to be the blueprint for Sartre's later comprehensive study of Flaubert,* L'idiot de la famille *(see Additional Bibliography), which also utilizes this method.]*

[Contemporary Marxism shows] that Flaubert's realism offers a kind of reciprocal symbolization in relation to the social and political evolution of the petite bourgeoisie of the Second Empire. But it *never* shows the genesis of this reciprocity of perspective. We do not know why Flaubert preferred literature to everything else, nor why he lived like an anchorite, nor why he wrote *these* books rather than those of Duranty or the Goncourt brothers. Marxism situates but no longer ever discovers anything. It allows other disciplines, without principles, to establish the exact circumstances of the life and of the person, and it arrives finally at demonstrating that its schemata have been once more verified. Things being what they are, the class struggle having assumed this or that form, Flaubert, who belonged to the bourgeoisie, had to live as he lived and to write as he wrote. What is passed over in silence is the signification of these four words, "belonged to the bourgeoisie." For it is neither his rental income nor the strictly intellectual nature of his work which first makes Flaubert a bourgeois. He *belongs* to the bourgeoisie because he was born in it; that is, because he appeared in the midst of a family *already bourgeois,* the

*A portrait of Elisa Schlesinger, for whom Flaubert harbored an infatuation throughout much of his life.*

head of which, a surgeon at Rouen, was carried along by the ascending movement of his class. If Flaubert reasons and feels as a bourgeois, this is because he has been made such at a period when he could not even comprehend the meaning of the gestures and the roles which were imposed upon him. Like all families, this family was particular. The mother was related to the nobility, the father was the son of a village veterinarian; Gustave's older brother, superficially more gifted, became very early the object of Gustave's hatred. It is, then, inside the particularity of a history, through the peculiar contradictions of *this* family, that Gustave Flaubert unwittingly served his class apprenticeship. Chance does not exist or, at least, not in the way that is generally believed. The child becomes this or that because he lives the universal as particular. This child lived, *in the particular,* the conflict between the religious ceremonies of a monarchist regime which was claiming a renascence and the irreligion of his father, a petit bourgeois intellectual and son of the French Revolution.

Considered in general terms, this conflict expressed the struggle of the former landowners against the purchasers of national property and the industrial bourgeoisie. This contradiction (masked, however, under the Restoration, by a temporary equilibrium) Flaubert lived for himself alone and by himself. His aspirations toward nobility and especially toward faith were continually beaten down by the analytical mind of his father. Consequently there was set up *inside him* this overwhelming father who did not cease, even after death, to destroy God, his principal adversary, nor to reduce the impulses of his son to bodily humors. The small Flaubert, however, lived all this through in darkness—that is, without gaining any real awareness, but in panic, flight, bewilderment, and within the limits of his material circumstances as a bourgeois child, well nourished, well cared for, but helpless and separated from the world. It was *as a child* that he lived his future condition through the professions which would be offered to him. His hatred of his older brother, a brilliant student at the Faculté de Médecine, barred the path to the Sciences; that is, Gustave neither wished nor dared to become a part of the "petit bourgeois" elite. There remained the Law. Through these professions, which he regarded as inferior, he had a horror of his own class; and this very horror was an once an attainment of awareness and a definitive alienation from the petite bourgeoisie. He lived also the bourgeois death, that solitude which accompanies us from the moment of birth, but he lived it by means of the family structures: the garden where he played with his sister was next to the laboratory in which his father practiced dissection; death, corpses, his young sister who was soon to die, his father's science and irreligion—all had to be unified in a complex and very particular attitude. The explosive mixture of naïve scientism and religion without God which constituted Flaubert, and which he tried to overcome by his love of formal art, can be explained if we understand that everything took place *in childhood;* that is, in a condition radically distinct from the adult condition. It is childhood which sets up unsurpassable prejudices, it is childhood which, in the violence of training and the frenzy of the tamed beast, makes us experience the fact of our belonging to our environment *as a unique event.* (pp. 57-60)

The Flaubert family was of the semi-domestic type; it was a little behind the industrial families which the father Flaubert cared for or visited. The father Flaubert, who felt that he was "wronged" by his "patron" Dupuytren, terrorized everyone with his own worth and ability, his Voltairian irony, his terrible angers and fits of melancholy. We will also easily understand that the bond between the small Gustave and his mother was

never determining; she was only a reflection of the terrible doctor. Thus we have before us an almost tangible cleavage which will often separate Flaubert from his contemporaries; in a century when the conjugal family is the type current among the wealthy bourgeoisie, when Du Camp and Le Poittevin represent children freed from the *patria potestas,* Flaubert is characterized by a "fixation" on his father. Baudelaire, on the other hand, born the same year, will be fixed all his life on his mother. And this difference is explained by the difference in their respective environments. Flaubert's bourgeoisie is harsh, new. (His mother, vaguely connected with the nobility, represents a class of landowners in process of liquidation; the father comes straight out of a village and wears strange, peasant clothing even at Rouen—a goatskin in winter.) This bourgeoisie comes from the country; and it returns there, too, since it uses its gradually won wealth to buy land. Baudelaire's family, bourgeois, urban for many years already, considers itself in some small way belonging to the new nobility (*la noblesse de robe*); it owns stocks and bonds. (pp. 62-3)

But we must be careful. Each one lives his first years, distracted or bewildered, as a profound and solitary reality. Here the internalization of the external is an irreducible fact. The "flaw" of the small Baudelaire is, to be sure, the widowhood and remarriage of a very pretty mother; but it is also a peculiar quality of his own life, a disequilibrium, an unhappiness which will pursue him until his death. Flaubert's "fixation" on his father is the expression of a group structure, and it is his hatred of the bourgeois, his "hysterical" crises, his monastic vocation. Psychoanalysis, working within a dialectical totalization, refers on the one side to objective structures, to material conditions, and on the other to the action upon our adult life of the childhood we never wholly surpass. Henceforth it becomes impossible to connect **Madame Bovary** directly to the political-social structure and to the evolution of the petite bourgeoisie; the book will have to be referred back to contemporary reality insofar as it was lived by Flaubert through his childhood. There results from this a certain discrepancy, to be sure; there is a sort of hysteresis on the part of the work in relation to the very period in which it appears; this is because it must unite within itself a number of contemporary significations and certain others which express a state recent but already surpassed by society. This *hysteresis,* always neglected by the Marxists, accounts in turn for the veritable social reality in which *contemporary* events, products, and acts are characterized by the extraordinary diversity of their temporal depth. There will come a moment at which Flaubert will appear to be *in advance* of his period (at the time of **Madame Bovary**) because he is *behind it,* because his book, in disguised form, expresses to a generation disgusted with romanticism the post-romantic despairs of a student of 1830. The objective meaning of the book—which the Marxists, as good disciples of Taine, take simply as conditioned by the moment represented in the author—is the result of a compromise between what this new generation of readers claims in terms of its own history and what the author can offer to it from his own; that is, it realizes the paradoxical union of two past moments of this intellectual petite bourgeoisie (1830 and 1845). It is in these terms that one will be able to *use* the book in a new perspective as a weapon against a class or a government. (pp. 63-5)

Let us suppose that I wish to make a study of Flaubert—who is presented in histories of literature as the father of realism. I learn that he said: "I myself am Madame Bovary." I discover that his more subtle contemporaries—in particular Baudelaire, with his "feminine" temperament—had surmised this identification. I learn that the "father of realism" during his trip through the Orient dreamed of writing the story of a mystic virgin, living in the Netherlands, consumed by dreams, a woman who would have been the symbol of Flaubert's own cult of art. Finally, going back to his biography, I discover his dependence, his obedience, his "relative being," in short all the qualities which at that period were commonly called "feminine." At last I find out, a little late, that his physicians dubbed him a nervous old woman and that he felt vaguely flattered. Yet it is certain that he was *not to any degree at all* an invert. Our problem then—without leaving the work itself; that is, the literary significations—is to ask ourselves why the author (that is, the pure synthetic activity which creates Madame Bovary) was able to metamorphose himself into a woman, what signification the metamorphosis possesses *in itself* (which presupposes a phenomenological study of Emma Bovary in the book), just what this woman is (of whom Baudelaire said that she possesses at once the folly and the will of a man), what the artistic transformation of male into female means in the nineteenth century (we must study the context of *Mlle de Maupin* [a novel by Théophile Gautier] etc.), and finally, just who Gustave Flaubert *must have been* in order to have within the field of his possibles the possibility of portraying himself as a woman. The reply is independent of all biography, since this problem could be posed in Kantian terms: "Under what conditions is the feminization of experience possible?" In order to answer it, we must never forget that the author's style is directly bound up with a conception of the world; the sentence and paragraph structure, the use and position of the substantive, the verb, etc., the arrangement of the paragraphs, and the qualities of the narrative—to refer to only a few specific points— all express hidden presuppositions which can be determined *differentially* without as yet resorting to biography. Nevertheless, we shall never arrive at anything but *problems*. It is true that the statements of Flaubert's contemporaries will help us. Baudelaire asserted that the profound meaning of **The Temptation of St. Anthony,** a furiously "artistic" work which Bouilhet called "a diarrhea of pearls" and which in a completely confused fashion deals with the great metaphysical themes of the period (the destiny of man, life, death, God, religion, nothingness, etc.), is fundamentally identical with that of **Madame Bovary,** a work which is (on the surface) dry and objective. What kind of person, then, can Flaubert be, must he be, to express his own reality in the form of a frenzied idealism and of a realism more spiteful than detached? Who can he, must he, be in order to objectify himself in his work first as a mystic monk and then some years later as a resolute, "slightly masculine" woman?

At this point it is necessary to resort to biography—that is, to the facts *collected* by Flaubert's contemporaries and *verified* by historians. The work poses questions to the life. But we must understand in what sense; the work as the objectification of the person is, in fact, *more complete, more total* than the life. It has its roots in the life, to be sure; it illuminates the life, but it does not find its total explanation in the life alone. But it is too soon as yet for this total explanation to become apparent to us. The life is illuminated by the work as a reality whose total determination is found outside of it—both in the conditions which produce it and in the artistic creation which fulfills it and *completes it by expressing it.* Thus the work— when one has examined it—becomes a hypothesis and a research tool to clarify the biography. . . . The work has revealed Flaubert's narcissism, his onanism, his idealism, his solitude, his dependence, his femininity, his passivity. But these qualities in turn are problems for us. They lead us to suspect at once both social structures (Flaubert is a property owner, he lives on unearned income, etc.) and a *unique* childhood drama. In short, these regressive questions provide us with the means to question his family group as a reality lived and denied by the child Flaubert. Our questions are based on two sorts of information: objective testimonies about the family (class characteristics, family type, individual aspect) and furiously subjective statements by Flaubert about his parents, his brother, his sister, etc. At this level we must be able constantly to refer back to the work and to know whether it contains a biographical truth such as the correspondence itself (falsified by its author) cannot contain. But we must know also that the work *never* reveals the secrets of the biography; the book can at most serve as a schema or conducting thread allowing us to discover the secrets in the life itself.

At this level, we study the early childhood as a way of living general conditions without clearly understanding or reflecting on them; consequently, we may find the meaning of the lived experience in the intellectual petite bourgeoisie, formed under the Empire, and in its way of living the evolution of French society. Here we pass over into the pure objective; that is, into the historical totalization. It is History itself which we must question—the halted advance of family capitalism, the return of the landed proprietors, the contradictions in the government, the misery of a still insufficiently developed Proletariat. . . . Beginning with an obscurely lived childhood, we can reconstruct the true character of petit bourgeois families. We compare Flaubert's with the family of Baudelaire (at a more "elevated" social level), with that of the Goncourt brothers (a petit bourgeois family which entered into the nobility about the end of the eighteenth century by the simple acquisition of "noble" property), with that of Louis Bouilhet, etc. In this connection we study the real relations between scientists and practitioners (the father Flaubert) and industrialists (the father of his friend, Le Poittevin). In this sense the study of the child Flaubert, as a universality lived in particularity, enriches the general study of the petite bourgeoisie in 1830. By means of the structures presiding over the particular family group, we enrich and make concrete the always too general characteristics of the class considered; in discontinuous "collectives," for example, we apprehend the complex relation between a petite bourgeoisie of civil servants and intellectuals, on the one hand, and the "elite" of industrialists and landed proprietors on the others, or, again, the *roots* of this petite bourgeoisie, its peasant origin, etc., its relations with fallen aristocrats. It is on this level that we are going to discover the major contradiction which the child, Gustave Flaubert, lived in his own way: the opposition between the bourgeois analytic mind and the synthetic myths of religion. Here again a systematic cross-reference is established between the particular anecdotes which clarify these vague contradictions (because the stories gather them together into a single exploding whole) and the general determination of living conditions which allows us to reconstruct *progressively* (because they have already been studied) the material existence of the groups considered.

The sum total of these procedures—regression and cross-reference—has revealed what I shall call the profundity of the lived. . . . The exploration of this profundity is a descent from the absolute concrete (**Madame Bovary** in the hands of a reader contemporary with Flaubert—whether it be Baudelaire or the Empress or the Prosecuting Attorney) to its most abstract conditioning. . . . Across **Madame Bovary** we can and must catch sight of the movement of landowners and capitalists, the evolution of the rising classes, the slow maturation of the Proletariat: everything is there. (pp. 140-46)

At this point in our research we have still not succeeded in revealing anything more than a hierarchy of heterogeneous significations: *Madame Bovary,* Flaubert's "femininity," his childhood in a hospital building, existing contradictions in the contemporary petite bourgeoisie, the evolution of the family, of property, etc. Each signification clarifies the other, but their irreducibility creates a veritable discontinuity between them. Each serves as an encompassing framework for the preceding, but the included signification is richer than the including signification. In a word, we have only the outline for the dialectical movement, not the movement itself.

It is then and only then that we must employ the progressive method. The problem is to recover the totalizing movement of enrichment which engenders each moment in terms of the prior moment, the impulse which starts from lived obscurities in order to arrive at the final objectification—in short, the *project* by which Flaubert, in order to escape from the petite bourgeoisie, will launch himself across the various fields of possibles toward the alienated objectification of himself and will constitute himself inevitably and indissolubly as the author of *Madame Bovary* and as that petit bourgeois which he refused to be. This project has *a meaning,* it is not the simple negativity of flight; by it a man aims at the production of himself in the world as a certain objective totality. It is not the pure and simple abstract decision to write which makes up the peculiar quality of Flaubert, but the decision to write in a certain manner in order to manifest himself in the world in a particular way; in a word, it is the particular signification—within the framework of the contemporary ideology—which he gives to literature as the negation of his original condition and as the objective solution to his contradictions.... [As] we move back and forth between material and social conditioning and the work, the problem is to find the *tension* extending from objectivity to objectivity, to discover the law of expansion which surpasses one signification *by means of* the following one and which maintains the second in the first. In truth the problem is to invent a movement, to re-create it, but the hypothesis is immediately verifiable; the only valid one is that which will realize within a creative movement the transverse unity of *all* the heterogeneous structures.

Nevertheless, the project is in danger of being deviated, like Sade's project, by the collective instruments; thus the terminal objectification perhaps does not correspond exactly to the original choice. We must take up the regressive analysis again, making a still closer study of the instrumental field so as to determine the possible deviations; we must employ all that we have learned about the contemporary techniques of Knowledge as we look again at the unfolding life so as to examine the evolution of the choices and actions, their coherence or their apparent incoherence. *St. Anthony* expresses the whole Flaubert in his purity and in all the contradictions of his original project, but *St. Anthony* is a failure. Bouilhet and Maxime du Camp condemn it completely; they demand that it "tell a story." *There* is the deviation. Flaubert tells an anecdote, but he makes it support everything—the sky, hell, himself, St. Anthony, etc. The monstrous, splendid work which results from it, that in which he is objectified and alienated, is *Madame Bovary.* Thus the return to the biography shows us the hiatuses, the fissures, the accidents, at the same time that it confirms the hypothesis (the hypothesis of the original project) by revealing the direction and continuity of the life. We shall define the method of

the existentialist approach as a regressive-progressive and analytic-synthetic method. It is at the same time an enriching cross-reference between the object (which contains the whole period as hierarchized significations) and the period (which contains the object in its totalization). In fact, when the object is *rediscovered* in its profundity and in its particularity, then instead of remaining external to the totalization (as it was up until the time when the Marxists undertook to integrate it into history), it enters immediately into contradiction with it. In short, the simple inert juxtaposition of the epoch and the object gives way abruptly to a living conflict.

If one has lazily defined Flaubert as a realist and if one has decided that realism suited the public in the Second Empire (which will permit us to develop a brilliant, completely false theory about the evolution of realism between 1857 and 1957), one will never succeed in comprehending either that strange monster which is *Madame Bovary* or the author or the public. Once more one will be playing with shadows. But if one has taken the trouble, in a study which is going to be long and difficult, to demonstrate within this novel the objectification of the subjective and its alienation—in short, if one grasps it in the concrete sense which it still holds at the moment when it escapes from its author and *at the same time* from the outside as an object which is allowed to develop freely, then the book abruptly comes to oppose the objective reality which it will hold for public opinion, for the magistrates, for contemporary writers. This is the moment to return to the period and to ask ourselves, for example, this very simple question: There was at that time a realist school—Courbet in painting and Duranty in literature were its representatives. Duranty had frequently presented his credo and drafted his manifestos. Flaubert despised realism and said so over and over throughout his life; he loved only the absolute purity of art. *Why* did the public decide at the outset that Flaubert was the realist, and why did it love in him *that particular realism;* that is, that admirable faked confession, that disguised lyricism, that implicit metaphysic? Why did it so value as an admirable character portrayal of a woman (or as a pitiless description of woman) what was at bottom only a poor disguised man? Then we must ask ourselves *what kind of realism* this public demanded or, if you prefer, what kind of literature it demanded under that name and why. This last moment is of primary importance; it is quite simply the moment of alienation. Flaubert sees his work stolen away from him by the very success which the period bestows on it; he no longer recognizes his book, it is foreign to him. Suddenly he loses his own objective existence. But at the same time his work throws a new light upon the period; it enables us to pose a new question to History: Just what must that period have been in order that it should demand *this* book and mendaciously find there its own image. Here we are at the veritable moment of historical action or of what I shall willingly call the misunderstanding. But this is not the place to develop this new point. It is enough to say by way of conclusion that the man and his time will be integrated into the dialectical totalization when we have shown how History surpasses this contradiction. (pp. 146-50)

*Jean-Paul Sartre, "The Problem of Meditations and Auxiliary Disciplines" and "The Progressive-Regressive Method," in his* Search for a Method, *translated by Hazel E. Barnes, Alfred A. Knopf, 1967, pp. 35-84, 85-166.\**

## JEAN ROUSSET   (essay date 1962)

*[The following excerpt is from Rousset's study* Forme et signification: Essais sur les structures littéraires de Corneille à Claudel,*

*published in French in 1962. Rousset analyzes Flaubert's use of narrative point of view. First, he discusses the beginning and end of the novel, where Flaubert adopts an external perspective, that of Charles, to introduce his main character. Next, he examines the shifts in point of view, praising them as smooth, gradual, and imperceptible. Rousset commends Flaubert's use of varying narrative perspectives that the author uses to alternate between intimate portraits of Emma's thoughts and panoramic perspectives that depict action. Highlighting the symbolic and thematic importance of windows in the novel, Rousset demonstrates their narrative function. For additional commentary on narrative perspective in* Madame Bovary, *see excerpts by Erich Auerbach (1942-45), Victor Brombert (1966), Leo Bersani (see Additional Bibliography, 1959), and Percy Lubbock (see* NCLC, *Vol. 2). Critics who discuss imagery in the novel include D. L. Demorest (1931), Martin Turnell (1950), Jean Pierre Richard (1954), Georges Poulet (1955), and Victor Brombert (1966).]*

[In the context of the development of the anti-novel], one feels compelled to stress the importance of Flaubert, the pure novelist critic, brought up from infancy on that greatest ancestor of all anti-novels, [Cervantes's] *Don Quixote.* His ambition, expressed when he starts **Madame Bovary,** is well known: "What I deem beautiful, what I would want to do, is a book about nothing, a book without reference outside itself . . . , a book that would be almost without a subject, or in which the subject would be almost invisible, if such a thing is possible" (January 16, 1852). And, a little later: "If the book on which I am working with such difficulty can be brought to a successful conclusion, its existence will at least have proven the following two truths which I consider to be self-evident: first, that poetry is entirely subjective, that, in literature, there is no such thing as a beautiful subject—hence, that Yvetot will do just as well as Constantinople; and that, consequently, it makes no difference what one writes about" (June 25/26, 1853).

This century-old declaration of war against the intrinsic importance of the subject clearly shows that the novel was felt to be in a state of crisis and revolt well before 1950. When today's "new novelists" are up in arms against the "traditional novel," they are attacking a novel that was itself rebelling against its predecessors. Differences exist, not only between the products of this rebellion but also, less obviously, between the models that are being rejected: the non-subject of one generation often becomes the subject to be rejected by their successors.

This does not prevent Flaubert's experiments from being particularly meaningful for us today; he is the first in date of the non-figurative novelists. The subject—and the psychology—of **Madame Bovary** certainly still play their part, albeit a muted one, in the concert of the novel, which could not exist without them. Yet, we have the right, and perhaps the duty, to ignore them and to echo Flaubert's statement to Goncourt: "As for the story, the plot of a novel—I couldn't care less." We can add to this the very modern-sounding statement of beliefs: "The works of art that I admire above all others are those in which there is an *excess of Art.* In a picture, it is Painting that I like; in a poem, Poetry." One could complete the statement: and in a novel, it is technique and style. Flaubert himself seems to invite us to read **Madame Bovary** as if it were a sonata. Thus we might escape the reproach he addressed to the greatest critics of his own time: "What shocks me in my friends Saint-Beuve and Taine is that they do not pay sufficient attention to *Art,* to the work in itself, to its construction, its style, all that makes up its beauty. . . ."

Flaubert does not explicitly mention a principle of composition which must have concerned him to the highest degree: the

"point of view" from which the novelist considers the events and the characters described in the novel. Is it the impartial and panoramic view of the ideal witness? One would expect this to be the case, remembering the author's declared intention in **Madame Bovary** to make himself as impersonal and objective as possible. This was, moreover, the usual technique in Balzac's novels. But Flaubert has no faith in impersonal knowledge. No such thing as objective reality exists for him; every vision, every perception is someone's particular illusion; there are as many "colored glasses" as there are observers. Does not this challenge the privileged position of the all-knowing author, endowed with divine and absolute vision?

The general organization of the book comes as a surprise: the main character is absent from the beginning as well as from the epilogue of the novel. This anomaly leads us directly to the problem of points of view.

The organization of the novel, which gives Charles Bovary a central position at the beginning and at the end, had been planned from the very first scenarios on. The only change that took place along the way is the growing importance of Homais in the final pages. These two characters are presented from the outside and from afar, almost as if they were things, opaque in their lack of self-awareness. The novel is thus framed by two episodes in which the point of view is very definitely that

*A portrait of Louise Colet, Flaubert's mistress and his "Muse," by Courbet.*

of the bystander watching the scene from a distance and from above, altogether detached from the inner motivations of characters which he treats as if they were puppets. At the one end, Charles first enters the field of our vision when he appears in the classroom observed by that curiously neutral "we" that will soon vanish from the novel; at the other end of the book, in a symmetrical construction so effective that it more than justifies the change in the original outline, we have the triumphantly grotesque exit of the pharmacist. At the two gates of his work, as he meets and as he leaves us, Flaubert has concentrated a maximum of sad irony and sarcasm, because these are the places in which his observation is most remote from its object. Thus the novel first moves from the outside inward, from the surface to the heart, from detachment to involvement, then returns from the inside to the periphery. Flaubert's first glance at the world always remains aloof, and only records the outside, the crust, the grotesque aspect of the mechanical gesture.

But soon enough he penetrates beneath the surface. Homais remains seen from the outside throughout, thus making it possible to use him for the concluding passage, but the same is not true for Charles. From the start, while he holds the center of the stage for a relatively long time, the author draws much nearer to him and takes the reader with him. The puppet becomes human: a brief flashback tells us about his birth, his childhood and adolescence, thus opening the way for a more sympathetic insight. It is nevertheless with some feeling of surprise that we suddenly find ourselves intimately close to him, sharing in his reverie: "On the fine summer evenings . . . he opened his window and leaned out. The river . . . flowed beneath him . . . Opposite, beyond the roofs, spread the pure sky with the red sun setting. How pleasant it must be at home! How fresh under the beech tree!" One almost suspects a mistake on Flaubert's part: such nostalgic dreams before the window, such reveries directed towards open space, are usually associated with his heroine. He could not resist this slight token of identification, this brief moment during which he espouses the point of view of his character. As a temporary protagonist, Charles is allowed some of the benefits of this position. But the moment of insight is brief; the author at once withdraws again to the proper distance. (pp. 440-43)

It is through Charles's eyes that we will first come upon Emma. Charles will be used as a reflector until the moment when the heroine, having been gradually introduced and then accepted, will occupy the front of the stage and become the central subject. But, like her future husband, she must first appear in the humbler guise of a character seen from the outside, as if she were a mere inanimate thing. Unlike Charles, however, the eye that perceives her is not critical, but dazzled, and the sensibility that reflects her image is familiar to us; the reader has even been allowed a glimpse of its inner workings, especially on the occasion of the doctor's early-morning visit to the Bertaux farm when, half asleep, we share in his split, double perceptions, just before Emma comes on the scene. Flaubert then uses Charles to introduce Emma, and to make us see her as she appears to him; we adopt strictly his point of view, his narrow field of vision, his subjective perception, as we follow him step by step in his discovery of an unknown woman. The author relinquishes the privileged position of the all-knowing novelist and gives us instead an image of his heroine that remains deliberately superficial and incomplete, in the sense that it records only successive and fragmentary impressions.

Charles arrives at the farm: "A young woman, in a blue merino dress, with three flounces, appeared on the threshold . . ." A blue dress is what he notices first of all, is all that he shows us. One page later, he notices the whiteness of her nails, then her eyes; somewhat later still, on talking with her, he notes the "fullness of her lips." When she turns her back on him, her hair on her neck swings in a movement "that the country doctor noticed there for the first time in his life." Instead of the full-sized portrait that exists out of time, and records what the author knows and perceives, as Balzac or, before him, Marivaux, would have given us, Flaubert draws a portrait composed of gradually emerging fragments—he lets such a portrait come into being from the pointillist observations of a character who is emotionally stirred and involved. Other encounters with Emma will add further touches, always similarly scattered, as they originate in the confused and troubled consciousness of a man who is falling in love. (pp. 443-44)

Flaubert doesn't rigorously adhere to the necessity of reflecting the limitations and distortions of his characters; he was still rather remote from Faulkner who locked himself hermetically within the interior monologue of a half-wit. Whether from lack of consistency or because he refuses to be over-systematic, Flaubert at times fills out Charles's usual perceptions, just as he sometimes puts in Emma's mind reflections or shades of irony that couldn't possibly be hers. The result is frequently a compromise in which it is difficult to discriminate between the contradictory viewpoints of the outside observer and the inner eye. Flaubert will not hesitate to commit the "error" for which Sartre so bitterly criticizes Mauriac (as if Mauriac were the first guilty of moving freely in and out of the consciousness of his characters): "As for Charles, he didn't stay to ask himself why it was a pleasure to him to go to the Bertaux," or else: "Was she speaking seriously? Emma probably didn't even know herself. . . ."

There can be no question, however, that throughout the prologue Charles is deliberately used as a center and as a reflector. He is never absent, and Emma is seen only through his eyes. All we know about her is what he finds out; the only words she speaks are those addressed to him. We don't have the slightest idea what she really thinks or feels. Emma is systematically shown us from the outside; Charles's point of view demands this. In this respect, Flaubert adheres strictly to his method. He even provides us with an extreme example: at the moment when the young girl makes the ominous decision to marry, a decision on which her entire miserable destiny and, therefore, the substance of the book hinges, the novelist hides her out of our sight; her conversation with her father, her inner reactions, and her answer are recorded indirectly and at great distance by Charles who is hiding behind the hedge and waiting for the window-blind to be pushed open against the wall. Only much later, when Flaubert moves closer to her and unlocks her thoughts, a set of refractions and juxtapositions will reveal something of what she thinks of Charles and her marriage, of her expectations, of what went on in her during that half hour. For the time being, however, she remains an opaque character contemplated from afar by Charles Bovary. All we know of her is what he knows—the outline of a face, a few gestures, a dress.

Soon enough, we discover what hides behind this surface and what kind of human being this young woman actually is, for the point of view is about to change. But Charles himself will never discover much more; to him, she will always remain that unknowable quantity that she will soon cease to be for us. He will never find out what hides behind this veil, for he totally lacks the novelist's power to penetrate into her inner self. From Chapter V on, the angle of vision slowly starts to revolve; from pure object, Emma becomes subject, the focus shifts from Charles to her, and the reader penetrates into a consciousness which, up till then, was as closed to him as it was to Charles.

This is probably the deeper reason for the country doctor's central position in the first chapters, as well as for the rigorous adherence to his point of view, including the occasional and surprising plumbing of his intimate self. Not only does it allow the reader to meet Emma first through a sensibility that is itself immersed in the flux of time; more than that, this organization of the perspective allows him to experience from the inside the type of knowledge that Charles will always possess of his wife. Thus prepared, the reader will remember it later, when Emma will have moved to the center, and this recollection will illuminate and enrich the fictional universe in which he immerses himself.

From Chapter VI on, Emma glides to the center of the novel, a place which she will never leave, except for some brief interruptions. There is nothing unusual about this. Balzac, master of the total and panoramic point of view, often chooses a central character, such as, for instance, Rastignac [in *Père Goriot* and other works of *La comédie humaine*], and organizes the action around him. Flaubert's originality resides in his combining the author's point of view with the heroine's. His perspectives alternate and interfere with each other, but the subjective vision of the character always predominates. His technical problem is to achieve the shifts in point of view and the transitions from one perspective to another without interrupting the movement, without disrupting the "tissue of the style."

Consider, for example, the transition from Charles to Emma, the gradual introduction, by almost unnoticeable steps, of the heroine's point of view. The point of departure and final destination of his itinerary are marked by the return of the same object, observed by two different sets of eyes: the garden of Tostes. "The garden, longer than wide, ran between two mud walls . . . to a thorn hedge that separated it from the field. In the middle was a slate sundial . . . ; four flower-beds . . . Right at the bottom, under the spruce bushes, a plaster priest was reading his breviary." This is a straightforward catalogue, an objective inventory of surfaces and materials, drawn up as by an outside observer, altogether detached—without any anthropomorphic participation in things, as [the French novelist] Robbe-Grillet would put it. The reason for this objectivity stems from the fact that Emma, when she is entering her new home, is still an utter stranger to whom Flaubert has not yet given us any access whatsoever. Thirty pages later, Emma's initiation accomplished, we come upon the same little garden, seen this time through the subjective glance of the disenchanted heroine, reacting fully to all the elements of stagnation, decline, and decay that reside in things: "The dew had left on the cabbages a silver lace with long transparent threads spreading from one to the other. No birds were to be heard; everything seemed asleep, the espalier covered with straw, and the vine, like a great sick serpent under the coping of the wall, along which, on drawing near, one saw the many-footed woodlice crawling. Under the spruce by the hedgerow, the curé in the three-cornered hat reading his breviary had lost his right foot, and the very plaster scaling off with the frost, had left white scabs on his face."

In the interval between the two passages everything has changed, not only in the situation and the mood of the heroine, but in the reader's position toward her as well. A skillful revolving movement has shifted the point of view, and the center of vision now gradually coincides with Emma's. We get a first glimpse into her dreams, followed, in flashback, by an analysis of the development that lead to her present sensibility. Flaubert's hand is very apparent throughout; at this point, none of these insights could have been Emma's own. Then comes a more revealing insight in her dreams of another honeymoon: "She thought, some times . . ." leading to the long reverie under the beech trees which is by now altogether subjective and richly endowed with all the characteristics of Flaubert's inner ecstasies.

Henry James, speaking of one of his novels, mentions "a planned rotation of aspects"; the expression could very well apply to Flaubert. It designates a subtle art of modulation in varying the point of view, an art of which Flaubert is a true master and which he puts to constant use. For if it is true that Emma never ceases to stand at the center of the novel, Flaubert nevertheless substitutes at times, for a brief moment, the outlook of another character. Such shifts are no easy matter to negotiate for an author who detests any trace of discontinuity, and wishes to avoid, at all cost, the tricks and manipulations of the novelist-stage director which abound in the first version of *The Sentimental Education*. When Flaubert relinquishes Emma's point of view in favor of that of Charles or Rodolphe, or gives the front of the stage for a moment to a minor character, he uses something resembling a closed-circuit system, without interrupting the flow of the narration. An example will show how the method works.

In the third chapter of Part II, immediately following the arrival at Yonville, Emma enters her new house; the reader goes with her, feeling "the cold of the plaster fall about her shoulders like damp linen. . . ." At this point, the novel has to impart miscellaneous bits of information about recently introduced characters such as Léon and Homais. Flaubert has to move away from the heroine without breaking the thread. He uses Emma's own outlook: "The next day, as she was getting up, she saw the clerk on the Square . . . Léon waited all day, etc. . . ."; the point of view has glided towards the clerk, where it stays for a while. From the clerk, whom M. Homais "respected for his education," we move almost imperceptibly over to the pharmacist, his habits, his attitude towards the new doctor, thus allowing a smooth transition to Charles. "Charles was depressed; he had no patients. . . ." Yet, in compensation, he rejoices in his wife's pregnancy. This glance cast by Charles on his pregnant wife closes the circle, returns us to Emma, happily concluding the full circuit of alternating viewpoints: "He looked at her undisturbed . . . Emma at first felt a great astonishment." Moreover, by juxtaposing the thoughts of Emma and Charles, Flaubert shows how distant they are from each other. He may, at times, deliberately forego his gradual transfers in order to reveal, as by a sudden gap, this divergence of their outlooks, the infinite distance that keeps them apart, even when they are sitting or lying side by side: "He saw himself dishonored . . . Emma, opposite, watched him; she did not share his humiliation, she felt another. . . ." But, as a rule, Flaubert puts a great deal of care in his art of modulation. Thus when Rodolphe and Emma end their last nocturnal dialogue, which the reader has experienced through the consciousness of the young woman:

> 'Till tomorrow then!' said Emma in a last caress.

And *she watched him go.*
He didn't turn around ... He was already on
the other side of the river, walking fast across
the meadows.
After a few moments Rodolphe stopped....

Again, carried by Emma's eye, the reader leaves her for the
object of her contemplation and joins Rodolphe; he hears him
think and sees him write the letter that puts an end to the affair.

This art of modulation, this concern with smooth and gradual
transition, reflects in a distinctive manner Flaubert's general
effort towards what he calls *style.* He conceives of style as a
binding agent which reduces the diverse to the homogeneous.
He strives for a unity of texture, as tight and even as possible,
in order to create continuity: "Style is made of continuity, as
virtue is made of constancy." (pp. 444-48)

[Without] leaving the questions of point of view and field of
vision with which we have been concerned, we should notice
the important part that windows play in **Madame Bovary.** [The
French critic] Léon Bopp has observed the importance of the
frequent presence of the heroine before open windows. This
allows for striking effects of depth perspective and panoramic
vision, corresponding to phases of maximum subjectivity and
extreme intensity.

Maria, in the story **November,** spent whole days at her window
waiting, keeping a vigil over the empty space in which a cus-
tomer might appear, or an event occur. The window is a favorite
place for certain Flaubert characters who, though unable to
move by themselves, are nevertheless swept away by the current of events. They are frozen by their own inertias while
their minds wander forever. Caught in the closed space in which
their souls dry up, they welcome the window as an escape
which allows them to expand into space, without having to
leave their chosen spots. The window combines open and enclosed space, represents an obstacle as well as an escape, a
sheltering room as well as an area of endless expansion, a
circumscribed infinity. Flaubert's main characters who, as
Georges Poulet has so well shown, are always absent from
where they live and present where they do not, vacillating
between contraction and expansion, are bound to choose for
their dwelling places borderline entities which allow for escape
in immobility; no wonder they select windows as the ideal
locale for their reveries. (pp. 449-50)

[Emma Bovary], locked within the walls of her cage, finds
before her window an "escape towards all horizons": "She
often stood there." In Tostes, she stands at the window to
watch the rain fall and the monotonous round of the village
days go by; in Yonville, the notary clerk as well as Rodolphe
are first observed from a window; standing in the garden window, Emma hears the ringing of the angelus bells that will
awaken a mystical longing in her, drawing her gaze upwards
to lose itself among the clouds or among the meanderings of
the river; the attic-window gives her the first dizzy temptation
toward suicide; and after her illness, when she resumes contact
with life, "they wheeled her arm chair by the window overlooking the Square...." They are the windows of despair and
of dreams.

On the other hand, we find in the novel closed windows, with
all curtains drawn during the rare moments when Emma is no
longer alienated from herself or from the place where she lives
and, consequently, feels no need to scatter herself into the
endless infinity of dreams. Instead, in the early and happy
moment of her passions, she makes herself into the center of

all things, as in Rouen, with Léon, "in the carriage with drawn
blinds ... more tightly closed than a tomb," then in the hotel
room where they live locked up all day long "all curtains
drawn, all doors locked ... in a hothouse atmosphere," as
one of the early scenarios expresses it. The same had happened
with Rodolphe when Emma, at the onset of their affair, paid
him surprise visits at la Huchette, in the room half-darkened
by "the yellow curtains along the windows." But this first
passion is generally a passion in the open air, in garden or
forest, where there are no windows at all. Flaubert thus contrasts the nature of the two lovers, while remaining faithful to
the thematic meaning of the windows in his novel.

In conjunction with their special significance for Flaubert's
characters, the windows provide the novelist-director with interesting technical opportunities in staging and ordering his
scenes. Flaubert uses them frequently to vary the narrative
perspective and to engineer interesting optical effects. The brilliant "symphonic" passage of the Agricultural Fair at once
comes to mind, in which the point of view is that of the two
future lovers, watching from the window on the second floor
of the town hall. The panoramic view here offers a double
advantage: in the first place, it reinforces the author's ironical
detachment towards the goings-on below and towards the budding idyll that he treats in juxtaposition to the fair; more important still, it reflects the upward motion, the more elevated
note struck at the moment of Emma's entrance upon the life
of passion. The tone is picked up in the following episode: the
same panoramic vision is used again a little later, during the
horse ride when Rodolphe completes the conquest begun on
the day of the fair. Arriving at the top of a hill, Flaubert gives
us a panoramic outlook over the land similar to the one that
Emma gains, at this same moment, over her life: "There was
fog over the land. Hazy clouds hovered on the horizon between
the outlines of the hills; others rent asunder, floated up and
disappeared. Sometimes through a rift in the clouds, beneath
a ray of sunshine, gleamed from afar the roofs of Yonville,
with the gardens at the water's edge, the yards, the walls and
the church steeple. Emma half closed her eyes to pick out her
house, and never had this poor village where she lived appeared
so small." The beginning of her love is marked by a rising
above the habitual level of existence; the place where this
existence occurred must first vanish before her eyes: Yonville
must shrink away into a distance made infinite by the bird's-
eye perspective, in order to make room for the imaginary space
in which her love will take place.... (pp. 450-51)

A few pages farther, on the evening of the same day, Emma
dreams of this new life that dawns upon her. As if the high
view of the afternoon had completely entered the inner landscape of her soul, she still thinks in terms of height and infinity,
united against the lowliness of her common existence: "She
was entering upon a marvelous world where all would be passion, ecstasy, endless rapture. A blue space surrounded her,
the heights of sentiment sparkled under her thought, and ordinary existence appeared only intermittently between these
heights, dark and far away underneath her."

Flaubert has made a different use of the same hilltop above
the village, at a moment that is not less decisive, though oriented in the opposite direction. Madame Bovary has seen Rodolphe for the last time and she returns to Yonville, utterly
dejected and about to kill herself. Instead of the ascent towards
the ecstasy of passion, we now have the descent towards suicide. During this hallucinated walk at nightfall, we meet her
at the top of a hill, the same perhaps as before. Suddenly, she
is shaken out of her spellbound state:

It all disappeared: she recognized the lights of
the houses that shone through the fog.
Now her plight, like an abyss, loomed before
her . . . she ran down the hill . . .

The return from the world of the imagination to the world of
reality is now a falling towards the village; this time, the village
appears out of the fog instead of hiding beneath it; it is a descent
into the abyss.

Thus, in two passages which, though quite far apart, are the
symmetrical opposites of each other, Flaubert has placed his
heroine, at the onset and at the end of her love-quest, in the
same dominating position and has made her command the same
panoramic outlook. It is up to the attentive reader to notice the
structural link that unites the two episodes and to discover the
wealth of meaning added by such a tightly controlled construction. One should compare to this another diptych, combining
this time the use of the window with that of the carriage (which
will play such an important part in the *Sentimental Education*):
the two views of Rouen, on the arrival and at the departure of
the stage coach, during Emma's Thursday encounters with
Léon. We are given one more panoramic view: "Thus seen
from above, the entire landscape seemed motionless like a
painting. . . ." And here again, the landscape, at first frozen,
will start to move, to vibrate and to expand under the impact
of an imagination driven by impending passion. There is one
important difference, however: instead of appearing remote and
hidden by a veil that makes it shrink into near oblivion, the
dwelling place of her desire will now, in a reverse optical
illusion, appear out of the mist and start expanding into an
immense capital—the only entity large enough to contain the
ever widening space she projects before her: "Her love grew
in the presence of this vastness, and filled with the tumult of
the vague murmuring which rose from below. She poured it
out, onto the squares, the avenues, the streets; and the old
Norman city *spread out before her like some incredible Capital, a Babylon into which she was about to enter*."

Windows and panoramic views, spatial reveries, opening up
into infinite perspectives, make up the crucial centers around
which the plot is organized; they are points of highest resistance
that stop the flow of the narrative. They coincide with the
adoption of a most unusual point of view: the author relinquishes his traditional god-like rights and leaves room instead
for a totally subjective vision. He places himself behind his
heroine and looks entirely through her eyes. Such moments
occur at significant points in the book. They are unevenly
distributed; entirely lacking during the periods of action, when
the play of passion is acted out, they are more frequent during
periods of stagnation and suspended waiting. So for instance
at Tostes, after the invitation to the ball, when for the first
time we see Emma, at the end of the evening, open the window
and lean out. From then on, in Tostes as well as in Yonville,
the reverie will never cease, till the moment when she embarks
upon her great adventure, returns to her husband, rejects him
again after the clubfoot episode, prepares her elopement, gets
involved in her financial dealings with Lheureux. After these
chapters of action and accelerated movement, the end of the
affair with Rodolphe brings back a slower tempo, a new period
of stagnation and inertia. Again, this change of pace is introduced by a window opening up before the heroine; this time,
however, the window is already a tragic one, suggesting the
dizziness and loss of consciousness that is a prefiguration of
the end. She reads Rodolphe's letter near the attic window,
"opposite, beyond the roofs, the countryside stretched out as

far as the eye could reach. . . ." She is about to return to a
world of regrets and frustrated desires, in which she will try
to expand beyond the limits of her confinement, to "float" in
the airy realm which is that of her reverie and of her panoramic
visions: "she was right at the edge, almost hanging, surrounded
by vast space. The blue of the sky invaded her. . . ."

Those repeated flights of reverie before the open window are
always followed by a fall, a return to earth: "'My wife! my
wife!' Charles called . . . and she had to *go down* and sit at
the table!" The book, like the inner life of the heroine, consists
of this rhythmical succession of flights and falls. Thus, at the
beginning of Chapter VI of the second part, the open window
through which the ringing of the angelus is heard leads to a
flow of memories and to an ascent into a weightless, suspended
state expressed by images of flight, of swirling feathers: "she
felt limp and helpless, like the down of a bird whirled by the
tempest"; then, on returning from church, "she let *herself fall*
into an armchair," recaptured by the heavy and confining world
of the room, by the monotonous weight of time, by the opaque
presence of creatures who "are there" as if they were pieces
of furniture: "the pieces of furniture seemed more frozen in
their places . . . , the clock went on ticking . . . little Berthe
was there, between the window and the sewing table . . . Charles
appeared. It was dinner time. . . ." Trying to reestablish contact with daily life, after the moments of escape towards the
beyond of the windows, is always an act of falling, a falling
back into confinement.

The same double movement recurs at other crucial passages,
such as the scene at the Agricultural Fair. Emma, stirred by a
smell of perfume and the "distant" sight of the stage coach,
unites in a kind of ecstasy lovers and experiences of the past
before she returns downward, to the crowd on the square and
the official oratory. Or again, in another ecstasy of a similarly
erotic nature, the scene at the opera in Rouen, which heralds
the beginning of the affair with Léon as the preceding one
began the affair with Rodolphe. The box from which Emma
looks "from above" over the stage is an exact equivalence of
the window, a new amalgamation, a synthesis of confinement
and expansion towards a space on which an imaginary destiny
is being acted out. This time, it is not her own destiny that is
being played out, but somebody else's being performed for her
benefit; yet it doesn't take her long to recognize her own plight,
to identify with the main feminine part, to join her in her desire
to "*fly away* in an embrace" and to see another Rodolphe in
the tenor part: "A mad idea took possession of her: he was
looking at her right now! She longed to run to his arms . . . ,
and call out 'Take me away!' . . . The curtain *fell* . . . and she
*fell back* into her seat. . . ." The sudden collapse of the dream
and of the aerial perspective is followed after the flight, by the
inevitable letdown. (pp. 451-54)

Moments of reverie, during which Flaubert's point of view
comes closest to coinciding with that of his heroine and which
allow us a glimpse into Emma's intimate self, abound in the
slowest-moving parts of the novel, during the periods of inertia
and spleen when time seems to stand still. They constitute the
most original and striking aspects of the novel, the ones, also,
that are most typical of Flaubert. During those moments, Flaubert relinquishes, to a considerable extent, the objective vision
of the universal observer.

On the other hand, at times when the action must move forward,
when new facts or characters have to be introduced, the author
reclaims his sovereign rights and resorts to a panoramic perspective. Restoring the distance between himself and his char-

acters, he can again show them from the outside. This happens, as we have shown, at the beginning and at the end of the novel, or in the opening chapters of a new part. Fresh beginnings demand the presence of the novelist-director, who sets the stage while introducing the cast of characters: so it is at the beginning of Part II, the big scene in the inn at Yonville or, in the introduction of Part III, the conversation between Emma and Léon in a Rouen hotel room, the rendezvous at the cathedral, the coach ride through the streets of Rouen. During the coach ride Flaubert takes advantage of the momentary distance that separates him from his heroine to achieve a surprising effect: the new lovers are in the coach, all curtains drawn, but the reader is not allowed to join them. In the foregoing pages, he was allowed no insight into their souls, but he could observe gestures and attitudes, catch the meaning of words that were spoken; here, even this privilege is taken from him—he can see nothing at all, and has to be satisfied with following the carriage from afar as it meanders through the streets. During this decisive episode, he finds himself confined to the narrowest point of view possible, that of the indifferent citizens of Rouen, for whom this woman is a total stranger. When she finally emerges from the carriage, he sees her in this very light: "a *woman* got out, walking with her veil down and without looking back." The effect is all the more uncanny since the reader has been allowed earlier intimate glimpses of Emma's soul, and this close knowledge makes it easy for him to guess what goes on behind the lowered veil.

A similar effect recurs somewhat later in the book, when the author adopts an equally distant point of view to narrate Emma's desperate call on Binet: the scene is shown through the eyes of the two prying neighbors as they watch through the attic window. We can hardly hear a word, we watch from afar;

*A daguerreotype of Louise Pradier, who critics believe was one of the sources for Emma.*

gestures and attitudes have to be guessed and interpreted—it is like a scene from a silent movie. One may assume that Flaubert, who has kept us in very close contact with his main character and made us share in her drama from the inside, feels so certain of our participation that he allows himself this sudden withdrawal to show us, for one brief moment, the heroine as she appears to the alien eye of the outside judge and observer. Immediately afterwards, we briefly lose sight of her altogether. The two gossips watch her disappear down the street in the direction of the graveyard, and we can only wonder with them what Emma is about to do. Then in a new and abrupt reversal, the novelist suddenly takes us back to Emma as she visits the nurse, letting us into her consciousness. Those violent manipulations of the reader, echoing the pathos that abounds in this part of the narrative, are the more effective since, at all other times, Flaubert, modulating and gliding from scene to scene in almost imperceptible transitions, has taken exactly the opposite approach.

In Flaubert's novel, the point of view and the subjective vision of the characters play a considerable part, at the expense of straightforward factual reporting. As a result, the importance of the slower movements increase as the outside impartial observer relinquishes his privileges, to a greater or lesser degree.

This slowness of tempo combined with the use of inner perspective constitute the novelty and the originality of Flaubert's novels. He is the novelist of the inner vision and of a slow, almost stagnant action. Admirable and distinctive as those qualities are, Flaubert himself nevertheless discovers them only gradually by trial and error, more by instinct than by design, and not without some serious misgivings. We read in his letters that there is no "action," no "movement," "fifty pages without a single event." His concern about the shape his novel is taking (almost in spite of itself) stems from the awareness of his difference from his predecessors. He is thinking primarily of Balzac, for whom all is action, drama, and suspense. Then he resigns himself: "One must sing in one's own voice: and mine will never be dramatic or seductive. Besides, I am growing more and more convinced that all this is a matter of style, or, rather, of appearance, a way of presenting things." The best he can do is to try to maintain a balance between action and inaction, between facts and dreams: "It will be a difficult task to make an almost equal division between adventure and thought."

Fortunately for us, he will never quite succeed in this. The dreamy nature of his heroine and the natural bent of his literary talent pull in the same direction. The nature of Flaubert's genius is such that he prefers the reflected consciousness of an event to the event itself, the dream of passion to the actual experience, lack of action and emptiness to presence. This is where Flaubert's art really comes into its own. What is most beautiful in his novels bears little resemblance to ordinary fiction. It is found not in the events—for, in his hand, they tend to crumble and disappear—but in what lies between events, those wide empty regions, the vast areas of stagnation in which no movement occurs. To succeed in charging emptiness with so much existence and substance, to conjure up such fullness out of nothing, is the miracle. But this reversal has still another consequence: in an objective narrative written in the third person, it magnifies the importance of the character's point of view and stresses the optics of his "thought"—the stage on which everything that matters takes place. (pp. 455-57)

*Jean Rousset, "'Madame Bovary': Flaubert's Anti-Novel," translated by Paul de Man, in "Madame*

Bovary'' by Gustave Flaubert: Backgrounds and Sources, Essays in Criticism, *edited and translated by Paul de Man, W. W. Norton & Company, Inc., 1965, pp. 439-57.*

## VICTOR BROMBERT  (essay date 1966)

*[Brombert's essay on technique in* Madame Bovary *contains five parts. Excerpted below are the sections on patterns of imagery and structure, irony, and point of view; not included are those covering the origins of the novel, Flaubert's use of symbolic detail, and the nature of Emma's tragedy. Here, Brombert begins by examining Flaubert's use of imagery. He contends that* Madame Bovary *is constructed around clusters of interrelated images that form cyclic themes and that characters and events in the novel consistently move from* ennui *to self-destruction. Brombert then identifies the author's perspective in* Madame Bovary. *After noting the connection between laughter, cruelty, and tragic absurdity in Flaubert's approach to comedy, Brombert contends that Flaubert uses a double perspective that renders him simultaneously inside and outside his characters. This results in the ambiguity of the authorial stance that allows Flaubert to project both ironic mockery and sympathetic understanding. For additional commentary on imagery and symbolism in the novel, see D. L. Demorest (1931), Martin Turnell (1950), Jean Pierre Richard (1954), Georges Poulet (1955), and Jean Rousset (1962). Critics who examine narrative perspective in* Madame Bovary, *include Erich Auerbach (1942-45), Jean Rousset (1962), Leo Bersani (see Ad-*

*ditional Bibliography, 1959), and Percy Lubbock (see* NCLC, *Vol. 2). Other discussions of structure and technique are provided by Henry James (1902), Erich Auerbach (1942-45), W. von Wartburg (1946), Martin Turnell (1950), Stephen Ullmann (1957), and Marcel Proust and Percy Lubbock (see* NCLC, *Vol. 2).]*

Flaubert takes cruel satisfaction in ironic contrasts. Many of them are set up in a somewhat obvious fashion: the Bovary dog-cart and the elegant carriages of the guests at the Vaubyessard ball; Charles' smugness and Emma's frustration; her exaltations and her moments of torpor; the alternations of ardor and frigidity; Emma's vibrating body still tingling from the caresses, while her lover, a cigar between his lips, is mending a broken bridle! At times, the antithesis tends to be more subtle: the knotty articulations of a peasant hand appear on the very page where the lovers' fingers intertwine.

These planned juxtapositions do, however, point to the heart of the subject. They emphasize the basic theme of incompatibility. Their implicit tensions stress a fundamental state of *divorce* at all levels of experience. But they also fulfill a dramatic function. If Charles' father happens to be a squanderer and an almost professional seducer, if Charles himself, while still married to his first wife, is drawn to Emma because she represents a forbidden and inaccessible love, these ironies are part of an effective technique of ''preparation.'' And these very anticipatory devices—whether prophetic in a straightforward or an ironic fashion—are in turn related to the theme of ''fate'' which Flaubert propounds with characteristic ambiguity. ''C'est la faute de la fatalité!'' is Charles' pathetic, yet moving final comment. But the notion of ''fatality'' is of course one of the most belabored Romantic clichés; Charles' exclamation carries its own condemnation, at the same time that it implies a debunking of the tragic ending of the novel. . . . Yet who is to deny that, in addition to elements of pathos, the novel constantly suggests an all-pervasive determinism: Emma's temperament, the character of Charles, the effects of heredity, the erosive quality of small-town life, the noxious influence of books, the structure of the novel itself?

Flaubert significantly devotes an entire chapter to Emma's education in the convent. Her private symbolism of love, mysticism and death is determined by this experience. The ''mystic languor'' provoked by the incense, the whisperings of the priest, the very metaphors comparing Christ to a celestial lover, predispose her to confuse sensuous delights and spiritual longings. The convent is Emma's earliest claustration, and the solicitations from the outside world, whether in the form of books which are smuggled in, or through the distant sound of a belated carriage rolling down the boulevards, are powerful allurements. As for Emma's reactions to the books she reads, the image of a female Quixote comes to mind. She too transmutes reality into fiction. Here, as in Cervantes' novel, literature itself becomes one of the strongest determinants.

Yet there is, in **Madame Bovary,** a necessity stronger even than the temperamental, social and intellectual pressures to which the protagonist is subjected. It is a necessity inherent in the inner logic and progression of Flaubert's own images. The very chapter on Emma's education . . . reveals a characteristic pattern. The primary images are those of confinement and immobility: the atmosphere of the convent is protective and soporific (''. . . elle s'assoupit doucement . . .''); the reading is done on the sly; the girls are assembled in the study, the chapel or the dormitory. Very soon, however, images of escape begin to dominate. These images are at first strictly visual. . . . Soon, however, the images become less precise, giving way to va-

*A caricature by Lemot of Flaubert dissecting Emma.*

porous dreams ("pale landscapes of dithyrambic lands"), and to an increasingly disheveled exoticism: sultans with long pipes, Djiaours, Bayadères, Greek caps and Turkish sabres. The suggested confusion of these images rapidly degenerates into indifferentiation and ultimately even chaos, as palm trees and pine trees, Tartar minarets and Roman ruins, crouching camels and swimming swans are brought into senseless juxtaposition. Escape seems inevitably to lead to a manner of disintegration, even to images of death (perhaps even a suggested death-wish), as the swans are transformed into dying swans, singing to the accompaniment of funereal harps, and Emma, infinitely bored by it all, but unwilling to admit it to herself, continuing her dreams by habit or by vanity, finally withdraws into herself, "appeased."

The chapter on Emma's education is revealing, not merely because it proposes a parable of the entire novel, but because the progression of images corresponds to a pattern repeated throughout the book: from ennui to expectation, to escape, to confusion, back to ennui and to a yearning for nothingness. But whereas the symbolic detail is often, with Flaubert, part of a deliberate technique, this logic of imagery associations, these recurrent patterns depend on the spontaneous life of images, on their mutual attractions and irremediable conflicts, on a causality which operates at an unconscious, *poetic* level. The novel as a whole is thus constructed around recurrent clusters of images, all of which are part of definable, yet interrelated cycles. These cycles, or cyclic themes, do parallel on a massive canvas the inevitable movement, from boredom to self-destruction, which characterizes *Madame Bovary* in its overall conception as well as in its detailed execution.

First the patterns of ennui. This begins early in the novel. The eternal sameness of experience is already suggested by the weekly letters to his mother which the boy Charles writes regularly every Thursday evening with the same red ink, and which he seals with the same three wafers. Charles' working habits are moreover compared to those of a mill-horse. The primary means for suggesting an anesthetizing routine are temporal. Emma gets into the habit of taking strolls in order to avoid the "eternal" garden. The days resemble each other (". . . the same series of days began all over"); the future seems like an endlessly dark corridor. And repeatedly, the mournful church bell punctuates the return of the monotonous hours and days with its characterless lament. The repeated use of the imperfect tense, with its suggestions of habitual action, further stresses the temporal reality of Flaubertian boredom. (pp. 52-6)

The underlying sense of hopelessness and monotony is also conveyed by means of liquid images. There is a great deal of oozing, dripping and melting in Flaubert's fictional world. During Charles' early courtship of Emma, the snow is melting, the bark of the trees is oozing, one can hear drops of water falling one by one. Later, when the bitterness of her married existence seems to be served up to her nauseatingly during their daily meals, Emma is aware that the walls are "sweating." These liquid images, suggesting erosion and deterioration, are of course bound up with a sense of the emptiness of Time. A steady *écoulement,* or flow, corresponds to feelings of hopeless waste and vacuity. These liquid images of an annihilating temporality will be even more pervasive in *L'Éducation sentimentale.* But *Madame Bovary* also brings out this immense sadness of time's undoing. . . . The steady flow becomes the very symbol of a chronic despair. . . . Finally, the monotony of existence is conveyed through a series of spatial images. The Norman

landscape near Yonville is "flat," the meadow "stretches," the plain broadens out and extends to the very horizon—"à perte de vue." This colorless landscape is in harmony with the lazy borough sprawling along the river banks. Emma, throughout the novel, scans the horizon. But nothing appears which would relieve the deathlike evenness.

This spatial imagery clearly constitutes the bridge between the theme of ennui and the theme of escape. Once again, the series of images can be traced back to the early pages of the novel which deal exclusively with Charles. Repeatedly, he opens his window, either to stare at the muddy little river which in his mind becomes a wretched "little Venice" and to dream of a yearned-for elsewhere, or to indulge in love reveries as he leans in the direction of the Bertaux farm. The window becomes indeed in *Madame Bovary* the symbol of all expectation: it is an opening onto space through which the confined heroine can dream of escape. But it is also—for windows can be closed and exist only where space is, as it were, restricted—a symbol of frustration, enclosure and asphyxia. Flaubert himself, aware that Emma is often leaning out the window, explains that "the window in the provinces replaces the theater and the promenade." . . . More, however, is involved than a simple taste for spectacle. Jean Rousset, in a brilliant essay, quite rightly suggests that the open window unleashes "mystical velleities" [see excerpt above, 1962]. In fact, the symbolic uses of the window reveal not only a permanent dialectic of constriction and spatiality, but an implicit range of emotions embracing the major themes of the novel.

Emma's characteristic pose is at, or near, a window. . . . The image, from the very outset, suggests some manner of imprisonment as well as a longing for a liberation. After her marriage, her daily routine brings her to the window every morning. When she goes through one of her nervous crises, she locks herself up in her room, but then, "stifling," throws open the windows. Exasperated by a sense of shame and contempt for her husband, she again resorts to the typical gesture: "She went to open the window . . . and breathed in the fresh air to calm herself." . . . The sense of oppression and immurement is further stressed after Rodolphe abandons her: the shutter of the window overlooking the garden remains permanently closed. But the imprisonment in her own boundless desire is intolerable. Emma's sexual frenzy, which reaches climactic proportions during her affair with Léon, is probably the most physical manifestation of her need to "liberate" herself. The window, as symbol, offers an image of this release. (pp. 56-8)

Chronic expectation turns to chronic futility, as Emma's élans toward the elsewhere disintegrate in the grayness of undifferentiated space. Velleities of movement and flight only carry her back to a more intolerable confinement within her petty existence and her unfulfilled self. But expectation there is. Just as the chatelaines in her beloved Gothic romances wait for the dashing cavalier on his black horse, so Emma lives in perpetual anticipation. "At the bottom of her heart . . . she was waiting for something to happen." . . . Flaubert insists, somewhat heavily at times, on this compulsive expectance of the conclusive event. (p. 59)

Images of movement reinforce the theme of escapism. Emma enjoys taking lonely walks with her greyhound and watching the leaps and dashes of the graceful animal. Restlessness and taste for aimless motion point to the allurement of a mythical *elsewhere.* Once again, the theme is ironically broached early in the novel, in pages concerned with Charles. "He had an

*Charles courting Emma at her father's farm. Mary Evans Picture Library.*

aimless hope. . . .'' Images of space and motion—the two are frequently combined—serve, throughout the novel, to bring out the vagrant quality of Emma's thoughts. Departure, travel and access to privileged regions are recurring motifs. The "immense land of joys and passions" exists somewhere beyond her immediate surroundings: the more accessible things are, the more Emma's thoughts turn away from them. Happiness, by definition, can never be *here*. "Anywhere out of the World"— the title of Baudelaire's prose poem—could sum up Emma's chronic yearning for the exotic. . . . By a skillful, and certainly far from gratuitous touch, Flaubert concludes Emma's initiatory stay at the Vaubyessard residence with a visit to the hothouses, where the strangest plants, rising in pyramids under hanging vases, evoke a climate of pure sensuality. The exotic setting becomes the very symbol of a yearned-for bliss. The "coming joys" are compared to tropical shores so distant that they cannot be seen, but from where soft winds carry back an intoxicating sweetness.

Travel and estrangement come to symbolize salvation from the immurement of ennui. Emma believes that change of abode alone is almost a guarantee of happiness. "She did not believe that things could be the same in different places. . . ." The unseen country is obviously also the richest in promises of felicity. Paris remains sublimely alluring precisely because—contrary to his original intentions—Flaubert does not grant Emma access to this promised land. Her first conversation with

Léon typically exploits the Romantic cliché of the "limitless" expanse of the ocean, which "elevates the soul" through suggestions of the ideal and of infinity. . . . The culmination of the travel imagery coincides with plans for Emma's elopement with Rodolphe . . . and with her visions of life in gondolas or under palm trees, to the accompaniment of guitars, in far-off countries with splendent domes and women dressed in red bodices. The very concept of emancipation is bound up with the notion of voyage. During her pregnancy Emma hopes to have a son, because a man is free: "he can travel over passions and over countries, cross obstacles, taste of the most far-away pleasures." And part of Rodolphe's prestige when she meets him is that he appears to her like a "traveler who has voyaged over strange lands." . . . Emma's tragedy is that she cannot escape her own immanence. "Everything, including herself, was unbearable to her." . . . But just as her walks always lead back to the detested house, so Emma feels thrown back into herself, left stranded on her own shore. The lyrical thrust toward the inaccessible leads back to an anesthetizing confinement.

The cycles of ennui and spatial monotony, the images of escape (window perspectives, motion, insatiable desire for the elsewhere), are thus brought into contrapuntal tension with an underlying metaphoric structure suggesting limits, restriction, contraction and immobility. The basic tragic paradox of *Madame Bovary* is unwittingly summed up during Emma's first conversation with Léon. They discuss the pleasures of reading: "One thinks of nothing . . . the hours slip by. One *moves motionless* through countries one imagines one sees. . . ." As for the sense of limitation, the very site of Yonville (the diminutive conglomeration in the midst of a characterless, undifferentiated landscape) suggests a circumscribed and hopelessly hedged-in existence. As soon as one enters the small market town, "the courtyards grow narrower, the houses closer together, and the fences disappear. . . ." The entire first chapter of Part II, which introduces the reader to Yonville, plays on this contrast between expanse and delimitation. The very life of Yonville suggests constriction. . . . The entire tragic tension of the novel seems to be summed up in this experience of spiritual claustrophobia. The sitting-room where Emma, in her armchair, spends hours near the window, is distinguished by its particularly "low ceiling." The predominant impression is one of entrapment or encirclement. (pp. 59-62)

This imagery of restriction and contraction is intimately related to the disintegrating experiences of sameness, interfusion and confusion of feelings, indiscrimination, abdication of will and lethal torpor. . . . The seduction scene at the *comices agricoles*—a chapter of which Flaubert was particularly proud— is almost a continuous exercise in telescoping of levels of reality. Everything tends to merge and become alike. Even the villagers and the peasants present a comical and distressing uniformity. "Tous ces gens-là se ressemblaient."

Confusion, whether due to oppressive monotony, moral drowsiness or spiritual anesthesia, is one of the leitmotifs in *Madame Bovary*. Once more, the opening pages are revealing. When Charles reads the list of course offerings at the medical school, he experiences a spell of "dizziness." Riding toward the Bertaux farm, he falls into a characteristic doze wherein his most recent sensations "blend" with old memories: the warm odor of poultices "mingled" in his brain with the fresh smell of dew. *Confondre, se mêler* are among Flaubert's favorite words. . . . Emma's ability to distinguish between levels of values dwindles as the novel progresses. "She confused in her desire the sensualities of luxury with the delights of the heart.''. . . Later, this commingling of sensations becomes increasingly habitual, until no clear notions at all can be distinguished.

Emma's lust, her longing for money and her sentimental aspirations all become ''confused'' in one single, vague and oppressive sense of suffering. While listening to Rodolphe's seductive speeches, she conjures up other images: the viscount with whom she waltzed at Vaubyessard, his delicately scented hair, Léon who is now far away. The characteristic faintness (''mollesse'') which comes over her induces an overlapping and a blurring of sensations which is not unlike a cinematographic fade-out. . . . But this psychological strabismus is not here a technique whereby the author creates suspense or modestly veils the action. It corresponds to an abdication of choice and will, and points to the very principle of disintegration. . . . The latent yearning for annihilation or nothingness is probably the most fundamental tragic impulse of Flaubertian protagonists. Not only does Emma dream of dissolving herself in an all-absorbing whole, but approaching death is described as a ''confusion de crépuscule.'' Ultimately, not only all desire but all pain is absorbed in an all-embracing and all-negating woe. Thus Charles' retrospective jealousy, when he discovers Emma's infidelities, becomes ''lost in the immensity of his grief.'' The frustration of all desire and of all hope is so great that nothing short of total sorrow and total surrender to nonbeing can bring relief.

A state of numbness or even dormancy is one of the chronic symptoms of *bovarysme. Mollesse, assoupissement* and *torpeur* are other favorite words of Flaubert. They refer most generally to a vague sensuous well-being, to a condition of nonresistance and even surrender. When Emma hears Rodolphe's flattering, if not original love declaration (he compares her to an angel), her pride ''like one who relaxes in a bath, expanded softly'' (''mollement''). The almost untranslatable *mollement* appears again, a few pages later, when Rodolphe puts his arm around Emma's waist and she tries ''feebly'' to disengage herself. Numbness and drowsiness occur almost regularly in a sexual context. During the nocturnal trysts in the garden, Emma, her eyes half closed, feels her emotion rise with the softness (''mollesse'') of the perfume of the syringas. Her physical submissiveness to Rodolphe is termed ''a beatitude that benumbed her'' (''une béatitude qui l'engourdissait'' . . .). And when she meets Léon again at the opera in Rouen, she is assailed by the ''torpor'' of her memories.

The pathological nature of such torpid states is strongly suggested. Early in the novel, her torpor follows moments of ''feverish'' chatter, and corresponds to periods when Emma suffers from heart palpitations. But the real pathology is of the spirit, not of the body. Just as the somnolence of the listeners at the agricultural show reflects the dullness of the speeches and the intellectual indolence of the townspeople, so Charles' congenital yawning symbolizes his inadequacy. When the coach arrives in Yonville, Charles is still asleep. During the evening at the Homais, he regularly falls asleep after playing dominoes. Such drowsiness seems contagious. Only Emma's takes on a more symbolic aspect. She suffers from an ''assoupissement de sa conscience'' . . .: her very conscience is made numb. And in this numbness there is not only the principle of despair, but of death. All desire, like Baudelaire's *ennui*, leads to an omnivorous yawn. (pp. 62-5)

This relentless deterioration of everything is very different from the Balzacian wear and tear which is most often the price man pays for his tragic energy. Flaubert's heroes not only have a

vocation for failure, but they fail independently of any investment of fervor. Charles' early fiasco at his examination foreshadows his entire career. Paradoxically, it could be said that unsuccess precedes the act of living. In Flaubert's world, life is not fought out and lost, but *spent*. It is only appropriate that Emma should be congenitally improvident. For she is a squanderer not only of money. In a strained but revealing simile, Flaubert compares her loss of illusions to a steady act of ''spending.'' ''Elle en avait dépensé à toutes les aventures de son âme. . . .'' But it is, in reality, her own self that she is dissipating, as though urged on by the desire to fade or melt away. Flaubert elsewhere speaks of death as a ''continuous swooning away'' (an ''évanouissement continu''). The death-wish is a permanent reality in the fictional world of Flaubert; it most often reveals itself through an almost mystical desire to vanish or be absorbed by a larger whole. On her way to Father Bournisien, Emma dreams of the ''disappearance'' of her entire existence. The longing for nothingness is often linked to religious or pseudo-religious images. In Emma's mind, it is most often associated with memories of the convent, with a desire to return to it, as one might to a maternal womb. The desire to stop living (''She would have liked not to be alive, or to be always asleep'' . . .) corresponds to a quasi-metaphysical fatigue, to the immedicable pain of having been betrayed by life itself. In the face of universal abandon, the Flaubertian heroine is driven to dissipation. She becomes the willing accomplice of all the forces of disbandment.

The convoluted fabric of images, often circuitous and apparently bound by an uncontrolled necessity, amply suggests that Flaubert is not indulging in a mere virtuoso exercise. The imagery, in *Madame Bovary*, appears almost self-generated: a determinism seems to preside over its pattern, and this pattern itself corresponds to the forms of the author's imagination, thus testifying to the all-importance of themes in his work.

This is not to deny the willed construction of the novel. . . . Flaubert's hesitations and ultimate decisions all bespeak an unrelenting concern for structure. The very strategy of Emma's adultery is revealing. In one of the earlier scenarios, Léon becomes her lover before Rodolphe. But very soon, Flaubert introduces a significant change: the love for Léon is to remain repressed. The reason for this repression is clear, and Flaubert himself has commented on it: Emma's ''fall'' with Rodolphe will become that much more *necessary*. Her successful defense against Léon fills her with the sadness of her own ''sacrifice,'' increases her resentment of her husband, and makes her an eager victim of any aggressive seducer.

Clearly, also, Flaubert took immense pains preparing and articulating his episodes. . . . Opening sentences often impose the very rhythm of Time. ''Ils recommencèrent à s'aimer''— the beginning of chapter 12 of Part II is a good example of the Flaubertian change of gears by means of which the unique act slips into a dreary continuum, and hope is transmuted into an unheroic despair. As for the almost unbearable acceleration toward the end of the novel, notably in chapter 7 of Part III, when, after the delirium of the senses, Emma frantically attempts to ward off financial disaster, it is brilliantly executed.

Yet the very care with which Flaubert proceeded resulted in a certain laboriousness: the novel, at times, seems a bit too ''constructed,'' the symbols appear perhaps just a trifle too obvious. With even a mild dose of ill will, one could easily magnify some characteristics of Flaubert's technique into significant defects. The exposition is indeed very slow, and occupies a good third of the novel. Not until chapter 9 of Part II does the dramatic action begin. (pp. 66-8)

[But] if the construction of the novel is indeed laborious and could be compared, as Flaubert himself might well have done, to the patient stacking of solid masses one on top of the other, this blocklike composition is also responsible for the admirable "scenes" which constitute the very anatomy of *Madame Bovary*. These scenes are themselves at times mere expository devices, such as, for instance, the beginning of Part II—the scene at Mme Lefrancois' inn—whose function it is to present a number of new characters (Binet, Léon, Homais, Bournisien, Hivert, Lheureux) and to introduce the reader to the atmosphere of Yonville. But most often the "scene" in Flaubert corresponds to a particular vision. The ambulant love scene in the cab . . . , where all the reader is granted is the view of the cab with its blinds drawn, now trotting quietly and then galloping furiously, driven by a puzzled and exasperated coachman, conveys—in its disordered movement as well as in its picturesque details—the very nature of Emma's erotic experience. The changes of speed, the dizzying crescendi, the torn letter scattered to the wind by an ungloved hand and falling on a field of red clover (an obvious reminder of the burning of her wedding bouquet), acquire a symbolic value. Indeed, all of Emma's life is a race ending in death (the cab is "shut more closely than a tomb"), and the lumbering machine into which Emma agrees to step because "it is done in Paris" is a grotesque but also malefic vehicle.

To be sure, the episode comes very close to being a tour de force. A relish for bravura similarly appears at the very conception of the famous *comices* chapter. The idea of having Rodolphe court Emma while prize cattle low and official speeches are declaimed, appealed to Flaubert because he was fond, in advance, of the "symphonic" effect he might achieve. As craftsman, he valued the challenge to create an animated triptych. The scene, ultimately, is far more than a clever display of technique: the comical juxtaposition and contrasts, the insistence on animality, as well as the general flow of meaningless words, not only bring out the vulgarity and stupidity of Emma's world, but constitute a parody, or rather a mockery of love. The central meaning of the novel is somehow conveyed in this chapter of futility and degradation.

But to enjoy Flaubert's art at its purest, that is where least tainted by the display of technical prowess, one should turn to another famous scene, though perhaps less spectacular than the *comices* chapter: Emma's visit to Father Bournisien. . . . Flaubert explained his intentions in a letter to Louise Colet: Emma, almost undergoing a religious crisis, seeks help from the inept and utterly pedestrian priest who, unable to intuit her anguish and aware only of physical suffering, remains totally deaf to her secret hope, and thus helps close the door to spiritual salvation. In the novel, however, analysis and commentary are totally absent. Language here carries the entire burden, and primarily the dialogue, which is the more effective for being used so sparingly in Flaubert's work. Emma's frustrating conversation with Bournisien rests almost entirely on a basic misunderstanding: she speaks of moral suffering, seeks solace and needs "no earthly remedy"; his mind turns exclusively to the discomforts of the flesh: the summer heat and the distress of indigestion. The very interruption of her sentences by Bournisien's irrelevant remarks stresses the fundamental lack of communication between them.

On one level, the scene is painfully comic. Flaubert almost indulges in caricature. The grease and tobacco stains on Bournisien's cossack, his noisy breathing, the shower of cuffs he distributes among his pupils, his thick laughter and cheap puns, all stress his coarseness and peasant mentality. He answers Emma's complaint that she is "unwell," with the admirable *mot de comédie:* "Well, and so am I." But there is a deeper irony in this passage. For the priest, reminding Emma that her husband is the "doctor of the body" (while he, Bournisien, is the "doctor of the soul"), is astonished that Charles Bovary did not prescribe something for her. After advising her to take some tea (always good for the digestion), he ends the conversation with a "Good health to you, madame" which is doubly ironic since he not only sends her back empty to an unbearable life, but specifically to a cohabitation with an incompetent husband-doctor. The very drama of incommunicability is summed up by this exchange:

> "But you were asking me something. What was
> it? I really can't remember."
> "I? Nothing . . . ! nothing . . . !"

A scene such as this involves the very nature of Flaubertian comedy. The intimacy between laughter, cruelty and tragic absurdity is indeed characteristic of Flaubert. Comedy, in *Madame Bovary*, appears on one level as a Molièresque farce. The ludicrous accoutrements (Charles' cap, Homais' costumes) are excellent illustrations of Bergson's theory of laughter: "le mécanique plaqué sur le vivant." Rigidity is here in conflict with life itself. Binet, the captain of the corps of firemen, wears a collar so high and stiff, a tunic so tightly buttoned, that his entire body, above his legs, seems paralyzed. The visor of his helmet, covering his face down to his nose, totally blinds him. This rigidity of attire and of body is paralleled by an equal stubbornness of mind which condemns the Flaubertian comic figures to an imprisonment within their ridicules, just as the Flaubertian "hero" becomes the quixotic victim of a perilous illusion. *Idées fixes,* misunderstandings, pedantry, boors and bores, the absurdities of medical practice and the humiliations of the flesh—all these are part of the tradition of comedy. What distinguishes Flaubert is the unusual stress laid on language itself, both as symptom and as an instrument of denunciation. This dual role of style is best exemplified in Flaubert's systematic exploitation of clichés. Homais' "opinions" (on weather, on hygiene, on women), his articles to the Rouen newspaper, are fundamentally as inane and as exasperating as Flaubert's lifelong entries into his *Dictionnaire des idées recues*, which, one suspects, he consulted repeatedly while writing *Madame Bovary*. The same almost perverse satisfaction occurs whenever he can weigh down a character under the load of his own unalterable ineptness.

Stylistic caricature and parody are among Flaubert's more obvious talents. But they correspond not merely to the author's desire to mock the mental foibles and the vulgarity of bourgeois society: too much has been made of Flaubert the *bourgeoisophobus!* This comedy of language reaches out to the very heart of the novel. When, for instance, Rodolphe writes his hypocritical, and fundamentally caddish farewell letter to Emma, and Flaubert studs this masterful missive with the most hackneyed Romantic thoughts and mannerisms, the author's attitude is critical, to be sure: Rodolphe is fully conscious of his own lies. But the irony of the passage reaches beyond the victim of seduction and the egoism of the seducer. It involves indirectly the very meaning of the novel: the tragicomedy of lies, ersatz and illusion. And it is characteristic of Flaubert that comedy is for him simultaneously an instrument of "meaning," an expression of his indignation and a technique of oblique intervention.

This raises the question of Flaubert's passionate "presence" in his own novel. The myth of the author's impassibility indeed crumbles as soon as the reader attunes his mind to the peculiar vehemence of Flaubert—a vehemence which most often, at least in his fictional work, takes the form of a contained wrath. A permanent, and to some extent artificially cultivated ire seems to be one of Flaubert's most fecund sources of inspiration. To the brothers Goncourt he once explained: "Indignation alone keeps me going. . . . When I will no longer be indignant, I will fall down flat." This propensity for anger reveals itself in the peculiar Flaubertian irony *at the expense* of his characters. We are here far from the tender, protective and lyrical smile of a Stendhal. Flaubert proceeds with an apparent absence of charity. Thus he has Charles almost push Emma into the arms of Rodolphe. This type of devastating irony is the common note. When Emma is about to ride off with Rodolphe, Homais' exhortation is like an invitation for trouble: "An accident happens so easily! Be careful! Your horses perhaps are impetuous!" (pp. 69-73)

This kind of irony is tragic by nature. It makes of the reader and accomplice of "destiny." Charles is the privileged victim of this cruel game. When Rodolphe invites Emma to go horseback riding with him, it is Charles who encourages her not to worry about public opinion: "Health before everything!" It is again he who thanks her for making a trip to Rouen to consult Léon on a business matter: "How good you are!". . . The entire episode of the club-foot operation is conceived and executed in order to humiliate Charles. One almost has the impression that Flaubert enjoyed destroying Charles professionally. (p. 73)

The author's presence is felt not only in such ironies of detail. Irony in the structure of the novel also points to the author's chronic "intrusion," and constitutes, so to speak, a built-in commentary. The most flagrant examples—though perhaps they show Flaubert at his most arbitrary—are the episodes with the Blind Man. The relationship between irony, the tragic spirit, and even a certain allegorical mood is nowhere more tightly drawn than in these passages. The Blind Man himself is a semigrotesque and semilugubrious figure, whose creation corresponds to Flaubert's taste for the pathological, and possibly also to memories of his trip to the Near East. A beggar afflicted with a horrible skin disease and with two huge, oozing empty eye-sockets, he appears at critical moments during the latter stages of Emma's life, like an embodiment of corruption and meaningless death. The first time Emma sees him is after one of the hotel-room meetings with Léon, and the ghastly contrasts between the innocent love ditty he sings and the leprous horror of his face is like a macabre emblem of all physical love. And it is significant that this first encounter takes place in the very chapter. . . which insists on Emma's moral corruption: her gluttony, her taste for lies, her walks through the red-light district, the voluptuousness and sadness of the hotel room with its faded elegance that reeks of decomposition.

The second meeting with the Blind Man. . . provides no less of a commentary on the action and moral situation. Emma is returning from a rendezvous with Léon during which she tried, with lascivious provocation, to convince her lover to steal money for her. This second scene with the Blind Man conveys an even more pungent and more terrifying symbolism. The ideas of Law and Society are invoked by Homais, who would like to see such intrusive beggars locked up. The pariah-like existence of the Blind Man is of course related to Emma's subjective feeling—particularly strong in this chapter—of being herself an outcast. Similarly, Homais' allusions to crime and penology are meant to resound in Emma's mind. But it is the Blind Man's revolting pantomine which most profoundly affects Emma: his head thrown back, his tongue sticking out, his hands rubbing his belly, his guttural cry are a repellent burlesque of all appetite and gratification, and more specifically a hideous mockery of the sex act. The scene ends with Emma's flinging to the beggar her last five-franc piece, as though money had exorcising virtues—an additional irony given the context of the novel.

The third appearance of the Blind Man—even more melodramatic than the others—coincides with the exact moment of Emma's death. The ditty he sings this time combines erotic and macabre motifs. The tragic elements of the scene are almost theatrical in a classical sense: the blind beggar is like an ancient chorus, present as an observer and as a mourner. His very blindness seems to endow him with supernatural vision, at the same time that it symbolizes a hopeless impasse in the face of the Absolute. His appearance, which interrupts the priest's prayers ("the muffled murmur of the Latin syllables"), did provoke the ire of the Imperial prosecutor. But it could be easily argued—as did Flaubert's lawyer, Maître Sénard—that far from representing a profanatory intrusion, the Blind Man is the living "reminder of her fault, remorse in all its horror and poignancy." Indeed, the arrival of the beggar not only coincides with her death, but seems to provoke it. The passage nonetheless remains characteristically ambiguous. The sinister laughter of Emma—a laughter which is described as "atrocious," "frenetic" and "desperate"—certainly does not bespeak the peace of a soul about to be released from human bondage. The laughter sounds much rather like a satanic expression of scorn in the face of life's ultimate absurdity, death.

The exact nature of the author's perspective remains one of the most puzzling questions in ***Madame Bovary***. Traditional interpretations insist either on frigid impassibility (the myth of objectivity) or on mordant satire (the double myth of the bourgeois-hater and the anti-Romantic). The truth is both more elusive and more interesting. For there is ambiguity not only in Flaubert's implicit commentary, but in the very method by which this commentary is textured into the fiction. Flaubert's almost exclusive instrument of intervention is style itself; it is this precisely which disconcerts the reader used to more formal, and more obvious techniques of intrusion. But this reliance on the resources of syntax enables Flaubert to be both "in" and "out" at the same time. This double perspective is nowhere better illustrated than in the countless examples of *style indirect libre*, of which Flaubert is a pioneer in French letters as well as the masterful practitioner, and which he utilizes not only as an elliptic abstract of conversation and as a subtle way of underlining clichés, but as an equivalent for interior monologue. Yet it is only an equivalent, for it allows him to formulate clearly that which, in the character's mind, remains unformulated or only half-formulated, and thus establishes a gap between what the characters feel and what the author understands. It is this somewhat elastic gap which represents the area of the author's personal commitment.

Some examples may clarify these remarks. First a rather simple illustration. When Emma lies naked in the sumptuous hotel-room bed, and Flaubert writes that "nothing in the world was so lovely as her brown head and white skin standing out against this purple color, when, with a movement of modesty, she crossed her bare arms, hiding her face in her hands". . . , this lovely pose is obviously appreciated both by Léon and by the author. But when Flaubert's style penetrates into the very consciousness of the protagonist, the focus becomes less clear: "But she—her life was cold as a garret whose dormer-window looks northward, and ennui, the silent spider, was weaving its web in the dark, in every corner of her heart.''. . . Who is thinking this? Is it a series of clichés to be attributed to the character, or is it the character's vague sensation that the author translates and elaborates into images? The same fundamental ambiguity presides over many comparisons and metaphors. "The future was a dark corridor, with its door at the end shut tightly.''. . . We are no doubt "inside" the character: it is Emma's sense of frustration and gloom that the metaphor conveys. But the metaphor also carries an "objective" value: it corresponds to the theme of claustration that Flaubert develops throughout the novel. This duplicity of the *style indirect libre* is perhaps most clearly illustrated in a passage where Emma dreams of an "impossible" love, while aware of the very principle of disintegration in her life:

> No matter! She was not happy—she had never been. Whence came this insufficiency in life— this instantaneous turning to decay of every- thing on which she leant?. . . But if there were somewhere a being strong and beautiful, a gen- erous nature, full at once of exultation and re- finement, a poet's heart in the form of an angel, a lyre with sounding chords ringing out elegiac epithalamia to heaven, why, perchance, should she not find him? Ah! how impossible! Noth- ing, anyhow, was worth the trouble of seeking it! Everything was a lie! Every smile hid a yawn of boredom, every joy a curse, all pleasure surfeit, and the sweetest kisses left upon your lips nothing but the unattainable desire for a greater delight. . . .

Clearly the passage fuses the character's interior monologue with the author's point of view. But even that point of view is not clear: Flaubert's pity blends with his caricature of Ro- mantic dreams, and nothing would be more difficult than to draw a line separating the two. Finally, even the caricature of the Romantic clichés remains ambiguous. On the one hand, the cliché—both as an intellectual and a stylistic *fausse mon- naie*— is the permanent object of Flaubert's scorn; but clichés are also, no matter how ludicrous and objectionable, the sur- prising and touching conveyors of the characters' "inno- cence." This is what neither the literal-minded reader nor a callous seducer such as Rodolphe is likely to understand. In one of the most curious passages of the novel, commenting on Rodolphe's insensibility to Emma's genuine emotion (he has heard the same expressions of love so often!), Flaubert explains that it is a grave mistake not to seek candor behind worn-out language, "as though the fullness of the soul did not at times overflow in the emptiest metaphors.''. . . And Flaubert, in what may appear like an *apologia pro domo*, suggests that nobody can ever give the exact measure of his needs and of his sorrows, that human speech is "like a cracked tin kettle on which we strike tunes fit to make bears dance, when we long to move the stars." This feeling that human speech cannot possibly cope with our dreams and our grief goes a long way toward explaining why so often, in the work of Flaubert, the reader has the disconcerting impression that the language of banality is caricatured and at the same time transmuted into poetry.

We are perhaps touching here on the very secret of Flaubert's lyrical achievement within a realistic framework. But the framework, or setting, should not blind us to the fact that Flaubert's temperament and practice, despite all the noise made around the substantive "realism," has little in common with the products of a Champfleury, a Duranty, or even a Daumier. "One need only read *Madame Bovary* with intelligence," writes Guy de Manupassant, "to understand that nothing is further removed from realism." And Maupassant goes on to explain that Flaubert's sentences soar above the subject they express, that in order to convey the stupidities of Homais or the silliness of Emma, his language assumes majesty and brilliance, "as though it were translating poetic motifs. . . ." One of the most striking features of Flaubert's art is indeed his ability to shift, without transition, from the trivial to the lyrical—or rather, to transmute the one into the other. This alchemy is not the result of chance: Flaubert was fully lucid about the dangers of a double "tone," and determined to bring about a poetic fusion. "The entire value of my book. . . will have been the ability to walk straight on a hair, suspended between the double abyss of lyricism and vulgarity (which I want to fuse in a narrative ananlysis)." (pp. 74-9)

A certain duplicity vis-à-vis his characters, a basic lack of solidarity with the world in which they move and suffer, and the insistence on the self-redeeming qualities of style, have made Flaubert vulnerable to the charge of having dehumanized the novel. The rift between the author's artistic, sophisticated vision and the insufficient, confused vison of the protagonist is probably responsible, as much if not more so than the Par- nassian aspects of Flaubert's prosody, for a certain rigid, in- animate quality. One misses, in Flaubert's work, those ap- proximations and hesitations, those imperceptible human tremors, thrusts and recoils which convey artistically the very drama of existence in the works of a Stendhal, a Dostoevsky or, in our own day, a Nathalie Sarraute. Yet it is precisely this rift, or rather the telescoping of two unrelated perspectives, which bestows upon the novel a unique beauty. A stereoscopic vision accounts in large part for the peculiar poetry and complexity of *Madame Bovary*.

This stereopsis is particularly evident in the beautiful landscape descriptions. (pp. 80-1)

During their "honeymoon" in Rouen, Léon and Emma take a boat to have dinner on one of the islands. . . . In approxi- mately ten splendid lines, Flaubert evokes the dockyard, the caulking mallets resounding against the hulls of the vessels, the smoke of tar, the large spots of oil undulating in the purple color of the sun—the very poetry of a river port. As they row toward the island, the city noises gradually grow distant. But the entire passage corresponds not merely to Flaubert's own attachment to the river—the permanent spectacle from his win- dows at Croisset; it also suggests Emma's transformation of the commercial port into a grandiose and lyrical image of de- parture, and her landing on the little island into an arrival in an exotic country of bliss. Similarly, the distant view of Rouen. . . involves double optics: the character's subjective, vague un- formulated feelings as the town appears "like an amphithe- ater," and the author's ability to see and to render the tableau. The personal poetry of the author and the reaction of Emma do not, of course, coincide. But the thematic validity of the passage depends almost exclusively on this very discrepancy which, once again, stresses the divorce between a reality per- ceived by the author (and by his accomplice, the reader) and the illusions of his heroine. The author describes the monot- onous landscape, "motionless as a picture," the anchored ships, the meanders of the river, the factory chimneys. But this ap- parently gratuitous description acquires its full significance once we become aware that Emma, looking at exactly the same panorama, experiences a giddiness, an inebriating sensation of space and infinite possiblity, as she is about to enter the rather dull provincial town which for her is an "enormous capital" and even a true Babylon!

This ability to be simultaneously "inside" and "outside" his characters leads to even greater complexities if one considers the poetry of adultery. Indeed Emma views adultery as a privileged condition. "I have a lover! a lover!" she keeps repeating to herself with a sense of wonder. It seeems to her like a long-awaited initiation to a mystery: "She was entering into a world of marvels. . . ." She feels surrounded by an azure infinity (the adjective "bleuâtre" occurs repeatedly in the novel) as she joins the "lyric legion" of the adulterous fictional heroines she so admires. . . . But Flaubert's attitude is by no means one of clinical detachment. It would be a misreading not only of the novel, but of Flaubert's entire work, to consider *Madame Bovary* a moral dununciation of conjugal infidelity! For the author also, adultery was a magic word. Ever since his adolescence the notion of adultery was endowed with a poetic and a tragic meaning. . . . To the entire generation reared on Romanticism—and Flaubert is as much a "victim" as Emma—adultery, because of its officially immoral and asocial status, acquired a symbolic value: it was a sign of unconventionality, rebellion and authenticity. But more important still—and here Flaubert the *troubadour* reworks one of the main themes of Western poetry—adultery holds out the promise of beauty precisely because it is the forbidden happiness, the inaccessible dream, that which always eludes: the Ideal. It is in this light that one should reread the juvenile works of Flaubert: *Mémoires d'un fou, Novembre,* the first *Éducation sentimentale*—where adultery is viewed as a "supreme poetry" made up of a mixture of voluptuousness and malediction.

The famous exclamation "Madame Bovary, c'est moi. . ." is thus not merely the sally of a writer irritated by seekers of sources and models. A curious symbiotic relationship exists between Flaubert and his heroine. The novelist, despite his practice of a double perspective, draws his fictional creature toward himself, and discovers himself in Emma even more than he projects himself into her. This complex relationship, in which the writer is to some extent playing hide-and-seek with himself, in which he punishes himself while granting himself a perspective that transcends the limits of his own temperament, makes it extremely difficult to assess the exact measure of personal involvement and to come to grips with the nature of this tragic experience. Emma's death exists, on the one hand, as a pathological fact, inevitable as the effects of the arsenic she swallows. But as she strains to kiss the crucifix, and as the priest gives the extreme unction to all those parts of her body that have lived, loved and suffered, an immense pity, an immense sadness and an immense fraternal understanding seem to emanate from Flaubert's text which will forever baffle those readers who view the novel principally as an anti-Romantic and antibourgeois satire. (pp. 81-3)

> *Victor Brombert, in his* The Novels of Flaubert: A Study of Themes and Techniques, *Princeton University Press, 1966, 301 p.*

### BENJAMIN F. BART   (essay date 1967)

[*Bart has written extensively on Flaubert. His full-length study, from which the following excerpt is taken, combines biographical detail, psychological investigation, and critical analysis. Here, Bart discusses the characterization of Emma.*]

*Rodolphe seducing Emma at the agricultural fair. Mary Evans Picture Library.*

Emma Bovary is a very ardent woman who knows passion briefly but who discovers that sensual pleasure alone (Flaubert's "terrestrial love") cannot produce a complete and durable love. She is Don Juan, but Don Juan transposed into the bitter, ironic key of the antiromantic. So long as, in romantic fashion, she seeks her own, individual satisfaction, she is necessarily doomed in Flaubert's eyes. Complete love he envisaged as aspiration, outgoing rather than self-centered. But he made Emma, from the very start, seek only a personal profit from any emotion, even from a landscape. This is what romanticism as she knew it in the convent invited her to desire. In facile, romantic novels the lover and his mistress are so much at one that all desires are held in common. Any romantic girl, Emma for instance, will then suppose that a lover is a man who wants what she wants, who exists for her. Nothing in Emma's character led her to doubt this, and nothing in her training could teach her otherwise. This, perhaps the most common and most serious of the romantic illusions, is at the core of *Madame Bovary* and helps to keep the book alive, for the succeeding years have not diminished the problem.

But Emma is more than that. Sensual, self-centered, vitiated by romanticism, she still carried to the grave some feeling of nobility and of grandeur. She has about her an aura of something extreme and rare. What she desires—furnishing her house, Léon, Rodolphe—may be petty, but her desire itself—to transcend Yonville—is neither tawdry nor wrong. The framework is akin to that of *Don Quixote*, in which Cervantes mocks the reality of what the knight wishes—the windmills, the real Dolores—but withholds his irony from the aspiration itself.

Flaubert once said that everything he was had its origin in *Don Quixote*, in which he admired the perpetual fusion of reality and illusion. But Don Quixote is deluded by his imagination; with Emma it is in large part her feelings which invalidate her perceptions. To some extent there is here a contrast between ideals and sentiments. Hence it is that Quixote's illusions have attained immortal life while Emma's feelings are forever damned. Quixote has misconceived reality but not his ideals; in some senses Emma misconceives both. Her surroundings are petty, it is true, but neither Léon nor Rodolphe is her equal; hence the objects of her desire are grotesque. Still, with the courage and violence of a Nero she drives toward her goals and gives of herself with generosity and grandeur, as Baudelaire points out. (pp. 317-18)

There is a further element to Emma, inherent in the determinism of Flaubert's philosophy. Since her specific fate is determined by her specific surroundings, it becomes possible to wonder whether other surroundings might not have let her have another fate. Contrast Don Quixote, who lives in a country with many windmills and no knights. Emma has no relatively harmless windmills against which to tilt and come out only bruised: she must confront Léon and Rodolphe and Lheureux. And Charles is so much of what she cannot stand: another husband might have alienated her less. Her child turns out to be a girl, when she longed for a boy. She could have had another priest than Bournisien. Homais's wife might have been a different sort of woman, capable of guiding her.

The issue the reader must decide is whether the determinism of *Madame Bovary*, the fated or inevitable quality the reader feels, depends in fact on a chance absence of anyone strong enough to break the chain of intellectual and moral conditioning. Flaubert was quite conscious of the problem and sought to transcend it by generalizing his portraits, by depicting not individuals but types. Bournisien is not a specific village parish priest, but the summation of all of them. Had he been more gifted, more sensitive, and hence more able to help Emma, his parish would no longer have been Yonville. Had he been less so, he would not have been in the priesthood. Similarly, Charles subsumes all possible husbands, Berthe all possible children. In each case the portrait is a type. For Flaubert the elements of Emma and Yonville were indispensable, but they had to be transcended. Emma is so real that she finally passes beyond immediate reality to become typical instead, and all specific examples of her type find themselves in her. And she is reacting to equally typical elements of provincial Normandy in her century. Finally, she reacts in a way which has thus far proved timeless.

The type Emma, as opposed to the person, is a strange one, relatively new in Flaubert's day and not to be confused with the woman whose problem is only that she has made the wrong marriage, a type common enough in all literature and especially frequent in Balzac and Mérimée in French fiction immediately preceding Flaubert. New in this novel, she has become steadily more common, once Flaubert gave her her classic formulation. She has sensuality, which is perennial. She has romantic illusions, which have shown no sign of disappearing. But she also has an uncontrollable desire for things, for material luxuries. And, with the lessening of her passionate involvement with Rodolphe and then with Léon, she finds less and less reason to control this latter passion. It is this, not her adulterous

love affairs, which brings about her downfall. She is, in fact, the victim of a moneylender, not of a lover or an irate husband. Her materialism, not her sensuality, causes her death, although she does not so understand it.

Flaubert here interweaves his threads to give to his tapestry that almost inextricable confusion which suggests reality. Emma is in fact hopelessly caught by Lheureux as she returns from her fruitless visit to Rodolphe: her household furniture is about to be sold, and her husband will be there either already knowing all about the financial catastrophe or sure to learn of it within hours. But this is not why Emma takes arsenic! Rather, hopelessly disillusioned by the discovery that neither of her lovers will save her, she measures the extent of their devotion more truly than she ever had before. In the face of this despairing calculation, she forgets the cause of her visit to Rodolphe; financial matters disappear from her ken, and she commits suicide because of a world in which it is no longer possible to love.

Emma defiantly faces her world of Yonville, proclaiming her values over against its conventions. So long as her fantasies are not fatal, she and not Yonville controls them. Even outside of herself she is so strong that, a giant in her surroundings, she can dare to pile Pelion and Ossa on Mount Olympus to scale her heaven, though it is the tragedy of the modern world that not Hercules but Lheureux brings this latter-day giant down. Before this, however, and for some little time it is she who is dominant, even illuminating those about her so that they take their color only in reference to her.

It is she and not Charles who makes him what he becomes. Charles is, as Emile Zola pointed out, an author's *tour de force*, a completely mediocre person whose presence is always there from start to finish. As Zola notes, in reality such men are gray or colorless, with nothing to bring them to one's attention; but Charles is constantly in our view. Partly Flaubert makes him important by observing him closely. But to a far greater extent it is Emma who is responsible for Charles, his role, his importance, and his fate. In and of himself he is inoffensive at worst, and frequently he is very good. His regret for the death of his first wife showed sweetness; his present of a horse for his wife may have been disastrously blind, but it was, again, a gentle and loving gesture. The absolute confidence which he reposed in Emma made possible her adulteries; but it, too, was a virtue. Unfortunately, placed in the specific context of the husband of Emma all these pale to unimportance beside her need for flaming romanticism. That what she wanted does not exist is not quite the problem here: what matters is that Charles is totally unable to help her, and hence his very virtues become terrible weaknesses facilitating or even bringing on the destruction of his wife and hence his own. His was a limited world, all of which he could compass; hers was limitless, but she wished to experience at least more of it than Yonville and marriage to Charles could allow. And so she had, in the end, to shatter the bounds which limited Charles' world and let him see that more lay beyond. That view would ultimately break him. (pp. 318-21)

Rodolphe, who initiates an inexperienced Emma into adultery, does eventually dominate her, except for a momentary lapse during which he, too, envisages running away. Despite Emma's illusions, he is in fact the cold and calculating seducer, not the flaming visionary that Emma was. And this she will ultimately be unable to control. Like Leporello, Don Juan's uncomprehending servant, Rodolphe imagines that all women are alike and all loves the same. Flaubert had intended that the vulgarity of Leporello should display the superiority of Juan and his search for the ideal. When Rodolphe almost casually abandons Emma, he is bringing out the same contrast. His nature dominates, but when it has and he leaves Emma, he returns to his own tawdry and uninteresting self: his existence as an exhilarating and exciting personality is in Emma's mind and imagination alone.

Léon, too, comes to rich and full existence for a time, but only by virtue of a special relationship to Emma. Afterwards he will be no more interesting than Charles or Rodolphe. At the precise moments that he and Emma meet, particularly on the second occasion, he can appear to be the person she imagines. Hence she will lend to him the coloring he needs to play the role. It is only when familiarity has rubbed off these borrowed hues that Léon will revert to mediocrity.

What then is Emma, this ardent woman who is doomed herself yet who is able to give to her husband and her lovers a life which they hardly possess but which is wholly theirs so long as they are hers? Flaubert was conscious that he had something particular and special to say in the book, an account of the profoundly sad aspect of modern man. (pp. 321-22)

Emma dies, damned by Yonville. At the touch of reality her dreams must necessarily shatter. To be sure, she is wrong to dream them, and Flaubert castigates her for them. But what of this society which has brought her up this way? What of Yonville, which damns her? We cannot infer that it is right because she is wrong. This is why Flaubert could not close his book on the death of Emma or even on the death of Charles. In Emma there was virile strength and the willingness to sacrifice for an ideal; in Charles there was simple goodness, too simple perhaps, but still goodness. Both had been destroyed. It remained for Flaubert to have his final say on the destroyers.

*Madame Bovary* is a tale of destruction. For when Emma and Charles have been destroyed by Yonville, that destruction means the triumph of people who had already destroyed everything fine and noble in themselves. *Madame Bovary* has in it the internal driving power of life itself: the reader can readily prolong it and imagine a sequel at will, which would display the triumphant success of Homais and of Lheureux. On the debris of Emma and of Charles, even of Léon, Homais and Lheureux will build their structures—and this, to Flaubert, was even worse. That a living Emma Bovary was weeping in twenty villages of France distressed him, but it enraged him that uncounted men such as Homais were building futures that would give them the Legion of Honor. And this was Flaubert's ultimate message. It may have been unfortunate that his hatred of the bourgeoisie outweighed his affectionate understanding of Emma, for understanding is more important than hatred. But the Emmas and those associated with them all over the world have been grateful for the understanding and have, in general, been content to laugh off Homais, who does not read books anyway and whose triumph in the last pages disappears, somehow, from the memory of readers, who are overwhelmed by the grandeur of Emma's death or the pathos of Charles. (pp. 322-23)

> *Benjamin F. Bart, in his* Flaubert, *Syracuse University Press, 1967, 791 p.*

## MURRAY SACHS   (essay date 1968)

[*Sachs examines the symbolic function of the blind beggar in* Madame Bovary. *In reviewing the writings of earlier critics who*

*characterize this figure either as a supernatural or a human figure, Sachs presents an opposing view: the blind beggar represents reality. After studying the three scenes in which he appears, Sachs describes the beggar's role as "the abrupt displacement of an illusion by the grim, ugly truth." For additional commentary on the role of the blind beggar in* Madame Bovary, *see excerpt above by Victor Brombert, 1966.*]

[The blind beggar is] unique in all of *Madame Bovary*, for it is the one symbol whose meaning is not immediately clear and understandable to all careful readers, and which has markedly divided the critics. Is this a deliberate vagueness on Flaubert's part, or perhaps a failure of his usually well-controlled art? Either view seems too uncharacteristic of the author to be plausible. Has the novel, then, been misread? Inasmuch as Flaubert's intentions, in creating the character of the blind beggar, emerge quite unmistakably from a careful scrutiny of the scenarios, the early drafts, and the novel itself, it is the contention of this essay that the novel has, on this point, been generally misread, and that because of that misreading the role of the blind beggar has, over the years, failed to be fully appreciated for what it adds to the structure and meaning of the novel as a whole.

The principal source of this persistent misreading is probably to be found in the fact that the death scene is undeniably the most important and memorable of the blind beggar's appearances in the novel and has pre-empted attention even though it is not the scene for which he was originally created nor the one in which the novelist's intended meaning is made most manifest. It has been an understandable tendency of critics and scholars to focus mainly on the death scene and to take, as the prime critical task, the problem of explaining the meaning of the symbol as it operates in that one scene alone. This tendency has the unfortunate consequence that other scenes in which the beggar appears are neglected, and that critical interpretations are thus constructed without due regard for the author's intentions. It is a fact that the text of the death scene contains not one word or phrase which hints at what the blind beggar is intended to symbolize. Diverse interpretations might seem therefore quite legitimate. But this spare writing in the death scene is neither deliberate nor accidental vagueness on Flaubert's part. It comes quite simply from the fact that he made his intentions quite clear regarding this symbolism in two earlier scenes and nothing additional should have been required to give the death scene its full force. While some exercise of the reader's subjective imagination is invited by the dramatic circumstances of the death scene, in interpreting the symbolic meaning of the blind beggar, no interpretation would be justified which is not a close and logical extension of the core meaning which Flaubert implanted in his symbol when he first created him. It is that core meaning which has been so neglected by the critics, and which can be clearly grasped only if one returns to an attentive reading of the scene for which the beggar was originally created.

The scene in question occurs in Chapter V of Part Three, wherein Flaubert is intent on giving the reader a general sense of the quality of Emma's experiences on those regular Thursday visits to Rouen to see her lover, Léon. The chapter begins, it will be recalled, with an account of Emma's morning preparations and the coach trip itself, culminating in the celebrated description of the first glimpse of the city, appearing in Emma's eyes as a glittering Babylon of pleasures. Here, as the journey ends, Emma's anticipations are at their highest.... After a day which inevitably falls short of these expectations, the blind beggar is pointedly introduced. He is the ugly and disturbing apparition that greets Emma as she begins her homeward journey in the coach. The contrast is deliberate: The Babylon of pleasures and the one hundred and twenty thousand souls palpitating with passion which fill her imagination in the morning have by late afternoon given way to a solitary, mutilated beggar, whose wailing song intensely distresses Emma. . . . The journey home at night is a sad, chilling counterpart to the exciting journey to Rouen she had made in the morning. The structure of the scene makes amply clear what the blind beggar's basic function is meant to be: he stands quite simply for reality. In limited, specific terms he represents the ugly truth of life in Rouen, after Emma's romantic illusions about it have been stripped away. By extension, he can symbolize the hard reality of life anywhere, the pitiable residue that remains after experience has deflated the dreams by which those with Emma's imaginative needs tend to embroider life. With his first irruption into Emma's line of vision, the blind beggar acts as a catalyst who precipitates the collapse of the last vestiges of her illusions and plunges her into a melancholy recognition of reality. But the beggar remains in her line of vision for an achingly long interval in this scene. Moreover, the imperfect tenses used throughout the scene convey the feeling of a scene repeated every Thursday over a considerable period of time. The beggar becomes, therefore, by his persistent presence, the eloquent, inescapable symbol of that reality in all its raw and brutal truth. And when he takes on this dimension, the blind beggar becomes a fully integrated symbol in the overall pattern of the novel, just as the scene itself, with its motif of the journey and return, continues the novel's basic movement and underlying theme: the determined flight from reality, followed by the inevitable descent back to the painful truth.

While the beggar's role in the death scene may well inspire such notions as the devil, damnation, degradation, or death in the reader's mind, no such extension of his core symbolic meaning seems needed for this scene in Chapter V which was the occasion for his original creation by Flaubert. His role is clear enough as the means by which Emma is forced to confront reality after one of her flights into illusion. . . . The earliest scenarios show no trace of any figure like the beggar, either in the death scene or in the proposed account of the Thursdays in Rouen. One does find already, in these initial outlines, the notion of contrasting the joy of the morning journey with the melancholy of the evening trip home, and, for the death scene, a reminder to include exact medical details for vividness. . . . Subsequently, when filling out the scene of the return journey with details, Flaubert made an interlinear addition as though it were a sudden inspiration: "mendiant dans la côte du Bois-guillaume.". . . It constitutes the first mention of the beggar in Flaubert's working papers. There is no comparable mention when the death scene is evoked in the course of this and other scenarios composed about the same time. The purpose the beggar is to serve in this first incarnation seems unmistakable: he is to be used as a visible external cause for Emma's plunge into melancholy at the end of the day. For as a conscientious artist who knows he must show rather than tell what is happening to Emma in this scene, Flaubert seeks ways to communicate the onset of this mood to the reader. Pondering this problem, he hits on the device of a beggar, whose appearance at the side of the road can plausibly occasion Emma's sudden melancholy. (pp. 73-5)

When he began to compose the death scene, Flaubert must have recognized that he found himself once more confronted by the same problem: how to plunge Emma back to the chill of reality. The situation is this: having swallowed poison, Emma

is dying, attended by Bournisien who administers the last sacraments. True to her nature, and inspired by the last sacraments, Emma expends her last resources of energy and will power to propel her imagination on a flight to that state of beatitude which she desires in death, as she has longed for it in life. For a brief moment she achieves a kind of serenity. But in harmony with the pattern of the whole novel, this flight into illusion must also end as had the others, in an abrupt return to the cruel truth. The problem was that this return must be forced while she is still conscious of what is happening. For a similar need, a similar solution: the blind beggar's song, if it could plausibly be made to reach Emma's ears at that moment in the action, would produce the desired effect. And the reader, already prepared by the blind beggar's previous appearance, would need no explanation of the effect this would have on Emma. It is surely by some such reasoning that Flaubert arrived at the conception of the blind beggar's role in Emma's death scene as we now have it. His appearance symbolizes, for Emma and for the reader, the abrupt displacement of an illusion by the grim, ugly truth. (p. 76)

Homais and Emma represent contrasting ways of coping with the crippling ugliness of life as symbolized by the blind beggar. Homais instinctively probes for ways to avoid giving the beggar money, and, better still, to exploit his very existence somehow for personal gain. Flaubert shows us Hoimais skilfully emloying the spectacle of the blind beggar to advertise his "progressive" social views, his medical skills and knowledge, and even his name and address. Emma, on the other hand, instinctively turns from the spectacle, hoping to shut it from her consciousness and pretend it isn't there, just as the reckless gesture of throwing the beggar her last coin is a desperate attempt to pretend that her financial problem isn't real. Emma flees reality, Homais exploits it. As a result, Emma will be destroyed, Homais will triumph. The blind beggar has thus proved to be for the reader a revealing touchstone of character and destiny. Fittingly, he will preside over the ultimate fate of each before the novel ends. Not only does Homais's offer bring him to Yonville in time for Emma's death, but in the last chapter of the book Flaubert further records Homais's final exploitation of the beggar and his consequent rise to power and prestige. . . . As the scene in Chapter VII shows, Homais is of that breed who batten on the misery of life and who are best equipped to triumph in an increasingly materialistic world, while Emma is of that opposite breed who are repelled by the misery of life, and who, in seeking irrationally to flee it, are in the end destroyed by it.

The contrasting destinies of Emma and Homais are, of course, at the heart of the novel's meaning. Flaubert's underlying purpose in the novel, as his subtitle indicates, was to depict provincial life, a pattern of existence he detested personally and which he felt to be growing more oppressively stifling daily. Homais and Emma complement each other, filling out the picture of provincial life as Flaubert saw it: how it destroys, what it takes to succeed in it. To dramatize these two sides of the same coin, Flaubert utilized the symbolic figure of the blind beggar in a brilliant series of eleventh-hour inventions. Thus, from an episodic character originally conceived for the purposes of one isolated scene, the blind beggar was transformed by Flaubert's creative imagination into a symbol of central significance for all of the novel's closing events and into a haunting and memorable presence by means of whom the ultimate meaning of the novel is revealed. (pp. 77-8)

*Murray Sachs, "The Role of the Blind Beggar in 'Madame Bovary'," in* Symposium, *Vol. XXII, No. 1, Spring, 1968, pp. 72-80.*

## LEO BERSANI    (essay date 1974)

*[Bersani examines the effects of popular nineteenth-century literature on Emma's conception of romantic love and sensual experience. To Bersani, she is a victim of literature. He defines the correlation between Emma's sensual experiences and the romantic novels on which she "gorges" herself as "an extraordinarily subtle dialectic between literature and sensation." Unaware of the differences between life and literature, Emma expects her experiences to mirror those of her heroines, never realizing that the novels she reads have no basis in reality. Thus, Bersani considers* Madame Bovary *"a critique of the expectations imposed on life by literary romances." For additional commentary on the novel's relationship to romanticism and realism, see excerpts by Paul Bourget (1897), Émile Faguet (1899), Henry James (1902), Martin Turnell (1950), Anthony Thorlby (see Additional Bibliography), and Charles Augustin Sainte-Beuve and Charles Baudelaire (see* NCLC, *Vol. 2).]*

The various sorts of intelligibility which literature brings to the life of the body are Flaubert's subject in **Madame Bovary.** Character has an interesting superficiality in the novel. Flaubert's intention of giving a realistic and inclusive image of bourgeois provincial life—the book's sub-title is **Moeurs de province**—partly disguises a certain thinness and even disconnectedness in his psychological portraits. True, the portrait of Emma Bovary is eventually filled in with an abundance of psychological and social details, but, during much of the narrative, she is nothing more than bodily surfaces and intense sensations. Emma first appears in Chapter 2; her personality begins to be analyzed in Chapter 6. For several pages, Flaubert's heroine is a patchwork of surfaces: a "blue merino dress with three flounces," excessively white fingernails, a thick mass of black hair, the moving reflections of the sun through her open parasol on her face, a tongue licking the bottom of a glass. (This attention to physical detail can of course be partly explained in terms of narrative strategy: Flaubert economically conveys the desires of the men looking at Emma by describing those aspects of her presence which stimulate them.) Not only do we thus see Emma as a somewhat fragmented and strongly eroticized surface; when we move to *her* point of *view,* we have an exceptional number of passages which describe the life of her senses. Mediocre in all other respects, as Brunetière wrote, Madame Bovary becomes a superior creature thanks to a rare *"finesse des sens."* (p. 17)

At moments of more overpowering sensuality there even emerges a "formula" for Emma's sensual intensities, a characteristic style of sensation which, as we know from Flaubert's other works, wasn't invented for Emma alone but rather seems to be a basic formula for Flaubertian sensation in general. Sexuality in Flaubert is frequently expressed in terms of a rippling luminosity. "Here and there," Flaubert writes as part of his description of Emma's first happy sexual experience (with Rodolphe in the forest near Yonville), "all around her, in the leaves and on the ground, patches of light were trembling, as if humming-birds, while in flight, had scattered their feathers.". . . The moon, during Emma's last meeting with Rodolphe in the garden behind her house, "cast upon the river a large spot, which broke up into an infinity of stars, and this silvery gleam seemed to writhe to the bottom of the water like a headless serpent covered with luminous scales. It also resembled some monstrous candelabra, with drops of molten diamond streaming down its sides.". . . While the experience of pleasure itself seems to include a vision of discreet points of light (the diamond light is perceived as distinct "drops"), the anticipation or the memory of sexual pleasure frequently diffuses these luminous points into a heavier, even slightly

oppressive atmosphere. In the garden description the brilliantly decorated serpent and the candelabra plunging into the water are hallucinated participations of the external world in Emma's sexual pleasure. At a certain distance from sex the thought of pleasure, or the images connected with it, makes for a less dazzling hallucination, and light now suffused with color becomes softer and thicker. After that first day in the forest with Rodolphe, Emma feels that "she was surrounded by vast bluish space, the heights of feeling were sparkling beneath her thought.". . . Much later, as she lies alone in bed at night enjoying fantasies of running away with Rodolphe, Emma imagines a future in which "nothing specific stood out: the days, all of them magnificent, resembled one another like waves; and the vision [cela] swayed on the limitless horizon, harmonious, bluish, and bathed in sun.". . . A world heavy with sensual promise (and no longer blindingly illuminated by sexual intensities) is, in Flaubert, frequently a world of many reflected lights blurred by a mist tinged with color. As the carriage draws her closer to her meetings with Léon in Rouen, the old Norman city seems to Emma like a "Babylon" of pleasure. She "pours" her love into its streets and squares; and "the leafless trees on the boulevards seemed like [faisaient] purple thickets in the midst of the houses, and the roofs, all shiny with rain, were gleaming unevenly, according to the elevation of the various districts.". . . Purplish masses of trees against an even darker background, millions of liquid light reflections which both brighten and obscure the city's outlines: this typical Flaubertian landscape recurs frequently during Frédéric's idle walks in Paris early in **L'Education sentimentale,** and, as in the case of Emma's Rouen, it seems to be what Flaubert's "hero" finds in the world when he looks at it with sensual longing. Desire has (or rather makes) its own *atmosphere* in Flaubert.

Now as soon as we speak of a characteristic formula of sensation or desire we are of course giving a certain intelligibility to what at first seemed to be the discontinuous and fragmented life of the body. But the intelligibility is all *for us;* nothing in **Madame Bovary** indicates that Emma has the slightest awareness of a durable and defining style in her sensuality. Furthermore, in the passages quoted in the last paragraph, it's by no means clear whether the images are meant to express what Emma is actually seeing or hallucinating in the world, or whether they are *Flaubert's* descriptive and metaphorical equivalents for sensations or states of mind to which they allude but which in fact don't include them. . . . [Even] if Emma does see the bejewelled candelabra in the river, that doesn't seem to be of any help to her in making sense of her sensations or in locating continuities in her experience. Of course, this is merely one aspect of her general mediocrity. She is inattentive even to that which makes her superior: the exceptional refinement of her senses. Emma's consciousness is intense, but it carries very little. She thinks in clichés, and, as far as her moral awareness goes, she is hardly less self-centered or more scrupulous than Homais. One has only to think how richly Jane Austen's and George Eliot's novels are nourished by all the ideas and principles of their heroes and heroines to appreciate the risk Flaubert takes in creating, to use a Jamesian term, such an insubstantial center of consciousness as Emma for his novel. (Indeed, James found Emma too thin a vessel to carry the weight of the novel's meaning [see excerpt above, 1902].) But the most interesting fact about Emma, as I've been suggesting, may be precisely that she has so little consciousness. For in spite of the fact that she is, after all, part of a realistic fiction in which characters have names, social positions and personalities, she almost succeeds in existing without what the realistic novel generally proposes as an identity. When she is not having intense sensations she does little more than *long for* sensations. Her principal activity is that of desiring. But what exactly is there for her to desire? In what images will she recognize a promise of happy sensations?

Love sublimates and novelizes sensation. The literature of romance on which Madame Bovary gorges herself is the only spiritualizing principle in her life. The dangers of this literature are so emphatically illustrated in Flaubert's work that we may tend to overlook the service it performs for Emma's intense but random sensuality. For a moment during the performance of *Lucia di Lammermoor* at the Rouen opera house, Emma manages to smile with a "disdainful pity" as she thinks of all the lies which literature tells about life; "she now knew," Flaubert adds, "how small the passions were which art exaggerated."... The next day, when Léon visits Emma at her hotel, they attempt, with the help of literary clichés, to recompose their past, to fit the quiet, uneventful love of the days in Yonville to an ideal of glamorously desperate passion. "Besides," Flaubert philosophically remarks, "speech is a rolling mill which always stretches out feelings."... But what alternative is there to the exaggerations and the extensions of language? In this same scene at the Rouen hotel Emma and Léon finally stop talking: "They were no longer speaking; but they felt, as they looked at each other, a humming in their heads, as though something audible had escaped from their motionless eyes. They had just joined hands; and the past, the future, reminiscences and dreams, everything was merged in the sweetness of this ecstasy."... In the same way Emma's sensual torpor as Rodolphe speaks to her of love on the day of the agricultural fair is a state in which "everything became confused" and the present merges with images from the past. Emma's consciousness is invaded by the odor of Rodolphe's pomade, the memory of a similar odor of vanilla and lemon which came from the viscount's beard as she waltzed with him at la Vaubyessard, the light from the chandeliers at that same ball, an image of Léon, and finally the smell of the fresh ivy coming through the open window next to which she and Rodolphe are seated.... As Jean-Pierre Richard has brilliantly shown [see excerpt above, 1954], a fundamental theme of Flaubert's "material" imagination is that of a fusion between the self and the world, as well as among all the elements of consciousness. Contours are blurred, boundaries disappear, and the great danger in Flaubert's imaginary world is that of being drowned in a kind of formless liquid dough, in a sea of thick, undifferentiated matter. I'll be returning to the dangers of fusion; for the moment I want to emphasize that even at moments of great sensual pleasure, as in the passage just quoted, the intense sensation tends *to break down differences* in **Madame Bovary**—differences between people, between the present and the past, and between the inner and outer worlds. Thus, not only does Flaubert present Emma as a patchwork of bodily surfaces; not only does he tend to reduce her consciousness to a series of strong but disconnected sensations; he also indicates that by its very nature sensation makes a mockery of the distinctions we invent in thought.

There is, however, the rolling mill of language to rescue us. Language *de*fuses; its conceptual nature attacks the intensity of sensations, and words unwrap the bundle of sensory impressions and extend them, as distinct and separate verbal units, along the "lines" of space and time. More specifically, in the case of Emma Bovary, stories of romance raise her sensations to the level of sentiment. They replace the isolated and anonymous body with couples sharply characterized socially, and they provide spatial and temporal elaborations—that is, a *story*—

*Emma at the Hôtel de Boulogne, at a clandestine meeting with Léon. Mary Evans Picture Library.*

for the ecstatic instant. But, interestingly enough, Emma recharges literary language by retaining only its inspirations for visual fantasies. Probably every reader of **Madame Bovary** has noticed that Emma "thinks" in tableaux. Indeed, the sign of desire in the novel is the appearance of a tableau. The desire for an ecstatic honeymoon is a mental picture of driving in the mountains, to the sound of goat-bells and waterfalls, toward a bay surrounded by lemon trees; the desire for an exciting existence in Paris is a group of neatly compartmentalized images of the different worlds of ambassadors, duchesses and artists in the capital; and the desire to run away with Rodolphe takes the form of an exotic travel fantasy through cities with cathedrals of white marble and finally to a picturesque fishing village. These desirable tableaux could be thought of as halfway between verbal narrative and the hallucinated scenes of intense sensations. As she indulges in them Emma enjoys a tamed version of bodily desires. There isn't a single original image in these romantic tableaux drawn from literature, but, perhaps because of that very fact, all the books which Emma has read collaborate to form a satisfyingly consistent love story, a highly intelligible cliché which imposes order on ecstasy.

Given the immensely useful function of literature in Emma's life, it is, in a sense, merely snobbish to complain about the inferior quality of the books she reads. But something does of course go wrong with the function itself. Emma is extremely demanding. She wants the intelligibility of literature *in the* ecstatic sensation. At the risk of making things overly schematic, let's say that we have followed her from disconnected sensations to the sublimating stories of art; how will she now return from art to life? There wouldn't be any problem if Emma could be satisfied with transposing literature into desirable mental tableaux. She is, however, engaged in a much more complicated enterprise, one which literature itself, to a certain extent, encourages. Literary romance gives a seductive intelligibility to the body's pleasures; but it perhaps also invites its readers to expect the body to confirm the mind's fictions. The lie of which Emma's novels are guilty is their suggestion that the stories which in fact modulate and dilute existential intensities are equivalent to them. It is as if writers themselves were tempted to ignore the abstracting nature of language and to confuse an extended novelistic fantasy with the scenes of hallucinating desire and sensation. Emma welcomes the confusion: she waits for experience to duplicate literature, unaware of the fact that literature didn't duplicate life in the first place.

This fundamental error naturally leads Emma into considerable trouble. For example, the books she reads (like all literature) make use of a conventional system of signs. Flaubert enumerates several of the gestures and the settings which signify love in the novels Emma read when she was at the convent: "[These novels] were filled with love affairs, lovers, mistresses, persecuted ladies fainting in lonely pavilions, postriders killed at every relay, horses ridden to death on every page, dark forests, palpitating hearts, vows, sobs, tears and kisses, skiffs in the moonlight, nightingales in thickets, gentlemen brave as lions, gentle as lambs, virtuous as no one really is, always well dressed, and weeping like fountains.". . . Love seems impossible to Emma unless it appears with all the conventional signs which constitute a code of love in fictions of romance. Since Charles doesn't respond to the romantic clichés she tries out on him, Emma, "incapable . . . of believing in anything that didn't manifest itself in conventional forms," decides that his love for her must be diminishing. . . . (Rodolphe, incidentally, makes the opposite mistake. . . : unable to see "the differences of feeling under the similarities of expression," he doubts Emma's passion because she uses formulas he has heard from so many other women.) There are particular words, costumes, gestures and settings which, so to speak, manufacture passion. As Flaubert says of Emma: "It seemed to her that certain places on the earth must produce happiness, like a plant indigenous to that soil and which would be unable to thrive anywhere else.". . . (pp. 17-22)

Furthermore, in seductive (and treacherous) fashion, the books which Emma reads attribute duration to the rapturous instant. Romantic love in literature may end tragically, but it is not likely to run out of emotional steam and end in boredom. Of course, all literature not only makes sense of the instant; it also makes time from the instant. The life of the body sublimated in time is the history of a person. But in Emma's favorite books history is glamorized as a succession of intensities. Romance conceptualizes sensation; furthermore, it suggests that time never dissipates sensations. Emma does experience sensations which seem to her to live up to her definitions of romantic ecstasy; but she learns that romantic ecstasy doesn't last. And we find the dramatization of this banal fact interesting only because it is made through a character who, quite remarkably, refuses to make any compromise at all with time. While Flaubert gives detailed attention to the modulations of feeling in time (I'm thinking, for example, of the chapter which summarizes the change in Emma between her return from la Vaubyessard and the move from Tostes to Yonville [and of the few pages]. . . which describe her agitated, rapidly changing feelings after she discovers that Léon loves her), his aristocratic

heroine expects each moment to repeat the rapture of a previous moment. But Emma's thrilling excitements are quickly submerged in ordinary time, and it is this shattering absence of drama which wears her out, which leads her to complain bitterly about the "instantaneous rotting away of the things she leaned on" and to feel that "everything was a lie!" (pp. 22-3)

Literature has served Emma very poorly indeed. It makes sense of experience for her, but experience doesn't confirm the sense she brings to it. And this is especially disastrous since Emma can't really return to literature. If *Madame Bovary* is a critique of the expectations imposed on life by literary romances, it is also a critique of the expectations which those same romances raise concerning literature itself. Flaubert's novel is an extraordinarily subtle dialectic between literature and sensation; the movement between the two creates a rhythm less immediately obvious but more profound than the alternation between exalted fantasies and flat realities. (p. 24)

> *Leo Bersani, "Flaubert and Emma Bovary: The Hazards of Literary Fusion," in* Novel: A Forum on Fiction, *Vol. 8, No. 1, Fall, 1974, pp. 16-28.*

## JEAN PACE   (essay date 1977)

[*Pace discusses Flaubert's image of women as outlined in his letters, juvenile work, and novels. Pace defines Flaubert's view as a paradox of "contempt for women in general coupled with a romantic idealization of one woman": Elisa Schlesinger, whom Flaubert idolized.*]

Among Flaubert's early, posthumously published works there is a fragment of considerable interest called *Une Nuit de Don Juan*. It is undated, but is referred to in letters written during his Egyptian tour in April, 1851. It is a sad little scenario on the impossibility of satisfaction and even of communication in love; and it contains this highly revealing passage: "Il y avait dans le jardin de mon père une figure de femme, proue de navire. Envie d'y monter. Il y grimpe un jour, et lui prend les seins. Araignées dans le bois pourri." [In father's garden there was a ship's figure-head of a woman. He longs to go up to it. He climbs up one day, and takes hold of her breasts. Spiders in the rotten wood.]

Although the note refers not to Flaubert himself but to Don Juan, a very different character (and the first partial publication of the fragment was due, appropriately enough, to Maupassant), one cannot avoid seeing in this image of desolation, disillusionment, and sexual revulsion a hint of something basic in the author's own personality. It is significant, moreover, that similar images recur elsewhere in his work: for instance in *Madame Bovary:* "L'ennui, araignée silencieuse, filait sa toile dans l'ombre à tous les coins de son coeur." [Boredom, a silent spider, spun its web in every corner of her heart], and later: "D'où venait cette insuffisance de la vie, cette pourriture instantanée des choses où elle s'appuyait?" [Why was life so inadequate, why did everything she leaned on immediately crumble away in rottenness?]

Such feelings, a general melancholia focused on sex and tending toward misogyny, openly expressed in his more personal writings and particularly in his voluminous correspondence, color his portrayal of women in the supposedly, and intentionally, impersonal novels and in particular in *Madame Bovary*.

More perhaps than any other great novel, *Madame Bovary* has been studied in detail as well as in depth; its structure and style, imagery, syntax, and sound have been examined with a scrupulous rigor equal to that of Flaubert himself, and with frequently illuminating results. It may thus seem almost irrelevant to approach this consummate work of art from a non-aesthetic point of view and without regard to the methods of thematists and structuralists. The fact remains that however much Flaubert wanted, or professed to want, to write a book "without a subject, which would stand up by itself through sheer force of style," the form in which he expressed himself here was neither abstract art nor pure poetry; it was a "realistic" novel about a middle-class, mid-nineteenth-century provincial Frenchwoman.

Emma Bovary is perhaps the first of a series of bored, frustrated, fictional heroines seeking vainly in dream an escape from the tedium and futility of their lives: the penalty of being a woman in nineteenth-century bourgeois society, one may think, remembering Florence Nightingale's bitter strictures on her own habit of daydreaming (and looking ahead to the women portrayed by Hardy, Ibsen, and Chekov). And as such, her portrait is unerringly truthful; the dreariness and vacuity of poor Emma's existence was familiar, as he'd known it would be, to more than one of his women readers—they wrote to tell him so. It is deliberately intensified in her case, of course, by the drabness of her provincial backwater, the mediocrity of all the people surrounding her; though one may wonder whether she would have been happier in the Chateau de la Vaubyessard than at Yonville! The flight into illusion is a natural enough weakness. Emma is presented as a born dreamer; as a girl she had indulged in every emotional and sentimental fantasy available to her, from the fervid religiosity of her convent days to the romantic extravaganzas inspired by novel reading; she has always been consumed by vague dissatisfaction, by the longing for elsewhere. But Emma does not merely daydream; she attempts, with what dire results we discover, to impose her dream upon life; she confuses illusion and reality, seeing herself as romantic heroine, the cynical sensualist Rodolphe and the feeble Léon as romantic heroes; she tries to act out her fantasies, and meanwhile horribly and irrevocably deteriorates. "Bovarysm," according to the critic Jules Gaultier, consists in "seeing oneself otherwise than as one is," a permanent state of self-deception, an inability to face reality.

Although the theme was topical enough in 1856, Bovarysm was no new phenomenon. Emma reincarnates an earlier figure; she reflects, as though in a distorting mirror, the victims of Romantic *weltschmerz*, like Chateaubriand's René, Goethe's Young Werther, Musset's *enfant du siècle* and a score of others, tormented by the contrast between what is and what might be, or ought to be. By the mid-nineteenth century, however, the Romantic hero was an outdated figure; he could no longer be the protagonist of a serious and truthful novel. (His anguish, indeed, could still be conveyed in poetry; Baudelaire's "spleen" shows it persisting in exacerbated form.) ... Woman, with her restricted education and opportunities and all the limitations of convention that crippled her, became a natural vehicle for the expression of such emotions. But Emma Bovary differs from her Romantic predecessors not only in the metamorphosis of sex but in the complexity and ambivalence of Flaubert's attitude toward his heroine.

"Madame Bovary, c'est moi" is perhaps the best known of all comments by an author on his creation. Whether or not Flaubert made the remark in so many words . . . , it is profoundly true at many levels. Superficially, it is the author's irritated reaction against all tiresome attempts to identify his characters with real people (was Emma based on Delphine Delamare, who was said to have committed suicide? or on Louise Pradier, who had lovers and got into debt? etc). In another sense it implies the imaginative identification that any artist must feel with his creation; the empathy summed up in Keats's "chameleon poet"; Louis Aragon quotes the phrase when describing Matisse's relation with his model, whether it be woman or still life. But in a deeper sense Emma is indeed Flaubert; "the heart I studied was my own," he wrote to his mistress Louise Colet. "How often at my best moments I felt the chill of the scalpel entering my flesh." It is not so much a portrait of the artist as a young woman, as a ruthless dissection of one important aspect of himself: the self that sought escape from a loathed reality in dreams, in exotic and impossible fantasies in the highly coloured and sadistic visions of *Salammbô* and *Saint-Julien l'Hospitalier.* (pp. 114-16)

[*Madame Bovary*] reveals, for all its objectivity, its rigid control and impeccable form, some important things about its author, and specifically about his attitude toward women. His very ambivalence toward his heroine is significant. When Flaubert chooses a woman to represent his own adolescent romanticism, he deliberately makes of it a diminished thing. He himself describes his heroine . . . as "a somewhat perverse nature, a woman of false poetry and false feelings." She is a bourgeoise in every sense of the word, and her dreams are second-rate and second-hand, mere *kitsch,* clichés from sentimental novels and the "keepsakes" of the time. More than that, which is after all a matter of circumstance: Emma herself is of shoddy stuff. She is utterly self-centered, incapable of feeling for anyone else or responding to another's feeling; poor Charles' devotion arouses only repugnance in her, and she ignores that of the boy Justin. Caring little for her child, she can assume the pose of maternal tenderness when it fits her temporary persona. She has no power of detachment, no breadth of sympathy or real imagination. "Incapable of understanding what she had not experienced, or of believing anything that was not expressed in a conventional form, . . . she needed to gain a sort of personal advantage out of things." Apart from her daydreaming faculty, the only genuine thing about her is her sensuality, which is implied from the very first descriptions of her. Its frustration in her marriage is a major cause of her neurosis. Unsatisfied, it assumes the form of self-indulgent longing for luxury, or the illusion of religious ecstasy (this is a major *leit-motiv* in her story, and indeed in the French nineteenth-century concept of woman in general). Emma has no honesty, no lucidity about her emotions: "she confused the sensuous enjoyment of luxury with the joys of the heart . . . sensual lust, cupidity and unhappy love were all intermingled. . . ."

The disintegrating effects of *ennui* have seldom been more powerfully conveyed than in Emma's capricious and inconsistent efforts to fill the void of her existence: now apathetic, now sentimental, now meticulously house-proud, now sunk in slovenly indifference, now dabbling in art or music or good works, pious by fits and starts. The story of her rapid decline and fall, after Rodolphe has aroused her sexually and then deserted her, follows the expected pattern, only now a new element in her personality has developed: her vague feelings have become sharpened and intensified, and with a kind of desperate strength she fastens on, and dominates, the spineless Léon. Flaubert's notes for *Madame Bovary* tell us: "She feels toward Léon as Rodolphe felt towards herself, she does not love him, she makes use of him—she does not love him for himself but *for her own sake.*" He is not a person to her, merely the object

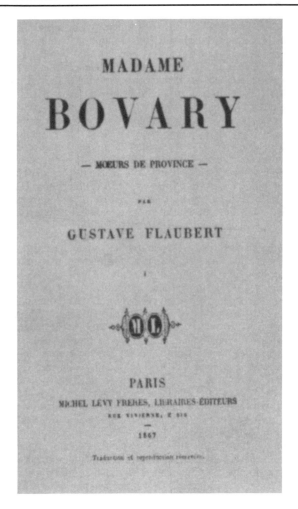

*The title page from the first edition of* Madame Bovary.

onto which she projects her own imaginings—as she had done, just before their reunion, with the tenor singing in *Lucia di Lammermoor* at the Rouen theater—and through whom she satisfies her desires. When their love cools, and adultery proves as dull as marriage, she tries to stimulate her dying feelings artificially by an effort of the imagination, just as when, a disappointed bride, she had tried to make herself feel love "according to what she took to be the right theories." She becomes avid, insatiable, ruthless, and reckless. Always adept at self-deception, she learns to deceive others, becoming involved in the most tangled web of duplicity. (pp. 119-20)

Studying Flaubert's attitude toward women—in his life and in his art—one is aware of certain paradoxes. The most immediately apparent is his contempt for women in general coupled with a romantic idealization of one woman [Elisa Schlesinger, Marie Arnour in *L'éducation sentimentale*]. . . . *Both* attitudes—the view of woman as irrational, sentimental, emotionally insincere, and the cult of the Madonna figure, the chaste and tender mother-figure—were widespread at this time. What is so odd as to be rather shocking is to find Flaubert, the scourge of the bourgeois, the despiser of *idées reçues*, accepting the conventional view of woman's nature; while conscious of the damaging role of her restricted education, he cannot see beyond its results; he uses the moral clichés of his time to confirm his own misogynistic prejudices. A further paradox relates to his art: the impersonality which was the

major tenet of his creed as novelist proves misleading. In his masterpiece, *Madame Bovary,* the tendencies that he pillories as being typically feminine are those that he resented and despised because he had felt and fought with them within himself. If only Flaubert, the supreme ironist, could have maintained enough detachment to note such contradictions, he might have found yet another occasion for a bitter laugh at *la bêtise humaine.* (p. 129)

> Jean Pace, "Flaubert's Image of Woman," in The Southern Review, *Vol. XIII, No. 1, January, 1977, pp. 114-30 [revised by the author for this publication].*

## ADDITIONAL BIBLIOGRAPHY

Allen, Woody. "The Kugelmass Episode." In his *Side Effects*, pp. 41-56. New York: Random House, 1980.
> A humorous short story in which Sidney Kugelmass, a twentieth-century Jewish professor from City College in New York, is transported into *Madame Bovary* and becomes Emma's lover.

Bart, B. F. "Aesthetic Distance in *Madame Bovary*." *PMLA* LXIX, No. 5 (December 1954): 1112-26.
> Examines the novel's "aesthetic distance," or in the words of David Daiches, "the distance from the object at which the reader must stand if he is to see it for what it is." Bart describes aesthetic distance in *Madame Bovary* as a reflection of Flaubert's attitude toward his material and as his method for governing the reader's reaction to the material.

Bersani, Leo. "The Narrator and the Bourgeois Community in *Madame Bovary*." *The French Review* XXXII, No. 6 (May 1959): 527-33.
> Contends that Flaubert's ambivalent attitude toward his material in *Madame Bovary* is reflected in his narrative stance.

———. "Flaubert and the Threats of Imagination (*Madame Bovary*)." In his *Balzac to Beckett: Center and Circumference in French Fiction*, pp. 140-91. New York: Oxford University Press, 1970.
> Explores the relationship in *Madame Bovary* between Flaubert's language and his depiction of imagination and reality.

Blackmur, R. P. "*Madame Bovary*: Beauty Out of Place." *The Kenyon Review* XIII, No. 3 (Summer 1951): 475-503.
> Focuses on structure, symbol, theme, imagination, and characterization in the novel to explain its "unexpected authority."

Bopp, Léon. *Commentaire sur "Madame Bovary."* Paris: Baconnière, 1951, 550 p.
> A comprehensive French-language study of Flaubert's literary technique that provides a close explication of *Madame Bovary.*

Bruns, Gerald L. "Flaubert, Joyce, and the Displacement of Fiction." In his *Modern Poetry and the Idea of Language: A Critical and Historical Study*, pp. 138-63. New Haven: Yale University Press, 1975.*
> Argues that Flaubert uses both metaphoric and metonymic language, or linguistic devices characteristic of both prose and poetry.

Carlut, Charles; Dubé, Pierre H.; and Dugan, J. Raymond. *A Concordance to Flaubert's "Madame Bovary."* 2 vols. New York: Garland Publishing, 1978.
> A concordance to a French edition of *Madame Bovary.*

Church, Margaret. "A Triad of Images: Nature As Structure in *Madame Bovary*." In her *Structure and Theme: "Don Quixote" to James Joyce*, pp. 61-80. Columbus: Ohio State University Press, 1983.
> A study of structure and imagery in *Madame Bovary*. Church contends that the novel's three-part structure corresponds to its triad of nature imagery, which is comprised of water, vegetation, and animals and insects.

Cortland, Peter. *"Madame Bovary."* In his *A Reader's Guide to Flaubert: An Analysis of the Texts and Discussion of Current Criticism,* pp. 17-82. New York: Helios Books, 1968.

An introductory guide to *Madame Bovary.*

Daniels, Douglas J. "The Evolution of Point of View in *Madame Bovary." Proceedings: Pacific Northwest Council on Foreign Languages* XXVII, Part I (22-24 April 1976): 50-2.

Documents the evolution of point of view in Flaubert's work from his juvenile writings, to early drafts of *Madame Bovary,* to that work's final published form.

Dauner, Louise. "Poetic Symbolism in *Madame Bovary." South Atlantic Quarterly* LV, No. 2 (April 1956): 207-20.

Treats *Madame Bovary* as a poem and outlines its major poetic symbols, which include the garden, water, Binet's lathe, and the blind beggar.

Du Bos, Charles. "On the 'Inner Environment' in the Work of Flaubert." In *"Madame Bovary" by Gustave Flaubert: Backgrounds and Sources, Essays in Criticism,* edited and translated by Paul de Man, pp. 360-71. New York: W. W. Norton & Co., 1965.

Analyzes excerpts from Flaubert's letters to uncover the "inner environment," or creative unconscious, in which his works originated.

Dumesnil, René. "The Real Source of *Madame Bovary."* In *"Madame Bovary" by Gustave Flaubert: Backgrounds and Sources, Essays in Criticism,* edited and translated by Paul de Man, pp. 298-301. New York: W. W. Norton & Co., 1965.

Demonstrates the parallels between the subjects of *Madame Bovary* and *Passion et vertu,* which Flaubert wrote in 1837. Dumesnil contends that the source for Flaubert's great novel lies in his earlier work and not in the story of the Delamarre family.

Engstrom, Alfred G. "Flaubert's Correspondence and the Ironic and Symbolic Structure of *Madame Bovary." Studies in Philology* XLVI, No. 3 (July 1949): 470-95.

Examines the ironic and symbolic structure of *Madame Bovary.*

Fairlie, Alison. *Flaubert: "Madame Bovary."* Great Neck, N.Y.: Barron's Educational Series, 1962, 80 p.

An introductory study of *Madame Bovary* that focuses on its anti-heroic subject, structure, characters, and values.

Festa-McCormick, Diana. "Emma Bovary's Masculinization: Convention of Clothes and Morality of Conventions." In *Gender and Literary Voice,* edited by Janet Todd, pp. 223-35. Women & Literature, n.s. vol. 1. New York: Holmes & Meier Publishers, 1980.

An interpretation of the symbolism of Emma's clothing. Festa-McCormick traces the connection between the masculinization of Emma's clothing and her rejection of social conventions.

Furst, Lilian R. "The Role of Food in *Madame Bovary." Orbis Litterarum* 34, No. 1 (1979): 53-65.

Investigates the symbolism of food in *Madame Bovary.* Furst contends that food functions as "an environmental factor, as a social indicator, as a means of characterization, and as a source of imagery."

Gill, Richard. "The Soundtrack of *Madame Bovary:* Flaubert's Orchestration of Aural Imagery." *Literature/Film Quarterly* I, No. 3 (July 1973): 206-17.

Points out the similarities between Flaubert's technique in *Madame Bovary* and that of modern film directors, with special attention to his use of sound.

Gray, Eugene F. "Emma by Twilight: Flawed Perception in *Madame Bovary." Nineteenth-Century French Studies* VI, Nos. 3 & 4 (Spring-Summer 1978): 231-40.

An analysis of Flaubert's description of light in *Madame Bovary.*

Haig, Stirling. "The *Madame Bovary* Blues." *The Romanic Review* LXI (1970): 27-34.

Traces the recurrence in *Madame Bovary* of the color blue, which Haig describes as a symbol for "our aspirations and our *ennui.*"

Harvey, Lawrence E. "The Ironic Triumph of Rodolphe." *The French Review* XXX, No. 2 (December 1956): 121-25.

A study of Rodolphe's role in the novel. Harvey contends that "Rodolphe is an alter-Emma, a liberated Emma who has achieved the sort of success she yearns for and fails to find." According to Harvey, Rodolphe succeeds where Emma fails in attaining the Romantic dream.

Kaplan, Harold. *"Madame Bovary:* The Seriousness of Comedy." In his *The Passive Voice: An Approach to Modern Fiction,* pp. 23-41. Athens: Ohio University Press, 1966.

An assessment of Flaubert's comic method in *Madame Bovary,* particularly in relation to his treatment of Emma.

LaCapra, Dominick. *"Madame Bovary" on Trial.* Ithaca, N.Y.: Cornell University Press, 1982, 219 p.

Examines the symbolic importance of the obscenity trial of *Madame Bovary.* LaCapra argues that "the study of a text's reception should be combined with an attempted critical reading of the text that provides intellectual and historical perspective on processes of reception." To that end, he discusses the trial to illuminate the relationship between literature and society.

Lapp, John C. "Art and Hallucination in Flaubert." *French Studies* X, No. 4 (October 1956): 322-34.

Traces the effects of Flaubert's nervous disease, which Lapp calls *petit mal* epilepsy, on the author's life and work. Lapp quotes passages from Flaubert's letters in which he describes his hallucinatory experiences during seizures and documents similar episodes in *Madame Bovary.*

Levin, Harry. "Flaubert: The Female Quixote." In his *The Gates of Horn: A Study of Five French Realists,* pp. 246-69. New York: Oxford University Press, 1963.

Appraises *Madame Bovary* as a realistic novel, focusing on its imagery, style, structure, and characterization.

————. "A Literary Enormity: Sartre on Flaubert." In his *Memories of the Moderns,* pp. 135-44. New York: New Directions Publishing Corp., 1980.

An analysis of Jean-Paul Sartre's treatment of Flaubert. Levin terms his essay a "counter-polemic" occasioned by the publication of Sartre's *L'idiot de la famille* (see annotation below). Sartre's study, according to Levin, is "the fulfillment of a lifelong vendetta" and "a hatchet-job."

Levine, George. *"Madame Bovary* and the Disappearing Author." *Modern Fiction Studies* IX, No. 2 (Summer 1963): 103-19.

Defines the term "objective" in relation to the novel and examines *Madame Bovary* in this light. Levine contends that Flaubert used authorial intrusions too extensively for his work to be considered objective.

Lowe, A. M. "Emma Bovary, a Modern Arachne." *French Studies* XXVI, No. 1 (January 1972): 30-41.

Examines imagery in *Madame Bovary* to prove that Emma was a modern incarnation of Arachne, a character from Greek mythology.

Man, Paul de, ed. *"Madame Bovary" by Gustave Flaubert: Backgrounds and Sources, Essays in Criticism.* Translated by Paul de Man. New York: W. W. Norton & Co., 1965, 462 p.

A new edition of *Madame Bovary* that includes a summary of critical response to the novel and a collection of what de Man considers a representative sample of the most important essays.

Maugham, W. Somerset. "Flaubert and *Madame Bovary."* In his *The Art of Fiction: An Introduction to Ten Novels and Their Authors,* pp. 163-88. Garden City, N.Y.: Doubleday & Co., 1955.

An appreciation of characterization and style in *Madame Bovary.*

Maurois, André. "Escape in Love—*Madame Bovary."* In his *Seven Faces of Love,* translated by Haakon M. Chevalier, pp. 175-208. New York: Didier, 1944.

Considers romantic love as depicted in *Madame Bovary* as a form of escape from reality.

Mein, Margaret. "Flaubert, a Precursor of Proust." *French Studies* XVII, No. 3 (July 1963): 218-37.*
    A comparison of *Madame Bovary* with the work of Marcel Proust.

Nabokov, Vladimir. "Gustave Flaubert: *Madame Bovary*." In his *Lectures on Literature,* edited by Fredson Bowers, pp. 125-78. New York: Harcourt Brace Jovanovich, 1980.
    An analysis of style, structure, and characterization in *Madame Bovary.* Nabokov devotes particular attention to Flaubert's "counterpoint method," which involves "parallel interlinings and interruptions of two or more conversations or trains of thought." To illustrate this method, Nabokov focuses closely on several scenes, including Emma and Rodolphe's conversation at the agricultural fair and Emma and Leon's first meeting.

Nelson, Robert J. "*Madame Bovary* As Tragedy." *Modern Language Quarterly* 18, No. 4 (December 1957): 323-30.
    Analyzes the structure of *Madame Bovary.* Nelson theorizes that the progression of action, and particularly the abrupt changes in the direction of the action, prove that *Madame Bovary* is a tragedy.

Nicholas, Brian. "The Novel As Work of Art: *Madame Bovary*." In *The Moral and the Story,* by Ian Gregor and Brian Nicholas, pp. 33-62. London: Faber and Faber, 1962.
    Addresses the morality of *Madame Bovary,* arguing that Flaubert satirically portrayed the *Moeurs de province* he cited in the subtitle.

Pascal, Roy. "The French Masters: Flaubert, *Madame Bovary*." In his *The Dual Voice: Free Indirect Speech and Its Functioning in the Nineteenth-Century European Novel,* pp. 98-112. Manchester, England: Manchester University Press, 1977.
    Closely studies the relationship between narration, style, and free indirect speech in *Madame Bovary.*

Sabin, Margery. "The Poverty of Nature in *Madame Bovary*." In her *English Romanticism and the French Tradition,* pp. 258-76. Cambridge: Harvard University Press, 1976.
    Examines the importance of nature to the French Romantic tradition and Flaubert's relation to that tradition.

Sabiston, Elizabeth. "The Prison of Womanhood." *Comparative Literature* XXV, No. 4 (Fall 1973): 336-51.*
    A comparative study of several provincial, isolated female characters, including the heroines of *Madame Bovary, The Portrait of a Lady* by Henry James, *Emma* by Jane Austen, and *Middlemarch* by George Eliot.

Sarraute, Nathalie. "Flaubert." *Partisan Review* XXXII, No. 2 (Spring 1966): 193-208.
    Emphasizes Flaubert's contribution to the modern novel and analyzes his handling of content and form in *Madame Bovary.*

Sartre, Jean-Paul. *The Family Idiot: Gustave Flaubert, 1821-1857,* Vol. 1. Translated by Carol Cosman. Chicago: University of Chicago Press, 1981, 627 p.
    Part one of *L'idiot de la famille: Gustave Flaubert de 1821 à 1857,* Sartre's comprehensive, three-part biography of Flaubert; volumes two and three are available only in French. Sartre terms this work a sequel to *Search for a Method* (see excerpt above,

1960). In this biography, he uses the method outlined in his earlier work, incorporating psychological, philosophical, and historical analysis.

Sherrington, R. J. "*Madame Bovary*." In his *Three Novels by Flaubert: A Study of Techniques,* pp. 79-152. Oxford: Clarendon Press, 1970.
    A detailed description of Flaubert's use of technique, and specifically point of view.

Starkie, Enid. *Flaubert: The Making of the Master.* New York: Atheneum, 1967, 403 p.
    A comprehensive study of Flaubert's life and work from his youth through the publication and trial of *Madame Bovary.* Starkie's approach combines "an analysis of the writer [with] a portrait of the human being." Starkie covers Flaubert's life from 1856 until his death in *Flaubert the Master: A Critical and Biographical Study (1856-1880).*

St. Aubyn, F. C. "Madame Bovary outside the Window." *Nineteenth-Century French Studies* I, No. 2 (February 1973): 105-11.
    Examines allusions to windows in *Madame Bovary* that depict Emma as an outsider looking in.

Tanner, Tony. "Flaubert's *Madame Bovary*." In his *Adultery in the Novel: Contract and Transgression,* pp. 233-367. Baltimore: Johns Hopkins University Press, 1979.
    A lengthy semantic study of *Madame Bovary* that outlines the dehumanizing effects of adultery as manifested in the novel.

Thorlby, Anthony. *Gustave Flaubert and the Art of Realism.* Studies in Modern European Literature and Thought. London: Bowes & Bowes, 1956, 63 p.
    Treats *Madame Bovary* as a realistic novel, with special emphasis on its style and form.

Thornton, Lawrence. "The Fairest of Them All: Modes of Vision in *Madame Bovary*." *PMLA* 93, No. 5 (October 1978): 982-91.
    Describes three modes of vision in *Madame Bovary*: descriptive, hallucinatory, and autoscopic, a narcissistic approach .

Wagner, Geoffrey. "Emma Bovary, the Usurper: With a Coda on Luiza of *Cousin Bazilio*." In his *Five for Freedom: A Study of Feminism in Fiction,* pp. 138-82. Rutherford, N.J.: Fairleigh Dickinson University Press, 1974.*
    A feminist interpretation of *Madame Bovary* in which the critic responds to earlier critical views of the novel as a negative portrayal of women. Wagner contends that Flaubert represented himself in the character of Emma and that he was, indeed, a feminist.

Wetherill, P. M. "*Madame Bovary*'s Blind Man: Symbolism in Flaubert." *The Romanic Review* LXI (1970): 35-42.
    Examines critical response to the blind man and analyzes his role in *Madame Bovary.*

Williams, D. A. *Psychological Determinism in "Madame Bovary."* Occasional Papers in Modern Languages, edited by Garnet Rees, No. 9. Yorkshire, England: University of Hull Publications, 1973, 81 p.
    Exposes the degree to which the characters and events of *Madame Bovary* are governed by fatality and determinism.

# Harold Frederic

## 1856-1898

(Born Harold Frederick. Also wrote under pseudonym of George Forth) American novelist, short story writer, and journalist.

Critics now consider Frederic one of the finest American novelists of the late nineteenth century, and his most popular work, *The Damnation of Theron Ware,* is a minor national classic. By combining elements of regionalism, naturalism, and romance in his short stories and novels, Frederic chronicled the changing mood of the country during the latter part of the nineteenth century. Such later writers as Stephen Crane, Frank Norris, Sinclair Lewis, and Theodore Dreiser were strongly influenced by Frederic's use of irony as a tool for psychological exploration and social commentary.

Frederic was born into a poor family in Utica, New York. His father, a freight conductor for the New York Central Railroad, died when Frederic was eighteen months old, and his mother remarried shortly afterwards. Because of the family's financial difficulties, Frederic worked from an early age. He demonstrated a talent for drawing and writing as a schoolboy, but his formal education ended with his graduation from the Utica Advanced School in 1871. Following employment as a photo printer and negative retoucher, Frederic departed for Boston in 1873. There he associated with bohemians and intellectuals and experimented with writing and painting. Frederic later wrote in his 1897 Preface to *In the Sixties* that his most important literary influences at this time were Nathaniel Hawthorne and the French historical writers Emile Erckmann and Alexandre Chatrian. He returned to Utica in 1875 and joined the staff of the *Observer,* where he advanced from proofreader to editor. During his career there, Frederic gained fame as a journalist. The paper also served as the first showcase for his talents as a short story writer. In 1877, Frederic married a neighbor, Grace Williams. The couple moved to Albany in 1882, when Frederic was invited to edit the *Albany Evening Journal.* During the next two years, Frederic transformed that newspaper into an important political organ and became involved both personally and professionally in Grover Cleveland's gubernatorial election campaign. However, a change in the *Albany Evening Journal*'s ownership and Frederic's subsequent ideological disagreement with the new owner prompted him to accept a post as London correspondent for the *New York Times.* Frederic spent the rest of his life in England, working simultaneously on his fiction and on journalistic assignments. His reputation as a correspondent was enhanced by a number of assignments which included an investigation into a cholera epidemic in France, a series of articles on the question of Irish Home Rule, an analysis of the persecution of Jews in Russia (later published as *The New Exodus: A Study of Israel in Russia*), and a study of Germany's Emperor William II (later published as *The Young Emperor William II of Germany: A Study in Character Development on a Throne*). In addition, his novels and short stories were serialized in leading magazines. During the 1890s he was also in demand as a reviewer and valued as an intellectual. He formed a close friendship with the American novelist Stephen Crane, who became one of Frederic's staunchest champions.

*From Dictionary of American Portraits, Dover Publications, Inc., 1967*

The 1890s also witnessed a dramatic change in Frederic's personal life. After the death of his son, Harold Jr., he began a liaison with Kate Lyon, an American expatriate. His wife, Grace, refused Frederic a divorce, and from 1890 on, he maintained two separate families—Kate and their three children in London, and Grace and their four children in a nearby suburb. The financial burden of supporting two families forced Frederic to work incessantly at his journalism and left him with little time for his fiction. In 1897, Frederic developed a heart condition, but refused to follow medical advice. Continuing his extremely demanding work schedule, he suffered a stroke in 1898 and died shortly thereafter. After his death, Grace Frederic initiated legal proceedings against Lyon, charging that Lyon, a Christian Scientist, contributed to Frederic's death by denying him medical treatment. Lyon was found not guilty, but only after a prolonged, scandalous, and well-publicized trial which, ironically, led to a surge in Frederic's popularity.

Frederic's first novel, *Seth's Brother's Wife,* was not a commercial success, but a number of critics praised its realistic style and open treatment of sexuality. The plot revolves around the interactions between an upstate New York politician, his journalist brother, and the politician's wife who is attracted to her brother-in-law. Reviewers considered Frederic's depiction of the hardships and monotony of rural life exceptionally frank. *In the Valley,* Frederic's next novel, is a historical epic which traces the lives of a group of Dutch settlers in New York's Mohawk Valley. Set primarily during the American Revolution, the novel is heavily symbolic; characterization, however, "remained shadowy," as Frederic later admitted. *In the Valley* received mixed reviews, but today some commentators credit Frederic with the revival of the genre of historical fiction in America. These two novels along with *The Lawton Girl*, a sequel to *Seth's Brother's Wife*, display Frederic's plan to create a consistent fictional setting with reappearing characters and settings. A controversial novel in its time, *The Lawton Girl* portrays the life of an unwed mother in the fictional town of Thessaly, New York, and articulates the problems faced by a village on the brink of becoming industrialized. In *The Return of the O'Mahony*, a romantic adventure novel about an American who inherits an estate in Ireland, Frederic uses satire and humor to convey his views about Home Rule for Ireland. *The Copperhead, Marsena*, and Frederic's two collections of short stories, *In the Sixties* and *The Deserter and Other Stories: A Book of Two Wars*, all set during the Civil War, deal in an unsentimental, objective fashion with personal and national conflicts of the period. Frederic's greatest popular and critical success was *The Damnation of Theron Ware* (published in England as *Illumination*). Here he traces the spiritual disintegration of Theron Ware, a rural Methodist minister who is beguiled by the progressive ideas and free behavior of his neighbors. With their encouragement, he abandons his stable way of life for theirs, only to be rejected as a "bore." While some critics lauded the novel as an example of a new realistic style in American literature, a brilliant exposé of small town and religious hypocrisy, and a probing psychological study of intellectual vanity, others deemed the study of a minister's corruption cynical and immoral. *The Damnation of Theron Ware* was the most popular and controversial novel of 1896. In the same year, Frederic also published *March Hares*, a romance based on his relationship with Kate Lyon, and *Mrs. Albert Grundy: Observations in Philistia*, a series of witty satirical sketches about contemporary London life. Most reviewers dismissed *March Hares* as unworthy of Frederic's talents, but others praised his light, humorous tone. Critics often refer to Frederic's posthumous novels, *Gloria Mundi* and *The Market-Place*, as his "English novels" because they are set in England and critique numerous aspects of English society. Generally regarded as one of Frederic's weakest productions, *Gloria Mundi* traces the problems faced by a young man who inherits a dukedom. *The Market-Place* follows the dealings of a ruthless businessman who later turns to philanthropy. Its hero, a type of Nietzschean superman, inspired both admiration and scorn. The novel has evoked lively critical reaction since its publication, and some critics now rank the work as second only to *The Damnation of Theron Ware*.

Assessment of Frederic's literary stature has undergone a remarkable transformation. Though his novels and short stories were praised by such influential nineteenth-century critics as Crane, William Dean Howells, and Gertrude Atherton, Frederic's contribution to American literature was largely ignored during his lifetime. In the early twentieth century, both Fred Lewis Pattee and Vernon L. Parrington declared some of Frederic's work "depressing" and "drab," setting the tone for later studies. Frederic was also criticized for applying journalistic standards to literature and for his frequently hasty composition. Since the 1960s, however, Frederic's works have undergone extensive revaluation. Modern critics commend Frederic's perceptive character studies, exploration of American values, and skillful interweaving of romance elements with sociological realism. His early New York state novels are ad-

mired for breaking through outmoded regionalist conventions and achieving a verisimilitude new to American literature. In addition, some critics compare Frederic's evocation of a fictional setting to William Faulkner's portrayal of Yoknapawtawpha County, and liken his exploration of American values to those of Hawthorne and Herman Melville. Today, *The Damnation of Theron Ware* is still considered Frederic's best work due to the intense psychological study of the novel's protagonist and his probing of the limitations of New World innocence. Though commentators still debate whether or not Theron's fall is too precipitous, almost all agree that the novel is valuable both as a literary work and as a social document. Many critics concur with Everett Carter, who placed *The Damnation of Theron Ware* "among the four or five best novels written by an American during the nineteenth century." Today, scholars are studying Frederic's writings with renewed interest and his reputation as an important nineteenth-century American novelist has been reaffirmed.

(See also *Dictionary Of Literary Biography*, Vol. 12: *American Realists and Naturalists*.)

## *PRINCIPAL WORKS

*Seth's Brother's Wife*   (novel)   1887
*The Lawton Girl*   (novel)   1890
*In the Valley*   (novel)   1890
*The Young Emperor William II of Germany: A Study in Character Development on a Throne*   (essays)   1891
*The New Exodus: A Study of Israel in Russia*   (essays) 1892
*The Return of the O'Mahony*   (novel)   1892
*The Copperhead*   (novel)   1893
*The Damnation of Theron Ware*   (novel)   1896; also published as *Illumination*, 1896
*March Hares* [as George Forth]   (novel)   1896
*Marsena*   (novel)   1896
*Mrs. Albert Grundy: Observations in Philistia*   (sketches) 1896
*In the Sixties*   (short stories)   1897
*The Deserter and Other Stories: A Book of Two Wars* (short stories)   1898
*Gloria Mundi*   (novel)   1898
*The Market-Place*   (novel)   1899
*The Harold Frederic Edition*. 2 vols. to date.   (letters and novel)   1977-

*Most of Frederic's novels were originally published serially in magazines.

---

*THE NEW YORK TIMES*   (essay date 1887)

Not only does the author give us the social aspect of a country family of some importance in New-York State [in **"Seth's Brother's Wife"**], but he presents, as one familiar with such subjects, their political aims and aspirations. . . .

Only close familiarity with the scenes he describes could have given Mr. Frederic the power to write as he does. **"Seth's Brother's Wife"** is something quite apart from other romances, being essentially American, and giving a phase of social political life in the country which has never been before written.

*"Mr. Frederic's Novel," in* The New York Times, *November 27, 1887, p. 14.*

## WILLIAM WALLACE   (essay date 1890)

*The Lawton Girl* is a strong story by the author of that remarkable book, *Seth's Brother's Wife.* One is reminded of [Nathaniel Hawthorne's] *The Scarlet Letter* by the sin of Jessica Lawton, which in this volume she nobly lives, and dies, down. But in no other respect does this book recall Hawthorne, whose influence cannot be traced in it. It is a book not so much of remarkable incidents—although Jessica Lawton's final act of self-sacrifice is a piece of powerful description—but of contrasts in character. Horace Boyce, selfish, weak, yet not irretrievably bad, is contrasted on the one hand with his honest, resolute, and sagacious though not astute partner, Reuben Tracy, and on the other with his own father, who, though more of a Bohemian, is less of a scoundrel than himself. He is even contrasted with the "superior fiends" in the form of mercantile swindlers in Thessaly and New York, who for a time utilise him. Then Kate Minster is contrasted at almost every third page with her mother, and Jessica both with her father and her sisters. Indeed, the one fault to be found with *The Lawton Girl* is that one is perpetually asked in it to look upon this picture and on this. It is, however, one of the best, most pathetic, and, in the highest sense, most humorous books which have come even from America within the past few years. It is, too, a decided advance, from the artistic standpoint, upon *Seth's Brother's Wife.*

> *William Wallace, in a review of "The Lawton Girl,"*
> *in* The Academy, *Vol. XXXVII, No. 941, May 17,*
> *1890, p. 333.*

## [WILLIAM DEAN HOWELLS]   (essay date 1890)

> *[Howells was the chief progenitor of American realism and the most influential American literary critic during the late nineteenth century. He was the author of nearly three dozen novels, few of which are read today. Despite his eclipse, he stands as one of the major literary figures of the nineteenth century: he successfully weaned American literature from the sentimental romanticism of its infancy, earning the popular sobriquet "the Dean of American Letters." Though he criticizes Frederic's inability to animate his historical novel,* In the Valley, *Howells comments favorably on* Seth's Brother's Wife *and* The Lawton Girl. *He emphasizes that Frederic's depiction of local politics is one of "the newest and best things in his story of* Seth's Brother's Wife."]

A fresh instance of the fatuity of the historical novel as far as the portrayal of character goes, is Mr. Harold Frederic's story, *In the Valley.* We do not mean to say that it is not very well written, and all that; it is uncommonly well written, and the whole *mise en scène* has verity and importance, for the valley of the Hudson, at the moment before the Revolution broke out, is new to romance, and it is certainly picturesque. But after we have owned the excellence of the staging in every respect, and the conscience with which the carpenter (as the theatrical folks say) has done his work, we are at the end of our praises. The people affect us like persons of our generation made up for the parts; well trained, well costumed, but actors, and almost amateurs. They have the quality that makes the histrionics of amateurs endurable; they are ladies and gentlemen; the worst, the wickedest of them is a lady or gentleman behind the scene.

We make the freer to say these things of Mr. Frederic's historical romance because it gives us the occasion to do grateful homage to his novels of contemporary life, which we have hitherto let go by. . . . It is a loss not to have known till now two books so robust, so sound, so honest as *Seth's Brother's Wife* and *The Lawton Girl.* They have to do with country, village, and minor city life in central New York, and they touch it at a great many points, both on the surface and below it. The metaphysics and ethics of the books are very good; the soul and its affairs are decidedly not left out of the account; and Mr. Frederic shows himself acquainted with the deeps as well as the shallows of human nature. But what seem to us the newest and best things in his story of *Seth's Brother's Wife* are his dramatic studies of local politics and politicians. These are rendered as we find them in the field of actualities, and as the newspapers, from which Mr. Frederic seems to have got his training for literature, know them. The Boss of Jay County, with his simple instinct of ruling and his invulnerability to bribes, is an example of Mr. Frederic's fidelity to conditions not much understood by people out of politics, which are managed by ambition rather than by money, as a general thing. Next to this in value is the truth, almost as novel, with which farm life, inside and out, is painted: it is so true that as you read you can almost smell the earthy scent of the shut-up country parlors; and the sordid dulness of those joyless existences lies heavy on the heart. The vigor with which the type of rustic murderer is worked out in the hired man Martin excuses the resort to the grand means for evolving character, which Mr. Frederic is rather apt to permit himself when they are not necessary. He shows a prentice touch in this more than in anything else, in both books; but in *The Lawton Girl* the characterization of the cheap young reprobate Horace Boyce is masterly; and the elder scoundrel, Judge Wendover, who uses him, is quite as satisfyingly good. In its way, the portrait of Mrs. Minster's respectability and mere wealthiness is excellent; and the decayed soldier in General Boyce is finely done. (pp. 800-01)

> *[William Dean Howells], in a review of "Seth's Brother's Wife" and "The Lawton Girl," in* Harper's New Monthly Magazine, *Vol. LXXXI, No. CCCCLXXXV, October, 1890, pp. 800-01.*

## FRANK DANBY [PSEUDONYM OF JULIA FRANKAU] (essay date 1896)

> *[Danby traces the critical reception of Frederic's novels in England. In her review of* Illumination, *she praises Frederic's portrayal of background and characterization, except for the character of Celia, who "is interesting but never absorbing."]*

As a novelist Mr. Harold Frederic has hitherto failed to receive in England the recogntion that is his due. **"Seth's Brother's Wife"** and **"The Lawton Girl"** may have been overestimated in the States, where they sold by their hundred thousand, and their author was acclaimed yet another American Dickens; but they were distinctly underestimated here, where they were only dribbled out to the circulating libraries in grudging dozens and half-dozens. Yet they are admirable stories, well told, well set. His next ventures in England in this line were **"In the Valley"** and **"The Copperhead."** Both dealt with unfamiliar types, set in unfamiliar scenes, but the author, notwithstanding his undeniable talents, lacked just that touch of genius which could have focussed them to illuminative and vivid points. But **"The Return of the O'Mahony"** was ten times as subtle, as humorous, as full of invention, characterization, and incident as, say, [Anthony Hope Hawkins's] "The Prisoner of Zenda"; yet in lack of popular success it shared the fate of its predecessors. It was never "talked about"; it excited no general interest; nobody wrote letters to the papers about its political signification or its moral tone; it inspired no parody in "Punch," and had not even the good fortune to offend the susceptibilities of the suburbs. Some explanation is necessary, then, to account for the comparative deadness of this capable novelist in the booksellers' world.

Such explanation seems to me to be twofold. The first is his lack of knowledge of the great art of *réclame.* . . . The second part of the explanation is that Mr. Frederic lacks the intuitive business faculties of our more prominent novelists. To use a Stock Exchange phrase, he "misses his market." **"The Lawton Girl"** was at least five years in advance of the "sexual question" mania, and the promiscuous intercourse of the sexes was not considered acceptable subject-matter for "copy" when the book appeared. His Irish book was given to the world just at the moment when the very name of Ireland stank stalely in the nostrils of press and people. . . . There was no Cuban revolt to stimulate interest in the American politicians of **"The Copperhead,"** nor Venezuelan Boundary Question to draw attention to **"In the Valley."**

Now it remains to be seen what **"Illumination"** . . . will do for its author's reputation. (p. 295)

The background has been wrought at with infinite care and precision, and commensurate success. Michael is a beautiful character, vividly and exquisitely painted. The Soulsbys, whose peculiar profession as "debt raisers" is unknown here, are creations who alone would make the book repay perusal. Levi Gorringe is a fine study. But there are loose ends in the story. Thereon, with the effect upon him of Celia's fascinations, is well realized; but Celia herself is imperfect; her relations with the priest are ill defined, her love for her brothers vaguely indicated, the motives which move her in her flirtation with Thereon less than intelligible. Perhaps Mr. Frederic intentionally portrayed her with the inconsistencies of her sex; if so, the mistake lies in the intention, otherwise in the execution, a fault less credible in so conscientious an author. Under the circumstances, his Circe is interesting but never absorbing; and this flaw in the principal character injures the book, which reflects in a measure the characteristics of the heroine.

To sum up with a prophecy, **"Illumination"** will not appeal to a sensation-loving and illiterate public, and it will fail to completely satisfy Harold Frederic's friends and admirers. It will not raise him to his due position among contemporary novelists, but it deepens the feeling we have that he is a very able man to whom fortune has been conspicuously unfair. (pp. 295-96)

*Frank Danby [pseudonym of Julia Frankau], "Mr. Harold Frederic's New Novel," in* The Saturday Review, *London, Vol. 81, No. 2108, March 21, 1896, pp. 295-96.*

**THE WAVE** (essay date 1896)

[*The reviewer considers* The Damnation of Theron Ware "*really an important novel," but questions "the truth of the situations" and the motivations of the characters. Too, the critic suggests that Theron's corruption is perhaps too "involuntary" to be truly convincing. This review was originally published in* The Wave *on April 25, 1896.*]

To the consideration of *The Damnation of Theron Ware,* the latest of Harold Frederic's novels, one brings the respect its announcements evoke. Certain critics have spoken of it as "the book of the year." It is really an important novel. (p. 281)

The elements, having combined the plot, move irresistibly onwards. (p. 282)

There seems no difficulty in the establishment of an understanding between this Methodist minister and the Irish daughter of Jerry Madden, and here is one of the weak points of the book. It but partially explains the condition which meets us, to say that the guilelessness of Theron Ware attracts these bolder spirits. However agreeable is intercourse with an innocent and kindly soul the pleasure inspired is contemplative rather than personal. Perhaps the girl's interest in the priest may be held to explain the sudden growth of her anomalous intimacy with the minister. The character of this interest, the manner of her relation with Father Forbes, is suggested so vaguely, so indefinitely, that one theory or another is tenable or confutable by the evidence of separate incidents. That Celia is sufficiently emancipated from conventionality to be friendly with whomsoever she chooses, may be true, but is not the selection of a Methodist parson as the object of devotion as improbable as the incident of a Catholic priest alluding in the presence of this same Methodist parson to the "Christ myth"? (p. 283)

From incident to event the author continues the narrative of Theron Ware's damnation. After [a] curious interview with Sister Soulsby he is introduced into the home of Celia Madden, whose character takes on a more inexplicable air as the book develops. The scene in her strangely furnished rooms however unreal is fascinating and highly dramatic, and in the modulation of the attitudes of minister and girl, there is the highest literary tact. Passing from this to the scene at Thurston's, and the interview with Doctor Ledsmar, to the camp meeting, which is as strong and graphic a situation as the Revival, to the dialogue between Ware, Celia, and Father Forbes in the wood, which culminates in Celia's kiss—then the warning of the dying Michael, who upbraids the minister's inconstancy and infidelity, and finally the trip to New York after Miss Madden and the priest—each accentuates the degeneration of poor Theron Ware. He is the victim of his own vain and hapless imaginings, a bubble on the wave of fate, tossed by events, and thrown, bruised and bleeding, against the rocks of worldliness.

The final scenes which follow the brutal awakening of the unfortunate Ware, when he flees, seeking to hide himself after the cruel speeches of the woman he so vainly adores, are expressed with rare power and restraint. Indeed, considering the book, there can be no question of its great ability, or of the vivid interest its narrative inspires. There is serious doubt, however, of the truth of the situations; we suspect the probabilities of such unconscious degeneration; it seems impossible that the conditions postulated should precipitate so involuntary a downfall. It seems so useless the game these various characters play against the unfortunate minister; his disillusion is so gratuitous, so merciless. One asks oneself what is the object of Celia's attentions and Father Forbes' interest—of Levi Gorringe's action?

Harold Frederic has left too many riddles.

*"A Degenerate Methodist," in* American Literary Realism 1870-1910, *Vol. 9, No. 3, Summer, 1976, pp. 281-84.*

**F. Y. ECCLES**   (essay date 1896)

*Illumination,* in spite of such obvious faults as a loose-jointed construction and a deluge of slang, is a really remarkable book. Theron Ware's character is developed with the most rigorous logic, and the complex Celia Madden is a genuine creation. Nor can one easily forget Sister Soulsby, the revivalist with a past, who receives the minister into her house after his catastrophe. The author deserves much praise for his restraint: to have devoted a large space to conversation on aesthetic and theological subjects without being tedious, and without giving an impression of desiring to "improve the occasion," or to do anything else but carry the story forward, is a considerable achievement in itself.

> *F. Y. Eccles, in a review of "Illumination," in* The Academy, *Vol. L, No. 126, July 4, 1896, p. 10.*

**THE ATLANTIC MONTHLY**   (essay date 1896)

[*The author of this review of* The Damnation of Theron Ware *expresses concern about the credibility of the novel because "Theron Ware damns himself, and his three accusers seem to get off scot-free."*]

The practiced novel-reader enters upon [*The Damnation of Theron Ware*] with keen anticipation of pleasure.... This feeling that he is in the hands of a master of fiction remains with him pretty much all through the First Part, which relates the experiences of a young Methodist minister and his wife, disappointed in their hopes of a flourishing parish, and shoved aside into a mean living in a large country town having a considerable Irish population. The description of the Conference in the opening chapter is graphic and quietly humorous, and the setting of the young couple in Octavius is so managed as to convey at once a good notion of a petty parish, in which the minister finds himself subjected to the ignoble tyranny of ignorant trustees. This minister, Theron Ware, with his ambition and his immaturity, is partially introduced; at least so the reader comes to think afterward, for on looking back, at the end of the story, he is reminded of the rather slight intimations given of Theron's native character before it is brought to the test. The novel, one premises from the title, has for its main purpose the disclosure of the history of a human soul. (p. 270)

The sharp contrast between Theron Ware's poverty-stricken surroundings and the richness of this Catholic world is set forth all the more admirably that the reader is not for a moment deluded into thinking he is to be invited to witness anything like conversion from the one faith to the other. Not this way does Theron Ware's damnation lie.... [The priest, the Irish girl, and Dr. Ledsmar,] by a sort of tacit agreement, amuse themselves with the innocent young parson. One of the felicities of the book is the skillful manner in which the reader's mind is drawn off from this view of the case until the dénouement, and his attention fixed upon Theron Ware as he subjects himself to the criticism of the three.

The real plotter against Theron's simplicity is the girl, Celia Madden, and it is in the relation between the two that the artificiality of the story appears. It is not impossible to concede the psychological facts of Theron Ware's slumping,—we can find no other single word to express the change from a conventionally good man into a noxious reptile,—but we question the naturalness of the means as elaborated by Mr. Frederic. He has conceived a man of some intellectual and emotional readiness, with a meagre education and very limited knowledge of the world; inoffensively virtuous through lack of opportunity for vice, but with no genuine foundation for his character. He has intended to make him not merely amiable, but rather attractive in his untried ingenuousness.... Mr. Frederic had a difficult task to perform in delineating a character which should seem [interesting] ... to persons with the angle of vision which the priest, Celia Madden, and Dr. Ledsmar had, and should at the same time be normal and ordinary enough to his wife and neighbors, while the reader was slowly to penetrate the real consciousness of the man. It is a task performed with unusual skill, and with a pardonable amount of open analysis; but in performing his task Mr. Frederic found it necessary to make Celia Madden play the part of fictitious temptress to this very feeble St. Anthony, and it is here that one feels the distortion of nature. It was well enough to present Celia Madden as rich, handsome, clever-mouthed, free with bravado; but to invest her with all the furnishings of her sybaritic apartment, to represent her as using the blandishments of dress upon poor Theron (effecting a change, by the way, in a period of time which would be brief for a variety actress), to make her try the effect of a sort of musical cathartic upon the minister's rigidly conventional conscience,—this portion of the story strikes one as very artificial and out of key. Nevertheless, one returns with the feeling that the scheme of the book is sound; that in the separate characters of the group of three as seen by the reader there is a latent quality which would account for their attitude toward the young minister; for the story in its unconscious intention is a damnation also of these three. Our contention is that in the half-sketch of Dr. Ledsmar there is too much left for us to guess, and that the part Celia has to play is illustrated by abnormal incidents; the priest alone is satisfactorily characterized.

There is one minor character, Celia's brother Michael, who deserves high praise. His outline is admirably drawn, and the scene in which he holds the mirror up to Theron Ware's face is most effective. As to the debt-raisers, Soulsby and Sister Soulsby, given the rather unbelievable premise of their past career, they are cleverly drawn and highly entertaining. The Methodist scenes throughout are very vivid, and though highly accented do not impress one as caricatures,—a statement not so surely made of Sister Soulsby. Most readers, we think, will say that the master stroke is in the last page, where Theron is shown, after his recovery from the shame of his exposure to himself, as just the same man he was in the beginning. It would be hard to find a sadder book, if one were looking for a pitiless illumination of a whited sepulchre. Nevertheless, we set it aside with the conviction that Mr. Frederic has overreached himself, for he leaves in the reader's mind an instinctive revolt against the fairness of the record. On this showing, indeed, Theron Ware damns himself, and his three accusers seem to get off scot-free; but in the higher court of human reason one feels that the upright judge would question more thoroughly the credibility of some of the evidence, as not agreeing wholly with the facts of human nature. (pp. 271-72)

> *"Mr. Frederic's 'The Damnation of Theron Ware',"* in The Atlantic Monthly, *Vol. LXXVIII, No. CCCCLXVI, August, 1896, pp. 270-72.*

**THE CRITIC,** New York   (essay date 1896)

[*In this positive review of* March Hares, *the critic asserts that the novel is Frederic's "declaration of independence" from realism.*]

Mint sauce is of no particular value unless it is associated with roast mutton, and Mr. Harold Frederic's new story, **"March Hares,"** is in itself a freakish and inconsiderable, though distinctly engaging, morsel of literature. Taken in connection with **"The Damnation of Theron Ware,"** however, it acquires sudden importance and affords the reader a delight which is not at all dependent upon its intrinsic merits and is perhaps disproportionate to them. It is said that the composition of Mr. Frederic's serious realistic novel about which all the world is still talking, required five years. The intimacy of the creative atmosphere is very exacting, and many readers of the book have wondered how the author endured the task of living with his interesting but most unlovable characters for so long a time. **"March Hares"** flatters us into believing that we have discovered this secret of the novelist's workshop. When his soul wearied of the dun-colored waste of Octavius, N.Y., and the degeneration going on there, he simply bundled that manuscript into a pigeon-hole and wrote a few pages of **"March Hares"** by way of giving himself an absolute change of scene. Nominally this little story is located in London, but its real setting is the New Arcadia. It owns no allegiance to reality, and the characters are only tied to this leaden world by their need for food and apparel. Consistency is not their jewel, and they pay no heed to the conventions of life. They meet and converse and part with the nonchalance and freedom of disembodied spirits. You may call them mad if you like. Their creator has discounted your scorn by his descriptive title; but their insanity is pretty and innocent and true to dreams, though direfully false to life.

The book is, in effect, a declaration of independence. Mr. Frederic might have written a prettier idyl, but not one which would more perfectly proclaim his freedom from the traditions of any school of literature. It is as if he put his hands in his pockets and said to the reader: ''The real world is a fine place, and it is the scene of our conflict, but come with me and see how good it is to get away from it for a while. I have proved that I know how to do realistic things as well as the next man, but I will be hanged if I am going to do them all the time!'' There is something refreshing and contagious about this attitude. Whether it produces literature or not, it commends itself as a mental gymnastic exercise, and certainly it would prevent a writer from taking himself too seriously in any one direction. Do all the earnest novelists have some similar method of relaxing, one wonders? Does Mr. Howells ever disport himself in Wonderland? Has even Mrs. Humphry Ward her hours of ease? Assuredly the habit ought to be universal, and copies of **"March Hares"** might well be distributed among those authors who are weighed down by their obligations to the actual, with the injunction, ''Realists, please copy!''

*A review of "March Hares," in* The Critic, New York, *n.s. Vol. XXVI, No. 764, October 10, 1896, p. 209.*

### THE NINETEENTH CENTURY    (essay date 1896)

[*In this appreciative review of* Illumination, *the English title of* The Damnation of Theron Ware, *the critic suggests that Theron's "better nature" was undermined by his "latent mean qualities" and urges the reader to decide whether the ending is indeed sad.*]

The moral deterioration of the Reverend Theron Ware [in Harold Frederic's **'Illumination'**], a young American Methodist minister in charge of a number of unpleasant souls who wanted 'straight-out, flat-footed hell' in their sermons, at Octavius,

U.S.A., is a singularly powerful study. It is interesting even in its weaker places, and notable for many of those pages of brilliant description which Mr. Frederic sometimes flashes before his readers just when they are beginning to discover they are bored. But in **'Illumination'** there are few opportunities for boredom, even though the local politics of a narrow and ignorant Methodist community, somewhere in the heart of New England, are not in themselves alluring, while the terrible Yankee jargon does, for all that may be said about its raciness, too often grate on English nerves. Theron Ware's history contains little enough of plot or action. He is treated badly by many people, and entirely demoralised by a pretentiously intelligent and unscrupulous woman, but his sufferings and wrongdoings are all of a subjective order. The interest of the book lies in the masterly drawing of this man's character, in the experiences which develop its latent mean qualities to the gradual subversion of his better nature, and of his happiness with his wife while dominated by an influence which he took to be a superior one.

It is the tale of the bull-frog over again, a poor little bull-frog who might have been good and happy if only a female vivisectionist had not encouraged him to attempt impossible feats of expansion and then abandoned him when the results were troublesome and uninteresting.

Celia Madden, the papist, began by playing Theron's soul away with her music and by the use of grosser arts in strange assortment with an assumption of personal distinction and refinement. She subsequently brought him 'illumination' in various disastrous forms, but on the whole she is a less convincing, more indefinite piece of character drawing than are the other women, the poor simple wife, who rings so true, and Sister Soulsby, that delightful mountebank who proves the Wares' good angel. It is not easy to realise her creator's intentions with regard to Celia, but most readers will accept her old friend Dr. Ledsmar's description of her in a moment of petulance, as more seriously accurate than he intended—'A mere bundle of egotism, ignorance, and red-headed immodesty . . . with a small brain addled by notions that she is like Hypatia, and a large impudence rendered intolerable by the fact that she has money.'

The interest of the reader is carried on from one striking scene or brilliant piece of description to another, with but little drooping over intermediate passages of lesser merit and more uncertain delineation. Amongst the most powerful must be named . . . the death of the workman, where Theron first meets Celia and sees the impressive last rites of the Roman Church; the revivalist meeting where, already half disillusioned, he watches with consternation his wife going through the process of conversion supported by Lawyer Gorringe, and last but not least the weird and semi-grotesque effects of the camp meeting in the forest. Whether the end be altogether unhappy the reader must decide for himself. Things might certainly have been many degrees worse both for Theron and his wife. (pp. 768-70)

*A review of "Illumination," in* The Nineteenth Century, *Vol. XL, No. CCXXXVII, November, 1896, pp. 768-70.*

### HAROLD FREDERIC    (essay date 1897)

[*In this preface to his* In the Sixties, *originally published in 1897, Frederic discusses his goals and methods in writing* In the Valley, Seth's Brother's Wife, The Lawton Girl, *and his Civil War stories.*]

[The stories of **"In the Sixties"**] were all, it is true, written in England, but they do not belong to the Old World in any other sense. In three of them, the very existence of Europe is scarcely so much as hinted at. The fourth concerns itself, indeed, with events in which Europeans took an active part; but what they were doing, on the one side and on the other, was in its results very strictly American.

The idea which finally found shape and substance in this last named book, **"In the Valley"**, seems now in retrospect to have been always in my mind. All four of my great-grandfathers had borne arms in the Revolutionary War, and one of them indeed somewhat indefinitely expanded this record by fighting on both sides. My earliest recollections are of tales told by my grandmother about local heroes of this conflict, who were but middle-aged people when she was a child. She herself had come into curious relation with one of the terrible realities of that period. At the age of six it was her task to beat linen upon the stones of a brook running through the Valley farm upon which she was reared, and the deep-hole close beside where she worked was the spot in which the owner of the farm had lain hidden in the alders, immersed to his chin, for two days and nights while Brant's Indians were looking for him. Thus, by a single remove I came myself into contact with the men who held Tryon County against the King, and my boyish head was full of them. (pp. 1-2)

[But in 1885] I realized that I had consumed nearly ten years in fruitless mooning over my Revolutionary novel, and was no nearer achievment than at the outset, simply because I did not know how to make a book of any kind, let alone a historical book of the kind which should be the most difficult and exacting of all. This determined me to proceed with the contemporary story I had begun—if only to learn what it was really like to cover a whole canvas. The result was **"Seth's Brother's Wife"**. . . . (p. 3)

At the time I thought of this novel almost wholly in the light of preparation for the bigger task I had to do, and it is still easiest for me to so regard it. Certainly its completion, and perhaps still more the praise which was given to it by those who first saw it, gave me a degree of confidence that I had mastered the art of fiction which I look back upon now with surprise—and not a little envy. It was in the fine flush of this confidence that I hastened to take up the real work, the book I had been dreaming of so long; and, despite the immense amount of material in the shape of notes, cross-references, dates, maps, biographical facts and the like which I had perforce to drag along with me, my ardor maintained itself to the finish. **"In the Valley"** was written in eight months—and that too at a time when I had also a great deal of newspaper work to do as well.

**"The Lawton Girl"** suggested itself at the outset as a kind of sequel to **"Seth's Brother's Wife"**, but here I found myself confronted by agencies and influences the existence of which I had not previously suspected. In **"Seth's Brother's Wife"** I had made the characters do just what I wanted them to do, and the notion that my will was not altogether supreme had occurred neither to them nor to me. The same had been true of **"In the Valley"**, where indeed the people were so necessarily subordinated to the evolution of the story which they illustrated rather than shaped, that their personalities always remained shadowy in my own mind. But in **"The Lawton Girl"**, to my surprise at first, and then to my interested delight, the people took matters into their own hands quite from the start. It seemed only by courtesy that I even presided over their meetings, and

that my sanction was asked for their comings and goings. As one of many examples, I may cite the interview between Jessica and Horace in the latter's office. In my folly, I had prepared for her here a part of violent and embittered denunciation, full of scornful epithets and merciless jibes; to my discomfiture, she relented at the first sight of his grey hair and troubled mien, when I had brought her in, and would have none of my heroics whatever. Once reconciled to the posture of a spectator, I grew so interested in the doings of these people that I lost sight of a time-limit; they wandered along for two years, making the story in leisurely fashion as they went. At the end I did assert my authority, and kill Jessica—she who had not deserved or intended at all to die—but I see now more clearly than anyone else that it was a false and cowardly thing to do.

There remains the volume of collected stories, long and short, dealing with varying aspects of home life in the North—or rather in my little part of the North—during the Civil War. These stories are by far closer to my heart than any other work of mine, partly because they seem to me to contain the best things I have done or ever shall do, partly because they are so closely interwoven with the personal memories and experiences of my own childhood—and a little also, no doubt, for the reason that they have not had quite the treatment outside that paternal affection had desired for them. Of all the writers whose books affected my younger years, I think that MM. Eckmann-Chatrian exerted upon me the deepest and most vital influence. I know that my ambition to paint some small pictures of the life of my Valley, under the shadow of the vast black cloud which was belching fire and death on its southern side, in humble imitation of their studies of Alsatian life in the days of the Napoleonic terror, was much more powerful than any impulse directly inspired by any other writers. By this confession I do not at all wish to suggest comparisons. The French writers dealt with a period remote enough to be invested with a haze of romance, and they wrote for a reading public vehemently interested in everything that could be told them about that period. These stories of mine lack these aids—and doubtless much else beside. But they are in large part my own recollections of the dreadful time—the actual things that a boy of from five to nine saw and heard about him, while his own relatives were being killed, and his school-fellows orphaned, and women of his neighborhood forced into mourning and despair—and they had a right to be recorded.

A single word in addition to an already over-long preface. The locality which furnishes the scenes of the two contemporary novels and all the War stories may be identified in a general way with Central New York, but in no case is it possible to connect any specific village or town with one actually in existence. The political exigencies of **"Seth's Brother's Wife"** made it necessary to invent a Congressional District, composed of three counties, to which the names of Adams, Jay and Dearborn were given. Afterwards the smaller places naturally took names reflecting the quaint operation of the accident which sprinkled our section, as it were, with the contents of a classical pepper-box. Thus Octavius, Thessaly, Tyre and the rest came into being, and one tries to remember and respect the characterisics they have severally developed, but no exact counterparts exist for them in real life, and no map of the district has as yet been drawn, even in my own mind. (pp. 3-6)

*Harold Frederic, in a preface to his* The Correspondence of Harold Frederic, *George E. Fortenberry, Stanton Garner, Robert H. Woodward, eds., Texas Christian University Press, 1977, pp. 1-6.*

## M. E. WARDWELL   (essay date 1897)

*[Wardwell favorably evaluates Frederic's style, but posits that Frederic "understands women less thoroughly than men." He contends that Frederic has the ability to write a significant American novel, but adds that to do so, Frederic would have to return to the United States.]*

Many astute reviewers have already pitched upon Mr. Frederic as likely in the course of his career to achieve the long-expected novel which shall do for the United States in a significant social study what the novels of Balzac and Tolstoi and Thackeray have already done for France and Russia and England; and it must be owned that his ventures in fiction have displayed qualities that give these prophets some foundation for their confidences. (p. 152)

[Mr. Frederic is] a worker with the brush, sketching one telling scene after another of the human comedy as they play it in Central New York, animated, often invested with genuine humor. There is never the glut of detail at which one rebels among the New England chroniclers: his style is marked by rare virtues of directness and simplicity, disclosing no superfluous or wasted word, and moreover he succeeds . . . in creating atmosphere which is altogether a different thing from local color. His best work is undoubtedly to be found in the stories of the Civil War. It seems unlikely that he will ever excel 'The Copperhead' . . . with its sturdily drawn central figure of the farmer Abner standing like a rock to his wrong opinions, while a storm of partisan feeling and excitement swept about him no less violent than at the front of battle. We have heard much lately of the actual hand-to-hand fighting in that dramatic contest between North and South, and with Stephen Crane's lurid descriptions still fresh in the mind, these reverse glimpses of the effect of war upon the stay-at-homes are most tellingly effective.

But . . . Mr. Frederic has his limitations. He understands women less thoroughly than men, and the feminine presence is too apt to be vague and shadowy. Sister Soulsby, in 'Theron Ware,' has a distinct personality; Jessica Lawton becomes real at times, and then fades away elusively; and Celia, above all a Celia in Thessaly, approaches the impossible. In 'Theron Ware,' too, that very subtle and delicate flavor of Americanism seems for the first time to have escaped him. It is American still beyond question, yet America tempered by alien influences, and the America of memory, not of present reality. Has he stayed too long in London? This latest performance shows the taint of cynicism, the tendency to epigram, the fatalism that never flourished in the simple wind-swept valley of the Mohawk. Perhaps a succession of yellow fogs has driven out of his mind the recollection of the bright and bracing air in which we Americans live. He should come back to his native soil if he wishes to fulfil the promise of his youth in one direction. An American novel he may write in Piccadilly or among the green lanes of Devon, but *the* American novel, never! (pp. 152-53)

M. E. Wardwell, "Harold Frederic," in The Citizen, Vol. III, No. 7, September, 1897, pp. 152-53.

## STEPHEN CRANE   (essay date 1898)

*[Crane was one of Frederic's closest friends and one of America's foremost realistic writers; his works have been credited with marking the beginning of modern American Naturalism. Briefly evaluating Frederic's novels, Crane laments the critical neglect of Frederic's contribution to American literature and comments on the significance of Frederic's life abroad.]*

[Frederic's] book, *In the Sixties,* which contains *The Copperhead, Marsena, The War Widow, The Eve of the Fourth,* and *My Aunt Susan,* breathes the spirit of a Titanic conflict as felt and endured at the homes. One would think that such a book would have taken the American people by storm, but it is true that an earlier edition of *The Copperhead* sold less than a thousand copies in America. We have sometimes a way of wildly celebrating the shadow of a mullein-stalk against the wall of a woodshed, and remaining intensely ignorant of the vital things that are ours. I believe that at about the time of the appearance of these stories, the critics were making a great deal of noise in an attempt to stake the novelists down to the soil and make them write the impressive common life of the United States. This virtuous struggle to prevent the novelists from going ballooning off over some land of dreams and candy-palaces was distinguished by the fact that, contemporaneously, there was Frederic doing his locality, doing his Mohawk Valley, with the strong trained hand of a great craftsman, and the critics were making such a din over the attempt to have a certain kind of thing done, that they did not recognize its presence. All this goes to show that there are some painful elements in the art of creating an American literature by what may be called the rattley-bang method. The important figures, the greater men, rise silently, unspurred, undriven. To be sure, they may come in for magnificent cudgelings later, but their approach is noiseless, invincible, and they are upon us like ghosts before the critics have time to begin their clatter.

But there is something dismally unfortunate in the passing of *Seth's Brother's Wife, In The Valley,* the historical novel, and *The Lawton Girl.* Of course, they all had their success in measure, but here was a chance and a reason for every American to congratulate himself. Another thing had been done. For instance, *In the Valley* is easily the best historical novel that our country has borne. Perhaps it is the only good one. *Seth's Brother's Wife* and *The Lawton Girl* are rimmed with fine portrayals. There are writing men who, in some stories, dash over three miles at a headlong pace, and in an adjacent story move like a boat being sailed over ploughed fields; but in Frederic one feels at once the perfect evenness of craft, the undeviating worth of the workmanship. The excellence is always sustained, and these books form, with *In the Sixties,* a row of big American novels. But if we knew it we made no emphatic sign, and it was not until the appearance of *The Damnation of Theron Ware* that the book audiences really said: "Here is a writer!" If I make my moan too strong over this phase of the matter, I have only the excuse that I believe the *In the the Sixties* stories to form a most notable achievement in writing times in America. Abner Beech, the indomitable and ferocious farmer, with his impregnable disloyalty or conscience, or whatever; Aunt Susan always at her loom making rag-carpets which, as the war deepened, took on two eloquent colors—the blue of old army overcoats and the black of woman's mourning; the guileless Marsena and the simple tragedy of his death—these characters represent to me living people, as if the book breathed.

It is natural that since Frederic has lived so long in England, his pen should turn toward English life. One does not look upon this fact with unmixed joy. It is mournful to lose his work even for a time. It is for this reason that I have made myself disagreeble upon several occasions by my expressed views of *March Hares.* It is a worthy book, but one has a sense of desertion. We cannot afford a loss of this kind. But, at any rate, he has grasped English life with a precision of hand that is only equaled by the precision with which he grasped Irish life, and his new book will shine out for English eyes in a way with which they are not too familiar. It is a strong and striking delineation, free, bold, and straight.

In the mean time he is a prodigious laborer. Knowing the man and his methods, one can conceive him doing anything, unless it be writing a poor book, and, mind you, this is an important point. (p. 359)

> *Stephen Crane, "Harold Frederic," in* The Chap-Book, *Vol. VIII, No. 9, March 15, 1898, pp. 358-59.*

## GERTRUDE ATHERTON   (essay date 1898)

*[Atherton was an American novelist, biographer, short story writer, historian, and a leading feminist. Her eulogy on Frederic stresses his intellectualism and expresses the opinion that Frederic was underrated.]*

[Harold Frederic's] style could hardly have been improved upon, and he was by far the most intellectual of the American writers of fiction. We have a half-dozen famous men novelists in the United States who are brilliant, witty, subtle, keen of observation, and graceful, even exquisite of style, but we have none left with the depth and strength of mind, the masculinity the unselfconsciousness, and the broad humanity of Harold Frederic. In place of the national cleverness he had the genuine intellect of the older races, and while not lacking in delicacy of touch, he had none of the irritating thinness which characterises the typical American product. He was not always an agreeable writer by any means, and in all fiction there is no character so remorselessly developed as Theron Ware. You despise the man almost from the beginning, and yet to skip a page of **"Illumination"** would be beyond the power of any serious reader; this in spite of the book's length and its lack of one humorous line or one loveable character.... [**"Illumination"**] is so admirably sustained and proportioned, the analysis so searching, the picture of the life treated so accurate, and therefore valuable, and the performance generally on so high a mental plane, that the intelligent reader is thankful for every line. Frederic was obliged to leave the United States and come to England for recognition; there he was overshadowed by the Littleists who have created a false standard of excellence. But now that he is dead, it is to be hoped that the country will realise what it has lost, and give him a place among its classics. If he had lived ten years longer there can be no question that he would have had the satisfaction of seeing tardy justice done to his large gifts, his books at the top of all lists of American authors; for his friends feel sure that he would in time have let some of the humour and geniality of his nature into his work.

> *Gertrude Atherton, "Harold Frederic," in* The Bookman, *London, Vol. XV, No. 86, November, 1898, p. 37.*

## WILLIAM MORTON PAYNE   (essay date 1898)

[We have read Frederic's **"Gloria Mundi"**] with disappointment, for it is inferior to several of Frederic's earlier books, and for a reason not far to seek. In attempting to write of English society—and particularly of a section of that society with which he had no intimate associations—he exceeded his powers, and allowed the journalist in him to get the better of the artist. But all the devices of the most resourceful and inventive journalism make a poor substitute for observation, and no amount of reading or talking about people, however earnestly or cleverly done, will suffice for depicting them as the

novelist should. The lords and ladies of this novel are lay figures merely; they are sketched from the outside and at a distance; they have nothing of the glow and the vitality of the figures in the author's American novels. Even the hero, in whose case something more closely approaching the creative effect has been reached, remains baffling and elusive; one never knows just what he thinks or what he is going to do. Nor is the story helped by the vein of didacticism that runs through it. A part of the narrative deals with a Ruskinian social system—the hobby of one of the minor characters—but of this we must say that either too much or too little is made. We cannot find out whether or not the author believes in it, yet the prominence given it warrants a reader in asking the question. What we have said should not be taken as a condemnation of the story; we mean simply that it is by no means as good a story as Harold Frederic knew how to write. But it is always an interesting, and, in some of its episodes, a brilliant piece of narrative invention.

> *William Morton Payne, in a review of "Gloria Mundi: A Novel," in* The Dial, *Vol. XXV, No. 300, December 16, 1898, p. 459.*

## THE SATURDAY REVIEW LONDON   (essay date 1899)

*[The author of this mixed review of* The Market-Place *expresses uneasiness about Frederic's attractive portrayal of a morally flawed character.]*

[We have read Frederic's **"The Market Place"**] with zest and amusement. (p. 107)

[The bear squeeze, the business manoeuvre on which the novel is based,] is not impossible: indeed it has been executed several times in the last few years. But it is getting every day more dangerous and difficult. We think that in this case the bears would have found out about the bogus allotment, and that the Stock Exchange committee would have refused a special settlement. But take the "corner" for granted, and the book is exciting, amusing, and full of strong descriptions of character, which are none the less interesting because some of them—notably the Marquis of Chaldon, chairman of the board—are easily recognisable as living portraits. Thorpe sells twice over a concession which he knows to be worthless, and he calmly meditates murdering his gardener, who ... is aware of these facts. Yet it is impossible not to admire his nerve, his tenacity of purpose, his resourcefulness, in a word, his brain power. The broker Semple comes to him in a cold sweat at the mere rumour of an Old Bailey prosecution, and Thorpe, having taken the precaution to ship off the only witness under the care of one of his dummy directors, calmly bids him "keep his hair on." One or two touches, however, which are meant for magnanimity, are, we think, unworthy of a master like Frederic. A great deal, for instance, is made of Thorpe's affection for his sister, who keeps a book shop in the Strand, and for his nephew and niece, who are superior young persons. We are even asked to admire his desire, when he is wealthy, to do something for the London poor. All this is in the last degree commonplace. Many a villain is fond of his family, and Jabez Balfour gave large donations to charity and religion. A far finer touch is his generosity to Lord Chaldon, his chairman, the ex-diplomatist, with soft manners and an eyeglass, whom he presents with a cheque for £30,000, under no compulsion whatever.... We will not spoil the pleasure of possible readers by telling how Lord Plowden tries to ruin Thorpe by producing the man to whom he had sold the concession in Mexico, and how Thorpe beats his lordship by superior brains and energy. We must however say that we do not see how Plowden who was clever enough to see through the "corner" would have been ass enough to try to blackmail Thorpe in a very clumsy way. Thorpe succeeds as completely as [William Shakespeare's] Macbeth. He has it all—the country place, the titled wife, the liveried servants, and the fleet horses.

> "Thou hast it now, King, Cawdor, Glamis, all."

Harold Frederic could draw a gentleman, of whom he knew many, but he could not draw a lady, of whom he probably knew very few. He is not successful with his American heiress or with Lady Cressage. He is curiously unequal in his phrases, and he has deplorable lapses into vulgarity. For instance, Miss Madden discussing Thorpe with Lady Cressage, asks, "Have you looked into his eyes—I mean when they've got that lacklustre expression? You can see a hundred thousand dead men in them." That is a fine phrase. But then Lady Cressage says of Lord Plowden, "He is too smooth, too well-balanced, too much the gentleman." That is a vile phrase. What a phrase for a woman who is by way of being *"très smart"*! The main object of a novel, however, is to make you read it and that end **"The Market Place"** achieves. (p. 108)

> *"A Stock Exchange Romance," in* The Saturday Review, *London, Vol. 88, No. 2282, July 22, 1899, pp. 107-08.*

## THE BOOKMAN, LONDON (essay date 1899)

[*The author of this review of* The Market-Place *acknowledges that the novel is "a great piece of work" and its atmosphere, despite the "vileness," is "healthy and moral."*]

**"The Market Place"** is a great piece of work, incomparably the best novel of the year, a literary legacy that will be remembered, almost a heirloom. The weakness of Harold Frederic's other work is the strength of **"The Market Place,"** for the book owes its very being to the rush and struggle and turmoil of existence that destroyed its creator. It throbs with the hum of life, and the wild, mad chorus of the market-place rises from its pages crescendo to a tremendous finale.

To transfer the "City" to the printed page is a wonderful achievement. In **"The Market Place"** his multitudinous, extravagant, corrupt, but extraordinarily fascinating "city" lives, moves, and has its being. Harold Frederic must have had intimate acquaintance with its secrets, for there is not an impossible incident in his novel, and much is a transcript from reality. To many **"The Market Place"** will seem the wildest of extravaganzas . . . and a stirring, exciting romance, too. To those who possess the key to the book it is a ruthless exposure, a merciless satire. Both as satire and romance it is splendid reading.

**"The Market Place"** has been described as an immoral book—immoral because a barefaced scoundrel holds the readers' admiration. We admit that we have identified ourselves with few heroes of fiction as with Thorpe, and we feel an agony of suspense when the success of his audacious and dastardly coup wavers in the hands of the Stock Exchange Committee. We admit the fascination of a Napoleonic personality, a man of infinite resource, infinite courage, infinite self-confidence. We admit our admiration for a swindler. But against this you must set the whole atmosphere of the book, which it seems to us is healthy and moral. The vileness, the bestiality of the absorbing

lust of gold stands out in its pages in hideous relief. It is not Thorpe the swindler that attracts, but Thorpe the man of iron nerve and will. Such a display of power would fascinate under any circumstances in any situation.

**"The Market Place"** is one of the few men's novels. From title-page to colophon it is compact of virility. As a study of characters it is supreme, for there is not one single failure in the book, and as a romance of the "City" it has no equal in modern fiction.

> *J.E.H.W., "A Literary Legacy," in* The Bookman, *London, Vol. XVI, No. 95, August, 1899, p. 136.*

## ROBERT MORSS LOVETT (essay date 1924)

[*Lovett focuses on Frederic's "technical competence" in* The Damnation of Theron Ware *and provides a brief analysis of theme, characterization, structure, and its "singularly national" traits.*]

[Frederic's] realistic method, from the outset uncompromising, results in his novels being branded unmistakably for what they are. (p. v)

**The Damnation of Theron Ware** stands out beyond all question as Harold Frederic's masterpiece. Compared with it his earlier work is experimental and, in the case of **In the Valley,** labored. His later work is stereotyped and conventional. But for a moment, at the height of his career, Harold Frederic was, with the exception of Henry B. Fuller, the most promising American novelist. **Theron Ware** appeared the year after Mr. Fuller's fine novel *With the Procession.* Both are realistic studies of American life. In *With the Procession* the emphasis is rather on background, in **Theron Ware** on character. Both are singularly complete in their structure, and show a mastery of the novel form which no contemporary novelist except Henry James had attained. It is a satisfaction to dwell on the technical competence of these books at a time when the American novel was a groping and wavering effort.

**The Damnation of Theron Ware** is definite in its theme, and extremely workmanlike in the way in which the theme pervades the story. The pattern is exact, from the moment when the Wares receive their first disappointment, in the Reverend Theron's failure to be assigned by the Methodist Conference to Tecumseh, to that in which they turn with new hope to real estate in Seattle. The material is perfectly distributed throughout the structure, with indeed a certain symmetrical opposition between Theron Ware's new companions and interests, and his home and his church. . . . The adaptation of means to ends is precise, and artistically economical. The effect upon Theron Ware of the intellectual world of Father Forbes and Doctor Ledsmar, and that of the aesthetic world through the artistic and sexual charm of Celia Madden, are calculated to a nicety, and the buckling of his character under stress and strain is like the answer to an architect's problem in the resistance of materials. The book has therefore the highest dramatic quality. Drama is the poetry of character, as Stevenson tells us. In **The Damnation of Theron Ware** everything is fixed in terms of character. Character is the meter of the piece, and events answer to one another as rhymes in human action—the right thing invariably falling out in the right place.

The character of Theron Ware is a masterpiece of intellectual analysis. The personages who surround him are more freely and impressionistically presented. In the Soulsbys one may suspect a touch of satire, but it is so gravely carried off that suspicion dies. Other characters round out expectation in a highly satisfactory manner. Father Forbes and his view of his ecclesiastical function furnishes one of the contrasts which emphasize the design of the book. Alice Ware and Levi Gorringe are literally *right,* pure American of their period. The elder Madden and Michael have about them the pathos of the older world and an older race. In Celia only do we feel a sense of incompleteness. We see of her all that Theron Ware sees, but his vision is too remote to satisfy. Yet it was a sure instinct which led Harold Frederic to attempt no filling in of the outline. He had told us all he knew. His revival of Celia Madden in *The Market Place* proves this.

If precision of structure and skilful character drawing represented the full extent of the claim of *The Damnation of Theron Ware* to survival, that claim would probably be dismissed. But *Theron Ware,* like *Main Street* and *Babbitt* of a later date, is singularly national in its quality, without the overemphasis which gives a certain bitterness to the former, and humor to the latter. In choosing a background for a serious discussion of American life, Frederic naturally selected religion, as Mr. Lewis in *Babbitt* selected business. Religion naturally provided the basis of Theron Ware's association with his fellow men, as business, of Babbitt's. Each succumbed to the peculiar temptations of the situation, Ware's fall being the more catastrophic as his moral edifice was more pretentious. In Theron Ware, indeed, Harold Frederic discovered a typical line of faultage in American character. The temptation to which Ware was subjected was one to which the American is peculiarly susceptible, when the superiority of the pioneer gives way to the inferiority complex of the provincial—the temptation of a culture which is beyond his understanding complicated as it often is with a sexual desire which is beyond his satisfaction. Henry James has dealt with this theme in various forms, always in the background of Europe. Frederic used his European understanding to develop the same theme in America. He found the Roman Church with its century old system and its cosmopolitan associations ready to his hand to set against the Nedahma Methodist Conference. It is a graphic picture of America and the world, and the part which Theron Ware plays in it is almost prophetic. His shining supremacy is gone as soon as he leaves his own sphere; and he falls like Lucifer, from angel to dupe, liar and bore. But Theron Ware is not all of America—there are the Soulsbys, vessels of that instinctive wisdom, of that unmatched genius for putting the most incongruous materials together into a workable whole, that amounts almost to a folk trait. The Soulsbys know, what we suspect Theron Ware never discovers even in Seattle, how to live in an actual world. They are never the victims of their own aspirations or the dupes of their instruments. Thus they are sent with a special mission to the Theron Wares—and they make the best of a bad job. If only Woodrow Wilson had taken Sister Soulsby to Paris! (pp. viii-xii)

> *Robert Morss Lovett, "Harold Frederic," in* The Damnation of Theron Ware *by Harold Frederic, Albert & Charles Boni, 1924, pp. i-xii.*

**VERNON LOUIS PARRINGTON**   (essay date 1930)

[*An American historian, biographer, and critic, Parrington is best known for his unfinished literary history of the United States,* Main Currents in American Thought. *Though modern scholars now disagree with many of his conclusions, they view Parrington's work as a significant first attempt at fashioning an intellectual history of America based on a broad interpretive thesis. Written from the point of view of a Jeffersonian liberal,* Main Currents *in American Thought has proven a widely influential work in American criticism. In this excerpt from that work, Parrington assesses* Seth's Brother's Wife *as "drab" and "bitter."*]

*Seth's Brother's Wife,* by Harold Frederic, is a drab tale of farm life in upper York State, as bitter as any tale of the western border. It is a story of defeat, of flight from country to town. The blight of failure is upon the farming community—a blight that embitters old and young; and the sketches of country louts, of soured lives, of broken men and women, do not make pleasant reading. No gentle idyllic light rests on the landscape such as Sarah Orne Jewett discovers on the fields and villages of New England. Sabrina Fairchild, an old maid embittered by the family failure, yet clinging to the family pride and hopeful that the family prestige will be restored, is a pathetic and desolate figure, gaunt and sharp-tongued; at mortal feud with another pathetic old woman, who with her husband had emigrated from Massachusettts years before, and held herself proudly above the mean and vulgar neighborhood in which they had settled. The slack servants, gossipy and impudent, the petty lives, the grasping ways unrelieved by any grace or beauty, and set in a world of petty machine politics, make a drab and unattractive picture. Harold Frederic quite evidently hates this countryside that bred him. He will not, like Hamlin Garland, take up the battle for it against the town. He sees no hope in political programs; he is no Populistic agrarian fighting for justice; he wants only to escape from it to the city, where life may be lived more generously. The "trail of the serpent is over it all," he remarks, "rich and poor, big and little. The nineteenth century is a century of cities; they have given their own twist to the progress of the age—and the farmer is almost as far out of it as if he lived in Alaska. Perhaps there may have been a time when a man could live in what the poet calls daily communion with Nature and not starve his mind and dwarf his soul, but this isn't the century . . . get out of it as soon as you can." (pp. 288-89)

> *Vernon Louis Parrington, "Literature and the Middle Border," in his* Main Currents in American Thought: The Beginnings of Critical Realism in America, 1860-1920, *Vol. III, Harcourt Brace Jovanovich, Inc., 1930, pp. 228-300.*

**ARTHUR HOBSON QUINN**   (essay date 1936)

[*An early twentieth-century American critic, editor, and biographer, Quinn was a strong advocate for his native literature before it gained widespread appreciation. He taught the first graduate course devoted to American literature and edited the first collection of national drama while a professor at the University of Pennsylvania. In addition, he wrote several comprehensive critical and historical surveys of American literature that are still respected for their accurate and original research. In this excerpt from his* American Fiction: An Historical and Critical Survey, *Quinn provides an overview of Frederic's novels and short stories, ranking his novels "far above the average."*]

[*Seth's Brother's Wife*] is an excellent picture of the hard, bare life of a New York farm, of politics in upstate New York, and of the seamy side of journalism. All these were drawn from his own experience. The effect of the loneliness of the farm life upon Isabel Fairchild, her passion for Seth, her brother-in-law, and the way she interferes with the growing love between Seth and Annie Warren by absorbing the credit for saving Seth's life, are told with a realism and a directness that are admirable.

Frederic strips from the country a false glamour that is sometimes given to it. (p. 449)

[*The Lawton Girl*] is faithful to the atmosphere of a small manufacturing town in New York; the conflict of capital and labor is not permitted to eclipse the interest in the central character. Jessica Lawton differs from the old-fashioned "wronged woman," for not only does she refrain from marrying the hero of the story but she also retains a certain amount of affection for her earlier betrayer and accepts a share of the responsibility for her own downfall. It is much better than Frederic's historical romance *In the Valley* . . . , laid in the Mohawk Valley before, during, and after the Revolution. The lack of incisive characters and his determination to prove that the defeat of St. Leger's campaign was the great fight of the Revolution are its principal defects. *The Return of the O'Mahony* . . . is an amusing fantasy retailing the adventures of a false and a real heir, both from America, to a poverty stricken estate on the west coast of Ireland. The two Americans are real enough, but most of the novel is comic opera.

When Frederic returned to his native State of a more recent time, he did much more important work. The Civil War was near enough for him to write of it, not as a romance of heroism but as a bitter struggle of conflicting opinion in the North. In *The Copperhead* . . . he drew a real character, Abner Beach, a farmer, a Democrat and an anti-abolitionist who refuses to change his opinions when war comes on. The hysteria of war, the intolerance that ostracizes Abner, first with petty tyranny and finally with the destruction of his house, is vividly portrayed. He is an individual who will not yield, and he pays the penalty meted out to many in that time. Frederic continued in his volume of short stories, *Marsena and Other Stories of the Wartime* . . . , to depict some of the less usual phases of the conflict. The scene in the surgeon's tent after Malvern Hill in which Julia Parmalee, an inconstant young woman whose war services are prompted by various motives, pulls her skirt away from a dying soldier because he is a mere private and then only dimly recognizes in the corpse a man with whom she had flirted quite violently at home, shows Frederic as a realist at heart.

It was in *The Damnation of Theron Ware* . . . , however, that Frederic wrote one of the best novels of the period. It was an ambitious theme, dangerous in fiction—the revelation of the fall of a Methodist minister from the simple sincere days of his early ministry until his degradation when, after a debauch, he is saved from utter ruin by Sister Soulsby, the revivalist, through her common sense, advice, and help. Frederic drew with skill the conflict between the emotionalism, the crudity, and the meanness of the small-town Methodist congregation, which even forces Ware's wife, Annie, to take the flowers out of her bonnet, and Ware's growing knowledge of his own ignorance and his desire to study and progress. But the novelist knew that this would not be enough. So he created in Celia Madden, the handsome, independent, pagan daughter of an Irish emigrant who has grown rich, the concrete influence which brings upon Ware his ruin. It is really his passion for Celia which makes him jealous of her friendship for Father Forbes, her pastor, and, while his admiration for the culture which Celia, Father Forbes, and his agnostic friend Dr. Ledsmar represent makes him discontented with his own limitations, Frederic shows well how Ware would and did square his ideals with the practical duty of earning a living. The forces which keep him from giving up his ministry, because of his disgust with the camp-meeting methods and emotional soul saving of the revivals, are represented by two well-sketched characters, Brother and Sister Soulsby. Sister Soulsby's conversation with Ware reveals the character of a woman who has been an actress and has almost been indicted for illegal practices, but who can influence a crowd of people through her dramatic appeal and who, moreover, believes she is doing an important job. It is, of course, the moral contrast again. Hearing that Father Forbes and Celia are going to New York, Ware jumps at the conclusion that they have illicit relations. He follows them, and realism has rarely gone farther than the description of his sordid ride in the day coach and his futile helpless pursuit of them to the Murray Hill Hotel, where they are trying to save her young brother from the consequences of his drunken debauch. Then when he forces his way into Celia's "parlor" she tells him the whole truth:

> "It is all in a single word, Mr. Ware," she proceeded, in low tones. "I speak for others as well as myself, mind you,—we find that you are a bore."

Frederic's understanding of racial and theological ideas is at times penetrating; for example, his analysis of the conflicting elements in the Irish character and his contrast of the Greek and the Hebrew ideal of life in Christianity. Frederic's picture of the Catholic Church is very interesting, but he is drawing with sympathy only one element in it, that of the man who loves its artistic side and is not concerned with dogma. He leaves out the devotional side of all the churches, and he seems to be the coiner of the phrase that in the Episcopal Church "nobody seems to have to believe particularly in anything except the beauty of its burial service." The general effect of this book is to paint religions as necessary concessions to human weakness. But, being an artist, he does this without descending into crude caricature as Sinclair Lewis does in *Elmer Gantry*. His people are real, and he never allows them to become shrill or disgusting, however he may be turning their souls inside out. His satire is therefore all the more effective. While *Elmer Gantry* is so obviously overdrawn that the instinctive reaction even by those who may dislike Methodism is a feeling in its favor, *Theron Ware* produces just the opposite effect.

In his last stories Frederic drew upon his knowledge of English life. *March Hares* . . . is a charming romantic novelette, with an illusion of reality. *Gloria Mundi* . . . is more important because, through the career of Christian Tower who by a series of sudden deaths becomes heir to the dukedom of Glastonbury, Frederic represented the strength and weakness of the English patrician system and the materialistic basis of its social structure, without satire, but as a contrast to the truer democracy of the Middle Ages. *The Market Place* . . . , a story of the interrelations of English society and the stock market, contains a very real character, Joel Thorpe, the promoter, who makes a fortune by a clever trick and proceeds ruthlessly to buy and force his way into the position of a country gentleman, only to be bored by a life for which he is not suited. While Frederic wrote at times with the easy facility of a journalist, he rose above it in his best work; his charming style, his natural dialogue, and his sympathy with the individual who is fighting against odds make his novels far above the average. (pp. 450-52)

*Arthur Hobson Quinn, "The Development of Realism," in his* American Fiction: An Historical and Critical Survey, *D. Appleton-Century Company Incorporated, 1936, pp. 433-71.*\*

## OSCAR CARGILL   (essay date 1941)

[Harold Frederic] discharged his weapon directly against the Methodist Church, then the largest Protestant sect in America. His *The Damnation of Theron Ware,* which arraigned the adventurer in religion, was the literary scandal of the year 1896. Though Comstock succeeded in persuading the Post Office Department to refuse it the mails, *The Damnation* reached a very large audience and materially undermined the influence of the lesser clergy in all Protestant sects. Frederic . . . drew a bold and merciless caricature of a snivelling divine and the members of his church board of trustees, then made an invidious comparison between his protagonist and the local Catholic father and his learned friends. As a result, the book is not lightly to be dismissed as agnostical—for while it filled certain Methodist bosoms with wrath, it struck more impartial readers as a just stricture on those who chose religion as a career without any inward signs of grace, and also as a bold plea for religious tolerance. Though *The Damnation of Theron Ware* is better at almost every point than Mr. Sinclair Lewis' *Elmer Gantry,* it has one glaring fault—the author's absurd notion of good taste, represented for us by the things with which a monied Irish hoyden, who takes Theron's fancy, surrounds herself in the tale. Frederic may be trusted when he draws the world he knew as a boy in upper New York State, but when he tries to impress us with his cosmopolitanism, he is far from successful. There is some good honest writing, though it is somewhat less ambitious, in his earlier tales, *Seth's Brother's Wife* . . . and *The Copperhead.* . . . (pp. 414-15)

> *Oscar Cargill, "The Intelligentsia," in his* Intellectual America: Ideas on the March, *The Macmillan Company, 1941, pp. 399-536.**

## ALFRED KAZIN   (essay date 1942)

[To Frederic, novel-writing] came too easily; though he wrote copiously, he never fulfilled himself. . . . In one of his most passionate novels, *Seth's Brother's Wife,* Frederic commented on the fact that American humor grew out of "the grim, fatalist habit of seizing upon the grotesque side," and his bitterness made the most of it. His most famous novel, *The Damnation of Theron Ware,* is a mischievously written museum piece, persistently overrated because it was among the first American novels to portray an unfrocked clergyman and to suggest the disintegration of relgious orthodoxy. But the unfrocked clergyman was to become as useful a symbol of the new era as the businessman, whom Howells defined so memorably as "the man who has risen." (pp. 35-6)

> *Alfred Kazin, "The Opening Struggle for Realism," in his* On Native Grounds: An Interpretation of Modern American Prose Literature, *1942. Reprint by Harcourt Brace Jovanovich, Inc., 1963, pp. 3-50.**

## PAUL HAINES   (essay date 1949)

[*Haines surveys Frederic's novels and short stories and concludes that Frederic's style progressed over the course of his career from "surface versimilitude" to mature individual and social portraiture.*]

Frederic's historical pieces stem from his boyhood enthusiasm for the surface realism of Erckmann and Chatrian, pathetic, archly witty, and charming. In several early stories he rather mechanically applied their device of the naive narrator to stiff love-stories in romantically remote settings. He worked for at least four years on his historical novel but could not complete it until the writing of the more personally reminiscent *Seth* had unleashed his pen. *In the Valley,* a Dutch picture of the deepening cleavage between Sir William Johnson's Tory descendants and the Dutch farmers of the Mohawk, culminating in the battle of Oriskany, is remarkable for its historical insights; though not exciting, it is charming and clear, which qualities are due largely to Frederic's telling the story as the recollections of a sober-minded Dutch patriot. Frederic, though little given to literary criticism, weighed the problems of local realism in his short story, **"The Editor and the Schoolma'am,"** . . . , in which he scouted the naturalism of Dostoievsky and Gogol as an absurd counter-romanticism; relishing the life of the American village and respecting the villagers, he would treat them without condescension, neither prettifying them nor regarding them with despondency or scorn. Some years later, in his Civil War stories, Frederic achieved just this tone, happily applying the familiar device of the naive narrator to materials drawn from his own reminiscence of early childhood. But he was mistaken in attributing his success to the pattern of Erckmann and Chatrian; it resulted from the perspectives of his own maturity, at once warmly sympathetic toward the village and humorously detached. The momentous personal issues of wartime, looming in the background, give the tales a weight of human dignity.

*Seth's Brother's Wife* was first conceived as a portrait of manners: of farm life, of town journalism, and of rural politics. The social sketches are humorous, robust, masculine, good-natured; Frederic does not present his own vigorous views on the political economy of New York agriculture. The political episodes and persons are closely patterned after those of the 1882 campaign, rearranged more simply to point the moral: the notion that the professional politician is necessarily corrupt and that one need only use money to succeed is a dangerous romanticism. But *Seth* is chiefly notable as a psychological study, a realistic comedy of good intentions and self-deceptions; thus it is incidentally a contribution to the current fictional discussion of the problem of evil. From the fact that error results merely from "the necessary conditions of the human mind," Frederic distils not gloom or pathos but tolerance and a sophisticated good cheer.—The development of *The Lawton Girl* which may be roughly traced in MS. notes, reveals Frederic's instinctive interest in the self-confident, not quite despicable blunderer; but this theme, which affords the wittiest writing in the novel, is blurred by more sentimental and dramatic elements. The novel provides a social panorama of the too suddenly industrialized village; but it lacks aesthetic unity.— In *The Damnation of Theron Ware,* Frederic's social and psychological interests are admirably fused, and the book is his masterpiece. . . . Frederic's picture of the Free Methodists is harsh but accurate; he is not, however, hostile to the cult: as he indicates, a social leader may and indeed must work within the evolved institutional forms. The protagonist, Theron Ware, an idealistic young Methodist preacher, is bruised by the crudities of his congregation and fascinated by the enlightenment of his new Roman Catholic friends. By steps so delicately motivated and justified that the reader cannot precisely censure him, he involves himself in hypocrisy and adulterous fancies. Frederic does not take this "damnation" seriously; the novel is not a study of the deterioriation of character but an account of the oral disturbances to be wrought by romantic misapprehensions, a comedy of innocence.

*The Return of the O'Mahony,* in plot a story of adventure and young love, reiterates the thesis of Frederic's Irish articles in the *Fortnightly Review:* whereas Ireland's worst exploitation has been at the hands of her own political romanticists, unscrupulous or merely irresponsible, an effective leader of the Irish must combine a practical and aggressive economic program with a shrewd but honest appeal to the national tradition; both elements are necessary, and the nationalism alone is dangerous. This gayest of Frederic's novels is also his most carefully integrated fictional statement of a political thesis.

The *Mrs. Albert Grundy* papers, subtitled *Observations in Philistia,* poke fun at the suburban British matron; *March Hares* is a frivolous love-story for hammock reading. In *Gloria Mundi* and *The Marketplace,* Frederic posed the question: granted power or the semblance of power, how may an individual exert it for the good of society at large? The hero of *Gloria Mundi,* a poor heir awaiting his inheritance, observes an experimental System: the organization of a self-supporting society in terms of medieval paternalism; he does not much like it. Then in London he witnesses the "dismal swamp of individualism," as the Systematizer calls the modern world of progress and free enterprise and disorder. The novel contains a number of careful sketches of English manners, but its hero arrives at no positive conclusions, and this failure is no satisfactory point after so long a quest. The protagonist of *The Marketplace,* a stronger novel less finely drawn, is the type of the new financier, making a fortune by an audacious paper operation in the stock market, chronicled in unedifying detail. Having achieved power for the sheer joy of struggle, he wearies of the game and settles down to enjoy his money. But idleness palls, and he at last faces the question of how to wield his power for the public good. He is no sentimental philanthropist but a man restless for action, ruthless to the point of murder, self-conscious among the aristocrats, awkward before his petty bourgeois sister, and impulsively generous. He projects a political reform movement, on which Frederic suspends judgment, so that this novel too is inconclusive, but the portrait is vigorous and convincing.

In sum, Frederic's work was thoroughly realistic. At first, his conscious concern was with not much more than surface verisimilitude; but from his first full-length novel on, he could handle portraiture and setting with the deftness and precision of Howells. His temperament and his political experience directed him also to a sociological realism, directed against romantic inability to understand and work within traditional social institutions, and to an ethical realism, directed against moral simplifications of virtue and vice and against naturalistic pother about the evil of the universe. Thus Frederic maintains the realistic position, as by anticipation, against later schools of fiction; and his novels, though not philosophically searching, are permeated with his geniality and his maturity of mind. For these reasons, they do not merely represent a moment in the evolution of American literature but merit a permanent place among the classics of that literature. (pp. 5-7)

> *Paul Haines, in his* Harold Frederic, *New York University, 1949, 13 p.*

### C. L. GOHDES    (essay date 1951)

[Harold Frederic] appears to have been an amoral, exuberant extravert, without firm convictions on the nature of humanity or of art. His chief purpose as a writer was merely money-making, and, seemingly, he contributed as readily to *The Youth's Companion* as to *The Yellow Book.* A farfetched romance about medieval Ireland caught his fancy as easily as an honest portrayal of a New York farmer. As a realist, he did his most

enduring work in connection with the life of the Mohawk Valley, which he knew best. He never surpassed the sturdiness of his first novel, though in *The Copperhead* and *The Damnation of Theron Ware* he contributed more memorable characters. The absence of the subjective note is apparent in his work, but, especially in *The Return of the O'Mahoney* and his final novels, he was at times as prone to idealize as Sir Walter himself. . . . Frederic is a good example of the seasoned veteran of the newspaper who knows how to reproduce what he has observed and who possesses no mean knowledge of human psychology but lacks both time and inclination to become an artist. We have had, more recently, many of his sort but few with better talent. . . . (pp. 745-46)

> *C. L. Gohdes, "The Facts of Life 'Versus' Pleasant Reading," in* The Literature of the American People: An Historical and Critical Survey, *edited by Arthur Hobson Quinn, Appleton-Century-Crofts, Inc., 1951, pp. 737-62.\**

### CHARLES CHILD WALCUTT    (essay date 1956)

[*In his* American Literary Naturalism, a Divided Stream, *a study of the naturalistic novel, Walcutt posits that Frederic's divided attitude toward his material in* Seth's Brother's Wife *and* The Damnation of Theron Ware *accounts for a failure in technique. Since Frederic was guided by ethical instead of naturalistic motivation, Walcutt argues, he ultimately reverted to conventional moral judgment.*]

[*Seth's Brother's Wife*] opens in a tone which suggests that the story is to deal primarily with the deadening effects of country life. . . . Not only do [anti-rural] passages go unanswered, so that they dominate the tone of the novel; they also reveal a plain and clear concept of determinism which is underlined when the "hero," Seth, is portrayed as ignorant, lacking in taste, and thwarted. The first hundred pages of the book call for an action that grows out of these miserable conditions.

But Frederic was unable to make such a story. The action of *Seth's Brother's Wife* swarms in and out of journalism, politics, murder, and not one but two love triangles. The writer, furthermore, is idealistic, polemical, and burning with moral indignation against the conduct of his rural people. . . . Frederic makes his reader hate the insolent servants who gossip in the kitchen. He forces the erring wife of Seth's brother (who through sheer boredom has engaged in epistolary flirtation with Seth to the point where he is ready to declare his love and elope with her) to confess that she is "a wicked woman!"

The crowning instance of ethical rather than naturalistic motivation appears when the corruption of the local political scene is corrected by the eleventh-hour conversion of the most vicious and powerful of political bosses into a pillar of righteousness. The change is not probable; it is not prepared for; it does not carry out the expectations of rural viciousness or backwardness that have been established in the rising action of the story. The spirit of this conversion endows a scoundrel with the "homely democratic virtues" that have been traditionally associated with the hard-working American farmer. Frederic begins the novel blaming the farm with unscientific indignation for what it has done to the poor farmer. Presently he is blaming the rural oaf for being a scoundrel. And finally he contrives the triumph of morality by what appears to be a completely unmotivated change of heart.

There were various more consistent ways of working out the possibilities of these materials. Frederic could have let his protagonist bring about his own destruction because his narrow background and lack of experience unfitted him for effective action or judgment in a crisis. It was probable that Seth should have become infatuated with his brother's wife—and probable that he should have got into inescapable difficulties with her. In another form, the material could have been developed as no story but a barren and dreary waste of futility in which nothing happened because the dreary environment paralyzed its people. A third form would have maintained a completely objective tone and presented the characters' thoughts and motives in a way that would have demonstrated their subjection to their environment without pretending to prove that the outcome of the story was inevitable. With complete objectivity and meticulous attention to the details of the background, such a story would have been massively consistent and convincing. In none of these forms does it appear that a happy solution is possible, for the conditions as given hold out no hope of any considerable improvement for anybody who is deeply involved with them.

But Frederic's idealism gets mixed into the action—early and earnestly. He is indignant with the deprivation of the rural life, and as he writes his way into the story he concentrates his outrage on what has happened to the people until—and the turn is not surprising when we see how it happens—he vents his wrath upon them. Finally, having damned them with his rage, he transfers the will-to-decency to the political boss and has him save the day with a story-book finish.

Frederic's literary technique was better fitted for exploring people than for demonstrating the large-scale operation of social forces. It is doubtless very presumptuous to undertake to read the minds of dead authors, but I am tempted to suggest that Frederic was frustrated by his inability to sustain a naturalistic technique, that this frustration turned into rage at his unmanageable materials, and that the rage expressed itself in the moral indignation which he directed at his characters. The initial vitality of **Seth's Brother's Wife** is impressive; it is a pity to see it diverted.

Frederic's more famous novel, ***The Damnation of Theron Ware: or Illumination*** . . ., although more mature, more interesting, and better written, falls into very much the same confusion. The opening sections of the book lead one to suppose that it will explore the blighting effects of fundamentalism and Puritanism upon the spirit of an eager young minister; it turns into a study, lacking in charity and compassion, of a mean spirit, a character who is condemned by his creator as both weak and vicious. (pp. 45-9)

The tone and manner, new and fresh, suggest the new era. The reader follows the adventures of Theron's decaying spirit with keen interest, and the other characters are very much alive. The spirit in which the setting is depicted—the moral and spiritual setting—suggests that the cause of Theron's disintegration must surely be that his Methodism and his limited social experience had failed to give him a cultural tradition upon which he could base his conduct. Thus when confronted with a new and attractive set of values in the outlooks of the priest, the girl, and the doctor, he had nothing to guide or restrain him. In these terms the novel could be a penetrating analysis of cultural forces. But this is not what comes out. One's judgment of Theron cannot be impersonal because his lack of background is not enough to account—to the reader's emotional satisfaction—for his contemptible weakness. This is laid to some personal failing within him, a failing which every line of the book suggests that he is ethically responsible for. The modern reader is apt to think, upon reconsideration, that Fred-

eric is too hard on Theron—that he fails to see how helpless Theron's meager outlook is before the first sophisticated people he has known. Frederic condemns instead of explaining.

Many elements of the American Dream appear in this strong novel and participate in its vitality. There is the flouting of mere conventional morality, the belief in a scientific or rationalistic view of man and his relations, and the earnest faith in intelligence, human dignity, and freedom. There is also, initially, a firmly monistic sense of the interdependency of nature and spirit: both the rasping piety of the community and the personal inadequacy of Theron are introduced as functions of the environment. But, just as in **Seth's Brother's Wife,** the stream of moral earnestness separates from the stream of scientific analysis, and presently it appears that Frederic has slipped back into the simple formula of orthodoxy which says that a person who displays moral weakness is one of the damned. What appears to be an intellectual confusion and inconsistency that leads to a complete reversal of attitude is probably not that but a failure of technique. The novel leaves the impression that Frederic was full of his subject and that he had thought long and earnestly upon it and reached fairly subtle conclusions. But again, as in **Seth,** he was unable to dramatize them into a demonstration of environmental forces at work. Instead he penetrated Theron's character so deeply that his moral earnestness became focused upon what he found there and he lost sight of the environment completely. What appears in the novel as the indignant condemnation of Theron for his moral deterioriation began as Frederic's moral indignation with the small town. Because he did not have the technique to lay out the whole spiritual landscape, he funneled his passion into the study of Theron—and there it appears, transformed but still providing the novel's vitality and interest. (pp. 51-2)

> *Charles Child Walcutt, "Adumbrations: Harold Frederic and Hamlin Garland," in his* American Literary Naturalism, a Divided Stream, *University of Minnesota Press, 1956, pp. 45-65.\**

**JOHN HENRY RALEIGH** (essay date 1958)

[*Raleigh discusses narrative structure, characterization, and what he terms "the paradox of 'Illumination-Damnation'" in* The Damnation of Theron Ware.]

The **Damnation of Theron Ware** is such an interesting novel and so neglected a minor classic that one hardly knows how to begin talking about it. Those who have read it sympathetically can only nod in wise agreement about the intricacies of its narration and its wry ironies, its humor and its ultimate terror. (p. 210)

[We] do not stand outside . . . and look down at the hero, always knowing more than he does; we are involved to a degree in Theron's own lack of perception. This is the detective-story aspect, although **The Damnation** is no mystery story either. All the proper evidence is there, but there are two sets of evidence, one for the appearance of things, and the other for the reality of things. Theron has only the appearance, and we see both; yet while we know what the reality is, the appearance beguiles us as well or, to put it another way, it keeps raising questions in our minds. For example, the novel was published in England under the title **The Illumination,** and when we put the English title and the American title together we have the paradox of "Ilumination-Damnation." For what happens to Theron is also an illumination that casts relentless and searching light on the illiberal fanaticism of his religion and on the paltriness and inflexibility of his upper-New York State rural background. (p. 211)

These ambiguities are further enhanced by the character of the protagonist himself, who is simultaneously likable and despicable. (p. 212)

Our lingering sympathy for him, despite the fact that he is a mountebank, a bore, and at the height of his illumination-damnation "the meanest man in town," results from two factors. First of all, he is incurably boyish. He brings out the mother-impulse of all the women in the book, who think of him as a nice young man of certain potentialities if only a wise woman can take him in hand. Thus his "damnation" is not final, but provisional, and he is still at the end a "boy," albeit a bit tarnished now. A second and deeper reason for our lingering sympathy arises out of the very method of narration, described above. According to Aristotle's formula, we feel pity and terror at the hero's fall—pity because a man has fallen, terror because he is a man like ourselves, and his misfortune could be ours. The pity is our objective, social reaction, in which our deepest self is not involved, while the terror is our subjective, personal reaction bound up with our deepest fears. In other words, through pity, we stand back from the tragic hero while, through terror, we identify ourselves with him. But in *The Damnation* the distancing factor, the superiority of our knowledge over that of Oedipus, is missing, for we are partially involved in his misperceptions. Further we are involved with a character whose misapprehension is not about a set of facts but about the nature of reality, which is our own deepest, most difficult, and most terrifying problem. Pity then is out of the question; we can feel only the terror. And indeed in the middle of the book the reader, if he be honest, begins to wonder about himself. I know of no other novel in which this device of involving the reader in the imperceptions of the protagonist is so artfully and so fairly done, and yet no other novel that is so puzzling, without being at all incomprehensible, in its earlier parts. So skilfully is it all done that even when we are sure that Theron is completely wrong and is "damned," even after trustworthy and perceptive characters in the novel tell him so, we still feel a lingering ambiguity and we still feel, against all evidence and all odds, that perhaps he *has* been illuminated and that Celia *does* love him. Only at the very end are all suspicions allayed. . . .

If *The Damnation* is unique in structure and psychology, it is unique as a cultural document as well. It exists on three historical and cultural levels: first, it emanates very clearly from late nineteenth-century America; second, it is also concerned with that perennial theme of much serious American literature: what is the identity and the nature of "the American" and what is his relationship to Europe? and, third, it is a metaphorical statement about the essential polarities of all human existence.

On the first historical level *The Damnation* is about how the powerful, relentless, experienced intellect of the late nineteenth century, combined with its love of "art for art," seduced, quickened, and finally damned the lingering intuitionalism and the reliance upon feelings, and the anti-aestheticism, which were the legacy of the early nineteenth and of which Theron Ware is the anachronistic embodiment. For Theron is the poor vessel for two outbursts of emotionalism that occurred in the late eighteenth and early nineteenth centuries: Methodism in the Protestant religion and the Romantic love of Nature. (pp. 212-14)

He is anachronistic, too, in that he is an Emersonian, a Romantic, a lover of nature, which he thinks somehow will sustain and fortify him. (p. 215)

On its second historical level *The Damnation* is concerned with the relationship of America to Europe; here again it is unique and for two reasons. First, it shows Irish Catholicism conquering American Protestantism, a happening without parallel in an important American novel, and, second, it has put together in the same book the respective viewpoints of Henry James and Mark Twain. (p. 217)

Sister Soulsby is the voice of shrewd, pragmatic wisdom and is possessed of a genius for getting things done. Her own private religion is simple, moral rather than theological: " 'I've got a religion of my own, and its got just one plank in it, and that is that the time to separate the sheep from the goats is on Judgment Day, and that it can't be done a minute before.' "

Her speech is right out of Mark Twain, as is her attitude. (p. 221)

Under the ministrations of the Soulsbys, . . . Theron, instead of committing suicide, is restored, partially at least, goes off to Seattle to start all over, wiser, if sadder. In this fact resides the genius of the Soulsbys; they don't expect anything or anybody to be perfect and merely try to salvage as much good as they can from the materials at hand. They represent a point of view that crops up in other places in American literature as well; it is usually expressed in prosaic metaphor, the imagery coming from the soil or hand-labor. . . .

Does this mean then that Sister Soulsby or what she represents is to be taken as the "moral" of the novel? The answer is "No," for hers is only one point of view, sane but grubby, in a novel that has no moral or message save the rather grim reminder that man is a poor creature, generally speaking, and is always being tempted to run off after pleasing illusions and to be blind to harsh realities. There is, nevertheless, a hierarchy of outlook and point of view, with some outlooks obviously more valuable and possessed of more strength than others. Theron's, of course, would be the lowest, while the respective attitudes of Father Forbes and Sister Soulsby would be the highest and strongest. (p. 223)

Primarily Father Forbes is the voice of Catholicism, although of a very heterodox and sophisticated kind. His deepest influence on Theron, however, is not religious but historical. (p. 224)

Man is a frightened wretch—half a savage—and there is nothing new under the sun: those two ideas provide the basis for everything that Father Forbes says. For Theron with his belief in progress and individualism and his notion that Protestant American man was the final flower of these processes and that the whole universe was ever creating itself anew with God smiling down upon it like the sun streaming down through the leaves of the tree, these ideas are profoundly unsettling. It is as if Father Forbes kept pulling back the successive curtains that cover the past, back and back through the abysses of time, and always the same tableau: the savages around the campfire, telling one another the same ghost stories. Thus the modern world that seems so new and unique is really a ghost-world ever re-enacting the primordial habits and thought-patterns of the dead ancestors and continually rebuilding the same structure on the ruins of the old one. (p. 225)

At the polar extreme from this grim and timeless picture of man that Father Forbes draws, we have the brisk, good-humored, and contemporary outlook of Sister Soulsby. If Father

Forbes regards men as potential savages, Sister Soulsby thinks of them as essentially good, although often misguided, boys. (p. 226)

Father Forbes, then, is the voice of history, of tragedy, of loneliness, of the unfathomable, of the mysteries that surround and encompass us, of our aboriginal fear of space and time, of the endless repetitions in which we are involved, of the point of view of "The Legend of the Grand Inquisitor"; while Sister Soulsby is the spokesman for the here-and-now, for life as a comedy, for the efficacy of common sense, for the sense of our common human solidarity, one linked to the other, for making do with what we have, no matter how insubstantial that equipment may be. . . . As psychological surrogates for Theron they are unmistakable: Father Forbes is the "father," while Sister Soulsby is the "mother." Thus in the last analysis the two forces represented by Father Forbes and Sister Soulsby are not antithetical but complementary. There is no real argument between them and there cannot be, for both are right. Father Forbes tells us what we *are;* Sister Soulsby what we must *do*. What happens in *The Damnation of Theron Ware* is that the protagonist, having experienced in his own person the lesson of Father Forbes, turns instinctively to Sister Soulsby to pull him out of the prehistoric depths, which she does. (pp. 226-27)

*John Henry Raleigh, " 'The Damnation of Theron Ware'," in* American Literature, *Vol. 30, No. 2, May, 1958, pp. 210-27.*

**EVERETT CARTER**   (essay date 1959)

[*In his introduction to* The Damnation of Theron Ware, *Carter considers the literary, cultural, and historical significance of the novel and characterizes Frederic's style as "a transition between the methods of verisimilitude and symbolism." This essay was written in 1959.*]

The American decade of the eighteen-nineties was an end and a beginning. . . . It was a time . . . of major change in American culture; Henry Steele Commager has termed it the great "watershed" in American intellectual history. And for these currents and countercurrents, these swirls and eddies of thought and action, where old faiths were meeting new doubts and artists were struggling to find the forms to contain this turbulence, Harold Frederic's *The Damnation of Theron Ware* is an illuminating literary document, and one of the most satisfying aesthetic forms.

This is a large claim for a work which has yet to be generally recognized as a major effort of the American imagination. (pp. vii-viii)

In an examination of the ways in which *The Damnation* was a work in the realistic tradition of Howells, and yet something more, we may come close to a description of its meaning and value for American literary history.

The novel is based on the realistic method. This called, first of all, for a fidelity to the life one knew, and all the better if this life were the life of a provincial area of American society, with its unique customs, and its local dialect and folkways. *The Damnation* is a rich example of an almost painstakingly documentary summary of life in a little-chronicled corner of America. . . . Its dialogue is a faithful transcription of the dialect of the region, and its conversational tone stays as close to the natural as possible. (pp. xii-xiii)

The novel, too, maintains the general sense of pragmatic attitude and morality that had dominated the realistic movement. Before Charles Sanders Peirce had invented the term, and long before William James popularized it, America's novelists instinctively were making pragmatism the philosophy of their fiction. . . . After rejecting the absolute, pragmatism went on to affirm experience as the test of truth and, indeed, as truth itself; it looked away from first causes to "fruits, consequences, facts"; it acknowledged that "truth independent . . . truth no longer malleable to human need, truth incorrigible. . . ." is simply nowhere to be found. And of all these pragmatic attitudes, Brother Soulsby, and most of all, his marvellous wife, Sister Candace Soulsby, are complete and exuberant embodiments. They could have been illustrations for James's text that truth is how we *act;* they are professional actors, mountebanks, performers. Their "act," their assuming of an outward demeanor, their making the appearance become a reality, seem almost a parable of James's insistence that an emotion literally is identical with its physical manifestation. (pp. xiii-xiv)

This hard-headed acceptance of the world of fact, operating through practical modes of behavior, is the central reality of the tale. For Sister Soulsby is described not as a "sister" but as a "mother," a healing and restoring madonna, a madonna in bangles and tights, to whom Theron instinctively turns after his other "mothers" prove inadequate or misleading. The stages of his journey to awareness are marked by his religious-sexual devotion, first to Alice, then to Celia, and finally to Sister Soulsby. Alice is described as the embodiment of golden innocence with which he enriched his youth; his association with her is described as a "daily communion" with this "most worshipful of womankind." Dissatisfied with his state of innocence, he turns to Celia, the representation of the absolute of beauty: the religion of art. He sees her pictured in the stained glass window of a cathedral, a halo about her head; her apartment is decorated with "variations of a single theme—the Virgin Mary and the Child." After his betrayal by Celia, he rises from the gutter to find himself at the entrance to a theater, under a poster featuring "a woman in tights"; at that moment he remembers Sister Soulsby and knows she is a friend, and the only one he has on earth. He comes straight to her, and, like a child, casts himself "on his knees at her feet," and abases his head "to bury it among the folds of the skirts at her ankles." She soothes him, "a motherly intonation in her voice," a "soft, maternal touch" in her hand. And then she gives him the basis in self-recognition of the new religion of modern pragmatic humanism: "You weren't altogether good a year ago, any more than you're altogether bad now." Theron Ware, in her maternal embrace, discovers his shabby humanity; as she tells Alice: "He isn't going to be an angel of light, or a saint, or anything of that sort . . . he'll be just an average kind of a man. . . ." Theron Ware turns his eyes to the future and to the West, and towards a new century, no hero, no "angel of light," but a man who has been told the homely, unpretty truth of the realistic, the pragmatic attitude towards life.

This attitude had been involved, in nineteenth-century American realism, with a sense of the comic rather than a vision of the tragic. . . . And in *The Damnation,* Frederic partakes of this sense of the comic, rather than the tragic perception of everyday reality. The hard, ugly Methodists of his congregation, Sister Soulsby reminds Theron, are no villains, but people with the usual admixture of good and evil. Theron does not end in physical and social disaster but is, after all, saved and soothed by Sister Soulsby, and reunited with his long-suffering wife.

But despite these hallmarks of the preceding age, the novel is, after all, the story of a damnation; its ending is uncertain and ambiguous; the healing of Theron seems no final salve to his soul, but a temporary repair to a shattered psyche prepared to face the twentieth century with only a sense of its own inadequacies. The subtitle of the American edition, and the title of the English, was *Illumination*; the term is bitter irony, of course. "I can use no word for my new state short of illumination," Theron tells Dr. Ledsmar, when he is well on the road to the dark hell of knowledge. The torment of Theron struck a new note: the note of a modern tragic irony which regards man and his society as mere delusive appearances, and the cosmos as hostile and malignant. For Theron, the world becomes all black, "plunged in the Egyptian night," and he finds himself "alone among awful, planetary solitudes. . . ." The universe holds him "at arm's length as a nuisance." His question at the end: "Was it a sham . . . . or isn't there any God at all,—but only men who live and die like animals?" introduces a terrible cosmic doubt. . . . And this was the new tone which began to insinuate itself into Frederic's depiction of the fall of intellectual America from innocence into knowledge.

[The fall] is specifically a sexual one; the story is, after all, the account of an errant husband. The strength of the work, however, lies in its merging of the sexual fall with the fall from innocence to experience in other kinds of knowledge as well: religious, scientific, and aesthetic. Frederic tries to make Theron's innocence typical: his features are described as "moulded into that regularity of strength which characterized the American Senatorial type in those far-away days . . . before the War." (pp. xv-xviii)

The first part of his fall is into the subtleties of theological truth. The overwhelming impact of the new biblical criticism, the entire conception of the symbolic rather than the literal truth of revealed religion is brilliantly presented by Father Forbes. Religious skepticism and the new criticism of the Bible was far from novel, of course; but the large popular awareness of the crumbling of fundamental faith in the solution of scientific skepticism was still to come. (p. xviii)

Theron's pitiful defense against this onslaught is his own naïveté and the contumacious fundamentalism of Brother Pierce: "What we want here, sir, is straight-out, flat-footed hell. . . ." It is scarcely sufficient armament. And when the attack is combined in the closest possible terms with the general impact of nineteenth-century science upon a mind of simple faith, the effect is overwhelming. Forbes's closest friend—so close that he feels the jealousy of a lover—is Dr. Ledsmar, and Ledsmar is the essence of experimental science. Such is his devotion to its cold ideal that he has given up a career as doctor of medicine, for to him healing was not truly scientific. Celia Madden is not far off when she bitterly denounces him and "his heartless, bloodless science." We see Ledsmar in his laboratory, experimenting upon animals, plants, and a man: a sleeping Chinese deep in an opium trance. The doctor explains that he is "increasing his dose monthly by regular stages, and the results promise to be rather remarkable." Heretofore, he goes on, to emphasize his abandonment of human sympathy, "observations have been made . . . on disease . . . subjects . . . This fellow of mine is strong as an ox. . . ."

With this description of Ledsmar, we have come to a turning point in the treatment of men of science by major literary sensibilities in America. (pp. xix-xx)

This double fall into religious and scientific knowledge is controlled by a third descent, embodied in the most alluring of the trio of seducers of innocence. It is, of course, Celia Madden. Much of the power of the novel derives from Frederic's projection, through her, of sex as a primary energy. Sex, he knew, was ". . . man's power to deal his only counter-blow against the enemy, death." It is, he stated with a bluntness and a perception rare in his age, "the mainspring of human activity." This bringing of the power of sex from the background to the foreground of realistic fiction was the most striking aspect of Frederic's break with his tradition. (p. xxi)

The Fall from sexual purity into sexual knowledge is the part of the fable that collects into itself all the other aspects of the tale, and makes the story a personalized unity.

Just as the novel pioneers in subject, so does it give evidence of shifts in technique away from the realistic and towards the symbolic and the mythical; away from the social and towards the individual. Frederic . . . found himself interested in primitive passions, unconscious stirrings, racial memories in a collective mind; and like these other writers of his generation, and like Henry James who would soon forge a new style to carry the load of his last fiction, Frederic began to experiment with techniques for revealing his fleeting insights into new dimensions of mind and character. The very title, in which the theme of the Faust legend advances from the dim recesses of allusion to complete overtness, signals these changes. . . . The play upon the function of seeing, and upon the word "light" has ambiguities enough to please the metaphysical poet: when Theron's eyes had been closed to knowledge, the Biblical heroes had glowed with a poetic light; when his eyes were opened, "this light was gone. . . ." As well as this paradox, there is an insistence upon the magic of numbers: "three" begins to be the pattern of experience much as it was in [Herman Melville's] *Moby Dick* or [Nathaniel Hawthorne's] *The Scarlet Letter.* Theron is involved with three women; the temptations presented to him are three. Nature and the seasons begin to play their part in this poeticizing of realistic prose fiction. Alice's garden is indeed a garden of the modern world; and when the serpent of knowledge comes into her life, "the gayety and color of the garden were gone, and in their place was shabby and dishevelled ruin." The presence of the diabolical is as clearly indicated as it had been in the romance: after Ledsmar witnesses the fall of Theron, he holds a lizard with a "pointed, evil head," and murmurs to it: "Your name isn't Johnny any more, It's the Rev. Theron Ware."

The technique of Frederic, then, was one of the landmarks in the change from a method which unobtrusively used symbols and allusions to reinforce the logical, natural surface of the narrative, to a "symbolism" which insists upon itself as the embodiment of a fable's otherwise obscure significance. With its attention to detail, its local color, its faithfulness to the life Frederic knew, *The Damnation of Theron Ware* points backwards to Howells; with its conscious use of heightened imagery it points forward to Norris, Henry James, and the "symbolic realism" that has become a major mode of the twentieth century. . . . As a transition between the methods of verisimilitude and symbolism . . . and as a depiction of America's necessary fall into sophistication, *The Damnation of Theron Ware* recommends itself as a continually interesting contribution to American sensibility. (pp. xxii-xxiv)

*Everett Carter, in an introduction to* The Damnation of Theron Ware *by Harold Frederic, edited by Ev-*

*erett Carter, Cambridge, Mass.: Belknap Press, 1960,
pp. vii-xxiv.*

## HORTON DAVIES   (essay date 1959)

[*Davies alleges in his* A Mirror of the Ministry in Modern Novels, *an exploration of the role of clergy in modern novels, that Theron's disintegration results from "vanity, in the form of intellectual ambition."*]

It is not surprising that [his] introduction to the world of esoteric scholarship and uninhibited thinking has an intoxicating effect on Theron Ware, particularly as his education has not equipped him to answer the challenge. What is far more disturbing is that his vanity should make him think that Celia Madden and her group should consider him as an equal. She adds to his perplexity by telling him that her cult is the Greek theology of the strong and the beautiful, and he foolishly believes that this emancipated woman wishes to leap into the shackles of an affair with him.

Already his liberation of mind is turning to an emancipation from loyalties. He finds the very idea of pastoral visitation a chore, but determines to concentrate on the worldlier members of his flock who would rather not talk shop, and for these he naïvely prepares by diligent newspaper reading!

His last moorings to the old faith are cut when he receives from Dr. Ledsmar a parcel of intellectual dynamite, consisting of six books, two of which were written by the celebrated modernist, Ernest Renan. He was particularly fascinated by *The Recollections of My Youth;* so intrigued, in fact, that he simulated sickness in order to avoid the prayer-meeting and keep on with the reading. This, too, is a sign of the disintegration of the man who once was honest. Yet while reading, Ware seems utterly unconscious of the fact that he is falling into the pit of a double intellectual standard—one for the humble believer and another for the rational, cultured man. Frederic comments, in a most perceptive analysis of the attractions of historical criticism and comparative religion:

> Somehow, the fact that the priest and the doctor were not religious men, and that this book which had so impressed and stirred him was nothing more than Renan's recital of how, he too, ceased to be a religious man, did not take a form which Theron could look square in the face. It wore the shape, instead, of a vague premise that there were a great many different kinds of religions,—the past and dead races had multiplied these in their time literally into thousands,— and that each no doubt had its central support of truth somewhere for the good men who were in it, and that to call one of these divine and condemn all the others was a part fit only for untutored bigots. Renan had formally repudiated Catholicism, yet could write in his old age with the deepest filial affection of the Mother Church he had quitted. Father Forbes could talk coolly about the 'Christ-myth' without even ceasing to be a priest, and apparently a very active and devoted priest. Evidently there was an intellectual world, a world of culture and grace, of lofty thoughts and the inspiring communion of real knowledge, where creeds were not of importance, and where men asked of each other, not 'Is your soul saved?' but 'Is

your mind well furnished? Theron had the sensation of having been invited to become a citizen of the world. The thought so dazzled him that his impulses were dragging him forward to take the new oath of allegiance before he had had time to reflect upon what it was he was abandoning.

Among the delights of [*The Damnation of Theron Ware*] are the set-pieces that Frederic introduces: the Methodist Conference, a Revivalist and Debt-cancelling Meeting, and a Camp-Meeting in the woods, which are remarkable for their accuracy and insight. In their way they are as reliable an account of social history and of disappearing practices in the older Methodism as Hale White's account of the nineteenth-century chapel versus church ethos of the ultra-sensitive Dissenters of the English midland counties. The hilarious account of how the debt-cancellers, Brother and Sister Soulsby, turn a revival meeting into a fund-raising campaign by playing off one trustee against another, after taking the precaution of locking the church doors, is also a means of introducing two shrewd but quite unpretentious Methodist lay people into the book. The Soulsbys prove in the end for all their lack of polish and culture to be the best friends of Ware and his wife when the bottom falls out of their world.

Ware's vanity leads him into one gaucherie after another. He tries to impress Celia that he is emancipated and, in fact, shocks her by saying that he has been reading a novel by George Sand. He makes a further *faux pas* when he tries to get Ledsmar to tell him if there is anything sinister in the association between Celia and Father Forbes.

His inner deteriorioration can be diagnosed from other signs. His preaching degenerates into mere flamboyant rhetoric, while his thoughts grow increasingly skeptical. He dallies with many aspects of the case against revealed religion 'from the mild heterodoxy of Andover's qualms to the rude Ingersoll's rollicking negation of God Himself,' considering himself free to postpone indefinitely the duty of selection. He lost all sense of right and wrong, and even bought a small book on the art of manicure! (pp. 74-6)

This novel, then, is not so much a study of the agonizing problem of correlating traditional faith with the new scientific and historical knowledge; it is chiefly a study of the disintegration of a minister through succumbing to vanity, in the form of intellectual ambition. If [Willaim Hale White's] *Robert Elsmere* and the *Mark Rutherford* novels are admirable case studies of honest doubt and its dilemmas, *The Damnation of Theron Ware* is a perceptive analysis of dishonest doubt. Both experiences may befall the minister who tries to be the interpreter of faith in a time of cultural crisis, and the warnings in these novels have not ceased to be relevant in our own time. (p. 78)

*Horton Davies, "Divines in Doubt," in his* A Mirror of the Ministry in Modern Novels, *Oxford University Press, 1959, pp. 51-80.*\*

## THOMAS F. O'DONNELL AND HOYT C. FRANCHERE   (essay date 1961)

[*In this excerpt from their biocritical study,* Harold Frederic, *O'Donnell and Franchere provide an overview of Frederic's major works and suggest that, in the twentieth century, he "has been rediscovered."*]

The reader who expects to find a steady, consistent line of development in Harold Frederic's fiction is bound to be puzzled at first by what he finds in *Seth's Brother's Wife*. In all the stories he had written before 1885 Frederic left seemingly clear indication that when at last he came to write a sustained work, it would be historical, romantic, derivative, and sentimental. But *Seth's Brother's Wife* is none of these. It is instead a powerfully realistic study of contemporary life in America, completely free from its author's perennial dependence upon Erckmann-Chatrian, and with little of the sentimentality and melodrama that mar his early short tales, both published and unpublished. *Seth's Brother's Wife* flatly defies explanation in view of Frederic's first exercises in fiction, for this first novel reflects life and hard-bitten experience in the real world of the 1870's and 1880's, and not the dim and history-bound one which existed only in the minds of two French story-tellers. (p. 73)

*Seth's Brother's Wife* is worthy of critical examination that goes beyond its two intertwined plots. Behind both are a background and an array of minor characters so richly and at times so grimly delineated that they sometimes distract the reader from the real point of the novel. For instance, Vernon Louis Parrington—one of the most formidable commentators of another generation—was so distracted that he read *Seth's Brother's Wife* as "a drab tale of farm life in upper York State, as bitter as any tale of the western border. It is a story of defeat," Parrington went on, "of flight from country to town. . . . The slack servants, gossipy and impudent, the petty lives, the grasping ways unrelieved by any grace or beauty, and set in a world of petty machine politics, make a drab and unattractive picture. Harold Frederic evidently hates this countryside that bred him" [see excerpt above, 1930].

This Procrustean observation, which trims *Seth's Brother's Wife* to fit Parrington's own brilliantly conceived thesis, actually mistakes the nonessentials for the novel itself. Bemused by the brilliance of Frederic's touches of local color, Parrington saw only the bleak setting and missed the drama proper, which is fundamentally comic in both plan and execution. Frederic, as the reader knows, had not been bred in the "countryside," and so the novel is no simple chronicle of the author's own "flight from country to town." Furthermore, Frederic would have been startled to hear that he "hated" the countryside that he described. Even as he wrote the final chapters of *Seth,* he was in fact happily planning a long vacation trip back to it. Nor is there any real "defeat" in *Seth's Brother's Wife* except for the carefully intended one of lax morality: of Isabel's plans for dalliance with her naïve young brother-in-law, and Albert's plans for a career built on chicanery and corruption. In this novel Frederic had a more positive purpose in mind than Parrington and other critics were able to see behind the portrayal of "slack servants" and a "drab and unattractive" farmyard. (pp. 76-7)

[The purpose of *Seth's Brother's Wife* when it] is read in the context of Frederic's other American fiction, is to show the gradual resurgence of the political integrity (synonymous to Frederic with public morality) of a community which has too long tolerated the arrogant machinations of corrupt and complacent public leaders—the "bad" in politics. He dramatizes this resurgence in his development of three characters representative of the regional population at three different organizational levels: Seth Fairchild, who survives attacks on his integrity not only as an individual but also as a member of a "county family" and as a newspaperman with a moral obli-

gation to his area; Abe Beekman, the incorruptible local "boss," the career politician who knows how to move the people to positive action; and Richard Ansdell, the inspiring "practical idealist" who—with the assistance of individuals like Seth and organizations like Beekman's—brings about the political (i.e., moral) regeneration of the community that had too long shown only apathy toward the need for integrity and morality in high public places.

In his first novel, Frederic was not concerned with political programs like the Populist agrarianism that Parrington looked for; unlike Hamlin Garland, Frederic was interested in *men*—in political leaders, rather than in political programs. The real social purpose of *Seth's Brother's Wife* was to demonstrate, in a tone of restrained optimism, that in spite of a certain drabness and apparent moral and spiritual laxity of life in upstate New York, the region could still produce from its own citizenry honest and devoted leaders who were capable of arousing the moral vigor of the public when such vigor was needed: men like Ansdell, whose zeal "often swayed despite themselves the politicians of his party who had least in common with him and disliked him . . . even when they were being swept along toward nobler purposes than their own small souls could ever have conceived, in the current of feeling which his devotion had created." (pp. 77-8)

Frederic's first novel is his affirmation of belief in the soundness of the political foundations and the underlying public morality of his own society. The affirmation is the more forceful because of his pejorative treatment of the unattractive social

*Drawing of Frederic by Austin Briggs, Jr., after a photograph taken by Frederic himself in 1896. Courtesy of Austin Briggs, Jr.*

characteristics that as a realist, temporarily at least, he felt bound to report. (pp. 81-2)

*In the Valley,* though not memorable for its banal love story, is important for the manner in which it traces the evolution of two groups of bitter and implacable enemies, the patriots and the Tories, within the mixed society that existed in the Mohawk Valley in the years leading up to the Revolution.

The novel is actually a dramatic treatment of Frederic's conviction that the Revolution in New York was really a civil war, with its own local dimensions: not a war of rebels against king, but of class against class. The population of the valley is a mixture of Germans, Dutch, Irish, Scotch, and English. "One cannot understand the terrible trouble which came upon us later," says Douw Mauverensen, the narrator, "without some knowledge of these race divisions." (p. 84)

Considered simply as an account of an episode in American political and military history, . . . *In the Valley* is successful. But Frederic was concerned with the social history of his valley as well, and so the novel abounds in authentic sidelights on the everyday life, customs, and traditions of the Mohawk Valley Germans and Dutch, in pre-Revolutionary days. Woven skillfully into the background, so that they become organically part of the fabric of the story, are Douw's reflections on such things as fur trading expeditions that are actually "coming-of-age" rituals, on the place of the Negro slave in colonial New York, on life in Albany when it was "almost as much in the wilderness as Caughnawaga." Not since the days of Cooper and James Kirke Paulding had life on the old Dutch-German frontier been recreated so carefully and lovingly.

For all its merits as dramatized history, however, *In the Valley* is hardly the great novel. . . . Through all the years of planning, and finally through the months of writing, Frederic was clearly more interested in the events of his story than in its characters. As a result, most of the fictional people in the novel (with the exception of occasional minor figures who are actually part of the setting) are too often mechanical, one-dimensional, and weakly motivated. Douw Mauverensen himself emerges as a character of some depth, although he sometimes talks like a device rather than like a human being. The others—Daisy, Philip Cross, Mr. Stewart—wear interesting costumes and move in the direction that the story demands; but they are not always convincingly real.

*In the Valley,* then, deserves praise as good reading, but not as distinguished fiction. (pp. 87-8)

As he had previously done in *Seth's Brother's Wife,* Frederic unfolds in *The Lawton Girl* a fast-moving but complicated story with slightly daring overtones. . . . (p. 90)

As a novel, *The Lawton Girl* is not so well constructed as *Seth's Brother's Wife.* The first novel has a compactness of organization, a unity and coherence, that *The Lawton Girl* lacks. As the author himself pointed out later [see excerpt above, 1871], his characters "took matters into their own hands quite from the start. . . . I grew so interested in the doings of these people that I lost sight of a time-limit." Jessica Lawton's death-scene in the final chapter, remarkable for its use of interior monologue and a curious mixture of pre-Freudian symbolism, is a gratuitous addition to the finished story. "At the end I did . . . kill Jessica," Frederic admitted, "she who had not deserved or intended at all to die—but I see now more clearly than anyone else that it was a false and cowardly thing to do." All in all, *The Lawton Girl* is the most discursive and disorganized of

Frederic's works, reflecting neither the long immersion in his background material that characterizes *In the Valley* nor the ability to stick to a clearly-defined plot like that of *Seth's Brother's Wife.*

Despite its faulty structure, *The Lawton Girl* is neverthleless the most ambitious of the first three novels that came in untiring succession from Frederic's pen. In it he attempted to cope with . . . "the problem," as Walter F. Taylor defines it, "of assimilating into a previously existent humane culture the disruptive forces of capitalistic industrialism." *The Lawton Girl* is Frederic's attempt to show the concrete manifestations of these forces as they operated within the very particular and specific framework of his own region. Theorists could talk abstractly about the dangers of industrialism in terms of Herbert Spencer's "Synthetic Philosophy" or John Fiske's "Cosmic Philosophy," or to take sides in William Graham Sumner's "holy war" against reformism, socialism, and government interventionism, or to look hopefully to the melioristic "dynamic sociology" of Lester Ward or the modified utilitarianism of men like E. L. Godkin. Frederic, however, saw the problem in the simple and concrete terms of a central New York village whose whole way of life is endangered when a group of scoundrels threaten to take over control of an ironworks.

In *Seth's Brother's Wife,* this same region had triumphed over political corruption; in *In the Valley* it had destroyed the threat of class tyranny; now, in *The Lawton Girl,* the region wins again—this time over economic despotism of the kind that Frederic saw to be inherent in the belief of social Darwinists like William Graham Sumner that "the social order is fixed by laws of nature precisely analogous to those of the physical order." And all three victories had been achieved under the leadership of men who were themselves able and intelligent products of the region. (pp. 95-6)

The story [of *March Hares*] is a sophisticated comedy of errors, of mistaken identity. It looks backward to Frederic's slight commentary on English mores in *Mrs. Albert Grundy* and it anticipates *Gloria Mundi* in its comment about the independent woman and about the improvidence of the British aristocrat. But it also displays Frederic's capacity for the light touch and for a widening range in the treatment of both subject and character. In other respects it is not a significant book. One should read it after putting one's self into Frederic's mood as it must have been at the time he wrote the fiction: a happily reminiscent mood tinted with the lighter shades of romance. (p. 120)

Though laced in a web of romance, *Gloria Mundi* nevertheless presents a remarkable, penetrating contrast between appearance and reality. But it effects this contrast with such eminent good humor that one almost thinks that the author took neither himself nor his subject seriously. That, of course, was not at all the case. To Frederic's mind, shaped as it was to regard democracy as both a political and a social structure, the power and significance of the British aristocracy was an illusion. To him, some of its members were obviously the victims of self-delusion and of the dry rot of caste privilege; some were broken financially; and others were sustained, if at all, by the importation of foreign-born and wealthy brides lured by titles. (pp. 121-22)

[It] should be said that although well-rounded characters do emerge from this novel and although the reader finds himself responding empathically, one is led to conclude that this was, in its author's mind, a novel of ideas—not satirical in intent, but evaluative. It is without question the most English of all

Frederic's works, not forgetting *March Hares.* The humor is sharper than that in *Mrs. Albert Grundy;* the romantic alliance is more serious than Mosscrop's in *March Hares.* (p. 123)

[The] current resurgence of interest in Harold Frederic is testimony to the durable quality of his fiction. He has been rediscovered. Today, one may say that *The Damnation of Theron Ware* is considerably more than a minor classic and is not by any means the only readable, even if it is the most significant, book that Frederic wrote.... Frederic had substance. The promise that he displayed in *Seth,* whatever crudities in it may be complained against, he lived up to in succeeding fictions. *Ware* was clearly the work of genius that only needed time for development. Skill and power were there. The broader canvas, the deeper plumbing of character, the higher finish in structure and style—these surely would have come had he not been stricken in mid-career.

As it is, Harold Frederic's stature among latter nineteenth-century American writers is today being recognized. He is taking his place, like Stephen Crane, in the vanguard of writers of that time. Though he did not possess all the natural endowments that Crane exhibited, he had many compensating facets of personality, among these a rich good humor that Crane did not often display. Crane had the greater artistry; Frederic had the greater warmth and human understanding. Crane had a vision of life and created its image; Frederic, perhaps lacking Crane's subtlety, saw life in the round and portrayed it that way. Crane was a man haunted, confused, and driven. Frederic had the vast hunger for life, and he lived it joyously and to the full. (pp. 162-63)

> *Thomas F. O'Donnell and Hoyt C. Franchere, in their* Harold Frederic, *Twayne Publishers, Inc., 1961, 186 p.*

## TOM H. TOWERS (essay date 1965)

[*Towers focuses on the theme of determinism in* Seth's Brother's Wife.]

The main critical questions touching *Seth* concern the nature and degree of determinism present in the novel....

Here, as in his later novels—e.g., *The Damnation of Theron Ware* ... and *The Market Place* ...—Frederic suspends his hero between conflicting elements. The hero does not choose his way so much as it is chosen for him by natural, social, and psychological forces outside his will.

First, there are those forces pulling Seth downward to brutality—the farm, the city, and his beautiful sister-in-law, Isabel. Opposed is the benevolent ministry of nature, often symbolized by Seth's eventual wife, Annie. We see the farm first, and its depressing, dehumanizing power is at once evident. The barns are "rickety," "patched," and "paintless." The barnyard is a "black mire" in which lean cows stand fetlock deep, feeding on "scant tufts of rank grass." All is "squalid," and not even the brilliant, warming sun can make the scene in any way attractive or "picturesque." Rather, the very purity of the sunlight makes the barns only "meaner," the cows only "dingier and scrawnier."

As we might expect, the setting exerts a degenerative influence on the farmer. (p. 362)

But mere escape from the farm does not insure either humanity or morality. In the city, Seth encounters destructive forces as powerful as the farm and more seductively attractive. In Te-

cumseh Seth is at first overwhelmed by the faceless crowd whose moral indifference allows free rein to the powers of corruption, and Seth's first friend in the city is the product and instrument of that corruption. (p. 363)

The city and its society ... offer Seth only examples of greed and selfishness, not models of rectitude; and running unchecked through society are the shaping forces of sensual depravity which initially ensnare Seth.

Isabel is the final destructive force in Seth's life. The farm works to actively destroy all but man's most brutish qualities; the city caters to these brute appetites and destroys by sating them. Isabel's is the most subtle corruption. She falsely appeals to what is potentially highest in Seth—his sense of beauty, his compassion, his intellect. But in this novel, as in *Theron Ware,* Frederic emphasizes the "wrongness" of aestheticism by associating it with carnality. All Isabel's talk of poetry and music and the higher life culminates in the invitation of her open bedroom door. In the end, Isabel acts as the city, fostering base desires in Seth at the expense of his integrity. She offers not beauty but fashion, not love but self-serving passion, not wisdom but wit.

These are the forces pulling Seth down. There is also ... the force of benevolent nature. Nature in this novel is not the nature of most naturalistic writers. Frederic's idea of natural determinism is much more traditionally Romantic. Nature for him resembles Wordsworth's "nature that never did betray the heart that loved her," but which man, to his great detriment, can forget or ignore.

Nature, as it operates on Seth, is wild nature, untouched by man and so uninfected by either farm or city. Indeed, life in nature is regularly opposed to the institutionalized existence we find elsewhere in the book. For example, Seth's life on the farm is wholly taken up with materialism and its attendant drudgery, but his experience in nature represents immediate escape from materialism. In nature he pursues leisure and the life of the spirit. (pp. 363-64)

The major interest of the novel lies in this conflict of contesting forces. But in Frederic's characterization of Seth as the object of those forces we discover the weaknesses of the novel. The idea of competing determinisms is forcefully presented in the crucial scenes, but in too many other instances Frederic's intentions seem ambiguous. In those scenes dominated by Abe Beekman—the nominating convention, the discovery and arrest of Milton—Frederic, probably drawing on his memory of Cleveland's gubernatorial campaign, becomes distracted from his theme to concentrate on political and social satire. Obviously social criticism is appropriate to Frederic's purpose, but he cannot fit the comedy of the Beekman sections to the Romantic tone of the rest of the work. In the Beekman scenes Seth's character becomes blurred; the "natural education" of the whole theme is diminished to an initiation into worldly, practical common sense. After Seth's spiritual ordeal has raised him far above all the characters except possibly Annie and Arthur Dent, Frederic allows John Fairchild and Beekman to go on treating him as the naive youngest son. And Seth is made to acquiesce in their attitude.

A decade later in *The Damnation of Theron Ware,* Frederic was able to make his religious setting an extension and symbolic reflection of his theme. There the religious debate embodies Theron's ordeal and illuminates it. But in *Seth* Frederic's political discussions stand outside the central spiritual conflict. Still, this weakness does not offset the basic value of the novel.

Frederic is a realist in his style, but an incipient naturalist in his vision of humanity. The effect in *Seth's Brother's Wife* is to make us aware of the awful, irresistible forces loose in man's life, and at the same time sensible of the drama and ultimate integrity of the individual life in which those forces operate. (pp. 365-66)

*Tom H. Towers, "The Problem of Determinism in Frederic's First Novel," in* College English, *Vol. 26, No. 5, February, 1965, pp. 361-66.*

## EDMUND WILSON   (essay date 1966)

[*Wilson is generally considered America's foremost man of letters in the twentieth century. A prolific reviewer, creative writer, and social and literary critic endowed with formidable intellectual powers, he exercised his greatest literary influence as the author of* Axel's Castle *(1931), a seminal study of literary symbolism, and as the author of widely read reviews and essays in which he introduced the best works of modern literature to the reading public. Wilson's criticism displays a fundamental concern for the historical and psychological implications of literary works. In the excerpt below, Wilson provides a brief overview of Frederic's Civil War stories and stresses their historical and literary importance.*]

[Harold Frederic's] stories of New York during the Civil War reflect the peculiar mixture of patriotism and disaffection which was characteristic of that region. . . . Due to this, these stories differ fundamentally from any other Civil War fiction I know, and they have thus a unique historical as well as a literary importance. The hero of the longest of them ["**The Copperhead**"]—really a short novel—is not merely a critic of Republican policies but a real out-and-out Copperhead, an upstate farmer whose ideas are rooted in the principles of the American Revolution and who believes that the South has the right to secede. He is ostracized and persecuted by his neighbors, but then, when the conflict is over, they realize they have injured a man who ought to have commanded respect, since he has stuck to his conviction of what is right and braved the hysteria of wartime, and they rebuild the house that has been burned as a result of one of their raids on him. (It was, and still is, a custom in that part of the world that when a house or barn has been burned, the neighbors must all lend a hand to rebuilding it.)

The other stories, too, in various ways, are true reports on the place and the time. They differ from most other fiction inspired by the Civil War not only in their honest description of the mixed feelings aroused by the war but also in their realistic focusing on the civilian population at home. There are very few glimpses of the armies in the field. "**A Day in the Wilderness**" is the only one—and it is not one of the best—that is entirely occupied with soldiers on active service. There is in general no melodrama, no romance, and very little sentiment. The anguish and bitterness caused by the disruption of domestic life and the discordance of once quiet communities is treated with sober and ironic restraint. The call of the bugle is heard but from afar and not always irresistibly. In "**The Deserter**," even the deputy marshal at home sympathizes with the boy who has been hired as a substitute and run away to look after his old father, and, pretending to shoot at the fugitive, allows him to take refuge in the forest. In "**Marsena**," one of those lethal coquettes who play such a role in Harold Frederic's fiction sends a mild and harmless suitor to his death when she challenges him to compete with a more vigorous and dashing rival, whom she had also egged on to enlist. When she has

got herself to the war as a nurse and finds them both seriously wounded, she hardly deigns to recognize them—though the weaker of the two is dying—in her snobbish preoccupation with a decorative and pretentious staff officer who has received a minor injury. (pp. xiii-xv)

But good though these stories are, it is strange to find the author of *Theron Ware*, undoubtedly his most brilliant achievement, declaring that they are "closer to my heart than any other work of mine, partly because they seem to me to contain the best things I have done or ever shall do, partly because they are so closely interwoven with the personal memories and experiences of my own childhood—and a little, also, no doubt, for the reason that they have not had the treatment outside that paternal affection has desired for them" [see excerpt above, 1897]. This reissue should give them the place that they deserve in American literature. Except for the juvenile element in those published in the *Youth's Companion*, they tolerate no Civil War clichés and they stand as acrid firsthand testimony to the delusions and lasting grievances implanted in American society by that fracture which, in the recent exploitation of the Civil War centenary, has been so much misinterpreted, so much melodramatized and romanticized. (pp. xv-xvi)

*Edmund Wilson, in an introduction to* Harold Frederic's Stories of York State *by Harold Frederic, edited by Thomas F. O'Donnell, Syracuse University Press, 1966, pp. xi-xvi.*

## LARZER ZIFF   (essay date 1966)

[*In his* American 1890s: Life and Times of a Lost Generation, *a study of the history, culture, and literature of America in the 1890s, Ziff examines* The Damnation of Theron Ware *in the context of changing American society.*]

Possessed of an imaginative knowledge of his home county, in which character was inseparable from ethnic, religious, historical, political, and social conditions, [Frederic] was able to follow Howells' lead in producing a fiction of the commonplace, yet to surpass the dean in rendering a sense of communal density. Not until Faulkner's Yoknapatawpha County did American literature have a region so fully and intimately explored as Frederic's fictionalization of his native area—the land around the invented cities of Tyre, Tecumseh, and Thessaly. In [*Seth's Brother's Wife, The Lawton Girl, In the Valley, The Damnation of Theron Ware,*] and several collections of short stories, Harold Frederic, sitting in London, detached from the immediate political maneuverings of upstate New York, brought into existence a fully articulated human community. The peculiar quality of rural brutality as well as rural speech, the way the political boss Beekman rules the countryside as well as the town, the relation of the best families to the processes of making public policy, the aldermanic view of responsibility, the contrasting social roles played by the Methodist and the Episcopal Churches, the Dutch resentment of the English settlers who had migrated from Massachusetts, and the code of the masculine small-town world as opposed to the public code of sexual morality, all emerge dynamically; they are, in Frederic's pages, so rich a context of action that the American would appear to be comprehensible only in terms of his dwelling place and the multifold allegiances and enmities that he has inherited with it.

The towns on Frederic's map, such as his Thessaly, appear to his imagination as the products of history and are criticized severely out of a genuine love. As a result, their past and their social structure engage the reader to a far greater extent than the actions of any of the characters. (pp. 209-10)

Frederic badly needed a habit of patience and reflection which would allow him to discover the themes inherent in his rich material. Nowhere in *Seth's Brother's Wife, The Lawton Girl,* or *In the Valley* does he trust to his material for form. Rather he adheres to the old plot lines of fallen women, conventional villains, and idealistic young heroes, and once having launched them spends his energies in setting forth the myriad subcultures within the community he is portraying, returning to his plots only occasionally and relying on melodrama or hackneyed conventions to wind them up. The result is novels in which amplitude of context is betrayed by the irrelevance of the action.

Running along as underdeveloped themes of greater interest than the actual plots of *Seth's Brother's Wife* or *The Lawton Girl* are questions about the relation of history to society and the inevitability of the Social Darwinist's thesis as opposed to one of social control. Frederic sees that the political boss, a usually vicious example of the fittest who survives, is also a demonstration that men can control society and that therefore they are not powerless in the grip of impersonal forces. He tentatively explores planned social management here, as he is later and more fully to do in his English novels. Another theme introduced to American literature by Frederic is that of the war as seen through the eyes of a child on the home front. *The Copperhead* . . . and *Marsena, and Other Stories of the Wartime* . . . are stories which, typically, are somewhat feeble in plotting, but which present a splendid picture of a Northern village while the men were away at the front, and serve as Yankee equivalents to the tales in Faulkner's *The Unvanquished.* Frederic here preserves the little insignificant details of those trying days which, in their smallness, give balance, proportion, and humanity to an otherwise misrepresented time. For him it is important, for instance, that "the outbreak of the war had started up the universal notion of being photographed."

*The Damnation of Theron Ware* . . . was the last of Frederic's New York State novels, and in it alone did he discover a plot which flowed naturally from his materials. It was recognized as worthy by book-buyers, who made it one of the ten best-selling books of the year, and after a submerged existence of half a century, during which it was read by writers but by few others, it is again prominent and seems assured of its deserved place as a minor American masterpiece. Frederic reached *Theron Ware* by way of the three earlier novels on the region. They equipped him with so full a sense of his scene as a representative area of America that he was freed to assume its history and its class structure as symbolic of the national career. He developed from them a plot which was intimately related to the region in which it took place, yet which at every step reverberated as a symbolic tale of America's progress to disunity in the latter half of the nineteenth century. (pp. 211-12)

Terribly unknowledgeable about the ways of the world, totally unread except in the Bible and fundamentalist manuals, narrow-minded, yet honest, sturdy, and likable in his upright simplicity, he is, in his wife's words, "a good, earnest, simple young servant of the Lord." (p. 212)

As the new aestheticism and the new science . . . flood in upon [Theron], the reader is pleased with this redemption of a basically likable country lad from the nastiness of small-town prejudices. But even when chronicling Theron's earlier social progress, Frederic had asked, "Was it, after all, an advance?" and now in the report of Theron's sense of his new self the

language is too highflown and vague to be trusted: "Born a Poet . . . child of light . . . brother to Renan and Chopin." The old ideality has failed; it cannot continue with influence in an America that has awakened to the implications of the Darwinist philosophy and the new historical and anthropological findings about organized religion.

But, as Theron's awakening shows, neither science nor aestheticism can replace what it has destroyed. Theron and the sympathetic reader, the American devoted to an advancing rush into the future, are tricked. In place of the honest Christian lad we do not have a refined, wise, and articulate adult; we have instead a pitiful creature who has betrayed the conditions of his breeding—his farming background and his idealistic legacy—in exchange for a grab bag of third-hand tastes, ill-digested ideas, and smirkingly cynical opinions about those who nourished and shaped him. Celia Madden can flee to Europe to indulge her taste for the new art; Father Forbes can control his knowledge of the psychological origins of religious feeling so as to be of greater service in his parish, even though he does not share the unqualified beliefs of his parishioners; Dr. Ledsmar can work out the implications of his science in antisocial isolation. But Theron cannot now turn back to the narrow ideals which have been killed, nor can he advance to a more meaningful life on the basis of the rag-tag and supercilious opinions he has purchased in exchange.

*The Damnation of Theron Ware* symbolizes the loss of innocent purpose in America. Theron, at the close, emerges from a period of disgrace and self-disgust to start life anew in the West. Now politics seems the best field for him, since in politics his ability to manipulate those who cling to the old beliefs, gained from his experience as a preacher, can be joined to his ability to follow the main chance, gained from his newly acquired set of shoddy modern opinions. It will be a thoroughly practical and usually despicable career. But it will not be pursued with any conscious hypocrisy, for the final irony is that Theron's new exuberance will ultimately lead him to believe the hollow phrases he will dole out, even as he earlier believed in his Sunday sermons.

Celia Madden reflects after his fall that what Theron (and the reader) took to be improvement was actually degeneration. This was the nineties' favorite word for its condition, the flag, as Nordau insisted, of its self-obsession. In *The Damnation of Theron Ware,* Harold Frederic created a masterpiece on the American variation of the theme. Since the Civil War his country had moved from a narrow-mnded loutishness, which was nevertheless illuminated by an honest devotion to the Christian rural ideal, to a shallow sophistication, unrelated to the needs created by the changes which had destroyed the ideal. Unity and innocence had degenerated into chaos and guilt. The new attitudes were not organic developments of what was worthy in the old, but betrayals of it, foulings of the nest.

The book, then, is dark, but not unrelievedly so, for if Frederic asserts that there is no turning back to the old innocence, he also suggests, though dimly, that there is a use for the new knowledge. In the Soulsbys he presents two characters who, on appearance, are as disagreeable as Theron is initially agreeable. They are professional fund-raisers, employed by the Methodist Conference to extract church funds from pinchpenny rural parishioners through carefully staged appeals. They sing old hymns to new tunes as they prepare the congregation for their appeals; none but the newly awakened Theron knows that one of their tunes is a simplification of a Chopin melody. In their appeals for money they mix the spice of carefully calculated titillation with the unguent of flattery, counting upon the pride and competitiveness of the small-town Methodists while verbally deploring these very traits and seemingly relying upon humility and brotherly love. They learned their tricks in show business, and they are immensely successful.

No characters are more qualified to be contemptuous of the mass and cynical about human ideals. But in point of fact the calculating Soulsbys do have souls. It is they who nurse Theron back from his self-destructive despondency when he realizes how mistaken he has been about his enlightenment, and it is they who outfit him for his trip West. In their experience as entertainers and near confidence men among the uneducated classes of American society they have . . . learned to manipulate greed and prurience for their own ends, but they have also developed a love for the people. Their manipulations are finally for the good of those manipulated, and if they have bastardized Chopin they have at least introduced his melodies to men who would never otherwise have heard them.

The Soulsbys represent the possibility of social control by a meritocracy of common-sensical people who sympathize with the masses and are knowledgeable enough to translate new intellectual developments into a tongue they can understand. They stand for what can be done on the American scene with the new knowledge that has destroyed innocence, and if they are manipulators of public opinion they at least derive their power to manipulate from intelligence and an identity with the manipulated rather than from a calculating contempt. They foreshadow the advertising man and the mass communicator with his wheedling explanation that without the 95 per cent trash he purveys nobody would get the 5 per cent of quality he offers, but they also foreshadow the social planner. They are Frederic's suggestion, in opposition to Social Darwinism, that men can control the future of their society if they but yield power to the able. The old Jeffersonian ideal must be modified to meet the realities of a world in which anti-social forces are increasingly centralized and must therefore be fought by centralization. (pp. 213-16)

For Frederic there is no turning back to simple democratic ideals. Just as Theron Ware, having lost his innocence, must learn to live with knowledge, so modern man should stop yearning—as did . . . the pre-Raphaelites, whose inadequacies are attacked in *Gloria Mundi*—for a simpler civilization. Rather, in an age of technology, the technocrat must be given power. Since he has gained all he could hope for from his private business activities, he should be trusted now to improve the condition of his fellow man rather then be hampered by public distrust, kept from power, and forced into only partly effective philanthropies. (p. 217)

> Larzer Ziff, "Overcivilization: Harold Frederic, the Roosevelt-Adams Outlook, Owen Wister," in his American 1890s: Life and Times of a Lost Generation, The Viking Press, 1966, pp. 206-28.*

## JAMES T. FARRELL (essay date 1967)

[*Farrell was an American novelist, short story writer, and critic who is best known for his grim Studs Lonigan trilogy, a series of novels which examines the life of a lower middle-class man of Chicago. Influenced primarily by the author's own Irish-Catholic upbringing in Chicago's rough South Side, and by the writings of Theodore Dreiser, Marcel Proust, and James Joyce, Farrell's fiction is a naturalistic, angry portrait of urban life. His literature explores—from a compassionate, moralistic viewpoint—the problems spawned of poverty, circumstance, and spiritual sterility. In*

*this appreciation of* The Damnation of Theron Ware, *Farrell maintains that its excellent characterization is also "a fine social characterization." This essay was written in 1967*].

[**The Damnation of Theron Ware**] is, to my mind, a very important American novel, one which stands up. The characterization of Theron Ware is an acute characterization: I think he is truly a character in American literature. His process of development is dialectical in character. What seems to be growth has within itself the seeds of disintegration. This is further influenced by the fact that Theron Ware takes the advice of Sister Soulsby, and plans to achieve his new life by a compromise, that of keeping within the folds of the faith on the one hand, and of living a rich personal and intellectual and emotional life on the other. Compromise is fatal to him, for the reason that his position as a minister doesn't permit that. It can only cause hypocrisy of a kind that eats into the roots of the soul. We see, but of such factors, how he becomes, instead of one who develops, a person whose development has tended to turn into fatuousness.

It is typical of many clerics that, in their first stages of discovering the possibilities of the world, they go forth to grasp these with a background of adolescent and naive emotions. Theron Ware is emotionally backward, and Harold Frederic is acute and incisive in the way that he concretely documents this aspect of Ware's personality. In a restrained way, the process of self-development of Ware tends to predict the so-called revolt of the twenties, with youth in seeking freedom, going to the extreme of seeking freedom, this being pure personal expression, which in turn becomes quite frequently mere gratification of impulse. The pattern is part of that which often characterizes young manhood and the last so-called stage of adolescence. Ware, on a restrained level, inasmuch as he is a minister, etc., follows through that pattern. Often, Frederic shows real subtlety in his grasp of such phases of Ware's character, and of his "development." Also, the conduct of the heroine, Celia, is extremely interesting to me. In essence, she acts like a rich girl, one who is whimsical, impulsive, concerned with gratifications and possessed of the means of achieving these. Often, such people—because they are beautiful as well as rich—develop without even thinking of it, an attitude which leads them to tamper irresponsibly with other people's lives. In essence, that is what this girl does with Theron Ware. He is basically sincere, and because of his sincerity and his inexperience, he takes things at face value. He doesn't understand the innuendoes, the qualifications, the conventions of expression and attitude of richer and more cultivated people, and he takes these at face and literal value. He acts on them. Herein, we see (a) an important cause of his disintegration, and (b) the role which Celia plays in messing up his life.

Frederic is often called a Populist writer. I wonder why. He is really sophisticated and grasped towards the gain of a sense of world culture. This, itself, makes the the book remarkable for its time, if we consider the character of American life when the Gilded Age was coming to its end and creating the material and social basis for the uprise of such human phenomena as that of, say, George Babbitt [in Sinclair Lewis's novel *Babbitt*].

Frederic illustrates the terrible backwardness of American life in this book. So much that is casually accepted by ordinarily experienced and sophisticated people of the city, so much is new, fresh, bewildering to Theron Ware. Just as he is personally immature, so is his whole background socially immature. While the book contains such an excellent characterization, that characterization is, in itself, a fine social characterization also.

The portrait of Dr. Ledsmar is very good. Ledsmar is close to Darwinism, the period of rampant Spencerian influence, the time when scientific discoveries were turned into generalizations about all of life and society, producing fatally incorrect conceptions of characters and events in society. That period, and the times preceding it, produced a rich variety of assumedly scientifically warranted generalizations which were narrow, and often cockeyed. We see something of this in Ledsmar. His attitude towards women, which he bases more or less on biology, is an instance. Ware's attitude towards Ledsmar is very revealing. There we see how out of ignorance, a simple idealistic way of looking at the world, and emotional immaturity, he takes Ledsmar at face value.

Much of what I say of Ware here further comes out clearly as the occupational effect on character. His very profession, Methodist minister, conditions this. Further, again and again, Frederic brings out the occupational effect on character of the sacred profession: Ware's tendency to meet situations of grief, nervous strain, etc., with a bromide; his ease in finding banalities to meet so many occasions; his reaction to the lawyer Gorringe; the kind of false confidence which he carries as a result of the dignity socially attached to his profession; his inclination to oratory, which is a kind of parallel on another level to his literal mindedness. He deals in words. They are his tools. He is a minister of a Christian religion which is literal in its acceptance of words, words in the Bible and the Discipline. This literalness utterly prevents him from grasping any subtleties of character and mind, brought out in human relationships. He understands his wife as badly as he does Celia, the Irish girl. For several centuries, education was purely verbal, a matter of words, and with this verbal type of education there was added authority—particularly and precisely the authority of the Holy Book itself. We see, in Ware's literalness, something of the concrete social meaning, the social cost, the concrete products of this type of education. So much, along these lines, is implied and stands behind the book.

In a very primitive and tentative way, we see in this book and in the times the first stages of change in religious life, mores, etc., that is—at a later time—documented by a type like Elmer Gantry [from Lewis's novel of the same name]. The influence of money, the pull of the town on the country, the growing hegemony of town over country, all these tendencies are reflected in the novel. There is more religious sincerity in this period, however; thus, Sister Soulsby is different from Reverend Monday.

There is a moral struggle in Theron Ware. By the time that Puritanism is pretty much overwhelmed in the post-war period, this moral struggle passes out. Just as everything that Babbitt buys is standardized. Moral problems don't hit often with acute thrusts. They are cushioned in standardization, in moral precepts and moral homilies. Moral solutions to problems are more or less commodities.

When protest again flares up in writing, it is protest against social conditions, against a general atmosphere which produces a life of spiritual poverty, protest which is, in one way or another, against society and against the cost of American development as that cost is reflected in its effect on individual destinies.

With this development, one theme in writing in America tends to drop out: the theme of self-discovery and self-development.

On the whole, American literature of the last fifty to sixty years had to be re-examined and rediscovered, studied with more perspective and more effort to relate it to the development of American society. If this is done seriously, *The Damnation of Theron Ware* will deserve a long, serious, and detailed analysis. (pp. 126-29)

*James T. Farrell, "Harold Frederic's 'The Damnation of Theron Ware'," in his* Literary Essays: 1954-1974, *edited by Jack Alan Robbins, Kennikat Press, 1976, pp. 126-29.*

**CLAYTON L. EICHELBERGER**   (essay date 1968)

[*Eichelberger discusses Frederic's negative view of philanthropy in* The Market-Place.]

Frederic's critical and satiric vision in *The Market-Place* embraces not only the buccaneer but also the philanthropist and tends to underscore a kinship between the two. The novel is concerned not only with the illegal and inhumane maneuvers of the buccaneer as he accumulates a fortune, but also with the self-interest which is sometimes an inherent part of the philanthropic pose. The people "'are hogs, right enough,'" Thorpe asserts to the Duke of Glastonbury, "'but they *are* "the people," and they're the only tools we've got to work with to make the world go round'".... Thorpe's "tenderness," his "munificence," his "democratic urge" are always so timed and so executed that he will himself reap the major benefit. Even in his vision of philanthropy he callously defends the validity of using one's fellow human beings for personal gain. (pp. 111-12)

Certainly in Frederic's vision, philanthropy was often dubious in efficacy and hypocritical in motivation. It is the motivation with which Frederic is particularly concerned. The buccaneer, if Thorpe is to be interpreted as representative, newly risen to the ranks of the wealthy, shares his booty for one of two main reasons . . . ; and neither of the two can be considered primarily benevolent or humanitarian. In the first place Thorpe is motivated by a sense of guilt. Charity motivated by guilt is not to be confused with conventional giving to assure social recognition or to mollify social insecurity. Thorpe is fully aware of the way in which he has used people for his own purposes, particularly in retrospect is he so aware, and he is conscious of the fact that sometimes the people he has used have been destroyed. In moments when unpleasant memories crowd into his mind, he rationalizes about his methods and attempts to hide his essentially immoral dealings beneath a blanket of goodness which is textured, at least in part, by charitable demonstrativeness. . . . As if to assure himself that such a naive separation were possible, that by the act of making one decision he might forever bury the evil nightmare of the past, he at this moment discovers as if by revelation and to his own amazement "that he intended to be a philanthropist." Even granting Thorpe's ferment of mind which precedes this climactic discovery, the sequential thought pattern in such tight temporal proximity to the nightmare is strongly suggestive of defensive concealing maneuvers.

A second negative motivation for philanthropy even stronger than guilt, however, is Thorpe's anticipation of the benefit he himself would derive from charitable display. While he was cornering the rubber market and, in doing so, accumulating a fortune, he reasoned that his ultimate goal was "unlimited leisure" and "power to enrich that life with everything money could buy." After "the last winnowing of the great harvest had been added to the pile,'' Thorpe, contemplating his future as a country gentleman, begins to form a ''beatific vision'' of himself:

> He would astonish the county by his charities, and in bad years by the munificence of his reductions in rents. Perhaps if there were a particularly bad harvest, he would decline all over his estate to exact any rent whatever. Fancy what a noble sensation that would make! . . .

For such charitable activity his reward would be the servile admiration and respect enjoyed by a noble patron. Of greater importance, however, would be the increased power he would win for himself: ''he did not waver at all from his old if vague conception of a seat in Parliament as a natural part of the outfit of a powerful country magnate.'' . . . (pp. 113-14)

Thus, in *The Market-Place* Frederic presents philanthrophy as an act of hypocrisy in which the generously outstretched hand seems to give—and is credited with giving—but in reality only buys the product of gratitude and ''humble subservience,'' and at bargain rates as well. The philanthropic act as it is represented here serves only as the means of Nietzchean extension and possible fulfillment. Once a man has with cunning and callowness amassed material power, he can, by seeming to give, buy his way into political power and so, as he will, ''transmute not only his own condition but also the very environment in which he lives.'' The picture of Thorpe, philanthropist, is equally as negative as the picture of Thorpe, buccaneer. (p. 115)

> Clayton L. Eichelberger, ''Philanthropy in Frederic's 'The Market-Place','' in American Quarterly, Vol. XX, No. 1, Spring, 1968, pp. 111-16.

**STANTON GARNER**   (essay date 1969)

[*In this general assessment of Frederic's novels, excerpted from his critical biography* Harold Frederic, *Garner suggests that Frederic's main achievement is* ''*the sensitivity and power with which he probed the naiveté and inconsistency of the American Dream.*'']

The main concerns [in *Seth's Brother's Wife*] are journalistic: the decay of New York State agriculture under the pressure of competition from the midwestern granaries, the operation and influence of a regional newspaper, and the power structure of a district political caucus. Frederic's style is similarly journalistic. Though tinged with Addisonian rhetoric, it is essentially colloquial and descriptive, substituting for elegance and wit a muscular, often crude prose. To readers who preferred the former, it appeared that Frederic was the victim of ''journalistic standards.'' Yet his painter's eye, his reporter's knack of getting directly to the point, and his raconteur's ability to create striking vignettes give vividness and pungency to his first novel.

The three principal concerns intersect in Seth Fairchild. Seth is threatened with a life of ignorance and despair on the ramshackle and dismembered Fairchild farm; he gains, almost loses, and then prospers in a newspaper career; and he opposes his brother Albert's cynical scheme to seize the district congressional nomination by bribery. Had Frederic had less insight into the weaknesses of men, had he not tested Seth's responses against suspicions about his own character, *Seth* might have gained in coherence while losing in significance and interest. But Frederic was unwilling to grant his protagonist the unqualified virtue which his heroic role demands. (pp. 14-15)

[His] humiliation disqualifies Seth as hero; his moral triumph is stillborn and he agrees to become Albert's political tool.

At this point Frederic's divided attitudes reach a fictional crisis. Is the democratic system capable of self-regulation through the virtues of its citizens and institutions, of frustrating the ambitions of the power-hungry who threaten to subvert it, or is the model Democratic Man naive and self-indulgent, powerless in his insufficiency? To put it another way, are the natural forces of probity capable of overcoming the forces of corruption, of evil, or are they themselves blighted by natural depravity? Seth, the instrument of Frederic's optimism, fatally disqualifies himself from action.

Yet Frederic is unwilling to accept the implications of Seth's failure. With the presumptive hero discredited, he moves outside of the social machinery he has created to salvage a positive resolution. A villain is made of an otherwise ineffectual farmhand, who preserves the integrity of the political process by murdering Albert, and an unexpected hero is made of a previously obscure third brother, John. John plays Fortinbras [a character in William Shakespeare's *Hamlet*], reassembling the scattered plot pieces by occupying the farm which is the family patrimony and demonstrating an integrity as editor of his weekly newspaper which Seth could not sustain. Thus the ''moral and spiritual laxity'' are embodied in Seth, and the ''honest and devoted leaders'' are peripheral and dramatically neutral figures. (pp. 16-17)

[*In the Valley*] is a response to Frederic's philosophical and fictional dilemma. Frederic sought the symbols of the past which might explain the present, and although *In the Valley* is scrupulously faithful to historical and geographical fact, it is nevertheless the most completely symbolic of Frederic's works. Many of the characters represent factions of the Valley population: Douw Mauverensen, the hero, the early European colonists; Philip Cross, his enemy, the arrogant English aristocrats. Daisy, the girl of indeterminate origin, is a symbol of the land itself for which the two groups compete. Even the geography is symbolic: the Mohawk Valley which divides the colonies culturally and strategically in two, and the gorge which separates Douw's home from Philip's, both represent the divisions between the settlers and between the Old World and the New, which resulted in warfare and were healed at last by brotherly reconciliation. (pp. 18-19)

America, Frederic concluded, is not simply a consequence of grafting an ideal system to a new unspoiled continent in which latter-day Adams and Eves started afresh under a new covenant. It is, in addition, a result of the melding of barely miscible ethnic elements on blood-tempered soil and the necessary catalyst is mutual tolerance. It is on this realistic foundation that the qualified promise of America stands. The implied danger, which tempts Douw, is that there may arise a new arrogance and intolerance which will invalidate the original victory. What is required, then, is manliness and unselfish responsibility which combine the best qualities of individualism with mutual understanding and respect between men. (p. 20)

*In the Valley* is not wholly successful. Though the scenic elements and dramatic passages are technically excellent, the total effect is of events and places seen through a remote haze, and except for Douw the main characters seldom attain more than symbolic life. Frederic admitted that ''their personalities always remained shadowy in my own mind.'' His style, elevated to meet the demands of an epic, loses force and stability in the process. Still, the novel is conceived with originality and deserves a prominent place in American historical fiction.

Following this Frederic traced the effects of independence during the period between Douw's growth to manly tolerance and Seth Fairchild's reversion to paralyzing self-indulgence. At precisely what point had the national experiment failed, if it had, and what could be learned from the subsequent experiences whch might illuminate and suggest remedies for the ills of the present? The Civil War had left vivid images of community apprehension and suffering on Frederic as a child, and to the maturing artist it attained a significance analogous to that of the War of Independence. Between these wars the nation had tested diverse political and social postures, had experienced waves of immigration, and, disturbingly, had begun to reorganize class distinctions. Great questions had remained unresolved: the relative supremacy of national and regional interests, and the willingness or unwillingness of individuals to suppress self-interest and tolerate divergent attitudes and ways in others. (pp. 20-1)

*The Damnation of Theron Ware* ... is a study of a new kind of American not-so-innocent, whose ancestors include both Huckleberry Finn [of Mark Twain's *Adventures of Huckleberry Finn*] and Faust [of Johann Wolfgang von Goethe's poem of the same name]. (p. 33)

In technique the novel is Hawthornesque, except for Frederic's deceptively realistic prose. Most of the proper names are heavily allusive and the passage of the seasons symbolizes a reversal of the regeneration of [Henry David Thoreau's] *Walden*. It moves from emblem to emblem, embodying meaning in those still-life pictures which have been characeristic of classic American fiction from its beginnings—Leatherstocking silhouetted against the sky, Dimmesdale standing bare-chested on a Boston scaffold, Bulkington glimpsed frozen to the *Pequod*'s tiller [in James Fenimore Cooper's *The Leatherstocking Tales*, Nathaniel Hawthorne's *The Scarlet Letter*, and Herman Melville's *Moby Dick*, respectively]. The decay of the modern ministry is displayed in the hierarchical arrangement of the assembly of the Methodist Conference; Theron's revulsion from the fundamentalists and his attraction to the sophisticates are repeated in his reactions to the squalor of his parsonage yard and the lush foliage next door; the foreign allure of Celia's paganized Christianity is reflected in the decor of her apartment; and Theron's youthful prejudice against Catholics is remembered in a ... cartoon of sinister priests.

When Theron meets Celia in a remote wood, halfway between the austere frenzy of a Methodist camp meeting and the Dionysian revelry of a Catholic picnic, they discover the novel's central emblem. "The path they followed had grown indefinite among the grass and creepers of the forest carpet; now it seemed to end altogether in a little copse of young birches, the delicately graceful stems of which were clustered about a parent stump, long since decayed and overgrown with lichens and layers of thick moss." The path lost and the solid beliefs of the past rotted way, tentative alternatives compete for dominance, though none now dominates. Theron is free to choose, but his choice must be sincere, positive, creative, rather than nihilistic. Above all, he must recognize that the new shoots are real and alive, not, as Sister Soulsby insists, illusory. When he does not, his damnation is assured. (pp. 36-7)

*Theron Ware* is a powerful masterpiece. It presents not only a brilliantly conceived and psychologically fascinating protagonist but a representative if unpromising man at the end of an

era of confidence and simple faith and the beginning of a darker era of complexity and doubt. It is only from the perspective of the present that we can see the full significance of what Frederic discerned at the end of the nineteenth century. The era to come—our era—would demand an inner strength much greater than had been required of men before. Deprived of the comforting assurances of the past, the modern man would be forced back upon the resources of his own character, his virtues, to use a nearly outmoded term, in order to make his way among the tangle of often questionable choices of the worldmaze. To look for stage machinery instead of truth is to invite degeneration, to confuse darkness with illumination, to strike a bargain with Satan, to lose what weed-grown Paradise is left in a diminished world.

Frederic's own slight version of Paradise, the solace he found in his mistress Kate Lyon, is the subject of a small, graceful novel written in reaction to the darkness of *Theron Ware*. Perhaps beauty in this world *is* stage illusion. In that case, a temporary stay against despair may be had by preserving the illusion. *March Hares* ... is the story of such protective self-deception, of failure and emptiness eluded by an escape into an artificial fairyland, embraced and substituted for distasteful truth. (p. 38)

Frederic's deft manipulation of point of view [in *The Market-Place*] makes severe demands on the reader's discrimination; one must be attentive to his road markers. Tension builds as the financial scheme alternates between apparent success and the constant danger of collapse, and as Thorpe's courtship is alternately frustrated and successful. The temptation to sympathize with an energetic figure who is also a scoundrel makes Thorpe's success all the more insidious. Evil appearing as evil is dangerous; evil masquerading as gumption, individualism, shrewdness, the American Dream, is a transcendent danger which can only be evaluated by the most exacting attention to humane principle. That is precisely Frederic's point. It is only by listening to the voice of principle, here that of Celia Madden (carried over from *Theron Ware*) and Thorpe's sister, that gross misreadings of the novel, such as attributing Thorpe's anti-Semitism to Frederic, can be avoided. There are numerous other pitfalls for the unwary, such as believing Thorpe's self-characterization at the end as a new man with new ideas. There is no new, humanized Thorpe; he is still a "man gathering within himself, to expend upon his fellows, the appetites, energies, insensibilities, audacities of a beast of prey." He is a twentieth-century political pirate, seizing power with stolen money. Celia's last analysis of him is accurate. "I shall always insist ... that crime was his true vocation."

Recognition came to Frederic late, and then for the wrong reasons. *Theron Ware* was read because of its scandalous impiety; *The Market-Place* because of the scandal surrounding his death. Soon thereafter, interest in his work subsided, and he has been a victim of the "effacing march of generations" which he dreaded. To a certain extent this neglect has been justified. Beginning with a journalistic conception of literature, and lacking Henry James's ability to theorize about the nature of fiction and to translate theory into practice, Frederic tended on occasion to write dramatized essays rather than novels. Not only that, but he was curiously inept with essay materials and in these novels he was often betrayed by the unresolved conflict between his ideology and the dramatic reality which embodied most faithfully his deepest understanding of the nature of men. It was only in his last three years that this conflict was resolved and his mature genius found expression. When it did, his achievement was too far in advance of current attitudes to be comprehensible to his public.

Nor has subsequent criticism been notably perceptive. Readers have classified him as a regionalist, as a realist, and as a naturalist, whereas his true descent from Hawthorne and Melville has largely gone unnoticed. Many sense the depth and power of *Theron Ware*, but find the source of his creative energy elusive.

Frederic's achievement lies in the sensitivity and power with which he probed the naiveté and inconsistency of the American Dream and announced its inevitable collapse in the face of the new order of complexity of the twentieth century. In this he surpassed all his contemporaries in his ability to dramatize, allegorize, and mythicize the coming fall from innocence. In addition, testing his vision against his own experience, he understood that a loss of innocence might not bring a dignified, saddened wisdom, but might transform youthful egotism into debased cynicism, and ultimately into predatory rapacity. Thus Frederic wrote for the twentieth century, not his own, and in his greatest works achieved a vigorous and alarming vision of the civilization to come which has, as we can now see, verified his worst fears and proved him to be one of the most perceptive and important novelists of his time. (pp. 44-5)

> *Stanton Garner, in his* Harold Frederic, *University of Minnesota Press, Minneapolis, 1969, 48 p.*

**AUSTIN BRIGGS, JR.**   (essay date 1969)

[*In this excerpt from his* The Novels of Harold Frederic, *the only full-length study of Frederic's novels, Briggs comments on style, characterization, and ideological content in several of Frederic's works. One of Briggs's central contentions is that he "treats conventional materials in a highly unconventional fashion."*]

[*Seth's Brother's Wife* is] a story that sounds as banal as a hero named Seth Fairchild. The novel itself, however, is far from what the conventional plot suggests. Here, as in his other fiction, Frederic makes witty use of what at first appear to be melodramatic situations, histrionic scenes, and stock characters. His technique is to put presumably predictable types in presumably predictable situations and then, in flashes of ironic illumination, reveal that the results were not predictable after all. The method requires readers with eyes sharp enough to see that the inconsistencies that Frederic's characters fall into are not the results of confusion in their author. They reflect his comic sense that people in real life seldom behave as they often do in books—as one expects them to.

One of the romantic conventions that Frederic plays with for comic ends is the duality between the brunette "bad" woman and the fair "pure" woman.... Superficially, he appears to resolve the contest between the two types in the classic fashion: Isabel does lose Seth to Annie, a schoolmarm; Reuben Tracy, the hero of *The Lawton Girl*, chooses Kate Minster, not Jessica, the fallen woman who worships him and sacrifices her life for him; at the end of *The Damnation* Theron Ware stands beside his wife, not the uninhibited Celia. The novels, however, show little real sympathy with the old formula. Most of Frederic's liberated young women, in fact, have already fulfilled the prophecy to which Henry James referred in "The Future of the Novel" ...: "It is the opinion of some observers that when women do obtain a free hand they will not repay the long debt to the precautionary attitude of men by unlimited consideration for the natural delicacy of the latter."

Isabel Fairchild, the young woman who "talks like a book," is a prime example. An exotic—or at any rate a liberated city girl transported to a farm; an adulteress in intent if not in act, a woman brought to the brink of ruin by her passions: these are the roles the beautiful Isabel plays. But they are roles, for though life has provided her with a woefully limited stage, Isabel is determined to live life as though it were opera. She is, Frederic says, "an artist." Having married young to gain what she calls "emancipation" from her family, she finds herself bored by a husband twenty years her senior. And as the novel opens she is trapped on a farm, more prey than ever to what John Fairchild (a third brother) identifies as the tendency of her "romantic mind to feed on itself".... Nowhere is this tendency more evident than in her epistolary flirtation with Seth after he leaves the farm for the city. He soon begins to find writing to his sister-in-law a "nuisance"; the best he can manage, usually after a good dinner or an evening spent viewing a romantic play, is a sentimental "force of sweet rhetoric." The lonely Isabel, however, treasures every line as "deeply, deliciously personal".... Although pathetic and even tragic possibilities lie in such self-delusion as Isabel's, Frederic never allows them to develop. If the portrait sometimes suggests Madame Bovary [the title character of Gustave Flaubert's novel] it usually contains comic touches that, if broadened, would bring to mind that other and different Emma who also confused life and literature—Twain's Emmeline Grangerford [from his novel *Adventures of Huckleberry Finn*].

Much as it might gratify her theatrical instincts, Isabel is neither a tragic figure nor a wicked one. On those occasions when she takes herself most seriously, Frederic is always at hand to upstage her and spoil the planned effect with an incongruous detail or an ironic aside. (pp. 29-31)

Isabel, not Frederic, would divide up womankind into the good and the bad, and generally she finds the latter role the more interesting. "Am I a wicked woman?" she asks herself late in the novel. Significantly, she debates the issue standing before her mirror, studying herself "with an almost impersonal interest".... She really does feel a good deal of remorse, though she alternates between blaming herself and others for her actions, but she never settles the question of her wickedness. Instead, she is suddenly distracted by the thought that although she has maliciously separated Seth and Annie they will eventually patch things up, marry, and—worst of all—forget her! And so she goes off to bring the young lovers together. She plays at sacrifice, Frederic makes amply clear, not to expiate any guilt she may feel but to make sure that Seth and Annie do not, in fact, forget Isabel. The scene is all she could wish. She gives her blessing to the couple with the light of a candle "glowing upon her throat and lower chin and nostrils and full, Madonna-like brows. Her face was at its best with this illumination from below. She would have been a rare beauty close before the footlights".... (pp. 32-3)

Seth Fairchild is nearly as contradictory as Isabel. He is the hero of the novel almost by default.... Seth is likable enough but a little dull. Until Isabel shows up and begins talking about the dreariness of rural life, he is the patient youngest son, resigned to caring for the plowing, the stock, and the old folks while his two brothers enjoy wider horizons. And with Isabel comes her husband—Seth's eldest brother—to take over the family responsibilities and send Seth off to "a chance in life," an editorial assistant's job on the Tecumseh *Chronicle*, a big city newspaper. It is at this point in the novel, when Seth arrives in the city and reaches "The Threshold of the World" as the chapter title puts it, that he really captures the reader's interest—and Frederic's as well, one suspects. (p. 33)

Like the Frank Courtneys, Harry Vanes, Robert Rushtons, and countless other [Horatio] Alger heroes before him, Seth has come to the city determined to be strong and steady, to be slow and sure, to strive and succeed. He discovers, however, that although "his head was full of negative information, of pitfalls to avoid, temptations to guard against . . . on the affirmative side it was all a blank". . . . (p. 34)

Having carefully prepared the reader to anticipate one more version of the success story that follows the rise of the good younger brother who makes his way in the city after serving out his time on the farm, Frederic turns his story upside down and relates the story of the good country boy who goes to ruin in the city, turns from Horatio Alger to the Prodigal Son. The conception is witty, and it is all the wittier for Frederic's ironic treatment of urban debauchery. Many an upstate New York farmer and villager, Frederic says, dreams wistfully of Tecumseh's "gilded temptations, its wild revels of sumptuous gayety, its dazzling luxuriance of life, as shepherd boys on the plains of Dura might have dreamed of the mysteries and marvels of Babylon". . . . For the sake of the occasional shepherd boy who made the trip, one dearly hopes that Babylon turned out to be better provided than Tecumseh. There may be real dens of iniquity here, but Seth does not find them. (p. 35)

After the series of chapters that send the hero virtually blindfolded and spinning from situation to situation, *Seth's Brother's Wife* loses a great deal of its comic momentum. The humbling of Isabel remains: she has yet to learn that Seth was not out till all hours killing her husband for love of her, but instead was proposing to Annie in the moonlight. The whole business of Albert's murder and the resultant mystery, however, is far from comic; it is in fact conceived as melodrama. But Frederic's comic sense never deserts him completely. Even Albert's murder cannot relegate the Comic Muse to a minor role for long. At the very moment the reader is asked to shudder at the spectacle of Albert's cold and broken corpse, he is distracted by a pair of rube vaudevillians—a lugubrious undertaker and a county coroner in the Dogberry tradition [from William Shakespeare's *Much Ado about Nothing*]. Just as the vast extent of the late Albert's political schemes is being fully exposed, it is also revealed that the villain has left the bulk of his vast fortune to his brothers—the greatest share by far to Seth.

The finer ironies of the closing chapters, however, are reserved mainly for the public rather than the private sphere of action. It develops that the real opposition to Albert's political ambitions has come not from aroused public morality, nor from crusading newspapers, nor from reformers (tea-drinking or otherwise). Richard Ansdell does finally win the congressional nomination and election, but he does so only with the leave and assistance of one Abram K. Beekman, known to all of upstate New York as "the Boss." Beekman is introduced late in the novel and may very well be an afterthought on Frederic's part. It is entertaining to imagine Frederic reading a novel about "An American Politician" like the one that so disgusted Albert and sitting down to produce Beekman. Afterthought or not, Frederic has painted a superb portrait of the tall, chin-whiskered politico who has worked his way up through local politics to a position of great, if obscure, power "by that process of exhaustion which we call the survival of the fittest," as Frederic wittily puts it.

From his first appearance Abe Beekman is fascinating. . . . An odd amalgam of homely democratic virtue and ruthless boss-ism, Beekman stands for neither the wonderfully monstrous corruption of Senator Ratcliffe in Henry Adams' *Democracy,* nor the monstrously wonderful virtue of [Booth] Tarkington's Gentleman from Indiana [from his novel of the same name]. He stands for—he is—a perplexing fact of American life. (pp. 44-6)

Beekman, in many ways a preliminary sketch of Brother Soulsby in *The Damnation,* makes possible a perfect comic resolution to the political matter of *Seth.* His role in the novel surprisingly and explosively confounds conventional expectations. On the one hand, he provides an ironic variation on the honest countryman who gives the rich city slicker his come-uppance; on the other, he plays hob with the tale of the young reformer who defeats the powers of political corruption. Frederic saves his parting shot until the last page but one. There he discloses that the Honorable Richard Ansdell, "the embodiment of Principle," is shortly to marry the gayest widow in Washington—who is, of course, Isabel Fairchild.

For a first novel, written by a young man not yet quite thirty who had published almost no fiction, *Seth's Brother's Wife* is an impressive performance. To those most concerned with following the rise of realism (the grimmer sort of realism, that is) the interesting pages of *Seth* will remain its early ones. Yet even in the bleaker pages of the novel Frederic's view was likely to shift suddenly and catch the humorous side of things. Into the gloomy picture of a farmhouse funeral, for example, Frederic could not resist introducing the comic discomfiture of soft little Father Turner, the Episcopal priest whose side whiskers reminded Isabel of baby brushes. Nor could he resist catching the neighborhood farm women at the funeral service as they furtively scraped their feet on the parlor carpet to test its nap.

The pages of *Seth* that capture the darker side of rural life are important, but it seems clear that those pages are neither the most notable nor the most characteristic of the work. Although it is possible to see in Frederic's first novel early stirrings of the movement toward the kind of realism that was soon to become dominant in American fiction, it is more reasonable to see the novel as continuing a tradition of comic realism that had already been vigorous for some time.

Frederic had the perception to see that "what the world knows as American humor" is "the grim, fatalist habit of seizing upon the grotesque side". . . . Yet he somehow managed to see life as humorous without finding it so terribly grim after all. He was, in an old-fashioned sense of the word, a humorist—one who delights in viewing the humors of others. The character in *Seth's Brother's Wife* who comes closest to functioning as a moral center for the book is John Fairchild. John, Frederic says, "had in almost unmeted degree that habit of mind which welcomes statements of both sides of a controversy". . . . Harold Frederic had that same habit of mind, no small virtue in a young man starting out to write novels. (pp. 47-8)

The faults of Frederic's [*In the Valley*] are Frederic's, and they are several. The dialogue, usually so strong in Frederic's fiction, is frequently weighted down with an eighteenth-century rhetoric more appropriate to the neoclassic essay than the daily conversation of colonial New York. And as for the characters, Frederic himself later confessed that "their personalities always remained shadowy in my own mind."

Saddest of all is the plot. (p. 53)

Frederic's fiction simply does not dramatize the historical truth as he sees it. His fiction calls for deeds of derring-do, for displays of freedom-loving heroism and goodness in conflict with Tory wickedness. His sense of the history of the Revolution, however, is far beyond such Whiggish simplification. The plot of brave New York patriots creating a brave history does not jibe with Frederic's instinctive feeling that the real story is of men shaped primarily by events. As fiction, *In the Valley* presents a personal conflict between a hero and a villain; as history, it presents civil conflict between ordinary men fighting for complicated motives of national origin (what Frederic calls "race"), class, economics, and prejudice.

If, like Scott at his best, Frederic had chosen for his hero a man relatively disengaged from the conflict he witnesses, *In the Valley* might have been a far more solid achievement. Instead, he chose to combine in a single character a partisan protagonist and narrator who must at times speak for Frederic's dispassionate and far from simple view of events. (pp. 54-5)

The convoluted lines of relationship among the characters . . . suggest that Frederic worked within romantic convention only with a certain confusion. He is unable to decide whether virtue or vice is to be assigned to dark-featured and plain-mannered seriousness, whether fine clothes and manners and fair good looks bespeak good or evil. Later he would unite the opposing qualities of his paired characters in single characters such as Theron Ware or Joel Thorpe. His interest in the simple external conflicts between the dark and the fair would give way to a mature concern for the complex internal struggles of individuals who contain within themselves both innocence and guilt, weakness and strength, good and evil. Unfortunately, when he set the plot and characters of *In the Valley* he committed himself to the conventions of his juvenile fiction, conventions that appear to have but poorly represented his sense of reality. (pp. 57-8)

One expects to be able to trace a line of development in Frederic, as in other artists, from the early to the late work. But it is surprising that Frederic seems to double back from this second novel to his first, *Seth's Brother's Wife*. Almost all of Frederic's modern-day critics, following the lead of Howells, have celebrated *Seth* as the triumph of a novelist finding himself as a realist, and have dismissed *In the Valley* as the failure of a realist temporarily seduced by historical romance. Although such a view does have some truth in it, it also has the unfortunate consequence of obscuring the similarities that do exist between the two novels. Completed and published after *Seth* and decidedly an inferior and very different work, *In the Valley* is nevertheless a prime source for *Seth's Brother's Wife*. Putting aside the very different ways in which Frederic treats his materials in the two novels, one is struck by how alike those materials are. As we have seen, Frederic had the story of *In the Valley* well in mind many years before he completed that novel or began *Seth*. When he temporarily abandoned *In the Valley* to work on *Seth*, the story and characters he used turned out to be variations on the story and characters that he had just laid aside. (pp. 60-1)

[Jessica in *The Lawton Girl*] is neither the harlot of lurid realism nor the victim of the conventional maid's tragedy. (p. 84)

The really odd thing about Jessica, what makes her so unconventional in her role of fallen woman, is that most of the time she is just what one expects to find in a conventional blonde heroine. The misery of her home life and a deadly boredom drove her into Horace's arms, but Jessica remains very much

as Reuben Tracy remembers her—one of the sweetest, hardest-working, best-behaved pupils he ever taught. In Frederic's fiction Jessica is not related to lush, free-mannered young women like Isabel Fairchild and Celia Madden [of *Seth* and *Theron Ware*, respectively], but to women like Annie Fairchild and Alice Ware [of *Seth* and *Theron Ware*, respectively], who combine a strain of patient endurance with a yielding weakness for men who are boyish, weak, and hypocritical. (p. 85)

Kate Minster is no more the stock Good Woman than Jessica Lawton is the Bad Woman. For one thing, Kate is sexually attractive, surprisingly more so than Jessica, the unwed mother and former prostitute. No frail blonde, Kate is a tall, forceful woman with raven hair, "softly luxuriant" olive skin, and "large, richly brown, deep-fringed eyes which looked proudly and steadily on all the world, young men included". . . . In the character of Kate Minster . . . , Frederic abandons the conventional heroine once and for all: Kate's portrait derives from Isabel, the bored vamp of *Seth*, rather than from the patient school-teacher Annie Fairchild.

Frederic manages with great skill to portray Kate as a passionate and spirited young woman while at the same time showing her almost entirely through the eyes of two suitors who sentimentalize her outrageously. (p. 86)

There is nothing of the Madonna or the fairy princess in Kate Minster, Reuben and Horace notwithstanding. She has inherited her father's boundless energy but has been able to find no satisfying outlet for it. (p. 88)

Kate Minster is obviously one of those New Women who were so much the talk in the nineties. There is something in her dilemma, however, that is common to both sexes. Frederic was interested in the New Woman . . . but he found that their problems were shared by the New Man as well. Later, in the career of Christian Tower, the hero of *Gloria Mundi*, he would work out with elaborate skill and interest the implications of the same question posed in his portrait of Kate: granted good will and power, what then? (p. 91)

Like most of Frederic's novels, *The Lawton Girl* treats conventional materials in a highly unconventional fashion. It begins with a cast that scarcely seems to require introduction: a poor but idealistic schoolmaster become lawyer; an unscrupulous and weak-willed lawyer out to marry and defraud a wealthy heroine; a fallen woman determined to redeem herself; a beautiful heiress who wishes to devote herself to philanthropy. As the novel progresses, however, it becomes increasingly clear that it is the characters' own ideas of themselves that are conventional and sentimental. To read *The Lawton Girl* simply as a realistic rendering of small town life is to overlook the more impressive achievement: Frederic's wry and good-natured exposure of the comic contrast between the grand roles that people plan for themselves and the roles they actually play. (p. 96)

*The Damnation of Theron Ware* . . . is what its English title and American subtitle suggest, a novel of illumination. Its opening and closing chapters alike contradict the view that it is a tale of spiritual innocence falling into corruption, a study of "degeneration" (to use a favorite word of the nineties). Nothing indicates more clearly how ignorant Theron is of his true self than his disposition to view his experience in the same mistaken fashion as so many readers of *The Damnation*. (p. 123)

It is common in speaking of Theron Ware's illumination to say that he is exposed to the new, to the new science of Dr. Ledsmar, the new theology of Father Forbes, and the new hedonism of Celia Madden, the New Woman. It is as much to the point, however, to observe that Theron is exposed to the old. When Father Forbes subjects Abraham and the Bible to scholarly examination, Theron asks, "But this is something very new?" Forbes replies, "Bless you, no!" and cites Epicurus and Lucretius as Darwinians. "As for this eponym thing," he adds, "why Saint Augustine called attention to it fifteen hundred years ago". . . . Dr. Ledsmar's one book is an anthropological history of serpent worship, and he is the foremost authority on Assyriology in the United States. Celia, when she is not playing Hypatia, wants to be a Greek pagan. "They were all there long ago," she says of the things she wants out of life, "thousands of years ago". . . . (p. 128)

Oliver Wendell Holmes speculated that science might substitute the Rise of Man for the Fall and so cause "the utter disintegration of spiritual pessimisms." As the twentieth century has appallingly shown, Dr. Holmes lacked proper confidence in the staying power of pessimisms. The new science which is so much the talk in *The Damnation* does dispense with the Fall, but it does away with the Rise of Man as well. Life becomes, as Sister Soulsby says, "a see-saw with all of us." In the novel only Theron expresses any faith in what Father Forbes terms the most "utterly baseless and empty" of all our myths, "this idea that humanity progresses". . . . (p. 129)

To Frederic's mind evolution meant not the progress of the race but, as he puts it in *Seth's Brother's Wife,* "that process of exhaustion which we call the survival of the fittest". . . . In a sense, Dr. Ledsmar suggests, ontogeny recapitulates phylogeny after birth as well as before: each man must pass through the barbarisms and blunders of all men throughout the history of the race. Undoubtedly *The Damnation* is a classic statement of beliefs and values in the latter nineteenth century, but there should be no doubt that Frederic sees the education of Theron Ware in a universal perspective. The new thought of Ledsmar and Forbes does not preach optimistically . . . on "the magnificent and well-nigh incredible conception of Change . . . gigantic, miraculous change, an overwhelming of the old in ruin and an emergence of the new." Instead, it holds out to Theron that awful vision of time, of all history. . . . "You see, there is nothing new," says Father Forbes to Theron: "Everything is built on the ruins of something else. Just as the material earth is made up of countless billions of dead men's bones, so the mental world is all alive with the ghosts of dead men's thoughts and beliefs, the wraiths of dead races' faiths and imaginings". . . . (pp. 129-30)

The ultimate irony in *The Damnation* is Frederic's disclosure that Theron's faith in his capacity for self-development remains undiminished and that he has learned nothing from even the last of his "illuminations." "We surmise that we have not heard the last of Ware," wrote one reviewer, and the speculation is as unsettling in its way as the one that closes [Herman Melville's] *The Confidence-Man:* "Something further may follow this Masquerade." That Frederic saw Theron's illusions in *The Damnation of Theron Ware* as comic, rather than tragic . . . detracts nothing from his achievement, one of the great achievements of American letters. (pp. 138-39)

*March Hares* opens approximately where *The Damnation* closes. Mosscrop gazes into the garbage-strewn Thames with much the same sense of personal waste and disgust that must have driven Theron Ware to the East River on the night he thought of committing suicide on the Brooklyn Bridge. Mosscrop is much closer to jumping than Theron was, however, for he has long lived with the sense of the past that Theron encountered for the first time in the remarks of Father Forbes and Dr. Ledsmar. "Never mind the dead men" is Sister Soulsby's advice to Theron. But, Frederic asks in *March Hares,* how does one forget them? What if the past will not die?

Mosscrop's dilemma is implicit not only in Theron's experiences but in those of the protagonists of the other works as well. The young men and women of Frederic's earlier novels struggle and strive to attain the sophistication and knowledge that Mosscrop has attained at thirty. Even at eighteen, Mosscrop jokes, "Confucius, John Knox, and Lord Bacon rolled in one would have been frightened of me". . . . Application, intelligence, and opportunity have taken him through the years of schooling that characters like Seth Fairchild lacked, until he now holds the most highly-endowed chair his university has to offer.

All his intelligence, all his learning, however, have left Mosscrop in a position as absurd as any the country boy heroes ever fell into. Thanks to the hobbyhorse of the man who endowed his university and his chair, he is doomed to lecturing on the crackpot thesis that the Culdees of ancient Scotland were the Chaldeans of the Bible. Mosscrop lectures on the Culdees three weeks a year to half-empty classrooms and has nothing more to do. When Vestalia asks him how he earns his living, he answers bitterly and honestly: "I am an habitual criminal by profession". . . . (pp. 154-55)

Even when *March Hares* does speak in the light-hearted tones that the reviewers heard to the exclusion of all else, sadness is not far away. The pleasant description of the first day Mosscrop and Vestalia spend together, for example, includes a somber backdrop of ruined temples, fragments of classical statuary, and ancient sarcophagi in the British Museum. Love finally does save Mosscrop, as love saves Alexander Waring in "The Editor and the School Ma'am." At the conclusion of that story, Waring abandons the Russian novels on which he has been feeding his gloom. Commenting on the suitability of [Nikolai] Gogol's realism for the American scene, he gives his office boy the money for a new overcoat; and casting aside his copy of *Dead Souls,* he says in the closing line, "let them go to their own funeral. I like to feel that I am alive." Even here there is a note of qualification: "I like to feel." So also in *March Hares* one senses a shadow of doubt beneath the high spirits of its brighter passages and right through to the conventional happy ending. (pp. 155-56)

One of the things that may have deceived readers about Frederic's true accomplishment in *Gloria Mundi* is that it harks back to many of the conventions of the mid-Victorian novel. . . . For his hero, Frederic went to that old standby, the lost heir; for one of his heroines he went to Dickens and came up with a Lady Edith Cressage who has been sold into a fashionable and disasterous marriage by her parents, as Edith Dombey [of Dickens's *Dombey and Son*] was sold by her mother and Major Bagstock.

Although the many echoes of the mid-Victorian may have persuaded some readers that Frederic, until then always the most up-to-date of authors, had regressed, *Gloria Mundi* is in the best sense a novel of its moment. (p. 161)

*Gloria Mundi* is a romance, but it is certainly not the light-hearted romance it has been taken to be. As his name suggests, it matters very little that Christian is an Englishman raised in France rather than an American raised in New York. . . . Frederic's young men and women are always deciding that the glass slipper fits, that they are born to something wonderful. . . . Whether their dream is the generous hope of public reform or the selfish egotism that mistakes self-cultivation for salvation, they are all true believers in the millennium. (p. 172)

All of Frederic's heroes might be said to be "lost heirs," and the dilemma they face when they come into their inheritance is cruel.

On the one hand, the heir can react like Theron. "He lacked even the impulse to turn round and inspect the cocoon from which he had emerged. Let the past bury the past. He had no vestige of interest in it". . . . But such egotism as this, which smugly confuses process with progress, seldom goes unpunished, and even if it does, it is contemptible. To Frederic the naiveté that is damning is that which looks upon its own former innocence and on the innocence of others without sympathy. On the other hand, if one learns the lesson of history, one is unlikely ever to stir far from his chair. Although humility is a safeguard against the excesses of egotistical enthusiasm, it is uncomfortably allied to paralyzing self-distrust in Frederic's thinking.

Christian comes to an understanding of life that the protagonists of the other novels never attain, but his discovery is implicit in all of the novels. "We learn only one thing from all the numberless millions who have gone before us," Christian says at the end of *Gloria Mundi,* "that man is less important than he thinks he is". . . . (p. 174)

All of the control that one perceives in the earlier fiction, however, does not prepare one for the degree to which Frederic sustains the pretense of moral neutrality throughout *The Market-Place.* One does not expect a sermon, a tract, or an exposé meant to shock . . . ; but one does expect some direct criticism. Frederic had always been primarily interested in those who deceive themselves rather than in those who deceive others. . . . Yet there had always been irony to spare for everybody. If the main concern in *The Damnation of Theron Ware* was with Theron's weak and petty hypocrisies born of self-delusion, the practiced and conscious hypocrisies of Brothers Winch and Pierce were not overlooked.

Knowing Frederic's earlier work, one opens *The Market-Place* with no expectation that Thorpe need fail in business or be carried off to jail, but one does anticipate that sooner or later the tycoon with the Midas touch will wake to find that he has grown ass's ears. One waits in vain. The shafts of irony are never loosed; the moment when one can laugh at the collapse of the millionaire's pretensions never comes. To be sure, the novel does end with laughter. In the last paragraph, Thorpe has just decided what new worlds to conquer. As he walks into his living room, one of his guests, Celia Madden, is speaking of him: "I shall always insist . . . that crime was his true vocation". . . . Thorpe laughs hardest of all—and laughs last. (pp. 182-83)

Although there is no reason to believe that Frederic had a pair of novels in mind when he began *Gloria Mundi,* he must have been aware by the time he finished it that he still had a great deal more to say about the uses of power and the possibilities of social reform. Unlike as the two novels at first appear to be, *Gloria Mundi* and *The Market-Place* are companion pieces, connected not only by the several characters they share but by their themes as well. Together the two works form a kind of dialogue. In *Gloria Mundi* Frederic's viewpoint is that of an older man, a man who has outlived the enthusiasms of his youth and for whom the glory of this world has passed away.

In *The Market-Place,* insofar as Thorpe's viewpoint controls the narrative, the world is seen through youthful eyes, delighting in the vigorous exercise of vulgar, vain, amoral energy. (p. 198)

*Gloria Mundi* follows hapless Christian Tower through to the numbing conclusion that man's dreams and hopes are impossible of fulfillment, are doomed to failure because of the brute resistance that life offers to any meaningful sort of change. *The Market-Place,* on the other hand, presents a hero possessed of an energy that men of self-distrustful conscience like Christian can scarcely conceive of. The supremely confident Thorpe seems a force in himself. He is an awesome embodiment of that raw vitality which Henry Adams found almost oppressive in Theodore Roosevelt: "the singular primitive quality that belongs to ultimate matter—the power that medieval theology assigned to God—. . . pure act."

Against *Gloria Mundi* and its evocation of Ecclesiastes—its sense of history as repetition—stands *The Market-Place* and its dynamic financier. Is Christian right when he protests to Thorpe that whether one leaves the world alone or not "it goes round just the same" . . .? Or is Thorpe right in his faith in his own vitality? He reminds Christian that there was a Thorpe among the judges who condemned Charles I; Christian counters by reminding Thorpe of the Restoration.

In *Gloria Mundi* and *The Market-Place* Frederic writes out of an acute sense of his historical moment. To what extent, he asks, will the age about to die determine the future? To what extent will the age about to be born depart from the past? Standing at the end of the nineteenth century, Frederic looks back upon nearly one hundred years of power garnered in the name of progress, and, turning to the century ahead, he asks just what that power implies. (pp. 199-200)

> *Austin Briggs, Jr., in his* The Novels of Harold Frederic, *Cornell University Press, 1969, 234 p.*

## EDMUND WILSON (essay date 1970)

[*Wilson briefly surveys most of Frederic's works in this excerpt, noting that, though his novels have attracted critical attention, "a certain sour flavor" has hampered their popularity. Further, Wilson asserts that Theron's fall at the end of* The Damnation of Theron Ware *seems improbable because of its swiftness and ease.*]

"**In the Valley**" has a certain interest for its picture of the hostile relations between the Dutch and the English colonists, and the strained situations that were peculiar at that time to New York, where a feudal tradition prevailed, as it did not do in New England, so that the farmers were driven to revolt, not so much against the King overseas as against the local Tory landowners. Harold Frederic makes this struggle come at last to a climax with the battle of Oriskany, near Utica, in which the aggrieved farmers confront and defeat the Tories, who had as allies the Mohawk Indians. But, as a story, "**In the Valley**" is wooden. It suffers from the stereotypes of its genre. The characters are all with such obvious design put through their historical paces that we never accept them as real individuals. (p. 114)

Frederic's two other early novels display a more interesting talent. . . . In "**Seth's Brother's Wife**" and "**The Lawton Girl**," he presents almost every kind of person that was to be found at that time in such a city as Utica: the moderately well-to-do farmer; the swindler and the crooked politician; the newspaper editor who was venal and the honest one who was zealous for reform; the serious-minded schoolteacher; the family of run-down ex-canallers; the family who had in one generation been made rich by the "knitting mills" and who lived in a large square mansion and cultivated what I used to like to call—partly deriving, as I do, from that region—their cold-storage Utica gentility. The life in these farmlands and villages is not shown in a particularly cheerful light, and though the landscape is accurately described, its ennobling grandeur and splendor are hardly done justice by Frederic, who had almost no sense of poetry, who said frankly that he could not read it, and that he had never written two lines of verse in his life. . . . You have, in these novels, the stultifying dullness of evenings on the old farm for a young man who has had to come back to it after working on a newspaper in the city; the embattled relations between workers and owners created by a lockout at the iron-works; the remorseless small-town machinations of confidence men and bankers. And Frederic very well conveys the nature of the life of a region which had only been settled at the end of the eighteenth century, where the communities had not wholly succeeded in finding their purpose and form. . . . In these novels, Harold Frederic has not yet been able entirely to free himself from the conventions of the fiction of the period. Though he always sticks conscientiously to real types and real conditions, he must not disappoint his readers by not having the stories come out right: the good man must get the good girl, morality must win in the end, and this is sometimes brought about in a way that is incongruous with the general tenor. On the other hand, as Frederic explains in the preface to the Uniform Edition of his fiction [see excerpt above, 1897], he has found himself being distracted from his tendency to plan too methodically, in order to demonstrate something, by finding that "to my surprise at first, and then to my interested delight, the people [in **'The Lawton Girl'**] took matters into their own hands quite from the start. It seemed only by courtesy that I even presided over their meetings, and that my sanction was asked for their comings and goings." He now confesses that it had been "a false and cowardly thing" to kill off, in deference to the current proprieties, the once fallen Lawton girl, who has so nobly rehabilitated herself and who is pathetically made to protest on her deathbed, "I tell you I *have* lived it down!" (pp. 114, 117-18)

[In **"The Damnation of Theron Ware,"** we] are still in upstate New York, but we are introduced to characters of a different kind from those who have figured in Frederic's earlier fiction. They are at once on a higher level—men of exceptional intellect, a woman of aesthetic sensibilities—and more mercilessly treated by the author, with an almost complete disregard of the contemporary literary conventions. The book attracted much attention both in England and over here. The story was run off with the smoothest skill; the author had been at work on it five years. It was amusing, absorbing, rather shocking. It dealt in the coolest way with those problems of religious faith which had already, with more emotion, been made the subject of novels and poems. It was the kind of book that everybody read. (pp. 123-24)

Many readers, including myself, though they have followed this novel with fascination, cannot help finding it rather repellent. A rereading makes the reasons for this plain. The three tempters, though Celia and the priest are presented not without sympathy, do really behave rather badly. They all put on performances for Theron in a way that shows little consideration for a green young man they are supposed to like. Why, for example, is Father Forbes, who is presented as the last word in Catholic sophistication and must know about Methodist doc-

trine, made to begin talking about "this Christ-myth" only the second time Theron has met him? This is surely neither behavior becoming a priest nor elementary good manners. . . . Celia Madden should surely have been able to size Theron up well enough to know that when she refers to "Meredith" he would hardly have known about George Meredith. He thinks she means Owen Meredith, the once popular author of "Lucile," of whom Theron *has* vaguely heard. When they see what is happening to Theron as a result of their "illuminating" him, all three wash their hands of him with cold contempt and without a word of pity or counsel. The "damnation," also, is made to take place with what seems improbable speed. Though Theron's weaknesses have been shown from the start—his cowardice and his impracticality—is it plausible that in a mere six months Theron's face, as Celia's brother is made to say, should have ceased to give the impression of "the face of a saint" and to seem "more like the face of a barkeeper"? When Theron follows Celia to New York City, full at the same time of nasty suspicions of her relations with Father Forbes and of daydreams of going with her to Europe on a yacht supplied, presumably, by her money, she dismisses him and crushes him in what is surely—though it has never been suggested that this rather conceited girl is remarkable for a kindly nature—an unnecessarily bitchy way. It is impossible, it seems to me, at the present time to agree with Harry Thurston Peck, who said when **"Theron Ware"** came out that it was "a literary event of very great importance." I doubt whether a great novel can be written around a central character who, having once been made sufficiently attractive for the reader to share his emotions, is in the end so abjectly humiliated. It is true that Sister Soulsby, the half-charlatan Methodist "debt raiser," whose sympathy and common sense provide the redeeming element among Theron's mischief-making friends, does rescue him from his "damnation" by finding him a job in Seattle, to which he sets out with visions of using his exceptional oratorical gifts to get himself elected to the Senate, but the effect of the book is unpleasant. It had appeared in Frederic's earlier novels that, unlike his respected Howells, he took a harsh sort of relish in producing confrontations which would give rise to quarrels and insults. Though Frederic, as his talent develops, is becoming more and more a master of a clear and impartial kind of comedy, there is a certain sour flavor in all his work, which perhaps, although certain of his books in their time could not fail to attract attention, has kept them from being much read since. (pp. 125-26)

It was for a long time a serious error on the part of American criticism to disparage Frederic's English novels. . . . But Frederic had evidently exhausted the material of the life he had known at home; he had nothing more from there to write about. Yet it is important to note that, in his subsequent novels, the central figure is, except in one instance (in whom, however, there is also an American element), either a transplanted American, an Englishman who has lived in the United States, or one who has grown up abroad and just come for the first time to England. Harold Frederic has simply gone on to utilize his own later experience. This is a Frederic now immersed in English life but still unmistakably American.

In the novels he is henceforth to write, Frederic's mimicry of English, Scotch, and Irish speech seems, at least to a non-British reader, almost as faithful as his expert rendering of the speech of his various kinds of New Yorkers. The little book **"Mrs. Albert Grundy: Observations in Philistia,"** which he published in 1896 in a series called **"The Mayfair Set"**—when he had been in England twelve years—is a curious tour de force. It exactly catches the tone—coy humor, snobbish chit-chat, light discussions of subjects of general interest—of the writings of G. S. Street, who also contributed to this series. At the other extreme of history, in a pair of short stories that are made to take place in the Middle Ages, Frederic brings to the Wars of the Roses the same kind of practical grasp and carefully exact description as he does to an Oneida County turkey shoot or a Methodist camp meeting. When he came, in **"The Market-Place,"** to deal seriously with modern England, I learn from Mr. Austin Briggs [the author of "The Novels of Harold Frederic"], it was the American reviewers, not the English, who complained that Frederic's knowledge of English life was only superficial. (pp. 130-31)

**"Gloria Mundi,"** is not of Frederic's best, but ambitious and rather surprising. Frederic is trying here to deal with the pressure of modern change on the hereditary structure of England. . . . The reader is left wondering what point Frederic wants to make. Is it simply that it is difficult for the landed nobility to dispossess themselves? . . . (pp. 131-32)

**"The Market-Place"** is connected with **"Gloria Mundi"** and evidently intended as a counterpart to it. Though Frederic has studied and documented himself on the life of the aristocracy, **"Gloria Mundi"** is rather unreal. **"The Market-Place"** is closer to what he has lived. It is perhaps, after **"Theron Ware,"** the best of Frederic's novels. (p. 132)

The merits of **"The Market-Place"** lie not only in its elements of adventure but also in the psychological interest of the specious rationalizations and the pseudo-benevolent sentiments with which the predatory Thorpe tries occasionally to justify to himself the more and more callous skulduggeries into which his drive for power is dragging him. (pp. 132-33)

> *Edmund Wilson, "Two Neglected American Novelists: II—Harold Frederic, the Expanding Upstater,"* in The New Yorker, *Vol. XLVI, No. 16, June 6, 1970, pp. 112-14, 117-19, 123-34.*\*

**JEAN FRANTZ BLACKALL** (essay date 1971)

[*Blackall thoroughly examines the characterization of* The Market-Place.]

The characterization of Joel Thorpe, hero of *The Market-Place* . . . , is Frederic's deepest and most provocative psychological portrait. If Thorpe is less the reflective man than Theron Ware of the *Damnation* . . . or Christian Tower of *Gloria Mundi* . . . , he causes the reader to reflect more upon his characteristics and behavior, because he is the active rather than the passive man, one who shapes the course of events rather than one whose fate depends largely upon an intellectual buffeting at the hands of other characters. Hence his story has more vitality; it has a cleaner plot line; and it moves more quickly than the other substantial late novels. Its ideational content is rendered more in organic terms, in what Thorpe is and does, and less by set speeches on the part of other characters. When one comes to consider how the behavior, the needs, the motivations, of Thorpe may be accounted for, however, his character proves to be far more complex than that of Theron Ware, who is essentially sophomoric, or that of Christian Tower, whose needs are more intelligibly commonplace. How Frederic feels about his character, and how he wants his reader to feel, are matters of considerable interest. Harold Frederic's ultimate statement about his hero is important not only in assessing the meaning and quality of this individual work, but also, I believe, because

his perplexities are corroborative of similar perplexities in other American nineteenth-century novelists in the valuation to be set upon the typical new man, the type of the capitalist entrepreneur, as conceived from an American writer's point of view. (p. 388)

Harold Frederic's dramatic rendering of the psychology of the tycoon in both public and private life is highly credible and complexly developed. Can we conclude, then, that the portrait was in itself Frederic's accomplishment . . .—that Thorpe is a full-length portrait, that it is a psychological as well as an objective one, that Thorpe's acts express in dramatic terms behavior appropriate to his psychology and role, and that Frederic found means to integrate the public and private life of such a figure into a plausible whole? This alone would seem to be a formidable accomplishment in coming to terms with the emergent nineteenth-century type of the financial buccaneer. Yet, taking a harder view, does one conclude that Frederic's stance as artist, like that of the news reporter, was primarily documentary, rather than reflective or interpretive in moral terms? Can one discern a moral assimilation of the tycoon under way in *The Market-Place* as well as an analytic understanding of the type? Such an attempt does reveal itself, I believe, in the fact that the major characters, including Thorpe himself, are perpetually made to reflect upon his nature and acts. (p. 396)

The idea of metamorphosis is in Thorpe's conception of himself from the beginning of the novel, and also, to some extent, in the terms in which Frederic characterizes him. When Thorpe is on the eve of success he symbolically rejuvenates himself, shaving off his beard, modifying his wardrobe and name ("Mr. Stormont Thorpe"), contemplating marriage for the first time. He is beginning life anew. Thereafter, modifications in Thorpe between the predatory figure of the market place and the triumphant man whom the predator has created are recurrently indicated by physical manifestations. In the one role he is monolithic, unkempt, lethargic, with a dull "lack-lustre" eye . . . that is the sphinxlike . . . mask for intense mental activity, the opaque eye in which Celia Madden sees dead men mirrored. . . . To others he appears a barbarian . . . or a pirate . . . or a criminal type. . . . Thorpe fluctuates between these two persons according to his fortunes, but basically, because he is successful, we see the figure characterized as a predatory animal or a primitive man yielding somewhat to the social animal. Superficially, Thorpe changes his clothes and his manners and for a time becomes too tame, a mere alderman in his wife's opinion. . . . More significantly he becomes identified with figures that integrate primitive qualities with accepted (albeit violent) social roles: a military leader, a dictator, a successful revolutionist. (p. 398)

Is Frederic asking a question, possibly, rather than giving an answer? Is Thorpe's moral portrait one in which good and evil are shown to coexist and the reader left to ponder the enigma? Or does Frederic press the reader toward some conclusive assessment? I think both things are true. Surely Frederic does judge Thorpe morally both through the remarks of reliable characters and by his own ironic implications. Yet, for whatever reason, calculated or unintentional, Frederic has created a portrait of variable effect.

If the condemnation of Thorpe was Frederic's primary objective, if Thorpe was meant to be taken as merely unscrupulous and ruthless, self-indulgent and lazy, whimsical and dangerous, and this represented Frederic's whole judgment of his character, then he has weighted his book in a way that works to obscure such a judgment. Despite Thorpe's disillusionment with success in the terms in which he had originally defined it, he is basically better off and happier at the end of his story, whether one judges him in the world's eyes or his own. He has made and secured his desired fortune, and this fortune enables him to choose freely another course of action. He has suffered no legal consequences of wrongdoing. Nor is he punished with remorse for his moral myopia. Thorpe wins the woman of his choice, not once but twice, and does this by being true to his character of buccaneer, not by forsaking it. (p. 399)

[Though] Frederic's granting an inner perspective on Thorpe may have the effect of revealing his unplumbed murky depths to the reader and his capacity for self-deception, it also has the effect of creating a sympathy for the *human* being, capable of fear, of fatigue, of self-doubt, of an idealistic love for a woman. If the book casts judgment on the symbolized type of the speculator, it does so more on Colin Semple than on Joel Thorpe because, compared with Thorpe, Semple is dehumanized and because his rudimentary money morality is inadequate even to Thorpe himself: "To the other's [Thorpe's] notion he seemed the personification of business—without an ounce of distracting superfluous flesh upon his wiry, tough little frame, without a trace of unnecessary politeness, or humour, or sensibility of any sort. He was the machine perfected and fined down to absolute essentials. He could understand a joke if it was useful to him to do so. He could drink, and even smoke cigarettes, with a natural air if these exercises seemed properly to belong to the task he had in hand. Thorpe did not conceive him doing anything for the mere human reason that he liked to do it".... Sentimentality, especially toward women, at times renders Thorpe mawkish; its manifestations are one aspect of his lack of sophistication. Nonetheless, sentimentality also justifies him in the author's view, judging especially by a pivotal instance in which Thorpe is forgiven for this quality by both Celia Madden and Lady Cressage.... Surely both plots, the terms in which the economic battle is defined, and certain aspects of characterization all work against the assumption that Frederic wholly condemns Thorpe.

The novel also posits a practical problem of how, after all, such a one as Thorpe is to live. If by fulfilling his impulses Thorpe is shown to sin against traditional moralities, he is likewise shown to sin according to his own understanding when he ceases to exercise his own peculiar impulse to power. From Thorpe's point of view he sins not by breaking the law or trampling on the economic condition of little people or using people to his own ends, but rather, by failing to fulfill the obligations that he understands power entails. (p. 400)

[Thorpe] is really a complex of three figures, which taken together elicit an ambivalent response in the reader and, I believe, in Frederic himself. There is the intelligent, persevering, daring, and successful Thorpe, hero of the mercantile plot, whose capacity for effective action speaks to the imagination. There is the doubting, fearful, perplexed, loving Thorpe, hero of the romantic plot, who addresses himself to the human sympathies. And there is the predatory Thorpe, whose destructive potential, whether in public or private life, provides the reflective substance of the novel. This multiplication of perspectives on Thorpe undoubtedly renders him a more rounded and a more interesting character, but Frederic's tendency so to perceive character, and the consequences, in terms of moral ambiguity, might fruitfully be compared with the same practice in Henry James. For the multilateral quality of Thorpe's characterization may also be seen to complicate, and possibly to obscure, the moral statement of the novel....

The problem in atittude that Frederic shared with other nineteenth-century writers is one elucidated by Henry Nash Smith and others, that the new type of the tycoon did arouse contradictory responses in his contemporaries. Thorpe speaks to the author's imagination as he does to that of characters in the novel. This is suggested by the detail and complexity of the portrait; by Thorpe's honest attempts at self-understanding and self-determination, which carry him far beyond the robot man Colin Semple; and by the metaphors used to characterize him, which convey both danger and grandeur. Frederic's novelistic interest in the *drama* of Thorpe's coup, which gives the book much of its impetus and vitality, is also a factor that tends to relax his judicial attitude. (p. 401)

Frederic genuinely seems to be pondering how to resolve the counterdemands—in fictional and also in moral terms?—of society and the tycoon. Thorpe's experience suggests that to live at all he must be himself; to sin is to violate an exceptional nature with its own oppressive fiats. Thorpe is portrayed as being something akin to a natural phenomenon, capable of arousing awe, fear, curiosity, or admiration, capable of good or evil effects, but nonetheless a vital force to be reckoned with as such, and one toward which traditional norms for assessing human behavior are shown to coexist with pragmatic ones. If this natural force, Thorpe's qualities and ambitions, can be harnessed, directed toward some constructive end such as amelioration of slum conditions, then Thorpe might belie Celia Madden's fears and justify his own sense of personal evolution toward the better man. It is true that elsewhere Frederic scorns characters who seek political power for personal reasons (e.g., Albert Fairchild in *Seth's Brother's Wife*), so we may assume that he distrusts Thorpe's aspirations and treats them ironically. It is also true that Frederic does not choose to end the novel, as he did *Theron Ware,* with a castigation of Thorpe for his misapprehensions and self-delusions, if that is what they are, but rather with a question, and this leaves the reader free to speculate. (p. 402)

Frederic does succeed in the body of his work in formulating a complex dramatic portrait of the type of the business entrepreneur that is a notable achievement for its time. And this portrait remains one of considerable depth and interest because it integrates elements of judgment with a probing inquiry into the unique nature of the tycoon, with its susceptibility to irrational impulse, its inherent demands upon the individual, its extraordinary capacity for practical effects, and its consequent imaginative impact on lesser men. (p. 404)

*Jean Frantz Blackall, "Perspectives on Harold Frederic's 'Market-Place'," in* PMLA, 86, *Vol. LXXXVI, No. 3, May, 1971, pp. 388-405.*

**JEAN FRANTZ BLACKALL** (essay date 1972)

[*Emphasizing Frederic's development of Christian's "inner experience," Blackall argues that* Gloria Mundi *is more a character study than it is "an account and judgment of" English society.*]

*Gloria Mundi* has not been taken very seriously by critics partly, I think, because it is cast in the form of a fairy tale with a rags-to-riches plot, and this form belies its serious matter. Or, it has been approached in its manifest aspect, as a work in which Frederic is struggling to acclimatize himself fictionally to his English environment in the role of social commentator. To view the novel as an evaluative portrait of English upperclass society, however justly, is also to contemplate its limited achievement as a novel of manners.... (p. 41)

What I would like to propose here is an emphasis that has been taken for granted in approaching both *Theron Ware* and *The Market-Place,* that the work is as much or more the story of the inner experience of its hero than it is an account and judgment of the world in which he moves. Like Theron, Christian Tower is cast in the role of an apprentice and observer, but because he is less naive than Theron, he does not so immediately translate the influence of others into overt blundering actions. Christian is a relatively subtle and complex figure, whose inner process of maturing is communicated to the reader frequently by dramatic means, but overt choices and dialogue, rather than by direct exposition. It is harder, therefore, for the reader to grasp this character, but, together with Theron Ware and Joel Thorpe of *The Market-Place,* he is one of Frederic's most highly developed and rounded figures, and rewards scrutiny.

In his role of apprentice and observer, Christian is portrayed as a tentative, susceptible, reverent and visionary sort of man rather than as one fully formed or boldly independent. These qualities make him relatively passive. . . . Nonetheless, Christian's sensibilities and responsiveness to others . . . make him an especially effective pivotal figure or sounding board. As the structural center of the novel he focuses and integrates its main ideas, both as these are severally articulated by the peripheral characters and as he himself reflects upon the views and upon his own experiences. To my sense the primary interest and accomplishment of *Gloria Mundi* lie, first, in the characterization of Christian and of several subordinate characters who function as mentors and antagonists and, secondly, in the carefully wrought structure of ideas through which these characters formulate the thematic statement of the novel. (pp. 41-2)

*Gloria Mundi* is a work of considerable substance and one that demonstrates a notable craftsmanship in its architectonic structure. Its plot is rudimentary. Christian inherits a dukedom and chooses a wife. Its action, however, is a story of inner maturing, which is communicated to the reader by a sequence of choices by Christian and the feminine protagonists among alternatives. The first three parts of the novel each examine one of Christian's theoretical alternatives: self-indulgence, philanthropy, and flight (or is it freedom?). Part IV represents Christian's own formulation of a role for himself, one which involves an acceptance of the sense of responsibility of the "good Torrs" profoundly modified by his own perception of the limitations of the individual. Meanwhile counterpointed against Christian's choices in the first three Parts are those of the three feminine protagonists, who variously represent these same alternatives as defined from a woman's point of view: that of a marriage for place, a marriage for love, or a feminist autonomy. In Part IV Frances Bailey also comes to a personal formulation. Like Lord Julius she is deflected from her sense of infinite individual capacity to master one's environment into taking refuge in a responsible but wholly traditional concept of value. He will be content with an heir; she, with a marriage for love. The experiences of all the characters, and of Christian and Frances in particular, coalesce in showing the inadequacy of individual human beings to master either their environment or their impulses wholly, so as to pursue courses of independent action. And the manifest distance between this image of human experience and the heroic concept of a great, glorious, autonomous human condition, which the Torrs' privilege, rank, and money would seem to assure, creates a dominating irony in the effect of the work as a whole. . . .

The primary weakness of the novel, so interpreted, is the failure of its theme to coalesce with its form. The pessimistic statement about man's nature and aspirations is obscured both by the fairy-tale character of Christian's experiences and by the conventional happy ending as regards plot, with Christian distributing largesse and winning the right princess. Frank is miscast in the role of princess, because her characterization as cranky, acid-tongued, and willfully independent is wholly at variance with the future she willingly embraces in this marriage. One might speculate that this disharmony between theme and plot is an ironic contrivance devised by Frederic to suggest the distance between things as they are and things as they seem to be. Surely such an irony is operative in the title of the novel. Such a dualism is likewise manifest in Frederic's two titles for *Theron Ware,* written immediately before *Gloria Mundi.* If, in a word, *Gloria Mundi* is pessimistic, and even deterministic, in formulation, is it intentionally or calculatingly so? Or does this novel exemplify an unresolved attitude in its author?

My own view is that *Gloria Mundi* illustrates an unresolved ambivalence toward the issue posed by all three of the principal women—and especially by Frances Bailey—that of female emancipation, and also a self-contradictory attitude in Frederic between his observations of human behavior and his will to believe in the possibility of human fulfillment. Furthermore, these problems of ambivalence as regards both topics are characteristic of his work more generally, and they account both for certain cruxes in individual works and for much of the intellectual interest and tension of the novels. An instance is Frederic's shifting moral attitude toward Celia Madden between *Theron Ware* and *The Market-Place.* The structure of *Gloria Mundi* is a negative example. We have here a portrait of human frustration upon which the will to be happy, to believe that love conquers or resolves all, is superimposed in the form of the fairy tale. The traditional resolution of the romance (with the inheritance, the title, and the marriage) partially obscures both the architectonic structure, the dialectical character, and the irresolution of the novel of ideas. (pp. 45-6)

> *Jean Frantz Blackall, "Frederic's 'Gloria Mundi'*
> *As a Novel of Education," in* The Markham Review,
> *Vol. 3, No. 3, May, 1972, pp. 41-6.*

### SAM BLUEFARB (essay date 1972)

[*In his* The Escape Motif in the American Novel, *Bluefarb discusses Theron's impulses to escape at various points in* The Damnation of Theron Ware *and characterizes his final flight as "a fortunate fall."*]

As the minister of a fundamentalist sect of the Methodist church, Theron Ware, in Harold Frederic's *The Damnation of Theron Ware* . . . , should have been adequately armed with such minimal theology as would have prepared him to recognize the sins of pride, lust, and cupidity; paradoxically, though, his innocence, which leads to his subsequent "damnation," lies in his unawareness of these self-defeating traits. Theron's pilgrimage toward the *terrestrial* city of self-knowledge, therefore, departs from a point in life when he is most ripe for a fall—a fall that will lead to his escape from Octavius and the ministry, and his flight to Seattle. We can thus look upon Theron Ware's escape, nonreligious though it is, as redemptive and partially cleansing in its effect, perhaps his one honest act in the novel. (p. 27)

Until his final escape from Octavius and the ministry, Theron's urges to flee have not been entirely unacted-upon. His early gestures, though tentative, have been made as far back as his boyhood on the farm. Born and reared on the farm, Theron has seen the ministry not merely as a dedication but as an escape from the drab monotony and drudgery of farm life. Thus, even as far back as his transition from farmer to minister, one can already see the seeds of discontent that will later blossom into the full flower of flight. For "neither his early strenuous battle to get away from the farm and achieve such education as should serve to open to him the gates of professional life, nor the later wave of religious enthusiasm which caught him up as he stood on the border-land of manhood, and swept him off into a veritable new world of views and aspirations, had been a likely school of merriment". . . . Even before his marriage to her, Theron sees in Alice a possible avenue of escape:

> She was fresh from the refinements of a town seminary: *she read books; it was known that she could play upon the piano.* Her clothes, her manners, her way of speaking, the readiness of her thoughts and sprightly tongue,—not least, perhaps, the imposing current understanding as to her father's wealth,—placed her on a glorified pinnacle far away from the girls of the neighborhood.

If, from the first moment of his arrival in Octavius, Theron has no *conscious* urge to escape, he has at least begun to give way to a wistful yearning. Discouraged by his first interview with the trustees of the Octavius church, Theron already feels like running away. On this occasion the trustees inform him where they stand on such matters as flower-bedecked "bunnits" and their antagonism toward "book-learnin' or dictionary words in [the] pulpit". . . . They go on to tell him that "no new-fangled notions can go down here. Your wife'd better take them flowers out of her bunnit afore next Sunday. . . . What we want here, sir, is straight-out, flat-footed hell,—the burnin' lake o' fire an' brimstone. Pour it into 'em, hot an' strong". . . . (pp. 36-7)

Theron's escapes, or what have thus far been proclivities, are as yet not consciously conceived in explicit physical terms or plans. He would like to "learn a trade," write a book, enjoy a certain solitude (as he actually succeeds in doing when he contracts some vaguely defined, probably psychosomatic, illness). But he does not even begin to contemplate an actual escape in terms of geographical flight until the end of the book, an escape that also coincides with the end of his year in Octavius.

For some months before his urge to escape becomes a conscious plan, Theron, still the minister, desires to make the best of both worlds: to enjoy his position as minister—with all of the respect and regard such a position exacts from others—and to indulge his whims. But this conflict of interests set him up as an excellent target for his own self-destructive urges. This kind of fence-straddling is then untenable. Sooner or later he must decide which it is to be—the "buried life" in Octavius or escape from it; sooner or later he must translate his urges into action.

His first plan is of course the dead-end plan of an escape with Celia. Yet, blind as it is, both as to its possibilities and consequences, it *is* one of the first signs that Theron is now consciously planning an escape of some sort; the circumstances of his wife and the church, both to whom and to which he is "married," lead him consciously into the practical considerations of such a projected flight:

But he could not enter upon this beckoning heaven of a future until he had freed himself. When Celia said to him "Come!" he must not be in the position to reply, "I should like to, but unfortunately I am tied by the leg." He should have to leave Octavius, leave the ministry, leave everything. He could not begin too soon to face these contingencies. . . .

(pp. 37-8)

In this early, consciously considered escape, then, we see what later turns out to be the great impulse that not only will take Theron Ware out of Octavius, but out of a way of life he had heretofore (until his arrival in the town) resigned himself to.

These early considerations of escape have taken three forms: first, his desire to escape from the church and its ministry; second, his desire to escape from Alice and what he feels to be an unfortunate marriage; and third, his desire to escape his former (innocent) self. Theron pleasurably indulges in one of these fantasies on the train that is taking him to New York City and to what he hopes will be a critical and successful reunion with Celia Madden. Peering out the window, he sees a rich man's yacht that will take them both to those happy isles of blissful irresponsiblity:

> Ah, how the tender visions crowded upon him! Eternal summer basked round this enchanted yacht of his fancy,—summer sought now in Scottish firths or Norwegian fiords, now in quaint old Southern harbors, ablaze with the hues of strange costumes and half-tropical flowers and fruits, now in far-away Oriental bays and lagoons, or among the coral reefs and palm-trees of the luxurious Pacific. He dwelt upon these new imaginings with the fervent longing of an inland-born boy. Every vague yearning he had ever felt toward salt-water stirred again in his blood at the thought of the sea—with Celia. . . .

(pp. 38-9)

If the yacht represents for Theron an escape from responsibility, it also suggests [an] Edenic idyll of innocence. . . . Of course, Theron's dream of escape with Celia on such a yacht (symbol of the ideal escape?) is in the realm of pure fantasy, because it is based on nothing more substantial than Theron's innocent vision of the world. Yet—and we might call this a fault of hyper-imagination in Theron—fantasy that it is, it nevertheless represents for this minister *manqué* a sharp and pleasant contrast to the drab-hued existence of his life in Octavius.

Throughout the year in Octavius—a year that for Theron represents a spiritual lifetime—the minister, whether he has known it or not, has been attempting to flee the mask toward his truer (perhaps better) self. Because Theron Ware had thought of himself as possessing a kind of Edenic goodness, when he finally discovers a side of himself that he had never thought existed, the knowledge almost kills him. As Sister Soulsby puts it, "Whatever else he does, he will never want to come within gunshot of a pulpit again. It came too near murdering him for that". . . . (pp. 39-40)

Theron Ware, having finally learned a lesson, can now turn his back on the past and look toward the future and a new way of life. Disabused of his outworn illusions, he can now face a new life in a new country. For Theron, the year has come full circle, and, looking toward the future, he can now decide to take his chance in the West—Seattle—where he will build a new life, perhaps even go into politics. To Alice, Seattle *"sounds like the other end of the world,"* which of course, in a sense, it is. And even more than that, Seattle represents for Theron not only the "other end of the world" but a new world. Like all of those escapers extending back into the American past, Theron is also in the tradition of the escaper who, if he is to survive as an individual and a human being, *must* strike out into the "wilderness" of a new life. For Theron . . . the restrictive settlements have closed in, and he must "light out," if he is to save himself from an even greater calamity than he has already experienced.

The final scene—that of Theron's departure for the West—takes place in the spring, signifying renewal and the rebirth of hope. . . . Theron will depart (or escape) in a season of promise. Thus, **The Damnation of Theron Ware,** though a story of a fall, is really the story of a fortunate fall (even if "fortunate" in a highly qualified sense). For Theron has left his greater innocence behind in Octavius; he has grown to larger manhood, with a more mature knowledge of the world—namely, a knowledge of his limitations. (pp. 40-1)

> Sam Bluefarb, " 'Theron Ware': The Fall from Innocence and the Escape from Guilt," in his The Escape Motif in the American Novel: Mark Twain to Richard Wright, *Ohio State University Press, 1972, pp. 26-41.*

## SAMUEL COALE (essay date 1976)

[*Coale examines Frederic's "communal and social vision" in* The Damnation of Theron Ware, *emphasizing his attempt to blend Hawthornian romance elements with "emerging American naturalism."*]

Harold Frederic's **The Damnation of Theron Ware** has puzzled critics ever since its appearance on the best-seller list in 1896. Most have chosen to look at it as yet another example of emerging American naturalism in the literary world. There are, indeed, reasons for this assumption, . . . , but Frederic was really trying to accomplish something else. (p. 29)

The communal and social vision, buttressed by Frederic's often pictorial and cinematic prose, accounts for the realistic texture of **The Damnation of Theron Ware.** Naturalistic details abound in the historical descriptions of village life in Octavius, of the Methodist Schism, the Catholic picnic, the debt-raising love-feast, and perhaps best of all the camp meeting. Sex, as *the* underlying instinct, underlies all, its primal thrust apparent in Celia's chambers, Theron's curiosity, Forbes's priestly powers, the supposed affair between Alice and Levi Gorringe, the quasi-phallic towers of the Catholic church, and the Madden house. With Celia beside him in the dark, Theron stares up at "the majestic bulk of the big silent house rising among the trees before them," which gives "him a thrilling sense of the glory of individual freedom," and declares, " 'I feel a new man already.' " And yet because we are locked, for the most part, inside Theron's point of view, his own brief comments upon the naturalistic and/or deterministic way of things seem merely casual attempts at self-justification, attempts to relieve himself of the personal sense of responsibility Frederic will not allow him to relinquish. He hungers for Celia and all she represents and thinks that "he was only obeying the universal law of nature—the law which prompts the pallid spindling sprout of the potato in the cellar to strive feebly toward the light." He justifies Alice's remonstrances and his fading affections for her by calling them "the accidents of life, the

inevitable harsh happenings in the great tragedy of Nature. They could not be helped, and there was nothing more to be said." Clearly in Frederic's mind natural determinism does neither explain nor excuse Theron Ware's behavior. It does not go to the roots of the dilemma.

In order to suggest broader and deeper causes of Theron's problem, Frederic must overcome mere sociological and historical causes and descriptions. He must grapple more deeply with the state of mind, the patterns of universal human experience, that Theron seems to represent. (pp. 34-5)

The world of **The Damnation of Theron Ware** is no longer one conceived in moral and ethical terms, at least in their socially rigid and/or traditional manifestations. Deeper urges fester beneath the surface here. . . . Consequently Frederic's use of or borrowings from Hawthorne are often inverted, undermined in the way he employs them. . . . There are no marble fauns transformed here, only illuminations which in themselves complete Theron's damnation. (p. 37)

[Frederic's characters] themselves fit the Hawthornian mold. Theron, of course, suggests the golden-tongued Dimmesdale [in *The Scarlet Letter*], though whereas Dimmesdale transforms himself into an allegorical object lesson of sin, Theron sheds ideas and sensations like clothes and ends as he began, secure in his cheerful, self-deluding "innocence." He recognizes nothing but marches to that self-deluding American Dream: "Go West, young man!" Lesmar is Chillingworth, Dr. Aylmer, and Dr. Rappaccini [in *The Scarlet Letter*, "The Birthmark," and "Rappaccini's Daughter," respectively] reborn, the heartless scientist, the cold observer. Celia might as well be a sister to Hester, Zonobia, and Miriam [in *The Scarlet Letter, The Blithedale Romance,* and *The Marble Faun,* respectively], though her overexaggerated paganism makes her the least believable character in the book. Father Forbes is a new voice on the scene, a Catholic figure with a perceptive historical sensibility. Hawthorne's priest in *The Marble Faun* could only hope slyly to seduce poor dove-haunted Hilda! The most interesting and misunderstood character may be Sister Soulsby. Does she represent some good amalgamation of necessary social control and common sense, or is she more evil in her effects on Theron Ware? Since all the characters remain somewhat ambiguous, and even confused, we cannot pin easy labels on them or as distinct a label as we could often pin on Hawthorne's characters. Yet it seems to me that Sister Soulsby is akin to Hawthorne's Westervelt in *The Blithedale Romance,* a representative of the modern manipulative world, not to be trusted, however practical and useful her tools of the trade. (p. 41)

[If egocentric innocence lies at] the heart of the novel, then all the romantic or Hawthornesque touches can only be self-justifications on Theron's part for his actions, as his comments on determinism must be, and we cannot take them seriously. The romantic elements, however inverted or transformed, can only be seen as the attempts of this comically ignorant creature to view his life in some broader and finally fraudulent perspective. Is he a romantic trapped in a naturalistic universe? It cannot be that simple, for Frederic's landscape, however relegated to Theron's own view of things, itself partakes of romantic allusions—the lights and shadows, the reversal of the seasons in relation to Theron's supposed growth toward self-knowledge, the names of the characters and their particular attitudes. These notions do not depend on Theron's point of view to exist in the novel. If we can believe in the wider representational aspects of Frederic's book, then what are we

*A caricature of Frederic. The Granger Collection, New York.*

to do with the naturalistic aspects of it—the role of sexual longings, primitive instincts, and uncharted yearnings? Can both the romantic and naturalistic elements be fused in the hypnagogic reality of Theron's experiences? And if that is true, why didn't Frederic make that reality more apparent, more visible to the reader?

The fault may lie in Frederic's original working title for the novel *Snarl*. He seems to have wanted to suggest both aspects, to invest his book with a cultural and social inevitability and at the same time with a more universal and representative allegorical framework that would develop beyond that more exclusive inevitability. In any case he did not succeed. The elements of Hawthorne, and they are several, just do not fuse with the historical realism of the novel. Even Hawthorne knew he had to create a mythic or legendary past, to get away from the present time and place, to allow his romantic and allegorical ideas to flourish.... The reader just cannot take Theron seriously. Society's roles and Hawthorne's significations battle each other instead of clarifying and absorbing each other. The fusion never takes place. Frederic was not an artist capable of such control or finesse.

But the fact remains. Frederic was trying to forge a newer "romanticism" in *The Damnation of Theron Ware,* trying to penetrate the simplistic and iron forces of a naturalistic universe to reach the primal forces of the human psyche, that dark realm which has always been the primal core of the best American literature. Perhaps *The Damnation of Theron Ware* reveals that there never really was a viable naturalist aesthetic at all, that the factual realism and accumulation of scientifically accurate force fields in the American novel were just not enough to get at the heart of the American experience. Is this why they were

abandoned so readily, why even the fiction of Theodore Dreiser, despite its Spenserian underpinnings, repeats and extends certain representational patterns of American experience that may be called romantic? Frederic clearly saw the roots he was after but he could not sufficiently blend or absorb them into the realistic caste of his fiction. They remained roots, snarled and confused, breaking loose from that fictional mold and hanging suspended in open space. It was left to a genius like Faulkner to accomplish finally the convergence of social and mythic patterns in the American psyche, to complete that attempt that had failed Hawthorne so utterly in *The Marble Faun*. Frederic may have sensed this need, this direction American literature would take, but he was not the artist to accomplish it. Perhaps the best way in which to view *The Damnation of Theron Ware* is not as an example of literary naturalism but as the midpoint between Hawthorne's allegories and Faulkner's myths.

Frederic did sense, however, the center of the haunted mind, that dark and pagan core from which all growth appears as mere illusion and experience can only be repetitious, cyclical, and eventually destructive. As Father Forbes, the closest character in the book perhaps to Frederic's own ideas, suggests: "'You see, there is nothing new. Everything is built on the ruins of something else. Just as the material earth is made up of countless billions of dead men's bones, so the mental world is all alive with the ghosts of dead men's thoughts and beliefs; the wraiths of dead races' faiths and imaginings.'" Perhaps Frederic penetrated to that dark central core of American literature in which "the world was all black again,—plunged in the Egyptian night which lay upon the face of the deep while the earth was yet without form and void. He was alone on it,—alone among awful, planetary solitudes which crushed him." From this perspective Father Forbes's description of the human race sounds strangely like a description of the continual images and emotions in our own literature: "The human race are still very like savages in a dangerous wood in the dark, telling one another ghost stories around a camp-fire." What Hawthorne shied away from, what Faulkner finally dealt with, Frederic had some awareness of, but he could not articulate that muted vision. It remained "like some huge, shadowy, and symbolical monument" with its roots in Hawthorne's aesthetic, its visible branches in the naturalistic atmosphere of his age, and its core somewhere between "giving forth from its recesses of night the sounds of screams and curses" and glowing like some "spectral picture of some black-robed, tonsured men, with leering satanic masks, making a bonfire of the Bible in the public schools." (pp. 43-5)

*Samuel Coale, "Frederic and Hawthorne: The Romantic Roots of Naturalism," in* American Literature, *Vol. 48, No. 1, March, 1976, pp. 29-45.\**

## ADDITIONAL BIBLIOGRAPHY

Bredahl, A. Carl, Jr. "The Artist in *The Damnation of Theron Ware*." *Studies in the Novel* IV, No. 3 (Fall 1972): 432-41.

   Suggests that the figure of the artist is a central image in *The Damnation of Theron Ware*. The numerous discussions about art in the novel, according to Bredahl, provide "a standard of judgment against which one can view Theron Ware."

Crowley, John W. "The Nude and the Madonna in *The Damnation of Theron Ware*." *American Literature* XLV, No. 3 (November 1973): 379-89.

A discussion of Theron Ware's relation to Alice, Celia, and Sister Soulsby. Because of his "Romantic delusion of pre-sexual innocence," Crowley contends, Theron remains unable to have a satisfactory relationship with any of the women, whom he views as either "sensual" or "maternal" figures.

Darnell, Donald G. "'Visions of Hereditary Rank': The Loyalist in the Fiction of Hawthorne, Cooper, and Frederic." *South Atlantic Bulletin* XLII, No. 2 (May 1977): 45-54.*
    Discusses Frederic's depiction of the Loyalist characters in *In the Valley.* Darnell describes Frederic's image of the Tory as "prideful and cruel," but adds that he also endows him with courage.

Donaldson, Scott. "The Seduction of Theron Ware." *Nineteenth Century Fiction* 29, No. 4 (March 1975): 441-52.
    Argues that it is Sister Soulsby who brings about Theron Ware's fall. As a result of her manipulation of Theron, Donaldson states, she succeeds in "indoctrinat[ing] him in her pernicious gospel of pragmatism."

Dooley, Patrick K. "Fakes and Good Frauds: Pragmatic Religion in *The Damnation of Theron Ware.*" *American Literary Realism* XV, No. 1 (Spring 1982): 74-85.
    Discusses Frederic's examination of pragmatic religion in *The Damnation of Theron Ware.* Dooley singles out Father Forbes and Sister Soulsby as characters who "are involved in the manufacture of religious emotions."

Earnest, Ernest. "The Flamboyant American: Harold Frederic." In his *Expatriates and Patriots: American Artists, Scholars, and Writers in Europe,* pp. 220-36. Durham, N.C.: Duke University Press, 1968.
    A study of Frederic as an expatriate. Citing evidence from his life and works, Earnest concludes that even after years of living abroad, Frederic's perspective in his writings remained "the melioristic one of American progressivism."

Fryer, Judith. "The Temptress: Celia Madden, the Temptress as 'Greek'." In her *The Faces of Eve: Women in the Nineteenth Century American Novel,* pp. 54-62. New York: Oxford University Press, 1976.
    A detailed discussion of the characterization of Celia in *The Damnation of Theron Ware.* Fryer suggests that Celia is a tempting figure for Theron not only because of her beauty and sociableness "but also because like Eve she represents knowledge." Fryer cites Celia's expression of "the superiority of the matriarchal over the patriarchal culture" as evidence that she "clearly exists outside the moral structure" of the community of Octavian Protestants to which Theron belongs.

Garner, Stanton. "Some Notes on Harold Frederic in Ireland." *American Literature* XXXIX, No. 1 (March 1967): 60-74.
    An analysis of Frederic's attitude toward Ireland. Though he actively advocated Home Rule in the 1880s, Garner states, Frederic's love for Ireland manifested itself largely in literary terms in the 1890s. Garner also traces Irish themes and subjects in Frederic's works.

Herron, Ima Honaker. "Heavenly Destiny." In her *The Small Town in American Literature,* pp. 146-89. New York: Pageant Books, 1959.*
    A survey of Frederic's novels which focuses on his treatment of small-town life. Herron praises his realistic style and "frank . . . presentation of provincial religious beliefs."

Johnson, George W. "Harold Frederic's Young Goodman Ware: The Ambiguities of a Realistic Romance." *Modern Fiction Studies* 8, No. 4 (Winter 1962-63), pp. 361-74.
    Assesses the realistic and romance elements of *The Damnation of Theron Ware* and concludes that, despite Frederic's "audacious" attempt to fuse them, "the book remains a literary near-miss."

Kane, Patricia. "Lest Darkness Come upon You: An Interpretation of *The Damnation of Theron Ware.*" *Iowa English Yearbook,* No. 10 (Fall 1965): 55-9.
    An examination of light and darkness imagery in *The Damnation of Theron Ware,* together with their biblical contexts. According

to Kane, Theron views himself as becoming "a child of darkness" because of his search for knowledge.

LeClair, Thomas. "The Ascendant Eye: A Reading of *The Damnation of Theron Ware.*" *Studies in American Fiction* 3, No. 1 (Spring 1975): 95-102.
    Explores the twin themes of seeing and being seen in *The Damnation of Theron Ware.* LeClair contends that Frederic's complex study of "the person as object of perception" as well as "perceiver of self and others" makes the novel a notable achievement.

Luedtke, Luther S. "Harold Frederic's Satanic Soulsby: Interpretation and Sources." *Nineteenth Century Fiction* 30, No. 1 (June 1975): 82-104.
    An analysis of Sister Soulsby's "serpentine character" and her role as the main corruptor of Theron Ware. In addition, Luedtke compares Sister Soulsby to Mrs. Jellyby of Charles Dickens's *Bleak House* and Lucy Soulsby, a nineteenth-century English reformer.

Miller, Linda Patterson. "Casting Graven Images: *The Damnation of Theron Ware.*" *Renascence* XXX, No. 4 (Summer 1978): 179-84.
    A study of various characters' search for moral and spiritual meaning in *The Damnation of Theron Ware.* Miller concludes that in Frederic's fictional universe "personal salvation" is impossible.

Ravitz, Abe C. "Harold Frederic's Venerable Copperhead." *New York History* XLI, No. 1 (January 1960): 35-48.
    Discusses the influence of New York Governor Horatio Seymour on Frederic's fiction. Ravitz suggests that Frederic's image of "the honest political maverick" derives from his familiarity with Seymour.

Sage, Howard. "Harold Frederic's Narrative Essays: A Realistic-Journalistic Genre." *American Literary Realism* 3, No. 4 (Fall 1970): 388-92.
    Explores the interplay between Frederic's journalistic and fictional prose. To Sage, his narrative essays represent a "compromise" between his expository and his narrative prose.

Stein, Allen F. "Evasions of an American Adam: Structure and Theme in *The Damnation of Theron Ware.*" *American Literary Realism* 5, No. 1 (Winter 1972): 23-36.
    Examines Theron Ware's pattern of evading responsibility for his actions. The pattern is perpetuated, Stein observes, because each instance concludes with Theron's "self-gratulation and self-delusion," which ensures that he will not learn from his mistakes.

Suderman, Elmer F. "*The Damnation of Theron Ware* As a Criticism of American Religious Thought." *The Huntington Library Quarterly* XXXIII, No. 1 (1969): 61-75.
    Traces Frederic's satirical use of several nineteenth-century religious conventions in *The Damnation of Theron Ware.* Suderman credits Frederic with "negative insights" into such religious beliefs as man's innate goodness and the possibility of conversion through revival meetings.

Vanderbeets, Richard. "Harold Frederic and Comic Realism: The 'Drama Proper' of *Seth's Brother's Wife.*" *American Literature* XXXIX, No. 4 (January 1968): 553-60.
    Maintains that Frederic's intended central focus in *Seth's Brother's Wife* was not politics but sociology. Vanderbeets cites as evidence an unpublished manuscript of Frederic's that presents the novel as a four-act drama in which politics is subordinate to social and character analysis.

Williams, David. "The Nature of the Damnation of Theron Ware." *Massachusetts Studies in English* II, No. 2 (Fall 1969): 41-8.
    Characterizes the damnation of Theron Ware as "the inability to live without a dream." Because he continues to hold on to his romantic notions, Williams contends, Theron is "damned to dream the dream" of perpetually possible salvation.

Woodward, Robert H. "Some Sources for Harold Frederic's *The Damnation of Theron Ware.*" *American Literature* XXXIII, No. 1 (March 1961): 46-51.

A description of Frederic's manuscript, notes, diaries, and clippings used in writing *The Damnation of Theron Ware*. Woodward concludes that Frederic was "forced into extensive study" so that his characters could reveal their intellectual selves as well as their personalities.

―――――. "Illusion and Moral Ambivalence in *Seth's Brother's Wife*." *American Literary Realism* 2 (1968): 279-82.

Suggests that the morally ambiguous world of *Seth's Brother's Wife* is similar to that of *The Damnation of Theron Ware*. Both novels, Woodward asserts, are "broadly stories of initiation" in which the characters are "lulled by illusions into false judgments of reality, into mistaken and dangerous loves and alliances, into questionable interpretations of themselves." However, Woodward adds that Frederic does ultimately believe in slow human progress toward knowledge.

# Eugène (Samuel Auguste) Fromentin

## 1820-1876

French novelist, critic, travel sketch writer, and essayist.

Fromentin was a minor French writer and painter whose oeuvre includes distinguished contributions in three areas: travel literature, the novel, and art criticism. He first achieved literary recognition as a travel writer in the late 1850s, publishing *Un été dans le Sahara* and *Une année dans le Sahel,* critically acclaimed travel sketches drawn from his artistic expeditions to North Africa. His next major production, the 1863 novel *Dominique,* is considered an engaging, gracefully written work that is often compared with such masterpieces of confessional literature as Benjamin Constant's *Adolphe* and Étienne Pivert de Sénancour's *Obermann.* Fromentin's last significant publication was a highly regarded 1876 study of Flemish and Dutch painting entitled *Les maîtres d'autrefois: Belgique, Hollande (The Old Masters of Belgium and Holland).* This work, in conjunction with *Dominique* and the travel sketches, forms the basis of Fromentin's reputation as a versatile and respected figure in nineteenth-century French letters.

Fromentin was born into a Catholic family and raised in the port town of La Rochelle. In addition to excelling in classical studies as a young man, he was deeply affected by an adolescent attachment to Jenny Léocadie Chessé, a summer companion who was four years his senior. His feelings for Chessé apparently crystallized when she married Émile Béraud in 1834, prompting Fromentin to visit her regularly until his parents interceded and sent him to Paris to study law in 1839. This interlude is generally regarded as Fromentin's principal source for the story of disappointed love and renunciation in *Dominique.* Fromentin's legal career was short-lived; abandoning law soon after obtaining his license in the winter of 1842-43, he turned to the study of art. He published essays on Eugène Delacroix, Alexandre Gabriel Decamps, and other French painters during this period and displayed an interest in Orientalist art that resulted in his first expedition to Algeria in 1846. Other trips to North Africa followed in 1847-48 and 1852-53 as he sought source material and inspiration for his paintings. The last expedition was especially significant, for Fromentin kept a journal during his trip that served as the basis for the travel books *Un été dans le Sahara* and *Une année dans le Sahel.* Responding to financial pressures, Fromentin first published *Un été dans le Sahara* in the journal *Revue de Paris* in 1854; *Une année dans le Sahel* was partially published as *Alger: Fragments d'un journal de voyage* in the journal *L'artiste* in 1857 and subsequently issued in its entirety in the journal *Revue des deux mondes* in 1858. Financial straits also provided the initial impetus for the creation of *Dominique;* the director of the *Revue des deux mondes* suggested to Fromentin that he augment his income by writing a novel. Fromentin produced the work with great difficulty, revising the manuscript extensively before it was serialized in the *Revue des deux mondes* in 1862.

Fromentin won a number of awards for his painting in the late 1850s and 1860s. He received a first place medal at the Salon of 1859, and he continued to prosper artistically in the 1860s, selling some of his most celebrated paintings at the Salon of 1863 and earning a first at the *Exposition universelle* in 1867.

In 1869 he traveled to Egypt with Théophile Gautier and Louise Colet as a member of the French delegation to the opening of the Suez Canal. However, his art career appeared to decline in the 1870s, as he struggled against the confinements of his reputation as a painter of Algerian desert scenes. In 1875, acting on a long-standing interest in writing art criticism, he embarked on a month-long tour of Belgium and Holland during which he took detailed notes on the paintings of the Flemish and Dutch masters. These notes provided the basis for *The Old Masters of Belgium and Holland,* which originally appeared in the *Revue des deux mondes* in 1876. Fromentin died following a sudden illness later in that year.

Of Fromentin's diverse body of writings, *Dominique* is at once his most popular and most problematic work. Recalling the author's youthful attachment to Chessé, the novel relates the story of Dominique de Bray's love for Madeleine de Nièvres, a young woman slightly older than he whose marriage to another man simultaneously incites and dooms their budding passion. Significantly, Dominique recounts this episode from his vantage point as an introspective, middle-aged gentleman-farmer given to solitary walks and self-depreciation. The import of the hero's perspective as a reflection on Romantic values has become the focal point of modern critical commentary on the novel: while such critics as G. J. Greshoff interpreted *Dominique* as a criticism of Romanticism, Ronald Grimsley and other commentators discerned a fundamental ambivalence in Dominique's attitude toward his Romantic past. Apart from this debate, however, critics generally agree that the sheer honesty and evocative power of Fromentin's writing make *Dominique* a compelling contribution to the field of confessional literature.

The travel books and *The Old Masters of Belgium and Holland* are also esteemed within their fields, although the latter book has several well-documented shortcomings. Largely accepted as a sound and frequently illuminating study of the Flemish and Dutch schools of painting, *The Old Masters of Belgium and Holland* is slightly flawed by the acknowledged disparity between Fromentin's treatment of the Flemish and Dutch masters Peter Paul Rubens and Rembrandt van Rijn. As Henry James and other critics have noted, Fromentin overestimates the powers of Rubens while misinterpreting and undervaluing the genius of Rembrandt. Fromentin himself admitted his difficulties with the Dutch artist, stating that "Rembrandt doesn't let me sleep."

Although George Sand, Gustave Flaubert, and other accomplished authors admired his writing, Fromentin was known to his contemporaries primarily as a painter. Contemporary critics praised his travel books, but his most ambitious literary effort, *Dominique*, was not particularly well received, and his reputation languished. With the exception of occasional reviews of *The Old Masters of Belgium and Holland*, Fromentin's works were largely overlooked until critics expressed renewed interest in *Dominique* in the 1950s. This resurgence of interest in the novel has led to the discovery of provocative new aspects of Fromentin and his work: Roland Barthes is one of several critics who have probed the reactionary, "bourgeois" values informing *Dominique*, while other commentators have proposed possible links between Dominique's inner conflicts and deep-seated polarities within Fromentin's psyche. Fromentin appears to be well served by such criticism, for appreciation of *Dominique* is central to his continuing recognition as a respected minor figure in French literature.

## PRINCIPAL WORKS

*Un été dans le Sahara*   (travel sketches)   1857
*Une année dans le Sahel*   (travel sketches)   1859
*Dominique*   (novel)   1863
 [*Dominique*, 1932]
*Les maîtres d'autrefois: Belgique, Hollande*   (criticism) 1876
 [*The Old Masters of Belgium and Holland*, 1882; also published as *The Masters of Past Time; or, Criticism on the Old Flemish and Dutch Painters*, 1913]
*Lettres de jeunesse*   (letters)   1909
*Correspondance et fragments inédits*   (letters and criticism) 1912

----

### THE NORTH AMERICAN REVIEW   (essay date 1858)

[*The critic reviews* Un été dans le Sahara, *praising Fromentin's poetic vision and lauding the book's strong sense of drama and characterization.*]

Never has the country which is now called "French Africa" been made so real to the reader as in this delightful little book

[M. Fromentin's *A Summer in the Sahara*]. . . . He brings before us all he sees, without any intermediary between it and us. We are with him in the Desert; and this is the master-charm of the book.

Like all really poetical works, *A Summer in the Sahara* deals with a very limited range of subjects, and its writer finds the springs of poetry in himself, and not in the objects around him. These *are* poetical, which is of small consequence; but he sees them poetically, which is the thing required. (p. 238)

[The book] is written *passionately*. You see in every line how intensely the writer has felt and loved what he has spoken of; and this, as it is in the nautre of all real passion to do, carries you away with it.

The Arab is painted as he really is, by M. Fromentin, and there is no fancy-dress work in his descriptions, but you see that he dwells more tenderly with nature than with man, and above all, as he himself says, with a certain phasis of nature, with the arid, burning-blue, sharp-outlined waste. The desert has secrets it reveals to him, and which he tells in turn. (p. 239)

The purely contemplative or poetic element is not the only one to be found in M. Fromentin's book. There is also a strong dramatic sense, and we would advise all who wish to seize the manners and customs of the Arab tribes to the life, to study well the descriptions of the siege of El-Aghouat, of the murder of the two poor Naylette girls, of the encounter with the caravan of a Bedouin Emir or prince, and of the arrest of the native servant who had stolen a purse. There are characters, too, in this little book that will live for ever; and the French Lieutenant, the ostrich-hunter, the flute-player Aouïmer, and the Kalifat Si-Chériff would be well placed by the side of the finest creations of Cooper or Walter Scott. (p. 240)

[We earnestly recommend M. Fromentin's] delightful little book to all who may wish to have a familiar idea of Arab life and of the strange attraction of the desert. (pp. 241-42)

> *A review of "Un Été dans le Sahara," in* The North American Review, *Vol. LXXXVI, No. CLXXVIII, January, 1858, pp. 238-42.*

### THE NORTH AMERICAN REVIEW   (essay date 1859)

[*The critic focuses on the originality and sense of immediacy informing Fromentin's description of Saharan desert life in* Une année dans le Sahel.]

In a former number we called attention to a small volume by M. Eugène Fromentin, entitled *Un Été dans le Sahara* [see excerpt above, 1858]; and while stating the deep impression it had made in France, we pointed out some of its numerous and striking beauties. Pictures like his regenerate the somewhat *blasé* world of letters in France, and make it young again by the virtue of admiration. *Une Année dans le Sahel* was written on this wise. One evening, as dusk is falling, our traveler meets a tribe of wandering Saharans, and the longing for the desert comes over him. Its unfathomable mystery tempts him, and he is irresistibly compelled to go forth. This it is which fascinates and compels the reader too. He is dragged beyond the bounds of all conventionalities, out of the narrow, noisy, meaningless life of every day, by a real genuine poet, in whom the poetic energy is such that it is impossible to resist him. Follow him you must. What he sees, you see, what he hears, you hear, and you live his life wherever he wanders,—in the tent, in the waste, . . . in all the scenes of Arab existence, which are as evident to you as if you had perceived them by the aid of your own senses.

This inspiration by the desert is so strong in M. Fromentin, that between the portion of his new book which precedes his excursion to the Sahara, and that which follows it, there is an almost immeasurable distance. There are beautiful passages in the first half, but they might have been written by any other equally talented writer and equally observant traveller,—whereas the latter half, after the return from the desert, is so thoroughly original, so unlike anything we have read, that we should not know where to find its parallel. It makes you think of Rubens,—it reminds you of Byron; but, better than all, it copies no one. Every page seems to bear the impress of the desert aspects. There is the sharp, pure outline, the fierceness of color that is yet harmonious, the breadth, the intensity, the saturation by sight, if it may be thus expressed, the silence, the grandeur,—but, above all, there is the poetry, inseparable from the whole, yet attainable only by those whose own latent poetry of soul draws out magnetically the same element from whatsoever surrounds them. (pp. 228-29)

> *A review of "Une Année dans le Sahel," in* The North American Review, *Vol. LXXXIX, No. CLXXXIV, July, 1859, pp. 228-32.*

## GEORGE SAND [PSEUDONYM OF AMANDINE AURORE LUCILE DUPIN DUDEVANT]   (essay date 1862)

[*Sand was one of France's most celebrated and controversial writers. Writing effortlessly, yet maintaining an impressive richness of style and unity of construction, she produced nearly sixty novels, a lengthy autobiography, numerous essays, twenty-five plays, and approximately 20,000 letters during her lifetime. Sand's flamboyant lifestyle interfered with serious critical assessment of her works from the beginning of her career; however, she eventually won acceptance as an artist by her contemporaries and is now noted for her bold exploration of such issues as sexual freedom and independence for women. Sand played an important role in fostering Fromentin's literary career. In addition to publishing several influential reviews lauding his travel books, she corresponded with Fromentin concerning his writing and offered suggestions for revising* Dominique *(see excerpt by Charles Morgan, 1949, for a summary of Sand's suggested revisions). In the passage below, originally published in her 1862 collection* Autour de la table, *Sand praises Fromentin's writing style in* Un été dans le Sahara, *maintaining that it "places him at one stroke in the very first rank of writers."*]

I know not what his palette has lent him, but what our language has furnished him of color and form is infinitely remarkable, and places him at one stroke in the very first rank of writers. His style has all the qualities that constitute a talent of the first rank. Grandeur and abundance in exquisite sobriety, the ardor of the artist and the spiritual and playful *bonhomie* of the young Frenchman, with the seriousness of a rare conscience; a touch energetic and delicate; what is just and true wedded to what is great and strong. These letters are destined to an immense success among artists, and as France is artistic, the success will be a popular one.

> *George Sand [pseudonym of Amandine Aurore Lucile Dupin Dudevant], in an extract from "Autour de la Table," translated by Eugene Benson, in* The Galaxy, *Vol. II, November 15, 1866, p. 533.*

## EUGENE BENSON   (essay date 1866)

[*Benson discusses the literary and artistic qualities of Fromentin's travel books. Noting that Fromentin is "not a traveler who writes, but an artist who travels and writes," he compares the author to Henry David Thoreau and George Sand and describes Fromentin as a writer "always dominated by the artistic spirit."*]

It is so seldom that books of travel have any distinguished literary charm, so rare that they are more than interesting or instructive narratives, that Eugène Fromentin's works, by the distinction of their style, and the dignity and serious traits of the personality which they reveal, fix the attention, and take the rank of a work of art in literature. (p. 533)

The first thing we remark in Fromentin is what we may call his uncommon and distinguished relation to nature; and it is this relation, so to speak, which determines the principal traits of ["**Un été dans le Sahara**"]. . . . He is not a traveller who writes, but an artist who travels and writes. His point of view is that of an artist—that is, a being of sensation, passionately seeking for the beautiful, quick to observe the picturesque, ready in his recognition of the human and natural. Where many writers describe, Eugène Fromentin may be said to depict; where others narrate, he expresses; where most moralize he simply contemplates. His conscience for the true may be compared to that of Thoreau; he is as accurate, he is as full, as vivid, and he has a grace derived from his sense of the beautiful, unknown to the sturdy soul of Thoreau. He is not aggressive like Thoreau, but he is as independent; he is less provincial and more artist.

Yet, artist as he is in his style, in his nature, and by his profession, I cannot forget that his literary form is not so ample and generous as that of George Sand; it is much more studied, much more minute, much more suited to the reserve and quiet of English taste than the ardent and ample utterances of the great master of French prose. His work is composed of a series of studies rather than what we would call pictures; it has the vividness, the truth, the local color, the interest of a study; for Fromentin has not roughly sketched life and nature in the East, he has *studied* it. (pp. 533-34)

To one in the least trained in the observation of nature from the artistic point of view, and wearied with the threadbare phrases and trite generalities of common seeing and common writing, Fromentin's *written* studies are delightfully fresh and win the compliment of repeated readings. We return to them again and again because of the poetic charm; the irresistibleness of the sentiment, which haunts us like music, and we remember it as some vague and dreamy revery of the mind's twilight. For instance, one day traversing the desert he meets a little boy leading thin camels. The next day, nothing. Then he recollects himself and says: "Yes, by the way, redbreasts and larks" (now remark the tenderness and sweetness of his thought), "sweet birds that make me see again all that I love in my country. What can they do in the Sahara, and for whom do they sing in the neighborhood of ostriches, in the mournful country of scorpions and horned vipers? Who knows? Without them there would be no bird to hail the rising sun."

When you make the acquaintance of Fromentin you will be struck with the fact that, unlike most travellers, and unlike most descriptive writers, he never seems to talk to advance himself; he has, as was well said, the art of existing fully in his work without dreaming to speak of himself. (p. 535)

[Fromentin] also made, for the Committee of Historical Monuments, archæological excursions, the results of which were published in pamphlets under the modest title of **"Artistic Visits or Simple Pilgrimages."** These writings I have not read: the two books which have introduced Eugène Fromentin to me are ["**Un été dans le Sahara**" and "**Une année dans le Sahel**"]. They are sufficient to make me cherish his influence and honor him as a serious, delicate and reserved man, a writer conscientious like Thoreau, easily capable of revery like Hawthorne, and always dominated by the artistic spirit. (p. 537)

> *Eugene Benson, "Eugène Fromentin," in* The Galaxy, *Vol. II, November 15, 1866, pp. 533-38.*

## EUGÈNE FROMENTIN    (essay date 1875)

[*Modestly describing himself as a "mere amateur" in the field of art criticism, Fromentin sets forth his methods and aspirations in writing* The Old Masters of Belgium and Holland. *His comments, dated 1875, were published in French in the preface to the 1876 edition of the work.*]

I have just been viewing Rubens and Rembrandt in their own homes, and at the same time the Dutch school in its unchanging frame of agricultural and maritime life, of downs, pastures, huge clouds, and low horizons.

Here are two arts, distinct, perfectly complete, entirely independent of each other, and very brilliant, which require to be studied at once by an historian, a thinker, and a painter. That the work should be properly done requires the union of these three men in one; and I have nothing in common with the two first, while as to the painter, however a man may have a feeling for distances, he ceases to be one in approaching the least known of the masters of these privileged countries. I shall traverse the museums, but I shall not review them. I shall stop before certain men: I shall not relate their lives, nor catalogue their works, even those preserved by their compatriots. I shall define simply as I understand them, as fully as I can seize them, certain characteristic sides of their genius or talent. I shall not grapple with too great questions; I shall avoid profundities and dark places. The art of painting is only the art of expressing the invisible by the visible. Whether its roads be great or small, they are sown with problems which it is permitted to sound for one's self as truths, but which it is well to leave in their darkness as mysteries. I shall only speak concerning certain pictures, of the surprise, the pleasure, the astonishment, and with no less precision of the vexation, which they have caused me. In all this I shall only translate with sincerity the inconsequent sensations of the mere amateur. (pp. xlii-xliii)

It is possible that some of my opinions may conflict with those generally received. I shall not seek, but I shall not avoid, any revision of ideas which may arise from these disagreements. I entreat you not to see in this any indication of a guerilla spirit, which seeks to distinguish itself by boldness, and which, while travelling the beaten path, would fear to be accused of observing nothing, if it did not judge everything differently from others. (p. xliii)

For the moment my method will be to forget everything which has been said on [the subjects of painters and painting]; my aim, to raise questions, to produce a wish to think about them, and to inspire in those who would be capable of rendering us such a service the curiosity to solve them. (pp. xliii-xliv)

> *Eugène Fromentin, in a preface to his* The Old Masters of Belgium & Holland, *translated by Mary C.*

*Robbins, 1882. Reprint by Schocken Books, 1963, pp. xlii-xliv.*

## [HENRY JAMES]    (essay date 1876)

[*James was an American-born English novelist, short story writer, critic, and essayist of the late nineteenth and early twentieth centuries. In addition to being regarded as one of the greatest novelists of the English language, James is admired as a lucid and insightful critic. As a young man he traveled extensively throughout Great Britain and Europe and benefited from the friendship and influence of many of the leading figures of nineteenth-century art and literature: in England, he met John Ruskin, Dante Gabriel Rossetti, William Morris, and Leslie Stephen; in France, where he lived for several years, he was part of the literary circle that included Gustave Flaubert, Émile Zola, Edmond de Goncourt, Guy de Maupassant, and Ivan Turgenev. Thus, his criticism is informed by his sensitivity to European culture, particularly English and French literature of the late nineteenth century. James was a frequent contributor to several prominent American journals, including the* North American Review, *the* Nation, *and the* Atlantic Monthly. *In the essay excerpted below, he commends certain stylistic features of* The Old Masters of Belgium and Holland *but otherwise cites the book as an example of the follies of "literary" art criticism. Chief among these faults, James contends, is overanalysis, which spoils the spontaneous nature of art appreciation. James also charges Fromentin with overestimating Peter Paul Rubens and misinterpreting Rembrandt van Rijn.*]

[M. Fromentin's *Les maîtres d' Autrefois: Belgique-Hollande*] is extremely interesting, but it strikes us as curious rather than valuable. We have always had a decided mistrust of literary criticism of works of plastic art; and those tendencies which have suggested this feeling are exhibited by M. Fromentin in their most extreme form. He would deny, we suppose, that his criticism is literary and assert that it is purely pictorial—the work of a painter judging painters. This, however, is only half true. M. Fromentin is too ingenious and elaborate a writer not to have taken a great deal of pleasure in the literary form that he gives to his thoughts; and when once the literary form takes the bit into its teeth, as it does very often with M. Fromentin, the effect, at least, of over-subtlety and web-spinning is certain to be produced. This over-subtlety is M. Fromentin's fault: he attempts to say too many things about his painters, to discriminate beyond the point at which discriminations are useful. A work of art has generally been a simpler matter, for the painter, than a certain sort of critic assumes, and M. Fromentin, who has painted pictures, ought to know that they are meant before all things to be enjoyed. The excess into which he falls is not of the same sort as that which is so common with Mr. Ruskin— the attribution of various incongruous and arbitrary intentions to the artist; it is rather a too eager analysis of the material work itself, a too urgent description of it, a too exhaustive enumeration of its constituent particles. Nothing can well be more fatal to that *tranquil* quality which is the very essence of one's enjoyment of a work of art. M. Fromentin, like most French writers on aesthetic or indeed on any other matters, abounds in his own sense. He can say so much so neatly and so vividly, in his admirable French style, that he loses all respect for the unsayable—the better half, we think, of all that belongs to a work of art. But his perception is extraordinarily just and delicate, and his power of entering into a picture is, in a literary critic, very rare. He enters too much, in our opinion, into the technical side, and he expects of his readers to care much more than should be expected even of a very ardent art-lover for the mysteries of the process by which the picture was made. There is a certain sort of talk which should be confined to manuals and note-books and studio records; there is something impertinent in pretending to work it into literary form—especially into the very elegant and rather self-conscious literary form of which M. Fromentin is master. It is narrow and unimaginative not to understand that a very deep and intelligent enjoyment of pictures is consistent with a lively indifference to this "inside view" of them. It has too much in common with the reverse of a tapestry, and it suggests that a man may be extremely fond of good concerts and yet have no relish for the tuning of fiddles. M. Fromentin is guilty of an abuse of it which gives his book occasionally a somewhat sickly and unmasculine tone. He is, besides, sometimes too inconclusive; he multiplies his descriptive and analytic touches, but we are at loss to know exactly what he has desired to prove.

This is especially the case in the pages upon Rubens, which contain a great many happy characterizations of the painter, but lack a "general drift," an argument. M. Fromentin indulges in more emotion on the subject of Rubens than we have ever found ourselves able to do, and his whole dissertation is a good example of the vanity of much of the criticism in the super-subtle style. We lay it down perplexed and bewildered, with a wearied sense of having strained our attention in a profitless cause. There is a limit to what it is worth while to attempt to say about the greatest artists. Michael Angelo and Raphael bid defiance to more than a moderate amount of "keen analysis." Either Rubens was a first-rate genius, and in this case he may be trusted to disengage himself freely from his admirers' impressions; or else he was not, and in this case it is not worth while to split hairs about him. M. Fromentin, speaking roughly, takes Rubens too seriously by several shades. There are fine painters and coarse painters, and Rubens belonged to the latter category; he reigned in it with magnificent supremacy. One may as well come to this conclusion first as last, for all the ingenuity in the world will not avert it. Rubens was in painting, an incomparable *improvisatore*; almost always a great colorist, often extremely happy in composition, he never leaves us without a sense that the particular turn the picture has taken, the cast of a certain face, the attitude of a certain figure, the flow of a drapery or the choice of a gesture, has been an accident of the moment. Hence we have in Rubens a constant sense of something superficial, irreflective, something cheap, as we say nowadays. His intentions had often great energy, but they had very little profundity, and his imagination, we suspect, less delicacy than M. Fromentin attributes to it. (pp. 29-30)

[M. Fromentin's] chapters upon Paul Potter, Cuyp, Ruysdael, Terburg, and Metsu are in our opinion the most felicitous in the volume; they are full of just discrimination and interesting suggestion. He ranks Ruysdael immediately after Rembrandt, a classification of this enchanting painter with which we have no quarrel; but we are not sure that with regard to him, too, he may not be accused of looking for mid-day (as the French say) *à quatorze heures*. But he characterizes him charmingly. He says very justly that there are a great many things which we should like to know about his life and person which it is impossible to ascertain; his history is obscure, and the questions are unanswerable. But would the idea come to us, he adds, of asking such questions about any of the other Dutch painters? "Brilliant and charming, they painted, and it seems as if this were enough. Ruysdael painted, but he lived, and this is why it is desirable to know how he lived. I know but three or four men who are to this degree personally interesting—Rembrandt, Ruysdael, Paul Potter, perhaps Cuyp. This is more than enough

to class them." Upon Rembrandt M. Fromentin expatiates largely and very ingeniously; but we should say of these chapters as of his remarks upon Rubens, that the author goes through a great critical motion without arriving at any definite goal. He strikes a great many matches, and often rather bedims the subject. The great picture at Amsterdam, best known by its French name of the "Ronde de Nuit," is a very strange work if you will, but nothing is gained by making it out stranger than it is and exhausting the vocabularly of hopeless aesthetic conjecture on its behalf. The note of M. Fromentin's view of Rembrandt is struck by his saying that he "revealed one of the unknown corners of the human soul," and by his adding, at the close of his remarks, that he was "a pure spiritualist—an ideologist." Some readers, doubtless, will be more struck with the felicity of this definition than we have been. It is not the unknown, we should say, that Rembrandt represents, but the known, the familiar, the common, the homely. His subjects, his scenes, his figures are almost all taken from common life, and where they are not they are brought into it. He was an alchemist: he presents them in that extraordinary envelope of dense light and shade which is the familiar sign of his manner; but in this it is the execution that is rare to our sense—incomparably rare, certainly—rather than the conception. But to whatever degree in detail M. Fromentin's readers may dissent from him they will do justice to the brilliancy of his work. Its acuteness and delicacy of perception are altogether remarkable and its manner most exquisite.It has a peculiar charm. (p. 30)

> [Henry James], "A Study of Rubens and Rembrandt," in The Nation, Vol. XXIII, No. 576, July 13, 1876, pp. 29-30.*

## EMMA LAZARUS  (essay date 1881)

> [Lazarus was a nineteenth-century American Jewish activist and writer who is best known as the author of "The New Colossus," her famous sonnet inscribed on the Statue of Liberty welcoming the "huddled masses yearning to breathe free" to the shores of the United States. She surveys Fromentin's writings in the essay excerpted below, reserving her highest praise for Un été dans le Sahara and Une année dans le Sahel.]

The distinguishing characteristic of Eugène Fromentin was refinement. Nothing issued from his pen or his brush that did not bear the stamp of a fastidious elegance of style and taste. . . . He had the courage of his opinions to a degree that amounted to little less than audacity in the minds of those who dissented from his conclusions, and both the quality and quantity of his literary and artistic achievement give evidence of a vigorous, indomitable will, no less than of a brilliant genius. . . . His literary work comprises four volumes—'The Old Masters,' a critical study of the Netherland schools of painting; 'Dominique,' a novel; 'A Summer in the Sahara,' and 'A Year in the Sahel,'—two books of eastern travel. 'The Old Masters' is essentially a painter's book, but it has an inestimable value and charm for the least technical reader. It holds indeed a unique place among art criticisms, and whatever indignant protests may be excited by its independence of judgment in regard to masters whose rank the world has already fixed, there can be but one opinion as to the force and grace of style and the sincerity of feeling with which its views are presented. However frankly Fromentin may dissent from the accepted verdict upon certain masterpieces (as for instance Rembrandt's 'Night-Watch'), there is never a trace of flippancy or arrogance in his expression. Without for a moment abdicating his prerogative of individual judgment, he approaches the works of genius in a spirit of reverence only too often lacking among modern critics. The tone of the book is one of serious and profound enthusiasm. He is equally successful in his detailed criticisms and in his brief summing up of an effect or a talent. . . .

'Dominique' is one of those rare novels which combine the beauty and grace of poetry with an autobiographical vividness and intensity. One is tempted to believe (all the more from its being the author's only work of fiction) that under the thin veil of his hero's imaginary name and circumstances he has made a study and confession of his own character. But if he has copied from life, we need scarcely say he has done so as an artist, not as a photographer. The record of the birth, development, and final renunciation of a forbidden passion, which forms the motif of the story, presents nothing new to the ordinary novel reader; it is in the originality of types, the picturesqueness of scene, the sincerity of accent, the trenchant or eloquent passages of reflection or criticism, the wonderful grace and tenderness of touch, that the peculiar charm of the book consists. Fromentin has expended all his art upon the principal character; the others are mere sketches, more or less shadowy. Madeleine, the unhappy object of Dominique's passion (which from the beginning resembles more a malady of the nerves than a healthy, genuine affection), is a highly poetic figure, but somewhat unreal or over-idealized. Perhaps this fault is inseparable from the method which Fromentin has adopted in making Dominique tell his own story; we never get a glimpse of Madeleine except through the rose-colored medium of her lover's sentiment. The author has evidently appreciated the morbid temperament and almost undignified situation of his hero, and has endeavored to palliate the occasionally unpleasant effect by representing him as extremely young, and by giving us from time to time the tonic counter-influence of a thoroughly healthy, intelligent, and practical man, M. Augustin. . . . It is needless to say, however, that all wise and kind counsels are thrown away upon a nervous, sentimental, poetical youth, who tortures himself with perpetual self-vivisection until he ends by thinking his commonplace woe something exceptional and tremendous, and by immolating upon the altar of his selfishness the pure and lovely creature whom he has pitilessly pursued from the moment when he knew her to be beyond his reach. It is all very human, very melancholy and singularly beautiful, and leaves an impression akin to that of Chopin's music, or of such a clear autumn evening as is described in the opening chapter, 'which typifies any moderate existence that is completed or concluded in a natural frame of serenity, silence, and regret.'

Among all of M. Fromentin's literary works those which bear the palm for originality and an almost magic fascination of style are the two volumes of Eastern travel with which he made his first appearance in literature. No other modern description of the Orient can be compared with these wonderful reproductions, not only of the color and line of Eastern landscape, figures, and costume, but of the secret glamour of the life and atmosphere. 'At first,' he says, 'you only perceive the variety of costumes; then you stop at the characteristic race-distinctions; you give to every individual the same family likeness of style, of insipid elegance and beauty. Only at a later period does the man appear under the lineaments of the Arab, and show that he has, like ourselves, his passions, deformities, and absurdities.' It was just this discernment of the human, the real, the eternal, under the strange and often bewildering mask of foreign types and customs, which enabled Fromentin to succeed in making us share his life through the long shadowless days of his desert sojourn. No fantastic pictures for us, but

real as personal experience are the enchanted oasis, glittering caravans, torrid, blinding wastes of sand, passionate, scintillating nights that 'come on like a swoon.' No 'splendid inanimate statues,' but breathing men and women are the Arab dervishes, servants, almehs, toilers at the loom, and merchants of the bazaar. (p. 364)

*Emma Lazarus, "Eugène Fromentin," in* The Critic, *New York, Vol. 1, No. 26, December 31, 1881, pp. 364-65.*

## HENRY ECKFORD   (essay date 1883)

[*Although he admires Fromentin's work, Eckford expresses reservations regarding several aspects of* The Old Masters of Belgium and Holland *and the travel books. In particular, he discerns confusion and timidity in Fromentin's criticism of Rembrandt van Rijn and notes the superficiality of the author's treatment of Eastern life and landscape.*]

["**Les Maîtres d'autrefois**"] is a series of brilliant studies of Rubens and Rembrandt, put together in an apparently hasty way and with a good deal of apology on the part of Fromentin. Here are, says he of the works of these two masters, two arts, distinct, perfectly complete, entirely independent of each other, and very brilliant, which require to be studied at once by an historian, a thinker, and a painter [see excerpt above, 1875]. That the work should be properly done requires the union of these three men in one; and I have nothing in common with the first two, while as to the painter, however a man may have a feeling for distances, he ceases to be one when he approaches the least known of the masters of these privileged countries. One may take Fromentin at his word, and yet derive the utmost pleasure from "**Les Maîtres d'autrefois.**" It is true enough that his study is incomplete; nay, it is often hasty and in minor points inaccurate; it is sometimes superficial. But there are abundant signs that both Rembrandt and Rubens—the latter, perhaps, more than the former—excited his critical faculties to the utmost, and in consequence his pages are alive with earnestness. One feels him groping for the truth, and groping not merely to show his skill in criticising masters whose work few critics dare to analyze; but with the zeal of a man who may have it on his mind to apply to his own painting some of the discoveries he made. Not the least curious thing in this book is to note the reaction on the style of the critic of the spirit of the master he was writing about. Thus, about Rubens the writing is bold and decided, like the work of that genius; but about Rembrandt it is comparatively timid and sometimes really confused. On the whole the effect of the book is not that of a product of a mind thoroughly informed with its subject and entirely settled in its conclusions. Fromentin distinctly avers this, and in part assumes it intentionally. Yet one cannot avoid the inference that if he had lived ten years longer, and allowed the effervescence of the powerful impressions made by the old Dutch masters on his lively, responsive, artistic temperament to subside, he would have made of this charming and brilliant series of sketches a work far more rounded, far more profound. We hesitate at his dicta about Franz Hals; we decline to go his lengths concerning Rembrandt as a painter, and even fancy that much that he writes about him is ill-digested and confused. It is picturesque, but not to be thoroughly trusted. Yet what are we saying? It sounds like a piece of flagrant ingratitude to quarrel with a book so full of delicate and independent research as "**Les Maîtres d'autrefois.**" When one reflects that the enthusiast, the sympathetic reporter of Oriental life in Northern Africa, is able to enter into and enjoy the entirely different art of Holland, respect must be felt for Fromentin's breadth of mind and acumen. (pp. 835-37)

His methods of work, both literary and artistic, may be seen in the fragmentary **"Voyage en Egypte,"** which . . . [constitute] the short, but apparently far from hurried, notes of a traveler. Only Hawthorne could have exceeded Fromentin in the minuteness of his record, and in the curious fashion of talking to himself in his notes, and jogging his own memory, telling himself to be sure not to forget this or that point. In every Egyptian town he visits the quarter of the Almehs, and jots down the shades of color in their brilliant dresses, notes the effect of the gold coins strung in their hair, and the glittering of their eye-balls and white teeth. The attention to colors is close and intelligent. This may be taken as a specimen from the Nile trip near Luxor.

> Very near the Libyan chain, lofty, rosy, fallow-colored, fully lit by the morning sun, magnificent in outline. The Nile is evidently lower. It has recovered its large banks—*(reflections entire)*. A pelican close by. Four shots at him—missed. The Nile like a mirror, all rose and *pale blue*. The greatest possible pallor. Banks should be ochre, bitumen, provided it is in the light. One little sail on a Nile boat shines white in the immensity of that blonde light. As strong as you will, so long as it is blonde, limpid, clear, flat, in every way pure. *Make it pure, never too much so!* Not to fear dryness, avoid it by the modeling of objects, choice of values, *thickness of tone*. Avoid reds. There are none. Measure distances by values, intensity of tones by one or two dominant spots, which are nothing but *blacks,* browns, blues; as a high light, a whitish blue, a cotton white. This on a pale river. Mountains *cendré* or rose, modeled or not, according to the hour. A soft sky. There is the whole of Egypt!

On the journey during which this was written he had the good fortune to witness the *fête* given by the Viceroy of Egypt to the Empress and the Emperor of Austria on the opening of the Suez Canal. The short, telling phrases bring the scenes before one quite as well as careful rewriting would. It shows how seriously Fromentin took both his writing and his painting. Nothing was neglected that could be done to make each perfect, and the result was that in art he approached the best of his contemporaries, and that in literature he has been placed with justice beside Alfred de Musset and Prosper Mérimée. (p. 837)

Nevertheless there are moments when one doubts whether Fromentin looked very deep into the life or the landscape of the East, notwithstanding the pleasant things said of him by his biographers and the delightful passages written by himself in more than one attractive volume. He was more occupied with externals than anything else. The colors of dresses made him give less attention to the expression of faces and the thoughts of the Orientals. The necessity to register in the memory changing effects of landscape scattered his observation still more. One is inclined to wonder often whether, after all, it was not a loss to Fromentin to have been so highly gifted in two directions; whether, in fact, he did not suffer from dividing his forces. (pp. 837-38)

*Henry Eckford, "Eugène Fromentin," in* The Century, *Vol. XXV, No. 6, April, 1883, pp. 829-38.*

## NORMAN HAPGOOD   (essay date 1900)

[*Hapgood characterizes Fromentin as a master art critic whose appeal is limited to the "cultivated few" by virtue of the technical orientation and stylistic precision of his criticism.*]

Of all the critics of painting whose knowledge is exact, [Eugène Fromentin] alone has high talent in literature; yet his one great book about pictures, **"Maîtres d'Autrefois,"** is little read by the public in France, and less elsewhere. It is, however, the mine for writers [on art]. (p. 278)

Among contemporary critics of painting Fromentin is recognised as pre-eminently the master. It seems impossible to meet his strength without surrendering. He floods and controls the mind, instead of spurring it to independent action. At first he subdues, and even on familiarity he hardly sets free, but continues a tyrant. This is because he does not indulge in what Professor James calls "fringe." There is no vague emanation, no mere personality, nothing which hitches his particular thought to a star, no moralisation to switch the reader's mind off into the ethical realms where disputants stand on more equal ground. . . . Whatever truths may have floated just beyond his reach he kept for his own private torture. He retains his superiority by remaining on that ground which he knows better than his reader. Nothing is committed to paper except what can be compressed into the solid technical moulds. Nor does he ever attempt, in the fashion of Emerson or Carlyle, to scare out a conception by pounding the bushes in which it has taken refuge. He strikes his victim or refrains, and although an exaggeration, it is not unfair to say that when he hits an idea that idea is dead. It has been put with such exactness that nothing is to be said. Thus we have a vivid example of the power and the weakness of a precision of style which includes only what it means.

Unless this technical concentration, this limitation to explaining what is unmistakably expressed and the methods of its expression, unless this definiteness left room for the personality of the painter criticised, Fromentin would not be the power he is. It is his own personality that is excluded. Of the artist expounded he gives what has gone into his work and no more. He does not imagine that the technique of the artist is unrelated to his nature, or avoid the task of explaining the texture of the soul. The meaning of workmanship is what he constantly gives. That Rubens "knows his trade like an angel" is a characteristic phrase. Form in substance and correctness in values and colours is life. He does not sharply divide the technical understanding of the painter from his spiritual insight. Rubens, he says, "is very earthy, more earthy than any among the masters whose equal he is, but the painter comes to the aid of the draughtsman and thinker and sets them free." He carries the principle that the man is revealed in his work to an almost illegitimate distance, but he practically means that as a critic of art he deals only with that part of the man which is the artist. (pp. 279-80)

Whether it be of Rubens, at the material extreme of the great painters, or of Rembrandt at the spiritual end, Fromentin can write sentences, beautiful in form and beautiful with the light of thought, with that air of finality which no other critic of painting has approached. One painter is depicted by pointing out what seem the most fundamental principles of art, yet the next inspires another set, different, yet equally convincing, never contradicting, but seldom over-lapping. You will scarcely find in the essay on Paul Potter any of the thought brought out by Van Dyck, and Ruysdael gives birth to a critical philosophy little related to that with which the essayist figured Rubens. (pp. 280-81)

[Of Ruysdael, Fromentin observes:]

> Had he joy, as he surely had bitterness? Did destiny allow him to love other things than clouds, and from what did he suffer most—if he did suffer—from the torment of painting well or of living? All these questions remain without response, and yet posterity is interested in them.

> Would it occur to you to ask as much about Berghem, Karel-Dujardin, Wouverman, Geyser, Terburg, Metz, Peter de Hoogh himself? All these brilliant or charming painters painted, and that seems enough. Ruysdael painted, but he lived, whence the importance of knowing how he lived. I know in the Dutch school but three or four men who are thus interesting for their personalities: Rembrandt, Ruysdael, Paul Potter, possibly Cuyp—which is already more than is needed to make them a class apart.

It is only because he does not among critics belong to this class that Fromentin's name is so seldom on the world's lips. What he was as a man seems irrelevant. "Grandeur and abundance in exquisite sobriety," George Sand found in him; "ardour, kindness, energy, and conscience." If a skilled reader can discern these human qualities they certainly seem to inhere in the work rather than to suggest the person behind the pen. Goethe said that any criticism not filled with the enthusiasm of partiality was empty. Fromentin's refined and unimpassioned justice takes him too far from average human nature. The public wishes not subtlety or exactness so much as flesh and blood. It was Fromentin's fate to prefer what he himself lacked. Public opinion, he says, is less fastidious than the critic, or more clairvoyant. Its paths are sometimes devious, sometimes direct, and its motives are not always the best, but it never reaches a conclusion which cannot be supported by the profoundest reasons. Why he is the guide of the cultivated few is suggested in what he says about the influence of Van Noordt: "Without that instructor would Rubens have been all that he is? Would not one accent have been wanting to him, one only, the plebeian accent which fastens him to the very heart of the people, and thanks to which he has been understood as well by them as by delicate minds and princes?"

So also with criticism, although it is not a popular art, yet to be great it must connect itself with the universal heart. One touch of nature makes the whole world kin, and that touch, in the opinion of Mr. Whistler, is vulgarity. Fromentin's critical intelligence kept him from saying that, and his tone is one of admission, almost of regret, when he puts the truth that what reaches only the cultivated falls short of greatness. He has imagination, but it is an imagination of science, distinct, psychological, compact, but not human. It is impossible to tell whether Fromentin the man had the sombre gravity and lonely earnestness of Ruysdael or not. If he had, they should have formed part of his art, even when that art was criticism, and they would have brought him into the intimacy of larger numbers. (pp. 281-82)

[In] his analysis, he, like most writers whose love of culture is too strong, weakens himself by leaning always in the direction of intellectual refinement. Perhaps the generalisation may be hazarded that any thought which takes the trained intelli-

gence in a vice is too severe for the larger uses of criticism. (p. 282)

Speaking of Raphael, Michelangelo, and Leonardo in contrast to Rubens, he says, "in truth there are in the world of the beautiful two or three spirits who have gone further, who have flown higher, who, consequently, have seen at closer range the divine lights and the eternal truths." That higher light and truth he hoped to point out to us, as he had revealed the natures of Rubens and Potter, of Ruysdael and the little masters, had not an early death cut him off. . . . When those who have seen how his pictures of the Dutchmen burned themselves into the minds of the leaders of art criticism remember that we have lost his thoughts about the artists whose flights he believed reached nearest to the summit of beauty, they feel a sadness surpassed by few broken destinies. "The only secret which belongs to him," Fromentin said of Rubens, "and which he has never given up, even to the most sagacious, even to the best informed—is this unproducible, unteachable point, this irreducible atom, this nothing, which in all the things of this world is called the inspiration, the grace, or the gift, and which is everything." This is the secret in every artist which haunted Fromentin and which he often makes us feel where none other can. He is too severe for the many, too rigidly exact, but for an important few there is in all the history of art criticism no book so valued as **"Maîtres d'Autrefois,"** and no loss so great as its author's untimely death. (pp. 282-83)

> *Norman Hapgood, "Eugene Fromentin," in* Contemporary Review, *Vol. LXXVII, February, 1900, pp. 277-83.*

### C. G. COMPTON    (essay date 1905)

[*Compton comments on* Dominique, *emphasizing Fromentin's gift for expressing emotion and intimacy and praising his depiction of the characters Dominique and Madeleine. Compton also notes that Fromentin withholds significant aspects of his own personality from his writings.*]

**"Dominique"**'s attraction lies in its intimacy. Like all the books—novels, diaries, or letters—which express the emotional experiences of an individual under a conventional disguise, it is effective by exactly so much as it makes us feel that the passion and sentiments had been felt by the writer. (pp. 509-10)

Fromentin writes about feeling without being sentimental or embarrassed. He is not ashamed of being in love, and he tells all there is to tell. It is, as the phrase goes, a boy and girl love affair, and for a love affair a boy and girl are the best. For a contract of marriage, a company director, an M.P. rising to an under-secretaryship, a Wesleyan solicitor, or something of that sort will do very well. But Fromentin was not a novelist, and he was treating the matter of poetry, and showing how the greatest of natural instincts is transformed by temperament. For, at the last, this is not the love affair of a boy who will become a company director. It is the passion of a fine and tenacious character of a man who has the nerves of an artist and the deep conservatism of a peasant. This sort does not take things lightly, and if they have known and loved a woman when she had just left the convent school, they will love her when she is married, and when they are married, like Dominique. He saw Madeleine first when she wore dresses that had the marks of kneeling on the convent floor; he had a great shock when she came back from a holiday and he saw her a young and beautiful woman, and he had a shock that lasted his life when she married. . . . Only a rare gift for refinements of emotion could have expressed and portrayed the growth and course of Dominique's passion, and only a sincere genius could have made it sympathetic. It is not the banal story of the other man's wife, nor the brief passion of puberty. It is a boy's companionship grown into a man's love, and the man's nature is strong and loyal with the strength and immutability of men whose fathers have lived close to the steadfast earth. And Dominique had found his right mate in Madeleine. At first a little abstracted and remote, in spite of her *gracieuseté* and a little of the saint enskied by a young lover, she is slowly revealed by the pressure of life. There are few women like her, but they are the women who would spend themselves to help their lover to endure his love. They would not know of their own danger, and they would suffer as she did. There is a true and singular pathos in the scenes where Dominique and Madeleine exchange their parts, where he has to strengthen her fortitude. The *mariage de convenance* has some admirable effects; it protects property and inspires comedy. But it is rather a tragic business when it leads to love instead of *galanterie*. That was never the alternative for Madeleine; she is, and always would have been, the *digne épouse;* the honoured mother, the woman who did not seek after love. But with these women it goes hard when love comes too late.

Fromentin has been as successful with Madeleine as with Dominique, perhaps more because she is individual, and there is a class for him. She is the kind of Frenchwoman who can make good sense charming, whose nature is kindly and gracious, who has principles and is intelligent. She belongs to the company of heroines who stay with us because they give the accent of their individuality to the general emotions. It is an achievement in any art to express truthfully the great passions, but the last distinction is to individualise the universal, to characterise emotion. (pp. 512-13)

Fromentin is delightful, exactly because in **"Dominique,"** as in **"Les Maîtres d'Autrefois,"** there is a constant interaction of feeling and intellect. His scenery is said to be too pictorial, addressed to the eyes instead of the mind. A painter who writes a novel must expect that sort of criticism, but if **"Dominique"** had been published anonymously, its pictorial precision would have been attributed to a novelist with eyes. Fromentin knew his country as Constable knew the valley of the Stour, and he expressed its calm, it homeliness, its grey skies, and grey seas with fond accuracy. The opening scenes have the breath of a Corot; the description of the *vendange* should be compared with Mr. Hardy's apple harvest. The scene by the lighthouse shows Fromentin's talent for giving a memorable picture in a few lines, and for rendering the atmosphere of place and time. (pp. 513-14)

In the books of travel, in the pictures, and in **"Dominique,"** we get Fromentin as the observer and the artist, and as the man who has felt, and can present, an emotion. They do not entirely reveal him. In the last resort there are, with few exceptions, no complete revelations. . . . The other sort who give themselves away are the egoists with vanity, Rousseau, Châteaubriand, Byron, invaluable documents for the psychologist, if the vanity could be precipitated. Montaigne talks about himself a great deal, Rabelais expresses himself in figures made in his own fashion, and we say that we know them. They know better, they have told us much, but they kept back, they did not yield the essentials. No one was less likely than Fromentin to reveal himself entirely, and as for doing so publicly, he would rather have gone to the stake. Ultra-sensitive natures

like his, which are at the same time sympathetic and intelligent and reflective, never give themselves away, but, having the malady of thought, they are driven to speech. Fromentin did, what people like him must do, he made confession to a few intimates whom he had tested and proved. If the opinion of these confessors, who were not directors, could be obtained, we should have the material for understanding Fromentin. As that is not possible, we must be content with the book which is, no doubt, to a large extent, a *résumé* of these intimate talks. (p. 514)

*C. G. Compton, "Eugène Fromentin," in* The Fortnightly Review, *n.s. Vol. LXXVII, No. CCCCLIX, March 1, 1905, pp. 508-19.*

**THE BOOKMAN,** LONDON   (essay date 1914)

[*The critic acknowledges the obsolescence of some parts of* The Old Masters of Belgium and Holland, *but defends the "essential justice" and acuity of Fromentin's criticism.*]

Eugène Fromentin wrote **"Les Maîtres d'Autrefois: Belgique-Hollande"** in 1875. That date and the address of "Brussels" appear at the head of the Preface [see excerpt above, 1875], in the first sentence of which is indicated the purpose of his travels and his book: "To see Rubens and Rembrandt in their own country, and at the same time the Dutch School in its natural setting." The field thus defined—for Fromentin in 1875 comparatively one of discovery—has since been worked over by innumerable students, many of them of indefatigable patience as well as acumen. Perhaps the most obvious change resulting from their researches is the sharpness of the distinction between the two divisions of the survey, North and South. No one now would bring the North and South Netherland painters under one rubric of the Dutch School. One does not say to-day that the Dutch School, meaning by that the North Netherland, begins with the first years of the seventeenth century, or that by a very slight abuse of dates we can fix the day of its birth. Had Fromentin written thirty years later than he did, his chapter on the origin, if not the character, of that school would have been expanded, and those on the forerunners of Rubens correspondingly modified. Both Lucas van Leyden and Jan van Scorel would have appeared more often, and more individualised, in his pages, and he would almost certainly have suggested some racial and spiritual affinity to Rembrandt in Geertgen tot S. Jans, whom as it is he does not mention at all. But the fact that Fromentin was imperfectly aware of distinctions made by recent scholarship, and wrote in ignorance of much that it has brought into the light since his day, does not affect the illumination which he cast upon the whole field as well, as upon particular figures in it. In especial, the pious and enthusiastic re-discovery of Rembrandt since he wrote, does not efface *his* discovery of him. One wonders, indeed, whether our newer knowledge is, after all, very essential. At any rate, it only brings into more relief the essential justice of the estimate which Fromentin's prescience enabled him to pronounce from the evidence under his hand.

That estimate is wonderfully satisfying—admiring, comprehensive and reasoned. Fromentin is never dogmatic. He is stimulating, by virtue of a method of raising questions suggesting answers both for and against the point he appears desirous of making. Yet he is always logical, and we must not complain if, with an artist's instinct for unity, he coerces his argument, and sometimes the facts, into a full charge in favour of a predetermined conclusion. Thus his well-known theory in regard to the domination and significance of *chiaroscuro* in Rembrandt's art rests (for him) on a series of props, not always quite secure, and the chief of them actually made a little wobbly by the restoration of the "Night Watch" and its removal from the *Trippenhius*. But even were they all to give way under it, there are others to take their place, and in any case the theory was brilliant psychology and is illuminating art-criticism. And then again, the point he makes in his character of Rembrandt, through the master's failure to found a school, is just as well as acute, even although Vermeer (under another name) is deliberately disconsidered, and Fabritius is left out altogether. Is one wrong in supposing that completely as Rembrandt conquered him, and his spirit flooded and moved him, the full homage was at first a little irksome to the author—that it chafed his professional amour propre ever so slightly to acknowledge a power which he was unable as a painter completely to explain? If so, he made ample amends, and possibly this slight constriction of his will renders in the end his elucidation of Rembrandt's difficult and original genius more comprehensive and acute. But, at the same time, we are aware how freely in comparison Fromentin moves in his survey of the genius of Rubens, whose character and work are so lucid, spontaneous and imperturbable, with nothing in either to hide, or profound enough to be hidden.

> *A review of "Les maîtres d'autrefois," in* The Bookman, *London, Vol. XLVI, No. 272, May, 1914, p. 92.*

### AARON SCHAFFER    (essay date 1923)

[*Schaffer praises Fromentin's prose style in* The Old Masters of Belgium and Holland.]

Fromentin's prose is marked by a style of such rich sonority that it must be read aloud in order that its beauties may be truly appreciated. There is a rhythm (and often even a rhyme) in his flowing periods and his crisp, concise phrases that make of him easily one of the masters of nineteenth-century French prose.

Nowhere do these qualities stand out in such brilliant relief as in *Les Maîtres d'autrefois*. . . . In this little volume, the artist sets out to record his impressions of a tour of inspection through the art galleries of Belgium and Holland. . . . A cursory reading of the book is alone sufficient to make one fairly ache with the desire to take this same trip. A more careful perusal of its three sections reveals an almost uninterrupted grandeur of style. Some of the chapters, as, for example, that in which Fromentin describes the Rubens *Saint Francis of Assisi* at Antwerp or that on Ruysdael, are veritable marvels of magnificent prose. (p. 372)

In the sixth chapter of his section on **"Holland,"** Fromentin asserts it to be his sincere opinion that "someone would render a true service by describing a tour about the Louvre, or, still less, about one of the salons, or, even less, a simple tour about a few paintings." He himself then becomes this "someone" by choosing three pictures upon which to expatiate, with the result that he opens our eyes to beauties which most of us certainly would never have discovered and, at the same time, in his description of the *Dutch Interior* of Pieter de Hooch, gives us one of the most remarkable of all the excellent appreciations which, literally, emblazon the pages of his little book. (p. 373)

The figures in these three paintings—the [*Gallant Soldier* of Terburg, the *Visit* of] Metzu, and the de Hooch—do not fail

to make an impression even during the first, more or less casual, examination; they produce just as deep an impression when studied in the finely-cutting words of Fromentin, though they may not have been seen at the Louvre; but they fasten themselves ineradicably in the memory of him who has studied them in the Louvre with Fromentin as commentary. All the greater, then, is the pity that the number of artists gifted with literary genius (and the reverse) is so limited. The union of music and poetry was effected ages ago; painting and poetry still remain, if you will, step-sisters of art. And what finer task could there be than that of giving to all the masterpieces of the world's painting, from the Italian and Flemish primitives of the Middle Ages down to the amorphous Degases and Picassos of our own day, the benefit of a treatment similar to that employed by Fromentin in his *Maîtres d'autrefois?* (p. 375)

> *Aaron Schaffer, "The Louvre and Eugene Fromentin," in* South Atlantic Quarterly, *Vol. XXII, No. 4, October, 1923, pp. 370-75.*

### FRANK HARRIS   (essay date 1927)

[*Harris was a highly controversial English editor, critic, and biographer who is best known as the author of a maliciously inaccurate biography of Oscar Wilde, a dubious life of George Bernard Shaw, and a massive autobiography in which he depicts Edwardian life primarily as a background for his sexual adventures. Many commentators maintain that Harris's greatest literary accomplishments were achieved during his tenure as editor of the* Fortnightly Review, Pearson's Magazine, *the* Evening News, *and the* Saturday Review *of London. His fame as a critic rests primarily upon his five-volume* Contemporary Portraits, *which contains essays marked by the author's characteristically vigorous style and patronizing tone. Here, Harris surveys Fromentin's principal works, defending* Dominique *against the condemnation of Charles Augustin Sainte-Beuve (see Additional Bibliography) and lauding* The Old Masters of Belgium and Holland *as "the best criticism of painting and painters in any language."*]

Taken strictly, we have only Rossetti in England and Fromentin in France who show that it is possible for a man to do first-rate work both in letters and in painting. Of these two Rossetti was far the more richly-endowed nature, the more gifted genius; but just because he reached greatness in both arts very easily he is not so interesting as Fromentin to the student. Fromentin is more self-conscious; his achievement more wilful; he deliberately defines both arts and outlines their respective spheres; and while as a painter he never reminds you of the man of letters, as a writer he never uses the brush instead of the pen. I cannot help thinking that Rossetti was by nature rather a painter than a writer. There is vision in him rather than thought; the souls fleet past *The Blessed Damozel* like "thin flames." While Fromentin is rather a writer than a painter, his finest essence is of the mind, and not of the eye. (pp. 179-80)

Fromentin's two books of travel and description ["**Un été dans le Sahara**" and "**Une année dans le Sahel**"] are masterpieces of their kind. No one has caught and rendered in words the characteristic beauty of the desert, the charm of its vast spaces of sky and plain, as perfectly as he has done. These books of his stand alone even in French descriptive writing. (pp. 181-82)

There is no seeking after rhetorical effect in his work, no trace of mannerism or trick; in both [painting and writing] he has the sincerity, the vision, the emotion of a master.

Again and again in Fromentin's life, as in his work, we are struck with proof upon proof of high intelligence. Not only does he understand the respective spheres of the two arts of painting and writing, but he knows his own powers as well, and his own limitations. He gives us two volumes of descriptive writing and not a word more; he gives a dozen masterly pictures, and hardly a poor or misused canvas. Now in the full midday of his powers, at the apogee of his singular and discreet renown, he enters a new field and dares a strange adventure [his novel "**Dominique**"]. . . . There is no trace of haste in the conception or in the writing—on the contrary, indeed. Yet "**Dominique**" fell flat—hardly a hint of praise anywhere. (p. 183)

It had the honour of being condemned root and branch in an article by Sainte-Beuve. . . . Sainte Beuve, we know, had an unhappy trick of marking his own limitations by sneering at his betters. Was "**Dominique**" then above his head, or had Fromentin, in spite of his high intelligence and his almost uncanny power of seeing himself from the outside, taken at length a wrong turning and misused his own talent? I should like, of course, to proclaim a masterpiece. It hurts me even to hesitate for a moment to appear to side with the Sainte-Beuves and the journalists against a creative spirit like Fromentin, to whom I owe many hours of exquisite and unalloyed delight. And, thank goodness, I am not compelled to in this instance. If "**Dominique**" is not a masterpiece, it certainly is not a failure, much less "an inept mistake." There are a couple of secondary characters in it which remain in the memory; the love-interest in it is unique and personal; there are descriptions of singular charm; but—I break off because I should have to spend much ink in order to describe "**Dominique**" as it deserves and classify it properly. One thing, however, must be said for it: it is of capital importance to any one who wishes to understand Fromentin or measure his talent; for he painted himself in it to the life, giving us his temperament in "**Dominique**" and his character in Augustin. But the two halves don't make a whole: the writer has told us at once too much and too little. (pp. 183-84)

I now come to his masterpiece ["**Les maîtres d'autrefois**"]. . . . I need say little about this book; it is the best criticism of painting and painters in any language—unique and singular; above discussion or praise; to be accepted by all with gratitude. I must just take one brick to show the wonder of the building:—

> The aim of Dutch painting (he says) is to imitate reality and *to make you love the imitation,* by putting before you vividly simple and sincere sensations. . . . The first condition of this style is to be natural, familiar, individual; it is the result of a union of moral qualities, simplicity, patience, perfect honesty. For the first time, what one calls *the domestic virtues* are revealed in the practice of an art.

Did any one ever see the truth more distinctly or find for it a more vivid and perfect expression? This work of Fromentin is one of the half-dozen books which I always carry about with me and read and re-read with ever new delight. If I were called upon to mark any limitation in it, I should be inclined to say that his admiration of the great craftsman, Franz Hals, is excessive in comparison with his measured praise of Rembrandt. Yet, all deductions made, this is one of the few modern books which deserve the praise Thucydides gave to his own history— "a possession for ever." (pp. 185-86)

*Frank Harris, "Eugene Fromentin: The Painter Writer," in his* Latest Contemporary Portraits, *The Macaulay Company, 1927, pp. 179-86.*

**EDWARD SACKVILLE-WEST**   (essay date 1947)

[*Sackville-West regards* Dominique *as a singular achievement in the realm of confessional literature. He cites "absolute sincerity of tone" as "one of the book's most permanently compelling qualities" and admires Fromentin's ability to imbue the novel with an elegiac sense of romanticism.*]

[The list of great novels in the genre of thinly veiled personal confession] is now fairly large; but I do not think an example exists more artistically flawless than Fromentin's *Dominique.* (p. 824)

As a novelist [Fromentin] owes much to George Sand and Sainte-Beuve, something to the Chateaubriand of *René* and the Balzac of *Le Lys dans la Vallée;* yet his method is in its wonderful refinement all his own, and so is the absolute sincerity of tone which is one of the book's most permanently compelling qualities. Fromentin has no need of the unusual, for the tragedy of his two chief characters is so touching in itself and so well set off by the surrounding figures, that it achieves the universal significance of a truly poetic conception. Dominique and Madeleine are pathetic and beautiful creations because Fromentin is scrupulously fair to them, in their weakness as in their strength. He is equally fair to Monsieur de Nièvres, who though he may be a little stiff and formal, perhaps a shade inhuman at times, is never shown as cruel or even unpleasant in the maintenance of his own and of his wife's dignity. And Madeleine herself is all the more real because, under the pressure of self-sacrifice, the level beauty of her nature begins to deteriorate, and she becomes peevish and moody. This is one of the most subtle strokes in the book. So many of the greatest novels have been written by men who either disliked women openly or loved them without really understanding or respecting the feminine character. To take extreme instances, neither Tolstoy nor Proust could endure what seemed to them the essential stupidity and perfidiousness of women. Not so Fromentin, whose single novel was not an act of tardy spite or of self-defence. Madeleine remained to him an object of esteem as well as of tenderness, and so he could afford to show her to us at her worst. To Dominique he had even less need to be indulgent, for Dominique was himself; in this character Fromentin—no doubt unconsciously—achieved the perfect portrait of a gentleman. The figure of Dominique de Bray is Fromentin's gesture of defiance against everything he despised in himself: his taste for the abyss, his tendency to melancholy inertia, to defeatism, to escape into fantasy.

The book as a whole possesses a wider significance. It is an affirmation of the will to happiness, and an exposition of how that will is a direct expression of the moral sensibility. *Dominique* is a clear testimony to all that was best in nineteenth-century civilisation. One thing, it seems to say, is certain— that Romanticism leads either to suicide or to misanthropy. And so it is no small part of Fromentin's achievement to have surrounded a story of uncompromising realism with an iridescent shimmer of that very quality in human nature the hopelessness of which he is concerned to establish. The sense of romance which lends beauty to memory, informs the style itself, as it were a piece of music tonally centred in two keys— a major and a minor. Such is the music of elegiac emotion— of that paradoxical sense of happiness which arises from the courage to bid a perpetual farewell, and renews itself, phoenix-like, from the ashes of the youthful heart. (p. 825)

*Edward Sackville-West, "Perfect Portrait of a Gentleman," in* The Listener, *Vol. XXXVIII, No. 980, November 6, 1947, pp. 824-25.*

MEYER SCHAPIRO   (essay date 1949)

[*Schapiro provides a comprehensive analysis of* The Old Masters of Belgium and Holland *that includes commentary on the book's structure and the author's style, tone, principles, standards, and judgments as an art critic. While Schapiro greatly admires Fromentin's searching empiricism, he also criticizes the writer's censorious treatment of Rembrandt van Rijn, ascribing it to Fromentin's feelings of inadequacy. Schapiro's essay, excerpted below from the* Partisan Review, *was also published in English as an introduction to a 1963 edition of* The Old Masters of Belgium and Holland; *Gallimard Press published his essay in French in 1983 in volume four of Schapiro's* Style, artiste, et société.]

*The Old Masters of Belgium and Holland* is the first and perhaps the only book of its kind: a critical study of painting by an accomplished artist who is also a first-rate writer. . . . But Fromentin's distinction does not lie simply in the fact that he combined the painter's experience with the writer's skill. . . . More than in its craft knowledge, the virtue of the book is in the sustained attitude of discrimination and judgment, resting on keen, tireless observation of the fabric of the painting as a sensory matter, like the musician's attentiveness to sounds, but penetrating at the same time with a wonderful power of sympathy into the artist's personality or moral nature, to use Fromentin's old-fashioned term. His exact notation of qualities, tones, rapports of colors and forms, is never just descriptive or analytic; it flows out of an instantaneous savoring of the whole which is prolonged and tested by further scrutiny of the work and aims also at a truer vision of the artist's physiognomy. There is nothing comparable for intensity of perception in the entire literature of art criticism.

Add to this a particular eloquence and devotion, a tone of vibrant enthusiasm, which art criticism had scarcely known before the modern period and which corresponds to an almost religious sentiment of the dignity of art.

Long before Fromentin, writers had seen that a painting is a personal object, but this insight had remained an unexplored generality. In *The Old Masters of Belgium and Holland* it becomes concrete, evidential, intimate, a field of problems and profound searching, as in the beautiful pages on Rubens and Ruisdael. Here, through repeated observations, we are made to see beyond doubt that the touch and the sensory stuff of a picture are spiritual things of the greatest consequence. The *facture* is a product of feeling, a result of the whole psychic disposition of the artist. What he does beyond his instinct, through acquired skill and calculation, depends on instinct too; even the artist's reason is marked with his character and appears in this book as a personal trait. Everything in the work of art— the attitude to the subject, the execution, palette, and forms— belongs then to the individual and is an expressive end as well as a means. This total conviction, with all that is vague and problematic in it, gives life to Fromentin's analyses and judgments. (pp. 25-6)

Fromentin's search for the personality in the painting sometimes suggests a scientific aim, as if he were looking for psychological laws. . . . Fromentin undertakes even to reconstitute the little known character of Ruisdael, in discreet touches and questions, from the peculiarities of his art. A painting, he thinks, is an infallible clue to the state of mind of its author at the moment of creation. And in this attempt he precedes, like other critics, the experimental psychologist who studies the individual aspect of motor behavior and fantasy.

But more important to Fromentin than genetic or diagnostic insight is the direct vision of the work itself as stamped with the qualities of a great individual. He can speak then of the execution or colors or arrangement as noble, generous, passionate or candid, as possessing, in short, the attributes of a superior humanity. (p. 27)

Throughout Fromentin's book we sense the full humanity of art and the critic's position as a man. His enthusiasm for Rubens is a judgment of a quality of human life. Fromentin has an image of man's greatness; he throbs and kneels when he encounters it in a painting. It is both in the conception of the subject and in the execution. It is the face and gesture of Saint Francis at his last communion and it is in the colors and brushwork of the naked body of Christ. Only a great man could have conceived and produced these things. The harmony of tones is matched by the moral perfection of a gesture. The interest of Fromentin lies in his power to make us see that the highest human values are involved in a patch of color, the bend of a line. (pp. 27-8)

Fromentin is not satisfied to judge that a work is good or bad. Few of the pictures he admires are perfect. He is too much a painter who has struggled with his canvas and suffered from the consciousness of its failings, even when it has been acclaimed a masterpiece, to approach the works of others with an all-or-none principle. Before Rubens he remains critical, attentive to the differences between one part and another. He sees the painter as a human genius of uneven powers, subject to the endlessly complex conditions of work. In a great painting the conception may surpass the execution, one figure may be masterly, another more relaxed in drawing, and all this variability of an artist arises from his character. Comparing Rubens' *Elevation on the Cross* with the *Descent*, Fromentin is able to say convincingly that the first is more progressive, more truly Rubens, but the other is more complete, more perfectly realized; or that his *Adoration of the Magi* in Antwerp is less accomplished than the one in Brussels, yet is the final expression of his knowledge of color and his dexterity. This is a profoundly objective kind of criticism which sees the modalities of an artist's achievement and is able to discern the differences not only between one work and another, but also between the aspects or parts of the same creation. (p. 28)

[Fromentin's] calling as a writer counted for something in the substance as well as style of his criticism. That unity of sensation and feeling, which is basic for his critical method, is also in his time a principle of imaginative writing, which represents the exterior world through a reacting sensibility. . . . He was, in fact, among the first to introduce into art criticism the standards of observation and of expression of sentiment developed by the French novelists and poets—the requirement of a direct encounter with the object, nuanced statement of feeling, and a rapid, flexible prose with a syntax and rich sensory language that could evoke the observed and the observer together, without dissolving the object in the sensation or mood. (p. 29)

As a piece of writing, *The Old Masters of Belgium and Holland* is original in form, recalling at the same time the Salon review, the travel book, the critical essay and the private journal. Like the Salons of Diderot and Baudelaire, it deals with what is immediately visible, the works exhibited in a particular place. Like the travel book, it follows an itinerary and conveys the impressions and feelings of Fromentin on a journey in the summer of 1875. It adds to these some vigorous pages of theory, it is concerned with principles and makes excursions into history and aesthetics. It builds up distinct images of artistic personalities. Finally, there is something of the intimate journal in its avowals, hesitations, enthusiasms and regrets, its monologue of artistic experience.

This variety of statement enables Fromentin to be more fully himself and to draw on more of his powers and interests than if he had adopted any one of the established forms of writing on art. It is a flexible medium for the complex culture and personality of the author. The restriction to what he has seen on a single trip and in Paris entails, of course, a disadvantage for a critic. It means that he must ignore important pictures of Rubens and Rembrandt in other countries although they were familiar to him through reproductions. And he cannot confront the work of an artist in its entirety to check his single judgments against a larger conception or in a perspective of the whole.

Nevertheless, the limitation was also an advantage; for it was precisely by restricting himself to the directly encountered paintings that Fromentin could liberate the criticism of past art from the established formalities and bookishness. We can see this better by a comparison with Delacroix's writings on art. In the great romantic's note-books there are long passages of the purest, most acute perception; but the articles on Gros, Poussin, Prud'hon and others that he published during his lifetime are written in another style: they are full-dress essays with much historical, biographic matter in a tone of public speech; the best qualities of his journal appear only faintly in these conventional works. Fromentin is the first writer to give to published criticism of the old masters the spontaneous personal character of this hitherto private, yet highly objective, discernment of art which must have been practiced by many artists. His relation to Delacroix is like that of Impressionist painting to its predecessors; it treats as self-sufficient and valid what had formerly been regarded as only a preparatory sketch or note, and it carries further the implications of that direct approach. Fromentin introduced as a governing principle into the studied criticism the immediacy of the unworked perception, while preserving all that came from analysis and prolonged meditation. (pp. 29-31)

What is astonishing and yet on reflection perfectly right is that the book is the fruit of a trip less than a month long in the Low Countries. . . . One of its main virtues is that it reads like a report of a month's journey, but a month of most intense and concentrated vision. If it has something of the quality of a travel book, it is by an explorer with a special purpose whose attention is fixed on his own objects, who knows his domain with a sovereign expertness, and in encountering certain things for the first time, brings to bear on them his entire personality as well as his knowledge of the field. Much that he has to say about Flemish and Dutch painting had been said before, at least in a general way; but in Fromentin's experience there is a liveness and sharp edge of appetite which we rarely if ever find in the older writers. . . . The chapters, designed in a seemingly formless way, with occasional repetitions, correspond for the most part to the order of the journey. And to maintain this direct vision and informality, he also describes the towns as he sees them, in finely nuanced, picturesque word strokes which call up images resembling certain of the paintings that he is to discover there and confirm for the reader both the local, rooted character of the art and the singlemindedness of the author who looks at the world and art with the same appreciating eyes. (p. 32)

In his certainty that the artistic fabric of a work is the final matter of judgment, [Fromentin] does not exclude other sides of art as irrelevant to critical decision. His practice is broader and more attractive than his theory. If only the artistic counts,

why so much trouble to envision the personality behind it? (p. 33)

Fromentin also gave to the subject of a painting more weight than his theory would allow. In his chapter on the subject in Dutch painting, where he noted the rarity of the anecdote and the historical theme in this art, he affirmed with the usual positiveness of modern critics that only the painting as an artistic work mattered. . . . If, however, the chapter had not been written and we undertook to discover through Fromentin's reactions to pictures precisely what counted for him, we would quickly learn that the conception of the themes and their meanings were important, that he sometimes responded to them with emotion, and that certain kinds of painting could be judged only in relation to the subject. In speaking of portraiture, he requires always that the nature of the sitter be expressed in the image; he explains the inferiority of Rubens' portraits to his other works by the painter's robust extraversion which made it impossible for him to concentrate on the inner life of others. On the other hand, if the *Saint George* ''is the pure essence of his genius,'' Fromentin believes that this is due to Rubens' affection for the subject. . . . It is clear that if Fromentin condemned the concern with subject as inartistic, he exempted from this criticism the religious and the epic theme for which he preserved the traditional respect. His attitude toward the theme of curiosity is not truly the modern one; he maintained rather the hierarchy of subjects taught by the old classical academicians. He could praise the still-life painter Vollon as a superior artist but only with the qualification that his genre was inferior. Like others of his time, he failed to see that although still-life and landscape were not subject-matters which had to be deciphered and ''understood,'' they embodied nevertheless an attitude to things no less significant philosophically than the religious or historical themes, and that like these they were individualized by the artists, so that one could discover in the choice of objects by Chardin a distinct personality and a relation to his mode of painting. (pp. 33-4)

[It] is a sign of his breadth that Fromentin, whose persistent critical concentration on the aesthetic offered what many had thought was lacking in Taine, should even concern himself with the milieu. He does not fear at all the charge that he might be reducing unique or ineffable facts of individual creativeness to social generalities, foreign to the nature of art. He regrets rather his insufficient knowledge of history, which is already considerable for a layman . . . and which guides him in his interpretations. . . . [In *The Old Masters of Belgium and Holland*,] the social basis of Dutch art, formulated with remarkable acumen by Hegel many years before and then elaborated by Taine in a less searching way, is presented as something not only fully evident, but also as necessary for the production and intimate character of the art. Read the curious, whimsical statement in the chapter on the ''origin and character of the Dutch School,'' where Fromentin remarks that Dutch art was so closely tied to the state of Dutch affairs that it issued promptly from the newly won Dutch independence as if ''the right to have a national school of painting'' were one of the stipulations of the treaty of 1609. . . . What interests us most in his vision of this Dutch complex is his view of the common qualities of the Dutch *school* as a true social accomplishment, an education of the individuals determining a high level of performance in the ordinary practitioners. To understand this view, one must contrast it with the current idea that the characteristics of a school are a mere taste or convention, without artistic value in themselves, serving only as a substratum for the achievements of the great masters. Bourgeois life at its best—and Holland was an example—had for Fromentin certain positive moral values: probity, patience, devotion to a task, reasonableness and regard for reality, which determine the character of lesser artists and give to their painting a seriousness and honesty that we must respect. In aristocratic Belgium, there are no interesting minor personalities around Rubens, only imitators or assistants; in Holland, Fromentin discovers a host of attractive individual minor painters, many of them artists who have also another profession or trade. (pp. 35-6)

[In] this apparently unplanned, unsystematic work with its varied impressions, encounters and free range of ideas, there is a structure, a large antithesis that underlies even the evaluations, shaping the latter into a drama of judgment. It is not a beautiful or great structure, but it is a form and that is important. On one side is the Flemish Catholic Rubens, the master closest to Fromentin's ideal—the exterior man, the synthesizer of the Italian and the Northern, the unproblematic genius who produces with an easy power like a force of nature; the more he is seen, the more he grows in mastery and grandeur; in his portraits alone he fails, but this task requires a sense for the inner world of personalities which is naturally denied him, being incompatible with his highest qualities. On the other side is the genius of Holland, the Protestant Rembrandt, an artist . . . rising above all the other Dutch painters whom Fromentin admires. His greatness emerges most clearly in portraiture, for Fromentin the most spiritual art of all. Yet Fromentin cannot take Rembrandt. Before some of his works—and these include the most famous, like *Dr. Tulp's Anatomy Lesson* and *The Night Watch*—he is repelled or uncertain. More than half his account of the artist is given to paintings that he rejects. Rembrandt, according to Fromentin, is a dual personality with conflicting aims that introduce fatal errors into his work. . . . [He] retained side by side in his work the antagonistic components of his nature; he wished to be both realist and idealist, the painter of the visible and the invisible. Where these appear separately, the results are the greatest masterpieces. Where he brings them together in a single work, as in *The Night Watch*, the painting is a failure. In only a few paintings, like *The Syndics,* are these opposites successfully combined.

Whatever we may think of this judgment of Rembrandt, the most debated and disturbing in the book, it is also an element of art in Fromentin's writing. It is as if Fromentin, having avowed his cult of Rubens in the first part, found it necessary to introduce and to play up as the major *motif* in the second part an opposite pattern of artistic personality, which in turn strengthens by contrast the intensity of his image of Rubens. (pp. 36-7)

One should not suppose therefore that all the analyses and judgments made within this antithetic framework are necessarily artificial and calculated for literary effect. The confrontation of unlike things, the search for contrasts, often bring out hidden characteristics which might otherwise escape us. Conflict is so basic in the growth of personality that the search for a dualism in the artist may be extremely fruitful for interpretation; much of recent criticism proceeds from this insight and the modernity of Fromentin's book lies partly in its dialectical approach. But the final image he gives us of Rembrandt is certainly distorted. We cannot accept his idea that Rembrandt preserved throughout his life two opposed styles; this is hard to reconcile with his known development as an artist. (pp. 37-8)

[The] importance he gives to the dualism of personality, whether resolved as in Rubens, or maintained as a permanent struggle,

as in Rembrandt, is more than a literary device; we suspect that it arises from a conflict within Fromentin, a consciousness of his own polarity. (p. 38)

The character of [Fromentin] is visible in the self-constraint of his delicate pictures; he is one of those who live below their means out of anxiety and unwillingness to take risks. He justified this attitude by underestimating his abilities, as if these were finally and fatally limited, instead of striving to surmount his admitted weaknesses. The same underestimation appears in the hero of his novel [*Dominique*] who is an image of the author: Dominique speaks of himself as a mediocrity, a failure, although his story and entire spirit mark him as a superior man. He is a defeated personality whose suffering arises from a hopeless romantic passion. To dominate himself after this unhappy love (which represents the great crisis of Fromentin's youth), he gives up poetry and intellectual ambition and retires to the province as a simple farmer in daily contact with the realities of nature and physical work. It is the common sense alternative to the romantic solutions: religion or travel—Fromentin's teacher, Cabat, after a crisis lived for a while in a Dominican monastery. Sainte-Beuve said of Dominique that he was not fully a poet nor fully a lover; as a lover, "he mistakes his fear for virtue and his natural timidity for a stoic effort." Even as a young man, more ardent and hopeful, Dominique is a timid dual being: his poems are published anonymously, but under his own name he writes a political treatise that gives him considerable prestige. Fromentin is haunted by his own duality and projects it constantly into his writing.

His attitude to Rembrandt may be seen then as a justification of himself. Scrupulous as he was in looking at the painting of the past, Fromentin could not escape his desires and least of all, his hidden regrets. They turn up often in this book which seems at first reading a triumph of disciplined observation and judgment. Event the account of Rubens is shaped by the inner needs of the deeply troubled artist. When he defines the Flemish master in a memorable phrase as a temperament *"sans orages et sans chimères"*—without storms and without vain dreams—he states the antithesis to his own youthful self which he had described fifteen years before in the person of Dominique as *"un coeur orageux.... et certainement martyrisé de chimères"*—a stormy heart and a martyr to chimerical dreams. Rembrandt too is acceptable to him only when he is free from those *"chimères";* the same word comes insistently to Fromentin's mind before the great portrait of the Burgomaster Six: *"personnage peu chimérique, une peinture sans chimère"*— a rather unfanciful personality, a painting without fancy. But Delacroix who adored Rubens no less than did Fromentin and placed Rembrandt above Raphael, on the contrary welcomed these chimerical fancies as the true source of art: "In taking his brushes in hand," he said "the artist abandons the easy and trivial course of everyday life to enter the world of noble fantasy (*chimères*), necessary for the creative fire." (pp. 39-40)

It is mainly in criticizing Rembrandt that Fromentin commits himself to laws and absolute stringencies in art. In Rubens he discovers an admirable *"mesure,"* but the Flemish master is no occasion for expounding rules. His art is a triumph of sheer genius, which by some miracle is in perfect harmony with good sense. Rembrandt is another story. With him Fromentin has to be unrelentingly censorious. The failures he reproaches in Rembrandt are due to no lack of genius or to unfavorable circumstance, but to the artist's willfulness, his disregard of plain logic as well as of the rules of art. (p. 41)

What are these rules that Rembrandt fatally disobeys? It is interesting for Fromentin's conscience that they not only command conformity as rules, but are themselves rules of conformity. If you paint reality, stick to reality; if you paint the visionary, stick to the visionary. Do not mix the two in the same work. But above all, conform to your theme. If it is a portrait, be faithful to the sitter; if it is a secular world, let it be recognizable as such in the costumes, the gestures, the proportions and the setting. *The Night Watch* is not religious or heroic; why then the disorder and fantastic gloom in a sober bourgeois assembly? With its shadows and lights, the picture is a mystification, not a transfiguration of reality. . . .

What makes us doubt Fromentin's reasoning in this case is that we have found in other great works a similar striving to unify the seemingly incompatible, to make the supernatural natural, and the natural unreal, to unite movement and stability, the surface pattern and depth. Indeed Fromentin discerns such oppositions in Rubens without asserting a problem. (p. 42)

As for the rules of color disregarded by Rembrandt, we recognize that they are the requirements of a particular style or tradition of which Fromentin is the anxious guardian against the heretics in his own day. His demand that the local color persist in light and in deepest shadow would be meaningless in an art unconcerned with a natural illumination; and even where sunlight is primary, as in Impressionism, there are great works that violate this rule and build upon the violation a novel beauty, not to mention a more precise suggestion of reality. It is surprising that in spite of his knowledge of history and of the marvellous variety of styles practiced with great art in different times and places, and in spite of his conviction that the man is the source of expression, inventing his appropriate means and fashioning his own kind of unity, Fromentin should wish to impose the conventions of his school as the prerequisite of all good art. This is the most common and inexpugnable error of criticism; and it turns up among those who have denounced it most firmly. (pp. 42-3)

What disturbed Fromentin in Rembrandt was not only the incorrectness of drawing and color, but a more far-reaching arbitrariness, an unwillingness to be reasonable and consistent. This fantastic Dutchman introduced bizarre elements into a painting of real life. He accepted the theme or convention of reality and then refused to abide by its conditions. Rembrandt, we have seen, is for him an anarchic master who undertakes the impossible, confounding the world of dreams and the world of reality. Fromentin feels in Rembrandt something profoundly unsocial that alarms him like the proposals of subversive revolutionary minds. Indeed the term *"chimère"* that he applies to Rembrandt was a common disparagement of socialist and utopian ideas in Fromentin's time; it had a repugnant sense for him in particular, because as a youth he had been attracted to the left just before the revolution of 1848. He opposed to it the concept of *"mesure"* as a social and not only artistic virtue, and came to regard this restraint as a positive, almost creative quality. Few words appear so often in Fromentin's criticism and his novel as *"chimère"* and *"mesure."* "Nothing chimerical. . . . a perfect equilibrium," he writes in *Dominique,* and in the same book, "a rare good sense, a perfect rectitude. . . .produces miracles." These are characterizations of Dominique's teacher, Augustin, who is like a little Dutchman in quality—sober, disciplined, honest, persevering, without great talent but effective through these domestic virtues; "the reasonable," he says, "is the inseparable friend of justice and truth." (pp. 44-5)

The more Fromentin criticizes Rembrandt, the more we are drawn to the Dutch painter and the more we feel sorry for Fromentin. What a turmoil in the Frenchman's heart as he pursues the old man so relentlessly in the name of reason, nature, law and the inherent necessities of art! With all his admiration for Rembrandt's portraits, he cannot wholeheartedly accept this crazy Hollander who dared to transfigure the real world. Grant his success and you have to grant also that Fromentin's art was possibly on a wrong path. Rembrandt's great inner liberty challenged and disturbed him as did nothing else. Fromentin wrote to his wife: "Rembrandt doesn't let me sleep." (p. 45)

[The] example of the Dutch painters had been a powerful argument [in the contemporary defense of Impressionism]. . . . It would have been impossible at this time to write about the Flemish and Dutch masters without hinting at the modern school.

Fromentin, whose art was exotic in theme and classicizing in mood, could only be embarrassed by this new trend. Where he refers to living painters, it is mainly to polemize against Manet and the emerging Impressionist art or to lament the general decay. . . . Manet disturbed him most, and in his letters he remarks with some ill-humor that all of Manet is already in Hals, but that the Frenchman has copied the weaknesses of Hals, the results of his senility. For us today those two works of Hals—the Regents of the Home for the Aged—are among his best and approach Rembrandt in their austere pathos and revelation of old age. Fromentin has judged them inferior because of his narrow standard of good *facture.* Besides, their relation to Manet is less obvious than he supposed; if they recall the modern painter in their bareness of tones and contrasts, the psychological insight of these exceptional, most mature works of Hals' old age is in spirit foreign to Manet. (pp. 47-8)

In attacking the unnamed Impressionists for giving an undeserved importance to sunlight and the open air, he seems to approach the criticism of this art made a generation later by a more advanced modern school; for one thing, he urges a return from this sketchy naturalism to pure painting, by which he means a more studied and constructed picture. But Fromentin's attack is too indiscriminate to convince us that he has looked at this contemporary art with the same care as at the old Dutch painting to which it corresponds. He is unable to see what is genuinely artistic in the originality of the Impressionists; that genteel discretion which forbids him to name living artists, also permits him to condemn entire schools *en masse* for violating his arbitrary rules of form. He excepts from his general condemnation a few artists: the old Corot, who had died in 1875, and two unnamed figures, Diaz and perhaps Jacque. Corot he admires chiefly in his weaker vaporous style and makes into an academic model by speaking of "the rules of value-painting" established and demonstrated by Corot in his works. On the other hand, in a criticism of the Salon of 1876, published under a journalist's name, Fromentin commended Puvis de Chavannes and Gustave Moreau as the true masters of his own generation and called Vollon "one of the rare good painters of our times." We are surprised that an artist who understood so finely Rubens and Ruisdael could prefer those academicians to their great contemporaries. That is the fatality of taste which owes both its strength and weakness to the complex stresses of personal needs. We learn from these pages of Fromentin how difficult his insight into a new contemporary art, especially if it belongs to a generation younger than one's own. (pp. 48-9)

With all its prejudices and errors, Fromentin's book remains a masterpiece of criticism. . . . We certainly prefer it to anything written about art by the defenders of Impressionism or Realism. Had he been sympathetic to these, Fromentin would no doubt have written more understandingly of Rembrandt too. But if he had possessed so daring and modern a mind as a painter, he would perhaps not have written at all. Yet the best qualities of his criticism are not far from the advanced contemporary arts in spirit. He is intensely empirical, in spite of his traditional norms. He knows how to see and explores the fabric and color of the old paintings with a sureness that has to do with the general movement of the new art toward a direct vision of things and a lyricism of color and light. His power of discerning the personality in the touch and the tone, as well as in the conception of the whole, corresponds to the self-consciousness of the modern artist as a responsive individual who represents only objects of immediate experience, who attends to his sensations and strives to make his pigment and brushstrokes and the surface of the pictures the evident carriers of his art. The progressive elements of Fromentin's criticism are inconsistent with the rules and standards that he applies to Rembrandt and his own time. I have suggested that these contradictions arise from conflicts within Fromentin; but it should also be said that he surpassed himself in the strength of his book. It is not the work of revery and poetic paraphrase of art, that we might expect from the author of *Dominique*, but grows out of a constant contact with human things, a tense effort of perception and judgment. The forceful qualities that he cannot realize in his studied painting of nature or in his sad autobiographical novel, surge up abundantly when he has to speak about art. In his encounter with the works of the past, he shows an energy of feeling denied him in daily life and in his own painting. The "unreal" world of past art is for him the fullest and richest reality, and the task of judging it, a personal liberation. (pp. 49-50)

> *Meyer Schapiro, "Fromentin As a Critic," in* Partisan Review, *Vol. XVI, No. 1, January, 1949, pp. 25-51.*

### CHARLES MORGAN　(essay date 1949)

[*Morgan focuses on the "uniqueness" of* Dominique. *After describing the lack of incident and dialogue in the novel as a peculiarity of the author's "extreme dramatic economy," he comments on the morality informing the work.*]

Fashion in literature is absurd; the masters, from Donne to Meredith, from Meredith to Kipling, from Baudelaire to Poe, always survive it; but it is temporarily formidable, and *Dominique* was held back by it. To-day, there is no reason that it should be held back among us, as it was when an earlier English translation appeared in 1932. The 'thirties marked the height of our own anti-romantic movement, but to-day even the cult of violence is almost spent, and whoever can listen to Chopin can read Fromentin.

And yet the parallel is inexact. Chopin, within the discipline of his form, had an urgency and a pressure that Fromentin had not. . . . [The] criticism of *Dominique* as slow-moving is justifiable. If it were to take rank as a love-story with Turgenev's *First Love* or *Torrents of Spring*, its narrative would have been strung, as Turgenev's narrative is, on quiet but lively incident, and character would have emerged, not primarily from analysis, but from luminous dialogue and action. But this is to say only that Fromentin had his limitations. The real question is:

what use did he make of them?. . . . Instead of saying what an author was not, instead of describing him in his relationship to other authors and to schools and tendencies, can we say what, in himself, he was? What was the peculiarity, the identity, of Fromentin? What is the uniqueness of *Dominique?*

Suddenly the word "uniqueness," used almost by chance in the sentence just written, emerges as the key-word in any criticism of *Dominique*. . . . Attempts are sometimes made by those who cannot be happy until they have sorted everything into categories to herd *Dominique,* as an autobiographical novel, into the same pen with Constant's *Adolphe* and even with Rousseau's *Nouvelle Héloïse,* but it will not do. The differences are overwhelmingly greater than the likenesses. In its merits and its demerits, *Dominique* stands alone. (pp. 221-22)

[It] is familiar neither in its motive nor in its method. Consider its method first. It begins with an account of Dominique as an ageing man living, with his wife and children, a retired life at Les Trembles, his country estate on the border of the Bay of Biscay. This is a long prologue, and a brief epilogue reverts to the same scene. In between is Dominique's own narrative of his boyhood, of his love for Madeleine, of his life with her and without her in the country and in Paris, and of the final crisis and parting.

George Sand, one of the book's friendliest critics, recognised that the opening was slow but also that it was too beautiful to be cut. Instead, she wanted the end to be elaborated, partly to give better proportion to the book, partly because she felt that the transition between Dominique's parting from Madeleine and our discovery of him tranquilly married to another woman, of whom we know almost nothing, was too abrupt. Rightly or wrongly, Fromentin, though he accepted minor revisions from her, disregarded her structural advice; rightly, we may believe, not because the advice itself was bad—on the contrary, it was extremely good—but because it was external to him, and he could not have given effect to it without destructive artificiality. The result is a book less competent than George Sand would have made it, but, for that reason the more, Fromentin's very own.

Its "slowness," its lack of incident and dialogue, may be seen, from another point of view, as an extreme dramatic economy. No writer knows better than Fromentin how to stop when he has made his point. For example, he describes with beautiful care a scene in a lighthouse. Dominique and his friend Olivier, Madeleine and her young sister Julie, who loves Olivier with hopeless, unrequited love, are on the platform gazing into the abyss.

> I knew instinctively that the tension was too great: sooner or later a string would snap. One of us would break down—perhaps not the one who was most deeply moved, but the one with least power of resistance. It was Julie.

Fromentin then tells how giddiness took her, how she almost fell, how Olivier put his arms round her. Then:

> A few seconds later she came to, with a sigh of distress that heaved the thin stuff of her bodice. "It's nothing," she said, reacting immediately from the fit of weakness that had been too much for her, and down we went.

Flaubert might have cut: "reacting immediately from the fit of weakness that had been too much for her." It is debatable. Otherwise the passage is flawless. (pp. 222-23)

His method has another quality peculiar to him which is an integral part of what is called his slowness. . . . [He] was a landscapist. It is therefore not surprising that he should have seen the background of his story with a painter's eye, but it is remarkable that, having this pictorial power, he was able to transcend it, to transmute it to serve his narrative purpose. When he describes a natural scene, as when he tells of a dramatic action, he writes always quietly, with economy, proclaiming no emotion, avoiding over-emphasis at all costs. And yet his descriptions of nature are a part of his dramatic method. Through them he communicates the moods, the sufferings, the delights and, above all, the tensions of his characters. In this special power, he has no superior, and takes rank even with Turgenev in his *Sportsman's Sketches*. The most ignorant townsman, who can find none of the pleasures of familiarity in descriptions of rural scenes, may be enthralled by Fromentin in this vein, for it is in his descriptions of nature that he continually reveals the essence of his characters. When Madeleine is lost and Dominique is returning to his old home, "hurrying on my miserable journey like a wounded animal losing blood and struggling to reach its hole before its strength gives out," Fromentin describes the young man's walk across the solitary marshes, "the peculiar rushing, rustling sound of wild-duck overhead," and his encounter with an old servant out shooting. It is a description not only of great beauty but of astonishing evocative power. It is too precious to abbreviate, too long to quote at length. Perhaps quotation is unnecessary. That little phrase about a wounded animal losing blood is evidence enough that, as a country poet, a country dramatist, Fromentin is unique.

His book is unique also in its motive. He has something to say about love and the responsibilities arising from it which has not been said elsewhere; and what he says about love has its bearing upon the whole conduct of life—upon all our hungers and not only upon that of desire; upon all our dedications and loyalties, and not only upon those of love; upon all our confusions, our deadlocks, our tormented oppositions of right to right, our cry that "nothing makes sense!" (pp. 223-24)

[Fromentin] assumes the existence and the over-riding validity of an absolute value which is not happiness. He assumes, further, that happiness itself cannot be obtained except by those who recognise this over-riding value. In the particular instance given by the novel, the concrete form of this absolute value happens to be the indissolubility of marriage, but the point of the novel is not to argue for this indissolubility, though the virtue of it is implied, but rather to suggest that life is unlivable in a world reduced to chaos by each man's and each woman's supposing that every impediment to his or her personal satisfaction is an intolerable injustice entitling him or her to break it down if possible and, in case of failure, to cry out: "Nothing makes sense!" We may, if we will, disagree with Fromentin on the subject of marriage if we accept other absolutes, belief in God or courage in battle or the sacredness of our given word—*something* from which we will not swerve in quest of our own ease or pleasure.

Fromentin, in effect, says: "No. Your unhappiness, even though it spring from no fault of yours, does not entitle you to take sides with chaos. Life which is not lived within a rule of law is not life, but death." When near the end of the book, Madeleine's and Dominique's love is fully recognised by them both, and Dominique, knowing that she is awake within, has come as far as her bedroom door, he turns away, not because it is expedient to do so, not in any consideration of conventional honour, but in obedience to an absolute law which is of the essence of Fromentin's story:

. . . Here I was, groping my way about the sleeping, unsuspecting house, in the middle of the night, drawn irresistibly to Madeleine's bedroom door, and bumping against it like a man in a dream. Was I merely an unhappy being with nothing left to sacrifice, blinded by desire, neither better nor worse than the rest of my fellow-creatures? or was I a criminal? This crucial question floated vaguely at the back of my mind without leading me to anything remotely resembling a positive choice between the alternatives of behaving like a man of honour, and deliberately planning an infamy. All that I knew beyond a doubt—and even that left me undecided—was that if Madeleine sinned it would kill her and that most certainly I shouldn't survive her an hour.

I can't tell you what saved me. All I know is that I found myself in the park. . . .

The important sentence is: *"La seule chose dont je ne doutais pas . . . c'est qu' une faute tuerait Madeleine."* The novel rests upon that basis of absolutism. Sainte-Beuve, who was prevented by the limitations of his genius from recognising absolutism when he saw it, while praising the novel on all other grounds, objected to this *denouement* which, he said, was not *entièrement d'accord avec la verité humaine*. He thought—and it is a typical of Sainte-Beuve—that Madeleine would have had good reason to despise Dominique for having brought her so far and then drawn her back, and Dominique himself, according to Sainte-Beuve, was a half-hearted lover "who mistook his natural timidity for stoicism." It is one of those unseeing and would-be worldly-wise comments which, in the work of a critic so masterly and so discerning on his own territory, make one blink. It misses the whole point of the book, which consists in its assumption that it was not open to the two lovers to argue with their appetites or to compromise with their separation. Their struggle from beginning to end is not to find a way round the truth as they see it, not to pride themselves on their stoicism or to despise each other for their abstentions, not to submit themselves to their satisfactions but to liberate themselves by their acceptances. It is this that Sainte-Beuve could not see when he wrote in 1864 and that we might not have been able to see in 1934. But to-day, when society is in peril of dissolving because the rejection of absolute values has resulted in chaos and chaos in violence, when we have come—to use Sainte-Beuve's words—*jusqu' au bord extrême du précipice*—we know that there are moments in life when it is necessary to stand absolutely and when *"une faute tuerait Madeleine."* That this is an enduring truth, independent of fashion, is a reason for **Dominique**'s survival through eighty years of tragedy in France. That it is a present truth, of mounting urgency in our own day, is a reason for thinking that there is a vast modern audience who would find their own intuitions of wisdom crystallised in Fromentin's story. (pp. 224-25)

*Charles Morgan, "An Old Novel Re-born," in* The Hibbert Journal, *Vol. XLVII, No. 3, April, 1949, pp. 219-25.*

**THE TIMES LITERARY SUPPLEMENT** (essay date 1950)

[*The critic surveys Fromentin's literary oeuvre, identifying the lyrical evocation of landscape and atmosphere as the paramount property of his art.*]

[Fromentin] wrote little, but what he did write—*Un Été dans le Sahara* and *Une Année dans le Sahel*, and the single novel *Dominique*—can be taken as a whole, as though they were three sections of a spiritual autobiography of the finest order. *Dominique* . . . is deservedly popular, in spite of its technical faults, but it is a melancholy book. . . . [In his two travel-books] we find Fromentin's sensibilities and powers of evocation at their best. They are works of art of a very high order; indeed, it would be difficult to find any book since written in this *genre* which could be compared to them. Put side by side, even Flaubert's travel notes seem remarkably insensitive, indeed brutal. *Un Été dans le Sahara,* certainly, cannot be bettered. . . . [In] Africa he found that peculiar vision, that sense of the "unattainable," for which his restless soul had been craving. Inevitably, since the whole of his personality was involved and not merely one part of it, his view of the Arab world was completely individual and expressed itself lyrically. . . .

Fromentin's art was not only lyrical, it was also governed by his peculiar ability to absorb the very smell and substance of an object or a scene which remained . . . as fresh some years afterwards as it had been at the original impact. Thus his two travel books are composed not of a series of dull facts and records of places visited but of intimate emotional outbursts which are as inconsequential as the mood in which he wrote them. He felt deeply and profoundly about many things—about birds, for instance, about a sunset, about the peculiar quality of the desert silence, about a French soldier sitting on a tree—but his feelings are never the expected. He gives few facts, and those that appear, as for instance his long description in *Une Année dans le Sahel* of Algiers, rear up like cold monuments in the warm atmosphere of his world. He saw the Sahara under a spell, and only rarely, and then somewhat peevishly perhaps, does his almost Calvinist upbringing break out with incongruous suddenness. . . . Then he is no longer the poet stirred to the depths of his being but the bourgeois of La Rochelle remembering the strict code of his home town. Yet the revelations, the sharpness of the impressions, the hymns in prose which celebrate the Arab world, all fuse into a polished mirror which reflects not only Africa but the essential Fromentin as well.

In his novel *Dominique* can be found exactly the same qualities as in his previous books, though the mood changes from serenity to a kind of nostalgic sadness, and febrile self-analysis is interspersed between the pages of evocation. . . . Unable to create a work of the purest imagination, he had to draw on what he had experienced; consequently *Dominique* really belongs to that limited *genre* which is partially fiction and mostly confession. His chief concern, it may be suspected, was not a desire to tell a story of a young man's hopeless love for a girl who became more and more unattainable (though that might have had some symbolic meaning) so much as a need to express all the memories of his past life as a young man and to release his buried emotion. The story, indeed, was merely the vehicle and, reduced to its bare bones, it is commonplace and banal enough. He was unfortunate, too, in choosing to write in the first person. This method requires of the author great skill, and Fromentin was not quite skilful enough to employ it successfully. Thus his narrative, through technical awkwardness, falls into three irreconcilable parts—a kind of preface, Dominique's story of his life, and an aimless epilogue which, while it needed to be inserted, was nevertheless an anti-climax.

Moreover, Fromentin's characterization betrays his lack of interest in human beings by themselves. His strongest point, hitherto, had been in the evocation of landscape and atmosphere—his travel books only briefly mention the people he met and then only in thumb-nail sketches—and when he came face to face with the necessity of creating a fully living being he tended to produce either an idealization or a sketch. Dominique himself, because, no doubt, so much a reflection of Fromentin, is successfully in the round. He is alive, in spite of a certain lack of focus here and there; and he dominates the book as Fromentin dominated everything he wrote. The tutor, too, is excellent. But the other characters, and in particular the heroine Madeleine, are not so happy. Madeleine, indeed, was probably pure fiction. Like many nineteenth-century heroines who are the personification of goodness, from Balzac to Zola, she is nothing more than a stylized agent whose presence is absolutely necessary, but whose depiction is no more rounded or credible than that of a cardboard figure. . . .

But though these criticisms must be made, they detract little from the book, for its emphasis and importance—both in literature and in history—lie elsewhere. . . .

[Fromentin's real success lay in his] ability to evoke the strongest and most delicate impressions of a lifetime, to fill his novel with impressions and landscape painting of the finest order. . . .

[The] substance of the book, with its tortured, adolescent atmosphere of mingled pain and the first intimations of beauty, is the very quality which makes it transcend its faults. Fromentin, as he confessed, has put into it "une bonne partie" of himself—more, perhaps, than even he had imagined. Not only do we find the smells and sounds of his far-off past rising like incense from the book—as well as the memory of his early years at La Rochelle—but also secret yearnings and painful self-criticisms. The need to "bury" himself in the country, to renounce the world and its fame and its temptations: above all, the humility, the constant self-abasement and the perpetual dissatisfaction Dominique is made to feel for his writings—are they not indistinguishable from Fromentin's own self-doubts and his own interior *malaise*? Certainly the portrait of Dominique contains many elements of unconcealed autobiography:

> A great concentration of mind: a habit of intense and active self-observation: the instinct to reach ever greater heights: and the endlessly vigilant self-control: the enthralling changes that life brings, and the determination to recognize the same self intact in each new phase: the voice of nature never silenced: the birth of emotions which soften the young heart feeding with callow egoism on its own substance: the name entwined with another name, the verses that slip from the sheath like a flower opening in spring time: frantic flights towards the lofty summits of the ideal: last of all, peace descending on this heart, so stormy, perhaps so ambitious and certainly tormented by [a] desire of the unattainable. . . .

It was, as it were, his own epitaph as well as his own portrait; for after *Dominique* (apart from his one work of art criticism) he was to stretch his creative and imaginative wings no more. But there lay his achievement. He had produced a work which possessed, in the fullest measure, the powers of intensity, emotion, feeling and sincerity. Seen from this point of view *Dominique*—which was written in an age as barren as our own, an age which the Goncourts aptly called "a period of transition''—represents the high-watermark of an exquisite sensibility emerging at its best, as George Sand indicated, in the descriptions of places and atmospheres. What distinguishes it from almost every novel of its time is what may be called its poetic content—the impact of which on the reader is often stronger, and better able to transmit imaginative truth, than a sense of action—and it is precisely this poetic content which, for the next fifty years or so, was so to decline in the art of the novel.

*"A Polished Mirror," in* The Times Literary Supplement, *No. 2507, February 17, 1950, p. 104.*

## MONK GIBBON (lecture date 1952)

[*Gibbon, who remarks on the distinctive honesty and evocativeness of Fromentin's writing in* Dominique, *discusses the novel's structure, plot, characterization, and style. Gibbon's commentary was originally presented as part of the Tredegar Memorial Lecture in November, 1952.*]

To me [Eugène Fromentin's ***Dominique***] seems an incomparably finer book than the much better known *Adolphe* of Benjamin Constant. In Constant's book the whole situation is rather artificial and the endless emotional transports have not even a telling background to lend them interest. It is a matter of indifference to most of us whether the young man finally deserts his mistress or not, and the fact that his sensibility seems to luxuriate in giving us the same exchange of reproaches over and over again, the same situation accompanied by the same lamentations, very soon calluses any sympathy we could possibly have felt for either party. We are at first irritated and finally bored. Fromentin never prolongs his anguishes and never bores us. (p. 6)

[The] book proceeds so modestly that one should suspend judgement on it during its early pages. But though it demands from its reader patience and that degree of surrender which only a masterpiece is entitled to ask, it rewards him proportionately. It is nonsense to say, as one English critic has done, that it is impossible to imagine anyone reading this book without skipping. It is far harder, to my mind, to imagine anyone, once fairly launched on its pages, wishing to miss a single word of it, or setting it down at the close without all that sense of nostalgic loneliness which overtakes us when we are expelled from a world in which we have lived happily for hours, or perhaps for days.

What strikes us at once is the sheer honesty of the writing and the evocative power of the descriptions.

> Evening was at hand. It was only a few minutes before the sun would reach the cutting edge of the horizon, and its long rays were lighting up with streaks of shine and shadow a wide, dreary woodless plain, chequered by vineyards, fallows, and marshland, with scarcely an undulation, and here and there a vista opening on the distant sea. Only a whitish village or two, with flat-roofed church and saxon belfry rising from a bulge of the plain and a few small lonely farms, each with a thin clump of trees and a huge stack of fodder by its side, gave life to this vast and monotonous landscape, whose picturesque poverty would have seemed complete but for the singular beauty conferred on it by the weather, the hour, and the season.

If we know France at all we see again mentally the whole scene, carried back to that country by these simple and straightforward sentences. Although it is written with great beauty, one is quite unconscious of any deliberate artistry when reading ***Dominique***. Such is its grave, calm sincerity that a strange thing happened when I once came direct from it to some of the later tales of Turgenev. It seemed to me that I had temporarily lost a little of my immense admiration for the Russian writer. His accomplishment was too evident. It was too obvious that he knew all the tricks of the trade. Despite his great skill one could detect that Turgenev was arranging his material, was presenting it. In the case of the French book, the flow of the narrative is easy and artless so that we have the feeling not of reading fiction at all, but of overhearing a genuine soliloquy. Its form grows naturally, shaped by some sense of inner compulsion. At his best, Turgenev can do the same—for example in *Torrents of Spring* and in *First Love*.

Fromentin's novel is patently sincere. Indeed its main structural defect may perhaps arise out of its author's anxiety to be honest with us. He wants us to know the end of his story before we know the beginning, he wants us to read the one in the light of the other. He employs the not very satisfactory literary device of the Chinese box—the story within the story—passing from one narrator in the first person to another, Dominique himself, who tells his own life story. It is a rather clumsy device, but it ensures that we shall see the hero's character in the right perspective. Having met the middle-aged Dominique, we are in a better position to understand him as a youth.

The plot is straightforward enough. Three young men face life and exchange their views on it, while they attempt to learn, or are forced to learn, some of its lessons. We are given a penetrating study of the introvert, the libertine, and the man of character. Equally sympathetically, Fromentin delineates the two sisters, the one suffering all the despair of love ignored, the other of a love ruled out by circumstance. His plot has a denouement and it is dramatic, but it is only psychologically dramatic. Indeed, psychological interest outweighs action throughout. Fromentin from the start hints to his reader that he is not going to be offered the spectacle of either seduction, adultery, or desertion. Dominique loses his heart mildly at sixteen to a girl a year his senior who is just back from her convent school. Soon after this she marries a man a good deal older than her and the rest of the book is largely concerned with the efforts of these two people to maintain their friendship in defiance of the impulse to love. One does not need to be an authority on platonics to realize that out of such a situation and the tension which it engenders may come a keen degree of suffering and self-awareness. (pp. 7-8)

Fromentin never elaborates unduly. His effects are always achieved with the utmost economy of means.

> We left Les Trembles in mid-November on a hoar-frosty morning. The carriages followed the avenue and drove through Villeneuve as I had done the time before. Madeleine was opposite me, and I looked alternately at the country disappearing behind us, and at her candid face.

It is all so simple as that, but in its context it is extremely telling: and, though a large proportion of his book takes place in Paris, Fromentin is a master of rural description:

> Only the winepresses had been left to ventilate the floor under the screws, and from one end of the village to the other the moisture of crushed

grapes and the hot exhalations of fermenting wine mingled with the smell of henhouses and stables. In the country beyond, no sound was to be heard but the crowing of the cocks, waking from their first sleep to announce that the night would be damp. Flocks of thrushes, carried on the east wind, birds of passage migrating from north to south, flew over the village, calling continually to one another like travellers on a road at night. Between eight and nine o'clock there was a sudden burst of festive sound which set all the farm-dogs barking. It was the shrill, rhythmical music of a bagpipe playing the tune of a country dance. . . .

All the descriptions are admirable. . . . But the characterization, although we are dealing with characters which might almost be called types—in the same way that Shakespeare's young girl, or Turgenev's young girl can be said to be types—is as vivid as the description, and *can* be extremely subtle. (p. 9)

In Madeleine's case, as in the case of nearly every individual in this quite short book, character transpires almost as slowly and gradually as in real life. For a long time she seems the very type of self-control and self-restraint, and her aspiration to play the part of elder sister to a promising young man, talented but ill-equipped with the quality of ambition, seems to us intelligible and absolutely genuine. It is genuine, and Fromentin's skill both as psychologist and storyteller emerges in the sudden, and yet extraordinarily simple and direct, incidental proof furnished to indicate her own surrender to a force from which she has been trying for so long to free another. For, as Dominique observes, 'of all maladies the one she had undertaken to cure me of was the most contagious'. Nothing could be more effective as a means of conveying pent-up emotion and a whole revolution in the attitude of one person to another than the episode of the torn bouquet as they return from the theatre and Madeleine's single anguished phrase, 'You're torturing me and breaking my heart.' This is all the more so if we have given due consideration to the relatively trivial circumstance which had held such significance for her and occasioned her distress earlier in the evening.

Fromentin's style, so far from seeming to exploit its material, gives the impression rather of having behind it a vast untapped emotional reserve, exercising a sort of tidal pull but never exhibiting its full force. He can risk simplicity which is just what a writer too conscious of his audience dares not risk. . . . (p. 10)

Under this restrained treatment—the emphasis almost of understatement—Madeleine may for a time seem a stick to us, but when she does, eventually and for an instant, show her feelings, the effect is tremendous. Again it is a matter of a single phrase.

> 'Help me to fold my shawl,' she said.

They fold the shawl, the fringe slips out of her hands, and suddenly she is in his arms,

> her head thrown back, her eyes shut, her lips cold, half-dead, and faint from my kisses. Then she shuddered with a violent spasm; she opened her eyes, stood on tiptoe to reach my height and threw herself on my neck with all her strength. And now it was she who kissed me.

That is all. An instant later they have separated. But we shall never think of her as a stick again. Or put beside this episode of the folded shawl her farewell to him next day, amazingly restrained until its final words, 'If you only knew how I love you! I couldn't have told you yesterday, but now I can admit it, because it is just the one forbidden word which is parting us.'

If all this seems great nonsense, then one can only say that it is from such nonsense that life in large measure derives its significance for us and that even a great poet like Shakespeare makes it again and again the pivot of his work. Even in a writer like Flaubert we get an admission of the significance of moral tension and a bare hint of the intrinsic significance of love. After that, the scientific heresy begins to creep into literature, man sees himself as an ape, and instead of love we get externalities like the frock coat, the brothel, and the libidinous kiss. (pp. 10-11)

> *Monk Gibbon, "Sir Edward Marsh's Translation of 'Dominique',"* in Essays by Divers Hands, *n.s. Vol. XXVII, 1955, pp. 1-20.*

## RONALD GRIMSLEY (essay date 1958)

[*Grimsley discerns the presence of both Romantic and anti-Romantic attitudes in* Dominique, *observing that while the hero takes public, anti-Romantic measures to resolve his Romantic conflicts, he nonetheless remains a Romantic in the private recesses of his "inner heart."*]

That **Dominique** is in many respects a strongly anti-romantic work is already evident from the very first paragraph, which confronts the melancholy self-absorption of the Romantic individualist with the self-effacement of a man who, in his own modest words, 'is no longer anything'. . . . This as yet unnamed hero, who loves to associate himself with the lives of ordinary, unknown people, does not claim—like so many of his Romantic predecessors—to be a 'genius' whose destiny is to teach 'humanity' some higher 'truth'. . . . He, for his part, has the quiet satisfaction of knowing that, as mayor of his commune and *vigneron*, he is carrying out his obligations to society and leading a rural life that is at least 'useful to some'. The 'narrow circle of this active, hidden existence' is in striking contrast to the restless wanderings of the rootless hero whose vain striving for the infinite makes him reject the conventional values of 'society'. Finally, against the unattainable Romantic ideal of perfect erotic love is set the instructive example of an unspectacular but happy marriage that expresses the universal moral values inherent in every fulfilled existence.

All these features are re-affirmed at the end of the narrative when the reader is in a much better position to understand the real character of Dominique de Bray. Particularly significant is the final appearance of 'that solid heart' and embodiment of 'reason' and 'will', Augustin, the tutor whose moral teaching and example Dominique has followed—'very late', as he admits, and 'with less merit and less courage than he', but ultimately 'with as much happiness'. Augustin stands for the triumph of firm courage and 'robust faith' over morally destructive self-analysis and a hopeless yearning for impossible chimeras. His judicious attitude is that of one whose resolute and optimistic pursuit of reasonable ambitions and down-to-earth happiness has reconciled him to existence and himself. If we add to all this a man's faithful attachment to his native province and the sane virtues of country life, **Dominique** certainly seems to offer a sound corrective to the insidious implications of Romantic passion and *ennui*.

Yet, at the very outset, Dominique's friend asks himself a question that will also be present in many readers' minds at the end of the story: was Dominique really sincere in his acceptance of this quiet, rural way of life. . . . Dominique himself is forced to admit that, in one sense, his resignation expresses a defeat that is not entirely free from all feelings of regret. As the story unfolds, this doubt is strengthened because Dominique—in spite of his insistence on the wisdom of his 'act of modesty, prudence and reason'—has had to contend with problems which, in their inception, were not very different from those of his Romantic predecessors. Already in these early pages our glimpses of him suggest a man whose lonely walks across melancholy and misty landscapes, full of 'serenity, silence and regrets', conceal a secret inner life that has not yet found complete fulfilment in terms of its actual concrete existence. This doubt receives still further confirmation when we learn of his habit of withdrawing to the quiet seclusion of the 'dangerous room' full of the ghosts of his past life. Even his friend is not sure whether he goes there in order to remember or to forget.

Scarcely has the narrator recorded Dominique's own anti-romantic observations when he uses an expression which immediately suggests a very close link between his hero and a fundamental Romantic mood. Dominique, he tells us, is 'épris de perfection'; his heart is 'martyrisé de chimères' . . . and he experiences 'des élans forcenés vers les hauts sommets de l'idéal'. Like so many young men of the earlier generation, he is haunted by an unattainable and, in many ways, confused ideal which, because it represents the self's absolute, infinite aspirations, makes the acceptance of everyday values meaningless and impossible.

As with the Romantics also, the frustration of this idealism tends to produce melancholy and *ennui* which are but the distorted expression of emotions that have found no outlet in the world of ordinary experience. Moreover, this perfectionist need seems to be the ineradicable characteristic of certain temperaments. . . . He suffers from an incurable 'natural infirmity'. From his earliest years Dominique reveals a young heart that is . . . constantly inclined to be more interested in its own feelings than those of other people. Admittedly this introspection is accompanied by genuine 'self-criticism' . . . and a perpetual 'self-distrust' . . . , as well as a total lack of 'self-esteem', but this kind of denigration simply helps to develop a very acute sense of self-awareness.

Dominique's introverted temperament ultimately confronts him with the same basic problem as had already tormented the Romantics—that of allaying a sense of irremediable solitude. . . . If this loneliness was reflected in the absence of any affectionate dependence on others, it was also tied to a special kind of *sensibilité* which, while separating him from his fellowmen, brought him into closer contact with his physical environment. . . . The sensations of adult life are . . . coloured by the influence of earlier memories so that he can never feel himself to be completely bound and circumscribed by the reality of immediate objects, which tend to become significant to him only in so far as they reverberate and re-echo in the depths of his own inner being.

The concrete reality of the physical world becomes imbued with the emotional overtones of his own personality; sensations derived from contact with physical objects take on a meaning only when they have been filtered through the stream of his own consciousness. . . . If the natural vistas are so often prolonged 'à l'infini', is it not because the hero himself yearns after some 'infinite' emotional satisfaction?. . . The proximity of the sea gives the impression that land and water form one infinite expanse. The sense of emptiness is also very remarkable. . . . The flat, empty landscapes are perfectly attuned to a nostalgic temperament that is ever ready to move away from what is to what is not. . . . When a precise physical sensation does stand out against this background, it always appears to carry some special emotional nuance, usually of a rather melancholy kind; it springs forth only to be re-absorbed into the silent source from which it so mysteriously came. Especially striking in this respect is Fromentin's frequent use of the motif of 'the cry', whether of man, bird or animal. (pp. 44-7)

[The] inner lives of the characters themselves seem to become permeated by the atmosphere of the physical world; Dominique has frequent recourse to nature metaphors to describe his own state of mind and the personality of Madeleine. (p. 47)

This relationship between Dominique and his surroundings recalls the Romantic conception of nature as 'un état d' âme'. . . . As far as the story is concerned, the effect is to reinforce the solitude and melancholy Dominique has experienced ever since his earliest years. In spite of his active, rural life he is constantly aware of the need to be alone. . . . Thus Dominique's essential problem is not very different from that of the early Romantics: he too is a lonely sensitive man who, being unable to find an adequate emotional outlet in his immediate environment, seeks refuge in the 'universal mother', Nature. His originality, however, is to have refused to allow this issue to emerge at the level of ordinary experience. Ostensibly he is a man who has turned his back upon Romantic day-dreaming in order to find salvation in the life of ordinary people. This decision has been facilitated by his modest, self-depreciatory character which causes him to conclude, at the end of his earnest endeavours to achieve a reputation as poet and writer, that he is nothing more than 'un homme distingué mais médiocre'. This conclusion seems all the more natural to him when he recalls that the main function of human life is not to be somebody' but to 'produce'. If a man lacks the creative power of the great genius, is he not bound to accept the obligations imposed on his fellowmen?

Nevertheless, when once a person has been vouchsafed a vision of higher beauty, it is not easy for him to become reconciled to the drabness of everyday life, even though he has acknowledged his own creative incapacity. In Dominique's case, the artistic urge to create, frustrated at the properly aesthetic level, forms part of a much more fundamental idealism which is really directed upon his absolute love for a particular woman. Indeed, Dominique's various literary activities are little more than substitutes for an idealistic impulse which can find no adequate outlet at the level of lived experience. His attitude towards Madeleine is in many ways similar to that of the aesthete inspired by some aspect of the physical world to dream of a beautiful masterpiece which he is unable to make real. His achievement remains in a state of permanent possibility. (pp. 47-8)

It is as though the intensity of Dominique's love partly depends on his feeling that it is inspired by an unattainable object. (p. 49)

Dominique's special *sensibilité* causes him to exclude the tangible reality of the loved person in favour of a more shadowy and elusive cluster of ambiguous sensations; it is as though he does not want to contaminate the purity of his love by any suggestion of physical desire. Although in one sense this attitude leads Dominique to unselfish idealism, it may also provoke a kind of narcissistic preoccupation with the objects of his own fancy. It is this feeling of being irretrievably separated from the loved person which makes the development of his emotions depend on the promptings of his own inner life rather than on the real qualities of the loved person herself. What he really loves is not Madeleine as she is—and indeed the reader perceives only a very dim image of her in [the novel's] early pages—but as she appears to him through the idealizing prism of his own subjective feelings. This subjectivism may assume a 'perfect' form, but it is a perfection born of solitude and not of the reciprocal interplay of two genuinely independent personalities.

This attitude is not consistently maintained, partly because the conditions making for a stable affection—even an 'ideal' one—are lacking, and partly because Dominique cannot completely subdue the more dynamic aspects of erotic love. Although Dominique's love for Madeleine is dependent on his particular *sensibilité,* and more especially on the kind of 'sensations' and 'impressions' experienced in the midst of nature, he had been forced at an early age to abandon his native province for the town of Ormesson where he felt lonely and uprooted. Consequently he is inwardly divided, and this tension reacts in its turn upon his love for Madeleine, making it more desperate and tormented. Not unnaturally, he seeks to relieve his suffering by allowing his *sensibilité* to express itself freely once more through a return to the scenes of his childhood. (p. 50)

It is in the remarkable eleventh chapter of the book that Dominique reveals the true nature of his feelings for Madeleine, since at Les Trembles he finds the only satisfaction possible in his ambiguous situation; there he experiences a fusion of his love for Madeleine and his feeling for nature. By taking her with him to his childhood home he hopes to establish between them a closer intimacy than was possible in Paris. He is careful to insist that his motive was not really 'seduction' because it involved no explicit 'calculation'; it was an instinctive impulse which led him to weave around them the delicate and almost invisible threads of mutual sympathy. Yet honesty compels him to admit that there was a certain element of forethought. . . . At the same time Dominique does not appear as a genuine 'seducer' because he is not consciously striving for possession; he remains a kind of spectator haunted by a static, contemplative ideal which abolishes the anxiety aroused by the attempt to satisfy physical desire in temporal existence. It is a mood without reference to the future (because he has no hope) or thought of the past (because he has no reason for regret). Throughout this idyll he enjoys a private, but in many ways unique experience, because, although it is in one way detached from normal desire, it also seeks to achieve a complete fusion of personalities which is 'de tous les instants', thus transcending separation in time.

The only moment of genuine anxiety experienced by Dominique and his friends during that perfect summer was on the occasion of their visit to the light-house. Perhaps it was there that Dominique achieved a sort of symbolic catharsis of a tumultous passion to which he had never been able to give conscious and outward expression. . . . As the great wind-swept tower sways on its base, it is not unreasonable to suppose that Dominique is being purged of all the dangerous emotions implicit in any abandonment to extreme erotic passion. (pp. 50-1)

From the very beginning of [the] holiday at Les Trembles Dominique is conscious of the inevitably ephemeral nature of this period of happiness. Even in the midst of his enjoyment, he realizes that it is passing from him and, by a curious reversal of normal psychological processes, he appears anxious to transform the living experience itself into a kind of memory; the present is already treated as past. Certainly the peculiar fascination of the present comes from the fact that this return to his childhood environment is enriched by the 'new feelings' derived from his love for Madeleine, and this circumstance makes the stay unique and unrepeatable. For all that, the element of memory is also strong. . . . A feeling of particular poignancy makes him eager to extract from this fleeting happiness some kind of durable essence which will fortify him against the day when the idyll of Les Trembles will exist no more and Madeleine will be lost to him for ever. In one way he is helped in this by his peculiar *sensibilité* and his special memory for sensations. It is not so much the isolated emotion as the memory of an emotionally tinged sensation which will remain alive within his personality. While treating the present as though it were already past, he seeks to collect and systematize what in actual experience may be confused and disordered. . . . (pp. 53-4)

The subsequent psychological development of the story is more conventional. As soon as he is forced to live in Paris again, his love which, during the summer at Les Trembles, had been for the most part tranquil and happy, is now transformed by solitude into a more aggressively erotic attitude. In spite of moments of remission when he regrets his anger and perversity, he is increasingly tormented by the awakening of passion. At first he is held in check by Madeleine's resistance and her courageous efforts to 'cure' him, but he slowly undermines her determination until she finally appears to be on the point of giving way. Then, at the instant of imminent triumph, he draws back, moved by a sudden pity for his 'prey.' Believing that dishonour will kill her, he cannot seize what is within his grasp. . . . To take her now would be to destroy for ever that love whose perfection derived from the unattainability of its object; the crude reality of physical possession would utterly shatter all his idealism. 'This purely instinctive commiseration', of which he speaks, was no doubt accompanied by more rational considerations such as the realization of the genuine degradation to which they would both be exposed by their action. But the basis of his behaviour is predominantly affective, and, after the first gesture of instinctive withdrawal, it is Madeleine—not Dominique—who has the moral courage to make an absolute break, for he is 'inerte, insensible et comme de sang-froid'. To some extent he still remains a victim of indecision and ambivalence. . . . For a long time Dominique remains inwardly divided and, in his original version, Fromentin proposed to incorporate a passage which showed his hero rebelling against his own generous impulse to spare Madeleine. . . . At first sight, it looks as though he is able to achieve victory over himself only with the help of a will stronger than his own; but this other will has had as its discreet and partly unwitting accomplice deeply rooted and barely conscious tendencies in his own nature; these had impelled him from the outset to replace a single-minded striving for physical possession by a more 'idealistic' attitude that demands, for its ultimate satisfaction, a permanent separation from the loved person, who henceforth remains an object of meditation and nostalgic reverie rather than of passionate desire. Through this final act of separation and renunciation Dominique's love can live on— perfect and intact in the diaphanous world of private memory, and yet still subtly related to that corner of nature which, for one brief summer, saw its tranquil blossoming.

Now happily married and integrated into the community he loves and respects, he can feel that he has overcome all the insidious moral dangers of his former passion. Nevertheless, while resting secure in the thought of his triumph over his own baser nature, he is free to gaze down the ever-lengthening corridor of time and see the memory of this idyllic love becoming more and more mysterious and beautiful. At the same time, these memories give him a kind of permanent essence with which his hidden self can henceforth be identified. All this creates a mood which is felt to be compatible with a zealous and apparently sincere devotion to the tasks of everyday life. Such is the final expression of a Romanticism which has overcome itself only to ensure its permanent survival in a more remote and hermetic form. Conquered and suppressed at the level of lived experience, this love is still worshipped in the secret recesses of Dominique's inner heart. (pp. 54-6)

> Ronald Grimsley, *"Romanticism in 'Dominique',"* in French Studies, *Vol. XII, No. 1, January, 1958, pp. 44-57.*

### G. J. GRESHOFF  (essay date 1961)

[*Emphasizing the importance of the narrative framework in validating the hero/narrator's growth and point of view, Greshoff contends that Dominique rejects his Romantic past as he grows toward maturity, thereby making the novel a "farewell to Romanticism."*]

[*Dominique*] is something more than just a romantic love story, although merely as such it would have survived. It has other meanings and themes: it is also the story of a young man's growth towards maturity, and it is also a farewell to Romanticism. This last aspect brings it very close to Flaubert's *L'Education Sentimentale.*

The book consists of a central episode, which is the confession proper of Dominique and in which he tells the story of his love. This episode is framed by two episodes of very different lengths: a prologue of thirty pages and an epilogue of five. These two episodes, which are told by an anonymous narrator, show us Dominique's present way of living: we see him solidly anchored in life, performing real social functions, surrounded by his family. By sandwiching the story of Dominique's love affair between two slices of 'real' life and thus contrasting past and present, Fromentin also makes clear that this painful love affair was but an episode in Dominique's life, a stage in his growth. When Chateaubriand writes an autobiographical novel, he does exactly the contrary, and in this way *René* is a truly romantic novel, which *Dominique* is not. The episode of *René* is sandwiched between scenes showing a world of unreal adventure lived in an unreal America amongst unreal Indians. With Chateaubriand we never leave the world of unreality, while with Fromentin we eventually come out into a real world.

The function of the prologue and of the epilogue is not only to show two sides of Dominique, to contrast past with present, to show what he was and what he has become; it also affords Fromentin the opportunity to show his character both from the outside, as seen by the narrator, and from the inside as told by himself. (pp. 166-67)

[When] we see Dominique for the first time, it is from afar. He is an impersonal shadow who is not really seen.

*Portrait of Fromentin as a young man drawn by the author.*

"Ah! voici M. Dominique qui chasse" me dit le docteur en reconnaissant à toute distance l'équipage ordinaire de son voisin. Un peu plus tard, nous l'entendîmes tirer et le docteur me dit: "Voilà M. Dominique qui tire". . . .

["Ah! here comes M. Dominique, who is out hunting," said the doctor who had recognised from this great distance the usual sporting dress of his neighbour. A little later we heard him shoot and the doctor told me: "That is M. Dominique shooting now".]

After this Dominique comes gradually closer: we meet him, then we see him as a farmer, as a host, as a mayor; later we see him surrounded by his family, in his daily life and finally we find ourselves inside Dominique's very mind and thought. The entire prologue of the novel is a gradual penetration into Dominique's privacy, until we finally reach his most hidden domain. (p. 167)

For an understanding of the prologue and indeed of the whole novel, the crucial passage is the description of Dominique's study, where the confession will take place. This room is not only the image of his past. . . . It is also the projection of Dominique's mind: by being inside the study we are inside Dominique himself. And finally the study is a projection of the novel itself. If one reads carefully, one recognises all the elements which we shall find later in the novel, all the meanings are hinted at, all the themes are indicated. What Fromentin has done in his passage is, in fact, what Proust will do many years later in the first part of *Du Côté de chez Swann*: to write a prelude which contains in embryo the entire novel.

The first object mentioned is the portrait of himself,

> jeune visage au teint rosé, tout papilloté de boucles brunes, qui n'avait plus un trait reconnaissable. . . .

> [a youthful, pink face surrounded by brown curly hair and in which not one trait was recognisable.]

We have here the major theme: the birth of a man out of childhood. This portrait in Dominique's study is the picture of a chrysalis. The books refer to his studious childhood under Augustin and to his period as a political writer. . . . With the geometrical figures, the 'chiffres enlacés', the poems written on the walls, we come into the centre both of Dominique's mind and of the novel. The poems refer to his awakening to poetry which accompanied his awakening to love, the quotation from Longfellow refers clearly to the period when Dominique, in a vain attempt to forget Madeleine, courts political and literary glory. The most important notations on the walls of Dominique's mind are the simple geometric figures.

> Ailleurs il y avait seulement une figure géométrique élémentaire. Au dessous, la même figure était reproduite, mais avec un ou deux traits de plus qui en modifiaient le sens sans en changer le principe, et la figure arrivait ainsi, et en se répétant avec des modifications nouvelles, à des significations singulières qui impliquaient le triangle ou le cercle originel, mais aves des résultats tout différents. . . .

> [Elsewhere there was only an elementary geometric figure. Beneath it, this same figure was reproduced with one or two lines added which modified its meaning without altering its basic shape. In this way, by being repeated with new modifications, the figure acquired strange meanings, all of which were linked to the original circle or triangle but with entirely different results.]

These geometrical figures refer to what I think is the deepest theme of the novel and the one which gives the entire work its meaning: the theme of identity. Dominique is in a way experimenting with himself—every adolescence is a period of experimentation—but whatever he does, he always remains in reality the same. He does not change, however much he may change superficially. In *Dominique* one must be on one's guard not to confuse apparent change with real change. The geometrical figures which clearly symbolise this aspect of the novel show this. For these figures, although changing, do not alter their identity; they are always identifiable as circle and triangle. These original elements are never lost. (pp. 168-69)

[There] is one more episode in the prologue: the return of his friend Olivier to *Les Trembles,* Dominique's country estate. Olivier was his school friend and the witness of his youth and of his love affair. After leaving Dominique, Olivier attempts suicide, but does not succeed. (p. 169)

The episode of Olivier's *suicide manqué* has two meanings, one which is clear but rather clumsy and literary. The suicide of Olivier is the precise parallel of Dominique's 'amputation' of his past. Both Olivier and Dominique are mutilated. This is . . . [an] example of Fromentin at his worst. Seen on this level, the sybolism is crude and obvious. But the episode has another and more subtle meaning: Olivier represents Dominique's romantic side. Olivier's suicide is the suicide of the romantic Dominique; it is only with this side of him silenced— not dead but disfigured and in exile—that Dominique can start his confession. (p. 170)

[*Dominique*] is the image of a romantic mind, but seen from a great distance. In this particular way *Dominique* resembles Constant's *Adolphe*. And a comparison of the two novels may bring out some of *Dominique*'s characteristics. What Constant gives us in his novel is the analysis of a situation; it is a perfectly static novel and quite unlike *Dominique,* for a very delicate but very real life flows beneath the apparently motionless surface of Fromentin's novel, which deals with the evolution of a love. It traces the subtle, imperceptible changes, the minute actions and reactions of two people to one another. . . .

Also the lighting of *Adolphe* and of *Dominique* is radically different. Adolphe receives a cold, sharp, blinding light which is reflected in Constant's thin, nervous, incredibly accurate and clear prose. *Dominique,* strictly speaking, is not lit at all. One wonders sometimes where the light comes from: it seems bathed in a very soft, grey light, rather monotonous and temperate. The diffuseness of lighting is not used by Fromentin to hide things. He is not trying to move us by nice, soft sentiments expressed in vague prose and which have no hard core of reality. The drawing of the experience is always firm and indirect; the lines are strong, and if at times they are slightly blurred, they nevertheless remain solid and substantial. In painting Fromentin would be closer to the firm gentleness of Corot than to the vague, hazy sentimentality of Carrère.

Finally, while Constant views romantic love ironically, there is not a trace of irony in *Dominique*. Fromentin keeps equally distant from the chilly, eighteenth-century irony of Constant and from the self-pity of the romantics. The novel reveals a genuine and generous understanding which does not in any way exclude severity.

I want now to turn to the characters and to the presentation of love in *Dominique*. (p. 171)

It is significant that [Dominique] becomes clearly aware of his love for Madeleine and that he formulates it for the first time when it is too late: 'Madeleine était perdue pour moi, et je l'aimais'. . . . He begins to love her only when he is quite certain that she is inaccessible. Dominique, like a good romantic, is masochistically in love with defeat, and because of this his love is sterile. It is shown as a painful, enervating, cruel and endless chase. (p. 172)

Fromentin, then, presents an almost identical situation to the one Flaubert treats in his *Education Sentimentale*. Here we find also a picture of a youthful, romantic love with all its unhealthy absorption in suffering and defeat. However, and here lies the great difference in the attitudes of Flaubert and of Fromentin: Frédéric, of *L'Education*, rests in his defeat, he never leaves his adolescence; he does not, like Dominique, emerge into reality and adulthood.

One thing, amongst others, which Frédéric and Dominique have in common, that is that neither is in love with a real person. Frédéric loves a ghost, a person he has made himself after the brief glimpse he caught of her on the boat from Rouen to Paris. Dominique also loves an imaginary creature. . . . [Fromentin initially describes Madeleine] as a young and still unformed person. . . , but he also describes a very commonplace, unremarkable girl without any real existence. The beautiful, firm Madeleine with whom Dominique is in love does not exist. In fact, he loves an image of Madeleine. This is brought out very clearly in the passage of the portrait. Dominique, having broken with Madeleine and not having seen her for a long time, comes across a portrait of her:

> Je restai annéanti devant cette effigie effrayante de réalité et de tristesse. . . . Madeleine était là devant moi qui me regardait, mais avec quels yeux! dans quelle attitude! avec quelle pâleur et quelle mystérieuse expression d'attente et de déplaisir amer. . . .

> [I stood dumbfounded before this image, frightening in its reality and in its sadness. Madeleine was before me, looking at me but with what eyes, in what an attitude. So pale and with a mysterious expression of expectancy and of bitter displeasure.]

What Dominique recognises in the painting is, of course, Madeleine in love. This is significant, for he discovers her love not by looking at *her,* but by looking at a picture of her. To this image of love Dominique immediately responds, and he makes love to the portrait:

> Je lui parlais, je lui disais toutes les choses déraisonnables qui me torturaient le coeur depuis près de deux années; je lui demandais grâce, et pour elle, et pour moi. Je la suppliai de me reçevoir, de me laisser venir à elle. . . .

> [I talked to her. I told her all the unreasonable feelings which tortured my heart for almost two years. I cried for mercy for both of us. I begged her to receive me, to let me come to her.]

One must remember that the object of this passionate outburst is a painting, and the effect is rather horrible. It has a nightmarish quality which is exactly in keeping with the kind of love Fromentin describes: the love for a dead image, not the love for a living person.

When Dominique and Madeleine are together, their relationship is not that of mistress and lover, but that of mother and child. Madeleine is older, but not much ('plus âgée d'un an à peu près'), she is stronger and she dominates Dominique because he wants her to. He enjoys this state of passive dependence, he relishes this mother-child relationship, and so does she. . . . [Even] if irony is absent, there is no absence of judgment. The picture Fromentin draws of romantic love is never complacent; on the contrary, he shows it as painful, but essentially unreal and childish. (pp. 173-74)

The love of Dominique, although puerile, does not remain a schoolboy love. It soon gets complicated by a violent sexual attraction. Fromentin's handling of sex is extremely discreet, so discreet that it seems to play no part in the novel, but it is nevertheless there; it is sex which gives the greater tension to the second half of the novel. Dominique's discovery of Madeleine as a woman is sudden. At a ball Madeleine gives, he sees her for the first time in evening dress:

> C'était la première fois que je la voyais ainsi, dans la tenue splendide et indiscrète d'une femme en toilette de bal. Je sentis que je changeais de couleur, et qu'au lieu de répondre à son regard paisible mes yeux s'arrètaient maladroitement sur un noeud de diamants qui flamboyait à son corsage. Nous demeurâmes une seconde en présence, elle interdite, moi fort troublé. Personne assurément se douta du rapide échange d'impressions qui nous apprit, je crois de l'un à l'autre que de délicates pudeurs étaient blessées. . . .

> [It was the first time I saw her dressed in the resplendent and indiscreet clothes a woman wears at a ball. I felt I changed colour, and that instead of answering her quiet glance my eyes were looking awkwardly at a diamond brooch which shone on her bodice. For a second we remained alone together, she disconcerted, I extremely embarrassed. Nobody, I am sure, suspected the quick change of impression which told both of us that a very delicate feeling of modesty had been hurt.]

This chapter is a turning point in the novel, and it opens with the revealing sentence:

> J'en avais fini avec les jour heureux. . . .

With sex a number of new experiences are introduced. Immediately after this 'échange d'impressions' Dominique discovers jealousy. . . . He also feels now the desire for possession:

> J'avais besoin de revoir Madeleine presque seul à seul, de la posséder plus étroitement après le départ de tant de gens qui se l'étaient pour ainsi dire partagée. . . .

> [I needed to see Madeleine almost alone, to possess her even more intimately after the departure of all these people who, as it were, had shared her.]
>
> (pp. 175-76)

However, Dominique's desire will not be gratified, in fact he is terrified at the thought that it might. Ostensibly he is afraid Madeleine will become a 'fallen woman' and cease to be 'une honnête femme'. His real fear stems from the knowledge that Madeleine's gift of herself will destroy precisely that quality of their love which they relish, its hopelessness and the sense of defeat on which it feeds.

Their relationship acquires now an enervating ambiguity.

> C'est alors qu'elle osa inventer des moyens de me voir hors de sa maison. Elle y mit une affrayante effronterie qui n'est permise qu'aux femmes qui risquent leur honneur, ou à la pure innocence. Bravement, elle me donna des rendez-vous. Le lieu désigné était désert, quoique peu éloigné de son hôtel. Et ne supposez pas qu'elle choisit, pour ces expéditions périlleuses, les occasion fréquentes où M. de Nièvres s'absentait. Non c'était lui présent à Paris, au risque de le rencontrer, de se perdre, qu'elle accourait à heure dite et presque toujours aussi

maîtresse d'elle-même, résolue que si elle avait tout sacrifié. . . .

[It was then she dared to find ways to meet me outside her home. She did this with the kind of frightening daring which is displayed only by innocence or by women who are willing to risk their honour. Courageously she gave me a rendez-vous. The place where we met was deserted, although not far from her house. And do not think that for these dangerous meetings she chose one of the numerous occasions when M. de Nièvres was away. Not at all, it was when he was present in Paris, running the risk of meeting him and of losing her honour, that she hastened to me at the appointed time, nearly always self-possessed and yet as determined as if she had wholly given herself.]

Few passages in the novel give a better reflection of the murky untidiness of Dominique's and Madeleine's love affair, and of its unhealthy atmosphere. The situation which Fromentin describes is, in actual fact, 'une situation galante', but emasculated, disembodied. It has all the stealth and expectancy of a secret affair without any of its content. It is horribly unreal: Madeleine is shown behaving like an adulterous wife, yet she remains pure. (p. 176)

In an obscene way they sleep together without touching each other. The scene in the 'loge' at the *Opéra* shows one of these episodes.

> Madeleine écoutait, haletante. J'étais assis derrière elle; aussi près que le permettait de dossier de son fauteuil, où je m'appuyais. Elle s'y renversait aussi de temps en temps, au point que ses cheveux me balayaient les lèvres. Elle ne pouvait pas faire un geste de mon côté que je ne sentis aussitôt son souffle inégal, et je le respirais comme une ardeur de plus. Elle avait les deux bras croisés sur sa poitrine peut-être pour en comprimer les battements. Tout son corps, penché en arrière, obéissait à des palpitations irrésistibles, et chaque respirations de sa poitrine, en se communiquant du siège à mon bras, m'imprimait à moi-même un mouvement convulsif tout pareil à celui de ma proper vie. . . .

> [Madeleine listened panting. I was sitting behind her, as near to her as the back of the chair on which I was leaning permitted. She was reclining, and thus from time to time her hair brushed my lips. She could not move in my direction without me feeling her uneven sighs, and I breathed them in as one more token of her love. Both her arms were crossed over her bosom as if she wanted to repress the beating of her heart. Her entire body, bent backwards, responded to uncontrollable palpitations, and every breath that she took touched my arm through the thickness of her chair and imparted to my body a convulsive movement which was like that of life itself.]

This is one of the climaxes of their relationship and what Fromentin shows is an 'accouplement' but, and this is what is important, it is a substitute one; for this is the only intercourse which can express their substitute love. When, towards the end

of the confession, they actually fall into each others' arms, they almost immediately shrink away in terror. (p. 177)

In the confession, the sea is clearly the symbol of wild, romantic passion which holds a terrible fascination for Dominique and tempts him. . . . Nowhere is this more clearly illustrated than in the scene of the lighthouse: Dominique, Julie, Madeleine and Olivier stand on top of a lighthouse and look at the sea and the sky:

> Chacun de nous en fut frappé diversément sans doute; mais je me souviens [que ce spectacle de l'immensité] eut pour effet de suspendre aussitôt tout entretion et que le même vertige physique nous fit subitement pâlir et nous redit sérieux. Une sorte de cri d'angoisse s'échappa des lèvres de Madeleine, et, sans prononcer une parole, tous accoudés sur la légère balustrade qui seule nous séparait de l'abîme, sentant très distinctement l'énorme tour osciller sous nos pieds à chaque impulsion du vent, attirés par l'immense danger, et comme solicités d'en bas par les clameurs de la marée montante, nous restâmes longtemps dans la plus grande stupeur, semblables à des gens qui, le pied posé sur la vie fragile, par miracle, auraient un jour l'aventure inouie de regarder et de voir au delà. . . .

> [Each one of us was, no doubt, struck in a different way; this spectacle of immensity . . . had the effect of suspending all conversation and . . . suddenly the same feeling of vertigo made us grow pale and serious. A cry of anguish came from Madeleine's lips and, without saying a word, our elbows leaning on the flimsy balustrade which alone separated us from the abyss, feeling clearly the enormous tower trembling at each tug of the wind, attracted and, as it were, sucked down by the rising sea, we remained quiet for along time like people whose feet while treading lightly on life, by a sudden miracle see beyond it.]

Later, after having related a sea trip of Dominique and Madeleine, Fromentin makes Dominique say:

> . . . je me rappelle aujourd'hui ces heures de prétendu repos et de langueur comme les plus belles et les plus dangereuses peut-être que j'aie traversée de ma vie. . . .

> [I remember now these moments of so-called restfulness and languor as the most beautiful and perhaps the most dangerous I have ever lived.]

The key word here, of course, is *dangereux,* and the idea of sea and danger are clearly linked. We have here, then, another theme of ***Dominique,*** the temptation of romantic passion: it is 'La Tentation de Saint Dominique'.

Dominique, however, does not give in to the romantic temptation, he does not throw himself into the sea and drown. He chooses the life of a gentleman farmer, he turns towards the shore. But nothing in this novel is final. Because he has resisted the temptation does not mean that the temptation is dead, it is constantly present: the sea, Fromentin tells us, is not very far from 'Les Trembles'; his daily rides take Dominique to its shores, and its noise can be heard from the house. (pp. 177-78)

Inseparably linked with the love theme, and perhaps more important, is the growth towards maturity: out of the puerile romantic will grow an adult person. Dominique turns his back to the sea and goes towards the shore. The novel, then, represents a rejection and therefore a criticism of romantic attitudes. It is a farewell to romanticism, but a nostalgic one written by a romantic. (p. 180)

In this rejection of romanticism Fromentin and Flaubert share a similar attitude, and the parallel with the *Education Sentimentale* is striking. On a bigger scale, but in a much more fragmentary way, Flaubert rewrote **Dominique**. While Fromentin gives us a vignette of a generation, Flaubert gives us a panorama. But the Dominique of the confession resembles Frédèric like a brother: the same attitude towards love, the same lack of will-power, the same tendency to be 'villéitaires' and never to achieve anything: they are both obsessed by the Great Romantic Ambitions: Love, Poetry, and Politics. Both **Dominique** and *L'Education Sentimentale* show young men at grips with their romantic past, but the outcome of this struggle is entirely different. Frédéric and Deslaurier are defeated by love and ambition because neither of these had a real object. At the end of Flaubert's novel we see them literally as 'old boys', reminiscing and regretting their past and saying of their first visit to a bordello: 'C'est ce que nous avons eu de meilleur.' This remark gives the exact measure of their failure. The picture drawn by Fromentin is quite different. Dominique is saved and not sucked under. Here we see, once again, the importance of the prologue and of the epilogue, which show Dominique turning towards the world outside him, towards an objective reality. He is no longer morbidly interested in his self. The different points of view from which he is seen, from the outside in the prologue and epilogue, from the inside in the body of the novel, reflect the profound change Dominique himself has undergone. (pp. 180-81)

It is in this context of Dominique's struggle with his romantic self that Olivier and Augustin become necessary and important. . . . Olivier is his confessor, Augustin is his master. Through the closeness of this bond they become part of Dominique's life, and eventually they seem to become part of Dominique himself. Roughly speaking, they are concrete representations of the conflicting ideas and sentiments which meet in Dominique. (p. 181)

[Throughout] the novel the drawing of Olivier is blurred. His actions are unpredictable and unreasonable; when playing cards he will suddenly throw his cards on the table and say: 'je m'ennuie'. All the actions in his life have the same quality. He is, of course, René, the romantic youth, old without being mature and who seems older than he is because he adopts, precociously and superficially, the manners, speech and outlook of his society:

> [il était] très-précose dans toutes les choses de la vie, aisé de gestes, de maintient, de paroles, ne sachant rien du monde et let devinant, . . . [il avait] une ardeur un peu singulière, jamais risible, . . . d'anticiper sur son âge et de s'improviser un homme à seize ans à peine. . . .

> [He was] very precocious with an easy manner, bearing and speech, knowing nothing of the world and instinctively responding to it. [He had] a strange, yet never ridiculous eagerness

to act beyond his years and to pretend to be a man when, in fact, he was only sixteen.]

Yet Olivier never grows older than sixteen and his suicide, a childish action, resembles that of the boy who flung his cards on the table and said: 'I'm bored.' Olivier has no will, no desires, he is tired of life before having lived, discouraged before having tried and devoured by a nameless *ennui*. Most of these traits of Olivier we will find again, in a modified form, in Dominique.

The drawing of Augustin is clear and the outline is firm. Because of this he emerges as rather flat and uninteresting. Augustin, unlike Olivier, has a tangible reality: his ambitions are real, he marries a real woman, he leads a 'visible' life. He emerges as a portrait of Taine as a young *Normalien*. Augustin, in short, is opaque, and this opacity strongly contrasts with Olivier's ghostliness.

Olivier and Augustin represent the two sides of Dominique's personality. It would be wrong, however, to think that Dominique is a mere addition of these two elements. Both Olivier and Augustin lack something. Fromentin says of Augustin that he was 'une personne incomplète', and the same can be said of Olivier. They both lack sensitivity. Olivier's apparent sensitivity is nothing more than a sort of tense morbidity; as for Augustin, we are told that he had 'une bonté d'âme réelle', which is not real sensibility either. They meet in the sensitive and sensible Dominique who contains them and complements them and who emerges, in the end, a more complete person than either.

The process of Dominique's growth towards maturity is shown as a growth towards identity. Once more the description of Dominique's study gives us a clue. I have already drawn the attention to the meaning of the geometrical figures and of the writings on the wall, but Fromentin, in the same passage, becomes more explicit:

> Puis, à dater d'une époque qu'on pouvait calculer approximativement par un rapprochement facile avec son mariage, il devenait évident que . . . il avait pris le parti de ne plus écrire. Jugeait-il que la dernière évolution de son existence était accomplie? Ou pensait-il avec raison qu'il n'avait plus rien à craindre désormais pour cette identité de lui-même qu'il avait pris jusqu-là tants de soin d'établir. . . .

> [Then from a certain date, which one could approximately calculate as coinciding with the time of his marriage, it became clear that he had decided not to write any more. Did he consider that the last phase of his evolution had been reached? Or did he think, with reason, that there was nothing more to fear for this identity with himself which he had taken such pains to establish.]

The deepest meaning of the novel lies here: Dominique reaches adulthood when he has found his identity, i.e., his sameness. . . . The sense of identity which Dominique acquires, is an awareness of resemblance; the notion which is opposed to this is not individuality, but sense of dissemblance, the awareness of being unique. What the young Dominique discovers, and for a long time is obsessed by, is his uniqueness. The experience which Fromentin describes in Dominique's confession is also an exploration of a self which implies a total absorption in one's self and leads to the discovery of one's singularity. The romantic mind, of which Dominique is such a clear reflection, is obsessed by what Malraux calls 'le fanatisme de la différence'. In this obsession the romantic mind is adolescent and immature. Maturity implies a loss of this fanaticism: one loses one's singular self in order to find one's identity. This is precisely what Fromentin shows in *Dominique*.

At the beginning of the novel, when the author gives us a brief glance inside Dominique, he makes him say, and this is the opening sentence of the book:

> Certainement je n'ai pas à me plaindre . . . car, Dieu merci je ne suis plus rien. . . .

> [Certainly, I have no grounds for complaints . . . for, thank heaven, I am no longer anybody.]

(pp. 182-84)

*G. J. Greshoff, "Fromentin's 'Dominique'—An Analysis," in* Essays in Criticism, *Vol. XI, No. 2, April, 1961, pp. 164-89.*

## HENRI PEYRE   (essay date 1963)

[*Peyre is a French-born critic who has lived and taught in the United States for most of his career. One of the foremost American critics of French literature, he has written extensively on modern French literature in works that blend superb scholarship with a clear style accessible to the nonspecialist reader. Peyre speaks of* Dominique *as an "aged" book in the essay excerpted below, explaining that the novel's unapologetic and unadorned provincialism disappoints the modern taste for intensity in art.*]

[The narrator in *Dominique*] is one more of those numerous Hamlets who proliferated in France even more than in Britain at the end of the romantic era and again after World War I. He longs for action and for the audacious conquest of the palpable advantages of life which seduced Balzac's heroes and a character, Augustin, who, in *Dominique,* serves as a foil to the introspective narrator and is offered by him as a model of shrewd practical wisdom. He loses no opportunity to offer a moral lesson on the vanity of revolt and on the need for discipline; that bourgeois didacticism is in part what has aged the book and causes us to prefer Fromentin's travel sketches in North Africa or his appraisal of Flemish and Dutch painters. Yet the novel, if less acutely lucid than [Benjamin Constant's] *Adolphe* and regrettably lacking in cruelty, is more courageously sincere—probably too much so, and its faults are those of the personal novel that refuses to lie in order to appear true.

Its supreme courage is in its acceptance of provincialism, unabashed and placid, in contrast with the attitude of young men like Julien Sorel [in Stendhal's *Le rouge et le noir*] and Rastignac [in Honoré de Balzac's *La comédie humaine*] who were drawn to Paris by the glittering splendor of the Second Empire and the newly opened possibilities for success in industrial and financial speculation. Few avowals are harder to make for a Frenchman than that of his inveterate provincialism. Equally few writers could be candid enough to reject all hypocrisy in love, all dramatization of their desires and of their feelings, every urge to pain or to vex or to dominate the young woman whom they know to be at their mercy. Neither religion nor ambition restrains the hero. But adultery would be, for that gentleman farmer, a violation of the laws of property, a reckless risk imposed upon the woman, since happiness could not lie in the acceptance of the natural and social order and in a clear

conscience. The reader is irked by such sincerity which stifles passion, eschews struggle, chooses the way of prudence, and dares praise chastity. (pp. 197-98)

Nothing is ever strained in *Dominique*. Even the novelist's bag of tricks, which Fromentin could easily have borrowed from his predecessors, remains unopened. Technical weaknesses are obvious, and accepted by the author. He describes himself with no pose whatsoever, no attempt to please or to transfigure. But a sincerity which thus fails to dramatize itself into anguish or to assume the extreme frankness of cynicism lacks the intensity that moderns appear to need in art. A lover who consents to abdicate is soon suspected of not loving ardently enough. "Lying," says Proust. . . , "is essential to mankind. It plays a part at least as large as the quest for pleasure; it is conditioned by that very quest. . . . We lie all our life long, even chiefly, perhaps solely, to those who love us." (p. 198)

*Henri Peyre, "The Personal Novel," in his* Literature and Sincerity, *Yale University Press, 1963, pp. 161-202.**

## ARTHUR R. EVANS, JR.   (essay date 1964)

[*In summarizing his findings in* The Literary Art of Eugène Fromentin: A Study in Style and Motif, *Evans identifies Fromentin's dominant literary impetus as the need for definition and resolution of problems, ascribing this imperative to his desire to harmonize discordant drives and dispositions within his personality. The critic places Fromentin with Gustave Flaubert, Joseph Ernest Renan, and other members of the generation born in the 1820s for whom the "search for form has become a discipline which saves them from the tragic consequences of a lived romanticism."*]

[Fromentin's] literary aims are motivated by a problem-seeking nature intent upon definition and solution. This is the dominating passion informing his work and giving to it a rigorous, pervasive unity of style. Painfully sensitive and sentimental, charmed by the past and hesitant as to the future, he is nonetheless urged on by an imperious need for quest and confrontation. Fromentin must see whole, steadfast, and clear. Just as the writer gives plastic form and relief to the chaos of the African scene, so the man is determined to discipline an inner life which threatens repeatedly to lose itself in sterile reverie and regret. He must master and make conform to his creative desires a sensibility in danger of being content with dilettantism and mere sensory excitation. Having grown up in the heartland of Huguenot France, grave and scrupulous, Fromentin is intent upon bringing into harmony contrary dispositions and drives, placating the opposing demands of bourgeois and aesthete. Within a stylized, somewhat academically classic form, he achieves a literary expression which is serious, sensitive, and eminently intelligent. In doing so, Fromentin shows that he did attain to such a harmony, which if not vigorous and assured, is nevertheless in the best traditions of French classicism. (pp. 145-46)

Each of the books is motivated by a single purpose which is patiently and exactly pursued. In the journals, the problem is aesthetic: that of composing from the novelty and complexity of the African experience a unique and harmonious composite of aesthetically significant moments. In *Dominique,* observation and description are turned inward and the problem becomes moral. An unstinting self-criticism explores the past history of the self, and finds it caught up in a conflict between reality and irreality: the suffering occasioned by a foredoomed love and a meretricious vocational success imposes upon Dominique the recognition of his own mediocrity. In the *Maîtres,* there is need for a direct confrontation with a great and neglected artistic tradition; but more than this we sense the critic's necessity of finding support and justification for his own notions as to what great art should be. Estranged from the experiments of contemporary painting, Fromentin can feel secure in clarifying and explaining to himself and to others the undeniable mastery of the Flemish and Dutch schools. The problem of the *Maîtres* then is at once critical, aesthetic, and moral. The initial attraction of the problematic and the eventual security in its solution can on deeper levels be exemplified by the symbolic pattern of winged flight and recurrent home-comings, that dialectic of departure and return which we find to be a constant in Fromentin's life, and which is typified in *Dominique* by the cycle, Trembles-Paris-Trembles.

The pursuit of the problem works toward a clarity and finality of resolution. Fromentin's art of narration moves forward by ''scenes,'' ''moments,'' and ''inquiries'' which are as so many stages in this process of ultimate definition; thus the mosaic of views in the African diaries, the Racinian elaboration of plot in *Dominique,* and in the *Maîtres* the synthesis of critical estimates. The attitude adopted is objective, contemplative, passive. This is reflected in the ideal of a timeless depiction of reality, the preference for heights, distant views, and total surveys; as well as the device of the dual narrators in *Dominique* and the dialectical modality of statement and counterstatement in the *Maîtres.* But perhaps the most pronounced evidence for this essentially contemplative attitude is the degree of stylization which Fromentin imposes upon his art of expression. Integral to such stylization is the reliance upon an affective memory which discriminates and highlights the materials for his art.

This elaboration is at once inclusive and selective. A cumulative, notational syntax strives to draw out, to comment upon, and to qualify all that is essential in a particular aspect of exterior or interior reality: a landscape, a mood, or the color composition of a painting. Descriptive art makes use of the ''microscopic eye,'' of the nuanced adjective, and of the illustrative image to further this same intensive but discriminating research.

In Fromentin, style and its psychological concomitants point to a classical culture in which artistic expression assumes the character of an ethic, as it were. As a bourgeois aesthete, Fromentin shares qualities of mind, temperament, and background with other writers of his generation, with Flaubert, Renan, and certain of the Parnassians. Romanticism was the formative climate of these men, and they were strongly affected by it; they sought in art and the life of the spirit the means of coming to terms with it. The forebears and masters of these fine and sensitive natures were men of great energy and vitalism, Balzac, Hugo, Michelet. In the generation of artists born in the 1820's, there is apparent a diminution of creative energy and a shying away from any ready, positive commitment to life. . . . For Fromentin and his contemporaries, refinement of feeling, subtlety in phrasing, and an intense reflection upon the craft of writing are qualities of expression which have tended to replace the freer, more vital, more spontaneous, though cruder and more uneven, productivity of the great romantics. The search for form has become a discipline which saves them from the tragic consequences of a lived romanticism, but they pay a price for it in that it cuts them off from the vitality which was inherent in romanticism. Their contemplative posture represents a moment of precarious balance prior

to the *fin-de-siècle* world weariness and retreat from life of the writers of the next generation: Verlaine, Huysmans, Villiers, and Mallarmé. (pp. 146-48)

*Arthur R. Evans, Jr., in his* The Literary Art of Eugène Fromentin: A Study in Style and Motif, *The John Hopkins University Press, 1964, 155 p.*

## BARBARA WRIGHT   (essay date 1965)

[*Wright, who is a leading Fromentin scholar, discusses the importance and originality of* Dominique *as revealed in the author's treatment of characterization, language, and the evocation of moods and impressions. Wright discusses the manuscript version of* Dominique *in her essay, reflecting her extensive research in preparing a scholarly, French-language edition of the novel (see Additional Bibliography for further details).*]

*Dominique* occupies a curious position in literary history: an acknowledged landmark in the development of the personal novel, its importance has not often been closely analysed nor its real originality apprehended. The very magic of the book, with its will-o'-the-wisp, gossamer-like quality, may well be an important factor in its subtle and evasive charm which so easily defies definition. For some, *Dominique* is even an exteriorized projection of a cherished period of their youth, a kind of fictionalized *journal intime.* . . . For others, Fromentin's novel is essentially '(une oeuvre) exquisement française', an attribute frequently used to explain, though not to excuse the fact that *Dominique* has remained so much apart from English literature. . . . It is, however, none the less true that, even in France, *Dominique* has not attained the full appreciation which it deserves and that part of the difficulty may be inherent in the very subtle and intimate nature of its beauty. (p. v)

Essentially, Fromentin aimed at concentrating the interest of his novel in a subtle portrayal of the human feelings involved, rather than in the development of any fictional plot or intrigue. . . . But though he disparaged fictional elements as such, Fromentin could never bring himself entirely to flout traditional literary requirements. On the contrary, he felt self-consciously inexperienced in this respect and was well aware of the difficulty involved in giving his work an individual imprint. (p. xii)

[It] is possible to detect in the evolution of *Dominique* a certain lack of spontaneous inspiration on the part of the author in relation to those incidents and scenes which were more closely linked with the literary heritage of the personal novel than with his own lived experience: the ball-scene, the theatre-scene, the flower-scene, the portrait-scene—to quote some of the principal examples. . . . For some of the . . . 'literary' scenes, the fragmentary plans which have been preserved reveal the author as casting around for fictional material to incorporate into the revised version of his novel. These notes, drafted in order to modify or complete the original manuscript before the emergence of the first published text, show that the earlier version of the theatre scene, for instance, was scheduled to be rewritten. Similarly, the note 'scène courte et violente à trouver' . . . heralds the advent of the flower-scene, and is shortly followed by the indication 'scène violente de Dominique en rentrant chez lui'. . . . The inventive weakness of Fromentin in relation to incidents of this kind contrasts sharply with the remarkable fluency of the earlier, more autobiographical passages. (pp. xiii-xiv)

Fromentin belonged to [the] generation of chastened Romantics and, like them, advocated a less declamatory and more restrained form of art. In working out the characterization of the principal figures in **Dominique,** he was clearly concerned to develop the anti-heroic subject and the quiet tone of his novel: Olivier's way of life, for instance, is intended to symbolize the dangers inherent in Romanticism, while the edifying example of Augustin is designed to inspire ethical strength and tenacious will-power. (pp. xv-xvi)

[An interesting] picture of Olivier emerges from the original manuscript of the novel. There, as well as displaying the mortal self-disgust and coldly disciplined distinction of the traditional dandy, he inspires an irrepressible element of sympathy, even though the fatal impasse of his way of life is clearly shown. In this respect, Fromentin has combined elements of both sincerity and cynicism in the characterization of Olivier, a complex juxtaposition reminiscent of the masterful interpretations of this theme by Musset, Gautier and Baudelaire. (p. xvi)

[Augustin owes something] to the heritage of Rastignac and Julien Sorel [characters, respectively, in Balzac's *Comédie humaine* and Stendhal's *Le rouge et le noir*], without attaining to such heights as these. At times, he seems rather too abstract and is almost insufferably right at every turn; yet the author appears reluctant to admit that this personality may have certain relatively unattractive aspects. Augustin, it is true, is shown to be not so much 'un grand homme' as 'une grande volonté'.... His is clearly a 'nature incomplète'.... But in the manuscript, the author came nearer to a more complex characterization for Augustin, in the following remark made by Dominique: 'J'admire Augustin qui, sans illusion, est devenu pour beaucoup de nos contemporains, un point de mire: mais je ne l'envie pas'.... This variant, however, and its many interesting implications, were omitted from the text, where Augustin, with his remarkable determination and unflagging will-power, presents an almost over-obvious contrast to Olivier's way of life. (p. xviii)

The unrequited love of Julie for Olivier emerges as a reversed parallel situation to that of Dominique. Julie is also doomed to the non-fulfilment of her desires, but again like Dominique, refuses to succumb to a Romantic catastrophe. She too reaches only a partial reconciliation with reality and, doomed to 'de longs jours misérables' ..., finds consolation in nature, returning from a walk during her convalescence, 'ranimée, rien que pour avoir respiré la senteur des chênes'.... (p. xix)

The gradual evolution of **Dominique** represents the implementation of one of the principal lessons contained in the novel, namely, the rejection of the follies and extravagances characteristic of the first Romantic generation. The transmutation of Olivier's letter at the end of Chapter II, from the setting of a monastic retirement, according to the more Romantic manuscript version, to that of the stark loneliness of his return home, as described in the final text ..., may perhaps give some indication of the author's intention in this respect. Yet, with Fromentin, as with many others who began by admiring Hugo and the early Romantics, traces of this initial affiliation remained beneath the surface.... In the characterization of Dominique, 'épris de perfection' ..., and with 'des élans forcenés vers les hauts sommets de l'idéal' ..., there is a Romantic idealism representing the highest spiritual aspirations, the non-fulfilment of which makes the acceptance of everyday reality, at best, a compromise saddened by regrets. (pp. xx-xxi)

Dominique's withdrawal has been seen by some readers as representing the solidity of bourgeois honour. Others have seen it as a self-righteous glorification of life in a provincial backwater.... (p. xxi)

All these interpretations, and more, are possible. Are we, for instance, to think of the fate of Dominique as representing a trial of strength or a lack of courage? Does it reveal a deep inner fulfilment or a cowardly desertion ... or both? The evidence of the manuscript and of the previous works and letters of Fromentin would tend to confirm that, in the elegiac nostalgia of Dominique's withdrawal, there are both negative and positive aspects: negative in the sense that a premature retirement of this kind is an admission of mediocrity, a shrinking back from the full-scale challenge of life; positive in the sense that a more circumscribed existence can lead to a higher degree of self-fulfilment within the framework of personal limitations. (pp. xxi-xxii)

It is clear that, for Fromentin, withdrawal did not necessarily involve any mental sclerosis. On the contrary, it implied ideally a vital and active existence within a narrow and limited framework. Previously, in **Une Année dans le Sahel,** he had described a way of life in which the impingement of external circumstances is reduced to a minimum, with repetition and routine playing a major part and even being somewhat glorified. Habit, which was anathema to most nineteenth-century writers, because of its tendency to foster an attitude of supine submission, nevertheless forms a central part of Fromentin's approach to withdrawal, despite his awareness of the moribund monotony of provincial life in the La Rochelle of his youth.... [The] functions of habit are implicit in many different contexts of **Dominique**. The concept of continuity, as abstracting from the succession of events all that appears to be most essential and meaningful, is fundamental to the fusion of memory and habit which takes place in the mind of the hero after the idyllic holiday at Les Trembles:

> ... cette vie de réminiscences et de passions, tout entière calquée sur d'anciennes habitudes, reprise à ses origines et renouvelée par des sensations d'un autre âge, ces deux mois de rêve, en un mot....

The emotions of Dominique, on leaving Les Trembles with Madeleine, are all the more deeply felt because they represent an almost exact replica of his earlier farewell when leaving, as a boy, for Ormesson. These memories combine with his present experiences, making the 'sentiments nouveaux ... bien autrement poignants'.... So far from finding, like Proust, with whom in other respects he has so much in common, that the operation of one's sensibility is facilitated by the 'cessation momentanée de l'Habitude', Fromentin maintained that sensations and experiences, when repeated, take on a new depth, like a theme which takes on a fuller meaning with each different variation. In a sense, this principle is symbolized by the inscriptions on the walls of Dominique's study, some of which consist of elementary geometrical figures, repeated with one or two changes of detail, modifying the pattern without altering the basic form of the design.... (pp. xxiii-xxiv)

For Fromentin, then, the initial creation of boundaries, in both work and life, did not necessarily imply any limitation in the final results and could, on the contrary, be most fruitful. These active potentialities in a life of withdrawal were just as real to him as the passive elements of escapism, though not perhaps so overtly presented. The manuscript, it is true, does suggest that, in retiring to Les Trembles, Dominique was responding to a 'cri vague de conscience' ..., an absolute value within himself, from which he could not depart in the interests of his own happiness and peace of mind. Again, in the manuscript, the author shows a very adult awareness of the concomitant elements present in the withdrawal of the hero: the fear of weakness and the realization of possible self-deception, stemming perhaps from 'un défaut de clairvoyance', or perhaps from 'un défaut de courage'. Fromentin had thus no complacent convictions as to the inherent virtue of such a withdrawal, but shows it rather as the necessary fulfilment of a deep, inner urge:

> Au reste, que ce soit illusion ou impuissance,
> qu'importe? puisque les résultats sont pareils.
> J'ai d'ailleurs obéi, sans me tromper, à une
> partie des nécessités qui résidaient au fond de
> mes origines. . . .

Had this complexity of approach been further developed, it might perhaps have disarmed those critics who found the subtle intangibility of the conclusion inadequate.

Linked with the theme of withdrawal and renunciation is, of course, the love-story of Dominique and Madeleine. . . . In relation to the love-story, as well as to the novel as a whole, Fromentin's work combines two tonalities, one major, one minor, suggesting poignant, haunting harmonies.

The gradual, hesitant beginnings of Dominique's adolescent love are most delicately described: his vague, indefinite longings, reminiscent of Chateaubriand's 'vague des passions'; his pre-Proustian sentimental receptivity acting as a prelude to falling in love; the growth of his love for Madeleine during her absence, or what Stendhal might have called the period of crystallization; the gradual emergence of Madeleine as the inaccessible idol of Romantic love, for whom the hero has an almost religious devotion. However, despite the dream-like qualities of Dominique's adolescent love and its later, more passionate and dramatic developments, many readers have been disappointed by the way in which it ends. Sainte-Beuve, for instance, complained of a sense of anti-climax in the behaviour of Dominique: 'Qu'avait-il à faire de souffler pendant des années le feu, pour se dérober et s'enfuir au moment où il voit la flamme?' From quite a different point of view, George Sand maintained that Fromentin needed to add 'quelques pages de plus entre le dernier adieu de Madeleine et le mariage de Dominique'. . . . So strongly did she feel on this question that she even advocated the inclusion of new material, the effect of which would have been to show the exasperation of the hero after parting with Madeleine, tantalized at having thrown away a unique opportunity in the false persuasion that renunciation represented strength, and at having 'agi comme un sot en n'agissant pas comme un maître'. . . . These suggestions were not, of course, adopted. They would have struck quite a false note in the context of Fromentin's light and delicate treatment of the love-story. (pp. xxiv-xxvi)

Yet, when set against the highest standards, the treatment of the love-story in **Dominique** is not entirely beyond criticism. The sense of anti-climax experienced by some readers might perhaps have been averted. It is true, of course, that the end is known in advance, but then some of the greatest tragic loves make this feeling of inevitability dramatic in itself, maintaining a razor-edge tension with the paradoxical illusion that the foreseen outcome may, even at the last moment, be reversed. The measure of their success is dependent on the intensity of the dramatic suspense, together with a careful presentation of how the foreseen end materializes. The first of these elements is

certainly present in Fromentin's love-story, where the tension and passion between the two central characters, particularly towards the end of the novel, is such that the reader is completely involved. The sense of anti-climax may possibly have its origin in the author's deliberate vagueness with regard to the *dénouement*. The position of Madeleine, for instance, has been unduly left out of account. So, too, has her attitude towards her husband. . . . (pp. xxvii-xxviii)

There is, furthermore, a need for some discussion of the real, not just the conventional problems involved in Dominique's love for Madeleine. The hero is clearly convinced that 'une faute tuerait Madeleine' . . . , and that this would mean both her death and his. Yet, of the many possible justifications for such an assumption, few are fully discussed in the novel. (p. xxviii)

Fromentin gives a delicate evocation of the voluptuous feeling of bitter-sweet experienced by the hero: the fascination exercised by the very impossibility of his love . . . and by the vertiginous thrill of hovering on the brink of disaster. . . . But the component elements in this feeling of 'âcre saveur' . . . , so cherished by Fromentin throughout his life, are not perhaps sufficiently analysed in the novel. The author might, for instance, have probed more deeply into the phenomenon of a subjective love, which depends for its existence on the very obstacles which stand in its way. . . . Again, if this impossible love is dependent for its very existence on the element of unattainability which originally inspired it, then it follows that effective possession would involve the destruction or defilement of that love. (pp. xxviii-xxix)

[Stylistically,] Fromentin sought to use words which, though in no sense strange or obscure, were normally associated with quite a different context and which, when transferred into their new surroundings, were immensely suggestive. This procedure . . . marks one of the most important respects in which the definitive text of **Dominique** has evolved from the original manuscript. The manuscript description of Ormesson, for instance, otherwise close in many respects to that in the text, contains no reference to its 'brouillards fiévreux' . . . , nor to its 'silence hargneux' . . . , phrases by which the text succeeds in conveying the sadness and monotony of Ormesson more effectively than by the factual statement, as made in the manuscript, that it was 'horriblement triste'. . . . Again, the manuscript account of Madeleine's room contains no reference to the 'étoffes de couleur sobre' . . . , or to the 'blancheur de l'effet . . . le plus recueilli'. . . . By means of this skilful interweaving of what Edmond Schérer described as 'un étrange contraste d'observation précise et de vagues contours', Fromentin succeeded in evoking those subjective impressions which so often perpetuate an experience in the memory. From this point of view, it is significant that most of his work was composed in retrospect since by writing from memory he claimed that he could achieve a balance, vital to his art, between precision and abstraction: precision, as recorded by his remarkably acute memory; abstraction, as evolved through the passage of time. (pp. xxxii-xxxiii)

Fromentin's technique comes close at times to that adopted by the Goncourt brothers, particularly in relation to the procedure commonly known as 'nominal syntax'. This procedure involves the use of a noun, where normal usage might have indicated an adjective or a verb; the noun, as a result, usurps the dominant position in the sentence and is made to suggest the desired impression.

Taking, first of all, the merging of adjectives into nouns, it may be said that, in the work of Fromentin, this technique involves the transference of an adjective from its position of secondary importance following the object which it qualifies, to the position of an abstract quality-noun dominating the phrase in which it appears. Thus, where one might have expected to find 'une statue blanche et inanimée', Fromentin instead has 'la blancheur inanimée d'une statue'. . . . (pp. xxxiii-xxxiv)

The full effect of this device may be seen by placing this fragment in its context. Dominique, having voluntarily exiled himself for some time from the world of Madeleine, suddenly returns to Nièvres on hearing that Julie is ill. In describing this return, Fromentin has faithfully retained the sequence of impressions in the exact order in which Dominique might have experienced them: getting down from the post-chaise in the dark, seeing first of all a blaze of lights and only identifying them afterwards, meeting some-one in the half-darkness of the hall and not realizing immediately that it was Madeleine herself. Even at this stage, the dominant impression experienced by the hero was one of whiteness, with Madeleine enveloped in 'la blancheur inanimée d'une statue'. Only gradually did his eye come to rest on the physical attributes of the heroine, as she clasped his hand. Fromentin's technique here is admirably suited to the suggestive effect of the passage, for two reasons. Firstly, the gradual unfolding of these impressions is a faithful reproduction of the order in which they would normally be experienced, and reflects a procedure vital to any form of art which seeks to enlist not merely the sympathy but also the collaboration of the percipient. Secondly, the quality is detached from the person or object which it describes and is given an independent existence—a technique which is an exact literary equivalent of the parallel device in Impressionist painting, whereby colour takes precedence over form. In both cases, the impressions are preserved with the utmost fidelity, from their first impact on the retina of the eye to their ultimate cerebral interpretation. (p. xxxiv)

The merging of verbs into nouns, equally a part of Fromentin's nominal syntax, takes the form of weakening the verb as much as possible and concentrating the main effect of the sentence into an abstract noun. In this way, it is possible to capture the most fleeting impressions, without interrupting their flow by the intrusion of any finite action. Thus, in describing Dominique's final return to Les Trembles, instead of 'des souvenirs tressaillirent en moi', Fromentin has 'il y eut en moi un tressaillement de souvenirs' . . . , a device by which the essentially passive nature of the experience can be more effectively conveyed.

This technique, whereby action-nouns can be introduced by 'avoir', has the advantage of enabling them to be used in the plural and, as a result, is particularly valuable in conveying lingering impressions. The description of the Seine, in the novel, owes much to this method, in the sentence which begins: 'La rivière avait des frissons de lumière qui la blanchissaient'. . . . The use of the plural here conveys an effect of prolonged shimmering and provides an admirable setting for the touch of colour contained in the final verb. (p. xxxv)

'L'originalité', Fromentin once wrote to his father, 'consiste moins dans le choix du sujet que dans la manière dont on l'interprète'. . . . In these words he might almost have been describing his own achievement in *Dominique,* for he brought to the age-old themes of the personal novel an individuality of treatment which was quite remarkable. The essence of his originality may be seen to lie in his evocative, suggestive art, and

his power to convey, by means of a few well-chosen touches, the inner moods of the characters. . . . (p. xxxix)

[For Fromentin,] the artistic rendering of subjective impressions reflects the physical sensations on which they were based. Synaesthetic transpositions, in the sense of analogies between one kind of physical experience and another, are not so common in *Dominique* as those between physical experiences and their mental attributes. In fact, the juxtaposition of the physical and the mental, the concrete and the abstract, is central to Fromentin's sensibility. . . . Physical sensations are evoked in *Dominique* together with their mental connotations, as for instance, the bitter-sweet reaction produced in the hero by the changing aspects of nature, 'tant de sensations dont j'étais traversé, délicieusement blessé dans tout mon être'. . . . Conversely, mental states in the novel are frequently suggested by means of associated physical sensations: Madeleine's wedding, for instance, is connected in Dominique's mind with a vivid memory of the acute physical pain which he experienced at the time, and which lingered on 'comme la trace d'inguérissables piqûres'. . . . Thus, not only was the author endowed with an unusually acute sensitivity, alert to physical impressions of which others were unaware; he was also immensely receptive to the subjective reactions thus stimulated in his own inner world:

> . . . je condensais, je concentrais, je forçais à
> ne plus jamais s'échapper, ce monde ailé, sub-
> til, de visions et d'odeurs, de bruit et
> d'images. . . .

This combination of dream and reality forms the very essence of *Dominique,* effecting what has been well described as 'cette continuelle correspondance entre le monde extérieur et les sentiments'. The physical sensation of touch, for example, is used to convey a deep union between the two lovers in the shawl scene. . . . 'Une odeur dit tout' . . . , as Fromentin himself observed, and this is exemplified in many different contexts throughout the novel, ranging from the 'odeurs de goudron' . . . associated with Ormesson, to the 'odeur exotique' . . . which forms so essential a part of Madeleine's charm. . . . [Fromentin's treatment of sound impressions in the work is also brilliant.] Even the background of silence takes on a certain resonance, against which sounds are echoed and re-echoed in their infinite complexity, forming 'un monde incalculable de rêveries'. . . . Indeed, the blending of sounds and inner harmonies forms so integral a part of the novel, that the final analogy of the blackbirds bringing the symphony to a close is particularly appropriate. . . . Above all, however, it is the sense of sight which emerges, in the work of Fromentin, as a means of opening up new horizons. . . . [The] juxtaposition of the visual and the mental recurs constantly throughout his work. In *Dominique,* for example, sunset is shown as invading the hero's room 'comme un flot de vie'. . . . Again, in the boat scene, the light of the noonday sun seems to produce a state of trance in the central characters, 'éblouis de lumière, privés de conscience . . .'. Indeed, such was the intensity of Fromentin's sense of sight that the praise which he formulated for Flaubert's *Salammbô* might equally well be applied in his own case, since he too was not merely 'un grand peintre', but also 'un grand *visionnaire,* car comment appeler celui qui crée des réalités si vives avec ses rêves et qui nous y fait croire?' (pp. xxxix-xli)

The achievement of Fromentin in *Dominique* has, on the whole, been rather unsatisfactorily related to the general literary trends of the nineteenth century. He has been thought of variously as a Romantic, a post-Romantic, a 'néo-classique' and a 'classique rajeuni', to mention only a few examples. Such classifications are of doubtful value, since though each one is valid, in that it describes individual elements in Fromentin's work, not one of these classifications conveys his achievement as a whole. (p. xliii)

[The] union between the outer and the inner world forms the basic pattern of the structure of *Dominique*. Such are the suggestive powers of the sensations which Fromentin evokes in his novel that, in their highest form, they seem to have the power to transport him beyond the bounds of external reality. The hero recalls, for instance, that at Les Trembles, during his childhood, he would sometimes ride on top of a hay-cart. There, lying flat on the hay, swayed by the movement of the cart, he would gaze out at the immensity of the wide, open countryside, all the more immense for being viewed from a greater height than usual. At times, this sense of vastness became so intensified that he was momentarily carried into another world. . . . (pp. xliii-xliv)

This fusion of the real and the imaginary has far-reaching consequences in the work of Fromentin. It underlies, first of all, his concept of affective memory. Dominique, like the author of the novel, was endowed with 'je ne sais quelle mémoire spéciale assez peu sensible aux faits, mais d'une aptitude singulière à se pénétrer des impressions' . . . , an attribute which suggests certain very striking analogies with Proust. Many of these parallels are discernible in Fromentin's novel: the power of 'une odeur subtile' . . . , for example, to evoke the memory of Madeleine during her absence with 'une lucidité surprenante' . . . , a sense of clarity and certainty not unlike that later described in *A la recherche du temps perdu*; the effortless, or as Proust would say, involuntary recollection of such little touches as the sound of Madeleine's voice, or her habit of twisting her hair; the revelation of a fuller perception of reality than at the time of the original experience, by means of new impressions hitherto unsuspected, 'impressions dont la nouveauté . . . paraissait exquise'. . . . For Fromentin, as also for Proust and many other writers concerned with the concept of affective memory, the recall of a physical sensation can open up new horizons for the imagination by playing on things absent or past, while, at the same time, the sensation itself is given a new freshness and vitality by being experienced in the present. (pp. xliv-xlv)

Despite [the] many analogies between Proust and Fromentin, it should, however, be pointed out that certain differences are also noteworthy in relation to their treatment of the concept of affective memory. It is, for instance, important that the celebrated distinction between the 'mémoire volontaire' and the 'mémoire involontaire' in the work of Proust does not have the same significance in the work of Fromentin. The author of *Dominique* did not find the 'mémoire volontaire' so unsatisfactory as did his illustrious successor. The signs and inscriptions on the walls of the hero's study, with sensations and impressions condensed into symbols, were effortlessly interpreted by him, 'comme s'il n'eût fait que traduire en paroles les mémoires chiffrés'. . . . Fromentin even goes so far as to suggest a conscious preparation of future memories, in the context of Dominique's determination to retain every detail of the idyllic holiday at Les Trembles. (p. xlvi)

Fromentin does not develop as fully as Proust the conquest of time in this context. The invasion by the past on the present, 'jusqu'à faire empiéter le passé sur le présent', is central to the Proustian discovery. For Fromentin, the point of emphasis

is entirely different: so far from the past invading the present, the percipient is nearly always transported back to a moment in the past—to Algiers, for example, or to a childhood environment, as in *Dominique*, by means of what the hero describes as 'réminiscences qui ont la puissance certaine de me rajeunir au point de me rendre enfant'. . . . The whole of Proust's attempt is to re-create the sense of immediacy in a recurrent impression, complete with its entire initial impact, and with time destroyed. Fromentin, on the other hand, presents his recollected impressions from a distance, simplified and strengthened by their long duration: 'Le temps les fortifie, la distance peut les prolonger indéfiniment sans les rompre'. . . . Thus, although Fromentin's memories, like those of Proust, are sharply recalled, they are set within the framework of time and not outside it. Essentially, then, these two approaches towards the concept of affective memory, although strikingly similar in many respects, differ in that for Proust the result is the conquest of time, and for Fromentin a resigned acceptance of its passing.

Fromentin's highly individual co-ordination of the physical and the extra-physical . . . also made him particularly well suited to treat the problem of adolescence in the personal novel. The complex theme of adolescence . . . presents many difficulties: all too often, youth is portrayed as viewed through adult eyes and with a consequent failure to re-create the characteristically turbulent emotions in all their spontaneity. Few before Fromentin had gone so far in paving the way for the later flowering of the French adolescent novel, and indeed this may well be one of the reasons for the particularly high esteem in which *Dominique* was held by the youth of the nineteen-twenties. Fromentin had captured something of the adolescent dream-world, in a fusion of acute sensibility and mental awareness, thus depicting the brief encounter of youthful feeling and adult maturity. (pp. xlvi-xlvii)

Finally, it should be pointed out that the close juxtaposition of the real and the imaginary can be traced back, in the case of Fromentin, to the very essence of his creative powers. Throughout his work, he has shown that, although physical sensations were of cardinal importance for him, frequently they were not enough in themselves and needed to be completed by a fuller mental awareness involving the entire personality, both body and mind. Fromentin, a self-avowed 'voluptueux en fait de sensations' . . . , was able to examine the subjective enjoyment of certain emotions with the detachment of a dispassionate observer, in a way reminiscent of Baudelaire's 'extase *faite de volupté et de connaissance*'. . . . In the context of *Dominique*, the lapse of time between the original experiences and their ultimate expression in the novel, enabled the author to reduce his own direct emotional involvement and, at the same time, to allow his imagination to work in a way which was to be immensely stimulating for his creative art. Fromentin, in other words, based his novel not so much on real emotions, which might have impeded his creativity, as on emotions experienced in the imagination. (pp. xlviii-xlix)

A similar fusion of feeling and thought is at the basis of Fromentin's concept of inspiration. . . . [In the] manuscript folios, Fromentin describes his moments of creative vision, his 'jours de vitalité particulière'. . . . These supreme pinnacles of his existence are a counterpart of the 'grands jours de soleil' described by Flaubert, or of the 'beaux jours de l'esprit' experienced by Baudelaire, during which 'les sens plus attentifs perçoivent des sensations plus retentissantes'. . . . At such times as these, the author, speaking through Dominique, feels his vitality so intensified that everything which he perceives seems to hold delight and meaning for him, striking his senses more strongly and bringing in its wake a new association of ideas. Such moments represent the height of creative power, appealing to man in his entirety, to his sensibility and to his intellect. . . . (pp. xlix-l)

Even in the earlier of the two manuscript versions, where the author describes his moods in a somewhat exaggerated Romantic terminology, the essential characteristic of these moments of creative vision appears to be a co-ordination between the processes of feeling and of thought:

> Exister c'était la demi-mort; en avoir la conscience /vive/ ardente, émue; . . . voilà qui me représentait . . . /un/ idéal de plénitude et la . . . /perfection/ du bonheur. . . .

'Vivre et me sentir vivre, être et me souvenir' . . . : this blending of sensation and awareness, which is central to Fromentin's inspiration, also underlies his whole achievement in suggestive art. He has, in the words of Banville, united 'le Visible et l'Invisible'. (pp. l-li)

> *Barbara Wright, in an introduction to* Dominique *by Eugène Fromentin, edited by Barbara Wright, Basil Blackwell, 1965, pp. v-li.*

## ROLAND BARTHES  (essay date 1971)

[*A French critic, essayist, and autobiographer, Barthes is considered a leading exponent of the French* la nouvelle critique *(new criticism) and one of the major critics of the twentieth century. His studies in semiology and literary analysis, such as the influential* S/Z, *ushered structuralism to the forefront of French intellectual thought in the 1960s.* Le degré zero de l'écriture *(Writing Degree Zero),* Barthes's most seminal work, outraged many prominent French academicians. In it Barthes presented his concept of* écriture, *the idea that the text has a meaning independent of, and possibly different from, the author's intentions. Contending that a completely objective style of writing (zero-degree writing) was the most desirable, Barthes urged that the reader and the critic see a text as a series of symbols that combine to form the meaning of the literary work. Critics have also praised Barthes's later works, in which he studies cultural phenomena using a semiological approach. The essay excerpted below, in which Barthes proposes to "draw from the text* [*of* Dominique] *at least all the polysemy it can yield," exemplifies this approach. The reactionary ideology of* Dominique *serves as the focus of Barthes's analysis, for he describes the novel as a "backward-looking" work and its hero as a "petty exploiter" of the peasantry. This essay was written in 1971 and first published as the preface to an Italian translation of* Dominique. *Barthes subsequently reissued these remarks in French in* Nouveaux essais critiques.]

[*Dominique* is] a punctilious novel, in which we recognize the founding values of a so-called bourgeois ideology, subsumed under an idealist psychology of the subject. This subject fills the whole book, which derives from him its unity, its continuity, its revelation; for convenience's sake, he says I, mingling—like every subject of bourgeois culture—his discourse and his consciousness, priding himself on this confusion under the name of *authenticity* (*Dominique*'s form is a "confession"); furnished with a transparent discourse and a consciousness without secrets, the subject can analyze himself at length: he has no unconscious, only recollections: memory is the sole form of dream known to French literature of this period; and even this memory is always "constructed": it is not an association, an irruption (as it will be in Proust), but a recall (yet

in Fromentin—and this is one of his charms—anecdotal reconstruction of the incident is often overwhelmed by the insistent, effusive recollection of a moment, a place). This pure subject lives in a world without triviality: everyday objects exist for him only if they can belong to a scene, a "composition"; they never have an instrumental existence, still less do they transcend such instrumentality to disturb the thinking subject, as will happen in later novels (Fromentin, nonetheless, would have been capable of trivial inventions: witness that bouquet of rhododendrons, their roots wrapped in wet cloth, absurd gift from the future husband to his young fiancée). Finally, according to standard classical psychology, every one of the subject's adventures must have a meaning, which is generally the way in which it comes to an end: *Dominique* involves a moral lesson, a so-called lesson in wisdom: repose is one of the rare possible felicities, one must have wit to limit oneself, romantic daydreams are blameworthy, etc.: the pure subject ends by prudently exploiting his lands and his peasants. Such is more or less what we might call *Dominique*'s ideological dossier. . . . (pp. 91-2)

This dossier is rather grim, but fortunately that is not all there is to *Dominique*. . . . [By] virtue of the very ambiguity of all writing, this ideological text includes certain interstices; perhaps it is possible to remodel this great idealist novel in a more material, more materialistic fashion: let us draw from the text at least all the polysemy it can yield. (pp. 92-3)

Even more than its "subject," a fiction's site can be its truth, because it is at the level of the site (scenes, odors, breezes, coenesthesias, weather) that the signifier is most readily articulated: the site may well be the figure of desire, without which there can be no text. In this regard, *Dominique* is not a love story but a novel of the Countryside. Here the Countryside is not only a setting (occasion of descriptions which doubtless constitute the most penetrating, the most modern element in the book) but the object of a passion ("what I can call my passion for the countryside," the narrator says: and if he permits himself to speak in this way, it is because it is really a passion which is involved, in the amorous sense of the word). The passion for the Countryside gives the discourse its basic metaphor, the autumn, in which can be read at once the melancholy of a character, the despair of an impossible love, the resignation the hero imposes on himself, and the docility of a life which, the storm once past, flows infallibly toward winter, toward death; it also gives the discourse its metonymies, i.e., certain cultural links so well known, so sure of their effect, that the Countryside becomes in a sense the obligatory site of certain identifications: first of all, the Countryside is Love, the adolescent crisis (associated, in how many novels, with the summer vacation, with youth in the provinces): a link favored by the metaphoric analogy of spring and desire, of sap and seminal liquor, of vegetal efflorescence and pubertal explosion (this is how we read the adolescent Dominique's wild excursion to the vicinity of his school town, one April Thursday); Fromentin has exploited this cultural link quite thoroughly: the Countryside is for his hero Love's eidetic site: a space eternally fated to contract and reabsorb him. Next, the Countryside is Memory, the place where there occurs a certain ponderation of time, a delicious (or painful) heeding of recollection; and insofar as the Countryside is also (and sometimes chiefly) the place of residence, a room there becomes a kind of temple of remembrance. Dominique, by a thousand notches and inscriptions, here practices "that mania for dates, figures, symbols, hieroglyphs" which makes Les Trembles into a tomb covered with commemorative seals. Lastly, the Countryside is Narrative; in it we can speak without a time limit, we confide our-selves to it, we confess to it; insofar as Nature is reputed to be silent, nocturnal (at least, in that post-romanticism to which Fromentin belongs), it is the neutral substance out of which can rise a pure, infinite discourse. Site of meaning, the Coun-tryside is opposed to the City, site of noise; we know how much, and how bitterly, in *Dominique,* the City is discredited; Paris is a producer of *noise,* in the cybernetic sense of the word: when Dominique visits the capital, the meaning of his love, of his failure, of his perserverance, is jammed; in contrast to which the Countryside constitutes an intelligible space where life can be read in the form of a destiny. This may be why the Countryside, more than Love, is the real "subject" of *Do-minique:* in the Countryside we understand why we live, why we love, why we fail (or rather, we resolve to understand nothing of all this, ever, but this very resolution soothes us like a supreme act of intelligence); we take refuge in it as in the maternal bosom, which is also death's embrace: Dominique returns to Les Trembles on the same disordered impulse which leads the gangster in [William Riley Burnett's] *The Asphalt Jungle* to escape the city and come to die at the gate of the country house he had once started from. Curiously, the love story Fromentin tells may leave us cold; but his desire for the countryside touches us: Les Trembles, Villeneuve at night, make us envious. (pp. 93-5)

*Dominique* is a reactionary novel: the Second Empire is that moment of French history when a major industrial capitalism developed with the violence of a conflagration; in this irre-sistible movement, the Countryside, whatever electoral con-tribution its peasants made to Napoleonic fascism, could only represent an already anachronistic site: refuge, dream, aso-ciality, depoliticization, here a whole falling off of History was transformed into an ideological value. *Dominique* stages in a very direct way (though through an indirect language) all the misfits of the great capitalist promotion, summoned, in order to survive, to transform into a glorious solitude the abandon-ment in which History leaves them ("I was alone, last of my race, last of my rank," the hero says).... Olivier, the pure aristocrat, ends by committing suicide, or, what is still more symbolic, by disfiguring himself (he even bungles his suicide: the aristocracy is discountenanced); and Dominique, also an aristocrat, flees the City (joint emblem of worldliness, finance, and power), and decays to the point of becoming a gentleman-farmer, i.e., a petty exploiter: a decay which the entire novel is concerned to consecrate under the name of wisdom, pru-dence, obedience—*sagesse,* which we must not forget consists of exploiting one's lands and one's workmen thoroughly; *sa-gesse* is exploitation without expansion. It follows that Do-minique de Bray's social position is at once moral and reac-tionary, sublimated in the features of a benevolent patriarchy: the husband is an idle man, he hunts and novelizes his mem-ories; the wife keeps the accounts; he strolls among the hired laborers, bent at their task and bending even lower to greet the master; her task is to purify property by distributions of be-nevolence ("She kept the keys of the pharmacy, of the linen closet, of the woodshed, the vine shoots," etc.): a complex association: on one side the book (the novel) and exploitation; on the other the books (of accounts) and charity, "all this quite simply, not even as a servitude, but as a duty of position, of fortune and of birth." The "simplicity" which the first narrator (who is more or less Fromentin himself) attributes to the lan-guage of the second is obviously no more than the cultural artifice by which it is possible to naturalize class behavior; this theatrical "simplicity" (theatrical because we are *told it*) is like the varnish under which are assembled the rituals of cul-

ture: the practice of the Arts (painting, music, poetry serve as references for Dominique's great love) and the style of inter-locution (the characters speak to each other in that strange language which we might call "Jansenist style," whose phrases are the product—whatever the object to which they are applied, love, philosophy, psychology—of Latin composition assign-ments and religious tracts; for instance: "withdraw into the effacement of one's province," which is a confessor's style). The high language is not merely a way of sublimating the materiality of human relations; it creates these relations them-selves: all of Dominique's love for Madeleine results from the anterior Book; this is a familiar theme of the literature of love, ever since Dante made the passion of Paolo and Francesca depend on that of Lancelot and Guinevere; Dominique is amazed to find his story in the book of others; he does not know that that is where it comes from. (pp. 95-7)

*Dominique* is a novel without sex (the logic of the signifier says that this absence is already inscribed in the ambiguity of the name which gives the book its title: Dominique is a double name: masculine and feminine); everything builds up, occurs, and concludes *outside the skin;* in the course of the story, there are only two moments of physical contact, and we can imagine what power of combustion they draw from the sensuously void milieu in which they intervene: Madeleine, engaged to Mon-sieur de Nièvres, rests "her two ungloved hands in the count's".... : here is the entire conjugal relationship; as for the adulterous relationship (which is not fulfilled), it produces only a kiss, the one which Madeleine grants and withdraws from the narrator before leaving him forever: a whole life, a whole novel for one kiss: here sex is subjected to a *parsimoni-ous* economy.

Blurred, decentered, sexuality goes elsewhere. Where? into emotivity, which can legally produce corporeal deflections. Castrated by morality, the man of this world (which is, by and large, the bourgeois romantic world), the male, is entitled to attitudes ordinarily reputed to be feminine: he falls to his knees (before the avenging, castrating woman, whose hand is phal-licly raised in a gesture of intimidation), he faints ("I fell headlong to the floor"). Once sex is debarred, physiology becomes luxuriant; two legal (because cultural) activities be-come the field of erotic explosion: music (whose effects are always described excessively, as if what was involved was an orgasm ("Madeleine listened, panting . . .") and excursions (i.e., Nature: Dominique's solitary strolls, the horseback rides of Dominique and Madeleine); we might well add to these two activities, experienced in the mode of nervous erethism, a final substitute, and a worthy one: writing itself, or at least—since the period did not accept the modern distinction between speech and writing—utterance: whatever the oratorical discipline, it is certainly sexual disturbance which passes into the poetic mania of the young Dominique and into the confession of the adult man who recalls and is moved: if there are two narrators in this novel, it is because, in a sense, *expressive practice,* a substitute for unhappy, disappointed erotic activity, must be distinguished from the simple literary discourse which is sub-sumed by the second narrator (the first's confessor and the book's author).

In this novel there is a last transfer of the body: the desperate masochism which governs the hero's entire discourse. This notion, fallen into the public domain, is increasingly abandoned by psychoanalysis, which cannot be content with its simplicity. If we retain the word here, it is precisely by reason of its cultural value (*Dominique* is a masochist novel, in a *stereotyped* fashion), and also because this notion is readily identified with the social theme of class disappointment, which we have mentioned . . . —what corresponds to the social frustration of a class (the aristocracy) which withdraws from power and buries itself *en famille* on its rural property is the doomed behaviour of the two lovers. . . .

Love, throughout this story, these pages, is, in fact, *constructed* according to a rigorously masochist economy: desire and frustration are united in it like the two parts of a sentence, necessary in proportion to the meaning it must have: love is born in the very perspective of its failure, it cannot be named (accede to recognition) except at the moment when it is acknowledged to be impossible: "If you knew how much I love you," Madeleine says; ". . . today I can confess it, since it is the forbidden word which separates us." Love, in this prim novel, is, in fact, an instrument of torture: it approaches, wounds, burns, but does not kill; its operative function is to *render infirm . . . ;* it is a deliberate mutilation inflicted within the very field of desire: "Madeleine is lost and I love her!" exclaims Dominique; we must read the opposite: I love Madeleine because she is lost: it is loss itself, in accordance with the old myth of Orpheus, which defines love.

The obsessional character of amorous passion (as it is described in Fromentin's book) determines the structure of the love story. This structure is composite, it combines (and this impurity perhaps defines the novel) two systems: a dramatic system and a ludic system. The dramatic system accommodates a structure of crisis; its model is organic (to be born, to live, to struggle, to die); born of the encounter of a virus and a terrain (puberty, the Countryside), passion is established, and pervades; after which, it confronts the obstacle (the beloved's marriage): this is the crisis, whose resolution is here death (renunciation, retreat); in narrative terms, every dramatic structure has as its mainspring *suspense:* how will this end? Even if we know from the very first pages that "this will end badly" (and the narrator's masochism announces this to us continuously), we cannot keep ourselves from experiencing the uncertainties of an enigma (will they end by making love?). . . . In *Dominique,* the question attached to any love story, any drama of love, is doubled by an initial enigma: what is it, then, which could have turned Dominique into a man buried alive? Yet—and this is a rather complicated aspect of the novel of love—the dramatic structure is suspended at a certain moment and permits itself to be penetrated by a ludic structure: this is my name for any *motionless* structure articulated on the binary oscillation of repetition—as we find it described in the *vort/da* game of the Freudian child: once passion is established and blocked, it oscillates between desire and frustration, happiness and misery, purification and aggression, the love scene and the scene of jealousy, in a literally *interminable* manner: nothing warrants putting an end to this interplay of appeals and rejections. For the love story to end, the dramatic structure must regain the upper hand. In *Dominique,* it is the kiss, resolution of desire (and how elliptical a resolution!), which puts an end to the enigma: for henceforth we know *everything* about the two partners: the knowledge of the story has joined the knowledge of desire: the reader's "ego" is no longer split, there is nothing further to read, the novel can, the novel must, end.

In this backward-looking novel, what is most surprising is, finally, the language. . . . This language is always *indirect;* it names things only when it can make them attain to a high degree of abstraction, to distance them beneath a crushing generality. What Augustin does, for instance, reaches the dis-

course only in a form which escapes all identification: "His will alone, supported by a rare good sense, by a perfect rectitude, his will worked miracles"; what miracles? This is a very curious method; a touch more here and there and it would be quite modern . . . : does it not consist in making the referent unreal and, so to speak, formalizing to extremes the novel's psychologism (a procedure which might, with a little boldness, have been able to depsychologize the novel altogether)? Augustin's actions remaining buried under a carapace of allusions, the character ends by losing all corporality, reduced to an essence of Labor, of Will, etc.: Augustin is a cipher. Hence *Dominique* can be read with as much stupefaction as a medieval allegory; the allusiveness of the utterance is taken so far that the latter becomes obscure, amphigoric; we keep being told that Augustin is ambitious, but we are told very late and in passing what the field of his exploits is, as if it were of no concern to us to know whether he wants to succeed in literature, in the theater, or in politics. Technically, this distance is that of the *summary:* there is no end to summarizing under a generic label (Love, Passion, Labor, Will, Dignity, etc.) the multiplicity of attitudes, actions, and motives. The language tries to return to its so-called source, which is Essence, or, less philosophically, genre; and *Dominique* is in this indeed a novel of origins: by confining himself to abstraction, the narrator imposes on the language an origin which is not the Fact (a "realistic" view) but the Idea (an "idealistic" view). We understand better then, perhaps, the considerable ideological advantage of this continuously indirect language: it honors all the possible meanings of the word "correction": *Dominique* is a "correct" book: because it avoids any trivial representation (we never know what the characters eat, except when they are of the lower classes, vineyard laborers who are served roast goose to celebrate the harvest); because it respects the classical precepts of good literary style; because it affords nothing but a discreet effluvium of adultery: that of adultery evaded; finally, because all these rhetorical distances homologically reproduce a metaphysical hierarchy, the one which separates the soul from the body, it being understood that these two elements are separated so that their eventual encounter may constitute a dreadful subversion, a panic Offense: against taste, against morality, against language.

"I beg you," Augustin says to his pupil, "never believe those who tell you that the reasonable is the enemy of the beautiful, because it is the inseparable friend of justice and truth": this kind of sentence is virtually unintelligible today; or, if we prefer to give our astonishment a more cultural form: who could understand it, after having read Marx, Freud, Nietzsche, Mallarmé? The anachronism of *Dominique* is certain. Yet, inventorying some of the distances which compose it, I have not necessarily meant that we must not read this book; I wanted, quite the contrary, by marking out the lineaments of a powerful network, somehow to liquidate the resistances which such a novel might provoke in a modern reader, so that there might then appear, during the actual reading—like the characters of a magic writing which, having been invisible, gradually become articulate under the effect of heat—the interstices of the ideological prison in which *Dominique* is held. This heat, producing an ultimately legible writing, is, or will be, that of our pleasure. There are in this novel many corners of pleasure, which are not necessarily distinct from the alienations we have indicated: a certain incantation, produced by the eloquence of the sentences, the voluptuous delicacy of the descriptions of the countryside, as penetrating as the pleasure we take in certain romantic paintings and, more generally, . . . the hallucinatory plenitude (I should go so far as to say: the eroticism) attached to every notion of withdrawal, of repose, of equilibrium; a conformist life is loathsome when we are in a waking state, i.e., when we are speaking the necessary language of values; but in moments of fatigue, of weakness, at the height of urban alienation or of the linguistic vertigo of human relations, a dream of bygones is not impossible: the life at Les Trembles. Then all things are inverted: *Dominique* seems to us a kind of illegal book: in it we discern the voice of a demon : a costly, culpable demon, since he invites us to idleness, to irresponsibility, to home; in a word, to *sagesse*. (pp. 98-104)

> Roland Barthes, *"Fromentin: 'Dominique',"* in his
> New Critical Essays, *translated by Richard Howard,*
> *Hill and Wang, 1980, pp. 91-104.*

## ROBERT LETHBRIDGE  (essay date 1979)

[*Lethbridge argues that Dominique's ambivalence regarding the life from which he has ostensibly withdrawn is less a reflection on Romanticism than a function of Fromentin's exploration of the conflict between the objectivity and subjectivity inherent in the* roman personnel, *or personal novel.*]

Fromentin's *Dominique* has provoked critical reaction framed largely within a single perspective: the novel has been measured against the imperatives of the *vraisemblable*. . . . Admirers and detractors . . . share a common tendency to judge the book according to the criteria of a reality outside, albeit reflected by, the consciousness of its central narrator. As *Dominique* is a notable representative of the 19th century *roman personnel*, its formal arrangement has certainly not gone unnoticed; but, considered as a traditional device to legitimize the story and shape the reader's response, the ironic distance obtained by juxtaposing the narrator's assertion of domestic contentment and the evidence which appears to contradict it, has been primarily discussed in the context of the hero's sincerity and the more general question of whether or not the book's explicit moral dimension makes it 'a farewell to Romanticism' [see excerpt above by G. J. Greshoff, 1961]. In other words, recognition of the importance of the *récit*'s structural organization does not alter the essentially mimetic status of *Dominique* as a fictional autobiography. The telling is thus seen to throw light, or alternatively ambiguous shade, on what is told. The aim of the present essay will be to invert such a relationship between narration and narrative to suggest the ways in which the tale itself, its characters, events and descriptions, dramatize the problematic nature of the form. It is clear, for example, that the novel's diversified perspectives create an ironic gap which is not the privilege of Fromentin's readers alone; for it is precisely the tension between subjective and objective perspectives, between self-expression and self-knowledge, which is, on a fictional level, at the heart of the protagonist's personal crisis. The novel's narrative strategies articulate both the distancing procedures affording a critical view of self and the erosion of critical distance in the process of self-reflection. As Fromentin explained to George Sand, 'le livre, en tant que livre, est un embryon'. For, in many ways, *Dominique* is less a static self-portrait retrospectively composed than a dynamic exploration of its own genesis.

We know that Fromentin himself was acutely aware of the problematic nature of the *roman personnel* and of the confessional mode he would adopt for *Dominique*. In his analysis of the work of Gustave Drouineau, the risks inherent in the genre are clearly underlined: 'le livre peut être des confessions. Qu'il en porte ou non le titre, il n'en sera pas moins le portrait de

l'auteur: portrait tantôt flatté, tantôt enlaidi, rarement sincère'. An avowed preference for a less direct self-portrait has prompted scholars to discern in a second type the formal model for *Dominique* itself:

> Il est d'autres livres qui, sans affecter la forme directe de la confidence avec le public, lui laissent entrevoir sous le masque de certains personnages, ou sous la fiction du conte, la physionomie morale, et les faits que l'auteur a par discrétion, par pudeur, ou par faux orgueil hésité à mettre à découvert.

'Il y a dans ces livres', Fromentin added, 'presqu'autant de vérité que dans les premiers, seulement elle est mieux dissimulée, et par conséquent moins facile à mettre à nu'. Nevertheless this did not eliminate the dangers of a compensatory enterprise motivated by vanity which would also undermine its claims to sincerity: 'N'y a-t-il pas dans le fait d'un homme qui écrit son histoire [. . . ] le plaisir que certaines gens éprouvent à essayer devant une glace l'effet d'un travestissement pittoresque, *et de caractère*, comme on dit?'. Placed alongside his later sceptical remarks on Rembrandt's 'rage de poser devant un miroir et de se peindre', this suggests, on Fromentin's part, a significant unease about the art of self-portraiture. (pp. 43-4)

Convinced of the relativisitic nature of truth and the synonymity of representation and interpretation, he is thus concerned above all with the problems of perception and point of view. And it is for this reason that aesthetic distance becomes a central preoccupation. As he argued in the 1874 Preface to *Un Eté dans le Sahara,* the artifice of the book's epistolary form afforded a paradoxically more authentic sense of reality than a more spontaneous account of his travels. . . . (p. 45)

At the same time, it is evident that Fromentin's prolonged meditation on self-expression is inseparable from his own anguished quest for self-reflection. Writing about *Une Année dans le Sahel* and *Un Eté dans le Sahara* at almost twenty years' distance, he makes the crucial point that it is less the portrait of himself as he then was than the 'certaine manière de voir' which assures a sense of permanence over the mutability of experience. . . .

It has sometimes been said that such immobility also forms 'the basis of his aesthetic ideal' [see C. B. West, Additional Bibliography]. But this is to fail to take account of the fact that, in turning to a literary mode, Fromentin perceived the possibility of realizing a *synthesis* of permanence and flux; painting, in his view, could not accommodate the latter: 'l'art n'est pas un récit, c'est uné expostion par la forme et par le fond d'une seule idée grande et belle'. Thus, in *Dominique,* he hoped to 'exprimer sous forme de livre une bonne partie de moi, la meilleure, qui ne trouvera jamais place dans les tableaux'. The earlier part of this oft-quoted response to George Sand's praise of the moral import of his novel is equally revealing: 'j'ai voulu me plaire, m'émouvoir encore avec des souvenirs, retrouver ma jeunesse à mesure que je m'en éloigne'; it not only outlines his hero's attempts to recreate the immediacy of his completed past from the vantage point of the shifting present, but is also an admission of the role of self-gratification in such self-reflection. So too, his remark that 'tout irait mieux, les hommes et les oeuvres, si on avait la chance de se bien connaître' advocates a self-conscious antidote to subjectivity which the fictional Dominique extends to his own narration. As we shall see, Fromentin's novel displays such a fascination with the processes of creative activity that it goes some way towards fulfilling his long-standing ambition to write a book whose subject would be 'comment se fait la production dans un cerveau'.

At one level evidence of such self-focusing is provided by the text's images of itself. . . . [One such image] is to be found in the geometrical patterns on the walls of Dominique's study:

> Ailleurs il y avait seulement une figure géométrique élémentaire. Au-dessous, la même figure était reproduite, mais avec un ou deux traits de plus qui en modifiaient le sens sans en changer le principe, et la figure arrivait ainsi, et en se répétant avec des modifications nouvelles, à des significations singulières qui impliquaient le triangle ou le cercle original, mais avec des résultats tout différents. . . .

Described as 'ce travail de réflexion sur l'identité humaine dans le progrès' . . . , such a search for an unchanging essence will receive its ultimate pragmatic expression in the character's glorification of habit within the perennial rituals of the seasons; but 'ces allégories dont le sens n'était pas impossible à deviner' also represent an idealized formal construction (with its triangular plot and circular structure) reconciling permanence and change. (pp. 45-7)

*Dominique* not only adopts a confessional mode as a well-tried literary device, but also elaborates the theme of confiding in its own right. . . . During the summer at les Trembles, Dominique shares with Madeleine 'comme une suite de confidences subtiles qui l'initiaient à ce que j'avais été, et l'amenaient à comprendre ce que j'étais' . . . , clearly not unaware of the ambiguity of the enterprise: 'j'y cédais assez ingénument pour n'avoir aucun reproche à me faire, si tant est qu'il y eût là la moindre apparence de séduction; mais que ce fût innocemment ou non, j'y cédais'. . . . The 'temptations' of the confessional mode are thereby made explicit; for while the narrative strives to create a distanced view of self as seen by others, the manipulative powers of the *récit* reduce this distance in the interests of an indulgent hearing, thus transforming an alienated image of self into a confirming self-reflection.

This is illustrated in almost exemplary fashion by Fromentin's exploitation of what we may call the 'external narrator' who introduces Dominique's own confession. The opening pages of the novel set up a critical distance from the hero, inviting the reader to question his reliability and alerting us to the virtual impossiblity of distinguishing between rationalization and avowed sincerity. . . . The novel's prologue sees the 'external narrator' gradually abandoning his objective stance and gaining access to Dominique's inner life, both as it is recounted and experienced, even to the point of staying in the latter's room and falling asleep to the sounds 'dont l'enfance de Dominique avait été bercée'. . . . By the end of Dominique's *récit* the initial critical distance has been forfeited so completely that Fromentin's readers have consistently pointed to the resulting confusion of moral and intellectual perspectives as one of his book's principal weaknesses. This presupposes, of course, that the 'external narrator' is intended to represent a genuinely autonomous point of view; it is difficult to believe, however, that the quite extraordinary parallels between this figure and Dominique himself are either simply fortuitous or further evidence of imaginative poverty. . . . [The] affective memory is a particular privilege they share . . . ; the beauties of nature excite a common senstivity . . . , and their descriptions of landscape are identical in their stylistic effects. . . . It is hardly by chance

that what brings them together is the object of a quest, and Dominique's apology for the necessity 'de me substituer à vous' . . . to prevent its loss. His reaction to his friend's dispassionate assessment of his verse is equally significant: 'voilà le poète jugé, dit-il, et bien jugé, ni plus ni moins que par lui-même'. . . . For the 'external narrator' can be more profitably considered as an externalised version of the novel's central narrative *persona;* inscribed within the main body of the *récit* as a mere rhetorical presence, he thus functions as an unquestioning mirror for Dominique's images of himself, as the complicity which characterizes their evolving 'relationship' is an allegory of the ways in which a prolonged intimate view of self works against the capacity for judgement.

Conceived essentially as a 'témoin' . . . , the 'external narrator' thus assumes a role in the drama of self-contemplation located in the hero: 'une active et intense observation de lui-même, l'instinct de s'élever plus haut, toujours plus haut, et de se dominer en ne se perdant jamais de vue'. . . . Such a preoccupation can properly be described as narcissistic, as Augustin warns him, in what is undoubtedly one of the key passages of the novel:

> Si d'une faculté créatrice, éminemment spontanée et subtile, vous faites un sujet d'observations, si vous raffinez, si vous examinez, si la sensibilité ne vous suffit pas et qu'il vous faille encore en étudier le mécanisme, si le spectacle d'une âme émue est ce qui vous satisfait le plus dans l'émotion, si vous vous entourez de miroirs convergents pour en multiplier l'image à l'infini, si vous melez l'analyse humaine aux dons divins, si de sensible vous devenez sensuel, il n'y a pas de limites à de pareilles perversités, et, je vous en préviens, cela est très-grave. Il y dans l'antiquité une fable charmante qui se prête à beaucoup de sens et que je vous recommande. Narcisse devint amoureux de son image; il ne la quitta point des yeux, ne put la saisir et mourut de cette illusion même qui l'avait charmé. Pensez à cela, et quand il vous arrivera de vous apercevoir agissant, souffrant, aimant, vivant, si séduisant que soit le fantôme de vous-même, détournez-vous. . . .

The Narcissus myth serves as a matrix for a number of images and themes central to an understanding of Fromentin's novel; but also of its formal design. . . . (pp. 48-9)

Dominique's narrative gives to his own activities as a writer a significance which it would be a mistake to ignore. . . . [He] sees in the creative imagination an instrument of self-projection. Mirroring the 'deux hommes en Dominique' . . . , 'une double bibliothèque, l'une ancienne, l'autre entièrement moderne' . . . reflects this duality in the midst of the 'attestations de lui-même . . . which fill his study. . . . Withdrawal to this figurative chamber leads to a frenetic burst of self-expression: 'd'une haleine, sans me relire, presque sans hésiter, j'écrivis toute une série de choses inattendues, qui parurent me tomber du ciel' . . . ; and, in burning his manuscripts, he is aware of 'cette destruction d'une autre partie de moi-même'. . . . On the other hand, it is equally important that such activities do not escape critical irony. . . . Above all, as Augustin never fails to remind him, the compensatory pleasures of the imagination are a source of illusory self-indulgence. . . . (p. 50)

Dominique's own *récit* is similarly structured, alternating between self-projection and narrative distance. On the one hand it is composed of a system of mirrors in which he is reflected. The secondary characters, unfailingly condemned by Fromentin's critics for their lack of psychological depth, are, in a sense, *created* by the narrator as subject doubles who become the means by which he is himself revealed. Augustin and Olivier thus incarnate Dominique's opposing selves, and are often brought together for purely comparative purposes.... Similarly [the secondary characters] act as a commentary on Dominique's own emotional situation or articulate his feelings; at Madeleine's wedding, for example, Julie 'pâle comme une morte' bears witness to his 'réelle douleur physique' ..., while Olivier's remarks 'me dispensait presque d'un aveu, il avait établi que nous nous comprenions au sujet de M. de Nièvres'.... Dialogue is often simply dramatized interior monologue.... (p. 51)

At the opening of Chapter III [Dominique] is distanced from his own story to the extent of not only setting the scene and introducing its *dramatis personae*, but also viewing himself as protagonist: 'un campagnard qui s'éloigne un moment de son village, un écrivain mécontent de lui qui renonce à la manie d'écrire, et le pignon de sa maison natale figurant au début comme à la fin de son histoire' ...; he is 'le personnage ambigu que vous connaîtrez plus tard'.... Interpolated references to the 'aujourd'hui' of the narration..., subversion of his own reliability as 'l'ingénieuse erreur d'un coeur malade'..., or mention of 'mon imagination, habile à tout transformer' ..., all have an analagous function to the external narrator's initial ironic perspective. But in both cases, as the fiction progressively effaces a differentiated point of view, so the 'presence' of narrator and listener serves merely to reinforce the authority of the *récit* itself.

The possibility of breaking out of this circle of illusion is offered by a further use of the secondary characters. For the fact that they are only partial reflectors gives them the status of living warnings and moral exemplars. Their somewhat arbitrary entrances and exits, either in the flesh or by correspondence, effect a temporary shift in narrative focus in introducing the voice of guidance and judgement which disrupts the subjective discourse....

[Such a technique allows for irony to be] internalized through the dialectics of sympathetic self-appraisal and the critical gaze of others.... 'Le regard', indeed, is the most striking feature of the minor figures in Dominique's narrative; but he flees the harsh light of such examination which is a prerequisite for self-knowledge liberated from introspection.... For 'le don cruel d'assister à sa vie comme à un spectacle donné par un autre' ..., in alienating him from himself, simultaneously engenders the need to reveal himself to others in his renewed quest for self-definition.

To confide in Madeleine is thus to leave him 'plus sûr de moi dans tous les sens' ...; but this is only possible in the contextual permanence of Les Trembles. She can assume 'ce rôle extraordinaire de confidente et de sauveur' by virtue of 'l'inaltérable douceur de son regard, la parfaite égalité de ce caractère composé d'or maniable et d'acier, c'est à dire d'indulgence et de pure vertu, cette nature résistante et sans dureté, patiente, unie, toujours dans l'équilibre d'un lac abrité'.... Narcissus gazing at himself in the smooth surface of his sheltered pool enacts the archetypal drama of self-delusion in a world untroubled by consciousness, sexuality and mortality. Self-awareness fractures such a stable unified image of the self

and brings Dominique face to face with 'un ennemi inséparable, bien intime et positivement mortel: c'était moi-même'.... Structurally and thematically the book articulates this crisis of differentiation—between land and sea, immobility and flux, timelessness and temporality, past and present. (pp. 51-3)

Differentiation is explored [in the relationship between Dominique and Madeleine] essentially in terms of a crisis of sexual difference. The narrative *dédoublement* in the figures of Olivier and Augustin thus appears as a dysfunctional attempt to cope with such a threat to the hero's own identity. As the sixteen-year-old Narcissus ('at once boy and man') flees the nymph's sexuality which defines his own, so the adolescent and androgynous Dominique is torn between the self-reflecting hesitant sexuality of Olivier and the virility of Augustin..., when confronted by the reality of Madeleine. At the moment she steps into adulthood, he becomes aware of 'la distance énorme' between them. For she is the profanated image of himself..., 'le fantôme de ma propre jeunesse, vierge, voilée et disparue'.... 'Madeleine est perdue, et je l'aime!' ... speaks of an idealization as illusory as the childhood portrait conserved in his room.... Complicity dissolves to reveal 'un être nouveau, bizarre, incohérent, inexplicable et fugace, aigri, chagrin, blessant et ombrageux'.... Passion leaves Dominique unable to recognize himself: 'la première glace où je m'aperçus me montra la figure étrangement bouleversée d'un fantôme à peu près semblable à moi, que j'eus de la peine à reconnaître'.... Their relationship therefore consists of alternating attempts to escape her fearful presence or transform her into a passive mirror in which he can see himself reflected as he would like to be; for Madeleine's identity is a function of his own.... To close the distance between them ... by consummating their relationship is, as surely as for Narcissus, inextricably associated with death; as the mythical youth is certain that 'both of us will perish together, when this one life is destroyed', so Dominique knows this would be the ultimate desecration.... Renunciation means solitude, sterility and petrification. Narcissus' lament ('I am cut off in the flower of my youth') provides Dominique with an image of his life: 'comme les arbres de courte venue, je l'ai coupée en tête'....

As Augustin suggests, Dominique's activities as a writer are to be inserted in the same psycho-sexual drama played out in this myth. Self-expression in the privacy of his room becomes, as it were, the auto-erotic substitute to which he has recourse after critical encounters with Madeleine, 'absolument comme un homme attiré par je ne sais quelle irrésistible entreprise qui l'épouvante autant qu'elle le séduit'.... Described as a frenzied 'manie', writing offers him 'un moment de plénitude'..., 'un mystère plein de jouissances', which has a therapeutic function: 'ce fut comme un trop-plein qui sortit de mon coeur, et dont il était soulagé au fur et à mesure qu'il se désemplissait'...; 'à l'effervescence excitée par une production prompte, entraînante, presque irréfléchie, succéda un grand calme'.... It is significant in this respect that we are told Dominique's giving up this habit coincides with the birth of his first child.... [Self]-analysis is ... the source of creative impotence. Only in the imagination can Dominique find the language of idealized self-reflection 'pour briser cet horrible écrou du silence', ... which simultaneously reveals himself to be the source of his own illusion. As withdrawal from Madeleine leads him to solitude, so renouncing the possibility of mediation through self-expression condemns him to silence.... (pp. 53-5)

[It] should not be forgotten, however, that the *récit* itself brings the drama of self-expression to a successful conclusion. The actual telling of the story can, in many ways, be considered the major 'event' in Fromentin's novel. (p. 55)

The novel opens with Dominique (designated as the huntsmanlike Narcissus) in a state of post-narcissistic 'repos', in solitude and silence, momentarily at one with himself in every sense. Olivier's letter provides the incidental justification for the *récit* in so far as it confronts him with a past self seemingly negated. This (literally disfigured) image provokes the renewed self-absorption of his tale, and can thus be seen to have precisely the same function as his earlier creative efforts. Unlike these, however, in breaking out of hermetic self-contemplation, the *récit* can also accommodate the paralyzing disjunctions of such self-reflection. It is recounted 'sans déguisements' but also 'non sans émotion'; Augustin's warning, in any case undermined by his own emotional sterility, goes unheeded: we are indeed given a view of Dominique 'agissant, souffrant, aimant, vivant'.... Above all, the form of the *roman personnel* ensures the survival of a narrative voice differentiated from the narrator's experience in so far as it enables the latter to be viewed within an overall pattern of meaning. The visit to the lighthouse, for example, is first relived and then reassessed.... Composed largely of past moments recreated by the memory and given the status of a timeless immediacy, the *récit* simultaneously ascribes significance to the past, conceived dynamically in its coherent relationship to the narrative present. Its 'faisceau d'évidences' ... can thus be compared to the geometrical shapes evoked in the prologue. For the shaping of the story is the key to self-knowledge.

Dominique's *récit* also has an expiatory motivation similar to that of his earlier writing, and in particular the 'balayage de conscience' designed to liquidate 'ces innombrables péchés d'un autre âge'... : 'Je m'imposai la tâche de fouiller ce vieux répertoire de choses enfantines et de sensations à peine éveillées. Ce fut comme une sorte de confession générale, indulgente, mais ferme, sans aucun danger pour une conscience qui se juge'..., but published 'sans signature' and with 'une préface ingénieuse' which speaks otherwise. In an earlier version of the final pages of the novel, Fromentin imagined Dominique giving instructions to have the inscriptions on the walls of his study obliterated: 'Encore un nettoyage dit-il quand le vieux André eut reçu cet ordre—et le dernier reprit-il avec un sourire'. The text in its present form is far more ambiguous, referring simply to the shadows filling in the space of the narration and bringing it to a close:

> L'ombre envahissait l'intérieur poudreux et étouffé de la petite chambre où se terminait cette longue série d'évocations dont plus d'une avait été douloureuse. Des inscriptions des murailles, on ne distinguait presque plus rien. L'image extérieure et l'image intérieure pâlissaient donc en même temps, comme si tout ce passé ressuscité par hasard rentrait à la même minute, et pour n'en plus sortir, dans le vague effacement du soir et de l'oubli....

Instead of ending with an unequivocal statement of triumphant self-expression, the novel's moral imperatives dictate renewed reference to 'le déserteur' and silent self-effacement. Fromentin's hesitations over whether to make the *récit* a definitive purging or the rebirth of a creative spirit leave the reader almost as unsure as at the beginning: the socially integrated *persona* outside the *récit* may be just as much 'une illusion des autres et de lui-même' ... as the self projected within it. Such confusion is, in a sense, a consequence of the thematics of *fusion*

*with* which structure the novel. Mediation overcomes the disjunction of self and other in literally bringing Dominique and the 'external narrator' together after the story is told. So too for the reader (for whom the latter is a surrogate), the decreasing emotional distance tends to subordinate narration to narrative: 'le récit très-simple et trop peu romanesque qu'on lira tout à l'heure' ... becomes a fully-fledged Romantic novel. As George Sand observed: 'Du moment que Dominique raconte, on est tout à lui'. For Fromentin himself, no doubt, **Dominique** was a personal expiation and a private pleasure; his awareness of the duplicity of language..., the rationalization inherent in the confessional mode and the fallacy of self-portraiture, suggests however that moral absolutes and questions of sincerity have no place in the drama of subjectivity played out in his text. A liquidation of past illusions is necessarily the (re)creation of a fiction. Narcissus can project himself only within the confines of his own repeated self-absorption, in the illusory reflection which is his *raison d'être* and its negation. (pp. 56-8)

> *Robert Lethbridge, "Fromentin's 'Dominique' and the Art of Reflection," in* Essays in French Literature, *No. 16, November, 1979, pp. 43-61.*

**EMANUEL J. MICKEL, JR.** (essay date 1981)

[*Mickel provides a detailed analysis of Fromentin's presentation of character in* Dominique, *an area often regarded as a weakness in the novel.*]

In the introduction to her critical edition [of **Dominique** (see excerpt above, 1965)], Barbara Wright laments that Fromentin, in an effort to make the contrast between Augustin and Olivier more pronounced, initiated changes in the text which made both characters less interesting as human beings and more like cardboard figures with only one-dimensional personalities. The criticism pertains basically to the secondary personages, of course, and not to the principal character.

Part of the difficulty lies in the use of a first-person narrator who has the disadvantage of knowing only what he perceives of the other characters. The secondary narrator might have added another perspective and other information, but Fromentin really makes very little use of him, except for a few comments about Dominique himself. Not given the opportunity to know the other characters personally, he is unable to comment on them independently. The reader and the narrator know only as much as Dominique tells them.

A second factor in the weakness of the other characters is the intense focus of the book on the relationship between Dominique and Madeleine. Fromentin could have broadened the roles of the secondary characters and given their lives an independent interest or had them play a larger role in forming the reader's opinion concerning the love relationship between Dominique and Madeleine. However, they are limited to the incidental role which Dominique gives them.

Beyond this one must say that there is very little development of anyone's personality in the manner of the classic nineteenth-century novel. Fromentin scarcely explores the intellectual interests or personal tastes of his characters. Rather he uses a traditional psychology which examines personal reactions to the moral issues of the text. Fromentin's aesthetic values drew him away from the individualization which became so prominent in post-eighteenth-century thought. One can see this in his travel literature. He was not interested in portraying the anecdote and peculiar details which characterized the North African Arab, but rather sought to capture the essential quality of North Africa and the people by eliminating what he considered superficial detail. The same motivation caused him to look within his characters to seek the central axis of their moral natures.

Even if one grants this premise, Fromentin's character presentation strikes one as too prescriptive. He does not allow his characters the freedom of individual action. Instead of allowing his characters to reveal themselves through their actions, he has Dominique simply describe their natures to the reader. One is told that Mme Ceyssac is serious and pious. She followed the laws of church and state and loved *des choses surannés* ("old-fashioned things"). The only actions which allow her to demonstrate this character are her pleasure in learning that Olivier is from a respected noble family and her reception of Dominique when he is returning to Trembles after his final separation from Madeleine. Madame de Bray is treated in a similar way. The narrator portrays her as an attractive woman and an excellent mother and wife. She has a kind nature, is gracious, has a good head for figures, and is adept at managing the estate. Her presence is important for what it says about Dominique's current life. It helps to answer the question concerning his failure or success and does not really focus on her as a character in her own right. Only her scene with Olivier permits the reader to evaluate her by her actions. She argues for marriage as a means of making one's existence worthwhile, in that it makes one's life useful to others. One might accuse her here of a certain insensitivity in treating Olivier so harshly. However, this is not really her intent. One is not focusing on her personality. Her role in the scene is to bring out the ideas which the author considers vital to the text's meaning. As such she is not really in conflict with Olivier personally. The important thing is that he will react to the ideas which provoke a crisis in his own life.

Perhaps the least satisfactory character is Julie. Dominique scarcely tells us enough about her to give any indication of her nature. This was probably his intent. It is clear that she was an enigma to Dominique, as he refers to her as being sphinx-like. One learns that she loves Olivier, is easily hurt by his indifference to her, and that she is disturbed when Madeleine is married. But one has no idea what she is like and Dominique does not seem to know what she thinks or feels about Olivier beyond his belief that she loves him. The impossible romance between Julie and Olivier does not serve well as a balance or parallel for the main story. Julie's own personality and personal struggle require more attention and development. Her participation is too limited for her unrequited love to serve as an effective counterpart to the relationship between Dominique and Madeleine. (pp. 113-15)

In chapter 3 Dominique makes an extensive summary of Augustin's personal qualities. The reader is told that Augustin is the epitome of honesty, courage, and kindness. He has excellent judgment, is modest, has lofty ideals, a strong will, and an infectious enthusiasm for life and his future despite personal difficulties. His lack of financial security forces him to have a practical turn of mind and even to be very ambitious. Dominique informs us that Augustin is well educated and that his learning is reflected in his judgment and wisdom.

Yet Augustin is not filled out as a character; he remains one-dimensional. Augustin's part is so dominated by his role as tutor that one does not see him much in other capacities. Dominique reads from some of the letters which Augustin wrote to him after their years at Trembles. The letters are full of advice urging Dominique to be diligent in his work and to live in reality. He warns him against the pitfalls of ennui and gently suggests the potential weaknesses in Olivier's character so as to alert him to the dangers there. But there is very little in these letters or in the future visit of Dominique to Augustin's home which gives a better idea of Augustin's personality. The reader knows that he attempted to write for the theater and then turned to journalism. To Dominique's eyes the life he lives is meager, although Augustin's wife seems happy enough and is confident that the future will satisfy her needs. The image of the life Augustin leads confirms our idea of a hard-working, worthy man whose will and tenacity may earn him a modest success. Yet one would like to know something of the kind of theater he tried to write and perhaps something about his dealings with the theatrical and journalistic worlds. One does not even know what Augustin thinks of his wife or his domestic life. Seeing him in various situations or in discussions of subjects which interested him might have helped to give a more rounded picture of Augustin.

One's only glimpse of an Augustin not in the tutor's role comes from almost insignificant items. When Dominique and Augustin separate at Ormesson, it is Augustin who shows the greater emotion and affection. Moreover, his genuine interest in Dominique is reflected in his continued correspondence and effort to be of help. He is willing to take the time to become acquainted with Madeleine, despite the pressures of his own busy life. One also sees a sensitive side to the practical Augustin. He early perceives the youth's love for Madeleine. Yet he is careful not to pry or to give any hint that he knows what lies behind the ennui and general disquietude reflected in Dominique's letters. And although he always uses phrases which indicate the difference in their ages, he is sensitive enough to vary the tone of his letters as Dominique grows older to make their dialogue more of a discourse between mature adults. (pp. 115-16)

Dominique himself called Augustin *une nature incomplète . . .*, obviously referring to the lack of a more spiritual side to his character. However, in changes he made to the manuscript, Fromentin diminished Dominique's personal aversion for his tutor. He did not wish to weaken Augustin's position opposite Olivier. Thus he removed the statement that Dominique himself had trouble liking Augustin. Professor Wright correctly points out that Fromentin did a disservice to the book in removing Dominique's own ambivalence for Augustin. It lessens the conflict within Dominique and reduces a side of his character which is already weak.

The character of Olivier seems drawn from the classic Romantic figure. . . . Dominique describes him as a handsome, somewhat delicate, blond individual who has the air of an aristocratic dandy, except that he has none of the taste for art or the artificial. Olivier loves the pleasures and grand life of Paris and he takes great care in his attire, although he does not continually attend to himself once he is dressed. Those who meet him invariably find him charming and attractive. He learns easily, although he reads little, and he finds Latin and literature boring. Questioning the use of it, Olivier scorns those who write books. He is so irregular in his habits and so undisciplined that he himself has no interest in study. At one time he traveled much, but he soon grew weary of it and returned to his provincial estate to live alone and withdraw from society. Even as a young man he was morose, filled with self-disgust, and gave the impression of being indifferent and blasé. Like his earlier Romantic counterparts, he was young and yet felt old at the same time.

Dominique notes that Olivier was his inferior in much that pertained to the intellect and that he was not nearly so advanced in his studies. Yet in mundane matters it is Olivier who is much more aware of the ways of the world. While Dominique is groping to understand his own feelings and is just beginning to realize that Madeleine has reached another stage in the process of maturing, Olivier already knows that Madeleine has reached a marriageable age. Dominique is unaware of the significance of the bouquet of flowers, whereas Olivier quickly seizes the attached card to take note of the sender's name. Dominique is only gradually awakening to the meaning of his strange feelings for Madeleine, while Olivier has already made advances to a married woman. In such matters Olivier is precocious. He understands the significance of Dominique's emotions well before Dominique himself perceives what they mean. In fact he sees so clearly into the situation that he outlines the scenario for the love affair between Dominique and Madeleine long before it occurs.

In his description of Olivier's character the author observes that he is an *aimable garçon* and that he has an attractive personality. When one analyzes his role in the text, however, there are few instances when this side of his character is revealed. Perhaps the only incident that shows the friendship which Olivier feels for Dominique occurs in chapter 6 when Dominique has entered Madeleine's room during her absence from Ormesson. Olivier returns before Dominique can exit and undoubtedly understands the reason for his presence. Olivier is sensitive to Dominique's plight and makes no reference to his presence there. Aside from this occasion one sees little evidence of the expression of intimacy and close friendship which would improve Olivier's role in the text. (pp. 116-18)

Of all the major characters one probably knows least about Madeleine. She suffers more than others from being seen only through Dominique's eyes. It is ironic, because Dominique watches her more closely and analyzes her every look and word with care. It is as if his great love for her hinders his ability to know her. Both Augustin and Olivier are quoted more extensively. . . . One often sees her react to Dominique's words and actions, but the meaning of her reactions is rarely clear and the interpretation of them by Dominique is open to question.

The introductory portrait of Madeleine reveals less about her character than her dress. Dominique stresses her upbringing in a convent and describes her dreary clothing as a reflection of this background. One only learns that she has the shyness and awkwardness of someone raised away from society and that she is deemed pretty. (p. 118)

[If] one analyzes the bits and pieces of dialogue and Madeleine's reactions apart from Dominique's interpretation of them, one finds that Madeleine's personality varies under stress and, at times, seems contradictory.

When Madeleine returns from her trip with her father, she appears changed, more mature to Dominique. At the awards ceremony and at the ball in chapter 12, Madeleine appears to be a person who enjoys society and the social life of Paris. She looks forward to the event, though she tells Dominique that it will be as much pain for her as for him, and during the evening she is described more than once as enjoying herself. This attitude accords with a few scenes in which she appears coquettish and provocative, but it contrasts sharply with the picture of suffering and courage seen throughout the text.

At Trembles, toward the end of their vacation, Madeleine surprises Dominique in the park and teases him about writing a sonnet. Dominique does not realize that Olivier has told her of his writing. He asks if she thinks him capable of writing poetry. She answers that he is capable of doing that. When he protests that Olivier should not have told her, she replies:

> Il a bien fait de m'avertir; sans lui, je vous aurais cru une passion malheureuse, et je sais maintenant ce qui vous distrait: ce sont des rimes.

Dominique stresses that she emphasized the word *rimes* in teasing him. Against the background of the preceding scene in which she seemed to become aware that Dominique loves her, one might see this as relief on her part that she was wrong. However, as much as she tries to avoid a situation in which he could declare his love, she seems, at times, to assume his love and to use the knowledge coquettishly. At the ball in chapter 12, Madeleine approaches the gloomy Dominique to inquire whether or not he intends to dance. When he answers negatively, she reproaches him: ''Pas même avec moi?'' One could take this as the remark of a friend, but it could be seen as the language of flirtation.

These moments of possible flirtation are in harmony with Madeleine's character in chapter 17, when Dominique sees her for the first time after a two-year absence. Unexplainably she momentarily assumes the role of a seductive, even provocative, woman in the famous scene where she insists that Dominique mount her husband's horse and accompany her on a wild ride into the country. Dominique must chase after her in fits and starts. Finally he catches up to her and insists that she stop this cruel game or he would commit suicide. She looks him straight in the eye and then returns calmly to the chateau and goes to her room. Given the nature of the ride and Madeleine's actions, one might well question whether or not Madeleine expected a different reaction from Dominique. Finally, just before the scene with the shawl, it appears as though Madeleine were looking for Dominique. How innocent is she in falling into his arms?

But this side of Madeleine, if one can even call it that, is scarcely visible when one considers the text as a whole. For the most part one sees Madeleine suffering silently, caught between friendship and a growing recognition of love. Although one sees her in a number of scenes where she is under attack from Dominique, who would like to force her to admit she loves him, not so much is learned about her character as one would hope. Just as the heroine in *La Princess de Clèves* [by Marie-Madeleine Comtesse de La Fayette], Madeleine must invent various means of avoiding a discussion that could permit Dominique to declare his love. For a while she answers ingenuously, as if she does not understand the innuendo or implication of Dominique's remarks. However, Fromentin does not recreate the situations but merely has Dominique report her strategy. This prevents a certain revelation of Madeleine's personality. Another means Madeleine uses is silence and the deflection of the conversation by a change of subject. And, finally, when Dominique refuses to be put off, she sits silently in grief and despair. Because her defense must be one of silence the opportunity for character analysis in these crucial situations is slight.

The minute analysis of Dominique's thoughts and emotions as he develops from adolescence to maturity remains within a classic framework. Although one sees him as a mature man and, through his own eyes, over a considerable span of time during his youth, one knows somewhat less than one might expect about his worldly interests and activities. Fromentin presents, rather, the classic struggle between Dominique's emotions and reason. The obstacle which prevents Dominique's love for Madeleine from coming to fruition represents the realities of life which often stand in the way of one's complete happiness. Fromentin sees the process of maturing and finding happiness in the ability to adjust one's sights and emotions to the realities of life. He does not see unmitigated joy as part of reality. If one is to find a measure of happiness in life, he must develop the possible pleasures and minimize the inevitable griefs. He who can come to accept reality and concentrate on the positive qualities of his existence can overcome the feeling that he has failed merely because he has not fulfilled all his dreams.

When one analyzes the opening statement by Dominique (as quoted by the narrator), one sees that he assesses his life in just this way. Dominique affirms that he is content with his lot and happy to have no longer the ambitions and desires which caused him so much grief. However, the initial statement is cast in such negative terms that one doubts the contentedness he claims. One wonders whether his subsequent statement is not that of someone trying to persuade himself that he is happy. (pp. 119-21)

It is the tension between regret and contentment in the frame story which makes the main narrative of such interest. Fromentin does not use the third-person narrative, as if the story had an objective reality. Rather, he has Dominique retell his own tale; he has him rethink the events, words, and gestures aloud just as he has done hundreds of times to himself. This allows one the vividness of reality as it is happening and also permits one to assess the emotional impact of the events on the narrator.

Dominique's analysis of the events really involves his own development as a human being from the young boy growing up among the peasants and his own private thoughts to the chagrined adult who deliberately returns to the peasants to make the best of life. In the process Dominique focuses on a few important periods of development. The picture of Dominique's carefree youth is concluded by the essay on Hannibal's departure. Dominique's own emotional response to the text represents his own feeling about leaving Trembles and entering the world. At Ormesson he is introduced to love. But the importance of Fromentin's psychological analysis is not in describing his conduct once in love, it is rather the portrayal of gradual recognition. Fromentin's analysis follows the process as slowly as if one were watching the physical growth of the adolescent. He moves from the desire to be alone through several incidents with Madeleine that, aided by comments from Olivier, eventually open his eyes to something which, to him, did not exist before. . . . When Dominique finally realizes that Madeleine is to be married, the shock is similar to his recognition of love. It had been there for some time; he simply could not perceive it until now. Fromentin carefully portrays the subsequent grief mixed with confusion. It is no wonder that Augustin reenters the text at this point. For the first time in his life, Dominique's reason must play a significant role. It must assess the situation and try to piece together a future suddenly shattered by reality.

While he listens to the counsel of Olivier and Augustin, another development is taking place within him. He is becoming a man, a fact which plays a major part in his treatment of Madeleine. From the moment he steps down from the platform at the awards ceremony, he discards a schoolboy's robes for a man's place in society. Fromentin subtly follows his development from the timid boy who is content to be near Madeleine to the sensual man who attempts to force Madeleine to confess her love. Despite the grief he causes her and his repeated repentance because of it, he returns to take pleasure in conversations and situations which end in Madeleine's grief and silence. In chapter 17 he gloats about his feeling of power over Madeleine, that she is finally in his power. After two years of public involvement, he returns for his final victory. But throughout this growth, there is within him the human feeling that causes him to repent of the misery he causes her. . . . The fully mature adult who had begun the process of rational assessment in chapter 16 now returns to Trembles to begin an existence controlled by reason rather than his senses. No longer will he try to live for his own pleasures and satisfaction. He will guide his life into a useful path which is compatible with his ability and with reality. (pp. 121-23)

> *Emanuel J. Mickel, Jr., in his* Eugène Fromentin, *Twayne Publishers, 1981, 166 p.*

---

## ADDITIONAL BIBLIOGRAPHY

Bremner, Geoffrey. "Ambivalence in *Dominique.*" *Forum for Modern Language Studies* V, No. 4 (October 1969): 323-30.
  Ascribes the defects in *Dominique* to a disparity between the didactic and emotional purport of the novel.

Charlton, D. G. "Fromentin's *Dominique.*" *Forum for Modern Language Studies* III, No. 1 (January 1967): 85-92.
  Responds to Barbara Wright's assessment of *Dominique* (see excerpt above, 1965), arguing that she and other commentators have "over-value[d]" the novel.

Cruickshank, John. "The Novel of Self-Disclosure." In *French Literature and Its Background: The Early Nineteenth Century*, Vol. 4, edited by John Cruickshank, pp. 170-88. London: Oxford University Press, 1981.*
  Comments on the relationship between art and self-disclosure in *Dominique* and three other introspective French novels: *Obermann*, by Étienne Pivert de Sénancour; *Adolphe*, by Benjamin Constant; and *Volupté*, by Charles Augustin Sainte-Beuve.

Gonse, M. Louis. *Eugène Fromentin: Painter and Writer*. Translated by Mary Caroline Robbins. Boston: James R. Osgood and Co., 1883, 280 p.
  Early biographical and critical study written with "sympathetic enthusiasm" for Fromentin and his works. The volume also includes two fragments by Fromentin—"The Isle of Ré" and "Un mot sur l'art contemporain"—and several letters from the George Sand-Fromentin correspondence.

Grant, Richard B., and Severin, Nelly H. "Weaving Imagery in Fromentin's *Dominique.*" *Nineteenth-Century French Studies* I, No. 3 (Spring 1973): 155-61.
  Discusses the use of weaving imagery as a thematic device in *Dominique*. According to Grant and Severin, this imagery reinforces the anti-Romantic lesson of Fromentin's story.

Hubert, Renée Riese. "Fromentin's *Dominique:* The Confession of a Man Who Judges Himself." *PMLA* LXXXII, No. 7 (December 1967): 634-39.
    Depicts Dominique as a character given to constant reevaluation concerning the usefulness of his activities. His decision to live and work at Les Trembles is thus cast as a conscious, psychologically consistent embrace of social utility rather than a regretful retreat from Romanticism.

Latiolais, F. M. " 'Not Quite a Masterpiece'—Fromentin's *Dominique* Reconsidered." *Mosaic* IV, No. 1 (Fall 1970): 35-48.
    An assessment of *Dominique* that includes commentary on the novel's narrative structure, themes, and characterization.

Magowan, Robin. "Fromentin and Jewett: Pastoral Narrative in the Nineteenth Century." *Comparative Literature* XVI, No. 4 (Fall 1964): 331-37.*
    Formulates a definition of pastoral that elucidates such nineteenth-century works as *Dominique* and Sarah Orne Jewett's *Country of the Pointed Firs.*

———. "*Dominique:* The Genesis of a Pastoral." *L'esprit créateur* XIII, No. 4 (Winter 1973): 340-50.
    Relates the pastoral character of *Dominique* to events in Fromentin's life.

Martin, Graham Dunstan. "The Ambiguity of Fromentin's *Dominique.*" *The Modern Language Review* 77, No. 1 (January 1982): 38-50.
    Argues that *Dominique* supports rather than assails certain aspects of Romanticism.

Mein, Margaret. "Fromentin." In her *A Foretaste of Proust: A Study of Proust and His Precursors,* pp. 143-60. Farnborough, Hants, England: Saxon House, 1974.*
    Explores Fromentin's affinities with the French novelist Marcel Proust. Mein maintains that "Fromentin's principal claim to rank as precursor of Proust lies . . . in his intense awareness of the bonds between memory and sensations—the latter to be interpreted in the sense of the minutest reactions to climate and setting—in fact, in his weather-vane propensity."

Mickel, Emanuel J., Jr. "Barbey d'Aurevilly and Fromentin: Classic Aesthetic Values in a Romantic Context." *Symposium* XXXV, No. 4 (Winter 1981-82): 292-306.*
    Demonstrates the contradictions within Romanticism by comparing two French writers associated with the Romantic tradition: Fromentin and Jules Barbey d'Aurevilly.

Rhodes, S.A. "Sources of Fromentin's *Dominique.*" *PMLA* XLV, No. 3 (December 1930): 939-49.
    Identifies the novel *Valérie* by Madame de Krüdener as the model for *Dominique,* contesting G. Pailhès's contention that *Edouard,* by Madame de Duras, served as the source of Fromentin's work.

Sackville-West, Edward. "An Elegiac Novel." In his *Inclinations,* pp. 182-88. 1949. Reprint. Port Washington, N.Y.: Kennikat Press, 1967.

Extols *Dominique* as the "supreme example" of the elegiac novel.

Sainte-Beuve, C.-A. "*Dominique.*" In his *Nouveaux lundis,* Vol. 7, edited by Calmann Lévy, pp. 102-50. Paris: Ancienne Maison Michel Lévy Frérès, 1883.
    Reprints the critic's French-language commentary on *Un été dans le Sahara, Une année dans le Sahel,* and *Dominique.* Sainte-Beuve's remarks were originally published in 1864 as part of his "Lundis," a celebrated series of newspaper articles that appeared every Monday morning over a period of several decades.

Sells, A. Lytton. "A Disciple of *Obermann:* Eugène Fromentin." *Modern Language Review* XXXVI, No. 1 (January 1941): 68-85.
    Argues that, through his novel *Obermann,* Étienne Pivert de Sénancour profoundly influenced Fromentin's novel *Dominique.*

Shanks, Lewis Piaget. "Eugene Fromentin—A Painter in Prose." *The Open Court* XXXIV, No. 11 (November 1920): 661-76.
    Eulogistic introduction to Fromentin's writings.

West, C. B. "Notes on *Dominique.*" *French Studies* IX, No. 2 (April 1955): 116-28.
    Focuses on the significance of memory, sound, and other sense impressions for Fromentin and his hero Dominique.

Wright, Barbara. "Fromentin's Concept of Creative Vision in the Manuscript of *Dominique.*" *French Studies* XVIII, No. 3 (1964): 213-26.
    Examines Fromentin's concept of creative insight as revealed in the original manuscript of *Dominique.*

———. "*Valdieu:* A Forgotten Precursor of Fromentin's *Dominique.*" *The Modern Language Review* LX, No. 4 (October 1965): 520-28.*
    Examines Armand du Mesnil's influence on *Dominique,* focusing on the affinities between Fromentin's novel and du Mesnil's *Valdieu.*

———. Introduction to *Dominique,* by Eugène Fromentin, edited by Barbara Wright, pp. vii-lxxiii. Paris: Librairie Marcel Didier, 1966.
    Important, French-language criticism of *Dominique.*

———. "Gustave Moreau and Eugène Fromentin: A Reassessment of Their Relationship in the Light of New Documentation." *The Connoisseur* 180, No. 725 (July 1972): 191-97.*
    Highlights the principal points emerging from *Gustave Moreau et Eugène Fromentin: Documents inedites,* a French-language study published by Wright and Pierre Moisy in 1972. Among other features, Wright reprints a passage from Moreau's notebook in which the painter attacks his friend Fromentin's views on Dutch and Flemish art.

———. *Eugène Fromentin: A Bibliography.* Research Bibliographies & Checklists, edited by A. D. Deyermond, J. R. Little, and J. E. Varey, no. 8. London: Grant & Cutler, 1973, 63 p.
    Bibliographic pamphlet listing significant publications by and about Fromentin. The bibliography is current through July 1972.

# Nathaniel Hawthorne

## 1804-1864

(Born Nathaniel Hathorne) American novelist, short story writer, and essayist.

The following entry presents criticism of Hawthorne's novel *The Scarlet Letter: A Romance.* For a complete discussion of Hawthorne's career, see *NCLC*, Vol. 2.

Critics have long acknowledged *The Scarlet Letter* as Hawthorne's greatest achievement and as a seminal work in American literature. Hawthorne's perceptive portrayal of the protagonists of *The Scarlet Letter*—Hester Prynne, the Reverend Arthur Dimmesdale, Roger Chillingworth, and Pearl—gave American literature four of its most memorable characters and set the standard for psychological realism for future generations of writers. Through his depiction of the consequences of Hester and Dimmesdale's adulterous union, Hawthorne explored the historical, social, theological, and emotional ramifications of sin, concealment, and guilt. Scholars characterize his handling of the pair's defiance of the Puritan community's laws of behavior as one of literature's most powerful treatments of the theme of the individual versus society. In addition, many praise the novel's intricate structure and evocative use of symbolism.

Hawthorne's lifelong fascination with New England social and religious history derived in part from his own family background. The Hathornes had lived in America since the early seventeenth century and were prominent until the nineteenth century, when their fortunes declined sharply. William Hathorne, the first family member to arrive in America, was involved in the persecution of the Quakers, and his son John played a key role in the Salem witchcraft trials of 1692. In addition to the stories passed down through his family, Hawthorne read widely about the Puritan era from Joseph Felt's *Annals of Salem,* Caleb Hopkins Snow's *A History of Boston,* John Winthrop's *Journal,* and the works of Cotton Mather. As a result, Hawthorne is frequently credited with portraying Puritanism in *The Scarlet Letter* in a remarkably authentic and convincing manner. Hawthorne also drew on his own work experience in writing "The Custom-House," the controversial introduction to *The Scarlet Letter.* From 1839 to 1840, he was employed as a salt and coal measurer in the Boston Custom House; he later held the position of Surveyor in the Salem Custom House from 1846 to 1849. Hawthorne's abrupt dismissal from that post, when Zachary Taylor's administration came to power, freed him to devote himself fully to writing. However, it also left him poor and embittered. Some commentators have claimed that his personal disappointment colored both his satiric comments in "The Custom-House" and the overall mood of the novel. Though Hawthorne alluded in his Preface to the second edition of *The Scarlet Letter* to the "unprecedented excitement" caused by his acrimonious remarks in "The Custom-House" against the new administration, he vigorously denied any "ill-feeling, personal or political," and subsequently republished it "without changing a word" (see *NCLC*, Vol. 2). Nevertheless, most critics have attributed the somber atmosphere of *The Scarlet Letter* to Hawthorne's dismissal and resultant concern about his family's dire financial situation as well as to his intense grief following the death of his mother in 1849.

Before *The Scarlet Letter,* Hawthorne had published three collections of short stories and *Fanshawe,* an unsuccessful novel written during his college years. His short stories, or tales, were widely acclaimed for their deft recreation of the past, insightful characterizations, and allegorical treatment of such themes as sin, guilt, and alienation. Critics believe that *The Scarlet Letter* served as a turning point between two phases of Hawthorne's career—the early tales and the later novels—for in this work, he succeeded for the first time in adapting his short-story writing skills to the demands of the novel form. Hawthorne described his novels as romances, or fictional works that range freely between imagination and reality and often focus on psychological exploration. In fact, *The Scarlet Letter* was first composed as a lengthy tale to be included in *Old-Time Legends: Together with Sketches, Experimental and Ideal,* a volume Hawthorne projected but never completed. The work's transformation from its earlier form into the carefully constructed novel testified to Hawthorne's ability to write longer fiction. His other romances—*The House of the Seven Gables, The Blithedale Romance,* and *The Marble Faun*—soon followed.

Prior to the appearance of *The Scarlet Letter* in 1850, Hawthorne had described himself as "the obscurest man of letters in America." His tales had won him critical attention, but

*Fanshawe* had been an artistic and financial disaster. *The Scarlet Letter*, however, permanently established Hawthorne's reputation. Though the novel was not an immediate popular success, many critics recognized its excellence. E. A. Duyckinck commended the novel's structure as "a drama in which thoughts are acts," E. P. Whipple stressed the "profound philosophy underlaying the story," and Anne W. Abbott extolled the elegance and clarity of Hawthorne's style. Certain commentators, including Abbott and the reviewer for *Littell's Living Age*, suggested that "The Custom-House" was perhaps the best section of *The Scarlet Letter* because of its pungent wit and lively tone. Yet others considered the introduction merely a manifestation of Hawthorne's malice against his political enemies. The harshest criticism was that its subject matter was morally objectionable. Abbott lamented that Hawthorne's choice of plot was "revolting," Orestes Brownson argued that Hester's crime "was not presented as loathsome enough," and Arthur Cleveland Coxe posited that *The Scarlet Letter,* in depicting the "nauseous amour" of a minister, encouraged "social licentiousness" and degraded American literature as a whole. Even those reviewers who were not outwardly hostile toward Hawthorne's theme complained about the novel's "morbid intensity," as Whipple phrased it. The *Blackwood's Edinburgh Magazine* critic expressed concern about the "unwholesome fascination" of *The Scarlet Letter* and its mood of "suppressed, secret, feverish excitement." Yet only two decades later, Anthony Trollope highlighted Hawthorne's curious detachment as an author and his "running vein of drollery." In contrast to many earlier critics, Henry James faulted Hawthorne's narrative method for its lack of passion, writing that "no story of love was surely ever less of a 'love story'" (see *NCLC*, Vol. 2).

Since the publication of *The Scarlet Letter,* critics have focused on several issues. They continue to discuss the structure of the novel, suggesting various ways of dividing *The Scarlet Letter* into sections or acts. They have also debated who functions as the novel's central figure—Hester or Dimmesdale—and whether Hawthorne condones their adultery. The roles of Chillingworth and Pearl, too, have sparked critical inquiry. Yet perhaps the aspect of the work that critics find most intriguing is its symbolism. Numerous studies of the novel's various symbols have appeared since its publication, with many focusing on possible interpretations of the letter A itself.

Most commentators agree that *The Scarlet Letter*'s symmetrical, compressed structure enhances the novel's unity and also illuminates a number of its main themes. As early as 1850, Duyckinck perceived a link between Hawthorne's "arrangement of scenes" and his psychological exploration of characters. Contemporary reviewers were willing to accept the internalized, static structure of the novel because they considered it a psychological romance rather than a novel of action. Since then, critics have outlined several interpretations of the work's structure. Malcolm Cowley suggested that *The Scarlet Letter* naturally falls into five dramatic acts so tightly interwoven that they "recaptured . . . the essence of Greek tragedy." Similar interpretations of the novel's structure were also proposed by John C. Gerber and Leland Schubert (see Additional Bibliography). In his Freudian reading of the novel, Régis Michaud posited that its structure derives from Hester and Dimmesdale's "abandonment to the freed libido." Turning his attention to Hawthorne's relationship to his work, Randall Stewart underscored the tension between Puritan and romantic elements in the novel, in relation to both its theme and Hawthorne's personal predilections, as the main structuring principle of *The*

*Scarlet Letter*. In an iconoclastic and controversial assessment, Ernest Sandeen contended that the work is shaped primarily as a love story. One of the most prevalent opinions, held by such critics as R. W. B. Lewis, Marius Bewley, A. N. Kaul, Nina Baym, and Michael Davitt Bell, is that *The Scarlet Letter* is organized around the conflict between the individual and society. Lewis termed the opening of the novel, which depicts Hester standing alone on the scaffold, as "the paradigm dramatic image in American literature." Bewley, Kaul, and Bell treated the implications of the individual's need to belong to a community and at the same time to be exempt from its strictures. Underscoring the largely patriarchal and utilitarian nature of the Puritan setting, Baym, on the other hand, investigated this theme in relation to Hester's predicament as a woman and an artist.

Most studies of characterization in the novel focus on Hester. Some scholars have suggested that Hawthorne might have modeled her character on the nineteenth-century Transcendentalist writer Margaret Fuller. But other critics regard this possibility as unlikely, since Hawthorne's journal entries indicate that he considered Fuller a "great humbug" and deficient in the "charm of womanhood." In fact, Hawthorne developed the prototype for Hester in his short story "Endicott and the Red Cross," written in 1837. Abbott and Brownson, whose reviews typify early critical response to the novel, condemned Hester for her pride and insufficient repentance. Brownson included Dimmesdale in this appraisal as well. Praising Hawthorne's realism in portraying the characters of *The Scarlet Letter,* W. D. Howells added that "in all fiction one could hardly find a character more boldly, more simply, more quietly imagined" than Hester. In contrast, the *Blackwood's* reviewer maintained that the characters in *The Scarlet Letter* are treated as "cases" rather than as human beings. John Macy regarded the novel's characters as symbols, while Carl Van Doren designated Hester a "type" in Hawthorne's allegorical scheme. Hawthorne's attitude towards Hester and, consequently, the attitude he intended the reader to adopt toward her, forms a major issue in evaluations of her character. At different times Hester has been interpreted as an immoral woman, a romantic heroine, an early feminist, and the prototypical pioneer woman. Many scholars, including Stewart and Frederic I. Carpenter, emphasized the ambivalence of Hawthorne's portrayal of Hester. Critics have also questioned whether she brings about change in the novel's Puritan community. Baym stressed that Hester's acceptance of the scarlet letter and her perseverance in continuing to live as a member of the community attest to her achievement of "a modest social change." Discussing this problem in historical terms, Bell differed from Baym in concluding that in *The Scarlet Letter,* "to repudiate the past . . . is only to repeat it." Dimmesdale's role in the novel, like Hester's, has also provoked lively critical exchange. Though Abbott found his final repentance unconvincing and his suffering "obstinate and inhuman," later critics have frequently provided a more sympathetic interpretation. Darrel Abel forcefully defended Dimmesdale's integrity and the sincerity of his confession and regeneration (see Additional Bibliography). Tempering this position, Hyatt H. Waggoner pointed out that Hawthorne neither condemned nor affirmed Dimmesdale's confession because Hawthorne himself did not know how to treat the question of atonement. Stewart asserted that it is Dimmesdale rather than Hester who serves as the "chief actor" in the novel because he represents Puritan theological beliefs; Sandeen offered an opposing argument, observing that Dimmesdale's role as the voice of Puritanism in the novel can only be viewed as ironic. Pearl's characterization, too, has puzzled critics of *The Scarlet*

*Letter.* Trollope and Howells termed her less than realistic, whereas Abbott praised her portrayal as "vivid and human." According to most scholars, Pearl embodies realistic and symbolic qualities and serves both an allegorical and a naturalistic function in the novel.

Many critics have extolled Hawthorne's carefully wrought imagery and symbolism in *The Scarlet Letter*. James, however, criticized what he considered the excess of symbolism in the work and reprimanded Hawthorne for "a want of reality and an abuse of the fanciful element—of a certain superficial symbolism" (see *NCLC*, Vol. 2). Several decades later, Macy pronounced the whole work "a prose poem" and classified each character as "a mood, a tone." In a similar vein, Yvor Winters highly praised Hawthorne's "cleanly allegorical" conception (see *NCLC*, Vol. 2). Many critical assessments center on the elements and sources of Hawthorne's imagery and symbolism. F. O. Matthiessen pointed out that Hawthorne's habit of creating "continual correspondence . . . between external events and inner significances" stems from a typically Puritan bent of imagination. On a similar note, Richard Chase categorized *The Scarlet Letter* as a "quasi-puritan allegory" which is "almost all picture" because Hawthorne relies on imagery and symbolism to carry the full thematic burden of the novel. Like Chase, Daniel Hoffman examined myth, folklore, and pagan and witchcraft imagery as an integral part of the novel's symbolism. Perhaps the most intriguing aspect of *The Scarlet Letter*, though, remains the function and meaning of the letter A. Various critics have speculated on its possible denotation; in addition to Adultress, some of the most prevalent interpretations are Admirable, Artist, Angel, Arthur, and America. Analyzing Hawthorne's strategy of using paradox and irony to suggest meanings for the A, Terence Martin theorized that the letter "encompasses and transcends all its individual meanings, and signifies, totally and finally, *The Scarlet Letter* itself."

Hawthorne's achievement in *The Scarlet Letter* can be measured by several different criteria, as the wide variety of critical approaches to his work affirms. Whether they interpret the novel as a love story, a realistic, historical piece, or, in the words of Q. D. Leavis, "a perfect sociological tragedy" (see *NCLC*, Vol. 2), almost all critics attempt to come to terms with the ever-shifting meaning of *The Scarlet Letter*. Scholars single out suggestiveness and ambiguity, best encapsulated in the polysemous scarlet A itself, as Hawthorne's greatest contributions to American literature. D. H. Lawrence sardonically termed this approach "perfect duplicity" (see *NCLC*, Vol. 2), and Winters coined the now-famous phrase "formula of alternative possibilities" to describe Hawthorne's method (see *NCLC*, Vol. 2). Most critics agree that Hawthorne succeeded in creating a work of impeccable unity accomplished through thematic focus, structural balance, and vivid characterization. Though debate about the merits of *The Scarlet Letter* continues, it has been championed as one of America's greatest masterpieces.

(See also *Dictionary of Literary Biography*, Vol. I: *The American Renaissance in New England* and *Yesterday's Authors of Books for Children*, Vol. 2.)

---

## NATHANIEL HAWTHORNE   (letter date 1850)

[*In this excerpt from a letter to a friend, written in February, 1850 shortly after the completion of* The Scarlet Letter, *Hawthorne*

*acknowledges that the main narrative "lacks sunshine," a trait which he believes will hinder its popularity. He also suggests that "The Custom-House" section may prove more appealing than the rest of the work—a prediction borne out by the comments of the anonymous critic for* Littell's Living Age *(1850) and Anne W. Abbott (1850).*]

[The publisher speaks of *The Scarlet Letter*] in tremendous terms of approbation; so does Mrs. Hawthorne, to whom I read the conclusion, last night. It broke her heart and sent her to bed with a grievous headache—which I look upon as triumphant success! Judging from its effect on her and the publisher, I may calculate on what bowlers call a ten-strike! Yet I do not make any such calculation. Some portions of the book are powerfully written; but my writings do not, nor ever will, appeal to the broadest class of sympathies, and therefore will not attain a very wide popularity. Some like them very much; others care nothing for them, and see nothing in them. There is an introduction to this book—giving a sketch of the Custom-House, with an imaginative touch here and there—which perhaps may be more widely attractive than the main narrative. The latter lacks sunshine. To tell you the truth, it is . . . positively a h-ll-fired story, into which I found it almost impossible to throw any cheering light.

> *Nathaniel Hawthorne, in an extract from* Hawthorne: The Critical Heritage, *edited by J. Donald Crowley, Routledge & Kegan Paul, 1970, p. 151.*

## [E. A. DUYCKINCK]   (essay date 1850)

[*A prominent nineteenth-century American editor and the co-author of the* Cyclopaedia of American Literature, *Duyckinck delivers high praise for* The Scarlet Letter. *He labels the novel "a psychological romance" and concludes that there is "no truer product of the American soil" than Nathaniel Hawthorne.*]

*The Scarlet Letter* is a psychological romance. The hardiest Mrs. Malaprop [from Richard Brinsley Sheridan's *The Rivals*] would never venture to call it a novel. It is a tale of remorse, a study of character in which the human heart is anatomized, carefully, elaborately, and with striking poetic and dramatic power. (p. 323)

It is a drama in which thoughts are acts. The material has been thoroughly fused in the writer's mind, and springs forth an entire, perfect creation. We know of no American tales except some of the early ones of Mr. [Richard Henry] Dana, which approach it in conscientious completeness. Nothing is slurred over, superfluous, or defective. The story is grouped in scenes simply arranged, but with artistic power, yet without any of those painful impressions which the use of the words, as it is the fashion to use them, "grouping' and "artistic" excite, suggesting artifice and effort at the expense of nature and ease.

Mr. Hawthorne has, in fine, shown extraordinary power in this volume, great feeling and discrimination, a subtle knowledge of character in its secret springs and outer manifestations. He blends, too, a delicate fancy with this metaphysical insight. We would instance the chapter towards the close, entitled **"The Minister in a Maze,"** where the effects of a diabolic temptation are curiously depicted, or **"The Minister's Vigil,"** the night scene in the pillory. The atmosphere of the piece also is perfect. It has the mystic element, the weird forest influences of the old Puritan discipline and era. Yet there is no affrightment which belongs purely to history, which has not its echo even in the unlike and perversely commonplace custom-house of Salem. Then for the moral. Though severe, it is wholesome, and is a sounder bit of Puritan divinity than we have been of late accustomed to hear from the degenerate succesors of Cotton Mather. We hardly know another writer who has lived so much among the new school who would have handled this delicate subject without an infusion of George Sand. The spirit of his old Puritan ancestors, to whom he refers in the preface, lives in Nathaniel Hawthorne. (p. 324)

Our literature has given to the world no truer product of the American soil, though of a peculiar culture, than Nathaniel Hawthorne. (pp. 324-25)

> [E. A. Duyckinck], "Nathaniel Hawthorne," in The Literary World, Vol. VI, No. 165, March 30, 1850, pp. 323-25.

### [E. P. WHIPPLE]   (essay date 1850)

[*Whipple praises* The Scarlet Letter, *highlighting Hawthorne's intensity and objectivity. However, he regards the novel's characterization as "too painfully anatomical"; a similar view is offered by* Blackwood's Edinburgh Magazine *(1855), and Brigid Brophy, Michael Levey, and Charles Osborne (1967).*]

In this beautiful and touching romance Hawthorne has produced something really worthy of the fine and deep genius which lies within him. . . . In **"The Scarlet Letter"** we have a complete work, evincing a true artist's certainty of touch and expression in the exhibition of characters and events, and a keen-sighted and far-sighted vision into the essence and purpose of spiritual laws. There is a profound philosophy underlying the story which will escape many of the readers whose attention is engrossed by the narrative.

The book is prefaced by some fifty pages of autobiographical matter, relating to the author, his native city of Salem, and the Custom House, from which he was ousted by the Whigs. These pages, instinct with the vital spirit of humor, show how rich and exhaustless a fountain of mirth Hawthorne has at his command. The whole representation has the dreamy yet distinct remoteness of the purely comic ideal. The view of Salem streets; the picture of the old Custom House at the head of Derby's wharf, with its torpid officers on a summer's afternoon, their chairs all tipped against the wall, chatting about old stories, "while the frozen witticisms of past generations were thawed out, and came bubbling with laughter from their lips"—the delineation of the old Inspector, whose "reminiscences of good cheer, however ancient the date of the actual banquet, seemed to bring the savor of pig or turkey under one's very nostrils," and on whose palate there were flavors "which had lingered there not less than sixty or seventy years, and were still apparently as fresh as that of the mutton-chop which he had just devoured for his breakfast," and the grand view of the stout Collector, in his aged heroism, with the honors of Chippewa and Fort Erie on his brow, are all encircled with that visionary atmosphere which proves the humorist to be a poet, and indicates that his pictures are drawn from the images which observation has left on his imagination. (pp. 345-46)

With regard to **"The Scarlet Letter,"** the readers of Hawthorne might have expected an exquisitely written story, expansive in sentiment, and suggestive in characterization, but they will hardly be prepared for a novel of so much tragic interest and tragic power, so deep in thought and so condensed in style, as is here presented to them. It evinces equal genius in the region of great passions and elusive emotions, and bears on every page the evidence of a mind thoroughly alive, watching pa-

tiently the movements of morbid hearts when stirred by strange experiences, and piercing, by its imaginative power, directly through all the externals to the core of things. The fault of the book, if fault it have, is the almost morbid intensity with which the characters are realized, and the consequent lack of sufficient geniality in the delineation. A portion of the pain of the author's own heart is communicated to the reader, and although there is great pleasure received while reading the volume, the general impression left by it is not satisfying to the artistic sense. Beauty bends to power throughout the work, and therefore the power displayed is not always beautiful. There is a strange fascination to a man of contemplative genius in the psychological details of a strange crime like that which forms the plot of **"The Scarlet Letter,"** and he is therefore apt to become, like Hawthorne, too painfully anatomical in his exhibition of them.

If there be, however, a comparative lack of relief to the painful emotions which the novel excites, owing to the intensity with which the author concentrates attention on the working of dark passions, it must be confessed that the moral purpose of the book is made more definite by this very deficiency. The most abandoned libertine could not read the volume without being thrilled into something like virtuous resolution, and the roué would find that the deep-seeing eye of the novelist had mastered the whole philosophy of that guilt of which practical roués are but childish disciples. To another class of readers, those who have theories of seduction and adultery modeled after the French school of novelists, and whom libertinism is of the brain, the volume may afford matter for very instructive and edifying contemplation; for, in truth, Hawthorne, in **"The Scarlet Letter,"** has utterly undermined the whole philosophy on which the French novels rest, by seeing farther and deeper into the essence both of conventional and moral laws; and he has given the results of his insight, not in disquisitions and criticisms, but in representations more powerful even than those of Sue, Dumas, or George Sand. He has made his guilty parties end, not as his own fancy or his own benevolent sympathies might dictate, but as the spiritual laws, lying back of all persons, dictated to him. In this respect there is hardly a novel in English literature more purely objective. (p. 346)

> [E. P. Whipple], in a review of "The Scarlet Letter, a Romance," in Graham's Magazine, Vol. XXXVI, No. 5, May, 1850, pp. 345-46.

### LITTELL'S LIVING AGE   (essay date 1850)

[*This review of* The Scarlet Letter *praises the novel as Hawthorne's best production and declares it "a genuine native romance" full of subtle terror. As Hawthorne predicted (see excerpt above, 1850), the reviewer considers the introduction, "The Custom-House," particularly appealing. Anne W. Abbott comments more extensively on this section (see excerpt below, 1850).*]

The weird and ghostly legends of the Puritanic history present a singularly congenial field for the exercise of Mr. Hawthorne's peculiar genius. From this fruitful source he has derived the materials for his most remarkable creations. He never appears so much in his element as when threading out some dim, shadowy tradition of the twilight age of New England, peering into the faded records of our dark-visaged forefathers for the lingering traces of the preternatural, and weaving into his gorgeous web of enchantment the slender filaments which he has drawn from the distaff of some muttering witch on Gallows-Hill. He derives the same terrible excitement from these legendary horrors, as was drawn by Edgar Poe from the depths of his own dark and perilous imagination, and brings before us pictures of death-like, but strangely fascinating agony, which are described with the same minuteness of finish—the same slow and fatal accumulation of details—the same exquisite coolness of coloring, while everything creeps forward with irresistible certainty to a soul-harrowing climax—which made the last-named writer such a consummate master of the horrible and infernal in fictitious composition. Hawthorne's tragedies, however, are always *motived* with a wonderful insight and skill, to which the intellect of Poe was a stranger. In the most terrific scenes with which he delights to scare the imagination, Hawthorne does not wander into the region of the improbable; you scarcely know that you are in the presence of the supernatural, until your breathing becomes too thick for this world, it is the supernatural relieved, softened, made tolerable, and almost attractive, by a strong admixture of the human; you are tempted onward by the mild, unearthly light, which seems to shine upon you like a healthful star; you are blinded by no lurid glare; you acquiesce in the necessity of the wizard journey; instead of being provoked to anger by a superfluous introduction to the company of the devil and his angels.

The elements of terror, which Mr. Hawthorne employs with such masterly effect, both in the original conception of his characters and the scenes of mystery and dread in which they are made to act, are blended with such sweet gushes of natural feeling, such solemn and tender relations of the deepest secrets of the heart, that the painful impression is greatly mitigated, and the final influence of his most startling creation is a serene sense of refreshment, without the stupor and bewilderment occasioned by a drugged cup of intoxication.

The "Scarlet Letter," in our opinion, is the greatest production of the author, beautifully displaying the traits we have briefly hinted at, and sustained with a more vigorous reach of imagination, a more subtle instinct of humanity, and a more imposing splendor of portraiture, than any of his most successful previous works. (p. 203)

[The "Scarlet Letter" is] a genuine native romance, which none will be content without reading for themselves. The moral of the story—for it has a moral for all wise enough to detect it—is shadowed forth rather than expressed in a few brief sentences near the close of the volume. . . .

The introduction, presenting a record of savory reminiscences of the Salem Custom House, a frank display of autobiographical confessions, and a piquant daguerreotype of his ancient colleagues in office, while surveyor of that port, is written with Mr. Hawthorne's unrivalled force of graphic delineation, and will furnish an agreeable amusement to those who are so far from the scene of action as to feel no wound in their personal relations, by the occasional too sharp touches of the caustic acid, of which the "gentle author" keeps some phials on his shelf for convenience and use. The querulous tone in which he alludes to his removal from the Custom House, may be forgiven to the sensitiveness of a poet, especially as this is so rare a quality in Uncle Sam's office holders. (p. 207)

*A review of "The Scarlet Letter," in* Littell's Living Age, *Vol. XXV, No. 311, May, 1850, pp. 203-07.*

## [ANNE W. ABBOTT]   (essay date 1850)

[*In the following excerpt, Abbott begins with a positive appraisal of "The Custom-House," saying she appreciates "the preface better than the tale." She then discusses style and characterization*

*in* The Scarlet Letter, *generally praising Hawthorne's artistic prowess. Though she faults Hester for her pride and contends that Dimmesdale and Chillingworth are unrealistic, she expresses delight in and approval of Hawthorne's depiction of Pearl. For a contrasting view of Pearl, see the excerpt by Anthony Trollope (1879). Abbott concludes that Hawthorne is a talented, picturesque writer, though she laments the "revolting subject" of his novel. Orestes A. Brownson (1850) and Arthur Cleveland Coxe (1851) arrive at similar conclusions.*]

["The Custom-House" chapter] is more piquant than any thing in the book; the style is racy and pungent, not elaborately witty, but stimulating the reader's attention agreeably by original turns of expression, and unhackneyed combinations of words, falling naturally into their places, as if of their own accord, and not obtained by far seeking and impressment into the service. The sketch of General Miller is airily and lightly done; no other artist could have given so much character to each fine drawn line as to render the impression almost as distinct to the reader's fancy as a portrait drawn by rays of light is to the bodily vision. Another specimen of his word painting, the lonely parlor seen by the moonlight melting into the warmer glow of the fire, while it reminds us of Cowper's much quoted and admired verse, has truly a great deal more of genuine poetry in it. The delineations of wharf scenery, and of the Custom House, with their appropriate figures and personages, are worthy of the pen of Dickens; and really, so far as mere style is concerned, Mr. Hawthorne has no reason to thank us for the compliment; he has the finer touch, if not more genial feeling, of the two. Indeed, if we except a few expressions which savor somewhat strongly of his late unpoetical associations, and the favorite metaphor of the guillotine, which, however apt, is not particularly agreeable to the imagination in such detail, we like the preface better than the tale.

No one who has taken up *The Scarlet Letter* will willingly lay it down till he has finished it; and he will do well not to pause, for he cannot resume the story where he left it. He should give himself up to the magic power of the style, without stopping to open wide the eyes of his good sense and judgment, and shake off the spell; or half the weird beauty will disappear like a "dissolving view." To be sure, when he closes the book, he will feel very much like the giddy and bewildered patient who is just awaking from his first experiment of the effects of sulphuric ether. The soul has been floating or flying between earth and heaven, with dim ideas of pain and pleasure strangely mingled, and all things earthly swimming dizzily and dreamily, yet most beautiful, before the half shut eye. That the author himself felt this sort of intoxication as well as the willing subjects of his enchantment, we think, is evident in many pages of the last half of the volume. His imagination has sometimes taken him fairly off his feet, insomuch that he seems almost to doubt if there be any firm ground at all. . . . (pp. 139-40)

Thus devils and angels are alike beautiful, when seen through the magic glass; and they stand side by side in heaven, however the former may be supposed to have come there. As for Roger Chillingworth, he seems to have so little in common with map, he is such a gnome-like phantasm, such an unnatural personification of an abstract idea, that we should be puzzled to assign him a place among angels, men, or devils. . . . Hester at first strongly excites our pity, for she suffers like an immortal being; and our interest in her continues only while we have hope for her soul, that its baptism of tears will reclaim it from the foul stain which has been cast upon it. We see her humble, meek, self-denying, charitable, and heart-wrung with anxiety for the moral welfare of her wayward child. But anon her humility catches a new tint, and we find it pride; and so a vague unreality steals by degrees over all her most humanizing traits—we lose our confidence in all—and finally . . . she disappoints us, and shows the dream-land origin and nature, when we were looking to behold a Christian.

There is rather more power, and better keeping, in the character of Dimmesdale. But here again we are cheated into a false regard and interest, partly perhaps by the associations thrown around him without the intention of the author, and possibly contrary to it, by our habitual respect for the sacred order, and by our faith in religion, where it has once been rooted in the heart. We are told repeatedly, that the Christian element yet pervades his character and guides his efforts; but it seems strangely wanting. "High aspirations for the welfare of his race, warm love of souls, pure sentiments, natural piety, strengthened by thought and study, and illuminated by revelation—all of which invaluable gold was little better than rubbish" to Roger Chillingworth, are little better than rubbish at all, for any use to be made of them in the story. Mere suffering, aimless and without effect for purification or blessing to the soul, we do not find in God's moral world. The sting that follows crime is most severe in the purest conscience and the tenderest heart, in mercy, not in vengeance, surely; and we can conceive of any cause constantly exerting itself without its appropriate effects, as soon as of a seven years' agony without penitence. But here every pang is wasted. A most obstinate and unhuman passion, or a most unwearying conscience it must be, neither being worn out, or made worse or better, by such a prolonged application of the scourge. Penitence may indeed be life-long; but as for this, we are to understand that there is no penitence about it. We finally get to be quite of the author's mind, that "the only truth that continued to give Mr. Dimmesdale a real existence on this earth, was the anguish in his inmost soul, and the undissembled expression of it in his aspect. Had he once found power to smile, and wear an aspect of gayety, there had been no such man." He duly exhales at the first gleam of hope, an uncertain and delusive beam, but fatal to his misty existence. From that time he is a fantasy, an opium dream, his faith a vapor, his reverence blasphemy, his charity mockery, his sanctity impurity, his love of souls a ludicrous impulse to teach little boys bad words; and nothing is left to bar the utterance of "a volley of good, round, solid, satisfactory, heaven-defying oaths," (a phrase which seems to smack its lips with a strange *goût!*) but good taste and the mere outward shell, "the buckramed habit of clerical decorum." The only conclusion is, that the shell never possessed any thing real,—never was the Rev. Arthur Dimmesdale, as we have foolishly endeavored to suppose; that he was but a changeling, or an imp in grave apparel, not an erring, and consequently suffering human being, with a heart still upright enough to find the burden of conscious unworthiness and undeserved praise more intolerable than open ignominy and shame, and refraining from relieving his withering conscience from its load of unwilling hypocrisy, if partly from fear, more from the wish to be yet an instrument of good to others, not an example of evil which should weaken their faith in religion. The closing scene, where the satanic phase of the character is again exchanged for the saintly, and the pillory platform is made the stage for a triumphant *coup de théâtre*, seems to us more than a failure.

But Little Pearl—gem of the purest water—what shall we say of her? That if perfect truth to childish and human nature can make her a mortal, she is so; and immortal, if the highest creations of genius have any claim to immortality. Let the author throw what light he will upon her, from his magical

prism, she retains her perfect and vivid human individuality. When he would have us call her elvish and imp-like, we persist in seeing only a capricious, roguish, untamed child, such as many a mother has looked upon with awe, and a feeling of helpless incapacity to rule. Every motion, every feature, every word and tiny shout, every naughty scream and wild laugh, come to us as if our very senses were conscious of them. The child is a true child, the only genuine and consistent mortal in the book; and wherever she crosses the dark and gloomy track of the story, she refreshes our spirit with pure truth and radiant beauty, and brings to grateful remembrance the like ministry of gladsome childhood, in some of the saddest scenes of actual life. (pp. 140-42)

We know of no writer who better understands and combines the elements of the picturesque in writing than Mr. Hawthorne. His style may be compared to a sheet of transparent water, reflecting from its surface blue skies, nodding woods, and the smallest spray of flower that peeps over its grassy margin; while in its clear yet mysterious depths we espy rarer and stranger things, which we must dive for, if we would examine. Whether they might prove gems or pebbles, when taken out of the fluctuating medium through which the sun-gleams reach them, is of no consequence to the effect. Every thing charms the eye and ear, and nothing looks like art and pains-taking. . . . One cannot but wonder, by the way, that the master of such a wizard power over language as Mr. Hawthorne manifests should not choose a less revolting subject than this of *The Scarlet Letter*, to which fine writing seems as inappropriate as fine embroidery. The ugliness of pollution and vice is no more relieved by it than the gloom of the prison is by the rose tree at its door. There are some palliative expressions used, which cannot, even as a matter of taste, be approved.

Regarding the book simply as a picture of the olden time, we have no fault to find with costume or circumstance. All the particulars given us, (and he is not wearisomely anxious to multiply them to show his research,) are in good keeping and perspective, all in softened outlines and neutral tint, except the ever fresh and unworn image of childhood, which stands out from the canvas in the gorgeously attired "Little Pearl." (pp. 146-47)

> [Anne W. Abbott], in a review of "The Scarlet Letter, a Romance," in The North American Review, Vol. LXXI, No. CXLVIII, July, 1850, pp. 135-48.

### [GEORGE B. LORING]   (essay date 1850)

> [After praising The Scarlet Letter *as an extraordinary work of art and "a vehicle of religion and ethics," Loring focuses on Hawthorne's depiction of Hester as a heroine whose courage and independence are fuelled by her strongly held moral convictions. Loring's critique is later noted by R. W. B. Lewis (1955) and Robert Penn Warren (1973).*]

No author of our own country, and scarcely any author of our times, manages to keep himself clothed in such a cloak of mystery as Nathaniel Hawthorne. From the time when his "Twice-Told Tales" went, in their first telling, floating through the periodicals of the day, up to the appearance of "**The Scarlet Letter,**" he has stood on the confines of society, as we see some sombre figure, in the dim light of the stage scenery, peering through that narrow space, when a slouched hat and a muffling cloak do not meet, upon the tragic events which are made conspicuous by the glare of the footlights. From nowhere in particular, from an old manse, and from the drowsy dilapidation of an old custom-house, he has spoken such oracular words, such searching thoughts, as sounded of old from the mystic God whose face was never seen even by the most worthy. It seems useless now to speak of his humor, subtile and delicate as Charles Lamb's; of his pathos, deep as Richter's; of his penetration into the human heart, clearer than that of Goldsmith or Crabbe; of his apt and telling words, which Pope might have envied; of his description, graphic as Scott's or Dickens's; of the delicious lanes he opens, on either hand, and leaves you alone to explore, masking his work with the fine *"faciebat"* which removes all limit from all high art, and gives every man scope to advance and develop. He seems never to trouble himself, either in writing or living, with the surroundings of life. He is no philosopher for the poor or the rich, for the ignorant or the learned, for the righteous or the wicked, for any special rank or condition in life, but for human nature as given by God into the hands of man. He calls us to be indignant witnesses of no particular social, religious, or political enormity. He asks no admiration for this or that individual or associated virtue. The face of society, with its manifold features, never comes before you, as you study the extraordinary experience of his men and women, except as a necessary setting for the picture. They might shine at tournaments, or grovel in cellars, or love, or fight, or meet with high adventure, or live the deepest and quietest life in unknown corners of the earth,—their actual all vanishes before the strange and shifting picture he gives of the motive heart of man. In no work of his is this characteristic more strikingly visible than in **"The Scarlet Letter;"** and in no work has he presented so clear and perfect an image of himself, as a speculative philosopher, an ethical thinker, a living man. Perhaps he verges strongly upon the supernatural, in the minds of those who would recognize nothing but the corporeal existence of human life. But man's nature is, by birth, *super*natural; and the deep mystery which lies beneath all his actions is far beyond the reach of any mystical vision that ever lent its airy shape to the creations of the most intense dreamer. (pp. 484-85)

[**"The Scarlet Letter"** is] extraordinary, as a work of art, and as a vehicle of religion and ethics.

Surrounded by the stiff, formal dignitaries of our early New England Colony, and subjected to their severe laws, and severer social atmosphere, we have a picture of crime and passion. It would be hard to conceive of a greater outrage upon the freezing and self-denying doctrines of that day, than the sin for which Hester Prynne was damned by society, and for which Arthur Dimmesdale damned himself. (p. 488)

[It was Puritan asceticism] which fixed the scarlet letter to the breast of Hester Prynne, and which drove Arthur Dimmesdale into a life of cowardly and selfish meanness, that added tenfold disgrace and ignominy to his original crime. In any form of society hitherto known, the sanctity of the devoted relation between the sexes has constituted the most certain foundation of all purity and all social safety. Imperfect as this great law has been in most of its development, founded upon and founding the rights of property, instead of positively recognizing the delicacy of abstract virtue, and having become, of necessity, in the present organization, a bulwark of hereditary rights, and a bond for a deed of conveyance, it nevertheless appeals to the highest sense of virtue and honor which a man finds in his breast. . . . It was as heir of these virtues, and impressed with this education, that Arthur Dimmesdale, a clergyman, believing in and applying all the moral remedies of the times, found himself a criminal. We learn nothing of his experience during

the seven long years in which his guilt was secretly gnawing at his breast, unless it be the experience of pain and remorse. He speaks no word of wisdom. He lurks and skulks behind the protection of his profession and his social position, neither growing wiser nor stronger, but, day after day, paler and paler, more and more abject. We do not find that, out of his sin, came any revelation of virtue. No doubt exists of his repentance,—of that repentance which is made up of sorrow for sin, and which grows out of fear of consequences; but we learn nowhere that his enlightened conscience, rising above the dogmas and catechistic creeds of the day, by dint of his own deep and solemn spiritual experiences, taught him what obligations had gathered around him, children of his crime, which he was bound to acknowledge before men, as they stood revealed to God. Why had his religious wisdom brought him no more heroism? He loved Hester Prynne—he had bound himself to her by an indissoluble bond, and yet he had neither moral courage nor moral honesty, with all his impressive piety, to come forth and assert their sins and their mutual obligations. He was, evidently, a man of powerful nature. His delicate sensibility, his fervor, his influence upon those about him, and, above all, his sin, committed when the tides of his heart rushed in and swept away all the bulrush barriers he had heaped up against them, through years of studious self-discipline,—show what a spirit, what forces, he had. Against none of these forces had he sinned. And yet he was halting, and wavering, and becoming more and more perplexed and worn down with woe, because he had violated the dignity of his position, and had broken a law which his education had made more prominent than any law in his own soul. In this way, he presented the twofold nature which belongs to us as members of society;—a nature born from ourselves and our associations, and comprehending all the diversity and all the harmony of our individual and social duties. Violation of either destroys our fitness for both. And when we remember that, in this development, no truth comes except from harmony, no beauty except from a fit conjunction of the individual with society, and of society with the individual, can we wonder that the great elements of Arthur Dimmesdale's character should have been overbalanced by a detestable crowd of mean and grovelling qualities, warmed into life by the hot antagonism he felt radiating upon himself and all his fellow-men—from the society in which he moved, and from which he received his engrafted moral nature? He sinned in the arms of society, and fell almost beyond redemption; his companion in guilt became an outcast, and a flood of heroic qualities gathered around her. Was this the work of social influences?

Besides all this, we see in him the powerlessness of belief, alone, to furnish true justification through repentance. (pp. 488-90)

[On Hester Prynne,] we see the effect of open conviction of sin, and the continued galling punishment. The heroic traits awakened in her character by her position were the great self-sustaining properties of woman, which, in tribulation and perplexity, elevate her so far above man. The sullen defiance in her, was imparted to her by society. Without, she met only ignominy, scorn, banishment, a shameful brand. Within, the deep and sacred love for which she was suffering martyrdom,—for her crime was thus sanctified in her own apprehension,—was turned into a store of perplexity, distrust, and madness, which darkened all her heavens. Little Pearl was a token more scarlet than the scarlet letter of her guilt; for the child, with a birth presided over by the most intense conflict of love and fear in the mother's heart, nourished at a breast swelling with anguish, and surrounded with burning marks of its mother's shame in its daily life, developed day by day into a void little demon perched upon the most sacred horn of the mother's altar. Even this child, whose young, plastic nature caught the impress which surrounding circumstances most naturally gave, bewildered and maddened her. The pledge of love which God had given her, seemed perverted into an emblem of hate. And yet how patiently and courageously she labored on, bearing her burthen the more firmly, because, in its infliction, she recognized no higher hand than that of civil authority! In her earnest appeal to be allowed to retain her child, she swept away all external influences, and seems to have inspired the young clergyman, even now fainting with his own sense of meaner guilt, to speak words of truth, which in those days must have seemed born of heaven. (pp. 493-94)

Her social ignominy forced her back upon the true basis of her life. She alone, of all the world, knew the length and breadth of her own secret. Her lawful husband no more pretended to hold a claim, which may always have been a pretence; the father of her child, her own relation to both, and the tragic life which was going on beneath that surface which all men saw, were known to her alone. How poor and miserable must have seemed the punishment which society had inflicted! The scarlet letter was a poor type of the awful truth which she carried within her heart. Without deceit before the world, she stands forth the most heroic person in all that drama. When, from the platform of shame, she bade farewell to that world, she retired to a holier, and sought for such peace as a soul cast out by men may always find. This was her right. No lie hung over her head. Society had heard her story, and had done its worst. And while Arthur Dimmesdale, cherished in the arms of that society which he had outraged, glossing his life with a false coloring which made it beautiful to all beholders, was dying of an inward anguish, Hester stood upon her true ground, denied by this world, and learning that true wisdom which comes through honesty and self-justification. In casting her out, the world had torn from her all the support of its dogmatic teachings, with which it sustains its disciples in their inevitable sufferings, and had compelled her to rely upon that great religious truth which flows instinctively around a life of agony, with its daring freedom. How far behind her in moral and religious excellence was the accredited religious teacher, who was her companion in guilt! Each day which bound her closer and closer to that heaven which was now her only home, drove him farther and farther from the spiritual world, whose glories he so fervently taught others. (pp. 495-96)

To those who would gladly learn the confidence, and power, and patient endurance, and depth of hallowed fervor, which love can create in the human heart, we would present the life of this woman, in her long hours of suffering and loneliness, made sweeter than all the world beside, by the cause in which she suffered. We dare not call that a wicked perversity, which brought its possessor into that state of strong and fiery resolution and elevation, which enabled her to raise her lover from his craven sense of guilt, into a solemn devotion to his better nature. She guided him rightly, by her clear vision of what was in accordance with the holiest promptings of her true heart. Aided by this, she learned what all his theology had never taught him—the power of love to sustain and guide and teach the soul. This bore her through her trial; and this, at that glowing hour when both rose above the weight which bowed them down, tore the scarlet letter from her breast, and made her young and pure again. (p. 498)

*Hawthorne with his publishers, James T. Fields (l.) and William D. Ticknor (r.).*

[*George B. Loring*], ''Hawthorne's 'Scarlet Letter','' *in* Massachusetts Quarterly Review, *Vol. III, No. XII, September, 1850, pp. 484-500.*

## ORESTES A. BROWNSON  (essay date 1850)

[*Brownson, an editor and writer, was one of the chief spokesmen for the American Transcendentalist movement; the following originally appeared in his* Brownson's Review, *October, 1850. Like Anne W. Abbott (1850) and Arthur Cleveland Coxe (1851), Brownson posits that* The Scarlet Letter *is morally objectionable because its characters are unchristian and unrepentant. Like George B. Loring (1850), Brownson views Hester as a spirited character, yet he denounces her convictions as prideful and therefore comes to a conclusion opposed to Loring's.*]

Mr. Hawthorne is a writer endowed with a large share of genius, and in the species of literature he cultivates has no rival in this country, unless it be Washington Irving. His *Twice-told Tales,* his *Mosses from an Old Manse,* and other contributions to the periodical press, have made him familiarly known, and endeared him to a large circle of readers. [*The Scarlet Letter*] is the largest and most elaborate of the romances he has as yet published, and no one can read half a dozen pages of it without feeling that none but a man of true genius and a highly cultivated mind could have written it. It is a work of rare, we may say of fearful power, and to the great body of our countrymen who have no well defined religious belief, and no fixed principles of virtue, it will be deeply interesting and highly pleasing. (p. 163)

Mr. Hawthorne, according to the popular standard of morals in this age and this community, can hardly be said to pervert God's gifts, or to exert an immoral influence. Yet his work is far from being unobjectionable. The story is told with great naturalness, ease, grace, and delicacy, but it is a story that should not have been told. It is a story of crime, of an adulteress and her accomplice, a meek and gifted and highly popular Puritan minister in our early colonial days,—a purely imaginary story, though not altogether improbable. Crimes like the one imagined were not unknown even in the golden days of Puritanism, and are perhaps more common among the descendants of the Puritans than it is at all pleasant to believe; but they are not fit subjects for popular literature, and moral health is not promoted by leading the imagination to dwell on them. There is an unsound state of public morals when the novelist is permitted, without a scorching rebuke, to select such crimes, and invest them with all the fascinations of genius, and all the charms of a highly polished style. In a moral community such crimes are spoken of as rarely as possible, and when spoken of at all, it is always in terms which render them loathsome, and repel the imagination.

Nor is the conduct of the story better than the story itself. The author makes the guilty parties suffer, and suffer intensely, but he nowhere manages so as to make their sufferings excite the horror of his readers for their crime. The adulteress suffers not from remorse, but from regret, and from the disgrace to which her crime has exposed her, in her being condemned to wear emblazoned on her dress the Scarlet Letter which proclaims to all the deed she has committed. The minister, her accomplice, suffers also, horribly, and feels all his life after the same terrible letter branded on his heart, but not from the fact of crime itself, but from the consciousness of not being what he seems to the world, from his having permitted the partner in his guilt to be disgraced, to be punished, without his having the manliness to avow his share in the guilt, and to bear his share of the punishment. Neither ever really repents of the criminal deed; nay, neither ever regards it as really criminal, and both seem to hold it to have been laudable, because they *loved* one another,—as if the love itself were not illicit, and highly criminal. No man has the right to love another man's wife, and no married woman has the right to love any man but her husband. Mr. Hawthorne in the present case seeks to excuse Hester Prynne, a married woman, for loving the Puritan minister, on the ground that she had no love for her husband, and it is hard that a woman should not have some one to love; but this only aggravated her guilt, because she was not only forbidden to love the minister, but commanded to love her husband, whom she had vowed to love, honor, cherish, and obey. The modern doctrine that represents the affections as fatal, and wholly withdrawn from voluntary control, and then allows us to plead them in justification of neglect of duty and breach of the most positive precepts of both the natural and the revealed law, cannot be too severely reprobated.

Human nature is frail, and it is necessary for every one who standeth to take heed lest he fall. Compassion for the fallen is a duty which we all owe, in consideration of our own failings, and especially in consideration of the infinite mercy our God has manifested to his erring and sinful children. But however binding may be this duty, we are never to forget that sin is

sin, and that it is pardonable only through the great mercy of God, on condition of the sincere repentance of the sinner. But in the present case neither of the guilty parties repents of the sin. . . . They hug their illicit love; they cherish their sin; and after the lapse of seven years are ready, and actually agree, to depart into a foreign country, where they may indulge it without disguise and without restraint. Even to the last, even when the minister, driven by his agony, goes so far as to throw off the mask of hypocrisy, and openly confess his crime, he shows no sign of repentance, or that he regarded his deed as criminal.

The Christian who reads *The Scarlet Letter* cannot fail to perceive that the author is wholly ignorant of Christian asceticism, and that the highest principle of action he recognizes is pride. In both the criminals, the long and intense agony they are represented as suffering springs not from remorse, from the consciousness of having offended God, but mainly from the feeling, especially on the part of the minister, that they have failed to maintain the integrity of their character. They have lowered themselves in their own estimation, and cannot longer hold up their heads in society as honest people. It is not their conscience that is wounded, but their pride. *He* cannot bear to think that he wears a disguise, that he cannot be the open, frank, stainless character he had from his youth aspired to be, and *she,* that she is driven from society, lives a solitary outcast, and has nothing to console her but her fidelity to her paramour. There is nothing Christian, nothing really moral, here. The very pride itself is a sin; and pride often a greater sin than that which it restrains us from committing. There are thousands of men and women too proud to commit carnal sins, and to the indomitable pride of our Puritan ancestors we may attribute no small share of their external morality and decorum. It may almost be said, that, if they had less of that external morality and decorum, their case would be less desperate; and often the violation of them, or failure to maintain them, by which their pride receives a shock, and their self-complacency is shaken, becomes the occasion, under the grace of God, of their conversion to truth and holiness. As long as they maintain their self-complacency, are satisfied with themselves, and feel that they have outraged none of the decencies of life, no argument can reach them, no admonition can startle them, no exhortation can move them. Proud of their supposed virtue, free from all self-reproach, they are as placid as a summer morning, pass through life without a cloud to mar their serenity, and die as gently and as sweetly as the infant falling asleep in its mother's arms. . . . Mr. Hawthorne seems never to have learned that pride is not only sin, but the root of all sin, and that humility is not only a virtue, but the root of all virtue. No genuine contrition or repentance ever springs from pride, and the sorrow for sin because it mortifies our pride, or lessens us in our own eyes, is nothing but the effect of pride. All true remorse, all genuine repentance, springs from humility, and is sorrow for having offended God, not sorrow for having offended ourselves.

Mr. Hawthorne also mistakes entirely the effect of Christian pardon upon the interior state of the sinner. He seems entirely ignorant of the religion that can restore peace to the sinner,—true, inward peace, we mean. He would persuade us, that Hester had found pardon, and yet he shows us that she had found no inward peace. (pp. 163-65)

Mr. Hawthorne mistakes the character of confession. He does well to recognize and insist on its necessity; but he is wrong in supposing that its office is simply to disburden the mind by communicating its secrets to another, to restore the sinner to his self-complacency, and to relieve him from the charge of cowardice and hypocrisy. Confession is a duty we owe to God, and a means, not of restoring us to our self-complacency, but of restoring us to the favor of God, and reëstablishing us in his friendship. The work before us is full of mistakes of this sort, in those portions where the author really means to speak like a Christian, and therefore we are obliged to condemn it, where we acquit him of all unchristian intention.

As a picture of the old Puritans, taken from the position of a moderate transcendentalist and liberal of the modern school, the work has its merits; but as little as we sympathize with those stern old Popery-haters, we do not regard the picture as at all just. We should commend where the author condemns, and condemn where he commends. Their treatment of the adulteress was far more Christian than his ridicule of it. (p. 166)

> Orestes A. Brownson, "Literary Notices and Criticisms: 'The Scarlet Letter'," in The Scarlet Letter: Text, Sources, Criticism by Nathaniel Hawthorne, edited by Kenneth S. Lynn, Harcourt Brace & World, 1961, pp. 162-66.

## [ARTHUR CLEVELAND COXE] (essay date 1851)

[Like Anne W. Abbott (1850) and Orestes A. Brownson (1850), Coxe disapproves of the subject matter in The Scarlet Letter. Coxe's harshness exceeds Abbott's and Brownson's, however, for he accuses Hawthorne of insidiously encouraging "social licentiousness" and degrading American literature. He adds that any woman would be insulted by the novel's suggestion of a role different from that described for her in the Gospel. The mention of Brook Farm refers to Hawthorne's six-month stay in this Transcendentalist commune in Roxbury, Massachusetts in 1841; the "late Convention of females" to which Coxe alludes was most likely the first national women's rights convention held at Worcester, Massachusetts in 1850.]

[In "The Scarlet Letter" there] is a provoking concealment of the author's motive, from the beginning to the end of the story; we wonder what he would be at; whether he is making fun of all religion, or only giving a fair hint of the essential sensualism of enthusiasm. But, in short, we are astonished at the kind of incident which he has selected for romance. It may be such incidents were too common, to be wholly out of the question, in a history of the times, but it seems to us that good taste might be pardoned for not giving them prominence in fiction. (p. 505)

And this brings inquiry to its point. Why has our author selected such a theme? Why, amid all the suggestive incidents of life in a wilderness; of a retreat from civilization to which, in every individual case, a thousand circumstances must have concurred to reconcile human nature with estrangement from home and country; or amid the historical connections of our history with Jesuit adventure, savage invasion, regicide outlawry, and French aggression, should the taste of Mr. Hawthorne have preferred as the proper material for romance, the nauseous amour of a Puritan pastor, with a frail creature of his charge, whose mind is represented as far more debauched than her body? Is it, in short, because a running undertide of filth has become as requisite to a romance, as death in the fifth act to a tragedy? Is the French era actually begun in our literature? And is the flesh, as well as the world and the devil, to be henceforth dished up in fashionable novels, and discussed at parties, by spinsters and their beaux, with as unconcealed a relish as they give to the vanilla in their ice cream? We would be slow to believe it, and we hope our author would not willingly have

it so, yet we honestly believe that "The Scarlet Letter" has already done not a little to degrade our literature, and to encourage social licentiousness: it has started other pens on like enterprises, and has loosed the restraint of many tongues, that have made it an apology for "the evil communications which corrupt good manners." We are painfully tempted to believe that it is a book made for the market, and that the market has made it merchantable, as they do game, by letting everybody understand that the commodity is in high condition, and smells strongly of incipient putrefaction.

We shall entirely mislead our reader if we give him to suppose that "The Scarlet Letter" is coarse in its details, or indecent in its phraseology. This very article of our own, is far less suited to ears polite, than any page of the romance before us; and the reason is, we call things by their right names, while the romane never hints the shocking words that belong to its things, but, like Mephistophiles, insinuates that the arch-fiend himself is a very tolerable sort of person, if nobody would call him Mr. Devil. (pp. 506-07)

[In] Hawthorne's tale, the lady's frailty is philosophized into a natural and necessary result of the Scriptural law of marriage, which, by holding her irrevocably to her vows, as plighted to a dried up old book-worm, in her silly girlhood, is viewed as making her heart an easy victim to the adulterer. The sin of her seducer too, seems to be considered as lying not so much in the deed itself, as in his long concealment of it, and, in fact, the whole moral of the tale is given in the words—"Be true—be true," as if sincerity in sin were virtue, and as if "Be clean—be clean," were not the more fitting conclusion. "The untrue man" is, in short, the hang-dog of the narrative, and the unclean one is made a very interesting sort of a person, and as the two qualities are united in the hero, their composition creates the interest of his character. Shelley himself never imagined a more dissolute conversation than that in which the polluted minister comforts himself with the thought, that the revenge of the injured husband is worse than his own sin in instigating it. "Thou and I never did so, Hester"—he suggests: and she responds—"never, never! What we did had a consecration of its own, we felt it so—we said so to each other!" This is a little too much—it carries the Bay-theory a little too far for our stomach! "Hush, Hester!" is the sickish rejoinder; and fie, Mr. Hawthorne! is the weakest token of our disgust that we can utter. The poor bemired hero and heroine of the story should not have been seen wallowing in their filth, at such a rate as this.

We suppose this sort of sentiment must be charged to the doctrines enforced at "Brook-farm," although "Brook-farm" itself could never have been Mr. Hawthorne's home, had not other influences prepared him for such a Bedlam. At all events, this is no mere slip of the pen; it is the essential morality of the work. If types, and letters, and words can convey an author's idea, he has given us the key to the whole, in a very plain intimation that the Gospel has not set the relations of man and woman where they should be, and that a new Gospel is needed to supersede the seventh commandment, and the bond of Matrimony. Here it is, in full: our readers shall see what the world may expect from Hawthorne, if he is not stopped short, in such brothelry. Look at this conclusion:—

> Women—in the continually recurring trials of wounded, wasted, wronged, misplaced, or erring and sinful passion, or with the dreary burden of a heart unyielded, because unvalued and unsought—came to Hester's cottage, demand-

ing why they were so wretched, and what the remedy! Hester comforted and counseled them as best she might. She assured them too *of her firm belief,* that, at some brighter period, when the world should have grown ripe for it, in Heaven's own time, *a new truth would be revealed, in order to establish the whole relation between man and woman on a surer ground of mutual happiness.*

This is intelligible English; but are Americans content that such should be the English of their literature? This is the question on which we have endeavored to deliver our own earnest convictions, and on which we hope to unite the suffrages of all virtuous persons, in sympathy with the abhorrence we so unhesitatingly express. To think of making such speculations the amusement of the daughters of America! The late Convention of females at Boston, to assert the "rights of woman," may show us that there are already some, who think the world is even now *ripe for it*; and safe as we may suppose our own fair relatives to be above such a low contagion, we must remember that to a woman, the very suggestion of a mode of life for her, as preferable to that which the Gospel has made the glorious sphere of her duties and her joys, is an insult and a degradation, to which no one that loves her would allow her to be exposed.

We assure Mr. Hawthorne, in conclusion, that nothing less than an earnest wish that his future career may redeem this misstep, and prove a blessing to his country, has tempted us to enter upon a criticism so little suited to our tastes, as that of his late production. (pp. 509-11)

> [Arthur Cleveland Coxe], "The Writings of Haw-thorne," in The Church Review, *Vol. III, No. 4, January, 1851, pp. 489-511.*

### *BLACKWOOD'S EDINBURGH MAGAZINE*  (essay date 1855)

> [*Commenting on the "unwholesome fascination" of* The Scarlet Letter, *this reviewer praises the novel's intense and exciting atmosphere while suggesting that Hawthorne depicts his characters in an overly clinical manner, "rather as a surgeon might exhibit his pet 'cases'." For similar views on Hawthorne's characterization, see the excerpts by E. P. Whipple (1850) and Brigid Brophy, Michael Levey, and Charles Osborne (1967).*]

The books of Mr. Hawthorne are singular books: they introduce to us not only an individual mind, but a peculiar audience; they are not stories into which you enter and sympathise, but dramas of extraordinary dumb show, before which, in darkness and breathless silence, you sit and look on, never sure for a moment that the dimly-lighted stage before you is not to be visited by the dioramic thunders of an earthquake, falling houses, moaning victims, dismay and horror and gloom. . . . *The Scarlet Letter* glows with the fire of a suppressed, secret, feverish excitement; it is not the glow of natural life, but the hectic of disease which burns upon the cheeks of its actors. The proud woman, the fantastic and elfish child, the weak and criminal genius, and the injured friend, the husband of Hester, are exhibited to us rather as a surgeon might exhibit his pet "cases," than as a poet shows his men and women, brothers and sisters to the universal heart. In this book the imagination of the writer has been taxed to supply a world and a society in accordance with the principal actors in his feverish drama. The whole sky and air are tropical; and instead of the gentle monotony of ordinary existence, its long, wearing, languid sorrows, its vulgar weariness and sleep, we have a perpetual strain of excite-

ment—a fire that neither wanes nor lessens, but keeps at its original scorching heat for years. The landscape is parched and scathed; the breeze is a furnace-blast; the volcano is muttering and growling in the depths of the earth; there is an ominous stillness, like the pause before a great peal of thunder. Nor is the air once clear, nor the fever dissipated, till, with a sigh of relief, we escape from the unwholesome fascination of this romance, and find ourselves in a world which is not always tending towards some catastrophe—a world where tears and showers fall to refresh the soil, and where calamities do not come from the blind and mocking hands of fate, but mixed with blessings and charities from the very gates of heaven. (pp. 562-63)

> "Modern Novelists—Great and Small," in Black-wood's Edinburgh Magazine, *Vol. LXXVII, No. CCCCLXXV, May, 1855, pp. 554-68.*\*

### ANTHONY TROLLOPE  (essay date 1879)

> [*A distinguished Victorian novelist, Trollope is best known for his "Barsetshire Chronicles," a series of novels that realistically and humorously depicts English provincial life. In his appraisal of* The Scarlet Letter, *excerpted below, he briefly discusses characterization; among other observations, Trollope notes that Hester is the only character with whom the reader can sympathize and that Pearl's "miraculous" personality is inconsistent with the rest of Hawthorne's characterizations in the novel. For a contrasting point of view on Pearl, see the excerpt by Anne W. Abbott (1850). More importantly, Trollope was one of the first critics to point out Hawthorne's ambivalent attitude toward his subject matter. Such later critics as Frederic I. Carpenter (1944), Richard Harter Fogle (1952), Hyatt H. Waggoner (1955), and Terence Martin (1983) discuss Hawthorne's ambivalence in greater detail.*]

[The personages in **"The Scarlet Letter"**] with whom the reader will interest himself are four,—the husband, the minister who has been the sinful lover, the woman, and the child. The reader is expected to sympathize only with the woman,—and will sympathize only with her. The husband, an old man who has knowingly married a young woman who did not love him, is a personification of that feeling of injury which is supposed to fall upon a man when his honor has been stained by the falseness of a wife. (p. 209)

With the man, the minister, the lover, the reader finds that he can have nothing in common, though he is compelled to pity his sufferings. . . . [Of Hester and Dimmesdale, he] is the greater sufferer. While shame only deals with her, conscience is at work with him. But there can be no sympathy, because he looks on and holds his peace. Her child says to him,—her child, not knowing that he is her father, not knowing what she says, but in answer to him when he would fain take her little hand in his during the darkness of night,—"Wilt thou stand here with mother and me to-morrow noontide"? He can not bring himself to do that, though he struggles hard to do it, and therefore we despise him. He can not do it till the hand of death is upon him, and then the time is too late for reparation in the reader's judgment. Could we have sympathized with a pair of lovers, the human element would have prevailed too strongly for the author's purpose.

He seems hardly to have wished that we should sympathize even with her; or, at any rate, he has not bid us in so many words to do so, as is common with authors. Of course, he has wished it. (pp. 209-10)

The fourth character is that of the child, Pearl. Here the author has, I think, given way to a temptation, and in doing so has not increased the power of his story. The temptation was, that Pearl should add a picturesque element by being an elf and also a charming child. Elf she is, but, being so, is incongruous with all else in the story, in which, unhuman as it is, there is nothing of the ghost-like, nothing of the unnatural. The old man becomes a fiend, so to say, during the process of the tale; but he is a man-fiend. And Hester becomes sublimated almost to divine purity; but she is still simply a woman. The minister is tortured beyond the power of human endurance; but neither do his sufferings nor his failure of strength adequate to support them come to him from any miraculous agency. But Pearl is miraculous,—speaking, acting, and thinking like an elf,—and is therefore, I think, a drawback rather than an aid. The desolation of the woman, too, would have been more perfect without the child. It seems as though the author's heart had not been hard enough to make her live alone;—as sometimes when you punish a child you can not drive from your face that gleam of love which shoots across your frown and mars its salutary effect.

Hatred, fear, and shame are the passions which revel through the book. To show how a man may so hate as to be content to sacrifice everything to his hatred; how another may fear so that, even though it be for the rescue of his soul, he can not bring himself to face the reproaches of the world; how a woman may bear her load of infamy openly before the eyes of all men,—this has been Hawthorne's object. And surely no author was ever more successful. The relentless purpose of the man, in which is exhibited no passion, in which there is hardly a touch of anger, is as fixed as the hand of Fate. (p. 211)

But through all this intensity of suffering, through this blackness of narrative, there is ever running a vein of drollery. As Hawthorne himself says, "a lively sense of the humorous again stole in among the solemn phantoms of her thought." He is always laughing at something with his weird, mocking spirit. The very children when they see Hester in the streets are supposed to speak of her in this wise: "Behold, verily, there is the woman of the scarlet letter. Come, therefore, and let us fling mud at her." Of some religious book he says, "It must have been a work of vast ability in the somniferous school of literature." "We must not always talk in the market-place of what happens to us in the forest," says even the sad mother to her child. Through it all there is a touch of burlesque,—not as to the suffering of the sufferers, but as to the great question whether it signifies much in what way we suffer, whether by crushing sorrows or little stings. Who would not sooner be Prometheus than a yesterday's tipsy man with this morning's sick-headache? In this way Hawthorne seems to ridicule the very woes which he expends himself in depicting. (pp. 212-13)

*Anthony Trollope, "The Genius of Nathaniel Hawthorne," in* The North American Review, *Vol. CXXIX, No. 274, September, 1879, pp. 203-22.*

## W. D. HOWELLS  (essay date 1901)

[*Howells was the chief progenitor of American realism and an influential American literary critic during the late nineteenth and early twentieth centuries. Although he wrote nearly three dozen novels, few of them are read today. Despite his eclipse, however, he stands as one of the major literary figures of the late nineteenth century; having successfully weaned American literature from the sentimental romanticism of its infancy, he earned the popular sobriquet "the Dean of American Letters." In this excerpt, How-*

*ells lauds Hawthorne's realistic characterization and his essential modernity. W. C. Brownell (1909) offers a similar view of Hawthorne's method, whereas John Macy (1913) provides a contrasting one.*]

From the first there is no affectation of shadowy uncertainty in the setting of the great tragedy of **"The Scarlet Letter."** As nearly as can be, the scenes of the several events are ascertained, and are identified with places in actual Boston. With a like inward sense of strong reality in his material, and perhaps compelled to its expression by that force in the concept, each detail of the drama, in motive, action, and character, is substantiated, so that from first to last it is visible, audible, tangible. From Hester Prynne in her prison—before she goes out to stand with her unlawful child in her arms and the scarlet letter on her breast before the Puritan magistracy and ministry and people, and be charged by the child's own father, as her pastor, to give him up to like ignominy—to Hester Prynne, kneeling over her dying paramour, on the scaffold, and mutely helping him to own his sin before all that terrible little world, there is the same strong truth beating with equal pulse from the core of the central reality, and clothing all its manifestations in the forms of credible, of indisputable personality.

In its kind the romance remains sole, and it is hard to see how it shall ever be surpassed, or even companioned. It is not without faults, without quaint foibles of manner which strike one oddly in the majestic movement of the story; but with the exception of the love-child or sin-child, Pearl, there is no character, important or unimportant, about which you are asked to make believe: they are all there to speak and act for themselves, and they do not need the help of your fancy. They are all of a verity so robust that if one comes to declare Hester chief among them, it is with instant misgivings for the right of her secret paramour, Arthur Dimmesdale, and her secret husband, Roger Chillingworth, to that sorrowful supremacy. A like doubt besets the choice of any one moment of her history as most specific, most signal. (pp. 164-65)

In certain things **"The Scarlet Letter,"** which was the first of Hawthorne's romances, is the modernest and maturest. The remoteness of the time and the strangeness of the Puritan conditions authorize that stateliness of the dialogue which he loved. The characters may imaginably say "methinks" and "peradventure," and the other things dear to the characters of the historical romancer; the narrator himself may use an antiquated or unwonted phrase in which he finds color, and may eschew the short-cuts and informalities of our actual speech, without impeaching himself of literary insincerity. In fact, he may heighten by these means the effect he is seeking; and if he will only keep human nature strongly and truly in mind, as Hawthorne does in **"The Scarlet Letter,"** we shall gratefully allow him a privilege which may or may not be law. Through the veil of the quaint parlance, and under the seventeenth-century costuming, we see the human heart beating there the same as in our own time and in all times, and the antagonistic motives working which have governed human conduct from the beginning and shall govern it forever, world without end.

Hester Prynne and Arthur Dimmesdale are no mere types of open shame and secret remorse. It is never concealed from us that he was a man whose high and pure soul had its strongest contrast in the nature

Mixt with cunning sparks of hell,

in which it was tabernacled for earth. It is still less hidden that, without one voluntary lure or wicked art, she was of a look and make to win him with the love that was their undoing. . . . They were both of their time and place, materially as well as spiritually; their lives were under the law, but their natures had once been outside it, and might be again. The shock of this simple truth can hardly be less for the witness, when, after its slow and subtle evolution, it is unexpectedly flashed upon him, than it must have been for the guilty actors in this drama, when they recognize that, in spite of all their open and secret misery, they are still lovers, and capable of claiming for the very body of their sin a species of justification. (pp. 167-68)

[In the forest scene, there is a greatness] which is unmatched, I think, in the book, and, I was almost ready to say, out of it. At any rate, I believe we can find its parallel only in some of the profoundly impassioned pages of the Russian novelists who, casting aside all the common adjuncts of art, reveal us to ourselves in the appeal from their own naked souls. Hawthorne had another ideal than theirs, and a passing love of style, and the meaning of the music of words. For the most part, he makes us aware of himself, of his melancholy grace and sombre power; we feel his presence in every passage, however deeply, however occultly, dramatic; he overshadows us, so that we touch and see through him. But here he is almost out of it; only a few phrases of comment, so fused in feeling with the dialogue that they are like the voice of a chorus, remind us of him.

It is the most exalted instant of the tragedy, it is the final evolution of Hester Prynne's personality. In this scene she

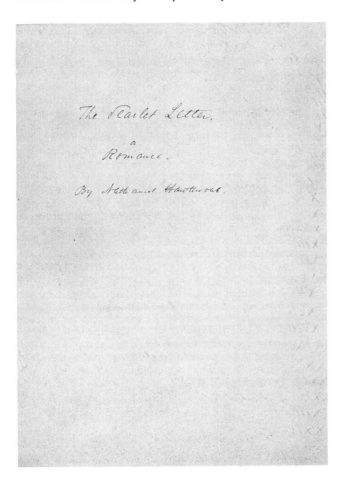

*Facsimile of the manuscript title page of* The Scarlet Letter.

dominates by virtue of whatever is womanly and typical in her, and no less by what is personal and individual. In what follows, she falls like Dimmesdale and Chillingworth under the law of their common doom, and becomes a figure on the board where for once she seemed to direct the game.

In all fiction one could hardly find a character more boldly, more simply, more quietly imagined. She had done that which in the hands of a feeble or false talent would have been suffered or made to qualify her out of all proportion and keeping with life. But her transgression does not qualify her, as transgression never does unless it becomes habit. She remains exterior and superior to it, a life of other potentialities, which in her narrow sphere she fulfils. What she did has become a question between her and her Maker, who apparently does not deal with it like a Puritan. The obvious lesson of the contrasted fates of Dimmesdale and herself is that to own sin is to disown it, and that it cannot otherwise be expropriated and annulled. Yet, in Hester's strong and obstinate endurance of her punishment there is publicity but not confession; and perhaps there is a lesson of no slighter meaning in the inference that ceasing to do evil is, after all, the most that can be asked of human nature. Even that seems to be a good deal, and in **"The Scarlet Letter"** it is a stroke of mastery to show that it is not always ours to cease to do evil, but that in extremity we need the help of the mystery "not ourselves, that makes for righteousness," and that we may call Chance or that we may call God, but that does not change in essence or puissance whatever name we give it. (pp. 173-74)

*W. D. Howells, "Hawthorne's Hester Prynne," in his* Heroines of Fiction, *Vol. I, Harper & Brothers Publishers, 1901, pp. 161-74.*

### W. C. BROWNELL (essay date 1909)

[*Like W. D. Howells (1901), Brownell applauds Hawthorne's realistic characterization in* The Scarlet Letter, *but considers his treatment of Chillingworth "a wasted opportunity." Further, Brownell comments that Hawthorne's exclusion of passion in order to focus on concealment "contributes to the originality and the perfection" of the narrative. He concludes by deeming* The Scarlet Letter *"the Puritan 'Faust'" because the work is distinguished by its superb use of allegory and symbolism. For a contrasting view of* The Scarlet Letter *see the excerpt below by John Macy (1913).*]

["**The Scarlet Letter**"] is not only an original work in a field where originality is the next thing to a miracle, but a work whose originality is in no wise more marked than its intrinsic substance.

It is not a story of adultery. The word does not, I think, occur in the book—a circumstance in itself typifying the detachment of the conception and the delicate art of its execution. But in spite of its detachment and delicacy, the inherent energy of the theme takes possession of the author's imagination and warms it into exalted exercise, making it in consequence at once the most real and the most imaginative of his works. It is essentially a story neither of the sin nor of the situation of illicit love— presents neither its psychology nor its social effects; neither excuses nor condemns nor even depicts, from this specific point of view. The love of Hester and Dimmesdale is a postulate, not a presentment. Incidentally, of course, the sin colors the narrative, and the situation is its particular result. But, essentially, the book is a story of concealment. Its psychology is that of the concealment of sin amid circumstances that make a sin of concealment itself. The sin itself might, one may almost say, be almost any other. And this constitutes no small part of the book's formal originality. To fail to perceive this is quite to misconceive it. As a story of illicit love its omissions are too great, its significance is not definite enough, its detail has not enough richness, the successive scenes of which it is composed have not an effective enough cohesion. From this point of view, but for the sacred profession of the minister and the conduct this imposes, it would be neither moving nor profound. Its moral would not be convincing. Above all, Chillingworth is a mistake, or at most a wasted opportunity. For he is specialized into a mere function of malignity, and withdrawn from the reader's sympathies, whereas what completes, if it does not constitute, the tragedy of adultery, is the sharing by the innocent of the punishment of the guilty. This inherent element of the situation, absolutely necessary to a complete presentment of it, the crumbling of the innocent person's inner existence, is absolutely neglected in "**The Scarlet Letter,**" and the element of a malevolent persecution of the culpable substituted for it. The innocent person thereby becomes, as I have already said, a device, and though in this way Hawthorne is enabled to vivify the effect of remorse upon the minister by personifying its furies, in this way, too, he sacrifices at once the completeness of his picture and its depth of truth by disregarding one of its most important elements.

He atones for this by concentration on the culpable. It is *their* psychology alone that he exhibits. And though in this way he has necessarily failed to write the *chef-d'oeuvre* of the general subject that in the field of art has been classic since monogamy established itself in society, he has produced a perfect masterpiece in the more detached and withdrawn sphere more in harmony with his genius. In narrowing his range and observing its limits he has perhaps even increased the poignancy of his effect. And his effect *is* poignant and true as reality itself. In confining himself to the concealment of sin rather than depicting its phenomena and its results, he has indeed brought out, as has never been done elsewhere, the importance of this fatal increment of falsity among the factors of the whole chaotic and unstable moral equilibrium. Concealment in "**The Scarlet Letter,**" to be sure, is painted in very dark colors. In similar cases it may be a duty, and is, at all events, the mere working of a natural instinct—at worst a choice of the lesser evil. But surely there is no exaggeration or essential loss of truth in the suggestion of its potentialities for torture conveyed by the agony of the preacher's double life. It is true his concealment condemned another to solitary obloquy. But if that be untypically infrequent and also not inherent in the situation as such, it is fairly counterbalanced by consolatory thought of the exceptional havoc confession would have wrought in his case. That is to say, if his remorse is exceptionally acute it is also exceptionally alleviated. On the whole the potential torture of remorse for a life that is flagrantly an acted lie is not misrepresented, either in truth or art, by the fate of Dimmesdale, though it is treated in the heightened way appropriate to the typical.

Concentration upon concealment further contributes to the originality and the perfection of "**The Scarlet Letter**" by eliminating passion. The sensuous element which might have served to extenuate the offence—since it is of its tragic essence that nothing can excuse it in anything like normal conditions—or if not that to render the story attractive and affecting, is rigidly excluded. (pp. 116-19)

[In "**The Scarlet Letter,**"] for once, with Hawthorne we have allegory richly justifying itself, the allegory of literature not that of didacticism, of the imagination not of the fancy, allegory neither vitiated by caprice nor sterilized by moralizing, but firmly grounded in reality and nature. Note how, accordingly, even the ways of the wicked fairy that obsessed him are made to serve him, for even the mirage and symbolism so dear to his mind and so inveterate in his practice, blend legitimately with the pattern of his thoroughly naturalistic fabric. The fanciful element is, at least, so imaginatively treated as to seem, exceptionally, to "belong." Hawthorne seems to have been so "possessed" by his story as to have conducted the development of its formal theme for once subconsciously, so to speak, and with the result of decorating rather than disintegrating reality in its exposition. At all events, to this "possession" (how complete it was in material fact all his biographers attest) two notable and wholly exceptional results are due. In the first place he *felt* his theme, as he never felt it elsewhere, and consequently presented it with an artistic cogency he never elsewhere attained. The story, in other words, is real and true. If it is thought to show a bias in pushing too far the doom of evil, to ignore the whole New Testament point of view, as it may be called, epitomized in the Master's "Go and sin no more," the answer is that though in this way it may lose in typical value, it gains in imaginative realism, since it is a story of that Puritan New England where it sometimes seems as if the New Testament had been either suspect or unknown. Besides, there is enough demonstration of its text on the hither side of what it is necessary to invoke the Puritan *milieu* to justify. Every erring soul may not suffer the extremity of Dimmesdale's agony, but it suffers enough, and the inevitability of its suffering was never more convincingly exhibited than in this vivid picture, softened as it is into a subdued intensity by the artist's poetized, however predetermined, treatment. For, in the second place, it is here alone that Hawthorne seems to have felt his *characters* enough to feel them sympathetically and so to realize them to the full. They are very real and very human. What the imagination of a recluse, even, can do to this end when held to its own inspiration and not seduced into the realm of the fantastic, may be seen in the passage where Hester pleads for the continued custody of her child. Pearl herself is a jewel of romance. Nothing more imaginatively real than this sprite-like and perverse incarnation of the moral as well as physical sequence of her parents' sin exists in romance. Her individuality is an inspiration deduced with the logic of nature and with such happy art that her symbolic quality is as incidental in appearance as it is seen to be inherent on reflection. . . . Chillingworth, the other symbolic character, is in contrast an embodied abstraction—the one piece of machinery of the book. But it cannot be denied that he performs a needful function and, artistically, is abundantly justified. As a Puritan parallel of Mephistopheles he is very well handled. "**The Scarlet Letter**" is, in fact, the Puritan "Faust," and its symbolic and allegorical element, only obtrusive in a detail here and there at most, lifts it out of the ordinary category of realistic romance without—*since nothing of importance is sacrificed to it*—enfeebling its imaginative reality. The beautiful and profound story is our chief prose masterpiece and it is as difficult to overpraise it as it is to avoid poignantly regretting that Hawthorne failed to recognize its value and learn the lesson it might have taught him. (pp. 121-23)

> *W. C. Brownell, "Hawthorne," in his* American Prose Masters, *Charles Scribner's Sons, 1909, pp. 63-132.*

## JOHN MACY   (essay date 1913)

*[Unlike such previous critics as W. D. Howells (1901) and W. C. Brownell (1909), who concentrated on the realistic aspects of* The

Scarlet Letter, *Macy views the novel as "a prose poem" in which each character "is a mood, a tone." Macy concludes that understood as such,* The Scarlet Letter *"is a perfect book in every detail."*]

Fictitious literary history is wont to regard Hawthorne as the chronicler and poetic embodiment of the Puritan spirit. The Puritans were gloomy and Hawthorne was gloomy; behold, the assimilation is perfect, the heredity is self-evident. In sooth, Hawthorne was the least Puritan of the New England writers; the spirit, the character, the history of his Puritan forefathers he did not know any better than he knew the history and characters of mediaeval Italians whose palaces and dungeons he gazed on without much enthusiasm. . . . The removal of Puritan inhibitions was a necessary condition of the beginning of anything like art in New England, and Hawthorne was notably free from the spirit of Puritanism. He was as far removed as Poe from any sort of ethical tradition that prevailed about him or that had prevailed before him. Indeed, he was the only one of the New Englanders who was purely artistic; and this fact is fundamentally related to the other fact that he was the only New England man of letters who was not deeply moved by black slavery or any of the burning issues of the time. He was interested in fanciful manifestations of the soul, not in genuine ethical problems; his home was fairyland, and he was especially fain of haunted woods and treacherous bogs.

He approached the Puritans just as he approached Greek Wonder Tales. **"The Scarlet Letter"** is in no sense a historical novel of Puritan life, any more than Macbeth is a study of the early history of Scotland. The problem of conscience is not for Hawthorne an aspect of the national mind or of the moral development of his "dear native land." It is a motive for story and legend to be wrought out in the purple colours of which he was master. The soul suffering from remorse is creepy and fascinating, and Hawthorne plays with it as Poe does, and as Stevenson does in "Markheim." People will continue to regard Hawthorne as the Blossom of Puritanism and to picture his handsomely melancholy face as a spiritual descendant of witchhangers. That is the *cliché* of the matter and it is in all the books. But Hawthorne, fortunately, was a mildly irreverent man, charmed by the colours of things, and somewhat sceptical of the intense beliefs of his contemporaries. The theme of **"The Scarlet Letter"** appealed less to his moral sense than to his pictorial imagination. He turned the symbol over and over, and embroidered his story with it. It is a red spot on a gray colonial dress. It is a bloody brand on a man's breast. It is a fiery portent in the sky. Hawthorne was enamoured of its hue and he designed it cunningly like a worker in tapestry against the tortured conscience of Dimmesdale, and against Chillingworth, the skulking ghost of revenge. They are two tones of blackish purple. Pearl is another colour, not a human child, but a symbolized flower of sin, a gem in the darkness. (pp. 83-4)

The story of Hester is not poignantly tragic, it is not even sentimentally pathetic like Goethe's story of Margaret. Hester Prynne is a "vaguely defined figure aloft on the place of shame." She does not live in the real world of the Rev. Cotton Mather, his "Magnalia," nor in the other real world of Thomas Hardy's "Tess." The development of her character, under suffering and the sweet influence of her child, is an abstract idea, beautifully suggested, but not the growth of a human heart in the breast of a flesh-and-blood woman. Dimmesdale is a voice, a clerical garment, a flat figure in a thin morality play, not a man whose passion has overcome a woman.

**"The Scarlet Letter"** is a prose poem, a development of the theme: "On a Field Sable, the Letter A, Gules." To regard it

as a novel of human character is to dissolve its enchantment. As well look for character in "The Eve of St. Agnes" or "Christabel," or "The Fall of The House of Usher." Each person in the story is a mood, a tone. Chillingworth's approach is like a change of the weather, a pervasive shadow darkening the sky. Dimmesdale and the gloom of the forest blend not as a living man with nature but as a sad theme of music with sombre under-harmonies.

So understood, **"The Scarlet Letter"** is a perfect book. No word, no suggestion, detail or scene, but is set in its place with sure artistry. Hawthorne knew thoroughly the nature and the methods of his art. He did not stumble into success, but worked with his eyes open. (pp. 85-6)

John Macy, "Hawthorne," in his The Spirit of American Literature, *Doubleday, Page & Company, 1913, pp. 77-96.*

## CARL VAN DOREN (essay date 1920)

[*Van Doren was a noted twentieth-century American critic, editor, historian, and biographer. Here, he explores the way in which the themes of* The Scarlet Letter *reflect Hawthorne's attitude toward Puritanism. According to Van Doren, Hawthorne's artistic treatment of sin transcends the boundaries and enriches the context of Puritan doctrine.*]

[When Hawthorne, in **"The Scarlet Letter,"**] gave the world the finest flower of three hundred years of American Puritanism, he passed quietly by the ordinary surfaces of life, not for lack of talent in portraying them, but for lack of interest in them. In thus being a Puritan to the extent that he rarely lifted his gaze from the human spirit in its sincerest hours, he was also a poet. During his long experimental stage as a writer of brief tales he had brooded over the confused spectacle of mankind, posing for himself one after another of the soul's problems and translating them into lucid forms of beauty; now he posed a larger problem on a larger scale. If his matter was at once that of the Puritan and that of the poet, so was his manner. The Puritan's parsimony in Hawthorne lies very close to the artist's passionate economy.

The impact which the story makes may be traced back of Hawthorne's art and personality to the old Puritan tradition which, much as he might disagree with it on occasion, he had none the less in his blood. Some ancestral strain accounts for this conception of adultery as an affair not of the civil order but of the immortal soul. The same strain in his constitution, moreover, makes of these circumstances more than the familiar triangle. A Frenchman might have painted the joy of Dimmesdale, the lover, with his forbidden mistress; an Italian might have traced the fierce course of Chillingsworth (*sic*), the husband, to a justified revenge; a German might have exhibited Hester, the offending wife, as actually achieving an outer freedom to match that one within. Hawthorne transfers the action to a different plane. Let the persons in the triple conflict be involved as they may with one another, each of them stands essentially apart from the remaining two, because each is occupied with a still vaster conflict, with good and evil as the rival elements which continually tug at the poor human creature. Small wonder, then, that the flesh, to which the sin was superficially due, should go unsung; that the bliss of the senses should hardly once be attended to. After such fleeting pleasures comes the inexorable judgment, which is of the spirit not of the body. To the Puritan imagination, journeys begin, not end, in lovers meeting. The tragedy of Dimmesdale lies in his defeat by evil through the temptation of cowardice and hypocrisy, which are sins. Chillingsworth tragically, and sinfully, chooses evil when he decides to take a treacherous vengeance into his own hands, though vengeance, he knows, is another's. Hester alone emerges from her guilt through her public expiation and the long practice of virtue afterward.

So far "The Scarlet Letter" agrees with the doctrines of the Puritans. Its broader implications critically transcend them. . . . In one respect [Hawthorne] seems sterner than the elder Puritans, for he admits into his narrative no hope of any providential intervention which might set these jangled bells again into accord. Dimmesdale will not encourage Hester to hope for a compensating future life even. The consequences of deeds live forever. At the same time, Hawthorne has drawn the action down from heaven's pavement, where Milton would have conducted it, to earth, and has humanized it to the extent that he centers it in human bosoms. (p. 649)

To the actual contemporaries of Hester and Dimmesdale it would have seemed a blasphemy worse than adultery for the lovers to agree, in their meeting at the brookside, that "what we did had a consecration of its own." These are Hester's words, and so it was to Hester that eventually "it seemed a fouler offense committed by Roger Chillingsworth than any which has since been done him, that, in the time when her heart knew no better, he had persuaded her to fancy herself happy by his side." Hester thus becomes the type—subtly individualized but yet a type—of the moving principle of life which different societies in different ways may constrain but which in itself irresistibly endures. Her story is an allegory of the passion through which the race continues. She feels the ignominy which attends her own irregular behavior and accepts her fate as the reward of evil, but she does not understand it so far as to wish uncommitted the act which her society calls a sin. A harder woman might have become an active rebel; a softer woman might have sunk passively down into unavailing penitence. Hester stands erect, and thinks. She asked herself whether women as life was constituted could be happy. "As concerned her own individual existence, she had long ago decided in the negative, and dismissed the point as settled." Yet her mind, though dismissing her particular case as a malady without hope, still ranges the universe for some cure for the injustice her sex inherits. "The world's law was no law for her mind." In this manner those whom the world crushes always take their surest revenge. Hester finds no speculative answer; and so she turns to action, plays her necessary part, and gives herself to the nurture of her child, no less a mother than if approved by every human ordinance. A universal allegory of motherhood, her story is also a criticism of the Puritan attempt to bind life too tightly. In the midst of the drab circumstances of Salem this woman of such radiance of beauty and magnificence of life rises up and cracks the stiff frame of the time. Great as her own suffering is, she has in some measure contributed to let a little light into the general tragedy of her sex. "The Scarlet Letter" is not merely a Puritan story. A spirit larger than Puritanism, as large as the whole world's experience, informs and ripens the book. (pp. 649-50)

[In a world, Hawthorne] asked himself, where human instincts are continually at war with human laws, and where laws, once broken, pursue the offender even more fiercely than they hedged him before, how are any but the more docile spirits to hold their course without calamity? The Puritan Fathers to the same inquiry, which they asked hardly more frequently than Hawthorne, could point in answer to election and atonement and divine grace. Hawthorne had inherited the old questions but not the old answers. He did not free himself from the Puritan mode of believing that to break a law is to commit a sin, or that to commit a sin is to play havoc with the soul; but he changed the terms and considered the sin as a violation less of some supernatural law than of the natural integrity of the soul. Whereas another romancer by tracking the course of the instincts which lead to what is called sin might have sought to justify them as native to the offender and so inescapable, Hawthorne accepts sin without a question and studies the consequences. He brought to his representation of the theme sanity without cynicism and tenderness without softness; he brought also, what is rarer than depth of moralism, an art finely rounded, a rich, graceful style, a spirit sweet and wholesome. He found a substance apparently as unpromising as the original soil upon which the Pilgrims established their commonwealth, and no less than they with their stony province he tamed and civilized it—going beyond them, moreover, by lifting it into an enduring loveliness. . . . (p. 650)

Carl Van Doren, "The Flower of Puritanism," in The Nation, *Vol. CXI, No. 2892, December 8, 1920, pp. 649-50.*

## RÉGIS MICHAUD    (essay date 1928)

[Michaud offers a brief Freudian interpretation of Hawthorne's "psychological realism" in The Scarlet Letter. Describing the theme of the novel as the dangers of inhibition, Michaud states that Hester and Dimmesdale, the victims of repression, find happiness "through their abandonment to the freed libido."]

Hawthorne's imagination was pagan. The two protagonists of "The Scarlet Letter", considered his most puritanical book, are thoroughly immoral. They begin in anguish through the suppression of their desires and end in happiness through their abandonment to the freed libido. (pp. 33-4)

I do not wish to introduce Doctor Freud everywhere, nor do I want to exaggerate Hawthorne's immoralism, but if there has ever been a piece of literature written to prove the dangers of the famous Freudian inhibition and to try to cure it, that work is certainly "The Scarlet Letter."

The wealth of psychological intuition in this novel is remarkable. It is the most human, the least moralizing (I was about to say the most personal of Hawthorne's novels), excepting of course the ending, edifying and conventional as could be desired, but which is neither better nor worse than all Hawthorne's endings. . . . Hawthorne is very canny in attributing to the Puritan Hester a rich, a voluptuous and almost "oriental" temperament. There does not exist, to my knowledge, even in Zola's famous description of the Paradou (in "La Faute de l'abbé Mouret") a more impetuous and eloquent burst of passion than the ending of "The Scarlet Letter", particularly the scene in the forest between the spirited Hester and the timid Dimmesdale whom she rescues from his hysterical inhibitions by her impassioned declarations.

An example of Hawthorne's psychological realism, still more characteristic than this case of Freudian evasion so exactly described, is the method which he used to wring from Hester's lover his secret. Dimmesdale's character is a masterpiece of intuition. He is a hypocrite but only through timidity, and in all, a tragic and pathetic figure, one of those weak and incomplete beings who have not even the courage to lie. . . . A victim, like Hester, of social conventions, but less courageous than she, less sure of himself in passion, Dimmesdale lacks very little to become the American Tartuffe [from Molière's play of the same name.]. But he is saved by Hester, who exorcises him at the end, and rescues him from repression. The minister's open confession on the pillory is an admirable scene. . . . It is an explosion of craving and of repressed passion. From the viewpoint of modern psychology this scene is natural and scientific.

But the most striking is the fashion in which Hawthorne endeavors to surprise Dimmesdale's secret. For that purpose he invented a very curious secondary character, Doctor Chillingworth. . . . [In Chillingworth's examinations of Dimmesdale,] Hawthorne shows himself again a very subtle psychologist and a precursor and pioneer of psychoanalysis. All the conditions in these scenes are so worked out that Dimmesdale's resistance takes on a truly Freudian aspect. Dimmesdale will release his secret for no consideration. In fact, to the very end, Chillingworth gets no further for all his trouble, but the cross-examination to which he subjects the Reverend is curious, and Dimmesdale has a narrow escape. (pp. 36-9)

[After his encounter with Hester and Pearl in the forest, the] transformation, the conversion of Dimmesdale freed from repression, is complete. It overthrows his whole philosophy of life. It makes of him an amoralist and a Nietzschean. (p. 44)

Hawthorne was one of the novelists best acquainted with man's conscience.

Less fecund than many, he had the wisdom and talent to concentrate his genius and thought upon the study of a preeminently human problem, that of evil and responsibility. Besides the genius of intuition he had that of symbolism. This realistic psychologist was a marvelous imagist. He himself has given us a striking formula of his art. Art, according to him, is the light of thought and imagination shining through what he called "the opaque substance of days." Like Emerson, he considered wonder as an essential human faculty. Intuitive sympathy alone, he believed, could solve the mysteries of existence. To come to truth one must possess the innocent and naive insight of a child. (p. 45)

> *Régis Michaud, "How Nathaniel Hawthorne Exorcised Hester Prynne," in his* The American Novel To-Day: A Social and Psychological Study, *Little, Brown, and Company, 1928, pp. 25-46.*

## F. O. MATTHIESSEN (essay date 1941)

[*Matthiessen, a literary critic and historian, was chiefly interested in the concept of cultural and literary tradition and is considered one of the foremost critics of American literature. In this excerpt, Matthiessen concentrates on Hawthorne's use of imagery and symbolism in* The Scarlet Letter, *especially his reliance on emblems and correspondences "between external events and inner significances" for conveying multiple meanings in the novel. Other critics who stress Hawthorne's imagery in* The Scarlet Letter *include Richard Chase (1957), Roy R. Male (1957), and Daniel Hoffman (1961).*]

[Beyond] any interest in ordering of plot or in lucid discrimination between characters, Hawthorne's imaginative energy seems to have been called out to the full [in ***The Scarlet Letter***] by the continual correspondences that his theme allowed him to make between external events and inner significances. Once again his version of this transcendental habit took it straight back to the seventeenth century, and made it something more complex than the harmony between sunrise and a young poet's

soul. In the realm of natural phenomena, Hawthorne examined the older world's common belief that great events were foreboded by supernatural omens, and remarked how 'it was, indeed, a majestic idea, that the destiny of nations should be revealed, in these awful hieroglyphics, on the cope of heaven.' But when Dimmesdale, in his vigil on the scaffold, beholds an immense dull red letter in the zenith, Hawthorne attributes it solely to his diseased imagination, which sees in everything his own morbid concerns. Hawthorne remarks that the strange light was 'doubtless caused' by a meteor 'burning out to waste'; and yet he also allows the sexton to ask the minister the next morning if he had heard of the portent, which had been interpreted to stand for Angel, since Governor Winthrop had died during the night.

Out of such variety of symbolical reference Hawthorne developed one of his most fertile resources, the device of multiple choice, which James was to carry so much further in his desire to present a sense of the intricacy of any situation for a perceptive being. One main source of Hawthorne's method lay in these remarkable providences, which his imagination felt challenged to search for the amount of emblematic truth that might lie hidden among their superstitions. He spoke at one point in this story of how 'individuals of wiser faith' in the colony, while recognizing God's Providence in human affairs, knew that it 'promotes its purposes without aiming at the stage-effect of what is called miraculous interposition.' But he could not resist experimenting with this dramatic value, and his imagination had become so accustomed to the weirdly lighted world of Cotton Mather that even the fanciful possibilities of the growth of the stigma on Dimmesdale did not strike him as grotesque. But when the minister 'unbreasts' his guilt at last, the literal correspondence of that metaphor to a scarlet letter in his flesh, in strict accord with medieval and Spenserian personifications, is apt to strike us as a mechanical delimitation of what would otherwise have freer symbolical range.

For Hawthorne its value consisted in the variety of explanations to which it gave rise. Some affirmed that the minister had begun a course of self-mortification on the very day on which Hester Prynne had first been compelled to wear her ignominious badge, and had thus inflicted this hideous scar. Others held that Roger Chillingworth, 'being a potent necromancer, had caused it to appear, through the agency of magic and poisonous drugs.' Still others, 'those best able to appreciate the minister's peculiar sensibility, and the wonderful operation of his spirit upon the body,' whispered that 'the awful symbol was the effect of the ever-active tooth of remorse,' gnawing from his inmost heart outward. With that Hawthorne leaves his reader to choose among these theories. He does not literally accept his own allegory, and yet he finds it symbolically valid because of its psychological exactitude. His most telling stroke comes when he adds that certain spectators of the whole scene denied that there was any mark whatever on Dimmesdale's breast. These witnesses were among the most respectable in the community, including his fellow-ministers who were determined to defend his spotless character. These maintained also that his dying confession was to be taken only in its general significance, that he 'had desired, by yielding up his breath in the arms of that fallen woman, to express to the world how utterly nugatory is the choicest of man's own righteousness.' But for this interpretation, so revelatory of its influential proponents, Hawthorne leaves not one shred of evidence.

It should not be thought that his deeply ingrained habit of apprehending truth through emblems needed any sign of miraculous intervention to set it into action. Another aspect of the intricate correspondences that absorbed him is provided by Pearl. She is worth dissecting as the purest type of Spenserian characterization, which starts with abstract qualities and hunts for their proper embodiment; worth murdering, most modern readers of fiction would hold, since the tedious reiteration of what she stands for betrays Hawthorne at his most barren.

When Hester returned to the prison after standing her time on the scaffold, the infant she had clasped so tightly to her breast suddenly writhed in convulsions of pain, 'a forcible type, in its little frame, of the moral agony' that its mother had borne throughout the day. As the story advances, Hawthorne sees in this child 'the freedom of a broken law.' In the perverseness of some of her antics, in the heartless mockery that can shine from her bright black eyes, she sometimes seems to her harassed mother almost a witch-baby. But Hester clings to the hope that her girl has capacity for strong affection, which needs only to be awakened by sympathy; and when there is some talk by the authorities of taking the wilful child's rearing into their own hands, Hester also clings to her possession of it as both her torture and happiness, her blessing and retribution, the one thing that has kept her soul alive in its hours of desperation.

Hawthorne's range of intention in this characterization comes out most fully in the scene where Hester and the minister have met in the woods, and are alone for the first time after so many years. Her resolution to save him from Chillingworth's spying, by flight together back to England, now sweeps his undermined spirit before it. In their moment of reunion, the one moment of released passion in the book, the beauty that has been hidden behind the frozen mask of her isolation reasserts itself. She takes off the formal cap that has confined the dark radiance of her hair and lets it stream down on her shoulders; she impulsively unfastens the badge of her shame and throws it to the ground. At that moment the minister sees Pearl, who has been playing by the brook, returning along the other side of it. Picked out by a beam of sunlight, with some wild flowers in her hair, she reminds Hester of 'one of the fairies, whom we left in our dear old England,' a sad reflection on the rich folklore that had been banished by the Puritans along with the maypoles. But as the two parents stand watching their child for the first time together, the graver thought comes to them that she is 'the living hieroglyphic' of all they have sought to hide, of their inseparably intertwined fate.

As Pearl sees her mother, she stops by a pool, and her reflected image seems to communicate to her something 'of its own shadowy and intangible quality.' Confronted with this double vision, dissevered from her by the brook, Hester feels, 'in some indistinct and tantalizing manner,' suddenly estranged from the child, who now fixes her eyes on her mother's breast. She refuses Hester's bidding to come to her. Instead she points her finger, and stamps her foot, and becomes all at once a little demon of extravagant protest, all of whose wild gestures are redoubled at her feet. Hester understands what the matter is, that the child is outraged by the unaccustomed change in her appearance. So she wearily picks up the letter, which had fallen just short of the brook, and hides her luxuriant hair once more beneath her cap. At that Pearl is mollified and bounds across to them. During the weeks leading up to this scene, she had begun to show an increasing curiosity about the letter, and had tormented her mother with questions. Now she asks whether the minister will walk back with them, hand in hand, to the village, and when he declines, she flings away from his kiss,

because he is not 'bold' and 'true.' The question is increasingly raised for the reader, just how much of the situation this strange child understands.

Thus, when the stiff layers of allegory have been peeled away, even Hawthorne's conception of Pearl is seen to be based on exact psychological notation. She suggests something of the terrifying precocity which Edwards' acute dialectic of the feelings revealed in the children who came under his observation during the emotional strain of the Great Awakening. She suggests, even more directly, James' *What Maisie Knew,* though it is typical of the later writer's refinement of skill and sophistication that he would set himself the complicated problem of having both parents divorced and married again, of making the child the innocent meeting ground for a liaison between the step-parents, and of confining his report on the situation entirely to what could be glimpsed through the child's inscrutable eyes. (pp. 276-79)

> *F. O. Matthiessen, ''Allegory and Symbolism,'' in his* American Renaissance: Art and Expression in the Age of Emerson and Whitman, *Oxford University Press, New York, 1941, pp. 242-315.**

### FREDERIC I. CARPENTER  (essay date 1944)

*[In this excerpt from his seminal study of* The Scarlet Letter, *Carpenter begins by considering the qualities that make it a lit-*

*Illustration of the first pillory scene from* The Scarlet Letter.

*erary classic. He then analyzes three different critical approaches
to the novel—the traditional, the romantic, and the transcendental—and the concept of sin inherent in each interpretation. Carpenter concludes that the work's greatest asset is the bold characterization of Hester, yet he also emphasizes that Hawthorne's
stance toward Hester was ambiguous: he was able to condone
her desire for freedom emotionally but not intellectually. The
novel's moralistic conclusion is consequently false, according to
Carpenter, because Hawthorne "damned the transcendental
character whom he had created, for being romantic and immoral." Other critics who focus on Hawthorne's ambivalent tone in*
The Scarlet Letter *include Anthony Trollope (1879), Richard Harter
Fogle (1952), Hyatt H. Waggoner (1955), and Terence Martin
(1983). Hawthorne's attitude toward romanticism and Puritanism
is also discussed by Randall Stewart (1958).]*

From the first *The Scarlet Letter* has been considered a classic.
It has appealed not only to the critics but to the reading public
as well. . . .

But in modern times *The Scarlet Letter* has come to seem less
than perfect. Other novels, like [Leo Tolstoy's] *Anna Karenina,* have treated the same problem with a richer humanity and
a greater realism. If the book remains a classic, it is of a minor
order. Indeed, it now seems not quite perfect even of its own
kind. Its logic is ambiguous, and its conclusion moralistic. The
ambiguity is interesting, of course, and the moralizing slight,
but the imperfection persists.

In one sense the very imperfection of *The Scarlet Letter* makes
it classic: its ambiguity illustrates a fundamental confusion in
modern thought. To the question "Was the action symbolized
by the scarlet letter wholly sinful?" it suggests a variety of
answers: "Yes," reply the traditional moralists; "Hester Prynne
broke the Commandments." But the romantic enthusiasts answer: "No; Hester merely acted according to the deepest of
human instincts." And the transcendental idealists reply: "In
part; Hester truly sinned against the morality which her lover
believed in, but did not sin against her own morality, because
she believed in a 'higher law.' To her own self, Hester Prynne
remained true." (p. 173)

The traditional answer remains clear, but the romantic and the
idealistic have usually been confused. Perhaps the imperfection
of the novel arises from Hawthorne's own confusion between
his heroine's transcendental morality and mere immorality.
Explicitly, he condemned Hester Prynne as immoral; but implicitly, he glorified her as courageously idealistic. And this
confusion between romantic immorality and transcendental idealism has been typical of the genteel tradition in America.

According to the traditional moralists, Hester Prynne was truly
a sinful woman. Although she sinned less than her hypocritical
lover and her vengeful husband, she nevertheless sinned; and,
from her sin, death and tragedy resulted. At the end of the
novel, Hawthorne himself positively affirmed this interpretation:

> Earlier in life, Hester had vainly imagined that
> she herself might be the destined prophetess,
> but had long since recognized the impossibility
> that any mission of divine and mysterious truth
> should be confided to a woman stained with
> sin.

And so the traditional critics have been well justified. *The
Scarlet Letter* explicitly approves the tragic punishment of Hester's sin and explicitly declares the impossibility of salvation
for the sinner.

But for the traditionalists there are many kinds and degrees of
sin, and *The Scarlet Letter,* like Dante's *Inferno,* describes more
than one. According to the orthodox, Hester Prynne belongs
with the romantic lovers of the *Inferno,* in the highest circle
of Hell. For Hester sinned only through passion, but her lover
through passion and concealment, and her husband through
"violating, in cold blood, the sanctity of the human heart."
Therefore, Hester's sin was the least, and her punishment the
lightest.

But Hester sinned, and, according to traditional Puritanism,
this act shut her off forever from paradise. Indeed, this archetypal sin and its consequent tragedy have been taken to symbolize the eternal failure of the American dream. Hester suggests "the awakening of the mind to 'moral gloom' after its
childish dreams of natural bliss are dissipated." Thus her lover,
standing upon the scaffold, exclaimed: "Is this not better than
we dreamed of in the forest?" And Hawthorne repeated that
Hester recognized the eternal justice of her own damnation.
The romantic dream of natural freedom has seemed empty to
the traditionalists, because sin and its punishment are eternal
and immutable. (pp. 173-74)

[All] the traditionalists agree that Hester's action was wholly
sinful. That Hester herself never admitted this accusation and
that Hester is never represented as acting blindly in a fit of
passion and that Hester never repented of her "sin" are facts
which the traditionalists overlook. Moreover, they forget that
Hawthorne's condemnation of Hester's sin is never verified by
Hester's own words. But of this more later.

Meanwhile, other faults in Hester's character are admitted by
the traditional and the liberal alike. Even if she did not do what
*she* believed to be evil, Hester nevertheless did tempt her lover
to do what *he* believed to be evil and thus caused his death.
And because she wished to protect her lover, she consented to
a life of deception and concealment which she herself knew to
be false. But for the traditional moralists neither her temptation
of her lover nor her deception of him was a cardinal sin. Only
her act of passion was.

Therefore Hester's passion was the fatal flaw which caused the
tragedy. Either because of some womanly weakness which
made her unable to resist evil, or because of some pride which
made her oppose her own will to the eternal law, she did evil.
Her sin was certain, the law she broke was immutable, and
the human tragedy was inevitable—according to the traditional
moralists.

But, according to the romantic enthusiasts, *The Scarlet Letter*
points a very difficult moral. The followers of Rousseau have
said that Hester did not sin at all; or that, if she did, she
transformed her sin into a virtue. Did not Hawthorne himself
describe the radiance of the scarlet letter, shining upon her
breast like a symbol of victory? "The tendency of her fate had
been to set her free. The scarlet letter was her passport into
regions where other women dared not tread." Hester—if we
discount Hawthorne's moralistic conclusion—never repented
of her "sin" of passion, because she never recognized it as
such.

In absolute contrast to the traditionalists, the romantics have
described *The Scarlet Letter* as a masterpiece of "Hawthorne's
immoralism" [see excerpt above by Régis Michaud, 1928].
Not only Hester but even the Puritan minister becomes "an
amoralist and a Nietzschean." "In truth," wrote Hawthorne,
"nothing short of a total change of dynasty and moral code in
that interior kingdom was adequate to account for the impulses

now communicated to the . . . minister.'' But Hester alone became perfectly immoral, for ''the world's law was no law for her mind.'' She alone dared renounce utterly the dead forms of tradition and dared follow the natural laws of her own instinctive nature to the end. (pp. 174-75)

Therefore, according to the romantics, the tragedy of *The Scarlet Letter* does not result from any tragic flaw in the heroine, for she is romantically without sin. It results, rather, from the intrinsic evil of society. Because the moral law imposes tyrannical restraints upon the natural instincts of man, human happiness is impossible in civilization. *The Scarlet Letter,* therefore, becomes the tragedy of perfection, in which the ideal woman is doomed to defeat by an inflexible moral tradition. Because Hester Prynne was so perfectly loyal and loving that she would never abandon her lover, she was condemned by the Puritans. Not human frailty, therefore, or any tragic imperfection of character, but only the inevitable forces of social determinism caused the disaster described by *The Scarlet Letter*—according to the romantic enthusiasts.

Between the orthodox belief that Hester Prynne sinned utterly and the opposite romantic belief that she did not sin at all, the transcendental idealists seek to mediate. Because they deny the authority of the traditional morality, these idealists have sometimes seemed merely romantic. But because they seek to describe a new moral law, they have also seemed moralistic. The confusion of answers to the question of evil suggested by *The Scarlet Letter* arises, in part, from a failure to understand the transcendental ideal.

With the romantics, the transcendentalists agree that Hester did wisely to ''give all to love.'' But they insist that Hester's love was neither blindly passionate nor purposeless. ''What we did,'' Hester exclaims to her lover, ''had a consecration of its own.'' To the transcendental, her love was not sinful because it was not disloyal to her evil husband (whom she had never loved) or to the traditional morality (in which she had never believed). Rather her love was purposefully aimed at a permanent union with her lover—witness the fact that it had already endured through seven years of separation and disgrace. Hester did well to ''obey her heart,'' because she felt no conflict between her heart and her head. She was neither romantically immoral nor blindly rebellious against society and its laws.

This element of conscious purpose distinguishes the transcendental Hester Prynne from other, merely romantic heroines. Because she did not deny ''the moral law'' but went beyond it to a ''higher law,'' Hester transcended both romance and tradition. As if to emphasize this fact, Hawthorne himself declared that she ''assumed a freedom of speculation which our forefathers, had they known it, would have held to be a deadlier crime than that stigmatized by the scarlet letter.'' Unlike her lover, she had explicitly been led ''beyond the scope of generally received laws.'' She had consciously wished to become ''the prophetess'' of a more liberal morality.

According to the transcendentalists, therefore, Hester's ''sin'' was not that she broke the Commandments—for, in the sight of God, she had never truly been married. Nor was Hester the blameless victim of society, as the romantics believed. She had sinned in that she had deceived her lover concerning the identity of her husband. . . . Not traditional morality, but transcendental truth, governed the conscience of Hester Prynne. But she had a conscience, and she had sinned against it.

Indeed, Hester Prynne had ''sinned,'' exactly *because* she put romantic ''love'' ahead of ideal ''truth.'' She had done evil in allowing the ''good'' of her lover to outweigh the higher law. She had sacrificed her own integrity by giving absolutely everything to her loved one. . . . True love is a higher law than merely traditional morality, but, even at best, human love is ''daemonic.'' The highest law of ''celestial love'' is the law of divine truth.

According to the transcendental idealists, Hester Prynne sinned in that she did not go beyond human love. In seeking to protect her lover by deception, she sinned both against her own ''integrity'' and against God. If she had told the whole truth in the beginning, she would have been blameless. But she lacked this perfect self-reliance.

Nevertheless, tragedy would have resulted even if Hester Prynne had been transcendentally perfect. For the transcendental ideal implies tragedy. Traditionally, tragedy results from the individual imperfection of some hero. Romantically, it results from the evil of society. But, ideally, it results from a conflict of moral standards or values. The tragedy of *The Scarlet Letter* resulted from the conflict of the orthodox morality of the minister with the transcendental morality of the heroine. For Arthur Dimmesdale, unlike Hester Prynne, did sin blindly through passion, committing an act which he felt to be wrong. And because he sinned against his own morality, he felt himself unable to grasp the freedom which Hester urged. If, on the contrary, he had conscientiously been able to flee with her to a new life on the western frontier, there would have been no tragedy. . . . To those who have never believed in it, the American dream of freedom has always seemed utopian and impossible of realization. Tragedy results from this conflict of moralities and this unbelief.

According to the orthodox, Hester Prynne sinned through blind passion, and her sin caused the tragedy. According to the romantic, Hester Prynne heroically ''gave all to love,'' and tragedy resulted from the evil of society. According to the transcendentalists, Hester Prynne sinned through deception, but tragedy resulted from the conflict of her dream of freedom with the traditional creed of her lover. Dramatically, each of these interpretations is possible: *The Scarlet Letter* is rich in suggestion. But Hawthorne the moralist sought to destroy this richness.

*The Scarlet Letter* achieves greatness in its dramatic, objective presentation of conflicting moralities in action: each character seems at once symbolic, yet real. But this dramatic perfection is flawed by the author's moralistic, subjective criticism of Hester Prynne. And this contradiction results from Hawthorne's apparent confusion between the romantic and the transcendental moralities. While the characters of the novel objectively act out the tragic conflict between the traditional morality and the transcendental dream, Hawthorne subjectively damns the transcendental for being romantically immoral.

Most obviously, Hawthorne imposed a moralistic **''Conclusion''** upon the drama which his characters had acted. But the artistic and moral falsity of this does not lie in its didacticism or in the personal intrusion of the author, for these were the literary conventions of the age. Rather it lies in the contradiction between the author's moralistic comments and the earlier words and actions of his characters. Having created living protagonists, Hawthorne sought to impose his own will and judgment upon them from the outside. Thus he described Hester as admitting her ''sin'' of passion and as renouncing her ''selfish ends'' and as seeking to ''expiate'' her crime. But Hester herself had never admitted to any sin other than deception and had never acted ''selfishly'' and had worn her scarlet letter triumphantly, rather than penitently. In his **"Conclusion,"** therefore, Hawthorne did violence to the living character whom he had created.

His artificial and moralistic criticism is concentrated in the **"Conclusion."** But it also appears in other chapters of the novel. (pp. 175-78)

[The] scene between Hester and her lover in the forest also suggests the root of Hawthorne's confusion. To the traditional moralists, the ''forest,'' or ''wilderness,'' or ''uncivilized Nature'' was the symbolic abode of evil—the very negation of moral law. But to the romantics, wild nature had become the very symbol of freedom. In this scene, Hawthorne explicitly condemned Hester for her wildness—for ''breathing the wild, free atmosphere of an unredeemed, unchristianized, lawless region.'' And again he damned her ''sympathy'' with ''that wild, heathen Nature of the forest, never subjugated by human law, nor illumined by higher truth.'' Clearly he hated moral romanticism. And this hatred would have been harmless, if his heroine had merely been romantic, or immoral.

But Hester Prynne, as revealed in speech and in action, was not romantic but transcendental. And Hawthorne failed utterly to distinguish, in his moralistic criticism, between the romantic and the transcendental. (p. 178)

Having allowed his imagination to create an idealistic heroine, he did not allow his conscious mind to justify—or even to describe fairly—her ideal morality. Rather, he damned the transcendental character whom he had created, for being romantic and immoral. But the words and deeds by means of which he had created her contradicted his own moralistic criticisms.

In the last analysis, the greatness of *The Scarlet Letter* lies in the character of Hester Prynne. Because she dared to trust herself and to believe in the possibility of a new morality in the new world, she achieved spiritual greatness in spite of her own human weakness, in spite of the prejudices of her Puritan society, and, finally, in spite of the prejudices of her creator himself. For the human weakness which made her deceive her lover in order to protect him makes her seem only the more real. The calm steadfastness with which she endures the ostracism of society makes her heroic. And the clear purpose which she follows, despite the denigrations of Hawthorne, makes her almost ideal.

Hester, almost in spite of Hawthorne, envisions the transcendental ideal of positive freedom, instead of the romantic ideal of mere escape. . . .

Hester Prynne embodies the authentic American dream of a new life in the wilderness of the new world, and of self-reliant action to realize that ideal. In the Puritan age in which he lived, and in Hawthorne's own nineteenth century, this ideal was actually being realized in practice. Even in our modern society with its more liberal laws, Hester Prynne might hope to live happily with her lover, after winning divorce from her cruel and vengeful husband. But in every century her tragedy would still be the same. It would result from her own deception and from the conflicting moral belief of her lover. But it would not result from her own sense of guilt or shame.

In *The Scarlet Letter* alone among his novels, Hawthorne succeeded in realizing a character embodying the authentic Amer-

ican dream of freedom and independence in the new world. But he succeeded in realizing this ideal emotionally rather than intellectually. And, having completed the novel, he wondered at his work: ''I think I have never overcome my adamant in any other instance,'' he said. Perhaps he added the moralistic **"Conclusion"** and the various criticisms of Hester, in order to placate his conscience. In any case, he never permitted himself such freedom—or such greatness—again. (p. 179)

*Frederic I. Carpenter, ''Scarlet A Minus,'' in* College English, *Vol. 5, No. 4, January, 1944, pp. 173-80.*

## RICHARD HARTER FOGLE (essay date 1952)

[*Examining Hawthorne's handling of light and dark imagery in* The Scarlet Letter, *Fogle discusses dramatic irony, moral ambiguity, and the possibility of multiple interpretations of themes in the novel. For other commentary on ambiguity in* The Scarlet Letter, *see the excerpts by Anthony Trollope (1879), Frederic I. Carpenter (1944), Hyatt H. Waggoner (1955), and Terence Martin (1983).*]

Interpretations of *The Scarlet Letter* have been almost startlingly various. This is not surprising, for Hawthorne has himself pointed the way to a wide range of speculations. The concluding words of *The Scarlet Letter,* however, summarily dismiss the more cheerful readings, of which there are a number. In describing the heraldic device on the common tombstone of Hester and Dimmesdale, they describe ''our now concluded legend; so sombre is it, and relieved only by one ever-glowing point of light gloomier than the shadow:—

'ON A FIELD, SABLE, THE LETTER A, GULES.'''

These words alone, in my opinion, are sufficient evidence for disproving the notion that *The Scarlet Letter* is ''about'' Hester Prynne the advanced feminist, or that the story can be satisfactorily summarized either by the moral which Hawthorne attaches to Dimmesdale, '''Show freely to the world, if not your worst, yet some trait whereby the worst may be inferred!''' or by the doctrine of *felix culpa,* ''the fortunate fall,'' that out of sin and evil comes good and that Hester is educated and refined by her wrongdoing. The sentiment is too darkly tragic to be appropriate to any of these conclusions, though Hawthorne at one place and another in *The Scarlet Letter* has suggested the possibility of all of them. The true conclusion of *The Scarlet Letter* is an unresolved contradiction—unresolved not from indecision or lack of thought but from honesty of imagination. Hawthorne gives the only answer that his formulation of the terms permits. If we consider that the problem of *The Scarlet Letter* is primarily the problem of Hester Prynne, the verdict is at best suspension of judgment after full examination of the evidence. And, as we know, Hester emerges from trial in better condition than her codefendants Dimmesdale and Chillingworth.

This is the contradiction, and a very widely representative contradiction it is: the sin of *The Scarlet Letter* is a symbol of the original sin, by which no man is untouched. All mortals commit the sin in one form or another, which is perhaps the meaning of ''your worst'' in the exhortation occasioned by the death of Dimmesdale. Hester, having sinned, makes the best possible recovery; and the crime itself is of all crimes the most excusable, coming of passionate love and having ''a consecration of its own.'' Yet the sin remains real and inescapable, and she spends her life in retribution, the death of her lover Dimmesdale having finally taught her that this is the only way.

This is the dilemma: human beings by their natures must fall into error—and yet it would be better if they did not.

The letter, an "ever-glowing point of light," is gloomier than the shadow of its background. The shadow, the "Field, Sable," is roughly the atmosphere of Puritanism, the "Letter A, Gules" the atmosphere of the sin. These are at odds, and no absolute superiority is granted to either. The Puritan doctors are no fit judges of a woman's heart; nor, on the other hand, is Hester to be absolved. The letter is glowing, positive, vital, the product of genuine passion, while the sable may certainly be taken as the negation of everything alive. Yet the letter is gloomier.

These shades are both of hell, and there is no hue of heaven in *The Scarlet Letter* which really offsets them. Sunlight is the nearest approach to it, and its sway is too fleeting to have any great effect. In the forest scene of chapters XVI-XIX sunshine, "as with a sudden smile of heaven," bursts over Hester and Dimmesdale, but this is merely a momentary relief. The hope which accompanies it is short-lived, delusory, and dangerous. A more steadfast light, "The sun, but little past its meridian," shines down upon Dimmesdale as he stands on the scaffold to confess his guilt. This is triumph, indeed, but little to counterbalance the continual power of the "bale fire" and "lurid gleam" of the letter. (pp. 104-06)

The problem of *The Scarlet Letter* can be solved only by introducing the supernatural level of heaven, the sphere of absolute knowledge and justice and—hesitantly—of complete fulfillment. This may seem to be another paradox, and perhaps a disappointing one. Without doubt *The Scarlet Letter* pushes *towards* the limit of moral judgment, suggesting many possible conclusions. It is even relentless in its search in the depths of its characters. There is yet, however, a point beyond which Hawthorne will not go; ultimate solutions are not appropriate in the merely human world. His sympathy with Hester and Dimmesdale is clear enough, but he allows them only to escape the irrevocable spiritual ruin which befalls Chillingworth. Figuratively his good wishes pursue them beyond life, but he does not presume himself to absolve them. Even in the carefully staged scene of Dimmesdale's death, where every impulse of both author and reader demands complete forgiveness, Hawthorne refuses to grant it. (pp. 106-07)

The intensity of *The Scarlet Letter*, at which Hawthorne himself was dismayed, comes from concentration, selection, and dramatic irony. The concentration upon the central theme is unremitting. The tension is lessened only once, in the scene in the forest, and then only delusively, since the hope of freedom which brings it about is quickly shown to be false and even sinful. The characters play out their tragic action against a background in itself oppressive—the somber atmosphere of Puritanism. Hawthorne calls the progression of the story "the darkening close of a tale of human frailty and sorrow." Dark to begin with, it grows steadily deeper in gloom. The method is almost unprecedentedly selective. Almost every image has a symbolic function; no scene is superfluous. One would perhaps at times welcome a loosening of the structure, a moment of wandering from the path. The weedy grassplot in front of the prison; the distorting reflection of Hester in a breastplate, where the Scarlet Letter appears gigantic; the tapestry of David and Bathsheba on the wall of the minister's chamber; the little brook in the forest; the slight malformation of Chillingworth's shoulder; the ceremonial procession on election day—in every instance more is meant than meets the eye.

The intensity of *The Scarlet Letter* comes in part from a sustained and rigorous dramatic irony, or irony of situation. This irony arises naturally from the theme of "secret sin," or concealment. "Show freely of your worst," says Hawthorne; the action of *The Scarlet Letter* arises from the failure of Dimmesdale and Chillingworth to do so. The minister hides his sin, and Chillingworth hides his identity. This concealment affords a constant drama. (pp. 110-11)

Along with this steady irony of situation there is the omnipresent irony of the hidden meaning. The author and the reader know what the characters do not. Hawthorne consistently pretends that the coincidence of the action or the image with its significance is merely fortuitous, not planned, lest the effect be spoiled by overinsistence. In other words, he attempts to combine the sufficiently probable with the maximum of arrangement. Thus the waxing and waning of sunlight in the forest scene symbolize the emotions of Hester and Dimmesdale, but we accept this coincidence most easily if we can receive it as chance. Hawthorne's own almost amused awareness of his problem helps us to do so. Yet despite the element of play and the deliberate self-deception demanded, the total effect is one of intensity. Hawthorne is performing a difficult feat with sustained virtuosity in reconciling a constant stress between naturally divergent qualities.

The character of Pearl illuminates this point. Pearl is pure symbol, the living emblem of the sin, a human embodiment of the Scarlet Letter. Her mission is to keep Hester's adultery always before her eyes, to prevent her from attempting to escape its moral consequences. Pearl's childish questions are fiendishly apt; in speech and in action she never strays from the control of her symbolic function; her dress and her looks are related to the letter. When Hester casts the letter away in the forest, Pearl forces her to reassume it by flying into an uncontrollable rage. Yet despite the undeviating arrangement of every circumstance which surrounds her, no single action of hers is ever incredible or inconsistent with the conceivable actions of any child under the same conditions. (pp. 113-14)

These qualities of concentration, selectivity, and irony, which are responsible for the intensity of *The Scarlet Letter,* tend at their extreme toward excessive regularity and a sense of overmanipulation, although irony is also a counteragent against them. This tendency toward regularity is balanced by Hawthorne's use of ambiguity. The distancing of the story in the past has the effect of ambiguity. Hawthorne so employs the element of time as to warn us that he cannot guarantee the literal truth of his narrative and at the same time to suggest that the essential truth is the clearer; as facts shade off into the background, meaning is left in the foreground unshadowed and disencumbered. The years, he pretends, have winnowed his material, leaving only what is enduring. Tradition and superstition, while he disclaims belief in them, have a way of pointing to truth.

Thus the imagery of hell-fire which occurs throughout *The Scarlet Letter* is dramatically proper to the Puritan background and is attributed to the influence of superstitious legend. It works as relief from more serious concerns and still functions as a symbol of psychological and religious truth. (p. 115)

Puritan demonology is in general used with the same effect. It has the pathos and simplicity of an old wives' tale and yet contains a deep subterranean power which reaches into daylight from the dark caverns of the mind. (p. 116)

This use of the past merges into a deep-seated ambiguity of moral meaning. Moral complexity and freedom of speculation, like the lighter ambiguity of literal fact, temper the almost excessive unity and symmetry of *The Scarlet Letter* and avoid a directed verdict. In my opinion the judgment of Hawthorne upon his characters is entirely clear, although deliberately limited in its jurisdiction. But he permits the possibility of other interpretations to appear, so that the consistent clarity of his own emphasis is disguised. Let us take for example the consideration of the heroine in Chapter XIII, **"Another View of Hester."** After seven years of disgrace, Hester has won the unwilling respect of her fellow-townsmen by her good works and respectability of conduct. From one point of view she is clearly their moral superior: she has met rigorous cruelty with kindness, arrogance with humility. Furthermore, living as she has in enforced isolation has greatly developed her mind. In her breadth of intellectual speculation she has freed herself from any dependence upon the laws of Puritan society. "She cast away the fragments of a broken chain." She pays outward obedience to a system which has no further power upon her spirit. Under other conditions, Hawthorne suggests, she might at this juncture have become another Anne Hutchinson, the foundress of a religious sect, or a great early feminist. The author's conclusions about these possibilities, however, are specifically stated: "The scarlet letter had not done its office." Hester is wounded and led astray, not improved, by her situation. Hawthorne permits his reader, if he wishes, to take his character from his control, to say that Hester Prynne is a great woman unhappily born before her time, or that she is a good woman wronged by her fellow men. But Hawthorne is less confident.

In the multiple interpretations which constitute the moral ambiguities of *The Scarlet Letter* there is no clear distinction of true and false, but there *is* a difference between superficial and profound. In instances where interpretation of observed fact fuses with interpretation of moral meaning, conclusions are generally relative to those who make them. (pp. 117-18)

There is also the ambivalence of the Puritans. It is easy to pass them by too quickly. One's first impression is doubtless, as Hawthorne says elsewhere, of a set of "dismal wretches," but they are more than this. The Puritan code is arrogant, inflexible, overrighteous; and it is remarked of their magistrates and priests that "out of the whole human family, it would not have been easy to select the same number of wise and virtuous persons, who should be less capable of sitting in judgment on an erring woman's heart. . . ." Nevertheless, after finishing *The Scarlet Letter* one might well ask what merely human society would be better. With all its rigors, the ordeal of Hester upon the scaffold is invested with awe by the real seriousness and simplicity of the onlookers. Hawthorne compares the Puritan attitude, and certainly not unfavorably, to "the heartlessness of another social state, which would find only a theme for jest in an exhibition like the present." And it is counted as a virtue that the chief of men of the town attend the spectacle without loss of dignity. Without question they take upon themselves more of the judgment of the soul than is fitting for men to assume, but this fault is palliated by their complete sincerity. They are "a people amongst whom religion and law were almost identical, and in whose character both were so thoroughly interfused, that the mildest and the severest acts of public discipline were alike made venerable and awful." By any ideal standard they are greatly lacking, but among erring humans they are, after all, creditable.

Furthermore, the vigor of Hawthorne's abuse of them is not to be taken at face value. They are grim, grisly, stern-browed and unkindly visaged; amid the gaiety of election day "for the

space of a single holiday, they appeared scarcely more grave than most other communities at a period of general affliction." In this statement the tone of good-humored mockery is unmistakable. Hawthorne's attacks have something of the quality of a family joke; their roughness comes from thorough and even affectionate understanding. (pp. 119-20)

Finally, the pervasive influence of Hawthorne's style modifies the rigorous and purposeful direction of the action and the accompanying symmetrical ironies. The style is urbane, relaxed, and reposeful and is rarely without some touch of amiable and unaccented humor. This quality varies, of course, with the situation. Hester exposed on the scaffold and Dimmesdale wracked by Chillingworth are not fit subjects for humor. Yet Hawthorne always preserves a measure of distance, even at his most sympathetic. The effect of Hawthorne's prose comes partly from generality, in itself a factor in maintaining distance, as if the author at his most searching chose always to preserve a certain reticence, to keep to what is broadly representative and conceal the personal and particular. Even the most anguished emotion is clothed with decency and measure, and the most painful situations are softened by decorum. (pp. 120-21)

*Richard Harter Fogle, in his* Hawthorne's Fiction: The Light & the Dark, *University of Oklahoma Press, 1952, 219 p.*

## R. W. B. LEWIS (essay date 1955)

*[Lewis, a prominent American literary critic and historian of ideas, locates the central theme of* The Scarlet Letter *in the interaction between the individual and society. He praises the complexity of Hawthorne's artistic vision, which enables him to dramatize society's power to both sustain and hinder the individual. For other analyses of the individual's relation to society in* The Scarlet Letter, *see the excerpts by Marius Bewley (1959), A. N. Kaul (1962), Nina Baym (1976), and Michael Davitt Bell (1980).]*

The opening scene of *The Scarlet Letter* is the paradigm dramatic image in American literature. With that scene and that novel, New World fiction arrived at its first fulfilment, and Hawthorne at his. And with that scene, all that was dark and treacherous in the American situation became exposed. Hawthorne said later that the writing of *The Scarlet Letter* had been oddly simple, since all he had to do was to get his "pitch" and then to let it carry him along. He found his pitch in an opening tableau fairly humming with tension—with coiled and covert relationships that contained a force perfectly calculated to propel the action thereafter in a direct line to its tragic climax.

It was the tableau of the solitary figure set over against the inimical society, in a village which hovers on the edge of the inviting and perilous wilderness; a handsome young woman standing on a raised platform, confronting in silence and pride a hostile crowd whose menace is deepened by its order and dignity; a young woman who has come alone to the New World, where circumstances have divided her from the community now gathered to oppose her; standing alone, but vitally aware of the private enemy and the private lover—one on the far verges of the crowd, one at the place of honor within it, and neither conscious of the other—who must affect her destiny and who will assist at each other's destruction. Here the situation inherent in the American scene was seized entire and without damage to it by an imagination both moral and visual of the highest quality: seized and located, not any longer on the margins of the plot, but at its very center.

The conflict is central because it is total; because Hawthorne makes us respect each element in it. Hawthorne felt, as Brown and Cooper and Bird had felt, that the stuff of narrative (in so far as it was drawn from local experience) consisted in the imaginable brushes between the deracinated and solitary individual and the society or world awaiting him. But Hawthorne had learned the lesson only fitfully apprehended by Cooper. In *The Scarlet Letter* not only do the individual and the world, the conduct and the institutions, measure each other: the measurement and its consequences are precisely and centrally what the novel is about. Hester Prynne has been wounded by an unfriendly world; but the society facing her is invested by Hawthorne with assurance and authority, its opposition is defensible and even valid. Hester's misdeed appears as a disturbance of the moral structure of the universe; and the society continues to insist in its joyless way that certain acts deserve the honor of punishment. But if Hester has sinned, she has done so as an affirmation of life, and her sin is the source of life; she incarnates those rights of personality that society is inclined to trample upon. The action of the novel springs from the enormous but improbable suggestion that the society's estimate of the moral structure of the universe may be tested and found inaccurate.

*The Scarlet Letter,* like all very great fiction, is the product of a controlled division of sympathies; and we must avoid the temptation to read it heretically. It has always been possible to remark, about Hawthorne, his fondness for the dusky places, his images of the slow movement of sad, shut-in souls in the half-light. But it has also been possible to read *The Scarlet Letter* (not to mention **"The New Adam and Eve"** and **"Earth's Holocaust"**) as an indorsement of hopefulness: to read it as a hopeful critic named Loring read it (writing for Theodore Parker's forward-looking *Massachusetts Quarterly Review*) as a party plea for self-reliance and an attack upon the sterile conventions of institutionalized society [see excerpt above, 1850]. One version of him would align Hawthorne with the secular residue of Jonathan Edwards; the other would bring him closer to Emerson. But Hawthorne was neither Emersonian nor Edwardsean; or rather he was both. The characteristic situation in his fiction is that of the Emersonian figure, the man of hope, who by some frightful mischance has stumbled into the time-burdened world of Jonathan Edwards. And this grim picture is given us by a writer who was skeptically cordial toward Emerson, but for whom the vision of Edwards, filtered through a haze of hope, remained a wonderfully useful metaphor. The situation, in the form which Hawthorne's ambivalence gave it, regularly led in his fiction to a moment of crucial choice: an invitation to the lost Emersonian, the thunder-struck Adam, to make up his mind—whether to accept the world he had fallen into, or whether to flee it, taking his chances in the allegedly free wilderness to the west. It is a decision about ethical reality, and most of Hawthorne's heroes and heroines eventually have to confront it.

That is why we have the frantic shuttling, in novel after novel, between the village and the forest, the city and the country; for these are the symbols between which the choice must be made and the means by which moral inference is converted into dramatic action. Unlike Thoreau or Cooper, Hawthorne never suggested that the choice was an easy one. . . . He acknowledged the dependence of the individual, for nourishment, upon organized society (the city), and he believed that it was imperative "to open an intercourse with the world." But he knew that the city could destroy as well as nourish and was apt to destroy the person most in need of nourishment. And

*Illustration of the last pillory scene from* The Scarlet Letter .

while he was responsive to the attractions of the open air and to the appeal of the forest, he also understood the grounds for the Puritan distrust of the forest. He retained that distrust as a part of the symbol. In the forest, possibility was unbounded; but just because of that, evil inclination was unchecked, and witches could flourish there.

For Hawthorne, the forest was neither the proper home of the admirable Adam, as with Cooper; nor was it the hideout of the malevolent adversary, as with Bird. It was the ambiguous setting of moral choice, the scene of reversal and discovery in his characteristic tragic drama. The forest was the pivot in Hawthorne's grand recurring pattern of escape and return.

It is in the forest, for example, that *The Scarlet Letter* version of the pattern begins to disclose itself: in the forest meeting between Hester and Dimmesdale, their first private meeting in seven years. During those years, Hester has been living "on the outskirts of the town," attempting to cling to the community by performing small services for it, though there had been nothing "in all her intercourse with society . . . that made her feel as if she belonged to it." And the minister has been contemplating the death of his innocence in a house fronting the village graveyard. The two meet now to join in an exertion of the will and the passion for freedom. They very nearly persuade themselves that they can escape along the forest track, which, though in one direction it goes "backward to the settlement," in another goes onward—"deeper it goes, and deeper into the wilderness, until . . . the yellow leaves will show no vestiges of the white man's tread." But the energy aroused by their encounter drives them back instead, at the end, to the heart of the society, to the penitential platform which is also the heart of the book's structure.

In no other novel is the *agon* so sharp, the agony so intense. (pp. 111-14)

> R. W. B. Lewis, "The Return into Time: Hawthorne," in his The American Adam: Innocence, Tragedy and Tradition in the Nineteenth Century, *The University of Chicago Press, 1955, pp. 110-26.*

## HYATT H. WAGGONER  (essay date 1955)

[*Like Anthony Trollope (1879), Frederic I. Carpenter (1944), Richard Harter Fogle (1952), and Terence Martin (1983), Waggoner probes Hawthorne's ambivalent treatment of sin and guilt in* The Scarlet Letter. *After discussing the dominant themes in the novel and the movement of the characters "up and down the lines of natural and moral value," he concludes that* The Scarlet Letter *is essentially a "dark tale" and that "Hawthorne's vision of death was a good deal stronger and more constant than his vision of life."*]

**The Scarlet Letter** is the most nearly static of all Hawthorne's novels. There is very little external action. We can see one of the evidences for this, and perhaps also one of the reasons for it, when we compare the amount of space Hawthorne devotes to exposition and description with the amount he devotes to narration. It is likewise true, in a sense not yet fully explored, that on the deepest level of meaning the novel has only an ambiguous movement. But in between the surface and the depths movement is constant and complex, and it is in this middle area that the principal value of the work lies.

The movement may be conceived as being up and down the lines of natural and moral value, lines which, if they were to be represented in a diagram, should be conceived as crossing to form an X. Thus, most obviously, Hester's rise takes her from low on the line of moral value, a "scarlet woman" guilty of a sin black in the eyes of the Puritans, to a position not too remote from Mr. Wilson's, as she becomes a sister of mercy and the light of the sickroom: this when we measure by the yardstick of community approval. When we apply a standard of measurement less relativistic—and all but the most consistent ethical relativists will do so, consciously or unconsciously, thoughtfully or unthoughtfully—we are also likely to find that there has been a "rise." I suppose most of us will agree, whatever our religion or philosophy may be, that Hester has gained in stature and dignity by enduring and transcending suffering, and that she has grown in awareness of social responsibility. Like all tragic protagonists, she has demonstrated the dignity and potentialities of man, even in her defeat.

Dimmesdale is a more complicated, though less admirable and sympathetic, figure. He first descends from his original position as the saintly guide and inspiration of the godly to the position he occupies during the greater part of the novel as very nearly the worst of the sinners in his hypocrisy and cowardice, then reascends by his final act of courageous honesty to a position somewhere in between his reputation for light and his reality of darkness. He emerges at last, that is, into the light of day, if only dubiously into that shining from the celestial city. We cannot help feeling, I think, that if he had had any help he might have emerged from the darkness much sooner.

As for Chillingworth, he of course descends, but not to reascend. As in his injured pride and inhuman curiosity he devotes himself to prying into the minister's heart, whatever goodness had been his—which had always been negative, the mere absence of overt evil—disappears and pride moves into what had been a merely cold heart, prompting to revenge and displacing intellectual curiosity, which continues only as a rationalization, a "good" reason serving to distract attention from the real one. He becomes a moral monster who feeds only on another's torment, divorced wholly from the sources of life and goodness. He is eloquent testimony to the belief that Hawthorne shared with Shakespeare and Melville, among others: that it is possible for man to make evil his good.

Thus the three principal characters move up and down the scale of moral values in a kind of counterpoint: Chillingworth clearly down, Hester ambiguously up, Dimmesdale in both directions, first down, then up, to end somewhere in the center. But this is not the end of the matter. Because there are obscure but real relationships, if only of analogy, between the moral and the natural (I am using "natural" in the sense of those aspects of existence studied by the natural sciences, which do not include the concept of freedom of choice among their working principles or their assumptions), because there are relations between the moral and the natural, the movements of the characters up and down the scale of moral values involve them in symbolic movements on the scale of natural values. The moral journeys are, in fact, as we have abundantly seen, largely suggested by physical imagery. Chillingworth becomes blacker and more twisted as he becomes more evil. Hester's beauty withers under the scorching brand, then momentarily reasserts itself in the forest scene, then disappears again. Dimmesdale becomes paler and walks more frequently in the shadow as his torment increases and his sin is multiplied.

But the moral changes are not simply made visible by the changes in the imagery: in their turn they require the visible changes and determine their direction. The outstanding example of this is of course Chillingworth's transformation. As we infer the potential evil in him from the snake imagery, the deformity, and the darkness associated with him when we first see him, so later his dedication to evil as his good suggests the "fancy" of the lurid flame in his eyes and the "notion" that it would be appropriate if he blasted the beauty of nature wherever he walked. So too the minister's moral journey suggests to the minds of the people both the red stigma which some think they see over his heart and the red A in the sky, with its ambiguous significance of angel or adultery. The total structure of the novel implies that the relation between fact and value is never simple: that neither is reducible to the other, yet that they are never wholly distinct.

All three of the chief characters, in short, exist on both of our crossed lines, the moral and the natural. They are seen in two perspectives, not identical but obscurely related. Pearl's situation, however, is somewhat different. She seems not to exist on the moral line at all. She is an object of natural beauty, a flower, a gem, instinctively trusted by the wild creatures of the forest. She is as incapable of deceit or dishonesty as nature itself, and at times as unsympathetic. She is not good or bad, because she is not responsible. (pp. 142-45)

Since "history" is created by the interaction of natural conditions and human choice, there is a significant sense in which Pearl has no history in the story. (p. 146)

But the others, including the Puritan populace, have histories and are involved in the larger movements of history created by all of them together existing in nature as creatures and moral beings. Hester might not have committed adultery had Chillingworth had a warmer heart, or perhaps even had he been younger or less deformed. He might not have fallen from a decent moral neutrality to positive vice had she not first fallen. Hester is forced to become stronger because the minister is so weak, and he gains strength by contact with her strength when they meet again in the forest. Chillingworth is stimulated by his victim's helplessness to greater excesses of torment and sin, and the Puritan women around the scaffold are stirred by Hester's youth and beauty to greater cruelty than was implicit in their inquisition anyway. History as conceived in *The Scarlet Letter* is complex, dynamic, ambiguous; it is never static or abstractly linear, as both simple materialism and simple moralism tend to picture it. St. Paul's "We are members one of another" could be taken as a text to be illustrated by the histories of human hearts recounted in the novel.

Yet with all this complex movement on two planes, with all this richness, this density, of history, when we ask ourselves the final questions of meaning and value we find the movement indecisive or arrested in one direction, continuing clearly only in the other. The Puritan people and Chillingworth are condemned, but are Hester and Dimmesdale redeemed? It is significant in this connection that Pearl's growth into womanhood takes place after the end of the story proper. It is also significant that though Hester bore her suffering nobly, it is not clear that she ever repented; and that, though he indulged in several kinds of penance, it is possible to doubt that the minister ever did. (pp. 146-47)

There is, then, despite Hester's rise, no certainty of final release from evil or of the kind of meaning to be found in tragedy, no well-grounded hope of escape from their sin for the sinners. The minister's dying words and the legend engraved on the tombstone both seem to me to make this clear. . . . Hawthorne, in this respect a man of his age, never formulated his religious feelings and attitudes into any clear-cut theology. If he had done so, he might have been puzzled by the question of how central and significant a place to give to the Atonement.

In this final theological sense then the work is static. On the natural plane, beauty and ugliness, red rose and pigweed, equally exist with indisputable reality. But on the moral plane, only evil and suffering are really vivid and indisputable. Hawthorne's constant exception to his ordinary characterization of the human heart, the spotless, lily-like hearts of pure maidens, will hardly bear looking into. The light around Mr. Wilson's head shines too weakly to penetrate far into the surrounding gloom. And the only light into which Dimmesdale certainly emerges is the light of common day. The novel is structured around the metaphor of bringing the guilty secret from the black depths of the heart out into the light. But it is suggestive not only of what went on in his own heart but of the poverty both of the Puritanism of which he wrote and of the Unitarianism which Puritanism became and which Hawthorne knew at first hand that Hawthorne could conceive of the need but not the existence or the nature of any further step. After confession, what then? "No great wrong is ever undone." Surely being "true," the one moral among many, as Hawthorne tells us, that he chose to underscore, is not enough. *The Scarlet Letter* sprang from Hawthorne's heart, not from his head.

The dominant symbols . . . are the cemetery, the prison, and the rose. The religious idealism suggested by the steeple-crowned hats is ineffective, positively perverted even, as the man of adamant's sincere piety was perverted by his fanaticism. The

clearest tones in the book are the black of the prison and the weeds and the grave, and the redness of the letter and the rose, suggesting moral and natural evil and natural goodness, but not moral goodness. "On a field, sable, the letter A, gules." Of the literal and figurative light, one, the sunlight, is strong and positive, while the other, shining, as St. John tells us, from the Light of the World, falls fitfully and dimly over minor characters or is posited in mere speculative possibility.

*The Scarlet Letter,* then, like the majority of the best tales, suggests that Hawthorne's vision of death was a good deal stronger and more constant than his vision of life. This is indeed, as Hawthorne calls it, a dark tale, and its mesh of good and evil is not equally strong in all its parts. Hawthorne was right in not wanting to be judged as a man solely by it, though I think he must have known, as we do, that it is his greatest book. For in it there is perfect charity, and a real, though defective, faith, but almost no hope. Unlike most of us today, Hawthorne was close enough to historic Christianity to know its main dogmas, even those he did not fully share. He preferred not to seem to be denying so central a part of the Christian Gospel as that men can be saved from their sins. (pp. 148-50)

> *Hyatt H. Waggoner, in his* Hawthorne: A Critical Study, *Cambridge, Mass.: The Belknap Press, 1955, 268 p.*

### MALCOLM COWLEY (essay date 1957)

[*An American critic, editor, poet, translator, and historian, Cowley has made valuable contributions to contemporary letters with his editions of the works of such American authors as Hawthorne, Walt Whitman, and Ernest Hemingway, his writings as a literary critic for the* New Republic, *and his chronicles and criticism of modern American literature. In the following excerpt, Cowley explores Hawthorne's handling of structure in* The Scarlet Letter *and posits that he accomplished a "truly important technical innovation" in the novel. By presenting the novel dramatically, as a series of scenes rather than as a continuous narrative, Hawthorne was able to develop each scene separately and to intensify characterization through dramatic juxtaposition of the protagonists. Two other critics who closely explore the structure of* The Scarlet Letter *are John C. Gerber and Leland Schubert (see Additional Bibliography).*]

[The first technical problem Hawthorne faced in writing *The Scarlet Letter*] was one of social background. The persons of Hawthorne's story existed in relation to a particular society, whose standards—which they fully accepted—intensified their guilt and lent drama to their atonement. How could the society be brought directly into the story—not merely talked about and explained by the author but presented in life?

Hawthorne's solution was to invent a few additional characters, not to be studied in depth, but merely to be put forward as representatives of the society in its essential aspects. (p. 11)

Except in the last chapter—which is an epilogue conceived in the expository manner of other early nineteenth-century writers—Hawthorne lets his characters act out their fates. No information is needed by the reader beyond that suggested by the behavior of the characters or imparted in their dialogues. The action of the novel is completely an *interaction* among four persons in a particular environment that is also presented in its own terms. Hawthorne had solved the problem of social background in a fashion that enabled him to write, for the first time in American literature, a novel that was a completely framed and self-subsistent work of art.

There was, however, another technical problem that required a more radical solution, arising as it did from the author's special experience and cast of mind. Until that time, the novel in all its forms had been essentially a chronicle of events and Hawthorne had no great talent or practice as a chronicler.... What he had learned from writing them was, among other lessons, how to work intensively in smaller forms and how to present his subjects as moral essays or allegorical pictures rather than as continually moving narratives.

His final problem, then, was to devise some method by which a larger theme could be adjusted to his training and personality as a writer. It was the solution he found, whether by reason or instinct, that became the truly important technical innovation in *The Scarlet Letter*. Instead of conceiving the novel as a single or double narrative moving ahead in a straight or zigzag line and revealing the social landscape as if to the eyes of a traveler on horseback, Hawthorne approached it dramatistically, almost as if his characters were appearing on a stage. Instead of dividing his book into narrative episodes—now the hero falls in love, now he fights a duel, now he escapes from prison—Hawthorne divided it into scenes, each of which is a posed tableau or a dramatic confrontation.

The advantage of the method for this particular author was that it enabled him to work on each scene intensively, as if it were a separate tale. Although there was little movement within the separate scenes, he could create a general sense of movement by passing rapidly from one scene to another, for example, from the marketplace at night to the seashore and thence to the forest. Unity of mood was not one of his problems—that had already been achieved by his years of brooding over the central symbol—but the method enabled him to give the book architectural unity as well, by balancing one scene against another and by ending the story where it really began, on the scaffold of the pillory. (pp. 11-12)

Hawthorne's knowledge of the drama came mostly from his reading, which—according to the records of the Salem Athenaeum—included all of Racine, besides other classical French dramatists; he had been familiar with Shakespeare's works since boyhood. It might well be argued that his cast of mind was not Shakespearean, as Melville thought, but Racinian. The fact is that *The Scarlet Letter* can be read, and gains a new dimension from being read, as a Racinian drama of dark necessity.

It is a novel in twenty-four chapters, but, considered as a tragic drama, it is divided into the usual five acts and subdivided into eight scenes. (One principle of division would be that an act may include two scenes if the second follows without any great lapse of time.) There are of course some chapters that fall outside the dramatic framework, since each of them deals with a single character (Chapter V with Hester, VI with Pearl, IX with Chillingworth, XI with Dimmesdale, XIII with Hester again, XX with Dimmesdale, and XXIV, the epilogue, chiefly with Hester), and since the method they follow is narrative or expository. These seven chapters serve as interludes in the dramatic action—or in one case as a postlude—and they provide some additional information about the characters that would have been difficult to incorporate into the dialogue. The essential chapters, however, are the other seventeen, in which Hawthorne is applying the scenic philosophy and method. Here is how they arrange themselves into rounded acts and scenes:

*Act I, Scene 1* (Chapters I to III) is laid in the marketplace of Boston, fifteen or twenty years after the founding of the city.

On the right, rear, is the enormous nail-studded door of the prison, with a wild rosebush growing beside it. On the left is the meeting house, with a balcony projecting over the stage. Under the balcony is the scaffold of the pillory, which will be the effective center of the drama. Hester Prynne emerges from the blackness of the prison, with the child on her arm not hiding the letter A in scarlet cloth pinned to her breast; in the whole scene it is the one touch of brilliant color. She moves through the gray crowd and climbs the scaffold. From the balcony overhead the Reverend Mr. Dimmesdale adjures her to reveal the father of her child. "Believe me, Hester," he says, "though he were to step down from a high place and stand beside thee, on thy pedestal of shame, yet better were it so than to hide a guilty heart through life." Hester shakes her head. Looking down at the crowd she recognizes her wronged husband, who had been missing for two years, but he puts a finger on his lips to show that she must not reveal his identity. All the named characters of the drama—including Governor Bellingham, John Wilson, and Mistress Hibbins—appear in this first scene; and there is also the Boston crowd, which speaks in strophe and antistrophe like a Greek chorus.

*Scene 2* of the first act (Chapter IV) is a room in the prison that same June evening. Here, after the public tableau of the first scene, comes a private confrontation. Hester and the child have fallen ill, a leech is summoned to care for them, and the leech is Chillingworth, the betrayed husband. He tells her that the scarlet letter is a more effective punishment than any he might have imagined. "Live, therefore," he says, "and bear about thy doom with thee." After revealing his determination to find the lover and be revenged on him, Chillingworth extracts one promise from Hester: that just as she has kept the lover's identity a secret, so she must keep the husband's.

*Act II, Scene 1* (Chapters VII and VIII) is laid in the governor's hall, three years after the events of the first act. Little Pearl is thought to be such a strange and willful child that there has been talk among the Puritan magistrates of taking her away from her sinful mother. When Hester, now a seamstress, comes to deliver a pair of embroidered gloves to Governor Bellingham, he holds an informal trial of her case. Chillingworth plays an ambiguous part in it, but Dimmesdale—when Hester demands that he speak—makes such an eloquent plea that she is allowed to keep the child. All the named characters are again present—down to Mistress Hibbins, who, at the end of the scene, invites Hester to attend a witches' sabbath in the forest. Hester refuses with a triumphant smile:

> "I must tarry at home," she says, "to keep watch over my little Pearl. Had they taken her from me, I would willingly have gone with thee into the forest, and signed my name in the Black Man's book, and that with mine own blood!"

This tableau and its brief epilogue are followed once more by a private confrontation. *Scene 2* of the second act (Chapter X) is set in Chillingworth's laboratory, among the retorts and crucibles. The old leech suspects Dimmesdale and has taken up residence in the same house, to continue all through the scene his relentless probing of Dimmesdale's heart. The minister will not confess, but, at the curtain, Chillingworth accidentally finds proof that he is indeed the guilty man.

*Act III* (Chapter XII) has only one scene, the scaffold of the pillory. Four years have passed since the second act. Subtly tortured by Chillingworth and finally driven half-insane, Dimmesdale has dressed in his ministerial robes and left his room at midnight, hoping to find relief in a private mimicry of public confession. Standing on the scaffold he shrieks aloud, but nobody recognizes his voice. Governor Bellingham and Mistress Hibbins both open their windows to peer into the night. On his way home from Governor Winthrop's deathbed, good John Wilson walks through the marketplace in a halo of lantern-light; he does not look up at the pillory. Then, coming from the same deathbed, Hester appears with little Pearl, and Dimmesdale invites them to join him. Holding one another's hands on the scaffold, they form what Hawthorne calls "an electric chain," and Dimmesdale feels a new life, not his own, pouring like a torrent into his heart.

"Minister!" Pearl whispers. "Wilt thou stand here with mother and me, tomorrow noontide?"

When Dimmesdale refuses, she tries to pull her hand away. At this moment a meteor gleams through a cloud, forming a scarlet A in the heavens while it also reveals the little group on the scaffold. It is another of Hawthorne's many lighting effects, based partly on his Emersonian belief that the outer world is a visible manifestation of the inner world, but also based partly on his instinct for theatre; one might almost speak of his staginess. While the meteor is still glowing, Chillingworth appears to lead the minister back to his torture chamber. This tableau, occurring at the exact center of the drama, is the turning point of *The Scarlet Letter;* from now the tempo will be quicker. The first half of the story has covered a space of seven years; the second half will cover no more than fifteen days.

*Act IV* is in two intimate scenes, the second of which is the longest in the drama. *Scene 1* (Chapters XIV and XV) is laid on the seashore, where Chillingworth is gathering herbs to concoct his medicines. While Pearl goes wading in a tidal pool, Hester accosts the old leech and begs him to release her from her promise not to tell Dimmesdale that he is the wronged husband. Chillingworth answers in a speech that reveals not only his own heart but the other side of Hawthorne's philosophy. The Emersonian side contributed to his stage effects, but it was his surviving Calvinism (in some ways close to Racine's Jansenism) that enabled him to conceive a tragic drama.

"Peace, Hester, peace!" the old man says. "It is not granted me to pardon. . . . My old faith, long forgotten, comes back to me, and explains all that we do, and all we suffer. By thy first step awry thou didst plant the germ of evil; but since that moment, it has all been a dark necessity. Ye that have wronged me are not sinful, save in a kind of typical illusion; neither am I fiend-like, who have snatched a fiend's office from his hands. It is our fate. Let the black flower blossom as it may! Now go thy ways, and deal as thou wilt with yonder man."

He goes back to gathering herbs. Hester calls to Pearl, who, as they leave the stage, keeps asking her, "Mother!—Why does the minister keep his hand over his heart?"

*Scene 2* of the fourth act (including four chapters, XVI to XIX) is set in the forest, which forms another contrast with the marketplace and helps to reveal the moral background of Hawthorne's drama. The forest, he tells us in what might almost be a stage direction, is an image of the moral wilderness in which Hester has long been wandering. But it was more than that for Hawthorne himself, and a close reading shows that the forest is the meeting place of those who follow their passions and revolt against the community. In this sense little Pearl, the natural child, is a daughter of the forest, and we observe in this scene that she is perfectly at home there. Witches like

Mistress Hibbins go into the forest to dance with Indian powwows and Lapland wizards, and Hester has been tempted to join them. When she meets Dimmesdale in the forest, although she intends only to warn him against Chillingworth, it is natural in this setting that she should also urge him to defy the laws of the tribe and flee with her to a foreign country. The minister agrees; they will take passage on a Bristol cruiser then moored in the harbor. For a moment Hester unpins the scarlet A from her dress and lets down her long black glossy hair; but Pearl, who has been called back from playing at the brookside, sulks until she pins the letter on her breast again.

On his way back to Boston (in Chapter XX) Dimmesdale meets Mistress Hibbins. "So, reverend Sir, you have made a visit into the forest," says the witch-lady, nodding her high head-dress at him. "The next time, I pray you to allow me only a fair warning, and I shall be proud to bear you company."

*Act V,* in a single scene (Chapters XXI to XXIII), takes place three days after the meeting in the forest and is the culmination toward which the drama has been moving. Once again it is laid in the marketplace, with all the named characters present, as well as the Bristol shipmaster and the Boston crowd that speaks with the voices of the tribe. Dimmesdale preaches the Election Sermon, the climax of his ministerial career, while Hester listens outside the meeting house. The shipmaster tells her that Chillingworth has taken passage on the same vessel; there will be no escape. Then Dimmesdale appears in a great procession of Puritan worthies and, instead of marching with them to the official banquet, he totters up the steps of the scaffold after calling on Hester to support him. At last they are standing together, in public, on the pedestal of shame.

"Is not this better," Dimmesdale murmurs, "than we dreamed of in the forest?" Facing the crowd he tears open his ministerial band and shows that there is a scarlet A imprinted on his own flesh. He has made his public confession and now, at the point of death, he feels reconciled with the community. As he sinks to the scaffold, Chillingworth kneels over him repeating, "Thou hast escaped me." Pearl kisses her father on the lips, and the tears that she lets fall are the pledge that she will cease to be an outcast, an embodiment of the scarlet letter, a daughter of the forest, and instead will grow up among human joys and sorrows.

I spoke of Hawthorne's kinship with Racine, but at this point, if not before, one begins to feel that his drama might have another ancestry as well, even though the author was not conscious of it. He has presented us with distinguished, even noble, characters who are inevitably brought to grief for having violated the laws of heaven and the tribe. He has presented "an action that is serious and also, as having magnitude, complete in itself . . . with incidents arousing pity and fear, wherewith to accomplish its catharsis of such emotions." The familiar quotation from Aristotle seems appropriate in a discussion of *The Scarlet Letter.* In telling his story by a new method, Hawthorne had done more than to extend the unity and economy of the brief tale into the realm of the novel; and more than to discover a new architectural form that would be rediscovered by Henry James and copied by scores of respectably talented novelists after him. It is not too much to say that he had recaptured, for his New England, the essence of Greek tragedy. (pp. 13-16)

*Malcolm Cowley, "Five Acts of 'The Scarlet Letter'," in* College English, *Vol. 19, No. 1, October, 1957, pp. 11-16.*

RICHARD CHASE    (essay date 1957)

[*Chase examines the origins and function of imagery in* The Scarlet Letter, *indicating that it derives from several different kinds of sources. Symbols in the work are unified, Chase asserts, when they are read as "projections of the faculties of the artist's mind and elements of a quasi-puritan allegory." For other studies of imagery in* The Scarlet Letter, *see F. O. Matthiessen (1941), Roy R. Male (1957), and Daniel Hoffman (1961).*]

*The Scarlet Letter* has in abundance that "complexity of feeling" often attributed to the American novel. At the same time, the foreground elements of *The Scarlet Letter*—the salient actors and events—have something of the two-dimensionality of actors and events in legend. What baffles our best understanding is how to make the mysterious connections between the rather simple elements of the book and what is thought and felt about them. (p. 67)

*The Scarlet Letter* is almost all picture. The adultery which sets everything going happens before the book begins, and it is never made believable. There are, to be sure, dramatic scenes—the three scenes on the scaffold; Hester and Pearl at the governor's mansion; Hester, Dimmesdale, and Pearl in the forest; and each of these scenes is exquisite and unforgettable.

Yet compared with the more immediate impact which in different hands they might have made on us, they seem frozen, muted, and remote. There is an abyss between these scenes and the reader, and they are like the events in a pageant or a dream, not like those of a stage drama. They are, in short, little differentiated from the pattern of the whole and they have the effect of being observed by the reader at second hand, of being reported to him, as in "picture." The author's powerfully possessive imagination refuses to relinquish his characters to our immediate perusal or to the logic of their own human destiny. This tight monolithic reticence is what gives *The Scarlet Letter* its unity and its mysterious remoteness. It is at every point the mirror of Hawthorne's mind, and the only one of his longer fictions in which we are not disturbed by the shortcomings of this mind but are content to marvel at its profound beauty.

Inevitably Hawthorne's symbol for the imagination was the mirror. . . . His fictions are mirror-like. They give us a static and pictorial version of reality. They are uncanny and magical, but they capture little of life's drama, its emergent energy and warmth, its conflict, crisis, and catharsis. (pp. 70-1)

What may be called the "grammar-school" idea of Hawthorne's novel supposes it to be a tale of sin and repentance. And this it certainly is, with strong stress on the repentance. More accurately, the subject of the book is the moral and psychological results of sin—the isolation and morbidity, the distortion and thwarting of the emotional life. From another point of view these are shown to be the results not of man's living in sin but of his living in a Puritan society, and thereby, to some extent, in *any* society. And yet it will not do to read *The Scarlet Letter* too closely as a comment on society, which is felt in its pages hardly more pervasively than sin.

To be sure there are elements of social comment in *The Scarlet Letter*. Is it not, for example, a feminist tract? So magically various is the book that one may sometimes think it is, even though a rich sensibility and profound mysteries are not usually associated with feminist literature. But doesn't Hester Prynne turn out to be rather like Hawthorne's sister-in-law Elizabeth Peabody, the emancipated reformer who became the prototype of Miss Birdseye in James's *The Bostonians*? Once a luxurious and passionate woman, Hester takes up a life of renunciation and service. Her life turns "in a great measure from passion and feeling, to thought." In an age when "the human intellect" was "newly emancipated," she assumes "a freedom of speculation," then common enough on the other side of the Atlantic, but which our forefathers, had they known it, would have held to be a deadlier crime than that stigmatized by the scarlet letter." Thus, in her lonely life, Hester becomes a radical. She believes that sometime "a new truth" will be revealed and that "the whole relation between man and woman" will be established "on a surer ground of mutual happiness." She even comes to think in feminist rhetoric, and one can hear not only Hester but Miss Peabody and Margaret Fuller talking firmly about "the whole relation between man and woman."

Undoubtedly, then, *The Scarlet Letter* does have a feminist theme. It is even a tract, yet on the few occasions when it is heard the tractarian tone is tempered by the irony of the author. The book may have other meanings of a social or political kind. Still, one makes a mistake to treat Hawthorne, either in *The Scarlet Letter* or *The Blithedale Romance,* as if he were a political or social writer. He is a very canny observer of political fact, as of all fact, and this is in itself an unusual distinction. But no coherent politics is to be derived from Hawthorne. . . . In *The Scarlet Letter* and Hawthorne's other works the people at large are sensed merely as a choric crowd and the few main characters are rather artificially grouped in a village square, an old house, a shop, an isolated farm community, a forest glade, or a garden. The settings do not seem to be permanently related to each other or to the actors who momentarily speak their pieces in them. (pp. 72-4)

[Hawthorne had] command over political theory or, what is more useful to a novelist, the instinct to dramatize politics in action. Hawthorne often gives the illusion of a systematic intellectual prowess, and this has led many readers to find in him an important moralist, political thinker, or theologian. It *is* an illusion, compounded of his hardheaded sagacity and his skepticism, his observance of elemental human truth. But the unities of his conceptions are first of all *aesthetic* unities, and Hawthorne tended to take an art-view of the world in so far as he took any consistent view at all. He stubbornly insisted that one could take such a view even in a democracy which appeared to have little use for aesthetic values. (p. 74)

Hawthorne undeniably has the historical sense. . . . [There] is no central unifying cultural "myth" in Hawthorne—only a clear perception of historical facts and an ability to endow these with beauty and significance. But the significance arises from the aesthetic harmonies of the composition as we find it from story to story, and although historical facts are observed, no theory or consistent view of history is presented. (p. 76)

[*The Scarlet Letter* is an allegorical novel and] the allegory both in form and substance derives from Puritanism. Let us add, also, that although no unifying myth is involved, the novel describes the loss or submergence of emotion involved in the abandonment of the Old World cultural heritage which had given human emotions a sanction and a manifold significance.

Neither in *The Scarlet Letter* nor elsewhere did Hawthorne ever make up his mind whether he approved of this loss and submergence. Purely as an artist he often felt dismayed and discouraged by what Cooper called "the poverty of materials" which the workaday, uniform life of democracy had to offer. And on one side of his moral character, Hawthorne had enough passion to make us feel the sadness and chill of the New

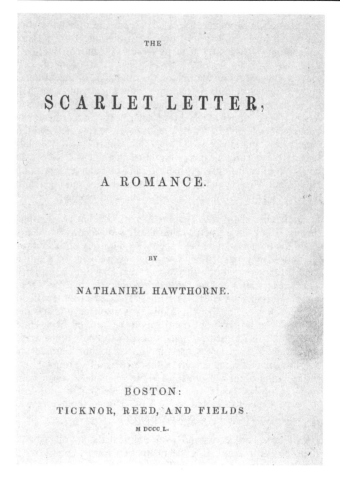

THE

## SCARLET LETTER,

### A ROMANCE.

BY

NATHANIEL HAWTHORNE.

BOSTON:
TICKNOR, REED, AND FIELDS.
M DCCC L.

*Facsimile of the title page of the first edition of* The Scarlet Letter.

World—for example, when Hester Prynne lets her rich black hair loose in the forest sunshine but then with her meek masochism hides it again beneath the gray cap. At the same time, the other Hawthorne, the Puritan conventionalist, permits himself a sigh of relief and rationalizes it by reflecting that after all we are disillusioned now, after our passage from the Old World to the New, and if a certain beauty disappears along with licentiousness and sin, that is the price we pay for our stern realism, our rectitude, and our practical sagacity.

If we are to hold to the idea that *The Scarlet Letter* is an allegory, we must assign meanings to the symbols of the story. . . . His symbols are broadly traditional, coming to him from the Bible, Dante, Shakespeare, Milton, Spenser, and Bunyan—the light and the dark, the forest and the town, the dark woman and the fair woman, the fountain, the mirror, the cavern of the heart, the river, the sea, Eden, the rose, the serpent, fire and so on.

Within the context of these symbols, the allegory proper may be, however, more peculiar to Hawthorne. The allegorical symbols are Puritan categories revised for Hawthorne's own purposes, and they can be assigned provisionally in the following manner.

Hester Prynne, about whom there is something queenly, imperious, and barbaric, as well as fallible and appealing and enduring, represents the eternal woman, perhaps, indeed, the eternal human. When she puts on her gray cap and becomes

a kind of social worker, her color and passion, her indeterminate, instinctual being is curbed and controlled. While this is going on Chillingworth and Dimmesdale are destroying each other. They are the two aspects of the will which confused Puritan thought in New England—the active and the inactive. From the beginning, Puritanism generated a strong belief in the efficacy of the will in overcoming all obstacles in the path of the New Israel in America, as in the path of the individual who strove toward Election. But at the same time the doctrine of Predestination denied the possibility of any will except that of God.

Chillingworth unites intellect with will and coldly and with sinister motives analyzes Dimmesdale. This is the truly diabolic act in Hawthorne's opinion. It is what he calls the Unpardonable Sin and it is worse than sins of passions ("He has violated, in cold blood, the sanctity of a human heart," says Dimmesdale. "Thou and I, Hester, never did so!"). Hawthorne is as close a student of those impulses which drive men to plunder and exploit the human heart as Cooper and Faulkner are of the impulses that drive men to plunder and exploit the land that Providence put into the trust of Americans. And for him as for them, violation, or impiety, is the worst of crimes.

Dimmesdale is intellect without will. He is passive; he is all eloquence, sensitivity, refinement, and moral scruple. What violence he has has long since been turned inward. He has preyed on himself as Chillingworth preys on him.

Little Pearl, one should say first, is a vividly real child whom Hawthorne modeled on his own little daughter Una. As a symbol as well as in life she is the offspring of Hester and an extension, as Hawthorne says, of the scarlet A. She represents the intuitive, lawless poetic view of the world. She is the eternal folk imagination, restored in every child, which is the fundamental element of the artist's imagination, and is outlawed by Puritan doctrine. "The spell of life went forth from her ever-creative spirit, and communicated itself to a thousand objects, as a torch kindles a flame wherever it may be applied." Ironically she conspires with everyone else in the tale to re-create the luxurious Hester in the puritan-democratic image. For it is she who insists that Hester shall replace the A and cover her hair with the gray cap.

As will be seen from the above, Chillingworth, Dimmesdale, and Pearl can be conceived as projections of different faculties of the novelist's mind—Chillingworth, the probing intellect; Dimmesdale, the moral sensibility; Pearl, the unconscious or demonic poetic faculty. Hester is the fallible human reality as the novelist sees it—plastic, various, inexhaustible, enduring, morally problematic.

From another point of view, we see that without becoming a myth, *The Scarlet Letter* includes several mythic archetypes. The novel incorporates its own comic-book or folklore version. Chillingworth is the diabolical intellectual, perhaps even the mad scientist. Dimmesdale is the shining hero or to more sophisticated minds the effete New Englander. Hester is the scarlet woman, a radical and nonconformist, partly "Jewish" perhaps (there is at any rate an Old Testament quality about her, and Hawthorne says that her nature is "rich, voluptuous, Oriental." Like many other American writers, Hawthorne is not entirely above the racial folklore of the Anglo-Saxon peoples, which tends to depict tainted women and criminal men as French, Mediterranean, or Jewish—as in Hawthorne's *Marble Faun,* Miriam is Jewish, in Melville's *Pierre* Isabel is French, and in *Billy Budd* Claggart is dimly Mediterranean). Pearl is sometimes reminiscent of Little Red Riding Hood or a forest sprite of some sort who talks with the animals. Later when she inherits a fortune and marries a foreign nobleman, she is the archetypal American girl of the international scene, like the heroines of Howells and James. The subculture from which these discordant archetypes emerge is evidently inchoate and derivative. The symbols do not cohere until they have been made into projections of the faculties of the artist's mind and elements of a quasi-puritan allegory. But to a receptive imagination, they connect *The Scarlet Letter* with universal folklore, as many other novels, good and bad, are connected. (pp. 76-9)

> *Richard Chase, "Hawthorne and the Limits of Romance," in his* The American Novel and Its Tradition, *Doubleday Anchor Books, 1957, pp. 67-88.*

**ROY R. MALE**   (essay date 1957)

[*Male focuses on what he terms the "Tongue of Flame" metaphor, which Hawthorne employs in* The Scarlet Letter *to stress the importance of uniting vision with utterance. For other studies of imagery in the novel, see the excerpts by F. O. Matthiessen (1941), Richard Chase (1957), and Daniel Hoffman (1961).*]

Perhaps the best way of returning to the flesh and blood of [*The Scarlet Letter*] is to consider its guiding metaphor, the Tongue of Flame. Hawthorne derives this figure from the description in Acts 2:3-4 of the descent of the Holy Ghost upon the chosen disciples: "And there appeared unto them cloven tongues like as of fire, and it sat upon each of them. And they were all filled with the Holy Ghost. . . ." However, Hawthorne interprets this gift in his own way. The tongues of flame symbolize not the power of speech in all languages but the ability to address "the whole human brotherhood in the heart's native language." . . . The Tongue of Flame is intuitive communication, the expression of "the highest truths through the humblest medium of familiar words and images."

I call this the crucial metaphor because ultimately the Tongue of Flame comes to be identical with the letter of scarlet, and its revelation consummates a process that goes on throughout the book. The quest for truth in *The Scarlet Letter* takes the specific and time-honored form of seeking to unite the Word and the Light in the Act. The Flame, or the Light, is vision—both insight and, as Sophia [Hawthorne] called it, "outsight"; it is the ability to see both the old universal patterns and the new particulars; and it is not only vision but revelation. The Word is the utterance and the investment; it comprises the tradition, the rhetorical and moral discipline, the communion, the surname; but it is also the new clothing, the new foliage, the new name. Both categories, therefore, contain the possibility of looking in opposite directions: backward and forward in time, inward and outward in space.

Thus *The Scarlet Letter* . . . is about ways of seeing. Many of the chapter titles—**"The Interview," "The Interior of a Heart," "The Minister's Vigil," "Another View of Hester"**—spring from the effort to gain a better perspective, a clearer view of the truth. Some of the book's key words retain vestiges of their original meaning in expressing this emphasis upon vision: "scene," "witness," "interview," "spectacle," "perspective," "speculation," "spectator," and "respectable." From the initial pillory scene, where Hester finds a "point of view," to the end, when she "glanced her sad eyes downward at the scarlet letter," the book deals with different kinds of vision.

But vision alone is insufficient as a means of conversion. To "be true," as the book's moral indicates, one must also "utter," make plain, "show freely" to others the secret of his identity. As the spirit is clothed in flesh and the flesh is clothed in garments, so ideas are clothed in words. (pp. 100-02)

The Light is a process of seeing and disclosing; the Word is a process of uttering and investing; the Act is the intuitive union of both. Truth comes as a reward for intellectual discipline and human sympathy, but the ultimate incarnation that unites light and letter, spirit and flesh can only *be*. This intuition may be simply a sign, like Pearl's gestures, or a facial expression, like Chillingworth's when he discovers the letter on Dimmesdale's breast. More significant expression is achieved in art: Hester's needlework, Chillingworth's psychiatric alchemy, and Dimmesdale's Election Sermon. The highest form of intuitive truth, however, is the life that is patterned as a work of art. To make one's life a parable is to be the word incarnate; from one perspective, Dimmesdale's final symbolic gesture approaches this saintly level.

The action of the book shows how the two major characters are transformed when they join the Word and the Light in their actions and their art. (pp. 102-03)

At the end we are left with the symbol into which the whole meaning of the book has been distilled. Around the letter have gathered not only the explicit associations of Adultress, Able, Affection, and Angel but also the myriad subtle suggestions of art, atonement, ascension, and the Acts of the Apostles. Here is the *A*, each limb of which suggests an ascension, with Pearl the link between the two; here is the sable background of the Puritan community; and fused in the entire symbol are the flesh and the spirit, the word and the light, the letter *A*, gules. Hawthorne seized upon the heraldic wording partly because of its rich poetic associations but also because "gules" is the perfect word with which to conclude the book. It means "scarlet," of course, but it originates from the Latin *gula*, meaning "throat." Here condensed in one word is the Tongue of Flame; here, joining the language patterns of vision and eloquence, is the perfect capstone for Hawthorne's symbolic structure. (pp. 117-18)

> *Roy R. Male, in his* Hawthorne's Tragic Vision, *University of Texas Press, 1957, 187 p.*

**RANDALL STEWART**   (essay date 1958)

[*In his exploration of Hawthorne's treatment of Romanticism and Puritanism in* The Scarlet Letter, *Stewart contends that the novel constitutes a criticism of both philosophies. For another inquiry into Hawthorne's attitude toward Romanticism and Puritanism, see the excerpt above by Frederic I. Carpenter (1944).*]

One of the chief thematic tensions in Hawthorne is the tension between the Puritan and the romantic tendencies. Hawthorne's writings lean in the Puritan direction. But he lived in a romantic age, and his work shows an awareness of the temper of that age. His work is in a sense a "criticism" of that temper, but it is not a criticism which is blind to the romantic fascination, or refuses it a sympathetic hearing.

In *The Scarlet Letter*, Hester is spokesman for the romantic view, and her argument carries weight with many readers. (p. 83)

Hester never felt that she had sinned, and her speech ["What we did had a consecration of its own. We felt it so! We said so to each other.''] is very appealing. Is not the book after all, some readers ask, an exposé of Puritan bigotry and intolerance? The answer is, Yes, to be sure; *The Scarlet Letter* is a criticism of Puritanism as well as of romanticism. But when the romantic apologist goes on to insist that the book is a vindication of individual impulse, the right of the individual to happiness, the sacredness of passion, it is necessary to demur. Does not Hester's view carry individualism a bit too far? Does it not translate ''the sacredness of the individual'' into ''the individual a law unto himself''? The book, taken as a whole, does not support the romantic view. I say this almost regretfully, because I like Hester and I sympathize (who does not?) with her frustrated love. But it is a ''romantic'' sympathy. *A consecration of its own?* ''Alas that ever love was sin!'' Hester is far removed from Chaucer's Wife of Bath (Hester is no wanton), but when thinking of her plight, one remembers the Wife's famous lament.

The tension between Puritan and romantic is especially emphasized in the forest scene. The symbolism is dualistic. The forest itself has a double significance: it stands for moral error, being the place where Hester and Arthur go astray; and it stands for natural innocence, for here little Pearl becomes a child of nature (in the romantic sense) and is recognized as such by the creatures of the forest. Pearl herself is also double: not only is she an innocent child of nature, but she is at the same time an agent of retribution (she insists that Hester replace the scarlet letter on her dress after having cast it aside). Hester's casting of the letter aside was her ''romantic revolt''; her replacing of the letter was her outward compliance with (not inward acceptance of) the Puritan law. Throughout the forest scene (perhaps the most richly symbolic scene in the book), Hester stands for romantic individualism, and Arthur for the claims of law and conscience.

For although Arthur, stimulated by the excitement of the moment, agrees to Hester's plan of escape, his experiences after leaving Hester force him back into the Puritan path. On re-entering the village, he was sorely tempted by the devil to say blasphemous things to the passers-by. On reaching his room, he destroyed the manuscript of the Election Sermon to be delivered on the following day, and furiously set about writing a fresh sermon. The author does not tell us exactly what went on in Arthur's mind at this point. To do so would be almost unavoidably to prepare us too well for the climactic scene, the public confession, and sacrifice the element of legitimate surprise and shock. But though we are not told explicitly, we can be sure that there was a struggle, and the minister was able finally to beat down Satan under his feet. It is axiomatic with Hawthorne that there can be no virtue without conflict and struggle. Only a great struggle can account for the minister's great heroism, and the greatness of the struggle came out of the greatness of his despair, his extremity.

I have said that Arthur stood for the claims of the Puritan law. ''Christian'' can be used here interchangeably (as so often in a discussion of this kind) with ''Puritan.'' The reader hardly needs to be told that the ''law'' broken by Hester and Arthur was the Seventh Commandment of the Decalogue, and that the Decalogue was not abrogated by the New Testament dispensation. Adultery continued to be a sin after Christ, as it had been before Christ. Jesus *forgave* the woman in adultery. The Puritans did not invent the Seventh Commandment, nor were they un-Christian in insisting upon its importance, though an uninformed reader might infer both of these notions from some of the commentaries on *The Scarlet Letter*. The Puritan com-

munity in Hawthorne's novel was un-Christian in its unforgiving attitude and behavior—its bigotry and cruelty—but it was not un-Christian in its doctrine.

Hester is a romantic heroine, a splendid one. She has been much admired, and justifiably. The richly embroidered A has been called by one of her modern admirers ''the red badge of courage.'' She was indeed courageous, and strong. Arthur, in comparison, has seemed pitiably weak, but justice, I think, has not been done to Arthur. Arthur's situation was much more difficult than Hester's. Her conflict was external. She was integrated within herself, and she set her solidly united self resolutely against the intolerant community. A fight like this can be inspiriting; it is fortifying, it builds one up. But Arthur's fight was with himself. His was a state of civil war, not war with the outside world. The community idolized him, but he had his internal troubles, and these proved to be serious. (Psychiatrists who happen to read *The Scarlet Letter* often express surprise that Hawthorne, in 1850, should have understood how serious internal conflicts can be.) If heroism is measured in terms of the magnitude and severity of the struggle which is undergone, then Arthur must be adjudged the more heroic of the two, for Hester never did anything which cost a tithe of the bloody sweat, the agony, which Arthur's public confession cost.

Hester is a noble, frustrated, pathetic figure, but she is not a tragic figure, because her mind is made up. . . . [She] is not the protagonist, the chief actor, and the tragedy of *The Scarlet Letter* is not her tragedy but Arthur's.

He is the persecuted one, the tempted one. He it was whom the sorrows of death encompassed, the pains of hell gat hold upon. His public confession is one of the noblest climaxes of tragic literature. Poor, bedevilled Arthur Dimmesdale, the slave of passion and the servant of the Lord, brilliant of intellect, eloquent of voice, the darling of his congregation, the worst of hypocrites, and the prey of endless rationalizations and sophistries! No veteran of the cavalry of woe was ever more battle-scarred or desperate than Dimmesdale as he stood on the scaffold, and began, ''People of New England!'' ''with a voice that rose over them, high, solemn, majestic.''

The confession was decisive. Its function in the novel is to resolve the action. It turned the scales in the great debate, though Hester, romantic heretic to the last, remained unconvinced, impenitent, unredeemed. She had at best an imperfect understanding of Arthur's problem. As for Arthur, he saw the problem all too clearly. He must make a public confession: ''Confess your faults one to another . . . that ye may be healed.'' There could be no salvation without that. Arthur was saved, yet as by fire. He was truly a firebrand plucked out of the burning. (pp. 85-8)

Thus in his profoundest character-creation, and in the resolution of his greatest book, Hawthorne has employed the Christian thesis: ''Father, not my will, but thine be done.'' And in the scene so constructed, we see the best illustration of what Melville called, perceptively, ''the ever-moving dawn that forever advances through Hawthorne's darkness, and circumnavigates his world.'' (pp. 88-9)

*Randall Stewart, ''Guilt and Innocence,'' in his* American Literature & Christian Doctrine, *Louisiana State University Press, 1958, pp. 73-106.**

**MARIUS BEWLEY** (essay date 1959)

*[Bewley suggests that in* The Scarlet Letter *Hawthorne sides neither with the Puritans nor with Hester. Instead, he is mainly*

*interested in examining the results of the act that alienates Hester, Dimmesdale, and Pearl from the rest of society. Other critics who study the interaction between the individual and society in* The Scarlet Letter *include R.W.B. Lewis (1955), A. N. Kaul (1962), Nina Baym (1976), and Michael Davitt Bell (1980).*]

[In *The Scarlet Letter* we] begin with an act that is destructive of that inner sphere of reality in which the human being finds his fulfilment through reciprocal sympathy, understanding, and love. The act, here presented superficially as a sexual transgression, is conventionally called a 'sin', but as the novel develops the reader is (or ought to be) left in some perplexity as to the exact nature of that 'sin' and who the real malefactors are. Even if the principal 'sinners' prove to be Hester and Dimmesdale, they are very different kinds of sinners, facing different moral problems. There is no question of vagueness here, but a miraculous control that can scarcely be surpassed. Hawthorne has recreated in his art the complex conditions of life itself; he has given us, in its shifting uncertainties, the bleak perspective of doubt in which the heart is compelled to search out its truth. We are concerned with adultery here only in a transient way. . . . [The act of which Hester and Dimmesdale are guilty] escapes easy definition, but we can begin by saying that its essence lies in the centrifugal nature of its effect. (pp. 161-62)

The act of which Hester and Dimmesdale are guilty is not only destructive, as we shall see, of interior fulfilment in private human relations, it is also destructive of social relationships in the largest sense of the word. But it is worth noting that . . . Hawthorne maintains our sense of ambivalence very subtly. If the scarlet letter creates a sphere of emptiness in the midst of which Hester stands, it has by this time become a 'mystic symbol' in relation to which the sin of society defines itself. If, in the beginning, the scarlet letter symbolized an act by which Hester violated her realtionship with her husband and society, the focus has now shifted and it is seen as a symbol of exclusion from reality of those whose intrusive curiosity violates the magnetic chain of humanity. The scarlet letter represents here a magic ring that can only be penetrated by selfless love. . . . (p. 162)

I do not wish, however, to exchange one simplification for another. Hawthorne does not end by pointing an accusatory finger at the intolerance of Puritan society while exonerating Hester and Dimmesdale. While condemning its intolerance, Hawthorne shows that it is also part of a larger human world against which the two protagonists have transgressed. The symbol lives in its various meaning at one and the same time. If Hawthorne gives us a society in which children play at whipping Quakers in the street, to leave it at this would be to elicit our sympathy and forgiveness for Hester and Dimmesdale far too easily. It would be to invite a disastrously facile moral judgement along 'liberal' lines, and to reduce the living complexity of art to the comparative vulgarity of a pat resolution. And so, while showing us the eccentric and fanatical side of the Puritan community, Hawthorne also gives it to us as a substantial microcosm of the great world. This sense of the microcosm is partly kept in the reader's mind by images suggesting the relationship between England and America. We are shown men whose dress and manners, and the order of whose minds, introduce echoes of another society beyond the seas. (pp. 162-63)

The essence of Dimmesdale's sin is concealment; Hester's is more complicated, but it is essentially a withdrawal from society on her part; for if Hester is banished, Hawthorne insists that she similarly banishes mankind from her own heart. The result is a living death. But in Chapters XVII and XVIII a rather extraordinary and un-Hawthornian thing happens. Meeting in the forest after their seven years of penitential misery, Hester persuades Dimmesdale to flee back to Europe with her: in other words, to re-establish their illicit union as a permanent thing. (p. 170)

Perhaps it would be too much to maintain that the husband of Sophia Peabody was arguing a case for adultery here, and he tries to cover any tracks he may have made in that direction by a discreet reference to 'higher truth'. But the passage clearly establishes that it is *not* adultery as such that constitutes the crime of *The Scarlet Letter*. The possible renewal of the adulterous union is seen here as a resurrection into life, and as a means of once again possessing, or entering into, the inner sphere of reality.

Hawthorne was always ruthless in the way he punished those characters who broke the magnetic chain of humanity. . . . One would not expect Hawthorne to let Hester off easily, then, if the essence of her sin was indeed that she had broken the magnetic chain. It is part of Hawthorne's artistic triumph in this novel, as contrasted with some of the others, that he is able to suggest (or make the reader believe that he does) the possibility of a final redemption for Hester. But the closing lines, which describe her grave, are far from the light-filled forest scene. . . . Hawthorne in the end emphatically rejects the possibility of escape which seemed to be offered there, and even in death Hester does not free herself from the awful symbol which shows more gloomily on her tombstone than it ever had on her breast. In the shadow of such a final paragraph all talk of redemption seems a little superfluous.

In view of the inexorable fate that overtakes the men and women who err in Hawthorne's stories and novels, his inability completely to forgive them, or to mark a termination to their punishment—in view of these things, it is tempting to say that Hawthorne's conception of human nature continued to be corrupted by Calvinism, even though, intellectually, it was unacceptable to him. The native defect of heart, or the inherited malaise of the will, which are so recurrent throughout Hawthorne . . . comes at last to impress one as some taint of the soul with which man is born, and for which, though hardly responsible, he must be endlessly punished. (pp. 171-72)

The most 'hopeful' part of *The Scarlet Letter* centres in Hester's little daughter, Pearl, and her role should be borne in mind as a necessary qualification of the pessimism I have emphasized in the conclusion. Pearl represents the wild, heathen nature of Hester's and Dimmesdale's love, which is symbolized by her intimate communion with the wild creatures of the forest. And simultaneously the little girl's hostility to society symbolizes the unconventional nature of their union—for Hawthorne explicitly presents Pearl as a symbol of their love in its full play of complex contradictions. The emotional transformation of little Pearl as she kneels by her dying father on the scaffold may be read to symbolize a kind of spiritual resurrection for both her parents. . . .

But all we can really be sure of is that the scattered parts of the magnetic chain are to be brought together once again in Pearl's life. For Hester and Dimmesdale the dark ambiguity remains, and almost the last words of Dimmesdale are, 'I fear! I fear!'

*The Scarlet Letter* has essentially the same meaning as nearly everything Hawthorne wrote—the same meaning, that is, if we resort to analytic paraphrase, for in *The Scarlet Letter* that

*Illustration of Hester Prynne and Pearl.*

recurrent meaning is incarnated in a symbolism that represents the highest triumph of his art. Hawthorne's inner sphere of reality is really little more than the quiet and pure communion of a human mind and heart with others in love and charity. Using the symbol of a magnetic chain of humanity which, in some ways, corresponds to the Christian idea of a mystical union among the faithful—using this symbol of spiritual fellowship, Hawthorne is always concerned to show the multiple and subtle ways in which the chain can be broken, and the effects this violation has on the human spirit. It is rather as if a Christian novelist were to set out to write a body of fictions dealing with the effects on the human heart of a fall from grace, of the subtle and hidden effects of sin on the soul. But with Hawthorne, the whole drama of which he writes, and which he analyses, is not conceived primarily in terms of sin, at least in the theological sense. His concern with the sanctity and purity of human relationships is ultimately as secular in nature as Henry James's. His interest is focused on an analysis of the barriers which arise between human spirits in a conventional society when its code has been transgressed, and of the subtle poisons that are generated because of those barriers. *The Scarlet Letter* is a study of isolation on the spatial plane. From Hester's and Dimmesdale's original transgression we see widening circles of isolation radiating outwards until Hester is left stranded in the midst of a terrible solitude which, to Hawthorne's thinking, is the negation of reality. Hester is simply cut off from

life. And yet, in the subtly woven novel, her guilt is shown to be balanced by that of the surrounding social medium, the intolerant element. The conflict between Hester and the community is the most poised statement Hawthorne ever made of the tension between solitude and society, and at no point does he simplify by allowing the guilt of the one to cancel out the guilt of the other. (pp. 173-74)

*Marius Bewley, "Hawthorne's Novels," in his* The Eccentric Design: Form in the Classic American Novel, *Columbia University Press, 1959, pp. 147-86.*

### DANIEL HOFFMAN   (essay date 1961)

*[Like F. O. Matthiessen (1941), Richard Chase (1957), and Roy R. Male (1957), Hoffman investigates Hawthorne's use of imagery and symbolism in* The Scarlet Letter. *He stresses the recurrence of pagan and witchcraft imagery and studies the role that elements of the oral tradition play in fostering alternative meanings in the novel.]*

In *The Scarlet Letter* the folklore of the supernatural is peculiarly appropriate to the development of Hawthorne's conflicts. The romance itself may be said to be based upon yet another myth, if we may consider as myth the Puritan doctrine which it is the fate of Hester, Dimmesdale, and Chillingworth to test. In his re-creation of Puritan society in this book, Hawthorne . . . takes pains to include superstition and witchcraft among the articles of popular belief. In fact the moral universe of *The Scarlet Letter* contains both the diabolical otherworld of **'Young Goodman Brown'** and the pagan paradise of Merry Mount [from **'The Maypole of Merry Mount'**]. These supernatural realms are metaphorically and inferentially significant, but the locale of the action, unlike that in these shorter tales, is literally the life of this world. Merry Mount was an Eden before the Fall, the Witches' Sabbath seemed a dream, but Governor Bellingham's Boston, with jail and scaffold at its very center, represents the actual world. It is just such a world through which the lovers expelled from Merry Mount would have to follow a 'difficult path,' though heaven be their destination.

The May-day paradise of Hester Prynne and Arthur Dimmesdale has been blasted and they expelled before the story of *The Scarlet Letter* begins. When we revisit the scene of what the Puritans called their sin but what the author terms their 'crime,' we are again in the forest. This was the site of both the Maypole and the witches' revels. The imagery of paganism and of witchcraft picks up these supernatural associations in *The Scarlet Letter.* Among a people to whom 'religion and law were almost identical,' superstition proves surprisingly nearer than dogma to spiritual truth.

While these uses of pagan and witchcraft belief are allusive and imagistic, there is yet a further role played by superstition in *The Scarlet Letter.* For his most characteristic device of style—which is to say, his way of looking at experience— Hawthorne took advantage of the folk tradition of the wonder. He makes the letter itself a supernatural providence; yet instead of evoking allegorical certitude it produces ambiguity on every side. Its significance is established by the conflicting testimony of several eye-witnesses. Popular tradition believes them all. Hawthorne's reliance upon the alternative interpretations which oral tradition gives to supernatural wonders proves to be a structural principle essential to his conception of *The Scarlet Letter.*

In Hawthorne's romance the scarlet letter itself serves as the controlling symbol of our thought, continually raising and defining problems which its inflicters did not acknowledge to exist. Those Puritan judges, sincerely pious but tragically restricted in their understanding of the soul, are unwittingly guilty of a sin more grievous than Hester's own. For they have taken it into their prideful hearts to pass absolute judgment upon a fellow-being, and to construct, for the supposed benefit of their own holy community, a man-made remarkable providence in imitation of God's wonders. Recalling Increase Mather's definition of the genre, we recognize Hester's 'A' as among the 'Remarkable Judgements upon noted Sinners' which comprised one of the varieties of his *Illustrious Providences.*

But if the Puritans in Hawthorne's romance are unaware of their own pride in presuming to judge Hester as God judges her, we are enabled to see their inadequacies as the letter works its influence in ways they had not dreamed. Not only that, but God Himself has passed a 'Remarkable Judgement' upon Hester. This judgment His zealous communicants are too blind to recognize, although it is just as plainly visible as the ignominy with which they brand her. For the actual 'Remarkable Providence' which God has brought about as a living emblem of Hester's sin is revealed in the same opening scene in which we first see the scarlet letter. Hester appears on the scaffold bearing her child in her arms: it is soon manifest that in the allegorical scheme of this romance, Pearl = 'A.'

It is through its similitude with Pearl that the scarlet letter can become endowed with life. Indeed, it seems to have a life of its own, as we shall see, in which the letter changes its relationship to the other characters as well as its meanings in itself.

But such a fluidity of meaning is of course intolerable in allegory. Hawthorne's artistic method is to use allegory to destroy the absolute certitude of the allegorical mind: by offering several certainties which any given phenomenon, wonder, or providence may be believed to represent, and by attributing to each of these alternatives a tenable claim to absolute belief, Hawthorne undermines the dogmatic monism of allegory itself. His reliance upon the folklore of providences as well as the theological absolutes of Puritanism made available to him the resources of this 'formula of alternative possibilities,' as Yvor Winters has termed it [see *NCLC,* Vol. 2]. Its first occurrence in *The Scarlet Letter* concerns the interpretation of a wild rose which has sprouted at the threshold of the first structure erected by the Puritans in the new colony—a prison:

> This rose-bush, by a strange chance, has been kept alive in history; but whether it had merely survived out of a stern old wilderness, so long after the fall of the gigantic pines and oaks that originally overshadowed it,—or whether, as there is fair authority for believing, it had sprung up under the footsteps of the sainted Ann Hutchinson, as she entered the prison-door,— we shall not take upon us to determine.

We note that the choice is unresolved between a botanical happenstance and a Divine providence—ironically, from the Puritan view, linking Hester to the heretical Mrs. Hutchinson and connecting both with a saint's legend.

This style seems indubitably Hawthorne's own. Its salient feature is the skeptical offering of the multiple meanings, each borne aloft by the clause of a rather formal periodic sentence. The tone of this style is curiously both detached and committed, both amused and serious, both dubious and affirmative. Its commitment, seriousness, and affirmation, however, all point to something other than the literal content of its assertions;

toward *that* the style indicates detachment, amused tolerance, dubiety. What is seriously affirmed is that *something* was signified by the rosebush. But the very presence, uncontradicted, of both alternatives quite compromises our willingness to believe unreservedly in either. Yet again, the fact that both are possible deters us from dismissing either one. Hawthorne uses his device of multiple choices to affirm neither the absolute claims of Puritan dogma nor the absolute claims of right reason. What it does affirm is, as one would expect of Hawthorne, a multiple truth larger than either of the partial truths offered by its alternatives: the world of fact *is* an hieroglyph of the spirit, and the language of the spirit is beyond the capacity of either unassisted belief or unassisted reason to read aright. Perhaps its reading requires the collaboration of both the intellect and the passions. (pp. 170-74)

It is apparent that the Puritans badly bungled the case of Hester Prynne. The scarlet letter they condemned her to wear was a self-evident judgment: A for Adultery. 'Giving up her individuality, she would become the general symbol at which the preacher and moralist might point, and in which they might vivify and embody their images of woman's frailty and sinful passion.' Hester would cease to be a woman, and be henceforth a living emblem in a morality play: guilt without redemption, suffering without end.

Yet in her first appearance the child at her breast made her, 'A' and all, resemble 'the image of Divine Maternity.' By midpoint in the tale we can be told that 'The scarlet letter had not done its office,' for her 'A' has taken on significations unintended by the judges. After some years of tending the sick as a 'self-ordained Sister of Mercy,' it was said that 'The letter was the symbol of her calling. . . . They said it meant Able, so strong was Hester Prynne, with a woman's strength.' Stranger still, it 'had the effect of the cross on a nun's bosom,' endowing Hester with 'a kind of sacredness.' Yet she herself tells Pearl that the 'A' is 'The Black Man's mark,' and when, in her forest rendezvous with Dimmesdale, she removed the scarlet letter, and shook loose her hair, she was at once transformed. 'Her sex, her youth, and the whole richness of her beauty, came back,' as sunshine flooded down in token of the sympathy of Nature—'that wild, heathen Nature of the forest, never subjugated by human law, or illumined by higher truth.'

But now Pearl does not recognize her mother. (pp. 177-78)

At one point Pearl amuses herself by mimicking her mother. She has been gazing into a pool in the woods, 'seeking a passage for herself into its [reflected] sphere of impalpable earth and unattainable sky.' Her attempt to merge herself into the elements is unavailing, and she turns to other tricks. She makes herself a mantle of seaweed, and, 'As the last touch to her mermaid's garb, Pearl took some eel-grass, and imitated, as best she could, on her own bosom . . . the letter A,—but freshly green instead of scarlet!' When Hester beholds her handiwork she says, 'My little Pearl, the green letter, on thy childish bosom, has no purport. But dost thou know, my child, what this letter means which thy mother is doomed to wear?' Pearl, with her preternatural intuition, answers 'Truly do I! It is for the same reason that the minister keeps his hand over his heart!' But Hester cannot bear to tell her what she seems already to know, and breaks off, saying, 'I wear it for the sake of its gold thread.'

This scene perhaps seems a digression which fails to advance our understanding of either Hester or Pearl. But in fact it comprises a metaphoric recapitulation and explanation of the nature of Hester's offense. Pearl's allegorical function brings into *The Scarlet Letter* the pagan values which Hawthorne had synthesized in **'The Maypole at Merry Mount.'** But in *The Scarlet Letter* the amoral freedom of the green natural world is viewed with yet greater reservations than was true of his story, written fifteen years earlier. We have already noticed that the forest is described, in Hester's rendezvous with Dimmesdale, as 'wild, heathen Nature.' The child will not let her mother cast the scarlet letter aside because Pearl herself is emblem of a passion which partook of that same heathen, natural wildness. 'What we did had a consecration of its own,' Hester assures Arthur, but that consecration was not a Christian or a moral sanctity. It was an acknowledgment of the life force itself. Consequently Pearl is endowed with the morally undirected energies of life. 'The spell of life went forth from her ever creative spirit, and communicated itself to a thousand objects, as a torch kindles a flame wherever it might be applied.' This spell is the power of fecundity, and its derivative power, that of imagination. 'The unlikeliest materials—a stick, a bunch of rags, a flower— were the puppets of Pearl's witchcraft. . . .'. These she brings to life, and she feels in herself kinship with life in every form. Although the forest is a place of dread and evil, the haunt of witches and of heathen Indian sorcerers, Pearl is at home among its creatures. It 'became the playmate of the lonely infant' and 'put on the kindest of moods to welcome her.' Squirrels fling their treasured nuts to Pearl, while even wolves and foxes take caresses from her hand. 'The mother-forest, and those wild things which it nourished, all recognized a kindred wildness in the human child.'

It was in this mother-forest that Hester had had her tryst with Dimmesdale, beyond human law and divine truth. Hester herself sees that 'The child could not be made amenable to rules. In giving her existence, a great law had been broken; and the result was a being whose elements were perhaps beautiful and brilliant, but all in disorder.'

What is lacking in Pearl of course is the imposition of that transcendent ordering principle which man, through grace, imposes upon Nature. Lacking this, she seems to the Puritans a 'demon offspring.' Mr. Wilson, the most humane among them, asks her, 'Art thou a Christian child, ha? Dost thou know thy catechism? Or art thou one of those naughty elfs or fairies, whom we thought to have left behind us, with other relics of Papistry, in merry old England?' Pearl is indeed an elf, a pre-Christian Nature-spirit in human form, whose soul must be made whole by submission to divinely ordered morality before it can be saved. Mistress Hibbins, the witch, is eager to attach Pearl to her legion, and tells her that her father is the Prince of the Air, just as she tells Dimmesdale to let her know when he goes again into the forest, for 'My good word will go far towards gaining any strange gentleman a fair reception from yonder potentate you wot of.' When Dimmesdale protests that he was only on his way to greet the Apostle Eliot.

> 'Ha, ha, ha!' cackled the old witch-lady. . . .
> 'Well, well, we must needs talk thus in the
> daytime! You carry it off like an old hand! But
> at midnight, and in the forest, we shall have
> other talk together!'
>
> (pp. 179-81)

The salvation of Pearl depends upon Dimmesdale. Until he acknowledges himself her father she can have no human patrimony, and must remain a Nature-spirit, untouched by the redemptive order that was broken in her conception. For Hawthorne, Nature is amoral but not malign. Witchcraft is not the

forest's nature; it comes into being when man repudiates God and chooses Satan. The forest, having no moral will, can shelter either the spirit of the Maypole or the self-damned coven of the Prince of Air. Hence Pearl, like the Maypole mummers, is not yet damned, because unfallen; but, like them, she is not yet wholly human either. Dimmesdale's confession wrenches her first kiss for him from Pearl, and her first tears. 'As her tears fell upon her father's cheek, they were the pledge that she would grow up amid human joy and sorrow, nor forever do battle with the world, but be a woman in it. Towards her mother, too, Pearl's errand as a messenger of anguish was all fulfilled.' (p. 183)

*Daniel Hoffman, "Hester's Double Providence: The Scarlet Letter and the Green," in his* Form and Fable in American Fiction, *1961. Reprint by Oxford University Press, 1970, pp. 99-220.*

## ERNEST SANDEEN   (essay date 1962)

*[Sandeen discusses* The Scarlet Letter *as a love story, pointing out that most critical appraisals ignore that dimension of the novel. Positing that Hawthorne acknowledged the fact that their adulterous love necessarily excludes Hester and Dimmesdale from Puritan society, Sandeen concludes that Hawthorne nevertheless encourages a sympathetic interpretation of them. For a contrasting view of the theme of love in* The Scarlet Letter, *see the excerpt by Leslie A. Fiedler (1966).]*

*The Scarlet Letter* has been interpreted as a story of sins and sinners for so long that this perspective has hardened into a convention. In Hester, Dimmesdale, and Pearl the sin of adultery and its consequences are seen; to Dimmesdale is added the further, less sympathetic sin of hypocrisy; and beyond the pale stands Chillingworth in his isolating sin of pride and self-consuming revenge. Once this standard point of view is assumed, it can be supported by what is incontrovertibly in the text, but if the angle of attention is shifted so that the novel is seen as a love story, that is, as a tragedy of the grand passion rather than as a tale of sinful passion, then certain features in our picture of the novel, obscure before, will leap into prominence and some of the previously more emphatic features will change their value in relation to the whole composition. Hawthorne's masterpiece may remain for us a haunted book, but it will be haunted by a mystery which we can identify as the mystery of erotic passion itself. It will be seen, in this perspective, that passion is the fixed reality throughout the novel and that it is "sin" which is the shifting, ambiguous term, as it is refracted in the many-sided ironies of the plot and of the narrative commentary. Further, from this point of view it becomes clear that the passion of the lovers is entering its most interesting phase when the story opens instead of being over and done with, except for its consequences, as is tacitly assumed in the conventional approach.

The more extreme and sentimental postures of "courtly love" do not appear in *The Scarlet Letter* since the setting, after all, is seventeenth-century Boston. Yet the initial situation involving a husband, his wife, and her lover is obviously "classic." Whenever marriage and passion come into conflict in the typical love story of our Western tradition—and they usually do— the claims of passion far outshine those of its humbler rival. Hester's marriage, in conformity with the tradition, is poor and mean compared to her love affair. In the prison interview Hester reminds her husband that from the first she had "felt no love, nor feigned any." Chillingworth, on his part, admits that he had married Hester simply because he had wished to kindle "a household fire" for his later years.

Far different from this passionless domestic arrangement is the love which unites Hester and Arthur. Although it is disastrous in that it wrecks all possibilities for happiness in their lives, it matures them morally and spiritually; under its influence they grow to a tragic height of character which they otherwise would probably not have reached. Yet the passion which works for their moral development is erotic and adulterous—a paradox which characterizes and might even be said to define the Western "heresy" of love.

Finally, however, it must be emphasized that Hawthorne in *The Scarlet Letter* was writing his own version of the traditional story of passion. In fact the patent features of the archetype which appear in the novel make his departure from the tradition appear all the more radical and dramatic. (p. 425)

The formal symmetry of *The Scarlet Letter* has often been commented upon, that is, the structural function of the three scaffold scenes placed precisely at the beginning, the middle, and the end of the story. The same rigorous symmetry can be seen also at a deeper level in the nice balance between the contending forces in the moral psychology of Arthur Dimmesdale, which is to say, the forces that define the basic dramatic conflict in the novel. Arthur's career up to the composition of his final sermon has demonstrated that he is deeply, genuinely committed both as a lover and as a minister and that therefore he cannot be true either to the passion he shares with Hester or to the society which condemns that passion unless he can somehow be true to both. Being what he is, he cannot fulfill his obligations to the one simply by abandoning his obligations to the other and still remain himself.

During the seven years between Hester's public humiliation and his meeting with her in the forest Arthur tries valiantly to give himself up entirely to his conscience as his loyalty to the theocracy would demand. But it proves impossible to be rid of his passion merely by running away from it and trying to ignore it. It is ever with him, frustrating his every attempt to arrive at the state of penitence his conscience requires. Then, in his private meeting with Hester, he resolves to try the opposite alternative; he will become wholly the lover and flee from all his obligations to the community. We can only speculate as to the consequences, had he and Hester been allowed to proceed with their plan to escape, but, in view of his character, it is unlikely that Arthur would have been any more successful in trying to run away from his conscience than he had been before in trying to run away from his passion.

Hester's dismay at Arthur's apparent withdrawal from their secret world when she sees him in the Election Day procession is well founded. She has believed that under her influence he has been converted to her own credo of love and thereby freed of his obligations as a man of God. But what she has done instead is to help him to reconcile the warring motivations in his soul. Through her the minister has been enabled to recognize and accept as the lover the self he had regarded before only as the sinner. Far from being destroyed in the process, the minister has found access to fresh inspiration and unsuspected energies which he has made use of in writing his sermon. Arthur has indeed become a new man but this new man is a synthesis of two selves, not a conversion from one self into the other. The new Arthur Dimmesdale has not at all shut Hester out of his world as she fears he has, but he has assumed a position of leadership in their relations. A dying man though

he is, Arthur dominates the confession scene as Hester dominated the forest scene.

Arthur's near attainment of inner wholeness not only makes possible a public "confession," but makes it imperative. Conscience and passion both demand a hearing. If Arthur in the final scaffold scene confesses his adulterous passion as a sin, he also bears witness to it as a power. A sinner, he feels shame before his fellowman and fear before his God. But he also conveys a feeling which could be called spiritual pride if it were expressed by the sinner and not by the lover. (pp. 432-33)

Arthur's physical dependence upon Hester dramatizes the fact that he is able to confess his sin only by making use of the strength given him by love. . . .

All the while that Dimmesdale has been clinging to Hester for support, he has also been clinging to the hand of his child Pearl. The whole tableau, as a result, has the appearance of a family group in which Arthur looks, finally, more like a husband and father than like a lover. In addition to a confession of sin and a testimony to love, this complex climactic scene may be said to include a marriage. Dimmesdale, by admitting his sin before God and before men, has not repudiated his passion, but has redeemed it, an effect which is registered in the change which comes over Pearl. . . .

As Pearl is brought into the human family by Arthur's act of public confession, so Roger Chillingworth is morally excluded. (p. 433)

If *The Scarlet Letter* preserved the tradition of true love in its classical purity, Hester Prynne and not Arthur Dimmesdale would emerge as the protagonist. Hester is, instead, more accurately described as one of the two principal antagonists in the drama, the Puritan community being the other. Arthur is the central character because the issue between Hester and the town comes to a focus in him. Committed to both he is caught between them and suffers their conflict in his own person. His final resolution of the struggle is made the climax of the novel and, in addition, it reveals how Hawthorne has shifted the point of view from which the story of true love is usually told to a more impartial perspective.

The Boston Puritans may be justified, from this balanced point of view, in trying to protect themselves against the social chaos of ungoverned passion, but the cruel sentence they impose on Hester Prynne, making her an outcast while she continues to live among them, shows their unwillingness to accept the human being in his totality. It indicates a disposition to revise human nature, to wish a part of it away altogether. Their moral zeal by its very rigor turns into a kind of hypocrisy. The severity of the public judgment of Hester implies a compensation is being made for the insecurity which the town feels in its own righteousness. Hints are not lacking in the story that many others in the colony, including some of the most respectable and venerable citizens, are guilty of the same sin as Hester.

But the irony of this inadequate view is that the town cannot do without the profoundly primitive part of human nature which it tries to suppress. It is an irony which we have seen illustrated by Hester's career after her condemnation as she begins gradually to fill a needed role in the colony. Pariah though she is, she comes, in time, to be referred to by the townspeople as "our Hester." The irony is even more pronounced in their attitude toward the Reverend Mr. Dimmesdale, for his edifying sanctity and his moving eloquence, which cause the town to regard him as a pillar of the theocracy, have their source in the passion which the town would outlaw. Yet the sanctity and eloquence are real enough. If it is ironical that the parishioners are deceived in their minister it is not only because *he* is hypocritical but also because *they* are.

The Puritans in their overrighteousness try to be superhuman and succeed only in becoming inhuman. From the detached narrative point of view, Hester, as the antagonist of the community, suffers from the opposite deficiency. The analogies with uncivilized nature which express how Hester feels and thinks imply that her "heresy" belongs to the pre-human. Hester's conviction that her love is self-sufficient, having a dedication of its own, independent of society and religion, stops short of the fully human condition. What the town through the arbitrary legal abstractions would dehumanize, Hester is content to leave incompletely humanized.

The conflict between Hester and the Puritan community is enacted on a smaller but more intense scale in the battle which Arthur Dimmesdale wages with himself, and here again the same psychological truth is stressed. Arthur becomes wholly himself only when the two selves warring within him are reconciled and fused. His self-illumination in the confession scene is a vision which transcends not only the townspeople's view of the passion that unites him with Hester but Hester's view as well.

In short, Hawthorne recognizes that the perennial heresy of love, through exclusion and overemphasis, makes a valid point which a society like that of colonial Boston might well ponder. Yet Hawthorne would agree with Chaucer's Franklin; he would have passion assimilated into the socially defined relations of marriage and family. Let lovers be husbands and wives, husbands and wives be lovers. In this connection the presence of Pearl in the story is of interest. This child of their passion is obstreperously conspicuous throughout the novel as a constant reminder to the lovers—and to the reader—of the social responsibilities involved in such a union as theirs. In contrast, though adulterous relations are more common than not in typical stories of the grand passion, it is remarkable that children seldom issue from them to distract the lovers in their pursuit of the pure Eros.

However, the formally structured moral perspective which Hawthorne maintains is not the whole of *The Scarlet Letter*. In its total effect the novel seems to be written from a point of view which is, to be sure, firmly impartial but at the same time compassionate and even tender. The richly evocative texture in which the drama and its personae are immersed gives an emotional distortion to the hard moral center. At the end, the reader's sympathies are not nearly as symmetrically balanced as the diagrammatic ordering of the moral conflict would seem to insure.

Hawthorne plays upon the sentiments of his reader in various and sometimes seemingly contradictory ways. For instance, in discussions of the lovers' thoughts and behavior, the narrative voice often takes on a tone of severity which makes it sound like the Puritan voice of the town itself, yet the method of presenting the antagonists produces a countercurrent of sympathy for the lovers. Although the Puritan society is felt to be a formidable opponent, it remains an abstract, collective force. It is given no spokesman who might appeal directly to our judgment and to our feelings. Such citizens and magistrates as are specified at all are played down as "flat," minor characters who, on the whole, strike us as vaguely unpleasant people. The wronged husband might conceivably become an effective

advocate for the community, but Hawthorne has made Chillingworth downright repulsive, physically and morally. In emphatic contrast, Hester and Arthur are the two characters we are allowed to know with such intimacy that they inevitably engage our warmest, deepest feelings, no matter how often the narrator's sober voice may remind us that they are sinners and no matter how often we may assent.

But whatever his methods may be, Hawthorne has not left us emotionally neutral in the struggle between the lovers and the town; in his own habitually somber way, he has honored the adage that all the world loves a lover. He has directed the bias of our sympathy toward Hester and Arthur—especially toward Hester, for if Arthur is the fulcrum of the dramatic conflict, Hester is the empathic center. Of course, our sympathy takes in Arthur too, for Hester's sake if not entirely for his own, and we like him most when he is most the lover. (pp. 434-35)

> Ernest Sandeen, "'The Scarlet Letter' As a Love Story," in PMLA, 77, Vol. LXXVII, No. 4, September, 1962, pp. 425-35.

### A. N. KAUL (essay date 1962)

[*In this excerpt, drawn from a doctoral dissertation presented in 1962, Kaul focuses on the broken family and Hester's relationship to society as the principal themes of* The Scarlet Letter. *The greatest sin committed against Hester, according to Kaul, is her forced alienation from the community. For similar discussions of this topic, see the excerpts by R.W.B. Lewis (1955), Marius Bewley (1959), Nina Baym (1976), and Michael Davitt Bell (1980).*]

[In *The Scarlet Letter,* Hawthorne's] attitude toward his subject suggests a complex relation rather than an intractable and artistically sterile distance. On account of his personal temperament, his artistic sensibility, and his family history, he could approach the seventeenth century as an insider, retaining at the same time the outsider's ability and freedom to judge and evaluate. Like so many great works of literature . . . *The Scarlet Letter* is a searching criticism of the world with which it deals precisely because it takes its stand firmly within that world. (pp. 174-75)

"Had Hester sinned alone?" Hawthorne asks in chapter 5, and goes on to describe how, though she struggles against such mysterious power, Hester's experience has given her the ability to recognize fellow sinners instinctively, and how, in token of such recognition, the emblem of sin on her bosom throbs sympathetically in the presence of magistrate, minister, sanctified matron, and spotless maiden alike. Hawthorne's criticism, at times muted and at others rising into open denunciation and satire, is directed fundamentally against the denial of this innate sense of human communion. If sin is the postulated basis of life, should its open manifestation be treated with understanding and compassion or with inhuman chastisement? The answer of the Puritan community to this question—posed concretely in their midst by Hester—is to put her upon the pillory, to make her bear permanently the stigma of her shame, and finally to excommunicate her. The most terrible part, the truly inhuman aspect, of Hester's fate is not that she is punished publicly but that her punishment takes the form of isolating her from the rest of the community. Even while she is standing in the center of the crowd in the marketplace, the letter A has "the effect of a spell, taking her out of the ordinary relations with humanity, and enclosing her in a sphere by herself."

*The Scarlet Letter* presents thus a highly complex variation on Hawthorne's general theme of human isolation and human community. In the drama of society and solitude which is enacted here, there is no doubt about the side on which the novel aligns our sympathies. Hester Prynne's isolation is inflicted upon her rather than willfully sought by her; and if it does not warp her moral personality, the reason is that she seeks throughout her life to re-establish a relationship with other human beings on a new and more honest basis—in other words, she is isolated by society but not alienated from humanity. The blame for her tragic predicaments falls heavily on the Puritan arbiters of her destiny. Even in terms of their own stern theory of sin, her excommunication . . . amounts to the banishment of a leper from a leper colony. But in reality the author's judgment of Hester is very different from that of the Puritan community. While not disputing the sinfulness of her deed, he presents her also as a source of new life and moral vitality and as a woman of the tenderest human sympathies in a cold and intolerant society. He provides her adultery with a background of long bondage in a loveless marriage, and invests the passion which leads to it with "a consecration of its own."

Hawthorne, in fact, uses the very symbol with which society identifies Hester, as a means of reversing its view of her. To the Puritans, with their allegorical habit of mind and their interpretation of life as though it were a Morality play, the meaning of the A is clear. But not so to a humane critic of the Puritan view of life. In an allegory the hidden meaning is easy to discover; indeed it is the allegory itself which superficially conceals it. The purpose of allegory is to strengthen, by an exercise of fancy, the received doctrine and the shared moral code. Symbols, on the contrary, put accepted meanings into doubt, introduce new ones, and finally create a radically different alignment of sympathies. Thus, while Hester becomes the sympathetic heroine of the novel, the society which persecutes her is revealed as not only bigoted and joyless but essentially evil; for to it belongs, equally with Chillingworth but without Chillingworth's personal justification, the unpardonable sin of violating in cold blood the sanctity of a human heart. (pp. 178-80)

[Hawthorne's image of New England, planted at the outset of the novel is that of] a society which claimed to have based itself on the highest principles of moral idealism but which turns out at the first test to be utterly lacking in the elementary Christian virtues of love and compassion. Its program of regeneration is in reality a mask for repression, and its intolerance and bigotry are worse than those of the European society from which it has, on that very account, separated itself. What its rulers seek assiduously is not the establishment of a republic of brotherly love but rather ruthless power over men. Their hypocrisy, the consequence of the wide divergence between their ideals and the practical aims of their enterprise, is insinuated everywhere, most strikingly in the contrast between the Puritan profession of austerity and the magnificence of the governor's residence which "might have befitted Aladdin's palace, rather than the mansion of a grave old Puritan ruler." Rich garments too are "readily allowed to individuals dignified by rank or wealth, even while sumptuary laws forbade these and similar extravagances to the plebeian order." This is indeed not the proclaimed city upon the hill—the refuge and sanctuary of oppressed generations and the future hope of mankind. On the contrary, the true hope of humanity lies in seeking refuge from rather than in it. "Begin all anew!" as Hester urges Dimmesdale in the forest. "Hast thou exhausted possibility in the failure of this one trial? Not so! The future is yet full of trial and success. There is happiness to be enjoyed! There is

good to be done! Exchange this false life of thine for a true one."

The challenge to break away from organized society is there in Hawthorne as much as in Cooper. It provides the backbone of the dramatic conflict in *The Scarlet Letter*. That this challenge is not successfully executed is due to what one can only call Hawthorne's greater historical and psychological realism—a realism which recognizes that the protagonists, Dimmesdale particularly, are themselves encumbered with the spirit of that same society against which they find themselves in rebellion. This is a tragic novel which ends in failure, waste, and death but which, like all true tragedies, affirms the very values that go down in defeat. The moral victory belongs to Hester. The future she talks about so passionately in the passage I have cited above is of course primarily her own domestic future. But nevertheless she comes to understand that such a future is intimately connected with the future of the whole society, and that true relationships cannot exist in the family unless they are also established in the civil community at large.

Hester's unavailing attempt to reconstruct her life forms the substance of the novel's action after her banishment from society. Although she is free to leave the colony altogether, she does not do so, but instead takes her stand at the farthest edge of the settlement. The reason for this, as given in chapter 5, is twofold. In the first place, while society has cast her off, she herself has not lost hold of the magnetic chain of humanity: "The chain that bound her here was of iron links, and galling to her inmost soul, but could never be broken." The deeper reason—the reason which, with her own consciousness of sin, she trembles to acknowledge even to herself—lies in the more intimate bond of love. "There dwelt, there trode the feet of one with whom she deemed herself connected in a union, that, unrecognized on earth, would bring them together before the bar of final judgment." Her relationship with the civil community is perforce of a marginal character. Being an outcast, and with her own judgment of society's institutions, she neither seeks nor is allowed a full place in it. Whether as a skillful embroiderer or a sister of mercy at scenes of grief and misfortune, her attitude is one of unobtrusive and undemanding sympathy. She is charitable to all alike, though, as Hawthorne says, the recipients of her kindness often bit the hand from which they received it.

By far the more interesting part of the novel, however, deals with the story within the story: the drama of broken family relationships within the larger drama of the protagonist's relation to society. The remarkable thing about the structure of *The Scarlet Letter* is the controlled integration of these two aspects of the theme, and the manner in which it connects the dominant principles of one sphere with the failure of human relationship in the other. The broken circuit of the family community thus reflects the absence of the magnetic chain of love and compassion in the civil community. (pp. 181-83)

*The Scarlet Letter* is a profound comment on the breakdown of human relationships in the society of the seventeenth century—a society which perhaps carried the seed of the dislocations more readily observable in our own. The force of individualism, which exerted itself on many spheres of experience, was at once its special glory and the cause of alientating man from man in it. Moreover, whether or not it was the age of dissociated sensibility, as presented in *The Scarlet Letter*, it reveals the beginnings of a disintegration in the individual psyche: a tendency for the life of the body, the mind, and the

*The Custom House in Salem, Massachusetts.*

soul to fall apart, somewhat like the broken and isolated lives of Hester, Chillingworth, and Dimmesdale. (pp. 188-89)

It is a measure of Hawthorne's historical and psychological insight that he recognized that the effort to achieve a well-integrated community life in such a world must lead to tragedy. The social principles of the Puritans, laudable in their idealism, become in reality a travesty of Christian aspirations. Hester's attempt to achieve a more wholesome family community ends in failure. What is left at the conclusion of the novel is a vague hope that, with her father's public acknowledgment of her, the curse is lifted from Pearl's alienated existence, and that in some distant land she "would grow up amid human joy and sorrow, nor forever do battle with the world, but be a woman in it." She will realize, in other words, the future that Hester had dreamed of in her interview with Dimmesdale. As for the tragic heroine herself, she gains the understanding that love cannot come to fruition in a world divided against itself, that the fortunes of the family community are intimately bound up with the character of the civil community in which it exists, and that, for the full realization of human happiness: "As a first step, the whole system of society is to be torn down, and built up anew." (p. 189)

> *A. N. Kaul, "Nathaniel Hawthorne: Heir and Critic of the Puritan Tradition," in his* The American Vision: Actual and Ideal Society in Nineteenth-Century Fiction, *Yale University Press, 1963, pp. 139-213.*

## LESLIE A. FIEDLER (essay date 1966)

[*An American critic, novelist, short story writer, essayist, poet, and editor, Fiedler is a commentator on American literature who has generated a great deal of controversy. Using primarily Marxist and Freudian perspectives, he attempts to uncover the origins of modern literature and show how myth is used in literature today. His critical works, which are often biographical and psychosexual in orientation, have been criticized for their sweeping generalizations. Though some have termed him "the wild man of American literary criticism," Fiedler is praised for his* Love and Death in the American Novel, *an insightful, provocative, highly individual landmark in literary criticism. In this excerpt from that work, Fiedler analyzes such elements as sexuality, incest, adultery, and the Fall in* The Scarlet Letter *and posits that the novel is Hawthorne's "treatise on the death of love." For a contrasting view of* The Scarlet Letter *as a love story, see the excerpt by Ernest Sandeen (1962).*]

Though sex is centrally present in **The Scarlet Letter** as it is not in our other great novels, it is there rendered reticently, incomprehensibly enough to seem, though not innocent, perhaps, as good as innocent. (p. 228)

The carnal act upon which adultery depends is not merely unnamed in **The Scarlet Letter;** it is further deprived of reality by being displaced in time, postulated rather than described. So displaced, that act becomes in the psychologist's sense, prehistoric; affects us much as the spied-upon primal scene (mother and father intertwined in bed), blurred by the amnesia of guilt. It is an original sin, more an "emblem" or a "type," in Hawthorne's terms, than a deed. "Ye that wronged me are not sinful," Chillingworth says to his wife and her lover, "save in a kind of typical illusion." In one sense, the postulated original sin seems merely a convenient explanatory device. Certainly, it accounts naturalistically for the existence of Pearl, the illegitimate daughter of Hester. But Pearl seems less a real child than an allegorical representation of the fruits of sin; and we are offered, as if jestingly, the alternative explanation that she is a by-blow of the Devil. In addition, Hester must be from the very beginning a mother, though she appears among men who are, within the time of the story itself, rendered as impotent. The impotence of Dimmesdale, however, must be felt as a punishment, the typical self-castration of the seducer, celebrated in the American novel from the time of [Susanna Rowson's] *Charlotte Temple;* and we are, therefore, asked to believe that at some point before the action begins he traduced Hester's innocence, thus unmanning himself. Actually, he is portrayed as one for whom sex is a remembered nightmare or a futilely longed-for hope; and he does not even kiss Hester at his moment of Satanic exhilaration in the forest.

If it is finally hard for us to believe *on a literal level* in the original adultery of Hester and Dimmesdale, this is because their whole prehistory remains shadowy and vague. Hawthorne's gestures at indicating the social backgrounds and historical contexts of his characters are half-hearted and unconvincing, a bow toward realism. And his book is finally dreamlike rather than documentary, not at all the historical novel it has been often called—evoking the past as nightmare rather than fact. It is, therefore, easier to believe in the diabolical transportation of Chillingworth from Germany than in any more rational theory of his arrival on the scene; just as it is easier to imagine Pearl plucked from a rosebush than carried for nine months within her mother. All the characters come into existence when the book begins and do not survive. Hester is simply not there until the prison doors open; and at that moment Chillingworth drops from the air. So born they must die with the action's close—contrary to the traditions of the Victorian novel. For all his desire to end his book like his contemporaries, Hawthorne finds it difficult to say simply that Pearl left the country and married well. He is much more comfortable with the end of Chillingworth, who withered away, as is quite proper for a protagonist regarded by his author as a "shadowy figure," one of a "tribe of unrealities," who cease to exist when he stops thinking of them.

Actors in a dark hallucination, Hawthorne's protagonists are aptly moved by a guilt as hallucinatory as themselves: a crime as vaguely defined, though as inescapable in its consequences, as the unknowable transgression in Kafka's *The Trial*. It is enough for Hawthorne to suggest the Oedipus situation: an equivocal mother, an evil father—and between them, Dimmesdale, who is described at first as "child-like" and at last as "childish." The whole action moves toward the climactic moment, when, after years of cowardly silence and a momentary temptation to flee, that child-figure totters into the noonday public square to confess his fault before the whole community. At that point, Oedipus-Dimmesdale blends with the image of Doctor Johnson standing in the Uttoxeter market-place to make public amends for an offense against his father. It is a story which obsessed Hawthorne all his life, which he wrote out as an exemplary tale for children and told himself in his diary, a story obviously representing to him some buried guilt of his own.

That guilt the prehistoric fall of *The Scarlet Letter* explains, too, in encoded form. It is incarnate in Hester, most "gor-

geous" of his Dark Ladies; for "gorgeous" is to Hawthorne a dirty word—a token of pollution. But why is gorgeousness a trap and love a crime, why beauty forbidden and joy banned to the nineteenth-century American? There was, *The Scarlet Letter* suggests, another fall in the Eden of the New World at precisely the moment at which the book unfolds, a communal fall to match Hester's private one. The very first page tells us that "whatever Utopia of human virtue and happiness" men may imagine in whatever land, they find it necessary "to allot a portion of the virgin soil as a cemetery, and another portion as the site of a prison." Before such a prison, Hawthorne's tale begins, and in such a cemetery, it comes to a close; and between, he attempts to explain how sin and death, for whose sake they exist, have come into the Puritan Commonwealth. Yet it is, finally, his own crisis of conscience that Hawthorne translates into a mythical history of America, his own experience of womanhood that he projects in Hester.

Sitting day after day beside the bed of his dying mother, confronted by his wife of whom she did not approve, and watching through the window his daughter Una playing the death scene to which she must eventually come—Hawthorne must have become aware with special poignancy of the web of femaleness in which we are involved from cradle to grave. But what this glimpse into the maternal mysteries did to him we do not know, except for the fact that he wept once when his mother died, again when he had finished the "hell-fired" book which is her memorial; and that somewhere between these two public betrayals of emotion, he suffered from what his family called "brain-fever."

The incest theme, however, even in its disguise of adultery, belongs primarily to the pre-plot of *The Scarlet Letter;* its plot is concerned with a second, quite different fall: a second temptation, in the face of which his characters, postulated as having been powerless before the "dark necessity" of their original fall, are portrayed as capable of free choice. Yet their freedom is ironic, for what they must learn freely to accept is the notion that freedom is the recognition of necessity. *The Scarlet Letter* is the most utopian of American books: not the Paradise Regained it seems at first, but only an Eden Revisited.

In the seeming Eden of the New World, a man and woman, who are still essentially the old Adam and Eve, deceive themselves for a moment into believing that they can escape the consequences of sin. The woman has served a prison term and bears on her breast the sign of her shame, and the man, who was the occasion of that shame, has lived secretly with his guilt and powerless remorse; yet in their deluded hope, they meet in the forest, plot a flight from the world of law and religion. For an instant, that hope seems to transfigure not only them, but the dark wood into which they have strayed. When Hester flings aside the scarlet letter and lets down her hair, the forest glows to life: "Such was the sympathy of . . . wild, heathen Nature . . . never subjugated by law, nor illumined by higher truth with the bliss of these two spirits. Love . . . must always create a sunshine that overflows upon the natural world."

Yet Hawthorne cannot grant these lovers even the mitigated bliss he earlier permitted the May King and Queen in **"The Maypole of Merry Mount"**; for between them lies the taboo of adultery, as real to him as to his ancestors. Hawthorne does not accept without qualification the judgment of his ancestors, though he condemns Hester's proposal of flight even as they would have, uses to describe it the Faustian metaphor. He is, after all, a modern, secular thinker, for whom nothing is self-evident, everything problematical; and he is being tempted as he writes to make a retreat from his own community very like Hester's. Yet, for all his quarrel with Puritanism and its persecuting zeal, he knows that no American can really leave behind the America which the Puritans have once and for all defined.

America represents for Hawthorne not only the marginal settlement, set between corrupt civilization and unredeemed nature, but also the rule of moral law in the place of self-justifying passion or cynical gallantry. In *The Scarlet Letter,* passion justifies nothing, while its denial redeems all. The fallen Eden of this world remains fallen; but the sinful priest purges himself by public confession, becomes worthy of his sole remaining way to salvation, death. Even Hester, though sin and suffering have made her an almost magical figure, a polluted but still terrible goddess, must finally accept loneliness and self-restraint instead of the love and freedom she dreamed.... Passion has opened up for her no new possibilities, only closed off older ones.

The relationship of Hester and Dimmesdale is not, however, the only passionate connection in the novel. Through the five years covered by the book's action (the unwritten pre-plot takes up two more, from the marriage with Chillingworth to the birth of Pearl, thus adding up to the mystic seven), one relationship grows in intimacy, depth, and terror. In it, Dimmesdale plays a key role once more, though this time a passive, feminine one, his tremulous hand laid to his heart. Between him and Chillingworth, grows an intense, destructive emotion (a "dark passion," Hawthorne calls it), compounded of the intolerable intimacy of doctor and patient, analyst and analysand, husband and wife, father and son, cuckold and cuckolder. (pp. 230-34)

The terms used to define the nature of their union are significant: "a kind of intimacy," a "paternal and reverential love," described by Dimmesdale's parishioners as the "best possible measure ... unless he had selected some one of the many blooming damsels to become his devoted wife." Hester, who has been the wife of one and the mistress of the other, yet never as close to either as they are to each other, says reproachfully to Chillingworth: "no man is so near to him as you.... You are beside him, sleeping and waking.... You burrow and rankle in his heart. Your clutch is on his life." "Burrow" is the key word for Chillingworth's penetration of Dimmesdale's heart: "burrow into his intimacy ... deep into the patient's bosom ... delving ... probing ... in a dark cavern." The climax comes with the exposure of the secret of Dimmesdale's bosom, his own scarlet letter, embossed (perhaps!) in the very flesh. "He laid his hand on his bosom, and thrust aside the vestment," Hawthorne says at the moment of revelation, portraying Chillingworth in an ecstasy, leaping into the air. He knows at last the ultimate secret of his dearest enemy; and knowing it, has possessed him, accomplished a rape of the spirit beyond any penetration of the flesh. "He has violated," Hester comments, ... "the sanctity of the human heart."

Hawthorne is not content, however, to leave the last word with Hester, answering her in his own voice, his own typically hypothetical manner:

> It is a curious subject of observation and inquiry, whether hatred and love be not the same thing at bottom. Each, in its utmost development, supposes a high degree of intimacy and heart knowledge; each renders one individual dependent for the food ... of his spiritual life

upon another.... In the spiritual world, the old physician and the minister—may, unawares, have found their earthly stock of hatred and antipathy transmuted into golden love.

Out of the ambivalence of love and hatred, the constitutionally double-dealing Hawthorne has distilled an equivocation which undercuts, at the last moment, the whole suggested meaning of his book. He has not, to be sure, committed himself finally; but his last qualification for the passion of Chillingworth and Dimmesdale is favorable, while his last word on that of Hester and Dimmesdale is quite the opposite. Though earlier Hester has boasted, "What we did had a consecration of its own," the only proof of her assertion she could offer was, "We felt it so! We said so to each other!" Dimmesdale does not demur in the forest, where he is temporarily mad; but he answers Hester in the market-place, at his moment of greatest insight: "It may be that we forgot our God—when we violated our reverence for each other's soul...."

As one bucket goes up, the other goes down; and we are left with the disturbing paradox (mitigated, to be sure, by Hawthorne's customary, pussyfooting subjunctives: "may have found," "may be that we forgot") that love may conceal a destructive impulse and work for ill, while hatred may be only a disguised form of love and eventuate in good. If on the one hand, *The Scarlet Letter* leads toward a Goethe-like justification of diabolism as an instrument of salvation, on the other hand, it insists, in a very American way, upon the dangers of passion. It is certainly true, in terms of the plot, that Chillingworth drives the minister toward confession and penance, while Hester would have lured him to evasion and flight. But this means, for all of Hawthorne's equivocations, that the eternal feminine does not draw us on toward grace, rather that the woman promises only madness and damnation. It is the eternal demonic—personified in the wronged husband—which leads Dimmesdale on; and saved by his personal Serpent, he can in turn save his Eve—his apparent weakness deliver her apparent strength.

There is, however, a turn of the screw even beyond this; for though Hester works, perhaps unwittingly, to destroy Dimmesdale, saps his courage and brings him to the verge of selling his soul, it is to her that he must turn for support. Morally, he is finally stronger than she, but physically he depends upon her as a child upon its mother. It is on her arm that he ascends the scaffold, on her breast that he rests his trembling head. "Is she angel or devil?" Hawthorne's wife had asked him of Beatrice Rappaccini [from **"Rappaccini's Daughter"**], when he was in the process of creating that prototype of Hester; and his answer was that he did not know! With Hester herself, he is still equivocal; she is the female temptress of Puritan mythology, but also, though sullied, the secular madonna of sentimental Protestantism.... (pp. 234-36)

*The Scarlet Letter* is, then, our only classic book which makes passion a central theme. Born into an age and a class pledged to gentility, Hawthorne was denied a vocabulary adequate to his subject, driven back on duplicity and cunning; and in the end, he seems to adorn that subject rather than present it, conceal it with fancy needlework, "so that the Capital A might have been thought to mean ... anything other than Adulteress." Indeed, the phrase from **"Endicott and the Red Cross,"** written some thirteen years before *The Scarlet Letter,* suggests that from the first the cryptic "A" may have represented to Hawthorne not only "Adultery" but "Art." Certainly, he regarded his own art as involving precisely that adornment of guilt by craft which he attributes to Hester's prototype: "sporting with her infamy, the lost and desperate creature had embroidered the fatal token with golden thread and the nicest art of needlework. . . ."

Unable to break through the limitations of his era or to repress the shame he felt at trifling with them, Hawthorne ended by writing in the form of a love story an elegiac treatise on the death of love. *The Scarlet Letter* is, in one of its major aspects, a portrayal of the attenuation of sex in America, the shrinking on our shores from Brobdingnagian parents to Lilliputian children. In a note in his journal, Hawthorne reminds himself that Brobdingnag, where Gulliver once sat astride the nipples of gross, lusty girls, was located on the coast of North America, home of the mid-nineteenth-century fleshless bluestocking! *The Scarlet Letter* is concerned not only with passion but also with America (another possible signification of Hester's letter), that is to say, it attempts to find in the story of Hester and Dimmesdale a paradigm of the fall of love in the New World. The Puritans who move through Hawthorne's pages belong to a first-generation community, which, despite its revolt against the paternal figures of kings and bishops, has not itself lost "the quality of reverence" or contracted "the disease of sadness, which almost all children in these latter days inherit along with the scrofula. . . ." The inhabitants of Hawthorne's seventeenth-century world still live in the Elizabethan afterglow; "for they were the offspring of sires . . . who had known how to be merry. . . ." It is the generation which succeeds them that made gaiety a "forgotten art" by darkening American life with "the blackest shade of Puritanism."

Hawthorne recreates these first ancestors not merely as merry rebels, but as mythical progenitors. Twice over he describes them as they pass ceremonially, a "procession of majestic and venerable fathers," among them his own ultimate "dim and dusky grandsire . . . grave, bearded, sable-cloaked and steeple-crowned. . . ." And the mothers who inhabit Hawthorne's dream are scarcely less overwhelming. "The women . . . stood within less than half a century of the period when Elizabeth had been the not altogether unsuitable representative of her sex. . . . The bright morning sun, therefore, shone on broad shoulders and well-developed busts, and on round and ruddy cheeks, that . . . had hardly grown paler and thinner in the atmosphere of New England." Hawthorne is, to be sure, somewhat ambivalent about the abundant fleshliness of these mothers of his race, suggesting that their "moral diet was not a bit more refined" than the beef and ale with which they satisfied their bellies. Yet there is something nostalgic, even rueful about his acknowledgment that since those early days "every successive mother has transmitted to her child a fainter bloom, a more delicate and briefer beauty, and a slighter physical frame. . . ."

To the world of such lush and substantial women, Hester unquestionably belongs. She is not an "ethereal" latter-day invalid like Sophia Hawthorne, but "lady-like . . . after the manner . . . of those days; characterized by a certain state and dignity, rather than by the delicate, evanescent and indescribable grace, which is now recognized as its indication." Dimmesdale, however, is no father, no mythic progenitor at all; after his love affair, at least (in which surely he was more seduced than seducing), he has been shrunken to Lilliputian size—seems a modern, alienated, anguished artist, transported into a more heroic age. He is not a Puritan, but a child of the Puritans, their diminished offspring, inheritor of melancholy, and the prototype of Hawthorne's own fallen generation. His fall from potency and his return to the maternal embrace just

before death constitute an "emblem" of the fate of the American male. (pp. 237-39)

> *Leslie A. Fiedler, "'Clarissa' in America: Toward Marjorie Morningstar," in his* Love and Death in the American Novel, *revised edition, Stein and Day Publishers, 1966, pp. 217-58.\**

### BRIGID BROPHY, MICHAEL LEVEY, AND CHARLES OSBORNE (essay date 1967)

[*In this negative assessment of* The Scarlet Letter, *Brophy, Levey, and Osborne treat the Puritanism of the novel as a reflection of Hawthorne's own limitations and prejudices. Their criticism of the work as "a document in obsession" echoes the comments of E. P. Whipple (1850), and* Blackwood's Edinburgh Magazine *(1855), who fault what they see as the morbid intensity of* The Scarlet Letter.]

There is undoubtedly a sort of clumsy power in Hawthorne, blacker than he probably realized and one which he seems to have been unable artistically to control. The tone of *The Scarlet Letter* is so profoundly Puritanical that the book becomes a document in obsession; it is indeed something which one hardly wants to think about afterwards. The result is certainly not a novel, but a case history of hatred of the flesh. A vicious joy keeps repeating that the scarlet letter 'sears' the bosom of Hester Prynne: red-hot iron is the next stage of this sort of cruelty, in which the author half shares, while at times standing back and speaking distantly of the gloom of the period in which he has chosen to set his story.

It is an indication of Hawthorne's divided nature that he thinks in terms of guilt, sin and retribution for Hester Prynne but has a rather different fate in store for her 'demon offspring', little Pearl. The mother has been dragged through the book suffering every form of physical and mental agony (including the child's cruelty to her in recognizing her as a mother only when she wears the hateful scarlet A) but Pearl inherits the kingdom of the New World, and reaps a typical reward in becoming 'the richest heiress of her day'. If there is a lesson here, it is that there is material benefit eventually in being the child of an adulterous union.

For those who have committed adultery, however, there is nothing but agony. Nor does Hawthorne question the judgement of an intolerant Puritan society and the vile punishment it inflicts. He cannot dodge out of the issue by pretending that he is telling a story which requires no intrusion by the narrator—for the book is full of historical references ('At that epoch of pristine simplicity . . .') which betray the narrator's presence. It is therefore without irony, and with an effortless assumption of the standards of the Puritan figures enshrined in the book, that Hawthorne speaks of little Pearl as 'a lovely and immortal flower, (sprung) out of the rank luxuriance of a guilty passion'. The excess of condemnation in the very language suggests Hawthorne's unconscious preference for such a passion. He cannot condone it—still less is he capable of understanding it—but it excites his imagination. It has a luxuriance, according to him, which presumably is lacking to a conventional marriage. (pp. 49-50)

The basic puritanism of *The Scarlet Letter* is the author's own. It is the reaction of the New England philistine—the same man who was shocked by nudity in antique Roman sculpture and disgusted by modern Roman behaviour. His mind was deliberately narrow, callow and frightened by prospects of pleasure, whether in art or life. He could not properly understand that the things he hated were things which dangerously appealed to him; in the violence of his rejection we have an indication of how intense was this appeal. Ambivalence is the mark of Hawthorne's own personal reaction to experience of every kind; but fear/love of the flesh is what underlies his character and his books. Secretly, and sometimes not so secretly, he is on the side of the persecutors of Hester Prynne. Women are dangerous, exotic creatures with white bosoms which can be cauterized only through the application of a scarlet A.

Hawthorne passes calmly under review every aspect of male intolerance, cruelty, emotional blackmail, repressed fears and secret emotions; aspects of life which are no doubt the more to be condoned as they lead to the accumulation of property and help to build a Godly, wealthy society. Women interrupt this harmony; they tempt men by beauty; they introduce sin into society. Hawthorne tacitly called up an army of male prejudice, while putting forward a vulgarly romantic idea of woman (or rather, Woman) which probably still remains the American dream. Passion and Affection—Hawthorne's capital letters—were no longer in Hester: 'Some attribute had departed from her, the permanence of which had been essential to keep her a woman.' But are passion and affection not essential to keep men as men? No. In Hawthorne's world they are too busy cutting up scarlet cloth so as to have plenty of letters ready to stick on the bosoms of the women they meet. And, very likely, that duty is the explanation which in America they give their wives for their habit of staring at other women's bosoms. (pp. 50-1)

*Brigid Brophy, Michael Levey, and Charles Osborne, "The Scarlet Letter," in their* Fifty Works of English and American Literature We Could Do Without, *1967. Reprint by Stein and Day Publishers, 1968, pp. 49-51.*

### ROBERT PENN WARREN   (essay date 1973)

[*Warren is considered one of the most distinguished men of letters in America today. His criticism is closely associated with two critical movements, the Agrarians and the New Critics. The Agrarians were concerned with political and social issues as well as literature, and were dedicated to preserving the Southern way of life and traditional Southern values. The New Critics comprised one of the most influential critical movements of the mid-twentieth century. Although the various New Critics did not subscribe to a single set of principles, all believed that a work of literature had to be examined as an object in itself through a process of close analysis of symbol, image, and metaphor. Warren's work is strongly regional in character, often drawing its inspiration from the land, the people, and the history of the South. While he often bases his themes on specific historical events, Warren successfully transcends the local to comment in universal terms on the human condition. Warren's deep interest in history and his conception that art is a vital force in contemporary society informs all his work. In the following excerpt, Warren discusses the tension between physical and spiritual desires in* The Scarlet Letter, *emphasizing what he calls the "irremediable askewness of life" depicted in the novel.*]

It is easy to see how, if a reader ignores all the characters except Dimmesdale, if he does not attend very closely to what Dimmesdale does and says, and if he accepts Dimmesdale's values as Hawthorne's, he can take *The Scarlet Letter* as *merely* a story of conscience and redemption. . . . [Some early readers, each] in his own way saw the tragic tensions, the pitiful instances of waste, the irremediable askewness of life which the story, taken as a whole, delineates.

*Taken as a whole:* that is the point. Even in Dimmesdale's story there are ambiguities. How much, for instance, is there of spiritual aspiration, and how much of fear of nature, fear of his own nature, sexual incertitude, and narcissism? But whatever Dimmesdale may actually be taken to be, he is only part of the pattern of the novel. Chillingworth, for instance, is a thematic and psychological counterpoint to him; and even, in the novel, a structural counterpoint, for the relation of each to Hester gives one principle of the action, and one principle of balance to the action. Psychologically and thematically, their rôles are even more significant. Both are men "outside" of nature, Chillingworth with his passion for study (to be directed, or course, to the good of mankind) and Dimmesdale with his aspiration to spirituality (so as to be a model for the redemption of mankind). When Chillingworth comes to the vital Hester he is already old, twisted, withered, and all but impotent, and if Dimmesdale discovers passion with her, there is inevitably the self-loathing we find expressed in the fact that part of his penance is to stare at his own face in a mirror. If Chillingworth, out of envy of what he takes to be the successful lover, and in his outraged vanity, devotes himself to the torture of Dimmesdale, then we find, as a parallel, Dimmesdale's obsessively gratifying process of self-torture. In the end, the two men are more important to each other than Hester is to either; theirs is the truest "marriage"—and a marriage of two perfect egotists.

Hester's story is one of penance, it is clear. She accepts her rôle as the outcast, the revulsion of society and the insults from even those unfortunates whom she succors, but she does this out of pride rather than humility. She has, in fact, stayed here for reasons having nothing to do with penance, to be near Dimmesdale and, perhaps more importantly, to fulfill some obscure sense of what Hawthorne calls the "unity" of her life and what we might call her identity. Further, her isolation has freed her mind to speculate about the nature of society, and to decide that society is not fixed by God in immutable law but is subject to change. This is not penance; and certainly not penitence.

Hawthorne says, indeed, that Hester had in her the making of a harsh prophetess who might attempt to create the future. It is this strain of coldness and harshness developed in her adversity, in her "battle" with the world, which he deplores, even as he admires her courage. This point is reinforced in the last scaffold scene. When Pearl, as though aroused by the "great scene of grief", comes out of the "spell" to kiss at last her father's lips, Hawthorne says that her tears "were the pledge that she would grow up in human joy and sorrow, nor forever do battle with the world, but be a woman in it"—unlike her mother.

The scaffold scene, then, would say that Hester has been forced to do battle with the world and that part of her tragedy lies in the consequent hardening of her womanliness; only in the meeting with Dimmesdale in the forest, where love is again "aroused", does her natural womanliness return: "Such was the sympathy of Nature—that wild, heathen nature of the forest, never subjugated by human law, nor illumined by higher truth."

Hester, strong, vital, beautiful, is indeed the wonderful "natural" creature, one of those dark, passionate temptresses that Hawthorne put into fiction and, apparently, flinched from in life; but even so, another source of her tragedy lies in the fact that she cannot be merely "natural". Here we must consider that the men she has accepted are not men we would reasonably expect as her sexual partners. We can argue that accident and social conditions may well have played a part here, and this is true; but *dramatically* regarded, what we have is the natural woman yearning, as it were, toward a condition beyond her "naturalness". Dramatically, psychologically, and thematically regarded, it is not an accident that Hester takes up with the old and twisted Chillingworth, and when she deserts him, it is for the pale, beautiful Dimmesdale and his pathologically sensitive conscience and narcissistic spirituality, instead of for some strapping officer of militia who would wear his religion more lightly, could gratify her appetites more single-mindedly, and could sleep better o' nights. From the very start there has been an askewness in her fate, an askewness that Chillingworth recognizes when he says, "hadst thou met with a better love than mine, this evil had not been." But what he does not recognize is the possibility that there may also be a reason why "naturalness" yearns beyond "nature".

The last chapter is balanced, as a kind of epilogue, against the first, which, as we have said, serves as a prologue. The climactic scaffold scene must, then, be regarded in the context of this conclusion. The meaning of Dimmesdale's confession is, in this epilogue, subjected to debate, and the mere fact qualifies the interpretation of the whole story. There is, too, considerable complexity in the way the story of Chillingworth is worked out. Deprived of the terrible meaning of his own life, he withers away, but in the very withering he provides means for Pearl to achieve her life. As heiress to his fortune, she goes to Europe, marries a nobleman, and, as we are given to understand, fulfills the prediction that she would not "do battle with the world, but be a woman in it". This may be taken as a happy normality coming out of the distorted lives—but if so, then with what illogicality, and after what waste! Pearl's happiness can scarcely be taken to discount the grief of all the others.

As for Hester, can the final meaning of her life be taken to discount the grief? She returns from Europe to resume her life in the withdrawn cottage and resumes, by her own choice, the scarlet letter—for only thus could she feel that her own life had found meaning. Now as she distributes comfort and counsel to women suffering from "wounded, wasted, wronged, misplaced, or erring and sinful passion", she assures them that a "brighter period" would come when the relation of man and woman would be "on a surer ground of mutual happiness". This, we must observe, is at the farthest remove from penitence, for the message that Hester, by implication, gives the suffering women is not that they are "sinners" in need of redemption, but that they are victims of a social order that violates nature.

How seriously are we, the readers, to take this prediction that would give to the novel, at least in a qualified way, a "happy ending"? Not very seriously, for, by a last strange irony, Hester, whose identity and vision have been made possible only by her "sin", can say that the prophetess of the new dispensation must be a woman "lofty, pure, and beautiful", and wise too, but, unlike Hester herself, not wise through a "dusky grief". This would be a world freed of all guilt, a world of natural joy. It is her dream, but scarcely the world Hawthorne envisaged.

In this connection, it may be recalled that, just as *The Scarlet Letter* was often misread as a cautionary tale of sin and conscience, it could also be misread as a tract in which Hester is primarily a martyr for the liberation of women—and of men, too—from a sexually repressive society. Such was the inter-

pretation in a transcendentalist discussion of the novel by a certain George Bailey Loring, a young physician, writing in Theodore Parker's *Massachusetts Quarterly Review*—transcendentalist in so far as the doctrine of "self-reliance" and the validity of "intuition" were taken to imply sexual release from the sanctions of both church and state [see excerpt above, 1850].

This element of conflict between the individual and society is clearly present in *The Scarlet Letter*, and it is reasonable to suppose that the influence of the Transcendentalists may have sharpened it in Hawthorne's mind. But Hawthorne's concern with the rigors of Puritan society, as with the complex tensions of sexual encounters, long preceded the initial meeting of earnest seekers in George Ripley's study that is usually understood to have officially ushered in the movement.

The meaning of *The Scarlet Letter* is far more tangled and profound than Dr. Loring ever imagined, and bears no simple relation to transcendental reformism. The concern of Hawthorne here, as in his work in general, lies in the tension between the demands of spirit and those of nature. Indeed, the Transcendentalists had insisted upon this issue, but Hawthorne's view, profoundly ironical as it was in seeing the tension between the two realms as the very irremediable essence of life, in its tragedy and glory and even comedy, was far different from anything that ever crossed a transcendental mind.

Even nature, which, in the novel, is thematically set against the sanctions of society, cannot be taken simply. The forest is a haunt of evil as well as of good, and the wishes of the heart may be wicked as well as benign. In the tale **"The Holocaust"**, for example, when all the marks of evil and vanity have been consigned to the flames, the world is not purged; there remains the human heart. In that world of ambiguities, there is, inevitably, a terrible illogic. Good and bad may be intertwined; good may be wasted; accident, not justice, rules. Man is doomed to live in a world where nature is denied and human nature distorted, and—most shatteringly of all—in a world where love and hate may be "the same thing at bottom", and even vice or virtue may represent nothing more than what Chillingworth calls "a typical illusion". But men must live by the logic of their illusions, as best they can—Dimmesdale by his, Hester by hers, and Chillingworth by his. That is their last and darkest "necessity". What compensation is possible in such a world comes from the human capacity for achieving scale and grandeur even in illusion—one might say by insisting on the coherence of the illusion—and from the capacity for giving pity. And here we must remind ourselves that Hawthorne found it "almost impossible to throw a cheering light" on the book.

So much for the hellfiredness of *The Scarlet Letter*. (pp. 106-11)

> *Robert Penn Warren, "Hawthorne Revisited: Some Remarks on Hellfiredness," in* The Sewanee Review, *Vol. LXXXI, No. 1, Winter, 1973, pp. 75-111.*

**NINA BAYM** (essay date 1976)

*[Baym indicates that Hester's adultery, which provokes a conflict between the values of "aging public males" and those of a young female, is treated by Hawthorne as a social rather than a theological crime. In addition, Baym proposes that Hester's predicament in* The Scarlet Letter *is analogous to that of Hawthorne as a romance writer in nineteenth-century America: both tried to resolve the inherent tensions between imaginative self-expression and the repressive "commonsense" forces of their society. For other treatments of* The Scarlet Letter *as a novel about the conflict*

*The house in which Hawthorne lived when he wrote* The Scarlet Letter, *in Salem, Massachusetts.*

*between the individual and society, see the excerpts by R.W.B. Lewis (1955), Marius Bewley (1959), A. N. Kaul (1962), and Michael Davitt Bell (1980).*]

In *The Scarlet Letter* Hawthorne defined the focus of all four of his completed long romances: the conflict between passionate, self-assertive, and self-expressive inner drives and the repressing counterforces that exist in society and are also internalized within the self. In this romance he also formulated some of the recurrent elements in his continuing exploration of this theme. In Hester he developed the first of a group of female representatives of the human creative and passionate forces, while in Dimmesdale he created the first of several guilt-prone males, torn between rebellious and conforming impulses. These two characters operate in *The Scarlet Letter* in a historical setting, which was not repeated in any of Hawthorne's later romances, but the historical setting is shaped according to thematic preoccupations that do recur. Nominally Puritan, the society in *The Scarlet Letter* in fact symbolizes one side of the conflict.

None of his many treatments of the Puritans depicted them in their own terms—that is, as a group bound together by a covenant among themselves and with God, to establish "a due form of government both civil and ecclesiastical," in accordance with "a special overruling providence." (pp. 124-25)

In *The Scarlet Letter*, unlike Hawthorne's stories about Ann Hutchinson, the Quakers, Roger Williams, or the Salem witches,

the Puritans are not punishing a heresy but an act that in its essence does not appear to quarrel with Puritan doctrine. What Hester and Dimmesdale have done is not a crime against belief but against the law. Many critics have maintained that, since the act violates one of the Ten Commandments, it is necessarily seen by Hawthorne as a crime against Divine Law. But in *The Scarlet Letter* he considers the act entirely as a social crime. Precisely because he does not take up the issue of whether the law broken is a divine law, the issues center on the relations of Hester and Dimmesdale to their community and to themselves as they accept or deny the judgment of the community on them. They differ from one another, not as beings more or less religious, more or less "saved," but as beings differently bound to the community and differently affected by it.

Such a thematic situation is created in *The Scarlet Letter* by the virtual absence of God from the text, and in this respect the romance is a very poor representation of the Puritan mental life as the Puritan himself would have experienced it. Divinity in this romance is a remote, vague, ceremonially invoked concept that functions chiefly to sanction and support the secular power of the Puritan rulers. And—another difference from Hawthorne's earlier formulation of Puritan psychology—these rulers are not transfigured by the zeal of a recovered faith burning like a lamp in their hearts. Remove the sense of communal purpose and service in behest of God, and a self-satisfied secular autocracy remains; this is what we find in *The Scarlet*

*Letter.* The Puritans of this community are sagacious, practical, realistic; they are lovers of form and display; they even tend toward luxury—consider Hester's many opportunities for fancy embroidery, and the elegance of Governor Bellingham's residence.

The ruling group is composed of old males, aptly epitomized in the Governor, "a gentleman advanced in years, and with a hard experience written in his wrinkles. He was not ill fitted to be the head and representative of a community, which owed its origin and progress, and its present state of development, not to the impulses of youth, but to the stern and tempered energies of manhood, and the sombre sagacity of age; accomplishing so much, precisely because it imagined and hoped so little." This patriarchy surrounds itself with displays of power, and when Hawthorne writes that this was "a period when the forms of authority were felt to possess the sacredness of divine institutions," . . . he makes the point, crucial for his story, that the Puritans venerate authority, not because it is an instrument in God's service, but because they believe secular authority itself to be divine. (pp. 125-27)

A community that embodies the qualities of aging public males must necessarily repress those of the young and female. Dimmesdale is a brilliant young minister who, in order to maintain himself as a favorite among the oligarchs, has repressed himself—made himself prematurely old by resolutely clinging to childhood. He "trode in the shadowy by-paths, and thus kept himself simple and childlike; coming forth, when occasion was, with a freshness, and fragrance, and dewy purity of thought, which, as many people said, affected them like the speech of an angel." . . . In this dewy innocent we recognize faint traces of Hawthorne's earlier men of fancy, and like them Dimmesdale does not so much want power as approval. He is a dependent personality. But he is still a young man, and to forgo the engagement with life characteristic of youth he must continually hold himself back. His "sin" is an impulsive relaxation of self-restraint and a consequent assertion of his youthful energies against the restrictions established by the elders. He does a passionate, thoughtless, willful thing. Precipitated out of his protected security as much by fear as by guilt, he must now confront the conflicts of adulthood. It is not only that he has been initiated into sex; it is less the sexual than the mental and emotional that interests Hawthorne, the inner rather than the outer aspects of the experience. Dimmesdale must now recognize and deal with previously hidden, subversive, and disobedient parts of himself.

Hester begins from no such position of security as Dimmesdale, and her relative lack of protection is at once a disadvantage and a blessing. He is the darling insider while she is in many ways an outsider even before her deed exposes her to public disgrace. She has been sent to Massachusetts by her husband, there to await his arrival; her own will is not implicated in her residence in the community. She thus has nothing like Dimmesdale's tie to the group at the outset. If, as the unfolding of the romance demonstrates, she is a far more independent character than Dimmesdale, her independence may be partly the effect of her relative unimportance in and to society and her consequent paradoxical freedom within it. To judge by the development of a certain feminist ideology in Hester's thinking over the years, it would seem that Hawthorne intended to represent a basic difference in the status of men and women within a patriarchal structure. Since women are of less account than men—are not fully members of the society—they are coerced physically rather than psychologically. Forced to wear a symbol

of shame in public, Hester is left alone behind that symbol to develop as she will.

The story of *The Scarlet Letter* evolves from the sin of omission that has occurred before the narrative begins to a much more important sin of commission that takes place in the same place seven years later. The original sexual encounter between Hester and Dimmesdale was an act neither of deliberate moral disobedience nor of conscious social rebellion. The characters had forgotten society and were thinking only of themselves. But seven years later when they meet again, they deliberately reject the judgment society has passed upon them. . . . Deciding to leave the community, they in effect deny its right to punish them. Hester is mainly responsible for this decision; seven years of solitude have made of her a rebel and a radical. . . . She undertakes alone the journey they had planned together and secures the fruit of her sin from the consequences of a Puritan judgment. Then, surprisingly, she returns.

But by returning, even though she takes up the scarlet letter and wears it until her death, she does not acknowledge her guilt. Rather, she admits that the shape of her life has been determined by the interaction between that letter, the social definition of her identity, and her private attempt to withstand that definition. Her life is neither the letter nor her resistance—neither the inner nor the outer—but the totality. But by again wearing the letter after her return—a gesture nobody would have required of her after so many years—and thus bringing the community to accept that letter on her terms rather than its own, Hester has in fact brought about a modest social change. Society expands to accept her with the letter—the private life carves out a small place for itself in the community's awareness. This is a small, but real, triumph for the heroine.

Hester and Dimmesdale work through their seven-year purgatory accompanied by alter egos, partly supernatural and parasitic beings related in several symbolic ways to their hosts: for Hester, Pearl; for Dimmesdale, Chillingworth. These subsidiary figures embody the sin that has been committed as it is felt and understood by each of the two actors; they are figures of the imagination made real. Since Hester and Dimmesdale imagine their act quite differently, the deed assumes a radically different shape in each one's inner life. Hester perceives her "sin" in the shape of the beautiful child, wild, unmanageable, and unpredictable, who has been created from it; Dimmesdale sees his in the form of the vengeful and embittered husband who has been offended by it.

Splintered off from the characters with whom they are associated, Pearl and Chillingworth indicate disharmony and disunity within Hester's and Dimmesdale's emotional lives, a direct result of the conflict between their sense of themselves and their awareness of how the community perceives them. Each character is alienated from a different part of his nature; crudely, Hester is tormented by her passions and Dimmesdale by his conscience. At the end of the romance the two shattered personalities become whole again and the symbolic characters disappear. Dimmesdale dies and so does Chillingworth; Hester, free at last from social stigma, becomes a whole person and so does Pearl. (pp. 127-30)

Two questions arise: what relation does the situation depicted in *The Scarlet Letter* bear to Hawthorne's idea of his own contemporary society? And what relation does the thematic design of the romance bear to his own function as an artist? Clearly, *The Scarlet Letter* is quite different from all of Hawthorne's earlier work, which had argued that the individual finds rich fulfillment when integrated into society, that society expresses the personality. Now although Hawthorne does not suggest in *The Scarlet Letter* that there is any joy in isolation, he does show that the individual pays a very high price to be a member of the group. The earlier fictions and sketches exhibited the imagination at work in the service of society; *The Scarlet Letter* makes it clear that imagination serves the self. The earlier works tended to define serving the self as obsession, egotism, or eccentricity; *The Scarlet Letter* asserts that the self has needs and claims that must be satisfied. The earlier works restricted the exercise of imagination to the surface of events, while *The Scarlet Letter* ties imagination to the life beneath appearances. Evidently, Hawthorne jettisoned the whole load of commonsense assumptions about imagination and art and replaced them with a romantic vision. (p. 142)

Hawthorne represents his romance, *The Scarlet Letter,* as originating in the attempts of his imagination to make itself felt and keep itself alive in the deadly atmosphere of the Custom House. His withdrawal from the tedium of the first-floor routine into the cluttered chambers of the upper story signifies Hawthorne's withdrawal into his own mind, his escape into fantasy. But in these circumstances, fantasy is an escape to freedom rather than a retreat from life. It is an affirmative rather than a denying gesture. In one of his flights of fancy, Hawthorne comes upon a roll of parchment enclosed within "a certain affair of fine red cloth" wrought "with wonderful skill of needlework" and "intended, there could be no doubt, as an ornamental article of dress." . . . Examination proves it to be a fabric representation of the letter *A*. (pp. 145-46)

In this electric moment, which many critics have recognized as central to both "**The Custom-House**" and *The Scarlet Letter,* Hawthorne senses with a mixture of fear and excitement that he has found his subject. The letter—a verbal sign, a symbol, and the channel of inspiration—becomes the type of Art.

Because in *The Scarlet Letter* the *A* signifies a social crime, Hawthorne suggests that the writing of his romance is in some sense an analogously guilty act. My analysis of *The Scarlet Letter,* stressing the self-expressive and passionate nature of Hester's and Dimmesdale's act, indicates why there is an analogy. For Hawthorne, the romance originated as expression of his own feelings of social defiance and discontent, as a reaction to the stifling position of surveyor in the Custom House at Salem. The decision to write the romance, or to try to write it, involves a transference of Hawthorne's allegiance from his Puritan conscience to his imagination, personified in "**The Custom-House**" by Surveyor Pue. Adopting this figure as his "official ancestor," Hawthorne accepts the former surveyor's charge that he publicize Hester's story. (p. 146)

Yet Hawthorne, in accepting Hester as his subject, does not return to the transcendentalists so much as go beyond them. She represents everything the transcendentalists believe and more besides, for in her Emerson's "Spirit" is transformed into Eros and thus allied to sex, passion, eroticism, flesh, and the earth. The Puritans seek to repress Spirit not only because of their dedication to permanence and form, but also because as shrewd men of hard experience they are aware of its sexual sources. Thus, the sin in *The Scarlet Letter* is sexual, and a sexual sin can symbolize Hawthorne's writing of romances. This is why Hawthorne epitomizes Puritan severity in a depiction of their persecution of women. In women they see the occasion of a dangerous passion. Their opposition to sex is not prudish but pragmatic. (pp. 147-48)

Hawthorne's servitude in the Custom House generated, as a reactive defense, the fantasy of the scarlet letter; his dismissal led to its creation. In both idea and execution, the romance is related to maladjustment between Hawthorne and his society. Miserable as Hawthorne had been in the Custom House, to be forced out of it represented an evident failure: "The moment when a man's head drops off is seldom or never, I am inclined to think, precisely the most agreeable of his life. . . . In view of my previous weariness of office, and vague thoughts of resignation, my fortune somewhat resembled that of a person who should entertain an idea of committing suicide, and, altogether beyond his hopes, meet with the good hap to be murdered." . . . Observe the ambivalence of the images. Hawthorne's thoughts of resigning from the Custom House are like thoughts of suicide. Why should this be, if the Custom House is so unpleasant? Obviously Hawthorne is torn.

Like Hester, he becomes a rebel because he is thrown out of society, by society. . . . (pp. 148-49)

*Nina Baym, in her* The Shape of Hawthorne's Career, *Cornell University Press, 1976, 283 p.*

## MICHAEL DAVITT BELL    (essay date 1980)

[*Discussing* The Scarlet Letter *in relation to Hawthorne's interpretation of New England social history, Bell focuses on the cycle of rebellion and repression implied in the novel's structure and themes. For other views on the interplay between the individual and society in* The Scarlet Letter, *see the excerpts by R.W.B. Lewis (1955), Marius Bewley (1959), A. N. Kaul (1962), and Nina Baym (1976).*]

*The Scarlet Letter* opens only twelve years after the initial migration [of the Puritans] to Boston, but the first "stir of spirit" has, clearly, already subsided. In spite of its historical youth, this community, as Hawthorne describes it, is principally characterized by age and rigidity. "The wooden jail," we are told, "was already marked with weather-stains and other indications of age. . . . The rust on the ponderous iron-work of its oaken door looked more antique than any thing else in the new world. . . . It seemed never to have known a youthful era." . . . By the opening of *The Scarlet Letter* the Puritans have themselves repeated the process against which they originally rebelled. Looking at the crowd around the prison door, Hawthorne notes "the grim rigidity that petrified the bearded physiognomies of these good people." . . . The Puritan impulse to repair the decay of things has only instituted another cycle of decay.

Set against this formal petrification is the vitality of Hester Prynne. She is early associated with the Catholic "image of Divine Maternity," . . . as Pearl will later remind Bellingham of court masques and Wilson of "the sun . . . shining through a richly painted window, . . . of those naughty elfs or fairies, whom we thought to have left behind us, with other relics of Papistry, in merry old England." . . . Like the rosebush outside the prison, Hester stands for the qualities of passion and imagination repressed by the Puritans and, in her case, literally imprisoned. The opening ceremony has a clear and deliberate import: Hester is being made to play the role of Adulteress in the allegorical social drama through which the Puritans maintain their community against, among other things, any further eruptions of the "spiritual mystery" that first established it.

Hester rebels, at first implicitly, then openly. This is the central "story" of *The Scarlet Letter.* As an artist, she transforms by her needlework what are meant to be badges of her shameful status—the letter and Pearl—into images of her passionate "individuality." She accordingly comes to incarnate the Utopian spirit lost to Boston as a whole:

> It was an age in which the human intellect, newly emancipated, had taken a more active and a wider range than for many centuries before. Men of the sword had overthrown nobles and kings. Men bolder than these had overthrown and rearranged—not actually, but within the sphere of theory, which was their most real abode—the whole system of ancient prejudice, wherewith was linked much of ancient principle. Hester Prynne imbibed this spirit.
>
> (pp. 176-77)

Hester's revolutionary sincerity is complicated, however, by a number of factors. Despite her status as victim of allegory, she often sublimates her own impulses into allegory, or projects them onto others, as rigidly as any Puritan. She stays in Boston, she tells herself, to work out her repentance. Is the hope of possible reunion with Dimmesdale among her motives? "She barely looked the idea in the face, and hastened to bar it in its dungeon.". . . What the Puritans do to Hester, as a figure of impulse, Hester does to her own impulses. . . . "What she compelled herself to believe," we are told, "—what, finally, she reasoned upon, as her motive for continuing a resident of New England,—was half a truth, and half a self-delusion.". . . Characters in *The Scarlet Letter* have a habit of projecting their secret motives onto others, and, if these others respond by uttering the secrets too openly, of demanding that they "hush." "Mother!—Mother!" Pearl implores, "Why does the minister keep his hand over his heart?" "Hold thy tongue, naughty child!" answers Hester. "Do not tease me; else I shall shut thee into the dark closet!". . . In such a spirit of mixed sincerity she sets out to meet Dimmesdale in the woods.

In the forest, to be sure, Hester utters openly what she has heretofore kept secret in the prison of her heart, but even here the light of revolutionary sincerity is clouded with irony. Chillingworth, argues Dimmesdale, "violated, in cold blood, the sanctity of a human heart." His sin was deliberate, Hester's and Dimmesdale's spontaneous. "What we did," pleads Hester, "had a consecration of its own. We felt it so! We said so to each other! Has thou forgotten it?" "Hush, Hester!" Dimmesdale replies before admitting: "No; I have not forgotten.". . . There is a deeper problem here than Dimmesdale's projective hypocrisy, his guilty "Hush!"; for Hester's call to spontaneous action fails to meet her own criteria. Maybe what she and Dimmesdale did, seven years before, was spontaneous, but to do it again, deliberately, could scarcely be equally so. This is the tragic inference behind the Utopianism both of Hester and of the now-formalistic community from which she seeks to escape. To act on the Utopian impulse—to express it or socialize it—is inevitably to allegorize and hence to falsify it. Hawthorne sees clearly the distinction between Dimmesdale's past capitulation to impulse and his present plan of escape with Hester. "This [past deed] had been a sin of passion, not of principle, nor even purpose.". . . To convert "passion" into "principle" or "purpose," in the world of *The Scarlet Letter,* is to trap life in an idea about life. The neutral territory between ideal and actual is a chasm after all.

At the close, Hester still hopes for some reconciliation, if not on earth then in Heaven. "Shall we not meet again?" she whispers. "Shall we not spend our immortal life together?" "Hush, Hester," Dimmesdale replies, "Hush!" And the rest

of his response is hardly more comforting: "The law we broke!—the sin here so awfully revealed!—let these alone be in thy thoughts!". . . Hawthorne's irony here is so devastating as to move from criticism into a kind of awe. As Dimmesdale forsakes overt hypocrisy for overt sincerity, he too falls into the trap of allegory, and in an especially hideous way. Even confronting the spiritual realm, the ultimate Utopia, he smothers what Edgar Huntly [the title character of a novel by Charles Brockden Brown] called "desperate suggestions" beneath "better thoughts" by projecting the former onto Hester, once again, with his admonitory "Hush." One suspects that, if Dimmesdale were the narrator of *The Scarlet Letter,* the book might sound a bit like a tale by Poe. Even God, in Dimmesdale's final vision, becomes a kind of allegorical double, manipulating on the stage of the world the symbols of the minister's guilty self-justification:

> "He hath proved his mercy, most of all, in my afflictions. By giving me this burning torture to bear upon my breast! By sending yonder dark and terrible old man, to keep the torture always at red-heat! By bringing me hither, to die this death of triumphant ignominy before the people! Had either of these agonies been wanting, I had been lost for ever! Praised be his name! His will be done! Farewell!"

Those readers who find Dimmesdale admirable in his confession should pay attention to his image of a God willing to damn Chillingworth in order to bring on the allegorical spectacle of Dimmesdale's "salvation." If the minister's self-serving sense of Providence is plausibly accurate to Puritan rhetoric, as it is, this is only to say that he shows how far the allegorical sublimation of forbidden impulse could go in seventeenth-century New England.

The historical action of *The Scarlet Letter* thus bears out [Hawthorne's conclusion in the short story] **"Main Street"**: the gradual discovery by Puritan society of "how like an iron cage was that which they called Liberty!" . . . Hester looks from an "estranged point of view at human institutions . . . ; criticizing all with hardly more reverence than the Indian would feel for the clerical band, the judicial robe, the pillory, the gallows, the fireside, or the church. The tendency of her fate and fortunes had been to set her free.". . . The irony of the last sentence should not go unnoticed. And Hester's repudiation of the outward language of culture—"the clerical band, the judicial robe," and the like—is finally as futile as the Puritans' original rejection of Anglican forms of worship. To repudiate the past, in *The Scarlet Letter,* is only to repeat it; for the past as it exists in the rigid formalism of Puritan Boston is but the petrified detritus of an earlier repudiation. Extreme gestures of sincerity, as Dimmesdale's case indicates, lead only to even more extreme formalism and repression. (pp. 177-79)

*Michael Davitt Bell, "The Death of the Spirit: Nathaniel Hawthorne," in his* The Development of American Romance: The Sacrifice of Relation, *The University of Chicago Press, 1980, pp. 168-93.*

**TERENCE MARTIN** (essay date 1983)

[*Martin's assessment of Hawthorne's overall artistic achievement in* The Scarlet Letter *emphasizes the work's deeply rooted ambiguity and ambivalence created through the use of paradox and irony. He also praises the intricate structure of the novel, asserting that it depends primarily upon the interplay and inter-*

*dependence of the principal characters. Other critics who highlight the importance of ambivalence in* The Scarlet Letter *include Anthony Trollope (1879), Frederic I. Carpenter (1944), Richard Harter Fogle (1952), and Hyatt H. Waggoner (1955).*]

The special quality of Hawthorne's achievement in *The Scarlet Letter* derives from the essential duality or ambivalence of his fictional world and its component parts. In a number of tales, of course, Hawthorne had explored modes of ambiguity and ambivalence. Goodman Brown's adventure with evil and Mr. Hooper's black veil resist any consideration that does not take their complexity into account; **"The Wedding-Knell"** and **"The Shaker Bridal"** counterpose—even in their titles—the ideas of marriage and death as aspects of the same ceremony. In *The Scarlet Letter*, however, Hawthorne sustains a vision of the ambivalent nature of reality beyond all he had done before and in a way he was never to do again. Hester, Dimmesdale, Chillingworth, the scarlet letter itself—all signify more than one thing; all must be considered in more than one way. To some readers, Hester Prynne seems a virtual saint, a woman who walks in humility and patience; to others, she is an unbending woman of pride, who glories in her sin. Hawthorne provides material for both portraits. He dramatizes the double (or multiple) nature of every important character, thing, and event in his romance. And one must take this doubleness into full account, must see that the coherence of Hawthorne's narrative emanates from duality, that only in terms of ever-deepening ambivalence is experience possible in the world of this romance. As a literary document which stands at a particular place in Hawthorne's career, *The Scarlet Letter* has all the finality, all the completedness, of a fact. As a masterpiece of literary art, however, it generates meaning by a technique of dynamic interrelationships, meaning that it is for the reader in a perpetual state of becoming.

The duality of experience in *The Scarlet Letter*—embodied in language, character, and theme—takes frequently the forms of paradox and irony. Hester Prynne, as we have seen, stands in the marketplace with a "burning blush, and yet a haughty smile"; her beauty shines out and makes "a halo of her misfortune"; on the scaffold she takes refuge in public exposure. Moreover, she has embroidered her letter fancifully; she has adorned the symbol of her sin almost as if she were parading that symbol and that sin before the public. Yet the young matron outside the jail whispers meaningfully that "not a stitch in that embroidered letter, but she has felt it in her heart." Hester, one sees, glories in her letter and suffers in her glory; and only by seeing the relationship between her suffering and glory does one do justice to Hawthorne's characterization of her. (pp. 117-18)

The penance imposed by the community has an ironic effect on Hester, changing her life "in a great measure, from passion and feeling, to thought." Alone and independent by decree, Hester's mind ranges widely, questing and probing into areas of thought concerning which the Puritan world would allow small latitude. (p. 118)

The world has ordained her a Sister of Mercy; to the world the *A* might mean Able or even Angel. But despite all these acts of helpfulness, despite a tenderness and sympathy unqualified in any way by Hawthorne's language, Hester is not contrite: "The scarlet letter," as he says, "had not done its office." The iron grace of Hester's life for seven years, a discipline bred on suppressed emotion, leads directly to the forest interview with Arthur Dimmesdale. The letter *A*, we see, might also stand for Arthur—which would double its meaning of

adultery and the ambivalence of Hester's attitude toward it. The community has pinned the initial of her lover on her breast, then wondered for seven years who he might be. (p. 120)

In the forest Hester removes her symbolic *A* (no need for the symbol when Arthur is alone with her, when they will redefine the very act by agreeing to run away), lets her dark hair tumble down, and demonstrates that seven years of ignominy have left her a resolute priestess of a private cult. Dimmesdale, the public priest, is seduced (perhaps again); tempted by winds of heresy, he enters again the private world of passion in a final psychic grab at identity.

Hester's decision to accompany Dimmesdale marks the culmination of a lengthy process in her life. (p. 121)

The consequences of the letter as penance are thus just the reverse of what the Puritan community thought they would be. A sin of passion, nursed by the memory of its sacredness, has blossomed into a sin of purpose. Hester, as we have seen, has virtually been preparing for such a moment of decision; but Dimmesdale, broken and ensnared by hypocrisy as he is, has never contemplated such a step in his wildest dreams. He embraces his sin once again, now willfully, with all the ardor of a convert to a new faith.

The ambivalence of Dimmesdale's position is part and parcel of the total ambivalence of the romance. Because of his sin, he has undergone excruciating penance; if Chillingworth lives to torture him, Dimmesdale lives to be tortured. Yet the fundamental falseness of his position yields an idiom of anguish that stands him very well in his professional life. His sermons, for example, are models of efficacy: the more he reviles himself as a sinner (in general terms, from the security of the pulpit), the more his congregation elevates him to new heights of spirituality and thinks comparatively of its own unworthiness. His anguish is convincing, compelling, and genuine, although it springs from and compounds his hypocrisy—even because of his knowledge that it springs from and compounds his hypocrisy. The irony is that Dimmesdale's sermons give spiritual assistance to everyone but himself. (pp. 121-22)

The psychological keenness informing Dimmesdale's transformation is of a high order. No matter what "religion" the minister professes, he serves ultimately the interests of one master—himself. Thus, in keeping with the brilliant economy of *The Scarlet Letter*, the moment at which Dimmesdale commits himself consciously to deadly liberating sin becomes the moment at which he secretly wishes to cap his public life with a final burst of eloquence on the most important occasion the Puritan community can offer.

Dimmesdale and Chillingworth, we may say, make each other possible in *The Scarlet Letter*. If Chillingworth were not present, it would almost be necessary for Dimmesdale to invent him. Conversely, with no Dimmesdale there could be no Chillingworth as we know him; the avenger requires the victim to make him what he is, just as the victim requires the avenger. (p. 124)

[Chillingworth, the] arch-sinner of *The Scarlet Letter* has victimized himself, has caught himself on a vicious blade of revenge which cuts two ways. Though there can be no getting even for Chillingworth, he must constantly intensify his torture; yet the more he intensifies his torture, the more he destroys himself. To shield himself from the bruising reality of the situation, he recalls his "old faith, long forgotten," which explains the entire action as a drama of "dark necessity." Yet

Chillingworth, for all his evil, admits to Hester that his was the first wrong—it was a mistake, he sees, to attempt to warm his heart and his hearth with a marriage to a young girl after committing himself to a life of solitude and thought. The mistake has terrible consequences, but since it arose from a sense of loneliness and incompleteness, from a human longing for warmth, Hawthorne cannot help providing a context for understanding it. Chillingworth, too, takes the first step to break down the silence and secrecy among the characters by releasing Hester from her promise of concealing his identity. Chillingworth personifies the Hawthorne antagonist in all his essential pride and monomania; but he comes into the romance trailing clouds of weakness; we understand his villainy (in all its complexity) all the more by seeing in him betrayed vestiges of humanity.

The complex interrelationships of Hester Prynne, Dimmesdale, Chillingworth, and the community yield a rich texture to the classic formal structure of *The Scarlet Letter*. . . . Hester, Dimmesdale, and Chillingworth, each of whom goes through much of the romance thinking fundamentally about himself, are what they are because of the uniqueness of the total dramatic situation. Each character takes his identity from the identities of the other characters and the community even as each contributes his identity to the identities of others and the community. One cannot discuss Hester, for example, at least with impunity, as if she were somehow liberated from the context out of which she takes her existence and to which she contributes. The same is true, of course, of any fully realized work of art. But the economy and complexity of *The Scarlet Letter* bring home the lesson with special clarity.

Taking its form in Hawthorne's imagination, the total context of *The Scarlet Letter* inheres in the letter itself. Invented by the community to serve as an unequivocal emblem of penance, the letter has frozen Hester into a posture of haughty agony, has brought Dimmesdale to a death of "triumphant ignominy" on the scaffold, has victimized the victimizer—Chillingworth. Hawthorne begins and ends with the letter, which encompasses and transcends all its individual meanings, which signifies, totally and finally, *The Scarlet Letter* itself. (pp. 125-27)

> Terence Martin, in his Nathaniel Hawthorne, *revised edition, Twayne Publishers, 1983, 221 p.*

*Photograph of Hawthorne taken by Matthew Brady in 1862-63. The Granger Collection, New York.*

———. "Hawthorne's Dimmesdale: Fugitive from Wrath." *Nineteenth-Century Fiction* II, No. 2 (September 1956): 81-105.
   An inquiry into Hawthorne's characterization of Dimmesdale. Arguing that Dimmesdale rather than Hester is the central figure of *The Scarlet Letter,* Abel discusses this character in terms of the Puritan concepts of sin and regeneration.

Bell, Michael Davitt. *Hawthorne and the Historical Romance of New England.* Princeton: Princeton University Press, 1971, 253 p.
   Explores Hawthorne's treatment of Puritan history. Bell's analysis of *The Scarlet Letter* focuses on Hester's adjustment to life in America and Dimmesdale's predicament as a second-generation New England Puritan.

Bell, Millicent. "The Obliquity of Signs: *The Scarlet Letter.*" *The Massachusetts Review* XXIII, No. 1 (Spring 1982): 9-26.
   An analysis of Hawthorne's attitude towards and use of various kinds of signs and symbols in *The Scarlet Letter.*

Boewe, Charles, and Murphey, Murray G. "Hester Prynne in History." *American Literature* XXXII (1960-61): 202-04.
   A survey of the historical sources Hawthorne used to create Hester.

Branch, Watson. "From Allegory to Romance: Hawthorne's Transformation of *The Scarlet Letter.*" *Modern Philology* 80, No. 2 (November 1982): 145-60.
   Documents Hawthorne's development of *The Scarlet Letter* from its short story form to its novel form. Branch terms the final version "an overlaying of a romance upon an allegory" and remarks that it evolved from "a rather limited though carefully wrought tale into an inexhaustible though flawed romance."

Brodhead, Richard H. "New and Old Tales: *The Scarlet Letter.*" In his *Hawthorne, Melville, and the Novel,* pp. 43-68. Chicago: University of Chicago Press, 1976.

## ADDITIONAL BIBLIOGRAPHY

Abel, Darrel. "Hawthorne's Pearl: Symbol and Character." *Journal of English Literary History* 18 (1951): 50-66.
   A discussion of Pearl's characterization and role in *The Scarlet Letter.* Abel contends that she embodies a mixture of Wordsworthian and Calvinist traits and that hers is a largely symbolic role in the novel.

———. "Hawthorne's Hester." *College English* 13, No. 6 (March 1952): 303-09.
   Examines Hawthorne's portrayal of Hester in *The Scarlet Letter.* Abel notes that Hester is presented sympathetically, but he also points out Hawthorne's implication that she is morally responsible for her sin.

———. "The Devil in Boston." *Philological Quarterly* XXXII, No. 4 (October 1953): 366-81.
   An analysis of Chillingworth's role in *The Scarlet Letter.* Abel maintains that Hawthorne's depiction of this character was influenced by seventeenth-century conceptions of sin, fate, and free will.

Examines Hawthorne's narrative style in *The Scarlet Letter*. In particular, Brodhead comments on Hawthorne's ideas about the form and function of romance writing.

Charvat, William. "Introduction." In *The Centenary Edition of the Works of Nathaniel Hawthorne: The Scarlet Letter*, Vol. I, by Nathaniel Hawthorne, edited by William Charvat, Roy Harvey Pearce, and Claude M. Simpson, pp. xv-xxviii. Columbus: Ohio State University Press, 1962.
    Provides valuable background information about the writing of *The Scarlet Letter*.

Cottom, Daniel. "Hawthorne versus Hester: The Ghostly Dialectic of Romance in *The Scarlet Letter*." *Texas Studies in Literature and Language* 24, No. 1 (Spring 1982): 47-67.
    Compares Hawthorne's narrative personality to the character of Hester.

Crews, Frederick. *The Sins of the Fathers: Hawthorne's Psychological Themes*. London: Oxford University Press, 1970, 279 p.
    Explores Dimmesdale's characterization using a psychoanalytic approach. Crews asserts that Dimmesdale equates his libidinal impulses with guilt and that his self-punishment "itself [becomes] a form of gratification."

Dauber, Kenneth. *Rediscovering Hawthorne*. Princeton: Princeton University Press, 1977, 235 p.
    Examines Hawthorne's novelistic technique. Dauber suggests that in *The Scarlet Letter*, Hawthorne emphasizes his novel's relation to history and "guards against over-psychologization."

Doubleday, Neal Frank. "Hawthorne's Hester and Feminism." *PMLA* LIV, No. 3 (September 1939): 825-28.
    Discusses Hester as a representative of feminism in colonial America and analyzes Hawthorne's attitude toward her in that role. Doubleday argues that Hester's feminism is presented as "the product of abnormal adjustment" to her predicament.

Feidelson, Charles, Jr. "*The Scarlet Letter*." In *Hawthorne Centenary Essays*, edited by Roy Harvey Pearce, pp. 31-77. Columbus: Ohio State University Press, 1964.
    Focuses on Hawthorne's narrative method, imagery, and characterization in *The Scarlet Letter*. Arguing that Hawthorne's approach is historical rather than moral, Feidelson notes that the novel is both "about" and "written out of" historical tradition.

Fogle, Richard Harter. *Hawthorne's Imagery: The "Proper Light and Shadow" in the Major Romances*. Norman: University of Oklahoma Press, 1969, 178 p.
    An in-depth study of Hawthorne's imagery. Fogle explores how Hawthorne's use of light and dark imagery in his characterization of Pearl accentuates her ironic and ambivalent personality traits.

Fryer, Judith. "The Temptress: Hester Prynne, the Dark Lady As 'Deviant'." In her *The Faces of Eve: Women in the Nineteenth Century American Novel*, pp. 72-84. New York: Oxford University Press, 1976.
    A study of Hester's role in *The Scarlet Letter*. Describing the work as "a novel about a failed community," Fryer contends that "Hester's life-giving but threatening sexuality [stands] for the hazard which individuality poses to the very survival of the community."

Garlitz, Barbara. "Pearl: 1850-1955." *PMLA* LXXII, No. 4 (September 1957): 689-99.
    Surveys critical interpretations of Pearl's characterization from the novel's publication to 1955.

Gerber, John C. "Form and Content in *The Scarlet Letter*." *The New England Quarterly* XVII, No. 1 (March 1944): 25-55.
    An analysis of structure in *The Scarlet Letter*. Gerber divides the novel into four parts and examines the relationship between cause and effect in each.

———, ed. *Twentieth Century Interpretations of "The Scarlet Letter": A Collection of Critical Essays*. Twentieth Century Interpretations, edited by Maynard Mack. Englewood Cliffs, N.J.: Prentice-Hall, 1968, 120 p.
    A collection of seminal essays on *The Scarlet Letter*. Topics discussed include the novel's structure and themes and Hawthorne's technique and sources. The editor provides a selected bibliography.

Gross, Seymour L. "'Solitude, and Love, and Anguish': The Tragic Design of *The Scarlet Letter*." *CLA Journal* III, No. 3 (March 1960): 154-65.
    Stresses the tragic theme in *The Scarlet Letter*. Gross asserts that the novel is not "merely moralistic or didactic," but rather an emotionally powerful tragedy because it ends in death and solitude.

———, ed. *A "Scarlet Letter" Handbook*. Wadsworth Guides to Literary Study, edited by Maurice Beebe. Belmont, Calif.: Wadsworth Publishing Co., 1961, 161 p.
    A collection of some of the most important essays on such topics as theme, characterization, symbolism, and structure in *The Scarlet Letter*. Gross also includes a selected bibliography of criticism on the novel.

Hall, Lawrence Sargent. *Hawthorne: Critic of Society*. Yale Studies in English, vol. 99. Gloucester, Mass.: Peter Smith, 1966, 200 p.
    Examines Hawthorne's ideas about society as reflected in his works. The major theme of *The Scarlet Letter*, Hall argues, is the importance of confessing one's sins in order to prevent the emotional isolation induced by guilt.

Hawthorne, Julian. "Problems of *The Scarlet Letter*." *Atlantic Monthly* LVII, No. CCCXLII (April 1886): 471-85.
    A defense of Hawthorne's narrative method, written by his son. Hawthorne contends that his father began the novel with the aftermath of Hester's adultery not because of propriety, but rather because "it is with the subjective consequences of a sinner's act that our understanding of him begins."

———. "The Making of *The Scarlet Letter*." *The Bookman* LXXIV, No. 4 (December 1931): 401-11.
    Provides an intimate account of the circumstances surrounding the composition of *The Scarlet Letter*.

Lathrop, George Parsons. *A Study of Hawthorne*. 1876. Reprint. New York: AMS Press, 1969, 350 p.
    An overview of Hawthorne's life and career, written by his son-in-law. While Lathrop criticizes *The Scarlet Letter*'s harsh tone, he praises the novel as a study of "a system of social discipline" and a depiction of "the capacity of sinning men and women for self-delusion."

Levin, Harry. *The Power of Blackness: Hawthorne, Poe, Melville*. New York: Alfred A. Knopf, 1958, 272 p.*
    A survey of Hawthorne's imagery. Levin examines blackness in *The Scarlet Letter* in terms of both light and dark imagery and the thematic role of tragedy.

McNamara, Anne Marie. "The Character of Flame: The Function of Pearl in *The Scarlet Letter*." *American Literature* XXVII, No. 4 (January 1956): 537-53.
    A study of Pearl's role in the plot of *The Scarlet Letter*. McNamara theorizes that it is Pearl "in her preternatural aspect" who brings about Dimmesdale's change of heart, which leads to his confession.

Porte, Joel. "Hawthorne: The Dark Blossom of Romance." In his *The Romance in America: Studies in Cooper, Poe, Hawthorne, Melville, and James*, pp. 98-113. Middletown, Conn.: Wesleyan University Press, 1969.
    Analyzes *The Scarlet Letter* in the context of the development of romance in American literature. Porte contends that as a writer of romance, Hawthorne resembles Hester, Dimmesdale, and Chillingworth because they all "convert passion into imaginative power."

Rahv, Philip. "The Dark Lady of Salem." *Partisan Review* VIII, No. 5 (September-October 1941): 362-81.

Discusses Hawthorne's use of "the dark lady," a type of heroine that appears in several of his writings. Explaining that this type of character "is a rebel and an emancipator," Rahv discusses Hester as an example and maintains that Hawthorne "wants to destroy the dark lady at the same time that he wants to glorify her."

Reid, Alfred S. *The Yellow Ruff & "The Scarlet Letter": A Source of Hawthorne's Novel*. Gainesville: University of Florida Press, 1955, 150 p.
    An analysis of a possible source for the plot of *The Scarlet Letter*. Reid suggests that the novel was based on an actual incident involving "adultery, revenge, murder, and concealed sin" that took place in seventeenth-century England.

———, ed. *"Sir Thomas Overbury's Vision" (1616) and Other English Sources of Nathaniel Hawthorne's "The Scarlet Letter."* Gainesville, Fla.: Scholars' Facsimiles & Reprints, 1957, 202 p.
    A companion volume to Reid's *The Yellow Ruff & "The Scarlet Letter"* (see annotation above). Reid assembles the actual documents he used in forming his theory about a seventeenth-century source for the plot of *The Scarlet Letter*.

Ringe, Donald A. "Hawthorne's Psychology of the Head and Heart." *PMLA* LXV, No. 2 (March 1950): 120-32.
    Focuses on the theme of evil in *The Scarlet Letter*. According to Ringe, Hawthorne's intention in the novel was "to show that man must fall if he is to rise to heights above the normal level of men."

Ryskamp, Charles. "The New England Sources of *The Scarlet Letter*." *American Literature* XXXI, No. 3 (November 1959): 257-72.
    Studies Hawthorne's method of recreating the historical past in *The Scarlet Letter*. Ryskamp surveys some of the historical sources that Hawthorne consulted as well as the ways in which he incorporated or digressed from the information he found there.

Schubert, Leland. *Hawthorne, the Artist: Fine-Art Devices in Fiction*. New York: Russell & Russell, 1963, 181 p.
    Discusses Hawthorne's use of such artistic devices as structure, design, rhythm, color, and sound in *The Scarlet Letter*. Schubert praises the novel's balance, symmetry, movement, and imagery.

Stein, William Bysshe. *Hawthorne's Faust: A Study of the Devil Archetype*. Gainesville: University of Florida Press, 1953, 172 p.
    A survey of Hawthorne's use of the devil archetype. Stein contends that this archetype directs the plot movement of *The Scarlet Letter* and provides a larger context for the novel. In terms of theme, Stein stresses that Hawthorne "elaborates the spiritual enlightenment engendered by experience with evil."

Stubbs, John Caldwell. *The Pursuit of Form: A Study of Hawthorne and the Romance*. Urbana: University of Illinois Press, 1970, 170 p.
    Explores the relationship between form and meaning in Hawthorne's works. *The Scarlet Letter*, Stubbs writes, presents "the human dilemma" in the form of a romance, allowing Hawthorne to delve systematically into the causes and effects of human action.

Van Doren, Mark. *Nathaniel Hawthorne*. The American Men of Letters Series, edited by Joseph Wood Krutch, Margaret Marshall, Lionel Trilling, and Mark Van Doren. New York: William Sloane Associates, 1949, 285 p.
    A critical biography. Van Doren contends that *The Scarlet Letter* is Hawthorne's masterpiece as well as "the high mark in American fiction" because it contains "the richest, most moving, most splendid things, put densely and inseparably together."

Wagenknecht, Edward. *Nathaniel Hawthorne: Man and Writer*. New York: Oxford University Press, 1961, 233 p.
    An overview of Hawthorne's life and career. Wagenknecht emphasizes Hawthorne's modernity in depicting Hester's "rich humanity [as] specifically rooted in her sexuality." In addition, he concludes that Hawthorne condemns her punishment because it "does not serve any useful purpose."

Warren, Austin. "*The Scarlet Letter*: A Literary Exercise in Moral Theology." *The Southern Review* I, No. 1 (January 1965): 22-45.
    A study of Hawthorne's themes and narrative method in *The Scarlet Letter*. Warren suggests that the main theme of the novel is the "dialectical nature of truth-finding and truth-reporting" and that each of the protagonists represents one aspect of the general truth.

Young, Philip. *Hawthorne's Secret: An Un-Told Tale*. Boston: David R. Godine, Publisher, 1984, 183 p.
    Examines the question of incest in Hawthorne's ancestry. Young's speculations, based on historical documents, lead him to attribute Hawthorne's confessional tone as well as his idea of the scarlet letter to an instance of incest among his relatives. The author also suggests that Hawthorne himself might have been suffering from secret guilt stemming from his incestuous feelings for his sister.

Ziff, Larzer. "The Ethical Dimension of 'The Custom House'." *Modern Language Notes* LXXIII, No. 5 (May 1958): 338-44.
    Examines the theory of romance that Hawthorne expressed in "The Custom-House." Ziff defines Hawthorne's concept of the romance as the intersection of the real and the imaginary and evaluates its aesthetic and ethical implications.

# Aleksandr Ivanovich Herzen

## 1812-1870

(Also transliterated as Alexander; also Hérzen, Hertzen, Gertsen; also wrote under pseudonym of Iskander) Russian novelist, essayist, and short story writer.

Herzen is recognized as one of nineteenth-century Russia's preeminent revolutionary thinkers. His writings provide a perceptive view of the Russian intellectual climate in the mid-nineteenth century, most notably in his extensive memoirs, *Byloye i dumy (My Past and Thoughts)*. Toward the end of his life, Herzen espoused an agrarian socialist philosophy that combined Slavophile and Western ideals. While he admired the Western values of individual freedom and progress, he also embraced the Slavophile love of country and emphasis on the collective. Herzen argued that a new social order, based on the peasant commune championed by the Slavophiles, should replace the bourgeois capitalist society that had corrupted Europe. This socialist philosophy formed the ideological basis for most of Russia's revolutionary activity in the 1850s, and though he had fallen into disfavor at the time of his death, critics today cite Herzen as one of the most significant figures in Russia's literary and political history.

Herzen was born out of wedlock to Ivan Yakovlev, a prosperous nobleman, and Luise Haag, a young German woman. Rather than give his son the family name, Yakovlev called him Herzen (from the German "herz," or heart). Guided by his father, Herzen studied world literature and developed an intense interest in Russian history. He was thirteen at the time of the unsuccessful Decembrist uprising against Nicholas I, and the incident affected him strongly; with his friend Nikolai Ogarev, Herzen vowed allegiance to the defeated rebels. In 1829, Herzen entered the University of Moscow, where he became the leader of a small group of students interested in radical politics and philosophy. While at the university, he studied the works of the French philosophers Claude Henri de Rouvroy Saint-Simon and Charles Fourier, whose socialist theories instilled in Herzen a great desire for political change. In particular, Herzen admired Saint-Simon's desire to end the exploitation of the individual by government institutions. From his study of Fourier, who sought to improve social conditions, Herzen derived his interest in cooperative societies that could accommodate the economic and personal needs of each group member.

In 1833, the year after Herzen's graduation, he and Ogarev were arrested and charged with subversion. The two were accused of publicly singing songs of adverse political content, which supposedly encouraged young people to rebel. Officials regarded both Herzen and Ogarev as dangerous and alleged that they had founded a secret anarchist society guided by the theories of Saint-Simon. Consequently, the two young men were exiled to the far provinces of Russia. During his confinement, Herzen turned to the works of the German philosopher Georg Wilhelm Friedrich Hegel. When he returned from exile, Herzen married and settled in Moscow, where he attended literary salons and took part in the debates between advocates of Western and Slavophile ideals. The philosophy of the Slavophiles, who supported Russian culture over that of Western Europe, was popular among many members of the

Russian intelligentsia. Like the Slavophiles, Herzen promoted the peasant *obshinas,* or village communes, and resented the domination of the individual by the Czarist government. He voiced this discontent in a number of polemical philosophical essays for local journals. Yet unlike the Slavophile purists, he also recognized the merit of such Western ideals as individual liberty and independence.

Herzen's father died in 1846, leaving his son a large fortune. Aided by this money, Herzen and his family went abroad to escape the tyranny of Nicholas I. Shortly before Herzen's departure, he published his didactic novel, *Kto vinovat? (Who Is to Blame?)*. Like other novels of the period, *Who Is to Blame?* presents social issues and a strongly independent hero patterned after the brooding "superfluous man" of Alexander Pushkin's *Eugene Onegin* and Mikhail Lermontov's *A Hero of Our Time*. Many critics believe that the style of the work reflects the influence of George Sand's novels concerned with contemporary social and philosophical problems, while its tone was inspired by the prevalent revolutionary mood against Nicholas I. At the time of its publication, a number of critics, most notably Vissarion Belinski, praised the novel's humanitarian spirit. However, because of its contemporary subject matter, *Who Is to Blame?* is of interest today primarily as a historical document.

After the publication of *Who Is to Blame?*, Herzen settled in Paris, though he soon grew disillusioned with the social and political climate. France was run by the bourgeoisie, a class which he considered little different from the Russian aristocracy he despised. Herzen had already observed unsuccessful rebellions in Russia and was deeply disappointed by the failure of the European revolutions of 1848 in Rome and Paris. Inspired by this discontent, Herzen wrote *Vom andern Ufer (From the Other Shore)*, a series of dialogues and essays that detail his unhappiness with his new home and probe the effect of revolution on society. In *From the Other Shore*, Herzen shared the lesson he had learned about European life: that the failure of revolutions indicated a general moral decline of the Western ideals he had cherished. As a result, he now believed Russia to be far more vigorous than any European nation.

In 1852, Herzen moved to London; his dissatisfaction with life on the European continent had been compounded by his wife's flagrant affair with the German revolutionary poet Georg Herwegh. Herzen's marital problems were still unresolved when, shortly after his move to England, his wife, mother, and son died within a period of several weeks. More than ever, Herzen needed a major project. He began writing his memoirs and used his inheritance to develop the first Russian free press abroad. Initially Herzen utilized the press in his appeal for the emancipation of the serfs and for fostering the spread of socialism. His first journal, *Polyarnaya Zvezda (The Polar Star)*, was devoted to Russian reform; in 1857, Herzen founded *Kolokol (The Bell)*, a weekly newspaper that became a primary political force in Russia even though it had to be smuggled into the country. Herzen's Russian success is thought to be due to his political tact. Though he refused to surrender his socialist tenets, he was willing to accept a monarchy if its intentions for reform seemed well founded. His office became well known and attracted a number of famous visitors, including Ivan Turgenev, Leo Tolstoy, and Thomas Carlyle. Dedicated to "the liberation of Russia," *The Bell* is now considered a major impetus in the liberation of the serfs in 1861. However, the journal's popularity waned after the failure of the Polish-Russian uprising of 1863. Herzen's pro-Polish position alienated more conservative followers and appeared outmoded to such younger radicals as Nikolai Chernyshevsky and Dmitri Pisarev, who felt that more violent measures were needed in order to bring about social change in Russia. Herzen moved to Geneva, where he sporadically published issues of *The Bell*, but the journal's reputation had irreparably declined, his followers continued to dwindle, and in 1868, *The Bell* ceased publication. Two years later, Herzen died of pneumonia after attending a political rally.

In the twentieth century, Herzen is remembered as a major political thinker. He has been championed by the Russians, whose political system ironically contradicts the very concepts Herzen espoused. Unlike his radical contemporaries, Herzen is primarily known for his judiciousness and fairness towards his opponents; most critics agree that he lacked the ruthlessness to be an effective revolutionary. He disdained the existing Russian social and political system and was one of the first to suggest a system of agrarian socialism based on the preservation of individual liberty. Inspired by these beliefs, his political writings endure as theoretical revolutionary documents. Of all Herzen's works, *My Past and Thoughts*—the memoirs that chronicle his philosophical and personal development—is considered his masterpiece. Shaped like a novel, *My Past and Thoughts* eloquently combines political discourse with personal anecdotes to detail Herzen's coming of age under the reign of

Nicholas I and his observations of the 1850s. Since its publication, commentators have consistently praised the memoirs as one of the great works of nineteenth-century Russian literature. Today, *My Past and Thoughts* is regarded as the most accurate and evocative portrait of Russian social and cultural history in the first half of the nineteenth century.

## PRINCIPAL WORKS

*Kto vinovat* [as Iskander]  (novel)  1847
   [*Who Is to Blame?*, 1978]
*\*Vom andern Ufer*  (essays)  1850
   [*From the Other Shore*, 1956]
*Le peuple russe et le socialisme*  (letter)  1852
   [*The Russian People and Their Socialism*, 1855]
*Byloye i dumy*  (memoirs)  1854
   [*Memoirs of Alexander Herzen* (partial translation), 1923;
      also published as *My Past and Thoughts*. 6 vols.,
      1924-27]
*Polnoe sobranie sochinenii*. 22 vols.  (novel, short stories,
      essays, and memoirs)  1919-25
*Selected Philosophical Works*  (essays)  1956

*This work was also published as *S togo berega* in 1855.

---

### V. G. BELINSKY  (essay date 1847)

[*Belinski is considered one of the most influential Russian literary critics of the nineteenth century. He initiated a new trend in critical thought by combining literary appreciation with an exposition of progressive philosophical and literary theory. His memorable contributions to Russian literature were produced during the latter part of his career when, as chief critic for the progressive review* Otechestvennye Zapiski (Notes of the Fatherland) *and later the noted liberal journal* Sovremenik (The Contemporary), *he embraced a form of humanitarian socialism and became the primary spokesman in the Russian intelligentsia's campaign against serfdom, autocracy, and orthodox religion. In the following excerpt from an essay that originally appeared in* The Contemporary *in 1847, Belinski analyzes* Who Is to Blame? *and praises its faithful depiction of society and sensitive portrayal of humanity.* Who Is to Blame?, *according to Belinski, consists of "a series of biographies" linked by the idea of "suffering, pain at the sight of unrecognized human dignity."*]

To regard the author of *Who Is To Blame?* as an uncommon artist signifies an utter failure to understand his talent. True, he possesses to a remarkable degree the ability of rendering a faithful picture of reality; his sketches are definite and clearcut, his pictures are vivid and immediately catch the eye. But these very qualities prove that his forte lies not in creativeness or artistic treatment, but in thought, profoundly cogitated, fully conscious, and developed thought. It is in the power of mind that the main strength of his talent lies; the artistic manner of faithfully portraying phenomena of actual life is a secondary, an auxiliary, force of his talent. Deprive him of the former, and the latter will prove incapable of original activity.

A talent of this kind is not something special, exceptional or fortuitous. No, such talents are just as natural as talents that are purely artistic. Their activities form a special sphere of art, in which imagination stands in the background and mind in the foreground. (p. 36)

What is the cherished idea of Iskander that serves as the source of his inspiration and, in his faithful depiction of the facts of social life, sometimes raises him almost to the height of art? It is the idea of human dignity debased by prejudice and ignorance, debased by the injustice of man to his fellow men, or by his own voluntary distortion of himself. The hero of all Iskander's novels and stories, however many he may write, will always be one and the same—man as a general and generic concept, man in all the fullness of this word, in all the sanctity of its meaning. Iskander is pre-eminently a poet of *humanity*. That is why his novel abounds in characters, most of them portrayed in masterly fashion, but there is no hero, no heroine.

In the first part, after winning our interest in the Negrov couple, he presents Krutsifersky as the hero of the novel and Lyubonka as the heroine. The hero of the episode written to link both parts together is Beltov, but Beltov's mother and his Swiss tutor interest the reader perhaps more than does he himself. In the second part the heroes are Beltov and Krutsiferskaya, and it is only here that the underlying idea of the novel, at first so puzzling in the title *Who Is To Blame?*, fully unfolds itself. We must confess, however, that this idea least of all interests us in the novel, just as Beltov, the hero, is in our opinion the least convincing personage of the whole novel. When Krutsifersky became Lyubonka's fiancé, Dr. Krupov said to him, "That girl is no match for you, say what you like—those eyes, that complexion, the tremor that sometimes passes over her face—*she's a tiger cub* that is not yet *conscious of its strength;* and you, what are you? You are the bride; you, brother, are like a German woman; you will be the wife—and that won't do." These words contain the plot of the novel, which, according to the author's intention, should have begun with the wedding instead of ending with it. (p. 38)

[In] the second part of the novel, Beltov's character is arbitrarily changed by the author. In the beginning, he was a man thirsting for useful activity and finding it nowhere, because of the wrong education the noble dreamer from Geneva had given him. Beltov knew a good deal and had a general conception of everything, but he was completely ignorant of the social milieu that was the only one in which he could make himself useful. All this is both said and shown by the author in masterly fashion. We think that the author might also have hinted at the nature of his hero, which was most unpractical and badly spoiled by wealth no less than by education. He who is born rich must be endowed by nature with a special propensity for some kind of activity if he is not to lead an idle life and be bored by inactivity. This propensity is not at all to be seen in Beltov's nature. His nature was extremely rich and versatile, but in this richness and versatility there was nothing that had deep roots. He was endowed with intellect, but an intellect that was contemplative and theoretical and not so much probed into things as glided over them. He was able to understand much, almost everything, but this very universality of sympathy and understanding prevents people like him from concentrating on one object and bending all their will to it. Such men have a constant urge for activity, endeavoring to find their path, but, of course, they do not find it.

Thus Beltov was doomed to languish in a craving for activity that was never satisfied, in a dejection born of inactivity. The author has given a masterly description of all his unsuccessful attempts to work in the civil service and later to become first a doctor, then an actor. If it cannot be said that he has fully depicted and explained this character, he has nevertheless given us a well-drawn, intelligible, and natural picture of the man.

In the last part of the novel, however, Beltov suddenly appears before us as a sort of superior nature, a genius, to whom life does not furnish a worthy career. This is quite a different man from the one whose acquaintance we had already made; this is no longer Beltov but something in the nature of [Lermontov's] Pechorin. Needless to say, the former Beltov was much better, like any man who plays his own role. The resemblance to Pechorin is decidedly not in his favor. We cannot understand why the author had to leave his own path and follow another! (pp. 39-40)

Krutsiferskaya, for her part, is of far more interest in the first part of the novel than in the last. It cannot be said that her character there was sharply drawn, but then her position in Negrov's house was sharply drawn. There she is a convincing figure, despite her silence and absence of any activity. The reader senses her although he hardly hears a single word from her. In describing her position the author has displayed an unusual mastery. It is only in passages from her diary that he makes her speak. We are, however, not entirely satisfied with this confession. Apart from the fact that the device of acquainting the reader with the heroines of novels through their diaries is out-of-date, worn threadbare and false, Lyubonka's diary entries smack somewhat of the spurious; at all events not everybody will believe that they were written by a woman. . . . Evidently here, too, the author has strayed beyond the limits of his talent. (p. 40)

Strictly speaking, *Who Is To Blame?* is not really a novel, but a series of biographies, written in masterly fashion and cleverly linked together externally into one whole through the medium of that idea which the author failed to develop poetically. But these biographies also contain an internal link, although the latter has nothing to do with the tragic love of Beltov and Krutsiferskaya. It is the idea that lay deep at their roots, breathed life and soul into each feature, each word of the story, that gave it the convincingness and interest that have the same irresistible appeal both to readers that sympathize and readers that do not sympathize with the author, to the educated and the uneducated alike. This idea manifests itself with the author as a sentiment, a passion; in brief his novel shows it to form the pathos of his life as well as of his novel. Whatever he speaks of, into whatever digressions he is drawn, he never forgets it, continually returns to it, and it seems involuntarily to speak for itself. This idea has become welded with his talent; herein lies his strength; if he cooled toward it, rejected it, he would instantly lose his talent.

What is this idea? It is suffering, pain at the sight of unrecognized human dignity, spurned with malice aforethought and still more without it. . . . (pp. 41-2)

It is this feeling of humanity that constitutes, so to say, the soul of Iskander's works. He is its proponent, its advocate. The characters he brings onto the stage are not ill-natured people—most of them are even good people, who torment and persecute themselves and others more often with good intentions rather than bad, more from ignorance than from malice. Even those of his personages whose feelings and odious acts repel us are shown by the author more as victims of their own ignorance and the environment in which they live than of their ill-nature. He describes crimes that are not challenged by existing laws and are qualified by most people as rational and moral behavior. He has few villains; in the three stories so far published it is only in the *Thieving Magpie* that a villain is depicted, but the kind of villain whom even today many would be prepared to consider a most virtuous and moral person.

Iskander's chief weapon, one that he wields with such amazing mastery, is irony frequently becoming sarcasm, but more often expressed with a light grace and most good-natured humor. Remember the kindhearted postmaster, who on two occasions very nearly killed Beltova, first with grief and then with joy, and who so good-naturedly rubbed his hands in anticipation of the surprise he was about to spring, that "there is not in the world a heart so cruel as could reproach him for this joke, and would not invite him to take a snack." Yet, even in this trait, in no way reprehensible, but only amusing, the author remains true to his cherished idea. Everything in the novel *Who Is To Blame?* that pertains to this idea is distinguished by its fidelity to actual life and a skill of exposition that is above all praise. It is here, and not in the love of Beltov and Krutsiferskaya, that the novel's brilliance and the triumph of the author's talent lie.

We have said above that this novel is a series of biographies linked together by a single idea, but infinitely varied, profoundly truthful, and rich in philosophical significance. Here the author is fully in his element. What is there better in that very part of the novel dealing with the tragic love of Beltov and Krutsiferskaya than the biography of the most worthy Karp Kondratich, his lively spouse, and their poor daughter Varvara Karpovna, called Vava for short—a biography included in the book as a mere episode? When are Krutsifersky and Lyubonka interesting in the novel? When they live in the Negrov house and suffer from their surroundings. Such situations lend themselves to the author's talent, and he displays unusual mastery in depicting them. When is Beltov himself of interest? When we read the history of his perverted and improper education, and then the history of his abortive attempts to find his way in life. This too is within the scope of the author's talent.

The author is pre-eminently a philosopher and a little of a poet besides, and he has availed himself of this to expound his concepts of life in the form of parables. This is best proved by his splendid story, *From the Work of Dr. Krupov "On Mental Ailments in General and Their Epidemic Development in Particular."* Here the author has not, by a single trait or word, overstepped the bounds of his talent, and hence his talent here is more clearly in evidence than in his other works. His idea is the same, but here it has assumed exclusively a tone of irony, for some, very gay and amusing, and for others, sad and painful; and only in the depiction of the squint-eyed Lyovka, a figure that would do honor to any artist, does the author speak seriously. In conception and execution this is positively the best work that appeared last year, although it did not make any particular impression on the public. However, the public is right in this case: in the novel *Who Is To Blame?* and certain works by other writers it found more intimate and hence more necessary and useful truths for itself, and the latter work has the same spirit and substance as the former.

In general, to reproach the author for being one-sided would mean not understanding him at all. He can represent faithfully only the world that comes within the range of his cherished idea; his splendid sketches are based on an innate power of observation and on the study of certain aspects of actual life. A receptive and impressionable nature, the author has preserved in his memory many images that had struck his imagination as far back as in his childhood. It is not difficult to understand that the characters he draws are not the sheer creatures of imagination, but rather skillfully finished, and sometimes even completely remodeled, materials taken wholly from reality. Have we not already said that the author is more of a philosopher and only a little of a poet? . . . (pp. 44-5)

V. G. Belinsky, "A Survey of Russian Literature in 1847: Part Two," in Belinsky, Chernyshevsky, and Dobrolyubov: Selected Criticism, edited by Ralph E. Matlaw, E. P. Dutton & Co., Inc., 1962, pp. 33-82.

**ALEXANDER HERZEN** (letter date 1849)

[*The following excerpt from a letter by Herzen is taken from his introduction to the Russian text of* From the Other Shore. *Written from Europe during a period of great social revolution, the essay expresses his sorrow at leaving his friends and explains his reasons for staying in Europe.*]

Do not, I beg you, make a mistake: it is not happiness, not distraction, not rest, not even personal safety that I have found here; indeed, I do not know who could find in Europe to-day happiness or rest, rest in the midst of an earthquake, happiness in the midst of a desperate struggle.

You saw sadness expressed in every line of my letters; life here is very hard, venomous malignity mingles with love, bile with tears, feverish anxiety infects the whole organism, the time of former illusions and hopes has passed. I believe in nothing here, except in a handful of people, a few ideas, and the fact that one cannot arrest movement; I see the inevitable doom of old Europe and feel no pity for anything that now exists, neither the peaks of its culture nor its institutions. . . . I love nothing in this world except that which it persecutes, I respect nothing except that which it kills—and I stay . . . stay to suffer doubly, to suffer my own personal anguish and that of this world; which will perish, perhaps, to the sound of thunder and destruction towards which it is racing at full steam. . . . Why then do I stay?

I stay because the struggle is *here,* because despite the blood and tears it is here that social problems are being decided, because it is here that suffering is painful, sharp, but *articulate.* The struggle is open, no one hides. Woe to the vanquished, but they are not vanquished without a struggle, nor deprived of speech before they can utter a word; the violence inflicted is great, but the protest is loud; the fighters often march to the galleys, chained hand and foot, but with heads uplifted, with free speech. Where the word has not perished, neither has the deed. For the sake of this open struggle, for this free speech, this right to be heard—I stay here; for its sake I give up everything; I give up you for it, a portion of my heritage and perhaps shall give my life in the ranks of an energetic minority of 'the persecuted but undefeated'.

For the sake of this freedom of speech, I have broken, or, better still, suppressed for a while my ties of blood with the people in whom I found so much response both to the bright and to the dark side of my soul, whose song and speech are my song and speech, and I stay among a people in whose life I am in deep sympathy only with the bitter tears of the proletariat and the desperate courage of its friends.

This decision has cost me dear . . . you know me . . . and you will believe me. I have stifled the inner pain; I have lived through the painful struggle and I have made my decision, not like an angry youth, but like a man who has thought over what he is doing . . . how much he has to lose . . . for months I have been calculating and pondering and vacillating, and have finally sacrificed everything to:

Human Dignity and Free Speech

The consequences are no affair of mine; they are not in my power, they are rather in the power of some arbitrary whim which has gone so far as to draw a capricious circle not only round our words but round our very steps. It was in my power not to obey—and I did not obey.

To obey against one's convictions when there is a possibility of not obeying—is immoral. Passive obedience becomes almost impossible. I have witnessed two upheavals, I have lived too long as a free man to allow myself to be chained again; I have lived through popular disturbances, I have become accustomed to free speech and I cannot accept serfdom again, not even for the sake of suffering with you. If it had been necessary to restrain oneself for the common cause, perhaps one might have found the strength to do so; but where at this moment is our common cause? At home you have no soil on which a free man can stand. How after this can you summon us? . . . If it were to battle—yes, then we would come: but to obscure martyrdom, to sterile silence, to obedience—no, under no circumstances. Demand anything of me, but do not demand duplicity, do not force me again to play at being a loyal subject; respect the free man in me.

The liberty of the individual is the greatest thing of all, it is *on this and on this alone* that the true will of the people can develop. Man must respect liberty in himself, and he must esteem it in himself no less than in his neighbour, than in the entire nation. If you are convinced of that, then you will agree that to remain here is my right, my duty; it is the only protest that an individual can make amongst us; he must offer up this sacrifice to his human dignity. If you call my withdrawal an escape and will forgive me only out of your love, this will mean that you yourselves are not wholly free. (pp. 9-12)

> *Alexander Herzen, in a letter to an unknown recipient on March 1, 1849, in* From the Other Shore *by Alexander Herzen, translated by Moura Budberg and* The Russian People and Socialism *by Alexander Herzen, translated by Richard Wollheim, 1956. Reprint by Oxford University Press, 1979, pp. 9-17.*

## T. CARLYLE (letter date 1855)

[*A noted nineteenth-century essayist, historian, critic, and social commentator, Carlyle was a central figure of the Victorian age. In his writings, Carlyle advocated a Christian work ethic and stressed the importance of order, piety, and spiritual fulfillment. Known to his contemporaries as the "Sage of Chelsea," Carlyle exerted a powerful moral influence in an era of rapidly shifting values. He met Herzen in England, and they corresponded sporadically. In the following excerpt from one of his letters, Carlyle responds to Herzen's proposed revolutionary ideas and comments that the Russians, more than any other people, possess "the talent of obeying."*]

I have read your eloquent Discourse on Russian revolutionary matters [*On the Development of Revolutionary Ideas in Russia*]; which manifests a potent spirit, and high talent, in various respects; and in which, especially, there is a tone of tragic earnestness not to be mistaken by the reader, nor to be judged lightly by him, whatever he may think of your program and prophecy as to Russia and the world.

For my own share I confess I never had, and have now (if it were possible) less than ever, the least hope in "Universal Suffrage" under any of its modifications: and, if it were not that in certain deadly maladies of the body politic, a burning crisis may be considered as beneficent, I should much prefer Tzarism itself, or Grand-Turkism itself, to the sheer Anarchy (as I reckon it sadly to be) which is got by "Parliamentary

Eloquence," Free Press, and counting of heads. . . . In your vast country,—which I have always respected as a huge dark "Birth of Providence," the meanings of which are not yet known,—there is evident, down to this time, one talent in which it has the pre-eminence, giving it potency far beyond any other Nation: the talent (indispensable to all Nations and all creatures, and inexorably required of them all, under penalties), *the talent of obeying*,—which is much out of vogue in other quarters just now! And I never doubt, or can doubt, but the want of *it* will be amerced to the last due farthing, sooner or later; and bring about huge bankruptcies, wherever persevered in. Such is my sad creed in these revolutionary times. (pp. 371-72)

> *T. Carlyle, in a letter to Alexander Herzen on April 13, 1855, in* The Romantic Exiles: A Nineteenth-Century Portrait Gallery *by Edward Hallett Carr, Frederick A. Stokes Company, 1933, pp. 371-72.*

## L. TOLSTOY (letter date 1861)

[*Tolstoy is regarded as one of the greatest novelists in the history of world literature. His* Voina i mir (War and Peace) *and* Anna Karenina *are considered all-encompassing documents of human existence and supreme examples of the realistic novel. Tolstoy admired Herzen's writing and corresponded with him extensively. In the following excerpt, Tolstoy contends that much of what Herzen writes is directed towards the intellectually gifted and courageous instead of the average citizen, arguing that most Russians are unable to comprehend the possibility of freedom.*]

I was going to write to you about *The Polar Star*, which I've only just finished reading properly. The whole volume is splendid, and that's not just my opinion, but the opinion of everyone I've seen. You keep saying, 'Give me a polemic.' What sort of polemic? . . . There are a lot of people and 99 Russians out of 100, who will be too afraid to trust your ideas (and let it be said in brackets that it's very easy for them, thanks to the tone of your article which is too flippant. You seem to be addressing yourself only to people who are clever and brave). These people, i.e. the ones who aren't clever and brave, will say that it's better to keep silent if you've reached these results—i.e. that such a result indicates that the path was wrong. And you give them some right to say this by the fact that in place of their shattered idols you put life itself, arbitrariness, or the pattern of life as you say. In place of tremendous hopes of immortality, everlasting perfection, historical laws etc., this pattern is nothing at all—a button in place of a colossus. So it would have been better not to give them this right, to have put nothing in their place—nothing except the force which overthrew the colossi.

Moreover, these people—the timid ones—can't understand that the ice cracking and breaking under their feet proves that man is advancing and that the only way not to fall in is to go on without stopping.

You say I don't know Russia. No, I know my own subjective Russia which I look at through my little prism. If the soap bubble of history has burst for you and me, this is also proof that we're blowing a new bubble which we can't yet see. And for me this bubble is the clear and sure knowledge of my Russia. . . . We practical people can't live without this. (pp. 144-45)

> *L. Tolstoy, in a letter to A. I. Herzen on March 26, 1861, in his* Tolstoy's Letters: 1828-1879, Vol. I,

*edited and translated by R. F. Christian, Charles Scribner's Sons, 1978, pp. 144-45.*

## IVAN TURGENEV   (letter date 1862)

*[Turgenev, a Russian novelist, dramatist, poet, and essayist, was greatly influenced by the literature, culture, and politics of Western Europe and promoted their acceptance in Russia. He was also a contemporary of Herzen, and the two corresponded frequently. In the following excerpt, Turgenev charged that Herzen's philosophical development is becoming clouded, that he is "whirling around in a fog." For additional commentary by Turgenev, see excerpts below, 1862 and 1876.]*

[You have] a German method of thinking; so do the Slavophiles. You are abstracting, from the barely intelligible and comprehensible substance of the people, the principles upon which you propose they construct their life. You are whirling around in a fog. What is most important is that essentially *you are repudiating revolution* because the people whom you kneel before are conservative *par excellence*. The people carry within themselves the embryos of just such a bourgeoisie [as you have depicted]; it is in their coats of tanned sheepskin, their warm and filthy huts, their bellies stuffed to the point of heartburn, and their aversion to every civic responsibility and independent action. All this goes far beyond the traits to which you have referred in your letters to characterize the western bourgeoisie accurately and faithfully. (p. 141)

*Ivan Turgenev, in a letter to Aleksandr Ivanovich Herzen on October 8, 1862, in his* Turgenev's Letters: A Selection, *edited by Edgar H. Lehrman, Alfred A. Knopf, 1961, pp. 140-42.*

## IVAN TURGENEV   (letter date 1862)

*[Here, Turgenev cautions Herzen against his zealous condemnation of contemporary European culture and argues that his new beliefs seem to contradict his earlier philosophies. For additional commentary by Turgenev, see excerpts above, 1862, and below, 1876.]*

The present letter has been evoked by your last letter to me in the *Kolokol.* . . . You diagnose contemporary mankind with unusual subtlety and sensitivity, but why on earth must this be *Western* man and not *bipèdes* in general? You are just like a physician who, having examined all the symptoms of a chronic illness, declares that the whole trouble comes from the patient's being a Frenchman.

An enemy of mysticism and absolutism, you bow down mystically before the Russian sheepskin coat, and see in it the grace, novelty, and originality of future social forms—*das Absolute*—in a word, the very same *Absolute* at which you jeer in philosophy. All your idols are smashed, but a man cannot live without an idol, so let an altar be erected to the new and unknown god (inasmuch as almost nothing is known about him), and you will be able again to pray, to believe, and to wait. The god does the complete opposite of what you are expecting from him; you think this is temporary, accidental, and forcibly grafted on to him by external power. Your god loves, to the point of adoration, what you hate and he hates what you love; he accepts just what you reject in his name; you turn your eyes aside, close your ears, and, with the ecstasy peculiar to all skeptics who have grown tired of skepticism—with that specific, ultra-fanatic ecstasy—you keep talking about "vernal freshness, beneficial tempests," etc. History, philol-

ogy, and statistics are nothing to you; facts are nothing to you even though, for example, it is undeniable that we Russians, both by language and by nature, belong to the European family—the *genus Europaeum*—and, consequently, by the most immutable delvings of physiology, must take the same road. I have never yet heard of a *duck*, belonging to the family of *ducks*, that breathed with gills like a fish. And meantime, because of your mental illness, your weariness, your thirst to place a fresh crystal of snow on a withered tongue, you attack everything that should be dear to every European, and therefore to us, too—civilization, legality, finally revolution itself. And, having filled young heads with your social and Slavophile home-brewed and unfermented beer, you allow [these] intoxicated and befogged [people] into a world where they will stumble at their first step. I do not doubt that you will do all this in good faith, honestly, and sorrowfully, with heated and sincere self-denial . . . but this does not help. [Do] one of two things: either serve revolution and European ideals as you did before, or—if you have reached the conclusion that they are worthless—have the spirit and the courage to look the devil in the eye, and say [you are] *guilty to all European mankind*—and not with evident or implied exceptions in favor of a Russian Messiah who is expected at any moment, and in whom you really and personally believe as little as you do in the Hebrew one. You will say: that is frightening—one can lose both popularity and the chance to continue one's activities. I agree, but on the one hand, to act as you are acting now is also fruitless; on the other, I am assuming in spite of you that you have enough spiritual strength to accept the consequences of your saying what you consider to be the truth. We shall wait a while, but for now this is enough. (pp. 143-44)

*Ivan Turgenev, in a letter to Aleksandr Ivanovich Herzen on November 8, 1862, in his* Turgenev's Letters: A Selection, *edited by Edgar H. Lehrman, Alfred A. Knopf, 1961, pp. 143-44.*

## FRIEDRICH NIETZSCHE   (letter date 1872)

*[Nietzsche is considered one of the most important philosophers of the nineteenth and twentieth centuries. His thought has influenced nearly every aspect of modern culture. Among his many achievements, he is acknowledged as a forerunner of existentialism, the first philosopher to recognize nihilism as a historical phenomenon, and an important psychological theorist. In the following excerpt from a letter written to the German translator of* My Past and Thoughts, *Nietzsche praises Herzen's memoirs, and calls him a "nobly fiery and persistent soul."]*

I was astonished at the aptness and vigor of expression [in Herzen's memoirs], and, tending to assume that Herzen possessed every distinctive talent, I had tacitly supposed that he had translated his memoirs from Russian into German himself. I have drawn my friends' attention to this work; from it I have learned to think about a number of negative tendencies much more sympathetically than I could until now—and I would not even call them negative. For such a nobly fiery and persistent soul could not nourish itself on negation and hatred alone. (p. 99)

*Friedrich Nietzsche, in a letter to Malwida von Meysenbug on August 27, 1872, in his* Selected Letters of Friedrich Nietzsche, *edited and translated by Christopher Middleton, The University of Chicago Press, 1969, pp. 98-9.*

**F. M. DOSTOIEVSKY   (journal date 1873)**

[*One of Russia's best-known novelists, Dostoevski is considered one of the most outstanding and influential writers of modern literature. His greatness as a fiction writer lies in the depth and range of his vision, his acute psychological insight, his profound philosophical thought, and his brilliant prose style. While best known for his novels* Prestuplenye i nakazanye (Crime and Punishment) *and* Brat'ya Karamazovy (The Brothers Karamazov), *his critical writings reveal his insight into the artistic process. In the following excerpt from his* Dvevnik Pisatelya (The Diary of a Writer), *Dostoevski indicates that Herzen was a paradoxical figure: he advocated revolution while embracing domestic tranquility and denied property while enjoying his own substantial inheritance.*]

On one occasion, conversing with the late Hertzen, I gave high praise to one of his books—*From the Other Shore*. . . . The book is written in the form of a dialogue between Hertzen and his opponent.

"And what I like most," I remarked . . . , "is the fact that your opponent is also very clever. You must concede that many a time he has pinned you to the wall."

"Why, that is the whole trick," said Hertzen, laughing. (p. 4)

[Hertzen] was a product of our noble class—a *gentilhomme russe et citoyen du monde* above all—a type which developed in Russia, and which could have sprung up nowhere but in Russia. Hertzen did not emigrate; he did not begin Russian emigration;—no, he was already born an emigrant. They all, akin to him, were ready-born emigrants, even though the majority of them never left Russia. During the hundred and fifty years of the preceding life of the Russian nobility, with very few exceptions, the last roots had rotted, the last ties with Russian soil and Russian truth had disintegrated. History itself, as it were, predestined Hertzen to embody, in a most vivid type, this rupture of the overwhelming majority of our educated class with the people. In this sense it is an historical type. (p. 5)

Hertzen had to become a socialist, and precisely after the fashion of a nobleman's son, that is, with neither need nor aim, but merely as a result of "the logical flux of ideas" and the heart-emptiness at home. He renounced the foundations of the former society; he denied family, and, it seems, was a good father and husband. He denied property, but at the same time he managed to arrange his affairs, and abroad he experienced with pleasure his financial independence. He engineered revolutions and incited other people to participate in them, and at the same time he loved comfort and family peace. He was an artist, a thinker, a brilliant writer, an extraordinarily well-read man, a wit, a wonderful conversationalist (he spoke even better than he wrote), and an excellent reflector. The reflex—the faculty of turning a most profound personal sentiment into an object which he set before himself, which he would worship and which, a minute later, he would ridicule—that faculty was highly developed in him.

Unquestionably, this was an unusual man, but whatever he may have been—whether he wrote his memoirs or published a magazine in collaboration with Proudhon; whether, in Paris, he mounted a barricade (which he so comically described in his reminiscences); whether he suffered, or felt happy, or was afflicted with doubts; whether, as in 1863, to please the Poles, he sent his proclamation to Russian revolutionists in Russia, even though he did not trust the Poles, and realized that they had deceived him, and knew that his appeal doomed hundreds

of these unfortunate young men; whether, with astounding naïveté he confessed to these things in one of his subsequent articles, failing to perceive in what light he had placed himself by such an avowal—invariably, everywhere and all his life, he was above all a *gentilhomme russe et citoyen du monde*, a mere product of former servitude which he hated and from which he descended, not only from his father, but precisely as a result of the severance with his native land and its ideals. (pp. 5-6)

> *F. M. Dostoievsky, in a journal entry of 1873, in his* The Diary of a Writer, *Vol. I, edited and translated by Boris Brasol, George Braziller, 1954, pp. 1-156.**

**IVAN TURGENEV   (letter date 1876)**

[*In the following excerpt, Turgenev describes his emotional response to* My Past and Thoughts. *For additional commentary by Turgenev, see excerpts above, 1862.*]

All these days I have been living with my impressions of the part of Herzen's manuscript for *Byloe i Dumy* in which he narrates the story of his wife, her death, etc. It was all written with tears and blood; it flames and burns. I am sorry that it cannot be published. He was the only Russian who could write like that. . . . (p. 284)

> *Ivan Turgenev, in a letter to Mikhail Evgrafovich Saltykov-Shchedrin on January 19, 1876, in his* Turgenev's Letters: A Selection, *edited by Edgar H. Lehrman, Alfred A. Knopf, 1961, p. 284.*

**K. WALISZEWSKI   (essay date 1900)**

[*Waliszewski praises* Letters on the Study of Nature *and* Who Is to Blame? *as skillfully delineated chronicles of intellectual development. However, he considers both inferior to* From the Other Shore, *which he terms "paradoxical" and "brilliant."*]

[*Letters on the Study of Nature*] contain a brilliant exposition of every philosophical system down to, and including, that of Bacon, together with a searching criticism of these systems from the point of view of contemporary knowledge. The work is interesting, but incomplete. Herzen's intention, no doubt, had been to develop his own cosmic ideas on this foundation, but other interests turned him from the undertaking. In *Whose Fault?* [*Who Is to Blame?*] we find, under the name of Beltov, the eternal "superfluous man," very much puzzled what to do with himself, until he meets with Liouba, who, by teaching him what love means, acquaints him with the secret of his destiny, but who is herself unfortunately bound to his friend Krouciferski. The struggle of emotions arising out of this situation is intended to indicate that the society producing it is badly constituted and needs a process of reconstruction. All the fault lies there. It is a work of social physiology and pathology, composed with extreme skill, and holds a position of capital importance in the history of the intellectual progress of that epoch. That personal and revolutionary fashion of regarding family and social relations, which Tolstoï was to make peculiarly his own, is already clearly indicated in its pages. From the aesthetic point of view, and in spite of the fact that the moral physiognomy of the little world of which it treats has been searchingly investigated by the author, the work has less value. The figure of Liouba, strongly marked out in the style of George Sand, is dry in drawing and poor in colour. Herzen shows himself less the painter than the surgeon, handling his instruments with impassive skill. The book owed the impression it made chiefly to the picture drawn in its earlier pages of the patriarchal life of ancient Russia, in its least honourable peculiarities, thanks to which Liouba, who is a natural daughter, and her mother, are both treated as *pariahs* in the house of Negrov.

Herzen was to do better work than this. . . . [*From the Other Shore,* a] collection of epistles and dissertations, composed under the combined influence of the revolutionary notions of the time, and of the doctrines of the Slavophil party, proclaimed, in somewhat audacious fashion, the near and inevitable end of the political and social organisation of the old European, Christian, and feudal world, and its regeneration by the agency of the Russian Community. Nothing else so paradoxical and so brilliant occurs in the revolutionary literature of the period. (pp. 302-04)

[Herzen's] character and his intellectual powers have been the subject of very contradictory judgments. His compatriots have taken him, at one time and another, to be either Hamlet or Don Quixote,—an idealist or a realist. . . . Herzen was, above all things, an exceedingly personal writer, very impressionable, and very apt to change his impressions. One only has been durable and dominant with him,—a deep love of his country, of his country's spirit, of its manner of existence and its methods of thought, joined with a profound feeling of sadness, the reason for which will be easily guessed. (p. 308)

> K. Waliszewski, ''The Controversialists—Herzen and Chtchédrine,'' in his A History of Russian Literature, 1900. Reprint by Kennikat Press, 1969, pp. 299-329.*

### PRINCE KROPOTKIN (lecture date 1901)

[*Kropotkin was a Russian sociologist, philosopher, geographer, essayist, and critic. Born of an aristocratic family, Kropotkin became an anarchist in the 1870s and later fled to Europe, where he composed several of his best-known works. Chief among these is his* Memoirs of a Revolutionist, *which is considered a monumental autobiographical treatment of the revolutionary movement in Russia. Kropotkin also composed several literary histories, including* Russian Literature, *which was drawn from a series of lectures he gave in the United States in the early 1900s. Here, Kropotkin assesses Herzen's career and focuses on his memoirs,* My Past and Thoughts, *which he considers ''one of the best pieces of poetical literature in any language.'' The following excerpt is taken from a lecture delivered by Kropotkin in March, 1901.*]

[Hérzen] felt a deep despair as regards Western civilisation altogether, and expressed it in most moving pages, in his book *From the other Shore.* It is a cry of despair—the cry of a prophetic politician in the voice of a great poet. (p. 273)

Apart from the historical value of [his memoirs *Past Facts and Thoughts*]—Hérzen knew all the historical personages of his time—they certainly are one of the best pieces of poetical literature in any language. The descriptions of men and events which they contain, beginning with Russia in the forties and ending with the years of exile, reveal at every step an extraordinary, philosophical intelligence; a profoundly sarcastic mind, combined with a great deal of good-natured humour; a deep hatred of oppressors and a deep personal love for the simplehearted heroes of human emancipation. At the same time these memoirs contain such fine, poetical scenes from the author's personal life, as his love of Nathalie—later his wife—or such deeply impressive chapters as *Oceano Nox,* where he tells about the loss of his son and mother. One chapter of these memoirs remains still unpublished, and from what Turguéneff told me

about it, it must be of the highest beauty. ''No one has ever written like him,'' Turguéneff said: ''it is all written in tears and blood'' [see excerpt above, 1876]. (pp. 273-74)

The works of Hérzen, even now, are not allowed to be circulated in Russia, and they are not sufficiently known to the younger generation. It is certain, however, that when the time comes for them to be read again Russians will discover in Hérzen a very profound thinker, whose sympathies were entirely with the working classes, who understood the forms of human development in all their complexity, and who wrote in a style of unequalled beauty—the best proof that his ideas had been thought out in detail and under a variety of aspects.

Before he had emigrated and founded a free press at London, Hérzen had written in Russian reviews under the name of Iskander, treating various subjects, such as Western politics, socialism, the philosophy of natural sciences, art, and so on. He also wrote a novel, *Whose Fault is it?* which is often spoken of in the history of the development of intellectual types in Russia. The hero of this novel, Béltoff, is a direct descendant from Lérmontoff's Petchórin, and occupies an intermediate position between him and the heroes of Turguéneff. (p. 275)

> Prince Kropotkin, ''Political Literature, Satire, Art-Criticism, Contemporary Novelists,'' in his Ideals and Realities in Russian Literature, Afred A. Knopf, 1915, pp. 263-318.*

### YULY AIKHENVALD (essay date 1913)

[*Aikhenvald, a Russian critic of the early twentieth century, provides a general appreciation of Herzen. While Aikhenvald calls Herzen an ''unmarshaled genius'' and a brilliant poet, historian, politician, and artist, the critic concludes that Herzen lacked focus and depth since he failed to create an original philosophy. The following is drawn from Vol. I of Aikhenvald's* Silučty russkikh pisatelel, *published in 1913.*]

Herzen belongs equally to Russian history and the Russian word. He is at one and the same time a doer and an observer, a politician and a poet. He was a participant in European events, and yet he did not lose the sense of lyricism and Romanticism which had been bequeathed to him by his Moscow circles. From the mountain heights of his social concern he would regularly return to himself, to the intimate life of his own heart. Politics did not reduce or dissipate him. He was never false to his own nature. A convinced Socialist, he did not cease to be an individualist, and he raised himself high over this apparent contradiction, not only in the sense that he went far beyond the constraining limits of a fixed doctrine, but also, and mainly, that the spiritual breadth of his own personality took precedence over any theories.

An ambassador-exile from Russia, a European who preached Russian Messianism, Herzen continued the tradition which had been begun by [Nikolai Karamzin's] *Letters of a Russian Traveler,* and perhaps that is why he cites Karamzin with sympathy so frequently. But everything that is superficial in Karamzin goes much deeper in Herzen, and he earned the right more than anyone to be a representative of his native land on foreign soil. This was precisely the role that suited him. He merged two worlds and overcame all boundaries, because from his youngest days culture had flowed into the thirsty and deep riverbed of his consciousness in rich waves. He was organically bound to be a European far and beyond Europe.

Herzen was never in any way provincial. Everywhere he showed himself to be higher than his milieu, and it was only because his disenchantment with the West was so deep and real that Western values and European ideals could be so much fuller and more real in his spiritual country than they were in their own geographical setting. This is why, in a sense, when he crossed the Russian border he arrived home. And that is also why he fell into the very center of things there, the more so because by his very nature he was always centralist. He never found himself in a secondary situation, never lost his head, and in no drama was he ever an "extra".

Herzen's intellectual sea always shone with a phosphorescent light. On its surface there was no still and no swell—nor was there, for that matter, the depth, the calm and quiet majesty, and the modesty necessary for true philosophical discoveries. He possessed all the attributes of high dilettantism, of genius which has not taken firm shape and focus. One may reproach him for his intellectual dissipation. There is, however, a beauty and wisdom of its own in this type of human ability, in this Herzenesque sort of unmarshaled genius. The creator of *My Past and Thoughts* is the personification of talent, but of talent in general. Herzen is a category unto himself. Many-sided but not motleyed, touching upon everything while being nowhere superficial, he had no specialty whatsoever. (pp. 105-06)

Although he was disposed to pluralism and counted his suns in the dewdrops, Herzen nevertheless was not eclectic. All his life he returned to one and the same questions, in which he was deeply involved and to which he brought every mite of his intellect and pathos. The founder of *The Bell* was a tribune, but not a tribune to the end; he was also an artist, but not completely; he was a remarkable thinker, but he did not leave an original philosophy. (p. 106)

An artist, he occupied himself with publicistic work. He was a publicist who did not wish the destruction of previous culture and declared that "not only does one feel sorry for people, but one also feels sorry for things, and *for some things more than some people*." This aristocratic heritage of Herzen's did not interfere with his civic work, did not hide from his view the existence of political and social problems, many of which he resolved in an incisive manner. If some of his expectations, such as faith in the Russian commune, have not ... been justified by history, this does not reflect upon his intellect and his power of prophetic guesswork, and one should sooner fault history than Herzen. It is clear in any event that he was uncomfortable and constrained in the sphere of politics alone and had no desire to bind himself to politics with all the fibers of his soul, would not have known how to do this even had he wanted to.

In exactly the same way, he was not fully an artist. His taste sometimes deceived him and craftily diverted him from an artist's strict line. An artist, or almost an artist, Herzen, telling about himself, converted his sins and weaknesses into literature. He treated events and feelings in such a way that their actual roughness and coarseness vanished, and in his hands many things acquired a sort of generalized, exaggerated, and romantic air. Fate furnished his aestheticism with a sufficient number of striking effects—he experienced the deaths of so many others before he had to experience his own, he had so many stunning impressions in his mind's eye; and he employed this material in his renowned chronicle in virtuoso fashion. Literature helped him bring his intimate and family affairs into public view, and he was right to blend the personal with the general. Herzen fused them into one panorama. He made his

personal life the subject of great interest to strangers, and the story of his life has become an obligatory page in the objective history of Russia. (pp. 106-07)

*Yuly Aikhenvald, "Yuly Aikhenvald on Alexandr Herzen," in* The Complection of Russian Literature: A Cento, *edited and translated by Andrew Field, Atheneum, 1971, pp. 105-07.*

### THOMAS GARRIGUE MASARYK   (essay date 1913)

[*Masaryk discusses the development of Herzen's philosophy which, the critic contends, changed little during his lifetime because Herzen never reevaluated or advanced beyond Ludwig Feuerbach's doctrine of positivism. According to Masaryk, Herzen failed to develop a full understanding of socialism because he limited his study to French socialists while ignoring the Russian developments of his day. His criticisms of society were too general, Masaryk argues, and Herzen failed to attain his goal as an objective philosopher and scientist. Masaryk concludes that Beltov, from* Who Is to Blame?, *aptly depicts Herzen's friends and himself. The following originally appeared in 1913 in* Russland und Europa: Studien über die geistigen Strömungen in Russland.*]*

Herzen, though he passed through a mystical period, grew up amid the liberal traditions of the eighteenth-century philosophy of enlightenment and humanitarianism; he soon became a radical, an admirer of the decabrists, and above all of Pestel; in the middle of the forties, as we have learned, he separated from the liberals and adopted socialist views.

Herzen became acquainted with the writings of the French socialists and with those of Weitling and Owen before he had studied the works of Hegel, but it was the influence of Hegel and Feuerbach which revolutionised his outlook and made him a socialist. He wrote a brief sketch of socialism in Russia, representing the Petraševcy and Černyševskii as precursors of socialism. After 1848 he discarded French and European socialism as futile, but he continued to term himself a socialist and to look forward to the true social revolution. In "Kolokol," especially in the later issues, the socialist note is extremely prominent, being stressed in polemic against the younger revolutionists who were dissatisfied with Herzen.

Herzen speaks of his socialism as "Russian." It is agrarian socialism, the socialism of the mužik and of the artel. But he advocated in addition municipal socialism, political socialism, and district socialism. Thus was Herzenism distinguished from Marxism, which looks chiefly to workers and proletarians for its fulfilment. Herzen's "Russian" socialism often spoken of as "Russian" communism, is further distinguished from Marxism by this, that Herzen, though a materialist, did not teach economic materialism. His own account of Marx in London shows, moreover, that Marx and the Marxists were to him personally uncongenial. He sided with Bakunin against Marx, and when the first edition of Marx's magnum opus was published in 1867, Herzen paid scant attention to it.

His primary demand, as has been recorded above, was for brain equality. He knew that civilisation is impossible to the hungry, and he knew that the civilisation of the minority depends on the physical toil of the majority. From Louis Blanc and others he learned of the class struggle in Europe, and he himself levelled accusations against the "Manicheism of society," but he was definitely opposed to the class struggle. He insisted that the function of socialism was not merely to put an end "to anthropophagy" and especially to capitalism, but above all to annihilate everything monarchical and religious.

Herzen looked to socialism for a new philosophy, and it seemed to him that Saint-Simon and Fourier had uttered no more than the first lispings of the future philosophy.

His socialism was based upon a positivist and materialist outlook. Shortly before his death, in *The Physician, the Dying, and the Dead,* he censured the socialism of his contemporaries as being still a religion, that is to say illusion, and from socialism of this texture he expected nothing but a new blood-letting, and not the true act of liberation.

In his demand for brain equality Herzen is no communist extremist. He does not suggest the complete abolition of private property, and would content himself with its investment by society in a manner analogous with that of the Russian mir. But it is plain that Herzen detests the capitalists more than the great landlords, and his views concerning the Russian aristocracy are recorded above. Throughout, Herzen's socialism remained essentially philosophic. He was little concerned about economic questions, and in this domain Proudhon was his leading authority. (pp. 417-19)

If Christianity as monotheism be regarded as embodying the essence of monarchism, Herzen's socialism, as materialistic atheism, may be regarded as predominantly antimonarchism.

This antimonarchism has the folk-state as its ideal. Herzen has an especial loathing for political centralisation, returning to this again and again, and declaring from time to time that the Slav is by nature opposed to centralisation, to the state. The language resembles that of Konstantin Aksakov. Herzen was afraid of the cultured and hypercultured absolutist state; he dreaded "Genghis Khan with telegraphs, steamships, and railways, with Carnot and Monge on the staff, his soldiers armed with Minié rifles and Congreve rockets, and led by Batu Khan."

In the *Letters to an Old Comrade* the abolition of the state is presented as an ideal, and we are told that the majority must attain to its full mental stature, since this is an essential preliminary to the abolition of the state. Proudhon's federalism and anarchism likewise find reiterated expression.

After his spiritual return to the Russia of the slavophils Herzen contented himself with the liberation of the peasantry in 1861, in place of the great and definitive social revolution which in 1848 he had contrasted with all previous revolutions. Either despotism or social revolution, had been Herzen's cry in the forties. The events of 1848 were to him a proof that Europe was incompetent for the social revolution. But in 1861 Russia taught him that she was capable of carrying through this revolution successfully, and of doing so without bloodshed. We must not forget that Herzen himself worked energetically on behalf of the liberation of the peasantry, and that he endeavoured to win over the aristocratic landowners to the idea of liberation. Truthfully and in moving terms he showed them how the free lords were themselves degraded by the institution of serfdom, writing: "We are slaves because we are masters. We are servants because we are landowners. We are ourselves serfs because we keep our brothers in servitude, those brothers whose origin, whose blood, and whose language we share."

The Russian mir has become for him the "lightning conductor" of revolution; and the supreme value of the mir consists for him in this, that the mir is not an abstract theory of cultured socialists, but a practical institution prevailing among a huge population—a population of illiterates.

The contrast between Herzen's views after 1861 and the socialism of his earlier phase will now be plain. The goal for Russia is no longer a social revolution but a political revolution, and the social revolution has become merely means to an end. Herzen now demands for Russia all that Europe possesses, the things which to Europe (according to his previous view) had been valueless. He demands civilisation, culture, and a parliament. (pp. 419-20)

Herzen was ever somewhat inclined to regard the masses from the outlook of a superior person. In 1850, when he demanded a socialist folk-state, the realisation of this ideal was deferred to a remote future. After 1861, however, he talks of immediate realisation, speaks favourably of the masses, not of the mužiks alone, but also of European operatives; and he even gives the intelligentsia its congé. How and why is the intelligentsia to disappear? Is it because Rousseau passed sentence upon civilisation—or does Herzen foresee the immediate organisation of brain equality?

According to the plan of 1862 the tsar in his Monomach crown is not to vanish, provided only that the sun rises unaccompanied by blood-tinged clouds, and it is plain that Herzen could readily contemplate the retention of the tsar, seeing that he did not consider the tsar to be a monarch in the strict sense of the term.

But what is the drift of this criticism? It is that Herzen did not whole-heartedly believe in the Russian saviour, and was never able completely to overcome his own scepticism. The task he assigned to Russia was far too great for him to hope that the Russian mir would ever be able to achieve it in its entirety.

The kernel of his philosophy of history is as follows. The old world was perishing beyond hope of rescue. Christianity, which had renovated the Roman world, was in process of decomposition. . . . The reformation and the great revolution had been no more than temporary expedients. Just as the aging Rome had rejected Christianity, so now did the aging Christian world reject socialism.

No doubt Herzen was quite in earnest when to the decrepit and dying Europe he represented Russia as the saving new world. He endeavoured to show that Russia and socialism were one and the same, and he desired to communicate the belief to Europe. Such was the chief aim of the letters he wrote in 1854, *The Old World and Russia.* But Herzen would not have been Herzen had he failed to recognise that the historico-philosophical analogy between socialism and Christianity was not convincing, and was the less convincing since, generally speaking, socialism was for him above all a new outlook. Were the Russian mir and the Orthodox mužik to constitute the new world, to embody the new doctrine? As early as the beginning of the thirties Herzen had made acquaintance with the works of Saint-Simon and with the attempts of the Saint-Simonian school to secure a new socialistic outlook; somewhat later Owen and the "new Christianity" came under his notice, and he now looked to this source for the doctrine of salvation. The study of Hegel and still more the study of Feuerbach strengthened these yearnings, and Feuerbach showed Herzen how the human being must develop out of the Christian. Is it possible to think that Herzen could without scepticism regard the mužik as the desired saviour? This is why he placed the operative beside the mužik, and this is why he became reconciled with the bourgeois. The approximation effected by Herzen was of Russia to Europe, not of Europe to Russia.

Herzen's career recalls the fate of Goethe's Eúphorion. Radiating light he rises, on high he shines, but he is dashed to pieces on the earth. In the fifties and in the early sixties Herzen was the spokesman of progressive Russia; after the liberation of the peasantry and after the Polish rising he became more and more isolated, increasingly lonely.

His criticism of Russia contributed much towards the realisation of the reforms before and after 1861; his influence upon all circles and strata of cultured Russia, not excepting the bureaucracy and the court, was powerful. (pp. 421-22)

Herzen was an awakener, his was the voice of one crying in the wilderness. Recognition is due to his character as well as to his literary activities. He said of himself that hypocrisy and duplicity were the two errors most alien to his disposition. Herzen could not be better portrayed.

Herzen helped the leaders of liberalism, such men as Čičerin, Kavelin, etc., to clarify their principles; the slavophils had to come to terms with Herzen; and even the reactionaries had to try conclusions with him.

His influence declined after the Polish rising of 1863. (p. 423)

I do not believe that the waning of Herzen's influence was solely due to his views upon the Polish rising. After 1861 his opinions and his policy forced him into a difficult position. Herzen's philosophy remained practically unchanged throughout life. Having become a Feuerbachian, a Feuerbachian he remained, as we learn from all his utterances down to the very last. Doubtless he mitigated his positivist disillusionment, and abandoned the Byronic Cain, but he held fast to his positivist materialism. It was natural that this philosophy should seem odious to conservatives and reactionaries, but some even of the liberals were repelled by it (Granovskii, Čičerin, etc.). Moreover, some of the liberals were antagonised by Herzen's socialism.

On the other hand, young men of socialistic and radical views considered Herzen too vague, and found his policy unduly conservative. The first proclamation issued by Young Russia reproaches Herzen for misunderstanding the situation and for conservatism. At this epoch, too, political endeavours were in the ascendant in Russia, where the leaders of the movement resided; publicist and political interests were concentrated in Russia; the powerful influence exercised by Černyševskii during the early sixties, if not the direct cause of the coolness felt towards Herzen, at least paved the way for its onset.

The reaction and repression which began in 1863, led to an increase in radicalism, and sent a new stream of refugees to Europe, refugees already unfriendly to Herzen. His removal from London to Geneva, the new refugee centre, availed nothing; an understanding was impossible. Not merely did Herzen remain estranged from the younger revolutionaries, but he was never able to harmonise his outlook with that of Černyševskii, though the two writers built on the same philosophical foundations.

Herzen knew and admitted that he had changed, but he had changed, he said, because the entire situation had altered. Modification of views is natural to a vigorously aspiring man, but the important question is, in what direction the modification occurs and by what it is determined. Much as I admire Herzen as author and as man, my liking for him has its reserves. (pp. 423-24)

For the very reason that Herzen appeals to us because of his many brilliant qualities we must endeavour to come to an understanding about his defects.

In philosophical matters Herzen's inadequacy was due to this, that he failed to criticise and recriticise the foundations of his philosophy, and that he uncritically continued to cling to Feuerbach and positivism. Marx and Engels advanced beyond Feuerbach, and even Stirner attempted to do so. At the outset Herzen passes on from Feuerbach upon the line of Marx towards revolution; he advances to crime, in Byronic fashion; but after remaining long content with breathing threatenings and slaughter, after prolonged "hesitation," he turns away to liberalism.

Now I, too, believe that Feuerbach's philosophy is defective. The identification of religion with myth is fallacious, and Feuerbach's materialism is of as little avail as materialism in general. Marx prudently transmuted it into economic materialism. Herzen deduced the political consequences of the Feuerbachian doctrine "homo homini deus"; but he remained too much on the abstract plane; he failed to undertake a precise analysis of the real relationships between religion and politics, between church and state; and he failed to secure any profounder insight into the nature of theocracy and into its development and forms.

To the last, Herzen remained an opponent of Orthodoxy, and yet he concluded a peace with the believing mužik and the old believers, to find the positively Russian in his folk-duma.

It was a grave defect, too, that Herzen failed to secure a better understanding of socialism, its true significance and its internal and external development. I am aware that it is by no means easy to arrive at clear views from a study of the writings of the French socialists. I admit, moreover, that the practical demands of these socialists were not such as most of us would consider practical (the Saint-Simonians, for example, wished to have all their clothing to button behind, so that it would be impossible for the individual to dress himself unaided, and his neighbour would be compelled to exercise the faculty of altruism!). But it was a weakness in Herzen that he failed to study Marx, that he did not observe the labour movement and the economic and social developments of his day, and that he did not grasp the influence that these changes were exercising in the political field.

Nor were Herzen's views of the mužik and the mir based upon close investigation of economic and social relationships. He says with justice of the slavophils that their holy-picture ideals and the fumes of incense made it impossible for them to understand the true condition of the people. But may we not say almost the same of Herzen's adoration of the mužik?

His knowledge of history was defective. Though he had a keen and profitable interest in the living present, he erred gravely through failing to undertake a thorough historical analysis of contemporary events. Unduly one-sided is the manner in which history is reduced to the biography of Herzen. In fact all Herzen's writings are extraordinarily subjective, far too subjective for a philosopher who desired to transcend German idealism and to escape its subjectivist pitfalls.

In the political field Herzen's subjectivism takes the form of anarchism, socialistic anarchism or anarchistic socialism—it does not matter which name we use. Herzen's anarchism derives from the defects of his subjectivism, and this is itself dependent upon Herzen's social position.

He was a refugee, stranger among strangers, economically and socially independent, living upon income drawn from Russia, an opponent of capitalism, but not necessarily an opponent of Rothschild, of whom he could make an adroit literary use in opposition to the fiscalism of the Russian government and the tsar. . . . In a word, this economic and social isolation made

Herzen unpractical. Helplessness in practical matters, becoming objective in the philosophic and literary fields, took the form of anarchism.

In course of time, lack of practical experience is apt to lead to contempt for practical experience. Herzen was inclined to share Plato's aristocratic disdain of politics and politicians, and the reason was the same in his case as in Plato's. To the philosopher, one who studies the ultimate principles of all being and life, and writes about these abysmal matters, the details of everyday politics seem petty; to him, officials, ministers, even the tsar, are no more than unimportant wage-earners appointed by the people. They can therefore be tolerated readily enough; it matters little whether we have to do with tsar or president, with one who wears Monomach's crown or a Phrygian cap. Thus abstract and theoretical anarchism becomes in practice legitimism, but it is natural that the real practitioners should look askance at this practical legitimism.

Herzen, moreover, has in his composition a considerable element of the anarchism peculiar to authors, and a brilliant and well-informed article seems to him more valuable and more important than all the tsars!

Herzen's futility in practical matters was the evil heritage of Russian absolutism. Tsarism, especially under Nicholas I, condemned to inactivity the best and the most energetic of the Russians, and for the refugee this inactivity was perpetuated and accentuated.

If, finally, we take into account the aristocratic factor in Herzen's mentality and his associations from childhood upwards, we have a sufficient explanation of his anarchism. Though at first he despised the bourgeois, he became reconciled later with "collective mediocrity" (he quotes Mill's phrase) and its "Chinesedom." He is sorry for the unfortunate bourgeois, and becomes reconciled with him after the manner of an aristocratic superior. In 1848 no less a man than Bělinskii thought it necessary to protect the bourgeoisie against Herzen's onslaughts. After a time, however, Herzen came to admit (1863) that Russia would perhaps traverse the bourgeois stage. Later still, he practically accepted this as inevitable. It was natural that Herzen should look upon the "autocratic masses" rather from the outlook of the aristocrat than from that of the historian or politician. He makes fun of the bourgeois because he buys his clothes ready-made, and because he replaces parks with orchards and palaces with hotels. As a romanticist Herzen detested the bourgeois; "accuracy and moderation" irritated him; he could see nothing in the bourgeois but indifferentism and stagnation; he despised "chameleopardism" devoid of strong racial and individual qualities, for all that was individual was typified for him in "the restless and the eccentric."

He achieved little with his conception of Byron's Cain as nothing more than the antibourgeois. Herzen did not adequately appraise the revolutionary defiance of Byron's Cain and Lucifer, and this is why his Cain capitulated to the bourgeoisie. Physical-force-anarchism was transmuted by Herzen into sermonising. In addition he adopted a positivistic categorical imperative, tincturing this with Schopenhauer's compassion.

Herzen was never able to transcend a paralysing scepticism; hence arose the "hesitation" which he so justly diagnosed in himself; and this is why Herzen did not become a permanent leader either in the theoretical or in the practical field. Louis Blanc was once branded by Herzen as a bourgeois in the following terms: "His intellectualist religiousness and his lack of scepticism surrounded him as with a Chinese wall, so that it

was impossible to throw within the enclosure a single new idea or a single doubt." (pp. 424-28)

At the outset of his literary career Herzen devoted much consideration to the relationship between scientific specialists and philosophers. He dreaded specialisation as unindividual; he was afraid of becoming such a man as Wagner in Goethe's *Faust;* and he therefore turned towards generalities, towards philosophy, although conversely he sufficiently recognised the dangers of dilettantism. He never attained to the goal of his desire, the perfect synthesis of these two extremes. Rather was it his privilege "to live a many-sided life," to embody both philosophically and politically the proverbial breadth of the Russian nature.

We involuntarily recall Beltov in *Who is to Blame?* where this "superfluous man" is ably and unsparingly analysed by Herzen. The Russian, who has received a thoroughly European education at the hands of Genevese Frenchmen, astonishes the German specialists by his versatility and astonishes the French by his profundity; but whereas the Germans and the Frenchmen achieve much, he achieves nothing. He has a positively morbid love of work, but he is unable to secure a practical position in relation to life, incompetent to make contact with an environment wholly foreign to him. He lives only in thoughts and passions, a frigid dreamer, eternally a child. Half his life is spent upon the choice of a profession, and again and again he begins a new career, for he has inherited neither culture nor traditions from his father, nothing but property which he does not know how to manage. Thus Beltov's life is the Russian active inactivity, and Beltov is only a generalised human being, a moral Caspar Hauser as it were.

Herzen here gives a masterly portrait of his friend Ogarev. Beltov desired to reveal the secret of the world, of its development and history, which was to be disclosed to astonished humanity in one of the most thorough and most profound philosophical works ever written; but he never got beyond the preface, and even this was not completed. Others of Herzen's friends besides Ogarev are figured in Beltov. Herzen considered that Stankevič, for example, was one of those who had achieved nothing. In a sense and to a degree Herzen limns himself, too, in Beltov. It is true that Beltov is only a caricature of Herzen, but the best portraits are really caricatures.

These considerations must not discredit the true and living interest which Herzen took in all the questions that stirred his time, the interest he took in all that was human. Herzen's many-sided interests converged in a single direction, upon a single object—Russia. (pp. 428-29)

*Thomas Garrigue Masaryk, "Aleksandr Herzen: Philosophical and Political Radicalism," in his* The Spirit of Russia: Studies in History, Literature and Philosophy, Vol. I, *edited and translated by W. R. Lee and Z. Lee, second edition, The Macmillan Company, 1955, pp. 384-429.*

## D. S. MIRSKY (essay date 1927)

[*Mirsky was a Russian prince who fled his country after the Bolshevik Revolution and settled in London. While in England, he wrote two important and comprehensive histories of Russian Literature,* A History of Russian Literature from the Earliest Times to the Death of Dostoyevsky (1881) *and* Contemporary Russian Literature. *These works were later combined and portions were published in 1949 as* A History of Russian Literature. *In 1932, having reconciled himself to the Soviet regime, Mirsky returned to the U.S.S.R. He continued to write literary criticism, but his work eventually ran afoul of Soviet censors and he was exiled to Siberia. He disappeared in 1937. In the following excerpt, which originally appeared in 1927 in* A History of Russian Literature from the Earliest Times to the Death of Dostoyevsky (1881), *Mirsky discusses Herzen's place in the history of Russian socialist thought and defines him as the innovator of Russian agrarian socialism. Mirsky also examines Herzen's political writings, the bulk of which, excluding* From the Other Shore, *he regards as propaganda. Like most critics, Mirsky considers* My Past and Thoughts *Herzen's masterpiece and points to "its freedom and obvious sincerity" as the work's greatest attributes.*]

Herzen was the pioneer in Russia of the positivist and scientific mentality of nineteenth-century Europe and of socialism. But he was deeply rooted in the romantic and aristocratic past, and though the content of his ideas was materialistic and scientific, their tone and flavor always remained romantic. The first stimulant of his thought was the French socialist Saint-Simon, and his gospel of the "emancipation of the flesh" from the traditional fetters of religion always remained one of Herzen's fundamental watchwords.

Socialism to Herzen was not so much a positive program as an incentive and a ferment that was to destroy the outworn civilization of the West and to rejuvenate the senescent tissues of European humanity. He was the first to lay the foundations of Russian agrarian socialism, which hoped to build a socialistic Russia not so much on a Europeanized proletariat as on the communistic tradition of the Russian peasant and the revolutionary initiative of an enlightened and generous minority. But he was always more political than social, and the inspiration of his thought was always liberty rather than equality. Few Russians have felt individual freedom and the rights of man as keenly as Herzen.

Herzen's socialism has a distinctly national coloring. He believed in Russia's vitality as he did not believe in that of the West, and he loved Russia with a passionate love. He hated the government of Nicholas I and the forces of reaction, but he loved not only the people, but also all that was sincere and generous in the intellectual classes; he had a warm feeling for the Slavophils, with whose Christianity he was in no sort of sympathy but from whom he derived much of his faith in the Russian people. In the West, though at one time he gave himself entirely to the European revolution, he had sympathy with the workman only, especially the French workman, in whom he saw a force that was to destroy the selfish bourgeois civilization he loathed.

What makes Herzen, however, much more than a mere teacher of revolutionary doctrines, and conciliates with him even those who are least inclined to share his aspirations, is his intellectual fairness and capacity for detachment. In spite of the extremeness of his views, he could understand his enemies and judge them by *their* standards. His historical intuition, his ability to see history in broad outline, to understand the significance of details and to *relate* them to the main lines, is marvelous. . . . He saw the "creativeness" of the process of becoming, the novelty of every future in relation to every past, and the pages he devotes to the confutation of all idea of predestination, all notion of an extrinsic *idea* guiding human history, are among the most eloquent he wrote. (pp. 220-22)

By far the most important of Herzen's political writings are his eight articles (three of them are in dialogue form) that compose *From the Other Shore*. The book was called forth by the failure of what Herzen had hoped would be the dawn of a

revolutionary and socialist Europe. Although distinctly dated in most of the details, it still reads as one of the most significant things ever written on human history and is perhaps particularly suggestive and appropriate reading in our own days, even though we find it often impossible to endorse Herzen's reading of historical facts. Alone of all Herzen's political writings, it was not written for propaganda purposes, and the edge of its irony is directed not against the old Europe, but against the idealistic optimism of revolutionaries, who expected too much and too early and were either too soon disillusioned or held too firmly to their errors and superstitions. To destroy the *religion* of revolution and socialism, with its rhetoric and its official optimism, and to replace it by a clear and sober *will* for revolution were Herzen's aim. It is here that his intuition of life receives full expression—a hopeful and active acceptance of the "stream of history" viewed as a *creative* process, not as preordained necessity, is the keynote of the book.

His other political writings are different in being primarily propaganda and written not in the disinterested pursuit of truth for itself, but with the aim of influencing other men's actions and opinions. It is in them, however, that Herzen's eloquence comes out especially well. It is a French and romantic type of eloquence—loosely built, spacious, varied, abundantly availing itself of repetition and purely emotional effects, never losing an opportunity to make a side stroke or score a point in a parenthesis or subordinate clause. The best example of this kind of writing is his letter to Michelet, on *The Russian People and Socialism,* an eloquent assertion of the difference between the people and the state and a defense of the former from all responsibility for the crimes of the latter, in particular in relation to Poland.

The same characteristics of his style, but in an even more unfettered and spontaneous form, still more like conversation and relatively free from rhetoric, recur in his autobiography, *My Past and Thoughts.* To the majority of readers it will ever remain his principal work. Its attraction lies above all in its freedom and obvious sincerity. Not that there is no pose in it—Herzen was too French and too romantic to do without a pose. He was, in fact, a rare example of a Russian not afraid of an obvious pose. The absence of self-conscious and excessive sincerity, the superficiality, the somewhat matter-of-course theatricality of *My Past and Thoughts,* are its essential charm to the open-minded reader. Apart from the tone of the voice, there is little self in Herzen's memoirs and less introspection. The relative conventionality of his psychology makes it all the simpler and truer, for he speaks of himself in universal and accepted terms. The best part of the book from this point of view is the wonderful account of his wife's love affair with the German revolutionary poet Herwegh. Here the impression of absolute human sincerity is attained precisely because Herzen openly and sincerely speaks of the relations in terms of current fiction; and this relating the true emotions of two real people to the accepted clichés of current psychological thinking produces that impression of universal humanity which no one who reads those pages can fail to have.

But the greater part of the book is not subjective, and its most frequently memorable pages are those in which he speaks of the outer world. Herzen is a great portrait painter, an impressionist—and the impressions he left of his father and other relations, of the Moscow idealists, and of the leaders of the European revolution are unforgettably vivid. His lightness of touch, which never insists and always moves on, gives them a wonderfully convincing mobility. Not the least remarkable passages of the book are those in which he gives a wider historical background to the narrative: the first parts devoted to his life before his exile contain the broadest, truest, and most penetrating view of Russian social and cultural history in the first half of the nineteenth century. They are a great historical classic. (pp. 222-24)

> *D. S. Mirsky, "The Age of Realism: Journalists, Poets, and Playwrights," in his* A History of Russian Literature from Its Beginnings to 1900, *edited by Francis J. Whitfield, Vintage Books, 1958, pp. 215-55.\**

## V. S. PRITCHETT   (essay date 1943)

[*Pritchett, a modern British writer, is respected for his mastery of the short story and for what commentators describe as his judicious, reliable, and insightful literary criticism. He writes in the conversational tone of the familiar essay, approaching literature from the viewpoint of an informed but not overly scholarly reader. In his criticism, Pritchett stresses his own experience, judgment, and sense of literary art, rather than following a codified critical doctrine derived from a school of psychological or philosophical theory. In the following excerpt, Pritchett praises the independence, confidence, and power of observation exhibited by Herzen in* My Past and Thoughts.]

I have read only one book of Herzen's: his *Memoirs*. This is one of the great autobiographies of the nineteenth century; indeed, I think a book of the highest rank. Of its style I can say nothing. I have read it only in French and in English, and in those translations the quality that comes out most strongly is the lack of dismay, the realism and the severe speculative independence of his mind. The *Memoirs* were written in middle age when he was bitterly conscious of "la logique impitoyable de la vie." That phrase may be, I suppose, one of those histrionic, autumnal cries which were heard in his time. Turgenev, also, liked to think of the leaves falling and the vanishing of youth; the cult of judgment and middle age, so typical of the nineteenth century and so established after 1848, had its root in politics. In Russia, Herzen himself notes that the Decembrists who came back from Siberia were "younger" than the generation that had grown up in their absence, and he was always the enemy of the spirit of an age where "tout devient mûr, affairé, c'est-à-dire bourgeois." But Herzen's judgment, and his truly remarkable sense of the world—especially remarkable in a revolutionary—had nothing to do with political fashion or historical accident. One simply has to say that they are natural to him. He had an intellect that masticated its experience. He was an adult.

Hence the stir of confidence we immediately feel when we pick up the *Memoirs;* and it is instructive to notice that precisely the quality of eclectic mastery prevents Herzen from being a considerable novelist. Herzen's sketches from life, his penetration of character and his hold on a story, come to nothing (I gather) in his one novel, *Whose Fault?* which is simply a verbose analysis of a triangular love story. A novelist does more—or less—than master his experience. He plays with his experience, he sets it against itself, or puts himself against it. He rearranges and unsettles. He substitutes revelation and mystery for expatiation. He seeks not one judgment but many. The instinctive novelist puts continual obstructions in the way of his own verdicts, and that obstruction is discovered to be life. From Herzen's *Memoirs* one can tell he was not that kind of writer. The force of personality was certainly stronger and more decisive in him than it is in most novelists.

Then, Herzen's independence: very quickly in his *Memoirs* we are struck by the writer's ability to stand on his own feet and to make his own observation. His power of observation is extraordinary. I do not mean merely that he sees things vividly or originally, but he tells you what he sees and how experience made him see it. His picture of his childhood in a dismal, aristocratic Russian household is not quite like anything else of the kind in Russian literature. I wonder does it owe something to Chateaubriand? The portrait of the hypochondriac father, with his arid cult of *savoir vivre* and the ceremony of his daily sarcasms and hourly habits, is the picture of a condition of mind and society as well as of a man. Herzen's memory particularises and generalises. We have a glimpse of the sad elder brother who is handed from surgeon to surgeon. We see the father assembling the servants and withering each one in turn with his mockery. We judge the different careers of the uncles and their finances. We catch the briefest sight of the passive German-Jewish mother suffocating among a host of female attendants in her room. We see the boy himself, neither Russian nor German, an exile from birth, wandering from room to room in his aunt's house where the silence is broken by the screech of a jacketed monkey and the scuffle of terrorised servants. The boy spends his time with the servants. Such a neglect might overwhelm the emotions of a boy; in Herzen it seems to have created the rebel, though (one suspects) it planted the seeds of hypochondria. The servants kept alive his natural affections. A large number of the sons of rich parents have been brought up among their family's servants, but Herzen is the only writer that I can remember who not only has described the servants he loved or disliked, but has troubled to analyse and generalise the subject. It is typical of Herzen to note that the cost of a household of servants in Russia in 1820 was a quarter of the cost in Paris. Where other writers of autobiography confine themselves to their personal life and private memory, Herzen appears already in boyhood to be documenting.

Herzen must have survived a lifetime as a refugee with dignity and indeed acquired his enormous European influence as a revolutionary pamphleteer, not because he was a rich man, but because he had learned exile in his own home. In his account of his imprisonment and exile in Russia as a student, we must be struck by his stoicism. How penetrating he is about his judges at the interrogations, how vivid are his descriptions of the long waits in the police headquarters and the anterooms. How shrewdly he judges the liberal men of influence who shuffled quickly out of trouble when he begged their help after young Ogarev's arrest. Herzen learned disillusion young, yet did not lose his heart. How dead on the mark are his notes on official society. The aristocracy had the indelicate task of persecuting the aristocracy; it was the period of the apologetic spy, the intermediary with the poker face and the hint. These things are unforgettable in the descriptions of Dostoevsky, too, but Dostoevsky [has] the artist's axe to grind—an axe apt to fly off the grindstone. Herzen succeeds in adding to reliable evidence a feeling of the deep animation that was hidden under the self-control of the educated man. He is adding all the time a sense of his intellectual development to the usual account of physical experience; he is cultivating what became his most important quality as a romantic writer and a revolutionary pamphleteer: his sense of situation. I suppose that is what I have been trying to get at: Herzen's gift for knowing not only what people are but how they are situated. How rare is the capacity to locate character in its time.

The great pamphleteers have always had a knowledge of the world, perhaps an underlying respect for it. Swift, Defoe, Cobbett certainly had. But Herzen's *savoir vivre* was not his father's. It is amusing to see the son using the same phrase . . . and we must suppose that Herzen's declaration that the English bourgeois did not know how to live was based on the beliefs of nobler days in both senses of the word. The feverish life of the frustrated revolutionaries, a life in which he joined, did not sustain him. Revolution must create. He liked to dream of a harmonious, co-ordinated life such as he had had in his first marriage, before the diseases of . . . Romanticism broke it up. In the end he fell back on "la logique impitoyable." To be disabused is itself a resource. That state of mind is more alive, at any rate, than the retreating mind of conventional orthodoxy. The son observed that *savoir vivre* in the father's sense meant a veritably religious observation of the conventions. Punctiliousness—a very bitter punctiliousness—became a grey drug; but after its doses, the orthodox heart shrank and faded. Melancholia was the price paid by Herzen's father, the procrastinating courtier, who killed himszelf by sneering at his own and everyone else's impulses.

There are many extraordinary chapters in the *Memoirs,* for Russia in that oppressed generation bred the isolated family in the isolated estate and people were left with nothing to do but to live off one another gluttonously, or to grimace in fantastic mental solitudes. . . .

I have sought to convey . . . the power of Herzen's character. His *Memoirs* are the autobiography of a European.

> *V. S. Pritchett, in a review of "Memoirs," in* The New Statesman & Nation, *Vol. XXV, No. 642, June 12, 1943, p. 387.**

### JANKO LAVRIN   (essay date 1947)

[*Lavrin is an Austrian-born British critic, essayist, and biographer. He is best known for his studies of nineteenth- and twentieth-century Russian literature. In such works as* An Introduction to the Russian Novel, *Lavrin employs an approach that combines literary criticism with an exploration into the psychological and philosophical background of an author. In the following excerpt, Lavrin provides a brief overview of Herzen's works. He reserves special praise for* My Past and Thoughts, *which he terms "a personal confession, as well as a cultural and social monograph of the entire epoch in which the author lived."*]

Herzen's contribution to literature consists of a problem novel, *Whose Fault* . . . , of a few stories, and above all of his voluminous masterpiece, *My Past and Thoughts*. . . . Beltov, the hero of the novel (which, by the way, shows more intelligence and observation than creative power) is a well-portrayed superfluous man and a Russian Hamlet of the 'forties. He returns from his wanderings abroad to his native place where he soon finds himself amidst all the pettiness and vulgarity of a provincial existence, described by the author in a good-humored satirical vein. After an unhappy love affair with the wife of his former schoolfellow, Beltov again leaves for abroad—this time feeling more superfluous than ever. The problem of the love tangle is mainly psychological and reflects the influence of George Sand. Herzen's few stories, one of which *(The Stealing Magpie)* is a passionate indictment of serfdom, are of less importance. This cannot be said, however, of his *My Past and Thoughts*—a classic of memoir literature. The author begins with his childhood, after which he describes, most vividly, the intellectual life in Moscow during his undergraduate years. We follow him into the dreary northern places of his exile, witness his romantic elopement with his cousin Natalie, and get to

know a whole gallery of people: Herzen's relatives, friends, various officials, and public figures. Later we are initiated into his exploits in France and England. Events and impressions keep on accumulating, all of them brimming with the author's wit, intelligence, and shrewd observation. The panorama ends with a few chapters from Switzerland and Italy, which make one regret that this long account of Herzen's life is not even longer. *My Past and Thoughts* is more than a free autobiography. It is a personal confession, as well as a cultural and social monograph of the entire epoch in which the author lived. And since he was in contact with such people as Garibaldi, Proudhon, Mazzini, Kossuth, Robert Owen, and Bakunin, his account of them is most valuable. He also presents them as vividly as he does the petty squabbles and jealousies of the political refugees in London.

Most of Herzen's other writings belong to the social-political thought, including his brilliant book of essays, *From the Other Shore* . . . , in which he gave vent to his loathing of Western Europe after 1848. "Social cannibalism"—this is how he defined the civilization he found in the bourgeois West. Aware of the dehumanizing tendency of capitalism, he now pinned his hopes for a better future to the working classes, and above all to the Russian people. It was in the Russian village commune, with its collective tenure of land, that he believed he had found a peculiar institution and an element of true socialism. Because of his faith in the innate socialist instincts of the Russian peasant masses, Herzen was one of those early populists or *narodniki,* their founder, in fact, who were responsible for the cult of the peasant among the Russian intellectuals. (pp. 48-50)

> *Janko Lavrin, "Fermentation of Ideas," in his* An Introduction to the Russian Novel, Whittlesey House, *1947, pp. 40-55.**

### ISAIAH BERLIN   (essay date 1956)

[*Berlin is a noted twentieth-century critic of Russian literature. In his writings, Berlin focuses on such revolutionary thinkers as Herzen and his contemporary Mikhail Bakunin and discusses the moral and social questions that they probed. In the following excerpt, which originally appeared in* Encounter, May, 1956, *Berlin outlines Herzen's philosophical development as detailed in* My Past and Thoughts, *a work that he maintains is informed both by Herzen's desire to preserve the liberty of the individual and his penetrating and sensitive understanding.*]

Herzen's most constant goal is the preservation of individual liberty. That is the purpose of the guerrilla war which . . . he had fought from his earliest youth. What made him unique in the nineteenth century is the complexity of his vision, the degree to which he understood the causes and nature of conflicting ideals simpler and more fundamental than his own. He understood what made—and what in a measure justified—radicals and revolutionaries: and at the same time he grasped the frightening consequences of their doctrines. He was in full sympathy with, and had a profound psychological understanding of, what it was that gave the Jacobins their severe and noble grandeur, and endowed them with a moral magnificence which raised them above the horizon of that older world which he found so attractive and which they had ruthlessly crushed. He understood only too well the misery, the oppression, the suffocation, the appalling inhumanity, the bitter cries for justice on the part of the crushed elements of the population under the *ancien régime,* and at the same time he knew that the new world which had risen to avenge these wrongs must, if it was given its head, create its own excesses and drive millions of human beings to useless mutual extermination. Herzen's sense of reality, in particular of the need for, and the price of, revolution, is unique in his own, and perhaps in any age. His sense of the critical moral and political issues of his time is a good deal more specific and concrete than that of the majority of the professional philosophers of the nineteenth century, who tended to try to derive general principles from observation of their society, and to recommend solutions which are deduced by rational methods from premises formulated in terms of the tidy categories in which they sought to arrange opinions, principles and forms of conduct. Herzen was a publicist and an essayist whom his early Hegelian training had not ruined: he had acquired no taste for academic classifications: he had a unique insight into the 'inner feel' of social and political predicaments: and with it a remarkable power of analysis and exposition. Consequently he understood and stated the case, both emotional and intellectual, for violent revolution, for saying that a pair of boots were of more value than all the plays of Shakespeare (as the 'nihilistic' critic Pisarev once said in a rhetorical moment), for denouncing liberalism and parliamentarism, which offered the masses votes and slogans when what they needed was food, shelter, clothing; and understood no less vividly and clearly the aesthetic and even moral value of civilisations which rest upon slavery, where a minority produces divine masterpieces, and only a small number of persons have the freedom and the self-confidence, the imagination and the gifts, to be able to produce forms of life that endure, works which can be shored up against the ruin of our time.

This curious ambivalence, the alternation of indignant championship of revolution and democracy against the smug denunciation of them by liberals and conservatives, with no less passionate attacks upon revolutionaries in the name of free individuals; the defence of the claims of life and art, human decency, equality and dignity, with the advocacy of a society in which human beings shall not exploit or trample on one another even in the name of justice or progress or civilisation or democracy or other abstractions—this war on two, and often more, fronts, wherever and whoever the enemies of freedom might turn out to be—makes Herzen the most realistic, sensitive, penetrating and convincing witness to the social life and the social issues of his own time. His greatest gift is that of untrammelled understanding: he understood the value of the so-called 'superfluous' Russian idealists of the 40s because they were exceptionally free, and morally attractive, and formed the most imaginative, spontaneous, gifted, civilised and interesting society which he had ever known. At the same time he understands the protest against it of the exasperated, deeply earnest, *révoltés* young radicals, repelled by what seemed to them gay and irresponsible chatter among a group of aristocratic *flâneurs*, unaware of the mounting resentment of the sullen mass of the oppressed peasants and lower officials that would one day sweep them and their world away in a tidal wave of violent, blind, but justified hatred which it is the business of true revolutionaries to foment and direct. Herzen understood this conflict, and his autobiography conveys the tension between individuals and classes, personalities and opinions both in Russia and in the west, with marvellous vividness and precision.

*My Past and Thoughts* is dominated by no single clear purpose, it is not committed to a thesis; its author was not enslaved by any formula or any political doctrine, and for this reason, it remains a profound and living masterpiece, and Herzen's greatest title to immortality. He possesses other claims: his political

and social views were arrestingly original, if only because he was among the very few thinkers of his time who in principle rejected all general solutions, and grasped, as very few thinkers have ever done, the crucial distinction between words that are about words, and words that are about persons or things in the real world. Nevertheless it is as a writer that he survives. His autobiography is one of the great monuments to Russian literary and psychological genius, worthy to stand beside the great novels of Turgenev and Tolstoy. Like *War and Peace,* like *Fathers and Children,* it is wonderfully readable, and, save in inferior translation, not dated, not Victorian, still astonishingly contemporary in feeling. (pp. 207-09)

*Isaiah Berlin, "A Remarkable Decade: Alexander Herzen," in his* Russian Thinkers, *edited by Henry Hardy and Aileen Kelly, The Viking Press, 1978, pp. 186-209.*

### THE TIMES LITERARY SUPPLEMENT   (essay date 1956)

[*The following excerpt is from a review of a single-volume edition of Herzen's work that contains* From the Other Shore *and* The Russian People and Socialism. *Here, the critic explores the reasons for Herzen's enduring reputation in Russia and interprets his philosophies as they are presented in these two works.*]

One or other or both of two political ideas dominated the minds of all serious writers in nineteenth-century Russia. One was that things simply could not go on as they were, either in Russia or in Europe; the other was that the Russian people alone, in spite of the Tsarist autocracy, contained within them the seeds of political and social redemption for the whole of Europe as well as themselves. . . . Herzen was dominated at different times of his life by both ideas, and they are respectively formulated in [**From the Other Shore** and **The Russian People and Socialism**] as clearly as anywhere: the first in **From the Other Shore** and the second in **The Russian People and Socialism**.

But it is still difficult at first sight to see from these political pamphlets alone why Herzen is regarded by so many qualified critics . . . as one of the supremely great figures of nineteenth-century Russia. Certainly he wrote brilliantly. . . . He also sometimes wrote inaccurately (even if not so inaccurately as the slipshod proof-reading in this case would lead one to suppose); but his polemics are none the worse for that.

What is not easy for the English reader to see is why the impact of his writing is thought to have been so important. He has certainly been much underrated in this country, as he was also in his lifetime, when he lived here for twelve years (1852-65) without making more of a mark on English opinion than that of just another *émigré* agitator. Yet this was the very period in which his periodical, *The Bell,* was reckoned by many Russians to wield a political power in Russia second only to that of the Tsar.

By 1870, when he died, his influence had almost entirely evaporated. The solutions which Herzen recommended to the problems of Russia and Europe had been repudiated by men of tougher mould. His faith in the Russian peasant and the peasant commune as the nucleus of a new socialist order, his preference of gradual reform to violence (though not necessarily to the exclusion of violence at the critical moment), and his willingness to see the Tsar as the head of a free federative State in place of the Russian Empire—all this set him at variance with almost every other revolutionary current then active in Europe. He quarrelled with Bakunin and abominated Marx; he disappointed the Poles, to whose cause he was devoted, and bitterly repudiated the nihilists, whom he regarded as having usurped a name to which they had no right; above all he detested Communism, which has nevertheless adopted him as one of its founding fathers. Mr. E. H. Carr has fairly described him as "the first Narodnik"—that is to say, the first to advocate the policy of reform by "going to the people." And this phrase is itself the measure of his apparent failure, for the policy proved to be a pathetic fiasco, and the title which embodied the claim to represent the people *(narod)* passed to men who believed in terrorism and assassination instead. . . . [Within] a decade of Herzen's death the course of the revolution had shifted to one diametrically opposed to his ideas—a course which led directly to October, 1917. Why did Herzen so fail, and why is he now so esteemed?

The pamphlets in the present volume show part of the answer to the first question. Herzen was equally compounded of heart and head; or at least equally enough to make his writings a perpetual battleground of unresolved struggle between the two. It was his heart which rejected as a cruel absurdity the doctrine, since fashionable among Communists, that the present generation must suffer for the benefit of the future. In the dialogue called **"Before the Storm"** (written in 1847, though no doubt given its title after 1848) he says:

> If progress is the end, for whom are we working? Who is this Moloch who, as the toilers approach him, instead of rewarding them, only recedes, and as a consolation to the exhausted, doomed multitudes can give back only the mocking answer that after their death all will be beautiful on earth?

It was his head, however, that completed the argument by pointing out that in any case

> the future does not exist: it is created by the combination of a thousand causes, some necessary, some accidental, plus human will, which adds unexpected dramatic *dénouements* and *coups de théâtre.*

And again:

> The future is worse than the Ocean—there is nothing there. It will be what men and circumstances make it.

It was also his head that acknowledged the difficult consequences of this line of argument. First, given vast social and economic inequalities, it leaves the "haves" with no possible inducement to sacrifice the smallest fragment of their blessings to the "have-nots." Incidentally, many of Herzen's revolutionary antagonists would have put to him with some bitterness the question he himself put to others:

> . . . Are they willing to lose all the comforts and charms of our existence, to have barbarian youth rather than civilized senility, untilled soil and virgin forests instead of exhausted fields and artificial parkland? Will they demolish their ancestral castle for the sole pleasure of helping lay the foundations of a new house which will be built, no doubt, long after our day?

Secondly, it is implicit in the passage from which these sentences are taken that the "old world" is doomed anyway. So what, in the upshot, is there for the intellectually honest re-

former to do but to recognize that things are as they are and will be as they will be?

Herzen's youthful training was in the natural sciences and Hegelian philosophy, and he never lost his taste for either. To his taste for scientific method he owed his positivist, non-moralistic attitude towards political events—even events which horrified him, like the crushing of the 1848 revolution in Paris. . . . And from Hegelianism he derived the almost mystical conviction that somehow the rational would eventually become the real, and everything would come right in the end, provided one did not try to do anything too abrupt before the critical moment came for the "dialectical leap."

These were the convictions to which his intellectual honesty led him. But his heart would not have it: his heart had its reasons, of which his reason had no knowledge. This tension and conflict between head and heart is no doubt the explanation of Herzen's use of the dialogue in several of the pieces composing *From the Other Shore.* . . . [The dialogues] read as if Herzen were communing with himself. This may be said to be almost self-evident in the piece called **"Consolatio,"** in which the disputants are a twenty-five-year-old girl and a middle-aged doctor. It is impossible to say that either speaks exclusively for Herzen: they speak antiphonally for his heart and his head.

The dispute between them is essentially a simple one. It is also everlasting and insoluble. One is concerned with what ought to be, the other with what is the case. One passes judgment and declares that this is right and must be promoted at all costs, that is wrong and must be fought. The heart asks angrily: "Why *should* they do this or want that?" The head replies that the important question is not why they *should* but why they *do;* for this is a practical question, and it can at least in principle be accurately answered (which the moral question cannot); and an accurate answer may lead to useful action, which moralizing never will do. These are the lines on which the doctor answers the girl's passionate protests at the "false dawn" of 1848—protests with which Herzen certainly sympathized himself—:

> I look at all this differently. I am accustomed to a doctor's point of view, which is totally contrary to that of a judge. A doctor lives in nature, in the world of facts and phenomena—he doesn't teach, he learns: he seeks not revenge, but the alleviation of pain.

But through another *persona* in another dialogue, Herzen insists that this attitude is not an abdication of the struggle:

> . . . . to understand is already to act, to achieve. You think that when you have understood what is going on, your desire to act will pass? But that would mean that what you wanted to do was not what was wanted.

Yet the very inconclusiveness of Herzen's dialogues suggests that in practice he did give way to his own theoretical optimism. If the Russian peasant commune was destined to redeem Europe, as he assured Jules Michelet in the open letter entitled *The Russian People and Socialism,* would it really be wise to interfere with the course of nature? What Herzen lacked to make him an effective revolutionary was the capacity for ruthless decision, which Bakunin and Chernyshevsky preached, and Trotsky and Lenin practised. He was a theoretical revolutionary whose theories contained the seeds of their own frustration: he set people thinking, and once they had started thinking, their thoughts were free to pursue other directions. . . . Herzen ended by preaching a Fabianism which played into the hands of tougher men. When he died, it appeared that his keen and brilliant perception was extinguished with him.

There remains, then, the question why his reputation stands so high three generations later? The answer is implicit in his works, including the two composing this volume, but it will not be found by reading them alone. Part of it is given in Mr. Berlin's introduction. [See excerpt below, 1979], which describes him in Paris as

> with Bakunin, the first denizen of the barbarous and frightening Russian Empire to be recognized as an equal by the political thinkers of the fabled West—as an equal intellectually, and not, like other liberal travellers from Russia, as a gifted and agreeable intellectual tourist, or an indolent and curious passer-by.

So much for his intellectual stature. But this recognition by the West would not have been enough had it not been for the coincidence that the great revolutions of 1848 followed within a year of his arrival. Because he witnessed the events of that year both in Rome and in Paris, and because he described them with a brilliant pen, his writings became almost the only first-hand account available in their own language to Russian socialists and revolutionaries of a later generation; and for the more European-minded among them the revolutions of 1905 and 1917 were the continuation and the consummation of the abortive revolution of 1848. They were consciously carrying on the same great struggle, and Herzen was their one dependable guide. (pp. 609-10)

> *"Heart of a Revolutionary," in* The Times Literary Supplement, *No. 2851, October 19, 1956, pp. 609-10.*

### FRANCIS B. RANDALL   (essay date 1968)

[*Randall argues that the diverse essays in* From the Other Shore *are unified by a "double system of imagery." The first uses images derived from the sea: the shore, a storm, and a ship. The second details the demise of ancient culture and the rise of Christianity, incorporating such Christian images as a dove and a weaver. According to Randall, these two systems merge in the "Vixerunt" section of the work in images suggestive of the Biblical deluge.*]

Books composed of essays originally written on diverse occasions are not usually noted for their unity and coherence. Why is *From the Other Shore* such a striking exception? The eight essays that constitute the text of the book were all written during one eighteen-month period, and all deal with one subject, albeit a large and complex one, the events of 1848-49. The first five essays were intended primarily for circulation in manuscript among Herzen's friends in the Russian capitals. Herzen had two occasions to revise his essays in the direction of unity, the publication of the German edition in 1850 and the publication of the Russian edition (in London) in 1855. All these circumstances no doubt contribute to the explanation.

But when one reads the finished book, over a century later, with an eye for form as well as substance, one is impressed by the degree to which the matter of the work is organized and expressed in a double system of imagery. The first system involves a sea, its shores, a ship, and a storm. The second involves the destruction of the ancient world and the rise of Christianity. The two systems are eventually combined in the imagery of Noah's ark and the Deluge. This double system of

imagery not only unifies and organizes the work; it is also the means by which Herzen expressed his sentiments on questions that he was too intellectually critical to answer outright. (p. 92)

The bulk of the introduction is taken up by a "Farewell" dated March 1, 1849 [see excerpt above]. It contains some of Herzen's most quoted libertarian outbursts: "I have finally sacrificed everything for 'human dignity / And free speech'." . . . "I cannot become a serf again, not even to suffer with you." . . . And "Freedom of the individual is the greatest thing; on this, and *only on this,* can the real will of the people be nurtured." . . . The Farewell also clarifies the problem of the ship, the sea, and the shores.

> I see the inevitable ruin of old Europe, and I have no regrets for anything here. . . . I love nothing in this world save what it persecutes. I respect nothing save what it kills—and I remain . . . I remain to suffer doubly, to suffer from my own anguish and from its anguish, to perish, perhaps, in the destruction and dissolution toward which it is racing at full steam. . . . I remain because the struggle is *here,* because in spite of the blood and tears, the social questions are being decided here. . . .

The reader is now in a position to master part of Herzen's complex image. A double focus is presented: the reader in Russia is still on the old-world shore of his native land, dark and bloody ground. He looks out to sea—that strange, unstable, unpredictable element which Russians above all other peoples were used to regarding as distant and alien—and he sees a ship, a symbol as rich as its referents are vague and shifting, as rich as the Europe that it stands for. It is an up-to-date, nineteenth-century steamship. Herzen is aboard it, and only the reader's imagination can tell him how many others. But the ship is headed for a storm, and in the course of the book will be swept by it and will emerge into scarcely less ghastly weather. And the other shore? Although Herzen had said, "The curious fate of Russians is to see farther than their neighbors" . . . , the other shore, the future beyond the storm, cannot be seen from Russia. For Russia the storm is the future.

On the other hand, the writer is in the middle of the European struggle, the middle of the ship, the middle of the storm. The sea air is exhilarating, even while it threatens and brings the tempest. Return to the past would be horrible as well as impossible. The image suggests the magnificence as well as the torment of European civilization. It explains as clearly as any of Herzen's straightforward statements why he remained in Europe. And the other shore? Is the European ship at sea any nearer to it than the Russian landsman? What will it be like, and how does one sail there? Not all questions can be answered in an introduction. The reader notices that the first essay of the work itself is called **"Before the Storm: A Conversation on Deck."**

The essay is dated December 1847, when many clever men and even a few wise ones laughed at the possibility of revolutions in 1848. (pp. 93-4)

The next essay turns out to be called **"After the Storm."** It is dated from Paris in the summer of 1848, and is chiefly a cry of horror at the ruthlessness with which the workers' rising, the "June Days," had been put down several weeks before. In this essay the storm was the sequence of events in Paris from February through June 1848. Herzen was well aware of the other European revolutions that were still going on, but the degree to which his interests were centered on France is made plain by his image here. The French struggle was the one major revolution of 1848 that did not involve what Herzen called ''the national question.'' France already had its independence and unity. Thus France was the most apt subject for Herzen's reflections in this book, in which he was concerned very little with nations and peoples but very much with the individual's quest for freedom and justice and with the future of European civilization as a whole.

The following essay, **''The Year LVII of the Republic, One and Indivisible,''** was ostensibly inspired by the ludicrous celebrations of the French radical republicans on September 22, 1848, New Year's Day according to the old Jacobin calendar, at a time when any radical impulse in France's Second Republic had long since been contained. This was all so mockingly horrible to Herzen that the thought of sailing to ''the other shore''—America—again presented itself. Again, it was not America but what America symbolized that attracted Herzen, a genuinely New World. (pp. 94-5)

This was about as far as Herzen could organize and express his thoughts through the imagery of the sea, its shores, a ship, and a storm. He did not have the temperament to be a dogmatic prophet. He was not certain of the next stage in history, and so there was nothing definite that he could convey by an image of the other shore. Consequently, from this depressed point on through the second half of the book, Herzen employs chiefly his second system of imagery, the destruction of the ancient world and the rise of Christianity.

The basic image of this second system can be expressed as a simple proportion: Christianity was to ancient Rome as socialism would be to modern Europe. But all simplicity vanishes when one thinks of the complex reactions that any element of this proportion inspired in most of Herzen's audience. Herzen was eager to force the ethical ambiguities on his readers.

> I place my wager on socialism. ''That's hard to imagine!''—It was hard to imagine that Christianity would triumph over Rome. I often think of the learned conversations Tacitus and Pliny had with their companions about that idiotic sect of Nazarenes . . . who came out of Judea with their vehement, half-insane speeches, or about the Proudhon of the time who appeared in Rome itself to preach the end of Rome. The Empire stood proud and powerful against these penniless propagandists—but it fell at last.
>
> Or don't you see the new Christians coming to build, the new barbarians coming to destroy? . . . When their hour comes, Herculaneum and Pompeii will disappear, the good and the bad, the just and the guilty, will perish side by side. That will be no judgment, no retribution, but a cataclysm, a revolution. This lava, these barbarians, this new world, these Nazarenes who are coming to finish off what is decrepit and weak and to clear a place for the fresh and the new, they are nearer than you think. . . .

Tacitus and Pliny *were* learned—and truly intelligent and highly civilized—yet their world perished. The Nazarenes *were* idiotic and half-insane; yet all of Herzen's audience—not only the believers—would have insisted that the Nazarenes had pearls beyond price. The socialists of 1848 were not regarded by Herzen as true sages. They *were* typified by Proudhon with all

his eccentricities and crackpottery. Yet the socialists *were* in the thick of the Paris June Days, which to Herzen seemed likely to prove the first shock of the cataclysm. He did not insist that the future would belong to the socialists—either the cataclysm or the new world—but he *would* say that he placed his wager on socialism. . . . The proletarians of Europe were to be the new barbarians and the new Vesuvius. The socialists were to be the new Christians. And there *was* to be a new catastrophe.

The parallel is pursued in the next essay, **''Vixerunt.''** The middle-aged man and the younger man of the first dialogue are brought together again on the streets of Paris, in November 1848. The young idealist is not impressed with any similarity between Christianity and socialism. The older man agrees in part.

> Christianity has remained a pious hope. Now on the eve of its death, as in the first century, it comforts itself with heaven. . . . To introduce the thought of a new life is very much harder in our times. . . . [Democracy] is still on the Christian shore. . . . The future is outside politics. The future soars over the chaos of all political and social aspirations and from them selects threads for its new cloth from which it will produce a winding sheet for the past and swaddling clothes for the newborn. Socialism corresponds to the Nazarene doctrine in the Roman Empire. . . .

This vein of imagery is again more precise in rejecting the past and the present—this still Christian shore—than in painting the future. The future soars? Over chaos? The dove, the Holy Spirit, moving on the face of the primeval waters of chaos? Herzen has made so much use of the image of a ship that we are easily led to think of the other dove, sent out by Noah over the waters of renewed chaos, the Deluge, from his ship, the ark of salvation. Christians had so often identified Noah's dove over the waters with the original soaring Holy Spirit that Herzen could readily draw on the association, and enrich it with his own suggestion that his ship of civilization is also Noah's ark. But first he switches to another traditional image of Christian rhetoric, the weaver and his winding sheet-swaddling clothes, vivid enough to a mid-nineteenth-century audience of Russians, whose babies were still swaddled and whose dead were still wound in much the same long roll of white cloth.

The younger man is still skeptical:

> If you remember what you just said about Christianity and extend the comparison, the future of socialism is not enviable. It will remain an eternal hope.
>
> But on the way [the older man replies] it will develop a brilliant period of history under its blessing. The Gospels were not realized; there was no need of that. But the Middle Ages, the ages of reconstruction, and the ages of revolution were realized. And Christianity permeated all these phenomena, participating in everything, guiding, showing the way. The fulfillment of socialism will exhibit the same unexpected combination of abstract doctrine and actual facts. . . .

The socialist future, then, will be at least as complex as the Christian past. Herzen was much too intelligent to predict it in detail and instead suggested it in these comparisons.

The flood of lava and barbarism, destroying that the world might be made new again, the future soaring over chaos, and the ship of civilization are now gathered up in the Biblical image that they have all suggested, the Deluge of Noah and his ark.... The Biblical Deluge is the union of Herzen's two systems of imagery. The ark is at once a ship that crosses from one fateful shore to another and the key to the transition from one stage of civilization through a cataclysm to another. The imaginatively agile reader can project himself from the hither shore that is by turns Russia, Europe, and the present, to the steamship of civilization that is also Columbus' caravel and the ark of salvation headed for the further shore that may be Europe or America or Christianity or socialism or sheer annihilation, amid the stormy, Turneresque sea that is at once the uncertain future and the certain future judgment and purification—and at some points the reader may have to project himself to the bottom of that sea.

One element is lacking on the modern side of Herzen's parallel. Who will soar over the face of *these* murky waters? No precise answer emerges from Herzen's arguments, but once more his imagery suggests his answer where his arguments remain silent. In the next essay, **"Consolatio,"** a discussion of human genius leads, as it so often did in the nineteenth century, to a paean of praise to Goethe.... The great man—Herzen felt he could do no more than to say a man like unto Goethe—would be the best substitute for God that humanity could expect in the advancing crisis. Having suggested as much, Herzen ends this dialogue-essay (the last of the five essays that made up the original *From the Other Shore*) rather ironically. His younger man mockingly proposes a false escape from the crisis, the emigration that he had seriously thought of in the first essay. (pp. 95-8)

[The last three essays in *From the Other Shore*] are bound somewhat less closely to the first five than the latter are to each other. Herzen's basic double system of imagery is not developed in any systematic way in the last three essays, but it is occasionally extended.

"There is *death*," Herzen remarks, "between the Rome of Julius Caesar and the Rome of Gregory VII." He quickly adds a footnote: "On the other hand, between the Europe of Gregory VII and the Europe of Martin Luther, the Convention, and Napoleon there is not death but development, transformation, growth." ... From such observations one gathers that Herzen subscribed to the common concept of cycles of civilization—a cycle for antiquity, a medieval-modern cycle, and the unknown cycle of the future. (p. 98)

The final essay of the book bears the curious title, **"Donoso-Cortés, Marqués de Valdegamas, and Julian, Roman Emperor."** Donoso-Cortés was a Spanish conservative, at that time ambassador to France who had made an alarmist speech in the Spanish Cortés that was being widely reprinted and praised in the right-wing Parisian press. The whole order of European society and religion, Donoso-Cortés stated at considerable length, was crumbling to dust. But Europe might yet be saved by pope, monarchy, and army, Donoso-Cortés declared, if England should return to Catholicism. Herzen contrasts the "accuracy" of the Spaniard's analysis with the fatuity of his "divine panacea." ... Donoso-Cortés inspired Herzen to add the last touch to his system of imagery. The ambassador, in Herzen's view, aspired to play the role of Julian the Apostate. Herzen, a reader of Gibbon, expresses great sympathy for Julian, who had done all that a man could do to restore the ancient world but had failed to realize—till his deathbed—that ancient civilization was unrestorable.

To Herzen, many of the would-be restorers of ancient Rome were intelligent, energetic, and appealing—in contrast to their modern equivalents. (p. 99)

In the century and a quarter since Herzen wrote, a number of Europe's greatest writers have used this technique, which Herzen was by no means the first to employ—the systematic comparison of certain aspects of modern life with their ancient counterparts in order to persuade the reader of the shabbiness of modernity when seen against the splendors of antiquity. As the ancient world fell, it could still produce Julian the Apostate, whose tragedy was magnificent. But to Herzen, modern Europe in its decline bred only Donoso-Cortés, whose blatherings were ridiculous. (p. 100)

Herzen, some say, fundamentally misconceived the situation he was living through. He thought he was living at the verge of a horrible and violent catastrophe that would annihilate Europe as it then existed, all this about 1850, when the industrial revolution was about to roll into high gear, lifting even the masses of Europe into a substantially higher standard of living, entailing the widespread achievement of national unity, constitutionalism, and parliamentary democracy. Even Herzen's beloved Russia was on the point of freeing its serfs and entering its period of Great Reforms and greater cultural outburst. Consequently, the unsympathetic reader might continue, Herzen expressed his fears and hopes in a series of images drawn from the most timeworn sources known to Europeans and kept shifting the meaning of his images, mixing and confusing them in a manner that illustrated his muddied outlook only too well.

Sympathetic readers find much more in *From the Other Shore.* Whatever the justice of Herzen's view of Europe's predicament around 1850, it has been harder to dismiss his apocalyptic forebodings in recent decades. Herzen went to Western Europe in time to witness the false hopes of the revolutions of 1848 and the bloody, melancholy repressions of the next few years. This horrified and depressed him; it seared his soul. Herzen's sensibility was nondogmatic. However much he might feel that his world was collapsing to give way to something new based on socialism, a totally new, incommensurably different, "pure" element in the Europe of his day, his intellectual ethic would not let him think that this was inevitably so in any mechanical way, much less write irritable dogmatic predictions, in the manner of some of his eminent socialist contemporaries. And so he used the method of dialogue to express contradictory views and suspend judgment, and he employed a complex system of imagery to denote only what he was willing to state, while connoting much of the tremendous range of his vision.

I believe that Herzen used a rich and compelling system of imagery. The stormbound steamship between two uncertain shores and the rise of Christianity in collapsing Rome are mingled in the ark of the Deluge, at once a ship in a storm and a destruction and renovation of society—but, as Herzen presented it, a stranger ark with no Noah to guide it, afloat on a more terrible deluge with no God to allay it. The viewpoint of the speaker, and hence of the sensitive reader, is constantly shifted. He moves from age to age and from shore to shore. The reader is pressed to broaden any previously narrow outlook and to realize some of the larger interconnections of the human enterprise.

The tone of the work is ultimately set by the invocation of early Christianity and the recurrence of images from the Bible. These impose an earnestness and a high seriousness on the discussion, whether readers are believers or not, that no merely political or mechanical imagery could have achieved. In the Europe of more than a hundred years ago, where no one was yet totally un-Biblical, Herzen chose the richest and most meaningful vein of imagery available, and illuminated thereby many areas of his troubled soul and his troubled world. Therein lies much of the secret of the real unity within the apparent diversity of his book. Therein lies some of the greatness of *From the Other Shore*. (pp. 100-01)

> Francis B. Randall, "Herzen's 'From the Other Shore'," in Slavic Review, Vol. XXVII, No. 1, March, 1968, pp. 91-101.

### R. V. SAMPSON  (essay date 1973)

[*Sampson provides a detailed assessment of the philosophical issues raised in* My Past and Thoughts *and contends that the work will endure as a literary classic because it is "still the best study in literature of the . . . pointless cruelties of tyranny." He also discusses Herzen's disillusionment with the Russian government, maintaining that Herzen was incapable of suggesting a solution to alleviate society's ills.*]

*My Past and Thoughts* is an essential source-book—the best we have for the climate of thought that shaped and was shaped by the generation of the 1840s in Russia. But it lives and will continue to live in the realm of literature because indirectly it is an astonishingly vivid self-portrait of a man remarkable for his integrity and truthfulness. It is, moreover, still the best study in literature of the atmosphere and social effects, the suffocating futility and pointless cruelties of tyranny. (p. 53)

Herzen had the best of reasons for understanding the significance of the spoken word in Russia. Everywhere truth has a peculiar power of its own, so that its statement in a world where it is not accustomed to frequent frank avowal does not go unnoticed. But in Russia under autocrats like Nicholas I and Joseph Stalin the truthfully spoken and, even more so, the written word achieved a special, almost holy status. As Herzen himself expressed it in his celebrated **Letter to Michelet** defending the Russian people: 'The terrible consequences of speech in Russia inevitably give it a peculiar force. A free utterance is listened to with love and reverence, because among us it is only uttered by those who have something to say. One does not so easily put one's thoughts into print when at the end of every page one has a vision of a gendarme, a troika, and, on the far horizon, Tobolsk or Irkutsk'.

Certainly Herzen's own words were effective in evoking the atmosphere of fear and suspense in the rigidly centralized police state administered by Nicholas and his gendarmes. If members of the ruling *élite* who stepped out of line by so much as a suspicion of a step, were dealt with so harshly and humiliatingly, it can be imagined what was the fate of the defenceless peasantry, the serfs. Herzen however does not leave it to our imagination. He gives chapter and verse to illustrate the only too justified terror of the peasants not so much of the arbitrariness of their masters, bad as that was, but from the processes of 'justice' itself. The victims, says Herzen, actually look forward to exile in Siberia, since what they have to endure at the hands of the authorities while awaiting trial is far worse.

Torture, he underlines significantly, was abolished by Peter III, Catherine II and Alexander I, much as successive American administrations abolished jobbing and corruption in the Civil Service or successive British administrations abolished the slums and intolerable housing conditions. Many instances of official brutality and persecution, sometimes of whole villages, are given. The directing hand at the apex of the pyramid, the hand that governed all Russia, the Tsar's chief gendarme, was Araktcheyev. . . . (p. 54)

Herzen illustrates his view of Russia's rulers under Nicholas with an account of Araktcheyev's conduct of the investigation of the murder of his mistress, a serf girl in Novgorod. One of those investigated, although entirely innocent, was ordered to be flogged. The police captain, hardened as he was, could not bring himself to flog a pregnant woman and broke down. But it made no difference. The woman was duly tortured and killed. With such examples set by those at the apex of power, what could be expected at the hands of a host of petty despots with powers of life and death over their serfs throughout Russia? Again, a single episode briefly alluded to by Herzen, although less spine-chilling than countless atrocities, conveys unmistakably something of the atmosphere in which it was possible for human beings, even children, to be so basely degraded. A servant in the family of a police colonel at Penza spilt a kettle of boiling water as a result of being bumped into by his mistress's child. The child was in consequence scalded. The mistress, determined that the punishment should fit the 'crime', ordered the servants' child to be summoned and duly scalded the child's hand from the samovar.

Living in a land where such things were possible, it is not surprising that Herzen was of the opinion that 'Man is cruel and only prolonged suffering softens him.' Nevertheless, there are degrees of cruelty and pathology; and life in Russia under Nicholas excited the revulsion of the world. . . . Herzen's loathing was simply more intense than most; he was exceptionally sensitive to injustice, and he had suffered in person. But Herzen was much too intelligent to suppose that the responsibility for the peculiar suffering of his countrymen could all be laid at the door of a single royal drill sergeant and his blood-stained henchmen. Herzen attempts a diagnosis and it is remarkably shrewd.

His analysis of the nature of the relations between aristocrats, peasants, house-serfs and children is interesting because it rests on the unstated assumption that all men (including children) are in everything that is *humanly* essential equals. He believes that the sadness of their behaviour results from the way in which that equality is violated by their life situation in a rigidly class-structured culture. For example, the house-serf spends his leisure drinking in the restaurant in order to attempt to restore his dignity outraged by the long hours of servility, waiting around below stairs or in the hall to obey any whim or caprice of his masters. In the restaurant for a moment the roles are reversed, and he too can savour the pleasure of giving orders and finding himself obeyed. The moral depravity of serfdom as an institution is illustrated in the lives of Alexey, his father's cook, and Tolotchanov, the feldsher, whose lives were ruined by the peculiar humiliations of serfdom. The cook saved assiduously in order to buy his freedom, the achievement of which for him constituted the great goal, indeed the meaning of his life. He succeeded at last only to find that his master refused to allow him to buy it. He gradually sank into drink and despair; his life was irretrievably wrecked. Tolotchanov led a prosperous, useful life until the day that his wife discovered that he was a serf. She was so appalled that in the anguish of her disappointed social aspirations she drove the feldsher to suicide. Good, valuable, honest lives totally ruined and for no purpose! Such is Herzen's reckoning with serfdom; and again the basis of the analysis is of course the assumption known to each one of us that, whatever the institutions under which we live, all men are equal. This same realization underlies his peculiarly shrewd analysis of the mutual attraction he observed frequently to obtain between servants and children under serfdom. (pp. 55-6)

Herzen sees perfectly clearly that the cause of the pathology in the system is the denial of equality in human relations at every point from top to bottom of the pyramid. And in the absence of the recognition of that which is most distinctively human, the system in its inhumanity requires the labelling of people, so that each will know how to behave to another according to his badge of rank. For human relations are substituted insolence and servility, in which each seeks to take turn and turn about in order to avenge on others weaker than himself the humiliations he has had to undergo at the hands of those more powerful than himself. (pp. 56-7)

Herzen, himself an aristocrat to his finger-tips, ascribes the arrogance of power in the person of the great dignitaries not to aristocratic sentiment—since the old-style grand gentleman was at any rate a genuine personality—but to the insolence of what he calls 'liveried and powdered flunkeys in great houses'—insolent to their inferiors, abject to their superiors. He gives a vivid portrait of one, Tyufyaev, the Governor of Vyatka, whom Herzen knew and suffered at first hand during the first period of his exile. An ex-copying clerk, who combined in his person a truly Byzantine servility with the total obliteration of personality required by official discipline, he meted out to his subordinates in full measure the portion of suffering which had been his own lot under the whip of the bureaucracy and the aristocracy. 'A true servant of the Tsar' is Herzen's description of him, void of all will, innocent of thought, a docile instrument in the hands of authority, but savage in oppression of those beneath him in the hierarchy. . . . People exist not so much as individuals as units of rank consciousness—soldiers, clerks, station superintendents, considering their claim to immunity from blows or insult or their right to administer same to derive not from personal identity, ability or courage but from the badge of office, the Anna, the Stanislav, the Vladimir ribbon— 'not for ourselves, not for ourselves . . . but for our rank!' Russia has become a gigantic regimental barracks in which individuality is replaced by the uniformity of Facelessness, of the neutrality of lifeless obedience, in which the ideal is neither to laugh nor cry, neither to rejoice nor grieve, neither to praise nor criticize, but simply to conform.

If Herzen understood quite clearly then that autocracy sprang not from the will of a single man, but was a vast network of human relations grounded in the arrogance of power and the humiliation of servility, how did he see the sociology of parliamentary democracy in the more liberal West? Essentially his view, like that of Pestel, the Decembrist martyr before him and like that of Tolstoy somewhat later, was that parliamentary democracy rested on military force no less than an Autocracy, but that the face of violence was better concealed and also less harsh in its application. Its relative ability to enforce a non-discriminatory rule of law sprang from a degree of administrative decentralization obtaining in countries like Switzerland, England and America, which contrasted sharply with the extreme centralization of Russia and to a lesser degree of the

Second Empire in France. He concedes the practical benefits of centralization in the organization and maintenance of posts and telegraphs, roads and currency; but for the rest warmly endorses the Swiss and Anglo-Saxon suspicion of the centralization of power. (pp. 57-8)

But if Herzen found the English suspicion of centralization to his taste, he was not at all disposed to accept the claims of parliamentary liberalism at their face value. He was deeply influenced at the most impressionable time of his youth by the trial of the Decembrists, which took place when Herzen was thirteen years of age. He described in lyrical terms the rapturous emotion with which Ogarev and he took the vow on the Sparrow Hills overlooking Moscow always to be faithful to the ideals for which the Decembrists had died. (p. 59)

[Herzen was also completely disillusioned] with Western liberal constitutionalism, which he [saw] as a mask to conceal the avarice of Protestant commercialism. The medieval world was possessed of a certain aristocratic dignity, symbolized in the figures of the knight and the feudal lord, whose position rested on the principle of *noblese oblige*. Even if the obligations were far from honoured in reality, the code of chivalry was understood, could be appealed to and provided a certain measure of mutual security. Catholicism even more obviously imposed clearly defined moral obligations which again, though more honoured in the breach than in the observance, set limits to natural extravagance and compelled those who lapsed to seek justification. This world could not survive because its structure rested on the classification of men according to status and this evoked the resistance of free men in the shape of the Reformation and the French Revolution. . . . In place of a medieval culture resting on ideals which were found wanting arose a culture involving no obligations, terrifying in its bankruptcy. The petty bourgeois culture is purely commercial—emancipated from absolute monarchy and serfdom, it is true—but resting on no sense of moral obligation, not even the obligation to serve in the army so long as voluntary mercenaries can be found and governments can be hired to ensure their fiscal and physical security.

> . . . Its gospel is brief: 'Heap up wealth, multiply thy riches till they are like the sands of the sea, use and misuse thy financial and moral capital, without ruining thyself, and in comfort and honour thou wilt attain length of years, marry thy children well, and leave an honoured memory behind thee'.

This is the spirit which informs the general atmosphere of European life with the result that where its principles are to be found most highly developed in the most industrialized, wealthy, cultured part of Europe, life is there at its most stifling, oppressive and insufferable.

In such a culture all conflict is inevitably canalized into two camps, contending with each other for property and power. On the one hand are the bourgeois property owners, who stubbornly defend their privileges and monopolies, and arrayed against them are the petty bourgeois, driven on by envy and avarice, possessed of no property but desperately anxious to wrest it from the bourgeoisie, if only they had the power. A man's role in life, the position he takes up on either side in the conflict is thus determined not by moral principle—since a conflict over possession is morally meaningless—but by the accident of birth and fortune, status or class position. These being the basic socio-economic conditions governing political conflict, the institutional political forms best suited to the working out of this spurious conflict are those of liberal parliamentary democracy. . . . [Of parliamentary government Herzen writes:]

> Parliamentary government not as it follows from the popular foundations of the Anglo-Saxon *Common Law*, but as it has taken shape in the law of the state, is simply the wheel in a squirrel's cage, and the most colossal one in the world. Could a show of a triumphant march forward whilst remaining majestically in the same spot be possibly achieved more perfectly than it is by the two English Houses of Parliament?

His contempt for parliamentary democracy is not confined to the conservatism of the English model. The system itself is fraudulent, providing an illusion of choice, of possible change, when the reality is one of greed administered by 'X' or 'Y' within the framework of the *status quo*. His analysis of Gallic republicanism on the other side of the Channel is accordingly on all fours with the scathing exposure of the Anglo-Saxon squirrel's wheel. 'Do you want political action within the present order?' he asks rhetorically. Do you really want to emulate the liberal politicians of the moment, the Marrats, the Odilon Barrots? Answering his own questions, he replies:

> You don't want this, you feel that any decent man is outside all politics, that he can't seriously concern himself with such questions as whether a republic needs or doesn't need a President, whether an Assembly may or may not send men to hard labour without trial, or, whether one should vote for Cavaignac or Louis Bonaparte? You may spend a month or a year thinking which of them is better; but you won't decide because they are, as children say, 'both worse'. All that is left for a self-respecting man is not to vote at all. Look at the other topics *à l'ordre du jour,* they are all the same, . . . death looms up behind them.

This entire soulless order of things is so irrational that it is doomed. Waste no pity on it; Tsarist autocracy and the so-called 'freedom' of bourgeois republics are alike condemned to death; for they are incompatible with genuine freedom and the ultimate aspirations of men. And what of the people? Although from time to time Herzen hurls an anathema in their direction, and although he is utterly contemptuous of the liberals' idealization of the people, fundamentally he looks to the people eventually to sustain the individualism, the love of independent character or personality, on which he sees freedom to be necessarily based. (pp. 59-62)

But there is a paradox for the individualist—one who believes in the right and duty of every man to realize his own identity and act it out with conviction or even stubborn persistence— if he also affects to despise the people, who after all are no more than a large number of separate individuals. Herzen is aware of this, and in more expansive and mellow mood, he comes to the defence of the people. He sees them as having been misunderstood and cast for an impossibly artificial and idealized role by the liberals themselves awakening from the uncritical torpor of their privileged existence. In this way he not only works off his exasperation with the liberals, the men who had persecuted his friend, Proudhon, but re-establishes

his identity and solidarity with the long-suffering, if ungrateful people. The people he sees as an elemental, majestic force which shapes history; to criticize the people is akin to criticizing the ocean or an earthquake. (p. 63)

But if Herzen has been tempered by years of disappointment, exile, crushed hopes, personal tragedies, he is of course never resigned in his own person to the evils that surround him, which he ceaselessly diagnoses with a view to struggling against and urging others to do likewise. For the inequalities, injustices and persecutions which he arraigns are not the end of the matter; their periodic outcome on the larger theatre of international relations is war. And the causes of war are shrewdly diagnosed in a short and little-known fragment which Herzen wrote on the occasion of the Austro-Prussian War in 1866. His view is that it is essential to recognize it as a morbid natural phenomenon in the sense that cholera is natural, and then on the basis of the evidence proceed to a scientific diagnosis of the causes of war as such—an attitude by no means common at that time. In the presence of cholera, we do not engage in futilities of justification or finding excuses; we do what is needful: bow our heads, treat the afflicted, bury the dead; but above all we seek the causes in the hope of eliminating them. Cholera, we know, has its origin in pits, awash with putrefying filth, where the germs breed. So these pits we clean out or rather, Herzen, always truthful, adds: 'we are always on the point of cleaning them'. Thus far, the analogy with war is exact save for one crucial difference. Whereas with cholera the rottenness is at the bottom of pits, in the matter of war the offending rottenness is to be found in the summits; and it is there that it is necessary to take our preventive measures.

He then makes an assertion which contains the two basic propositions on which Tolstoy was to erect his giant edifice of *War and Peace,* namely, *(a)* the elemental fatalistic character of war as a great natural, historical phenomenon, and *(b)* the fact that this fatal *motif* rests on lack of conscious responsibility on the part of the masses and unscrupulousness on the part of their leaders. In Herzen's own words:

> For the masses War has that self-same fatalistic, unconscious character as the sea. It is only powerful through the absence of consciousness at the bottom and the absence of conscience and truth at the top.
>
> (p. 65)

Herzen allowed for the possibility of moral development and never abandoned his faith in it; but, as he grew older, he had to struggle with a growing sense of pessimism and gloom. He speaks of the 'childishness of the human brain' which is accordingly unable to accept the truth in all its simplicity, but which requires a muddled complexity, incomprehensibility and irrationality of explanation to match its own confused incoherence. Nor, he insists, is he speaking of the uncultivated masses, but of the learned, the literary, juristic, governmental and revolutionary would-be governmental people who vie with one another in 'maintaining the innate senselessness of mankind'. Injustice, irrationality, absurdity must in the nature of things always prevail over their contraries, since the contending forces are so hopelessly unequal. (p. 66)

[Herzen] saw with piercing clarity what was wrong and diagnosed it brilliantly. But he was less sure of himself when it came to prescription. He had the sharp insight of one who truly understood and valued freedom, but, an atheist to the end, he had no solid metaphysical base on which to stand, and was accordingly driven back on to the shoals of relativism. This is also seen in the fact that, although his warm-hearted, sustained sincerity is never in doubt, he failed himself to live up to his own best insights. He rejects wealth and privilege as inconsistent with equality, as the fruits of avarice or the cause of envy and as corrosive of the simplicity of the human spirit at its best, but he justified his own wealth on the grounds that money is power, a weapon, and it would be stupid to throw away a weapon in time of war. 'It would be hypocritical to affect to despise property in our time of financial disorganization'. (p. 67)

The difficulty with Herzen is that he has nothing to offer to the individual as to why he should make sacrifices to attempt to stand fast against . . . overwhelming pressures. Consciousness of being right or hoping that somehow or other things will improve in the future are reasons which do not seem entirely convincing. He has outlived the romanticism of the revolutionaries, he tells us; he has put behind him the mystic belief in progress to which he had remained wedded longer than 'other theological dogmas'. All this is admirable if a sure anchorage is found at last. But what was there left? Nothing, he confesses, except a passionate, what he calls 'religious' belief in the individual, in the human will, by which he means a confidence in himself and faith in two or three friends. What is this ultimately other than the individualism of, say, John Stuart Mill, stripped of the utilitarian rhetoric? As he himself candidly admits, there were inner contradictions in such a position, and this fundamental contradiction between absolute and relativist values he never did resolve. It is the fatal flaw, the Achilles heel in Herzen.

He is quite explicit in avowing his relativism. In answer to the question: 'Is there not an eternal morality, one and indivisible?' he answers categorically, 'No'. Such an absolute morality necessarily could have no existence outside the realm of theory and abstract thought. . . . [There] is no Truth, only new values gradually forged to replace old ones which have ceased to carry conviction and are found wanting. (pp. 68-9)

Ultimately the profoundest and best side of Herzen's nature identifies quite unequivocally with the free spirit of man, capable of emancipating itself from the determining influence of appetite and environment. He believes in the ineluctable freedom to choose inherent in each and every individual. If history is determined, it is not inexorably so. The existing form of the State is doomed; nothing, he believes, can stand in the way of socialism eventually. But the forms of development will be determined in detail by the will of individuals. Progress is possible, albeit very slow. He likens it to the movement of Alpine glaciers. Every summer the ice crust melts, every autumn it begins to freeze again a little thinner. Meteorologists can reckon how many aeons of time will be needed for the summer finally to beat the winter and melt all the ice; the historians have not as yet made their parallel calculation. In fact, they could not do so, as Herzen in his non-scientific mood, well understands. For there is nothing inevitable about progress. As he himself points out, the power of evil as of good is dependent on the will and work of individuals. 'It is possible to lead astray an entire generation, to strike it blind, to drive it insane, to direct it towards a false goal. Napoleon proved this'. And in our own time Hitler proved it even more decisively.

If there is freedom for evil, there is certainly freedom for good. The mistake people make lies in yielding too easily to the power of the external world; they give in without really willing it and

thus find their independence, their most priceless possession, forfeit. Once we cease to rely upon ourselves, 'the fatal power of the external becomes invincible; to enter into battle with it seems madness'. To reject the sway of the temporal and material forces that seem to dominate our lives is, Herzen knows, not easy; frequently it requires long arduous trials in which a man feels himself sore beset. When dogged by misfortune he comes close to despair, and then at last when most at odds with the world, he feels confident not only that he understands it but that he understands himself; that he is no longer dependent on the world, because he knows that to struggle against it against all the odds is somehow indubitably right. There then arises in the soul the simple liberating question: 'Am I really so fettered to my environment in life and death that I have no possibility of freeing myself from it even when I have in fact lost all touch with it, when I want nothing from it and am indifferent to its bounty?'

From that moment a man is free, no longer herding together with his brethren for warmth and security, but alone, a stranger, an alien outside the gates, at war for ever with the City of Destruction, alone but standing on 'open, manly ground'. On this ground alone is nourished the inner spiritual freedom to advance humanity in defiance of the pressures of the power of autocracy above and of the masses below. Everything good comes from the individual, standing his ground, unafraid, yet humble enough to know that he is called upon to wage an unending struggle within himself as well as with a hostile, external world. (pp. 70-1)

*R. V. Sampson, "Alexander Herzen," in his* The Discovery of Peace, *Pantheon Books, 1973, pp. 49-71.*

**WILLIAM CANNON WEIDEMAIER**    (essay date 1981)

[*Weidemaier considers Herzen a forerunner of atheistic existentialism. After outlining the seven elements he considers central to this philosophical movement, including the denial of God, rejection of metaphysical beliefs, and a general hatred of bourgeois values, he traces the occurrence of these ideas throughout* From the Other Shore.]

Although no unanimously accepted definition of atheistic existentialism exists, most scholars would stress at least seven interrelated ideas: (1) a denial of God and of all God substitutes; (2) a rejection of metaphysical systems and an insistence that reality is completely devoid of any transcendent meaning or purpose; (3) a disbelief in objective values, accompanied by a claim that values exist only to the extent that they are first created and then sustained by free individual choice; (4) an extreme, uncompromising individualism that stresses personal fulfillment and individual freedom not only from such external restraints as the state and the crowd but also from the deceptions of an unauthentic self; (5) a contempt for the modern world because of its alleged impotency and its high levels of anxiety; (6) a loathing of bourgeois values with their worship of progress and their indiscriminate leveling of taste; and (7) a sense of anguish over the spiritual loneliness created by the preceding conditions and over the inevitable suffering believed to accompany life and knowledge. Separately, of course, each of these seven ideas can be found outside of atheistic existentialism; it is only when all seven are fused into a single world view, to become a protest against depersonalizing modern social and intellectual systems, that they delineate a distinct movement in the history of ideas.

The first of these seven points, the denial of God, seems obvious enough in Herzen. He lacked in his youth any strong religious influence and, following a brief flourish of religiosity during his first provincial banishment, easily abandoned all religious belief in a soul or its immortality. In *From the Other Shore*, written in his mid-thirties, he condemned God to the same fate as Louis XVI, declaring both theological and political absolutism to be incompatible with the sovereignty of reason. If Herzen's atheism never attained quite the degree of metaphysical loneliness Nietzsche achieved when he announced the death of God and sent man "straying as through an infinite nothingness," Herzen certainly approached this in claiming that "there is no master craftsman, no design, only a foundation, and we are entirely alone."

It is important not to confuse Herzen's outlook with the atheism which was becoming increasingly common in European intellectual circles as materialism and positivism gained ground in the nineteenth century. In fact, Herzen was contemptuous of the complaisant atheism he found in his contemporaries. "As if atheism were enough to abolish religion," he scoffed. What was needed was to root out the religious urge itself. It distressed him that there seemed to be "no logical abstraction, no collective noun, no unknown principle or uninvestigated cause that might not be, if only for a short time, divine or sacred." He could not understand how, "having discarded positive religion, we have retained all the habits of religion." Against such habits he preached a total iconoclasm: "Down with all idols." "Sincerity and independence are my idols." This desire to eradicate all compulsion to worship—including the secular theorist's compulsion to turn political and moral abstractions into divine surrogates—is reminiscent of Nietzsche, who warred against the "theologian's instinct" as the "most widespread, really *subterranean*, form of falsehood found on earth," and of Stirner, who upon reading Feuerbach's call to love man rather than God replied: "Haven't we the priest again there? Who is his God? Man with a great M! . . . It is nothing more or less than a new—*religion*."

The second feature of atheistic existentialism, its rejection of all metaphysical systems and teleological scenarios, can be found in Herzen's mature thought just as surely as can his atheism. His antipathy toward philosophical system building began with his well-known revolt against German idealism, particularly Hegelianism. As early as 1841 he wrote of his longing for "the development of philosophy into life." By the mid-1840s he was complaining of how difficult it was to get at reality in a straightforward way because "our imagination is so corrupted and saturated with metaphysics." He increasingly detected in German philosophers a compulsion "to impose an artificial structure on history." Eventually he would decide that life simply "does not coincide with the dialectic of pure reason." (pp. 559-60)

In examining Herzen's break with German idealism certain scholars have seen little more than a Russian version of Left Hegelianism. Up to a point there is indeed a parallel. But what is frequently overlooked is that Herzen, unlike the Left Hegelians, was not interested in constructing a systematic materialistic philosophy, whatever its inherent political advantages, but in abandoning systematic philosophy entirely. . . . In the end his antipathy toward systematic philosophy led him to reject materialism as thoroughly as he had earlier rejected idealism.

Herzen's hostility to everything systematic, while in sharp contrast to the mainstream of nineteenth-century thought, is typical not only of atheistic existentialism but religious existentialism as well.

A further aspect of Herzen's rebellion against metaphysical system building is his complete break with all teleological conceptions of history. In his mature world view, history has no purpose or goal, a conclusion seemingly forced upon him less by philosophical reflection than by the long series of tragedies that marred his personal and political life. With each new blow he inched ever closer to a nihilistic perspective of a meaningless universe governed largely by chance and will. As late as 1836 the idea that reality was ruled by chance still seemed to him "an absurdity concocted by disbelief. "But by 1842, following his second provincial banishment and the deaths of several of his children, he was ready to curse "the outrageous power of chance." (p. 561)

In the West Herzen developed fully his views on "the delirium of history" and "the plasticity of nature." *From the Other Shore* undoubtedly offers the most extreme expression of this ateleological outlook and marks the termination of Herzen's earlier efforts to grapple with the problems of history and metaphysics. In *From the Other Shore*, the future simply "does not exist"; nothing is inevitable since "everything can happen." What then of human destiny? Why do people live?

> Just so, they are born and they live. Why does anything live? This I think is the limit of all questions. Life is both the means and the end, the cause and the effect. . . . In the past people used to look for answers in the clouds or in the depths, upwards or downwards, but they found nothing, because all that is essential, and important, is here on the surface.

The early date at which Herzen asserted this doctrine of the total self-sufficiency of human existence—that it neither has nor requires any transcendent purpose or explanation—is the strongest single reason for insisting on his place among the founders of atheistic existentialism. This belief that life is its own first principle is the final result of atheistic existentialism's metaphysical revolt. . . .

Metaphysical nihilism led Herzen to yet a third trait found in atheistic existentialism—the denial of absolute moral values. Having found no God, no purpose, and no overriding necessity, he could find no basis for an absolute system of values either. "Absolute morality," he decided, "must share the fate of everything which is absolute—outside of theories, outside of abstractions, it does not exist." "Indeed, the free man *creates* his own morality." (p. 562)

But assuming one is free to create one's own morality, what features should it possess? Herzen's answer to this question constitutes his fourth link with the existential revolt—an extreme, uncompromising individualism. He would use his moral freedom to establish, as an ethical first principle, the absolute sanctity of the individual. He claimed to have devoted his entire life to this one idea, to a war "against every kind of deprivation of freedom, in the name of the absolute independence of the individual." If there is a categorical imperative in his writings it is his advice "to begin an independent, self-reliant life, which would find salvation within itself even were the whole world around us to perish." The defense of this principle could be entrusted to no party, ideology, or political system: "we shall find no haven but in ourselves, in the consciousness of our unlimited freedom, of our autocratic independence." Herzen's concern here goes well beyond nineteenth-century liberalism's defense of individual liberty to a deeper concern with the sanctity of the person:

> To understand the personality of man; to understand all the sacredness, all the breadth of the actual rights of the individual, is the most difficult task, and, except for special cases and exceptions, it was never solved by any of the past historical forms; for this a greater maturity is needed than man has attained.

This belief in the immaturity of his own age best explains another feature of Herzen's individualism that is typical of the existential thinker—a loathing of the crowd. Even Herzen's earliest writings exhibit this dislike. "People! People! Wherever you are everything is spoiled," he exclaimed at age twenty-one. (p. 563)

Residence in the West only intensified this contempt. Here Herzen discovered "a passive mass, an obedient herd." At one point he dismissed nearly the entire population of Europe as "orangutans." He was particularly harsh on the French, accusing them of trying "to subject individuality to the herd." Throughout his Western writings, but especially in *From the Other Shore,* he contrasted the crowd not only with the individual but with truth:

> I said that truth belongs to the minority.... In the present as in the past, I see knowledge, truth, moral strength, craving for independence, love of beauty in a small group of men, antagonistic, unsympathetic to the majority, lost in their milieu.

Such condemnations of the crowd are one of the most familiar features on both sides of the existential revolt. (pp. 563-64)

It would be misleading of course to stress Herzen's condemnation of the crowd while ignoring his sympathetic portraits of Russian peasants or his repeated demands for social justice. Clearly his hatred for the crowd was not an aristocratic contempt for the lower social orders but a recognition of the dangers that public opinion presents to individual integrity. What Herzen despised was the herd mentality, whatever its social form, while what he admired was the ability to stand independently, to accept complete responsibility for the defense of one's own rights and ideas....

[His] extreme "aristocratic" individualism was often accompanied by a pronounced egoism typical of atheistic existentialism. While contemptuous of petty vanity, Herzen extolled a "healthy vanity" of the sort found in "a man in the fullness of his power and activity." ... (p. 564)

However existential Herzen's egoism and his contempt for the crowd may appear, his individualism must meet an additional requirement. Ever since Kierkegaard, major contributors to both the religious and atheistic sides of existentialism have stressed that true individualism requires a victory over self-alienation, an inner liberation from an unauthentic self, and a rediscovery of a supposedly authentic core of the personality from which one has become alienated by internalizing and unconsciously accepting the values of one's surroundings.

Did Herzen share this concern with self-liberation? At first glance it is easy to see in him only the social polemicist warring against the evils of the external world. But closer examination reveals that the concept of an inner liberation was actually central to his other beliefs. His very notion of revolution came

to rest on the idea of self-liberation, on the belief that "one cannot liberate a people outwardly any further than they have freed themselves inwardly." (p. 565)

Herzen's fifth affinity with existentialism—his conviction that the mind and spirit of the modern world were nearly bankrupt—was evident even before he left Russia in 1847. He had already sensed by then that the modern age was one of anxiety. This insight, like everything in his writing, attained its fullest expression only after his experiences in the West and his encounter there with what he described as "the perpetually torn, agitated, agonized soul of modern man." Anxiety, however, was only a symptom. For Herzen modern man's fundamental problem was his lack of creative power.... Though basically a reasonable person, Herzen at times attacked modernity with those extremes of irrational overstatement and disregard for veracity common to existentialism:

> I am truly horrified by modern man. Such absence of feeling, such narrowness of outlook, such lack of passion and indignation, such feebleness of thought.... But when, how did these people waste their lives? When did they have time to dissipate their strength? They were corrupted at school and befuddled there. They went to pieces, with their existence of beer shops and wild student squalor. They lost their strength in petty, dirty amours. Born and bred in a sickroom atmosphere, they never had much energy and withered before they blossomed. They were exhausted, not by passion but by dreams of passion. Here again, as always, these *litterateurs,* idealists, theorists practiced debauchery in their minds and passion in books. Really one sometimes bitterly regrets that a man cannot turn himself into some other species of animal—obviously to be a donkey, a frog, or a dog is more pleasant, more honest, nobler than to be a man of the nineteenth century.

It could be argued, of course, that these indignant and emotional charges are not a product of existentialism so much as the legacy of a romanticism Herzen falsely claimed to have abandoned. (pp. 565-66)

But if Herzen never completely escaped his early romanticism, this fact in no way eliminates him from the ranks of the existential rebels. Many early participants in that revolt, their numerous disclaimers notwithstanding, had deep roots in the romantic movement.... (p. 566)

The sixth of Herzen's seven existential traits is his scathing contempt for the bourgeoisie. What links Herzen to the existential revolt in this regard is that his own contempt for the bourgeoisie rested less on the deep concern with economic exploitation that one expects from a socialist than on an essentially aesthetic condemnation of the bourgeois personality. The bourgeoisie had a flawed character; it lacked "expansiveness" and "higher interests"; it was insufferably mediocre. Its "Philistinism" inhibited culture by destroying all respect for quality. (pp. 566-67)

Like other participants in the existential revolt, Herzen ridiculed the bourgeoisie's adoration of progress. Indeed, he denounced the idea of progress not only as a middle-class value but as a revolutionary ideal as well. Much like Camus, who refused to discuss reform in terms of "that evil toy called progress," Herzen saw progress as a dangerously beguiling idol and opposed those who would sacrifice present generations to it in the name of future happinesss. Instead he preached devotion to the individual of the present: ''Is it not simpler to understand that the individual lives not for the *fulfillment of destiny,* not for the incarnation of an idea, not for progress, but only because he was born, and was born *for* (however unsatisfactory the word is) . . . the present.''

The seventh and final intellectual trait that justifies placing Herzen among the founders of atheistic existentialism is the deep sense of anguish that pervades his mature writing. ''Is it possible,'' he asked as early as 1843, ''that the whole of life should consist in torment and agony?'' Life and suffering appeared inseparable. ''What grounds are there,'' he wanted to know, ''for the idea that people are happy anywhere, that they can or ought to be happy?'' Only his distrust of the abstract prevented the mature Herzen from professing ''a new type of Manichaeism,'' a belief in a world possessed of ''rational (that is, purposeful) evil.''

The principal source of Herzen's anguish, in addition to his tragic personal life, was his conviction that knowledge invariably led to misery. As early as *Dilettantism in Science,* in 1843, he suggested that the sight of naked truth could cost a man ''his life and his finest hopes.'' In *From the Other Shore* he spoke of the need to choose between ''the bliss of lunacy'' and ''the unhappiness of knowledge.'' A confirmed skeptic, he could never bear skepticism with the ease of Montaigne, Voltaire, or Hume. For Herzen doubt was never easy: ''You think that doubt, calm on the surface, is easy, but can you know what a man, in a moment of pain, weakness, exhaustion, might not be ready to give for a belief?'' (p. 567)

[The] joining of misery and knowledge is one of the most recurrent themes in existential thought, especially on its atheistic side. ''I swear to you, gentlemen,'' sneers the Underground Man, ''to be overly conscious is a disease, a real thoroughgoing disease.'' . . .

Herzen's works offer abundant evidence for placing him among the earliest precursors of atheistic existentialism. (p. 568)

But if Herzen was an existential thinker, care should be taken nonetheless in comparing him with Western thinkers of that tradition. . . .

If a likeness to some Western figure in the existential tradition must be found, then perhaps it is best to compare Herzen to the least purely philosophical of those figures—Albert Camus. Camus meets all seven points of our earlier definition of atheistic existentialism and, like Herzen, expressed his philosophic views almost entirely as a literary by-product of his attempts to wrestle with the immediate problems of life and politics. Neither he nor Herzen allowed his intense individualism to degenerate into that extreme subjectivity which points so much of existential thought down the road toward solipsism. (p. 569)

> *William Cannon Weidemaier, ''Herzen and the Existential World View: A New Approach to an Old Debate,'' in* Slavic Review, *Vol. 40, No. 4, Winter, 1981, pp. 557-69.*

## NICHOLAS RZHEVSKY (essay date 1983)

[*In this overview of Herzen's fiction, Rzhevsky analyzes the early short stories and* Who Is to Blame? *Among the works discussed are* ''The Legend,'' ''Elena,'' ''The Notes of a Certain Young Man,'' ''The Thieving Magpie,'' *and* ''Doctor Krupov.'' *Rzhev-*

*sky assesses their style, structure, and content, as well as the literary influences informing each work.*]

[''**The Legend**'' was Herzen's] first work of fiction, and a largely unnoticed attempt to bring an older genre tradition of Russian Christian culture into nineteenth-century literature. The principal source of ''**The Legend**'' was a *Cheti Minei* or church calendar reading of saints' lives. Herzen's particular choice is St. Theodora; he does not leave the original structure of her vita intact, however, but adds a surprise ending, mysterious flashbacks, and other narrative devices meant to liven up the genre's rigid form. The stylistic changes, designed to appeal to a modern reader, reinforce the short story's intellectual purpose by making contemporaneous the moral intensity of religious values expressed in St. Theodora's noble sacrifice and spiritual heroism.

One such contemporary technical innovation—suggested, in all likelihood, by prior readings in the autobiographical styles of Rousseau, Heine, Goethe, and Karamzin—was the use of the first person in combination with an omniscient point of view. The narrator of the first part of the story, as Herzen himself during the writing of the primary draft, is in a prison which overlooks Moscow. Glancing down into the city he thinks of the constant polarity of good and evil, ''holy minutes of ecstasy'' and ''the poisonous essence of licentiousness,'' which affect the urban life of the present. The ringing church bells of Simon Monastery remind him of the derisive ''whistles and laughter'' which greet religion in the nineteenth century and lead him to think of past spiritual heroism which could provide examples for the present. A lengthy footnote at the conclusion of the passage explicitly formulates Herzen's intentions. In it he asks why it is necessary to retell the life of a saint already available in the old church text and suggests a response which clearly postulates the need for bringing a religious message into the contemporary world: the compiler of saints' lives did his work in the tenth century, while ''it is now the XIX.''

The latter part of the narrative shifts into a third person account of St. Theodora's life. The plot is full of flashbacks and interruptions at key moments; a number of puzzling questions are answered only in the shattering dénouement when it is finally revealed that the humble monk Theodore is really Saint Theodora. . . . Initially, the reader is faced with the enigma of Theodore's motives and origins before entering the monastery: the youth is noble and handsome but deeply troubled by something. At about midpoint in the story Herzen adds a second key puzzle when the half-naked daughter of an abbot attempts to seduce Theodore and the passage is tantalizingly interrupted before we find out if she succeeds. Soon afterward, however, a newborn child is brought to the monastery; accused of its paternity, Theodore is ostracized by the monks. Suspense is maintained by the implicit question of why a character till then portrayed as the noblest and purest of men would fall into such extreme temptation, and, moreover, why he would lie to his mentor about his sins. The last is a particularly heinous act on the face of it, because Theodore and the Abbot establish a near sacred friendship in which they set out together on a spiritual quest to find the true meaning of religion.

The intellectual motifs of the story are expressed mainly in the protagonists' theological dialogues. Theodora, as much in action as in words, stands for kenotic values; she willingly accepts suffering and martyrdom to achieve a moral triumph over injustice and humiliation suffered at the hands of the monks. The abbot, on the other hand, defends a metaphysics based on theosis; through Christ, he argues, man has the means of expressing his free will and divine destiny. Close as such ideas are to the ones offered in **"On the Place of Man in Nature,"** Herzen does not allow Christianity to be idealized. The failings of the church (in addition to the monks' shortsightedness and the potential for religious corruption represented by the seductress) are hinted at in a passage on the Inquisition and in the overly heated rejection of women and sensuality which the abbot—all ironic ignorance—proposes to Theodore. The abbot also notes a more positive religious role, however, by pointing to monastic life as a model of brotherhood and equality for the future. The direction indicated is toward the religious foundations on which utopian socialists would build their plans. At the same time, by having the monks reject Theodora, the writer suggests his favorite dilemma of the individual standing against the crowd. Socially progressive as it may be, monastic life thus indicates the future concern for uncomfortable conditions in the phalanstery that Herzen would later show in his defense of individuality. (pp. 35-7)

The progression from religious motifs and values to a contemporary literary perspective continues in Herzen's second complete work of fiction, **"Elena."** ... (p. 37)

**"Elena"** unites three narrative tonalities, repeating in a somewhat less successful fashion the fictional experiments begun by Alexander Pushkin and Nikolai Gogol in the 1830s. The primary stylistic line involves wordplay, sudden reversals in meaning, cutting metaphors, satire, and irony. Not unlike Pushkin's "Little House in Kolomna" (1830), Gogol's "Nose" (1836) and "Nevsky Prospect" (1835), a jocular and often mocking narrative voice jolts the reader's sensibilities and expectations. The opening sentence, "In a small house on Povarsky street lived a man who was of small height," establishes an irreverent tone which continues throughout. The description of a room is made in these terms: "The whole study was a continuation of this table, or better, the table was an abbreviation of the study." A bust of Socrates with an "upturned nose" stares at a bust of Cardinal Richelieu with "drooping cheeks." The life of one protagonist is described as "peaceful," but a phrase is added to the effect that cemeteries are peaceful too. An old woman's face is described to be a "coffeepot," while her neighbor's face "did not even have the appearance of a coffee-pot." The major character, who is to become thoroughly mad at the end of the story, declares in his first dialogue that "[he] is not mad," and so on. In contrast, a second narrative line provides a straightforward description of the protagonists' strong passions and tragic destinies. The Prince's "gnawing conscience" is declared to "tear asunder [his] soul." When he begs his mistress to be calm in the face of their impending separation, the argument used is that "every tear falls as molten lead on my heart." Sensing the inevitability of her lover's departure the young woman exclaims in all seriousness, "Is it not happiness to die now on your chest remembering our [first] meeting!" A servant is described praying before an icon of the Holy Mother with a comment that "the simple girl was so noble at this moment." From the narrator's point of view, in short, there is nothing funny in such prayers, in the high seriousness of true emotions, or in the fate of the abandoned Elena.

The two narrative modes evolve out of separate literary traditions. The mocking, satirical treatment is partially reminiscent of Voltaire's short fiction, partially indebted to Pushkin's irreverence, and partially written in the style of 1830s "clerk" literature of which Gogol created the most talented examples.

The description of high emotions, on the other hand, extends back to the genre based on saints' lives and the sentimental and romantic writings of Rousseau, Karamzin, and Goethe. A further complication is a third influence—evident in the Prince's madness and in some hints of the supernatural—of romantic writers such as Hoffmann, Zhukovsky, and Novalis. **"Elena"** is among the first Russian works after Gogol's to raise difficulties of interpretation arising from the use of such different literary traditions in one text. As a result of the narrative mixture the reader is likely to be uncertain where the author himself stands.

One cause of this uncertainty in perspective is the abandonment of a protagonist—similar to St. Theodora—who can directly present the writer's ideas and who can be used as an example of moral heroism and dignity. Herzen's growing awareness of literary craft undoubtedly suggested to him the clumsiness of the straightforward argumentation of the earlier pattern. ... An increasing familiarity with new fictional modes led the young author to introduce his beliefs not in the speeches or heroic acts of a central, positive character, but through experiments with different prose situations. Because of its rough edges in fact, **"Elena"** can be said to be most interesting for its probative nature; Herzen appraises and reformulates various literary traditions in the course of the narrative and tentatively starts off on an independent course appropriate to his own maturing thought.

Although the Prince comes from a long line of romantic heroes, and Elena suffers the fate of a typical sentimental character, neither is allowed the luxury of remaining within their literary tradition. A pivotal scene which can be expected to jolt and frustrate expectations of readers accustomed to established narrative schemata occurs at the story's end. The Princess comes to Elena's grave to beg absolution for her sick husband. Her touching speech—"... forgive him, he is suffering, tormented, unhappy in my embraces, and I do not dare to console him without making up with you"—is answered by a beautiful chorus of women's voices heard through an open church window. Apparently the prayers have some effect, for "a small cloud which had covered the sun dissipates." In the next scene the Prince indeed awakens a changed man; it would seem that a miracle has occurred. "He again felt his strength and his health," comments the narrator, but in this case from a deliberately unreliable and ironic perspective: the change is really in the direction of total madness. The Prince jumps out of bed only to start composing insane projects and to receive his wife, just arrived from Elena's place of repose, as a petitioner for government favors.

The ending mocks a number of conventions. Those readers who tended to view Elena as the innocent, suffering victim out of sentimental fiction are now faced with the unpleasant possibility—hinted earlier in her rather self-centered outbursts—that she is dispensing revenge rather than meekness and forgiveness from beyond the grave. Beguiled by the deceitful narrator, those readers who had placed their hopes in the efficacy of prayer and in some form of divine intervention are now confronted with a jeering providence that ridicules their expectations. Finally, the readers anticipating a noble or tragic resolution of the Prince's grief are left with a ludicrous madman scribbling incoherent projects.

The mocking narrative construction is not an end in itself, however, but serves a larger purpose supported by Herzen's feelings of guilt over Medvedeva, his contacts with Natalia and Witberg, and the attempt begun in **"The Legend"** to reformulate certain religious values in contemporary literary terms. Most of the traditional literary meanings of the characters and their actions are made unsteady by the narrative perspective, with one notable exception: the moral reality of the Prince's madness. By invalidating peripheral literary situations the narrator concentrates attention on the central motif which he does take seriously. Herzen's ideas on free will and man's dignity, as we have seen, would predispose him to view unfavorably either a simplistic religious faith in divine intervention or an elevation to heroic proportions of sentimental characters who do not control their fate. Since the element of moral triumph shown by St. Theodora is practically nonexistent in Elena, and since there is nothing of high exemplary value in her suffering or in that of the Princess, it is fully in keeping with his vision of individualism to maintain a narrative distance between himself and these characters and to have a bit of fun at their expense. The protagonist's madness, on the other hand, is neither the simplistic hope of supernatural intervention felt by his wife nor the sentimental fate of his mistress, but rather an expression of self-generated feelings of guilt. (pp. 37-40)

In subsequent works Herzen continued to look to religious material not only for moral reference but also for historical subject matter and for reinforcement of his sociocultural theories. The extent of his religious commitment can be judged by **"From Roman Scenes"** . . . and **"William Penn."** . . . Although the original texts are lost, two remaining sketches of these verse dramas include a number of telling rhetorical passages.

The first piece is set in pre-Christian Rome and consists mainly of a debate between the down-to-earth Meveii and his visionary friend Licinius. Licinius anticipates new eras not yet clearly seen and agonizes over the influence time and space have on human destiny: "The consciousness of my moral freedom, my eternal life lies in (my) heart, while I am limited on all sides by my body." In a formulation reminiscent of **"On the Place of Man in Nature,"** he argues for the absurdity of putting a soul in man if he is only a "hairless monkey." Feeling himself to be a disbeliever in pagan religions he senses, nevertheless, that "man must be connected to God, [must find] peace in him, [rise] up to him in love." At the sketch's end a fulfillment of this vision is hinted in the coming of Christ. Plebians brought on stage to explain the new era give it both a social resonance in keeping with French progressive theories—"God sent his son to save the world, to save the oppressed and poor"—and a supernatural meaning—"and the blind have begun to see, and the dead are resurrected." Many of the same religious motifs are present in "William Penn." The Quaker, in Herzen's interpretation, is reminiscent of the heroic kenotic image of St. Theodora brought close, it is true, to utopian socialist standards. Moreover, the protagonist and his mentor, George Fox, show the visionary qualities of Licinius; they too are willing to sacrifice their lives for "social, progressive religion."

In **"The Notes of a Certain Young Man"** . . . elements of the "clerk" literary tradition are combined with autobiographical, romantic, and sentimental components. As in the prior pattern, a core motif is the high spiritual destiny and the importance of the individual. "Life is my natural right," Herzen writes from the first person, "I am the master in it. I press forward with my 'I.' . . . I struggle. I open my soul to all. Through it I suck in the whole world." In large measure the reference here is to the pantheistic corner of German idealism in which the ultimate attainment of personality was understood to be the merger of man with nature. The tone of the quotation, however, is more indicative of authorial intent than the pantheistic message in the abstract. For throughout the sketch Herzen's core argument is not for subjugation to nature or to anything else, but for the assertion and spiritual fulfillment of the "I" to be brought about by a frontal attack on the obstacles to its existence.

Herzen's style, therefore, is again sharp with irony, bright with sarcasm, and colored with youthful exuberance; he is full of insolent jokes, puns, and slapstick incidents which explode in all directions. (pp. 41-2)

Herzen reverts to animal metaphors reminiscent of Gogol's symbolic technique to indicate . . . spiritual inadequacy. . . . [The] main vehicle for such an effect is a cruel, grotesque caricature of the baseness, whining servility, and blind obedience of an archetypal petty man, the Russian clerk. Herzen, in short, is agonizingly aware of the low thing that human beings make of themselves, and his principal intent is to force the reader to confront and reject this type of personality. (pp. 42-3)

***Who Is to Blame?*** reflects the major premises of the essays and private writings. Herzen's characters are all psychologically inadequate in some way, and their respective failures to rise up to high levels of "egoism" provide readers with clues to the novel's meaning. The first important clue, of course, is the unusual title. The personal pronoun evokes a sense of individual responsibility—precisely "who" and not "what"—while the form of a question shapes the entire text into a response invited from the audience.

As in the case of his earlier fiction, Herzen uses a number of different prose traditions. Each of the protagonists—the teacher Krutsifersky, his wife Liubon'ka, and the nobleman Bel'tov—derive from a separate literary world. Krutsifersky belongs to the clerk and natural schools of writing; Liubon'ka to sentimentalism; and Bel'tov to romanticism. The literary styles and motifs are not inviolate, however, but are juxtaposed for purposes of parody, irony, and the expression of Herzen's own literary ideas. In a more complex version of **"Elena's"** literary structure, the narrator stands outside the characters and events he describes. It is largely through his intervention that the different literary traditions are used to focus the intellectual presuppositions Herzen wants to criticize and to establish the principal sources of responsibility for what occurs. (pp. 51-2)

Herzen cleverly highlights the new issue of women's rights by refracting it through an older literary tradition based on feminine helplessness. The circumstance of Liubon'ka's background—a peasant mother, illegitimacy, the insults she endures in Negrov's household—place her in the typical victim role of the emotionally high-strung and suffering heroine favored by sentimental writers. Such a literary destiny is impossible in her case, however, because it is anticipated and caricatured through another character, Liubon'ka's stepmother. Madame Negrova comes out of a similar mixed-class marriage between a merchant-woman and a count. (pp. 52-3)

Herzen uses the common background of Liubon'ka and Negrova to show the younger woman's potential triumph over the sticky and degrading female role played out in her stepmother's caricatured sentimentalism. Liubon'ka, the narrator takes pains to point out, is unaffected by sentimental and romantic fiction because she develops intellectually on her own. The "barren environment" of country life, rather than being a hindrance, contributes to her mental and spiritual development by throwing her back on internal resources. She feels a sense of alienation, and this independent perspective enables her to rise above the laziness and vulgarity of the Negrovs. The one sentimental, romantic expectation she does share with Negrova, however, proves to be decisive. In this regard, Krutsifersky performs the same damaging function for her that her father earlier served for his wife, for the men are a form of escape that turns into another, ultimately defeating loss of freedom. (p. 53)

In Krutsifersky Herzen combines philosophical and psychological concepts he explored in his essays wth the clerk and natural-school literary traditions. . . . Meekness and daydreams place Krutsifersky in a position in which he is totally incapable of self-assertion, and such a failure of egoism in turn leads him to the debased life of an alcoholic. A complementing factor is Krutsifersky's ponderous fatalism; Herzen has him constantly parading the belief that all things, including his marriage (and assumedly Liubon'ka's affair with Bel'tov) are predetermined and cannot be controlled by human beings.

Krutsifersky's life, not unlike Liubon'ka's, follows the narrative heritage of his parents. The father, a poor doctor, is aged prematurely not by "passions" but by an "endless, crushing, petty, humiliating battle with need." . . . It is not surprising, therefore, that Krutsifersky becomes an alcoholic in compliance with a traditional pattern of the natural school, the literary world most reminiscent of such misfortunes. Any pathos or compassion that could be evoked by the young teacher's fate, however, is deliberately undercut by the comical and absurd tone of the narrative voice.

Part of this effect is created through the ironical juxtaposition of Krutsifersky with sentimental and romantic predecessors. . . . What is required from Krutsifersky for survival, it is made plain, are action and daring rather than the bouts of crying and readings from Zhukovsky of which he is fond. Liubon'ka, the sentimental heroine who rises above her literary prototype almost to the point of a complete break, can only note with bewilderment her husband's fixation in a similar role of a helpless, unmanly victim. She never thought a man could cry so, she writes in her diary.

The mockery of sentimental effusions is, at times, quite cruel. In one characteristic scene, the boorish and dim-witted Negrov acts as a tool of deflation when he accidentally receives Krutsifersky's love note to Liubon'ka. His slow reading, in a "heavy, bookish pronunciation" of Krutsifersky's poetical outpourings ("Be my Alina [Zhukovsky heroine]. I love you mindlessly, passionately, with exulation; your very name is love . . .'') provides one of the more humorous scenes in the novel. (pp. 54-5)

The mockery and victimization of the unhappy tutor in such passages would be a senseless cruelty on the part of the narrator if the character was indeed shown to be helpless and crushed by the environmental circumstances which affect his family. Krutsifersky, however, has more than ample opportunity to break out of the sad degradation of his life. In Part II Herzen gives him and Liubon'ka the means to a happy if not luxurious existence supported partially by her dowry and partially by his teacher's salary. Constricting environmental conditions are casually dismissed by the narrator as "external history," and emphasis is placed on the inner drama of ego and morality played out by the Krutsiferskys and Bel'tov. In this situation, the major issue is clearly Krutsifersky's character, and it is in such a realm of spirit and personality that he is conclusively shown to be inadequate; he can neither defend his rights to

Liubon'ka's love, nor sustain attempts at noble self-sacrifice (labeled "unnatural" by the narrator). (pp. 55-6)

Bel'tov, Krutsifersky's rival for Liubon'ka's love, continues the evolution of the romantic hero begun in Herzen's earlier works. On the whole, critics have tended to place him among the "superfluous men," in keeping with the character typology developed out of Pushkin's term by the radical publicist and editor of *The Contemporary,* Nicholas Dobroliubov. (p. 56)

Herzen's principal contribution to Russian literary characterization through Bel'tov, in fact, lies in his development of the "superfluous" protagonist's spiritual qualities. We know that the literary origins of the superfluous man lie partially in a stock situation of romanticism, a positioning of central hero against social milieu or "the crowd" that can be seen in Byron, Goethe, and Pushkin. In original form the romantic hero— mystic, poet, artist, or madman—stands outside of society or mere social categories since he represents the much more important contact of man with the nontemporal and divine. Bel'tov, in fact, reads Lord Byron and has the dignity, pride, and capacity for intense passions that separate him from the everyday community and link him with his literary predecessors. But if Childe-Harolde's, Aleko's, Onegin's, and Pechorin's negative moral and psychological traits are partially diminished and blurred by the attractiveness of their separation from the crowd and by the meanness and vulgarity of the society they abandon, Bel'tov's ideas and conscious judgments are focused by Herzen and found to bear the major responsibility for his condition. (p. 57)

[Bel'tov] stands in roughly the same relationship to Krutsifersky as Liubon'ka stands to her stepmother; the sentimental typology is preempted in both instances by its caricature in the clearly inferior characters. Krutsifersky's maudlin nature, absurdly passionate letters, and readings of Zhukovsky made it impossible for Bel'tov to be received as an idealistic, pure soul ruined by fate and society, just as it is impossible for Liubon'ka to be read sentimentally after the satiric depiction of Madam Negrova. . . .

Bel'tov's life, in the same way as Liubon'ka's and Krutsifersky's, is flawed by an inability to project and express his personality in the world. Educated by a Genevan tutor, a hopelessly idealistic and impractical man, he fails to pursue any one activity to its end. His biography is a succession of defeats, first in government service, then in medicine, art, local politics, and finally in love. The chief intellectual source of these difficulties, along with the sentimental-romantic literary typology, is anticipated and caricatured in Krutsifersky. Just as the tutor, Bel'tov does not believe in free will and refuses to recognize an independent sphere of action for man; but unlike Krutsifersky, Bel'tov is provided with unusual intelligence and talent so that the pathos of unfulfilled promise stands out in much stronger relief against his consciously accepted fatalism. (p. 58)

In the pattern of the other protagonists, Bel'tov is thematically linked to family history. Of particular interest, because it indicates what Bel'tov himself could have undertaken in the affair with Liubon'ka given a more resolute frame of mind, is the life of his father. The reader first encounters Bel'tov's parent, a profligate nobleman, during his attempt to seduce Sofia, a governess in his mother's household. Although she manages to escape his advances, gossip that arises out of the elder Bel'tov's careless remarks dishonors the young woman and makes it impossible for her to find a decent source of livelihood. Having reached the point of extreme poverty and despair, she decides to spend her last few pennies on a letter to vent her outrage over Bel'tov's dishonorable behavior. Bel'tov, who has entirely forgotten his unfortunate victim, is deeply affected by this correspondence and it generates an intense moral crisis in him. He radically changes his sense of values, goes off to find Sofia, and finally marries her.

The point of this key episode is that the elder Bel'tov's life is redeemed by his moral conversion; having served his function, in fact, Bel'tov dies soon after his marriage. It is not the society or economic forces that transform this protagonist, but an inner struggle and his own will to change his life. Such a moral confrontation, with oneself suggests, in turn, the proper solution to the dilemma of Bel'tov's son and Liubon'ka Krutsifersky. Bel'tov and Liubon'ka are at fault much more than the society they inhabit because they allow themselves to be victimized by the social institution of marriage instead of asserting the moral prerogative of their love. The absence of such assertion lies at the heart of their tragic separation and indicates that "blame" and responsiblity, in Herzen's view, must rest finally with the individual, his internal makeup, and his ethical choices. (p. 59)

["**The Thieving Magpie**"] is undoubtedly the most "social" of his published fiction in that it focuses on the abuses of serfdom and the brutal treatment of peasants by the infamous Prince Kamensky. A central motif is the triumph of human spirit and dignity in noxious conditions of oppression. ["**Doctor Krupov**"] is more complex and interesting for it provides a synoptic view of the literary technique and ideas we have been observing. In compact form, the story includes most of the essential points of transition from Herzen's religious and idealistic influences to the aesthetic culmination of his fictional work.

The two protagonists of "**Dr. Krupov**" are Levka, a feeble-minded boy serf, and the doctor himself, a character Herzen had already introduced in his novel. Levka is the last transformation of the positive, religious hero that Herzen began with St. Theodora. Anticipating somewhat Tolstoy's Platon Karatayev and Dostoevsky's Myshkin, he is the *iurodivyi* (holy fool) familiar to the Greeks as a *salos* and encountered frequently in Orthodox saints' lives and the kenotic tradition. In original form the *bozhii chelovek* (person of God), as he is also known, provided a reminder of nonearthly involvements and a divine moral standard for laymen through his rejection of material goods and commonsense pursuits of happiness. The *iurodivyi's* saintly disorientation and prophetic talents, as demonstrated by the holy fool who jolts Boris Godunov's conscience in Pushkin's play, served to suggest the presence of a transcendental measure in the universe; and Herzen, while hardly believing in prophecy or miraculous forces by now, uses Levka in essentially the time-honored fashion. The character's madness is really a form of moral worth and the means to indict the "banal ritual" and "same dull repetition not leading anywhere" of everyday, mundane life. (p. 60)

The key to Levka's madness is his individuality: he refuses to follow the norms and conventions of society and the humiliations and mockery he suffers result from a reluctance to abandon his own inclinations for a common measure. The people who surround Levka, Krupov decides, are as weakminded as he is, but they dislike the boy because he is "weak-minded not in their way but in his own." This independence, as we last see Levka, takes a traditional form of moral positioning found in the saints' lives; he retreats to the forest, lives on fruit and berries, and is befriended by animals whose natural

state enables them to respond to the innate spiritual worth rejected in civilization. An added, still-vibrant intellectual nuance of such withdrawal from society, of course, was provided to Herzen and his readers by Rousseau's exploration of secular sainthood.

If contemporary social and literary motifs in combination with religious prototypes suggested the metaphor for a positive spiritual condition in an ostensibly unbalanced mental state, madness also offered a technical resolution to the problem of depicting a positive hero in the desentimentalized and deromanticized conditions of 1840s literature. By separating Levka from the normal course of events—his withdrawal to the forest is not unlike that of another sublime idiot type, Prince Myshkin, who can only survive in the ethereal heights of Switzerland—Herzen is able to make his protagonist bear the burden of positive qualities without disturbing the skeptical and unsentimental narrative tone. Levka's incorruptible and timeless attributes are thus not imposed on the way things are understood to be in reality, and are used to measure the real against the ideal without didacticism or overly rhetorical gestures on the author's part.

The intermediary between Levka and society is Doctor Krupov, who serves as narrator and a figure of deliberate historical and religious reference in his own right. The two roles are interconnected: as the narrator, Krupov's function is to contrast Levka's timeless spiritual dignity to the society at large; as a character with his own literary meaning Krupov represents one concrete social form of the transition from religious to secular moral values. He is a priest's son who receives his higher education in a seminary, a fictional model of those many teachers, radicals, and men of letters who entered Herzen's cultural milieu by way of ecclesiastical training or background. Krupov's decision to interrupt his study of "spiritual subjects" in order to turn to the "earthly subject" of medicine is undoubtedly a form of commentary on the shifts of religious-moral impulses in Russia. (pp. 61-2)

The thematic structure is closely related to this underlying sense of movement in ideas from religious to secular concerns. If the work's first section includes Krupov's clerical background and a description of Levka's spiritual state, in the second Herzen shifts to a madhouse in which Krupov works and then to society at large. The narrative line incorporates, in miniature, the course of Herzen's writing from directly religious subjects, to supernatural-ethical issues explored in psychological form, to the secular sociopolitical expression of core religious moral standards. An essential omission in literary reference is perhaps as telling an indication of this fictional evolution as what is included. For both "**Dr. Krupov**" and the larger pattern of Herzen's literary development show a progression out of religious subjects and modes without the typical Western recourse to the picaresque. The structure of the picaresque—a series of unrelated characters and events connected by the secular point of view of the rogue—was certainly well known to Herzen through the related depiction of world madness in Voltaire's *Candide* and through the works of Fadey Bulgarin and Alexander Vel'tman. It was this structural arrangement which was used by Gogol in *Dead Souls*, although the religious crisis planned for Chichikov in Part II of the novel called for a moral transformation of the picaro which appears to have been unsuccessful. Rather than attempting such an awkward change in the rogue's essential secular properties or using the picaro at all for a thematic center, Herzen rejects the rogue's outside positioning, it can be hypothesized, because he recognizes that the totally alienated and cynical perspective could not adequately express his own strong commitments. Krupov, however, provides such a required narrative center by expressing native standards related to spiritual dignity, individualism, and moral vitality through his seminary-student-turned-doctor point of view. The character expresses both criticism and conviction, and thus allows Herzen to formulate his disagreements with the way things are without falling into complete disillusionment.

Although Krupov's examination of madness is the uniting thread of the two sections, in the second part a potential source of confusion is that instead of representing the positive attributes of Levka's individuality, madness is used to describe the *negative* qualities of various social types Krupov encounters. The reason for this transition from positive to negative nuances is not at all obvious in a superficial reading and has not really been explained in literary scholarship. It is one key, however, to Herzen's fictional treatment of the moral-psychological condition in modern society and opens his principal address to his readers.

In the lunatic asylum the causes of madness are still as clear as in Levka's case: madness originates in the inadequate recognition and nourishment which the committed are able to find for their "proud individuality." By humouring the inmates—i.e., addressing one as the Chinese emperor he imagines himself to be rather than administering the prescribed treatment—Krupov is much more successful than his medical colleagues. His cure, as can be expected, involves the acceptance of each patient's right to a particular existence and vision of self. In the outside world, however, lunacy is as prevalent as in the asylum, although the causes are much less clear to Krupov. (pp. 62-3)

The underlying explanation of the new negative shades of meaning . . . comes out of a continued exploration of psychic imperatives, particularly the drive to assert and fulfill one's individuality, dignity, and moral worth, that we have already observed. For if in the instances of Levka and the psychiatric ward patients, madness is presented as a clearly symbolic and abstract statement of such spiritual needs, in the everyday world the same moral-psychological forces are shown to prevail but in the actual self-defeating forms created for them by Herzen's contemporaries. . . . The metaphor of madness in both sections is addressed to self-interest and individuality . . . and its negative denotation represents those instances when individuals veer away from the high norms of dignity and morality that Herzen envisions to be the proper form of self-fulfillment.

Herzen's intellectual future is prefigured in the remaining observations made by Krupov. Among other modern forms of madness he mentions religion and romanticism, and characterizes the last as a "spiritual scrofula" that fosters "revulsion for everything real (and) practical." The remark anticipates Herzen's total shift from core Orthodox and romantic ideas to new sociopolitical interests. In later works, he would abandon entirely religious subjects and motifs, although their influence would remain in the deep-seated values and moral intensity of his memoirs and his political and historiocultural writings. One such metamorphosis would be evident in the writer's defense, undertaken in the court of Western liberal thought, of Russia's unique spiritual destiny. Herzen would never give up his conviction that the native Russian sense of communality and brotherhood offered the best hope for a historical model of morality and goodness and, at the same time, he would remain adamantly opposed to the notion that history is predetermined to

some such inevitable future. The vision of a free and irrational world evolution in which the individual's sphere of action is of primary value would form the basis of his historical and political speculations, and would be accompanied by an unbroken faith in moral choice and individual dignity, even in the face of the high-powered materialism and utilitarianism that would prevail in the 1850s and 1860s on the Russian political left.

Continuity would be preserved between Herzen's fiction and later political essays in one other constituent element of his writing. His abandonment of literature as a medium, in fact, was most likely made in response to an intensification of the long-active impulse to confront and affect his readers; the shift to total political rhetoric and historical argument was part of an attempt to reach the audience even more directly than in the earlier prose. Before the balance and distancing required of fiction was lost, however, (although not entirely, since a full range of important narrative skills were clearly put to work in *My Past and Thoughts*) Herzen once again signaled his particular concern for readers in the introduction to a novel he left uncompleted, *Duty Before All* (1851). "I do not know what goal could be nobler for an author than to educate and improve morals," he writes. "This is the duty of everyone who takes pen in hand, for what can be more pleasant than to teach others and to raise them up to *our* level of perfection." Characteristically, the ironic tone is complemented by a serious literary purpose, for what follows is a differentiation between "dry" didacticism and a morality decorated by "fancy" which Herzen proposes "to develop in a tale of moral education." The hoped-for spiritual education of the reader proceeding through literary fancy can be seen to be a core meaning of the fiction we have examined from its beginnings. It is in terms of such an aesthetic catalysis of the readers' responses to the transcendental standards of their selves, then, that we can discard affective fallacies and speak of Herzen's own affective verity. (pp. 63-5)

*Nicholas Rzhevsky, "Herzen's Fiction: An Affective Verity," in his* Russian Literature and Ideology: Herzen, Dostoevsky, Leontiev, Tolstoy, Fadeyev, *University of Illinois Press, 1983, pp. 29-65.*

---

## ADDITIONAL BIBLIOGRAPHY

Annenkov, P. V. *The Extraordinary Decade: Literary Memoirs.* Edited by Arthur P. Mendel. Translated by Irwin R. Titunik. Ann Arbor: University of Michigan Press, 1968, 281 p.*

    Memoirs of the decade in Russia beginning in 1839, written by a prominent Russian critic of the mid-nineteenth century. Annenkov was an intimate friend of Herzen, and his book is scattered with anecdotes about Herzen that illuminate his development as a socialist thinker.

Barghoorn, Frederick C. "Russian Radicals and the West European Revolutions of 1848." *Review of Politics* 11, No. 3 (July 1949): 338-54.*

    Describes the circumstances that led to the European revolutions of 1848. Barghoorn focuses on the recreation of these events in the writings of Nikolai Chernyshevsky and Herzen, whom he refers to as "those two greatest of Russian pre-Marxian social thinkers."

Carr, Edward Hallett. *The Romantic Exiles: A Nineteenth-Century Portrait Gallery.* New York: Frederick A. Stokes Co., 1933, 391 p.*

    An account of Herzen's life after he left Russia. Carr focuses on the personal aspects of those years and extensively discusses Herzen's wife's affair with the German poet Georg Herwegh.

Dziewanowski, M. K. "Herzen, Bakunin, and the Polish Insurrection of 1863." *Journal of Central European Affairs* 8, No. 1 (April 1948): 58-78.*

An analysis of the roles played by Herzen and Mikhail Bakunin in the unsuccessful Polish uprising of 1863. The critic also examines how the two men's participation in the insurrection affected their political and literary careers.

Lampert, E. "Alexander Herzen (1812-1870)." In his *Studies in Rebellion*, pp. 171-260. London: Routledge and Kegan Paul, 1957.

A discussion of Herzen's role in the history of Russian revolutionary thought during the second quarter of the nineteenth century. Lampert considers Herzen, Vissarion Belinski, and Mikhail Bakunin the three outstanding socialist thinkers whose work developed and matured during that period.

Malia, Martin. *Alexander Herzen and the Birth of Russian Socialism: 1812-1855*. Cambridge: Harvard University Press, 1961, 486 p.

A biography of Herzen's life from his birth in 1812 until the death of Czar Nicholas I in 1855. Malia writes that he selected these dates because it was during this period that Herzen exerted his greatest influence as a formulator of socialist thought. In addition to analyzing Herzen's political philosophy, Malia explores what he considers the three most important topics in early-nineteenth-century Russian intellectual history: the emergence of socialism, the influence of romantic idealism on socialism, and the development of ideological nationalism.

Partridge, Monica. "Herzen's Changing Concept of Reality and Its Reflection in His Literary Works." *Slavonic and East European Review* XLVI, No. 107 (July 1968): 397-421.

Examines the influence of Herzen's early fiction on the development of the realistic novel in mid-nineteenth-century Russian literature.

Pritchett, V. S. "Books in General." *The New Statesman & Nation* XXV, No. 644 (26 June 1943): 419.

An analysis of Herzen's personality and life as revealed in his memoirs.

Slonim, Marc. "Westerners and Slavophiles." In his *The Epic of Russian Literature: From Its Origins through Tolstoy*, pp. 143-58. New York: Oxford University Press, 1950.*

Focuses on Herzen's role as a leader of the Russian intelligentsia during the 1850s and his initial opposition to Slavophilism.

Venturi, Franco. "Herzen." In his *Roots of Revolution: A History of the Populist and Socialist Movements in Nineteenth Century Russia*, translated by Francis Haskell, pp. 1-35. New York: Alfred A. Knopf, 1964.

A study of Herzen's role in the development of Populism in Russia during the reign of Czar Nicholas I.

Zenkovsky, V. V. "A. I. Herzen." In his *A History of Russian Philosophy*, Vol. I, translated by George L. Kline, pp. 271-98. Columbia Slavic Studies, edited by Ernest J. Simmons. New York: Columbia University Press; London: Routledge & Kegan Paul, 1953.

Discusses the influence of the German philosopher George Wilhelm Friedrich Hegel upon the thought of Herzen.

# Victor Marie Hugo

## 1802-1885

French novelist, poet, dramatist, and critic.

The following entry presents criticism of Hugo's novel *Les misérables* (1862). For a complete discussion of Hugo's career, see *NCLC*, Vol. 3.

*Les misérables* is considered one of the most memorable novels in nineteenth-century literature and the maturest expression of Hugo's lifelong interest in the problems and sufferings of the poor. Described by Hugo as a religious epic "moving around a great soul, which is the incarnation of all the social misery of the time," *Les misérables* is the story of a released convict, Jean Valjean, whose bitterness is alleviated by the kindness of the saintly Bishop Myriel. Valjean's tragic history is an indictment of unfair legal penalties, and his life in the underworld of Paris illustrates Hugo's conviction that social evils were created and fostered by existing laws and customs. Written in praise of the masses and offering the victims of society's injustice the hope of redemption, *Les misérables* achieved international popularity and was influential in the movement for legal and social reform in nineteenth-century France.

Various incidents in Hugo's life informed the creation of *Les misérables*. Hugo was born into a military family in Besançon, France. He traveled extensively during his childhood, and his early education took place in Italy, Spain, and Corsica. After his parents' separation in 1814, Hugo lived with his mother and two older brothers in Paris; he later immortalized the idyllic garden surrounding his home there in the "L'idylle rue Plumet" section of *Les misérables*. Although Hugo's parents urged him to join the military, he early declared his ambition to be a writer. In 1819, he founded an influential literary magazine, *Le conservateur littéraire,* and his first collection of poetry, *Odes et poésies diverses,* appeared three years later. *Odes et poésies diverses* earned Hugo a pension from Louis XVIII that enabled him to marry his childhood sweetheart, Adèle Foucher, and devote his time exclusively to writing.

Hugo's literary career continued to flourish, but his personal life deteriorated when Adèle fell in love with his best friend, the renowned critic Charles Augustin Sainte-Beuve. Although Hugo and his wife remained married, he was devastated by her infidelity and found solace in a number of romantic liaisons. He formed his deepest and most enduring attachment to Juliette Negroni Drouet, an actress he met in 1833. In addition to transcribing the manuscript of *Les misérables,* Drouet drew upon experiences of her convent upbringing to provide Hugo with details for the novel's lengthy description of the cloistered life.

Hugo's literary achievement was recognized in 1841 by his election to the Académie française and in 1845 by his elevation to the peerage. During the latter half of that decade, he devoted most of his time to politics. In accordance with his desire to represent "the camp of the convicts" rather than any political party, Hugo delivered a number of impassioned speeches in the Chamber of Peers in which he condemned the legal system and society's persecution of the poor—subjects he had treated in the novels *Le dernier jour d'un condamné* (*The Last Day of the Condemned*), *Notre Dame de Paris* (*The Hunchback of*

*Notre Dame*), and *Claude Gueux.* These themes also dominated a work in progress whose title, *Les misères,* was eventually changed to *Les misérables.* As Hugo became increasingly disenchanted with monarchism, he interrupted the composition of *Les misérables* to participate in the revolution of 1848. In 1849, he was elected to the L'assemblée nationale and publicly espoused republicanism. Because of his uncompromising opposition to Louis Napoleon's dictatorial ambitions, he was forced to leave France following the *coup d'état* of 1851. He initially fled to Belgium, but finally settled on the island of Guernsey, where he remained unitl 1870. While in exile, Hugo wrote several volumes of poetry before completing *Les misérables* in 1861.

A ten-volume novel, *Les misérables* was published in installments between April and June, 1862. The action of the book, which is set in Paris and its environs during the first half of the nineteenth century, primarily revolves around Valjean's adventures, though the story involves many other characters whose lives intersect with his. Early in the novel, Hugo indicates his scorn for legal justice by contrasting the insignificance of Valjean's crime—stealing a loaf of bread for his sister's children—with the severity of his punishment: nineteen years of imprisonment and hard labor in the galleys. The sentence transforms Valjean from an honest laborer into a vindictive scoundrel. Succeeding portions of the novel focus on

Valjean's regeneration through the kindness of Bishop Myriel, his struggles with the police officer Javert, and his attempts to help a poor working woman named Fantine and her illegitimate daughter, Cosette. Valjean's story, as well as that of the other characters, exemplifies what Hugo outlines in his preface as the "three great problems" of the nineteenth century: "the degradation of man in the proletariat, the subjection of women through hunger, the atrophy of the child by darkness." Hugo elaborates on these ideas and details his political and religious beliefs in several lengthy digressive sections seemingly unrelated to the plot. These portions of the novel describe, among other subjects, the Battle of Waterloo, the lives of street urchins, and the Paris insurrection of 1832.

Upon its appearance, *Les misérables* received world-wide popular acclaim and equally strong critical reprobation. Contemporary commentators almost unanimously condemned Hugo's argument against existing social institutions and customs. Algernon Charles Swinburne complained that Hugo exaggerated society's responsibility for crime, and Jules-Amédée Barbey d'Aurevilly described the novel as a "long-drawn-out piece of sophistry." One of the most vehement attacks leveled against the work was written by Caroline de Peyronnet, who warned of the dangerous influence of Hugo's "pernicious" social and political doctrines. Early critics greeted *Les misérables*'s discursive elements with almost as much disdain, contending that they were extraneous and an impediment to the narrative. This argument was also advanced by George Saintsbury early in the twentieth century, but more recent commentators have judged them less harshly. Elliott M. Grant praised the digressions for their accurate reflection of nineteenth-century social and political concerns. Later, John Porter Houston also defended these sections of *Les misérables,* stating that they contributed to the novel's realism and heightened the interest of the narrative.

Twentieth-century crititism of *Les misérables* focuses on the work's autobiographical elements and historical documentation as well as its unrealistic characters and plot, a topic noted by Edmond and Jules de Goncourt in the nineteenth century. Numerous commentators, including Madame Duclaux, Grant, and André Maurois, have examined the relationship between Hugo's life and the characters in *Les misérables.* They frequently observe that Marius, Cosette's lover, undergoes a political conversion similar to Hugo's and that his courtship with Cosette parallels that of the author and his wife. Critics also note that much of the content of *Les misérables* is historically accurate. In discussions of the novel's genesis, both Grant and Matthew Josephson contended that actual accounts of an early nineteenth-century French bishop who welcomed a liberated convict into his home inspired Hugo's portraits of Bishop Myriel and Valjean. While acknowledging Hugo's attempt to create a realistic novel, most later critics cite *Les misérables*'s stylized characters and improbable plot as evidence that he failed. However, opinions on the work's lack of realism vary. Robert Lynd maintained that improbabilities in the story's plot and characterization were artistically justified because they created suspense and helped to convey Hugo's social and political philosophy. Conversely, Joseph Warren Beach argued that the work's melodramatic plot accounted for both its success as an adventure story and its failure as an example of "serious" novel writing. Similarly, Maurois singled out *Les misérables*'s theatricality as one of its greatest faults, but praised its exciting narrative, pronouncing the work an "extraordinarily adroit detective novel."

Although critics generally agree that *Les misérables* is artistically flawed, they also consistently admire its broad vision of humanity, emotional power, and penetrating study of the consequences of crime. With few exceptions, Hugo's evocation of the theme of redemption through charity and his presentation of Valjean as a symbol of human perfectibility have met with resounding approval. In addition, recent critics praise the book's universality, echoing Denis Saurat's assertion that it is "a fusion of almost all the known kinds of novel." Perhaps the best explanation for the work's enduring popularity was offered by Grant, who stated that *Les misérables* is "great above all because a profound human sympathy animates its every page."

---

**VICTOR HUGO**   (essay date 1862)

[*The following is Hugo's widely discussed preface to* Les misérables, *first published in 1862, in which he underscores the social and humanitarian implications of the novel.*]

While through the working of laws and customs there continues to exist a condition of social condemnation which artificially creates a human hell within civilization, and complicates with human fatality a destiny that is divine; while the three great problems of this century, the degradation of man in the proletariat, the subjection of women through hunger, the atrophy of the child by darkness, continue unresolved; while in some regions social asphyxia remains possible; in other words, and in still wider terms, while ignorance and poverty persist on earth, books such as [*Les misérables*] cannot fail to be of value. (p. xiii)

> *Victor Hugo, in a preface to his* Les Misérables, *Vol. I, translated by Norman Denny, The Folio Press, 1976, p. xiii.*

**CHARLES BAUDELAIRE**   (essay date 1862)

[*A French poet and critic, Baudelaire is best known for his famous collection of poems* Les fleurs de mal (The Flowers of Evil), *which is ranked among the most influential works of French poetry. In* The Flowers of Evil *Baudelaire analyzes, often in shocking terms, his urban surroundings, erotic love, and conflicts within his own soul. Underlying these topics is Baudelaire's belief that human beings are inherently evil. Only that which is artificial can be construed as absolutely good. Poetry, according to Baudelaire, should in turn serve only to inspire and express beauty. This doctrine forms the basis of both his poetry and his criticism. In the following review of* Les misérables, *Baudelaire expresses admiration for Hugo's convincing characterization of Fantine and skillful handling of Valjean's struggle with his conscience in the chapter entitled "Tempête sous un crâne." However, he complains that Hugo's portrait of Javert is somewhat unrealistic. In portions of the essay not excerpted below (see* NCLC, *Vol. 3), Baudelaire applauds the social philosophy advanced in* Les misérables. *Later commentators frequently note the hypocritical nature of this review, pointing out that after its publication in* Le boulevard *in April, 1862, Baudelaire remarked in conversation that he had been guilty of a lie in praising the "unspeakably foul and stupid book."*]

[The chapter in *Les Misérables* entitled **"Tempête sous un Crâne"** which recounts Valjean's struggle with himself], with its hesitations, its mental qualifications, its paradoxes, its false consolations, its desperate attempts to cheat, contains pages in which not only French literature but even the literature of thinking Humanity may forever take pride. It is glorious for Rational

Man that these pages should have been written! One would have to look a great deal and a long time, a very long time, to find elsewhere pages equal to those which expose in so tragic a manner all the appalling Casuistry inscribed from the Beginning in the heart of Universal Man.

In this gallery of suffering and catastrophic events there is a horrible, repugnant figure—the gendarme, the police sergeant, strict, inexorable justice, uncritical justice, the law that is not interpreted, savage intelligence (can it be called intelligence?) that has never understood attenuating circumstances, in a word the Letter without the Spirit, the abominable Javert. I have heard some fairly sensible people say of Javert: "After all, he is a decent fellow; and he has his own greatness." This is certainly the time to say with de Maistre: "I don't know what an honest man is." At the risk of being considered guilty ("those who tremble feel themselves guilty," said that madman Robespierre), I confess that for me Javert seems an incorrigible monster, as starved for justice as a wild animal for raw flesh, the absolute Enemy in a word.

And then in this connection I should like to make a small criticism. However enormous, however emphatic in outline and movement the ideal figures of a story may be, we must suppose that they had a beginning, like people in real life. I know that man may be more than zealous in every profession. He becomes a hunting dog, a fighting dog in everything that he does. That is certainly a form of beauty that has its origin in the passions. Thus one can be a policeman *with enthusiasm;* but does one join the police as *a result of enthusiasm,* and is it not, on the contrary, one of those professions which one may enter only under the pressure of certain circumstances and for reasons that have nothing to do with fanaticism?

I assume that it is not necessary to recount and explain all the tender, heartbreaking beauty which Victor Hugo has lavished on the character of Fantine, the fallen shopgirl, the modern woman, caught between the fatality of poorly paid work and the fatality of legal prostitution. We have long known how skillful he is in expressing the cry of passion in the abyss, the groans and furious tears of the lioness deprived of her young! Here, by a very natural liaison, we are led to recognize once again the sureness and lightness of touch with which this vigorous painter, this creator of colossi, colors the cheeks of childhood, enlivens their eyes, and describes their lively and ingenuous movements. You might say Michelangelo taking delight in vying with Lawrence or Velásquez. (pp. 287-88)

> *Charles Baudelaire, " 'Les Misérables'," in his*
> Baudelaire As a Literary Critic, *edited and translated*
> *by Lois Boe Hyslop and Francis E. Hyslop, Jr., The*
> *Pennsylvania State University Press, University Park,*
> *1964, pp. 280-89.*

## [ALGERNON CHARLES SWINBURNE] (essay date 1862)

[*Swinburne was an English poet, dramatist, and critic. Though renowned during his lifetime for his lyric poetry, he is remembered today for his rejection of Victorian mores. His explicitly sensual themes shocked his contemporaries: while they demanded that poetry reflect and uphold current moral standards, Swinburne's only goal, implicit in his poetry and explicit in his critical writings, was to express beauty. Swinburne reviewed each of* Les misérable'*s five parts in separate essays that appeared in the* Spectator *between April, 1862 and October, 1862. His conviction, presented in the following review of the first part, "Fantine," and in his last essay on* Les misérables *(see excerpt below), that the novel*

*rests on a false philosophical basis is shared by most contemporary commentators.*]

[*Les Misérables*] is a remarkable attempt to examine social problems from the artistic point of view. It has some features which are very open to criticism. The mere idea of presenting a picture of human life in its greatness and in its weakness through ten volumes of an encyclopaedic romance seems to argue a curious confusion of scientific and artistic possibilities; the translator of Shakspeare ought, one would think, to have known better that the depths of the heart are searchless. . . . [M. Victor Hugo's] strange love of the supernatural and the grotesque . . . [reappears in the first part of *Les Misérables,* "Fantine,"] where the *dramatis personae* are a patriarchal bishop, a saintly burglar, a narrow-natured inspector of police, and a self-sacrificing Magdalene. Revolt against society and systems is the principle proclaimed in the preface, and taught in every incident of the story. Yet withal Victor Hugo is no vulgar rebel against authority; no mere blaspheming Capaneus; but a Titan stealing light that he may impart it. Age has mellowed without impairing his inspiration, and an unquenchable faith in the good of human nature has finally triumphed over the fervid political animosities of the man, who began life as a Legitimist and is now in exile as a Republican. It need scarcely be said that his style has a nameless charm of language, or that his story always interests, though it may fail to convince. To those who can allow themselves to forget that M. Victor Hugo's system of the world is not ours, and that he has another heaven and another earth, the exquisite finish of every detail, the nature thrown into every little touch, will give, partially at least, the effects of actual and very beautiful life. It is like music and familiar voices that have blended with the fantastic tracery of a dream. (p. 410)

It is difficult to criticize an unfinished work where the next few volumes may correct all that we find one-sided and imperfect in ["Fantine,"] but the question to what purpose is this picture of human misery and short-comings remains to our mind the great argument against M. Victor Hugo's book. He himself says [in the preface to *Les Misérables*] that it is one of a class which can never fail to have a use "so long as there shall exist through laws and manners a social damnation creating artificial hells in the midst of civilization, and complicating destiny, which is divine, with a human fatality" [see excerpt above, 1862]. No doubt much of this is true. Our imperfections do often reproduce themselves in a ghastly progeny of crime, with which we seem to be unconnected, and which only God can father on its true parents. The philanthropy that teaches us to educate that we may not have to correct, and to make reform the great object of punishment, can never be out of place. But surely it is false to infer that laws and manners do in any eminent degree create a social damnation. Allowing that Jean Valjean was punished beyond his due, and so brutalized by punishment, we may yet fairly say that the era of Draconian legislation is passed, and that, after all, we must in this world look chiefly to acts, and leave the question of intention to Heaven. The true preventive for all crimes that arise from necessity is the simple expedient of an efficient poor law, which M. Victor Hugo, like most Frenchmen not men of science, would probably regard with horror. For the man who, having the workhouse at hand, prefers stealing to breaking stones and a temporary separation from his family, we confess we have little pity. The case of Fantine's ruin and desertion is no doubt more difficult. The problem how to keep a young girl, who can earn a scanty but sufficient living by her needle, from preferring to live idly, expensively, and at the cost of her self-respect, with a young man whose dress and manners fascinate her, because they seem to indicate superiority, is one which no legislation can solve. But M. Victor Hugo is untrue to morality and to art when he entitles the latter period of Fantine's career "the Descent." He seems to imply that if her seducer had pensioned her, and she had been able to live on without selling herself, taking her old sin as a matter of pleasant memory, she would have been a higher woman than she was as the street Pariah. To ourselves, Fantine, mutilating herself, sacrificing life and shame for her daughter, is on a higher moral level than Fantine dining happily at St. Cloud with her seducer and his friends. Nor can we see that matters would be much mended if the inequalities of social life could by any miracle be so far levelled that a woman's love of refinement and indolence should no longer be inducements to her to prefer concubinage to marriage. Without reference to the fact that great disparity in the number of the sexes seems to lead under any circumstance to illicit connexions, or to the argument that inequalities must always remain, and that a woman may as well sell herself for refinement or even for money as for physical beauty, we object absolutely to the idea that we can extirpate vice by removing its opportunities. We want the morality of men, not the faultless movements of puppets, and the feeble innocence of the boy unacquainted with evil or unattracted by it is of less value than the firm will that has learned in much suffering to be its own law. (p. 411)

> *[Algernon Charles Swinburne], "Victor Hugo's New Novel," in* The Spectator, *Vol. 35, No. 1763, April 12, 1862, pp. 410-11.*

## EDMOND DE GONCOURT AND JULES DE GONCOURT (journal date 1862)

*[French diarists, novelists, historians, and critics, the Goncourt brothers were literary innovators who are noted for their diverse contributions to the world of letters. Their best-known work,* Journal des Goncourt: Mémoires de la vie littéraire, *a diary that contains a detailed record of the literary society of Paris during the second half of the nineteenth century, is considered an invaluable account of contemporary development in art and literature. In this excerpt from their journal, the Goncourts point to* Les misérables's *inflated style, its poor construction, and, above all, its unrealistic characters and plot in asserting that the work diminishes Hugo's reputation as a novelist. Their assessment of* Les misérables *is discussed by Norman Denny (1976). Additional commentary on the novel's lack of realism is provided by Joakim Reinhard (1899), Robert Lynd (1932), Joseph Warren Beach (1932), and André Maurois (1960).]*

Hugo's *Les Misérables* [is] a great disappointment to us. I leave out of account the moral of the book—there is no morality in art—the novel's humanitarian point of view is nothing to me. Besides, on thinking it over, I find it rather amusing to make two hundred thousand francs—which is the true figure of the sales—by pitying the miseries of the people!

Let us leave that and go on to the work itself. It makes Balzac greater, it makes Sue greater, it diminishes Hugo. Title not justified: no wretchedness, no hospital, prostitution barely touched on. Nothing living: the characters are of bronze, alabaster, everything except flesh and bones. Lack of observation obtrudes and irritates one throughout. Situations and characters: Hugo has constructed his whole book with the appearance of reality instead of the real, without that truth which completes all things and all men in a novel by providing the unexpected element. There lies the fault and the profound wretchedness of this work.

As for its style, it is inflated, strained, breathless, unsuitable to what he is saying. It is like Michelet on Sinai—no order, half of it irrelevant. Hugo is no novelist; he is always Hugo! Fanfare and no music. No subtlety. A predilection for the coarse and the too highly colored. Flattery and fawning on vulgar opinion: a saintly bishop, and a Bonapartist and republican Polyeucte; craven concern for success which goes so far as to deal gently with the honor of innkeepers.

That is the book from which, when we opened it, we expected revelation; when we closed it, we realized it was merely a commercial speculation. In a word, a novel for the lending library written by a man of genius. (pp. 66-7)

> *Edmund de Goncourt and Jules de Goncourt, in a journal entry of April, 1862, in their* Paris and the Arts, 1851-1896: From the Goncourt "Journal", *edited and translated by George J. Becker and Edith Philips, Cornell University Press, 1971, pp. 66-7.*

## [C. KNIGHT WATSON] (essay date 1862)

*[In the following mixed review of* Les misérables, *Watson represents the novel as the work of two writers, "the one a poet, the other a system-monger." Watson attributes* Les misérables's *artistic unity and vivid language to Hugo the poet; to Hugo the system-monger he ascribes the novel's nonsensical social and political digressions. Watson is joined by Caroline de Peyronnet (1863) and George Saintsbury (1917) in condemning* Les misérables's *digressions.]*

It is not, we believe, very generally known that *Les Misérables* is the work of two writers—the one a poet, the other a system-monger; the one richly endowed with feelings of the highest order, which come to him as naturally as instincts (and herein is he a poet); the other sententiously parading the crudest notions, the product of no thought, the result of no experience, as the very foundations of Law and Order, as the only conditions on which the happiness of a nation can be secured, and the victory over Sin and Misery completed. The one great on the smallest theme—the gambols of an infant: the other small on the greatest theme—the relation of the Individual to the State, and the condition of the Dangerous Classes. This literary partnership has been productive of all the mischief which might be expected from the collaboration of two minds of so opposite a character. It is not only that we are indebted to it for the infliction of nearly one thousand pages of digressions with which we could well have dispensed, but these digressions mar the interest by interrupting the sequence of the story, which they do nothing to develope, and everything to retard. So great, indeed, is the injury which the social and political quack has done to his colleague the poet, that many critics have been thrown, it would seem, off the scent; have been unable to reunite that thread of the story which these interminable episodical essays are ever breaking, and have thus denied to Victor Hugo the poet that artistic skill of which Victor Hugo the quack has done so much to mask the grandeur and to mar the effect. (pp. 273-74)

[Amid] all its defects, this work has something more than the beauties of an exquisite style, and the 'word-compelling' power of a literary Zeus, to recommend it to the tender care of a distant posterity: . . . in dealing with all the emotions, passions, doubts, fears, which go to make up our common humanity, M. Victor Hugo has stamped upon every page the hall-mark of genius, and the loving patience and conscientious labour of a true artist. We sit here as utterly dispassionate judges. (p. 274)

[The first volume of *Les Misérables*] gives the keynote to the whole: it is here, too, we may observe, that our author has put forth his greatest strength. Critics have prated much about the want of unity in the work, and have stigmatised it as a mere congeries of episodes. They have not seen, or have been slow to acknowledge, that on the revulsion of feeling and of character which took place in that eventful October [when Jean Valjean encountered the good Bishop] all the sequel of the story may as truly be said to hang as on the wrath of Achilles the tale of Troy divine. In every critical juncture of his life, on every occasion in which Jean Valjean dared to be greatly good, we seem to hear those parting words of the Bishop, and to recall the day when he wrestled so bravely with all that was bad within him and ceased not till he had won the mastery. Again and again, throughout the story, this struggle has to be renewed; again and again he has to choose between doing what was right and courting what was safe; between having a stain upon his conscience and keeping a mask upon his face. It is this great epic of a conscience at war with itself—it is this choice of Hercules which M. Victor Hugo, if we read him aright, has set himself to unfold as he traces the career of a despised convict—it is this which imparts to the work a far higher order of unity than any mere external connexion of incidents can supply. (pp. 283-84)

[If *Les Misérables* be] a wondrous maze, it is not without a plan which witnesses to the artistic power of its author. It seems to us that nothing but the inconsiderate hastiness with which modern criticism is in the habit of tossing off a judgment on the works, great or small, which come under its ken, can account for the blindness which, so far as we know, has everywhere been shown respecting the leading idea which forms as it were the trunk-line of the work. But the merits of *Les Misérables* do not merely consist in the conception of it as a whole; it abounds, page after page, with details of unequalled beauty. We feel bound to say that we know of nothing in the whole compass of French literature which can even be compared with such chapters as those entitled '**Le dedans du désespoir,**' '**L'onde et l'ombre,**' and '**Petit Gervais,**' in the first volume; '**Une tempête sous un crâne**' and '**Bâtons dans les roues,**' in the second volume; '**La cadène,**' in the seventh volume; '**Buvard, bavard,**' in the eighth; and '**Immortale Jecur,**' in the tenth. The power which they so transcendently display is not merely different in degree, it is different in kind, from anything in the language at any period of its history. Michelet, indeed, in some passages of his 'Histoire de France,' suggests a parallel, but on closer examination it will be found that one cardinal distinction prevents us from pursuing the parallel any further. The process which presided over the cradle of all language, and which embodied the abstract emotions of the mind in terms borrowed from the concrete material world, is one which also presides over that inexhaustible fund of imagery with which every page of Victor Hugo is rife. His metaphors are almost uniformly the *carrying over* of the invisible into the visible world. With Michelet it will be found the converse is the case; and this difference so affects the style, that Victor Hugo is still left without any one to whom we can liken him. By no writer since the time of Rabelais have the capabilities of the French language been set forth to such advantage—never before have so much bone and muscle been laid bare. Some French critic—M. Cuvillier Fleury, if we remember right—has said that, in the presence of the author of *Les Misérables,* his readers must feel like the Lilliputians in the hands of Gulliver. The comparison is a very just one. Victor Hugo's mind is essentially Titanic; he is more at home, shows more power, where he is dealing with conceptions of a su-

perhuman character, than when he dwells among ordinary men. And yet the tenderness, the grace, the pathos which he brings to bear on his description of children, are no less wonderful than the grandeur of his style and the majesty of his gait when dealing with the colossal and the superhuman. But, while thus at home with pigmies and giants, he seems at times to be lacking in what Pascal somewhere calls 'l'entredeux.' His creations of men and women, such as we meet with in everyday life, lay themselves open to criticism, as being types of a class rather than individuals with definitely marked outlines of their own. (pp. 302-03)

On the social and political opinions of which [the] numerous digressions are made the vehicle, it is difficult for an Englishman to speak without impatience and surprise;—impatience at the amazing ignorance of the rudiments of social and political philosophy which even such a man as Victor Hugo displays in every line; surprise at the stolidity which prevents the author from seeing that the events which are either the pretext or the cause of his becoming and remaining an exile were but the natural and only possible fruit of those doctrines, which are paraded with so much emphasis and apparent sincerity. Not often has greater genius been placed at the service of greater nonsense. . . . Whatever may be the blemishes observable in this work—and we have not been slow to point them out—it bears undoubted traces of having been the produce of much honest toil, and many noble aspirations. Qualities such as these are not of such common occurrence that we should treat their possessor with sarcasm and contempt because he indulges at times in extravagances which test the patience of the reader. (p. 306)

> *[C. Knight Watson], in a review of "Les Misérables," in* The Quarterly Review, *Vol. CXII, No. CCXXIV, October, 1862, pp. 271-306.*

### [ALGERNON CHARLES SWINBURNE]   (essay date 1862)

> [*In his fifth and last review of* Les misérables, *from which the following excerpt is drawn, Swinburne relates the antithetical style of the novel to its philosophical teachings. According to Swinburne, Hugo's social and political philsosophy is flawed by its reliance on "crises of lightning or eclipse" and its inattention to "the petty growths which make up nearly the whole of life." In an earlier essay (April, 1862), Swinburne also faulted the philosophical doctrines advanced in* Les misérables.]

[*Les Misérables*] is very much more than a work of art, and . . . it seems not unfitting to criticize the general drift and inner creed of a book which touches, on almost every side, the principles of human life and progress,—of ethics, of society, of politics, of religion, of civilization. (p. 1193)

The title chosen by Victor Hugo for this great work is not only unjust to its spirit, but a disguise for its philosophy. Misery, properly so called, we doubt if Victor Hugo could understand. His philosophy is in this respect, dependent on his art; and as his art is largely penetrated with the spirit of antithesis, so his philosophy blends light and darkness with far more than the usual force of artistic contrast. In this lies the secret fault of his individual social and political philosophy, as well as the wonderful power and effectiveness of his artistic touch. He speaks incidentally of God as "delighting in antithesis," which seems to us rather to mean that he himself delights in discovering or imagining it. At all events, this tale is not a tale of the blackness of misery, but rather of the conflict between light and darkness; and the only fault of its philosophy is that it scarcely believes in the finite and the gradual at all, except as artistic foils for the infinite and the ultimate. Though with all the skill of a great artist Victor Hugo paints the infinitesimal limitations and littlenesses of human character and human institutions, we feel at every step that he is not prepared to accept them, or to admit them within his creed and convictions; they exist for him only to bring out the background of gloom or glory on which they are painted; and though he is happy therefore to paint them, he will not commit himself to any faith or philosophy which would give them a *right* to exist. Victor Hugo's faith and philosophy are all derived from the great crises of individual social or political life; it is, like one of the old geological theories, a *catastrophic* philosophy, which draws its conception of ordinary life from the study of revolutionary eras. But in any case it is not a philosophy founded on pain, limitations, or darkness; it is rather a rendering of Rembrandt into the moral world. The story opens with a bright light, which sends a stream of soft illumination, like the path of the moon upon the sea, down its course to the very close, effectually effacing any overpowering sense of wretchedness. In the picture of the simple, humble, and serene Bishop of D— we have, though not the most vivid and graphic portrait of the book, a clear transparency of apostolic trust and goodness, which is just consistent with a definite human character, and no more; for we constantly wonder how any light so mildly diffused and homogenous, which seems to be a mere lunar reflection of the Light of the World, how a charity so completely dominant, a self-forgetfulness that, within certain French limits, appears to melt away all the distinguishing lines of human personality, is yet somehow reconciled with distinct feature, clear outline, and individual tone. That it is so shows the genius of the artist— for this opening picture is essential not merely to the art, but to the philosophy of the book. Without the silver lustre of the Bishop of D—'s character, neither the story would hang together nor the philosophy. It supplies the great initial force of the narrative, and the centre also of the social theory. In his view of human life and character, whether individual, social, or political, Victor Hugo never allows anything for gradual growth. He paints character in equilibrium, and he paints character in revolution; but he does not paint, and probably scarcely believes in, those small modifications made day by day by which the greater changes of life are really effected. Hence for his original moral force he needs a character in its way nearly perfect, sending forth a light which can reach the deepest depths of a convict's degradation, and at once as he himself says, "transfigure" rather than transform. Similar, too, is his conception of the whole framework of human society. He sees in it an immense store of divine light and an immense shadow of ignorance and evil. He mixes these lights and shadows in almost every proportion, but whenever any progress is made at all in the encroachment of either light on shadow or shadow on light, it is by sudden starts or lapses. He does not seem to believe in the power of infinitesimal, or even of small changes. He absolves and condemns on the largest considerations of ruling motive, and will scarcely believe in a sin proceeding from an interior of self-denying love, or in a virtue that is alloyed with selfishness. Thus, the "infinitely little" which, in real life, is of such vast importance, is to him morally, absolutely zero,—though he retains it and values it for the sake of the artistic distinctness which it gives to his painting. Every one must be either in the full sunshine or the deep shadow— and what he loves best is to picture the upheaving force which transfers from one to the other. The greatest efforts of his book are studies of the strange blending between the infinitely great and the infinitely little,—of the details which rise like air-

bubbles to the surface of a deeply agitated mind,—the trivialities which float on the tide of revolution,—the insignificancies which measure the swiftness of a social gulf-stream. (pp. 1193-94)

[It] is when this antithetic creed of the great artist touches social and political life that we see its deficiencies most. Human institutions if they do not rest on the finite as well as the infinite—if they do not embody the actual as well as the ideal— if they do not adapt themselves to men's limitations as well as to his indefinite capacity for progress, are not in any sense historical or fit to be historical. Yet Victor Hugo evidently would provide for men institutions that could only work if wielded by an infinite compassion in the cause of human misfortune and misery. The main purpose of this book is, perhaps, to plead for a profound and limitless compassion as the basis of the criminal system—which if it could be really compassion of so divine a kind as the Bishop of D—'s would, no doubt, be in effect justice as well as compassion, because it would rend the conscience of the convict, and so bring with it the only penalty which is certain cure. But to base any system of criminal justice on the spurious compassion of ordinary administrators, who in their secret heart see the guilt more in the social consequence than in itself, would assuredly be even less safe than to base it on the present rude but definite sense of law and social justice. (p. 1194)

Again, in politics, Victor Hugo looks at the national life as if it were always, or even generally, the great self-conscious unity which, in luminous moments of great political excitement, it becomes. . . . He can see real progress only in those lucid moments of national vigilance in which, as he says, "the whole people are dilated into the sublimated individual;" in which "there is no poor man who, having his right, has not also his radiance;" in which "the man dying of hunger feels within himself the honesty of France." Hence, he makes it the glory of the First Napoleon to have been in some sense, and in his best moments, "the Man-people as Christ was the Man-God." And this is obviously the measure by which he tries political institutions; do they really gather up and glorify the life and heart of the people? We should say, that, in this sense, it is not often even desirable that they should. There are various true causes and springs of national unity which are not meant to *express* the popular life, but rather to guide and educate it. Of these, monarchy and aristocracy, so far as they are elastic and capable of yielding to the progressive pressure of the popular life beneath them, are some of the most important; and these, because they do not express the infinite and absolute truth, but only the finite and temporary forms of political life, Victor Hugo clearly despises. He can accept a Napoleon who is France incarnate, but not even a Louis Phillipe,—just and gentle as he is to him,—who is only a centre of government and a symbol of law.

The fault of Victor Hugo's philosophy seems to us to be throughout a disposition to ignore the small responsibilities, the little movements, the petty growths which make up nearly the whole of life, and to concentrate his attention on the crises of lightning or eclipse. The consequence is that while he has the keenest of eyes for the *internecine* stages of the strife between good and evil, compassion and misery, liberty and slavery, he passes over in contempt those smaller and more limited agencies by which,—whether in the field of the individual life or that of the State and the nation,—the space is bridged between crisis and crisis, and lands us in the characteristic paradox of an "antithetical God." (pp. 1194-95)

[Algernon Charles Swinburne], ''Victor Hugo's Philosophy,'' in The Spectator, Vol. 35, No. 1791, October 25, 1862, pp. 1193-95.

## THE BOSTON REVIEW (essay date 1863)

[*Like Elliott M. Grant (1945) and John Porter Houston (1974), this anonymous reviewer argues that* Les misérables's *digressions, particularly those on conventional life and the Battle of Waterloo, are instructive and do not impede the narrative. The critic praises Hugo's portrayal of the male characters in* Les misérables *and his penetrating study of crime, but condemns the social and political philosophy advanced in the novel.*]

'Les Miserables' is an elaborate work of art. It sparkles and throbs with genius. It is full of high creative imagination. Diffuse in its general style, it gathers itself into occasional passages of condensed force like Erie rushing through the cut of Niagara. Its prolixity is seldom wearisome, for it is the unforced exuberance of the play of the liveliest of fancies, combined with a wealth of learning singularly curious and recondite. One is quite willing to stop in mid route of this engrossing story to let the author talk through whole chapters of the mysteries of the Parisian *argot,* the language of outlaws, ''always in flight like the men who use it,'' and of the yet darker and deeper sewerage of that city. These long digressions can hardly be called irrelevant to the plot, and convey much valuable information. The writer gives us the statistics and thoughts of a statesman, as well as the scenes of a dramatist.

His descriptive power is admirable. He catches the salient points of his subject, and makes his picture with a few bold strokes, or with the most minute filling up, as the occasion demands. He is equally at home in the most contrary and disonant surroundings; as, for example, in painting the tropical luxuriance and bewitching moonlights of the sequestered gardens of Le Rue Plumet, and the splendors of a June morning after a night of rain. . . . (p. 53)

[It is worth comparing Hugo's magnificent description of the battle of Waterloo] with Thackeray's feeble handling of the same engagement, in 'Vanity Fair,' . . . to note the superior genius of our author for grasping and grouping and giving life and movement to such a tempest of war as burst over that memorable spot. The terrors of ''the sunken road of Ohain'' burn a furrow into one's memory which lasts like the vision of a seething volcano. (p. 54)

This writer shows a yet greater skill in delineating human character. The opening portrait of the good old Bishop Bienvenu is a charming study, well limned and shaded, of a Romanist Oberlin in charge of . . . a rude and even savage people. He overflows with love almost to a feminine softness; and yet his visit to the dying ''Conventionist,'' and his tour among the mountains of robbers, display a passive courage which is more saintly than masculine. He is a great bundle of amenities very creditable to the heart and head of his creator. We admire his quiet, compassionate philosophy with a half doubt if it is not rather over mixed with mucilage. His practical kindliness runs into the widest improbabilities, as in the affair of the thief and the silver candlesticks; but these, so that they do not slide into absolute impossibilities, are a legitimate and important part of the novelist's capital. (pp. 54-5)

The female actors in this melodrama are its weakest. Except Cosette, they attract but little interest and less admiration. Is the quality of French society responsible for this? We think not; although, on the scale of things which this novel repre-

sents, the women of that country are not generally good subjects for minute delineation. Cosette enlists our feelings, at first, of painful pity, then of pleased participation in her improving fortunes. But she gets scarcely beyond the butterfly or the singing-bird development when the curtain drops, and nowhere shows much strength. The other sex is the author's forte. Here he is at home. The group of young republicans, in ''**Marius,**'' is certainly a drawing from life. The logical idealist, Enjolras, the exponent of the divine right of revolution, and the philosophic reasoner, Combeferre, the exponent of its human right, are the works of none but a great master of mental analysis. (p. 55)

Historical personages pass along these pages as breathing and earnest flesh and blood. Napoleon, the genius of war, stands for a striking outline *vis-a-vis* the imperturbable, mathematical Wellington. (p. 56)

Louis Philippe is minutely dissected. His accession to power is detailed with the studied accuracy of a personal witness, and his variously, not to say contradictorily, composite character, is analyzed; not with any degree of admiration, yet with a manly fairness. (p. 57)

The portions of this work in which the romancer gives place to the publicist are of uncommon interest. This change is continually varying the hue of the story. You see the hand of the acute man of affairs, the impulsive orator, the enthusiastic reformer, the sagacious observer of historical revolutions, everywhere appearing. The book is a mirror of modern society, a repertory of ideas concerning human life and progress. It is a panorama of French society and civilization for more than a generation past, by one who was there to see. It is a drama on the boards of a vast theatre, with the grandest of scenery enveloping and interpreting its action. The plot is simple and easily remembered, through which a multitude of figures come and pass on, with what hopes and aspirations and burdens and reliefs we are curious and anxious to discover. (p. 58)

The author shows his profound study of crime and its consequences in the picture of the condemned and hopeless [Jean Valjean] gradually sinking down to the instincts of a ferocious brute. That unsuccessful struggle of an awakening moral sense against the acquired force of life-long habits of felony, while the harassed Valjean prowls through the bishop's unprotected apartments at midnight, and at last flies with his booty, is full of tragic power. (p. 59)

We cannot of course give even an idea of the changing lights and shades of the novel, nor more than allude to some of its finer passages. But here we remark one lesson of the whole which is awfully impressed at a hundred points—that however a man may repent of crime and outlive its legal sentence, he can never throw off the dishonor of its commission. ''Liberation is not deliverance. A convict may leave the galleys behind, but not his condemnation.'' Poor Valjean must carry the scar of that deep wound to the grave. Healing the gash does not obliterate its mark. Almost at the last, this woe is hunting his steps like a hungry hound. ''It is true, then? the soul may be cured, but not the lot. Fearful thing! an incurable destiny!''

But who is responsible for the destiny? There opens a wide field of questionings and cross-questionings, amid the tangled thickets of which more theorists than our author have been lost. We intimate our prime difficulty with this book. It merges individual responsibility in public wrongs and oppressions. It makes the State accountable for the crimes which imperil it. We are not denying the extenuating circumstances of the vicious ignorance which swarms through our densely populated centres, which is everywhere in appalling distribution. Once for all, give these their largest claims of a humane and a Christian charity. We are anxious to make the mantle as broad as possible. But after this is done, the truth stands firm as the eternal hills that the sinner is guilty of his sin, the transgressor of his transgression. This our author is perpetually denying in implication and direct assertion. This sophism shapes his conclusions respecting the spirit of justice, the punishment of felonies, and the social science generally. It crops out in the old bishop so early as page sixteen of the first part. He has attended officially a capital execution. To his eyes "the scaffold is a sort of monster, . . . the accomplice of the executioner—it devours, it eats flesh, it drinks blood." "I did not believe that it could be so monstrous. It is wrong to be so absorbed in the divine law as not to perceive the human law. Death belongs to God alone. By what right do men touch that unknown thing?" A fallacy into which a bishop should not slide. There is no conflict of laws here. The human is the divine. The execution of law to its ultimate severities is the divinely human. But not on our author's doctrine of personal irresponsibleness. That makes it unjust, cruel. Yet he himself defends war as necessary and benevolent, with all its havoc of life. (pp. 59-60)

[According to Hugo,] "Society is culpable in not providing instruction for all, and it must answer for the night which it produces. If the soul is left in darkness, sins will be committed. The guilty one is not he who commits the sin, but he who causes the darkness." True and false: a sound premise and a non sequitur. Society is guilty and suffers; so with the culprit, thief or murderer. Again: "My friends, remember this, that there are no bad herbs, and no bad men; there are only bad cultivators." This is shallow to a degree. Monsieur, the reclaimed mayor, has succeeded in getting out of the nettle a filament like flax, from which cloth can be manufactured. Therefore nettles are not nettles because capable of useful applications. So poison is not poison because it can kill bugs. And bad men are a fiction because they are convertible to goodness. But what if they are never converted?

We wonder that a writer, who could conduct the conscience of M. Madeline (the former and the later Jean Valjean) so unswervingly through that fearful self-conflict, when it summoned him to Arras to liberate from conviction a suspected criminal by exposing and denouncing himself to the judges, when every personal and social consideration pleaded against that self-sacrifice, save simple righteousness; we wonder that the creator of this most thrilling and harrowing scene, should have tripped so unconsiously at other points of his ethics. That struggle in a strong man's soul is worthy of Shakespeare's dramatic power. It is a study in morals of a microscopic penetration and lucidity. He makes the prosperous and irreproachable mayor, whom no one suspects of former wrongdoing, go and place himself, as a malefactor, under arrest, to save a villain from the unjust charge of being an escaped convict, which act remands him to the galleys, and seemingly ruins all his hopes. A triumph this such as no battle-field of nations ever wreathed around a monarch's brow:

> let us bear our weights,
> Preferring dreary hearths to desert souls.

But how could a judge who could thus carry through this interior trial, perpetrate such heresies as these? Fantine is a courtesan who has lived for years with a paramour, and is the mother of an illegitimate child. She has been greatly injured, and may be a penitent. Granted. But what is this as a ground

of the deliberate and solemn absolution which the author certainly intends as his own opinion. "Listen. I declare to you from this moment, if all is as you say, and I do not doubt it, that you have never ceased to be virtuous and holy before God." So when the detective Javert asks the nun who never told a lie, if Valjean was within, and, while this person was directly behind the door, she answers, "No"; we have this comment: "She lied. Two lies in succession, one upon another, without hesitation, quickly, as if she were an adept in it. . . . Oh, holy maiden! for many years thou hast been no more in this world; thou hast joined the sisters, the virgins, and thy brethren, the angels, in glory; may this falsehood be remembered to thee in Paradise." That *no* was natural enough in the circumstances; one would not make it a very heinous fault perhaps. But this canonization of it, as a positive meritoriousness, and fount of grace, is worse than absurd. We do not blame, we honor and love, the author's kindliness towards all sorts of erring ones; but this becomes itself vicious when it sanctifies immoralities small and large.

The vitiating element of this book takes another form. Javert, the policeman, a very marked character, is studiously set up as the impersonation of the attribute of punitive justice. He is a rectilinear man who has but two ideas—detection and retribution. He has no heart, and no conscience save what the statute-book has made for him. Vengeance is his proper name and function; and by and by, when he has almost been compelled to set a supposed criminal free who has saved his life, he goes and drowns himself in the Seine because he has done an official misdemeanor, or, as the author puts it, is "off the track"—that is, of judicial retaliation. He has just unearthed a long-hunted *suspect* . . . :

> He thought it natural that certain infractions of the written law should be followed by eternal penalties, and he accepted social damnation as growing out of civilization. . . . He was compelled to recognize the existence of kindness. This convict had been kind; and he himself, wonderful to tell, he had just been kind. Therefore, he had become depraved. . . . To be granite, and to doubt! To be the statue of penalty cast in a single piece in the mould of the law, and to suddenly perceive that you have under your breast of bronze something preposterous and disobedient which almost resembles a heart!
>
> (pp. 61-3)

The picture is complete and is very carefully executed. But it is a broad caricature of everything which deserves the august and benign name of justice, whether in heaven or on earth. Justice—no heart? and forsooth must turn suicide when it begins to mistrust that its bosom is not a solid ice-house! The falsity needs no other refutation than an exclamation-point. Nor are even 'eternal penalties' the proof of a revengeful spirit in Him who inflicts them. His gospel denies the charge. We are sorry for a country whose philosophers and philanthropists have got no farther than such conclusions. We cease to wonder at almost any exhibition of drivelling sentimentalism, even when so brilliant a pen as Victor Hugo's pleases thus to moralize, or, rather, *de*-moralize over a brood of already lost wantons: "Sad creatures without name, without age, without sex, to whom neither good nor evil were any longer possible, and for whom, on leaving childhood, there is nothing more in this world, neither liberty, nor virtue, nor responsibility!"

A true picture of Parisian life could hardly be made up without the details of a sort of gallantry and dissipation which can only pollute the page on which they are written: therefore, we think the picture would better be left imperfect than to expose such orgies as the **"Double Quatuor"** and **"Four to Four"** amours and conversations in **"Fantine."** The blasphemies of the drunken Grantaire are as little edifying. . . . We must leave these flaws in this fine crystal, uselessly regretting their existence, but guarding, as we hope, some reader against mistaking them for the true veinings of the gem. We have yet to note the exact type of human progress which our author so eloquently advocates.

A single sentence might almost incline us to suspect that he finds the beginnings of our low estate in a preëxistent fall from virtue. "Who, alas! are we ourselves? Who am I who speak to you? Who are you who listen? Whence do we come? and is it quite certain that we did nothing before we were born? The earth is not without resemblance to a jail. Who knows that man is not a prisoner to divine justice?" But be this as the "Conflict of Ages" may settle it; the starting-point is low and dark enough. **"Les Misérables"** proves it. Its doctrine is—the want of knowledge has ruined the race. "The true division of humanity is the luminous and the dark." . . . "Destroy the cave Ignorance, and you destroy the mole Crime." Partially, without doubt, but not wholly or necessarily. "What is required to exorcise these goblins? Light. Light in floods. No bat resists the dawn. Illuminate the bottom of society." The analogy is not perfect. To a certain distance it holds; at a certain point it breaks down. It is less firm than specious. We are suspicious of our author's understanding of the elements of this great social and spiritual problem—what light is, and to what he would have it conduct us. He says—

> The work of the eighteenth century is sound and good. The encyclopaedists, Diderot at their head; the physiocratists, Turgot at their head; the philosophers, Voltaire at their head; the utopists, Rousseau at their head; these are four sacred legions. To them, the immense advance of humanity towards the light is due. They are the four vanguards of the human race going to the four cardinal points of progress: Diderot towards the beautiful, Turgot towards the useful, Voltaire towards the true, Rousseau towards the just.

A "glittering generalization" emphatically, but a decoying lantern, too, into the defiles of the dark mountains. In no sense is this statement correct. Three of these men, at least, were anything but the ministers of the beautiful, the true, the just. These terms are insulted by such an association. Nor was the work of "93' a sound and good work, but horribly atheistic and wicked, notwithstanding social benefits may have come from it. The world has small need of such light and progress, in either hemisphere. Yet it does need a right illumination, and this is its guide out of the shadows. History will not reverse its verdicts at the dictation of even so able a special pleader as this, demanding the men of September and the tumbrils to be accepted as the pioneers of the world's "Edenization," and because "this holy, good, and gentle thing, progress, was pushed to the wall," then they turned themselves into savages, "terrible, half naked, a club in their grasp, and a roar in their mouth." It is fanciful to write of those demi-demons: "They proclaimed the right furiously; they desired, were it through fear and trembling, to force the world into paradise. They

seemed barbarians, and they were saviours. With the mark of night, they demanded the light." This is an extravagant idealization. We are not yet far enough from the fell triumvirate, Marat, Danton, Robespierre, nor from their philosophic sympathizers, for distance to lend any such enchantment to that view.

A naturalistic illumination is not sufficient to clear the bats out of that old cavern of Ignorance. Here is where this theory fails. There is not Christianity enough in it to save it. That kind of enlightening leads to Voltairism in politics and religion. Grace must use wisdom to restore humanity; else pride, presumption, infidelity, heartlessness, destruction. Our author, in a single place, seems to feel it, and to recoil from his positiveness as a mental illuminator. "But he who says light does not necessarily say joy. There is suffering in the light: in excess it burns. Flame is hostile to the wing. To burn and yet to fly, this is the miracle of genius." It is more than this. Genius does not insure this safety. It did not in the Voltaireans. It does not in any school of intellectual illuminati. It cannot, in humbler seekers after rest. An earnest, spiritual faith in Christ alone performs this miracle. This was Valjean's trouble. There was a thorough ethical regeneration in the old convict's nature. His conscience wrought well and was purged by the action into exceeding rectitude. But no peace possessed his spirit even to the last moment. He was all his lifetime subject to the inner bondage as well as the outer. Love, in its Christian holds and hopes, as connecting the forgiven sinner, through the one Redeemer, to God, was what he needed to cast out fear and torment. All that a mental and legal renovation could do for him was done. His moral transformation needed to be touched with Christ's holy chrism. So does society's, to secure to it repose. That would have rid him of the 'secret monster, the disease which he fed, the dragon which gnawed him, the despair which inhabited his night.' If one, then many, then all. (pp. 63-6)

M. Hugo disports himself with evident satisfaction in several important political questions, the study of which has formed a large part of his life-work. He is at home in the philosophy of revolutions, which he calls 'a vaccination for people-quakes,' a disease which taken naturally is apt to be fatal. . . . He is . . . witty upon the philosophy of political reaction, as in the pausing of the revolution of 1830 to seat Louis-Philippe on the throne. It is of the nature of a "compromise." It is the pleasant not-too-fast of a cautionary moderation. "Between cold water and warm water, this is the party of tepid water. This school, with its pretended depth, wholly superficial, which dissects effects without going back to the causes, from the height of a half-science, chides the agitations of the public square." "Sometimes the stomach paralyzes the heart." The work of 1830 was a halt midway in a march. The nation sat down to rest and take refreshments. The people-giant must be wrapped in flannel and hurried to bed, under a mild, anti-febrile diet. Hercules must be medicated. The point is finely made, and is sharp and long enough to puncture in other spots as well. He is caustic upon our current utilitarianism, less patriotic and chivalric than cunning and thrifty. "The modern spirit is the genius of Greece with the genius of India for its vehicle; Alexander upon the elephant." (pp. 66-7)

The picture [which Hugo gives of the deteriorating and demoralizing tendencies of conventual life] is delicate, tender, appreciative, but full of the dark, dismal, deathlike, nightmare repulsiveness of that most unnatural mode of existence. Valjean escaping from Javert finds a safe shelter in one of these Parisian solitudes. The passage is among the most thrilling of the story. This opens the way to an analysis, searching and repellant to every human instinct, of the cloister-community. Not the least striking part of it is, Valjean's comparison of it with the unlike yet similar life of the galley-slave. The parallels are run with telling effect. Sentimental young ladies might do well to study this section of the novel before taking that particular kind of veil. It is a sad story of puerility and servitude, wherever it finds its repetition—an utterly abnormal violation of humanity, and robbery of God, under pretence of his especial honor. It is only another form of '**Les Misérables**,' and not the least miserable of them all. This book is rightly named. It is a chronicle of misery, every day ploughing its furrows through society to sow new harvests of sorrow; still there is sunlight enough in it to remind us that,—

> —howsoe'er the world goes ill,
> The thrushes still sing in it.

We wish that the author had opened to us more adequate sources of hope and consolation. We take what he offers, but are glad that we are not limited to these. (pp. 67-8)

> *"Victor Hugo's 'Les Miserables',"* in The Boston
> Review, *Vol. III, No. 13, January, 1863, pp. 52-68.*

### [CAROLINE DE PEYRONNET]  (essay date 1863)

[*Peyronnet vigorously condemns* Les misérables *on both moral and artistic grounds. She criticizes the novel's "totally irrelevant" digressions, discordant, antithetic style, and "pernicious" social and political philosophy. For similar commentary on* Les misérables's *digressions, see the excerpts by C. Knight Watson (1862) and George Saintsbury (1917).*]

'This book is a drama of which the first personage is The Infinite; Man is the second.' It would be difficult for any criticism, however concise, to give, in as few words, so just an idea of M. Victor Hugo's style and pretensions as this brief quotation from '**Les Misérables**' conveys. Innumerable sentences of the same nature scattered over the work, and the acquiescence in them, generally, of the critical press of France, are well calculated, it will be admitted, to awaken some diffidence in a reviewer about to grapple with four thousand pages of heterogeneous and unconnected matter. Have we been mistaken? Can this series of improbable adventures, this incongruous collection of rambling disquisitions and contradictory amplifications, be the great prose epic of the nineteenth century, as it has been proclaimed to satiety on the other side of the Channel? Is our intellect so obscured that we should have mistaken for the misshapen and monstrous phantasmagory of a political showman, the effulgent mirror of Truth held up by the hand of Genius to reflect the social deformities of the age? Is it possible that a work, which our sober judgment obliges us—notwithstanding the indisputable power and beauty of many passages—to condemn, on moral grounds, as a gross and unscrupulous appeal to popularity, and in a literary point of view as the receptacle of every gaudy piece of rhetoric and paradox which during a long course of authorship may have remained on hand;—is it possible, we say, that such a work should have been admitted by conscientious judges to be a faithful record of 'progress from evil to good, from injustice to justice, from falsehood to truth, from darkness to light, from lust to conscience, from rottenness to life, from bestiality to duty, from Hell to Heaven, from nothingness to God?' For this second pompous definition we are again indebted to M. Victor Hugo himself; and it is not one of the least curious features of our task that when seeking to exemplify the excessive praise which has been bestowed on this work, we should unconsciously be tempted to have recourse to the author's own estimate of it. Or is it, after all, merely a 'sensation novel' of great pretensions, in which taste, nature, and truth are sacrificed in every page to the desire of exciting violent emotions of sympathy, perplexity, aversion, and disgust?

If the value of a book were to be measured by the curiosity it has excited, by the number of its readers, or even by the eulogies which hail its first appearance, we might indeed feel misgivings, for we have failed to discern the justification of these paeans in '**Les Misérables**.' . . . (pp. 208-09)

All France at the present moment is imbibing the doctrine that if men steal and murder, and if women fall into the lowest depths of infamy, it is no fault of theirs: the sin lies at the door of that collective abstract being called Society. The accusation not only results from the whole book, but M. Victor Hugo expresses it in explicit terms [in his preface to '**Les Misérables**' (see excerpt above, 1862)]. (p. 211)

The discrepancies and contradictions which abound in the tale of '**Les Misérables**' are venial faults in comparison with the invention or even the inflation of social wrongs, when they are made the ground-work of a specious accusation. That the penal code, even of the most civilised nations of Europe, retains some vestiges of barbarism; that the production and distribution of wealth is regulated by imperfect laws; and that society, in spite of daily reforms and indefatigable exertions, has still its outcasts who are not always its worst criminals, none will venture to deny. But M. Hugo seems to forget that there may be such a thing as bearing false witness even against the guilty. The most obvious and not the least unfortunate result of such a course is to damage irrecoverably the true testimony which may be mixed up with so much baseless crimination. That these distortions or exaggerations were necessary to heighten the interest of the narrative is not an available excuse in this instance, as it might be in the case of an ordinary novel. It is no fault of ours if M. Victor Hugo, by his pretensions, has made himself amenable to two tribunals. Neither can absolve him. As a social philosopher, he stands convicted of having pressed into the service of his cause incidents and characters which could only be tolerated in the wildest work of fiction. As a novelist, every literary judge must condemn him for having degraded his pen into a mere instrument of party warfare; for having defiled his pages with indecent pleasantries, and burdened them with ponderous pedantry; for having placed on the brow of his Muse—the Muse of the '**Orientales**' and '**Hernani**'—the red cockade of the Socialist demagogue, and compelled her to gather up in her once brilliant robes the unclean sweepings of Parisian corruption. Who, in the coarse jester and the unscrupulous partisan of '**Les Misérables**,' would recognise the author of the fanciful but elevating theory, of 'Art for its own Sake'? . . . (pp. 211-12)

The story, although not easily told, is by no means so long as the sight of ten octavo volumes would lead one to suppose. It is interrupted by digressions of such length, that were they struck out, and the book divested of all its superfluous white paper, '**Les Misérables**' would scarcely be more substantial than the customary three-volumed English novel of the present day. One hundred and fifty pages on the battle of Waterloo have no other connexion with the main plot than the introduction of an obscure plunderer of the slain, one of those vultures in human shape which hover over all battle-fields. More than a hundred pages on monastic institutions, and as many on the sewers of Paris, are introduced with as little reason; and the history of the barricades of 1832, magnified into an epic, would form a volume in itself. If to these are added an elaborate portrait of Louis-Philippe, a dissertation on the slang language of French thieves, a glorification in sixty pages of the Parisian *gamin,* and a few other disquisitions dragged in under the most trifling pretexts, we shall be within the mark in saying that '**Les Misérables**' contain about a thousand pages of totally irrelevant matter. (p. 212)

There are . . . but three characters in the whole work really deserving of careful analysis: the Bishop, Jean Valjean the hero, and the Inspector of Police, Javert,—the saint, the convict, and the thief-catcher. These have evidently been studiously worked up by M. Victor Hugo, and are the embodiment of certain principles. Fantine, Marius, and Cosette, although they give their names to three of the parts into which '**Les Misérables**' are divided, are mere lay-figures adorned at times with that splendid drapery which M. Hugo knows so well how to throw over his most unnatural conceptions, but more frequently decked out with tawdry finery. (p. 213)

No chapter in '**Les Misérables**' shows M. Hugo in a better light as a novelist than that in which Valjean's first adventure on quitting the Bishop is related. One cannot but feel indignant with a writer who, having the power to paint such a scene as that with Petit-Gervais in a few simple words, ransacks at other times the whole vocabulary, and indeed often goes beyond it, in search of violent contrasts and laboured effect. (p. 225)

This meeting with Petit-Gervais is not, as most readers might suppose, a mere episode, charmingly told, and introduced to show the death-struggles of ferocious instincts in a hardened criminal, it has been made by M. Hugo, in defiance of all probability, the turning-point of his story. For this insignificant theft which had no witness but a frightened child, whose testimony would scarcely find credence, Valjean is to be condemned to death at the expiration of eight years! Indeed, from this point the whole work is but a series of impossibilities. (p. 226)

The author, not his critics, must be held responsible for the disproportionate share of attention which [the first two volumes of '**Les Misérables**'] have universally attracted. They contain the real interest of his story, and the spirit of his doctrine. If we may be allowed so homely a comparison, we would liken '**Les Misérables**' to an enormous kite: there is a large wide head, and a long—a very long—narrow tail, composed of detached bits of learning, paradox or pathos, as the case may be, tied up and connected with a slight thread of adventure. These appendages of strangely-variegated hue have been very useful in flying the socialist machine which M. Hugo has sent up so triumphantly into the highest regions of popularity. Every now and then the story seems to come fluttering, flapping, and diving downwards to the ground; but, with one sharp pull at the string, and a brisk lyrical run into the domain of history or poetry, the author soon gets it up again. His flattering portrait of Louis-Philippe,—his praise of Napoleon I.—his outbursts of sentimental *religiosity,*—to borrow a very useful French neologism,—and, above all, his account of the battle of Waterloo, so palatable to popular feeling in France,—have served, in great measure, to balance the obnoxious theories which form the framework of the book. (pp. 236-37)

The style in which . . . ['**Les Misérables**' is] written is a piece with the disordered violence of the intellect which gives [it] birth. The one step which is said to divide the sublime from

*Frontispiece of an 1889 edition of* Les Misérables.

the ridiculous has no terrors for M. Hugo. He stands perpetually, Colossus-like, astride on the frontier, with one foot in either domain. At all times the chief characteristic of his diction has been a great propensity to startling antithesis and paradox. Success and advancing years have produced their usual result, and magnified the defect into a deformity. His writing now consists in a strain of screaming discords, both of form and matter. Black is laid upon white—great things are opposed to small—beauty to hideousness—excessive sanctity to excessive crime—pompous terms are applied to trivial things—and homely expressions to the most lofty ideas. (pp. 239-40)

M. Hugo has no claim to indulgence. He is a poet, an orator, and a master of language in his way. No writer of the present day has a greater command of words; and yet he has taken with his native language—of all modern languages the least tolerant of disrespect—liberties which have never been equalled. . . .

We shall not, however, discuss any further M. Hugo's literary sins. Our severity has not been called forth by them. English critics are not bound to avenge his outrages on the French language. It is his influence as a social and political teacher—it is the world-wide circulation of his pernicious book, translated, as far as such jargon is translateable, into all languages—that have imposed on us the duty of judging him. We are tempted, in concluding, to paraphrase freely his preface to '**Les Misérables,**' and to account for our review in very nearly the same words that he has used to account for his book.

So long as there shall exist, by reason of certain political and literary laws, writers creating artificially in the midst of civilisation an imaginary social damnation, and complicating with evil passions and class hatred our destiny, which is divine, so long criticism such as our may not be utterly useless.

(p. 240)

[Caroline de Peyronnet], "Victor Hugo's 'Les Misérables'," in The Edinburgh Review, Vol. CXVII, No. CCXXXIX, January, 1863, pp. 208-40.

### THE SOUTHERN LITERARY MESSENGER  (essay date 1863)

[In contrast to most contemporary critics, this anonymous reviewer grants Les misérables unqualified praise, pronouncing it second only to Johann Wolfgang von Goethe's Wilhelm Meister's Apprenticeship among nineteenth-century novels.]

[Les Misérables] is the greatest and most elaborate work of Victor Hugo's fruitful genius.... A novel, in the ordinary acceptation of that term, [Fantine] is not. The ordinary novel, according to Carlyle, is a "tale of adventures which did not occur in God's creation, but only in the Waste Chambers, (to be let unfurnished,) of certain human heads, and which are part and parcel of the Sum of No-things; which, nevertheless, obtain some temporary remembrance, and lodge extensively, at this epoch of the world, in similar still more unfurnished chambers." These productions have wonderful plots and still more wonderful machinery. Fantine has simply dramatic situations, and therefore Fantine is no novel. They are remarkable for many words and few ideas; every page of Fantine contains some beautiful thought, poetically expressed, or some brilliant passage upon Life, Law, Religion, or Philosophy; hence Fantine is not a novel. People with waste chambers, (to let unfurnished,) need not read it; it was never written for them. But to the thinker it will be a solace and delight, albeit its lessons may excite some saddened reflections in sympathetic minds.

We have stated that Fantine had not the plot of the ordinary novel; but dramatic situations, instead. Let us add, that the work is composed of a series of brilliant pictures, boldly touched off by a master-hand, as in the case of the great works of Niccola Poussin and Claude Loraine.... There is not in the literature of fiction a finer portraiture than that given of [M. Charles François Bienvenu Myriel, Bishop of D—]. His every trait of character, objective and psychological, is elaborately depicted. It is, for several pages of the book, a lone sketch, nothing to heighten the interest thereof save two old virtuous ladies of his household; who are about as important to the theme, as the occasional and indifferent tree in some of Raphael's paintings. It is quite as powerful and much more elaborate, yet not quite so fearful or mysterious, but far more genial and beautiful in type than, Byron's grand portrait of Lara; and equally well sustained in power throughout. But the character of Lara is dark and gloomy; that of M. Myriel radiant with spiritual beauty. We are permitted to look, not only upon the objective form and actions of the man, but as if his mind were spread open to view, we have a full revelation of his psychology—we gaze into the divine depths of his immortal soul. Indeed so beautiful is the moral portraiture of that simple but good man, that one of our contemporaries has pronounced such a being an impossibility! We cannot think so—and if mistaken, our historic lessons, standard of ideal virtue, and belief in the true, beautiful and good, must have rested upon shifting

sands.... But conceding the supposed fact, that we err—surely it is highly creditable to the genius of M. Hugo, that out of the depths of his contemplation he could create an Ideal Character, so perfect as to be an impossibility in humanity; a concession which, however, must greatly reflect upon, and detract from, the boasted grandeur of the human soul.

But, be this as it may, two personages of opposite opinions are brought in contact with the Bishop—one, a Senator, and the other, a Conventioner, persecuted by the ruling power which succeeded to the French Revolution. The former is a kind of little Atheist—a scoffer at the established forms of religion, after the manner of Voltaire. The latter is a bold intellectualist; a master of the syllogistic forms of logic; a dogmatic denunciator of legitimacy and royalty; and a mystic in Deism. In detailing the particulars of M. Myriel's interviews with these men, Victor Hugo has carried to its highest point of delicacy, that civilization in Art, which pervades modern French authorship. The Atheist's sneers against revealed religion, is treated with respectful silence, or returned only with Christian pity. The bold sallies and loud declamations of the old Conventioner, are met with pastoral humility until he is half subdued. And when death is about to close his eyes, the good Bishop is his only friend—the only witnesser of his spirit's flight. It is as if the Lion had made of the Lamb its confidant and friend. This is the place to remark, however, that Senator and Conventioner, are simply machinery whereby lessons upon life, history, and morality are promulged; as with many of the seemingly nonessential characters in Goethe's Faust. (pp. 435-36)

[We] do not hesitate to pronounce [Les Misérables] the ablest novel—after Goethe's Welhelm Meister—of this century.

Certain supercilious young gentlemen, of most questionable principles, and certain publicists of still more questionable morals, think it fashionable and brilliant to decry Les Misérables as an immoral book; simply because they have not the brains to understand it. To us, it is a Bible in the fictitious literature of the nineteenth century. To them, it is merely a translation of a French novel; and all France is but their second Sodom: we know that France is not morally worse than America. To them, it is a production by Victor Hugo; to us it is a protest of genius against universal crimes—the plea of one who advocates, in the face of obloquy and contumely, the cause of the Life-Wretched. To them, it is a proclamation of war against society; to us, it is a grand sermon in behalf of primitive Christiantiy—a splendid endeavour to have Christendom permeated by the rules and regulations of the "Church and House Book of the Early Christians," and of the "Law-Book of the Ante-Nicene Church." To them, it is massive, grand, unusual, and incomprehensible; to us, it is beautiful as the Iliad of Homer—real as a play by Shakspeare. Les Misérables is an event—it is a new jewel in the literary crown of our century. (pp. 442-43)

[Les Misérables] should awaken the conscience of society from its dismal lethargy of evil. For it is profound, straight-forward, and marvellously eloquent. "But then, it is a French novel"—say its critics. So much the better, is our response; because it is greater than all of the English novels, gathered together and massed into one, which have appeared during the past quarter of a century. "But," repeat its critics, "it contains exaggerations." No doubt of it; we admit the fact. But are there not exaggerations in all novels? Was there ever one printed that contained them not? Are there not ... more absurdities and vulgar caricatures in [Dickens's] Great Expectations, than there could be found in so many of such books as Les Misérables, as would sink the Great Eastern? *A French novel!* Is this phrase used as a term of reproach, applicable to the literature of the most civilized and cultivated empire upon the globe? If so, is the novel, or its ignorant assailant, to be blamed—and which? Why the latter. Who is the French Novelist, and what is the French Novel? The one, is a scholar of genius and refinement; the other, a reflex of life and society. What English writers— what American writers—can be compared with such authors, in points of power and art, as Victor Hugo, Alfred de Musset, Alphonse Karr, Edmund About, Emile Souvestre, Octave Feuillet, Alexander Dumas, Michelet and Sue? Here are no contortionists—no forced humorists—no retailers of vulgar and far-fetched wit—no writers of dreary, idealess wilderness-pages; but gentlemen of power, large and well digested observation, polished wit, noble satire, keen irony, and great Philosophy. . . . [To] such as find fault with Hugo's humble characters, we would say: first remove Reynold's Dunghill, or clean out Dickens's Augean stables. If they think that the Frenchman crushes society, why, let them the more enjoy Thackeray's crunching and mastication of it. Or if they dislike Jean Valjean, because he was a reformed criminal, then let them revel in the irreclaimable hideousness of Bulwer's Villains. For there are no graceless scamps or vagabonds in the chambers of M. Hugo's mind. His most infamous creation has some principle of homogeneity left; but the vagabond of one English novel, like the sinner of Jonathan Edwards' theology, is past redemption. In short, the French novel is civilization; the English novel affectation—semi-nude barbarism. It is not, however, much to the credit of our vaunted enlightenment, that the greatest of recent Fictions—this very *Les Misérables*—should have been but poorly received by the press. . . . [It] is safe to say, at the least, that another so grandly brilliant a book, of its class, will not appear in the lifetime of the youngest of this generation! (pp. 445-46)

> *T.W.M., in a review of "Les Misérables—Fantine," in* The Southern Literary Messenger, *Vol. XXXV, No. 7, July, 1863, pp. 434-46.*

**CYRUS REDDING** (essay date 1866)

**"Les Misérables"** is styled an extraordinary work. It really is so, if thus denominated for its display of high talent wasted, and the natural course of things outraged. (p. 90)

[A] writer of so vigorous a fancy, and gifted with such a genius, never surely perverted both, nor committed such gross mistakes as [Hugo has done in **"Les Misérables,"**], by intermingling the most striking scenes in powerful language with the improbable, immoral, inconsistent, unconnected, and incoherent. Likely enough to attract the attention of the groundlings, and astonish those who have no taste nor judgment, but who are for the most part proof against the writer's real merits,—such may be charmed with scenes or passages which set nature at defiance, endeavour to reconcile what is irreconcilable, and startle by novelty. (pp. 90-1)

In every part [of **"Les Misérables,"**] truth, probability, and simplicity are violated, while virtue and vice are confounded. Every reader not a lunatic must see that the events stated to have taken place never could do so by any chance in human affairs, that they are out of all nature and fitness, and that this new romantic school of drama and romance no more resembles the romantic drama of Shakspeare or of Calderon, or the tales of the English or Germans, written in the modern romantic, than it equals the Arabian Nights in extravagance and in want

of harmony with truth and nature. The drama and romance of the author—the designation of the present work being of the former class—are up to certain mark as in the verisimilitude of their details, and in an adherence to truth, nature, and moral effect exactly the same, however different on other points, beside their unnatural character, improbability, and extravagance.

We are not strangers to the fallacious pleas of sympathy for the vicious, and to that false pity which is put forth as the excuse for the frailties of one sex and the vices of the other, but in reality for a make-weight to cover powerful descriptions of vices, startling from novelty, and creating false sympathies. Appeals are thus made to our compassion to cover what else could not have currency or be admissible by good taste, while, besides familiarising vice, it is innocent, through numerous anomalies, of imparting any acceptable acquisitions of a pure character to amuse, instruct, or elevate the mind of the reader.

That a powerful genius should pervert the true course of things, and for the sake of surprising cease to paint nature and fact, preferring to have recourse to unfaithful delineations of exaggerated vices, seeking to cozen unworthy sympathy by an untruthfulness of portraiture, is lamentable, and positively injurious to morals. Hugo has ability for nobler, more elevated, and more endurable results. The present work wants moral feeling, veracity, good taste, and a respect for public morality. Before long this school will disappear, but we fear not without leaving evil effects. (p. 94)

> *Cyrus Redding, "Victor Hugo," in* The New Monthly Magazine, *Vol. CXXXVIII, No. DXLIX, September, 1866, pp. 81-95.*

**FRANK T. MARZIALS** (essay date 1888)

[The **"Misérables"** had been begun] even so far back as in the days anterior to 1848, and had afterwards been gradually worked upon, added to, altered. And it bears in some respects the mark of this slow fitfulness of growth. Not that there is any want of unity of effect or purpose. That is very far from being the case. But the unity, to use a very old image, which, however, is here so apposite that I must be forgiven for making it do service once more—the unity is that of a Gothic cathedral, and quite compatible with all kinds of episodical additions and outgrowths. These, in the **"Misérables,"** are of very diverse interest and value. It would be too much to affirm that a description of the battle of Waterloo was essential to the book. No doubt the father of Marius, the second hero, is all but slain in that "king-making victory," and Marius himself greatly influenced in after years by the manner of his father's rescue. But to hold it necessary on this ground to give a full account of the battle is taking a very liberal view of the novelist's functions. Nevertheless few of us would wish Victor Hugo's description unwritten. It may or may not be strategically exact—of this I am no judge. It is at least a fine effective piece of battle painting, and not to be spared. But when Marius in turn is rescued, and the novelist thereupon thinks it incumbent upon him to give an account of the origin and history of the sewers through which the wounded youth is borne,—why then we feel inclined to use the reader's privilege of "skipping." Except to a specialist, the sewers of Paris, regarded in their historical aspect, can scarcely have an interest for any one; and the specialist would probably regard Victor Hugo's erudition as not beyond cavil. (pp. 175-76)

[How] by any weak process of epitome or analysis, convey to the reader any impression of the power of this great book? There are chapters upon chapters in it that for grandeur and pathos cannot be surpassed. Such is the chapter . . . entitled **"Une tempête sous un crâne,"** describing the storm in Jean Valjean's brain when he is debating whether he should deliver himself up to justice. Such are the chapters relating to poor little Cosette,—her terrified walk in the dark to the village well—her little broken wooden shoe put out on Christmas eve in the hope that some Santa Claus might pass that way—though, heaven knows, no Santa Claus had ever put anything into it on previous occasions. Such—I am quoting almost at hazard—is the short chapter comparing Jean Valjean's position to that of a man lost and sinking in mid-ocean. And everywhere the descriptions live, the events move. We see it all. Each scene is present to us. And the characters live too. Bishop Myriel, apostolic as he may be, is no lay figure. Jean Valjean is a man of very real flesh and blood. Poor Fantine one seems to know; and Cosette most certainly; and Marius as a "jeune premier" of a very French type. Marius' royalist grandfather, M. Gillenormand, is also genuine enough, is somewhat caricatured. And there are two characters that live not only as individuals, but as types. These are, Javert, the ideal policeman, whose life is wrecked on finding that Jean Valjean, though a convict, is not a scoundrel;—and Gavroche, the little street arab, the town sparrow of Paris. (pp. 179-80)

The publication of the **"Misérables"** was an event. . . . The power and pathos of the book were unmistakable. Vigour in the painting of the scenes, admirable effectiveness in narration, real vitality in the characters, intense sympathy with the downtrodden and suffering, a style such as no other contemporary, and but few writers of any other time could handle—when a novel possesses qualities like these, it is a very great novel. (p. 181)

> *Frank T. Marzials, in his* Life of Victor Hugo, *Walter Scott, 1888, 224 p.*

### JOAKIM REINHARD   (essay date 1899)

[*Like Edmond and Jules de Goncourt (1862) and André Maurois (1960), Reinhard emphasizes Hugo's limited powers of characterization. He argues that the most convincing figures in* Les misérables *are those modeled on characters from the works of such novelists as Honoré de Balzac and Gustave Flaubert. "Without the guidance of borrowed pattern," Reinhard contends, Hugo created men and women who are "nothing more than arrangements in color, or rattling strings of sonorous antitheses."*]

Hugo described best such things as he had never seen and could never have seen with his bodily eye. Not that his memory was not retentive of real, palpable traits—a description like that of Little Picpus in **"Wretches"** [**"Les Misérables"**] shows that it was—but the impression undeniably produced by the chapters about this famous convent is to a very considerable degree due to their accumulation of historical and technical items concerning conventual life heretofore zealously guarded behind the walls of the cloister or confined within the forbidden covers of Latin ecclesiastical treatises. The author's avowed and indubitable intention of dealing fairly with the subject raises these chapters high above the level of the greater part of what has been written on topics of this kind—Julien's seminary life in Stendhal's "Red and Black," for instance. And although Hugo should by no manner of means be understood to have penetrated to the core of convent life, nor treated it with that unlimited understanding which proceeds from spontaneous sympathy alone,

it is nevertheless certain that his Little Picpus has enough of the air of reality round it to justify the marked attention it has always attracted. (p. 35)

It constituted Hugo's strength that in an age when to most people—particularly such as write—things had become words, to him words remained things; things affecting his sight, hearing, smell, taste, every one of his senses. The sound of the syllable "cold" causes him to shiver, at the word "night" his heart quakes within him as it does in a child unexpectedly let into a dark room. When coming to relate that little Cosette is obliged to go to the woods after water, late in the evening, he is seized with dizziness.

> Darkness [he exclaims] makes you giddy. Man needs brightness. Whosoever becomes ingulfed in the reverse of daylight feels his heart sink. When the eye sees black the spirit sees confusion. . . . No one walks alone in the nighttime through a forest without trembling.
>
> (p. 37)

[A] faculty for abstract reasoning, though not, if properly controlled, injurious to a novelist, is by no means indispensable. Hugo managed to get along very well without it, precisely because the instincts of a painter and stage manager had so strong a hold on him. He always knew where and when to relieve the monotony of a sermon by treating his audience to a picture exhibition. Farther than that, however, he was unable to go. He never rose to the creation of live men and women. He nowhere even came near it. In all his novels we recognize shadows of other men's offspring. . . . The influence not only of Sue and Dickens, but of other contemporary novelists, is very evident in Hugo's later productions, **"Wretches"** in particular. Bishop Myriel possesses hardly a modicum of commendable originality to those acquainted with Balzac's Father Bonnet [from "The Country Parson"]. Even such a figure as Thénardier, the vulgar innkeeper who quotes Voltaire and has pretensions to freethinking and materialism, seems an anaemic repetition of Balzac's vile middle class specimens or Flaubert's Homais [in "Madame Bovary"]. (pp. 38-9)

[Still, Jean Valjean has] at least some vague semblance of life. It is when Hugo tries character drawing without the guidance of borrowed pattern that his failure becomes hopelessly obvious. What he would pass off as portraits are nothing more than arrangements in color, or rattling strings of sonorous antitheses. Cosette's whole person, for example, was "*naïveté,* ingenuity, transparency, whiteness, candor, a ray [*rayon*]. One might have said of Cosette that she was *clear.*" Cosette was "a condensation of the light of dawn in woman's form." The detective Javert in the same novel was

> composed of two sentiments, very simple and relatively very good, but made all but evil by his exaggeration of them—respect for authority and hatred of revolt. . . . His whole life might be comprised in these two words: wake and watch. He had introduced the straight line into the most tortuous circumstances of life.

In this latter achievement, it should be observed, Javert had but imitated his literary lord and master, Victor Hugo. Hugo's personages are all constructed of a few lines running either straight hellward or straight heavenward. (pp. 39-40)

Like the Egyptian priests of old who vaticinated to the faithful through the open mouth of the deity's hollow statue, thereby saving the deity much trouble, Hugo is so merciful to the people whom he parades across his pages as to do all their talking for them.

When the former galley slave, Jean Valjean, sees the impending collapse of the noble structure of honesty and social respectability which he has slowly and laboriously reared for himself under an assumed name, does he then hurl at the court and the people in the courtroom a few simple, manly, passionate words, the cry of an upright, unfortunate, outraged soul? Far from it. From between his lips Hugo declaims in his name:

> It is true what has been told you that Jean Valjean was a very wicked and unfortunate man. But perhaps it was not all his fault. . . . The jail makes the jail bird. Remember this, if you please. Before the bagnio I was a poor unintelligent peasant, some sort of idiot; the bagnio changed me. I had been stupid, I became wicked; I had been fuel, I became flame.
>
> (pp. 40-1)

Hugo's personages, being wholly devoid of innate individuality, yield to the requirements of his plots as readily as martinettes to the touch of their manipulator's fingers. A man as wise and experienced as the seventy-five-year-old bishop Myriel in the beginning of **"Wretches"** is said to be could not avoid long ago forming a well-grounded conviction regarding the main issues of the French revolution, and yet a volley of phrases fired at him by a dying ex-member of the convent transforms his view entirely and forces him down on his knees to beg the old radical for his blessing. Nothing is less probable than that Jean Valjean, on being caught with the Bishop's plate, should think of pretending that it had been given him as a present by that ecclesiastic. But Hugo needed this improbability (or rather impossibility) for the climax, where the Bishop saves Jean by corroborating his statement. The unlikelihood of Fantine's leaving her adored baby with those human monsters, the Thénardiers, is painfully glaring, but Hugo was bound to procure material for the affecting tableau of an innocent child in the lair of wild beasts. (pp. 41-2)

[Hugo] felt exactly as the larger portion of his contemporaries did, or as they fancied they ought to feel, and he expressed his feelings better, to be sure, than they could ever dream of doing, yet never so far better as to become hard of comprehension. In no other respect was there anything essentially modern in his mental composition. The nineteenth century is over and over again spoken of as the age of exact science, but there never lived a man who cared less for exact science, or comprehended more imperfectly what the term meant, than Hugo. (p. 44)

> *Joakim Reinhard, "Victor Hugo's Novels," in* The Sewanee Review, *Vol. VII, No. 1, January, 1899, pp. 29-47.*

## LYTTON STRACHEY (essay date 1912)

[*Strachey was an early twentieth-century English biographer, critic, essayist, and short story writer. He is best known for his biographies* Eminent Victorians, Queen Victoria, *and* Elizabeth and Essex: A Tragic History. *Critics agree that these iconoclastic reexaminations of historical figures revolutionized the course of modern biographical writing. Like his biographies, Strachey's literary criticism is considered incisive. Although he wrote on a wide variety of topics, his discussions of French literature are*

*regarded as his most insightful. In Strachey's opinion, there is little to be said in* Les misérables's *favor; he cites its rhetorical style, inadequate characterization, melodramatic plot, and disorderly construction in pronouncing it a "magnificent failure."*]

**Les Misérables** is the consummation of the romantic conception of fiction which Rousseau had adumbrated half a century before. In that enormous work, Hugo attempted to construct a prose epic of modern life; but the attempt was not successful. Its rhetorical cast of style, its ceaseless and glaring melodrama, its childish presentments of human character, its endless digressions and—running through all this—its evidences of immense and disordered power, make the book perhaps the most magnificent failure—the most 'wild enormity' ever produced by a man of genius. (p. 115)

> *Lytton Strachey, "The Romantic Movement," in his* Landmarks in French Literature, *1912. Reprint by Oxford University Press, 1969, pp. 103-20.\**

## GEORGE SAINTSBURY (essay date 1917)

[*Saintsbury was an English literary historian and critic of the late nineteenth and early twentieth centuries. A prolific writer, Saintsbury composed a number of histories of English and European literature as well as several critical works on individual authors, styles, and periods. Here, Saintsbury points to* Les misérables's *protracted narrative, poorly drawn characters, and lengthy, irrelevant digressions in asserting that it fails as a novel. C. Knight Watson (1862) and Caroline de Peyronnet (1863) also censure* Les misérables's *digressions.*]

It was no doubt lucky for [**Les Misérables**'s] popularity that it fell in with a general movement, in England as well as elsewhere, which had with us been, if not brought about, aided by influences in literature as different as those of Dickens and Carlyle, through Kingsley and others downwards,—the movement which has been called perhaps more truly than sympathetically, "the cult of the lower [not to say the criminal] classes." In France, if not in England, this cult had been oddly combined with a dash of rather adulterated Romanticism, and long before Hugo, Sues and Sands . . . had in their different manner been priests and priestesses of it. In [Hugo's] own case the adoption of the subject "keyed on" in no small degree to the mood in which he wrote the **Dernier Jour** and **Claude Gueux,** while a good deal of the "Old Paris" mania (I use the word nowise contumeliously) of **Notre-Dame** survived, and even the "Cour des Miracles" [an area of Paris famous for its disreputable population] found itself modernised. . . .

I know that, to me, [**Les Misérables**] is the hardest book to read through of any that I know by a great writer. (p. 111)

It is as if Victor Hugo had said, "You shall read this at your peril," and had made good the threat by dint of every blunder in novel-writing which he could possibly commit. With his old and almost invariable fault (there is a little of it even in **Les Travailleurs de la Mer,** and only **Quatre-Vingt-Treize** avoids it entirely), he delays any real interest till the book, huge as it is, is almost half way through. Twenty pages on Bishop Myriel—that rather piebald angel who makes the way impossible for any successor by his fantastic and indecent "apostolicism" in living; who tells, *not* like St. Athanasius, an allowable equivocation to save his valuable self, but a downright lie to save a worthless rascal; and who admits defeat in argument by the stale sophisms of a moribund *conventionnel*—might have been tolerable. We have, in the compactest edition I know, about a hundred and fifty. The ruin and desertion of Fantine would have been worth twenty more. We have from fifty to a hundred to tell us the story of four rather impossibly beautiful grisettes, and as many, alas! too possible, but not interesting, rascals of students. It is difficult to say how much is wasted on the wildly improbable transformation of Jean Valjean, convict and pauper, into "M. Madeleine," *maire* and . . . millionaire, through making sham jet. All this, by any one who really knew his craft, would have been sketched rapidly in fluent preliminary, and subsequent piecemeal retrospect, so as to start with Valjean's escape from Thénardier and his adoption of Cosette.

The actual matter of this purely preliminary kind extends . . . to at least three-quarters of an average novel of Sir Walter's: it would probably run to two or three times the length of a modern "six-shilling." But Hugo is not satisfied with it. A point, an important point, doubtless, but one that could have been despatched in a few lines, connects the novel proper with the Battle of Waterloo. To that battle itself, even the preliminary matter in its earliest part is some years posterior: the main action, of course, is still more so. But Victor must give us *his* account of this great engagement, and he gives it in about a hundred pages of the most succinct reproduction. For my part, I should be glad to have it "mixed with much wine," even if the wine were of that luscious and headachy south-of-France character which he himself is said to have preferred to Bordeaux or Champagne, Sauterne or even Burgundy. Nay, without this I like it well enough and quarrel with nothing in it, though it is in many respects (from the famous hollow way which nobody else ever heard of downwards) very much of a dream-battle. Victor does quite as much justice as any one could expect him to do . . . to English fighting; while if he represents Wellington as a mere calculator and Napoleon as a hero, we can murmur politely (like a Roman Catholic bishop, more real in many ways than His Greatness of Digue), "Perhaps so, my dear sir, perhaps so." But what has it all got to do here? Even when Montalais and her lover sat on the wall and talked for half a volume or so in the *Vicomte de Bragelonne* [by Alexandre Dumas, *père*] . . . , the superabundance, though trivial, was relevant: this is not. When Thénardier tried to rob and was no doubt quite ready to murder, but did, as a matter of fact, help to resuscitate, the gallant French Republican soldier, who was so glad to receive the title of baron from an emperor who had by abdication resigned any right to give it that he ever possessed, it might have been Malplaquet or Leipsic, Fontenoy or Vittoria, for any relevance the details of the battle possessed to the course of the story.

Now relevance (to make a short paragraph of the kind Hugo himself loved) is a mighty goddess in novelry.

And so it continues, though, to be absolutely just, the later parts are not exposed to quite the same objections as the earlier. These objections transform themselves, however, into other varieties, and are reinforced by fresh faults. The most inexcusable digressions, on subjects as remote from each other as convents and sewers, insist on poking themselves in. . . . The gamin Gavroche puts in a strong plea for mercy, and his sister Eponine, if Hugo had chosen to take more trouble with her, might have been a great, and is actually the most interesting, character. But Cosette—the cosseted Cosette—Hugo did not know our word or he would have seen the danger—is merely a pretty and rather selfish little doll, and her precious lover Marius is almost ineffable.

Novel-heroes who are failures throng my mind like ghosts on the other shore of the river whom Charon will not ferry over; but I can single out none of them who is, without positively

evil qualities, so absolutely intolerable as Marius. Others have more such qualities; but he has no good ones. His very bravery is a sort of moral and intellectual running amuck because he thinks he shall not get Cosette. Having, apparently, for many years thought and cared nothing about his father, he becomes frantically filial on discovering that he has inherited from him, as above, a very doubtful and certainly most un-"citizen"-like title of Baron. Thereupon (taking care, however, to have cards printed with the title on them) he becomes a violent republican.

He then proceeds to be extremely rude to his indulgent but royalist grandfather, retires to a mount of very peculiar sacredness, where he comes in contact with the Thénardier family, discovers a plot against Valjean, appeals to the civil arm to protect the victim, but, for reasons which seem good to him, turns tail, breaks his arranged part, and is very nearly accessory to a murder. At the other end of the story, carrying out his general character of prig-pedant, as selfish as self-righteous, he meets Valjean's rather foolish and fantastic self-sacrifice with illiberal suspicion, and practically kills the poor old creature by separating him from Cosette. When the *éclaircissement* comes, it appears to me—as Mr. Carlyle said of Loyola that he ought to have consented to be damned—that Marius ought to have consented at least to be kicked.

Of course it may be said, "You should not give judgments on things with which you are evidently out of sympathy." But I do not acknowledge any palpable hit. If certain purposes of the opposite kind were obtruded here in the same fashion—if Victor (as he might have done in earlier days) had hymned Royalism instead of Republicanism, or (as perhaps he would never have done) had indulged in praise of severe laws and restricted education, and other things, I should be "in sympathy," but I hope and believe that I should not be "out of" criticism. Unless strictly adjusted to the scale and degree suitable to a novel—as Sir Walter has, I think, restricted his Mariolatry and his Jacobitism, and so forth—I should bar them as I bar these. And it is the fact that they are not so restricted, with the concomitant faults which, again purely from the point of view of novel-criticism as such, I have ventured to find, that makes me consider *Les Misérables* a failure as a novel. Once again, too, I find few of the really good and great things— which in so vast a book by such a writer are there, and could not fail to be there—to be essentially and specially good and great according to the novel standard. They are, with the rarest exceptions, the stuff of drama or of poetry, not of novel. That there are such exceptions—the treacherous feast of the students to the mistresses they are about to desert; the escapes of Valjean from the ambushes laid for him by Thénardier and Javert; some of the Saint-Merry fighting; the guesting of the children by Gavroche in the elephant; and others—is true. But they are oases in a desert; and, save when they would be better done in poetry, they do not after all seem to me to be much better done than they might have been by others—the comparative weakness of Hugo in conversation of the kind suitable for prose fiction making itself felt. That at least is what the present writer's notion of criticism puts into his mouth to say; and he can say no other. (pp. 111-16)

*George Saintsbury, "Victor Hugo," in his* A History of the French Novel (to the Close of the 19th Century): From 1800 to 1900, Vol. II, *1917. Reprint by Russell & Russell, Inc., 1964, pp. 96-132.*

**MADAME DUCLAUX** (essay date 1921)

[*Duclaux's discussion of* Les misérables *focuses on the novel's genesis, literary models, elements of realism, and social impli-*

*cations. For a fuller treatment of* Les misérables*'s origins and developments, see the excerp: by Elliott M. Grant (1945).]*

[*Les Misérables*] is conceived in the same key as [*La legende des siècles*]; it also is a progression towards an apotheosis. But where the poem is legend or prophecy, the prose epic touches reality and moves in our sphere. Marius, the hero, is the contemporary, and indeed the double, of Victor Hugo—the son of a Royalist mother and a father who had served in Napoleon's armies, like General Hugo.

Marius, too, had been young in 1830, had lived on the barricades of a revolution, had married, after endless difficulties, the girl whom all his young will and passion were bent on obtaining. Marius is an image of Hugo's youth. But is Marius the hero of *Les Misérables*? No. Evidently their real hero is Jean Valjean, the convict, the criminal who steals the cherished treasure of his benefactor, who cheats the boy-sweep of his florin; who then, repenting, is transformed into a man of honesty and honour. (p. 203)

There is, no doubt, a sort of moral paradox, an amplification like that produced by the fumes of opium, in this conception of a hardened criminal shattered by remorse because he has stolen two francs from a little boy, and giving himself up to justice in order to save an innocent man wrongly accused. Hugo is incurably sentimental. We must accept him as he is. His virtuous thieves and angelic prostitutes are, after all, but the transposition into modern art of figures sufficiently familiar in the Gospels. Hugo was as intimately convinced as any priest that the heart of man is complex, never wholly good nor wholly bad, and that there is no sin which may not be redeemed. In *Les Misérables* he gives life and substance to those theories of expiation and atonement which he has preached consistently enough in his play of *Marion de Lorme* and in his poems of *Les Contemplations.*

Jean Valjean is a double nature, such as suited the genius of Hugo, that unrepentant Manichee: Jean Valjean wears, as it were, two pouches; in one he has the experience of a convict, in the other the instincts of a saint; and his thoughts and deeds are extracted, as he goes through life, sometimes from the one, and sometimes from the other.... When Jean Valjean stole the Bishop's plate, there was something hidden with it in his sack, as surreptitiously as the silver cup in Benjamin's wallet; and that was Salvation. For kindness, charity, courtesy, though betrayed, and finally a free forgiveness, accomplished that which years of cruel repression had failed even to suggest. In an earlier book—which all lovers of *Les Misérables* should read—in *Claude Gueux,* Hugo had already incriminated the injustice of human justice. Tolstoi, I think, must have thought of *Les Misérables* when he wrote *Resurrection.*

In his former great novel, in that tragic, bitter, dilettante *Notre-Dame de Paris,* Hugo, his heart wrung by the deep disappointment of his marriage, had preached the hopeless doctrine of Fatality. We are all, said he, subject to Necessity.... But *Les Misérables* is a generous recantation, a palinody full of faith in the soul's liberty and in social progress.... Fatality is a monster of the Middle Ages. Monsters evolve and develop into angels. From the dead cocoon of Necessity a soaring and glittering being issues, shedding hope and love from its radiant wings; and Fraternity illuminates the Future.... [In *Les Misérables* Hugo] celebrates the times when there shall be no more wars, no more classes sunk in misery, no more ignorance, no more crime, no more indigence. Here Hugo wanders in Utopia; but he does not ignore, in his novel, the terrible problem

of crime. Besides Jean Valjean, the criminal-made, he sets Thénardier, the criminal-born, whom nothing can redeem; who, when unexpected prosperity gives him, in a new country, a new lease of life, employs his unhoped-for capital as a fund to start himself in business as a slave-dealer. There is not one single noble instinct in Thénardier.... [Round] Thénardier gravitates a system of thieves and bullies, criminal by a bent of their nature, from laziness, or brutality, or sheer malice, as well as from mere love of adventure. For nine-tenths of these, surely, there is little to be hoped in this world or the next. All we can admit is their annihilation, since Evil has no immortal soul. Hugo the novelist knows the depths of human nature more profoundly than Hugo the philosopher. The root of Crime is not mere Ignorance. There exists a mysterious natural depravity. Was not the vile Thénardier, who had studied to be a priest, less ignorant than Jean Valjean? (pp. 204-05)

*Misérables* is a word with two meanings, for *misérable* means "wretch," and also merely "wretched"—wretchedly poor. Victor Hugo had never been able to forget the condition of Lazarus at his gates; pity for the poor no less than love of liberty had made him a revolutionary; and the question of how to purify the dregs of society was seldom long absent from his mind. Something noble and magnanimous in his temper prevented him from acquiring the indifference of the pure aritst, and at sixty years of age he rebelled as indignantly against injustice, oppression, or the hard and starving misery which infests the slums of great cities as any generous youth in his first fresh contact with reality. If I had to translate the title *Les Misérables,* I think I should call it: The Dregs of Society. In our common round of life we scarcely notice these dregs, fallen to the bottom; the draught we drink is clear and sweet. But sometimes the Hand of God takes up the glass and shakes it rudely. Then there is a revolution and the dregs mix with the wine, and give their acrid flavour to the whole.

*Les Misérables* is a study of those first years after 1830, when the people of France, resenting the tricks of legerdemain, thanks to which Louis-Philippe had put their revolution in his royal pocket, broke out again and again in useless insurrections.... It was [Hugo's] memories of the street-fighting of 1851 which enabled him in *Les Misérables* to vivify his picture of the life of a barricade, and to show that mutual exaltation, that more than individual existence, that incorporate and unanimous mind, in which a trench or a barricade—any body of men so much in earnest as to make light of death and pain—can live a sublimer life than their separate components ever know. *Les Misérables* is an epic of insurrection, the development of an obscure and immanent force, that tends to the light, striving to destroy the tyranny which would keep it plunged in the abyss. Both the tyranny and the resurgent force ... are charged with the fetters of the Past. Their clash is the conflict of two powers alike doomed to perish; for who lives by the sword shall perish by the sword; but, out of their ruined violence, a new order shall arise, which shall not seek to repress or punish, but to reform and to elevate; which shall attempt not to grasp but to share, and not to dominate but to love.

Such is the gospel of *Les Misérables;* but a novel lives less by its general ideas than by the characters which it exhibits and the pictures it represents. Hugo has never been so happy in his personages as in these volumes. Marius and Cosette move through these scenes of riot and upheaval haloed in a blue and tender gleam as wonderful as that more golden haze which irradiates the figure of a girl in Rembrandt's "Ronde de Nuit"; for he sees them in the light of his own youth—still infinitely fair and intimately real, in spite of Life's disenchantment. Cosette is just a girl in love—a type more than an individual—and she has borrowed something from either of the two women that Hugo loved with the two valves of his double heart. . . . [It] is not so much the woman that we see as the charm that emanates from her, the dawn-like, delicious, girlish radiance that suddenly transfuses and transfigures the lean, lanky, sallow grasshopper of a girl to whom Marius had paid scant attention. Cosette is a haunting strain of music, an almond-branch in flower, a delight we should be sorry to have missed. But Marius is a person, for Marius is Victor Hugo, and the study of Marius unbares the poet's heart. (pp. 206-08)

There are pages in *Les Misérables*—the charming idyll of Marius and Cosette in the Luxembourg Gardens; the struggle in the soul of Jean Valjean when he hears that an innocent man has been arrested for his crime; his dream; his drive to Amiens; and the scene in the Courts; or again the magnificent recital of the suicide of Javert, with its view of Paris at night seen from the quai de la Mégisserie—there are pages which, I suppose, are unmatched in nineteenth-century fiction except perhaps by certain passages in the great novels of Tolstoi or George Eliot. And yet at this supreme point commences Hugo's decadence. For his age betrays him: that proliferation of tissue which is a sign of degenerescence, that senile amplification which more and more will gain upon our poet, are already incipient. . . . (p. 209)

> *Madame Duclaux, in her* Victor Hugo, *Henry Holt and Company, 1921, 268 p.*

## ROBERT LYND (essay date 1932)

[*In the following commentatory assessment of* Les misérables, *Lynd argues that improbabilities in the story's plot and characterization are artistically justified because they create suspense and help to convey Hugo's social and political philosophy. Lynd notes* Les misérables's *superiority among novels that are half "tract" and half "'thriller'," but acknowledges that its appeal to modern readers is limited by its didactic and sensational elements. Additional discussion of* Les misérables's *lack of realism is provided by Edmond and Jules de Goncourt (1862), Joakim Reinhard (1899), Joseph Warren Beach (1932), and André Maurois (1960). Lynd's essay first appeared in 1932 in* John o' London's Weekly.]

Among the novelists Victor Hugo has suffered more than ordinary loss of reputation. There is probably no critic writing to-day who would say of him, as Swinburne once did, that he was 'the greatest writer born in the nineteenth century.' His rhetoric has faded with time; his propaganda is the propaganda of a past age; his characters belong to melodrama rather than to the fiction of human nature; and his sentimentality is as unpalatable to many modern readers as that of a tract. As a result, though long critical studies of most eminent novelists, ranging from Balzac to Peacock, appear from time to time, it is difficult to imagine one of the younger critics spending his labour on a study of Victor Hugo.

Even so, when I re-read *Les Misérables* recently I found it as enthralling as ever. As one reads it, one feels certain that, if Hugo had been born in the present century, he would have been one of the greatest of all writers for the films. He is a master of suspense: he is also a master of the scenic; and the super-abundance and variety of his imaginative force are among the most remarkable products of nineteenth-century literature.

*Les Misérables,* by Hugo's own confession [in the preface to the work (see excerpt above, 1862)], is an attack on three great evils—'the degradation of man by poverty, the ruin of woman by starvation, and the dwarfing of childhood by physical and spiritual night.' 'So long as ignorance and misery remain on earth,' he declares in his preface, 'books like this cannot be useless' [see excerpt above, 1862].

At the same time, Hugo aims at our conversion, for the most part, not as a preacher but as a story-teller. He sets out to win our sympathies for his merciful creed by compelling us to sympathize with three human beings—Jean Valjean, the convict; Fantine, the outcast woman; and Fantine's daughter, Cosette, the enslaved household drudge, who at length brings sweetness into Valjean's life.

At first, it is true, it is a little difficult to believe in Jean Valjean. We can easily believe that more than a hundred years ago it was possible for a man to be sentenced to five years in the galleys for stealing a loaf of bread to feed his sister's children. We can believe that, because he made four attempts to escape, his sentence was prolonged to nineteen years. We can believe that, owing to his past, he was turned from the doors of even the meanest lodging-houses, and was refused permission to sleep in a stable. What we can scarcely believe, however, is that when the Christ-like bishop of D— took him into his house, fed him at his table, and gave him a bed, Jean rose in the night and stole his benefactor's silver. Being what he was, a fundamentally honest man, who could not even tell the bishop a lie about himself, Jean could not, in my opinion, have committed that particular crime.

Imaginative writers, however, must be given a certain licence to strain our credulity. Shakespeare strains it by allowing King Lear to behave as he does to Cordelia at the beginning of the play, and, in the result, we do not complain. Similarly, Jean Valjean's theft is artistically justified by the noble behaviour of the bishop when the convict is brought back by the police. It is not surprising that the scene in which the bishop pretends that he has given Valjean the silver, and adds the silver candlesticks to the haul, remains as vividly and as movingly in the reader's memory as almost any scene in fiction.

Without the theft, this Tolstoyan charity would have been impossible, and without the Tolstoyan charity of the bishop, Jean Valjean would not have been transformed from an embittered ex-convict into a saint and martyr. (pp. 156-57)

[After Jean Valjean's] two revengeful crimes, the robbery of the bishop and of the little boy, he is transformed into a successful manufacturer who, in spite of his attempts to avoid distinction, has been appointed mayor of his town. This, too, is a little difficult to believe, but it is necessary for Hugo's titanic fable of the inhumanity of justice. Living under the name of M. Madeleine, Valjean is widely loved and respected, not only as a successful man, but as a supremely good man and the friend of the poor and miserable. Thus, it is not merely a rich man but a saint whom the law pursues with its lust for destruction. (p. 158)

When Valjean . . . escapes from the galleys in circumstances which convince everybody that he is drowned, he again finds himself Javert's quarry. The story of his having kidnapped Cosette puts Javert on his track, and we find another great flight along with Cosette, in which impossible walls are scaled, and Valjean has to allow himself to be carried out of a nunnery in a coffin and listen to the earth being flung on the lid in the graveyard in order to escape. Again a little incredible. But we believe it as we read, and are as apprehensive for the safety of Valjean as though he were not fabulous. We feel the terror of Javert's pitiless eye more than Valjean felt it.

There is no development in Valjean's character after his conversion: there is development only in his adventures. He is really a magnificent Henry Irving character conceived in the spirit of Dickens and Tolstoy. Or, if there is any development in his character, it is a greater softening that comes with his love for the child, Cosette. Possibly he ceases to be an entirely perfect saint for the moment, when Cosette grows up and he grudges her her happiness with her young lover. But on the whole he is a static figure representing innocence in the toils of justice—goodness hounded down by civilized society. It is because of the beauty of his character that we read with such excitement the story of his ceaseless perils. . . . (pp. 158-59)

Possibly the novel that is half a tract and half a 'thriller' belongs to an outworn convention. The modern world does not seem to produce writers who are at once great preachers and great sensational story-tellers, as Victor Hugo and Charles Reade were. Among all the novels written with this double genius *Les Misérables* is surely the greatest; and among all the characters who have been created in such novels the most memorable, it seems to me, is Jean Valjean, the ex-convict. (p. 159)

*Robert Lynd, "Jean Valjean," in his* Books and Writers, *J. M. Dent & Sons Ltd., 1952, pp. 156-59.*

## JOSEPH WARREN BEACH   (essay date 1932)

[*Beach contends that* Les misérables's *melodramatic plot accounts for both its success as an adventure story and its failure as an example of the art of "serious" novel writing. In portions of the essay not excerpted below (see* NCLC, *Vol. 3), Beach elaborates on this idea, arguing that* Les misérables *is artistically flawed, particularly because of its unconvincing characterization, and that it is primarily a vehicle for Hugo's social ideas.*]

[It] must be said that, so far as story goes, [**"Les Misérables"**] is very well done. In a narrative involving many characters drawn from the most diverse *milieux*, the author follows the excellent method of establishing one group of characters very solidly before introducing another group which is eventually to be closely linked with them. It is a well-ordered story, free from the innumerable fussy little interruptions and changes of center that spoil so much of Balzac's story-telling. Hugo has many high qualities in the *manner* of doing it. Such is the excellent objectivity with which, at one point and another, he shows us a character in action, especially Jean Valjean. In general the story is notable for its bold modeling, its dramatic intensity. I know nothing in the whole range of fiction which goes faster where it does go, which holds the reader in a tighter grip of suspense. Is there anything more exciting than Jean Valjean's flight through Paris that ends with his scaling the convent wall, or his adventure in the underground labyrinth of sewers?

It is true that this fine story-telling is the good side of a vicious method, since it is made possible, for one thing, by the author's election to narrate only the most exciting moments of the history, to "hit" only the "high spots." The moments of ordinary life are neglected altogether or treated in hasty survey. There is none of the patient following of small incidents such as make up the staple of most lives and such as Thackeray and the French realists excel in. In other words, this is, on the side of action, a pure adventure story. It is one long tissue of coincidences, of extraordinary and well-nigh incredible happen-

ings, of impudent clever *coups de théâtre,* which, taken all together, amount to simple melodrama. Everywhere the author depends for effect on surprise and on the "noble gesture." (pp. 57-8)

When examined closely, few scenes are found to be well done save on the side of suspense and drama, and where the theatrical element is not strongly present it is hard to realize the situations imaginatively. Compared with the work of the really serious artists, this is simply chromo, and in his story Hugo may be said to have altogether neglected what the novelist proper—whether of the rank of Tolstoy and Flaubert, or that of George Moore or George Gissing—regards as of the essence of his craft. (p. 59)

*Joseph Warren Beach, "Philosophy: Hugo," in his* The Twentieth Century Novel: Studies in Technique, *The Century Co., 1932, pp. 55-64.*

## ALBERT THIBAUDET   (essay date 1936)

[*Thibaudet was an early twentieth-century French literary critic and follower of the French philosopher Henri Bergson. He is often described as versatile, well-informed, and original, and critics cite his unfinished* Histoire de la littérature française de 1789 à nos jours, *from which the following excerpt is drawn, as his major critical treatise. In this work, first published in 1936, Thibaudet classified authors by the generations of 1789, 1820, 1850, 1885, and 1914-1918, rather than by literary epochs. Here, Thibaudet describes the reasons for* Les misérables's *popular appeal.*]

The triumph of *Les Misérables* was immense and immediate, and it is still going on. It was through *Les Misérables* that the poet maintained contact with the crowds. . . . It deserved this popularity. Here, at the forge of a Cyclops, Hugo hammered out the novel of Paris, the novel of adventures, the detective novel, the novel of human pity, the heroic novel. Certainly *Les Misérables* would no more have existed without the July monarchy than *Notre-Dame* without Walter Scott. The fact is that Hugo was carried along by his time. But his creations have no resemblance to those of anyone else, even those of nature. It does not shock us that his characters are all of a piece, that Javert is all policeman, that Thénardier is all the wicked man, that Marius and Cosette are all youth: their life outside time is a life. And it was in part as a result of this procedure that Hugo achieved that unique success in the novel—the creation of a saint, Monseigneur Myriel. He incorporated into the novel that theme that Lamartine had entrusted to the epic: the rise of a soul, the liberation of man the galley slave by the spark of goodness, of sacrifice; and in truth *Les Misérables* turns its back on the heroes of novels in order to become almost a novel of heroes. Another paradox: novels are women; the success of novels is made by women. Now *Les Misérables* is a novel without women: I mean without other love affairs than the incidental and the conventional, like those of Marius and Cosette. In this respect Hugo's masculine genius viewed the novel in the terms in which Corneille viewed the theater. The heroic novel is a virile novel. (pp. 224-25)

*Albert Thibaudet, "The Novels of the Poets," in his* French Literature from 1795 to Our Era, *translated by Charles Lam Markmann, Funk & Wagnalls, 1968, pp. 221-26.\**

## ELLIOTT M. GRANT (essay date 1945)

*[In his approbatory assessment of* Les misérables, *Grant delineates the reasons for the novel's success, citing its well-drawn characters, suspenseful plot, and memorable historical accounts of the Battle of Waterloo and the Paris insurrection of 1832. Grant also discusses the novel's genesis and elements of realism; he points out those of its characters that are drawn from life and notes that in 1861, Hugo altered the original manuscript of* Les misérables *to accommodate his changed political and religious opinions. Expressing particular admiration for* Les misérables's *attention to nineteenth-century social and political concerns, Grant argues that the novel's digressions accurately reflect the problems and beliefs of Hugo's era. For other positive appraisals of* Les misérables's *digressions, see the unsigned essay from the* Boston Review *(1863) and the excerpt by John Porter Houston (1974); Madame Duclaux (1921) provides additional commentary on the work's genesis.]*

"Dante," said Victor Hugo, "created a hell out of poetry; I have tried to create one out of reality." In these words the great exile underlined the realistic import of his mighty novel, **Les Misérables,** conceived early in his career and gestated over a period of nearly thirty years. Yet, in spite of characters taken from real life, in spite of the minute evocation of certain milieux, in spite of the importance given to the underprivileged classes of society, in spite of the sordidness which the author did not hesitate to depict, **Les Misérables** cannot be considered as an exclusively realistic novel. (p. 246)

[Perhaps] we need not worry too much about the exact classification of Victor Hugo's novel. Let us be satisfied that the book is great; great because it contains certain characters who have achieved world-wide fame, great because it reflects so admirably some of the problems and beliefs of the nineteenth century, great because it relates so stirringly certain historical events, great above all because a profound human sympathy animates its every page. Once again we discover that, wittingly or not, Victor Hugo has gone beyond the limitations of any one school.

The splendor of **Les Misérables** has been frequently obscured by the abbreviations inflicted on the book by well-meaning editors and moving-picture producers. In school texts and the cinema emphasis has been laid on action, and the melodramatic conflict between Jean Valjean and Police Inspector Javert has taken the center of the stage. That conflict, of course, is not unimportant in the complete version, but there it is reduced to its proper proportions; there, it takes its place beside other elements of equal or even greater significance. The man-hunt . . . is not permitted to outbalance the rest. (p. 247)

Except for the *Comédie humaine,* nothing like [**Les Misérables**] had been seen in France. **Les Misérables** is, of course, more limited in scope than Balzac's series, yet the work surpasses in size any one of the Balzacian novels. The number of characters created is, within the given limits, on the Balzacian scale. To some extent, like the *Comédie humaine,* it is a history of the Restoration. And to some extent, again like the *Comédie humaine,* the struggle for existence is as important a theme as love. But there, it must be admitted, the comparisons come to an end. **Les Misérables** can hardly be considered the great *roman de moeurs* which is one of the *Comédie humaine's* claims to eternal fame. Balzac's work entirely lacks the essentially religious idea which animates **Les Misérables.** The social and political philosophy of the two authors is almost diametrically opposite.

Among the book's great characters the greatest and best-known are, of course, Bishop Myriel and Jean Valjean, who symbolize two of Victor Hugo's deepest convictions: the essential goodness of man and the reality of human redemption. In Bishop Myriel the author has given us a picture, [modeled on the life of Mgr de Miollis, Bishop of Digne] . . . , of the good and just man, the ideal Christian, charitable, kind, forgiving, self-sacrificing, and sincere. This marvelous portrait would have won unanimous applause save for a few odd details. It is surprising to hear a Catholic bishop come very close to expressing belief in metempsychosis; it is positively startling to see him kneel before an old Revolutionary of 1793 and ask his benediction. Quite understandably, conservative Catholics were scandalized by such things and their protests were vehement. . . . The truth is that Bishop Myriel is not merely a reflection of Mgr de Miollis, but also of Victor Hugo himself. If Myriel's career is, for the most part, like that of the benign bishop of Digne, his ideas are certainly very similar to those of the novelist. Like Victor Hugo, Myriel believes in free and universal education; like Victor Hugo he condemns capital punishment and is horrified by the sight of the scaffold; like Victor Hugo he believes in the possibility of human redemption. Of course these ideas were widespread. But the notion of metempsychosis and the attitude of the Bishop before the old Revolutionary are perhaps more markedly Hugolian. They were added by the poet many years after he had sketched the original portrait. In 1861 he included traits which he would not have thought of in 1845 or earlier. During that interval he had elaborated his personal philosophy and during that interval the features of Mgr de Miollis had doubtless grown dimmer in his mind. The final picture of Bishop Myriel may be displeasing to the hidebound; it is nonetheless one of Victor Hugo's admirable creations.

Jean Valjean is even more the product of Hugo's imagination and his art, for the model, Pierre Maurin, served merely as an initial stimulus. The case of Maurin, plus Hugo's documentation, also serves to exculpate the novelist from the accusation of exaggeration. Immediately after publication of the book in 1862 it was charged that no one would ever be sent to the galleys for stealing bread and would certainly not be kept there for five years, subsequently stretched into nineteen by attempted escapes. But Hugo, concerned with the problem of realism, had consulted the *Code pénal des Chiourmes* which completely supports his narrative. Jean Valjean committed his "crime" in 1795 at a time when the law did not provide for extenuating circumstances. If such evidence were deemed insufficient, the case of Pierre Maurin is there to prove the realism of Hugo's story. (pp. 250-52)

[Jean Valjean's] conversion is skillfully manipulated. It does not come too soon. His reception by Bishop Myriel obviously impresses him. But he is still far enough from virtue to steal the Bishop's silverware. When Myriel makes him a present of his theft, gives him his silver candlesticks to boot, and frees him from the officers who had caught him, Jean Valjean is again obviously impressed. But he is still not wholly converted, and he steals a piece of money from a child, Petit Gervais. It is only when the realization of what he has done sweeps over him that the full import of the Bishop's parting words, "It is your soul I am redeeming. I withdraw it from black thoughts and from the spirit of perdition and I give it to God," overcomes his resistance, breaks down his defenses, and for the first time in nineteen years he weeps. (p. 253)

[Such a life as Jean Valjean's] might have been presented with nauseating sentimentality. Victor Hugo successfully avoided that pitfall. He has described Jean Valjean's paternal love— for the relationship between him and Cosette is essentially that of father and child—with the same moving simplicity which distinguished the poems of *Pauca meae* in *Les Contemplations.* Posterity as well as Hugo's contemporaries recognized the greatness of the portrait. Jean Valjean is known the world over as the type of the redeemed man, saved by Christian charity from evil, and transformed into a character of exemplary goodness and kindness.

In Cosette and Marius we see a reflection of Victor Hugo's own youth. Cosette is to some extent modeled on the Adèle Foucher whom Victor Hugo loved and married in 1822. But in the beginning she is just a little girl in need of kindness and protection. Later, she blossoms out into a beautiful adolescent. It is then, of course, that she resembles Adèle: it is then that she becomes quite the nineteenth-century *jeune fille française* [young French girl], a combination of grace, charm, and innocence. There is really not much more to be said about her.

Marius, on the other hand, is an interesting character in whom Hugo depicts much of his own youthful aspirations and political idealism. . . . [The] poverty which Marius endured after his break with his grandfather resembles Hugo's own poverty in the rue du Dragon after his mother's death. When the author said of Marius' privations that "destitution engenders greatness of soul and mind" he knew from personal experience what he was talking about. After Marius meets Cosette, he worships her in the same ultra-romantic fashion that the twenty-year-old Victor Hugo worshiped Adèle Foucher. . . . And yet in spite of this sentimental recolleciton of his courting of Adèle, Victor Hugo chooses as the wedding day for Cosette and Marius the date of February 16, 1833! Thus their nuptial night coincides with the beginning of Victor Hugo's liaison with Juliette Drouet. A strange man, Hugo. (pp. 254-55)

Other memorable characters grace the pages of *Les Misérables.* Javert, thanks to the abbreviators and to motion pictures, is as well known as Jean Valjean, perhaps better known than he deserves to be. [The French critic] Edmond Biré admired him inordinately, but to the present writer he is a far less interesting character than many others in the book. Among them is M. Gillenormand . . . , a salty, pigheaded, tyrannical old royalist—an altogether admirable, lively portrait. Then there is the immortal Gavroche, the *gamin de Paris,* witty, impudent, and clever; heroic, too, as his death before the barricades amply reveals. There is Enjolras, the young political idealist, who nobly fights and nobly dies in the insurrection of 1832. There is M. Mabeuf, church warden . . . , naturalist and scholar, a gentle soul, indifferent to political disputes, who also dies on the barricades, red flag in hand, after poverty has driven him to sell his last beloved volume. There are Thénardier and his ugly wife, as consummate evildoers as have ever appeared in fiction. By one of those quirks of heredity which now and then occur, they have produced some children of a different stamp. Gavroche is one of them. So are those two little boys who suddenly find themselves adrift in Paris with no lodging for the night. Momentarily taken in tow by Gavroche who is quite unaware of their identity, they later glide across the scene and their worried, childish faces wring one's heart. And the elder daughter of Thénardier, Éponine, is one of Hugo's most brilliant and moving creations. To the present writer she seems more real than Fantine, the seduced and abandoned girl. In the latter's situation, pitiful as it may be, there is something so obviously conventional, or perhaps one should say trite, that in comparison with the Thénardier girl she touches the reader

less. But Éponine, as terrible a victim of environment as can be imagined, the hapless daughter of a mean father and a vicious mother, is a genuine flower growing on a dunghill. Not unspotted, to be sure, but fundamentally still unspoiled. Her hopeless, self-sacrificing love for Marius provides one of the really tragic moments of this extraordinary book.

The action in which all these characters are engaged is, of course, complex and rather loosely knit. . . . [We] frequently lose sight of one group of characters while the author turns his spotlight on another. The central action of *Les Misérables* involves Jean Valjean and those who come importantly into contact with him. It is frequently melodramtic: the man-hunt, the ambushing of M. Fauchelevent by Thénardier, the rescue of Marius, are a few of the exciting elements of the action. But while the melodrama of *Les Misérables* is not always credible, indeed, at times because of the accumulation of coincidences quite unbelievable, it nevertheless seems on the whole more rational than the melodrama of *Hernani* or *Notre-Dame de Paris.* The antitheses seem more natural. Certainly the reader is far less conscious of artificiality. Merely as a novel of action or adventure *Les Misérables* stands up under critical scrutiny fairly well.

This central action is almost submerged in a flood of digressive and episodic material which swells the work to four fat volumes. For this Victor Hugo has been severely censured. . . . But, except for some fanatical abbreviators, I know few readers who would willingly sacrifice the description of the battle of Waterloo, or the convent episode, or the insurrection of 1832, or the two brilliant pages in which Hugo describes the death of a man in quicksand, or even the chapter on the sewers of Paris.

The brilliance, color, and movement of Waterloo recall the text of "L'Expiation." Here the canvas is larger and, therefore, allows more details—details which Hugo got from many sources, from his own observation while staying at Mont St. Jean, from the *Histoire du Consulat et de l'Empire* of Charles de Lacretelle, from diverse maps, from his personal researches in the Royal Library of Brussels. In spite of these conscientious efforts to relate the truth, he did not succeed in putting together a narrative which completely satisfies the historian. The general effect is nevertheless sound. Perhaps the French cavalry did not fall in confusion into the sunken road of Ohain . . . as Hugo claims, but they did charge with unbelievable fire and courage. What cannot be contested is that Hugo has caught the essential drama of that fateful June Sunday. As in "L'Expiation" he sees that the destiny of a man, Napoleon, the destiny of a country, France, the destiny of a continent, Europe, were at stake. And as the cuirassiers of Milhaud make their headlong charge, as the Imperial Guard marches majestically into the fray, as the tide of battle turns, and the Grande Armée tastes the bitter brew of defeat and utter rout, the reader realizes that then as today there are great moments in history that consitute important turning-points. In these pages of Victor Hugo he is in the presence of one of them. Who would willingly suppress these pages?

The convent episode, *Le petit Picpus,* is not thrilling, but it has undeniable charm. . . . [The] principal charm of this episode lies in its tranquility, its calmness, its peace. After the tempest of Waterloo and the excitement of Javert's pursuit, the respite is welcome. The reader feels that Jean Valjean deserves a little relief from his ordeals and the reader himself is not unwilling to linger a bit in this port in a storm.

As for the insurrection of 1832, it is definitely one of the important episodes in the book, almost impossible to eliminate. Indeed, it would be monstrous to eliminate it. . . . [The narrative's] general authenticity is well established. . . . [Hugo] read attentively the carefully documented novel by Rey-Dusseuil, *Le Cloître Saint-Méry,* published in September 1832. In this book (which was quickly suppressed) Hugo found a complete account of the insurrection, from the funeral of General Lamarque and the rôle of policemen as agents provocateurs to characters who served as models for Enjolras and Gavroche. But the color and drama of Hugo's narrative are essentially his own. The means by which he linked this episode to the rest of the book is both skillful and original. Paul Meurice was not an impartial critic, but he was, I think, right in saying: "It is a sublime idea to have brought together there on the barricades, all these sufferings in the midst of all these ideas, Marius, Mabeuf, Éponine, Jean Valjean with Enjolras, the friends of the A B C, and Javert." The tragic and beautiful deaths of Mabeuf, Éponine, Gavroche, and last of all Enjolras heighten the sacrifice which the inevitable failure of the insurrection demanded of all its participants. Far from being an inconsequential episode, a kind of hors d'oeuvre, the **Épopée rue Saint-Denis** becomes, thanks to Hugo's skill, an integral, almost a central part of the book.

Few critics have objected to the use of the Parisian sewer-system as a means of escape for Jean Valjean and Marius. It may be unusual, but it is perfectly logical. Criticism has centered on the chapters collectively entitled **"L'Intestin de Paris."** And, indeed, those chapters are anything but appetizing. Hugo's argument on the efficacy of sewerage as a fertilizer may interest the agriculturist, may even amuse the sardonic reader, but the average reader, impatient to get on with the tale, is doubtless repelled. The history of the sewer system, carefully documented from a *Statistique des égouts,* following this initial discussion is more pertinent and it certainly helps the reader to appreciate Jean Valjean's feat in emerging successfully from this foul labyrinth. Once, he almost succumbed, for he ran into a *fontis* (a kind of pocket of slime and filth without a firm bottom). This provoked the brilliantly written comparison of the man fatally bogged in quicksands, a *morceau* [excerpt] which has appeared in numerous anthologies and which is justly famous. Without the sewers, we might not have had this celebrated description.

Stripped of all its digressions *Les Misérables* would still be an interesting book, containing an essentially great lesson, but it would be much less a book extraordinarily representative of the nineteenth century. In its final form it gives us not only the lesson of Jean Valjean, but it gives us some of the great deeds and important ideas of the century. For in this definitive version it is more than a novel of action and character, it is also and above all a novel of ideas. (pp. 255-60)

What is the rôle of religion in the scheme of *Les Misérables?* The author's ideas are presented through the characters of Bishop Myriel and Jean Valjean and in the episode of *Le Petit Picpus.* They are summed up in the sentence: "We are for religion against religions." The phrase reveals . . . that the novelist was a genuinely religious man but one quite indifferent, even hostile, to religious forms and ceremonies, to religious organizations, to orthodox dogmas. Bishop Myriel, as we have already seen, is a personification of this attitude, always excepting the fact that he was an officer of an established church. Apart from that anomaly his views were similar to Victor Hugo's. He could, therefore, kneel before the Conventionnel of '93,

*An illustration of Jean Valjean. Historical Pictures Service, Chicago.*

something which no ordinary orthodox Catholic could conceivably do. It may be said that there is no real contradiction between Victor Hugo's anticlericalism and his sympathetic portrait of Bishop Myriel, for he has in reality painted a picture of the kind of bishop he admired but who, for that very reason, could not exist. Perhaps that was what he meant when he denied having used any living person for the portrait and claimed that the Bishop was entirely his own creation.

Nor is there any great contradiction between Hugo's picture of the convent and his hostility to religious institutions. For he always recognized that such institutions had a noble side. He says as much in his text:

> When we speak of convents, those homes of
> error but of innocence, of wanderings from the
> true path but of good intentions, of ignorance
> but of devotion, of torture but of martyrdom,
> we must almost always say yes and no.

And Hugo recognizes the beneficial influence of the convent on Jean Valjean when he said: "Everything that had entered his life (Valjean's) during the past six months, led him back to the Bishop's sacred injunctions, Cosette by love, the convent by humility." This recognition of convents' virtues makes the author's condemnation of their limitations and dangers all the more effective.

Although the central idea of the book, redemption of human nature by charity and goodness, is an essentially religious idea, political questions play as large a part in the composition of *Les Misérables* as does religion. . . . [As] the book developed political ideas were given progressively greater weight. The point of view naturally shifted, for the exiled republican held quite different opinions from the Peer of France. Not that Hugo entirely repudiated his past. His portrait of Louis-Philippe, composed in 1861, shows that he had not forgotten the associations and loyalties of the forties. (pp. 261-62)

The political opinions of the exiled Hugo are to be found in the portrait of Marius and in the discussion of the Amis de l'A.B.C. Marius and his swing to Bonapartism existed, of course, in the early version of *Les Misères*. So did the characters Enjolras, Courfeyrac, and Combeferre. But the *Friends of the Under-dog* . . . were introduced later in 1861, and they play a vital rôle in Marius' final evolution to democracy. When Marius in his new enthusiasm for Napoleon asks what can be greater than the emperor's achievements, Combeferre replies simply: *To be free!* Years before, Hugo had revealed essentially the same attitude in "L'Expiation," for if the poem glorifies the emperor, it nonetheless condemns the *Dix-huit Brumaire* as a crime to be expiated. Hugo's position, then, is fundamentally compatible with his political record. (pp. 262-63)

*Les Misérables* breathes forth the ardent republicanism and the deep humanitarianism of the great exile. Like *La Légende des siècles* the book reposes on an undying faith in human progress. Like *Les Contemplations,* it is infused with genuine religious sentiment, unorthodox, but profoundly sincere. These conceptions and these sentiments are not only set forth as abstractions, but are illustrated in concrete form by characters remarkable for their vitality and credibility. Conceptions, sentiments, and characters are involved in an action doubtless loosely knit, at times over-melodramatic, perhaps too often interrupted by digressions, but an action which nevertheless holds the reader's interest to the end. If *Les Misérables* is not, as Paul Meurice with pardonable enthusiasm said, *the* book of the nineteenth century, it is indubitably one of the great books of that productive era, and it remains singularly alive and significant today. . . . (pp. 265-66)

> *Elliott M. Grant, in his* The Career of Victor Hugo, *Cambridge, Mass.: Harvard University Press, 1945, 365 p.*

### DENIS SAURAT (essay date 1958)

[*Saurat underscores the variety of* Les misérables*'s appeal, analyzing it as a detective, military, love, realistic, and philosophical novel.*]

*Les Misérables* is a fusion of almost all the known kinds of novel. It is, first, a detective novel, with one of the best 'sleuths' invented by fiction—Javert. Jean Valjean's adventures with the police, and especially his escape through the sewers of Paris, put all later crime stories in the shade. Incidentally, the description of the sewers of Paris in the early nineteenth century is in itself a masterpiece of realism . . . .

But Hugo rises (and note the date: before 1862) to the most sublime discovery of the detective *genre*. He discovers and exemplifies the law that in good police work the victims should always be arrested first. This must be read to be believed, yet is unanswerable ('**Marius,**' Chap. XXI).

To balance the detective novel (which is a story of conflict within an organized community) Hugo gives us a military novel. Again, within this military *genre*, there are two complementary aspects. The old orthodox idea of a battle is magnificently presented in his narrative of the battle of Waterloo—probably the best description of the action that has been written—with an interpretation of the greatness of both sides, while for those of us who have had enough of great battles, Hugo draws in another part a picture of a revolutionary civil war. Many critics hold that the best part of *Les Misérables* is the story of the barricades in Paris under Louis Philippe, the story of the fight of the people of Paris against the army. Heroism and failure are artistically blended, and any would-be revolutionary wishing to discover what went wrong and why the people were defeated on that occasion could study these pages with profit.

Needless to say, we also have a love novel here—was there ever a real novel without love as a main motive? Marius and Cosette are among the great lovers of the world. The naïveté and the depth of first love have never been so well described as in this idyll. But Hugo cannot be taxed with overall naïveté, for a cynical picture accompanies the simple-minded love story. Nor have the faults of the lower classes, 'the noxious poor,' been anywhere else so well analysed as in '**Les Thénardiers**'; and although Hugo remained an unrepentant believer in the potentiality for progressive improvement of the human race, he comes to the conclusion here that with some specimens of humanity there is nothing to be done. So it is that at the end of *Les Misérables* he sends Thénardier over to America to become a gangster.

A detective novel, a novel of war and revolution, a sentimental novel, a cynical and realistic novel—all in one; but over and above all these, giving them a common life and unity, there is a great philosophical religious novel. Let not the words *philosophical* and *religious* awe those readers who look for entertainment. So long as they are not averse from a little cerebral exercise, they will get their entertainment, for Hugo's ideas are nothing if not original.

First of all, he faces philosophically the great constructional problem of the novelist; the problem of coincidence, which most writers try to camouflage or by-pass. Jean Valjean runs away from the police, with little Cosette in his arms. He is trapped in a cul-de-sac in the middle of Paris. His only escape is by climbing over a wall into a garden. On the other side he finds the grounds of a convent, which the police cannot search—and at the foot of the wall a gardener, a man whose life he, Jean Valjean, had saved. No reader will accept that as a likely story. So Hugo, facing the reader and the problem, blandly states that God Himself, who takes a great interest in Cosette and Jean Valjean, has arranged it so. God arranges *everything,* without interfering with our freedom—enhancing it, in fact. Surprisingly enough, Balzac holds the same view, and states it clearly at the end of *Eugénie Grandet.* A new function is discovered for theology: to help the novelist in a quandary.

But let us not succumb to the temptation of too easily deriding Hugo's philosophy. He has many stimulating ideas. In Part I, Book V, Chap. V he explains at leisure the very queer relationship between mankind and the animals. The brute creation, in all its monstrosity, is only a picture made by God symbolizing the virtues and vices of mankind wandering about the earth. 'God shows them to us to make us reflect'; hence they are incapable of education, which implies a strange view also of the powers of education.

There are many other such 'ideas,' exciting in themselves, no doubt, but chiefly departure platforms for our own ideas.

But Hugo's highest piece of philosophizing is his demonstration of the 'personality of God'—surely a surprising thing to find in a novel. Yet the novel as a *genre* is, more than any other human exercise, an imaginative study of the variations of personality; why, then, should the novel remain silent about God? In Part II, Book VI, Hugo gives us a fascinating account of a religious community of women devoted to perpetual adoration, and this alone would give immortal value to *Les Misérables.* Adoration of what?—of God. What is God? Hugo takes the two ideas of infinity and personality, often accounted to be in contradiction. He points out that this contradiction is solved every day in the human soul; a human being is, properly and literally, infinite in its possibilities of feelings, of ideas, of actions, and at the same time is a personal self-conscious unit. Since this happens in man it happens in God: there is a 'self' in the infinite above, as there is a 'self' in the infinite below. . . . I am not sure that professional theologians and psychologists should not look carefully at those pages of *Les Misérables.* There is often truth in the dreams of a poet.

So much for *Les Misérables.* The book goes beyond literature. Perhaps it goes even beyond human nature. And yet it is instinct with a feeling of pity for all human suffering—which its untranslatable title fully indicates—as of a god preparing to come down and bring some peace to man's sufferings. At the same time it is full of the joy of young love, which it brings to a successful issue. For it is also that rare thing: a novel, not of failure, but of success. (pp. vii-x)

> *Denis Saurat, in an introduction to* Les Misérables, Vol. 1 *by Victor Hugo, translated by Charles E. Wilbour, 1958. Reprint by Dutton, 1968, pp. vii-xi.*

## ANDRÉ MAUROIS (essay date 1960)

[*Maurois was a versatile French man of letters who made his most significant contribution to literature as a biographer. Although he finds* Les misérables's *depiction of human nature unfaithful, Maurois praises the novel's language and, especially, its portrayal of Valjean's redemption. Edward Sagarin (1981) takes exception to Maurois's interpretation of* Les misérables; *other critics who discuss the novel's lack of realism include Edmond and Jules de Goncourt (1862), Joakim Reinhard (1899), Robert Lynd (1932), and Joseph Warren Beach (1932).*]

The complex events in *Les Misérables,* the various flights and disguises, make of the book, by certain of their aspects, an extraordinarily adroit detective novel. There lies one of the reasons for its enduring success. Victor Hugo proved a worthy disciple of Eugène Sue. But, beyond a mere tale of adventure, Hugo wrote a poem of repentance, of the redemption of the individual, of the power of love. Jean Valjean is materially and spiritually saved by the good works of the bishop, Fantine by those of Jean Valjean. And when even Javert dies, he is touched by some obscure grace.

Christianity, in Hugo's mind, is commingled with Jacobin and revolutionary doctrines. When he shows the agreement . . . between an old revolutionary and Bishop Myriel, doubtless the give and take of the dialogue resound in Hugo's own soul.

It is easy to understand why most French readers loved a book written in praise of the masses and offering the unfortunate such high hopes of rehabilitation. These simple, gentle ideas moved the crowds of readers for the same reasons as Tolstoy's

did later in Russia. But Tolstoy, an aristocrat by birth, and well-acquainted with the élite, gives us a more equitable picture of it than Hugo. It is perhaps valid to find moral greatness in a convict and in a prostitute! it is certainly naïve and quite false to imagine that moral grandeur can be found in them alone. (p. xiii)

The author of *Les Misérables* clings to a partisan prejudice which always proves dangerous for the novelist and which was bound to lead Hugo into obvious improbabilities. One might, at a pinch, admit the rehabilitation of Jean Valjean; but how does it happen that *nothing whatever* of the primitive Jean Valjean remains in Monsieur Madeleine? How could a police inspector be so stupidly obstinate as Javert? How can an ex-convict, in an environment as mistrustful as the French provinces provide, become mayor of his city? It would be easy to multiply such questions.

*Les Misérables* is a generous book, and that is a good deal; but it does not paint, as Balzac and Stendhal do, a faithful picture of human nature. Hugo's romantic work might, in its epic character, be more readily compared to Zola's. But even the epic cycle of the Rougon-Macquarts would appear more realistic than that of *Les Misérables.* There is in Hugo the novelist a theatrical side, a need to surprise the reader by the violence of contrasts and the glitter of dialogue. These prove to be serious faults.

Such criticism must inevitably be made. Yet when all is said and done, the fact remains that the book touches and moves us in a peculiar way.

*First of all because of its literary qualities.* The moment Hugo avoids prophetic declamation, he writes admirable French. Not only is he a true poet, but an excellent prose writer as well, brought up on the classics and capable of creating vast historical frescoes in the most vigorous style. Read in *Les Misérables* the striking painting Victor Hugo gives of society under the Restoration in the year 1817; read, too, the celebrated description of Waterloo. The French language never has been moulded with greater vitality.

*But especially because of its moral qualities.* It is wholly true that never a convict on land or sea resembled Jean Valjean, that never a police inspector resembled Javert, that never a bandit resembled Thénardier, that never students spoke as Marius and his friends speak. Yet more than one saint has resembled Monseigneur Myriel; and it is saints rather than average humans that Victor Hugo attempted to depict in *Les Misérables.* Now the lives of many men . . . are but a painful quest of heroism and of sanctity. Doubtless in this quest almost all men fail; but it is precisely because of their personal failures that they like to meet, in a noble book, heroes who, better than they themselves, have conquered their basest passions.

There are some books whose reading debases the reader; he emerges from it the foredoomed victim of every exterior force. There are others, on the contrary, which give him greater confidence in life and in himself. *Les Misérables* belongs to the category of books which speak more to man, as Spinoza said, "of his liberty than of his slavery," and we must congratulate ourselves to-day upon seeing this deservedly illustrious novel take a new lease on life. (pp. xiv-xv)

> *André Maurois, in an introduction to* Les Misérables: A Novel *by Victor Hugo, translated by Lascelles Wraxall, The Heritage Press, 1960, pp. ix-xv.*

**JOHN PORTER HOUSTON** (essay date 1974)

[*Houston defends* Les misérables's *digressions, stating that they contribute to the novel's realism and provide variety in the interest and pace of the narrative. In addition, he traces subterranean imagery in the work. For additional positive commentary on* Les misérables's *digressions, see the unsigned essay from the* Boston Review *(1863) and the excerpt by Elliott M. Grant (1945).*]

[What] cannot be readily conveyed and yet gives such a characteristic color to [*Les Misérables*] is not so much the number of events as the involved moving back and forth between characters and situations—all within a carefully worked out time scheme—and the abundant digressions on matters of momentary concern to the plot. The battle of Waterloo episode is the most famous of these, partly because of its length and partly because, seen in one light, it has little relevance to the novel. However, Marius's whole awakening to political and social questions is dependent on his and the reader's awareness of the Napoleonic era. Other digressions are not always intended to create a sense of history so much as to give a feeling of a special institution, like the convent where Cosette is placed, or of some peculiarity of Parisian life like argot. The city, in fact, is depicted with particular care for the character of out-of-the-way areas in it. Hugo's own brand of realism assures an elaborate grounding of the novel in place as well as in time.

The digressive pattern of *Les Misérables* is far more prominent than that of *Notre-Dame de Paris,* which is a matter both of length and of the infinitely richer mass of material which Hugo could take from a historical period he himself had lived through. But, as a glance at the immense table of contents shows, the discursive essays are carefully placed to provide variety in the interest and pace of the novel. They do not at all resemble the interminable and seemingly (at a first reading at least) directionless digressions of Balzac's less harmoniously constructed novels; although Hugo's plan was conceived on a very large scale, the details were not neglected. Furthermore, as was the case in *Notre-Dame de Paris,* there is a stylistic unity in the authorial voice whether it be narrating or expounding.

Modern interest in *Les Misérables* has focused both on the genuine elements of realism in it and, more notably, on the thematics of the work. It has often been observed that this story of rehabilitation and social redemption parallels *La Fin de Satan*: It is the exoteric, contemporary, and realist version of the esoteric myth. At the same time, *Les Misérables* contains elements of symbolism, which, for many, counterbalance the slightly unsubstantial quality of the major (but not the minor) figures. The parallelism with *La Fin de Satan* is, as it has been remarked, somewhat imperfect, since the crime which Jean Valjean expiates is a petty one; however, in society's eyes his guilt is nonetheless considerable for having been a convict at all. His redemptory acts are, as it were, penance for crimes of which life in prison had made him capable even though he did not commit them. Hugo manages thus to give some psychological verisimilitude to his character.

Richard B. Grant has noted a goodly number of Christological references in regard to Jean Valjean, since his self-redemption is accomplished through saving others [see Additional Bibliography]. However, the dominant impression the novel gives is more somber. It is noteworthy that in the first version, *Les Misères,* the landscapes tend to be crepuscular or nocturnal, to reflect a gray and dreary purgatory. Despite the flamboyance of some later additions, much of this tonality survives in *Les Misérables;* it is not a novel in which light or nature in its sumptuousness plays a major role. The Parisian life of Jean

Valjean is largely passed in self-claustration, in semihiding. Furthermore, there is a recurrent imagery of the subterranean: An especially striking example of this comes at the beginning of Part III, Book 7, where, under the title of **"Mines and Miners,"** Hugo develops an image of society as a vast underground structure. Human thought and endeavor extend downward beneath the "hovel and marvel" of civilization to the point where good becomes dubious and begins to take on an evil, lurid coloring, as it approaches the ultimate abyss. The Ugolino of humanity, just one of Hugo's references to Dante's descending circles, lies near the bottom, and it is in this milieu of crime that an important central part of *Les Misérables* takes place. But the most important reference to hell is its embodiment in the sewers of Paris, through which Jean Valjean carries Marius, as the ultimate part of his journey through death to resurrection. Like the pane of glass separating man from God in *Notre-Dame de Paris,* there is a grill covering the outlet to the sewers, which Jean Valjean finally makes his way to, but this time salvation takes place—through the ironic intervention of Thénardier, Jean's enemy, who, not recognizing him, opens the locked grating. (pp. 144-46)

> *John Porter Houston, in his* Victor Hugo, *Twayne Publishers, Inc., 1974, 165 p.*

**NORMAN DENNY** (essay date 1976)

[*In his introduction to* Les misérables, *from which the following excerpt is drawn, Denny takes as his point of departure the evaluation of the novel by Edmond and Jules de Goncourt (see excerpt above, 1862). Here, Denny complains that the Goncourts failed to recognize* Les misérables's *imaginative realism which accounts for its "depth of vision and underlying truth, its moments of lyrical quality and of moving compassion" and secures its place among the "great works of Western literature." Denny allows, however, that the brothers were correct in their assertion that Hugo was unsuccessful in his attempt to create a factually realistic novel.*]

The Goncourts were both right and wrong [in their assessment of *Les Misérables* (see excerpt above 1862)], right in the narrow sense but not in the large one. They were right about the realism which Hugo strove so laboriously and, on the whole, so unsuccessfully to achieve. No one could have worked harder at it. He read and read, he pored endlessly over maps and documents, and the fruits of his researches so encumber his book that many readers besides the Goncourts must have found themselves unequal to the effort of pursuing it. but this factual realism is constantly at war with the oet. Imaginative realism is another matter. *Les Misérables,* with its depth of vision and underlying truth, its moments of lyrical quality and of moving compassion, is a novel of towering stature, one of the great works of Western literature, a melodrama that is also a morality and a social document embracing a wider field than any other novel of its time, coeived on the scale of [Leo Tolstoy's] *War and Peace* but even more ambitious.

That is the trouble. The defects which the Goncourts saw, and which no one can fail to see, since they are as monumental as the book itself, may be summed up in the single word, extravagance. hugo, although as the final result shows he was masterly in the construction of his novel, had little or no regard for the discipline of novel-writing. he was wholly nrestrained and unsparing of his reader. He had to say everything and more than everything; he was incapable of leaving anything out. (pp. viii-ix)

*Norman Denny, in an introduction to* Les Misérables, Vol. 1 *by Victor Hugo, translated by norman Denny, The Folio Press, 1976, pp. vii-xii.*

### KATHRYN M. GROSSMAN  (essay date 1981)

[*Grossman examines the relationship between* Les misérables's *ethical structure and the cognitive capacities of Valjean, Javert, and Thénardier. According to Grossman, Thénardier's and Javert's limited notions of justice are indicative of their narrow perceptions of both themselves and others. In contrast, Grossman argues, Valjean's broad view of his intellectual and moral self, particularly his recognition of his potential for both good and evil, results in his altruism and enables him to pursue a virtuous existence beyond normal legal boundaries. Grossman concludes that, to Hugo, Valjean symbolizes a literary as well as a moral ideal; she maintains that Valjean is the embodiment of "truly synthetic, creative, passionate, humanitarian—i.e., romantic—literature."*]

[There exists a link between *Les Misérables*'s] ethical structure and the cognitive capacities of [Jean Valjean, Javert, and Thénardier]. In two of the best-known books of *Les Misérables*—"L'Affaire Champmathieu" . . . , and "Javert Déraillé" . . . for example, Jean Valjean and Javert both find themselves torn apart by a moral dilemma which forces them to look not only outward at where they ought to be going but also inward at who they really are. This moment of crisis and ultimate truth culminates, in the case of Jean Valjean, in victory. By achieving a synthesis of his past and present identities in one persevering self, he is also able to transcend the limitations of his ethical quandary and choose a proper solution. In the case of Javert, it leads to humiliation, despair, and death. Jean Valjean opts for a life of self-effacement. Javert decides to efface himself entirely by committing suicide. Thénardier, on the other hand . . . , misses any similar transfiguration and ends as miserably as he begins.

It would appear then that, for Hugo, there exists a close affiliation between the cognitive and the ethical domains; that "conscience," as both conscience and consciousness, the apprehension of the self in the midst of its actions, is better equipped to deal with complex matters than either the legal code or pure lawlessness; and that the conversion born of moral crisis involves a radical, discontinuous transformation of being, a leap which may be transcendent or suicidal in nature. While Thénardier's sense of justice is entirely self-centered, Javert manages to be more disinterested, pursuing his duty for the sake of society. Neither ethos can fathom the actions of Jean Valjean, who cleaves to self-imposed but impartial principles of a broadly humanitarian scope. (pp. 471-72)

In perusing the passages of *Les Misérables* pertaining to Thénardier and his milieu, the reader is immediately struck by several salient features: a morality of gratification, exchange, and revenge; a limited notion of identity; and a confusion by the criminal of everyone else's motives with his own. The egoistic relativism of Thénardier and his cronies translates into a notion of justice and equality that permits only the exchange of favors or blows. (p. 473)

At the same time that he so selfishly affirms his own needs, however, Thénardier appears to lack both a solid sense of himself and an ability to understand any other mode of being. . . . Ironically, the excessive affirmation of the self results in its dissolution. The "chaos" . . . that the lawless hope to wreak upon society reflects their own inner anarchy. Thus, while Mme. Thénardier perceives in her husband a "grand ac-

teur" . . . , his many aliases and disguises actually derive from a shattered personality that can never know intellectual or moral wholeness. . . . His eternal schemes, the product of a twisted, tangled mentality in which he himself is lost, end by weaving a directionless and purposeless existence. . . . [He] and his friends in Patron-Minette will spend their lives revolving in vicious circles, without any core identity to guide them.

That Thénardier's egocentricity masks a basic ignorance is a theme that runs throughout *Les Misérables*. . . . [He] is shown by Hugo to possess as narrow a vision of others as of himself. In this way, Jean Valjean's impoverished exterior and generous acts at the inn lead Thénardier to speculate that he is some sort of "voleur." . . . Later on in Paris, he tries to persuade his reluctant victim that they are brothers in crime. . . . This lip service to their supposed confraternity, and therefore to the favors they owe each other, is reiterated at the exit to the sewers, where Thénardier mistakes Jean Valjean for the assassin and thief of the unconscious Marius. . . . His reduction of every human act to one of simple exchange—be it for vengeance or profit—reveals the shallow nature of both his intelligence and his notion of brotherhood. . . . He will never know or even imagine the kind of internal discord and moral anguish which threaten to destroy Javert and Jean Valjean, simply because he deems himself to be the only real actor, and his needs the only reality, in the drama of life.

This blindly egotistic world view and the anarchic "rebellion" and "chaos" it engenders may seem far removed from the mentality of the novel's heroes. Nevertheless, from a temporal perspective, it does constitute an early moment in each character's biography. Such . . . is the case with Javert's hereditary milieu (he is even born in prison), but it should be noted as well that Jean Valjean's own tale begins with the rather dull-witted theft of a loaf of bread. More important, however, is the structural role of this apparent origin of both cognition and morality. For, just as each successive logical stage reconstructs and entails those which precede it, the way the cube entails the square, the square the line, and the line the point, so can this initial level be considered an intimate, *present* part of Jean Valjean and Javert alike, despite the latter's vehement efforts to deny it. The way in which these personages deal with the old Adam, the Thénardier, buried deep within them should, therefore, elucidate the differences between their respective destinies.

Now, while the many superficial traits that Jean Valjean shares with the real criminals of *Les Misérables* do not prevent the reader from discerning his true virtue, it is important to recognize that this virtue is not entirely pure. The hatred that he nurtures in the galleys still suffuses his glance at Marius in the sewers, even as he is saving his life. To love his enemy thus, he has first had to learn to understand and love himself. The intimate relationship between "conscience" as conscience and as consciousness—particularly self-consciousness—is one of the major *topoi* of the novel, and Jean Valjean excels in the development of both. His radical "transfiguration" . . . from sinner to saint, a conversion that he must renew daily, requires the continual stripping away of the subtle layers of hypocrisy and egotism that so often warp one's judgment. Thus, as M. Madeleine, he does his best to erase and forget the "face sinistre" . . . of his past self, only to have it resurge during the Champmathieu affair. But his denial, in "Une tempête sous un crâne," that he is still Jean Valjean . . . is doubled by a growing awareness that there is no correct solution to his moral dilemma, that whether he opts to save Champmathieu on the one hand or Fantine, Cosette, and his community of workers on the other he will be forced to sin grievously against someone. It is no coincidence that his decision to accept the responsibility for all his actions is accompanied by the sudden reaffirmation of his true identity, first to himself, then at Arras: ''Je suis Jean Valjean.'' . . . (pp. 474-75)

Although his subsequent flights from the law necessitate, as with Thénardier, a series of aliases and disguises, Jean Valjean is never bewildered amid these fictive personalities. Instead of shattering into a myriad of false appearances, he learns to embrace everything he has been, is, and might be. This recognition of a single, enduring self whose potential for evil as well as good is fully acknowledged enables him to pursue moral existence beyond the normal legal bounds. . . . [His] conscience-consciousness keeps him on the right inner and outer track, avoiding the pitfalls of despair and pride alike. He locates Arras, the Petit-Picpus convent, and an exit from the sewers, despite overwhelming odds. . . . In all these mazes, the symbol of the labyrinthine paths of ''conscience,'' he finds himself by losing himself: his self-sacrifice bestows, paradoxically, an acute awareness of who he is and where he is going.

In this way, Jean Valjean's outwardly chaotic existence is in fact ordered by the autonomous, reflexive, self-imposed principles of a lofty virtue. . . . [He] has become a law unto himself. . . . Yet, it should be added, he is no Zorro or Robin Hood, no popular hero who robs from the rich to give to the poor. Actually, for the most part, he is scrupulously law-abiding, not unlike Javert. Moreover, all forms of vengeance, even the most justified, have been banished from his horizon, replaced by an ethic of love that begins within and proceeds outward to include everyone else. This emphasis on the supreme value of life is revealed, for instance, when he risks his own to save Champmathieu, then Cosette, then Javert, then Marius. His sense of the brotherhood of man, by way of contrast with Thénardier's treacherous fellowship of thieves, views all men as ends in themselves, to be treated with equal compassion. (This theme of the essential brotherhood of all, beyond conventional appearances, is echoed in the minor mode in Gavroche's treatment of Magnon's two lost children as if they were his own siblings—which, indeed, they are.) (pp. 475-76)

[Jean Valjean's] ability to perceive the fundamental truth of a situation . . . in no way alters this universal altruism. The ''acceptation de personnes'' . . . which so stuns Javert merely reflects Jean Valjean's awareness of all the real and potential selves he carries within his own being. However, by thus surpassing society's dictates to follow those of conscience, he remains, in his own way, as far outside the law as any ''bandit.'' His refusal to sanction any evil means toward even the best of ends—the violence of revolution, for example, in the service of progress—restricts his relationships to a one-on-one format which, on the surface at least, resembles the exchange-revenge structure previously observed in Thénardier's dealings with others. The exception here is that Jean Valjean renders good for evil and expects nothing in return.

This ethic of self-abnegation in the name of humanity implies, of course, potentially anti-social, but highly principled, behavior. On the cognitive level, Hugo's ex-convict succeeds in combining the role of impartial judge with that of active participant in any given conflict by depersonalizing himself to the point of seeing his own needs in no more interested or passionate a manner than he views everyone else's. Thus does he undertake, in the Champmathieu affair, to do what he must for Champmathieu at once, for Fantine and Cosette later, and

for the good of his soul in both cases. . . . In condemning himself . . . Jean Valjean eventually ceases to have any discernible social identity whatsoever. (pp. 476-77)

Javert, who can deal with more complex ethical and cognitive matters than Thénardier, but less adequately than Jean Valjean, typifies the conventional mentality that continually misreads and misinterprets such a radically unorthodox mode of being. That he views himself as champion of the highest good, that is, of law and order, is clear enough. (p. 477)

[His] ''conversion'' from self-confidence to self-destruction, detailed in **''Javert Déraillé''** but prepared throughout the novel, again demonstrates the close affiliation for Hugo between the cognitive and ethical realms. For, just as Javert's view of himself is yoked to an intense awareness of his stature as a moral agent, so does his ability to form sound ethical judgments depend on his capacity for reasoning in general. . . . Javert long believes in the simplicity of truth. . . . His unwavering devotion to absolute truthfulness, to the law as a code of ethics, and to social order in general are really just so many attempts always to remain logically consistent—within a limited axiomatic framework, of course. (pp. 477-78)

This faith in the limpid, straightforward truth he considers revealed by the letter of the law is completely uprooted when Javert finds himself suddenly owing his life to one he has always judged his archenemy. He discovers, to his amazement . . . , that legal dogma can never cover all exigencies. In fact, it has completely led him astray, causing him, like Thénardier, to misconstrue Jean Valjean's motives and actions for years. For, in his orderly, classical world, everyone has been typecast and no one may ever step out of character. At every point in the past where he might have recognized that the ex-convict's continual challenge—even outrage—to his logic implied the existence of a higher truth and a more complex moral order, he could see only the chaos of evil. In this way, Jean Valjean's need for aliases, flight, and hideaways has been constantly confused with the machinations of common criminals such as Thénardier. Even his kindness to Fantine seemed to Javert no more than the solicitude of one outlaw for another, a part of the underworld buddy system, instead of a gesture of pure human compassion. . . . The ''victim'' of Jean Valjean's generosity in Montreuil-sur-Mer and at the barricades, he cannot explain to himself how such a contradiction of his whole logically structured world can possibly be. (pp. 478-79)

[In a struggle] within the very center of his being, Javert apprehends but one essential truth: the irrefutable venerability of Jean Valjean and the relative value of his own existence. It is this intolerable vision of a world gone crazy, where he no longer represents the highest authority, that eventually culminates in his suicide. . . . (p. 479)

[The identity crisis that Javert undergoes] causes him to doubt his very being. His revised self-image, a decidedly humiliating one, closely resembles that revealed to Jean Valjean following his theft from Petit-Gervais. . . . Javert is forced to compare himself with the man who has just saved his life. . . . His sense of being so abruptly and irrevocably diminished, he decides to vanish entirely, rather than try to change his way of life as does the ex-convict. (pp. 479-80)

Javert is unable to represent, even to himself, the dazzling and wholly admirable union of opposites which Jean Valjean succeeds in living throughout his life. Whereas his superior cognitive/ethical position in relation to Thénardier and Patron-Minette permits him to understand the intricacies of the criminal mind, his complete denial of any such old Adam in himself obfuscates his new vision of Jean Valjean in **"Javert Déraillé."** What he fails to perceive is that his foe's rare morality derives from the dynamic, conscious subsuming of egotistic desire *under* the categorical laws imposed by an autonomous conscience, not just from a static juxtaposition of equally powerful, but contrary, tendencies that end by cancelling each other out.

Nowhere does Hugo attempt to define explicitly the nature of Jean Valjean's towering virtue. Nevertheless, he makes possible for his reader the same intuition of the sublime which so moves Javert by depicting a whole gamut of ethical modes and continually playing them off against each other. It is in comparison with the tortuosity of Thénardier and the rigidity of Javert, for example, that Jean Valjean's true merit comes into focus. Moreover, the ex-convict's perpetual struggles with the potential evil within himself prevent him from becoming too exemplary—and therefore inhuman—a figure. Strangely enough, the emphasis on his satanic roots makes his progress to sainthood and martyrdom all the more apprehensible. Thus does Hugo overcome, like Dante before him, the problem of rendering the sublime as palpable as the infernal. (pp. 481-82)

But this *thématique* of a superior moral sphere, so persistently and coherently developed throughout the novel, raises a whole new set of questions. Given the ambiguous status of the sublime as both an ethical and an aesthetic concept, might we not discern in Jean Valjean an emblem of the literary, as well as the moral, ideal? Would not the cognitive/ethical modes of Thénardier and Javert then also invite an aesthetic analogy? A rereading of these three personages readily confirms this hypothesis.

It is certainly not difficult to discover in Javert, for instance, the epitome of the classical temperament. His excessive love of logic, rules, authority—in brief, of order—and his corresponding fear of anything resembling chaos, rebellion, or emotion depict the specific negative characteristics of the literary tradition with which Hugo broke in his youth. On the other hand, if the poet's aesthetic hierarchy does indeed parallel the cognitive/ethical one, it becomes evident that he much prefers this type of art to the fraudulent, anarchic, facile, over sentimental sort of literature (so frequently mislabeled "romantic") that Thénardier must typify. (p. 482)

In the apparent resemblence between Thénardier and Jean Valjean we have, then, a lesson on the various kinds of art which lies outside the normative domain delineated by conventional notions of beauty and good taste. The bad thief is, of course, the prototype of the bad artist, whose manipulative, self-serving fictions are entirely devoid of any underlying form or rules. . . . Nevertheless, this seed of chaos, of nothingness, along with Javert's respect for the law, is integrated into the higher aesthetic realm connoted by the all-embracing, self-imposed morality of Jean Valjean. Consequently, the good thief also authors a variety of fictions, most notably the idea that all men are brothers. And this metaphorical "lie," like the premises founding all utopias, is actually truer, grander, and more beautiful than any "reality" a Javert might believe in. (pp. 482-83)

[Jean Valjean's] ability to project himself into the viewpoints of other people, to play many roles via an imaginative leap of compassion, clearly exemplifies the writer's ability to people a whole fictive universe. Thénardier's many aliases and maudlin sentimentality merely cast, in this light, the negative shadows of the truly synthetic, creative, passionate, humanitarian—i.e., romantic—literature embodied by Jean Valjean. By the

same token, the ex-convict's uncommonly disciplined existence, which superficially resembles Thénardier's chaotic meanderings, reflects the hidden structure of a novel that continues to assert its coherence through a veritable labyrinth of digressions. (p. 483)

*Kathryn M. Grossman, "Hugo's Romantic Sublime: Beyond Chaos and Convention in 'Les Misérables',"* in Philological Quarterly, *Vol. 60, No. 4, Fall, 1981, pp. 471-86.*

### EDWARD SAGARIN   (essay date 1981)

[*Sagarin interprets* Les misérables *as an indictment of society rather than as a study of human rehabilitation. In opposition to André Maurois (1960), who values Valjean's heroic conquest of ignoble passions, Sagarin argues that Valjean fails as a symbol of redemption because his crime—stealing a loaf of bread for his sister's children—was not a sin but an act of altruism.*]

[What delineates Jean Valjean in *Les Misérables*] is the essential innocence of the man. If he were innocent only in the sense of having been falsely accused, his would be a different tale, and probably one with far less significance for us. Jean Valjean does indeed commit the act that sends him to the galleys and that is the beginning of his downfall. Hugo's supreme indictment of society—for this *is* an indictment of society (he was a forerunner of Zola and other novelists who saw themselves as social critics)—lies in the nature of the act which his hero has perpetrated and for which he is imprisoned. Literally, Jean Valjean is guilty of stealing a loaf of bread.

It would appear that such an act would ordinarily evoke only sympathy and hence require no further mitigation in order for an author to exculpate his "criminal" and to paint him as the purest and most saintly of all beings (one is almost compelled to use quotation marks around *criminal*, so that Hugo's relentless efforts to remind the reader of Valjean's goodness are rendered with integrity). To this end, the taking of the loaf of bread is an almost perfect transgression, and the breaking of the law is justified or at least extenuated by the forces of hunger, poverty, and the execrable social conditions that followed the counterrevolution in France. But Hugo goes even further than this, and in so doing betrays a weakness not only in the literary work but in the social criticism: it is not for himself and his own stomach that Jean Valjean commits a theft. He does not even so much as expect to taste a morsel of the stolen bread. It is for his sister's children, young, fatherless, and hungry, that he becomes a thief. So two factors are here at work, and as they follow the reader throughout the five volumes that make up this novel, they detract from each other rather than act symbiotically to strengthen the motifs: there is the social indictment, and there is the criminal as saint. (pp. 60-1)

Starting with the criminal as victim, Hugo continues with the criminal (or more accurately the exconvict) as the embodiment of virtue. He is the penitent incarnate, but he has never done wrong and has nothing for which to repent. Over and over he redeems himself. Without a blemish on his past, however, the redemption is ill-placed. What emerges, from the viewpoint of the social critic, and in contrast with other great literary images of the transgressor, is a series of unintended ambiguities, with messages not as clearly drawn as are even the one-dimensional characters who inhabit the novel. (p. 61)

If Jean Valjean is going to be painted as pure and saintly, and he is, the theft from the bishop and a subsequent incident with a little boy from whom he takes a coin are the blemishes—

these, and not the stealing of the loaf of bread. Through the many years to follow until the last moments of his life, and through the countless pages and the episodes, coincidences, acts of strength, heroism, and sacrifice, there will be nothing but these two acts that are short of Christlike purity. What is Hugo telling us, then, when so good a person as his hero steals first from the bishop and then from the boy Gervais? That it is prison that brings out all that is worst in man, that turns the potentially best into the most wretched, that leaves one bitter and angry, seeing all humanity, even a man of God and a child, as enemy. . . .

In the message of Hugo, it is kindness, in its most extreme and unexpected form, that alone can bring reform or even instant rehabilitation, not through guilt or expiation but through rebirth and resurreciton. Love, Victor Hugo is telling us: love, and the wretched mass of humanity will be redeemed. Man is essentially good, more than good, he is pure and heavenly, he needs only to be shown the other cheek and he will embrace and kiss it, not rebuff and repel it. Jean Valjean is the embodiment of this, but how universal, or how convincing even in his own instance, is a matter of dispute. . . .

[After Jean Valjean's encounters with the bishop and Gervais, we] are given a glimpse of a man in the process of conversion, of the forces of good and evil struggling within him, each seeking victory over the other, the classic theological battle for possession of a man's soul between the devil and God's angels. . . . (p. 63)

[Hugo catches] his character in the very act of change, at the moment of duality when he is traveling from evil to good and both are present as adversary forces. He is neither one person nor the other, neither the convict hardened, gloomy, and bitter against the world nor the redeemed man who has had a vision of the beauty that resides in the good and is beckoned to it. He is neither in the pure sense, because he remains both, as anyone at a moment of change must be. For Hugo, he is one of the two persons (or personalities) in his impulses, instincts, and habits, and he is the other in the intellect which is freeing him (or seeking to do so) from the nineteen years of the constant formation of an evil self. When his intellect sees what his habits have brought him to, he recoils, he denies that it is he (the eternal evasion of responsibility, it was not I, it was something in me, something that drove me), he repents and seeks to undo the act. It is Schopenhauer's eternal enmity between the worlds of will and idea, and it is a forerunner of Freud and the struggle between the unconscious and the intellect. In Valjean, the idea and the intellect will triumph.

Now he must run, run endlessly, for as a second offender, he will, if seized, be returned to the galleys for life. Hugo implies some condemnation of the judicial and penal systems, their harshness and cruelty, but essentially they are tangential to his story and even occasionally interfere with it. The galleys are not filled with Jean Valjeans but with men whose delicts are far more serious than the theft of a loaf of bread, and there is not a great deal that Hugo has to say about these men or their conditions of servitude. Here and there a word suggests suffering and cruelty, but Hugo seems to have known little about the actual conditions prevailing for prisoners, and his book falls short as an important indictment. If it is not an example of successful rehabilitation, for there was no evil in the protagonist but only in the society that condemned him, it nevertheless contradicts the strongly believed tenet that prison itself corrupts. All that is necessary for Jean Valjean to make his

way in society is to conceal that he is an exconvict and, as the event with the chid makes him, a fugitive as well. (pp. 64-5)

Had Valjean been a different person, or had there been others from the galleys like him, he might have symbolized what Hugo seems haltingly to be suggesting at times: the criminals are the saints, and their jailers are the sinners. But Thénardier and many others are evil criminals, and aside from Valjean himself there are none that epitomize goodness. Only one man has risen, and in the end he is one who had never fallen. (p. 67)

André Maurois has written glowingly of this work [see excerpt above, 1960]. He praises its literary qualities, the excellent prose, the historical frescoes (the description of the Battle of Waterloo, and a more detailed one of the barricades on the streets of Paris in 1832). It is, however, a narrow view, for while *Les Misérables* has these virtues, Maurois ignores its faults—how ill-drawn the characters are, how absurd the plot, how unsubtle the unweaving of the story, as one compares it with the works of the giants of the French novel who came just before Hugo and during his lifetime: Balzac, Stendhal, Gautier, and particularly Flaubert. But then Maurois finds in it great moral qualities, the painful quest of heroism and sanctity. . . . It is an interesting evaluation, and heroism and sanctity are indeed here present—frequently, selflessly, passionately, unmistakably. No reader can fail to discern the message. There is satisfaction in finding in another these qualities that one cannot attain oneself, but a reader must wish that there really were base passions in Valjean, and that he had actually conquered them and not merely overcome a momentary bitterness that arose because of the inhuman treatment he was accorded following the theft of the single loaf. If only there had been sin, there might have been redemption. Valjean never rises from the basest passions because he had never descended. The thefts of the bishop's silver plates and of the child's two-franc coin, whch he sought to return: these and the loaf of bread are all that we have against him; for these he must spend a lifetime of expiation.

Yet there is expiation. I am not sure, as Maurois contends, that this is the sort of book that gives one "greater confidence in life and in himself." Maurois writes of *Les Misérables* that it speaks more to man of "his liberty than of his slavery." Yes and no, but it depends largely upon the willingness of the reader to suspend confidence in the universality of almost all other characters and utilize the hero as symbol of humanity. For Valjean does have liberty to rise, despite the pursuit by Javert, innumerable social pressures, and the social conditions that caused hunger and virtual thralldom.

Victor Hugo evidently gave great importance to the loaf of bread, and *Les Misérables* has left a legacy to the language of irony, that in the world of unequals he who steals a million dollars becomes a prime minister or an industrial tycoon while he who steals a loaf of bread ends up in prison. Jean Valjean spent nineteen years as a galley slave for his theft, about which Hugo writes in one of the passages in which he departs from his role of novelist and becomes essayist, social commentator, or historian:

> This is the second time that, during his essays on the penal question and condemnation by the law, the author of this book has come across a loaf as the starting-point of the disaster of a destiny. Claude Gueux [in the short story "**Claude Gueux**"] stole a loaf, and so did Jean Valjean, and English statistics prove that in

London four robberies out of five have hunger
as their immediate cause. . . .

(p. 68)

Here is Hugo as the critic of society: it is a world populated
by prisoners of starvation, and it drives good men to crime. It
is a world of cruelty and injustice, and it determines the destiny
of men such as Jean Valjean. His, the author's and the hero's,
is a cry from the depths of despair. Yet the message of Hugo
actually is that all that is good in man cannot be destroyed by
the prison air . . . , not *all* that is good, and not in *all* good
men. It can only be driven beneath the surface as one hardens
in the struggle for survival.

If this is a story, or even the story, of man rising to heights
from the lowest depths, it is also a story of man seeking to
escape from a past, to conceal it, to find a manner of starting
life anew without pursuit from others and without the cloak
that must be worn if one's stigma is to remain invisible. In the
first instance, one almost wishes that the rise to heights were
to places somewhat less lofty. Maurois is understating when
he draws attention to the inability of the reader to fulfill a
similar quest for heroism and sanctity. The fact is that Jean
Valjean is just too good to be true, and this becomes literal
for the reader who cannot immerse himself only in the man as
symbol and wants to see him as a living person and to be
confronted with greater verisimilitude with his fate.

Hugo's artistry, nonetheless, with all its shortcomings, does
present us with an individual who captures our interests; very
much as in the old-fashioned cinemas that were continued from
week to week, as the hero or heroine hung from the cliffs while
the enemy was in hot pursuit, so we read breathlessly and
applaud inwardly as Jean Valjean narrowly escapes doom.
(pp. 68-9)

Jean Valjean is a sympathetic symbol, but more than a symbol.
At times he does emerge as a meaningful personality, even if
no one else in the novel has the same good fortune. As symbol,
however, Valjean is never at the lowest depths, never has been,
and here Hugo fails us. Essentially, Valjean was not converted,
especially since his first crime had not been anything other
than an act of sacrifice, of altruism, of goodness. Raskolnikov
[in Dostoevsky's *Crime and Punishment*] did murder, he killed
the pawnbroker and her sister with a hatchet; he planned the
murder, and his was an act of baseness. And . . . Lord Jim [in
Conrad's *Lord Jim*] did abandon ship, as no captain or mate
ever should, leaving aboard the sinking vessel the men under
his command in contravention of his vows and the moral order
of the sea. Moll Flanders [in Defoe's *Moll Flanders*] stole and
stole and stole. But what Hugo has given us is more of a
condemnation of society (as his aside on the subject of four
out of five English crimes would indicate), and for that reason
his novel cannot rank as a study in human redemption. There
was really no crime, or so little of one. Valjean had never been
a Raskolnikov; Raskolnikov could never have been canonized
by Dostoevsky.

Like Lord Jim, Jean Valjean is seeking to escape from a past,
but there the analogy ends. Lord Jim never wants to be faced
by anyone who has learned of his misdeed because it was an
act of infamy; it is really from himself that he wishes to find
refuge. An impossible task: there are no worlds without mirrors. So while Lord Jim's secret protects him from inner persecution, Valjean's secret must guard him from the outer world,
for two reasons: first, because the world will demand a penalty
if he is apprehended and his identity disclosed; and second,

because the world will never cease condemning an exconvict. . . . [In the world of Hugo, man,] once condemned, is
forever condemned; he may be released from the bagnes, the
galleys, the walls and bars, but he remains always in prison
once he has been there. There is no Christian world that forgives
anyone, not even this man for whom there is nothing to forgive.
One pays forever, and at best can live only by concealment.
The biography is there and cannot be rewritten, but it does not
have to be told, or it can be falsified (and the two are essentially
one). In this sense, if there is a message that Hugo wants us
to learn from the life of Jean Valjean, the book is still very
much alive. Ask any exconvict, in France or the United States
and probably most other countries of the world, and they will
tell you that the world of Jean Valjean remains almost unchanged among us. If these exconvicts were to be sanctified,
it would give them as little solace as it did Hugo's central
figure, for where is the audience that would believe the glor-
ifiers, or perform the canonization rites, except perhaps a century and a half after their death?

The departures that the author takes from his novel in order to
offer social commentary often have only tangential reference
to the plots and subplots of the book, but they are significant
in themselves. Hugo is, as it were, reminding himself that he
is writing a story of the wretched, not of one individual, and
even if the two clash it does not concern him. ''All the crimes
of the man begin with the vagabondage of the lad,'' he states . . . ,
although it was hardly true of Jean Valjean and there is little
evidence of it in the criminal underworld elements with whom
Valjean comes into contact at certain points in his adventures.
(pp. 69-71)

A passage that refers to the underworld, the literal criminal
underworld though it might be equally applicable to the world
of fear of exposure in which Jean Valjean lives, summarizes
perhaps as well as any in this novel what Hugo has to say
about crime:

> The social evil is darkness; humanity is iden-
> tity, for all men are of the same clay, and in
> this nether world, at least, there is no difference
> in predestination; we are the same shadow be-
> fore, the same flesh during, and the same ashes
> afterward; but ignorance, mixed with the hu-
> man paste, blackens it, and this incurable
> blackness enters man and becomes Evil there. . . .

It is more than Jean Valjean that Hugo is discussing when he
writes that the social evil is darkness, it is humanity. If only
humanity could accept the brotherhood of man, know that we
come from nothing and will return to nothing, that the short
time between need not be wretched for the millions of poor,
*les misérables,* then we could live in harmony and low on
earth. Have no illusions: we are not predestined, Calvinism
notwithstanding, to eternal damnation or endless bliss. We all
have the same future, the darkness of the grave, and if we
could lift ourselves from the ignorance that does not accept
this, we could bring light into a world of somber shadows.
This is Hugo's hope for salvation, but it is a meager hope, and
in the end only Jean Valjean finds this salvation, only one
unusual soul among millions of ordinary folk. Our sins are
greater than thefts of loaves of bread for the hungry and the
young, and we will not be able to fulfill en masse the hopes
that Hugo expresses so eloquently in this passage. (pp. 72-3)

*Edward Sagarin, ''Jean Valjean: For Stealing a Loaf*<br>*of Bread,'' in his* Raskolnikov and Others: Literary

*A photograph of Hugo taken in 1882. The Granger Collection, New York.*

Images of Crime, Punishment, Redemption, and Atonement, *St. Martin's Press, 1981, pp. 60-76.*

---

## ADDITIONAL BIBLIOGRAPHY

Carrera, Rosalina de la. "History's Unconscious in Victor Hugo's *Les misérables*." *Modern Language Notes* 96, No. 4 (May 1981): 839-55.
  A Freudian interpretation of *Les misérables*.

Carrière, J. M. "A Seventeenth Century Precursor of Mgr Myriel." *The French Review* X, No. 4 (February 1937): 285-92.*
  Points out resemblances between Monsignor Myriel and Monsignor Nicolas Pavillon, a seventeenth-century French bishop whose career is documented in Claude Lancelot's *Relation d'un voyage d'Aleth*. Carrière is unable to determine whether Hugo read Lancelot's work, but he states that it is not "altogether unreasonable" to assume that he did.

Davidson, A. F. "1856-1862." In his *Victor Hugo: His Life and Work*, pp. 237-53. London: Eveleigh Nash, 1912.

Briefly contrasts the portraits of Monsignor Myriel in *Les misères* and *Les misérables*.

Downs, Robert B. "Romantic Humanitarianism: Victor Marie Hugo's *Les misérables* (1862)." In his *Molders of the Modern Mind: 111 Books that Shaped Western Civilization*, pp. 289-91. New York: Barnes & Noble, 1962.
  Views *Les misérables* as a vehicle through which Hugo expressed his social ideas.

Grant, Richard B. "Myth and Society: *Les misérables*." In his *The Perilous Quest: Image, Myth, and Prophecy in the Narratives of Victor Hugo*, pp. 154-76. Durham, N.C.: Duke University Press, 1968.
  Discusses Hugo's use of Christological imagery in *Les misérables*.

Hooker, Kenneth Ward. "*Les misérables* in England (1862-1863)." In his *The Fortunes of Victor Hugo in England*, pp. 143-58. New York: Columbia University Press, 1938.
  A bibliographical essay in which Hooker assesses coverage of *Les misérables* in the British press from 1862 to 1863.

Josephson, Matthew. "*Les misérables*." In his *Victor Hugo: A Realistic Biography of the Great Romantic*, pp. 438-64. Garden City, N.Y.: Doubleday, Doran & Co., 1942.
  Describes the genesis of *Les misérables* and summarizes its plot.

Maurois, André. "Part Nine, The Fruits of Exile: *Les misérables*." In his *Victor Hugo*, translated by Gerard Hopkins, pp. 379-85. London: Jonathan Cape, 1956.
  Examines the circumstances surrounding Hugo's composition of *Les misérables* and recounts the facts on which he based much of the novel. In addition, Maurois briefly describes contemporary French response to *Les misérables*.

Meredith, George. "Letter to Captain Maxse." In his *Letters of George Meredith: 1844-1881, Vol. 1*, edited by W. M. M[eredith], pp. 75-6. New York: Charles Scribner's Sons, 1913.
  A frequently quoted letter dated June 23, 1862 in which Meredith states that *Les misérables* is "conceived in pure black and white."

Moore, Olin H. "Realism in *Les misérables*." *PMLA* 61, No. 1 (March 1946): 211-28.
  Documents a progression toward photographic realism in the successive stages of the composition of *Les misérables*. In charting Hugo's "*drift* towards *reportage*," Moore relies mainly upon Hugo's unpublished correspondence.

Rosselet, Jeanne. "First Reactions to *Les misérables* in the United States." *Modern Language Notes* 67, No. 1 (January 1952): 39-43.
  Excerpts liberally from several early American reviews of *Les misérables*.

Spencer, Philip. "A Note on Paul Meurice and *Les misérables*." *The Modern Language Review* LI, No. 4 (October 1956): 566-68.*
  Suggests that Paul Meurice's *Léonard Aubry* provided the inspiration for the episode of the dying revolutionary in *Les misérables*.

Sumichrast, F. C. de. Introduction to *Les misérables,* by Victor Hugo, pp. xiii-xxvii, Boston: Ginn & Co., Publishers, 1896.
  Defends the originality of *Les misérables* by pointing out themes in the novel that Hugo had examined in his earlier works. Sumichrast also briefly discusses the characters in *Les misérables* that are drawn from life.

# Charles Lamb

## 1775-1834

(Also wrote under pseudonym of Elia) English essayist, critic, poet, dramatist, and novelist.

A well-known literary figure in nineteenth-century England, Lamb is chiefly remembered today for his "Elia" essays, a series renowned for its witty, idiosyncratic treatment of everyday subjects. Through the persona of "Elia," Lamb employed a rambling narrative technique to achieve what many critics regard as the epitome of the familiar essay style. Lamb's elegant prose has delighted generations of readers, and his literary criticism also testifies to his versatility and perceptiveness. However, since their first appearance in print, Lamb's opinions on drama have been the subject of controversy. Though recent commentators affirm Lamb's importance in the history of criticism, they also fault his unsystematic critical method. Despite these reservations, most scholars agree that Lamb's writings on drama helped bring about a revival of interest in the Elizabethan playwrights in England during the early part of the nineteenth century.

Lamb was born in London, the youngest of seven children, of whom only three survived into adulthood. His father was a law clerk who worked in the Inner Temple, one of the courts of London, and wrote poetry in his spare time. Almost nothing is known about Lamb's mother. In 1782, Lamb was accepted as a student at Christ's Hospital, a school in London for the children of poor families. He excelled in his studies, especially in English literature, but the seven years away from home proved lonely. Later, Lamb wrote that his solitude was relieved only by his friendship with a fellow student, Samuel Taylor Coleridge. At this time Lamb also began to experiment with verse. Since his family's poverty prevented him from furthering his education, Lamb took a job immediately upon graduation. Working first as a clerk, he became an accountant at the East India Company, a prestigious trade firm, where he remained until retirement in 1825. During his career there he read widely and corresponded frequently with such friends as Coleridge, William Wordsworth, and Robert Southey. It was at Coleridge's insistence that Lamb's first sonnets were included in Coleridge's collection *Poems on Various Subjects,* published in 1796.

Near the end of 1795, Lamb collapsed and committed himself to a hospital for the mentally ill. Though biographers are uncertain as to the exact cause of his breakdown, they believe it might have been precipitated by unrequited love. Lamb's sister, Mary, who was also mentally ill, stabbed her mother to death in 1796—an event that completely transformed Lamb's life. His father, nearly senile, and his brother, John, wanted to commit Mary permanently to an asylum, but Lamb succeeded in obtaining her release and devoted himself to her care. From then on, Mary enjoyed long intervals of sanity and productivity as a writer, but these were inevitably punctuated by breakdowns. Biographers attribute Lamb's bouts of depression and excessive drinking to the stress of worrying about Mary, to whom he was very close. During her lucid periods, however, she and Charles lived peacefully and even adopted a young girl.

In 1820, the editor of the *London Magazine* invited Lamb to contribute regularly to his periodical. Lamb, eager to supplement his meager income, wrote some pieces under the pseudonym of "Elia" for the magazine. With the success of these essays, Lamb became one of the most admired men in London. He and Mary presided over a weekly open house, which was attended by his many literary friends including Coleridge, William Hazlitt, Leigh Hunt, and Henry Crabb Robinson. Besides his diverse friendships, Lamb found his chief pleasure in writing, which consumed his evenings and holidays. After his retirement from the East India Company, he devoted more time to his favorite occupation. Lamb was still at the peak of his popularity as an essayist when he died suddenly from an infection in 1834.

Lamb's first published works were his sonnets, which critics praised for their simple diction and delicate poetic manner, but he quickly discovered that his talent and inclinations lay elsewhere. His first serious work in prose, *A Tale of Rosamund Gray and Old Blind Margaret,* appeared in 1798. A short experimental novel, *Rosamund Gray* displays the influence of Henry Mackenzie and Laurence Sterne. Lamb, always an avid theater-goer, decided to try his hand at drama next; however, *John Woodvil,* a tragedy in the Elizabethan style, was neither a popular nor critical success. Most reviewers criticized the play for its archaic style and static structure, but a few praised

Lamb's clear dialogue and effective handling of characterization. His next two projects also testify to his love of Elizabethan literature. In 1807, he and Mary collaborated on *Tales from Shakespeare,* a prose version of Shakespeare's plays which was intended for children. The *Tales* were generally well received and the Lambs were commended for expanding the scope of children's literature in England, though a few critics regarded the *Tales* as distorted renderings of the plays. That same year, Lamb completed his *Specimens of English Dramatic Poets, Who Lived About the Time of Shakspeare,* an anthology that included selections from the plays of such Elizabethan dramatists as Christopher Marlowe, John Webster, George Chapman, and Thomas Middleton. Since many of these works were previously unavailable to readers, Lamb's anthology was an important reference source. Each author entry was supplemented with explanatory notes that are now considered his most important critical work. Lamb further elaborated on his views in "On the Tragedies of Shakespeare Considered with Reference to Their Fitness for Stage Presentation." In this essay, he argued that the best qualities of Shakespeare's plays can be fully appreciated only through reading; according to Lamb, stage performances often diminish the plays' meanings, and individual performers often misinterpret Shakespeare's intended characterizations.

Though he initially achieved prominence as a drama critic, Lamb's greatest fame came through his "Elia" essays, first written for the *London Magazine* between 1820 and 1825. When *Elia: Essays Which Have Appeared under That Signature in the "London Magazine"* was published in 1823, Lamb was already one of the most popular writers in England. He composed sketches in the familiar essay form, a style popularized by Michel Eyquem de Montaigne, Robert Burton, and Sir Thomas Browne. Characterized by a personal tone, narrative ease, and a wealth of literary allusions, the "Elia" essays enjoyed unparalleled success. Critics were enchanted with Lamb's highly wrought style and his blending of humor and pathos. Never didactic, the essays treat ordinary subjects in a nostalgic, fanciful way, and one of their chief attractions for readers of both the nineteenth and twentieth centuries is the gradual revelation of "Elia's" personality.

Lamb's importance as a critic has been much debated. Some scholars, most recently René Wellek, have denigrated his prejudices and his lack of consistent critical methodology. Lamb's thesis in "On the Tragedies of Shakespeare" is considered especially controversial. Because Lamb theorized that Shakespeare's works were best unperformed, such critics as T. S. Eliot held Lamb personally responsible for what Eliot termed the detrimental distinction between drama and literature in the English language. Conversely, such diverse critics as Henry Nelson Coleridge, Algernon Charles Swinburne, and E.M.W. Tillyard have proclaimed Lamb's historical importance and hailed his *Specimens* as a critical landmark. No such controversy surrounds the "Elia" essays, and they have been universally extolled by reviewers ever since their initial appearance. Although some scholars considered his style imitative of earlier English writers, the majority now accept that quality as one of "Elia's" distinctive hallmarks, along with his fondness for the obscure and other idiosyncrasies. Stylistic studies by Walter Pater, Arthur Symons, A. G. van Kranendonk, and Donald H. Reiman explore diverse aspects of Lamb's artistry as evidenced in the essays. Both early and recent critics, including Thomas De Quincey, Bertram Jessup, and Gerald Monsman, have probed the "Elia" persona—proof that readers' curiosity about Lamb's personality has not waned. In one

of the most recent studies of Lamb, Monsman has written that the creation of "Elia" was an "exorcism" of his troubled family past. While most critics acknowledge Lamb's contribution to the rediscovery of Elizabethan drama in nineteenth-century England, his reputation rests on the "Elia" essays, whose enduring humor and spontaneity continue to capture the imaginations of modern readers.

## PRINCIPAL WORKS

*Poems on Various Subjects* [with Samuel Taylor Coleridge] (poetry) 1796
*A Tale of Rosamund Gray and Old Blind Margaret* (novel) 1798
*John Woodvil* (drama) 1802
*Tales from Shakespeare* [with Mary Lamb] (short stories) 1807
*Specimens of English Dramatic Poets, Who Lived About the Time of Shakspeare* [editor] (dramas) 1808
*Elia: Essays Which Have Appeared under That Signature in the "London Magazine"* [as Elia] (essays) 1823
*The Last Essays of Elia* [as Elia] (essays) 1833
*\*The Works of Charles and Mary Lamb.* 7 vols. (essays, novel, short stories, poetry, and dramas) 1903-05
*The Letters of Charles Lamb.* 3 vols. (letters) 1935

*\*This work includes the essays "On the Genius of Hogarth," "On The Tragedies of Shakespeare Considered with Reference to Their Fitness for Stage Presentation," and "On the Artificial Comedy of the Last Century."

---

**[THOMAS BROWN]** (essay date 1803)

[*In this scathing review of Lamb's drama* John Woodvil *and some accompanying fragments, Brown deems the play an example of "drama in its state of pristine rudeness."*]

We have often regretted, in perusing the dramatic compositions of the ancients, that we do not possess any of those earlier specimens of the art in its state of rudeness, from which the merit of succeeding dramatists might best be determined. It is always a consolation to badness, that there is something worse; and the greater number of our tragic writers have therefore a just ground of complaint against the fraud of the stages of antiquity, which, by transmitting only their best productions, have deprived them of the power of looking back to pieces inferior to their own. We have dramas of Eschylus indeed; but Eschylus, 'pallae repertor honestae,' had already raised poor barefoot Tragedy on buskins, and given her a comfortable cloak to her back. (p. 90)

[Mr. Lamb's *John Woodvil*] may indeed be fairly considered as supplying the first of those lost links which connect the improvements of Eschylus with the commencement of the art. (p. 91)

The whole is indeed almost uniformly venerable, and will be justly appreciated by all who are desirous of possessing a complete specimen of the drama in its state of pristine rudeness.

The tragedy is accompanied with two little pieces, a 'balad [*sic*] from the German, which, though it have not made Schiller more pathetic, has certainly, in converting him to Methodism, made him much more pious; and **'Helen'**, a song, in which, though we sometimes discerned the manner of that person of quality who assisted the Wits of Queen Anne's reign, we thought, till we had read the appended fragments of Burton, that it was in every respect an original piece, and an original of more value, from the probable rarity of any future productions which might resemble it. It is addressed to a lady, whose love the author is supposed to have long fought in vain, and for whom, when at length compliant, he finds that his love has perished. But the most singular circumstance is, that, with love surpassing that of Pygmalion, he still weeps to the picture of her whom he scorns, 'nor ever sleeps, complaining all night long to her.' Such violence of distress must be merely the continuance of an old habit: and it is perhaps only physically, because her tenderness would interfere with this habit, that he no longer feels regard for the *living* Helen. The real reason of his coolness he leaves us to guess, by putting it in the form of a query.

> Can I, who loved my beloved
>      But for the scorn was in her eyes
> Can I be moved for my beloved,
>      When she returns me sigh for sigh?

We own, that we do not discover the reason of this impossibility. That any one should love scorn *merely as scorn,* is inconceivable; and her sympathy is certainly no reason for the change, unless he prefer his own solitary grief to her for whom he grieves. If he had frankly owned, that she was now not so lovely as when younger, we should at least have understood his meaning; but, in that case, he would not have been enamoured, till the very moment of her melting, as the deteriorations of age must have been gradual, and not dependent on a single smile. The two lines which close the poem,

> Helen grown old, no longer cold,
> Said, "You to all men I prefer."

are most singularly placed. At the beginning they would have been very communicative; but at the conclusion they tell us nothing; since the fact, without the knowledge of which the preceding verses must have been unintelligible, was therefore graciously expressed before. Mr. Lamb had perhaps heard, that poems of this kind should end with a point; and wisely reflecting, that the beginning of any thing is as much a point as its end, was too good an economist of his time, to consume it in elaborating and polishing an useless conclusion.

The extracts from a common-place book of Burton, are recommended only by their quaintness and party-coloured learning. There is one sentence which Mr. Lamb introduced perhaps as descriptive of his own compositions.

> The fruit, issue, children, of these my morning meditations, have been certain crude, impolite, incomposite, hirsute, (what shall I say?) verses.

If this was really intended by him, we must add to the praise we have already given him for poetic talent, our still higher commendation of the justness of his criticism. . . . (pp. 95-6)

> [Thomas Brown], "Lamb's 'John Woodvil'," in The Edinburgh Review, *Vol. II, No. III, April, 1803, pp. 90-6.*

## THE CRITICAL REVIEW    (essay date 1807)

[*This brief early review of* Tales from Shakespeare *focuses on the work's didactic potential.*]

[We have compared Lamb's *Tales from Shakespeare*] with many of the numerous systems which have been devised for rivetting attention at an early age, and insinuating knowledge subtilly and pleasantly into minds, by nature averse from it. The result of the comparison is not so much that it rises high in the list, as that it claims the very first place, and stands unique, and without rival or competitor, unless perhaps we except [Daniel Defoe's] *Robinson Crusoe,* with which it has one excellence in common, vis. that although adapted to instruct and interest the very young, it offers amusement to all ages.

In these times of empiricism and system-building, the world has been too credulous to the professions of old women of both sexes, who hold the reins of government over the education of children. We have grown so very good of late, that none but devotional books or moral tales, as they are called are entrusted into the hands of our children. The former teach all the cant, without any of the mild spirit of religion; the latter, all the cold austerity, without any of the amiable urbanity of virtue. They both in general represent some one little being, who has committed an error in the wildness of youth, some unlucky child, as an object for the eternal abhorrence and persecution of what are called the upright and pious. Their morality and religion tend alike to give a child of good disposition a distaste for both; or, if he be a convert, to render him an unforgiving hypocrite. We will not scruple to say, that these little volumes are more calculated to conquer the distaste in children for learning, than any, excepting the excellent work of De Foe above mentioned which have yet appeared. . . .

[In reading the *Tales,*] the child would not only be instructed in language, but in the usage of terms the most simple, vigorous, and expressive. His mind, stored with the images and words of our greatest poets, would turn with disgust from the sordid trash with which the minds of children are usually contaminated. (p. 98)

[And when] advantages that accrue to the heart, morals, and manners, are united to the soundness of head and beauty of language, which they equally promote, we confess ourselves at a loss to find any character more perfect than that which has been formed in such a school. We heartily subscribe our opinion to that of the author, and feel confident that all those beneficial effects which he has proposed to himself will be answered wherever his book shall be adopted. (p. 99)

> *A review of "Tales from Shakespeare, Designed for the Use of Young Persons," in* The Critical Review, *Vol. XI, May, 1807, pp. 97-9.*

## BLACKWOOD'S EDINBURGH MAGAZINE    (essay date 1818)

[*Surveying the collected works of Lamb, this reviewer provides a balanced assessment of Lamb's poetry, dramas, essays, and criticism. The critic focuses on Lamb's originality, pathos, and critical acumen.*]

Mr Lamb is without doubt a man of genius, and of very peculiar genius too; so that we scarcely know of any class of literature to which it could with propriety be said that he belongs. His mind is original even in its errors; and though his ideas often flow on in a somewhat fantastic course, and are shaded with no less fantastic imagery, yet at all times they bubble freshly from the fountain of his own mind, and almost always lead to truth. It is pleasant to know and to feel that we have to do with a man of originality. Much may be learned even from the mistakes of such a writer; he can express more by one happy word than a merely judicious or learned man could in a long dissertation; and the glimpses and flashes which he flings over a subject, shews us more of its bearings than a hundred farthing candles ostentatiously held up by the hands of formal and pragmatical literati. . . .

His mind has not a very wide range; but every thing it sees rises up before it in vivid beauty. He is never deceived by mere seeming magnitude. He tries every thing by the standard of moral worth. Splendid common-places have no charm for the simplicity of his mind. He has small pleasure in following others along the beaten high-road. He diverges into green lanes and sunshiny glades, and not seldom into the darker and more holy places of undiscovered solitude. . . . There is in him a rare union of originality of mind with delicacy of feeling and tenderness of heart. His understanding seems always to be guided by the kindliest affections, and they are good and trusty guides; so that there is not in these two volumes a single sentiment or opinion which does not dispose us to love the pure minded and high-souled person who breathes them out with such cordial sincerity. (p. 559)

The style of his prose seems to us exceedingly beautiful; sometimes, perhaps, savouring of affectation, or at least of too studious an imitation of those rich elder writers of ours; but almost always easy, simple, graceful, and concise. . . . It is a style well worthy of all commendation in these days, when grace, elegance, and simplicity, have been sacrificed to false splendour and an ambitious magnificence. (pp. 599-600)

He is far indeed from being a great Poet, but he is a true one. He has not, perhaps, much imagination; at least he takes but short flights, but they are flights through purest ether. There is a sort of timidity about him that chains his wings. He seems to want ambition. In reading his Poems, we always feel that he might write far loftier things if he would. But in his own sphere he delights us. He is the very best of those Poets who are Poets rather from fineness of perception, delicacy of fancy, and pure warmth of heart, than from the impulses of that higher creative power what works in the world of the imagination. (p. 600)

Before we leave Mr Lamb's Poetry, however, we must remark, that there can be no greater folly than to talk of him as being one of the Lake School of Poets. He has a more delicate taste, a more graceful and ingenious turn of mind, than any one of them; but he bears no resemblance to Southey, Wordsworth, Coleridge, or Wilson, in those peculiar talents, peculiar theories, and peculiar poetical habits of life, in which all these poets agree, and which have given to their compositions a character so easily distinguishable from all the other Poetry of the age. (p. 601)

[The Tragedy of *John Woodville*] is, throughout, deficient in vigour, and now and then so very simple as to be almost silly, though even in the worst passages there is a redeeming charm in the diction and versification. It seems to have been written when its author's mind teemed with the fresh beauties of the ancient drama, and many of those beauties are transfused into the piece. Nothing can excel the delicate skill with which he has imitated the finer under tones of the best old dramatists, and many of its scenes are eminently distinguished by tenderness and pathos. The tragedy is founded on a tale of domestic sorrow, and the only female character, Margaret, is conceived and drawn in a manner worthy of Massinger himself. . . . We wish Mr Lamb would write another tragedy. Let him put a little more force into it—widen the range of his action and

characters—be less under the constraint of imitation—and dismiss a few little womanish affections and weaknesses—and he really has so much tenderness, delicacy, nature, and even passion, that if he gives himself fair play, he is sure to produce a domestic tragedy that would universally touch and affect the minds of men. . . .

Mr Lamb's humour, though always somewhat original, is often very forced and unnatural. When he gets hold of an odd and outrageously absurd whim or fancy, he is beside himself, and keeps in an eternal dalliance with it till it is absolutely pawed into pieces. This fault infects all his humorous epistles more or less. That, **"On the Inconveniency of being Hanged,"** has some capital strokes, but it is overlaboured. (p. 602)

Mr Lamb has also written a farce, called *Mr. H.,* which was damned. He has done unwisely, we think, in publishing it. The hero has so ugly a name, that he calls himself by the initial letter H., and lives in constant trepidation lest his real name be detected. On this trepidation the farce hinges. Detected it is at last,—*Hogsflesh!* Men of genius are apt, very apt, to mistake their talent. The author has every reason to be ashamed of this farce, yet we fear he plumes himself greatly upon it. The prologue is worth the farce itself ten times over. (p. 604)

But by much the best part of Mr Lamb's book is his serious Essays, and more especially his **"Characters of Dramatic Writers contemporary with Shakspeare,"** the Essay on the **"Tragedies of Shakspeare,"** and that on the **"Genius of Hogarth."**

We observe that a writer in this Magazine has occasionally quoted passages from the first of these, in his Analytical Essays on the Old English Drama, and therefore we need not now give any additional extracts. But we cannot help remarking, that Mr Lamb, from his desire to say strong and striking things, and to represent the objects of his enthusiasm as deserving even of his idolatry, has often pushed his panegyrics on the ancient English Dramatists beyond all reasonable bounds. In some few cases, his extravagant zeal has led him into expressions of his feelings most indefensible and offensive. Mr Lamb is, we know, a man of virtue, and, we doubt not, a man of religion. He ought not, therefore, in speaking of mere human feelings and passions, ever so far to forget himself as to hazard allusions to the awful mysteries of Christianity, which, when brought into contact with our sympathies for mere humanity, cannot but wear an air of irreverence. Thus, when speaking of the "Broken Heart," by Ford, he says, in reference to the death of Calantha, "the expression of this transcendant scene almost bears me in imagination to Calvary and the cross; and I seem to perceive some analogy between the scenical sufferings which I am here contemplating, and the real agonies of that final completion to which I dare no more than hint a reference." Mr Lamb has here dared to hint a great deal too much—far more than Ford himself would have hinted, or Shakspeare. Such a passage must shock every heart; and we implore Mr Lamb, for whom we entertain sincere respect and affection, to obliterate, in a future edition, this most unadvised, irreverent, and impious allusion. He is a Christian: let him therefore beware of offending his fellow Christians—of offending his God. (pp. 604-05)

In his **"Essay on the Tragedies of Shakspeare,"** he adopts a paradox, namely, "that they are less calculated for performance on a stage than those of almost any other dramatist whatever." (p. 605)

Much as we admire such speculation as this, we cannot think that Mr Lamb has at all made good his point. It is true, that in Shakspeare's tragedies there are innumerable beauties,—more by far than in any other dramas,—which must be lost or marred in stage-representation. But grant this; and do not more and higher beauties still remain, fit for such stage-representation, than in any other plays? Shakspeare wrote for the stage, and no man ever saw so profoundly as he did into the natural laws and boundaries of the scenic world. His poetical soul lavished in profusion over all his dramas the etherial flowers of poetry, and these, it is possible, may sometimes be too delicate, or too gorgeous, to endure an abiding place in the broad glare of a theatre. Their native air, under which they most beautifully bloom and most fragrantly breathe, may be that of seclusion and peace. Yet, even on the stage, probably where they may seem but little congenial with the character of much that surrounds them, these divine beauties of poetry startle us into sudden delight; and we feel, while they come glistening and shining upon us, as if conscious of a purer and heavenly life. With respect, too, to those nicer and finer shades of character and passion which Mr Lamb thinks cannot be expressed by any actors,—we have frequently glimpses even of them; and though there are many of these in Shakspeare that can never be brought over the form or the face, nor into the voice or eye of any human being, yet the soul of every enlightened auditor in a great measure conceives them for himself, and they accompany him silently, and perhaps unconsciously, throughout all the scenes of the acted drama. It would, we humbly think, be a little unreasonable to maintain, that in real life, Grief weeping and wailing before us, was not so affecting as some imagined tale of distress might be,—because that in grief there are thoughts that lie too deep for expression of voice or feature, and that, therefore, real sufferers are in fact but indifferent actors, give us only imperfect symbols—general representations of human calamity. Shakspeare gives us in his plays all that is in the power of human actors to express, every variety of human passion that can by shewn by the voices, countenances, or bodies of men. If he gives us a great deal more than this, so much the better; but we are at a loss to conceive why that should make his plays worse fitted for representation. We agree with Mr Lamb, that Shakspeare's plays read better in the closet than those of any other writer, and this is all that his argument seems to us to prove: we cannot see, that merely because they read better in the closet, they should *therefore* act the worse on the stage. (p. 607)

*A review of "The Works of Charles Lamb," in* Blackwood's Edinburgh Magazine, *Vol. III, No. XVII, August, 1818, pp. 599-610.*

## WILLIAM HAZLITT   (lecture date 1818)

*[One of the most important commentators of the Romantic age, Hazlitt was an English critic and journalist. He is best known for his descriptive criticism in which he stressed that no motives beyond judgment and analysis are necessary on the part of the critic. A critic must start with a strong opinion, Hazlitt asserted, but must also keep in mind that evaluation is the starting point—not the object—of criticism. Hazlitt's often recalcitrant refusal to engage in close analysis, however, led other critics to wonder whether in fact he was capable of close, sustained analysis. Characterized by a tough, independent view of the world, by his political liberalism, and by the influence of Samuel Taylor Coleridge and Charles Lamb, Hazlitt's style is particularly admired for its wide range of reference and catholicity of interests. Though he wrote on many diverse subjects, Hazlitt's most important critical achievements are his typically Romantic interpretation of characters from William Shakespeare's plays, influenced by the German critic August Wilhelm Schlegel, and his revival of interest*

*in such Elizabethan dramatists as John Webster, Thomas Haywood, and Thomas Dekker. In the following excerpt, originally delivered as a lecture at the Surrey Institution in 1818, Hazlitt attributes the flaws of* John Woodvil *to Lamb's attempt to imitate Elizabethan dramatists, but praises the drama's general delicacy and profundity, especially as evidenced in the characterization of Margaret. For Hazlitt's later assessment of Lamb, see excerpt below, 1825.]*

Mr. Lamb's '**John Woodvil**' may be considered as a dramatic fragment, intended for the closet rather than the stage. It would sound oddly in the lobbies of either theatre, amidst the noise and glare and bustle of resort; but "there where we have treasured up our hearts," in silence and in solitude, it may claim and find a place for itself. It might be read with advantage in the still retreats of Sherwood Forest, where it would throw a new-born light on the green, sunny glades; the tenderest flower might seem to drink of the poet's spirit, and "the tall deer that paints a dancing shadow of his horns in the swift brook," might seem to do so in mockery of the poet's thought. Mr. Lamb, with a modesty often attendant on fine feeling, has loitered too long in the humbler avenues leading to the temple of ancient genius, instead of marching boldly up to the sanctuary, as many with half his pretensions would have done: "but fools rush in, where angels fear to tread." The defective or objectionable parts of this production are imitations of the defects of the old writers: its beauties are his own, though in their manner. The touches of thought and passion are often as pure and delicate as they are profound; and the character of his heroine Margaret is perhaps the finest and most genuine female character out of Shakspeare. This tragedy was not critic-proof: it had its cracks and flaws and breaches, through which the enemy marched in triumphant. The station which he had chosen was not indeed a walled town, but a straggling village, which the experienced engineers proceeded to lay waste; and he is pinned down in more than one Review of the day, as an exemplary warning to indiscreet writers, who venture beyond the pale of periodical taste and conventional criticism. Mr. Lamb was thus hindered by the taste of the polite vulgar from writing as he wished; his own taste would not allow him to write like them: and he (perhaps wisely) turned critic and prose-writer in his own defence. (pp. 195-96)

*William Hazlitt, "On the Spirit of Ancient and Modern Literature—On the German Drama, Contrasted with That of the Age of Elizabeth," in his* Lectures on the Dramatic Literature of the Age of Elizabeth, *Lemma Publishing Corporation, 1972, pp. 195-218.*

## [LEIGH HUNT]   (essay date 1819)

*[An English poet and essayist, Hunt is remembered as a literary critic who encouraged and influenced several young Romantic poets, especially John Keats and Percy Bysshe Shelley. Hunt produced volumes of poetry and critical essays and, with his brother John, established the* Examiner, *a weekly liberal newspaper. In his criticism, Hunt articulated the principles of Romanticism, emphasizing imaginative freedom and the expression of a personal emotional or spiritual state. Although his critical works were overshadowed by those of more prominent Romantic critics, such as his friends Samuel Taylor Coleridge and William Hazlitt, his essays are considered both insightful and generous to the fledgling writers he supported. Reviewing the first edition of Lamb's collected works, Hunt compliments Lamb on the simplicity of his poetry, but acknowledges that his originality is better expressed in his critical writings. In addition, Hunt commends Lamb's ability to invest his dramatic poetry with moral lessons.]*

We fear indeed, that by every body but the author, we have been thought culpably negligent, in not noticing [*The Works of Charles Lamb*] before; but will credit be given to us when we say, (we! who have been hardy critics for a number of years, man and boy), that we felt diffident in writing upon the subject? Yes; those will believe us, who know, that great liking is often as hesitating a thing as delay itself; and that there are subjects, before which the stoutest encounterer of all the rougher topics of life, feels himself taken with a bland and enjoying stillness, which he is almost afraid to break by expressing his sense of it.

If these are refinements, they are such as the work before us is well calculated to produce. There is a spirit in Mr. Lamb's productions, which is in itself so *anti-critical*, and tends so much to reconcile us to all that is in the world, that the effect is almost neutralizing to every thing but complacency and a quiet admiration. . . .

That the poetical part of Mr. Lamb's volumes . . . is not so striking as the critical we allow. And there are several reasons for it;—first, because criticism inevitably explains itself more to the reader; whereas poetry, especially such as Mr. Lamb's, often gives him too much credit for the apprehensiveness in which it deals itself;—second, because Mr. Lamb's criticism is obviously of a most original cast, and directly informs the reader of a number of things which he did not know before; whereas the poetry, for the reason just mentioned, leaves him rather to gather them;—third, because the author's genius, though in fact of an anti-critical nature (his very criticisms chiefly tending to overthrow the critical spirit) is also less busied with

creating new things, which is the business of poetry, than with inculcating a charitable and patient content with old, which is a part of humanity:—fourth and last, because from an excess of this content, of love for the old poets, and of diffidence in recommending to others what has such infinite recommendations of it's own, he has really, in three or four instances, written pure common-places on subjects deeply seated in our common humanity, such as the recollections of childhood . . . , the poem that follows it, and one or two of the sonnets. But he who cannot see, that the extreme old simplicity of style in *The Three Friends* is a part and constituent recommendation of the very virtue of the subject;—that the homely versification of the *Ballad noticing the Difference of Rich and Poor* has the same spirit of inward reference,—that the little Robert Burton-like effusion, called *Hypochondriacus*, has all the quick mixture of jest and earnest belonging to such melancholy,—and that the *Farewell to Tobacco* is a piece of exuberant pleasantry, equally witty and poetical, in which the style of the old poets becomes proper to a wit overflowing as theirs,—such a man may be fit enough to set up for a critic once a month, but we are sure he has not an idea in his head once a quarter. (p. 187)

The tragedy of *John Woodvil* has this peculiarity,—that it is founded on a frailty of a very unheroic nature, and ends with no punishment to the offender but repentance. Yet so finely and humanly is it managed, with such attractions of pleasantry and of pathos, that these circumstances become distinguishing features of it's excellence; and the reader begins to regret that other poets have not known how to reconcile moral lessons, so familiar and useful, with the dignity of dramatic poetry. (p. 189)

> [Leigh Hunt], in a review of "The Works of Charles Lamb," in The Examiner, No. 586, March 21, 1819, pp. 187-89.

## THE MONTHLY MAGAZINE, London    (essay date 1823)

[*The following is the first review of the* Essays of Elia.]

[The pleasure afforded by the *Essays of Elia*] is in a great measure weakened, and sometimes destroyed, by a disagreeable quaintness and affection. The author's style is founded on the writers of Queen Elizabeth's time, and with many of their beauties he has a still greater proportion of their defects. In some of his papers he will delight the reader by the originality of his subjects, and his pleasant manner of treating them, whilst, in others, he will absolutely disgust by their revolting indelicacy and sometimes by their ridiculous puerility. (pp. 62-3)

> A review of "Essays of Elia," in The Monthly Magazine, London, Vol. 55, No. 378, February 1, 1823, pp. 62-3.

## WILLIAM HAZLITT    (essay date 1825)

[*In this general appraisal of Lamb's style, Hazlitt posits that Lamb's mannerisms, idiosyncrasies, and love of the old-fashioned are the hallmarks of his writings. Though he admits that Lamb's style borrows from earlier writers, Hazlitt stresses that Lamb's sentiments are his own. For Hazlitt's earlier assessment of Lamb, see excerpt above, 1818.*]

Mr. Lamb has raked among the dust and cobwebs of a . . . remote period, has exhibited specimens of curious relics, and pored over moth-eaten, decayed manuscripts for the benefit of the more inquisitive and discerning part of the public. Antiquity

*Watercolor portrait of Lamb by William Blake. The Bettmann Archive, Inc.*

after a time has the grace of novelty, as old fashions revived are mistaken for new ones; and a certain quaintness and singularity of style is an agreeable relief to the smooth and insipid monotony of modern composition.

Mr. Lamb has succeeded, not by conforming to the *Spirit of the Age,* but in opposition to it. He does not march boldly along with the crowd, but steals off the pavement to pick his way in the contrary direction. He prefers *bye-ways* to *highways.* When the full tide of human life pours along to some festive show, to some pageant of a day, Elia would stand on one side to look over an old book-stall, or stroll down some deserted pathway in search of a pensive description over a tottering doorway, or some quaint device in architecture, illustrative of embryo art and ancient manners. Mr. Lamb has the very soul of an antiquarian, as this implies a reflecting humanity; the film of the past hovers forever before him. He is shy, sensitive, the reverse of every thing coarse, vulgar, obtrusive, and *common-place.* He would fain 'shuffle off this mortal coil'; and his spirit clothes itself in the garb of elder time, homelier, but more durable. He is borne along with no pompous paradoxes, shines in no glittering tinsel of a fashionable phraseology, is neither fop nor sophist. He has none of the turbulence or froth of new-fangled opinions. His style runs pure and clear, though it may often take an underground course, or be conveyed through old-fashioned conduit-pipes. Mr. Lamb does not court popularity, nor strut in gaudy plumes, but shrinks from every kind of ostentatious and obvious pretension into the retirement of his own mind. (pp. 262-63)

This gentleman is not one of those who pay all their homage to the prevailing idol: he thinks that

New-born gauds are made and moulded of things past,

nor does he

Give to dust that is a little gilt
More laud than gilt o'er-dusted.

His convictions 'do not in broad rumour lie,' nor are they 'set off to the world in the glistering foil' of fashion, but 'live and breathe aloft in those pure eyes, and perfect judgment of all-seeing *time.*'

Mr. Lamb rather affects and is tenacious of the obscure and remote, of that which rests on its own intrinsic and silent merit; which scorns all alliance or even the suspicion of owing any thing to noisy clamour, to the glare of circumstances. There is a fine tone of *chiaroscuro,* a moral perspective in his writings. He delights to dwell on that which is fresh to the eye of memory; he yearns after and covets what soothes the frailty of human nature. That touches him most nearly which is withdrawn to a certain distance, which verges on the borders of oblivion: that piques and provokes his fancy most, which is hid from a superficial glance. That which, though gone by, is still remembered, is in his view more genuine, and has given more 'vital signs that it will live,' than a thing of yesterday, that may be forgotten to-morrow. Death has in this sense the spirit of life in it; and the shadowy has to our author something substantial in it. Ideas savour most of reality in his mind; or rather his imagination loiters on the edge of each, and a page of his writings recals to our fancy the *stranger* on the grate, fluttering in its dusky tenuity, with its idle superstition and hospitable welcome!

Mr. Lamb has a distaste to new faces, to new books, to new buildings, to new customs. He is shy of all imposing appearances, of all assumptions of self-importance, of all adventitious ornaments, of all mechanical advantages, even to a nervous excess. It is not merely that he does not rely upon, or ordinarily avail himself of them; he holds them in abhorrence; he utterly abjures and discards them and places a great gulph between him and them. He disdains all the vulgar artifices of authorship, all the cant of criticism and helps to notoriety. He has no grand swelling theories to attract the visionary and the enthusiast, no passing topics to allure the thoughtless and the vain. He evades the present; he mocks the future. His affections revert to, and settle on the past; but then even this must have something personal and local in it to interest him deeply and thoroughly. He pitches his tent in the suburbs of existing manners, brings down the account of character to the few straggling remains of the last generation, seldom ventures beyond the bills of mortality, and occupies that nice point between egotism and disinterested humanity. No one makes the tour of our southern metropolis, or describes the manners of the last age, so well as Mr. Lamb: with so fine and yet so formal an air: with such vivid obscurity: with such arch piquancy, such picturesque quaintness, such smiling pathos.

How admirably he has sketched the former inmates of the South-Sea House; what 'fine fretwork he makes of their double and single entries'! With what a firm, yet subtle pencil he has embodied **Mrs. Battle's Opinions on Whist!** How notably he embalms a battered *beau;* how delightfully an amour, that was cold forty years ago, revives in his pages! With what well-disguised humour he introduces us to his relations, and how freely he serves up his friends! Certainly, some of his portraits are *fixtures,* and will do to hang up as lasting and lively emblems of human infirmity. Then there is no one who has so sure an ear for 'the chimes at midnight,' not even excepting Mr. Justice Shallow; nor could Master Silence himself take his 'cheese and pippins' with a more significant and satisfactory air. With what a gusto Mr. Lamb describes the Inns and Courts of law, the Temple and Gray's-Inn, as if he had been a student there for the last two hundred years, and had been as well acquainted with the person of Sir Francis Bacon as he is with his portrait or writings! It is hard to say whether St. John's Gate is connected with more intense and authentic associations in his mind, as part of old London Wall, or as the frontispiece (time out of mind) of the *Gentleman's Magazine.* He haunts Watling-street like a gentle spirit; the avenues to the playhouses are thick with panting recollections; and Christ's-Hospital still breathes the balmy breath of infancy in his description of it! Whittington and his Cat are a fine hallucination for Mr. Lamb's historic Muse, and we believe he never heartily forgave a certain writer who took the subject of Guy Faux out of his hands. The streets of London are his fairy-land, teeming with wonder, with life and interest to his retrospective glance, as it did to the eager eye of childhood; he has contrived to weave its tritest traditions into a bright and endless romance!

Mr. Lamb's taste in books is also fine; and it is peculiar. It is not the worse for the little *idiosyncrasy.* He does not go deep into the Scotch Novels; but he is at home in Smollett or Fielding. He is little read in Junius or Gibbon; but no man can give a better account of Burton's *Anatomy of Melancholy,* or Sir Thomas Brown's *Urn-Burial,* or Fuller's *Worthies,* or John Bunyan's *Holy War.* No one is more unimpressible to a specious declamation; no one relishes a recondite beauty more. His admiration of Shakespear and Milton does not make him despise Pope; and he can read Parnell with patience and Gay with delight. His taste in French and German literature is somewhat defective; nor has he made much progress in the science of Political Economy or other abstruse studies, though he has read vast folios of controversial divinity, merely for the sake of the intricacy of style, and to save himself the pain of thinking.

Mr. Lamb is a good judge of prints and pictures. His admiration of Hogarth does credit to both, particularly when it is considered that Leonardo da Vinci is his next greatest favourite, and that his love of the *actual* does not proceed from a want of taste for the *ideal*. His worst fault is an over-eagerness of enthusiasm, which occasionally makes him take a surfeit of his highest favourites. Mr. Lamb excels in familiar conversation almost as much as in writing, when his modesty does not overpower his self-possession. He is as little of a proser as possible; but he *blurts* out the finest wit and sense in the world. He keeps a good deal in the background at first, till some excellent conceit pushes him forward, and then he abounds in whim and pleasantry. There is a primitive simplicity and self-denial about his manners and a Quakerism in his personal appearance, which is, however, relieved by a fine Titian head, full of dumb eloquence! (pp. 264-67)

The style of the *Essays of Elia* is liable to the charge of a certain *mannerism*. His sentences are cast in the mould of old authors; his expressions are borrowed from them; but his feelings and observations are genuine and original, taken from actual life or from his own breast; and he may be said (if any one can) 'to have coined his heart for *jests,*' and to have split his brain for fine distinctions! Mr. Lamb, from the peculiarity of his exterior and address as an author, would probably never have made his way by detached and independent efforts; but, fortunately for himself and others, he has taken advantage of the Periodical Press, where he has been stuck into notice; and the texture of his compositions is assuredly fine enough to bear the broadest glare of popularity that has hitherto shone upon them. (p. 268)

> William Hazlitt, "*Elia—Geoffrey Crayon,*" in his The Spirit of the Age; or, Contemporary Portraits, 1825. Reprint by Oxford University Press, 1947, pp. 262-71.

## [HENRY NELSON COLERIDGE]  (essay date 1835)

[*The nephew of Lamb's lifelong friend Samuel Taylor Coleridge, Henry Coleridge focuses here on Lamb's contributions as a literary critic. He defends Lamb from the charge that his style was affected and praises his originality and sense of humor. According to Coleridge, Lamb is important as a critic because he renewed popular interest in Elizabethan dramatists. Other critics who favorably assess Lamb's criticism include Algernon Charles Swinburne (1885), E.M.W. Tillyard (1923), Arnold Henderson (1968), George Watson (1973), and Joan Coldwell (1978).*]

Charles Lamb was not the greatest, nor equal to the greatest, among his famous contemporaries, either in splendour or in depth; but he was, perhaps, the most singular and individual. He was one of nature's curiosities, and amongst her richest and rarest. Other men act by their faculties, and you can easily distinguish the predominance of one faculty over another: A.'s genius is greater than his talent, though that is considerable; B.'s talent is beyond his genius, though that be respectable;— we dissect the author, take so much of him as we like, and throw the rest away. But you could not so deal with Lamb. He was all-compact—inner and outer man in perfect fusion,— all the powers of the mind,—the sensations of the body, interpenetrating each other. His genius was talent, and his talent genius; his imagination and fancy one and indivisible; the finest

scalpel of the metaphysician could not have separated them. His poems, his criticisms, his essays,—call them his *Elias,* to distinguish them from anything else in the world,—these were not merely written *by* Lamb,—they *were* and *are* Lamb,—just the gentle, fantastic, subtle creature himself printed off. In a library of a thousand volumes you shall not find two that will give you such a bright and living impress of the author's own very soul. Austin's, Rousseau's,—all the Confessions on record, are false and hollow in comparison. There he is, as he was, the working or the superannuated clerk,—very grave and very wild,—tender and fierce at a flash,—learned enough, and more so than you thought,—yet ignorant, may be, of school-boy points, and glorious in his ignorance,—seeming to halt behind all, and then with one fling overleaping the most approved doctor of the room; witty and humorous. But Lamb's wit requires a word or two of analysis for itself. Wit is not humour, nor is humour wit. Punning is neither, and the grotesque is a fourth power, different from all. Lamb had all these, not separately each as such, but massed together into the strangest intellectual compound ever seen in man. And even besides these he had an indefinable something,—a *Lambism,*—about him, which defied naming or description. He stammered,— the stammer went for something in producing the effect; he would adjure a small piece for the nonce,—it gave weight;— perhaps he drank a glass of punch; believe us, it all told. It follows that Lamb's good things cannot be repeated. (pp. 58-9)

[Lamb's readers are sometimes] struck with a certain air and trick of the antique phrase, unlike anything in the style of any contemporary writer. This manner has been called affected; many think it forced, quaint, unnatural. They suppose it all done *on purpose*. Now nothing can be farther from the fact. That the cast of language distinguishing almost all Lamb's works is not the style of the present day is very true; but it was *his* style nevertheless. It is altogether a curious matter, one strongly illustrating the assimilative power of genius—that a man, very humbly born, humbly educated, and from boyhood till past middle life nailed, as a clerk, to a desk in the South Sea or India Houses, should so perfectly appropriate to himself, to the expression of his own most intimate emotions and thoughts, the tone and turn of phrase of the writers, pre-eminently the dramatic writers, of the times of James and Charles I. Their style was as natural to him as the air he breathed. It was a part of his intellect; it entered into and modified his views of all things—it was the necessary dialect of his genius. (pp. 62-3)

In his dedication of the two volumes of his works published in 1818, Lamb speaks of his having 'dwindled' into criticism. It was doing himself very great injustice. Nor is it enough to say, that the various critical essays contained in his works are beautiful in themselves—they are little text-books of sound principles in the judgment of works of literature and general art; equally profound, discriminating, and original. It is to these essays, and his judicious selection of *Specimens* . . . that we are pre-eminently indebted for the exhuming of the old dramatic writers of the Shaksperian age, and the restoration of the worthiest of them at least to their most deserved station in our literature. (p. 64)

Lamb's criticism partook largely of the spirit of Coleridge— not, indeed, troubling itself with any special psychological definitions, nor caring to reconcile all the varying appearances upon some common ground of moral or intellectual action— the everlasting struggle and devotion of Coleridge's mind— but entering, with a most learned spirit of human dealing, into the dramatic being of the characters of the play, and bringing out, with an incomparable delicacy and accuracy of touch, their places of contact and mutual repulsion. The true point of view Lamb always seized with unerring precision—a high praise for a critic of any sort—and this led him, with equal success, to detect the real centre, whether a character or an event, round which the orb of the drama revolved. Hence he was one of the most original of critics, and threw more and newer light upon the genuine meaning of some of the great masterpieces of the theatre than any other man; and yet we do not remember a single instance in which any of his positions have been gainsaid. Like all critics who have a real insight into their subject, Lamb helps you, in a few words, to a principle—a master-key—by which you may work out the details of the investigation yourself. You are not merely amused with a brilliant description of a character or passage, but become a discerning judge in the light of your own perceptions and convictions. (p. 65)

[The practical excellence of Lamb's essay **"On the Artificial Comedy of the Last Century"**] is such, that, when you have once read it, you are inclined to wonder how you could ever have methodized your feelings and taste upon the subject without the light which it has imparted. It sets you right at once and for ever. One consequence of its pregnant brevity was that a swarm of imitators fastened upon it, sullying its purity and caricaturing its manner,—writers who added nothing to what Lamb had shortly yet adequately done, but who materially injured his fame by being vulgarly associated with him; and whose showy, disproportioned, rhapsodical essays upon Shakspeare and the contemporary dramatists, disgusted all persons of sound judgment, and went very far to bury again under a prejudice what their discriminating leader had but newly recovered from oblivion. We have been more earnest in bringing forward, in the prominent light which they deserve, Lamb's merits as a critic and restorer of much of our most valuable old literature, not only to vindicate them from a derogatory association, but because they have been greatly overlooked in the more general popularity which attended and will, we predict, constantly attend the miscellaneous essays of Elia. From the same cause, and in more than an equal degree, his poetry, exquisite as much of it is, is really almost entirely forgotten; in fact, *nocuit sibi*,—just as the transcendant popularity of Waverley, Guy Mannering, and Old Mortality made the world almost lose sight for a time of the splendid chivalry, the minstrel ease, the *Homeric* liveliness of the Lady of the Lake, the Lay, and of Marmion. Lamb's poems are comparatively few in number and inconsiderable in length; but in our deliberate judgment there are amongst them some pieces as near perfection in their kinds as anything in our literature,—specimens of exceeding artifice and felicity in rhythm, metre, and diction. His poetic vein was, we think, scanty, and perhaps he exhausted it; he was not what is called *great,* yet he was, if we may make such a distinction, eminent. He has a small, well-situated parterre on Parnassus, belonging exclusively to himself. He is not amongst the highest, but then he is alone and aloof from all others. (pp. 68-9)

Lamb excelled in drawing what he himself delighted in contemplating—and indeed partly in *being*—a veritable Ben Jonsonian Humor. The extreme delicacy of his touch in such sketches is particularly admirable; he very seldom, indeed, slips into caricature; it is rather by bringing out the otherwise evanescent lines of the character than by charging the strong ones, that he contrives to present such beautifully quaint excerpts from the common mass of humanity. His **'Captain Jackson,'** in [**The Last Essays of Elia**], is a masterpiece; you have no sense or

suspicion of any exaggeration; the touches are so slight in themselves, and each laid on so quietly and unconcernedly, that you are scarcely conscious, as you go on, how the result is growing upon you. Just before you come to the end of the essay, the entire creation stands up alive before you—true in every trick to the life, the life of the Fancy. You may not have met exactly such a personage in society, but you see no reason why you should not meet him. You cannot doubt Lamb's own intimate acquaintance with him. Indeed, you perceive he was a relation. Poor Elliston was another of Elia's happiest subjects. Elliston was of the true blood of the *humorous,* and Lamb has him in enamel, alive and dead. (p. 74)

Many of Lamb's best essays were worked up from letters written by him to his friends. **'The Superannuated Man'** was a letter, if we mistake not, to Mr. Wordsworth. **'The Two Races of Men,'** the **'Dissertation on Roast Pig,'** and one or two others, were letters. Sometimes he bettered the original thought—sometimes a little overlaid it (as in the essay on Munden's acting)—and sometimes his letters, not otherwise used by him, are as good as his printed efforts. (p. 77)

[Henry Nelson Coleridge], in a review of "The Last Essays of Elia," in The Quarterly Review, Vol. LIV, No. CVII, July, 1835, pp. 58-77.

## WILLIAM WORDSWORTH   (poem date 1835)

[*An English poet and critic, Wordsworth was central to English Romanticism. Wordsworth's literary criticism reflects his belief that neither the language nor the content of poetry should be stylized or elaborate and that the value of a poet was to feel and express the relation between man and nature. A friend and frequent correspondent of Lamb, Wordsworth composed this poem shortly after Lamb's death. It was originally published in 1835.*]

To a good Man of most dear memory
This Stone is sacred. Here he lies apart
From the great city where he first drew breath,
Was reared and taught; and humbly earned his bread,
To the strict labours of the merchant's desk
By duty chained. Not seldom did those tasks
Tease, and the thought of time so spent depress,
His spirit, but the recompence was high;
Firm Independence, Bounty's rightful sire;
Affections, warm as sunshine, free as air;
And when the precious hours of leisure came,
Knowledge and wisdom, gained from converse sweet
With books, or while he ranged the crowded streets
With a keen eye, and overflowing heart:
So genius triumphed over seeming wrong,
And poured out truth in works by thoughtful love
Inspired—works potent over smiles and tears.
And as round mountain-tops the lightning plays,
Thus innocently sported, breaking forth
As from a cloud of some grave sympathy,
Humour and wild instinctive wit, and all
The vivid flashes of his spoken words.
From the most gentle creature nursed in fields
Had been derived the name he bore—a name,
Wherever Christian altars have been raised,
Hallowed to meekness and to innocence;
And if in him meekness at times gave way,
Provoked out of herself by troubles strange,
Many and strange, that hung about his life;
Still, at the centre of his being, lodged
A soul by resignation sanctified:

And if too often, self-reproached, he felt
That innocence belongs not to our kind,
A power that never ceased to abide in him,
Charity, 'mid the multitude of sins
That she can cover, left not his exposed
To an unforgiving judgment from just Heaven.
O, he was good, if e'er a good Man lived!

(pp. 272-73)

*William Wordsworth, "Epitaphs and Elegiac Pieces: Written After the Death of Charles Lamb," in his* The Poetical Works of William Wordsworth, *edited by E. de Selincourt and Helen Darbishire, Oxford at the Clarendon Press, Oxford, 1947, pp. 272-76.*

## HENRY T. TUCKERMAN  (essay date 1836)

*[In this appreciation of Lamb's "Elia" essays, Tuckerman extolls Lamb's sincerity and the spontaneity and freshness of his prose style. Tuckerman regards Lamb's writings on drama as informed by his "deeply felt [recognition of] its importance to modern society." The qualities which Tuckerman relishes most in Lamb's essays are their intimate tone, attention to detail, and ability to render the ordinary interesting. This article was originally published in the* American Quarterly Review *in March, 1836.]*

[The writings of Lamb] are obviously the offspring of thoughtful leisure; they are redolent of the *otium;* and in this consists their peculiar charm. We are disposed to value this characteristic highly, at a time which abounds, as does our age, with a profusion of forced and elaborate writings. It is truly delightful to encounter a work, however limited in design and unpretending in execution, which revives the legitimate idea of literature,—which makes us feel that it is as essentially *spontaneous* as the process of vegetation, and is only true to its source and its object, when instinct with freshness and freedom. No mind, restlessly urged by a morbid appetite for literary fame, or disciplined to a mechanical development of thought, could have originated the attractive essays we are considering. They indicate quite a different parentage. A lovely spirit of contentment, a steadfast determination towards a generous culture of the soul, breathes through these mental emanations. Imaginative enjoyment,—the boon with which the Creator has permitted man to meliorate the trying circumstances of his lot, is evidently the great recreation of the author, and to this he would introduce his readers. (p. 653)

Much of the interest awakened by [The *Essays of Elia*] has been ascribed to the peculiar phraseology in which they are couched. Doubtless, this characteristic has had its influence; but we think an undue importance has been given it, and we feel that the true zest of Elia's manner is as spontaneous as his ideas, and the shape in which they naturally present themselves. If we analyse his mode of expression, we shall find its charm consists not a little in the expert variation rather than in a constant maintenance of style. He understood the proper time and place to introduce an illustration; he knew when to serve up one of his unequalled strokes of humor, and when to change the speculative for the descriptive mood. He had a happy way of blending anecdote and portraiture; he makes us see the place, person, or thing, upon which he is dwelling; and, at the moment our interest is excited, presents an incident, and then, while we are all attention, imparts a moral, or lures us into a theorising vein. He personifies his subject, too, at the appropriate moment; nor idealises, after the manner of many essayists, before the reader sympathises at all with the real picture. Lamb's diction breathes the spirit of his favorite school. He need not

have told us of his partiality for the old English writers. Every page of Elia bears witness to his frequent and fond communion with the rich ancient models of British literature. Yet the coincidence is, in no degree, that which obtains between an original and a copyist. The tinge which Lamb's language has caught from intimacy with the quaint folios he so sincerely admired, is a reflected hue, like that which suffuses the arch of clouds far above the setting sun; denoting only the delightful influence radiated upon the mind which loves to dwell devotedly upon what is disappearing, and turns with a kind or religious interest from the new-born luminaries which the multitude worship, to hover devotedly round the shrine of the past. If any modern lover of letters deserved a heritage in the sacred garden of old English literature, that one was Charles Lamb. Not only did he possess the right which faithful husbandry yields, but his disposition and taste rendered him a companion meet for the noble spirits that have immortalised the age of Elizabeth. In truth, he may be said to have been on more familiar terms with Shakspeare, than with the most intimate of his contemporaries; and it may be questioned whether the Religio Medici, that truly individual creed, had a more devout admirer in its originator, than was Elia. He assures us that he was "shy of facing the prospective," and no antiquarian cherished a deeper reverence for old china, or the black letter. Most honestly, therefore, came our author by that charming relish of olden time, which sometimes induces in our minds, as we read his lucubrations, a lurking doubt whether, by some mischance, we have not fallen upon an old author in a modern dress.

There is another feature in the style of these essays, to which we are disposed to assign no inconsiderable influence. We allude to a certain confessional tone, that is peculiarly attractive. There is something exceedingly gratifying to the generality of readers in personalities. On the same principle that we are well pleased to become the *confidant* of a friend, and open our breasts to receive the secret of his inmost experience, we readily become interested in a writer who tells us, in a candid, *naïve* manner, the story not merely of his life, in the common acceptation of the term, but of his private opinions, humors, eccentric tastes, and personal antipathies. A tone of this kind, is remarkably characteristic of Lamb. And yet there is in it nothing egotistical; for we may say of him as has been said of his illustrious schoolfellow, whom he so significantly, and, as it were, prophetically, called "the inspired charity boy;"—that "in him the individual is always merged in the abstract and general." Writers have not been slow to avail themselves of the advantage of thus occasionally and incidentally presenting glimpes of their private notions and sentiments; indeed, this has been called the age of confessions; but with Elia, they are so delicately and yet so familiarly imparted, that they become a secret charm inwrought through the whole tissue of what he denominates his "weaved up follies." There are passages scattered through this volume, which exemplify the very perfection of our language. There are successive periods, so adroitly adapted to the sentiment they embody, so easy and expressive, and, at the same time, so unembellished, that they suggest a new idea of the capabilities of our vernacular. There are words, too, at which we should pause, if they were indited by another, to institute a grave inquiry into their legitimacy, or, perchance, prefer against their author the charge of senseless affectation. But with what we know of Elia, in catching ourselves at such a process, we could not but waive the ceremony, and say of it as he said on some equally heartless occasion—"it argues an insensibility."

Another striking trait of the *Essays of Elia*, is the familiarity of their style. In this respect they frequently combine the freedom of oral with the more deliberative spirit of epistolary expression. We have already alluded to one effect of this method of address; it annihilates the distance between the reader and author, and, so to speak, brings them face to face. Facility in this kind of writing, is one of the principal elements in what is called magazine talent. It consists in maintaining a conversational tone while discussing a topic of great interest in a humorous way, or making a light one the nucleus for spirited, amusing, or instructive ideas. (pp. 654-55)

Lamb is not singular in his attachment to minutiae; it is characteristic of the literature of the day. In former times, writers dealt in the general; now they are devoted to the particular. In almost every book of travels and work of fiction, we are entertained, or rather the attempt is made to entertain us, with exceedingly detailed descriptions of the features of a landscape, the grouping in a picture, or the several parts of a fashionable dress. By such wearisome nomenclature, it is expected that an adequate conception will be imparted, when, in many cases, a single phrase, revealing the *impression* made by these objects, would convey more than a hundred such inventories. Lamb, by virtue of his nice perception, renders details more effective than we should imagine was practicable. In a single line, we have the peculiarities of a person presented; and by a brief mention of the gait, demeanor, or perhaps a single habit, the ceremony of introduction is over; we not only stand and look in the direction we are desired, but we *see* the object, be it an old bencher, or a grinning chimney sweep; an ancient courtyard, or a quaker meeting; a roast pig, or an old actor; Captain Jackson, or a poor wretch in the pillory, consoling himself by fanciful soliloquies. We have compared essays, in their general uses, to a set of cabinet pictures. Elias' are peculiarly susceptible of the illustration. They are the more valuable, inasmuch as something of the mellow hue of old paintings broods over them; here and there a touch of beautiful sadness, that reminds us of Raphael; now a line of penciling, overflowing with nature, which brings some favorite Flemish scene to mind; and again, a certain softness and delicate finish that whisper of Claude Lorraine.

There are two points in which Charles Lamb was eminent, where tolerable success is rare; these are pathos and humor. He understood how to deal with the sense of the humorous and pathetic. He seems to have been intuitively learned in the secret and delicate nature of these attributes of the mind; or rather, it would appear that his own nature, in these respects, furnished a happy criterion by which to address the same feelings in others. We cannot analyse, however casually, the humor and pathos of Elia, without perceiving that they are based on a discerning, and, if the expression may be allowed, a sentimental fellow-feeling for his kind. So ready and true was this feeling, that we find him entering, with the greatest facility, into the experience of human beings whom the mass of society scarcely recognise as such. He talks about a little chimney sweep, an aged mendicant, or an old actor, as if he had, in his own person, given proof of the doctrine to which his ancient friend, Sir Thomas Browne, inclined, and actually, by a kind of metempsychosis, experienced these several conditions of life. His pathos and humor are, for the most part, descriptive; he appeals to us, in an artist-like and dramatic way, by pictures; we are not wearied with any preparatory and worked up process; we are not led to anticipate the effect. But our associations are skilfully awakened; an impression is unostentatiously conveyed, and a smile or tear first leads us to inquire into the nature of the spell. It is as though, in riding along a sequestered road, we should suddenly pass a beautiful avenue, and catch

a glimpse of a garden, a statue, an old castle, or some object far down its green vista, so interesting that a reminiscence, an anticipation, or, perchance, a speculative reverie, is thereby at once awakened. Endeavors to touch the feelings or excite quiet mirth fail, generally, because the design is too obvious, or a strain of exaggeration is indulged in, fatal to the end in view. Frequently, too, the call upon our mirthful or compassionate propensities is too direct and strong. These feelings are not seldom appealed to, as if they were *passions,* and to be excited by passionate means. Indignation, enthusiasm, and all powerful impulses, are doubtless to be roused by fervent appeals; but readers are best *allured* into a laugh, and it is by gentle encroachments upon its empire, that the heart is best moved to sympathy. In drawing his pictures, Lamb indulged not in caricature. It is his truth, not less than his quaintness and minute touches, that entertains and affects us. He avoids, too, the vulgar modes of illustration. Not by descriptions of physiognomy or costume, does he excite our risible tendencies, nor thinks he to win our pity by over-drawn statements of the insignia and privations of poverty. Elia is no poor metaphysician. He comprehends the delicacy of touch required in the limner who would impressively delineate, even in a quaint style, any element or form of humanity. By what would almost seem a casual suggestion, we often have a conception imparted worth scores of wire-drawn exemplifications. (p. 656)

The drama was a rich source of pleasure and reflection to Lamb. During a life passed almost wholly in the metropolis, the theatre afforded him constant recreation, and the species of excitement his peculiar genius required. It was to him an important element in the imaginative being he cherished. By means of it, he continually renewed and brightened the rich vein of sentiment inherent in his nature. To him it addressed language rife with the meaning which characterised its ancient voice,—full of suggestive and impressive eloquence. Deeply versed in the whole range of dramatic literature, master of the philosophy of Shakspeare, and overflowing with a highly cultivated taste for the dramatic art, the drama was ranked by Elia among the redeeming things of life. He did not coldly recognise, but deeply felt, its importance to modern society. (p. 657)

Notwithstanding his partiality for theatrical representations, few play-goers entertained a more just idea of their frequent and necessary inadequateness. He recognised the limits of the dramatic art. He realised, beyond the generality of Shakspeare's admirers, the impossibility of presenting, by the most successful performance, our deepest conception of his characters. He knew that the wand of that enchanter dealt with things too deep, not only for speech, but for expression. He was impatient at the common interpretation of Shakspeare's mind. In the stillness of his retired study, the creations of the bard appeared to him, as in an exalted dream. In the attentive perusal of his plays,—the delicate touches, the finer shades, the undercurrent of philosophy, were revealed to the mind of Lamb with an impressiveness, of which personification is unsusceptible; and few of his essays are more worthy of his genius than that which embodies his views on this subject. It should be attentively read by all who habitually honor the minstrel of Avon, without being perfectly aware why the honor is due. It will lead such to new investigations into the mysteries of that wonderful tragic lore, upon which the most gifted men have been proud to offer one useful comment, or advance a single illustrative hint. . . .

One of Lamb's most winning traits is his sincerity. The attractiveness of this beautiful virtue, even in literature, is worthy

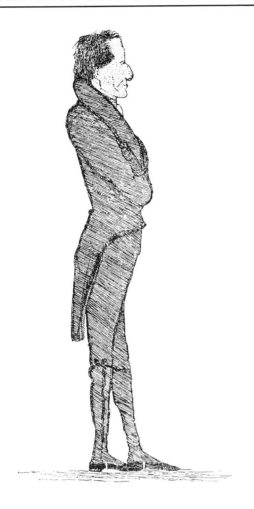

*A caricature of Lamb at age fifty.*

of observation. It seems to be an ordination of the intellectual world, and a blessed one it is to those who cherish faith in a spiritual philosophy—that truth of expression shall alone prove powerfully and permanently effective. . . .

Lamb endeavored not to express what he did not feel; he wrote not from necessity or policy, but from enthusiasm, from his own gentle, sweet, yet deep enthusiasm. He had a feeling for the art of writing, and therefore he would not make it the hackneyed conventional agent it too often is; but ever regarded it is a crystalline mould wherein he could faithfully present the form, hues, and very spirit of his sentiments and speculations. (p. 658)

There is a unity of design in the essays of Elia. Disconnected and fugitive as we should deem them at first sight, an attentive perusal reveals, if not a complete theory, yet a definite and pervading spirit which is not devoid of philosophy. After being amused by Lamb's humor, interested by his quaintness, and fascinated by his style, there yet remains a more deep impression upon our minds. We feel that he had a specific object as an essayist; or, at least, that the ideas he suggests tend to a particular resuit. What, then, was his aim? As an author, what mission does he fulfil? We think Charles Lamb is to life, what Wordsworth is to nature. The latter points out the field flowers, and the meadow rill, the soul's most primal and simple movements, the mind's most single and unsophisticated tendencies;

the former indicates the lesser, and scarcely noticed sources of pleasure and annoyance, mirth and reflection, which occur in the beaten track of ordinary life. . . . He seems to have broke away from the bondage of custom and to have seen all things new. One would think, to note the freshness of his perceptions in regard to the most familiar objects of London, that in manhood he was for the first time initiated into city life—that he was a newcomer in the world at an advanced age. . . .

We never rise from one of his essays without a feeling of contentment. He leads our thoughts to the actual available spring of enjoyment. He reconciles us to ourselves; causing home-pleasures, and the charms of the wayside, and the mere comforts of existence, to emerge from the shadow into which our indifference has cast them, into the light of fond recognition. The flat dull surface of common life, he causes to rise into beautiful *basso-relievo*. In truth, there are few better teachers of gratitude than Lamb. He rejuvenates our worn and weary feelings, revives the dim flame of our enthusiasm, opens our eyes to actual and present good, with his humorous accents, and unpretending manner, reads us a homily on the folly of desponding, and the wisdom of appreciating the cluster of minor joys which surround and may be made continually to cheer our being. (p. 659)

*Henry T. Tuckerman, ''Characteristics of Lamb,'' in* The Southern Literary Messenger, *Vol. VI, No. 9, September, 1840, pp. 652-60.*

**[THOMAS DE QUINCEY] (essay date 1848)**

[*An English critic and essayist, De Quincey used his own life as the subject of his best-known work,* Confessions of an English Opium Eater, *in which he chronicled his addiction to opium. De Quincey contributed reviews to a number of London journals and earned a reputation as an insightful if occasionally long-winded literary critic. At the time of De Quincey's death, his critical expertise was underestimated, though his prose talent had long been acknowledged. In the twentieth century, some critics still disdain the digressive qualities of De Quincey's writing, yet others find that his essays display an acute psychological awareness. Discussing the shortcomings of Lamb's prose, De Quincey posits that Lamb avoided ''sustained'' and ''elaborate'' narrative in favor of stylistic simplicity because he ''had no sense of the rhythmical in prose composition.'' For De Quincey's later assessment of Lamb, see excerpt below, 1851.*]

[Lamb], by native tendency, shrank from the continuous, from the sustained, from the elaborate.

The elaborate, indeed, without which much truth and beauty must perish in germ, was by name the object of his invectives. The instances are many in his own beautiful essays where he literally collapses, literally sinks away from openings suddenly offering themselves to flights of pathos or solemnity in direct prosecution of his own theme. On any such summons, where an ascending impulse, and an untired pinion were required, he *refuses* himself (to use military language) invariably. The least observing reader of *Elia* cannot have failed to notice that the most felicitous passages always accomplish their circuit in a few sentences. The gyration within which his sentiment wheels, no matter of what kind it may be, is always the shortest possible. It does not prolong itself, and it does not repeat itself. But in fact, other features in Lamb's mind would have argued this feature by analogy, had we by accident been left unaware of it directly. It is not by chance, or without a deep ground in his nature *common* to all his qualities, both affirmative and negative, that Lamb had an insensibility to music more absolute

395

than can have been often shared by any human creature, or perhaps than was ever before acknowledged so candidly. The sense of music, as a pleasurable sense, or as any sense at all other than of certain unmeaning and impertinent differences in respect to high and low—sharp or flat—was utterly obliterated as with a sponge by nature herself from Lamb's organization. It was a corollary from the same large *substratum* in his nature, that Lamb had no sense of the rhythmical in prose composition. Rhythmus, or pomp of cadence, or sonorous ascent of clauses, in the structure of sentences, were effects of art as much thrown away upon *him* as the voice of the charmer upon the deaf adder. We ourselves, occupying the very station of polar opposition to that of Lamb, being as morbidly, perhaps, in the one excess as he in the other, naturally detected this omission in Lamb's nature at an early stage of our acquaintance. Not the fabled Regulus, with his eyelids torn away, and his uncurtained eyeballs exposed to the noontide glare of a Carthaginian sun, could have shrieked with more anguish of recoil from torture than we from certain sentences and periods in which Lamb perceived no fault at all. *Pomp*, in our apprehension, was an idea of two categories; the *pompous* might be spurious, but it might also be genuine. It is well to love the simple: *we* love it; nor is there any opposition at all between *that* and the very glory of pomp. But, as we once put the case to Lamb, if as a musician, as the leader of a mighty orchestra, you had this theme offered to you—"Belshazzar the king gave a great feast to a thousand of his lords"—or this, "And on a certain day, Marcus Cicero stood up, and in a set speech rendered solemn thanks to Caius Caesar for Quintus Ligarius pardoned, and for Marcus Marcellus restored,"—Surely no man would deny that, in such a case, simplicity, though in a passive sense not lawfully absent, must stand aside as totally insufficient for the *positive* part. Simplicity might guide, even here, but could not furnish the power; a rudder it might be, but not an oar or a sail. This, Lamb was ready to allow; as an intellectual *quiddity*, he recognised pomp in the character of a privileged thing; he was obliged to do so; for take away from great ceremonial festivals, such as the solemn rendering of thanks, the celebration of national anniversaries, the commemoration of public benefactors, &c., the element of pomp, and you take away their very meaning and life; but, whilst allowing a place for it in the rubric of the logician, it is certain that, *sensuously*, Lamb would not have sympathized with it, nor have *felt* its justification in any concrete instance. (pp. 194-95)

[*Thomas De Quincey*], "*Charles Lamb and His Friends,*" in The North British Review, *Vol. X, No. XIX, November, 1848, pp. 179-214.*

## THOMAS DE QUINCEY   (essay date 1851)

*[In this brief analysis of Lamb's "Elia" essays, De Quincey predicts that Lamb's works will remain "for ever unpopular, and yet for ever interesting." Praising Lamb's originality and mixture of seriousness and whimsy, De Quincey also stresses the crucial role of personality in the essays. For De Quincey's earlier assessment of Lamb, see excerpt above, 1848.]*

[Charles Lamb] ranks amongst writers whose works are destined to be for ever unpopular, and yet for ever interesting; interesting, moreover, by means of those very qualities which guarantee their non-popularity. The same qualities which will be found forbidding to the worldly and the thoughtless, which will be found insipid to many even amongst robust and powerful minds, are exactly those which will continue to command a select audience in every generation. The prose essays, under

the signature of *Elia*, form the most delightful section amongst Lamb's works. They traverse a peculiar field of observation, sequestered from general interest; and they are composed in a spirit too delicate and unobtrusive to catch the ear of the noisy crowd, clamoring for strong sensations. But this retiring delicacy itself, the pensiveness chequered by gleams of the fanciful, and the humor that is touched with cross-lights of pathos, together with the picturesque quaintness of the objects casually described, whether men, or things, or usages, and, in the rear of all this, the constant recurrence to ancient recollections and to decaying forms of household life, as things retiring before the tumult of new and revolutionary generations; these traits in combination communicate to the papers a grace and strength of originality which nothing in any literature approaches, whether for degree or kind of excellence, except the most felicitous papers of Addison, such as those on Sir Roger de Coverley, and some others in the same vein of composition. (pp. 168-69)

Everywhere, indeed, in the writings of Lamb, and not merely in his *Elia*, the character of the writer coöperates in an undercurrent to the effect of the thing written. To understand in the fullest sense either the gayety or the tenderness of a particular passage, you must have some insight into the peculiar bias of the writer's mind, whether native and original, or impressed gradually by the accidents of situation; whether simply developed out of predispositions by the action of life, or violently scorched into the constitution by some fierce fever of calamity. There is in modern literature a whole class of writers, though not a large one, standing within the same category; some marked originality of character in the writer becomes a coëfficient with what he says to a common result; you must sympathize with this *personality* in the author before you can appreciate the most significant parts of his views. (pp. 169-70)

To appreciate Lamb, therefore, it is requisite that his character and temperament should be understood in their coyest and most wayward features. A capital defect it would be if these could not be gathered silently from Lamb's works themselves. It would be a fatal mode of dependency upon an alien and separable accident if they needed an external commentary. But they do *not*. The syllables lurk up and down the writings of Lamb which decipher his eccentric nature. His character lies there dispersed in anagram; and to any attentive reader the regathering and restoration of the total word from its scattered parts is inevitable without an effort. (pp. 171-72)

*Thomas De Quincey, "Charles Lamb," in his* Biographical Essays, *1851. Reprint by Ticknor and Fields, 1861, pp. 167-226.*

## [SIR EDWARD BULWER-LYTTON]   (essay date 1867)

*[An English novelist, dramatist, poet, and essayist, Bulwer was one of the most versatile and popular writers of the nineteenth century. Though his works are rarely read today, his success once rivaled that of Charles Dickens and his novels were considered the epitome of fashionable style. Bulwer singles out charm as a main characteristic of Lamb's technique, but also stresses his naturalness and humor. Maintaining that Lamb's reputation rests on the "Elia" essays, Bulwer discusses their general merits and compares Lamb's sense of verbal balance in prose to Horace's sense of balance in verse.]*

Lamb is one of those rare favourites of the Graces on whom the gift of *charm* is bestowed. . . . (p. 17)

He is not without something of charm, even in those compositions in which his genius appears to the least advantage. As a Drama, 'John Woodvill' has almost every defect that a Drama can have, and it is only in very rare passages that some happiness of expression or grace of versification atones for the general tameness of the language and the dissonance of the rhythm—yet still the work leaves a pleasing impression. We are not moved by the action of the play, but we are contented to enjoy in repose and calm the contemplation of that amiable mind which reflects itself in the current that quietly flows before us. 'Rosamond Gray' is a story which in ruder hands would have been disagreeable and painful, and, brief as it is, while aiming at the simplest form of narrative, it wants the truthfulness of incident essential to genuine simplicity. . . . Lamb's special genius was as little adapted to romantic narrative as it was to dramatic character and passion. Yet, with all its faults, 'Rosamond Gray' has an attraction which many a good novelist might envy, because there is in it that nameless sweetness of sentiment which constitutes the master-spell of the author.

But neither in these departments of literature nor in those minor poems—which are rather evidences of an exquisite poetic sensibility than achievements of poetic power—did the true genius of Charles Lamb find its natural scope. It is not on these that he rests the enduring reputation of 'Elia.' Happily for us and for him, he found in the pages of a Magazine precisely the field best suited to exercise, without overstraining, the faculties in which he excelled. As an Essayist, following the bent of his own mind—stamping on all that he wrote the vivid impression of his own rare individuality—he gave to the varieties of mankind a new character and left to his language a new style. As the character given was his own, so the style bequeathed was, with all its mannerism, perfectly natural to the man. It was no style invented and built up for a literary purpose. We have only to read his delightful correspondence to see that the quaint diction of 'Elia' was that in which he habitually expressed himself in familiar commune with his friends. Hence, artificial though it seem at the first glance, he is much more at his ease in it than when he writes in a style more natural to other men. In the last he forfeits originality, and gains nothing to compensate in exchange. The brevity to which he was compelled by the limited space that a Magazine allots to a contributor was favourable to Lamb's peculiar genius. It compelled him to concentrate his thoughts, and out of that concentration comes the pause of reflection which is propitious to felicity in wording; so that his essays are really marvellous for terseness of treatment and nicety of expression. 'Elia' is never verbose, yet never incomplete. You are not wearied because he says too much, nor dissatisfied because he says too little. In this inimitable sense of proportion, this fitness of adjustment between thought and expression, the prose of 'Elia' reminds us of the verse of Horace. Nor is the Essayist without some other resemblance to the Poet: in the amenity which accompanies his satire; in his sportive view of things grave; the grave morality he deduces from things sportive; his equal sympathy for rural and for town life; his constant good fellowship and his lenient philosophy. Here, indeed, all similitude ceases: the modern essayist advances no pretension to the ancient poet's wide survey of the social varieties of mankind; to his seizure of those large and catholic types of human nature which are familiarly recognizable in every polished community, every civilized time; still less to that intense sympathy in the life and movement of the world around him which renders the utterance of his individual emotion the vivid illustration of the character and history of his age. Yet 'Elia' secures a charm of his own in the very narrowness of the range to which he limits his genius. For thus the interest he creates becomes more intimate and household.

Humour in itself is among the most popular gifts of genius; amiable humour among the most lovable. The humour of Charles Lamb is at once pure and genial; it has no malice in its smile. His keenest sarcasm is but his archest pleasantry. It is not of the very highest order, because the highest order necessitates the creation of characters self-developed in the action of romance or drama. Lamb is not Cervantes nor Molière. . . . Yet if it be not of the highest order, its delicacy places it among the rarest. A proverb has been defined to be the wisdom of many in the wit of one. There is much in the humour of Charles Lamb, and the terseness of style into which its riches are compressed, that would merit this definition of a proverb. As Scott's humour is that of a novelist, and therefore objective, so Lamb's is that of an essayist, and eminently subjective. All that he knows or observes in the world of books or men becomes absorbed in the single life of his own mind, and is reproduced as part and parcel of Charles Lamb. If thus he does not create imaginary characters . . . , he calls up, completes, and leaves to the admiration of all time a character which, as a personification of humour, is a higher being than even Scott has imagined, viz., that of Charles Lamb himself. Nor is there in the whole world of humorous creation an image more beautiful in its combinations of mirth and pathos. (pp. 17-20)

> [Sir Edward Bulwer-Lytton], "Charles Lamb and Some of His Companions," in The Quarterly Review, Vol. CII, No. CCXLIII, January, 1867, pp. 1-29.

### WALTER H. PATER  (essay date 1878)

[A nineteenth-century essayist, novelist, and critic, Pater is regarded as one of the most famous proponents of aestheticism in English literature. Distinguished as the first major English writer to formulate an explicitly aesthetic philosophy of life, he advocated the "love of art for art's sake" as life's greatest offering, a belief which he exemplified in his influential Studies in the History of the Renaissance and elucidated in his novel Marius the Epicurean and other works. Pater's evaluation of Lamb as a humorist is considered a seminal essay in Lamb criticism. Expressing his admiration for Lamb's delicacy and perceptiveness, Pater especially praises the tone of intimacy and self-revelation which Lamb creates in his works. He concludes by asserting that Lamb's writings "are an excellent illustration of the value of reserve in literature," for he successfully sublimates tragedy to the humorous and the everyday.]

[In the making of prose Charles Lamb] realises the principle of art for its own sake, as completely as Keats in the making of verse. And, working thus ever close to the concrete, to the details, great or small, of actual things, books, persons, and with no part of them blurred to his vision by the intervention of mere abstract theories, he has reached an enduring moral effect also, in a sort of boundless sympathy. Unoccupied, as he might seem, with great matters, he is in immediate contact with what is real, especially in its caressing littleness, that littleness in which there is much of the whole woeful heart of things, and meets it more than half-way with a perfect understanding of it. What sudden, unexpected touches of pathos in him!—bearing witness how the sorrow of humanity, the *Weltschmerz*, the constant aching of its wounds, is ever present with him; but what a gift also for the enjoyment of life in its subtleties, of enjoyment actually refined by the need of some thoughtful economies and making the most of things! Little arts of happiness he is ready to teach to others. The quaint remarks of children which another would scarcely have heard, he preserves,—little flies in the priceless amber of his Attic wit,—and has his **"Praise of chimney-sweepers,"** . . . valuing carefully their white teeth, and fine enjoyment of white sheets in stolen sleep at Arundel Castle, as he tells the story, anticipating something of the mood of our deep humourists of the last generation. His simple mother-pity for those who suffer by accident, or unkindness of nature, blindness, for instance, or fateful disease of mind, like his sister's, has something primitive in its bigness; and on behalf of ill-used animals he is early in composing a **"Pity's Gift."**

And if, in deeper or more superficial senses, the dead *do* care at all for their name and fame, then how must the souls of Shakspere and Webster have been stirred, after so long converse with things that stopped their ears above and below the soil, at his exquisite appreciations of them; the souls of Titian and of Hogarth also; for, what has not been observed so generally as the excellence of his literary criticism, Charles Lamb is a fine critic of painting also. It was as loyal, self-forgetful work for others, for Shakspere's self first, and then for Shakspere's readers, that this too was done; he has the true scholar's way of forgetting himself in his subject. For though "defrauded," as we saw, in his young years, "of the sweet food of academic institution," he is yet essentially a scholar, and all his work mainly retrospective, as I said; his own sorrows, affections, perceptions, being alone real to him of the present. "I cannot make these present times," he says once, "present to me."

Above all, he becomes not merely an expositor, permanently valuable, but for Englishmen almost the discoverer of the old English drama. "The book is such as I am glad there should be," he modestly says of the ***Specimens of English Dramatic Poets who lived about the time of Shakspere:*** to which, however, he adds in a series of notes the very quintessence of criticism, the choicest aromas and savours of Elizabethan poetry being sorted and stored here with a sort of delicate intellectual epicureanism, which has had the effect of winning for these, then almost forgotten poets, one generation after another of enthusiastic students. Could he but have known how fresh a source of culture he was evoking there for other generations, all through those years, in which, a little wistfully, he would harp on the limitation of his time by business, and sigh for a better fortune in regard of literary opportunities!

To feel strongly the charm of an old poet or moralist, the literary charm of Burton, for instance, or Quarles, or Lady Newcastle; and then to interpret that charm, to convey it to others,—he seeming to himself but to hand on to others, in mere humble ministration, that of which for them he is really the creator,—that, is the way of his criticism; cast off in a stray letter often, or passing note, or lightest essay or conversation; it is in such a letter, for instance, that we come upon a singularly penetrative estimate of the genius and writings of Defoe.

Tracking, with an attention always alert, the whole process of their production to its starting-point in the deep places of the mind, he seems to realise the but half-conscious intuitions of Hogarth or Shakspere, and develops the great ruling unities which have swayed their actual work; or "puts up," and takes, the one morsel of good stuff in an old, forgotten writer. There comes even to be an aroma of old English in what he says even casually; noticeable echoes, in chance turn and phrase, of the great masters of style, the old masters. Godwin, seeing in quotation a passage from ***John Woodvil***, takes it for a choice fragment of an old dramatist, and goes to Lamb to assist him in finding the author. His power of delicate imitation in prose and verse goes the length of a fine mimicry even, as in those

last essays of Elia on Popular Fallacies, with their gentle reproduction or caricature of Sir Thomas Browne, showing the more completely his mastery, by disinterested study, of those elements in the man which are the real source of style in that great, solemn master of old English, who, ready to say what he has to say with a fearless homeliness, yet continually overawes one with touches of such strange utterance from things afar. For it is with the delicacies of fine literature especially, its gradations of expression, its fine judgment, its pure sense of words, of vocabulary,—things, alas! dying out in the English literature of the present, together with the appreciation of them in our literature of the past,—that his literary mission is chiefly concerned. And yet, delicate, refining, daintily epicurean, though he may seem, when he writes of giants such as Hogarth or Shakspere, though often but in a stray note, you catch the sense of awe with which those great names in past literature and art brooded over his intelligence, his undiminished impressibility by the great effects in them. Reading, commenting on Shakspere, he is like a man who walks alone under a grand stormy sky, and among unwonted tricks of light, when powerful spirits might seem to be abroad upon the air; and the grim humour of Hogarth, as he analyses it, rises into a kind of spectral grotesque; while he too knows the secret of fine, significant touches like theirs.

There are traits, customs, characteristics of houses and dress, surviving morsels of old life, like those of which we get such delicate impressions in Hogarth, concerning which we well understand, how, common, uninteresting, or worthless even, in themselves, they have come to please us now as things picturesque, when thus set in relief against the modes of our different age. Customs, stiff to us, stiff dresses, stiff furniture,—types of cast-off fashions, left by accident, and which no one ever meant to preserve, we contemplate with more than good-nature, as having in them the veritable accent of a time, not altogether to be replaced by its more solemn and self-conscious deposits; like those tricks of individuality which we find quite tolerable in persons, because they convey to us the secret of life-like expression, and with regard to which we are all to some extent humourists. But it is part of the privilege of the genuine humourist to anticipate this pensive mood with regard to the ways and things of his own day; to look upon the tricks in manner of the life about him with that same refined, purged sort of vision, which will come naturally to those of a later generation, in observing whatever chance may have saved of its mere external habit. Seeing things always by the light of some more entire understanding than is possible for ordinary minds, of the whole mechanism of humanity, and the manner, the outward mode or fashion, always in strict connexion with the spiritual condition which determines it, a humourist like Charles Lamb anticipates the enchantment of distance; and the characteristics of places, ranks, habits of life, are transfigured for him, even now and in advance of time, by poetic light; justifying what some might condemn as mere sentimentality, in the effort to hand on unbroken the tradition of such fashion or accent. "The praise of beggars," "the cries of London," the traits of actors just "old," the spots in "town" where the country, its fresh green and fresh water, still lingered on, one after another, amidst the bustle; the quaint, dimmed, just played-out farces, he had relished so much, coming partly through them to understand the earlier English theatre as a thing once really alive; those fountains and sundials of old gardens, of which he entertains such dainty discourse,—he feels the poetry of these things, as the poetry of things old indeed, but surviving as an actual part of the life of the present, and as something quite different from the poetry of things flatly gone from us and frankly antique, coming back to us, if at all, as entire strangers, like Scott's old Scotch-border figures, their oaths and armour. Such gift of appreciation depends, as I said, on the habitual apprehension of men's life as a whole; its organic wholeness, as extending even to the least things; of its outward manner in connexion with its inward temper; and it involves a fine perception of the congruities, the musical accordance of humanity with its environment of custom, society, intercourse of persons; as if all that, with its meetings, partings, ceremonies, gesture, tones of speech, were some delicate instrument on which an expert performer is playing.

These are some of the characteristics of Elia, one essentially an essayist, and of the true family of Montaigne, "never judging," as he says, "system-wise of things, but fastening on particulars;" saying all things as it were on chance occasion only, and as a pastime, yet succeeding thus, "glimpse-wise," in catching and recording more frequently than others "the gayest, happiest attitude of things;" a casual writer for dreamy readers, yet always giving the reader so much more than he seemed to propose. There is something of the follower of George Fox about him, and the quaker's belief in the inward light coming to one passive, to the mere way-farer, who will be sure at all events to lose no light which falls by the way; glimpses, suggestions, delightful half-apprehensions, profound thoughts of old philosophers, hints of the innermost reason in things, the full knowledge of which is held in reserve; all the varied stuff, that is, of which genuine essays are made.

And with him, as with Montaigne, the desire of self-portraiture is, below all more superficial tendencies, the real motive in writing at all,—a desire closely connected with that intimacy, that modern subjectivity, which may be called the *Montaignesque* element in literature. What he designs is to give you himself, to acquaint you with his likeness; but must do this, if at all, indirectly, being indeed always more or less reserved for himself and his friends; friendship counting for so much in his life, that he is jealous of anything that might jar or disturb it, even to a sort of insincerity, of which he has a quaint "praise;" this lover of stage plays significantly welcoming a little touch of the artificiality of play to sweeten intercourse.

And, in effect, a very delicate and expressive portrait of him does put itself together for the duly meditative reader; and in indirect touches of his own work, scraps of faded old letters, what others remembered of his talk, the man's likeness emerges; what he laughed and wept at, his sudden elevations and longings after absent friends; his fine casuistries of affection and devices to jog sometimes, as he says, the lazy happiness of perfect love; his solemn moments of higher discourse with the young, as they came across him on occasion, and went along a little way with him; the sudden, surprised apprehension of beauties in old literature, revealing anew the deep soul of poetry in things; and still the pure spirit of fun, having its way again,— laughter, that most short-lived of all things, (some of Shakspere's even having fallen dim,) wearing well with him. Much of all this comes out through his letters, which may be regarded

*Drawing of (l.-r.) Leigh Hunt, William Hazlitt, Lamb, and Thornton Leigh Hunt, drawn by the latter.*

as a part of his essays. He is an old-fashioned letter-writer, the essence of the old fashion of letter-writing lying, as with true essay-writing, in the dexterous availing oneself of accident and circumstance, in the prosecution of deeper lines of observation; although, just as in the record of his conversation, one loses something, in losing the actual tones of the stammerer, still graceful in his halting, (as he halted also in composition, composing slowly and in fits, "like a Flemish painter," as he tells us,) so "it is to be regretted," says the editor of his letters, "that in the printed letters the reader will lose the curious varieties of writing with which the originals abound, and which are scrupulously adapted to the subject." (pp. 468-72)

The writings of Charles Lamb are an excellent illustration of the value of reserve in literature. Below his quiet, his quaintness, his humour, and what may seem the slightness, the merely occasional or accidental character of his work, there lies, as I said at starting, as in his life, a true tragic element. The gloom, reflected at its darkest, in those hard shadows of **Rosamund Grey**, is always there, though restrained always in expression, and not always realised either for himself or his readers; and it gives to those lighter matters on the surface of life and literature, among which he for the most part moved, a wonderful play of expression, as if at any moment these light words and fancies might pierce very far into the deeper heart of things. In his writing, as in his life, that quiet is not the low flying of one from the first drowsy by choice, and needing the prick of some strong passion or worldly ambition, to stimulate him into all the energy of which he is capable; but rather the reaction of nature, after an escape from fate, dark and insane as in old Greek tragedy; following which, the mere sense of relief becomes a kind of passion, as with one who, having just escaped earthquake or shipwreck, finds a thing for grateful tears in the mere sitting quiet at home, under the wall, till the end of days. (pp. 473-74)

*Walter H. Pater, "The Character of the Humourist: Charles Lamb," in* The Fortnightly Review, *No. XVI, September 1, 1878, pp. 466-74.*

### J. BRANDER MATTHEWS   (essay date 1883)

[*Matthews, a prominent American dramatist and critic, begins his commentary on Lamb by speculating on the reasons for his remarkable popularity with American readers. In his assessment of* John Woodvil, *Matthews faults Lamb's dramaturgy and asserts that the play is more rewarding as literature than in performance. Matthews also defends* Mr. H., *a play by Lamb which received overwhelmingly bad notices in England.*]

Americans take a peculiar delight in the humor of Charles Lamb, for he is one of the foremost of American humorists. On the roll which is headed by Benjamin Franklin, and on which the latest signatures were made by "Mark Twain" and Mr. Bret Harte, no name shines more brightly than Lamb's. It may be objected by the captious that he was not an American at all; but surely this should not be remembered to his discredit: it was a mere accident of birth. Elia could have taken out his naturalization-papers at any time. . . . He had humor, high and dry, like that which England is wont to import from America in the original package. At times this humor has the same savor of irreverence toward things held sacred by commonplace humanity. Charles Lamb never hesitated to speak disrespectfully of the equator, and he was forever girding at the ordinary degrees of latitude and longitude. His jests were as smooth as they seemed reckless. He had a gift of imperturbable exaggeration; his inventive mendacity was beyond all praise; he

took a proper pride in his ingenious fabrications; and these are all characteristics of the humor to be found freely along the inlets and by the hills of New England and on the prairies and in the sierras of the boundless West. He had a true sense of his high standing as a matter-of-lie man. Moreover, he had a distaste for the straight way and the broad road, and he had a delight in a quiet tramp along the by-path which pleased him personally,—a quality relished in a new country, where a man may blaze out a track through the woods for himself, and where academic, and even scholastic, methods have hard work to hold their own. Even his mercantile training, in so far as it might be detected, was in his favor in a land whose merchants are princes. And behind the mask were the features of a true man, shrewd, keen, and quick in his judgments, one who might make his way in the New World as in the Old. There is something in the man, as in the writer, which lets him keep step to a Yankee tune. (p. 493)

Lamb's humor has an Oriental extravagance to be expected in one who signed himself "Of the India House," but his phrase had always a clerkly and clean-shaven precision not a little deceptive. In him, as in any other humorist, unusual allowance must be made for the personal equation. A humorist sees things as no one else does. He notes a tiny truth, and he likes it, and straight-way he raises it to the *n*th, and, lo! it is a paradox. . . .

Lamb's liking for the drama and for all things pertaining to the drama was second only to his love for Shakespeare. . . . To Lamb, more than to any other, is due the revival of interest in the Elizabethan dramatists. It was the fresh discovery of these old dramatic poets that gave him the impulse to write **"John Woodvil."** (p. 494)

[Théophile Gautier] said that the skeleton of every good drama is a pantomime. Action, of course, is only the bare bones of a play, and must be covered with the living flesh of poetry. There can be no true life in a piece unless it has a solid skeleton; a play may exist even—as we see in vulgar melodramas—with a scant clothing of verbiage; but the finest poetry cannot give life to a drama unless the bones of its story are well knit and well jointed. This is what the Elizabethans intuitively understood, in spite of the rudeness of their stage. This is what Lamb seems never to have grasped as a vital truth. In externals, **"John Woodvil"** is at times strangely like a minor work of a minor fellow-dramatist of Shakespeare's. . . . In internal structure, however, there is nothing Elizabethan in **"John Woodvil;"** there is no backbone of action; the story is invertebrate. (p. 495)

The minor characters reveal themselves in their deeds, and they are grouped skilfully to set off the hero. But the hero himself is not a man of action; he is an elegant conversationalist. . . . There is not much to act in **"Woodvil:"** the man does little or nothing; he talks, and stalks, and talks again; once he seems about to get drunk, which might enliven the story somewhat; and once he fights a duel, but, as he spares his adversary's life, even this pleasing incident lacks finish. The end of the drama is tame beyond endurance on the stage.

If, however, we put down our opera-glasses and read **"John Woodvil"** quietly by the fireside, there is much to reward us. The character of Margaret is beautifully presented and developed. She is akin to Shakespeare's women both in character and in adventure. Even the manly disguise she dons is a frequent Elizabethan—and, indeed, Shakespearian—device. The dialogue throughout is full of the tricks of the older dramatists,—especially a frequent dropping into rhyme.

At the time Lamb wrote "**John Woodvil**" he was in the fresh flush of his delight in the plays of Beaumont and Fletcher and Marlowe. In the joy of his discovery of these poets and of their fellows, and the imitative fever it gave him, consciously or unconsciously, he wrote, besides the tragedy, a dramatic sketch called "**The Witch.**" This fills a scant three pages in the collected edition of his poems, but it is an extraordinary production. . . . It has the secret black and midnight atmosphere. "**The Witch**" is as Elizabethan as "**John Woodvil**" in external language, and even more so in the internal feeling and thought. (p. 497)

The consensus of British criticism is that "**Mr. H.**" was too slight for the stage and too wire-drawn in its humor, and that its failure was what might have been expected. From this view an American—for reasons to be given hereafter—feels called upon to dissent. No doubt "**Mr. H.**" is not one of the author's richest works. Nor, on the other hand, is it as barren and bare as its critics have declared. To my mind, "**Mr. H.**" is not at all a bad farce,—as the farces of the time go. In 1806 popular farces were not required to be as substantial and as instructive as a tragedy. . . . It is "well cut," as the French phrase it,—well planned, well laid out. In the first act is the wonder, the perplexity, the guessing, the questioning as to the name hidden behind the single aspirate. In the second we have the unexpected disclosure, the general repulse, and the happy deliverance. The dialogue is actable,—it is fairly good stage-dialogue, lending itself to the art of the actor; and, while it is not in Lamb's best manner, it is of far higher literary quality than can be found in the faded farces of that time—or of this. The fault of the piece, the fatal fault, was the keeping of the secret from the spectators. To keep a secret is a misconception of true theatrical effect, an improper method of sustaining dramatic suspense. An audience is interested not in what the end may be, but in the means whereby that end is to be reached. (p. 498)

> *J. Brander Matthews, "Charles Lamb's Dramatic Attempts," in* Lippincott's Monthly Magazine, *Vol. V, No. 29, May, 1883, pp. 493-99.*

## ALGERNON CHARLES SWINBURNE (essay date 1885)

> [*Swinburne was an English poet, dramatist, and critic. Though renowned during his lifetime for his lyric poetry, he is remembered today for his rejection of Victorian mores. His explicitly sensual themes shocked his contemporaries: while they demanded that poetry reflect and uphold current moral standards, Swinburne's only goal, implicit in his poetry and explicit in his critical writings, was to express beauty. In the following excerpt, Swinburne spiritedly praises Lamb's humor, compassion, refinement, and the spontaneity of his style. However, he concludes that Lamb's greatest contribution to English literature is "the revelation and the resurrection of our greatest dramatic poets after Shakespeare." Other critics who favorably assess Lamb's criticism include Henry Nelson Coleridge (1835), E.M.W. Tillyard (1923), Arnold Henderson (1968), George Watson (1973), and Joan Coldwell (1978).*]

The most beloved of English writers may be Goldsmith or may be Scott: the best beloved will always be Charles Lamb. His claim and his charm, for those who can feel them at all, are incomparable with any other man's. . . . [In Lamb's works there is something] of so intimate a tenderness, a devotion so personal and private, an affection so familiar and so grateful, that the translation or the transference of such impressions into definite speech seems hardly more difficult as a task than indelicate as an attempt. The exquisite humour, the womanly tenderness, which inform and imbue each other with perfect life and faultless grace beyond reach of any art but that which itself is nature; the matchless refinement of his criticism, the incomparable spontaneity of his style; all these it is easy, if it is not impertinent, to praise: the something within or beyond all these which possibly may appeal but to few can assuredly be defined by none. A more acceptable service than any futile attempt at definition of the indefinable is rendered by any one who gives us but one grain or one drop more from the siftings of his granary or the runnings of his well: provided that these have in them the pure and genuine flavour of the special soil. A very few relics—two or three at most—have been preserved, and even foisted into certain recent editions, with which his truest lovers would be the readiest to dispense. But these are not among the spontaneous effusions of his natural mind: they are avowedly and obviously the forced products of unenjoying labour or of merriment for once uninspired. Cancel these, with a few imitative sentimentalities of his earliest versifying days, and there will remain of him nothing that may not be treasured and enjoyed for ever. (pp. 66-7)

[We] find a homely magic in the name of Lamb, a special fragrance in the fame of it, such as hardly seems to hang about the statelier sound of Coleridge's or Wordsworth's or Shelley's. No good criticism of Lamb, strictly speaking, can ever be written; because nobody can do justice to his work who does not love it too well to feel himself capable of giving judgment on it. And if such a reader as this should undertake to enter the lists against any of Lamb's detractors, or to engage in debate with any of his half-hearted and semi-supercilious partisans, he would doubtless find himself driven or tempted to break all bounds of critical reason in his panegyric of a genius so beloved. . . . Let me not be suspected of any desire to maintain this thesis if I avow my enjoyment and admiration of Lamb's tragedy, his comedy, and his farce. Of his essays and letters, humorous or pathetic, prosaic or fantastic, erratic or composed, what is there to be said but that it would be a feat far easier to surpass all others than to approach the best of these? But the truth is simple and indisputable that no labour could be at once so delightful and so useless, so attractive and so vain, as the task of writing in praise of Lamb. Any man or any child who can feel anything of his charm utters better praise of him in silence than any array of epithets or periods could give. . . . No man ever had less about him of pretention, philosophic or other, than Charles Lamb: but when he took on him to grapple in spirit with Shakespeare, and with Shakespeare's fellows or followers, the author of *John Woodvil*, who might till then have seemed to unsympathetic readers of that little tragedy no more than the 'moonshine shadow' of an Elizabethan playwright, showed himself the strongest as well as the finest critic that ever was found worthy to comment on the most masculine or leonine school of poets in all the range of English literature. With the gentler natures among them—with the sweet spirit of Dekker or of Heywood, of Davenport or of Day—we should naturally have expected him to feel and to approve his affinity; but even more than towards these do we find him attracted towards the strongest and most terrible of all the giant brood: and this by no effeminate attraction towards horrors, no morbid and liquorish appetite for visions of blood or images of agony; but by the heroic or poetic instinct of sympathy with 'high actions and high passions,' with the sublimity of suffering and the extravagance of love, which gave him power to read aright such poetry as to Campbell was a stumbling-block and to Hallam foolishness. . . . Truly and thankfully may those whose boyish tastes have been strengthened with such mental food and quickened with such spiritual wine—the meat so carved and garnished, the cup so tempered and poured out, by such a master and founder of the feast—bear witness and give thanks to so great and so generous a benefactor; who has fed us on lion's marrow, and with honey out of the lion's mouth. To him and to him alone it is that we owe the revelation and the resurrection of our greatest dramatic poets after Shakespeare. . . . He alone opened the golden vein alike for students and for sciolists: he set the fashion of real or affected interest in our great forgotten poets. Behind him and beneath we see the whole line of conscientious scholars and of imitative rhetoricians: the Hazlitts prattling at his heel, the Dyces labouring in his wake. If the occasional harvest of these desultory researches were his one and only claim on the regard of Englishmen, this alone should suffice to ensure him their everlasting respect and their unalterable gratitude: and this is as small a part as it is a precious one of his priceless legacy to all time. The sweet spontaneous grace of his best poetry has never been surpassed: for subtle and simple humour, for tender and cordial wit, his essays and letters have never been approached: as a critic, Coleridge alone has ever equalled or excelled him in delicacy and strength of insight, and Coleridge has excelled or equalled him only when writing on Shakespeare: of Shakespeare's contemporaries Lamb was as much the better judge as he was the steadier, the deeper, and the more appreciative student. A wise enthusiasm gave only the sharper insight to his love, the keener edge to his judgment: and the rare composition of all such highest qualities as we find scattered or confused in others raised criticism in his case to the level of creation, and made his lightest word more weighty than all the labouring wisdom of any judge less gracious, any reader less inspired than Charles Lamb. (pp. 88-91)

> *Algernon Charles Swinburne, "Charles Lamb and George Wither," in* The Nineteenth Century, *Vol. XVII, No. XCV, January, 1885, pp. 66-91.\**

### THE SPECTATOR (essay date 1885)

[*In this review of an edition of* Mrs. Leicester's School, *the critic compliments Charles and Mary Lamb on the timeless style and content of their stories and favorably compares them to Jane Austen's works.*]

[In Charles and Mary Lamb's *Mrs. Leicester's School* there] is the staid, decorous treatment of Miss Austen, reminding us, and not unpleasantly, that this is no new Christmas book, and proving to us that there can be standard stories for the young as well as standard novels for the adult; stories which have stood the test of time, and which will rivet the attention of many a little circle of children to-day, as they held that of their fathers and grandmothers before them. . . . The lonely child, Maria Howe, who, in the **"Witch Aunt,"** relates the experiences of a solitary and misunderstood child-life, with its weird and morbid fancies, falls little short of deserving the adjective powerful. The stories from **"Glanvil on Witches,"** preying upon the impressionable mind till the night-hours become a terror; the creeping out of bed into the old aunt's room to find her mumbling and nodding over her prayer-book, with spectacles tottering on her nose; the instant confusion between the *praying backwards* of Glanvil's wicked witches and the innocent old lady's evening petitions, are, indeed, "inimitable." . . . This, and **"First going to Church,"** are from the pen of Charles Lamb, and we hardly know which we like the best. A little girl, living in the Lincolnshire Fens, and knowing nothing of a church till after she is six years old, save what the distant bells and a child's prodigiously active fancy can

supply, is a theme in dealing with which Lamb is very happy. . . . Mary Lamb's **"The Changeling"** is full of cleverness and quiet fun. The account of the drawing-room play written by a child, and acted by herself and her little companions, is simply lifelike. We seem to see the little boy of five who has to rehearse "many times over," though in undertaking the part of an anxious father he has only to say *"How does my little darling do to day?"* And the climax is equally good,—*"The curtain drops, while the lady clasps the baby in her arms and the nurse sighs audibly."*

To this series the brother contributed three stories, and the sister seven; and their style and treatment is so akin, we could not without assistance decide the question of their separate authorship. It is very pleasing and very natural that it should be so, for it was no common bond that united the hearts and lives of Charles and Mary Lamb. They had one darling pursuit, and they lived under the pressure of one common and terrible fear. (pp. 1621-22)

But is there not something especially pathetic in the knowledge that this gifted and sorely tried pair, in the intervals of sanity for the one, and of comparative ease of mind for the other, gave themselves [in writing *Tales from Shakespeare*] to the task of bringing the greatest of English writers within the ken of that vast and by no means unimportant public,—the little children?. . .

In this age of reprints and fac-simile editions it will be welcomed, more especially by those who associate these stories with their childhood, and who at least of the quaint little figures reproduced in these pages will no longer have to say, with their poor author,

> All, all, are gone,—the old familiar faces.

(p. 1622)

> *"Charles and Mary Lamb's Tales for Children," in* The Spectator, *Vol. 58, No. 2997, December 5, 1885, pp. 1621-22.*

### AUGUSTINE BIRRELL (essay date 1886)

[*Birrell reassesses Lamb's reputation in the light of the tastes of a new generation of readers. Stating that Lamb's humor is "modish," he also argues that Lamb's style is not overly elaborate if his works are considered as a whole. Birrell notes a forthcoming edition of Lamb's letters and terms them the most thorough commentary on the author's life.*]

Lamb's popularity shows no sign of waning. Even that most extraordinary compound, the rising generation of readers, whose taste in literature is as erratic as it is pronounced . . . , read their Lamb, letters as well as essays, with laughter and with love.

If it be really seriously urged against Lamb as an author that he is fantastical and artistically artificial, it must be owned he is so. His humour, exquisite as it is, is modish. It may not be for all markets. . . . Lamb's elaborateness, what he himself calls his affected array of antique modes and phrases, is sometimes overlooked in these hasty days, when it is thought better to read about an author than to read him. To read aloud the **'Praise of Chimney Sweepers'** without stumbling, or halting, not to say mispronouncing, and to set in motion every one of its carefully swung sentences, is a very pretty feat in elocution, for there is not what can be called a natural sentence in it from beginning to end. Many people have not patience for this sort of thing; they like to laugh and move on. Other people again like an essay to be about something really important, and to conduct them to conclusions they deem worth carrying away. Lamb's views about indiscriminate alms-giving, so far as these can be extracted from his paper **'On the Decay of Beggars in the Metropolis,'** are unsound, whilst there are at least three ladies still living (in Brighton) quite respectably on their means, who consider the essay entitled **'A Bachelor's Complaint of the Behaviour of Married People'** improper. But, as a rule, Lamb's essays are neither unsound nor improper; none the less they are, in the judgment of some, things of naught—not only lacking, as Southey complained they did, ''sound religious feeling,'' but everything else really worthy of attention.

To discuss such congenital differences of taste is idle; but it is not idle to observe that when Lamb is read, as he surely deserves to be, as a whole—letters and poems no less than essays—these notes of fantasy and artificiality no longer dominate. (pp. 276-77)

Lamb's letters from first to last are full of the philosophy of life; he was as sensible a man as Dr. Johnson. One grows sick of the expressions, ''poor Charles Lamb,'' ''gentle Charles Lamb,'' as if he were one of those grown-up children of the Leigh Hunt type, who are perpetually begging and borrowing through the round of every man's acquaintance. Charles Lamb earned his own living, paid his own way, was the helper, not the helped; a man who was beholden to no one, who always came with gifts in his hand, a shrewd man capable of advice, strong in council. Poor Lamb indeed! (p. 277)

Of the [works of Charles Lamb] we can say deliberately what Dr. Johnson said, surely in his haste, of Baxter's three hundred works, ''Read them all, they are all good.'' Do not be content with the essays alone. It is shabby treatment of an author who has given you pleasure to leave part of him unread; it is nearly as bad as keeping a friend waiting. Anyhow read **'Mrs. Leicester's School;'** it is nearly all Mary Lamb's, but surely it is none the worse for that.

We are especially glad to notice that . . . [a volume of Lamb's letters is now being prepared]. . . . Lamb's letters are not only the best text of his life, but the best comment upon it. They reveal all the heroism of the man and all the cunning of the author; they do the reader good by stealth. Let us have them speedily, so that honest men may have in their houses a complete edition of at least one author of whom they can truthfully say, that they never know whether they most admire the writer or love the man. (p. 279)

> *Augustine Birrell, ''Charles Lamb,'' in* Macmillan's Magazine, *Vol. LIV, May, 1886, pp. 276-79.*

### THE METHODIST REVIEW   (essay date 1887)

[*The writer of this review suggests that the value and charm of Lamb's essays lie not in their didactic content, but rather in their quaint, rambling style and ''infectious'' spirit.*]

Lamb wrote his [**''Essays of Elia''**] in the first person, thereby giving them a somewhat egotistic aspect. But his egotism was not, like Montaigne's, the expression of offensive vanity, but only of a genial friend talking to you about matters of common interest, with a good-natured familiarity which puts you at your ease and commands your confidence. In kindliness of temper Elia reminds one of the *Spectator*, as he does also in the quiet humor which exhales from evey page like fragrance from flowers, and which, though rarely provoking a downright laugh, yet keeps the lips of an appreciative reader constantly rippling

with smiles. Elia's genius was not creative like Addison's. Hence in his essays there is no such realistic embodiment of humor as the immortal Sir Roger de Coverley. Neither is there any thing so deeply thoughtful as Addison's essays on the ''Immateriality of the Soul,'' on ''Good Intentions,'' etc.; for though Elia had flashes of deep thought, he was neither a profound nor a continuous thinker. Continuity ''teased'' him, he said. To instruct, to moralize, or to reform society was not his aim. But he loved to ramble in the realm of his eccentric fancy, and to gather such facts and fictions, light jests, shrewd observations, and tender recollections as might, says Mrs. Oliphant, ''transport his readers in a moment all unwittingly from laughter into weeping, and to play upon all the strings of their hearts.'' Hence the charm of his essays lies in the quaintness of his fancies, in the oddity of his phrases, in the tenderness of his pathos, in the perspicuity and variety of his style, in his humorous delineations of character, in occasional gleams of penetrative thought, in keen criticism, and in his power of graphic description. These qualities, animated by a sweet, gentle, and sometimes frolicsome spirit, make his essays delightful reading, not perhaps to general and superficial readers, but to such as have the sympathies and the tastes, intellectual and esthetic, necessary to the appreciation of their peculiarities. (pp. 384-85)

To unhappy *individuals* with whom he was brought into personal contact he was kind even to a fault, but the range of his affections, like the sphere in which he moved, was narrow. It comprehended individuals, not classes. He was humane, but not a humanitarian. We see this limitation in his essay entitled, *The Praise of Chimney Sweepers*, and also in one on *The Decay of Beggars in the Metropolis*. In the former he revels with frolicsome delight over the humorous side of the wretched lives of the child sweeps, whom he designates ''dim specks, poor blots, innocent blacknesses,'' and describes an annual feast given them by his merry friend, James White, in London; but, unlike Sydney Smith in his essay on the same subject, he utters no protest against that heartlessness of society which suffered little boys to be subjected to the tortures inseparable from their daily task of ascending blindfold the crooked flues of soot-begrimed chimneys. He makes no plea for a law forbidding such unpardonable cruelty. Not that he is without sympathy with the unhappy little wretches. He looks upon them kindly. He seeks to stir like sympathies in the breast of his reader, saying to him, ''If thou meetest one of these small gentry in thy early rambles, it is good to give him a penny. It is better to give him twopence. If it be starving weather, and to the proper troubles of his hard occupation a pair of kibed heels (no unusual accompaniment) be superadded, the demand on thy humanity will surely rise to a tester.'' This is the language of a kind heart stirred to feeling by the actual sight of individual suffering, but it is not the expression of a mind that sees humanity degraded in the subjugation of little children to such shocking treatment. Moreover, by making merry over the ludicrous side of the poor sweep's character, Lamb fails to call forth more than superficial sympathy with his woes. His humor did not ally itself to the broad aims of philanthropy.

In like manner, his essay *On the Decay of Beggars*, viewed as a bit of humor, is exquisite. It clothes the mendicant in the robes of Harlequin, transmutes his rags into the toga of a freeman, and with unreasoning short-sightedness denounces the laws framed to prevent mendicity as edicts for the persecution of innocents! It is not, therefore, the utterance of a philanthropic mind seeking to reform and elevate humanity, but of a mind whose sense of the grotesque was stronger than its repugnance to a habit of vagrancy which was as demoralizing to those who adopted it as it was annoying to the community which permitted it.

But though these objections hold good against a few of his essays, yet, taken as a whole, they are as sound and healthful as they are entertaining. In a literary sense they are also profitable reading. If not deeply thoughtful, they yet quicken thought by their many suggestive observations. If they add little to one's stores of knowledge, they do nevertheless warm the imagination, mellow the sympathies, excite kindly affections, and give birth to pleasant emotions. They relieve the weary mind and beguile it into a condition of pleasant restfulness. Their spirit, now quaintly playful and then tenderly pathetic, is infectious, and he who once learns to appreciate their peculiar qualities never loses his relish for them. (pp. 388-89)

Among the most touchingly beautiful but least humorous of these essays are the *Dream Children*, and *The Child Angel*. The former he calls a ''revery,'' the latter ''a dream.'' Both are remarkable for simplicity of statement and delicacy of feeling. . . .

In *Grace before Meat* Lamb gives us a humorous satire on the irreverence involved in asking the divine blessing at a richly laden table while the thoughts of the hungry guests are more intent on the steaming viands than on Him whose approval they affect to crave. But for the doubt it casts on the propriety and duty of an ancient and beautiful Christian custom, this essay might be esteemed as a deserving rebuke of those to whom asking a blessing at the table is little else than a form of thankful speech which, not being begotten of gratitude, is irreverent mockery. (p. 390)

Among Lamb's most humorous essays must be reckoned that almost universally known bundle of incongruities called *A Dissertation upon Roast Pig*. Equally amusing, perhaps, though less grotesque in its humor, is his sketch of *Captain Jackson*, whose philosophy taught him, though ''steeped in poverty up to the lips, to fancy himself all the while chin-deep in riches.'' His essay on *Modern Gallantry* is a sharp satire on men who, while conventionally polite to women of wealth and social standing, habitually treat poor women with contemptuous disrespect, thereby showing that they have not that genuine reverence for womanhood itself which breathes in the spirit of this essay. (p. 391)

*''Charles Lamb's Essays,'' in* The Methodist Review, *n.s. Vol. LXIX, May, 1887, pp. 382-97.*

### ARTHUR SYMONS (essay date 1905)

[*Symons was an English critic, poet, dramatist, short story writer, and editor who first gained notoriety in the 1890s as an English decadent. Eventually, he established himself as one of the most important critics of the modern era. Symons provided his English contemporaries with an appropriate vocabulary with which to define the aesthetic of symbolism in his book* The Symbolist Movement in Literature; *furthermore, he laid the foundation for much of modern poetic theory by discerning the importance of the symbol as a vehicle by which a ''hitherto unknown reality was suddenly revealed.'' In the excerpt below, Symons surveys Lamb's writing career and terms Lamb's verse unsuccessful because his natural simplicity prevented him from transforming his material into poetry. Asserting that Lamb's best work is often ''accidental,'' Symons praises his prose style for its breadth and elegance. He also notes the interplay between order and disorder, harmony and interruption, and focuses on digression as one of the most prominent qualities of Lamb's style.*]

The name of Lamb as a poet is known to most people as the writer of one poem. ''**The Old Familiar Faces**'' is scarcely a poem at all; the metre halts, stumbles, there is no touch of magic in it; but it is speech, naked human speech, such as rarely gets through the lovely disguise of verse. It has the raw humanity of Walt Whitman, and almost hurts us by a kind of dumb helplessness in it. A really articulate poet could never have written it; here, the emotion of the poet masters him as he speaks; and you feel, with a strange thrill, that catch in his breath which he cannot help betraying. There are few such poems in literature, and no other in the work of Lamb.

For Lamb, with his perfect sincerity, his deliberate and quite natural simplicity, and with all that strange tragic material within and about him (already coming significantly into the naïve prose tale of ''**Rosamund Gray**'') was unable to work directly upon that material in the imaginative way of the poet, unable to transform its substance into a creation in the form of verse. He could write about it, touchingly some times, more or less tamely for the most part, in a way that seems either too downright or too deliberate. ''Cultivate simplicity, Coleridge,'' he wrote, with his unerring tact of advice, '' or rather, I should say, banish elaborateness; for simplicity springs spontaneous from the heart, and carries into daylight its own modest buds and genuine, sweet, and clear flowers of expression. I allow no hot-beds in the gardens of Parnassus.'' This simplicity, which was afterwards to illuminate his prose, is seen in his verse almost too nakedly, or as it it were an end rather than a means.

Lamb's first master was Cowper, and the method of Cowper was not a method that could ever help him to be himself. But, above all, verse itself was never as much of a help to him as it was a hindrance. Requiring always, as he did, to apprehend reality indirectly, and with an elaborately prepared ceremony, he found himself in verse trying to be exactly truthful to emotions too subtle and complex for his skill. He could but set them down as if describing them, as in most of that early work in which he took himself and his poetry most seriously. What was afterwards to penetrate his prose, giving it that savour which it has, unlike any other, is absent from his almost saltless verse. There is the one inarticulate cry, the ''**Old Familiar Faces**,'' and then, for twenty years and more, only one or two wonderful literary exercises, like the mad verses called ''**A Conceipt of Diabolical Possession**,'' and the more intimate fantasy of the ''**Farewell to Tobacco**'' (''a little in the way of Withers''), with one love-song, in passing, to a dead woman whom he had never spoken to.

The Elizabethan experiments, ''**John Woodvil**,'' and, much later, ''**The Wife's Trial**,'' intervene, and we see Lamb under a new aspect, working at poetry with real ambition. His most considerable attempt, the work of his in verse which he would most have liked to be remembered, was the play of ''**John Woodvil**.''. . . As a play, it is the dream of a shadow. Reading it as poetry, it has a strange combination of personal quality with literary experiment: an echo, and yet so intimate; real feelings in old clothes. . . . The writing has less of the Elizabethan rhetoric and more of the quaint directness, the kindly nature, the eager interest in the mind, which those great writers whom Lamb discovered for the modern world had to teach him, than any play written on similar models. I am reminded sometimes of Heywood, sometimes of Middleton; and even when I find him in his play ''imitating the defects of the old writers,'' I cannot but confess with Hazlitt that ''its beauties are his own, though in their manner'' [see excerpt above,

1818]. Others have written more splendidly in the Elizabethan manner, but no one has ever thought and felt so like an Elizabethan.

After one much later and slighter experiment in writing plays "for antiquity," Lamb went back to occasional writing, and the personal note returns with the **"Album Verses"** of 1830. Lamb's album verses are a kind of amiable task-work, done easily, he tells us, but at the same time with something painfully industrious, not only in the careful kindness of the acrostic. The man of many friends forgets that he is a man of letters, and turns amateur out of mere geniality. To realise how much he lost by writing in verse rather than in prose, we have only to compare these careful trifles with the less cared for and infinitely more exquisite triflings of the letters. The difference is that between things made to please and things made for pleasure. In the prose he is himself, and his own master; in the verse he is never far enough away from his subject to do it or himself justice; and, tied by the metre, has rarely any fine freak or whimsical felicity such as came to him by the way in the mere turn of a sentence in prose.

More than of any poet we might say that a large part of his poems were recreations. We might indeed, but with a different meaning, say as much of Herrick. To Herrick his art was his recreation, but then his recreation was his art. He has absolute skill in the game, and plays it with easy success. Lamb seems to find playing a task, or allows himself to come but indifferently through it. His admiration for "Rose Aylmer" was not surprising, for there, in that perfectly achieved accident, was what he was for ever trying to do.

*Portrait of Mary and Charles Lamb in 1834.*

Yet, at times, the imprisoned elf within him breaks forth, and we get a bubble of grotesque rhymes, as cleverly done as Butler would have done them, and with a sad, pungent jollity of his own; or, once at least, some inspired nonsense, in parody of himself, the

> Angel-duck, Angel-duck, winged and silly,
> Pouring a watering-pot over a lily;

together with, at least once, in the piece of lovely lunacy called **"The Ape,"** a real achievement in the grotesque. His two taskmasters, **"Work"** and **"Leisure,"** both inspire him to more than usual freedom of fancy. And it is among the **"Album Verses"** that we find not only those "whitest thoughts in whitest dress," which, for the Quakeress, Lucy Barton,

> best express
> Mind of quiet Quakeress,

but also the solemn fancy of the lines **"In My Own Album,"** in which a formal and antique measure is put to modern uses, and the jesting figure of "My soul, an album bright," is elaborated with serious wit in the manner of the "metaphysical" poets. And it is under the same covers, and as if done after the same pattern, that we find the most completely successful of his poems, the lines **"On an Infant Dying as Soon as Born."** The subject was one which could not but awaken all his faculties, stirring in him pity, compassionate wonder, a tender whimsicalness; the thought of death and the thought of childhood being always sure to quicken his imagination to its finest utterance. There is good poetical substance, and the form, though not indeed original, is one in which he moves with as natural an air as if he were actually writing two hundred years ago. It was in this brief, packed, "matterful" way, full of pleasant surprises, that his favourite poets wrote; the metre is Wither's, with some of the woven subtleties of Marvel.

With Lamb, more than with most poets, the subject-matter of his work in verse determines its value. He needs to "load every rift with ore," not for the bettering, but for the mere existence, of a poem. . . . He was a poet to whom prose was the natural language, and in verse he could not trust himself to rove freely, though he had been born a gipsy of the mind.

Even in his best work in verse Lamb has no singing voice. The poetry of those lines **"On an Infant Dying as Soon as Born"** is quite genuine, and it has made for itself a form adequate to its purpose; but the verse, after all, is rather an accompaniment than a lifting; and "la lyre," it has been rightly said, "est en quelque manière un instrument ailé." He speaks in metre, he does not sing; but he speaks more delicately in metre than any one else not born a singer.

There is something a little accidental about all Lamb's finest work. Poetry he seriously tried to write, and plays and stories; but the supreme criticism of the **"Specimens of English Dramatic Poets"** arose out of the casual habit of setting down an opinion of an extract just copied into one's note-book, and the book itself, because, he said, "the book is such as I am glad there should be." (pp. 38-44)

He had begun, indeed, deliberately, with a story, as personal really as the poems, but, unlike them, set too far from himself in subject and tangled with circumstances outside his knowledge. He wrote **"Rosamund Gray"** before he was twenty-three, and in that "lovely thing," as Shelley called it, we see most of the merits and defects of his early poetry. It is a story which is hardly a story at all, told by comment, evasion, and recurrence, by "little images, recollections, and circumstances of past pleasures'' or distresses; with something vague and yet precise, like a dream partially remembered. Here and there is the creation of a mood and moment, almost like Coleridge's in the ''Ancient Mariner''; but these flicker and go out. The style would be laughable in its simplicity if there were not in it some almost awing touch of innocence; some hint of that divine goodness which, in Lamb, needed the relief and savour of the later freakishness to sharpen it out of insipidity. There is already a sense of what is tragic and endearing in earthly existence, though no skill as yet in presenting it; and the moral of it is surely one of the morals or messages of **''Elia''**: ''God has built a brave world, but methinks he has left his creatures to bustle in it how they may.''

Lamb had no sense of narrative, or, rather, he cared in a story only for the moments when it seemed to double upon itself and turn into irony. . . . Narrative he could manage only when it was prepared for him by another, as in the **''Tales from Shakespeare''** and **''The Wanderings of Ulysses.''** Even in **''Mrs. Leicester's School,''** where he came nearest to success in a plain narrative, the three stories, as stories, have less than the almost perfect art of the best of Mary Lamb's: of **''The Father's Wedding-Day,''** which Landor, with wholly pardonable exaggeration, called ''with the sole exception of the 'Bride of Lammermoor,' the most beautiful tale in prose composition in any language, ancient or modern.'' There is something of an incomparable kind of story-telling in most of the best essays of **''Elia,''** but it is a kind which he had to find out, by accident and experiment, for himself; and chiefly through letter-writing. ''Us dramatic geniuses,'' he speaks of, in a letter to Manning against the taking of all words in a literal sense; and it was this wry dramatic genius in him that was, after all, the quintessential part of himself. ''Truth,'' he says in this letter, ''is one and poor, like the cruse of Elijah's widow. Imagination is the bold face that multiplies its oil: and thou, the old cracked pipkin, that could not believe it could be put to such purposes.'' It was to his correspondents, indeed to the incitement of their wakeful friendship, that he owes more perhaps than the mere materials of his miracles.

To be wholly himself, Lamb had to hide himself under some disguise, a name, **''Elia,''** taken literally as a pen name, or some more roundabout borrowing, as of an old fierce critic's, Joseph Ritson's, to heighten and soften the energy of marginal annotations on a pedant scholar. . . . Few of the letters, those works of nature, and almost more wonderful than works of art, are to be taken on oath. Those elaborate lies, which ramify through them into patterns of sober-seeming truth, are an anticipation, and were of the nature of a preliminary practice for the innocent and avowed fiction of the essays. What began in mischief ends in art. (pp. 44-6)

In Lamb [the] love of old things, [the] willing recurrence to childhood, was the form in which imagination came to him. He is the grown-up child of letters, and he preserves all through his life that child's attitude of wonder, before ''this good world, which he knows—which was created so lovely, beyond his deservings.'' He loves the old, the accustomed, the things that people have had about them since they could remember. ''I am in love,'' he says in the most profoundly serious of his essays, ''with this green earth; the face of town and country; and the sweet security of streets.'' He was a man to whom mere living had zest enough to make up for everything that was contrary in the world. His life was tragic, but not unhappy. Happiness came to him out of the little things that meant nothing to others, or were not so much as seen by them. He had

a genius for living, and his genius for writing was only a part of it, the part which he left to others to remember him by. (pp. 46-7)

To read Lamb makes a man more humane, more tolerant, more dainty; incites to every natural piety, strengthens reverence; while it clears his brain of whatever dull fumes may have lodged there, stirs up all his senses to wary alertness, and actually quickens his vitality, like high pure air. It is, in the familiar phrase, ''a liberal education''; but it is that finer education which sets free the spirit. His natural piety, in the full sense of the word, seems to me deeper and more sensitive than that of any other English writer. Kindness, in him, embraces mankind, not with the wide engulfing arms of philanthropy, but with an individual caress. He is almost the sufficient type of virtue, so far as virtue can ever be loved; for there is not a weakness in him which is not the bastard of some good quality, and not an error which had an unsocial origin. His jests add a new reverence to lovely and noble things, or light up an unsuspected ''soul of goodness in things evil.'' (p. 52)

Lamb's defects were his qualities, and nature drove them inward, concentrating, fortifying, intensifying them; to a not wholly normal or healthy brain, freakish and without consecution, adding a stammering tongue which could not speak evenly, and had to do its share, as the brain did, ''by fits.'' (pp. 53-4)

[In Montaigne and Lamb,] one sees precisely what goes to the making of the essayist. First, a beautiful disorder: the simultaneous attack and appeal of contraries, a converging multitude of dreams, memories, thoughts, sensations, without mental preference, or conscious guiding of the judgment; and then, order in disorder, a harmony more properly musical than logical, a separating and return of many elements, which end by making a pattern. Take that essay of ''Elia'' called **''Old China,''** and, when you have recovered from its charm, analyse it. You will see that, in its apparent lawlessness and wandering like idle memories, it is constructed with the minute care, and almost with the actual harmony, of poetry; and that vague, interrupting, irrelevant, lovely last sentence is like the refrain which returns at the end of a poem.

Lamb was a mental gipsy, to whom books were roads open to adventures; he saw skies in books, and books in skies, and in every orderly section of social life magic possibilities of vagrancy. But he was also a Cockney, a lover of limit, civic tradition, the uniform of all ritual. He liked exceptions, because, in every other instance, he would approve of the rule. He broke bounds with exquisite decorum. There was in all his excesses something of ''the good clerk.''

Lamb seemed to his contemporaries notably eccentric, but he was nearer than them all to the centre. His illuminating rays shot out from the very heart of light, and returned thither after the circuit. Where Coleridge lost himself in clouds or in quicksands, Lamb took the nearest short-cut, and, having reached the goal, went no step beyond it. (pp. 54-5)

He was the only man of that great age, which had Coleridge, and Wordsworth, and Shelley, and the rest, whose taste was flawless. All the others, who seemed to be marching so straight to so determined a goal, went astray at one time or another; only Lamb, who was always wandering, never lost sense of direction, or failed to know how far he had strayed from the road.

The quality which came to him from that germ of madness which lay hidden in his nature had no influence upon his central sanity. It gave him the tragic pathos and mortal beauty of his wit, its dangerous nearness to the heart, its quick sense of tears, its at times desperate gaiety; and, also, a hard, indifferent levity, which, to brother and sister alike, was a rampart against obsession, or a stealthy way of temporising with the enemy. That tinge is what gives its strange glitter to his fooling; madness playing safely and lambently around the stoutest common sense. In him reason always justifies itself by unreason, and if you consider well his quips and cranks you will find them always the play of the intellect. (pp. 55-6)

Arthur Symons, ''Charles Lamb,'' in Monthly Review, *Vol. XXI, No. 62, November, 1905, pp. 38-56.*

## PAUL ELMER MORE (essay date 1905)

[*More was an American critic who, along with Irving Babbitt, formulated the doctrines of New Humanism in early twentieth-century American thought. The New Humanists were strict moralists who adhered to traditional conservative values in reaction to an age of scientific and artistic self-expression. In regard to literature, they believed that the aesthetic qualities of a work of art should be subordinate to its moral and ethical purpose. More was particularly opposed to Naturalism, which he believed accentuated the animal nature of humans, and to any literature, such as Romanticism, that broke with established classical tradition. His importance as a critic derives from the rigid coherence of his ideology, which polarized American critics into hostile opponents (Van Wyck Brooks, Edmund Wilson, H. L. Mencken) or devoted supporters (Norman Foerster, Stuart Sherman, and, to a lesser degree, T. S. Eliot). He is especially esteemed for the philosophical and literary erudition of his multivolumed* Shelburne Essays *(1904-21). In the following excerpt, More discusses what he terms Lamb's ''unsubstantiality'', both in his imaginative writings and in his criticism. He also maintains that Lamb's verse style imitates that of the ''lesser poets'' of the Elizabethan era, who were more concerned with effect than substance.*]

There is an exquisite make-believe about [Lamb's] essays, like the quieting unreality of country scenes to one whose life has been ''in populous cities pent.'' No doubt a vein of pathos runs through them all, but it is of a mocking kind and makes no appeal to the *lacrimarum fons.* **Christ's Hospital Five and Thirty Years Ago** was in reality a school of hard discipline; passed through the alembic of Lamb's fancy, it becomes unreal and very beautiful, a memory of dreams. He goes to **Oxford in the Vacation,** and that city of scholars and gay livers is suddenly transformed into a refuge of ghosts. . . . The same dissolving power of the fancy is turned upon **The Old Benchers of the Inner Temple,** and the place is forever haunted by those three *revenants,* Thomas Coventry, Samuel Salt, and Peter Pierson, walking not with arms linked together—''as now our stout triumvirs sweep the streets''—but with hands folded behind their backs, strange figures that are very much of this earth, yet somehow unconcerned with its prosaic business. He writes of those ''dim specks'' of the London streets, the childish **Chimney-Sweepers** ''blooming through their first nigritude,'' who ''from their pulpits (the tops of chimneys), in the nipping air of a December morning, preach a lesson of patience to mankind''; and their sermon is a quaint echo of the Shakespearian,

> Golden lads and lasses must,
> As chimney-sweepers, come to dust.

Or he takes the beggars of the metropolis for a theme, and in place of the brutal and hideous pictures which a modern ''nat-

uralist'' would give us, he turns to muse on the idyllic tenderness of Vincent Bourne's blind vagrant and dog:

> Hi mores, hæc vita fuit, dum fata sinebant.

Again, he gathers up into an essay the bereavements and long abnegations of his bachelor life, and instead of the bitter arraignment of Thomson's outcast in *The City of Dreadful Night* or the half-renounced envy of Christina Rossetti—

> While I? I sat alone and watched;
> My lot in life, to live alone
> In mine own world of interests,
> Much felt but little shown;—

instead of these, he has woven his regrets into **Dream Children, a Reverie,** where the pathos is as aërial and undisturbing as the shadows that fall from smoke.

And his critical disquisitions, fine and penetrating as they are in many respects, have to my mind something of the same unsubstantiality. I read of Shakespeare in Lamb's essays, and I do not seem to be in the presence of the great constructive dramatist who carried the weight of human experience in his brain, but of some sovereign alchemist skilled to convert the leaden cares of life into golden leaf. It is characteristic of Lamb's paradoxical spirit and half-conscious irony that he should have found Shakespeare more fitted for the cabinet, where the reader's fancy had freer license to sport, than for the stage with its closer confinement of realism. The whole Elizabethan drama, which he so loved and which he did so much to restore to general favour, attracted him chiefly by its salient points of light, and the plays of the Restoration were avowedly dear to him because they carry us into a region ''beyond the diocese of the strict conscience,'' into the vision of that ''pageant where we should sit as unconcerned at the issues, for life or death, as at a battle of the frogs and mice.''

Much of Lamb's poetry is of a frankly ephemeral sort, album verses for importunate young ladies and the like, but even in those poems that are in a way dedicated to the severer muses the same note of fanciful unreality, concealing a basis of discarded emotions, may be heard as in the letters and essays. I think this note can be detected in his tragedy of **John Woodvil,** in his lament over **The Old Familiar Faces,** written, be it observed, when he was scarcely out of his teens, and in those lovely stanzas to **Hester,** whose close rises higher in poetic grace perhaps than he anywhere else attained. . . . (pp. 94-7)

[The charm of Lamb's verses] is of the Elizabethan school, but they follow the models of the lesser poets who turned from the direct expression of the emotions and from the language of power to the more wanton light of the fancy. It would be interesting, if not too technical, to carry this contrast into the very mechanism of Lamb's style and show how it is based on the Euphuistic school and on the metaphysical writers who cared more for the lambent play of the intellect than for directness and depth of impression. His language does not flow, but moves with a continual eddy; the interest is in the quaintness of individual words and phrases rather than in sustained harmony. The effect is delightful, piquant, tantalising, and at times, it must be confessed, a little *saccadé* and even wearisome. We remember this criticism which Lamb pronounced on **Elia,** ''The informal habit of his mind, joined to an inveterate impediment of speech, forbade him to be an orator,'' and we wonder whether this impediment does not now and then manifest itself in a certain retardation of his written, as well as his spoken, utterance. Unique and exquisite as his more artificial language often is, I confess to like even better those occasional passages where he forgets his mannerism and speaks out with simple straightforwardness. As an illustration of this chaster style I would select that vindication of his friend in the letter of *Elia to Robert Southey*. . . . The passage, thus inviting a comparison with Hazlitt, would have the further merit of calling attention to the widely different traditions which, coming down side by side in English literature from the beginning, have divided the aims of these two friends. Hazlitt, with his passion and force and weight of utterance, descends by direct inheritance from Marlowe and Hooker and Milton; Lamb, with his quaintness and emphasis on phrase and word, is a later-born brother of Lyly and Sidney and Quarles and Fuller. (pp. 97-8)

> Paul Elmer More, "Charles Lamb," in his Shelburne Essays, second series, *G. P. Putnam's Sons, 1905, pp. 87-103.*

### GEORGE SAINTSBURY   (essay date 1912)

[*Saintsbury was an English literary historian and critic of the late nineteenth and early twentieth centuries. A prolific writer, Saintsbury composed a number of histories of English and European literature as well as several critical works on individual authors, styles, and periods. The following excerpt is a brief analysis of Lamb's style, which Saintsbury labels "a perfectly achieved conglomerate."*]

When we come to Lamb, we come to one of the exceptions [to English prose style]. That he could have written paragraphs—that he did write sentences—exquisitely rhythmical, is certain. But it was scarcely ever his humour to do the first, and not often to do the second. His faithful and constant following of the Elizabethans in the wide sense (to say that he was not "a sedulous ape" of Browne and Burton and Fuller is, I think, a mistake) must, to some extent, have interfered with any such production, by distracting his view. But the very certainty and success with which he assimilated the products of this imitation, and combined them with that of others, especially Sterne, proved this still more. His style is a perfectly achieved *conglomerate,* the particles conglomerated being perceptible, but indissolubly united, and in fact unified, by the mortar of his own idiosyncrasy. Yet in actual continuity of sound, as distinguished from sense, the whole is too much broken up to achieve the highest rhythmical results. They are, it may be said, not wanted; and I heartily agree. But there are some excellent people who, when you say that something is not somewhere, resent the statement, as if "and it ought to be" were implied. The uniquely broken bits of Lamb's composition would be ill exchanged for fresh examples of a continuous harmony which we can find elsewhere. In the middle style, moreover—that which aims at and achieves concinnity of rhythm without going higher,—he was, in his less fantastic moods, an absolutely consummate master. There is nobody like him (unless it be Goldsmith) between Addison and Thackeray, and I do not myself care to place the four in order of merit. (p. 362)

> George Saintsbury, "Miscellaneous Prose, 1820-1860," in his A History of English Prose Rhythm, *1912. Reprint by Indiana University Press, 1965, pp. 347-90.**

### HUGH WALKER   (essay date 1915)

[*In this overview of Lamb's work, Walker emphasizes the inherent wisdom expressed in Lamb's essays. In addition, Walker discusses the elements which contribute to Lamb's individuality as a writer and deems his imitation of such seventeenth-century writers as Sir Thomas Browne and Robert Burton to be successful.*]

[The evidences of Lamb's] wisdom are to be met with everywhere. It is the essence of Lamb's criticism. No one but a man endowed with the very genius of common sense could have been so uniformly right as he. Taste alone will not do, for taste is apt to have a bias—Lamb's certainly had for the quaint and the antique. But good sense makes him substantially right even where his own preferences do not guide him; and where they do guide him he has, at his best, as in the essay *On the Genius and Character of Hogarth,* a marvellous power of comprehension and interpretation which can be explained only as the fruit of a rare wisdom. Again, *The Old and the New Schoolmaster* is the work of a man who has looked upon life with the shrewdest and most penetrating eye. There is a sound philosophy of life in *Old China,* and excellent principles of education are laid down in *Recollections of Christ's Hospital.* The author of *Modern Gallantry* had delved beneath shows to reality; and *The Tombs in the Abbey* is as just in thought as it is vigorous in style. *Grace before Meat* is from beginning to end instinct with wisdom. It also illustrates well the reason why this quality in Lamb has so often passed undetected. There is a playfulness in it that turns the mind from the expectation of serious thought. But the serious thought is there. He flings down a profound truth in a phrase—"true thankfulness (which is temperance)." And in this lies his whole philosophy of the grace, beautiful at a poor man's table, less beautiful at a rich man's, and not beautiful at all at a city banquet. "When I see a citizen in bib and tucker, I cannot imagine it a surplice." "You are startled at the injustice of returning thanks—for what?—for having too much while so many starve?" "The proper object of the grace is sustenance, not delicacies; the means of life, and not the means of pampering the carcass." It is unanswerable; the profoundest thinker could have taught no more. Take again the essay on *A Quakers' Meeting*—the Quakers, by the way, are pronounced to have more right to a grace than their neighbours, because "they are neither gluttons nor wine-bibbers as a people." Though Lamb includes the Quaker with the Caledonian, the Jew and the Negro among his "imperfect sympathies," the Quaker essay is a model of comprehension, and sympathetic comprehension too. There is no better test of wisdom. To be able to comprehend and do justice to that which is widely different from ourselves is one of the things most difficult of achievement. (pp. 231-32)

Comprehension of that which is different from self is one test of Wisdom; self-knowledge is another—the last and highest, according to the Delphic motto as it is commonly interpreted. No one stands the test better than Lamb. . . . Much the same view of himself is given again in *Mackery End:* "Out-of-the-way humours and opinions—heads with some diverting twist in them—the oddities of authorship please me most." But the best evidence is to be found in the fine *Character of the late Elia,* in which Lamb, under the guise of "a friend of the late Elia," stands aloof and criticises himself with far subtler comprehension than any contemporary ever showed. He, and he alone, knew exactly the significance of his own jests and apparent irrelevancies. He writes about Elia's conversation, but the words are applicable no less to his writings: "He would interrupt the gravest discussion with some light jest; and yet, perhaps not quite irrelevant in ears that could understand it. . . . He would stutter out some senseless pun (not altogether senseless, perhaps, if rightly taken) which has stamped his character for the evening." Such was Lamb's way of hinting that there was method in his madness. But even his friends could not fully and at all times believe it. And how delicately in the same preface (as became a friend writing of the dead) he hints at the infirmity which he exaggerates in the **Confessions of a Drunkard:** ''He was temperate in his meals and diversions, but always kept a little on this side of abstemiousness.''

A man may, however, be most sagacious and yet fail to win love, as Lamb won and still retains it. The secret of that is the nobility of nature which the facts of Lamb's life so eloquently attest, the gentleness of heart which Coleridge praised, not in error, but in the wrong way, the goodness to which Wordsworth bore his emphatic testimony. This too is graven deep upon the essays. They are full of phrases that reveal it. What but the kindliest of hearts could have thought as Lamb did about a kindly face? ''When a kindly face greets us, though but passing by, and never knows us again, nor we it, we should feel it an obligation.'' In his thoughts on his own childhood we see the genesis of this spirit of his manhood: ''The solitude of childhood is not so much the mother of thought, as it is the feeder of love, and silence, and admiration.'' There are whole essays irradiated with it—the two just quoted, **Grace before Meat, The Praise of Chimney-Sweepers, Captain Jackson.** There is an unaffected gusto in the story of Jem White in the **Chimney-Sweepers.** The economic wisdom of **A Complaint of the Decay of Beggars** may be dubious: we know that Burn, the author of the history of the Poor-Law, would even have made it penal to give to beggars. But there can be no doubt of the charity of the heart that wrote: ''Shut not thy purse-strings always against painted distress. Act a charity sometimes.'' But perhaps the most impressive of all proofs of the boundless kindliness of Lamb is to be found in **Captain Jackson.** If the character were read a little differently, what a subject for **The Book of Snobs!** Notwithstanding his reputation for cynicism, Thackeray was no unkindly man; but he could never have looked upon a Captain Jackson with the large-hearted charity of Lamb. Genteel poverty is treated in **The Book of Snobs** too; but what we see there is the pretentious host lifting the pretentious cover from the dish where lie two or three lean chops. In Lamb, imagination conquers reality, the remnant rind of cheese becomes a generous meal, ''the sensation of wine was there,'' though no wine, and ''you reeled under the potency of his unperforming Bacchanalian encouragements.'' ''You saw with your bodily eyes indeed what seemed a bare scrag—cold savings from the foregone meal— remnant hardly sufficient to send a mendicant from the door contented. But in the copious will—the revelling imagination of your host—the 'mind, the mind, Master Shallow,' whole beeves were spread before you— hecatombs—no end appeared to the profusion.'' (pp. 233-35)

There is nothing affected or insincere about this. In his own way Lamb was a champion of the poor as well as Dickens, and one hardly less catholic in his sympathies or less tolerant. (p. 235)

In point of style Lamb is not wholly a modern. His exquisite but mannered English was based upon the prose masters of the seventeenth century, men like Browne, and Burton of the *Anatomy,* and Fuller. To them he was drawn by a natural kinship. Their thoughts were largely his, their quaintnesses and conceits fitted in with his humour, their antique flavour pleased his critical palate. This natural affinity, combined with the thoroughness of Lamb's knowledge of them, made the imitation— if a thing so natural can be called by that name—successful, and explains the genesis of a style at once unique and, for the purposes to which it is turned, unsurpassed in effectiveness.

Though itself based upon models in the past, it is obviously an extremely unsafe style to imitate. No one could advise the student to give his days and his nights to Lamb, if the purpose was to learn how to write English. An imitation of Lamb, to be successful, would require a conjunction of three qualities. First, there must be the same natural affinity to the seventeenth-century writers; and of this there has been probably no example for a hundred years except Lamb himself. Secondly, there must be the same thorough knowledge; which, though attainable, is nevertheless both rare and difficult. Thirdly, there must be that unfailing tact, that instinct for style which Lamb possessed; and where that is present the possessor will find his own way without advice.

Lamb's style is inseparable from his humour, of which it is the expression. His ''whim-whams,'' as he called them, found their best expression in the quaint words and antique phrases and multiplied and sometimes far-fetched yet never forced comparisons in which he abounds. Strip Elia of these and he is nothing. Neither the brilliancy of Hazlitt, nor the harmony of De Quincey, nor the vigour of Macaulay, nor the eloquence of Ruskin, nor the purity of Goldsmith could for a moment be thought capable of expressing the meaning of Lamb. In argumentative passages no doubt one or other might suffice. Hazlitt might have maintained the thesis of **The Artificial Comedy** with equal skill. But when we come to the most characteristic essays, such as **The Two Races of Men** and **Poor Relations** and **A Chapter on Ears,** what style is conceivable except that in which they are couched? Of no one else is the saying that the style is the man more true than of Lamb. In the deepest sense therefore his style is natural and all his own. Its basis in the seventeenth-century writers is, after all, not so much imitation as the expression of his natural affinity to them. (pp. 238-39)

> *Hugh Walker, ''The Early Magazines of the Nineteenth Century,'' in his* The English Essay and Essayists, *E. P. Dutton & Co., 1915, pp. 222-65\**

## W. L. MacDONALD   (essay date 1917)

[*Arguing for Lamb's primacy among the world's essayists, MacDonald favorably compares him with the sixteenth-century essayist Michel Eyquem de Montaigne and the seventeenth-century essayists Francis Bacon, Joseph Addison, and Sir Richard Steele. MacDonald posits that the most distinctive attributes of Lamb's style in the ''Elia'' essays are versatility, wit, and the ability to surprise.*]

Lamb's genius was suited for the essay. Whatever virtues **Rosamond Gray** and **John Woodvil** possess, they unquestionably show that the author was deficient in constructive powers as well as in capacity for character drawing in story and drama. For one kind of character sketching he had . . . a peculiar felicity, but this aptitude merely points with other finger-posts along the highway of the essay.

To get a complete idea of Lamb the essayist, attention must not be centered entirely upon the **Elia** collections. No doubt these contain what Lamb considered the best of his contributions to the London Magazines, but it is difficult to understand some of the omissions. When, for instance, he saw fit to include **On the Artificial Comedy of the Last Century** and **Barrenness of the Imaginative Faculty,** why did he not reprint **On the Tragedies of Shakespeare,** . . . as he did the **Bachelor's Complaint,** written in the same year? **Edax on Appetite, Hospita on Immoderate Indulgence,** and **On the Custom of Hissing at the**

*Theatres,* not to mention a dozen other pieces which are now included in the Miscellaneous Prose, are all worthy of a place in the collection which will be Lamb's passport on the day of Judgment.

"My Essays," wrote Lamb to his publishers, "want no preface; they are *all preface.* A preface is nothing but a talk with the reader; and they do nothing else." This is exactly the attitude of all the earlier essayists. Nothing in Lamb—not even the autobiographical element—is so suggestive of Montaigne as the jovial contempt he frequently shows for any sort of unity in his essays. They are, as all the older essays professed to be, only "imperfect offers, loose sallies of the mind, irregular or undigested pieces," that "rather glaunce at all things with a running conceit, than insist on any with a slowe discourse." *In Praise of Chimney Sweepers,* is a good example of what an essay subject may become,—a mere starting point from which various related or unrelated ideas may be developed. With the exception of the last two pages, the *Praise* is so attenuated as to be as near *nil* as can be. The text, *Old China,* is again a mere starting point, the real subject of the piece being the joys of easy poverty as against the cares of affluence. Like Montaigne and Cornwallis, Lamb refuses to "chain himself to the head of his chapter." In the very last lines the original situation, the imaginary theme, is recalled as a joke by the essayist. Of course, an author who indulges in such vagaries may write at any length according to his mood, the allotted space, or the fecundity of his mind. (pp. 554-55)

That Lamb, both consciously and unconsciously, modelled his writings on those of the old masters of English prose there is ample evidence. He has the characteristic attitude of the essayists toward what is old. His predecessors of the seventeenth century were never tired of quoting the classics; Lamb is constantly quoting the old English classics. The names of Sir Thomas Browne, Fuller, Butler, Marvel, Shakespeare, and the old dramatists are those which most often appear in the essays, and quotations from their writings are to be found in abundance. Classical references of course are numerous, but as has been pointed out, the general reading public of Lamb's day was no longer the kind to respond to such an appeal; moreover, Lamb was thoroughly convinced that his own native English contained stores as rich as any to be found in the literature of Greece and Rome. Not only in the matter of literature does this respect for antiquity, or the antiquated, and neglect of the contemporary appear. The passing of the sun-dial, the change in readers, who no longer read for pleasure as they did thirty years ago, the deterioration in acting, the decay of beggars and schoolmasters, are all subjects of complaint, though of course the complaint must be taken only half seriously. Attention has already been called to the fact that there is but one distinct reference to the Napoleonic wars in all the essays.... References to contemporaries like Hunt, Hazlitt, and Coleridge fall in a different category, being inevitable in autobiographical essays.

Lamb carries on the tradition of Bacon and Addison, yet in a sense he is greater than either. Elia's aphorisms are frequently as wise as Bacon's, but they are not so closely packed together as to form the tissue of the essay. One always feels that Bacon has something very wise to say, that the proper thing to do is to listen attentively. Lamb, on the other hand, frequently startles his readers by some profound observation in the midst of seemingly trivial talk. Frequently it is apparent that Lamb has little or nothing to say, and then he performs the *tour de force* of holding his reader by saying nothing in a clever, interesting

way. *The Convalescent* is an instance. Contrast with this the very next piece *On The Sanity of True Genius.* The former is spun out of mere nothing; in the latter the essayist grapples with a real text. Did Bacon ever sound more profound depths of wisdom than Lamb on the subject of oaths (*Imperfect Sympathies*) or ceremony (*Bachelor's Complaint*)? Whether the answer is "Yes" or "No," there are few readers that will not find Lamb's offering more acceptable than Bacon's. The latter teaches *ex cathedra,* the former inveigles us into the ways of wisdom.

Like Bacon, Lamb occasionally talks in abstract terms, as for example in *Stage Illusion;* more frequently, however, the subject is opened in a general way and illustrated by an interesting anecdote, much in the manner of Fuller's *Holy and Profane State.* Examples of this kind of essay are *Witches and Other Night Fears, The Old and New Schoolmaster* and *The Two Races of Men.* But one cannot say that Lamb has any particular method of treatment. He uses every method. In fact, it is Lamb's versatility, his protean temper, his facility of surprise both in individual pieces and in successive essays, that make the *Essays of Elia* supreme amongst their kind. . . . None of the other essayists, excepting Steele occasionally, writes with such pathos as permeates *Dream Children* and underlies *The Wedding.* The nice balance preserved between the light and the pathetic in the last named essay is an instance of the danger in declaring that one special mood gives the key to any individual composition of Lamb's. When we speak of satire we think of Lamb in relation to the eighteenth-century periodical essayists. Like Addison's, the satire of Lamb is always light, never vindictive

*Jones rathersh unwell*

*Ch⁵ Lamb*

*A caricature of Lamb drawn by Daniel Maclise.*

or canine, as is usually the case in Hazlitt's essays. In the *Imperfect Sympathies* the writer suggests that perhaps the imperfection is in himself. *On the Custom of Hissing at the Theatres, Hospita on the Immoderate Indulgence of the Pleasures of the Palate, Edax on Appetite, A Vision of Horns,* and others, are very much in the style of the *Tatler* and *Spectator*. The essay last named immediately suggests Addison's *Vision of Justice* in form and substance, but as compared with the latter is crude and ineffective. Addison's infallible decorum allows him to handle a delicate subject in such a way that only the humor of the satire is impressed upon the reader. Lamb is not always decorous, and in this instance there is something repulsive, a lack of nice taste, which probably persuaded him to omit the piece from the *Elia* collection.

Epigram and aphorism, the stock in trade of the older essayists, are abundantly present everywhere in Lamb, but in using them the nineteenth-century writer has improved upon his masters. Lamb's purpose is to entertain his readers, not to provide an exercise in mental gymnastics. Bacon parades his witticisms and profound general truths in massed battalions. Lamb's method is to lead them out in extended order—a more effective if less imposing arrangement. The occasional epigram gives a fillip to the intellect and raises the commonplace to a higher plane without forcing the mind to be constantly on the alert. The usual way with Lamb, as with all essayists, is to open up the subject with a striking statement that immediately arrests attention. "The human species," thus he begins *The Two Races of Men*, "according to the best theory I can form of it, is composed of two distinct races, *the men who borrow* and *the men who lend*." "I have no ear—" are the opening words of *A Chapter on Ears*. Wealth of allusion, apt metaphor and simile are qualities of style that every prose writer requires who wishes to be interesting. Lamb's felicity in this respect is too obvious to be insisted upon here; every critic of the essayist has discussed these elements of his style. The peculiar effect of Lamb's style is best expressed in the word "unexpectedness." He can be grave and gay, dignified and playful, grandiose and simple, rhetorical and pathetic in successive compositions and sometimes in the same essay. The style is as whimsical as the mood which produces it, and the exact correspondence of the two constitutes the special charm of Lamb's essays. In this respect he is far superior to all his predecessors. Bacon seldom if ever unbends. The eighteenth-century periodical writers, to whom Lamb is much more nearly allied, are always dignified. (pp. 557-61)

The seventeenth-century "character" is a form nearly related to the essay.... The normal character is a brief composition consisting of sententious, epigrammatic, often paradoxical statements, defining and describing a person or thing not as an individual but as representative of a class. The essential difference from the essay lies in the concrete treatment of the character and the satirical mood of the writer. (p. 562)

As a writer of characters in the seventeenth-century meaning of the word, Lamb is an adept. But just as he was too versatile an essayist to conform to any particular mould, so in character writing he is too great an adept to confine himself to any form or any particular mood. Sympathy with his fellow-men and his kindly nature would not allow him to indulge in the mordant, satirical humor that ordinarily gives pungency to the seventeenth-century character. Moreover, interest in the life around him forbade his dwelling on the abstract qualities of a class when he saw only the concrete eccentricities of an individual. At the same time Lamb does write characters of the older kind.

His versatility is amazing. Nothing makes greater demand upon the "sheer wit" of an author than a character sketch that consists only of happy epigrams; and nothing of the same length in all Elizabethan and Jacobean literature is more clever than the first three paragraphs of *Poor Relations*. (pp. 562-63)

*Rosamond Gray* and *John Woodvil* prove pretty conclusively that Lamb lacked the capacity for showing the gradual development of character through action and conflict. His genius was not suited to such a task. No character excepting that of Bridget Elia recurs in the essays, and it seems entirely improbable that Lamb had the intention of giving any sort of unity to the *Elia* pieces by this device. (p. 564)

Many of Lamb's essays are not in the dispassionate essay mood. Frequently the *indignatio saeva* is merely affected, as for instance when he makes his bachelor's complaint against the display of married happiness, or when he warms his wrath against the "sea-charmed emigrants" from town who, trained in the pit of the London concert halls, pretend to find a pleasure in the music of the waves—because it is the fashion. But in *Readers against the Grain* his anger, if not white hot, is genuine, because the offence is simulated, half-hearted, empty loyalty to a sovereign who, according to Lamb's way of thinking, demands whole-souled allegiance or none at all. And this brings us to the subject of Lamb's literary criticism, not the excellence or limitations of it,—that has been treated often enough already,—but its place in Lamb's essays.

When the question is one that concerns literature or any allied subject in which Lamb has a special interest, painting or acting, he never pretends to assume a detached attitude,—that is one of the reasons why his remarks are so readable. *On the Genius and Character of Hogarth* was written quite frankly for the purpose of combating the "vulgar notion" respecting the artist. *The Tragedies of Shakespeare* was inspired by the inscription to Garrick in the Abbey which practically puts the actor on a par with the dramatist. This aroused Lamb's ire and became the occasion of one of the most famous passages in literary criticism. But Lamb overstated his own case and was led by his passion into uttering a paradox. The same thing happened in the essay *On the Artificial Comedy of the Last Century*. Lamb loved paradox; he loved to shock conventionality. "I like a smuggler," he says in *The Old Margate Hoy*, "he is the only honest thief." He does not approve of the crusade against Beggars, "the oldest and honourablest form of pauperism." Frequently whole passages give the effect of paradox, although he is not stating paradoxes. *Popular Fallacies* witness to the same predilection for the unpopular side. So in the two famous critical pieces mentioned above, he has just been led to utter a paradox and afterwards forced to bolster his thesis with special pleadings. For while there is much truth in every part of these two essays, the total impression that remains after seeing a good performance of one of Shakespeare's tragedies is that they are fitted for presentation on the stage; and after reading many of the comedies of the eighteenth century, one is forced to conclude that the dramatists of that period did take delight in shocking the ordinary views of morality. (pp. 565-66)

In the foregoing discussion an attempt has been made to show in outline that the English essay has had an almost unbroken career as a literary form from the time of Bacon to the late nineteenth century, and in particular that the *Essays of Elia* are lineal descendants of ancestors that flourished in the seventeenth and the eighteenth centuries. And not only are Lamb's essays in the main current of what may be called the "literary essay," but precedence may fairly be claimed for them over any other similar collection in English. Lamb used all styles of essay-writing, and in the words of Johnson's epitaph on Goldsmith, he touched nothing which he did not adorn. In skilful handling of the materials with which essayists have worked, aphorism, epigram, character-writing, literary criticism, etc., he has proved himself second to none, and in versatility, whether of style, mood, or wit, superior to all the rest. (p. 572)

> W. L. MacDonald, "Charles Lamb, the Greatest of the Essayists," in PMLA, 32, Vol. XXXII, No. 4, December, 1917, pp. 547-72.

### E. M. W. TILLYARD  (essay date 1923)

[Tillyard, one of the most influential twentieth-century Shakespearean critics, examines Lamb's role as a critic, noting that he ranks among the greatest English masters of applied criticism. He contends that Lamb's weaknesses as a critic were his narrow range of expertise and lack of systematic thought; however, these were balanced, according to Tillyard, by his modesty and originality. Other critics who assess Lamb's criticism favorably include Henry Nelson Coleridge (1835), Algernon Charles Swinburne (1885), Arnold Henderson (1968), George Watson (1973), and Joan Coldwell (1978).]

The position a man will give to Charles Lamb as a literary critic depends on what he believes the highest criticism to be. Does he seek information or enlightenment of it? Should it persuade him by argument or like the Sublime of Longinus transport him by its power? For if he goes to it chiefly for facts, for arguments, for masterly comparisons, for sustained intellectual effort, he will find Lamb deficient, disagreeing probably with several of Lamb's contentions and condemning his critical writings as occasional, unmethodical and fragmentary; but if he goes to it for something that by some subtle means brings him closer to certain works of art than he has been able to get unaided, for something that creates in his mind the right receptive mood, then he will put Lamb among the very greatest of critics. (p. viii)

Of English masters of theoretical criticism Coleridge is the greatest, of applied, in a sense, Lamb.

To exalt Lamb so high may seem rash in view of the comparatively small bulk of his work and of his being so obviously an amateur, not, like Hazlitt, a professional critic; and if one were to judge Lamb as any kind of critic other than the creative, the claim would be preposterous. But the fact is that the bulk of criticism that is both a high work of art in itself and tells the truth about what it deals with is remarkably small and correspondingly precious. This should not be in the least surprising, if we consider the qualities that must go to the making of a great critic of authors. (p. ix)

Now it is the first and greatest glory of Lamb's criticism that not a little of it has got [the] quality of indispensableness . . . Nor is this quality confined to a few famous places: it meets us again and again. (p. x)

But if it is impossible to analyse the essence of Lamb's most memorable passages, there is one obvious contributory reason why he succeeded in penetrating so near the centre of truth; namely that his very faults, his amateurishness and lack of range, helped him to concentrate the more intensely on what he loved, and to reach a more intimate sympathy with it. There are men, of whom Dryden and Hazlitt are conspicuous among the English, who react with vitality to almost any good literature that they meet, men with quick initial perceptions and strong immediate judgments. Their very versatility prevents quite that close intimacy which is such a peculiar property of Lamb. Not that they are open to the charge of superficiality, but that they have not the faculty of brooding over what they read as Lamb had. You feel that in them there is always present the desire to express in words what they feel about the books they read, and that they are always a little restless until they have expressed themselves. But when Lamb is 'hanging over (for the thousandth time) some passage in old Burton, or one of his strange contemporaries,' his mood is one of unspoiled serenity, and the waters of his spirit receive the perfect reflection of what he reads, unstirred by any wind of restlessness.

It is very easy to exaggerate the 'quaintness' of Lamb's writings in general, and it is positively wrong to use the word as peculiarly descriptive of his criticism. Nobility and high seriousness are terms that can more fittingly be applied to his greatest, modesty and simplicity to his lesser, and originality to all his criticism. There is nobility, high seriousness and a passionate emphasis in the essay *On the Tragedies of Shakespeare* and even in the mutilated review of *The Excursion*. Moreover Lamb's fundamental concern was with the literature of human action rather than of fancy, and could not have coexisted with a fundamental quaintness. 'The plays which I made choice of,' he writes at the beginning of the *Characters of Dramatic Writers, Contemporary with Shakspeare*, 'were, with few exceptions, such as treat of human life and manners, rather than masques and Arcadian pastorals, with their train of abstractions, unimpassioned deities, passionate mortals—Claius, and Medorus, and Amintas, and Amarillis. My leading design was, to illustrate what may be called the moral sense of our ancestors.' These are not the words of one whose quaintness is fundamental: the spirit in which they are written would not have been disowned by Matthew Arnold. This concern with human action is nowhere better seen than in the admirable review of Keats' *Lamia* volume, in which Lamb with an instinct perfectly true to himself, though not necessarily truer than the instincts of those who have thought otherwise, prefers *Isabella* with its greater insistence on action, human feeling and dramatic qualities generally to all the splendour of the pictorial writing in *The Eve of St. Agnes*. He could never have shown this preference, had his critical turn of mind been above all things quaint.

Lamb's modesty and simplicity . . . are evident with the rarest exceptions throughout his letters, from his earliest criticisms of Coleridge to his latest of Moxon. He never tries to be clever; he never in the slightest degree lords it over those who have delivered themselves into his hand by showing him their works. What he criticises and how he can help it are everything, his own glory as critic nothing. The same qualities are to be found in the passage on Sir William Temple in *The Genteel Style in Writing*. I can imagine no more perfect introduction to a writer than this. Lamb works here largely by quotation, but every now and then delicately adjusts the reader's mood by a judicious remark. At the end we have forgotten the critic, and are left with an inexplicably vivid impression of Temple and a vehement desire to learn all there is to know about him. How many a modern review do we read with the feeling that the reviewer is a very clever fellow, but that we are not particularly drawn to learn more of his subject! (pp. xi-xii)

Of Lamb's originality it is superfluous to speak: it meets us everywhere in the good and the bad alike. He had no master, his tastes were entirely native, and there is hardly a line of his criticism that anyone else could have written.

Lamb's defects as a critic were frankly implied by himself in more than one confessional passage. . . . (p. xiii)

Lamb confesses in ***Imperfect Sympathies*** that his mind is desultory, sadly lacking in system, 'suggestive merely' and 'content with fragments and scattered pieces of Truth.' Granted that he was true enough to his nature to make out the worst case he could against himself, we must admit that his self-accusation is substantially true. It is impossible to deny that Lamb was lacking in range, that his attainments as a scholar were not great, that his knowledge of foreign literature depended mostly on translations and even so was not wide, that he read what he liked, not what he ought, and so on. But is lack of range such a very serious fault? Cannot the virtue of immense reading be exaggerated? The total amount of great literature extant in the world is very large. A few supermen, uniting a high vitality with powerful eyesight, prodigious memories, a highly developed patience of sitting in chairs and a small desire for sleep, may gain more than a superficial acquaintance with most of it, and retain their faculty for appreciation. But I cannot believe that such range is desirable except for a few, or that those few can have the intensity of appreciation of a Lamb. Those who exact vast range in a critic underestimate the expenditure of emotional force that must go to a great appreciation of a masterpiece. It is futile to expect any one man to enjoy the accumulated out-pourings of the great minds of many ages in any worthy degree of intensity.

Then there is the charge brought by Hazlitt in his essay *On Criticism in Table Talk* that Lamb has an invincible predilection for the obscure, and cannot appreciate anything that appeals to the multitude. That Lamb was attracted by the curious and the out-of-the-way, and that he liked to feel that he was appreciating something neglected by others or appreciating in an unusual way something known, cannot be denied. It was a pleasure to him to appreciate Wither, the luckless butt of ignorant Augustan abuse, and he gets peculiar pleasure in saying in his essay on him, 'Whoever expects to find in the satirical pieces of this writer any of those peculiarities which pleased him in the satires of Dryden or Pope, will be grievously disappointed.' He has in fact got very strongly the antiquarian delight of collecting rarities. Yet this delight is not fundamental, but an added zest. Primarily he seeks what he likes; if what he likes happens to be rare, if he can work his way through a little dust to some neglected piece of human passion, so much the better; but he does not allow mere antiquarianism to affect his tastes. He is, as it were, a man who in 1860 admires Chippendale chairs, not an original who in 1923 deliberately adorns his house with the furniture of 1860: even in 1923 he would have liked Chippendale chairs, though with just a trifle less relish. It is as wrong to consider Lamb's occultism and antiquarianism as his most important characteristics as it is to exaggerate his quaintness. His chief concern was with great literature, in particular with Shakespeare, but when, to use the phrase of literary appreciation, he took 'an airing beyond the diocese of the strict conscience' (and who can live for very long at a stretch in the rarefied atmosphere of the great masterpieces?) his antiquarian instincts asserted themselves. (pp. xiii-xiv)

[But when all is said and done, Lamb's defects] are quite innocuous. He made mistakes: he admired Southey overmuch; he spoke contemptuously of [Goethe's] *Faust;* he did not give Shelley a chance. But his mistakes are not such as mislead; sheep and goats in his criticism require no divine aid in the separation. If he states one side of a question only, as in the

essay on ***Shakespeare's Tragedies*** and ***The Artificial Comedy of the Last Century,*** he in no way makes us forget that there is another side, and withal gives us high criticism that entirely transcends the nominal issue. His native frankness and sincerity keep his most questionable assertions from being in the least more dangerous than Dr Johnson's enchanting strictures on *Lycidas.* (p. xv)

> *E.M.W. Tillyard, in an introduction to* Lamb's Criticism: A Selection from the Literary Criticism of Charles Lamb *by Charles Lamb, edited by E.M.W. Tillyard, 1923. Reprint by Greenwood Press, Publishers, 1970, pp. viii-xvi.*

## WALTER RALEIGH   (essay date 1926)

[*In this brief appreciation Raleigh praises Lamb's comic detachment and focuses on the melding of humor and seriousness in his writings.*]

Charles Lamb was not a poet, or essayist, or critic—he was a person. His works are a fortunate accident. They consist of:—

(1) Sayings.
(2) Letters.
(3) Poems and Essays.

—to be valued, I think, in that order. To anyone who lived so much in his affections as Lamb did, company is more than letters, and letters more than books.

There is an odd kind of privacy in Lamb's works—like *family* literature. His plays are like charades. He never took himself quite seriously, as we say, but "played at literature" with the glee of a child who dresses up and acts a part. He never dreamed of pitting himself against the gods of his idolatry. It is impossible to think of him as a "writer of books"—he stammers confidences, and has not the voice for public utterances. Sometimes he seems a kind of brownie, for fun and shy helpfulness: if you offer him wages, he will be off. At other times, by his sound sense and fearless clear judgment on human affairs, he seems as stalwart and robust as a grenadier. (pp. 120-21)

Lamb's sayings are not robust jests, like those of his friend (was it?) to whom he said, "When *you* make a joke, it's no laughing matter." Some of them are light, irresponsible nonsense, and as nonsense is the purest form of jesting, so Lamb's is the best kind of nonsense. Others are extraordinarily incisive. It has been said that all his wit was gentle; it would be truer to say that it often cut, but did not hurt. In this matter he enjoyed the privileges of an angel—as those often do who wish no ill to anyone. He had a right to jest. Heartlessness he needed not to fear. The putting off responsibility and cheapening things by jests was impossible to him. He did not offer a joke in lieu of a helping hand. But wherever the joke is realler and truer than the solemnity—there he jested.

Lamb's puns may seem to need an apology. The pun is almost dead. It was the fashion of Lamb's age; to make the best pun of the evening was fame. Punsters of repute were hunted in society. Perhaps the best puns have all been made; we have to get on as best we can with the inverted commonplace, the paradox, and the transferred initial consonant.

Lamb almost raised the pun to a higher power. His puns very often *mean* something. A pun is like one of those scientific toys that rotate in a vacuum: he almost made it do work.

There never was such a *taster* of literature as Lamb. He has fixed the values, and left it to more learned historians to arrange them, and talk of cause and effect.

It does not matter much when Great Authors die. Their lives were the process which gave us their Works. The death of Homer, or Voltaire, or Goethe, is like the death of a rich uncle; not so much went out with them as went out with Charles Lamb. He left works, it is true, but he left something more fragrant and subtle than works—a memory; so that his death is like the death of a child, which can never happen (Adam Smith remarks) without rending asunder the heart of somebody. Even as an author he makes a more private appeal than almost all other authors, and keeps his ragged regiment of friends about him. (pp. 122-24)

> *Walter Raleigh, "On Some Writers and Critics of the Nineteenth Century: Lamb," in his* On Writing and Writers, *edited by George Gordon, Edward Arnold & Co., 1926, pp. 120-24.*

## JAMES O'DONNELL BENNETT   (essay date 1927)

[*Bennett extols Lamb's works and asserts that the appeal of the "Elia" essays is timeless.*]

[Lamb's] style is as fragrant to us, his topics as appealing, and his approach as sociable as if he were one of us. In truth, he is. Not only did he never grow old; he never *has* grown old. The boon he asked for himself—for his physical body and his social soul—in the fifth of the first series of Elia papers, has been bestowed upon his books: they live on in pleasant, permanent companionships, as he wished to live. (p. 230)

Charles Lamb was so original a mind and so deft a stylist that he could make an essay on anything come laughing to him—and crying, also, for the lachrymae rerum ever were close behind his smiles. He could, and did, make a ten-page essay on roast pig a classic. It is the twenty-fourth paper in the first Elia series, and contains the perfect pun, "'Presents,' I often say, 'endear Absents.'"

He made an essay on a game of whist a classic. He did the same with old china, with a Quaker meeting, with poor relations, with chimney-sweepers, and with a needy man who could convincingly play-act opulent hospitality. The commonplaces of every day, some would call them, but he made them the distinguished things of all the days. (p. 231)

Lamb wrote other essays more in the academic strain; he wrote poems and tales (collaborating with his sister Mary in the stories from Homer and from Shakespeare), and he left a mass of letters unsurpassed—one would say unequaled save that remembrance of Horace Walpole tugs—in our language for wit and vivacity.

But he wrote nothing so thoroughly Lamblike, so gracefully, daintily frisky as the fifty-one Elia papers which lure by their effect of complete spontaneity. Had that spontaneity, however, been actual the essays would have lapsed into twaddle. It was not actual. We know that he rewrote and rewrought the little articles. . . .

Merits far more general in their appeal than expert craftsmanship have kept men friends with Elia for a century. There is in his writing the warmth of a cheerful heart which had been ennobled by bitter trial. There is the essence of a tutored and sensitive mind. There is the tang of a sharp individuality. These

are made known with the distinction of a fine style. Thus are the topics of every day made literature.

Lamb looked at life with the eyes of whimsical pity. His sympathies were as tender as they were gay. He had the delicacy of perception which converted the ludicrous not into the ridiculous but touched it with a soft and fleeting yearning that I like to think of as a smiling reverence. He knew the touchstones of kinship. (p. 232)

> *James O'Donnell Bennett, "Lamb's 'Essays of Elia'," in his* Much Loved Books: Best Sellers of the Ages, *Boni and Liveright Publishers, 1927, pp. 230-35.*

## A. G. VAN KRANENDONK   (essay date 1932)

[*In this discussion of Lamb's style in the "Elia" essays, van Kranendonk argues that Lamb did not imitate Elizabethan authors, nor did he exhibit typically Romantic characteristics. Through a close examination of diction and technique, van Kranendonk concludes that Lamb's style was not artificial, as some critics have claimed, but rather a highly individualistic blend of various traits.*]

[The influence of Elizabethan authors on Lamb's] work was but slight. He never imitated them, not even in single passages, at least not in the *Essays of Elia*. Naturally a curious old word or turn of phrase remembered from his favourite authors often stood him in good stead, when he wanted to suggest an atmosphere of antiquity, but mostly he used the old words, the deliberately pompous expressions, for various other purposes of his own.

In some respects his work follows the tendencies of his age; he may be said to belong to the romantic movement by his feeling and imagination, his sense of the mystery and wonder of life, his love of the quaint and the grotesque, his interest in the literature of the past, but essentially he stands alone and unrelated. (p. 5)

And unlike many of the romantic writers, who in their quest after the ideal fled away from reality, he did not send his imagination wandering, but kept it within narrow bounds. Preference and necessity made him restrict himself to the actual, to everyday life, to the town. . . . In most of the *Essays* he indeed makes little things of importance, he does talk magnificently about trifles, seeing them with the eye of the artist, discovering a hidden significance, a strange beauty in the simple and commonplace.

But he was at the same time conscious of his limitations, he did not allow himself to be deceived by his own fancies. He knew that it was after all mostly about trifles that he talked, and talked magnificently, but far from dispelling the charm, this self-consciousness, leading as it does to an exquisite play of humour and pathos, greatly adds to the enchantment. Little things, commonplace scenes and personages assume a certain dignity, a hitherto unsuspected beauty and importance, but at the same time there is in this vision splendid nearly always a peculiar, somewhat wistful humour to be discerned, a sadness dissolving into smiles, a gentle mockery at the glamour of romance his own imagination has cast over the theme. (pp. 5-6)

It was a pleasurable but not at all an easy task for him to express within the narrow compass he allowed himself all the ideas, perceptions and emotions a theme awakened in him. "I experience at all times the greatest difficulty of finding words to express my meaning", he says in his *Confessions of a Drun-*

*kard,* but in his best work he has shown himself a master in the "potential use of words," in perfectly expressing his individual vision and mode of feeling. His style is nearly always richly suggestive. . . . To render his uncommon and complex vision it is but natural that he should occasionally have to use uncommon words or even to coin new ones. That this was not a mere whim, a mannerism, a mechanical habit may already be gathered from the fact that in a considerable part of his writings his language is perfectly simple. He could do without uncommon figures of speech if he thought fit, and still write excellent prose. In most of his letters there is hardly any trace of the little eccentricities associated with his name, neither is there much of it in his *Popular Fallacies* or even in several of the *Essays* themselves. We need only remind the reader of *Dream Children* in which the exquisite effect is almost exclusively attained by simple means, and in nearly all the other famous *Essays* there are passages showing that he was quite capable of restraint. Whenever in his best work he had recourse to an unusual turn of phrase, to old, quaint words, there were excellent reasons for it. Not only did they do him signal service in rendering the odd and the antique for which he had such a marked preference, but by means of them he achieved a variety of other effects, chiefly humorous, ranging from the comic or the purely farcical to the highest forms of humour where it is blended with original thought or deep pathos, his keen sense of humour always saving him from dropping into the sentimental.

By rendering the homely in terms of the heroic a curiously comic effect is produced. Throughout his work we find isolated examples of this practice, often in the midst of a serious discussion or descriptive passage, and in the delightful *Dissertation upon Roast Pig* we have a familiar example of its consistent use; a less famous, but to my mind an even more brilliant one, in *The Praise of Chimney-sweepers*—or rather of their apprentices: "tender novices blooming through their first nigritude"; especially in the digression on a kind of tea made from "the sweet wood yclept sassafras", which young sweepers are said to favour. The incongruity between the grandiloquent phraseology and the humble, commonplace theme makes this passage—too long to quote—irresistibly comic.

The device of solemn, ornate over-statement cannot, however, entirely account for the remarkable result he attained in passages like this. It is partly due to his power of observation, to his gift of finding concrete picturesque details to illustrate and enrich a thought, a description; partly also to the extensive vocabulary he had at his disposal and his wonderful sense of the value of words: his high rhetoric is in itself supremely good; it is an agent of fun, but also sheds a lustre on the fooling, it "ennobles" a joke. (pp. 6-7)

In passages of a more serious character, where the humour is blended with graver thoughts and feelings, the style is no less suggestive, the old, ornate diction calling up various associations. In *New Year's Eve* for instance, in a passage already referred to, where he confesses how deeply he is in love with life, he also says he cannot understand how people can ever become reconciled to death by the consolations of philosophy. This at least is the gist of the paragraph and if rendered in simple language the reflection would have been commonplace enough. Instead we find him using a somewhat stilted diction and this seemingly unnecessary transposition makes the passage convey by implication much more than the simple reflection it primarily expresses. When, for instance, after saying: "I have heard some profess an indifference to life", he

adds: "Such hail the end of their existence as a port of refuge and speak of the grave as some soft arms in which they may slumber as on a pillow . . . those metaphors solace me not. . ." etc., the sentences mirror the high-flown language of the old moralists, and the imitation implies a sly mockery at their traditional tags; "those metaphors solace me not", suggests at once: as they are reputed to have done the ancients; and in the whole passage there is also an undertone of playfully pretended dissatisfaction at his own inability to follow their example, as well as of doubt whether the "ancients" were after all really so stoically brave and philosophically-minded as is often supposed.

There are several other parts in the *Essays* where by the adaptation of an old conventional idiom he slily scoffs at pompous moralists and at the stock-phrases used by them.

At other times the lofty words have a somewhat more serious connotation, as in the reminiscences of his youth. They lend a certain grandeur, a glow of romance to the incidents recorded, which makes us realize, better than any direct statement could have done, how important they were to the youthful minds of his companions and himself, how terrifying a sad experience can be to a child, how blissful a pleasant one. And when he speaks in the same spirit of the sorrows or difficulties of a later period in his life, the words also convey a sense of the consolation there lay in the possibility of seeing them thus important, as in *The Superannuated Man,* where, for instance, in referring to the time spent at the office he uses such terms as "durance", "thraldom" etc.; or in *New Year's Eve,* when the theme reminds him of his unhappy love-affair: "Methinks it is better that I should have pined away seven of my goldenest years, when I was thrall to the fair hair, and fairer eyes, of Alice W—n, than that so passionate a love-adventure should be lost". He had conquered his suffering, he could now afford to smile a little at his old self, to speak of the time of his youth with gentle irony in lofty terms; yet there was something consolatory too in dramatising the past in this way, and the wistfully humorous words also subtly express the lingering tenderness, the deep regret he still felt. (pp. 8-9)

There was indeed much of the actor in Lamb, and it came quite natural to him to dramatize the incidents of every-day life and his own experiences, to represent them as events of historic importance, worthy to be handed down to posterity in dignified, flowery language. He does it in a playful mood, always remaining conscious of the discrepancy between the real significance of the subject and the temporary glory his imagination has conferred on it, a consciousness, humorously expressed, by which all sentimentality is dissolved or sublimated. Yet there is in this humour, whether it is tinged with melancholy or hilariously comic, always a poetic quality; it does not obscure or counteract what is essentially true in the vision splendid, it only modulates the expression of it.

We find him use the same characteristic method in his comic portraits of contemporaries, drawn with such deep, sympathetic insight, especially in those of his old colleagues in *The South Sea House.* They are individually strikingly different, these old clerks, yet they have one trait in common, a characteristic which as a matter of fact we may observe in the great majority of men: humble, commonplace though they are, each of them possesses, or thinks he possesses, a gift, a quality on which he can pride himself, which in his own opinion distinguishes him from the common herd, gives him the flattering feeling that in this one respect at least he stands above his fellow-men. This craving for distinction, unconscious though it usually re-

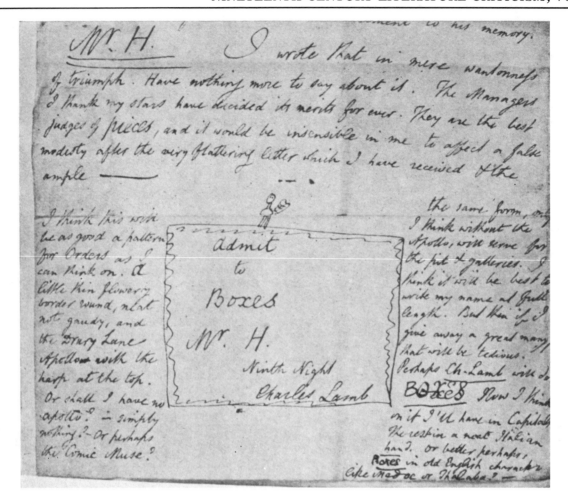

*Facsimile of a letter from Lamb to William Wordsworth.*

mains, must needs be satisfied in some way or other. Lamb does not mention this weakness, this very real need of human nature, he shows it in its typical, sometimes singular, manifestations. And the high-flown terms in which he describes the qualities on which the old people pique themselves are well-calculated to make us realise the importance they attach to them and to poke gentle fun at their innocent vanity. Often he uses with great effect a sort of indirect quotation of some one's secret thoughts, couched however in words that convey at the same time the author's own view of the man.

John Tipp is proud of his ability as an accountant and of his profession in general. When we read that "he was indeed equal to the wielding of any the most intricate accounts of the most flourishing company in these or those days," we feel that the sentence does not—as it slily purports to do—give Lamb's estimate of his old colleague, but that it is rather a paraphrase of Tipp's own thoughts, the quaint mode of expression suggesting the pride Tipp took in his ability and especially in the importance of his task, whilst also gently ridiculing his self-complacency.

Evans was a melancholy man who believing himself to be a brilliant conversationist, found consolation in social chat at meal-times. We are made to see him as a man of great dignity, struggling against his constitutional melancholy, which seems a gloom scarcely to be borne; and when the author, instead of saying he had a sad face, speaks of his "tristful visage", this may seem mere affectation, in reality the pompous words are perfectly justified, because they chime in with the purposely exalted tone of the passage and heighten the comic contrast intended. . . . (pp. 9-10)

But his mockery at these simple souls is never in the least malignant; it does not undermine but stimulates our affection. Lamb makes us love them not in spite of, but because of their failings. His attitude to them is not one of passive tolerance, but rather one of active advocacy; only of course his pleading is not direct, but implicit and its persuasive force is the stronger for it. He understood them so well; he saw that they too, though on an immeasurably lower plane than himself, sought consolation in little things, and were probably concealing equally bitter sorrows. He sublimated their very faults even while ridiculing them, his mockery is suffused with a deep, compassionate understanding. (p. 10)

Equally excellent is the portraiture in *The Old Benchers of the Inner Temple,* as it is indeed everywhere else in the *Essays* which contain sketches of real or imaginary persons.

It is an amiable, many-sided, exceptionally interesting personality that talks to us in the *Essays* with such a wonderful blending of humour and essentially poetic feeling, and in almost every sentence we are surprised by the felicitous, graphic and picturesque mode of expression, by a supreme craftsmanship that triumphs over all difficulties. I might go on quoting—Elia is indeed notorious for enticing one to it—but no detached examples can do full justice to the unique quality of his work, the charm of which escapes analysis. If I have still ventured to give a few quotations and comments it was only with a hope to show that there is more behind the peculiarity of his style than a mere mannerism, that it cannot in justice be called artificial. (p. 10)

> A. G. van Kranendonk, "Notes on the Style of the 'Essays of Elia'," in English Studies, Vol. 14, No. 1, February, 1932, pp. 1-10.

## F. J. HARVEY DARTON   (essay date 1932)

*[Darton provides an overview of children's works by Charles and Mary Lamb. This work was originally published in 1932.]*

[The Lambs' children's books] were written for the market. On the other hand, the authors personally, like Blake and, in a less degree, Oliver Goldsmith, are apt to be a little one-sidedly viewed in this connection. Lamb, of all men, was least of any period, even when he was spinning his own epoch out of himself in delicately shot silk. England under George III contained him, but did not produce him—so far as Elia the man is concerned. If he lived today, he would not have to write or think differently to win the suffrages of the judicious (not that he ever sought them). But if he and his sister wrote their children's books, today, they might very well not find an eager publisher.... You can see small gleams of timeless genius in the interstices of the Lambs' juvenile books, but they are rare glints in a drab not of their own creating.

It is very difficult to rid oneself of the confusion between affectionate appreciation of the writer for 'grown-ups' and a transferred uncritical affection for the same writer when he is not creating spontaneously. But love of Lamb as an essayist, and the inextricable love of himself and Mary as human figures, must not conceal the fact that their children's books neither were nor are of much value in the evolution of their kind. Except that one of the productions may have led some children to read Shakespeare, they inspired nothing, they showed no fresh point of view, they won no wide hearing as compared with workaday stuff by other writers with like aims and no claims on the adult intelligence. All their seven 'juveniles' (the coarse trade term is used on purpose) must be considered here simply as common objects by the wayside of social history, not museum pieces or personal treasures.

(They have, however—to step still further aside—this value: that they show, if it were necessary, that children's books were no longer a very minor by-product of general literature; and to that extent they direct to the special subject persons who might otherwise ignore it.)

The first of the series was Lamb's own—*The King and Queen of Hearts*.... It was not meant to be anything more than a trifle. The ancient rhyme—whose origin has been frequently discussed without much definite result—has not been ousted by this version which seems to have had no noticeable contemporary life. (pp. 196-97)

*Tales from Shakespear. Designed for the Use of Young Persons* ... is an altogether different matter. It was the first joint work of Charles and Mary, who received sixty guineas for it. The greater part was by Mary. Charles did *Lear, Macbeth, Timon, Romeo, Hamlet* and *Othello,* and probably some passages in

other tales—'groaning all the while, and saying he can make nothing of it'. (p. 198)

Lamb may have found the task-work—for it was that—a matter for groaning, and not everyone today, perhaps, would affirm with complete conviction that the *Tales* either represent Shakespeare accurately or provide all modern children with spontaneous pleasure. They are written 'down' rather obviously and are often laboured.... On the other hand, they have, even if they *were* groaned over, a kind of earnestness and faith which grows into charm and gradually fastens upon even a careless reader. Often one might well guess at the personalities behind them (and not guess wrongly) if one knew merely the period and not the authorship. The English, as language, is more than a means of expression; it is an expression in itself. And in one respect the *Tales* were unique. No one had hitherto attempted anything of the kind. The Lambs gave to children and simple folk something like a reality of the Elizabethan spirit which at that time they could not otherwise obtain.... The *Tales* have many defects, and they are not the finest Elia nor yet the best that Mary could do. They bear unmistakable traces of the period's morality and commerce (a Janus god), for that very reason. But they are also to some extent a revolt against the traffic in didactics.... [The *Tales*] provide a defence of poesy by a kind of nursery introduction to it in prose.

The next Lamb children's book was by Charles alone. In this too he gave a prose specimen of Elizabethan literature, for his *Adventures of Ulysses* ... is based on Chapman's translation, not on Homer. It was a vast advance on the dismal morality of Fénelon's *Telemachus,* then still very rife in translations for juvenile readers. Though Chapman, to unsophisticated minds, may appear a little tortuous or crabbed in his roughness, Lamb achieved the strange feat of getting some of the *Odyssey*'s glorious ease into what might almost be simple Elizabethan prose. There are a few slightly pedagogic asides here and there ('Ulysses, of whose strength or cunning the Cyclop seems to have had as little heed as of an infant's'—you should never explain the obvious), but the whole runs with a gracious Homeric speed and smoothness. There was a little disagreement with Godwin over slight details, but it came to nothing. In freedom of description Lamb went some distance from the continuation of Fénelon which he originally intended, and from the opinions he stated in his preface.

*Ulysses* is a refreshing oasis in the moral desert, but it does not seem to have caused much excitement. The next in the Lambs' list was an unassailably moral tale, or rather set of moral tales, of the approved substance, but a little more distinguished in manner than the ruck, and gentler in outlook. *Mrs. Leicester's School* ... is nearly all by Mary Lamb. In this 'History of Several Young Ladies, Related by Themselves', three stories only—*Maria Howe, Susan Yates (First Time of Going to Church),* and *Arabella Hardy, or, The Sea Voyage*— are related by Charles himself, and they are more serious and meditative than most of the others, though they also contain Elian touches of fantasy. In Mary's work there is a weakish humour and a very real tenderness, with something of the same sudden vision here and there. The morality, throughout, is not rampant. Possibly that is one reason why, to be honest, the tales as a whole are dull. They are often too contemplative and also too flickering, with brief intuitions and withdrawals taking the place of experience and action. They had some contemporary success because they were near enough to the market standard; a ninth edition was called for by 1825. They have remained in print and in middling repute rather through the general love of their authors than by their own vitality.

To go for a moment out of chronological order, **Prince Dorus, or Flattery Put Out of Countenance** . . . , ought to be mentioned briefly, but only in justice to its author. It is neater than some of the 'nonsense' stories in rhyme, pseudo-nursery rhymes, which by then were epidemic, and to which I come later. It was reasonably moral in a crude fashion: the slight fashion of a stage pantomime, a mode which its plot might suit. But it has no historical and not much literary value unless it be as a variant telling of a tale by Mme le Prince de Beaumont, 'Le Prince Désir', which appeared in the *Magasin des Enfans* in 1756. Nor need **Beauty and the Beast** . . . detain us, for it is disputably Elian. At that time there were plenty of cheap editions of the famous tale on the market.

The remaining work has a great deal of small significance (authorship apart), as much by what it fails to do as by what it succeeds in doing. . . . Lamb said the poems [in **Poetry for Children**] were written to order, by 'an old bachelor and an old maid'. They are a most curious and unequal mixture, perhaps what one might have expected when the old bachelor was a man of genius—but still an old bachelor—and the old maid that haunting figure whom we know, so closely yet so distantly, as Mary Lamb. It is stretching language very far to believe that Charles's **'Queen Oriana's Dream'** is either good poetry or good children's verse; and many other arch pieces creak audibly in the mechanism, apart from the old bachelor and old maid point of view. Yet simplicity sometimes wins. The opening lines of **'Cleanliness'** (attributed to Charles):

> Come my little Robert near—
> Fie! what filthy hands are here—
> Who, that e'er could understand
> The rare structure of a hand,
> With its branching fingers fine,
> Work itself of hands divine. . .

begin like Jane Taylor and run into something like Blake. When the poems are definitely of the moral type, they are overweighted by length, and they sometimes reveal a sense of humour . . . deeply asleep. . . . Practically none has the real intimacy which a child could draw into a friendly embrace and keep warm in memory. Few show the quick imaginative simplicity of wonder, to be grasped at one splendid leap, the quality that is in Blake, in *The Forsaken Merman*, in *Goblin Market*. They are poems about children (not, indeed, about moral dolls, which is something to be thankful for), or about what the authors would like children to be thinking in their moments of infant contemplativeness, with their mortal span just becoming visible in front of them; not poems *for* children, except in so far as a socio-commercial demand envisaged the child.

In its day the **Poetry** had no great vogue. In fact, it almost disappeared. It went out of print in England—the United States had an edition in 1812—and seems to have survived, for a time, only fragmentarily, but suitably, in 'Mylius's Reading Books', compilations made for use at Christ's Hospital [the school Lamb attended as a child]. (pp. 198-201)

> *F. J. Harvey Darton, "The Moral Tale: Persuasive; Chiefly in Verse," in his* Children's Books in England: Five Centuries of Social Life, *Cambridge at the University Press, 1932, pp. 182-204.\**

## LYN LL. IRVINE (essay date 1932)

[*Irvine analyzes Lamb's idiosyncratic style as revealed through his correspondence and compares it to that of such other letter-writers as Lady Bessborough, Horace Walpole, and William Cowper.*]

Swift and Lamb were both men of peculiar individuality; they swam against the stream. Swift could be excellent company, but he could be vile company too. Lamb was charming, but he must have his joke at a funeral. . . . The reactions to social stimuli of Lamb or Swift could not be relied on; a contrary spirit dwelt within them and awoke when it was least welcome and least expected. With geniuses of this type humour may take strange forms, it may be, as with Lamb, one of the chief means which the spirit within has of expressing its contrariness. (p. 203)

To compare Lamb and Falstaff is of course absurd, but he has the Falstaffian flow of language and images, too ready to be merely an imitation, and Falstaff's nimbleness in wit, the lightning changes from one side to another in his argument; above all things Falstaff's love of a hoax—"a bite, a palpable bite!"— and his gift for making himself the source of laughter. (p. 206).

But Lamb had also the capacity for a more sophisticated sort of humour. He was not a country recluse like Cowper, and although he lived in a very different circle from his contemporary Lady Bessborough, he constantly met people and varieties of people. Lamb was a cockney and had the quick eye and the command of slang characteristic of the pure-bred cockney. (p. 207)

Lamb, like Swift, is so familiar a part of our general ideas, so nearly a truism of the past, that we imagine everything must be known about him. But actually, Lamb is hard to know, even more so than Swift. We can form no conception of the kind of self he might have revealed in love letters, and since he was never separated from Mary Lamb except by her fits of madness we cannot now discover anything about the language of affection and familiarity which they may have used. Most of Lamb's friends were literary people and so much of his early correspondence consists of discussion word by word of early literary excursions that, as human documents, their value is as small as those of any specialist wrapped up in the technicalities of his work.

Moreover, Lamb became an essayist by profession, and he seldom forgot it. Often in his letters he started an idea, gave it a trial run, then caught it and put it in his tail pocket for future use. And in the real extemporising of his letters he practised the simulated extemporising of his essays. (p. 210)

Several of the essays are to be found foreshadowed in the letters and if the letters lack the elaborate allusiveness, the supreme fancy, the finished absurdity of the essays, they have sometimes a directness and spontaneity not always to be found in the corresponding essay. This double-harnessing of letter-writing and essay-writing became in Lamb's letters a literary preoccupation which puts them in a place apart. A born letter-writer— Walpole, Mme de Sévigné or even Fitzgerald—can be relied upon never to forget either himself or his correspondent, never to rhapsodise, never to concentrate too long or too fervently upon any subject. The manners of letter-writing are the manners of polite conversation, and in these Lamb continually defaults. The superiority of the town over the country strikes him, he remembers the charms of an actress or the flavour of a favourite dish, and he is off, absorbed and lost in his subject, and nothing will recall him until inspiration runs dry. In this as in his style of writing he is peculiarly masculine. The feminine mind is what Bacon called "bird-witted", its attention is the most mobile thing about it, and therefore the feminine mind, whether owned by a man or a woman, is excellently suited to letter-writing. (p. 211)

It is worth remembering that he disliked biographies. "What damn'd Unitarian skewer-soul'd things the general biographies turn out," he wrote, and clever as he was at making copy from his own life, he avoided disclosing his most personal feelings. What he said in letters to Wordsworth, Coleridge or Manning was seldom more intimate than what he said in his essays. Moreover, he had not much gift for reporting conversations or gossip; he was sociable indeed at times, but with the worker's hatred of people as constituting interruptions to the real business of life. . . His humorous references to the trials of friendship had sometimes a sub-acidity even more forcible than Swift's plain cynicism upon the constancy of his enemies. (p. 212)

Lamb was town bred and a town dweller. He belonged more to the nineteenth than to the eighteenth century. Cowper at Olney, Gray at Cambridge, Walpole and Swift in their small eighteenth-century worlds did not have the same need to underline their individuality. In the country or in a small familiar group of people the individual has little struggle to assert himself. But in cities and as population increases, a superficial similarity clothes men and women, and it requires either gross or courageous egotism for one man in a community of millions to believe in his distinction and to assert it. Except in rare cases it also requires some skill, the ability to frame a thesis about oneself and to make that thesis intelligible to strangers. All sorts of exaggerations and absurdities are committed by people sensitive to social codes and determined at all costs not to be mistaken for anyone else. Lamb was one of the first people to realise the necessity of emphasising all the points upon which he differed from other people. His essay-writing stimulated him to emphasise them still more, and he allowed his professional manner to permeate his private life—either that, or he elaborated his private manner for professional ends. Lady Bessborough or Gray would not have thought it good style to make so much of personal idiosyncrasies.

As Lamb distinguished himself, so he distinguishes his friends. He picked out characteristics that identified them for ever beyond fear of confusion. (pp. 215-16)

When Lamb turned his attention from his friends to those he disliked, his capacity for exaggeration gathered strength and brilliance and the infusion of acid grew more marked. (p. 216)

But no one doubts that Lamb's ferocity about [people he disliked] behind their backs was redeemed by mildness and courtesy to their faces. Lamb rode in the van of the crusade against bores, but in his case as in so many others the crusade turned into a martyrdom. The greater the bore the greater his invulnerability, and in making proof of the enemy's imperviousness the assailant must often suffer the last extremities of boredom. . . .

So Lamb dealt with people, far more subtly than Walpole did in his letter-chronicles, while still looking upon the world as consisting of people and dominated by people, just as Walpole had looked upon it. To neither of them did it occur that the mind could be more fittingly occupied than in the pleasure-duty of reducing the mob of humanity to some order, whether by narrative and description, or by putting a finger upon the significant idiosyncrasy—"He ate walnuts better than any man I ever knew"—or by proscription. (p. 217)

*Lyn Ll. Irvine, "Lamb," in her* Ten Letter-Writers, *Hogarth Press, 1932, pp. 202-19.*

## ALICE LAW　(essay date 1934)

[*In her assessment of Lamb's reputation, written on the centenary of Lamb's death, Law writes that his eternal youthfulness and "whimsicality," as well as his "broad humanity," have guaranteed Lamb's enduring popularity.*]

Lamb, with a naïveté justified by his genuis, assumes from the first that his readers are with him, that they are interested in his personal thoughts and affairs. And, chiefly from the way in which these thoughts and feelings are presented to us, we are interested the moment we open his pages. The matters dealt with are, perhaps, ordinary enough, but it is the individual appeal that holds us. Lamb talks directly to his reader, strolls about with him in his mind, taking his arm and pointing out this or that way of looking at things in a manner no one has ever assumed with us before. His gaiety is irresistible. We smile and nod with him, feeling the glow of his rich mind, and hurry to pick up the *largesse* he throws continually about him. His charm is indefinable. It partakes largely of the quality of the unexpected. All the delicate fabric of his imagination is spun out of himself, and is shot with a luminous sheen of the most delicate humour. But the material defies analysis; it cannot be handled any more than gossamer. One might as well hope to capture quick-silver as to fix or define the particular genius of Charles Lamb between ruled lines or pages. He winds in and out of his conceits and fancies like a mischievous, sparkling boy, leading us through a labyrinth, yet triumphantly bringing us out with peals of laughter at the end.

A boy! Ah! Here we have the clue! Charles Lamb never grew up! To the very end of his days, despite the well-known tragedies and agonies of his life, he retained the joyous heart of a boy. Equally this same youthful spirit made him detest all literary starch and buckram. . . . Yet for all this, though he was never stiff or ponderous, Lamb himself, in some of his rarer passages, could rise to a height of lyrical prose that proclaims him no unworthy pupil of the great sixteenth- and seventeenth-century prose writers in whose works he loved to steep himself. (pp. 706-07)

His whimsicality is perhaps nowhere better illustrated than in his essay on *The Convalescent*. It is a subject that appeals to most of us, and is as fresh in its humour as if written yesterday, for he is always more than usually delightful when he is airing a grievance. (pp. 707-08)

Yet, beneath all the spirited, brave, almost boyish fun and laughter, beneath all the sparkling wit and brilliance, there is in the writings of Charles Lamb a deep, sad humour, a mood of tragic suffering entailed by the circumstances of his life, by the recurring madness of his beloved sister Mary, by those breakdowns in their domestic harmony that again and again broke up the home, and left him intermittently a disconsolate mourner at a lonely fireside. (p. 709)

Apart from some weak sentimentality—which he shared with some of the great poets of his day—Lamb's critical judgment was sound. He admired Defoe, and was one of the first to be impressed by the as yet unrecognised genius of William Blake. Byron he did not like, nor did Shelley appeal to him, but from the first years of their coming together he was conscious of the greatness of his friend Coleridge. . . .

Lamb's dramatic criticism is invaluable and outstanding, witness his discourse upon *The Artificial Comedy of the Last Century,* where he estimates for us the greatness of Congreve's Art. Also how delicious is his fine irony in respect of Sheridan's

*The East India House.*

portrayal of the respective characters of Joseph and Charles Surface. What, again, can be more subtle than his analysis of the parts of Iago or Malvolio. Yet to realise fully Lamb's greatness as a critic it is necessary to peruse his essay on *The Tragedies of Shakespeare*, in which he puts forth the original and daring theory that "the plays of Shakespeare are less calculated for performance on a stage than those of almost any dramatist whatever. . . . There is so much in them which comes not under the province of acting, with which eye, and tone and gesture have nothing to do." (p. 711)

Many of his letters are almost as entertaining as his *Essays*, and reveal to us the man as he moved, thought and lived. . . .

Gentle and sensitive to an exceptional degree, Lamb was characterised by a deep and broad humanity which finds eloquent expression in many of his essays: his plea for those small, unhappy children who, a century ago, were employed in the sweeping of chimneys, will be remembered. Elsewhere, also, as in his study of *The Genius and Character of Hogarth*, in his *Reflections in the Pillory*, or in his ironical comments upon the *Gallantry* of his day, are voiced his occasionally scathing protests against many of the social abuses of his time—protests which undoubtedly influenced the public opinion of the England of a hundred years ago. The evils he condemned have been swept away, not so his humane and courageous condemnation of them. These outbursts, together with his wit, his fine critical appreciations, his happy pleasantries and delightfully humorous reflections upon life as he knew it, remain, and have secured for Charles Lamb an undisputed literary immortality. (p. 712)

*Alice Law, "Charles Lamb," in* Contemporary Review, *Vol. CXLVI, December, 1934, pp. 706-12.*

**DENYS THOMPSON**　　(essay date 1934)

[*In this largely negative evaluation of Lamb's style and stature, Thompson criticizes Lamb for his "undiscriminating" admiration of Elizabethan dramatists and his misrepresentation of Shakespeare's plays in* Tales from Shakespeare. *Lamb's style, Thompson maintains, has been a "Bad Influence" on students of English prose. Furthermore, the "fake personality" of "Elia" serves only to ingratiate Lamb with his public, whom Thompson calls "the uneducated reader with vestigial pretensions to literacy."*]

If one wanted to be unkind to Lamb, one would scrutinize his dramas, his poetry and his novelette; and his other work seems to me not more valuable. His revival of Elizabethan dramatists was as undiscriminating as his admiration for Burton and Browne. In the *Tales from Shakespeare,* he has like most popularizers done his author a disservice, by stressing inessentials, and promoting the idea that poems are reducible to statements of plot and character, which any sensible person would have written in prose, the poetry being added as a flavouring of magic. . . . The process inevitably involves distortion—Hamlet is sentimentalized into a nice young man who only needed to be kept straight—and it is not apparent that what the Lambs did is much different or more justifiable than the potted versions of the World's Greatest Stories which appeared in the *News of the World* over the signature of the Rt. Hon. Winston Churchill. It has also been claimed for Lamb that given a better opportunity he might have done creditable work. He certainly had a sardonic vein which cropped up when he was not sober. On Wordsworth's boast that he could write like Shakespeare if he had the mind, he commented, 'It is clear that all he lacks is the mind'.

It seems more useful to inquire how a writer so trivial should, any more than half a dozen of his contemporaries, have survived, to be accorded extravagant eulogy and the greater tribute of exploitation for profit in his centenary year. Perhaps that 'trivial' ought to be substantiated, since a mummified Lamb is an important exhibit in our primers of literature. The official verdict ('the splendid range of his veiled mind, the freedom of his sympathies, his command of human experience and his intuitive adventures in the visionary or abstract') seems so preposterous and so unrelated to fact, that one can hardly take it seriously or find a point to engage controversy. In the panegyrics it is Lamb the essayist who is advertised: Lamb a successor of Addison—here, perhaps, is a possible approach. (pp. 200-02)

Lamb, the droll and sentimental, and Addison, serious and witty, rarely converge in their topics of discussion. Lamb's jocularity is feeble and intolerable, and he never (with possibly a unique exception in *Modern Gallantry*) requires his reader to re-orientate himself. If one is offended in reading his essays, it is by the tone; it is often so exacerbating that one wants to shout 'don't breathe in my ear'. He is remote from the centrality reached by Addison and his readers. (p. 203)

The Essays in his lifetime did not reach a second edition, and he seems to have been little read in the century—in the inspection for other purposes of a number of nineteenth-century biographies, I have come across no mention of Lamb among extensive reading lists. . . . Lamb owes his canonization to the heartier journalists and professors of the last thirty years, and a sentence from *Fiction and the Reading Public* indicates the reason: 'After many centuries of unquestioning assent to authority the natural man has asserted himself'. And for him has been provided a *faux-bon* literature, with new and specialized forms. Lamb's gravitation upwards and final shelving with the classics is due to his having chanced upon a recipe peculiarly satisfying to the uneducated reader with vestigial pretensions to literacy. Elia offers him experiences acceptable because they are already in stock, and the exaggerated (because compensatory) gestures of Lamb suit readers without much capacity for living of their own. Lamb gives no shock to self-satisfaction, flattering instead the man who does as he likes, reassuring him that he's right to preserve his irrationalities, foibles and prejudices. The unthinking man in the street shares a number of Lamb's tastes and interests—drink, gastronomy and smoking.

The suitable reader of Lamb nowadays is the 'representative man', proudly ignorant and hostile to serious art and intelligence. . . . Admirers of Elia have a sapless, inherited respect for literature, conceived as uplift and unrelated to living. This accounts for the respect shown for Lamb's Style, an assumed and easily assimilable bag of tricks, little literary touches which give the illiterate something predigested for toothless gums to mumble, and cheat him into believing that he is in contact with great thoughts. Thus the uneducated when they wish to be impressive in writing will resort to the affectation, archaisms, circumlocution, allusions, puns and other tokens of immaturity put into currency by Lamb. . . . Lamb's genius was to call a letter-box 'the all-swallowing indiscriminate orifice of the common post'. The ordinary man is easily impressed by something he cannot immediately understand, so long as he feels that he's flank to flank with a 'warm core of humanity'. In his letters Lamb wrote much better, when this embarrassing confectionary manner was not required for posturing; the contrast is illuminated when little bits of innocent chat in the letters are worked up later into an essay. . . . (pp. 205-08)

Elia has been a Bad Influence. The conception of style, *voulu*, an end in itself, proved serviceable to writers who needed something impressive to conceal their own indigence of mind. . . . In schools especially, where he is imposed as a classic and pattern of writing by the examination system, Lamb's influence is pernicious. 'If this is Literature, I'll take Science' is the reaction of the intelligent young. In this connection a schoolmaster reports that his pupils 'must also be taught hypocrisy. They must be taught, in short, what are the conventional judgments, and how best they may be reproduced. One set book was a selection of Lamb's *Essays*. What is one to say of a boy who finds *Dream Children* repulsive? I found myself obliged to give him a hypocritical note on ''Lamb's Sentiments'' to learn by heart (he got the question and passed). . . .' Lamb and his successors are the worst writers that could be held up for admiration in schools.

But our chief debt to Lamb is not Style. It is the fake personality. In these days, when literature is regarded as suspect and aloof, the popular writer must be wary of being too consistently literary, if he is to have a wide audience. His best way is to identify himself with the reader, comply with him, and strike attitudes which he can share. (pp. 209-11)

*Denys Thompson, ''Our Debt to Lamb,'' in* Determinations: Critical Essays, *edited by F. R. Leavis, Chatto & Windus, 1934, pp. 199-217.*

### T. S. ELIOT   (essay date 1934)

[*Eliot, an American-born English poet, essayist, and critic, is regarded as one of the most influential literary figures of the first half of the twentieth century. As a poet, he is closely identified with many of the qualities denoted by the term Modernism, such as experimentation, formal complexity, artistic and intellectual eclecticism, and a classicist view of the artist working at an emotional distance from his or her creation. As a critic, he introduced a number of terms and concepts that strongly affected critical thought in his lifetime, such as his concept of the ''objective correlative,'' which he defined in his Selected Essays as ''a set of objects, a situation, a chain of events which shall be the formula of (a) particular emotion in the reader.'' His overall emphasis on imagery, symbolism, and meaning and his shunning of extratextual elements as aids in literary criticism helped to establish the theories of New Criticism. Eliot, who converted to the Anglican Church in 1928, stressed the importance of tradition, religion, and morality in literature. In the following excerpt, Eliot briefly discusses the impact of Lamb's dramatic criticism. For another negative assessment of Lamb's criticism, see the excerpt by René Wellek (1955).*]

The accepted attitude toward Elizabethan drama was established on the publication of Charles Lamb's *Specimens*. By publishing these selections, Lamb set in motion the enthusiasm for poetic drama which still persists, and at the same time encouraged the formation of a distinction which is, I believe, the ruin of modern drama—the distinction between drama and literature. For the *Specimens* made it possible to read the plays as poetry while neglecting their function on the stage. It is for this reason that all modern opinion of the Elizabethans seems to spring from Lamb, for all modern opinion rests upon the admission that poetry and drama are two separate things, which can only be *combined* by a writer of exceptional genius. The difference between the people who prefer Elizabethan drama, in spite of what they admit to be its dramatic defects, and the people who prefer modern drama although acknowledging that it is never good poetry, is comparatively unimportant. For in either case, you are committed to the opinion that a play can be good literature but a bad play and that it may be a good play and bad literature—or else that it may be outside of literature altogther. (pp. 8-9)

> *T. S. Eliot, "Four Elizabethan Dramatists," in his* Elizabethan Essays, *Faber & Faber Limited, 1934, pp. 7-20.\**

## H.V.D. DYSON AND JOHN BUTT  (essay date 1940)

[*Generally commending Lamb's originality, Dyson and Butt focus their remarks on the author's style. According to these critics, Lamb's writings mirror his personality: both are "allusive, whimsical, remote, familiar and almost wanton."*]

Lamb's personality is [strong] and many of his admirers are apt to treat him as a personal friend. They claim that to get the best from Lamb one must develop a personal allegiance to him. Either one knows him intimately or not at all. He has no acquaintances. This insistence on his personal character, well known to us from memoirs and letters, rather than on his authorship has been of doubtful advantage to his fame. But it is not inexcusable. It is true that Lamb, when he writes about what he cares for, gives us rather a way of looking at objects than objects to look at. Hazlitt is more wary. Despite his eagerness to share his pleasures and his admirable power of communicating his enthusiasm, his attitude is often a defiant one, and he appears to enjoy what so many of his fellows enjoy despite the fact that he is not quite at home with them. Hazlitt initiates his readers; Lamb adopts them into his strange family. You have to utter his passwords, to respect his reserves. Lamb was a fairly persistent minor poet and has two or three fine things to his credit. But it is as 'Elia' that he is chiefly read and as 'Elia' that he lives. Not that his *Tales from Shakespeare* . . . are not by far the most effective retelling of this sort that has been done. His notes to his *Specimens of English Dramatic Poets who lived about the time of Shakespeare* . . . show knowledge and insight, as well as appreciation of a class of literature that he, like Coleridge and Hazlitt, was doing so much to bring back into fashion. But 'Elia' is Lamb. His best criticism, his tenderest reminiscences, his rarest appreciation are here, in the two series of essays. He adjusts his memories as an antique dealer does his wares. They are not for all markets; to be given away to his friends; to be sold to the connoisseur; to be withheld from the stranger. We *do* come back to the personal relationship after all. If you do not know Lamb and, perhaps, care for him, his stock is not for you, and you will make a bad bargain. Like so many of his contemporaries, there is an eternal immaturity about him. None of them made this often irritating quality so rich a source of delight. Lamb is always looking back; to his old quaint favourites among authors, Burton, Fuller, Margaret, Duchess of Newcastle, and to his own experiences in extreme youth which he had shared with his sister. He understood childish terrors as none before him and few since, and he can still shudder at their recollection. He never lost the taste of childish enjoyments that long ago caressed his palate and he can persuade us that we too know their elusive flavour. The threatening shadows on the nursery wall and the long-expected, long-deferred treat, the expedition to play or countryside, form some of his best material. He was most at home in his imagination amidst the years when terrors and pleasures alike spring from slight matters and endure long. He reminds us that our childhood was real and is not quite extinguished.

His style is like himself, allusive, whimsical, remote, familiar and almost wanton. As Hazlitt is perhaps . . . [a good] model

for English prose, . . . so Lamb is perhaps the worst. To repeat his magic is to turn it to folly. His English written by others, who have neither his knowledge nor his limitations, is one of the most irritating languages that ever affronted the sensibilities with obsequious and mannered parade of quaintness. (pp. 95-6)

> *H.V.D. Dyson and John Butt, "Romantics," in Augustans and Romantics: 1689-1830, by H.V.D. Dyson and others, 1940. Reprint by The Cresset Press, 1961, pp. 72-99.\**

## WALTER E. HOUGHTON, JR.  (essay date 1943)

[*Houghton analyzes Lamb's essay "On the Artificial Comedy of the Last Century" to illuminate Lamb's views on the theory of comedy. Weighing what he considers the positive and negative aspects of that essay, Houghton concludes that it "is a highly sensitive interpretation" of Restoration comedy.*]

[In **"On the Artificial Comedy of the Last Century"**] Lamb is not discussing artificial comedy by itself, but only by contrast with another type of comedy which he goes on at once to define in the opening paragraph of article two. The direct connection is shown by the parallel phrasing. In a modern play, he says, whether sentimental comedy or the "drama of common life," "the moral point is every thing"; and "instead of the fictitious half-believed personages of the stage (the phantoms of old comedy) we recognise ourselves, our brothers, aunts, kinsfolk, allies, patrons, enemies,—the same as in life." The habit of reception thus formed in the modern spectator tended to incapacitate him for the correct and utterly different response to artificial comedy. What he did was to see the latter as he was accustomed to see the former, and hence distort the artificial into the natural. "We substitute a real for a dramatic person, and judge him accordingly. We try him in our courts, from which there is no appeal to the *dramatis personae,* his peers." And Lamb shows that this perversion was facilitated by the actors themselves. . . . At every point, this basic comparison is in the front of Lamb's mind, always qualifying the meaning of such terms as "unrealize" or "realization" by the implied "in contrast with." If his remarks on artificial comedy are pulled out of this context, as they have always been, they are naturally misunderstood. . . . Lamb, never called the world of Wycherley and Congreve "unreal," or a fiction, or a dream, or a fairyland—except in comparison with the drama of common life.

The criticism of [William Congreve's] *Love for Love* starts from a fact of consciousness. Lamb notices (1) that his moral sense was untouched by Bannister's performance of Ben; and (2) that it would be touched, or had been touched, most definitely by another actor—namely one who would play the rôle in the modern mode. Why was this so? The answer, he decided, was the *relative degree of reality,* which meant in turn a relative degree of moral implication. Far from forgetting the relation between art and life, . . . Lamb is preoccupied with the different extent of that very relation in two types of comedy. Just before the comments on Ben, he says that "in the more highly artificial comedy of Congreve or of Sheridan especially, *the absolute sense of reality . . . is not required,* or would rather interfere to diminish your pleasure." And again, "you do not believe" in their characters, but you do not disbelieve in them either. Ben is not literally a "phantom": he is a creature "dear to half-belief" and a phantom only by comparison with an honest-to-goodness Jack Tar. Specifically, Ben is a "dreamy combination of all the accidents of a sailor's character—his contempt of money—his credulity to women," and so on; but he is not a strict metaphrase, not the downright concretion of a Wapping sailor.

Now Lamb has put his finger squarely on the source of this difference. It is the suppression—not the extinction—as contrasted with the thrusting forward of the sensibilities, both by the playwright and the actor. And therefore the further difference in the moral reaction of the audience—either negative or positive. So long as the emotional side of human nature is largely excluded, the moral sense is hardly affected, and certainly not wounded. A man without a heart can only act heartlessly, and for that reason we never think the worse of Ben. But given a real warm-hearted Jack Tar, and his callousness will at once shock the moral feelings.

This may be put from a more subjective angle. If the characters of artificial comedy are essentially creatures of wit, if their appeal remains broadly on the level of the intellect, then our own emotions, whether "good" or "bad," are scarcely implicated. . . . Lamb is concentrating, we notice, on his own reaction. He does not say he could not *connect* these sports with real life, whether of the Restoration or his own time, but rather with his own real life. It is because the first connection does not include the passions, that it is not sufficiently real to rouse his own passions. Because the sports are witty, they cannot be an effective temptation. Hence the characters are creatures, not of fairyland but of "a world of themselves" *like* "fairy-land"—that is, almost equally neutral in its moral effect upon him, and equally opposite to the effect of modern comedy, where his conscience is at once called into action. (pp. 65-9)

It is true enough that in his desire to check the increasing exclusion of Restoration comedy from the stage on moral grounds, Lamb brought forward another argument which is quite unsound, and which therefore blurred his real thesis. The sound defense against the Evangelical prudery was to center, as we have just seen, on the quality of reaction produced, or not produced, by Wycherley and Congreve. But Lamb went on to claim that the plays themselves were free from any immorality because the characters have got out of Christendom into a world where morality doesn't exist. . . . Surely he knew that Restoration comedy was not only gay, but bold and bawdy. Perhaps with his mind acutely aware of the everlasting moral pressure of the new comedy, and yet aware also of no immoral response in himself to the old comedy, he slipped half-consciously into the notion of two worlds, one moral, the other non-moral. More probably his desire to save Wycherley and Congreve from threatened extinction made him the less critical of an argument that the plays themselves lay outside the moral sphere, when in point of fact that was true only of the spectator's reaction. (pp. 69-70)

Had Lamb spoken of a privation of moral *effect,* and of deformities which now are none because we *feel* them none, he would have expressed his meaning more precisely. But the meaning is Wycherley's, though conveyed by another vehicle of contrast. Wycherley argues, in effect, that he didn't introduce a single gush of *immoral* feeling, having in mind the type of decadence which later appears in Vanbrugh and Farquhar. But Lamb's point of reference being modern comedy, what he sees lacking is any gush of *moral* feeling. In both cases, however, the effect is the same: given the feeling of whatever kind, and the judgment is inevitably called back to actual life and actual duties. Subtract the feeling, leave the characters little more than shadows in a Utopia of wit, with only enough flesh and blood for dramatic illusion, and the moral sense is hardly touched.

When we free ourselves from the critical tradition, when we go back to Lamb's text, and read all that he says in all of its context, including the essay **"On Some of the Old Actors,"** we reach a theory of comedy that needs no apology. It might have been expressed with more downright precision; it is slightly blurred; it does not apply equally to all the plays—no theory does; and even as a theory we need not think it infallible, nor accept it blindly. But it is not fantastic or dreamy; it is not a trick or a paradox. It is a highly sensitive interpretation of **"The Artificial Comedy of the Last Century."** (pp. 71-2)

> *Walter E. Houghton, Jr., "Lamb's Criticism of Restoration Comedy," in* ELH, *Vol. 10, No. 1, March, 1943, pp. 61-72.*

**BONAMY DOBRÉE** (essay date 1946)

[*Dobrée characterizes Lamb as an impressionistic critic who excels at reminiscence and offers his personal views of various subjects. Praising the playfulness of Lamb's diction, Dobrée also compares his essays to those of Michel Eyquem de Montaigne.*]

It is the fashion nowadays to decry Lamb as being too mannered, too fanciful, altogether too egotistical and whimsical: but that is largely because his imitators—and people still imitate Lamb—have imitated the wrong thing. Imitators usually do. Because of his way of writing, a theory has grown up that the less an essay is 'about' the more perfect it is. . . . Lamb's essays, nevertheless, are very definitely about something other than himself, though he seems always to be writing about himself alone. If one wanted to make a contrast between him and the usual run of eighteenth century essayists, one would say that whereas they were moralists, he was impressionistic; indeed he goes back further, and his style is Temple's rather than Addison's, though he has a literary sense and tact unknown to the retired ambassador.

He is egotistic in the sense that rather than seem to be uttering great truths about things, he gives his own feelings about them, and in the main he treats of small things (which after all make up most of our lives), preferring, as Hazlitt said of him, byeways to highways. But out of these small things he developed thoughts which spread over the whole of a personal life. Great issues do not figure in his titles; one is invited to read, rather, on subjects such as roast pig, or chimney sweepers, or Mrs. Battle's opinions on whist, but what you find implicit in what follows is an attitude towards life. He is at his best when he is reminiscent, while much of his writing is pervaded by a tenderness towards the helpless, the weak, or the oppressed, a tenderness which some find sentimental, but which, all the same, is invariably controlled. Steeped as he was in seventeenth century literature, he loved the strange striking word so much that its use almost became a vice with him. Yet how apt it seems, how it gives just that turn of whimsicality which is a defence against sentimentality, a whimsicality which it must be confessed itself sometimes came perilously near to being a vice. Yet look at the word 'nigritude' in the opening paragraph of his **"In Praise of Chimney-Sweepers"**:

> I like to meet a sweep—understand me—not a grown sweeper—old chimney-sweepers are by no means attractive—but one of those tender novices, blooming through their first nigritude, the maternal washings not quite effaced from the cheek. . . .

Similar effects crop up everywhere.

But whatever archaic mannerisms (sometimes friendly parodies), or irrelevant eccentricities may here and there a little irritate you in Lamb, he is among the most intimate of our essayists; he really is like Montaigne. Although he was the close companion of the greatest literary figures of his day, we never feel as we read him that he is anything but a lovable ordinary man, lovable because he appreciates our actions, understands our feelings. (pp. 25-7)

As compared with his predecessors, with him we feel delightfully free of what he called the perpetual coxcombry of our moral pretensions.

Not that Lamb was always personal; his critical essays reach out beyond his own affairs, memories, and idiosyncrasies, to general principles, which are based, as all good criticism ultimately is, on what he feels he knows in his bones to be good. The essay on **"The Artificial Comedy of the Last Century"** was a landmark in the criticism of Restoration Comedy, for though its argument is false, it is freshly thought and eagerly argued. Perhaps Lamb is the sort of writer you either warm to very much, or ought to leave severely alone. (p. 28)

> *Bonamy Dobrée, "The Personal Essay," in his* English Essayists, *Collins, 1946, pp. 25-31.*\*

### BERTRAM JESSUP   (essay date 1954)

[*Treating "Elia" as a philosopher, Jessup delves into Lamb's views on reality, religion, taste, and aestheticism as formulated in the essays. Overall, he praises the antiformalism and breadth of Lamb's ideas.*]

Elia is a philosopher—and one of the tough-minded rather than the tender-minded variety. He stands firmly in the tradition of British empiricism, a relativist and anti-absolutist. He believes in the truth of sensation, and in larger matters distrusts anything beyond probabilities. His romantic, sentimental reputation notwithstanding, he thinks as well as dreams—and when he dreams he knows it. His dreams are not metaphysical. (p. 247)

"I am in love with this green earth," says Elia, "the face of town and country; the unspeakable rural solitudes, and the sweet security of streets. I would set up my tabernacle here." Neither transcendental logic nor mystic vision could for Elia produce convincing or satisfying substitutes for the robust realities of here and now—of the

> Sun, and sky, and breeze, and solitary walks, and summer holidays, and the greenness of fields, and the delicious juices of meats, and fishes, and society, and the cheerful glass, and candle-light, and fireside conversations, and innocent vanities, and jest, and *irony itself*—

Believing in life as it comes leads Elia to believe also in life as it goes. He accepts the simple tragedy of its evanescence. He is no two-worlds man. Life is real and good and the loss of it is real and evil. "Do these things go out with life?" he asks. And he finds nothing in the metaphysicians or the divines to show that they do not—no reason, no evidence. Instead, only dry metaphors borrowed from popular self-delusion, which, says Elia, "solace me not, nor sweeten the unpalatable draught of mortality." "I am not content to pass away 'like a weaver's shuttle.'" "I care not to be carried with the tide, that smoothly bears human life to eternity." And ghosts, he is quite sure, are ghosts. "Can a ghost laugh, or shake his gaunt sides when you are pleasant with him?"

For Elia death is real because life is real. (pp. 247-48)

Like Elia, Lamb was in love with life with its full factual and concrete immediacy. His taste for life was strong and not squeamish or finicky. He liked things unassorted as they come—all that he demanded was that they be alive—and human. (p. 248)

Quite consistently with his essential naturalism, which regarded this world and this life as sufficient unto themselves, both intellectually and emotionally—or if not, that there was no mending—Elia does not go in for religious belief or religious morality. (pp. 249-50)

Elia knew quite well that the dogmatism of religion and the religion of religion are all the same thing as far as claims to knowledge and principles of virtue are concerned. In the **"Imperfect Sympathies"** his simple logic makes the plain point which should have but hasn't disposed once for all of the canting notion that between sects and doctrines there should be the kind of tolerance which is proper to inquiry and hypothesis. Religion is dogmatic and absolute. "The reciprocal endearments," between dogmatists—he speaks here of Jew and Christian—"have to me, something hypocritical and unnatural in them. I do not like to see the Church and Synagogue kissing and congeeing in awkward postures of an affected civility. If *they* are converted, why do they not come over to us altogether?" And if they are not, he leaves us to think further for ourselves, why tolerate them at all? If we believe our religion let's believe it religiously—that is, dogmatically and intolerantly, and if we don't, let's proceed hypothetically altogether and admit our beliefs to empirical tests and reason.

On the matter of religious morality, Elia operates with the same quiet logic—when he considers it at all, which is not often. In **"Grace Before Meat,"** which offended Dorothy Wordsworth, he speaks of the practice of saying grace. "You are startled at the injustice of returning thanks—" he asks, "for what?—for having too much while so many starve. I have seen it," he adds,

> in clergymen and others—a sort of shame—a sense of the co-presence of circumstances which unhallow the blessing. After a devotional tone put on for a few seconds, how rapidly the speaker will fall into his common voice, helping himself or his neighbor, as if to get rid of some uneasy sensation of hypocrisy.
>
> (p. 250)

On the question of small mercantile or employment virtues, which in Victorian times as now were supposed to add up to a kind of material godliness, [Lamb was] . . . latitudinarian. For instance, he was, so he says, accustomed to do all his private correspondence on company time at his desk in the East India House. "I have the habit of never writing letters but at the office; 'tis so much time cribbed out of the company."

Subtracting jest, whimsy, and exaggeration, there is enough remainder in passages such as these, when added to directer statements of belief which we occasionally find from Lamb, to characterize his serious ethical views. He is firm in opposition to formalism of any kind or degree. Life, he believes, is too complicated to reduce to principles, and it is too individual to warrant anyone's setting himself up as guide or judge. Particular cases always elude rules. Constrained conformity is a gall. "Damn virtue that's thrust upon us!" His social ethics and his personal are fairly well summarized in the following two paragraphs:

> If one is to secure a reasonable degree of happiness in life as it is, one must first of all not expect too much of human nature, and not forget that even the best of men and women have their weaknesses (like oneself).
>
> I am determined to lead a merry life in the midst of sinners. I try to consider all men as such, and to pitch my expectations from human nature as low as possible. In this view, all unexpected virtues are God-sends and beautiful exceptions.

The anti-formalism which characterizes Charles Lamb's ethical thought, is reflected in a more comprehensive form in the anti-rationalism of the mind of Elia. Rationality in the sense of reasonableness in respecting facts and not confusing them with wishes or habits, he regards highly and follows with singular consistency. But rationalism in the sense of believing that man's thinking legislates the facts, or that facts are the body of man's mind, he disallows completely. (pp. 252-53)

Not only does Elia, however, stand with the traditional empiricists against the absolutists and apriorists in holding the problematic nature of all truth; he goes quite beyond them in being skeptical of the regular increase in probability of particular beliefs. Progress in thinking, he seems to suspect, consists often in an exchange of superstitions. Superstitions are quite natural to man, and not the result of bad up-bringing. Belief in witches, for example, was formerly reasonable; given the postulates, the evidence for their existence followed quite conclusively.... Even reason, the implication is, has its limits, and to pursue it without limit is pretense and superstition at the roots, it is rationalism.

This rationalism is particularly rank in what is modernly known as matters of value as distinguished from matters of fact, or in Elia's terms, in matters of preferences, sympathies and criticism. In such matters, he is clear, likes are facts. (p. 254)

In holding the position that in matters of value, likes are the primary facts and preference the ultimate standard, Elia is quite contemporary. Whether it recommends him to you or not belongs in the company of the relativists, and the emotivists.

One consequence of holding consistently to his position, will not, I am sure, recommend him or his theory to the social liberalism which is currently correct. The position itself is contained unmistakably in the **"Imperfect Sympathies,"** and abstractly it is that there is a limit beyond which reasoned likes cannot go. The limit is at any time for any individual his stubborn basic preferences which arguments can't change. Elia calls them, with frank admission of their irrationality, "imperfect sympathies." To have imperfect sympathies, the observations suggest, is simply to be human—to find things different in one's affections. *Perfect* sympathy would be to like nothing at all. (pp. 254-55)

The question of taste leads naturally to a further general and strong Elian characteristic of mind and attitude—one which also brings up points of possible division between him and some of us. It is his aestheticism. The position is not indefensible, however. It is the conviction that what matters finally is the qualitative immediacy of things, that the best and surest way of getting hold of anything—whether an antique clock in the temple square or a city full of people, is to feel them in their unique quality, and not through round about and translated abstractions—intellectual, moral, critical, logical, etc. If it is

*Illustration of Hamlet, Horatio, and the grave digger from the first edition of* Tales from Shakespear.

a matter of worth it is a matter of immediacy. It is the kind of direct savoring typical of Lamb as literary critic. . . . (p. 256)

Not only literature and works of art and concrete things to be looked at lend themselves to this kind of rendering, but institutions and social aggregations and systems as well—and this is Lamb's way—or Elia's. A system of ideas or a set of attitudes sits well or it doesn't—that is the final test. And so of other things. A slum or a social practice like "modern gallantry" or "grace before meat" may be dissected into unacceptable consequences and implications, but finally they or their consequences are or are not an affront to sensibility, and are or are not ugly to immediate contemplation. More systematic and intellectually more reputed philosophers than either Elia or Lamb have held at least a part of the same view, and have been listened to. Even Plato allowed Beauty to be the immediate way to truth and goodness. In such good company Elia's aestheticism may pass respectably enough.

But his aestheticism takes another direction, in which the company is not so good—or vanishes altogether. If there are those who take the same direction, *they* commonly take a more devious and secret route, while Elia takes the short and open way. This aestheticism in its frank Elian form is a moral aestheticism, which accepts in principle everything, even the socially ugly and the privately sore, as possibly interesting—something of its own unique quality, which can be suffered or attacked, on the one hand, or which can be savored and enjoyed, on the other. (pp. 256-57)

[In **"The Praise of Chimney-Sweepers"** and **"A Complaint on the Decay of Beggars in the Metropolis,"**] both chimney-sweeps and beggars are feelingly recognized as unfortunate victims of society, but at the same time they are prized as part of the aesthetic landscape. They are an interesting species, for whose loss we would be the poorer in immediate quality. Elia sets himself against reforming them out of existence. "I do not approve," he says in the Beggars essay,

> of this wholesale going to work, this impertinent crusado, or bellum ad exterminationem, proclaimed against the species. . . . The mendicants of this great city were so many of her sights, her lions. I can no more spare them than I could the Cries of London. No corner of a street is complete without them.

This is the point, most of us would probably protest, at which the incommensurability of values would have to take hold—and the aesthetic give way somewhat tragically to the moral. Perhaps Elia needs again to put his tastes in order. But so do some of us, who "enjoy" slumming in the big cities.

My final observation on the Mind of Elia reverts to something upon which I have already touched, and which might be called—if it were not ascriptive pretension—Elia's theory of reality. Elia, I have said, is an empiricist and a particularist. No Platonist, rationalist or mystic, he believes in the fleeting and varied particular, in what his senses give him or attest. In literature, he anticipates the line of Flaubert, and Proust, and Howells—the observationalists. He is interested in life, in things and places and persons as they are or have been; he is not interested in the pale perfection of the absolute or the transcendent. He likes Hogarth and the robust Elizabethans, and dislikes the dreaming Shelleys and the denying Byrons. He likes the concrete, the thing of qualities and the specific human act, and not the spirit of Beauty or the bloodless voice of duty absolute.

Things are many, they change and they differ. This, Elia, seems to say, is the first truth about reality. In that he rests and from that derives his aestheticism. It turns him to the unique, the irregular, the odd—even to the contradictory. . . . Lamb confirms the taste in his friend. . . . (pp. 257-58)

This belief that the real and important is unique and individual rather than general and universal is revealed too in the way he dwells on the functionally non-essential in the persons he remembers and describes, as for example, in The South Sea House, the old clerks. Each is a character all himself, except for being a clerk, and that counts little. They were "humorists . . . of all descriptions . . .

> not having been brought together in early life . . . but for the most part, placed in the house in ripe or middle ages, they necessarily carried into it their separate habits and oddities. . . . They formed a sort of Noah's ark. Odd fishes.

One, the cashier, was a hypochondriac, "melancholy as a gibcat." Another, John Tipp, scraped the fiddle most abominably. Several shared an eccentric passion for tootling flutes. So were they defined, uniquely and non-essentially, except for one common passion, which might be held to be professional—the love of figures and exact balances, quite apart from and indifferent to profits. "To a genuine accountant the difference of proceeds

is as nothing, the fractional farthing is as dear to his heart as the thousands which stand before it . . . he is the true actor."

This attachment to the unique and particular, it should be noted finally, is consistent with his uncommon devotion to the past, on account of which he has often been called an escapist and non-realist. But he is in fact no escapist. It is only that his realism has a wider temporal range than the present and the practical. His realism is an "aesthetic realism." It includes as equally real whatever comes to present experience, whether from the temporal present or the past. There is, to be sure, a certain preference for the bygone. But this is explainable within his realism. The present thing or person always tends to become categorized, functionalized or generalized in abstractions. Once safely in the past, if it visibly or otherwise concretely survives in fact or memory, it becomes itself again. It is no longer a sign of something or a use for something. The inactivated, the memory the superannuated, the outdated—these are all qualities once more—immediacies. In his way, Elia is not amiss in counting them real and in prizing them. In his way, he knows *what* things are better than most men. He likes reality but he likes it broad. He likes almost everything that can be put fast to be looked at—past or present. This to him is the way—it is life, and to him, as Coleridge said, "No sound is dissonant which tells of life."

If this is philosophy, then Elia is a philosopher. If it isn't, then he still is a philosopher in the sense in which the philosopher has been described as one who is possessed of an "intellectual force and depth," a "firm, clear, quiet intelligence" which arms him who has it "against humbug and quackery." Much of the humbug and quackery of conventional belief and vested attitude he—Elia or Lamb, as you now wish—stripped away, deviously, charmingly and mockingly, but with frequent finality and rare precision. (pp. 258-59)

> *Bertram Jessup, "The Mind of Elia," in* Journal of the History of Ideas, *Vol. XV, No. 2, April, 1954, pp. 246-59.*

## RENÉ WELLEK   (essay date 1955)

[*Wellek's* A History of Modern Criticism, *from which the following is drawn, is a major, comprehensive study of the literary critics of the last three centuries. His critical method, as demonstrated in* A History, *is one of describing, analyzing, and evaluating a work solely in terms of the problems it poses for itself and how the writer solves them. Here, Wellek credits Lamb with initiating the "evocative" method of criticism in England, but argues that his comments are not historically important since they are unsystematic and recorded mostly in the form of marginalia. Surveying some of Lamb's remarks on drama and poetry, Wellek concludes that "Lamb's most 'creative' criticism is his most indirect." For another negative assessment of Lamb's criticism, see the excerpt by T. S. Eliot (1934).*]

Whatever the obscure origins of the [critical method which uses evocation, metaphor, and personal reference] may be, Lamb was the original initiator in England. It seems hard, however, to agree to the extravagant claims which have been made for his general importance in a history of criticism. . . . We can see the germs of Lamb's method in early informal letters dating back to 1801. Speaking of Walton's *Angler* he says: "Don't you already feel your spirit filled with the scenes?—the banks of rivers—the cowslip beds—the pastoral scenes—the neat alehouses—and hostesses and milkmaids." As we have read so much of this kind of evocative criticism, we may not be impressed, but it would be hard to find earlier instances in English. Nor could one find pure instances of criticism by metaphor earlier than in Lamb. Thus, speaking of Jeremy Taylor, Lamb enumerates the similes and allusions "taken, as the bees take honey, from all the youngest, greenest, exquisitest parts of nature," and then calls Taylor's imagination "a spacious garden, where no vile insects could crawl in; his apprehension a *Court* where no foul thoughts kept 'leets and holydays.'"

These casual pronouncements become a method in the remarks commenting on individual plays and passages in Lamb's *Specimens of English Dramatic Poets* . . . and in scattered essays, of which two, **"On the Tragedies of Shakespeare Considered with Reference to Their Fitness for Stage Representation"** . . . and **"On the Artificial Comedy of the Last Century"** . . . , are best known and most admired. But these essays are not impressive for their general arguments. The view that the "plays of Shakespeare are less calculated for performance on a stage, than those of almost any dramatist whatever" can hardly be taken seriously except as a means of drawing our attention to the greatness of Shakespeare's poetry and the diverse shortcomings of the stage in the time of Lamb. Nor are we likely to be convinced by the argument that Restoration comedy leads us into the "land of cuckoldry, the Utopia of gallantry" which "has no reference whatever to the world that is." We must take it as a protest against the literal-minded moralism of the time, as an assertion of the conventionality of the stage, not as a serious argument against relations between literature and life, drama and society. Lamb, on occasion, can drive home a single well-taken point: he argues against strict stage-illusion in comedy, "for a judicious understanding, not too openly announced, between the ladies and gentlemen—on both sides of the curtain." He is good in praising the sanity of true genius, an argument of peculiar poignancy in his own case. But for the most part Lamb's criticism must be described as "detached thoughts on books and reading," as *marginalia*. They deserve our admiration because they are finely phrased and reveal a literary taste new at that time, shared only by Coleridge and a few others: a taste for the 17th century, its quaintness and baroque grandeur, for Browne and Burton, for Fuller and Jeremy Taylor. But it seems impossible to claim for these marginalia great significance in a history of criticism.

*Specimens of English Dramatic Poets* was an influential anthology of the non-Shakespearean drama, which at that time had been only partially reprinted and had elicited mostly antiquarian interest. Lamb was one of the very first to appreciate these plays for their poetry. His enthusiasm for Webster was new, and one can understand the feelings of a discoverer that led Lamb to call Thomas Heywood "a sort of prose Shakespeare" and to place John Ford in the "first order of poets." But as criticism the comments are usually little more than exclamation marks, mere assertions of enthusiasm. Even such a longer passage as the comment on the torture scenes in [Webster's] the *Duchess of Malfi* amounts to little more than an enumeration of the details of the action and the doubtful claim that Webster has conveyed the horror with dignity and decorum. It is the kind of personal unargued criticism whose irrelevance to the text becomes most obvious when Lamb speaks of [Cyril Tourneur's] the *Revenger's Tragedy.* "I have never read it but my ears tingle, and I feel a hot blush overspread my cheeks." It is the criterion of the thrill down the spine, the bristling of the beard, the rise in the pit of the stomach, which A. E. Housman has in our time proclaimed to be the test of true poetry. This exclamatory criticism has its function in the notes to an anthology: it serves in lieu of the inverted commas used by Pope to mark off the "beauties of Shakespeare."

Much of the rest of Lamb's criticism is a kind of pointing to fine passages: the essays on Thomas Fuller and George Wither especially are little more than anthologies. Only in the piece on the sonnets of Sidney is there an attempt at actual criticism: in opposition to Hazlitt, who thought them frigid and cumbrous, Lamb considers them "full, material and circumstantiated." But it seems doubtful whether the verse of these sonnets "runs off swiftly and gallantly," or whether "it might have been tuned to the trumpet; or tempered (as he himself expresses it) to 'trampling horses' feet.'" There is small relation between such a metaphor derived from a knowledge of Sidney's life and martial experiences, as suggested by Sidney's remarks on [the anonymous ballad] *Chevy Chase,* and the sonnets which Lamb himself quotes as his favorites: "With how sad steps, O Moon, thou climb'st the skies"; "Come, Sleep, O Sleep, the certain knot of peace." What have such lines to do with trumpets and trampling horses' feet? This is impressionistic criticism which has lost all contact with the text.

Lamb's formal reviews, such as that of Wordsworth's *Excursion* and of Keats' *Lamia* volume, are largely strings of extracts with pronouncements of preferences. The much admired review of Keats, which selects fine passages from a poet then quite unrecognized, still comes to the false conclusion that *Isabella* is better than *Lamia, The Eve of St. Agnes,* and the odes on the ground that "an ounce of feeling is worth a pound of fancy." This and many other judgments show Lamb's emotional romanticism, the view that passion is "the all in all in poetry."

Lamb, of course, *wanted* to point out fine passages and convey his own enthusiasm to his readers. He knew that he was no theorist and not even a regular critic; with his usual modesty he speaks of his "inability of reviewing, of giving account of a book in any methodical way." "I can vehemently applaud, or perversely stickle, at *parts:* but I cannot grasp at a whole." At the same time he recognized the deficiencies of all selections, all snippets: "how beggarly and how bald even Shakespeare's princely pieces look when thus violently divorced from connection or circumstance! . . . Everything in heaven and earth, in man and in story, in books and in fancy, acts by Confederacy, by juxtaposition, by circumstance and place." Lamb also understood Wordsworth's and Coleridge's theory of the imagination, of which he said (earlier than any of their extensive discussions in print) that it "draws all things into one . . . makes things animate and inanimate, beings with their attributes, subjects and their accessories, take one color, and serve to one effect."

Some of Lamb's *obiter dicta,* scattered over the essays and letters, may seem to us mistaken, but his dislike of Shelley and Byron, his description of Goethe's *Faust* as "a disagreeable canting tale of seduction," his approval of Wordsworth's opinion about the dullness of Voltaire's *Candide* cannot surprise if we know the political and social context. Nevertheless, we must agree with him when he praises [Coleridge's] the *Ancient Mariner* or chides Wordsworth for his overt didacticism and for "continually putting a sign post up to show where you are to feel." Lamb's most "creative" criticism is his most indirect. His pastiches and imitations of Burton and Sir Thomas Browne's "beautiful obliquities" show that he had a true feeling for their style even though he was unwilling or unable to define or analyze it intellectually. (pp. 191-95)

René Wellek, "Hazlitt, Lamb, and Keats," in his A History of Modern Criticism, 1750-1950: The Romantic Age, Vol. 2, 1955. Reprint by Cambridge University Press, 1981, pp. 188-215.\*

**DONALD H. REIMAN** (essay date 1965)

*[Reiman traces Lamb's method of developing thematic unity in his essays, arguing that to avoid preaching to his readers he imbued ordinary, even "trivial" events with lessons about philosophical and moral issues.]*

As I hope to show by analyzing systematically **"Mrs. Battle's Opinions on Whist," "The Two Races of Men,"** and **"Old China,"** the essays attributed to Elia achieve their thematic and artistic integrity by exploring everyday events and trivial opinions that suggest, analogically, larger philosophical issues. Focusing his ideas around an unpretentious symbol, Lamb could remain nondogmatic and skeptical through the light tone appropriate to this ostensible subject and, by ironically understating his conclusions, could avoid all trace of the "mental bombast" that, according to Coleridge, occasionally marred Wordsworth's poems of high seriousness. (pp. 470-71)

Though Mrs. Battle did not take whist at all lightly, Elia seems to treat his old companion and her favorite game with some detachment. At the end of the essay, however, Elia confesses himself so dedicated to cards that he wishes his game of piquet with Bridget could go on forever. Is this mere whimsy? Or do the card games in this essay assume significance beyond innocent amusement? One should note in the opening paragraph that old Sarah Battle, "now with God," "loved" one thing better than "a good game at whist": "her devotions." This pairing does not seem to be simply an ironic juxtaposition of the cosmic and the trivial in the values of an eccentric old woman: the author tells us nothing to indicate that Mrs. Battle's religion was shallow or sentimental; on the contrary, the sole reference to the result of her piety—"now with God"—suggests the opposite conclusion, that there was some defensible relation between Mrs. Battle's devotions and her whist-playing, the two most important things in her life.

Mrs. Battle, indeed, considered that playing whist "was her business, her duty, the thing she came into the world to do,—and she did it." . . . It was "her noble occupation, to which she wound up her faculties." Whist was, in other words, Mrs. Battle's "vocation," that to which she had been called, that in the proper performance of which she could win salvation. Not that Elia or Mrs. Battle would care to translate the analogy as I have just done—assert rather than suggest—but this unmistakable suggestion governs the entire essay. (pp. 471-72)

As the name "Mrs. Battle" itself suggests, and as Elia repeatedly emphasizes, the old lady considered card games to be a kind of warfare: "She loved a thorough-paced partner, a determined enemy. . . . She fought a good fight: cut and thrust." (pp. 472-73)

In short, Mrs. Battle believed that "man is a gaming animal" and that "this passion can scarcely be more safely expended than upon a game at cards" in which, "during the illusion, we *are* as mightily concerned as those whose stake is crowns and kingdoms." Whist is "quite as diverting, and a great deal more innoxious, than many of those more serious *games* of life, which men play, without esteeming them to be such." . . . Mrs. Battle thus makes explicit the larger analogy and the ramifications of her vocation. To one skeptical of the objective

value of religious, philosophical, political, or even aesthetic dogmas and slogans, to one for whom every endeavor seemed a commitment to an illusion, complete dedication to the game of whist might serve to develop one's character and purify the soul as surely as would devotion to any other cause or creed.

In the concluding paragraphs Elia, having already established the differences between his character and that of Mrs. Battle, remarks that he sometimes finds card games stimulating even if there is no stake, no reward to be won. Sometimes, when he is "in sickness, or not in the best spirits," he plays "a game at piquet *for love* with my cousin Bridget—Bridget Elia." Though he breaks all of Mrs. Battle's stern injunctions, he yet manages to enjoy the game: "I wished it might have lasted for ever, though we gained nothing, and lost nothing, though it was a mere shade of play: I would be content to go on in that idle folly for ever." For Elia the aesthetic enjoyment of the game is its own reward. He need not vanquish his "enemy" nor anticipate a reward. The game of life has value in the present moment quite apart from subsequent developments, which might, indeed, prove as painful as "the gentle lenitive to my foot, which Bridget was doomed to apply after the game was over. . . ."

Lamb in this essay . . . developed the rationale for the elevation of sports and games as symbols or parables of human life's serious occupations, and Hemingway's billiard players, fishermen, and bull fighters are distant relations of Mrs. Battle.

**"The Two Races of Men"** exhibits a subtler, more ambitious interweaving of theme and subject. The ostensible topic under discussion is the classification of "the human species" into "two distinct races, *the men who borrow,* and *the men who lend.*" After setting forth the thesis in two introductory paragraphs, Lamb explores it through two subsequent divisions of the essay: six paragraphs ironically chronicle the activities of those members of "the *great race*" who, like Ralph Bigod, Esq., specialize in borrowing money, and the remaining six paragraphs center on that "class of alienators more formidable" ("to one like Elia")—"your *borrowers of books.*" Chief among these scavengers is "Comberbatch" (Coleridge), "matchless in his depredations."

Elia, one sees immediately, distinguishes between these two classes of borrowers almost as sharply as he does between borrowers and lenders. He who "borrows" from his purse steals, not trash (Elia's refutation of the popular fallacy **"That Enough Is as Good as a Feast"** forbids this interpretation), but something that, once gone, is unlikely ever to return. (pp. 473-75)

The real theme of **"The Two Races of Men"** is, then, that there is indeed a Great Race of borrowers, men exemplified by Alcibiades, Falstaff, Sir Richard Steele, and Richard Brinsley Sheridan . . . and by Coleridge; these borrowers, in their turn, contribute much to the world's welfare—not, perhaps, in a material way, with money or physical books, but through intellectual contributions to mankind in general and to their friends and companions in particular. Such men are those to whom Elia and all wishing to avoid combining the "penalties of Lazarus and of Dives" . . . (poverty and parsimony) should open their hearts and their libraries and receive the rewards of their magnanimity from truly great-minded men.

The theme of **"Old China"** seems obvious enough, except for the apparent irrelevance of the remarks on old china with which the essay begins and concludes. The main body of the essay consists of Cousin Bridget's elegy on the passing of the good old days of poverty, and Elia's unsentimental, hard-headed reply: "It is true we were happier when we were poorer, but we were also younger, my cousin. . . . Competence to age is supplementary youth; a sorry supplement indeed, but I fear the best that is to be had." . . . Both Elia and Bridget regret the loss of their youth and its humble adventures, but whereas Bridget tries to externalize the problem and blame the loss of past joys on the accumulation of wealth, Elia more realistically recognizes that the difficulty lies within himself and Bridget, subject to the gentle ravages of Fate, Time, Occasion, Chance, and Change.

Elia's love for old china is one of those tastes "of too ancient a date to admit of our remembering distinctly that it was an acquired one. I can call to mind the first play, and the first exhibition, that I was taken to; but I am not conscious of a time when china jars and saucers were introduced into my imagination." . . . In the symbolic world of this essay, then, Time governs the plays and pictures which Bridget mentions in her elegy for lost happiness and which thereby become symbols of the decay of human faculties (much as do beauties of nature, seen but no longer felt, in Coleridge's "Dejection: An Ode"). Because the love of old china is not, however, associated with any particular moment in the past, this attachment participates in a timeless world that mutability cannot affect. (p. 476)

Bridget bemoans the loss of human youth and novelty and joy against the backdrop of a world where Beauty *can* keep her lustrous eyes and where youth does *not* grow pale, and specter-thin, and die. Like Keats's Grecian urn, Yeats's lapis lazuli sculpture, or T. S. Eliot's Chinese jar, Elia's china tea-cups present a still point amid a world of flux and, at the same time, a stimulus for the human imagination both of him who creates and him who contemplates them. Elia turns back to the china, therefore, at the end of the essay, in order to retain his hold on the values of a summer world that he feels slipping away from him. . . . Could the world of human affairs, even the great world of Croesus and the Rothschilds, retain its values, man might find his ultimate meaning in worldly activity—in the affairs of the East India Company, for example. But because Elia feels this to be impossible, he turns instead to a world of fragile art that proves to be a never-fading source of delight—as we, for example, turn to the essays of Elia.

Lamb, as I have said, intentionally avoided the kind of overt moralizing that I have explicated from his hints and analogies. Once the thematic unity of an essay becomes clear, however, one can return to Lamb's writings with a new appreciation of the perfectly balanced tone that suggests deeper meanings without committing Lamb or his reader to the logical analyses or marshaled facts that must have accompanied a discursive development of the thesis. Lamb, the humane skeptic, preferred not to dogmatize—or even to speculate systematically—on the nature of the state of being that must inevitably follow "that last game" of piquet he played with his "sweet cousin," but he was not unwilling to set forth his opinions on the game of life and the stakes for which a man ought willingly to play. He therefore created a symbol-world through which he could explore universal human problems in a truly imaginative way; like the pastoral world of Robert Frost's best poetry, the trivial universe of Elia and Bridget, of whist games, borrowed books, and frail china tea-cups, provided a language for one who truly desired both to teach and to delight. (pp. 477-78)

*Donald H. Reiman, "Thematic Unity in Lamb's Familiar Essays,"* in The Journal of English and Germanic Philology, *Vol. LXIV, No. 3, July, 1965, pp. 470-78.*

**GEOFFREY TILLOTSON** (essay date 1966)

[*Tillotson focuses on Lamb's essay "Witches and Other Night Fears." He credits Lamb with being "one of the first writers to discover the child's psyche as a substantial matter for literature" and to explore the effect of the child's imagination on the adult mind.*]

[One of Lamb's] most profound essays is **"Witches and Other Night Fears."** It contains the best extended account in our literature of child psychology (on several of its sides, not merely the horrific) that exists before Dickens. Lamb is one of the first writers to discover the child's psyche as a substantial matter for literature. His essay serves to show that the subject as Lamb discovered it qualifies for treatment in prose. Lamb discovers the child's psyche for what it is, not for what it is conveniently believed to be by the sentimental and the avuncular. Indeed, there cannot have been many of his many successors in this field who have dared to tell autobiographical truths so little to the author's credit. Clearly as a *British* child Lamb was a failure. (p. 96)

The truth of Lamb's account of his own horrors (I am assuming that the essay is autobiographical) is evinced by two things in particular: (1) the detail of the mantle [from Stackhouse's illustrated *History of the Bible*]—it is shown billowing wildly in the engraving, and we all remember that horror is worst when its hugeness is concentrated in a detail; and (2) the picture, nowadays at least, would not seem to be more than mildly disturbing—in other words Lamb, as he well knew, contributed horror from his own capacity to create it. If not shaped by Stackhouse's illustrator, his horror would have come, as he says, "self-pictured". . . . (pp. 98-9)

["**Witches and Other Night Fears**"] ends with one of those long codas where, as not infrequently in Lamb's essays, the tension is eased, or the mood lifted or depressed to a different level. Up to now, we have been attending to the child, though always from the point of view of maturity—the man has been remembering the child and his double interest in himself, and it has been kept before us by means of a series of short inserted comparisons. . . . But now at the close, we abandon the child and take a look at what remains in the adult of the child's great power of gruesome imagination. The turn affords an opportunity that Lamb has the genius to take. (p. 103)

He claims very little for his own dream. Though it began in grandiose fashion, it ended in a way that no poet of this time—unless he were that uncommon thing at this date, a poet who could freely alternate or interpenetrate the comic and sublime—would have dared to describe. (p. 104)

To characterize Lamb's mind as shown in the essays, we should have to invoke something between the mind of novelist, critic, and poet. . . . [Novelists] represent life as it is; and this is what Lamb's essays do, though they may be pretending to do something else. In the mid-nineteenth century, there was a strong movement toward taking truth as the first virtue of a fiction writer; and among its predecessors, Lamb stands prominent. (pp. 111-14)

[There] was a poet in Lamb. He did, in fact, write poetry in meter, and some of the results are admirable. But his most remarkable poetry is embedded in his prose. Some of it is the poetry of fancy, but in that description of the dream, and in a score or two of comparable passages there is poetry of a deeper sort, which we should be the more ready to allow because we have recently returned to admire and marvel at the poetry of Pope. It is poetry that is flexible in its operation—of the sort that Hazlitt discerned in the *Rape of the Lock,* and did not know whether to laugh or cry over. It mixes beauty and commonplace, richness and dinginess, and those two things which, according to Thackeray, make humour when combined—wit and love. (pp. 115-16)

> Geoffrey Tillotson, "The Historical Importance of Certain 'Essays of Elia'," in Some British Romantics: A Collection of Essays, *James V. Logan, John E. Jordan, Northrop Frye, eds., Ohio State University Press, 1966, pp. 89-116.*

## BRIGID BROPHY, MICHAEL LEVEY, and CHARLES OSBORNE   (essay date 1967)

[*Brophy, Levey, and Osborne address the discrepancy between Lamb's private traits and the public narrative persona of "Elia." According to the critics, underneath the innocent, quaint veneer of "Elia," Lamb was actually "a knowing old sheep."*]

There is something in the author's very name that has a bleating irritation about it, a sort of coy pulling of wool over the eyes, a consciously innocent, over-innocent, association—all of which is quite unfair, of course, to Charles Lamb. Or is it? Lamb was by most accounts such an amusing, good-hearted—and brave—man that one would like to let the question rest, were it not for the literary work. (p. 39)

The essay form is one of the weakest plants in literature's garden. It promises very little, is powered by a barely creative urge, and pushes up only a few pale sprouts, leaves that are seldom accompanied by anything as positive as a flower. In some ways it is—to change the metaphor—a sort of intellectual tatting for those not strong enough to embark on a full-scale piece of work. There is Montaigne, of course, and there is Bacon. Neither perhaps, however historically or personally interesting, is quite sufficient to wipe away the stigma left by Johnson's definition of what he too wrote, the essay: an irregular, ill-digested piece. The essay's dependence on the essayist's personality is rather frightening: it never quite cuts free—as does a work of art—and gradually seems to demand more and more sustenance from the personality. It hovers on an intimacy which is false; it encourages the essayist to construct a public *persona,* usually self-deprecatory, whimsical, a lover of little things, a bit of an oddity but well aware of the literary value of being an oddity. Ultimately it becomes a genteel striptease which, while insisting on its artistic qualities, is aware of being sustained by vulgar human curiosity.

This makes for some uneasy moments. It is not possible to be totally guileless, candid and fully intimate in something intended as a work of art. . . . Lamb seems to think first of his audience and then to perform suitably in front of it, dressed up as 'Lamb', an automaton which becomes a stereotype—trailing before us his family, his friends, his foibles ('a foolish talent of mine'), until it is obvious that he is not at all guileless. Underneath is a knowing old sheep: one who is shrewd enough always to touch the audience's chord of sentimentality, shamelessly doing so in expressing an irrational love—a weakness, reader, but who without it?—for all that is past. Impossible to count the number of times emotive use is made of the word *old:* applied to china, Margate Hoy, benchers of the Inner Temple, libraries, plays, and of course friends.

*Illustration of the witches in* Macbeth *from the first edition of* Tales from Shakespear.

This sentimental conservatism extends to the harsher facts of the world. There is no vein of Swiftian irony in Lamb's '**A Complaint of the Decay of Beggars in the Metropolis**'; he is seriously sentimental about the picturesqueness of going in rags. Although even his admirers shy away from the pathetic yet mawkish '**Dream Children**', they should really be more deeply disturbed by the essay on young chimney-sweepers. There was no Shaftesbury in the genteel, whimsical, ever-popular Lamb who enjoyed the sight of 'these young Africans of our own growth', and thought himself charitable in urging his readers to give them a penny. By a typical sloppiness he could not even get Shakespeare right when quoting him apropos chimney-sweeps, but had to soften the verse to read 'Golden lads and lasses must . . .'. Lamb is one of those people (still richly present among us) who will defend a wrong by appealing to hallowed custom, praising the colourfulness of inequality and ever-ready to condemn as 'drab' anything that banishes poverty or child-labour.

It may be thought that Lamb was too unworldly to bother about such things; quite the opposite is the case. He was profoundly worldly and, outside his own interests, basically indifferent, even cruel. The obverse of the sentimental claptrap is a nasty joy manifested in the '**Bachelor's Complaint**'. The prose has lost its facetious frills and usual coy periphrases, a welcome loss which only emphasizes the sour comment on children: 'how often they turn out ill, and defeat the fond hopes of their parents'. There is more in the same mood as we seem about to stumble the author's real nature. It is an abrupt revelation, and there are others of varying kinds. The Lamb who warmly praised Titian's *Bacchus and Ariadne* in a published Essay, wrote privately to Wordsworth that he was by no means an absolute admirer of the picture—it had merely served as illustrative of a point he wished to make.

Perhaps ultimately one prefers the private person, whatever his faults, to the increasingly rouged, positively by the end simpering, public performer whose chief stylistic contribution to English prose was to think up arch and not always intentionally funny wrapping paper to put round naked words and facts. What began as strip-tease ended up as a sort of gift shop, equipped with china ornaments of pouting children, some old brass candlesticks, and a fancy line in poker-work mottoes. The occupant of that is exactly the person to speak with inimitable roguishness, about 'that little airy musician—the lark'— and ponder where he 'doffs his night gear'. (pp. 39-41)

> *Brigid Brophy, Michael Levey, and Charles Os-
> borne, "'The Essays of Elia',"* in their Fifty Works
> of English and American Literature We Could Do
> Without, *1967. Reprint by Stein and Day Publishers,
> 1968, pp. 39-41.*

## ARNOLD HENDERSON (essay date 1968)

*[Henderson's essay is an in-depth analysis of Lamb's critical precepts and technique. He comments that Lamb was "an alarmingly personal critic," rather than a theoretician, who displayed a great range of dramatic knowledge and who understood the theater from the point of view of the audience. For other positive assessments of Lamb's criticism, see the excerpts by Henry Nelson Coleridge (1835), Algernon Charles Swinburne (1885), E.M.W. Tillyard (1923), George Watson (1973), and Joan Coldwell (1978).]*

Charles Lamb was an alarmingly personal critic, ready not only to examine an author but to love him and exclaim over him. He wanted no critical system to rein him in: "I do not lay claim to much accurate thinking. I never judge system-wise of things, but fasten upon particulars." He attempted no comprehensive theories, and his criticism is scattered among essays, letters, and the notes to his *Specimens of English Dramatic Poets.* He has made it too easy for later students to take up each of his literary opinions in isolation from the rest. His opinions on drama in particular have seemed to some, erratic impulses rather than natural conclusions from premises. These premises may not be explicitly defined each time they are invoked, but are implicit in the principles and working methods constant throughout his criticism. When they are sifted out it should become clearer that he has a definite critical position, and that it lies, not in the realm of Fantasy, but in that particular region of the realm of Realism whence the *Lyrical Ballads* [of Wordsworth and Coleridge] also sprang. (p. 104)

Lamb—like Coleridge, particularly in the lectures—presents his personal sympathetic reactions to literature as models for all readers. He is thus what Northrop Frye calls a "public critic" who "represents the reading public at its most expert and judicious." If personal reactions are to be valid models for others, such a critic must have a sympathy neither too idiosyncratic, for then he can represent only himself in his odd likings, nor too confined, for then he can represent the public in its reaction to only a few works and authors. Both flaws can be found, in moderation, in Lamb.

Lamb sometimes is idiosyncratic in displaying more sensibility than most of us. He finds Malvolio's situation in *Twelfth Night* capable of exciting "a kind of tragic interest." . . . But most of us identify less with Malvolio than with his detractors, and the "tragic interest" he might excite is washed away in his absurdity. Lamb shows that the play is more than farce, but he does not show why it remains comedy. Or again, he calls the end of *The Broken Heart,* where Calantha hides her grief by dancing, "so grand, so solemn." . . . [John] Ford presumably did intend the audience to share and admire Calantha's emotional struggle. But the problem with the play is that few of us *can* react that way, so artificial is the situation and so inadequate is her motive. If we think Lamb wrong, it is not because he has abandoned principles for spur-of-the-moment impulses, but because he has followed his principle of sympathy all too energetically.

The success of Lamb's principle of sympathetic reading is also hampered by the second sin of public critics, a failure of sympathy for certain works and authors. The problem is more that of gaps within his range than of a too-narrow range: he was one of the few persons of his time to appreciate both [Alexander] Pope and Wordsworth, both Sir Philip Sidney and Bernard Barton, both Sir Thomas Browne and William Hazlitt. He can immerse himself in such varied authors because he modulates his attitudes to suit what each demands. If, for example, he finds a Massinger deficient in dramatic power, yet he opens himself to sense the purity of his writing style. . . . He is a chameleon who takes on the colors of the authors upon whom he sits in judgement. But however wide his range, it was discontinuous: certain authors fell in the gaps. If he was a chameleon, he was a chameleon with, to mix metaphors, a limited palette. He could not turn Byron color or [Johann Wolfgang von] Goethe color or, except for one minor poem, [Percy Bysshe] Shelley color. He agrees, for example, with Barton on Shelley: "I can no more understand Shelley than you can. His poetry is 'thin sewn with profit or delight.'"

But despite gaps, Lamb ranged over an astonishingly diverse selection of authors, giving each the sympathy he might to a favorite. In this continual exploration he was spurred on by a publicist streak, a desire to introduce readers to neglected works, particularly, though not exclusively, old, undeservedly forgotten ones. Shakespeare aside, most of the authors Lamb treats were obscura to his day, though many, such as [Christopher] Marlowe, [John] Webster, Sir Thomas Browne, or [Izaak] Walton, are more familiar now. Even when treating well-known figures, Lamb tends to treat their lesser-known works. (pp. 105-06)

Comparison was especially natural in the *Specimens of English Dramatic Poets,* where Lamb addressed an audience who knew little Elizabethan-Jacobean drama aside from Shakespeare, [Philip] Massinger, [Francis] Beaumont and [John] Fletcher, and perhaps Jonson. Coleridge himself had first-hand knowledge of only these. The known authors, especially Shakespeare, naturally became Lamb's landmarks. Thus "Chapman perhaps approaches nearest to Shakespeare in the descriptive and didactic, in passages which are less purely dramatic" . . . , while "Heywood is a sort of *prose* Shakespeare. His scenes are to the full as natural and affecting. But we miss *the Poet.*" . . . But Lamb regularly uses the comparative method even outside the *Specimens.* By bringing together Shakespeare, Massinger, and [Robert] Southey, he gives Coleridge his feelings about Beaumont and Fletcher. . . . [Robert] Burns illuminates [George] Wither . . . , and modern drama is foil to Restoration comedy. . . . Once, in a single sentence Lamb served up two Shakespeare plays, *Venice Preserved,* one Beaumont and Fletcher play, and a painting by Titian—all to illustrate [William] Hogarth! (p. 107)

This comparative method has both dangers and virtues. The *Specimens* . . . [praised] old drama whenever it was better than current drama in doing the same things, such as quarrel and reconciliation scenes, without regard to whether or not these things were intrinsically worth doing. Lamb himself once "recanted" and apologized for publishing a false comparison. . . . But this recantation did not stop the flow of comparisons— and fortunately so. By regularly trying his reaction to one work against his reactions to others, Lamb ties his criticism together without the need many critics feel for conscious system.

The historical method further frees Lamb's personal judgments from the limitations of his time and temperament. Of course Lamb was no historian: he read the [David] Garrick plays in random instead of chronological order, and he was silent on biography on the grounds that "My business is with their poetry only." . . . But he does modify his standards according to the era of a work. (pp. 107-08)

This check-and-balance of the historical method versus personal reactions or principles is common in romantic criticism. (p. 108)

Three things stand out as being consistently praised by Lamb— and, for that matter, Coleridge and others—and used as touchstones for excellence: depth of feeling, moral worth, and truth to nature. For all the airy grace of Elia's essays, Lamb was no worshiper of pure ornament, but insisted on depth of genuine feeling. (p. 109)

Lamb, like Wordsworth, demands a natural decorum of feeling. He praises the ending of *King Lear* for restraint, and prefers the old ballad of the "Nut-Brown Maid" to Prior's heightened and pretentious version. . . . In the *Specimens* he praises the intensity of *The Duchess of Malfy* while also praising its restraint. . . . Feeling must not be wrenched into sensationalism beyond the natural capacity of men. (p. 110)

Although Lamb was not as prone as Coleridge to draw explicit rules of moral conduct from literary examples, he as characteristically judges a work by its moral effect on the audience or by the character of the ideals embodied in it. He praises Kent in *Lear* as "the noblest pattern of virtue which even Shakespeare has conceived." . . . This, incidentally, may have been an observation of Coleridge's, whose marginalia on *King Lear* include the remark: "Kent [is] the nearest to perfect goodness of all Shakespeare's characters. . . ." It is on moral grounds that Lamb preferred Marlowe's *Dr. Faustus* to Goethe's *Faust,* which he saw as "a disagreeable canting tale of Seduction." . . . Shelley, too, is morally dubious: "For his theories and nostrums they are oracular enough, but I either comprehend'em not, or there is miching malice and mischief in 'em." . . . Moral nobility makes Wordsworth better than [Lord] Byron: "Why, a line of Wordsworth's is a lever to lift the immortal spirit! Byron can only move the Spleen." . . . Though he could like a work of just good fun, he praised most highly works which bettered the men who read them.

Truth to nature, Lamb's third regular criterion of value, means primarily truth to human nature. He praises Ford as "of the first order of Poets. He sought for sublimity, not by parcels in metaphors or visible images, but directly where she has her full residence in the heart of man; in the actions and sufferings

of the greatest minds." . . . Truth to nature is what Fletcher lacks: "He is too mistrustful of Nature; he always goes a little to one side of her. Shakespeare chose her without a reserve: and had riches, power, understanding, and long life, with her, for a dowry." . . . A scene in [Thomas] Middleton's *Women Beware Women* is "one of those scenes which has the air of being an immediate transcript from life." . . . (pp. 110-11)

But Lamb distinguishes between inner and external truth—he wants realism, but not necessarily literalism. In his notes on Fuller, the opposed terms are the "essential verities" and "truth of the fact." . . . In his essay **"Sanity of True Genius,"** he rebukes a novelist whose characters and incidents were outwardly ordinary but inwardly so false to human nature as to be "innutritious phantoms, . . . the improbable events, the incoherent incidents, the inconsistent characters, or no-characters, of some third-rate love intrigue." This writer he contrasts to [Edmund] Spenser with his seemingly unreal characters in whose "inner nature, and the law of their speech and actions, we are at home and upon acquainted ground." . . . For Lamb, true geniuses give the order of inner truth, and so, however disjointed the surface of their works may appear, these geniuses are in a sense more sane than ordinary imperceptive people, who can give only incoherent accounts of human nature. However dreamlike a passage in Spenser, its inner truth stands being tried by the "waking judgment." . . . Though sometimes called a dreamer, he was concerned not with the dream as dream, but with its inner truth to nature.

Certain of Lamb's opinions on drama have seemed to some neither realistic nor serious; they have appeared to lack concern for either truth to nature or moral worth. But here, too, we must distinguish between inner and outer. Lamb does indeed oppose contemporary stage practice as both too literally true to nature and too insistent on clear moral elevation. In the essay **"Stage Illusion"** he argues that actors should violate the illusion of being real people, and more so in comedy than in tragedy. . . . Here he seems to abandon realism and truth to human nature, but he does so to avoid alienating the audience. In real life certain sorts of characters—cowards, misers, irritable old men—would be offensive, and so such characters are made palatable in comedy by presenting "just enough of a likeness to recognise, without pressing upon us the uneasy sense of reality." Comic stage quarrels become disturbing if acted too earnestly; they should "seem half put on." If one character seems too realistically earnest, "his real-life manner will destroy the whimsical and purely dramatic existence of the other character." Thus Lamb wants less illusion for the sake of more illusion, for the sake of more participation by the audience in the inner experience of the play. Greater outward illusion would block sympathetic participation: the audience would be offended by comic flaws and frightened by comic dangers.

In his essay **"On the Artificial Comedy of the Last Century,"** he applies this theory to specific works. He fears that an audience accustomed to modern plays where every tinge of immorality is to be despised could not bear to witness Restoration comedy—where the heroes may philander and hope to live idly on inherited wealth. If the audience is to sit through the play in comfort, they must leave ordinary morality outside the playhouse. (pp. 111-12)

In the essay **"On the Tragedies of Shakespeare"** Lamb again argues for artificiality of outward representation in order to give the audience greater penetration into the characters: "The elaborate and anxious provision of scenery, . . . which in comedy, or plays of familiar life, adds so much to the life of the imitation, in plays which appeal to the higher faculties, positively destroys the illusion which it is introduced to aid.'' . . . Our busy senses distract our imagination, as Lamb humorously points out elsewhere of a blind man at a play: ''Having no drawback of sight to impair his sensibilities, he simply attended to the scene, and received its unsophisticated impression.'' . . . Following the train of logic, Lamb concludes that (at least for readers as sensitive as himself) it is best to read the play if one wants the all-important inner drama of human emotions: ''On the stage we see nothing but corporal infirmities and weakness, the impotence of rage; while we read it, we see not Lear, but we are Lear,—we are in his mind, we are sustained by a grandeur which baffles the malice of daughters and storms; in the aberrations of his reason, we discover a mighty irregular power of reasoning.'' . . . Both Lamb's suggestions, using less elaborate scenery, and reading instead of or in addition to seeing the plays, are intended to increase audience participation in the ''human'' aspects of the drama. Thus when Lamb opposes external illusion, he does it for the sake of inner illusion. He is trying to bring the audience closer to the experience of the play.

Achieving the proper degree of illusion in watching a play seems to have been a problem for Lamb. With his perhaps extreme sensitivity to suffering, he seems to have come sometimes perilously close to the old position attacked by Coleridge, and in theory by Lamb himself, that in viewing a play we should be deluded into thinking the actors really are the persons they portray. Lamb admits that he feels called upon to shelter Lear from the storm. What backwoodsman, seeing a stage-play for the first time and leaping up to thrash the villain, could do more? In the essay on Shakespeare he suspects that presenting a play on stage must have such effects, and, since they would mask the particular qualities of Shakespeare, he abandons the stage, seeking in the reading experience the highest realization of the author's intent. In the later essay on Restoration drama he modifies this despair of the stage, Restoration plays being more tractable than Shakespeare's. Here, instead of abandoning the stage when the highest understanding is sought, he asks it to reform. The audiences are to recognize historical relativism by forgetting their code of morality, and the actors are to use a slight artificiality. As a result, no one is to feel called upon to leap up to rebuke a philanderer—or help an old man to shelter. But a twentieth-century, post-Coleridgean (and post-Brechtian!) audience rarely has the delusion Lamb seeks to cure by reducing stage illusion, or banishing morality, or sending the audience home to read for themselves. Lamb, living in a time of differing stage conventions, and naturally more sensitive than most people, more prone to enter passionately into an illusion almost to the point of delusion, now seems extreme in recommending cures for a problem we feel less. (pp. 113-14)

This emphasis on the experience of the audience runs through all of Lamb's criticism. Depth of feeling is depth of feeling evoked in us. A noble or morally valuable character is one who stirs what is noble in us, and a work has moral worth not in adhering to rules but in bettering us. Lamb's very working method, compiling and publishing his likes and dislikes, emphasizes the reaction to a work as distinct from the process of its creation, the audience more than the author of the work discussed. While a recognized characteristic of romantic criticism is . . . its tendency to refer literary questions back to the author's mind, Lamb more typically looks to the audience (frequently himself), though he does sometimes refer back to

the author, praising, for example, the personal qualities he assumes Shakespeare must have had to produce his works. That he does not do so more often betrays no disagreement with Wordsworth's making the very definition of poetry depend on the author's emotions. Nor does it controvert Coleridge's characteristic method of approaching the qualities in a work from the faculties of the author's mind, leading to such generalizations as those concerning ''Shakespeare's mode of conceiving characters out of his own intellectual and moral faculties.'' Lamb is talking about a different link in the literary chain: the reaction to a work, not the process of its creation. A full theory would perhaps have touched more upon origins, and Lamb might have seemed more like his friends. But in one respect his different emphasis serves, not to set him off from the others, but to throw added light on them. Where we find them sharing his concerns we must recognize those concerns as characteristically romantic, at least in that combination, for many of these principles and working habits can be found in isolation or different groupings in earlier criticism. Concern for moral elevation, truth to nature, depth of feeling, the principle of sympathetic reading, and the historical method are in varying degrees common concerns of Wordsworth, Coleridge, Lamb, and their circle. The fact that Lamb shows these characteristics so prominently without as much expressed concern for the psychology of the author helps dramatize their presence—and importance—in the others of his group.

Lamb, then, is a thinker of a particular school, despite his refusal to develop a formal critical system. Though he gives free rein to his likes, dislikes, and personal reactions, his criticism, even where it is perhaps not fully correct, is neither random nor inexplicable. Each opinion proves compatible with general principles and values common to all. We would not, of course, look to Lamb for the theoretical exposition of those principles and values. There, Coleridge is the romantic master. Even within practical criticism, Lamb is of less use for ranking various authors one against the other than for giving a sense of what a given author is about. He plays favorites and, instead of being the impartial judge of all writers, is the champion of favorite or neglected ones. If we were to ask him who, after Shakespeare, was the best Jacobean tragic dramatist, he would be likely to reply, not that Webster, or Middleton, or whoever, was the best, but that Fulke Greville and George Chapman were better than most people realize. Furthermore, since he cannot feel his way into some authors—Byron, Shelley, Goethe—he cannot judge them by the same penetrative method that he uses for others—Wordsworth, Coleridge, Marlowe. He could not rate all on the same scale. But for criticism that tries to define the particular qualities of an author, that tries to characterize a work and show how it operates on us, Lamb's eccentricity and partiality are no hindrances. Lamb wrote about works he liked, and he remains helpful for them even if he might not have been helpful had he tried to interpret Shelley. Lamb was a keen observer of what went on inside himself, and if he reacts to a work at all, he can give a clear, even a stirring, account of what his reaction is. His lesson for those practising criticism in these days of objectivity is perhaps that the subjective need not be banished when one tries to talk sense, that if one is interested in those mortals who write and those who read literature, then it is no disadvantage if the critic himself happens to be a human being. (pp. 115-16)

*Arnold Henderson, ''Some Constants of Charles Lamb's Criticism,'' in* Studies in Romanticism, *Vol. VII, No. 2, Winter, 1968, pp. 104-16.*

## GEORGE WATSON   (essay date 1973)

[*Evaluating Lamb's stature as a critic, Watson suggests that his approach may be closer to that of the eighteenth-century critics, who stressed morality over imagination, than to that of his contemporaries. Watson posits that although Lamb's criticism does exhibit some traits of Romanticism, probably as a result of the influence of Samuel Taylor Coleridge, he is more of "a sound Johnsonian critic" than a Romantic. For other positive assessments of Lamb as a critic see the excerpts by Henry Nelson Coleridge (1835), Algernon Charles Swinburne (1885), E.M.W. Tillyard (1923), Arnold Henderson (1968), and Joan Coldwell (1978).*]

Lamb's criticism, almost all descriptive apart from a late essay on **'Stage Illusion',** is tiny in its scope. It could be collected—and has been collected—into a slim volume of less than fifty thousand words, and survives as something altogether desultory, scattered through his letters, the apparatus of the *Specimens* . . . and other editions of his favourite authors, the monthly and quarterly reviews, and of course *The Essays of Elia*. . . . Unmistakably Coleridgean in its subject-matter—it concerns itself overwhelmingly with such favourite subjects of Coleridge's as Elizabethan and Jacobean drama, the prose of Sir Thomas Browne, Jeremy Taylor, Fuller, and Walton, and contemporary romanticism—it looks timid and cautious when set beside the revolutionary assertions of some of his contemporaries. Everything points to a lack of confidence. But Lamb is one of those rare authors who can make a virtue of timidity and amateurishness. Throughout his long clerkship in East India House . . . he would never have pretended to be an 'important' critic, and only asks that he should be seen lucidly for what he is: a good friend and a good disciple whose critical intuitions possess, at the best, a delicacy unknown to more vigorous and ambitious intelligences than his own.

There are moments, none the less, when we feel that Lamb's real mentor is not Coleridge but Samuel Johnson, and it comes as a start, in view of Lamb's reputation as leader of the nineteenth-century vogue for the quaint and the baroque, to watch him inveigh as heavily as Johnson might have done against medieval and Tudor extravagances, both literary and moral. The following judgement against Marlowe could easily belong to some neoclassical critic:

> Tamburlaine . . . comes in, drawn by conquered kings, and reproaches these 'pampered jades of Asia' that they can 'draw but twenty miles a day'. Till I saw this passage with my own eyes, I never believed that it was anything more than a pleasant burlesque of mine ancient's. But I can assure my readers that it is soberly set down in a play which their ancestors took to be serious.

and

> Barabas the Jew, and Faustus the conjurer, are offsprings of a mind which at least delighted to dally with interdicted subjects.

Only the 'quaint' reference to 'mine ancient' belongs to the beloved Lamb of the Elians, forever tolerant and (in spite of personal tragedy) forever good-humoured. The sentiments belong to the world of Johnson's sound Anglican moralism that makes no bones about being shocked and will have no truck with the fanciful. There is much more of this sort of thing in Lamb than is commonly rememberd. The moral assumptions of his criticism are not exactly stern. But they are conventional,

a part of that continuum of English prudery that has its roots in eighteenth-century piety and looks forward to the great Victorian self-censorship. The fact is that his taste for Renaissance quaintness is only a degree or two more developed than Johnson's, and hardly different at all from that of the Wartons or of his friend Coleridge. It is rather a symptom of the growth of popular historicism, of the vogue for the 'Gothic' past, than of any determined critical analysis. Lamb's taste for the seventeenth century is sentimental, and scarcely more than sentimental: he could no more abide the Metaphysical conceit than Coleridge could, and preferred Wither, who 'lays more hold of the heart', to Quarles's 'wretched stuff'. . . . On the other hand, he can see virtues in Renaissance poetry less baroque than the imagery of Quarles, and yet too particular to have appealed to Johnson. Sidney's sonnets struck the mean that he loved best, 'full, material, and circumstantiated', in healthy contrast to late eighteenth-century verse, where there are too many 'vague and unlocalized feelings'. Poetry *may* number the streaks of the tulip, in Lamb's view—perhaps ought to do so. The Johnsonian term 'Nature' resounds through his criticism, but it is a Nature strangely elastic in its scope, and includes even the matter of visions and of waking dreams. (pp. 122-24)

A sound Johnsonian critic, then, partly romanticized by his reverence for Coleridge: this seems an apter summary of Lamb's quality as a critic than any view that conceives of him as the

*Illustration of King Lear and the Fool from the first edition of* Tales from Shakespear.

perfect prototype of the romantic critic. Wordsworth, Coleridge, Hazlitt, and De Quincey are all more romantic critics than Lamb, and all of them reject more firmly than he did the 'Aristotelian' criteria of critical judgement. Compared with them, Lamb's position seems wavering and uncertain, and his belief in a clear, moral light and his affection for the obscure and Cavalier are often in mild, unworried conflict. But he is not the kind of critic who takes himself seriously or thinks consistency to be any sort of virtue, and the doubleness of his vision is on the whole a matter for complaisant pride. His attitude to Restoration comedy provides a perfect illustration. He has no doubt that, ultimately, it deserves the moral condemnation it had already received ('The business of their dramatic characters will not stand the moral test'). But, on the other hand, 'I am glad for a season to take an airing beyond the diocese of the strict conscience ... I come back to my cage and my restraint the fresher and more healthy for it. I wear my shackles more contentedly for having respired the breath of an imaginary freedom.' The spiritual tourist is all the better for his little spree, though even on his day out he observes some essential rules, abandoning himself to Congreve and drawing the line at Marlowe. Such tolerances would not have been admitted by Addison or Johnson: but they have a future, they make sense in Victorian terms, in the liberal morality of Leslie Stephen, Walter Pater, and the Bloomsbury Group.

Lamb's attraction to Jacobean tragedy, which he sought to revive through the slightly bowdlerized *Specimens of English Dramatic Poets Who Lived about the Time of Shakespeare* . . . , is all of a piece with this readiness to enjoy new and alien experiences. The attraction is one of opposites. Lamb's very gentleness is drawn to the Webster of *The Duchess of Malfi*. . . . The distance between Lamb and Webster is so vast that it is surprising he can see him even with a telescope; yet he describes Webster's essential quality with notable accuracy, if by generalities. Lamb's analysis is rarely more particular than this, and its chief virtue is the virtue of sound characterization. He loves to tell you, in a few phrases, what a whole author is like. And the taste that moves him is conservative but self-indulgent, in love with quaintness if it is not too quaint, and romanticism if it is not too romantic, but above all impressed by the abiding worth of sober virtue. (pp. 124-26)

> *George Watson, "Lamb, Hazlitt, De Quincey," in his* The Literary Critics: A Study of English Descriptive Criticism, *second edition, The Woburn Press, 1973, pp. 122-33.\**

## GEORGE L. BARNETT   (essay date 1976)

[*In the excerpt below, taken from his study of Lamb's life and works, Barnett surveys Lamb's essays, the strengths and weaknesses of his dramatic criticism, and his art criticism. He asserts that "the Elia essays represent the culmination of Lamb's attainment in the familiar essay."*]

[The] Elia essays tend to fall into three subject categories: the specifically personal, concerned with an observation, self-reference, experience, or dream; places; and people. The difficulty of categorizing lies in determining the emphasis in a particular essay and in the fact that some essays, such as **"The South-Sea House"** and **"Mackery End, in Hertfordshire,"** partake of all three of these rather arbitrary areas. There is also a unifying tendency toward reminiscence and the past which militates against division into groups: the titular use of "Old" is found in **"The Old Benchers of the Inner Temple,"** primarily devoted to people; in **"The Old Margate Hoy,"** concerned

ostensibly with a coasting vessel associated with a place; and in **"Old China,"** which basically belongs to the first of the categories distinguished.

To this variety of subject is added a variety of treatment, involving sometimes narrative, as in **"Amicus Redivivus"** and **"A Dissertation upon Roast Pig"**; sometimes description, as in **"Blakesmoor in H——shire"**; sometimes exposition, as in **"Imperfect Sympathies."** Permeating them all is the autobiographical tone that qualifies them as personal or informal essays. Since the relationship of the incidents, circumstances, and people of Lamb's own life to those of the essays of Elia has intrigued readers and engaged the attention of critics, it is important to determine the extent of this relationship.

Correcting an alleged misrepresentation of Samuel Salt as a bachelor, Lamb provided for future errors in a postscript to **"The Old Benchers,"**: "Henceforth let no one receive the narratives of Elia for true records! They are, in truth, but shadows of fact—verisimilitudes, not verities—or sitting but upon the remote edges and outskirts of history." Factual data are often incorporated with imaginary names and incidents to lend credence to an essay. Another purpose of this fusion of fact and fiction was the gratification of his characteristic love of mystifying his readers. On August 16, 1820, just before the appearance of his first Elia essay, **"The South-Sea House,"** he wrote to Barron Field that "You shall have soon a tissue of truth and fiction impossible to be extricated, the interlacings shall be so delicate, the partitions perfectly invisible, it shall puzzle you till you return, & I will not explain it."

This form of humor, dependent on some alteration or shading of truth, which we saw Lamb practicing in his letters, reached its zenith in his spurious **"Biographical Memoir of Mr. Liston"** and his **"Autobiography of Mr. Munden,"** both of which were published in the *London* during 1825. Of the first, Lamb exulted to Sarah Hutchinson on January 20, 1825, that, "Of all the Lies I ever put off, I value this most. It is from top to toe, every paragraph, Pure Invention; and has passed for Gospel, has been republished in newspapers, and in the penny playbills of the Night, as an authentic Account. I shall certainly go to the Naughty Man some day for my Fibbings."

In Lamb's preface to **The Last Essays of Elia**, he pointed to another form of mystification: "what he tells us, as of himself, was often true only (historically) of another." Again, while thinking particularly of **"Christ's Hospital Five and Thirty Years Ago,"** which portrayed Lamb through the eyes of Coleridge, Lamb often identified himself with others in his essays. Furthermore, we recall his remonstrances with the reviewer who placed a literal interpretation on his earlier **"Confessions of a Drunkard."** Obviously, a reader must not confuse Elia—or the persona of the non-Elian essays—with Charles Lamb. (pp. 98-100)

Elia's characteristic and pervasive preference for the past is a quality of Romanticism. . . . Recollection of the past provides a contrast with the present, as in this essay, and a dramatic tension is produced.

The prevalent use of the dream in the poetry of the time finds its prose counterpart in several of Lamb's essays; **"The Child Angel"** is subtitled **"A Dream,"** and **"Dream-Children"** is **"A Reverie."** Together with the focus on the past, Lamb's dreams have sometimes been interpreted as an escape. They are, rather, a utilization of life—the natural result of an inward-looking mind that is conditioned by scenes of the past and that has a feeling of kinship with the past through reading. Charged with an affected style, Lamb protested in the Preface to *The Last Essays of Elia* "that a writer should be natural in a self-pleasing quaintness." In like manner, the past and the dream were to him natural extensions of reality on a wider temporal or mental scale than is consciously recognized by the practical mind.

For Lamb, the worlds of dream and of the past stabilize and immortalize the transitory reality of the present. It is easy for those who regard the essays as escape to overemphasize the role of the imagination; it is equally easy for those who focus on Lamb's personality to overemphasize the reality. . . . Lamb, like Wordsworth and Coleridge, learned that reality had to be made meaningful through the imagination. Thus, his departures from actuality are not escapist but for positive, esthetic ends; the desideratum is achieved in **"Old China," "The Old Margate Hoy,"** and **"Distant Correspondents."** . . .

Lamb's art progresses beyond a mere admixture of illusion and reality. He creates a dramatic situation, as in **"Dream-Children,"** wherein the calculated interruptions of his narrative by the imaginary John and Alice serve a purpose similar to that enunciated by De Quincey's "On the Knocking at the Gate in Macbeth": they keep us mindful of the present—or the would-be present—and perpetuate a tension between the real and the ideal that is cathartically resolved at the end. Both time and reality are involved here. In **"Old China,"** the tension of the drama is temporal; and it is similarly created by structure and contrast. (pp. 101-02)

The place of memory in poetry—including the memory of places—may have been confirmed in Lamb by Wordsworth; but his life and temperament were such that he could have independently recognized its value in his prose lyrics. Nostalgic contemplation of places remembered and scenes revisited is the basis of several essays. As usual, the autobiographic association is obvious in such pieces as **"The South-Sea House," "Christ's Hospital Five and Thirty Years Ago," "Mackery End, in Hertfordshire,"** and **"Blakesmoor in H——shire."** The last-named essay exemplifies the equally pervasive alteration of names that is one part of the distinction between Lamb and Elia: Blakesmoor was really Blakesware in, of course, Hertfordshire. In similar fashion, **"Oxford in the Vacation"** was actually Cambridge, which Lamb, "defrauded in his young years of the sweet food of academic institution," loved to visit. However, there is considerably less attempt to disguise the identity of places than there is to conceal the names of the originals of his characters. (p. 103)

Lamb's intense interest in people and his deep attachment for his many friends—he could never hate anyone he had once met—are reflected throughout his letters and essays in the numerous character portrayals that have a solid basis in the reality of his own relatives or friends. The abundance of such sketches in his letters testifies to his fondness for describing them. In the essays, they furnish entertainment; and none of the social reform motive so evident in Addison and Steele appears. Even in essays primarily otherwise oriented, character sketches appear as, for example, in **"The Old Margate Hoy,"** where chance acquaintances are described: or in **"Mackery End,"** where his cousin Bridget, as Mary is called by Elia, comes in for laudatory analysis; or in **"Modern Gallantry,"** which centers upon his example, Joseph Paice, a real person by that same name. Such a profusion of characters is another reason for the difficulty we have in listing certain essays as concerned with people. Indeed, Lamb's influence on the personal essay consists largely of his increased emphasis on character in the Elia essays. (p. 104)

Many essays are particularly character-oriented, with some focusing on type: **"The Old and the New Schoolmaster," "The Convalescent," "The Two Races of Men"**; some on a genre: **"The Praise of Chimney-Sweepers," "A Complaint of the Decay of Beggars in the Metropolis"**; and some on one or more individuals: **"Mrs. Battle's Opinions on Whist," "My Relations," "The Old Benchers of the Inner Temple," "Captain Jackson," "Amicus Redivivus," "Barbara S——"**—the list is endless. It is surprising how often an essay that sets out to portray a type—or even to discuss a place or a concept—comes round imperceptibly to an individual characterization. Thus, **"Poor Relations"** begins by describing the type, expands to consider a female Poor Relation, and them goes off on a lengthy discussion of "Poor W——." "I do not know how, upon a subject which I began with treating half seriously, I should have fallen upon a recital so eminently painful; but this theme of poor relationship is replete with so much matter for tragic as well as comic associations, that it is difficult to keep the account distinct without blending. The earliest impressions which I received on this matter. . . ." And then, momentarily occupied in digesting Lamb's half apology, the reader is swept unawares by the attractive reality into an even longer narration about Mr. Billet, another Poor Relation. (pp. 104-05)

More typical of Lamb's own period, of course, is the greater concern with individual personality; his sympathetic understanding of people enabled him to distinguish their peculiarities and to raise the commonplace to a position of compelling interest. The techniques of his predecessors in the essay would not have sufficed without the perceptive creativity of the author. So, **"The Convalescent,"** while detailing characteristics of the type, is personalized by the framework of self-reference; and **"The Gentle Giantess"** fascinates us with the personality of a highly individualized woman. In **"A Bachelor's Complaint of the Behaviour of Married People,"** the narrator takes issue with the ways of his married acquaintances; in so doing, he reveals by implication his envy and so draws the reader's creative attention, just as it is drawn by the speaker in a monologue by Robert Browning. Another difference that underscores Lamb's originality is his use of the character or of the character sketch as a portion—often introductory—of an essay, rather than as an end in itself. Thus, **"The Character of an Undertaker"** serves as the second part of the essay **"On Burial Societies; and the Character of an Undertaker." "The Good Clerk"** is introductory in the essay **"The Good Clerk, a Character; with Some Account of 'The Complete English Tradesman.'"** And the type description of **"Poor Relations"** draws us into accounts of individuals of the species.

Of equal importance to interest in the individual in an enumeration of Romantic characteristics is the glorification of childhood, an attitude shared by Lamb with Blake, Wordsworth, and Coleridge. The appeal of youth to Lamb was so strong as to appear a weakness to him. . . . Nowhere is Lamb's love of children more evident than in his essays in which he transforms the stuff of his own early life and that of others into characterizations. Only a lover of children could have created the "tender novices" of **"The Praise of Chimney-Sweepers,"** the "young maiden" of **"Valentine's Day,"** the eleven-year-old girl of **"Barbara S——,"** the "angelet" of **"The Child Angel: A Dream,"** and the little Alice and John of **"Dream-Children."** The close association of Lamb's interest in childhood with his preoccupation with dreams is pointed up in

**"Witches and other Night Fears,"** where he testifies that he has outgrown the child's propensity to dream: "and I have again and again awoke with ineffectual struggles of the inner eye...."

"Crude they are—I grant you—a sort of unlicked, incondite things—villainously pranked in an affected array of antique modes and phrases. They had not been *his,* if they had been other than such; and better it is that a writer should be natural in a self-pleasing quaintness, than to affect a naturalness (so called) that should be strange to him." Lamb's typically modest and self-denigrating description of his essays in the Preface to *The Last Essays of Elia* contains a basic truth that is essential to an accurate appraisal—that the quaintness is natural; that the essays are genuine, not affected.

Style cannot be separated from content in a genre such as the personal essay, whose effect is just as dependent on the manner, if not more, as on the matter. Still, we are no longer reluctant to examine the concomitants of the manner, as were the Victorian appreciators, who claimed that Lamb's style defied analysis or who feared to destroy its delicacy by examination. The individuality of the style complements that of the content and is achieved through variety, diction, structure, allusion, and especially tone....

That Lamb himself was conscious to a high degree of his own style is evident . . . from his never-ending revisions, in manuscript and afterwards. It is also evident from comments on his style in his letters. Of course, the essays differ from the letters stylistically: the letters are more personal in tone, sometimes more spontaneous, less unified, and less steadily progressive; the essays are more deliberate, more elaborately allusive, more finely finished. Still, both forms of expression share the familiar and conversational tone and method, including second thoughts and parenthetical additions. Such apparent mannerisms in the essays are revealed by the letters to be characteristic. The difference is that the essays appear to be unpremeditated; the letters actually are. (pp. 106-08)

Lamb's careful choice of words was dictated in large part by their connotative value. As a confirmed lover of food and drink, he naturally drew heavily from culinary terminology to enrich the emotional appeal of his descriptions; "feed," "nourish," "suck," and similar terms are applied throughout his essays to activities and concepts unrelated to physical ingestion. Observing the preponderance of such language and the apparent suppression of sex and maternal memory, a modern commentator wonders if this preoccupation has a psychoanalytic explanation. It is doubtful if that question can ever by answered, but there is no doubt that Lamb's "gastronomic language" adds immeasurably to the apprehension of meaning through the introduction of a physical sense of flavor and texture. One result of Lamb's felicitous diction is compression. . . . Perhaps Lamb's lifelong habit of proportioning his letters, of which he wrote so many, to a length accommodated by a sheet of paper may also have exerted an influence.

Yet structural brevity did not militate against structural freedom, both in the essay as whole and in individual sentences. "The order of our thoughts," wrote Lamb, in an undated letter to Patmore, "should be the order of our writing." As a consequence of this theory, his essays begin with one subject only to become something entirely different. So **"Oxford in the Vacation"** quietly departs from his enthusiastic response to the walks and the old library and devotes the last third to a description of his good friend "G. D. [George Dyer]—whom,

by the way, I found busy as a moth over some rotten archive...." Yet, the framework device is calculated, artistic digression; for Lamb returns to the frame at the end. In **"Old China,"** similarly, he soon leaves the titular pretension of the essay to present a sketch of Mary and their earlier life together, returning only with the last sentence to the ostensible subject.... (pp. 109-10)

Sentences also exhibit an apparent looseness indicated by a profusion of dashes, which are carefully calculated to suggest an informality—the beautiful order of subjective experience—freed from the more delicate precision marking poetry; as Lamb phrased it to Hone on March 20, 1827: "prose feeds on grosser punctualities." Frequent use of iteration of thought in successive phrases, with no progression but rather for emphasis and from a teeming brain, such as we find in the opening lines of **"Poor Relations,"** recalls a similar practice in the work of Fuller and Browne. (pp. 110)

The prevailing tone of Lamb's essays is indicated by the title of a collection of extracts from Lamb's essays, letters, and reported conversation: *The Wit and Wisdom of Charles Lamb.* The juxtaposition of these two qualities is characteristic of the dichotomy in his writings and in his personality....

Unlike Lamb's contemporary Romantics, he was seldom genuinely confessional and almost always humorous. Of mirth or wit in variety of forms, we have abundance; mystification and misrepresentation in the essays parallel the falsification in the letters. In both, the humor lies in the puckish enjoyment that the author takes in the temporary shock and discomfiture of the reader. His inveterate punning belongs more to the brevity of conversation than to the permanence of print. But his pathos, as exemplified in **"Dream-Children,"** helps to distinguish his essays from those of his contemporaries as well as those of the eighteenth century and is compatible with his pervasive nostalgia and reminiscence. In this essay, Lamb created . . . a psychologically ordered movement of consciousness rather than a rationally ordered sequence. The manipulation of the three worlds of the past, of supposition, and of reality creates the illusion that the children are real; from this illusion the effect derives. (p. 112)

Also informing the tone of the essays is . . . apparent simplicity.... We know from the evidence of his extant manuscripts that his essays wear the look of careless ease paradoxically because he labored endlessly over his phrasing. By this effort, he eschewed the dignity of the eighteenth-century periodical essayists; in its place is a measure of egotism but an inoffensive, even attractive, egotism that is qualified by modesty and self-effacement. As with other aspects of Lamb's writing, this subjective, conversational informality was practiced and perfected in the correspondence; it emerges in the essays to give a sense of their having been written for a friendly reader, not an impersonal public.

As we have seen, the Elia essays represent the culmination of Lamb's attainment in the familiar essay. His imaginative portrayal of scenes, of individuals, and of personal experience—all typically of the past—formed a subject matter with a timeless and universal appeal. His ability to infuse these materials with his personality but without any offensive egotism reaches its perfection here in the effective dramatization of the Elian intellect, with its wisdom, human sympathy, and essential genuineness. Blended inseparably with this substance is a unique style that conveys an illusion of confidential discourse. His nostalgic tone, expressed in "antique modes and phrases," in allusions, and in half-recollected quotations, strikes a chord of familiar sentiment that responds to the theme of lost childhood and to the enticement of the dream. Finally, the humor conjured up to soften the melancholy and lighten the tragedy of reality adds its effect to the lyricism that characterizes the best of Lamb's familiar essays. (p. 113)

> George L. Barnett, in his Charles Lamb, *Twayne Publishers, 1976, 172 p.*

## JOAN COLDWELL  (essay date 1978)

[*Coldwell examines Lamb's contribution to Shakespearean scholarship. She discusses Lamb's reasons for considering certain plays unsuitable to stage performance. She deems Lamb's sensitive studies of Shakespeare's characters his greatest critical contribution and expresses admiration for the "clear and forceful narrative" of* Tales from Shakespeare. *For other positive assessments of Lamb's criticism see the essays by Henry Nelson Coleridge (1835), Algernon Charles Swinburne (1885), E.M.W. Tillyard (1923), Arnold Henderson (1968), and George Watson (1973).*]

Long before he found his own creative form in the familiar essay, Charles Lamb had developed a solid, if limited, reputation as a Shakespearean critic. . . .

Lamb's influence as a Shakespearian began in talk and, in spite of his bad stammer, it was through memorable phrases, astute shafts of wit and pithy summaries that his reputation developed. He had neither the desire nor the capacity for sustained critical argument, claiming that he was temperamentally unsuited to a methodical approach to literature. Perhaps this was a reaction to the routine of his East India House clerkship, work which certainly left him little time for preparing any substantial commentary. Most of his published criticism came out first as periodical pieces and there is only one essay, apart from theatre reviews, devoted entirely to Shakespeare. The rest is fragmentary, a passage here or there in general essays or letters, and always the tone of the conversationalist is maintained. Indeed, one virtue of Lamb's criticism is precisely the virtue of fine talk: by flashes of perception, neatly worded and founded on complete familiarity with the subject, the reader is challenged to articulate his own responses and test his own judgment. But the fact that Lamb's comments on Shakespeare are scattered throughout his work has made them relatively inaccessible and his reputation as a critic has inevitably suffered. (p. 11)

feature of the Romantic absorption in Shakespeare was feeling of personal involvement with him, the belief in an initiate's intuitive grasp of his meaning. Lamb was by no means alone in his sense of almost mystical identification with Shakespeare. Keats provides perhaps the most familiar examples of this kind of empathic response and a passage in one of his theatre reviews admirably illustrates the coterie spirit: 'The acting of Kean is Shakesperian;—he will fully understand what we mean.' When Wordsworth attempted to shift the god Shakespeare from his pinnacle, Lamb rose to the challenge with a response that, in spite of its humour, is typically possessive and personal: 'after one has been reading Shaksp. twenty of the best years of one's life, to have a fellow start up, and prate about some unknown quality, which Shakspere possess'd in a degree inferior to Milton *and somebody else*!!' While such passion and enthusiasm have little validity as a rational base for criticism, it is nevertheless true that, in the work of men who are in addition in-

formed, well-read and intelligent, they give rise to an invaluable extra dimension of insight. (pp. 11-12)

Like Coleridge, Hazlitt and De Quincey, Lamb held that Shakespearean drama is best appreciated in the reader's own imagination and can only suffer diminution on stage. He knew that his views were shaped in part by the far from ideal conditions of the early nineteenth century theatre, where Shakespeare's own texts were seldom if ever used, where costumes and settings either lacked design or strove too hard for 'realism' and where oratorical method emphasized the artificiality of such conventions as the soliloquy and the aside. But Lamb could not apparently visualize any theatrical style in which the plays could be performed to his ideal standards. This was not so of all drama; Lamb does not argue against theatre in general but he distinguishes between types of play suited to stage performance. The distinction is based on characterization. Some playwrights draw their characters from life, as in the comedy of manners, and real human beings fittingly personate them on stage. But Shakespeare's characters, in the Romantic view, are products of the poet's imagination, not imitations of 'those cheap and everyday characters which surrounded him, as they surround us.' Therefore, as characters of imagination, they will most nearly be approached through the imagination of a reader. They are abstract, and to give them visible form is, in Lamb's view, to bring down 'a fine vision to the standard of flesh and blood.' To Lamb an actor can only be an obstruction between Shakespeare's concept of the character and his own perception of it; everything about stage performance distracts, costume, gesture, style of speech, even the actor's own personality ('we speak of Lady Macbeth, while we are really thinking of Mrs. S.[iddons].') It is the visual aspect that is most disturbing because it draws attention away from the intellectual and inner to the outward and superficial parts of a character.

The imaginative understanding of character is Lamb's chief contribution to criticism and he was one of the first to explore the many-sidedness of Shakespeare's characters. His most original and perceptive study is of Richard III, a plea for the playing of a human Richard instead of a melodramatic monster. One can trace the gradual development of Lamb's view from the time he saw Cooke's performance of the role in 1801 through successive rethinkings to a simple summary in the essay on the tragedies ten years later. His analysis of Malvolio, in whose fall he sees a 'kind of tragic interest', is more controversial but again it illustrates a method of looking at character in depth, for human comprehensiveness rather than as stage caricature. In this Lamb may be said to have foreshadowed the concerns of modern psychological criticism.

Lamb knew himself to have been a pioneer in studies of Shakespeare's fellow dramatists. In his autobiographical sketch he wrote: 'He also was the first to draw the Public attention to the old English Dramatists in a work called **"Specimens of English Dramatic Writers who lived about the time of Shakespeare"**.' Lamb's interest in this drama was fostered by his love of old books. He owned, among many rare volumes, a folio edition of Beaumont and Fletcher, already virtually unattainable by 1804, and he copied extracts from this and others into his letters so that friends might share his delight. This was the chief motive behind his decision to publish extracts from the collection of old plays in the British Museum, but he was also concerned, as he wrote in the Preface, to show 'how much of Shakespeare shines in the great men his contemporaries, and how far in his divine mind and manners he surpassed them and all mankind.' Lamb's notes to the plays touch on comparative themes, such as the contrast between Richard II and Marlowe's Edward II, to be developed by twentieth century critics.

In yet another area Lamb, together with his sister, did pioneering work and in this case it has not been bettered. *The Tales from Shakespear* are clear and forceful narrative condensations of the plays, which do not talk down to their young audience but show, in their skilful paraphrasing, a firm mastery of Shakespeare's complex language and thoughts. Lamb was responsible for the tragedies and in his selection of details and emphases one can observe the influence of his general critical approach. The Macbeth story provides a good illustration. Although Lamb intended to make only such alterations as were necessary to provide 'easy reading for very young children', he here seems rather to introduce changes to fit his own interpretation of the tragedy.

We know from a conversation recorded by H. C. Robinson that Lamb considered Lady Macbeth a 'hardened being', 'one of Shakespeare's worst characters'. Thus in the tale she is forcefully categorized as a 'bad, ambitious woman'. Lamb goes further than Shakespeare in making her actively evil. For instance, his Lady Macbeth plans from the beginning to murder Duncan herself. This is possibly a justifiable reading of her:

> What cannot you and I perform upon
> Th' unguarded Duncan.

When the resemblance to her father shakes her courage she returns to Macbeth 'and with the valour of her tongue she so chastized his sluggish resolutions, that he once more summoned up courage to the bloody business.'

To increase the sense of Lady Macbeth's villainy, Lamb alters the episodes so that Macbeth does nothing evil of his own planning. He does not kill the grooms, nor does he plan the murder of Banquo without his wife's connivance. 'Be innocent of the knowledge, dearest chuck', he says in the play, but in Lamb's story 'they determined to put to death both Banquo and his son.' The sleep-walking scene is omitted, lest sympathy for the queen develop, and Lamb simply says that the two 'had their sleeps afflicted with terrible dreams.' (pp. 13-15)

[Lamb] had a very clear awareness of his own critical strength, as the following anecdote illustrates. Lamb was once at a dinner with De Quincey, whose essay 'On the knocking at the gate in *Macbeth*' is probably more widely known than any of Lamb's criticism. Pointing to De Quincey, Lamb said: 'Do you see that little man? Well, though he is so little, he has written a thing about Macbeth better than anything I could write;—no— not better than anything I could write, but I could not write anything better'. It is for such qualities of honesty, clearsightedness and a confidence based on knowledge and experience that Lamb's criticism is still to be valued. (p. 16)

> *Joan Coldwell, in an introduction to* Charles Lamb
> on Shakespeare *by Charles Lamb, edited by Joan
> Coldwell, Colin Smythe, 1978, pp. 11-16.*

## GERALD MONSMAN (essay date 1984)

[*Monsman explores Lamb's complex "Elia" persona, examining
its relation to Lamb's psychological history and the trauma of his
mother's death. He suggests that for Lamb, "Elia" served as an
alter ego which made possible "a therapeutic psychic exorcism
or catharsis derived from the act of writing itself."*]

*Illustration of Othello from the first edition of* Tales *from*
Shakespear.

Unlike Enlightenment rationalists, who were inclined to locate meaning in a transcendent or absolutist system of valuation, the romantics and, increasingly, the Victorians typically wavered between a commitment to the traditional idea of a time-transcending, eternally complete Absolute and a fascination with the notion of a gradually self-realizing World-Spirit. By de-emphasizing metaphysical and theological interpretations of history in favor of a critical study of the principal modes of experience, the nineteenth century tended to locate the productive force for the creation of values, ideals, and purposes within the temporal and historical structure of human life. Not surprisingly, the century encountered increasing difficulty in reconciling its new emphasis upon the density and reality of finite human life with the catastrophic character of life-in-time.... If the human condition typified an inauthentic or "allegorical" unreality, then the symbol, entangled as it is within a divine reality, promised to rescue man from his moribund selfhood. Yet the hallmark of the century's maturer aesthetics is the recognition that even when the literary work tries to annihilate temporality, it embodies in its basic character an ontological commitment to the life of man in time. The issue that [Lamb's] Elia persona addresses most trenchantly is the presumptuous pride of the artistic voice which denies that the regnant role of its language of symbols is to redeem or rehabilitate the "allegorical" images of this our phenomenal world. (pp. 3-4)

"My poor dear dearest sister in a fit of insanity has been the death of her own mother. I was at hand only time enough to snatch the knife out of her grasp. She is at present in a mad house, from whence I fear she must be moved to an hospital. God has preserved to me my senses,—I eat and drink and sleep, and have my judgment I believe very sound." . . . With these sad words to his old schoolmate Coleridge, Charles Lamb in effect prefaces his future domestic life, the personal circumstances of which will prove fully as bizarre as that of any English author. (p. 12)

More than Lamb himself could ever know, the creation of his Elia persona enclosed the memory of September 22, 1796, that moment of primal horror seemingly imported direct from some antique Grecian myth or tragic drama: the young Charles just entering the door from work; the frenzied sister with the bloody knife still in her hand, snatched from the table laid for dinner; the mother across her chair, dead and bloody, stabbed to the heart; the senile father gouged in the forehead by a savagely thrown fork, blood-spattered and numbly whimpering; the aged aunt possibly unconscious full-length upon the floor; the servant girl hysterically screaming. This sudden tableau climaxed a series of reverses that had affected the fortunes of the family and of Lamb in his early maturity. . . . But in Elia he breaks free from the trap of circumstance and gains public esteem by writing an autobiographical prose without confessing, as he did privately in his letters, the starker, more fearsome truths of his own life. The essence of Lamb's persona is the absence of any explicit narrative of that pivotal "day of horrors" . . . which nevertheless everywhere informs the contours of Elia's essays. Elia is the result of Lamb's having confronted an emotional catastrophe and turned that primal horror back upon a host of other moments and memories forged by loss, each enriched and deepened emotionally by the others. He thus employs that death-blow against itself to produce his covertly confessional persona. (pp. 13-14)

Like Lamb's letters, the essays of Elia reflect the undogmatic and skeptical processes of Lamb's idiosyncratic mind. They are, says Phil-Elia, "unlicked, incondite things" . . .—crude little bear cubs awaiting their dam to lick them into shape. Their seemingly unmethodical form precisely matches Lamb's studied indifference toward and inconsistent opinions pertaining to such areas as politics ("Public affairs—except as they touch upon me, and so turn into private, I cannot whip up my mind to feel any interest in" . . .) or religion ("I am determined my children shall be brought up in their father's religion, if they can find out what it is" . . .) or literary criticism ("**Detached Thoughts on Books and Reading**" is the revealing title of one Elia essay) or philosophy ("Nothing puzzles me more than time and space, and yet nothing puzzles me less, for I never think about them" . . .). Unlike the shapeless flesh and fur of the mythic cubs attended by their "watchful Bruin" who, in Pope's words, "forms, with plastic care, / Each growing lump, and brings it to a Bear," Elia's essays never fall heir to any wholly authoritative principle of ordering. If the essays at times seem to be patterned almost mathematically around a central scene, most undercut their form ironically or trail off, ambiguously unresolved. (p. 15)

Not surprisingly, the prose of Elia resembles most closely the more direct and personal reflective verse of Wordsworth or Coleridge, especially the so-called conversation poems of Coleridge in which the contradictions of Coleridge's life allow either only the most precarious "reconciliation of opposites" or defeat it altogether. Lamb's baffling lack of logical system

or methodical presentation implies neither helpless confusion nor unoriginality, nor does it void the subtle artistic contours of his compositions over which, as he told Robert Southey, he labored "as slow as a Fleming painter." . . . Indeed, when Elia's essays are compared with the poems of his contemporaries, Wordsworth and Coleridge, they appear to be sly critiques of the central dogmas of romanticism. If . . . aspects of Lamb's aesthetic program can be defined in nearly the same terms as that of [Coleridge and Wordsworth's] *Lyrical Ballads,* the application of its aims in practice leads Lamb to qualify sharply the Coleridgean notion of the reconciliation of opposites and the Wordsworthian and romantic doctrine of *presence*—the claim that hidden places of power are open to the imagination under certain circumstances. Although in "Elegiac Stanzas" the supremacy of the poetic imagination is questioned by Wordsworth as a "fond illusion," the predominant note of Wordsworth's metaphysics is faith in the possibility of reproducing privileged "spots of time." The predominant note of Lamb's view of life and of the imagination, however, is a skepticism built on the notion that any wholly straightforward correspondence between the self and ultimate reality is a hoax. The final truth of any object or event is its hairsbreadth escape from outright ontological fraudulence. (pp. 16-17)

[In the essays,] "deception" means that Lamb's personality is reproduced in Elia as an idealized aesthetic mask or façade that disguises his darker double. Yet Lamb knows the sad truth which he confesses in an indirect manner through Elia's figurative language. When, for example, Elia remarks of Laurence Sterne's "fine Shandian lights and shades" that "I must limp after in my poor antithetical manner, as the fates have given me grace and talent" . . . , Elia imports as a figure of speech into his theory of compositional practice a personal idiosyncracy of the actual Charles Lamb. Already in his early personae—in Pensilis, the Drunkard, and Edax—he gives voice to his own doubts, fears, sorrows, and guilts by exteriorizing or objectifying his inner states, a mode of dramatic detachment that creates a double who can cry out upon the world with the full force of his corrosive misery. To interpret these personae as serving a covertly confessional role is to class Lamb's creative enterprise as essentially autobiographical. Although life histories of an author by himself, like artists' self-portraits, are coeval with language and literature, the term *autobiography* was first used in English a few months after Lamb's "day of horrors," in the writings of Lamb's friend and sometime adversary, Southey—an indication that suddenly Lamb and his contemporaries found the self *in relation to* what is written, the connection between a life and the act of telling or recounting it, to be of interest. (pp. 17-18)

In every autobiography the three key elements are *autos,* the remembering self of the author, *bios,* the life that lies at the center of the noun, and *graphē,* the textual inscription wherein the simulacrae of past and present experience are reified. The *autos* can be given a variety of written forms—letter, diary, journal, narrative, deposition, memoir, or that of Lamb's personae, confession. In the *graphē* designated confession, the *bios* is Lamb's inner and most private thoughts, not the external dramatic events of standard autobiographical narration. Although spiritual confessions such as Augustine's often begin in intense desolation or spiritual torment, most are concerned with finding some faith in an organized system of belief or in an intuitive mystical moment of revelation producing peace, joy, power, and triumph. Lamb's class of secular confession, however, avoids direct personal experience of revelation and absolution. In contrast to the classical Augustinian confession that achieves closure, the romantic Rousseauistic confession presents intrusive or repetitive images or impulses against which the *autos* struggles—fears and sins not to be assuaged. Confession, originally undertaken to obtain absolution by the priest, here becomes for Lamb a therapeutic psychic exorcism or catharsis derived from the act of writing itself; but instead of explicit unmasking, Lamb weaves his liabilities into a figurative language and compositional structure that serve as metaphors both of his central guilt and of its exorcism. . . . [Words] for Lamb are never able to re-create the child's original illusion of plenitude without some degree of "superfoetation" . . . , but by turning the Elia persona back upon the guilty profile of his own life in a transforming and purgative act, Lamb catches within his verbal net a limping reflection of his now absent original wholeness. This paradoxically idealized but limping alter ego becomes the voice that frees his guilty self from the fallenness of time and space in order that he may cry out from the depths of his self-contradiction and name that innocence outside his power to command. (pp. 18-19)

> *Gerald Monsman, in his* Confessions of a Prosaic Dreamer: Charles Lamb's Art of Autobiography, *Duke University Press, 1984, 165 p.*

---

## ADDITIONAL BIBLIOGRAPHY

Ades, John I. "Charles Lamb, Shakespeare, and Early Nineteenth-Century Theater." *PMLA* 85, No. 3 (May 1970): 514-26.
　　Examines how Lamb's familiarity with the theater of his day influenced his Shakespearean criticism. Lamb's disillusionment with the staging of the author's plays, Ades argues, led him to conclude in "On the Tragedies of Shakespeare" that reading Shakespearean tragedy is preferable to witnessing performances.

Ainger, Alfred. *Charles Lamb.* English Men of Letters, edited by John Morley. New York: Harper & Brothers, Publishers, 1882, 182 p.
　　A critical biography. Ainger discusses Lamb's style in the "Elia" essays and his importance as a critic, noting that Lamb's poetic talents were "at the root of his greatness as a critic."

Barnet, Sylvan. "Charles Lamb's Contribution to the Theory of Dramatic Illusion." *PMLA* LXIX, No. 5 (December 1954): 1150-59.
　　A discussion of Lamb's essay "Stage Illusion." Barnet concludes that his concept of dramatic illusion was "the most sophisticated, the most discriminating, and the most accurate treatment of the problem in the history of English dramatic theory."

Barnett, George L. *Charles Lamb: The Evolution of Elia.* Indiana University Humanities Series, edited by Edward D. Seeber, no. 53. Bloomington: Indiana University Press, 1964, 286 p.
　　A biography focusing on those elements of Lamb's early life that influenced his later development as a writer, particularly as the author of the "Elia" essays.

――――. "The History of Charles Lamb's Reputation." *Charles Lamb Bulletin,* n.s. No. 10 (April-July 1975): 22-33.
　　Surveys critical response to Lamb's works in England and America.

――――, and Tave, Stuart M. "Charles Lamb." *The English Romantic Poets & Essayists: A Review of Research and Criticism,* rev. ed., edited by Carolyn Washburn Houtchens and Lawrence Huston Houtchens, pp. 37-74. New York: New York University Press, 1966.
　　An annotated bibliography of works by and about Lamb.

Blunden, Edmund, ed. *Charles Lamb: His Life Recorded by his Contemporaries.* Biographies through the Eyes of Contemporaries, vol. I. London: Hogarth Press, 1934, 256 p.
　　A compilation of contemporaneous writings about Lamb.

Boas, F. S. "Charles Lamb and the Elizabethan Dramatists." In *Essays and Studies by Members of the English Association,* Vol. XXIX, pp. 62-81. London: Oxford University Press, 1944.
　　Determines the extent to which Lamb's *Specimens of English Dramatic Writers, Who Lived About the Time of Shakspeare* contributed to the revival of interest in Elizabethan drama in nineteenth-century England. Boas contends that Lamb's greatest innovation in the anthology was to present episodes from the plays not merely as pleasant passages but "as specimens of dramatic quality."

Bradford, Gamaliel. "Charles Lamb." In his *Bare Souls,* pp. 169-204. London: Jonathan Cape, 1925.
　　A brief "psychography" of Lamb in which Bradford studies the author's letters for the light they shed on his life and career.

Coldwell, Joan. "The Playgoer As Critic: Charles Lamb on Shakespeare's Characters." *Shakespeare Quarterly* XXVI, No. 2 (Spring 1975): 184-95.
　　A survey of Lamb's Shakespearean criticism. Asserting that Lamb's critical method was typically Romantic, Coldwell praises his character studies and contends that they were colored by his knowledge of the theater.

Haven, Richard. "The Romantic Art of Charles Lamb." *Journal of English Literary History* 30, No. 2 (June 1963): 137-46.
　　An in-depth examination of "Old China" and "The Old Benchers of the Inner Temple." Using these two essays, Haven traces Romantic elements in "Elia's" style, and he deems Lamb "no mean master of the romantic idiom."

Hayden, John O. "Out of School: Charles Lamb." In his *The Romantic Reviewers: 1802-1824,* pp. 226-32. Chicago: University of Chicago Press, 1969.
　　An overview of early critical response to Lamb's works, with attention to the changes in his overall reputation during the first part of the nineteenth century.

Johnson, Edith Christina. *Lamb Always Elia.* London: Methuen & Co., 1935, 288 p.
　　Traces the evolution of Lamb's "Elia" persona.

Lake, Bernard. *A General Introduction to Charles Lamb Together with a Special Study of His Relation to Robert Burton, the Author of the "Anatomy of Melancholy."* Leipzig: Dr. Seele & Co., 1903, 91 p.*
　　A brief survey of Lamb's life and career. Lake also examines the influence of the seventeenth-century English essayist Robert Burton on Lamb's style.

Law, Marie Hamilton. "Seventeenth and Eighteenth Century Influences in the Essays of Hunt, Lamb, and Hazlitt." In her *The English Familiar Essay in the Early Nineteenth Century,* pp. 57-123. New York: Russell & Russell, 1965, 238 p.*
　　Discusses seventeenth- and eighteenth-century influences on Lamb's "character" sketches. Law compares Lamb's mastery of this form to that of the famous eighteenth-century English essayists Joseph Addison and Sir Richard Steele.

Lucas, E. V. *The Life of Charles Lamb.* 2 vols. London: Methuen & Co., 1905.
　　The standard biography.

Mulcahy, Daniel J. "Charles Lamb: The Antithetical Manner and the Two Planes." *Studies in English Literature* 3 (1963): 517-42.
　　Analyzes Lamb's method of "interweav[ing] with his tapestry of illusion a thread of reality" as it is illuminated by two essays, "Witches, and Other Night-Fears" and "Blakesmoor in H-Shire." Arguing that Lamb conceived of life as existing on two planes—the real and the imaginative—Mulcahy concludes that the term "escapism" does not apply to Lamb's artistic intent.

Nabholtz, John R. "Drama and Rhetoric in Lamb's Essays of the Imagination." *Studies in English Literature* XII, No. 4 (Autumn 1972): 683-703.
　　Examines a group of Lamb's "Elia" essays that focus on the role of the imagination in the creative process. Nabholtz argues that, in terms of rhetoric, syntax, and structure, the essays "are the

working out . . . of the experience of imaginative liberation it-self.''

Park, Roy. ''Lamb, Shakespeare, and the Stage.'' *Shakespeare Quarterly* 33, No. 2 (Summer 1982): 164-77.
Probes the relationship between Lamb's theories of drama in ''On the Tragedies of Shakespeare'' and his experiences with the theater of his day. Park suggests that Lamb's argument against the performance of Shakespeare's plays was never meant to be proscriptive.

Patterson, Charles I. ''Charles Lamb's Insight into the Nature of the Novel.'' *PMLA* LXVII, No. 4 (June 1952): 375-82.
A study of Lamb's attitudes toward the novel. Patterson explores Lamb's ideas about narrative and the way he used them in *Rosamund Gray* and *The Reminiscences of Juke Judkins*, an unfinished novel he started in 1826.

Prance, Claude A. *Companion to Charles Lamb: A Guide to People and Places, 1760-1847*. London: Mansell Publishing, 1983, 392 p.
A compendium of information related to Lamb's life and career. Prance includes such features as a map of London and an index to actors, actresses, dramatic critics, and plays popular during Lamb's lifetime.

Praz, Mario. ''The Letters of Charles Lamb or Religio Burgensis.'' *English Studies* 18, No. 1 (February 1936): 17-23.
A negative review of Lamb's *Letters* in which Praz argues that the author's correspondence illustrates his ''narrowness of interests.''

Priestley, J. B. ''Some 'Characters'.'' In his *English Humour*, pp. 49-58. New York: Stein and Day, Publishers, 1976.*
An appreciation of Lamb's humor. Priestley places Lamb in the company of Samuel Johnson, whom he considers the greatest humorist of the eighteenth century.

Randel, Fred V. *The World of Elia: Charles Lamb's Essayistic Romanticism*. Kennikat Press National University Publications, Literary Criticism Series, edited by John E. Becker. Port Washington, N.Y.: Kennikat Press, 1975, 170 p.
An in-depth analysis of the ''Elia'' essays focusing on Lamb's handling of style, imagery, narrative voice, and the concepts of time and space.

Scoggins, James. ''Images of Eden in the Essays of Elia.'' *Journal of English and Germanic Philology* LXXI, No. 2 (April 1972): 198-210.
An analysis of Lamb's use of the theme of innocence in the ''Elia'' essays. According to Scoggins, the implied object of the essays is to recapture childhood happiness, ''those vestiges of Eden that have remained behind.''

Williamson, George. ''The Equation of the Essay.'' *Sewanee Review* XXXV, No. 1 (January 1927): 73-7.
Examines the relationship between Lamb's letters and essays that treat the same subject. Williamson maintains that in his letters, Lamb's language is that of ''statement,'' whereas in the corresponding essays, it is that of ''suggestion.''

# Eduard (Friedrich) Mörike

## 1804-1875

German poet, novella and fairy tale writer, novelist, and dramatist.

Mörike is regarded as a major nineteenth-century German lyricist. Although he wrote in several genres, his reputation rests primarily on his varied collection of verse, *Gedichte,* which he revised and expanded throughout his career. His poetry defies categorization, though it is often compared to the verse of the German Romantic movement, Classical period, and the post-Romantic *Biedermeier* school. Because of his distinctive blend of styles, Mörike holds a singular place in the history of German literature.

Mörike was born in Ludwigsburg, Swabia (later Germany). After his father's death in 1817, his family moved to Stuttgart and Mörike was sent to a preparatory school in Urach to study German literature and the Greek and Latin classics. He later entered the seminary in Tübingen. While there he had a love affair with Maria Meyer, who inspired the five poems known as the "Peregrina" cycle. In 1826, Mörike completed his studies and was assigned to the first of many parishes. As a young pastor, he often neglected his duties in favor of literary pursuits. He briefly left the curacy in 1828 to write for the Stuttgart *Damenzeitung,* although he soon returned to religious life. In 1833, Mörike settled with his mother and sister Klara at the vicarage in Cleversulzbach, where he continued his literary activity, producing fairy tales and poems as well as translations of classical Greek and Latin verse. During this period, he published the first volume of *Gedichte.* Shortly after his mother's death in 1841, Mörike received a small pension that allowed him to retire from his work as a minister, and he and his sister moved to Mergentheim, where he met his future wife, Margarete von Speeth. After their wedding, they moved to Stuttgart, where Mörike taught literature and composed poetry, fairy tales, and a novella, *Mozart auf der Reise nach Prag (Mozart on the Way to Prague).* The marriage was unhappy, however, and the Mörikes divorced in 1873, two years before Mörike's death.

Though best known for his poetry, Mörike also composed a number of works in prose. *Maler Nolten,* his first prose work, is a semi-autobiographical novel that is often compared to *Wilhelm Meisters Lehrjahre* by Johann Wolfgang von Goethe. Mörike incorporated in his narrative lyric poems (including the "Peregrina" cycle), letters, diaries, and a drama, and employed such devices as replacing the names of people and places with asterisks and dashes and using the narrator as an editor who supplies important details. While this work has been criticized for its archaic style, fragmentary nature, and excessive length, critics do acknowledge the psychological depth of its characters, particularly Larkens and Elisabeth. Mörike also composed short prose works, including the fairy tales *Das Stuttgarter Hutzelmännlein* and *Die Hand der Jezerte.* These works, with their descriptions of local customs, manners, and renderings of local dialect, demonstrate his affinity for Swabian folklore. Mörike was so skilled in creating fairy tales, in fact, that his contemporaries frequently suspected him of borrowing from existing folk literature.

Of all Mörike's prose works, his novella *Mozart on the Way to Prague* is the most popular. In this work, he depicts a journey made by the composer Wolfgang Amadeus Mozart and his wife, Constance. Although *Mozart on the Way to Prague* is not historically accurate, many commentators agree that Mörike successfully captured the essence of Mozart's personality and the tenor of his age. They also praise the skillful characterizations, whimsical humor, and simple, direct narration of the work and suggest that Mozart, because of his rich imagination and seemingly effortless composition, was Mörike's artistic idol.

Mörike's lyric poetry in *Gedichte,* his best-known work, demonstrates the influence of several distinct currents in German literature, including Romanticism, Classicism, *Biedermeier,* and folk poetry. Mörike's subject matter is most often Romantic, revolving around such personal themes as solitude, transience, and parting. His nature poems are considered Romantic for their depiction of the poet's mystical relationship to nature, as are his love poems, particularly the "Peregrina" cycle, for their portrayal of tragic love. While the content of Mörike's verse is predominately Romantic, the form is Classical. Influenced by German Classical writers and by his readings of ancient Greek and Latin verse, Mörike adopted a style characterized by simplicity, plasticity, clarity, and balance. Critics praise his mastery of form, citing his deft handling of traditional rhythms and meters. Mörike is also linked with the *Biedermeier* poets, whose work is noted for its nostalgic tone and glorification of provincial life. His evocations of Swabia, which display his humor and knowledge of human nature, are said to derive from this tradition. To a lesser degree, Mörike's poems reflect the influence of the German folk tradition. In his *Volkslieder,* or folk songs, Mörike often adopted the traditional ballad form to present his adaptations of popular legends and to create new tales. Like his fairy tales, they demonstrate the ease with which he assimilated popular culture. When considering Mörike's entire poetic output, critics often praise his sensitivity, imagination, rich vocabulary, musicality, and technical mastery.

Response to Mörike's work has varied widely. During his lifetime, his achievements were overshadowed by the poetry of the *Jung Deutschland* group, who, unlike Mörike, focused on political and social topics. In the 1880s, however, his popularity grew when the German composer Hugo Wolf set fifty-three of his poems to music. Although Mörike's works were studied extensively in Germany, they remained virtually unknown outside his native land for many years. Only in the 1950s did they begin to attract the attention of English-language critics, who have since published many analyses of *Maler Nolten* and *Mozart on the Way to Prague,* as well as numerous studies of individual poems from *Gedichte.* While critics continue to debate his exact placement within the German literary tradition, there is little doubt that Mörike made a significant contribution to German lyric poetry.

## PRINCIPAL WORKS

*Maler Nolten* (novel) 1832
*Gedichte* (poetry) 1838; also published in revised form as
     *Gedichte,* 1848, 1856, 1867
*Klassische Blumenlese* [translator] (poetry) 1840
*Idylle von Bodensee; oder, Fischer Martin und die*
     *Glockendiebe* (poetry) 1846
*Die Hand der Jezerte* (fairy tale) 1853
*Das Stuttgarter Hutzelmännlein* (fairy tale) 1853
*Mozart auf der Reise nach Prag* (novella) 1856
     [*Mozart on the Way to Prague,* 1934]
*Briefe Mörikes.* 2 vols. (letters) 1903-04
*Sämtliche Werke.* 3 vols. (poetry, novel, novellas, fairy
     tales, dramas, translations, and libretto) 1918
*Poems* (poetry) 1959
*Sämtliche Werke.* 3 vols. (poetry, novel, novellas, fairy
     tales, dramas, translations, and libretto) 1967

---

**WILLIAM GUILD HOWARD** (essay date 1904)

[*The following is an appreciative survey of Mörike's poetry and prose that illuminates his relationship to the literature of his age. Howard considers Mörike's lyric poetry his best work.*]

Mörike is greatest as a lyric poet. The gentle notes in his little volume of *Gedichte* in 1838, were, to be sure, drowned out by the thunder of the political poets; his homely sentiments could make no headway against the rush of enthusiasm for the tropical monsters of Freiligrath; and when this fever had abated somewhat, men sought refreshment rather . . . in the trickling meadow-brooks of Geibel than in the hidden spring of Mörike's verse.

Nevertheless, it may be said that no German poet since Goethe wrote so nearly in the master's spirit as this fellow-countryman of Schiller and Uhland. Mörike did not, like the other Suabians, delight in ballads and the treatment of historical themes. He expressed more personal emotions, reacting on the experiences of his daily life, or uttering the thoughts which assumed plastic form while he wrote, like Wordsworth, with his eye on an object in nature. The fertility of his fancy, which conceived even the most familiar events in figures of striking novelty and significance, the roguishness of his humor, the depth and wholesomeness of his feeling make of Mörike's occasional pieces—and his poems were to a greater degree even than Goethe's inspired by particular occasions—a singularly charming history of what life brought to the soul of this man. If he gave no poetic embodiment to the forces that collide in the social struggles of men, he enobled with the sense of beauty the impressions made upon his individual personality by contact with the world. His life was more contemplative than active. He was a dreamer and a seer of visions; he loved the seclusion of the picturesque valleys of his native land. Like Kerner a believer in mystic bonds between the world of sense and the world of spirits, Mörike outdid in imaginativeness even the traditional lore of the German folk, and discovered new realms for the creatures of faerie. Across the boundary of the region lying somewhere between day and night Mörike was particularly fond of straying. But whether we follow him thither, or wander with him among the wooded hills of Württemberg, we are made to feel equally at home. Simplicity, heartiness and naturalness prevail in the end over the supernatural.

Simplicity and naturalness are also the chief characteristics of the form of Mörike's verse. He may sing in the artless strain of the *Volkslied* or speak in more complicated measures, his diction is unsurpassed for classic inevitableness on the one hand and the effects of musical cadence on the other. Uhland often seems to be experimenting in metres—successfully, indeed, but with too great desire for variety. This is never true of Mörike, and the very suggestion of following a fashion . . . he would have abhorred. One feels that the children of his imagination were born in comely shape. (pp. vi-vii)

Mörike's prose is no less artistic than his verse, and in respect to subject and treatment, his prose writings form a worthy counterpart to his poetry. *Maler Nolten* is a story of the fortunes in love, friendship and artistic endeavor, of a young painter; a story written partly after the model of [Goethe's] *Wilhelm Meister,* but bearing no resemblance to Tieck's imitation of the same model, *Franz Sternbald.* It is no accident that Mörike's hero is a painter—Mörike was himself too much of a painter for that. He does not, however, like Tieck, undertake to describe the education and development of a painter. Nolten might have been a sculptor or musician, or even a poet, and the decisive elements of the situation in which he finds himself would have been unchanged. Mörike's wish was to throw light on this situation. The novel is less encyclopedic than either Goethe's or Tieck's, but more poetic than either, more fanciful, more delicate in tracing the subtle forces that determine character and conduct. Mörike gives no such picture of the contemporary world as Goethe draws, nor such a panorama as Keller unfolds in his scenes from the life of a painter, *Der grüne Heinrich.* The eye surveys only a small field in *Maler Nolten* . . . ; but within this field, the author shows a familiarity with social ranks high and low, and a power of interpreting human actions, surprising enough in a rural vicar of eight and twenty. The atmosphere of the tale is romantic. The figure of a gypsy girl lurks like fate personified constantly in the background; letters, diaries, lyrical poems, and a fantastic masque *Der letzte König von Orplid* are incorporated in the narrative; and a certain voluntary fragmentariness, that appears both in the episodic composition and the abrupt conclusion,—all these things are romantic characteristics. On the other hand, Mörike is powerfully influenced by Goethe's *Wahlverwandtschaften,* both as to the idea of elective affinity and as to the conception in ideal forms of figures taken from real life and made more significant, but not different, by the touch of poetry.

Besides the *Maler Nolten,* which Mörike called at first *Novelle in zwei Teilen,* but which is really a *Roman,* and is so called in the second, much altered edition . . . , Mörike wrote half a dozen *Novellen* and *Märchen,* some of them sheer plays of exuberant fancy, others psychological studies of a keenness and power to which only the tales of Kleist are comparable. In these short narratives, Mörike's delight in whimsical conceptions and weird situations appears at its best. He never excelled in the marshalling of the incidents of an extended action. Given a single incident, however, and he makes of it all that can be made. To the charm of a vivacious and fluent story-teller he adds, as it were, the esthetic sanction of a poet accustomed to weigh his words.

*Mozart auf der Reise nach Prag* . . . is Mörike's ripest work and at the same time his last considerable product, his most successful effort in pure narration, in the exposition of a character which was indeed his own conception but which he presented as an objective fact, and without any suggestion of mystery or magic. Mozart the musician was for Mörike inseparable from Mozart the man, just as in his own case the poet and the man were one and the same; and no musician has ever been more fully and sympathetically understood or more humanely portrayed than the composer of *Don Giovanni* by Mörike in this story of the trip to Prague. Even to the smallest details the portrait is complete; from trivial incidents of domestic life to moments of supreme inspiration we see the master musician in all his amiability and unpractical greatness. It is as if the soul of music took human shape, and harmony and melody acquired a new significance through the endowment of articulate speech. We breathe the very air of an autumn day in 1787 as we accompany the travellers in their old-fashioned carriage. . . . The story is not historical in the sense of recounting a real event in Mozart's life; truth and poetry are inextricably intermingled, and one is no truer than the other. Such as they are here described were indeed the men and women for whom *Don Giovanni* was as yet an unrealized expectation, and in whom [Goethe's] *Werthers Leiden* had as yet struck no sympathetic chord. Mörike makes himself one of them. Simply and directly, but in a slightly archaic style, and with a sprinkling of Italian and Austrian idioms, he tells his tale of a bright and happy day, towards the end of which, however, the clouds of the future already cast their ominous shadow. (pp. viii-x)

> *William Guild Howard, in an introduction to* Mozart auf der Reise nach Prag *by Eduard Mörike, edited by William Guild Howard, D. C. Heath & Co., Publishers, 1904, pp. v-x.*

### T. M. CAMPBELL  (essay date 1917)

[*Campbell discusses the content and style of Mörike's verse, particularly that of his nature, folk, and domestic poetry.*]

Mörike is in no sense a "modern" poet. There are no problematic themes in his collection [*Gedichte*]. He is not philo-

sophical, nor even intellectual, but rather a writer of delicate feeling and unusual susceptibility to sensuous beauty. "A thing of beauty seems blessed in itself." Such was the instinct of the youth, such the confession of the mature poet. His themes are simple and transparent, though treated with infinite variety. If he writes of nature, it is the approach of spring, a swim in the river, a walk through the woods, midnight, a September morning. There is no titanic yearning for comprehension of the innermost soul of nature, such as the Faust in Goethe knew, or if it is there, it is a rare and transient mood. And if he writes of love, his subjects have the simplicity of the Volkslied: love's beginning, love's joys, forsaken love. Or else he falls with unexcelled grace into the anacreontic vein, which must be graceful or nothing. The poem in which Amor sells the poet ink, thereby converting every letter into a love-letter, is conceded to be a rival of Goethe's *With a Painted Ribbon.* Mörike's success in this direction bears witness to a sure taste, a vivacious fancy, and a delicate humor.

Among the more obvious characteristics of his style is a clear, poetic vision of sensuous beauty. His writing is graphic to a degree rare even among poets. Of the German poets none can equal him in this respect except Goethe, and perhaps Keller in his prose, while of the English poets Keats may furnish us with a fair comparison. Many of his lyrics show us a heart full of the ecstasy of living, expressing itself in joyous buoyant language. Their vocabulary is rich in words of tone and color, which lead us gently and unaware into a radiant atmosphere. This singular clarity of vision pervades the entire range of his work, whether the subject be beautiful or grotesque. Without apparent effort, with a swift and facile imagination he finds the fitting word. If he wishes to contrast the birch-tree with the oak, he can put in two lines the qualities of heavy and open foliage, of strength and grace, of resistance and motion, of man and maiden, of darkness and light. This style excludes what is fantastic, but does not restrict the imagination. It is graphic without being tedious.

A closer consideration of Mörike's nature-poems reveals several general methods of expression. Sometimes the sensuous vision above characterized extends throughout the poem, practically unmixed with emotion. That is, the lyric is as nearly objective as any expression can be after passing through the mind. The view of nature given us serves no emotion, it is an end in itself. The poet, while he is the maker of that particular scene, no longer seems entangled in what he portrays. His soul is clarified into a simple medium of beauty. Some of these unemotional poems are varied, however, by the use of personification, which is guided by an unerring taste. Noteworthy among poems of this type is *Midnight,* which is otherwise remarkable for sound, rhythm, and color. Night descends calmly on the land, and leans in meditation on the mountain-sides. Her eye sees the golden balances of time rest with equal scales. The springs rush forth, and sing to their mother, Night, their story of the day that has passed:—

> The old primeval slumber-song,—
> To her it is too old, too long;
> To her the Heaven's blue hath sweeter sound,
> The fleeting hours with even-balanced round.
>
> [Das uralt alte Schlummerlied
> Sie achtet's nicht, sie ist es müd';
> Ihr klingt des Himmels Bläue süsser noch,
> Der flücht'gen Stunden gleichgeschwung'nes Joch.]
>
> (pp. 176-77)

Mörike is, however, as fully master of the emotional values of nature as of her more indifferent moods. The extent to which he allows his individual emotion to penetrate his lines varies greatly. Now the emotion is slight and indirect, now the main object, as when it is used as a foil to love. Sometimes the symbol and the thought run side by side, touching only by implication—an old, approved method of the masters. A good example is the second strophe of the verses entitled *Advice of an Old Woman:*—

> I was young too—
> I know a few things.
> And now I am old,
> Hence heed my word.
>
> Fine ripe berries
> Hang on the branches;
> Neighbor, there's no use
> Fencing your garden,
> Mischievous birds
> Will find out the way.
>
> But you, my lassie,
> Let me advise you—
> You keep your sweetheart
> Full of affection,
> Full of respect. . . .

The parallelism is, however, often much more complex, so that the lines of thought and symbol wind in gradually, like the lines of a volute, about the central effect. Where mere parallelism would be too pensive to express the emotion, Mörike intensifies the inner mood by the outer situation. Such a poem is *Homesickness,* which contains one of the finest lines in his work:—

> Hier scheint die Sonne kalt ins Land.

Another example is furnished by the most popular of his shorter songs, *The Forsaken Girl,* where the stroke of art is in depicting despair at the dawn of day, when any emotion is likely to be keenest. . . . [Few] poets could have made such an effort succeed as Mörike did.

Mörike's art, like that of Goethe and Heine, is marked by its affinity with the folksong. The gardener and his hidden love for the princess, the young hunter kissing the king's daughter, the song of the soldier's girl wishing her lover home from war—such are among his subjects. To a striking degree, also, he possesses the personifying, myth-making powers that are serviceable in this genre. Though he uses some of these inventions in ballads, his style in general is not energetic enough for ballads of great spirit. The charm of his ballads lies in their lyric quality, in situation and mood. Attention has been called by Professor Mayne [the noted Mörike critic] to the interesting fact that Mörike differs from Uhland, an excellent writer of ballads, in inventing his stories rather than accepting them from tradition. This shows that his strength lay in emotional shading. As far as these narrative poems illustrate his myth-making talent they are in great part grewsome or weird, in old Germanic fashion, personifying the forces of nature as malicious: the witch, as a beautiful woman, ensnaring the king's son and throwing his body into the sea; the Daughter of the Heath threatening to take vengeance on her faithless lover; Frau Donne drowning two lovers; the seven nixies destroying the prince.

In other myth-poems, however, Mörike is on more friendly terms with nature. In them he preserves the genuine spirit of the friendly fairy-tale. He loved to lie in the woods, listening

to the wood-cutter's axe—familiar sound in Grimm—reading that "dearest of books" until he felt himself to be legendary. From this intimate association with nature sprang poems like the *Elfsong.* . . . Here should also be mentioned the grotesque Sure-Man (Sicherer Mann), a hero of unique qualities. A rude forest giant, born just after the flood, he has hair and beard like bristles, and all day long he does nothing but idle away his time, talking aloud to himself, or venting unreasoning hatred on the mile-posts, which he destroys with a single kick. (pp. 178-79)

Some idea of the range of Mörike's fancy is had by making the transition from the grotesque world of the Sure-Man to the classic beauty of Orplid, the mystic island of his imagination [in *Maler Nolten*]. Orplid, presided over by the Goddess Weyla, is a land of calm serenity. From its bright strand ascend the mists moistening the cheeks of the gods, primeval waters laving those shores grow young again, and kings are its priests and guardians. It is as if Mörike had expressed in *Weyla's Song* his dream of a paradise unrevealed to mortal eyes. Orplid becomes his Avalon. This song, only eight lines in length, is the very height of lyric perfection. It expresses the same yearning for beauty as an end in itself as we find in *Midnight* and the elegiac lines *To an Æolian Harp.* (p. 180)

Besides the general classifications above given of Mörike's verse we find many poems written to his friends, to some favorite poet or scientist, or in honor of some special occasion, such as a birthday, a party, or a wedding. Being, as one of his friends remarked, "poet all day long," he wrote hundreds of "house-verses" for his acquaintances, never intending or allowing the majority of them to find a place in his authorized edition. These domestic verses are remarkable for their cleverness and grace, and bring us personally nearer to the poet's lovable spirit. Of poems expressing more or less directly his attitude to life, we find a very few. Here Mörike gives us a glimpse of himself: his aversion to all affectation, official self-complacency, and chill stoicism; his dislike of formal social functions, as in the amusing poem to Eberhard Lempp, begging off from such an occasion, and representing himself as tormented by the worst of furies, Agrypnia or Sleeplessness, since accepting the invitation; his humorous inhospitality to insolent critics, whose departure from his house he would like to hasten "with a gentle kick." Or again, in *Seclusion,* is revealed the tendency in his nature, deep-laid and increasing with age, to escape from the glare of the world into the solitude of his own heart. And if what a man asks for is characteristic, the *Prayer,* in nine lines, shows us a modest soul, wishing to be overwhelmed with neither joy nor pain. "Gracious contentment lies in the middle." The transitoriness of all human life finds occasional expression in his verse. The lines to Kepler pass into admiration of the stars as inaccessible to the vicissitudes of human passion, and in the sonnet *Too Much* the poet, under the same influence, takes refuge from the "rapturous conflict in his heart" to descend into the abyss of contemplation, where for him, as for Keats, "love and fame to nothingness do sink." (pp. 180-81)

*T. M. Campbell, "Eduard Mörike: A Neglected German Classic," in* The Sewanee Review, *Vol. XXV, No. 2, Spring, 1917, pp. 171-86.*

**THE TIMES LITERARY SUPPLEMENT** (essay date 1951)

[*The following is taken from an anonymous review of* Eduard Mörike, *a study by the German scholar Benno von Wiese. The reviewer discusses the generally accepted interpretation of Mörike as a morbid, melancholy poet and suggests that his verse has not been appreciated sufficiently. In conclusion, the critic states that Mörike "is indeed one of the few German poets of the nineteenth century whose work can be placed beside that of his English contemporaries."*]

[The poems of Mörike's *Gedichte*] "are melancholy and even morbid in character, but distinguished by a love of Nature not unlike that of Wordsworth." This typical encyclopaedia judgment would appear to be borne out by the selection from Mörike given in the *Oxford Book of German Verse*. Yet on turning back to the volumes of his collected works . . . one looks for, and sometimes thinks that one finds, a more robust figure than the handful of his most familiar poems had led one to expect. They had presented a comfortable Biedermeier figure, the pastor of a snug little Swabian village, a lazier Herrick pausing sadly over his pipe and beer to dwell on the flaxen-haired beauties of his student days who are now the matrons of his Sunday congregation. . . .

There is something more, perhaps, than a gentle melancholy about the pastor's musings. A sickness in the blood suggests rather a Poe or a Lenau than Wordsworth reflecting on the singing of his Solitary Reaper. But so various is his achievement, such his obvious delight in the labour of creation, that he almost succeeds in concealing the worm which gnaws at his heart. Surely there is nothing but pure lyricism, tinged with a little mild regret, in such a celebration of the country joys as **"Auf eine Wanderung."** . . .

[There] is a solemnity in its metre that suggests a transience hardly even implicit in its words. It is not difficult, however, to find joy—though a more earthy joy—in Mörike's poetry. He knew little of the pleasures of love fulfilled, nor did Nature grant him, as she did to Wordsworth, intimations of an abiding pattern beneath her seeming multiplicity. But he rejoiced in lowlier things: in the quirks of peasant humour that went to the making of his mythical creatures, more pagan than Christian, to those rumbustious giants who stampede through his unanthologized poetry; and also in the homely delights of food and neighbourliness and childhood memories. Of such motives his less-known poems are full. Defeated, like other Romantics, in his quest for the ineffable experience that would give life an unchanging significance, he found passing compensation, not in his religion but in the creation, out of earthly stuff, of a private world founded on the Swabian scene yet rich with unexpected possibilities of escape from the here-and-now. Lacking a true vision of Heaven, he created his own [in **"Der alte Turmhahn"**] and peopled it with such fairy-like creatures as the old, ruminating weathercock, taken down from the church tower to hang over the pastor's stove in his study at Cleversulzbach. . . .

[Even] in the peace of his study Mörike could capture no undiluted joy. For though the weathercock might count over the snug delights of a country pastor's life, it is a life cut off from more than an occasional glimpse of the snow-clad hills, of which a weathercock, high on a church-tower, has an uninterrupted view. However close the poet drew his chair to the winter fire he was disconcertingly aware of something missing from his life for which no snugness could compensate him. Perhaps he derived his deepest pleasure from creating those genial, clumsy monsters who, like Mr. Robert Graves's ogres, could score off the gods and get away with it. Through them he could take vicarious revenge on those intangible forces that robbed him of a true joy in the world. Never is Mörike's verse more vigorous than when he is celebrating Suckelborst [in **"Erbauliche Betrachtung"**]. . . . Mörike was a master of such shambling narrative verse. Indeed he was a master of so many metres and devices that the best comparison might be, not with Wordsworth at all, but with his contemporary William Barnes. Like Barnes, he concealed wide reading and much conscious experiment behind an apparent artlessness. He shared his Dorset contemporary's regional loyalty and his affection for dialect, though he confined his use of Swabian to occasional words. Yet there was a profound difference between the two men. Barnes's regionalism and his devotion to his craft were based on a conservative independence of mind; he had loved and lost, but the earth was firm under his feet. Mörike, on the other hand, was conscious of the loss of something he had never known. His invention and his industry betray an overriding sense of insecurity. He is like a man who whistles a little too gaily in a dark wood.

It is perhaps for this reason that, in spite of the perfection of his best lyrics, in spite of the raciness of his narrative style, it is never possible to think of Mörike as a major poet. There is about so much that he wrote a fatal inconsequence, which is at its most pronounced in his long prose fairy-tale, **"Das Stuttgarter Hutzelmännlein,"** but which is equally present in his seven-canto poem, **"Die Idylle von Bodensee."** The Idyll is in the style of [Goethe's] *Hermann und Dorothea* and tells, among other things, of an old fisherman's practical joke, played upon two tailors whom he persuades to steal a bell that does not in fact exist. However, though the belfry is empty it has once housed a bell of ill-omen, cast long ago from the metal of a heathen altar. The tale of its casting and of its exorcism by a Franciscan friar, who wrestles for nine hours with the devil inside it, occupies almost a canto; and the narrative is interrupted by a further unrelated incident concerning the practical joker's son and the revenge which his friends take on the girl who jilts him. Herr von Wiese is at pains to proclaim the **"Idylle"** a unity. The whole thing, he asserts, is held together by its charming humour, which can absorb anything, however small, into the tissue of jest and earnest that makes up the story. But this is most disputable. For the incident of the pagan bell had a far more profound significance for the poet than the fanciful inventions of the other six cantos. Mörike was throughout his life obsessed with certain memories of his youth, deeply painful to him, which he was for ever trying to render innocuous by accepting them into the present in the form of myth. The purpose of his writing was, in some sense, to compose fictions in which the painful could be transmuted into legend, in which the old bell could be exorcised of its devil and prove to be of the same world as the merry fisherman and the pranks he played on his neighbours. But the two levels do not combine, and the reader is never convinced that the belfry is really empty, that there is nothing more there for the tailors to steal than the fisherman's old hat. It is this failure to reconcile the conflicting strands of his experience in any sustained poem that invalidates such claims to greatness as Herr von Wiese is emboldened to make on Mörike's behalf. . . .

The theme of abandonment, associated with his first and perhaps only genuine experience of love, recurs constantly in Mörike's poetry; it was, in Herr von Wiese's opinion, Maria's desertion that opened his eyes to that "Bodenlosigkeit des Lebens" which all his life long he could never forget. She is the Peregrina of the poems interpolated in *Maler Nolten*. . . .

Mörike's immediate reaction to the loss of his Peregrina was to compose with his friend Ludwig Bauer the great Orplid myth, the fantasy of a world which partook both of fairy-tale and saga in which these young men lived. . . . Memories of Orplid, the legend of which was elaborated during two years, carry the same emotional overcharge in Mörike's poetry as those that recall Peregrina. None of his poems, indeed, is so richly dyed with the misty greys of Romantic legend as the "Gesang Weylas," which was written as a gentle farewell to that island of the gods, upon which Weyla was the only goddess. . . . But the Orplid myth was not Mörike's only alternative to the realities with which he could not come to terms. Weyla's song is a pure distillation, comparable with [Coleridge's] "Kubla Khan" or Hölderlin's "Hälfte des Lebens," of longing for a land of heart's desire, which in Mörike's case . . . was a world of death. . . .

Mörike's melancholy and the vein of morbidity suggested by the encyclopaedia note are indeed the predominant strains in his character. The robustness that one seems to find on turning from an anthology to his collected works is illusory. The clatter of Suckelborst's seven-league boots does not conceal the menacing silence of the abyss that yawns at the poet's feet. But his fear of confronting his own emptiness made him a prodigious inventor, and except for that rather too cosy piece of Biedermeier, the story of "Mozart auf der Reise nach Prag," almost all that he wrote is still fresh and delightful. He is indeed one of the few German poets of the nineteenth century whose work can be placed beside that of his English contemporaries.

*"Eduard Mörike," in* The Times Literary Supplement, *No. 2598, November 16, 1951, p. 730.*

### R. B. FARRELL   (lecture date 1953)

[*In this excerpt, drawn from the English summary of his German-language lecture given in 1953, Farrell discusses the content and tone of Mörike's Romantic poems, or those dealing with "Nature, love and the mysterious and inexplicable stirrings of his inner life." For commentary by Farrell on Mörike as a Classical poet, see excerpt below, 1955-56; see also Additional Bibliography.*]

Mörike's poetic work exhibits a variety of subjects and tones unknown to the romantics and to his contemporaries—distinct worlds, even if in the last analysis they all float in an atmosphere that belongs unmistakeably to their creator. For a long time he was regarded as the idyllic Biedermeier poet who recounted pleasantly and humorously the little happenings of daily life in the rural surroundings of the village of Cleversulzbach, where he was a very unwilling pastor. Later research has attached greater importance to the romantic elements of his poetry, to its cosmic vision, its awareness of the demonic, its Nature magic, so that the early picture of him as a poet who loved to spend his mornings in bed sipping tea and nibbling biscuits and forgetful of his pastoral duties had to be adjusted to include that side of his being which at the same time listened to voices from the cosmos. A third side of his genius unfolds in his classical poems, where, like Goethe, he is able to evoke the world of objects and of art for the senses, particularly for the eye. One thing, however, is noticeably absent: all reference to the social and political events of the times. An introvert, sensitive to the point of morbidity, shunning society, a visionary who not only could feel himself attuned to the harmony of the cosmos but saw into its abyss, one who at times preserved his human equilibrium by escape to an idyllic rustic world of trivial and humorous happenings and by contemplation of beauty in art and in other visual objects—such is the picture of the

man that emerges from his life and that we divine behind his work. (p. 22)

To concentrate on the predominantly romantic group [of Mörike's poems], the great spheres of life which he presents are Nature, love and the mysterious and inexplicable stirrings of his inner life.

Mörike conjures up the many coloured garment of Nature, the green forest, the blue sky, the glittering freshness of morning, with a sensuous power unrivalled except by Goethe. While Eichendorff sees Nature as a green shimmering sea and floats through or above it like a disembodied spirit, Mörike, without losing his sense of the whole, perceives the smallest and most inconspicuous objects and absorbs them, so to speak, through every pore, as in **Besuch in Urach,** where, though driven onwards in his quest for the soul of Nature and almost overwhelmed by the luxuriant landscape, he nevertheless opens himself lovingly to the meanest flower that blows. His sensuousness extends to bodily sensations as the feeling of water in **Mein Fluss** or the sweat of an early morning walk up hill and down dale in **Fussreise,** and can pass over into intense sensual feeling as in **Erstes Liebeslied eines Mädchens,** where the girl, as the experience overpowers her, thinks she must be clutching at a snake or a sweet eel slipping down her breasts. Which sense, however, enjoys pride of place it is difficult to say, whether the ear which perceives such august harmonies in the cosmic poems or the eye which everywhere and above all in the classical group renders emotions in terms of visual imagery. (pp. 22-3)

Yet it is no static landscape that Mörike portrays; his inner eye, piercing externals, perceives the life-force of Nature in ceaseless activity. (p. 23)

[*Septembermorgen*] is typical in its conception of autumn as a dynamic force and in that from beginning to end it evokes a process, in much the same way as the emotions portrayed by the poet are a changing or fluctuating course rather than a constant state. In the poems of night and early morning it is the pulse, the circulation of cosmic life that the poet hears, ecstatic and rapt in the object of his contemplation. Characteristically, such poems begin with purely sensuous material, often with a concrete situation, and then soar into cosmic realms. In **Gesang zu Zweien in der Nacht** the opening image of the night breeze softly grazing the meadow is followed by that of the forces of earth pressing upwards into the air, which quivers like a web, until the music of the spheres is heard and the soul of creation ecstatically enfolds the lovers. A picture of the movement and harmony of the cosmos is evoked in the first half of **Nacht** with its vision of the play of the night sky. In **An einem Wintermorgen vor Sonnenaufgang** the natural phenomenon is expanded to the creative process itself, merging the creativeness of the self with that of the cosmos.

But it is by no means always the harmony and majesty of the cosmos that Mörike reveals; he was no less aware of its powers of destruction. . . . The demonic forces of life can raise man to the heights, but they can also sweep him into the abyss. He is threatened by the cosmos which withholds its secret from him and thrusts him back into the uncertainties of human existence. Confronted by this dual face of Nature, Mörike is overcome by fluctuating feelings, ecstasy suddenly giving way to melancholy and wistful memories or even to a shattering of his whole emotional life. Helplessness arising out of a conflict between the desire to merge with the universe and the fear of thereby losing his human self is the thought expressed in the second part of *Nacht* and is the experience elaborated in prose in the final section of *Mozart auf der Reise nach Prag.* (pp. 23-4)

The convulsion and disintegration of the self no less than the transcending of human limits and fusion with the harmony of the universe can be brought about by the passion of love. If in *An die Geliebte* the self hears "Die Quellen des Geschicks melodisch rauschen" and hearkens to the "Lichtgesang" of the "Sterne", in *Peregrina* we find the record of its devastation by a hopeless conflict of intense attraction and repulsion. Apart from the classical group, which in the manner of Goethe portrays sensual passion as a heightened and delighted perception of sensuous charms, sometimes with a touch of roguish humour, love generally appears as an unhappy unrequited passion, particularly in the guise of woman's love.

This brief and inadequate account of Mörike's major themes is necessary for an understanding of the inner attitude out of which the emotional tone and the characteristics of his form and style are born. I am referring to a tone audible in his work, not to a condition of creative effort. We are first struck by a passivity of soul which accepts fate rather than defying it or making demands of it. It manifests itself as humility and resignation and, furthermore, as absence of the will and of desire, even where the theme is unhappy love or the destructive power inherent in Nature. The everyday, all too human self with its desires and purposes is silent and submissive to the object to the point of self-forgetfulness; love which seeks nothing for self takes its place. To present another aspect of this attitude: the poet's soul resembles the aeolian harp, the music of which Mörike describes so movingly. Life plays whatever tune it will on the unresisting soul, which reflects with absolute purity the nature of the object. Selflessness we may call this. . . . (p. 24)

Mörike's selflessness may thus be simply the imagination that informs all great poetry. On the other hand, it appears intensified by reason of its fusion with a contemplative passivity, whereas with Goethe it is instinct with the buoyant spirit of activity. Pure existence or experience, that is, free from all purposes and desires, is revealed in Mörike's poetry. . . . At bottom, Mörike's purposelessness is akin to play and thus to the nature of the child. It accounts, too, for the impromptu and unpremeditated effect of so much of his poetry. The play element in this exhibits a wide range of forms and tones—from the roguish and whimsical jest and the pretty Rokoko compliment to the play of the soul over an abyss. Everywhere he describes play of various kinds. The *Idylle am Bodensee* tells of one practical joke after another, while many of the Biedermeier poems with a mingling of hilarity and tenderness relate humorous incidents. Some of the idylls, as e.g. *Wald-Idylle,* suggest a delighted escape from society or the burden of duty and a playful, childlike abandonment to the world of imaginings of the Märchen. Or we are reminded of the ball game with oranges on the bay of Naples described in the Mozart story [*Mozart auf der Reise nach Prag*] and the memory of which inspired the composer with a number for his *Don Giovanni;* indeed, of the whole festive atmosphere and the playful arabesques of this work, however much they may be intertwined with the motives of transience and death. Even the activity of the cosmos Mörike experiences as play, as the purposeless and desireless unfolding of itself made manifest in the sublime and harmonious spectacle of the night sky. . . .

[An] impression of purposeless play arises no less from Mörike's style, which never seems to advance in a straight line but to be a weaving, an interlacing, sometimes of remote ele-

ments "leichtfertig verknüpft" as he himself says of the Märchen in *Wald-Idylle.* The many pictures linked by "indessen", the frequent use of "oder", the fondness for parentheses are a few of the visible signs of this style. (p. 25)

[A] Mörike poem reveals a defenceless attitude of the self to its world, a course of feeling which often begins with a concrete situation and purely sensuous perception and develops impromptu-like with sudden fluctuations, sometimes with a transcendent or demonic world opening up, at other times keeping well within the bounds of everyday life but transfiguring this with humour. Always there is a submission to the object, which in the last analysis explains why Mörike in his classical poems could evoke objectively the sensuous charm and beauty of the visible world and, approaching the manner of the ancients, even if he is too tender to be completely antique, render inner states of being in visual imagery. (pp. 25-6)

> *R. B. Farrell, "The Art of Eduard Mörike," in* Proceedings of the Australian Goethe Society, *Vol. IV, 1952-53, pp. 22-6.*

## R. B. FARRELL    (lecture date 1955-56)

[*In the following excerpt from a lecture delivered in 1955-56, Farrell discusses Mörike's translations of Greek and Latin poetry as well as the influence of Classical poetry on Mörike's verse. For commentary by Farrell on the Romantic qualities of Mörike's poetry, see excerpt above, 1953; see also Additional Bibliography.*]

[Mörike's] constant devotion to and understanding of the Greek and Latin lyric are shown in the three volumes of translations from these languages, published in 1840, 1855 and 1865 [*Klassische Blumenlese*; *Theokritos, Bion und Moschos*; and *Anakreon und die Sogenannten Anakreontischen Lieder*]. By no means all the renderings are his own, and he in fact modestly disclaimed all credit except for working over what his predecessors had already done. The handling of classical measures and the close study of their style in general must have brought him near to the spirit of the ancients. I am not competent to judge the subtleties of the translations, but in their re-production of the meaning and the style of the original they do seem to me to be faithful renderings, and read, moreover, despite occasional metrical laxness, naturally. From the Greek he translated a few Homeric hymns, war-songs by Callinus and Tyrtaeus, pieces by Theognis, specimens of Anacreon and of his followers, and above all a number of the idylls of Theocritus, the poet who, more than any other, was dear to his heart; from the Latin, selections from Catullus, Tibullus and Horace. That section of his own work in which his debt to the spirit and the style of antiquity is clearest consists of poems in the epigrammatic manner recalling the Greek Anthology and Goethe's epigrams; then longer pieces where the influence is less direct and more difficult to disentangle, such as the idylls and the humorous and satirical treatment of every-day incidents, sometimes in the form of epistles or descriptions of this and that which also read like letters. Understandably, he wrote almost nothing of this kind during his twenties, a certain intimacy and harmony with the world of men and women about him being a pre-requisite. His early poetry, dominated by a sense of the power and the beauty of the cosmos, shows him alone with Nature and hardly less alone in his experience of passionate love, and although these themes were not later abandoned entirely, they were no longer presented directly, but, so to speak, under the surface in a human setting. No parallel with Goethe's development however, can be drawn. In no sense can we in

Mörike's case speak of a period of classicism as a consistent view and way of life, a classicism which with Goethe was also reflected as 'Bildung' in the content of his work no less than in its form. The classical spirit stirred Mörike to creative effort at irregular intervals, the years 1837, 1845 and 1846, however, witnessing a particularly rich harvest. (pp. 43-4)

In the literature of antiquity he found objectivity and a sense of oneness with life, even where painful emotions are described. And his choice of poets for translation shows where his sympathies pre-eminently lay: less with the heroic and the monumental than with the idyllic, the playful and the wise, not the philosophically wise, but mellow practical wisdom. Harry Maync, his chief biographer, sees in Homer the source of the narrative flow, of the looking backwards and forwards and of the general reflective passages in the *Idylle am Bodensee*. But if Mörike studied Homer's technique, and no doubt he did, his application of it is so original as to constitute a difference in kind. . . . [His] narrative verse contains a lyrical element, which in the Bodensee idyll takes the form of a mood of mingled delight, whimsicality, tenderness and also jest, prompting him to digress as the fancy takes him, even to the point of constructing the work as two almost unconnected stories; to intervene and address at length the characters dear to his heart; and finally to make the hexameter glide and hover as though it had wings. Of greater significance, I should say, was Theocritus. . . . In his idylls Theocritus not only invests his descriptions of small things with charm but gives pictures of people absorbed in their world, whether of every-day affairs or of passionate love; and, above all, he can make his characters prattle delightfully about these things. But when Mörike took over something of the manner and the devices of another poet he generally added an element of his own: a tendency to abandon himself to a mood of delight or of grotesque, sometimes capricious, humour. His debt is mainly to the spirit of ancient literature, but he occasionally borrows a situation, a motif or simply a hint which he then heightens in this way; as he obviously did with the playful suggestion he found in the Greek anacreontic poem, which in his translation he calls *Das Bild des Bathyllos*. . . . It is the motif of the painter painting a double image of the beloved on the same canvas and appears in a more grotesque form in Mörike's *Das Bildnis der Geliebten*. In a similar way his *Lose Ware* heightens and elaborates the playful element that he found in the Greek poem called in his translation *Besuch des Eros*. . . . (pp. 50-2)

The most cursory comparison of Mörike with the ancients makes it clear what possibilities of theme and treatment their study must have opened up to him in his search for objectivity and harmony with life. And yet there is a far-reaching difference. His harmony has little of the natural sense of oneness of the Greeks and little of the good-sense and matter-of-factness of the Romans. Rather does it come as a rush of high spirits, as play, which is somehow aware that it exists only in the imagination. Whether as idyllic delight or as whimsical or grotesque humour, his play by its very abandon mostly betrays itself as a sudden and momentary impulse of the imagination and in consequence, I should think, as lacking that stable feeling of oneness with life which we associate with the classical spirit. I cannot read this section of Mörike's work without sensing his relief at escaping from pressure and without thinking of this kind of play as a role he was able to slip into. (p. 56)

*R. B. Farrell, "Mörike's Classical Verse," in* Publications of the English Goethe Society, *n.s. Vol. XXV, 1955-56, pp. 41-62.*

*Mörike at age nineteen. A pencil drawing by J. G. Schreiner.*

### HARVEY W. HEWETT-THAYER    (essay date 1957)

[*Hewett-Thayer discusses the conventional literary techniques that Mörike used in* Maler Nolten *to compensate for his inexperience as a prose writer. He examines, in particular, Mörike's use of the omniscient narrator, lyric inserts, and interpolated manuscripts, as well as his reluctance to name people and places. For further commentary by Hewett-Thayer, see Additional Bibliography.*]

[At its publication], *Maler Nolten* was in certain technical aspects already somewhat old-fashioned, and the revised version appearing in 1877, though considerably altered, must have seemed doubly so, for at that time the nineteenth century had begun its last quarter, and the trend of fiction had been toward a greater concentration, a tighter control of material, and the elimination of the superfluous. A close reading of the story, especially of the first version, shows the author struggling and at times fumbling with the technique of story-telling. (p. 259)

In view of his inexperience, Mörike inevitably, though doubtless unconsciously, adopted the technical modes of fiction of the preceding periods. He published *Maler Nolten* as a "Novelle," and it seems probable that his conception of the genre was influenced by, if not derived from, Ludwig Tieck, one of his favorite authors. . . . In the second place Goethe was Mörike's master, the Goethe of *Wilhelm Meisters Lehrjahre* and *Die Wahlverwandtschaften*. Mörike follows Tieck rather than Goethe in not dividing his story into chapters; even the division into two parts is not structurally significant.

For the most part Mörike narrates consistently in the third person. He is the omniscient story-teller who is present on all occasions, knows to the letter what the characters say, records and interprets their inmost thoughts, and analyzes their motives. . . . [In] numberless passages he reveals the inner emotional world of Nolten, Agnes, and Konstanze. At times, however, Mörike strays into another type of fictional technique, one extremely common in earlier novels. The novelist is an interested spectator or a secondary participant in the happenings; he has gathered material together, perhaps through interviews with other spectators, and thus fills in the gaps to form a complete narrative. This is a variant of the novelist as editor: in one way or another, manuscripts, letters, or diaries have fallen into his hands, and, recognizing their interest, he then arranges the material for publication; of this method [Goethe's] *Werther* is an obvious example. The titles or subtitles of numerous eighteenth-century novels give evidence of this technique. It is, of course, a transparent device to heighten the seeming actuality of the story. (pp. 259-60)

Characteristic of the [first version of *Maler Nolten*] was the personal narrator, in contrast with the later preference for the purely objective chronicle. The practice seemed to invite a more intimate relation with the reader and assumed an interest in the fortunes of the characters; that is, the reader is invited to be a companion of the novelist. Thus throughout the story Mörike speaks of "unser Maler," "unser Freund," "unsere Gesellschaft," as Goethe of Wilhelm Meister as "unser Held". In the management of the material the novelist takes the reader into his confidence, tells him what he is going to do and the reason for it. . . . (pp. 260-61)

Mörike's dependence, however unconscious, upon earlier conventions in fiction is illustrated by his reticence in naming places and people. In *Wilhelm Meister,* for example, whatever inferences may be drawn from localities with which Goethe was familiar, the topography is left utterly indefinite. Mörike's story abounds in descriptions of places, often of deep feeling and great poetic beauty; the places may often be identified in terms of his own Swabian homeland, but he avoids mention of actual names. . . .

In one passage the novelist seems almost under a spell in his maintenance of this tradition. The avoidance of names of places is forced and unnatural. There is discussion of plans for the journey northwards; Nolten wishes to go by a roundabout route in order to visit some German cities that are worth seeing. A map is spread out on the table, but no towns are mentioned. . . . (p. 261)

Similarly traditional is the treatment of personal names. . . . Among the chief figures of the story the reader never learns Agnes' last name or Larkens' first name; Raymund might be either a first or last name; Amandus, Leopold, and Ferdinand are without family names. . . .

Thus Mörike follows the practice of his predecessors either in evasion or in the use of initial letters, asterisks, and dashes. One recalls Gellert's *Das Leben der schwedischen Gräfin von G.* or the numerous characters in Goethe's novels known only by a single name, first or last, or by a mere title. In earlier novels the fashion was often a mere trick for increasing the illusion of reality; the actual identity of people and places is discretely concealed. Mörike adheres to the tradition almost as if it were an unwritten law in fiction.

As a lyric poet, Mörike naturally copied his predecessors in the use of lyric inserts in his prose narrative. Some of them have a demonstrable function in the development of the story: as a prisoner, Nolten hears the warder's daughter singing the

song of the forsaken maiden; Agnes sings first **"Der Jäger"** and then, by fateful choice, the **"Rosenzeit"** with its concealed application. The **"Peregrina"** poems and the cycle **"An L."** illumine retrospectively inter-relationships between characters in the story. In the case of **"Der Feuerreiter"** a suspicion might arise that the episode of the Albanikirchturm is craftily manipulated to provide for its inclusion. But generally Mörike supplies a natural or understandable context for the inserted poems. (p. 262)

In *Maler Nolten* the novelist is frequently skillful in disclosing significant details in the past life of the characters by unobtrusive and natural means. The young artist at his meeting with Tillsen would be more or less under obligation to tell something of himself; Nolten's wistful reminiscences on his return to Neuburg are by no means unnatural or obviously contrived for the enlightenment of the reader, even though what he says is already part of his hearers' memories. In some cases the necessity for imparting such information tends to inject an awkward interruption in the flow of the narration.

Mörike uses, however, a traditional device in disclosing the one outstanding experience of Nolten's youth, following older models by introducing an interpolated manuscript. This story, **"Ein Tag aus Noltens Jugendleben,"** has come into being in a rather dubious way: Nolten has told his friend Larkens of his youthful encounter with the Gypsy girl, and Larkens has written it out afterwards in literary form as a third-person narrative. Though, as an actor, Larkens may have had a phenomenal verbal memory, even a casual reading stamps the attribution to Larkens' authorship as a questionable expedient. And more disturbing still, in the latter part of the story Mörike allows Larkens to assume the role of the omniscient story teller and relate in great detail what Nolten could not have told him, for the boy was in bed asleep; that he heard all this later from his sisters is an untenable assumption. As Nolten's boyhood meeting with the Gypsy is crucial for the whole development of the story, it must have been in Mörike's mind from the outset. With considerable plausibility one may speculate that Mörike wrote the **"Tag"** narrative as the beginning of the story, intending at that time to employ the chronological order of events. Later he plunged *in medias res,* probably in the interest of mystery and suspense, and accordingly had to find a method for introducing this essential episode at a later point of the story. He had to invent a subordinate authorship for the inserted tale and reasons for its appearing where it did.

The method of attaching this material at a later point in the action also seems decidedly inept. Larkens is in prison, and the police have confiscated all his papers. With Leopold, who has been permitted to visit him there, he talks of Nolten, and on the street at night Leopold has recently seen the Gypsy with the face of Nolten's "Organ-player." This naturally leads to the manuscript, which Larkens has lent to an unnamed friend— conveniently indeed, so that it is now available and not in the hands of the police. Larkens gives Leopold a note to this friend; Leopold obtains the manuscript and reads it; thus it is made known to the reader. It seems highly improbable that Larkens would have lent this intensely personal document even to an intimate friend. One may surmise that Mörike, having decided against the chronological order of narration, continued in the writing of his story beyond the point of the double arrest of Larkens and Nolten, and then, becoming aware that the material of **"Ein Tag"** was overdue, inserted it at this place. This necessitated the rather lame invention of the loan of the manuscript.

The conjecture that "**Ein Tag**" was originally written as the beginning of the novel receives support from the inclusion in it of extracts from the diary of Nolten's uncle, Friedrich Nolten, who was also an artist. The use of letters and diaries was part of the stock-in-trade of the earlier novelists, and Mörike had naturally no hesitation in employing the device. These excerpts are inserted in the latter part of the "**Tag**" narrative, in the evening after the disappearance of the Gypsy. The father has disclosed her identity and now by way of supplying further information tells to his eldest daughter Ernestine, who was more his companion than the younger children, the story of his brother's life; he has the diary before him, but pushing it aside relates the events without reference to it. . . . [At] the end of the passages from the diary the impression is given that the father was reading them. . . . The "**Tag**" narrative includes further an account of the remainder of the evening and of the following morning and a brief statement of Nolten's fortunes after his father's death. That is, the excerpts from the diary are imbedded in the narrative of "**Ein Tag**." But the novelist fails to account in any way for the presence of this material in Larkens' possession; this would seem to be obligatory in the case of Larkens' authorship, but no explanation would be required, if "**Ein Tag**" were simply the first chapter or section of the novel. (pp. 263-65)

From the technical point of view a critic of the late nineteenth century would censure not only the narrative "**Ein Tag**" as a "flash-back" awkwardly and unconvincingly introduced, but even more the inclusion of a drama in prose and verse which occupies nearly one tenth of the whole novel. He would note that the play contributes to the story—in the narrower sense—to the plot, one single element. As economy of means to an end, even in novel writing, had been established as a principle, the critic would insist that the novelist should have been able to provide for this element at less cost, particularly since it is present only in parts of the drama. Further, the discussions and digressions violated the doctrine of strict economy in the use of materials. In one of his predecessors, Heinrich von Kleist, Mörike might have observed an exponent of such economy, . . . but he did not take Kleist as a model.

It is doubtless superfluous to say that no one reads *Maler Nolten* as an example of technical mastery in the art of fiction. . . . (p. 266)

*Harvey W. Hewett-Thayer, "Traditional Technique in Mörike's 'Maler Nolten'," in* The Germanic Review, *Vol. XXXII, No. 4, December, 1957, pp. 259-66.*

### CHRISTOPHER MIDDLETON (essay date 1969)

[*In the excerpt below, Middleton briefly treats Mörike's translations of ancient Greek and Latin verse as well as the classical characteristics of his original poetry. For further criticism by Middleton, see Additional Bibliography.*]

Germanists are prone to quote Gottfried Keller's remark about Mörike being a "son of Horace by a sophisticated Swabian woman": and his poems do have distinctive classical qualities, even when his feeling is most "personal," even during the period when his motifs might least promise them (1824-1837). The qualities in question (and they make Mörike perhaps the purest of German lyric poets) are: balance, plasticity, clarity, and a high-spirited play of instinct. Nowhere in his poems does one find the bookish or postured classicizing which occurs sometimes even in Goethe, and often—closer to Mörike's time—in Platen. He also had a different and quite new conception of

classical *scale*. His work revokes all grandiosity of the kind which had bedeviled German classicizing. . . . Not magnitude but wholeness of structure was Mörike's concern, a wholeness best achieved by relating close-knit resonant surfaces of minimum expanse. (p. 404)

His first book of translations was the *Classische Blumenlese* of 1840, which began with some Homeric Hymns and ended with Tibullus. His own poems of the 1840's have a concentrated crisp warmth which is due in no small measure to the vivacity of their classical meters (senarius, elegiac distichs, and hexameter) and to their graceful kinds of tension. These poems include his miniature pastoral epic *Die Idylle vom Bodensee,* a poem which contains some of the most "organic" (and mimetic) hexameters ever written in German. The Theocritus translations were certainly the outcome of a profoundly felt commitment to the idyll as a genre and to a poet whom Mörike loved second only to Homer. They reveal, too, his fondness for the forms of energy in which classical art answers human need: order and symmetry, intricacy and harmony.

Hölderlin and Nietzsche command the nineteenth century as far as German literary exploration of the Greek world is concerned. They were the myth-makers, one at the start of the century, the other at its end. Between them, chronologically, comes Mörike. Not an idealist, not an iconoclast, still Mörike shared the mad streak which destroyed the other two men and which was a primary force in the tensions shaping the sensibilities of all three. And Mörike, too, brought back to life, by his acts of imagination, in his own undemonstrative way, some of the voices in the Greek polyphony.

Introducing his translations, Mörike made no bones about admitting that he had built on [earlier translations from the works of Theocritus]. . . . Mörike also wrote that his concern had been to avoid the ineptitudes of the earlier versions, and to preserve the "natural delivery" of the originals. Even if it meant relaxing the meter somewhat, he had looked for a "form that would be homogeneous and adequate to the spirit of the German language." In effect, his hexameters have an economy and elegance which make ordinary talk a marvel of directness. (pp. 404-05)

*Christopher Middleton, "Theocritus through Mörike," in* Arion, *Vol. 8, No. 3, Autumn, 1969, pp. 398-406.*

### MARTIN LINDSAY (essay date 1969)

[*In this excerpt from his descriptive survey of Mörike's poetry and prose, Lindsay maintains that Mörike's verse, including his Biedermeier, Volkslied, mystic, Romantic, and supernatural poems, "reflects the many facets of his complicated personality." Lindsay contends that Mörike's powerful poetic vision "sets him apart from lesser poets" and concludes that he was a "lyric poet of almost unparalleled range and virtuosity, who has written a large number of the best poems in the German language."*]

Mörike's poetry reflects the many facets of his complicated personality. The aspect which he most willingly displayed to the world of the comfortable, slightly humorous poet of Swabian domesticity, the very incarnation of *Biedermeier* poetic art, the parson poet composing verses cosily in his study while outside the bees hummed and the local rustics carried on contentedly with their seasonal tasks undoubtedly forms part of the truth. . . . [He] reflects the rural Swabia of a century or so ago in an often slightly idealising manner. . . . His profession as a rural vicar, however unenthusiastically exercised, has thoroughly acquainted him with the lives of all sorts of Swabians and he views their occupations, interests and foibles with tolerant, understanding interest. The most famous poem he wrote in this vein is **Der alte Turmhahn** which tells in agreeable near-doggerel of his sentimental purchase of the old weathercock from his church tower. He placed it on top of the stove in his vicarage study. The poem purports to be spoken in the first person by the weather cock, which tells of its own life and that of its new owner; it also seems to have observed the doings of the local people with a good deal of sly humour. Mörike evidently surveys his own life and doings with considerable detachment and even ironic superiority. (p. 212)

Among other poems in the same vein one remembers **Häusliche Szene,** a humorous dialogue in hexameters between an eccentric middle-aged schoolmaster with an obsession for brewing vinegar and his good-natured and long-suffering young wife. Mörike very evidently knows his people and regards them with kindly understanding but he is far from blind to their shortcomings. His humour can also take a less kindly and tolerant form; in **Abschied** he allows himself the luxury of kicking his reviewer downstairs after the reviewer has paid a social call and commented on the size of his nose. This poem is attractively written in rhyming couplets with lines of varying length; the undignified descent of the reviewer is well communicated in the last few jerky and bumpy lines. A few poems take the peasants sharply to task for their less endearing ways, for instance **Pastoral-Erfahrung** and **Gute Lehre.** The former poem rather affectionately describes the naïve naughtiness of Mörike's parishioners, who steal his lettuces on a Saturday night, and in church on Sunday expect the sermon to provide them with the sharpness of vinegar and the smoothness of oil—a perfect dressing for the lettuce. **Gute Lehre** exposes the ungraciousness and philistinism of the people who are not capable of appreciating the beauty or the rights of other creatures in nature. All these poems and many others like them exemplify one facet of Mörike's chameleon-like personality; the detached, kindly, generally humorous observer of other men's foibles and peculiarities, who sets down his experiences in a fluent and entertaining form which, however, seldom raises these poems above the level of charming trifles.

Mörike can strike the *Volkslied* note most authentically, too. From the German Romantic poets he may well have inherited his interest in and love of folk poetry, but he also had a great love of his fellow human beings, a natural affinity with the sources of popular poetry and a sensitive appreciation of the joys and sorrows, the range of experience and the forms of expression of ordinary people. **Das verlassene Mägdlein,** a poem in four short stanzas, perfectly expresses the distress of the deserted servant-girl, sorrowing over her faithless lover as she makes the fire. Because the poet can fully appreciate the girl's emotional situation as well as the circumstances of her job, because he deals in absolutely simple language with things familiar to her like cockcrow, the stars and flying sparks, this poem has a truth and aptness which surpass other poets' more ambitious but less genuine attempts to imitate the manner of the *Volkslied.*

Mörike was also well versed in popular legend and traditions, and in one poem after another he either retells familiar legends or invents new ones akin to them. Some of these poems have a force and vitality which demand reading aloud or a musical setting if they are to have their full effect. **Der Feuerreiter,** the legend concerning a mad young man who is attracted by any fire in the neighbourhood, is a case in point. This poem, with its swift, staccato movement, and the emphatic refrain "Hinterm Berg", changing in the last strophe to "Ruhe wohl" after the excitement of the fire is past, has a daemonic force which again suggests that even the compulsion which draws the *Feuerreiter* to the scene of the blaze is not wholly incomprehensible to the poet. As so often in Mörike's poetry, one senses that the poet is aware of the susceptibility of human conduct to domination by irrational and uncontrollable forces. Even if one views **Der Feuerreiter** in isolation something of the urgent compulsion of which the young rider is a victim comes across unmistakably.

Another famous poem dealing with a legend is **Die Geister am Mummelsee.** . . . This poem opens with a question on a carefree, unsuspecting note; the speaker clearly has no idea of the ghostly ritual that is about to take place. The mounting sadness of the supernatural spectacle is skilfully evoked by the poet's cunning use of rhyme and rhythmic resources—especially the very short penultimate line of each stanza has an incantatory force which adds greatly to the effect of the poem. . . . The reader, enthralled by the poetic power of these verses, finds himself at the least strongly aware of the hostile and dangerous forces threatening Man's existence; the poem conveys a sense of menace and insecurity akin to that induced by Goethe's *Erlkönig or Der Fischer.*

Other poems give expression to less frightening and disturbing legends. **Schön-Rohtraut** forms an enchanting variation on the age-old theme of the princess who loves her gamekeeper—and surely most readers will agree that the fulfilment of this shy and modest young man's dream of kissing the princess leaves more to the imagination and is therefore aesthetically more satisfying than D. H. Lawrence's ruthlessly comprehensive narration of a gamekeeper's amorous exploits with his employer's wife. Here, as often, Mörike uses archaic and traditional forms of expression from the folk ballad in the most natural way. In a different vein altogether are the two songs of the robber chief, Jung Volker, the **Gesang der Räuber** and **Jung Volkers Lied.** These are gay, wild, abandoned songs, full of amoral energy and drive, not really quite what one would expect from the pen of a young clergyman. Once again, as so often, in the **Gesang der Räuber** Mörike uses an alliterative refrain . . . to striking effect.

All the poems so far mentioned show Mörike treating themes and employing verse forms which had often been used before; he is on the whole not breaking new ground, although his superior poetic talent makes his imitations of folk songs and ballads based on folk motifs far more natural and seemingly organic growths than those of, for example, his fellow-countryman and contemporary, Ludwig Uhland. The next group of poems for discussion shows Mörike in a very different light, and indeed illustrates an aspect of his poetic personality which was for many years not generally recognised. Mörike is more aware than most poets of both the heights and the depths of human experience. His poetic vision can be and quite often is of an intensity and power which sets him apart from lesser poets and justifies his claim to be regarded as Goethe's near poetic kinsman. The Germans like to call this area of human experience "dämonisch", but in a way this is begging the question, and we should try to isolate those elements in Mörike's poetry which place him in a special, very high category among German poets. Perhaps this can best be done by looking more closely at certain examples of his work.

**An einem Wintermorgen vor Sonnenaufgang,** written when he was scarcely twenty-one, represents one of Mörike's rare attempts to communicate a moment of preternatural illumination. The glad sense of release, the sudden brightness and the unexpected, dramatic merging of various elements of Christian and pagan religious experience, which are linked by the emotion of joy,—all this is sparked off by the sensation of awakening, on a dark winter morning. Mörike, a poet generally given to understatement, startles us into closer attention here by using such powerful expressions as ''Wollust'' and ''glühe'', words which might indeed be small coin in the hands of certain poets, but which when used by him must certainly convey a very powerful meaning. (pp. 212-15)

[For Mörike in **Wintermorgen**], all the distorting and discolouring elements have been removed and his soul is directly exposed to some most sublime influence. . . . [He] uses images akin to those employed by Goethe, Donne or Wordsworth to communicate the incommunicable. We may not be able fully to apprehend the exquisitely exciting experience which prompted this poem, but in the various striking images used by Mörike we gain at least some inkling of its power and immediacy. (pp. 215-16)

From the higher reality of his morning vision the poet returns to the ordinary world in the final stanza. Yet even the ordinary world has acquired some reflected glory from the higher reality, as we realise from Mörike's description of dawn. The poet has been greatly moved, whether by the subconscious memory of a past blessed state or by the promise of such a state in the future he cannot say. He cannot retain the magic of that unexpected, marvellous moment; but the day's awakening has given him both strength and ability to go on living. Mörike is always acutely responsive to nature, but it is often solitude and darkness or semi-darkness which can most readily stir his being.

Another poem in which the reader becomes aware of Mörike's acute sensitivity to Nature is **Die schöne Buche**. . . . This is a much later poem, and differs from the **Wintermorgen** and many other poems inspired by Nature in that it actually describes fairly closely the beech tree which is its subject. . . . One has the impression that the description of the scene is offered only as a preliminary to the festal moment of full appreciation, when the poet's breath is taken away by the beauty of the scene and he is overcome by the sheer beauty of this magic circle. On this occasion Mörike does not endeavour to communicate by any approximately suggestive image what the aesthetic experience is like, yet one realises that although the experience has been brief it has been of rare intensity. The poem is written in most harmonious hexameters, which fittingly contain the almost religious emotion of Mörike's aesthetic experience. Mörike was capable at fairly frequent intervals of moments of ''exaltation and ecstasy'', and when these came upon him he willingly surrendered himself to the thrill of enhanced awareness and forgot this world.

Another poem from the same middle period of his life is **Auf eine Christblume**. Here Mörike becomes ever more intensely preoccupied with the nature of the flower and succeeds well in communicating his reflections. The innermost essence of the flower is hard to apprehend, but Mörike strives to get as near it as possible. His whole endeavour is here directed to grasping the particular magic of the Christmas rose, not to describing its physical aspect only but its individuality and its spiritual meaning. The rose yields up its innermost secrets to the close observer; through the eye the poet can feel himself into the very heart of his subject. Once again we realise how much the flower matters to the poet; for a time it has constituted the exclusive focus of all his attention to the point where the

fusion between subject, poet and universe becomes complete. Mörike's dedicated contemplation has not only enabled him to write a beautiful poem, but it has also helped him to transcend the limitations of his own individuality through complete absorption in something else. On this occasion he uses rhyming iambic pentameters to achieve a perfect formal setting for his musings on the nature of the flower. Many years before Rilke Mörike was already using with complete mastery the techniques with which we are familiar in the *Neue Gedichte*.

Mörike's love for Maria Meyer . . . [produced a] direct poetic harvest in the form of several poems, the most famous of which are the cycle of five poems printed for the first time in **Maler Nolten** as **Peregrina**. . . . Even the first short poem in its unambitious metre soon begins to express the ambivalence of Mörike's feeling for Maria, his fear of becoming involved with her set against the almost irresistible attraction of her personality. The poet's mixed feelings about this girl are drastically conveyed in the final line of the poem:

> Reichst lächelnd mir den Tod im Kelch der Sünden.

The second poem of the cycle forms a sort of daemonic epithalamion. Perhaps expressing the poet's wild, uncontrollable emotion, the metre becomes much freer, although still strongly rhythmical. . . . [After the account of the wedding feast, the] couple go in to the banquet in the decorated hall and presently slip away to enjoy one another's love in idyllic natural surroundings—this description of love's fulfilment is both restrained and wonderfully effective. Despite the bride's strange choice of colours for her dress—red is the harlot's colour, not the bride's—nothing at this stage diminishes the pure joy of their love, and the last line of this poem shows the poet setting the seal on the relationship by taking the girl to live in his house.

The third poem, still in free verse, tells of the horrors of discovery and disillusionment. Mörike's use of strong terms:

> *Schaudernd* entdeckt' ich verjährten *Betrug*,

indicates the strength of his feeling of outrage and injured innocence. And yet he senses, despite his harsh judgment and condemnation of the girl, that she loves him and that a special, indissoluble relationship will always exist between her and him. . . . The see-sawing of the poet's emotions is well expressed in the fluctuations of length and rhythmical beat of the verse lines. He knows he could not resist her if she returned to him.

The fourth poem, written in rhyming, more regular lines, reveals the power that the poet's love still exercises over his heart. It tells of an imaginary return of the girl to her lover; they sit for a time grieving and wounding one another by their silence; then suddenly he weeps and the ice is broken.

The fifth poem, a sonnet, sums up and records the whole experience. Intellectually, the poet is fully aware of his beloved's weakness; he even admits that she was mad. Yet even this knowledge by no means impairs his love for her. He knows now that she can never love him wholly and solely, that she will leave him and never return again and the knowledge pains him ineffably. It is as though he needed to contain his intellectually accurate analysis of the situation in lines which at the same time are charged with anguish. (pp. 216-18)

[The **Peregrina** poems] illustrate very fully and movingly Mörike's awareness and fear of passion on the one hand, and the irresistible fascination for him of the mysterious and daemonic.

In spirit they are very close to the novel *Maler Nolten,* of which they form part, yet they form a completely characteristic expression of the poet's early torment, an aspect of his inner life and personality just as much as the rare moments of insight and inspiration underlying poems like *An einem Wintermorgen vor Sonnenaufgang.*

Mörike's reaction to the strain and excitement of experiences like that of *Peregrina* was to pray for freedom from these harrowing stresses. He preferred to avoid exposing his soul to these hazards, no doubt from a feeling that he was not certain of being able to emerge from them unscathed. Certainly his love for Maria Meyer enriched his whole life and broadened his sympathies in the end—*Maler Nolten* leaves us in no doubt about this, but it also hurt him, and he could not bear the thought of a repetition. This explains the tone of the famous and utterly characteristic little *Gebet* . . . , in which Mörike, in all faith and piety prays God to give him no excess of joy or sorrow but to let his life be marked by gracious contentment; he is content to take whatever destiny God sends, but he would rather avoid the extremes of human experience.

On the whole Mörike wrote very little directly religious verse, although it is clear from the fervid tone of many nature poems that he does not distinguish between specifically religious verse and nature poetry. A poem such as *Auf eine Christblume* has a religious intensity which has more to do with an extreme reverence for Nature and a sensitive appreciation of her beauties than with any orthodox religiosity. However, Mörike did write, in addition to the *Gebet* already mentioned, a handful of other religious poems. Examples that readily spring to mind are *Zum neuen Jahr* [and *Neue Liebe*]. . . . It is fair to observe that despite the almost baroque charm of the New Year poem and the genuine devotion and piety which so clearly informs *Neue Liebe* there is not a trace of Protestant or even any Christian belief in either poem. They both show trust in God and a complete willingness to accept His purposes but unlike so much confessional poetry they at no point presume to interpret these purposes. (p. 219)

Mörike sometimes wrote of elves and fairies, spirits and goblins and such trappings of the Romantic world of the imagination. He handles this delicate material with a light touch and enough humour to make us abandon our rational objections to this evidently unreal world. Examples of this kind of poem are *Elfenlied, Nixe Binsefuß, Der Zauberleuchtturm* and the *Mausfallen-Sprüchlein.*

Some of Mörike's poetry has a very strongly sensuous quality, which is scarcely found in any other German poet. Perhaps *Mein Fluß* . . . exemplifies this aspect of Mörike's poetry more strikingly than any other poem. The highly developed tactile sense of the poet here becomes the principal agency through which he apprehends the whole of nature with almost mystical power. What begins as a hymn to the delightful coolness of the river in summer becomes a general song of joy in the universe and in love. Water, the single element, becomes the key to the poet's whole sense of belonging within a more general scheme of things. Another poem in which sensation plays a striking part is *Erstes Liebeslied eines Mädchens,* in which the daemonic, uncontrollable nature of love is communicated by means of the most arrestingly sensuous image. (pp. 219-20)

As a young man still feeling his way in the profession of literature Mörike wrote his only novel, *Maler Nolten* . . . , which reflected his own life up to the age of about twenty-five

or six. *Maler Nolten* is a tormented book and in writing it Mörike was plainly getting his own doubts and disharmonies under control. . . . The plot of *Nolten* is complicated but fragmentary, and the narrative technique falls short of what would normally be regarded as necessary in a novel nowadays. . . . [The] reader's interest is maintained by the insight shown by the author into disordered and diseased states of mind. The action is constantly interrupted by elements which are not properly integrated into the work as a whole—poems, flash-backs, very detailed and rather indigestible descriptions of works of art, long reflective excursions, sections describing supernatural experiences and even a short drama. All this extraneous material makes the book too long and it suffers from a total lack of organisation. On the credit side, however, the work contains several very well-observed characters. . . . The court in early nineteenth century Germany rings true, and individual parts of the book show clearly that Mörike was a natural but undisciplined prose stylist of high quality. The poems in the book include some of Mörike's best—the *Peregrina-Lieder,* for instance, and the sonnets to Luise Rau, the *Feuerreiter* and more than a score of others. Mörike simply included within the text of the novel under one pretext or another the poems which he had written but not yet published elsewhere. It would be idle to pretend that *Nolten* is a very great work of literature; it owes something to [Goethe's] *Wilhelm Meister* and to Hölderlin's *Hyperion* and to the German Romantic novel and can be compared to Keller's *Der grüne Heinrich* which appeared just over twenty years later. However, the novel is so much less organized and complete than Keller's that it suffers by comparison; also, the reader must admit that despite bright and interesting sections the total effect of *Nolten,* in which every major character dies in more or less depressing circumstances, is hardly calculated to provide entertainment or edification. Not surprisingly *Maler Nolten* had little success, although a few perceptive critics saw that a considerable talent lay concealed behind its romantic horrors and loose structure. For Mörike the writing of *Maler Nolten* was in the nature of a therapeutic exercise, which enabled him to get out of his system tendencies to mental illness. Nolten and Larkens die so that their author may live. (pp. 220-21)

Mörike occupies a special place among German poets of the nineteenth century. He is a lyric poet of almost unparalleled range and virtuosity, who has written a large number of the best poems in the German language. His exceptional sensitivity to nature and music and his responsiveness to every human situation are wedded to an altogether unusual mastery of the forms of poetic expression. More than any other nineteenth century German poet he succeeds in assimilating and rendering personal to himself the world of folksong and folklore, but . . . he is equally at home in the very demanding arts of sonnet-writing and translation. . . . We must not allow ourselves to be misled by his seemingly insignificant and unsuccessful life into underrating his genius; Mörike is a great and universal poet who possesses the cardinal attribute of being a ''vates'' as well as a master of form. This quality has nothing to do with worldly success or even having a strong character or being in any obvious sense one of the world's leaders, but it has a habit of being increasingly recognised with the passage of time, so that Mörike has now come to be regarded as one of the handful of poets who have most generously enriched German Literature. (p. 223)

*Martin Lindsay, ''Eduard Mörike,'' in* German Men of Letters: Twelve Literary Essays, Vol. V, *edited by Alex Natan, Oswald Wolff, 1969, pp. 209-25.*

**HELGA SLESSAREV** (essay date 1970)

*[In her book-length study,* Eduard Mörike, *Slessarev provides biographical information and discusses Mörike's poetry and prose. The following excerpt is an examination of his fairy tales.]*

In 1836 Mörike published **"Der Schatz"** (**"The Treasure"**), which he designated as a "novella." Three years later, however, in the foreword to the second edition, he used the term "fairy tale." The ambiguity of the title is related to the story, which also is ambiguous. Again and again, one feels the author's effort to [psychologically] explain his hero's dreams and experiences on the trip to Frankfurt. . . . But on the other hand, the principal characters are so strongly guided by their faith in the existence of certain legendary figures that the supernatural seems to project into real life. Legendary or fairy tale figures, like ghosts, dwarfs, and speaking animals appear to the characters in the story when they are either under the influence of alcohol, are ill (scarlet fever), or when they are asleep. Everything that happens to the hero in **"The Treasure"** could be naturally explained and the story would then be correctly termed a novella, i.e., a narration of unheard-of events. But the characters themselves believe in the supernatural and make it a force that must be reckoned with and which influences the course of events. Thus the faith in the one hundred rules—and a few additional ones for special occasions—which the hero, on the day of his confirmation, finds in the little book called "Jewel-box," runs through the story like a red thread. The good luck of the hero, who wins his bride and an envied position in society without any effort simply because he was born on an Easter Sunday, transposes us into a fairy tale world. (pp. 127-28)

**"The Stuttgart Hutzelmännlein"** was published in 1852, during the early happy stage of Mörike's married life in Stuttgart. More than any other work, this fairy tale breathes his love for the simple people, for his native country, and for fairy-tale motifs. It is related to the **"Idyl from Lake Constance,"** which mirrors the life of shepherds and fishermen. But in the **"Idyl"** the heroic meter (the hexameter) gave the simplicity a touch of the exemplary or classical, while the prose of the **"Hutzelmännlein"** is so mixed with words and rhymes from the Swabian dialect that it comes realistically close to the popular language. . . . (p. 132)

[This fairy tale contains motifs] so natural and so closely related to popular tales that Mörike's friends were convinced the author had made use of an already existing folk legend. But Mörike denied having any knowledge of similar traditions. We must, therefore, attribute the wealth of his inventions in the **"Hutzelmännlein"** once more to his gift of inventing myths of a kind that are otherwise known as property of the people. That is true also of the following details of his story: upon their farewell, the *Hutzelmännlein,* who reaches only to the waist of the hero, hands Seppe a *Hutzelbrot* that will always grow again, as long as he does not eat the last bit. Other objects with magic power are the two pairs of shoes he is given, one for himself and one for leaving somewhere to be found by the girl who will some day bring happiness to him. The shoes were made by the *Hutzelmännlein,* the patron of the craft of the shoemakers, and are supposed to bring good luck to whoever wears them. (p. 134)

[With the] ending, Mörike diverges from most other fairy tales in which the heroes find happiness and wealth far away from home. The world he portrays in his tale thus appears more limited—it is at the same time more concrete and realistic. The same tendency can be observed throughout the tale. While folk fairy tales give indication of being abstractions by stressing a magic number (for example, by testing the hero three times), Mörike was carried away by his love for details and forgot all about the abstractions. . . . Mörike also acquaints us with his characters much more closely than fairy tales, which usually stress only one trait. He weaves so many folklore elements into his story that it can be read as a chapter in a description of customs and manners in Swabia at the time of the famous Count Eberhard. The story is a glorification of the life and people in Swabia. Yet we should not understand it in too narrow a sense. Like the other fairy tales, it is also a mirror of the world, of its joys and troubles, of love and crime, trickery and generosity, life and death, good and evil.

In 1853, one year after **"The Hutzelmännlein"** was published, there appeared another, much shorter work from Mörike's pen, **"Die Hand der Jezerte"** (**"The Hand of Jezerte"**). He himself called it "a kind of fairy tale in archaic style." What did he mean with the designation "archaic"? Did the work again describe the customs of earlier times like **"The Hutzelmännlein"**? Or was he referring not to content but to form? (p. 138)

*Mozart contemplating the count's orange garden. From* Mozart on the Way to Prague, *by Eduard Mörike. Translated by Walter and Catherine Alison Phillips. Illustrated by Eliane Bonabel. Copyright 1947 by Pantheon Books, Inc. Reprinted by permission of Pantheon Books, a Division of Random House, Inc.*

Upon learning of the content of this work, the reader must feel reminded of the usual folk fairy tales, probably more so than in the case of **"The Hutzelmänlein."** It is a tale of a king and his love, fair judgment, and his mistress' love and jealousy. The characters are types rather than persons with whom the reader would identify. . . . It seems as if the story were not fixed in time or place and remained abstract like a paradigm. But upon a closer look, we notice motifs that do point to a certain historical period during the Middle Ages when Germanic, Christian, and Oriental beliefs and customs were fused. . . . The *Gesta Romanorum,* a Latin collection of anecdotes and tales compiled in the late thirteenth or early fourteenth century, reflect the fusion of classical and oriental stories with Christian legends which must have been common property of people of the time. It abounds in motifs similar to the ones found in Mörike's story. . . . [The] story of Jezerte is set in an atmosphere similar to that of Erinna in Mörike's poem **"Erinna to Sappho."** Both works describe the morning toiletries of the girls, mention precious oils and byssos web, details which, in Mörike's mind, must have constituted a certain classical flavor.

A glance at the dates of the conception and publication of the fairy tale affords us an explanation of this classical influence. The first draft of the beginning of the story accompanied a letter to Hartlaub in 1841, the year after the publication of the *Anthology of Classical Poetry [Klassische Blumenlese]*. Mörike completed the fairy tale in 1853, two years before he finished the translation of idylls by Theocritus. . . . The tale thus stems from a period in which he occupied himself intensely with the ancient tradition and wrote most of his poetry in classical meter. **"Erinna to Sappho"** was going to be a very late fruit of this harvest in 1863. By that time, the figure of the girl whom Death called from the joys of Youth had been transformed in the poet's mind from the beloved of a young king into a young poetess loved and mourned by the famous Sappho. Retaining the elements of the girl's preoccupation with her appearance and her predilection for precious ointments and clothes, he had transformed her into a symbol of even deeper value by adding the gift of poetry to the themes of beauty and love. At the same time, he intensified his story by simplification when he omitted the array of characters surrounding Jezerte and the king and concentrated on the story of love and death, without distracting from it through a phase of doubt, as the one induced by Naïra in the tale of Jezerte.

The content of the story, then, is a combination of the classical and medieval. Mörike's description of it as "archaic" is, therefore, justified. The tale is written in a highly stylized prose that is only one step removed from the free rhythm of **"Erinna to Sappho."** One can see this if he follows the beginning of the story:

> Before the early light appeared in the king's garden, the leaves of the myrtle tree stirred and it said:
>
> "I sense the morning wind in my branches; I am drinking sweet dew already: when will Jezerte come?"
>
> And with a whisper the nut-pine answered:
>
> "Already I see her through the graceful screen of the lower window, the gardener's youngest daughter. Soon she will step out of the house, climb down the steps to the well and bathe her face, the beautiful girl."

And the well replied:

> "The dear child has no balm, no attar of roses; she dips her hair into my clear blackness, she draws my water with her hands. Hush! I hear the lovely girl come."
>
> And the gardener's daughter came to the well, washed herself and combed and braided her hair.
>
> And behold, it so happened that Athmas, the king, went forth from the palace to enjoy the morning-coolness before the coming of the day; he walked hither the wide path on yellow sand and noticed the girl, came closer and stopped in amazement because of her beauty; he greeted the frightened girl and kissed her forehead.
>
> Since then she was dear to Athmas and stayed close to him day and night; she wore precious garments of byssos and silk and was honored by the king's cousins for she was loving and modest with the great and the humble; and she gave much to the poor.
>
> After a year, however, Jezerte fell ill; no help was possible, and she died in her youth.
>
> Then the king had a tomb built for her at the edge of the palace garden where the well sprang up; and above it a small temple, and he had her image placed in it made of white marble, showing her full figure as if alive, a miracle of the arts. And the people held the well sacred.

The style of this tale appears somewhat forced, at times, when the reader becomes conscious of the fact that it is a combination of the naïve and simple tone of folk fairy tales and boasts a vocabulary that suggests a Southern or Middle Eastern setting. It is as precious as the style of the fairy tales written by Goethe and Novalis who wanted to reveal mythological content in highly select style. The tendency toward the oriental in Mörike's work, however, reminds us also of the style of Platen and Rückert, his contemporaries, whose scholarly knowledge of oriental literature was reflected in their own poetry. We know that Mörike considered their poetry stilted and unnatural. He may have applied the same criticism to **"The Hand of Jezerte"** and thus decided not to write any more in the same vein. The experiment with this style, however, still bore fruit in his later writings, when he employed some of its vocabulary in such works as **"Erinna to Sappho."** (pp. 140-42)

*Helga Slessarev, in her* Eduard Mörike, *Twayne Publishers, Inc., 1970, 173 p.*

**J. P. STERN**  (essay date 1971)

[*Stern examines the distinguishing characteristics of Mörike's lyric poetry. Specifically, he considers Mörike's "inward re-creation of the past" and his themes of parting, solitude, and loss. Stern finds in Mörike's verse an underlying belief in "the connectedness of the human and the divine," and concludes that his poetry is "an expression of the world . . . as a creation of God."*]

The area of experience charted by the lyrical poetry of Eduard Mörike . . . is not difficult to delimit. Its settings are rural, provincial, uncontaminated by contact with the great world. At its most memorable it is concerned with intimate personal encounters and their evanescence. Its tranquility and its deep emotions are those of a solitary soul; only the ineluctable passage of time, not faction and strife, intimates the common lot of man. Mörike excels at showing man in contact with the natural world; Nature often acts as a consoler, a giver of meaning to human relations; sometimes she echoes and confirms man's essential solitude. Those readers in Germany and abroad who, until a generation ago, saw the finest achievement of nineteenth-century German literature in its lyrical poetry, justly recognised in Mörike its finest representative. But even if, as one suspects, this view has now become something of a cliché, his achievement remains assured. Among the critics Mörike has no enemies. He has been subjected to the mystagogic treatment with its all-too-ready appeal to 'demonic powers', for no better reason than that much of his poetry issues from unhappy emotional tangles. As against that, there is his warm yet not uncritical humanity, laced with a dose of Swabian humour, or again his considerable influence as a craftsman and as a quiet guardian of intimate personal values. His spirituality is uncontentious, wholly undogmatic and free from all strenuous antitheses, yet it has a reassuring strength all its own.

In the word 'Erinnerung' the German language underlines the inwardness of memory or recollection, its re-creative intimation, and critics have often pointed to the special place that lyrical poetry has in this inward re-creation of the past. In this sense Mörike is a German lyrical poet *par excellence*. What makes him into a modern European poet is the fact that in many of his poems such a re-creation no longer takes the form of a story or fable but of an extended image transfixed in a moment of time.

The freshness and apparent simplicity of his poetic utterance gives one the impression that several decades of strenuous aesthetic debate have left no trace on his verse, that idealism, industrialism, and the social movements of his time have passed him by, unconsidered. Thus one of the most famous of his poems, *Verborgenheit* (*Withdrawal* . . .) expresses a gentle resignation, a contentment with that which the heart has already experienced, and a renunciation and apprehension of further turbulent emotions; yet its first and last stanza begin with the line 'Laß o Welt, o laß mich sein!', and it is as a renunciation of the *world* that this poem has commonly been read. We know from Mörike's lively correspondence with writers fully involved in contemporary controversies that he knew that world, vicariously perhaps, but well enough. But we also know that, for all his personal vacillations and unresolved conflicts, he firmly exercised his choice as a poet, and consciously resisted being drawn into the arena. (pp. 76-7)

Such a consciousness of withdrawal, it is clear, is hardly compatible with that simplicity of diction for which Mörike is often praised. He is not the 'naïve' poet of Schiller's definition. His poetry is an artifact that neither vaunts nor hides its essential character. The consciousness that enters his poetry is mainly confined to personal feelings. It expresses not so much a deliberate withdrawal from the issues of the contemporary world as an apprehension of and a withdrawal from the things around him, from some of the *données* of private experience, in order to portray a subtle state of mind in which joy and sorrow combine; yet the themes of parting and solitude predominate. The apparent simplicity of his finest poem [*Verborgenheit*] is a measure of his success in conveying the consciousness of loss by converting it fully into poetic story and image—the result, it may be, of a complex creative process; but we have no means of telling as the process of transformation leaves

little or no trace in the poems. They do not readily lend themselves to a reconstruction of his inner biography. (p. 77)

Mörike began writing in the age of Goethe and in the heyday of German Romanticism. Yet he was a contemporary of Baudelaire, and his last poems overlap the poetry of Verlaine and the Symbolists. His work intimates some of the changes that lyrical poetry underwent during his lifetime; and it does so more clearly than his retired existence in a Swabian backwater would lead one to expect. Implicitly challenging the traditional notion of poetry as an 'Nacheinander' . . ., Mörike's poetry turns from story to meaningful image for its most characteristic effects. He wrote no theoretical statement of his aims, and only a reader who saw his work through anachronistic preconceptions could persuade himself that Mörike wrote poems about the writing of poems. . . . He has extended the area of German poetry, both in the direction of emotional depth and also by placing imaged artifacts, including works of art, at the centre of some of his finest poems. But his discoveries seem to have been largely intuitive: the consciousness that informs his poems is not a literary selfconsciousness. The artifact is, for him, not a symbol of the aesthetic experience but, being itself an object hallowed by human use, it becomes a repository of deep, nonliterary emotions. . . . (p. 78)

The tradition in German literature which recent criticism has dwelt on contains no traces of Mörike's serenity. Fragmentariness, visions of the extremes of the human condition, exposure to the daemonic forces of Being, and an unnerving search for the roots of that Being accompanied by dread and *Angst*, a longing for the unconditioned and a lack of accommodation in the real world—these make up our current image of German poets. Having few of these traits, Mörike's poetry questions our assumption that depth is always the depth of despair, or that the depth of despair must always resort to the fragmentary or visionary manner for its expression. He has fully considered the dark side of the world, he too knows that the world of the unhappy man is different from the world of the happy. Yet his creativeness bears him on, all the way to the completed form, to the point where discord is transmuted into the harmony beyond. Yet again, this is no aestheticism, no triumph of perfect form over base, irredeemable matter. On the contrary, underlying his poetry and occasionally made explicit in it is a belief in the connectedness of the human and the divine. Art for him is not an expression of the ineffable. It is an expression of the world (or at least of a small, intimate part of the world) as a creation of God. . . . (pp. 78-9)

*J. P. Stern, "Eduard Mörike: Recollection and Inwardness," in his* Idylls & Realities: Studies in Nineteenth-Century German Literature, *Frederick Ungar Publishing Co., 1971, pp. 76-96.*

**M. B. BENN** (essay date 1972)

[*Benn outlines the historical inaccuracies in Mörike's portrait of Mozart and his age in* Mozart on the Way to Prague. *Yet despite these inaccuracies, Benn praises the construction, humor, and "stylistic delicacy" of the novella and maintains that its concluding section demonstrates not merely talent, but "genius."*]

To a much greater degree than is usual in literary works of art, the value of *Mozart auf der Reise nach Prag* depends on the *truth* of its portrayal of the hero. For this Novelle is essentially a historical portrait, a portrait not only of Mozart but also of the age in which he lived, and it has therefore only a limited freedom to deviate from the historical reality. The limits are set by the knowledge of the hero and of his age which the public can be presumed to have. . . . [We] know more about Mozart than about almost any historical figure. . . . Any misrepresentation of a character so well known to us and so highly valued must be felt as a violation, and it is for this reason that the demand for essential truth in Mörike's portrayal of Mozart is inescapable. . . . [By] his own account Mörike is—naturally and properly—unconcerned about the details of Mozart's biography: he places him in 'freely invented situations'. Nor does he claim to give equal prominence to *all* the elements in Mozart's character; the brighter qualities are to be fully illustrated, the darker merely suggested. But whatever the disposition of light and shade in the picture, it is clearly a portrait of the real Mozart that Mörike is professing to offer us. . . . It is legitimate, therefore, to ask whether the Mozart of Mörike's portrayal is, in fact, essentially true. And, incidentally, this confrontation of Mörike's Mozart with the historical Mozart seems likely to be fruitful not only for its bearing on our critical estimation of the Novelle but also for the light it may throw on its style and inspiration—for the help it may give us in seizing the true character of the work. (pp. 369-70)

[Slight] distortions in the representation of Mozart's character have the effect of making him appear to belong much more closely and unreservedly to the aristocratic rococo culture of his time than was in fact the case. Mozart is presented not only as a devoutly loyal subject of the Emperor but as whole-heartedly accepting, and being whole-heartedly accepted by, the kind of privileged society represented by Count Schinzberg and his family. However much he may transcend that society by virtue of his artistic genius, in ethos and attitude he appears to be in complete accord with it. . . . [Mörike's] Mozart represents an end, not a beginning—the decline of an incomparable life and of a whole culture. And it is characteristic of Mörike that even Mozart's art appears to him as the summing up and conclusion of a period rather than as a discovery of new directions. (pp. 371-72)

[All] this is a misreading of Mozart's position, both socially and artistically. Mozart's life and work were at least as much vernal as autumnal. No doubt his style—like every artistic style—was transitory; but he has remained, more than almost any other artist, a source of inspiration to later musicians, and at least one of the most valuable developments in European music would have been unthinkable without him: the development of German opera. (p. 372)

[The] most revealing indication of the difference between the historical Mozart and the hero of Mörike's Novelle is to be found in the description of the fête in the Bay of Naples. . . . It will be remembered how, in this episode, a number of handsome youths with an equal number of charming girls provide a wonderful display of gymnastic and juggling skill by throwing oranges from one boat to another to the accompaniment of a potpourri of Sicilian melodies. . . . But what a 'Verniedlichung' of *Figaro* that is! At the time when Mozart chose this dangerous theme as the subject of an opera, Beaumarchais' play was banned in Vienna as being politically and morally subversive. . . . The grace and verve of Mozart's opera, its musical brilliance and beauty, should not blind us to its satirical implications, to [its] 'social undertones'. . . . Mörike, having to express in literary terms the daring and ironical beauty of this musical masterpiece, offers us the spectacle of some boys and girls tossing oranges to each other on the water.

And if *Figaro,* in Mörike's presentation, seems 'verniedlicht', must we not also say that *Don Giovanni* seems emasculated?

While Kierkegaard sees the hero of this opera as the demonic genius of sensuality and seduction, as 'flesh incarnate, or the inspiration of the flesh by the spirit of the flesh' . . . , Mörike achieves the astonishing feat of presenting Don Juan without any allusion whatever to sex! He describes the dreadful retribution that overtakes Mozart's hero, but not the sins and crimes that have provoked it. Not, of course, that Mörike was blind to the sensual element in *Don Giovanni*. . . . But in the Novelle this essential aspect of the opera is completely suppressed. (pp. 372-74)

[In] the final section of the Novelle, where we leave behind us the description of rococo manners and fashionable trivia and enter the sublime world of eternal art, we find ourselves hardly prepared for such a sudden and steep ascent. We may fully agree with Mörike's contention that *Don Giovanni* ranks with [the] great tragic masterpieces . . . ; we may fully grant the claim of the historical Mozart to have earned a place beside Sophocles and Shakespeare; but we may wonder whether the Mozart *whom Mörike has shown us*—a Mozart subject to so many social, intellectual and moral restrictions—could conceivably have created a work comparable with [Sophocles's] *Oedipus* and [Shakespeare's] *Macbeth*. Yet we are almost inclined to waive the objection in our admiration of this concluding section of the Novelle. Every reader must feel that these pages are of a different and rarer quality than those preceding them. Up to this point Mörike has displayed his talent—a certain histrionic gift, a stylistic delicacy and resourcefulness, a whimsical humour and fancifulness almost reminiscent of Charles Lamb, an impressive skill in construction, moreover, and the ingenuity to develop much out of little. But now it is not only talent he shows, it is genius. However hampered he may have been by the circumstances in which he had to live and work, Mörike had the heart and the imagination to appreciate the grandeur with which Mozart invests the last moments of Don Juan, and the poetic inspiration to express that terrible beauty in words. And having achieved this level, he maintains it to the end—in the sad irony of the Mozarts' cheerful farewell to the Count, in the forebodings of the solitary Eugenie, and in the perfect lyric with which the Novelle closes. In all this Mörike is drawing upon his own experience—that peculiar sense of the omnipresence of death which is so strikingly expressed in the poem *Erinna an Sappho*. But it is an experience which Mozart too had known, and Mörike's expression of it is felt to be not only profound and beautiful but to ring true in its application to his hero. . . . (p. 375)

> M. B. Benn, ''Comments of an 'Advocatus Diaboli' on Mörike's 'Mozart auf der Reise nach Prag','' in German Life & Letters, n.s. Vol. XXV, No. 4, July, 1972, pp. 368-76.

**URSULA MAHLENDORF** (essay date 1976)

[*In the following excerpt from her analysis of* Mozart on the Way to Prague, *Mahlendorf links Mörike's depiction of the stages of Mozart's creative process with his psychosexual development and distinguishes three "distinct but interlinked" creative episodes within the novella. She suggests that in each incident "Mörike describes a different originating impulse, at a different development level (oral, phallic, oedipal), resulting in a different mode of expression (lyrical-idyllic-intimate; festive-social-humorous; tragic-elegiac-sublime)." Mahlendorf maintains that such an explication of "the symbolic structure of the tale" provides insight into Mörike's understanding of the creative process. Within this discussion she also examines Mörike's treatment of the symbolism*] *of quest and paradise, the social function of art, and the Don Juan theme.*]

For romantics as much as for post romantic authors, such as Mörike . . . , Mozart was the paradigm of the exuberant and effortless creator. In his Mozart novella, Mörike telescopes the composer's entire life into the narrative space of some seventy pages and into the compass of a single day. It is an autumn day two years before the French revolution and four years before Mozart's early death. On that day, the thirty-one year old composer, still at work on his *Don Juan,* travels by coach through Bohemia to Prague. As a consequence of the telescoping technique, each detail of the narrated day stands for a fundamental aspect of the composer's life. (p. 304)

From among the distinct but interlinked episodes of the day, three stand out as moments during which the composer creates. We shall look closely at the symbolism in these episodes in order to shed light on Mörike's insights into the different motivations, stages, and results of creativity. In each of the three incidents, Mörike describes a different originating impulse, at a different development level (oral, phallic, oedipal), resulting in a different mode of expression (lyrical-idyllic-intimate; festive-social-humorous; tragic-elegiac-sublime). The modes of expression which Mörike attributes to Mozart correspond to his own three favorite moods. The story is of special interest to the student of creativity because in it we find not merely one wellspring of creativity but clearly differentiated sources, occasions and products of creativeness. (p. 305)

On the symbolical level, Mozart's journey to Prague is a quest whose expressed aim is the composition and performance of *Don Juan.* It is a quest in several stages, three of which result in artistic creation. . . . By explicating the symbolic structure of the tale, we gain insight into Mörike's conscious and unconscious knowledge of the creative process and into his awareness of primary and of secondary process. In the structure of the tale, realistic detail, narrator's comment, allegory and symbol supplement each other. (p. 308)

Mozart travels on his journey to Prague in order to work on and to see his *Don Juan* performed. In describing the effect of the opera, Mörike compares the work to two other works of similar stature, namely [Sophocles's] *Oedipus* and [Shakespeare's] *Macbeth.* . . . By so doing, he draws our attention to the theme they share, namely the killing of a father-figure by the protagonist son. All three works deal with variations on the oedipal problem. By choosing this journey of Mozart's when he was composing this particular opera, Mörike portrays the artist's quest as an attempt to resolve his conflict with various forms of paternal authority.

The quest itself takes place in a world which Mörike sees as a maternal world. The women are mother and sister figures in various disguises. The males who possess and guard the paradise represent paternal and fraternal authority. The artist's life journey involves both mother and father; his creative process in turn involves the self-forgetting in the maternal ground and identification with paternal authority, discipline and form; the creator needs both to be open to primary process and to form its affects, energies and content through secondary process. In following the quest which Mörike attributes to Mozart, we move back and forth between the two worlds and the two processes in various patterns of interchanges between them.

The symbolism of the first creative episode, the first stage of the journey, is that of the oral stage of development. The composer stops for a noon rest in a village nestled in a fertile valley. The garden where the composer finds the orange tree with its 'golden apples' contains a circle of orange trees, laurels, and oleanders surrounding the large, oval basin of a fountain, with an arbor opening upon it. On the allegorical level, Mozart jokingly refers to the Garden as "Paradise" where I "like Adam" have "eaten the apple." . . . The ironic reference only thinly disguises the truth of the matter. For the place where his inspiration occurs is, on the symbolical level, a maternal paradise, a place protected and protecting, round and sensual. (pp. 308-09)

On the symbolic, unconscious level, the scene unites elements of infantile enjoyment at the mother's breast with elements of a sexual union. The composer experiences here a moment of regression to a polymorphous perverse state. The oceanic bliss experienced at this stage finds its joyous outpouring in song. . . . [The early], primal memory of reunion with the mother provides the first driving impulse of the musical inspiration and its richness of tone. Mozart himself says of the melody that it is "a tune which seemed to flow into the words." . . . (p. 310)

As the intruding male, Mozart is totally unconscious of his actions, aims and motives. He wanders into the garden aimlessly, finds the orangery by chance, caresses the orange absentmindedly and inadvertently breaks it off. Lost in his revery, he cuts the orange open. He hears the music which is to become the wedding song. His inner eye gazes at a scene of twenty years ago. He is open to all sense impressions (all six are specifically mentioned) and awake to internal mental-emotional processes. He is totally dominated by primary process: Boundaries between inner and outer experience, between present and past cease to exist. . . . (pp. 310-11)

The description of the unity of inner and outer event supports Freud's later notions of a primary ego-feeling, of a limitless narcissism enjoyed by the infant and recalled in artistic and mystic trance. This reactivation of narcissistic libido is, to use [the American philosopher and sociologist Herbert] Marcuse's formulation, the beginning of the creative process. In this incident, Mörike describes a creator whose "productivity . . . is sensuousness, play and song," who experiences being as "gratification, which unites man and nature," who is dominated by the pleasure principle.

In its demonstration of paradisiac happiness, Mörike's novella runs counter to the mainstream of German letters of post romanticism which is given to the praise of the performance principle. Mörike is different from the romantics who earlier extolled narcissism in that his paradise, the actual garden where Mozart sits, has an unromantic concreteness, sensuousness, and realism. Mörike achieves this richness of sensuous gratification for the reader by the technique of telling the event twice, each time from a different perspective. In the analysis given above, I have blended the outer with the inner events as they are experienced by Mozart. The reader who reads the story for the first time, however, first observes Mozart in a sensuous environment. Nothing distracts from the reality of the senses. A few pages later, the reader relives, in the composer's narrative and from his inner perspective, the events in the garden, the memories, and the significance of both to the creation of the composition. Moreover, the memory and the garden scene share many sensuous features so that all sensations appear doubled.

Given over to the pleasure principle as he is, Mozart, awakened from his revery by the gardener, reacts as if caught in a shameful act. ". . . visibly flushing" he wants to hide the orange

but then puts it down in full sight "with a . . . defiant flourish."
. . . The gardener appears to him a "big, broad-shouldered
man" . . . , a "monster." . . . Giving a joking allegorical meaning
to him, he calls him a Nemesis, a man who in cruelty is like
the Roman emperor Tiberius. The terror he feels at the gardener's appearance seems to him out of keeping with the situation. . . . He imagines, in joking retrospect, even further
terrors from being caught by the authorities. "If the man looks
like that, . . . what will the master look like." . . . The count
is, by this description, established as an authority, as a father
figure, in the story and the actual gardener, who caused Mozart
such terror is never mentioned again. The oedipal core of the
scene, namely that being in paradise means union with the
mother, is confirmed by the gardener's appearance and by the
protagonist's reactions to him. The experience of sensuous
pleasure as much as the rape of the tree is a transgression
against the father's property and authority. The fear it arouses
is fear of castration, hence the reference to the sword of Nemesis. (pp. 311-12)

While the inspiration for [Zerlina's wedding] song comes during the actual erotic-sensuous, narcissistic experience, the writing down of the music, the utilization of the sublimation, is
an act of restitution and a different event. The work of art owes
its existence as an actuality outside of the composer's mind to
his wish for gaining pardon for the transgression against the
father's world. It expresses his need for winning acceptance
in the father's world. (p. 313)

The act of restitution follows a different law than the act of
inspiration. Inspiration occurs under the sway of primary process. Putting the inspiration on paper involves thinking, planning, "all the rules of his art" . . . , technique and mastery of
form, that is the secondary process. Inspiration binds the composer to the maternal sphere; by elaboration he integrates himself into the paternal sphere by using a mental process which
his culture holds to be paternal. Mörike, in this novella, gives
considerable space to these paternal processes, to presenting
Mozart as a craftsman knowledgeable and disciplined. Mozart
performs and composes to make a living. Despite his restlessness, he follows a regular work schedule with hours set aside
for composition. . . . His attitude to composing is professional
and methodical. (pp. 313-14)

The end product of the creative process, this particular work
of art [the wedding song], owes its existence to the continuum
of experience which begins with oceanic feeling, regression to
the oral stage of development, and ends with an act of restitution. The work of art which has its inception in the oral stage
bears the marks of this origin. It is characterized by a folk-
songlike simplicity, repetitiveness, and the onomatopeic infantile "tra la" of the stanza refrain. It is an idyllic country
air and dance, pleasant, joyous and sensuous. As the composer
puts it "the smiling beauty of the Bay of Naples joined in"
the song. . . . (p. 314)

The success of the restitutive measure depends on the culprit's
finding a receptive audience. It is the charm of the Mörike tale
that all the participants in the festivities at the manor, father
and brother, mother and friend, bride and groom accept and
enjoy the gift. All of them understand its allegorical significance; the bride intuits its symbolical meaning. . . . Because
the male audience enjoys and utilizes Mozart's gift, they come
to share in his creativeness. Beginning with the count, Max
and Mozart, and only joined by one of the women, an elderly
aunt with a "cracked soprano" . . . , they spontaneously compose a humorous canon in praise of the artist and his work.

*Mozart performs a love song for the count's niece, Eugenie.
From* Mozart on the Way to Prague, *by Eduard Mörike.
Translated by Walter and Catherine Alison Phillips. Illus-
trated by Eliane Bonabel. Copyright 1947 by Pantheon Books,
Inc. Reprinted by permission of Pantheon Books, a Division
of Random House, Inc.*

During this festive scene, which abounds as did the earlier
solitary creative episode with sensuous-erotic stimulation, the
father figure is no threat to the frolic but rather a participant
in it. (pp. 314-15)

On the symbolic level, Mozart creates in the manor house a
second, a social paradise. . . . During the festivities, we seem
to see a non-repressive society emerge with the composer playing the role of a catalyst of interaction. His ability to sublimate,
that is to transform libidinal energy into symbol, is contagious.
Breaking forth into spontaneous song, he brings the male world
to participate in his creativeness. Even the count, father figure
and symbol of unspontaneous order, discovers, to his own
surprise, that he can sing and rhyme "inspired only by himself." . . . In this episode, father—"count" and "artist"—
son identify with each other, work together in a common endeavor and thus advance the culture, improve their environment, and strengthen their bonds with each other. Their earlier
enmity is transcended in their new society.

The active participants in the second episode are the males.
The exuberance and expansiveness which dominate this scene,
the emphasis on masculinity and male identification places this
scene in the phallic stage of development. (pp. 315-16)

In his narration of the third creative experience of the day on
the occasion of Mozart's performance of the opera's piano

score, Mörike directly confronts the father-son theme which he earlier dealt with in a light, playful, even comic manner. While the first creative episode concerned the oral stage, and the second moved forward on the developmental ladder to the phallic stage, the third with its expressed parallelism to *Oedipus Rex* deals in all earnestness with the oedipal phase. How serious this matter is to narrator and composer alike appears from their both using delaying tactics in order not to get to Don Juan and his rebellion. (pp. 316-17)

[At the] point in the narrative when the rebellion breaks into the open, both author and composer break through the literary and social conventions which held them earlier. With his many digressions and with his playfulness in the preceding scenes, Mörike has but ill prepared the unsuspecting reader for the violence and passion which now erupt. Similarly, the composer casts his drawingroom audience, by the symbolic gesture of extinguishing the candles, into darkness and confusion. Unprepared and their defenses weakened, audience and reader are forced into an identification with the rebel. Mörike expends some of his most moving sentences on the greatness of this rebellion. (pp. 317-18)

At the Don's rebellion and refusal to atone, audience and reader experience a "mingled delight and terror" (*Lust und Angst*). . . . Mörike substitutes for the Aristotelian 'pity and fear' which we expect in a discussion of tragedy, the unexpected and hence startling "delight and terror." He thus emphasizes that theirs and ours is no intellectual or pitying sympathy with the rebel but that it is rather a passionate, lustful (*Lust*) identification.

Still in the throes of identification with the protagonist, [the] composer, narrator, and audience share in his death struggle. As he is killed for his rebellion, each experiences the rebel's death as the death of his own rebellious self, as a symbolic self-sacrifice. The symbolic self-sacrifice is the restitution offered to the father. The completion of the death scene means, for the composer, that he has attained his maturity, that now he can contemplate his own future death and be at peace. . . . (pp. 318-19)

By the symbolic self-sacrifice, a new relationship to the father and his order becomes possible. . . .

Mörike strengthens the reconciliation between father and son in a further symbolic episode. Don Juan's rebellion is unproductive; the artist's rebellion is productive in a double sense. His portrayal of the rebellion heals the artist and his audience of their rebelliousness. Even further, it wins the artist the respect and admiration of the father. Mörike expresses this newly gained paternal respect by the symbolism of the count's— father's—parting gift to Mozart, a coach. (p. 319)

The work of art of the oedipal phase proper is deeply serious, passionate and tragic in its outcome. It is a classical work in the sense that it deals with weighty subject matter in a weighty style; it is the composer's mature achievement. Mörike sees him acquire, by this work, that characteristically Mozartian lightness and social grace which the reader sees him demonstrate earlier in the narrative. Mörike seems to say that only an artist who has made this symbolic self-sacrifice can, through his art, contribute to his culture. (p. 320)

At the end of the story, Mozart's quest continues, for the opera is not yet completed. This appears to mean, on the symbolical level, that the quest of life, the self-realization of the artist in society, the self-actualization of man in society, is a continuous process. On the formal level, Mörike indicates the continuity

of the process by the interrelationships he established between the first and the third creative episodes. The reader fully understands the first only after he has appreciated the third. Since the quest of the artist is a circular process, the artistic paradise is neither a land in the past nor a goal in the future but rather an ever-present possibility of life everyone, the artist more readily than others can attain. As we have seen in the second creative episode, the artist can show other men how to realize themselves, how to create the heightened paradisiac estate in their own lives. This is his mission and gift. (p. 321)

> *Ursula Mahlendorf, "Mörike's 'Mozart on the Way to Prague': Stages and Outcomes of the Creative Experience," in* American Imago, *Vol. 33, No. 3, Fall, 1976, pp. 304-27.*

---

## ADDITIONAL BIBLIOGRAPHY

Adamson, Carl L. "The Problem of Romanticism: Three Poems." *The University of South Florida Language Quarterly* XIII, No. 3-4 (Spring-Summer 1975): 49-52.*
> Employs the poems "Nachts" by Joseph von Eichendorff, "Sprich aus der Ferne" by Clemens Brentano, and "An einem Wintermorgan vor Sonnenaufgang" by Mörike to illustrate the characteristics of Romanticism, "late-Romanticism," and "post-Romanticism."

Belmore, H. W. "Two Romantic Poems of Solitude: Leopardi and Mörike." *German Life and Letters* XXXI, No. 4 (July 1978): 313-18.*
> Compares Mörike's poem "Die schöne Buche" to "L'Infinito" by Giacomo Leopardi.

Browning, R. M. "Mörike's 'Auf eine Christblume'." *The Germanic Review* XLII, No. 3 (May 1967): 197-214.
> A detailed interpretation of "Auf eine Christblume." Browning also discusses previous readings of this work by Christopher Middleton (see annotation below) and by the German critics Benno von Wiese (see annotation below), Gerhard Storz, and Bernhard Boschenstein.

Closs, A. "Droste-Hülshoff: Eduard Mörike." In his *The Genius of the German Lyric: An Historic Survey of Its Formal and Metaphysical Values*, pp. 350-54. London: George Allen & Unwin, 1938.
> A concise appreciation of Mörike's verse.

Crichton, Mary C. "A Goethean Echo in Mörike's 'An eine Äolsharfe'." *Seminar: A Journal of Germanic Studies* XVI, No. 3 (September 1980): 170-80.*
> Suggests that "An eine Äolsharfe" was inspired in part by a passage in *Italienische Reise* by Johann Wolfgang von Goethe.

Dallett, Joseph B. "Symmetry in Mörike's Poetry." *Carleton Germanic Papers* V (1977): 1-28.
> A discussion of the rhythmic, thematic, and visual symmetry of Mörike's poetry.

Dieckmann, Liselotte. "Mörike's Presentation of the Creative Process." *The Journal of English and Germanic Philology* LIII, No. 3 (July 1954): 291-305.
> Discusses Mörike's conception of the creative process as evidenced in *Maler Nolten, Mozart on the Way to Prague*, the *Spillner* fragment, and his letters.

Doerksen, Victor G. "Was auch der Zeiten Wandel sonst hinnehmen mag (The Problem of Time in Mörike's Epistolary Poetry)." In *Deutung und Bedeutung: Studies in German and Comparative Literature Presented to Karl-Werner Maurer*, edited by Brigitte Schludermann, Victor G. Doerksen, Robert J. Glendinning, and Evelyn Scherabon Firchow, pp. 134-51. The Hague: Mouton, 1973.
> Introduces Mörike's epistolary poems and examines their dominant theme: time.

Farrell, R. B. "German Themes: Mörike and Hölty." *Affinities: Essays in German and English Literature Dedicated to the Memory of Oswald Wolff (1897-1968)*, edited by R. W. Last, pp. 246-55. London: Oswald Wolff, 1971.*

Compares Mörike's verse with that of the eighteenth-century German poet Hölty (pseudonym of Ludwig Christoph Heinrich).

Feuerlicht, Ignace. "Mörike's 'Jilted Girl'." *The Germanic Review* LV, No. 1 (Winter 1980): 22-6.

A detailed structural and thematic analysis of "Das verlassene Mägdlein."

Field, G. Wallis. "Silver and Oranges: Notes on Mörike's Mozart-Novelle." *Seminar: A Journal of Germanic Studies* XIV, No. 4 (November 1978): 243-54.

An analysis of the use of color and symbolism in *Mozart on the Way to Prague*.

Fuerst, Norbert. "Old Germany: Gotthelf and Mörike." In his *The Victorian Age of German Literature: Eight Essays*, pp. 55-9. University Park: Pennsylvania State University Press, 1966.*

Compares Mörike to one of his contemporaries, the Swiss novelist Jeremias Gotthelf.

Graham, Ilse. "Orpheus Looks Back: Movement and Meaning in Three Poems by Eduard Mörike." *The German Quarterly* LII, No. 2 (March 1979): 218-26.

Argues that the metrical patterns of "Das verlassene Mägdlein," "Denk es, o Seele!" and "Gebet" shed light on the poems' meanings.

Hewett-Thayer, Harvey W. "Mörike's Occultism and the Revision of *Maler Nolten*." *PMLA* LXXI, No. 3 (June 1956): 386-413.*

A discussion of the 1877 revision of *Maler Nolten* undertaken by Mörike and posthumously completed by his friend Julius Klaiber. Hewett-Thayer explores the influence of the German poet and physician Justinus Kerner on Mörike's interest in the occult and how it affected this revision.

Immerwahr, Raymond. "Apocalyptic Trumpets: The Inception of *Mozart auf der Reise nach Prag*." *PMLA* LXX, No. 3 (June 1955): 390-407.

Explores the genesis of *Mozart on the Way to Prague* by studying the events from his own life that Mörike associated with Mozart and particularly with his opera *Don Juan*.

———. "Narrative and 'Musical' Structure in *Mozart auf der Reise nach Prag*." In *Studies in Germanic Languages and Literatures in Memory of Fred O. Nolte*, edited by Erich Hofacker and Liselotte Dieckmann, pp. 103-20. St. Louis: Washington University Press, 1963.

An analysis of the manner in which Mörike used symbolism to express thematic polarities in *Mozart on the Way to Prague*.

Jennings, Lee Byron. "Mörike's *Maler Nolten*." In his *The Grotesque Element in Post-Romantic German Prose: 1832-1882*, pp. 148-219. Ann Arbor, Mich.: University Microfilms, 1956.

A Ph.D. dissertation from the University of Illinois that focuses on Mörike's use of the grotesque.

———. "Mörike's Grotesquery: A Post-Romantic Phenomenon." *Journal of English and Germanic Philology* LIX, No. 4 (October 1960): 600-16.

An examination of Mörike's art and creative process condensed from his "Mörike's *Maler Nolten*" (see annotation above).

Kneisel, Jessie Hoskam. *Mörike and Music*. n.p., 1949, 236 p.

A detailed study of music in Mörike's life and thought. Kneisel treats the composers who set Mörike's poems to music, the musical elements in his *Gefühlslyrik*, and his importance in the development of the *Lied*. Kneisel also provides a bibliography of Mörike's songs.

Mare, Margaret. *Eduard Mörike: The Man and the Poet*. London: Methuen & Co., 1957, 276 p.

The only book-length biography of Mörike in English.

Maync, Harry Wilhelm. *Eduard Mörike: Sein Leben und Dichten*. Stuttgart: Cotta, 1944, 610 p.

A biography in German by a major Mörike scholar.

Middleton, Christopher. "Mörike's Moonchild: A Reading of the Poem 'Auf eine Christblume'." In his *Bolshevism in Art and Other Expository Writings*, pp. 190-208. Manchester, England: Carcanet New Press, 1978.

A close explication of the poem "Auf eine Christblume" that draws from the interpretation by the German critic Gerhard Storz.

Pascal, Roy. "The Troubled Poet." *The Sunday Times*, London, No. 7026 (12 January 1958): 9.

Briefly discusses Mörike's mental instability and its effect on his works.

Prawer, S. S. "Poetic Realism: Mörike, 'Mein Fluss'." In his *German Lyric Poetry: A Critical Analysis of Selected Poems from Klopstock to Rilke*, pp. 167-74. London: Routledge & Kegan Paul, 1952.

A close analysis of the poem "Mein Fluss."

———. "Mignon's Revenge: A Comparative Study of *Maler Nolten* and *Wilhelm Meister*." In *Papers Read Before the Society in 1955-56*, edited by Elizabeth M. Wilkinson, pp. 63-85. Publications of the English Goethe Society, n.s. vol. XXV. Leeds, England: W. S. Maney & Son, 1956.*

Explores the influence of Johann Wolfgang von Goethe, and particularly his novel *Wilhelm Meisters Lehrjahre*, on *Maler Nolten*. Prawer suggests that *Maler Nolten* begins where *Wilhelm Meisters Lehrjahre* ends—with the hero's initiation into aristocratic society and his love for a noblewoman.

———. "Mörike's Second Thoughts." *Modern Philology* LVII, No. 1 (August 1959): 24-36.

Examines the evolution of some of Mörike's best-known poems, including "Auf einer Wanderung," "Um Mitternacht," "Erinnerung," and the "Peregrina" cycle.

———. "The Threatened Idyll: Mörike's *Mozart auf der Reise nach Prag*." *Modern Languages* XLIV (1963): 101-07.

A discussion of seldom-treated characteristics of *Mozart on the Way to Prague*, including inflections, angles of vision, and shifts in imagery.

Rolleston, James. "Time Structures: A Reading of Poems by Mörike, Rilke, and Benn." *The German Quarterly* LIII, No. 4 (November 1980): 403-17.*

An analysis of "Die schöne Buche" by Mörike, "Todes-Erfahrung" by Rainer Maria Rilke, and "Eingeengt" by Gottfried Benn. Rolleston demonstrates how the poets' conceptions of time affect the structure of their poetry.

Rowley, Brian A. "A Long Day's Night: Ambivalent Imagery in Mörike's Lyric Poetry." *German Life and Letters* n.s. XXIX, No. 1 (October 1975): 109-22.

Explores day and night imagery in Mörike's verse.

Sammons, Jeffrey L. "Fate and Psychology: Another Look at Mörike's *Maler Nolten*." In *Lebendige Form: Interpretationen zur deutschen Literatur, Festschrift für Heinrich E. K. Henel*, edited by Jeffrey L. Sammons and Ernst Schürer, pp. 211-27. Munich: Wilhelm Fink Verlag, 1970.

An interpretation of the dual motivation in *Maler Nolten*. Sammons studies psychologically motivated and fated actions to demonstrate Mörike's ambiguous attitude toward fate.

Schier, Rudolf D. "Natural Objects and the Imagination: Mörike's View of Poetic Language." *Modern Language Quarterly* XXVIII (1967): 45-59.

A discussion of "An eine Äolsharfe," "Die schöne Buche," "Auf eine Christblume," and "Auf eine Lampe."

Snow, Frank E. "Moerike's 'Firerider' and an Interpretative Tale." *Modern Language Journal* XXVIII, No. 1 (January 1944): 590-96.

A close explication of the poem "Der Feuerreiter" ("The Firerider") based on interpretations by the German scholars Jakob Baechtold, Karl Fischer, and Harry Maync.

Thayer, Terence K. "Knowing and Being: Mörike's 'Denk es, o Seele!'" *The German Quarterly* XLV, No. 3 (May 1972): 484-501.

A close textual analysis of "Denk es, o Seele!"

''Eduard Mörike.'' *The Times Literary Supplement,* No. 2901 (4 October 1957): 585-86.

A discussion of Mörike's folksongs and classical verse. The anonymous reviewer maintains that Mörike favored classical rhythms over native ones when ''the direct, almost mystical, contact with the spirit of nature made way for deep, absorbed, impersonal contemplation.''

Wiese, Benno von. *Eduard Mörike.* Tübingen, Germany: R. Wunderlich, 1950, 304 p.

A biography in German by a principal Mörike scholar.

Williams, W. D. ''Day and Night Symbolism in Some Poems of Mörike.'' In *The Era of Goethe: Essays Presented to James Boyd,* pp. 163-78. Oxford: Basil Blackwell, 1959.

Elucidates the significance of day and night symbolism in Mörike's poetry.

Woods, Jean M. ''Memory and Inspiration in Mörike's *Mozart auf der Reise nach Prag.*'' *Revue des langues vivantes* XLI, No. 1 (1975): 6-14.

Discusses the biographical nature of *Mozart on the Way to Prague.* In particular, Woods links the orange tree episode in the work to one of Mörike's own sensory experiences.

Yates, W. E. ''Mörike's Conception of an Artistic Ideal.'' *Modern Language Review* LXXIII, No. 1 (January 1978): 96-109.

Traces the evolution of Mörike's concept of aesthetic perfection from one of Romantic to Classic inspiration.

# Johann David Wyss

## 1743-1818

Swiss novelist.

Wyss was the author of the beloved children's book, *Der Schweizerische Robinson; oder, Der schiffbrüchige Schweizerprediger und seine Familie (The Swiss Family Robinson)*. In writing this work, he fashioned a tale whose immediate popularity was succeeded by enduring renown as a classic of children's literature. Borrowing from and enlarging upon Daniel Defoe's *Robinson Crusoe*, Wyss created a work at once imitative and innovative, a universally appealing story whose pedagogical intentions are transcended by its idealized portrayal of hard work, family life, and adventure in a benign paradise.

Little is known about Wyss's life. Born in Bern, Switzerland, he became a chaplain in the Swiss Army in 1766 and was later the pastor at Bern's Reformed Protestant Cathedral. The patriarch of a close family, Wyss led an active outdoor life with his four sons, fishing, hunting, and hiking in the Swiss countryside. These shared experiences helped to shape the plot of *The Swiss Family Robinson*, and the members of the Wyss family played an important part in the evolution of the work from fireside story to published book.

*The Swiss Family Robinson* originated as a story told by Wyss for the education and enjoyment of his sons. Fond of travel literature and adventure stories, the family was naturally attracted to Defoe's *Robinson Crusoe*, published in 1719. After hearing a factual account of a Russian ship's captain who had discovered a Swiss pastor lost with his family on an island near New Guinea, Wyss began to narrate a story to his own family, placing them in a similar predicament.

Defoe's tale of a man stranded on a desert island had produced a host of imitations and sequels, so many that the term "Robinsoniad" was coined to describe them. Wyss's contribution to the body of this genre was distinguished by the idyllic character of his island. In contrast to the rugged environment in which Defoe had placed Crusoe, Wyss chose a lush paradise for his castaways, featuring plant and animal life from every corner of the earth. Scarcely does the family find a need for something before nature provides the article. There is also a strong didactic element in the story, most obvious in the frequent asides on subjects ranging from natural history to mechanics and moral digressions on the virtues of perseverance under difficult circumstances. The tale proved a great success with his children, and eventually Wyss began to write it down. With the entire family contributing their own ideas, characteristics, and episodes, the manuscript grew to 841 pages, including sixty illustrations by Wyss's third son, Johann Emanuel.

While the exact dates of *The Swiss Family Robinson*'s composition are unknown, the details of its publication—though also somewhat obscure—have gradually become clear. Wyss had received encouragement to publish the work from friends who had heard it read aloud, but it was his second son, Johann Rudolf, who at age thirty determined to publish the manuscript. A professor of philosophy at the University of Bern, Johann Rudolf had authored the Swiss national anthem and had also published works on travel, history, and Swiss folklore. The

first edition of *The Swiss Family Robinson* appeared with his name on the title page; however, in a preface to the second volume of the work he credited his father with "all that is original, instructive, and best in this book." Johann Rudolf's precise contribution to the text is therefore uncertain. Various critics state that he edited, adapted, and revised the work, though the original manuscript is in his father's handwriting.

Subsequent to its original publication, *The Swiss Family Robinson* was translated and freely adapted into numerous languages. Most of the hundreds of editions of the book have been based on the French translation and continuation of the story made by the baroness de Montolieu in 1816. Critical reaction to *The Swiss Family Robinson* has focused on its edifying qualities as a work for children and the playful absurdity inherent in the island's unlikely collection of flora and fauna. The influence of Jean Jacques Rousseau on the instructive, moralizing purpose of the narrative has also been noted by a number of commentators. While early reviewers applauded the educational and moral virtues of the book, recent critics have taken a different approach, asserting that though the tone of the work often becomes pious and pedantic, it does not detract from Wyss's imaginative achievement.

An immensely popular work from its publication, *The Swiss Family Robinson* has charmed generations of readers with its unique blend of fanciful romance and moral imperative. The most successful of an enormous number of ''Robinsoniads,'' Wyss's adaptation of the *Robinson Crusoe* story has itself inspired numerous imitations. Although Wyss's name is virtually unknown to readers, *The Swiss Family Robinson,* with its celebration of family life and ingenuous improbability, remains one of the most notable works for children written in the nineteenth century.

(See also *Something about the Author,* Vols. 27 and 29)

## PRINCIPAL WORKS

*Der Schweizerische Robinson; oder, Der schiffbrüchige Schweizerprediger und seine Familie* (novel) 1812-13
  [*The Family Robinson Crusoe; or, Journal of a Father Shipwrecked, with His Wife and Children, on an Uninhabited Island,* 1814; also published as *The Swiss Family Robinson,* 1818]

---

### CHARLES NODIER (essay date 1837)

[*This introduction, originally written in French, appeared in an 1837 edition of* The Swiss Family Robinson *edited by Elise Voïart.*]

[Wyss did not arrogate to himself the merit of Daniel Defoe's ''Robinson Crusoe'']—he accepted it, he built upon it, he proclaimed himself an imitator and a copyist of an immortal model; but to imitate, as M. Wyss has done, is even better than to invent; it is to apply a recognized invention to the most important of all possibly useful objects; it is to inspire with a soul this artist's figure of clay; it is to give life to Pygmalion's statue. ''Robinson Crusoe'' will ever remain a good and a noble book; but the ''Swiss Robinson'' merits, perhaps, the first place among all the works of imagination designed for the instruction of men as well as children, manhood no less than youth. Seek neither in romances, nor in the most special treatises which a tender philanthropy enlightened by science has inspired, a code of physical, moral, and intellectual education preferable to it! I wish you could discover such an one, but you will not. (p. 9)

The ''Swiss Robinson'' of M. Wyss is ''Robinson Crusoe'' in the bosom of his family. Instead of the rash and obstinate sailor who struggles against death in a prolonged agony, it is a father, a mother, and their charming children, so different in age, character, and mind, who engage our interest. Do not imagine that interest is diminished because it is divided. It is multiplied, on the contrary, by all the sympathies which a family inspires. The new author's combination has changed the entire economy of his fable; it transports you from the final abode of a solitary adventurer to the cradle of human society. It puts before you the growth of communities when enlightened by God's wisdom and succoured by His providence. Crusoe's island expands before your eyes; and you may study there the progress of a rapid civilization which embraces every period of the world's history.

The Swiss Robinson is one of those men who has learned much from the simple but laudable design of gathering knowledge, and whom Necessity, that imperious ruler of minds, suddenly compels to transform all his theories into practice. Over man

in a natural and uncultivated condition he has the advantage of instruction; like Adam, he knows the names and properties of things—a marvellous boon, which our species possessed in its primitive state, which it lost after the Fall, and which it does but slowly recover by collecting the discoveries and ideas of past generations; but this precious labour of an exalted intelligence our hero has undergone. All that can be known, he knows; all those mysteries of creation which are comprehensible and useful, have been revealed to him; and that knowledge which springs of God while accumulating in a judicious and submissive mind, has contributed to strengthen his religious faith. It is such a man as this who is called upon to shelter a wife and children—to feed, to clothe, to lodge them in a manner suitable to their habits—with the scanty resources of the desert; it is this man who succeeds in so great a task by means of arduous labours, indefatigable exertions, and a devout confidence in the unlimited goodness of the Master. His history embodies, then, the entire history of man, and even of society; it is space enclosed within a narrow boundary; it is time summed up in a brief succession of years—the prolonged and patient toil of humanity set forth in the internal economy of a small household. It is the peculiarly attractive and readable summary of an encyclopædia, conceived by men of true wisdom, and adapted to our actual needs.

A moment's reflection suffices to show that M. Wyss's plan embraces a complete Educational Course, and that it conducts the author, in a single generation, to the reasonable limits of *Progress,* understanding the latter word in its exact value—that is, without regard to the extravagant pretensions of those impious sophists who are always building Babel! The Swiss Crusoe asks of Nature all the help which Nature can give to man, and Nature refuses him nothing, because all creation is at the service of humanity. To laborious patience nothing is wanting, to inventive industry nothing is wanting, but those things whose need has not yet been experienced, and shall we say that aught is really deficient which is not necessary? It is true that the Swiss Crusoe's island is more than usually favoured in its natural products; but that we do not find the same resources wherever we cast our glances or plant our feet is due to imperfect inquiry, or, if we may so speak, to the absence of any absolute and imperious need. Who ''in populous cities pent'' has not trodden disdainfully on the much-contemned nettle and bracken, never reflecting that these could supply him with an agreeable and wholesome food, a tissue not inferior to that of hemp, a paper far preferable to that which we manufacture at present from cotton, a savoury bread, a brilliant transparent crystal? Truly we are very heedless and very ungrateful! But the Swiss Crusoe avails himself of all the gifts of God, while referring the glory of them to God; he studies, and he learns in company with his pupils, which is an excellent method of teaching; every discovery leads to an experiment, every experiment creates some art or suggests some handicraft; each day bears its own fruit; all these discoveries, all these successes, are so many acts of gratitude to the great Creator. See how this life is animated by wholesome pursuits, by useful and strengthening labours, by pious aspirations towards a merciful Father, by a sweet and tender emulousness who shall most contribute to the happiness of all! Show me anywhere a system of primary instruction which surpasses this, and whether it comes from Locke, Rousseau, the philosophers, or the University, I promise it beforehand my warmest praises! (pp. 9-11)

*Charles Nodier, in an introduction to* The Swiss Family Robinson; or, Adventures of a Shipwrecked Family on a Desolate Island *by Johann Wyss, translated by*

*W.H.D.A. [W. H. Davenport Adams], T. Nelson and Sons, 1871, pp. 7-11.*

## W[ILLIAM] D[EAN] HOWELLS   (essay date 1909)

[*Howells was the chief progenitor of American realism and an influential American literary critic during the late nineteenth and early twentieth centuries. Although he wrote nearly three dozen novels, few of them are read today. Despite his eclipse, however, he stands as one of the major literary figures of the late nineteenth century; having successfully weaned American literature from the sentimental romanticism of its infancy, he earned the popular sobriquet "the Dean of American Letters." In the following introduction to* The Swiss Family Robinson, *Howells explores the enduring attraction of the book for readers who delight in the author's portrayal of family life and his "art of telling something fresh on every page." He concludes by expressing regret that "there is no especial scope given for the imaginations of the girl readers of the book."*]

[If] it had not been for *Robinson Crusoe* **The Swiss Family Robinson** would not have been written, just as *Robinson Crusoe* would not have been written if it had not been for the narrative of Alexander Selkirk. But for the present the children need not take this very much to heart. It is good to have had **The Swiss Family Robinson** on any terms; and, as the children will learn later on, there is no new thing under the sun—a saying which was not new when Solomon said it. What puts this book before the greater book that went before it is the author's art of telling something fresh on every page, or, rather, freshly presenting something. For him no day passes without its difficulty overcome, its danger escaped, its adventure happily ended. In reading the book I have not been able to place on the map the sea where the island is on which this excellent family was wrecked, and which they made their happy home for so long, and where the story leaves nearly all of them. What I know is that almost every wild animal that can be tamed, or that ought to be killed, is found in it; that every beautiful or eatable or companionable bird nests there; that every strange or familiar fruit and vegetable grows on the trees or above or under the ground. In these happy pages there is never any want of work or play, never any lack of sport; there is no wanton slaughter of harmless creatures for pleasure, and such as do not supply the table are left unharmed unless they danger the lives of those excellent Robinsons. The children need not be told outright that the morality is admirable, that the old-fashioned piety is beautiful, and that the gentle, early nineteenth-century humanity is such as the early twentieth century would be the better for embracing. When the boys and girls come back from ramping and rummaging through the happy island, they will have some sense of this, and I would not have it borne in too strongly upon them. I would not have many sermons preached to them about the lovely family life of the Robinsons, which is never insipidly sweet, but is full of true affection and willing subordination. The children, who are different enough in other things, are alike in loving their father and mother, as the Good Book bids them, and the father is worthy through his wisdom and prudence, the mother through her glad providence and tender vigilance. The father leads the boys in their adventures and enterprises; the mother welcomes them home and spreads the table with rich and wholesome abundance. For the honest-hearted, home-loving boy, it is like being under his own roof, with a boundless range of field, forest, and sea, and every harmless delight of them.

I should like to invite the elders to join me in observing the good behavior of the wreck, from which the Robinsons draw

*A depiction of the family's journey from the shipwreck to the island, in a boat made of casks.*

every needed supply not afforded by their island or contrived by their ingenuity. I really did not make out whether that kind wreck ever broke up; but almost any boy could tell me. What I really grieve for, and it is the only thing, is that there is no especial scope given for the imaginations of the girl readers of the book. That English girl coming in at the last moment with her rescue and her return home will hardly do; and if I did not feel that girls nowadays had more and more the tastes of boys, but not tomboys, and so must enjoy the book almost as much as boys, I should, the very first thing, myself write a sequel to **The Swiss Family Robinson,** tracing the experiences of a family of American Robinson Girls to every fortunate conclusion. (pp. xi-xiii)

*W[illiam] D[ean] Howells, in an introduction to* The Swiss Family Robinson; or, The Adventures of a Shipwrecked Family on an Uninhabited Isle Near New Guinea *by [Johann] David Wyss, translated by Mrs. Henry H. B. Paull, Harper & Brothers, 1909, pp. xi-xiii.*

## RICHARD BUTLER GLAENZER   (essay date 1911)

[*Glaenzer comments briefly on the differences between* The Swiss Family Robinson *and Daniel Defoe's* Robinson Crusoe. *He also discusses why Defoe's work, while intended for adults, actually appeals to a younger audience than does* The Swiss Family Robinson.]

The story of the family that built a house in a tree: such is the memory which most people retain of *The Swiss Family Robinson,* while to the same, *Robinson Crusoe* recalls a desert island, Friday, and a footprint on the sand. There is nothing extraordinary about a house or a footprint on the sand; but a house built in a tree is as fascinating in its suggestion as a Spanish castle, and a footprint on the sand of a desert island is as terrible as a voice in an empty tomb. The one spells Romance, the other Realism. Therefore is it futile to discuss the comparative merits of the two books. The first was narrated to the young; the second was written for the old: the former, at an epoch when many of the young were becoming sceptical; the latter, at a period when some of the old were still credulous.

*Robinson Crusoe* has suffered the fate of Horace, a fate even less dignified, since it is held unworthy of the schoolroom. It is termed a classic by lexicographers and authoritative critics. It is much sought after in its earliest editions by bibliophiles and by them guarded like a treasure. But, as reading matter, it is reserved for children of a tender age—that age for which everything is debased to words of one syllable. *The Swiss Family Robinson,* on the other hand, still holds the audience for which it was written, but without realising the author's purpose; for the "benefits of intelligence, industry and a well-ordered mind" are uninteresting if indisputable facts to the average boy of to-day, so that his possible appreciation of noble precepts and the beneficence of Providence palls before a lively enjoyment of the spirited adventures in which the book abounds.

Here rises the inevitable question. Why is it that *Robinson Crusoe,* a piece of fiction written primarily for adults, appeals so strongly to young children, to younger children, in fact, than its successor? That this appeal is at least a century old is evidenced by Sir Walter Scott in his edition of Defoe:

> There is hardly an elf so devoid of imagination as not to have supposed for himself a solitary island in which he could act "Robinson Crusoe," were it but in a corner of the nursery.

But this does not answer the question. "It happened one day, going toward my boat," says Crusoe, "I was exceedingly surprised with the print of a man's naked foot on the shore. . . . I stood like one thunderstruck, or as if I had seen an apparition. . . . I slept none that night."

In the religion of childhood there are two great realities, fear and the mother; and it depends largely on the mother which shall be the greater. But no mother in the world can save her little one from fear. She can save him from the thing feared, but from fear itself nothing can save him. To him, tiny egoist, blended of sublime self-satisfaction and blind dependence on others, the world of his narrow vision is an island—a desert island by night, when its shore discloses many a dreadful footprint and apparitions that not even a mother can explain away. May not this be the secret of childhood's sympathy with the lonely mariner?

The day arrives when a child outgrows fear or rather makes a great show of having done so; when he not only parades his disbelief of Santa Claus but pities or despises the faithful. To him, Jack of the Beanstalk becomes silly because his beanstalk is incredible and Prince Charming, an effeminate milksop because he is forever making love to some Princess. In short, legendary heroes, giants and fairies and their marvellous deeds

appear too improbable to invite imitation, while the symbolism behind them—tops and marbles are the symbols of these first days of adolescence! It is at this point that *Robinson Crusoe* begins to lose its hold on the imagination, not in this case because Crusoe is unreal or because his adventures are impossible, but because he is too cheerless a figure to serve as a model. Boys are only happy when they can identify themselves with their heroes or envy them, and very rare are the boys that lead an isolated life and fewer are they that wish to do so. But that is not all. The small child battles with his own fears. The big boy must inspire awe in others. He must be one of a company of boys, the leader or potential leader of it, for it is the joy of wresting victory from his peers or the hope of doing so that is the breath in his nostrils. If at this stage he craves any kind of reading, *The Swiss Family Robinson* satisfies the want; for it celebrates conspicuously the good-natured rivalry of four healthy boys.

That this is the side of the book which attracts more especially the youthful mind cannot be doubted, and though its author intended it to be the means to an end rather than the end itself, all credit is due him for his excellent choice of means. Since his object was the instruction of his four sons, it may be argued that it was to give each a rôle to play that he introduced the same number of boys in his story. This is as self-evident as the identity of the father of the boys with the narrator himself, but the following will show that it was not his only reason. When Ernest, the more reticent of the lads, appeared to wish to be left alone on a newly discovered islet "like a real Robinson Crusoe," his father reproved him thus: "Thank God, my boy, that He has not gratified your wish. . . . God created man for society, and although the entertaining story of Robinson Crusoe is embellished with poetic fancies, quite delightful to read, yet his lonely position must have been full of sadness. We can look upon ourselves as a whole family of real Robinsons, but far better off, because we have each other for companions." The beginning of which sounds solemn enough, but allowance should be made for the fact that the speaker was a Swiss pastor who in spite of his frequent genuflections and thanksgivings—embarrassing, no doubt, to a public which indulges itself but one day in seven—was own cousin to common sense, a friend of Canary sack, and as much comrade as father to his children. (pp. 139-40)

Page after page of . . . incidents in which the impossible seems to merge into the commonplace may point to dry reading, but such is not the case. Each day in the lives of these kindly folk has its vexed problems as well as its innocent pastimes; but it is always as a family, a truly sympathetic little group, that they accept both. Their courageous, almost joyous way of grappling with difficulties, their perseverance in the face of disaster and disappointment, and their gentle unquestioning faith are full of tender inspiration. Situations which should prove ridiculous are charming through their very ingenuousness, and details which should weary by repetition form in reality a background of substantial and satisfying homeliness. There is no sham about these simple people, however absurd may be the scene of their adventures. But whether for this reason or for that— real reasons being so imperceptible—*The Swiss Family Robinson* appeals, as it must, to every manly boy and every man who has been a real boy, both will agree that none could have expressed their feelings better than Mr. Howells when he remarked in that quiet little way of his: "This is one of the dearest old books in the world." (p. 142)

*Richard Butler Glaenzer, "The Books of Our Youth, I: 'The Swiss Family Robinson',"* in The Bookman,

*A 1909 illustration showing the approximate location of Wyss's imaginary island.*

*New York, Vol. XXXIV, No. 2, October, 1911, pp. 139-42.*

## SOLOMON EAGLE [PSEUDONYM OF J. C. SQUIRE]  (essay date 1922)

[*Eagle declares that* The Swiss Family Robinson, *despite its improbabilities and summarizing,* " *is a classic beyond all dispute.*"]

["**The Swiss Family Robinson**"] is a superb book. It is easy to make fun of it. Everybody when he remembers it remembers it with a smile; but it is usually a smile of affection. The style . . . is the greatest example of naive pomposity which we possess. The improbabilities (over and above the great obvious improbability of every kind of bird and beast in the Zoo being concentrated on a single island) follow each other without a break, and no edifying story-teller on record ever pumped out his edification with so little attempt at concealment. Here is no education in parenthesis and no moralising by implication: the morals are expounded in sermons, and the facts, mainly zoological, are handed out in large wads, accompanied by frankly informative illustrations. By all the rules of story-telling, as expounded by critics and observed by conscious artists, this book was bound to fail; the most innocent child must inevitably be bored by it. But the point is that it didn't fail. I do not think that I was more addicted to sermons than any other child or less fond of being educated; but I do clearly remember that I was thrilled by this story, and that the irrelevant

details here never struck me as irrelevant. It seemed the most natural thing in the world for the author, when mentioning an ant-eater, to digress in order to tell all about ant-eaters; and I happened to be interested in ant-eaters. With the exception of [John Bunyan's] "The Pilgrim's Progress" (which is on a much higher literary plane), I do not remember any book in which so large a didactic element is so successfully conveyed in a story. And the author managed it because he was a man of extraordinary simplicity, sweetness, goodness, and curiosity, a man with much of the child in him, who went straight ahead as he felt inclined, and never thought at all of himself or of art. . . . This *is* a classic beyond all dispute. (pp. 199-200)

> *Solomon Eagle* [*pseudonym of J. C. Squire*], *"An Edifying Classic," in his* Essays at Large, *George H. Doran Company, 1922, pp. 196-200.*

## JAMES O'DONNELL BENNETT   (essay date 1927)

[*Bennett praises* The Swiss Family Robinson *as "an epic in little of civilization."*]

["**The Swiss Family Robinson**"] is one of the books that once read remain a permanent possession. Whether that is because we read it first in childhood, when the mind is uncluttered, or because Johann David Wyss was a genuine artist in the effective disposition of extensive material, I know not. His material is immense, and one thing is certain: A sensible boy, having attentively read the story, has learned more about processes, contrivances, and the nature of things, animate and inanimate, than most adults who have not read "**The Swiss Family Robinson**" ever learn. That fact is a remarkable tribute to a book which librarians catalogue as a juvenile. But this book is much more than that. It is an epic in little of civilization—a romance of the varied contrivings by which man has raised himself from the state of nomad to the state of developer, controller, and— more or less—of perfecter. A book should be read in relation to life. If it cannot be so read, it is no book. This book is all life. The multitude and variety of incident are astounding. . . . Invariably they are things that have to do with life as it must be lived if man is to get through it with decency, comfort, usefulness, and a fair degree of distinction. (pp. 190-91)

But it is not in its unfolding of "most disastrous chances and moving accidents by flood and field" that the essential charm of this story lies. The charm lies in the presentation of man as a contriving animal—a building animal plus the genius for readily, subtly, and independently varying his contrivances to suit new conditions and sudden exigencies, which is one of the capacities distinguishing him from the lower animals. That capacity has made a great story ever since man first came out of his cave and began to build in the open. You may see evidence of the fascination of it any day in the throng loitering in front of a building in process of erection. Persons deficient in imagination sneer, and call the lookers-on idlers, and wonder whether they have naught better to do. Naught *else* to do they may have, but aught more entertaining they could hardly find. They are answering to the same spell that carries a child so eagerly and attentively through the 600 pages and the ten years of incidents of "**The Swiss Family Robinson**." (p. 193)

> *James O'Donnell Bennett, "Johann David Wyss's 'Swiss Family Robinson'," in his* Much Loved Books: Best Sellers of the Ages, *Boni and Liveright, Publishers, 1927, pp. 190-96.*

**JOHN HENRY GROTH**  (essay date 1929)

[*In this excerpt from his introduction to a 1929 edition of* The Swiss Family Robinson, *Groth briefly discusses the relation between Wyss's novel and the philosophy of Jean Jacques Rousseau.*]

"The Swiss Family Robinson" belongs to the class of stories which became popular throughout Europe in the eighteenth century after the publication of Defoe's "Robinson Crusoe" in 1719. The unprecedented success of Defoe's book naturally called forth a host of imitators who wished to share in his good fortune. (p. xi)

"Robinson Crusoe" also came to play a rôle in the field of education and gave rise to a juvenile educational literature of large proportions. It is in this category that the "Swiss Family Robinson" belongs. The impulse toward the production of this literature was given by the French philosopher, Rousseau. Regarding civilization as the root of all evil and extolling man as he is by nature, Rousseau could not fail to be keenly interested in Defoe's story. It did not escape his eye that Robinson was obliged to learn precisely as he believed children should learn. Nature was the teacher, and Nature was kind to Robinson. (p. xiii)

In "The Swiss Family Robinson" the pastor, his wife, and four young sons are the only survivors of a shipwreck upon an unknown tropical coast. While their situation is insecure enough to render the story interesting, they are really much better off than Crusoe. . . . The father reveals a wide knowledge of nature. He is able to identify every herb, tree, and flower, and he always knows what to do next. Moreover, he is eager to impart his knowledge to the boys. Whenever it is possible, he employs the Socratic method and allows them to find the answer to their questions for themselves. . . . Each day has its new experiences and its new lessons. Each difficulty must give up its own solution. There are no text-books, except "Robinson Crusoe," and that is consulted only when everything else fails. Indeed, instruction plays so prominent a part that the action is sometimes retarded. In the last chapter the father gives the manuscript of his journal to the sons who are about to depart for Europe and asks them to have it printed. His remarks on this occasion admirably reflect the purpose of the book as well as eighteenth-century ideas of religion and morality. (pp. xiv-xv)

Since the days of Rousseau the production of juvenile didactic literature in story form has been nothing short of enormous. The Robinson motif was only one among many themes employed. . . . Although the first editor of "The Swiss Family Robinson"—for it is no doubt Johann Rudolf Wyss speaking here—disavows "the conceit of the learned educator" and declares that he "followed no definite plan of education," the author yet moves in the Rousseauistic atmosphere. The very lack of method in the training of the boys, the mild rationalism of the religion of the pastor, and the emphasis upon the "useful" and the "practical," would have had the approval of Jean Jacques. On the whole, "The Swiss Family Robinson" is a characteristic product of the late eighteenth century. It embodies its outlook upon science, religion, and ethics presented in accord with the ideals of its greatest educational philosopher, and it employs the name and the motif of its most widely read book. But, like "Robinson Crusoe," "The Swiss Family Robinson" has in a modest way something about it that is not of the eighteenth century, nor of any century. By virtue of this "something" it continues to appeal to the class of readers for whom it was intended. (pp. xvii-xviii)

*John Henry Groth, in an introduction to* The Swiss Family Robinson *by Johann David Wyss, edited by John Henry Groth, The Macmillan Company Publishers, 1929, pp. xi-xviii.*

**VINCENT STARRETT**  (essay date 1940)

[*Starrett lauds the charm and "philosophy of contentment" of* The Swiss Family Robinson.]

Outstanding and pre-eminent among *Robinson Crusoe's* descendants is that pious and alluring juvenile long known to English readers as the *Swiss Family Robinson*. . . . Its opening lines are among the most memorable to be found on that special shelf of island literature which is in the forefront of all youthful recollection. Has there been anything quite like them since?

> The storm, which had lasted for six long and terrible days, appeared on the seventh to redouble its fury. We were driven out of our course, far to the southeast, and all trace of our position was lost. Sailors and passengers alike were worn out with fatigue and long watching; indeed, all hope of saving the ship had disappeared. The masts were split and overboard, the sails rent, and the water in the hold from

A CASTLE IN THE AIR

*A 1909 drawing of the family's house in a tree.*

many leaks, made us expect every moment to be swallowed up in the waves.

There is something oddly effective in those fine old mixed-tense openings of a century ago, which plunge us instantly into the heart of the commotion. Reading them, today, one suspects that somewhere along the years the art of narration has been lost. At any rate, there have been few such opening paragraphs since, and few such books as the *Swiss Family Robinson,* more's the pity.... Crusoe owes his ultimate comfort to his own exertions; but the enviable Robinsons become the tenants of a tropical Eden in which everything is provided by a beneficent natural goodness. An island where, it has been written, "all may be had for the asking; where figs grow on thistles, and apples on thorn-trees, and roasted pigs are crying out, 'Oh, eat me, if you please!'" And Eden is precisely the word, for nearly all the animals of the garden, surely, are ultimately discovered and harnessed to man's needs. No member of the smug, delightful circle ever stirs an inch beyond that memorable treetop home—later there was a grotto, was there not?—without finding some new wonder of nature intended to make existence more idyllic. The end is an Utopian dream come true. (pp. 42-3)

Through this paradise strides good Father Robinson, a natural scoutmaster, attended by the members of his remarkable family. Sententious and Socratic and not a little pedantic, if the truth be told—a living textbook of universal knowledge—he loses no opportunity to impart a bit of improving information, right out of the encyclopaedia, or read a little sermon on the divine goodness that has made possible this perpetual Presbyterian picnic. In the very act of escaping from the wreck, it will be recalled, he paused to explain the principal of the lever—"as well as I could in a hurry"—and promised to have a long talk on the subject of mechanics when opportunity offered. It is easy to be satirical at the expense of the Robinsons, and always a temptation. At any moment one half expects the precocious Ernest to stumble upon a field of growing musical instruments, with which the happy castaways will start a family band. Or a whisky-and-soda tree. But the charm of the old tale is beyond dispute. And there is a quality of busy kindness in it that I have never encountered to the same degree in any other book. It projects a philosophy of contentment that is perhaps the most sentimental and seductive in island literature. (pp. 43-4)

*Vincent Starrett, "Of Castaways and Islands," in his* Books Alive: A Profane Chronicle of Literary Endeavor and Literary Misdemeanor, *Random House, 1940, pp. 33-60.**

**WILLIAM GOLDING**   (essay date 1960)

[*Golding is one of the major English novelists of the period following World War II, and in 1983 won the Nobel Prize in literature for the body of his work. In the following essay, which was originally published in the June 10, 1960, issue of the* Spectator, *the novelist explores the unique appeal of* The Swiss Family Robinson, *and asserts that the "great strength" of the book lies in Wyss's ability to evoke the spirit of close family life.*]

Has anyone ever resisted the charm of the Swiss Family? Indeed, can anyone think of it as just another book? Someone once likened Chaucer's stories to an English river, slow, quietly beautiful, and winding all the way. In the same terms, *The Swiss Family Robinson* is like a mountain lake. It is contained and motionless. It does not go anywhere. It has no story.

WE ENTERED
THE GROTTO

*An illustration from a 1909 edition of* The Swiss Family Robinson.

Details, and detached incidents, are looked at separately without regard to what is coming next. This is how children live when they are happy, and this is why children will read *The Swiss Family Robinson* backwards and forwards and not bother about the end. To the adult eye, very little seems intended for out-and-out realism. When father Robinson puts together his boat of tubs with the ease and speed of a Popeye who has just eaten spinach, we, and children too, accept a literary convention. Nor are the vague people at all convincing. For Johann Wyss began, not by writing for a wide public but for his children who knew him and his wife and themselves too well to bother about characterization, even if he had been capable of it. Having isolated his characters, Wyss used the book from then onwards as a sort of holdall for conveying moral instruction and scientific information. He did not foresee the outcome of the book. One feels that the lively and capable Miss Montrose was brought in at the end because Wyss's eldest son had got engaged and Wyss wanted to bring his fiancée into the family. The charm of the book, then, lies precisely in the absence of story. The days are endless and time has no meaning. We sink completely into the milieu of these people who are not going anywhere and do not mind. Time is bright and uncomplicated as holidays spent by the sea in childhood.

At the back of the book stands the determination of Wyss to make and keep his family secure. How safe the Swiss Family

Robinson is! That omniscient and omnipotent father, God's representative on earth to his family; that mild, womanly and devoted mother who is nevertheless so competent in her defined sphere—there is no hint that they can be anything but perfect. There is no flaw in their parental authority. (pp. 106-07)

[The] children take a child's place. There is simply no possibility of juvenile delinquency. The guiding hand is gentle but adamant. The children are not allowed to overshadow their parents and save the day, perhaps because these are not the sort of days that have to be saved. We should no more expect Fritz to succour his father and mother than we should expect Jim Hawkins [in Robert Louis Stevenson's *Treasure Island*], conversely, to stay in the stockade and allow Doctor Livesey to take top place. It may be that the convention of children knowing more than their parents, being heroic and returning to a saved and admiring father, was a reaction against that gentle but adamantine hand. You can have too much of a good thing after all; and sometimes even a child's eye detects the absurdities in that godlike father-figure.

But no one, either child or adult, laughs at Johann Wyss without affection. He achieved more than he hoped or imagined possible. He gave his own family, and a good slice of European youth, total security between the covers of a book. For the great strength of *The Swiss Family Robinson* is not the brilliantly evoked spirit of place (the crystal cavern, the lobster pools, the grove of trees); it is not even the details held up to the eye and exactly observed (the tools and weapons, the plants and rocks, the good, earned meals). What Wyss captured effortlessly because it was so familiar to him was that family sense—the period when children are no longer babies and not yet young men: the period when a family, if it is lucky and emotionally stable, can look in on itself and be a whole world. (pp. 107-08)

> *William Golding, ''Islands,'' in his* The Hot Gates and Other Occasional Pieces, *Faber and Faber, 1965, pp. 106-10.**

## ROBERT CUSHMAN MURPHY (essay date 1963)

[*In the following excerpt from his introduction to a 1963 edition of* The Swiss Family Robinson, *Murphy first discusses possible sources for the novel. He then comments briefly on Wyss's attitude towards women projected in the novel as well as the work's ''impossible conglomeration'' and didacticism.*]

[When Wyss] wrote *Der Schweizerische Robinson* in collaboration with his four young sons, this imaginative family stood halfway between an age of Eden-like romance and the rapidly developing age of purposeful global discovery. This is not to deny that sober description of faraway regions had long antedated the clergyman's pen, nor to imply that works of untrammeled geographic fancy ended with his book. As to the first, Wyss was soaked in reading—wide and deep. As a scholarly Swiss theologian, he presumably knew at least six languages, ancient and modern. He could quote the naturalists from Aristotle to Linnaeus. He repeatedly reveals his familiarity with such classics as the *Voyages* of Captain James Cook, published 1773-1784, and the stirring circumnavigation of Lord Anson (1748). But his text refers equally to fantasies like [Swift's] *Gulliver's Travels*, which appeared in 1726. And it was of course *Robinson Crusoe* (1719) that supplied the title for his family yarn. Epic fiction in the manner of Defoe's masterpiece was in that period known on the continent of Europe as a 'robinsoniad.' (p. v)

Even such varied antecedent texts as the several mentioned by no means uncover all the roots of *The Swiss Family Robinson*. Reading shrewdly, we can make out uncredited sources of ideas, among them Rousseau's discourse of 1754 on the origin of human inequality. In this the French philosopher pictured 'natural man' as a pure and innocuous animal. Only after the arrival of industry was equality doomed to vanish. This tenet, together with Diderot's popular concept of the 'noble savage,' had a vast influence on romanticism—and Wyss was eminently a romantic, albeit a pious one. We may be certain that he warmly disapproved of Rousseau, but he had pored over his pages nonetheless. In expressing the effect of nature on human feeling Rousseau was unsurpassed, and love of nature was obviously a compelling trait in Wyss. We recognise the influence of Rousseau in the complete removal of an entire family from the workaday world, and its segregation on an island beyond all horizons. It is reflected also in the frequent allusions to savage or 'natural' men who, unlike Crusoe's Man Friday, never materialise. Still again we see it in the comically innocent pre-courtship antics of Fritz and Emily, when an outsider, and a young female at that, is at last hauled improbably into the family narrative. The thoughts of Wyss were those of an educator; in a sense, he was writing his own version of [Rousseau's] *Emile*. (pp. v-vi)

[Wyss] was a companionable father, fond of long hikes with his boys, and devoted to fishing and gunning. Days afield in the Alps seem to have had evening counterparts in the living-room, where all hands sojourned at the antipodes and each contributed most implausible adventures which the father integrated on the burgeoning pages. (pp. vi-vii)

If Papa Wyss was the undeniable pal of his sons, let us not forget that he was likewise a pedantic patriarch who never harboured a doubt that all responsibility centered in himself alone. No reasonable and harmless proposals by well-grown young men could be carried out without specific fatherly approval. 'I consented,' he is continually writing about matters that anyone else would take for granted. As applied to him the adjective 'unfeminist' would be understatement. He stresses the modest reluctance with which Mother—let's whisper it!—shed her normal garb and donned the clothes of a sailor for the first trip ashore by raft. Elsewhere she exhibited 'courage and resolution far beyond her sex.' A palanquin, of course, had to be built for her in the wilderness. 'I and my wife' is an expression the author sometimes employs (but this may be a matter of semantics rather than etiquette: probably the pronoun and noun should, in justice, be reversed in English idiom). At any rate, the aim of the benevolent tyrant never fails to be high. 'Gentle measures,' commended half a century later by Jacob Abbot of the 'Rollo books,' gradually transform the separate and individual faults of the sons into their opposite virtues. Mother, naturally, had only virtues. At the end of ten years in their exclusive little insular universe, all the Wysses are utterly harmonious as well as healthy, wealthy, and wise. They no longer pine to be discovered and transported home.

In general opinion the fame of *The Swiss Family Robinson* rests more upon impossible conglomeration than anything else. If the juxtaposition of plants and animals from all zones sometimes turns out to be not impossible, it is only by accident. For example, the shipwrecked family is greeted at its deliverance on an unknown shore by the clamour of penguins and flamingos. This *could* happen at the Galápagos Archipelago, or on the coast of central Peru where the writer of this Introduction once encountered flamingos and penguins within sight and sound of one another. But Father Wyss knew nothing of that; to his credit be it said that he very rarely makes the mistake of being correct. Let us admit, too, that he and his sons knew this as well as we do. (pp. vii-viii)

The chief author was no doubt fully aware of the whimsicality of much of his tale. But as regards moral purpose, he was in dead earnest. It is altogether too easy to overlook the fact that the aim is didactic and that the personalities and aptitudes of the fictional Fritz, Jack, Ernest, and Francis are those of the living sons in a conventional Bernese home. The boys grew up as their father would have them, thanks to his own educational philosophy. *The Swiss Family Robinson* is primarily a success story, a pre-Victorian 'Horatio Alger,' and an apotheosis of the dime novel.

Good books are for diverse use. One reading may be enough for even some of the greatest. Others, such as [Carroll's] *Alice in Wonderland,* yield a new crop of fruit even at the nth reading. *The Swiss Family Robinson* should be read at least twice—the first time when one is so young as to want to believe it all, the second in much later years when its heart beats more loudly than the nonsense on the surface. (p. ix)

> *Robert Cushman Murphy, in an introduction to* The Swiss Family Robinson *by Johann Wyss, The Heritage Press, 1963, pp. v-ix.*

## ADDITIONAL BIBLIOGRAPHY

Allen, Francis H. "News for Bibliophiles." *The Nation* XCV, No. 2462 (5 September 1912): 210-11.
> Chronicles the early history of *The Swiss Family Robinson*'s publication, including the endings contributed by the Baroness de Montolieu to later editions.

Becker, May Lamberton. Introduction to *The Swiss Family Robinson,* by Johann Wyss, edited by William H. G. Kingston, pp. 11-14. Cleveland: World Publishing Co., 1947.
> Focuses on the origins of *The Swiss Family Robinson* and the use of its popular subject matter by later authors.

Bosworth, Allan R. Introduction to *The Swiss Family Robinson,* by Johann Wyss, pp. vii-xii. New York: Harper & Row, Publishers, 1966.
> Explores the influence of Daniel Defoe's *Robinson Crusoe* on *The Swiss Family Robinson* and the appeal of Wyss's work as a product of the oral tradition of storytelling.

Wyss, Robert L. "The Real Swiss Wysses." *Life* 37, No. 26 (27 December 1954): 63-4.
> Discusses the question of *The Swiss Family Robinson*'s authorship, as well as the history of how it came to be written and published. The critic is a descendant of the author and owns the original manuscript.

# Appendix

The following is a listing of all sources used in Volume 10 of *Nineteenth-Century Literature Criticism*. Included in this list are all copyright and reprint rights and acknowledgments for those essays for which permission was obtained. Every effort has been made to trace copyright, but if omissions have been made, please let us know.

**THE EXCERPTS IN NCLC, VOLUME 10, WERE REPRINTED FROM THE FOLLOWING PERIODICALS:**

*The Academy,* v. IV, July 1, 1873; v. XII, July 7, 1877; v. XXXVII, May 17, 1890; v. L, July 4, 1896; v. LIX, July 28, 1900; v. LXI, December 14, 1901; v. LXI, December 21, 1901; v. LXIX, December 23, 1905.

*American Imago,* v. 33, Fall, 1976 for "Mörike's 'Mozart on the Way to Prague': Stages and Outcomes of the Creative Experience" by Ursula Mahlendorf. Copyright 1976 by The Association for Applied Psychoanalysis, Inc. Reprinted by permission of the Wayne State University Press and the author.

*American Literature,* v. 30, May, 1958; v. 48, March, 1976. Copyright © 1958, 1976 by Duke University Press. Both reprinted by permission.

*American Quarterly,* v. XX, Spring, 1968 for "Philanthropy in Frederic's 'The Market-Place' " by Clayton L. Eichelberger. Copyright 1968, Trustees of the University of Pennsylvania. Reprinted by permission of the publisher and the author.

*American Quarterly Review,* v. XIX, March, 1836.

*The Antioch Review,* v. XXXV, Winter, 1977. Copyright © 1977 by the Antioch Review Inc. Reprinted by permission of the Editors.

*Arion,* v. 8, Autumn, 1969 for "Theocritus through Mörike" by Christopher Middleton. Copyright © 1969 by the Trustees of Boston University. Reprinted by permission of the publisher and the author.

*The Athenaeum,* n. 3223, August 3, 1889.

*Atlanta Monthly,* v. 76, November, 1895; v. LXXVIII, August, 1896.

*Belgravia,* v. XLVII, April, 1882.

*Bentley's Miscellany,* v. XL, 1856.

*Blackwood's Edinburgh Magazine,* v. III, August, 1818; v. XXX, November, 1831; v. LXXVII, May, 1855; v. CXXXVI, November and December, 1884.

*The Bookman,* London, v. XV, November, 1898; v. XVI, August, 1899; v. XLVI, May, 1914.

*The Bookman,* New York, v. XXXIV, October, 1911.

*The Boston Review,* v. III, January, 1863.

*The Century,* v. XXV, April, 1883.

*The Chap-Book,* v. VIII, March 15, 1898.

*The Church Review,* v. III, January, 1851.

*The Citizen,* v. III, September, 1897.

*College English,* v. 5, January, 1944/ v. 19, October, 1957 for "Five Acts of 'The Scarlet Letter'" by Malcolm Cowley. Copyright © 1957 by the National Council of Teachers of English. Renewal copyright © 1985 by Malcolm Cowley. Reprinted by permission of the author./ v. 26, February, 1965 for "The Problem of Determinism in Frederic's First Novel" by Tom H. Towers. Copyright © 1965 by the National Council of Teachers of English. Reprinted by permission of the publisher and the author.

*Contemporary Review,* v. LXXVII, February, 1900; v. CXLVI, December, 1934.

*Country Life,* v. CLXVII, January 17, 1980 for "Keep the Home Fires Burning" by Marghanita Laski. © copyright 1980 by Marghanita Laski. Reprinted by permission of the author.

*The Critic,* New York, v. 1, December 31, 1881; n.s. v. XXVI, October 10, 1896.

*The Critical Review,* v. XI, May, 1807.

*The Dial,* v. II, July, 1841; v. III, July, 1842; v. III, April, 1843; v. IV, July, 1883; v. X, November, 1889; v. XXV, December 16, 1898.

*The Eclectic Review,* v. VI, April, 1810.

*The Economic Journal,* v. XXV, September, 1915.

*The Edinburgh Review,* v. II, April, 1803; v. LIV, September, 1831; v. CXIV, July, 1861; v. CXVII, January, 1863; v. CLXI, January, 1885.

*ELH,* v. 10, March, 1943.

*Encounter,* v. 6, May, 1956./ v. XXXVI, March, 1971 for "Walter Bagehot; or, The Political Journalist as Entertainer" by Henry Fairlie. © 1971 by Encounter Ltd. Reprinted by permission of the publisher and the author.

*English Studies,* v. 14, February, 1932.

*Essays by Divers Hands,* n.s. v. XXVII, 1955.

*Essays in Criticism,* v. XI, April, 1961. Reprinted by permission of the Editor of *Essays in Criticism.*

*Essays in French Literature,* n. 16, November, 1979. © Department of French Studies, The University of Western Australia. Reprinted by permission.

*The Examiner,* n. 586, March 21, 1819.

*The Fortnightly Review,* n. XVI, September 1, 1878; n.s. v. XXVII, April 1, 1880; n.s. v. XLII, December 1, 1887; v. LXII, July 1, 1897; n.s. v. LXXVII, March 1, 1905.

*Fraser's Magazine,* v. IV, September, 1831; v. V, May, 1832; v. LXXVI, August, 1867; n.s. v. XIX, March, 1879.

*The French Quarterly,* v. VII, September & December, 1925.

*French Studies,* v. XII, January, 1958. Reprinted by permission.

*The Galaxy,* v. II, November 15, 1866.

*German Life & Letters,* n.s. v. XXV, July, 1972. Reprinted by permission.

*The Germanic Review,* v. XXXII, December, 1957.

*Graham's Magazine,* v. XXXVI, May, 1850.

*Harper's New Monthly Magazine,* v. LXXXI, October, 1890.

*The Hibbert Journal,* v. XLVII, April, 1949.

*Hispania,* v. XXXIV, February, 1951.

*The Journal of English and Germanic Philology,* v. LXIV, July, 1965 for ''Thematic Unity in Lamb's Familiar Essays'' by Donald H. Reiman. © 1965 by the Board of Trustees of the University of Illinois. Reprinted by permission of the publisher and the author.

*Journal of the History of Ideas,* v. XV, April, 1954. Copyright 1954, renewed 1982, Journal of the History of Ideas, Inc. Reprinted by permission.

*LeBeau Monde and Monthly Register,* v. II, November, 1809.

*Lippincott's Monthly Magazine,* v. V, May, 1883.

*The Listener,* v. XXXVIII, November 6, 1947.

*The Literary World,* v. VI, March 30, 1850.

*Littell's Living Age,* v. XXV, May, 1850; v. LV, October 17, 1857.

*The London Mercury,* v. IX, March, 1924.

*Macmillan's Magazine,* v. XLIII, December, 1880; v. LIV, May, 1886; v. LXVII, March, 1893.

*The Markham Review,* v. 3, May, 1972. Reprinted by permission.

*Massachusetts Quarterly Review,* v. III, September, 1850.

*The Methodist Review,* n.s. v. LXIX, May, 1887.

*The Monthly Magazine,* London, v. 55, February 1, 1823.

*Monthly Review,* v. XXI, November, 1905.

*The Nation,* v. XXIII, July 13, 1876; v. XXVIII, June 26, 1879; v. XXXII, June 16, 1881; v. XL, February 5, 1885; v. CXI, December 8, 1920.

*The National Review,* London, v. XXXV, August, 1900.

*The New Monthly Magazine,* v. CXXXVIII, September, 1866.

*The New Stateman & Nation,* v. XXV, June 12, 1943; v. XXVIII, July 29, 1944.

*New York Herald Tribune Weekly Book Review,* June 15, 1947. © 1947 I.H.T. Corporation. Reprinted by permission.

*The New York Times,* November 27, 1887.

*The New York Times Book Review,* April 29, 1928; October 17, 1948; April 25, 1982. Copyright © 1928, 1948, 1982 by The New York Times Company. All reprinted by permission.

*The New Yorker,* v. XLVI, June 6, 1970 for ''Two Neglected American Novelists: II—Harold Frederic, the Expanding Upstater'' by Edmund Wilson. © 1970 by The New Yorker Magazine, Inc. Reprinted by permission of the Literary Estate of Edmund Wilson and Farrar, Straus and Giroux, Inc.

*The Nineteenth Century,* v. XVII, January, 1885; v. XL, November, 1896.

*The North American Review,* v. LXXI, July, 1850; v. LXXXVI, January, 1858; v. LXXXIX, July, 1859; v. CXXIX, September, 1879.

**THE EXCERPTS IN NCLC, VOLUME 10, WERE REPRINTED FROM THE FOLLOWING BOOKS:**

Aikhenvald, Yuly. From ''Yuly Aikhenvald on Alexander Herzen,'' in *The Complection of Russian Literature: A Cento*. Edited and translated by Andrew Field. Atheneum, 1971. Copyright © 1971 Andrew Field. All rights reserved. Reprinted with the permission of Atheneum Publishers, Inc.

Auerbach, Erich. From *Mimesis: The Representation of Reality in Western Literature*. Translated by Willard R. Trask. Princeton University Press, 1953. Copyright 1953, renewed © 1981, by Princeton University Press. Excerpts reprinted with permission of Princeton University Press.

Barnett, George L. From *Charles Lamb*. Twayne, 1976. Copyright © 1976 by Twayne Publishers. All rights reserved. Reprinted with the permission of Twayne Publishers, a division of G. K. Hall & Co., Boston.

Bart, Benjamin F. From *Flaubert*. Syracuse University Press, 1967. Copyright © 1967 by Syracuse University Press, Syracuse, N.Y. All rights reserved. Reprinted by permission.

Barthes, Roland. From *New Critical Essays,* translated by Richard Howard. Hill and Wang, 1980. Copyright © 1972 by Editions du Seuil. Translation copyright © 1980 by Farrar, Straus and Giroux, Inc. All rights reserved. Reprinted by permission of Hill and Wang, a division of Farrar, Straus and Giroux, Inc.

Barzun, Jacques. From an introduction to *Physics and Politics; or, Thoughts on the Application of the Principles of ''Natural Selection'' and ''Inheritance'' to Political Society*. By Walter Bagehot. Knopf, 1948. Copyright 1948, renewed 1975, by Alfred A. Knopf, Inc. All rights reserved. Reprinted by permission of the publisher.

Baudelaire, Charles. From *Baudelaire as a Literary Critic*. Edited and translated by Lois Boe Hyslop and Francis E. Hyslop, Jr. Pennsylvania State University Press, University Park, 1964. Copyright © 1964 by The Pennsylvania State University. All rights reserved. Reprinted by permission.

Baym, Nina. From *The Shape of Hawthorne's Career*. Cornell University Press, 1976. Copyright © 1976 by Cornell University. All rights reserved. Used by permission of the publisher, Cornell University Press.

Beach, Joseph Warren. From *The Twentieth Century Novel: Studies in Technique*. The Century Co., 1932. © 1932, renewed 1960. Adapted by permission of Prentice-Hall, Inc., Englewood Cliffs, NJ 07632.

Béguin, Albert. From ''On Rereading 'Madame Bovary','' in *''Madame Bovary'' by Gustave Flaubert: Backgrounds and Sources, Essays in Criticism*. Edited and translated by Paul de Man. Norton, 1965. Copyright © 1965 by W. W. Norton & Company, Inc. Reprinted by permission of W. W. Norton & Company, Inc.

Belinsky, V. G. From ''A Survey of Russian Literature in 1847: Part Two,'' in *Belinsky, Chernyshevsky, and Dobrolyubov: Selected Criticism*. Edited and translated by Ralph E. Matlaw. Dutton, 1962. Copyright © 1962 by E. P. Dutton. All rights reserved. Reprinted by permission of the publisher, E. P. Dutton, a division of New American Library.

Bell, Michael Davitt. From *The Development of American Romance: The Sacrifice of Relation*. University of Chicago Press, 1980. © 1980 by The University of Chicago. All rights reserved. Reprinted by permission of The University of Chicago Press.

Ben-Israel, Hedva. From *English Historians on the French Revolution*. Cambridge at the University Press, 1968. © Cambridge University Press 1968. Reprinted by permission.

Bennett, James O'Donnell. From *Much Loved Books: Best Sellers of the Ages*. Boni & Liveright Publishers, 1927. Copyright 1927 by Boni & Liveright, Inc. Renewed 1954 by James O'Donnell Bennett. Reprinted by permission.

Bewley, Marius. From *The Eccentric Design: Form in the Classic American Novel*. Columbia University Press, 1959. © 1959, Columbia University Press. Reprinted by permission.

Bluefarb, Sam. From *The Escape Motif in the American Novel: Mark Twain to Richard Wright*. Ohio State University Press, 1972. Copyright © 1972 by the Ohio State University Press. All rights reserved. Reprinted by permission.

Brenan, Gerald. From *The Literature of the Spanish People: From Roman Times to the Present Day*. Cambridge at the University Press, 1951.

Briggs, Austin, Jr. From *The Novels of Harold Frederic*. Cornell University Press, 1969. Copyright © 1969 by Cornell University. All rights reserved. Used by permission of the publisher, Cornell University Press.

Brombert, Victor. From *The Novels of Flaubert: A Study of Themes and Techniques*. Princeton University Press. 1966. Copyright © 1966 by Princeton University Press. All rights reserved. Excerpts reprinted with permission of Princeton University Press.

Brophy, Brigid, Michael Levey, and Charles Osborne. From *Fifty Works of English and American Literature We Could Do Without*. Stein and Day, 1968. Copyright © 1967 by Brigid Brophy, Michael Levey, Charles Osborne. All rights reserved. Reprinted with permission of Stein and Day Publishers.

Brownell, W. C. From *American Prose Masters*. Charles Scribner's Sons, 1909.

Brownson, Orestes A. From "Literary Notices and Criticisms: 'The Scarlet Letter'," in *The Scarlet Letter: Text, Sources, Criticism*. By Nathaniel Hawthorne, edited by Kenneth S. Lynn. Harcourt Brace & World, 1961.

Buchan, Alastair. From *The Spare Chancellor: The Life of Walter Bagehot*. Chatto and Windus, 1959. © copyright Alastair Buchan 1959. © Copyright Alastair Buchan 1960. Reprinted by permission of the author and Chatto & Windus.

Cargill, Oscar. From *Intellectual America: Ideas on the March*. Macmillan, 1941. Copyright 1941 by Macmillan Publishing Company. Renewed 1968 by Oscar Cargill. All rights reserved. Reprinted with the permission of Macmillan Publishing Company.

Carlyle, T. From a letter to Alexander Herzen on April 13, 1855, in *The Romantic Exiles: A Nineteenth-Century Portrait Gallery*. By Edward Hallett Carr. Frederick A. Stokes Company, 1933.

Carter, Everett. From an introduction to *The Damnation of Theron Ware*. By Harold Frederic, edited by Everett Carter. Cambridge, Mass.: Belknap Press, 1960. Copyright © 1960 by the President and Fellows of Harvard College. All rights reserved. Excerpted by permission.

Chase, Richard. From *The American Novel and Its Tradition*. Doubleday Anchor Books, 1957. Copyright © 1957 by Richard Chase. All rights reserved. Reprinted by permission of Doubleday & Company, Inc.

Coldwell, Joan. From an introduction to *Charles Lamb on Shakespeare*. By Charles Lamb, edited by Joan Coldwell. Colin Smythe, 1978. Copyright © 1978 by Colin Smythe Ltd. Reprinted by permission.

Croce, Benedetto. From *European Literature in the Nineteenth Century*. Translated by Douglas Ainslie. Alfred A. Knopf, 1924. Reprinted by permission of the Literary Estate of Benedetto Croce.

Croker, John Wilson. From a preface to *Familiar Epistles to Frederick J---s, Esq., on the Present State of the Irish Stage*. J. Barlow, 1804.

Crossman, R.H.S. From an introduction to *English Constitution*. By Walter Bagehot. Collins, 1963. © in introduction R.H.S. Crossman, 1963. Reprinted by permission of the Literary Estate of R.H.S. Crossman.

Darton, F. J. Harvey. From *Children's Books in England: Five Centuries of Social Life*. Cambridge at the University Press, 1932.

Davies, Horton. From *A Mirror of the Ministry in Modern Novels*. Oxford University Press, 1959. Copyright © 1959 by Oxford University Press, Inc. Reprinted by permission.

Demorest, D. L. From "Structures of Imagery in 'Madame Bovary'," in *"Madame Bovary" by Gustave Flaubert: Backgrounds, Sources, Essays in Criticism*. Edited and translated by Paul de Man. Norton, 1965. Copyright © 1965 by W. W. Norton & Company, Inc. Reprinted by permission of W. W. Norton & Company, Inc.

Denny, Norman. From an introduction to *Les Misérables, Vol. 1*. By Victor Hugo, translated by Norman Denny. The Folio Press, 1976. © copyright The Folio Society Limited 1976. Reprinted by permission.

De Quincey, Thomas. From *Biographical Essays*. Ticknor, Reed, and Fields, 1851.

Dobrée, Bonamy. From *English Essayists*. Collins, 1946.

Dostoievsky, F. M. From a diary entry in 1873, in *The Diary of a Writer, Vol. 1*. by F. M. Dostoievsky, edited and translated by Boris Brasol. Charles Scribner's Sons, 1949. Copyright 1949 Charles Scribner's Sons. Copyright renewed © 1976 Maxwell Fassett, executor of the Estate of Boris Brasol. All rights reserved. Reprinted with the permission of Charles Scribner's Sons.

Driver, C. H. From "Walter Bagehot and the Social Psychologists," in *The Social & Political Ideas of Some Representative Thinkers of the Victorian Age*. Edited by F.J.C. Hearnshaw. George G. Harrap & Company Ltd., 1933.

Duclaux, Madame. From *Victor Hugo*. Henry Holt and Company, 1921.

Dyson, H.V.D., and John Butt. From *Augustans and Romantics: 1689-1830*. By H.V.D. Dyson and others. The Cresset Press, 1940.

Eagle, Solomon. From *Essays at Large*. George H. Doran Company, 1922.

The Earl of Balfour. From an introduction to *The English Constitution*. By Walter Bagehot. Oxford University Press, London, 1928.

Eden, Anthony. From an introduction to *The Semi-Attached Couple*. By Emily Eden. Houghton Mifflin, 1947. Copyright 1947 by Anthony Eden. Copyright © renewed 1975 by Anthony Eden and Susanne Suba. Reprinted by permission of Houghton Mifflin Company.

Eden, Anthony. From an introduction to *The Semi-Detached House*. By Emily Eden. Frederick A. Stokes Company Publishers, 1928.

Eden, Emily. From a preface to *The Semi-Attached Couple*. Bentley, 1860.

Eliot, T. S. From *Elizabethan Essays*. Faber and Faber, 1934.

Evans, Arthur R., Jr. From *The Literary Art of Eugene Fromentin: A Study in Style and Motif*. The Johns Hopkins University Press, 1964. © 1964 by The Johns Hopkins Press. Baltimore, MD 21218. Reprinted by permission.

Faguet, Émile. From *Flaubert*. Translated by Mrs. R. L. Devonshire. Houghton Mifflin Company, 1914.

Farrell, James T. From ''Harold Frederic's 'The Damnation of Theron Ware','' in *Literary Essays: 1954-1974*. By James T. Farrell, edited by Jack Alan Robbins. Kennikat Press, 1976. Copyright © 1976 by Kennikat Press Corp. All rights reserved. Reprinted by permission of Associated Faculty Press, Inc., Port Washington, NY.

Fiedler, Leslie A. From *Love and Death in the American Novel*. Revised edition. Stein and Day, 1966. Copyright © 1960, 1966 by Leslie A. Fiedler. All rights reserved. Reprinted with permission of Stein and Day Publishers.

Flaubert, Gustave. From extracts from nineteen letters to Louise Colet from October 23, 1851 to January 2, 1854, in *The Letters of Gustave Flaubert: 1830-1857*. Edited and translated by Francis Steegmuller. Cambridge, Mass.: Belknap Press, 1980. Copyright © 1979, 1980 by Francis Steegmuller. All rights reserved. Excerpted by permission.

Fogle, Richard Harter. From *Hawthorne's Fiction: The Light & the Dark*. University of Oklahoma Press, 1952. Copyright 1952 by the University of Oklahoma Press Publishing Division of the University. Reprinted by permission.

Fox-Lockert, Lucía. From *Women Novelists in Spain and Spanish America*. The Scarecrow Press, 1979. Copyright © 1979 by Lucía Fox-Lockert. Reprinted by permission.

Frederic, Harold. From a preface to *In the Sixties*. By Harold Frederic. Charles Scribner's Sons, 1897.

Fromentin, Eugene. From a preface to *The Old Masters of Belgium and Holland*. By Eugene Fromentin, translated by Mary C. Robbins, J. R. Osgood and Company, 1882.

Garner, Stanton. From *Harold Frederic*. University of Minnesota Press, Minneapolis, 1969. American Writers Pamphlet No. 83. © 1969, University of Minnesota. All rights reserved. Reprinted by permission.

Gohdes, C. L. From *The Literature of the American People: An Historical and Critical Survey*. Edited by Arthur Hobson Quinn. Appleton-Century-Crofts, Inc., 1951.

Goncourt, Edmond de and Jules de Goncourt. From journal entries of December 10, 1860 and April, 1862, in *Paris and the Arts, 1851-1896: From the Goncourt ''Journal.''* By Edmond de Goncourt and Jules de Goncourt, edited and translated by George J. Becker and Edith Philips. Cornell University Press, 1971. Copyright © 1971 by Cornell University. All rights reserved. Used by permission of the publisher, Cornell University Press.

Grant, Elliott M. From *The Career of Victor Hugo*. Cambridge, Mass.: Harvard University Press, 1945. Copyright © 1945, renewed 1973, by the President and Fellows of Harvard College. Excerpted by permission.

Groth, John Henry. From an introduction to *The Swiss Family Robinson*. By Johann David Wyss, edited by John Henry Groth. The Macmillan Company Publishers, 1929.

Haines, Paul. From *Harold Frederic*. New York University, 1949. Copyright 1949 by New York University. Reprinted by permission of the publisher and the author.

Harris, Frank. From *Latest Contemporary Portraits*. The Macaulay Company, 1927.

Hawthorne, Nathaniel. From *The Scarlet Letter*. Ticknor, Reed, and Fields, 1850.

Hazlitt, William. From *Lectures Chiefly on the Dramatic Literature of the Age of Elizabeth*. Stodart and Steuart, 1820.

Hazlitt, William. From *The Spirit of the Age; or, Contemporary Portraits*. H. Colburn, 1825.

Herzen, Alexander. From a letter to an unknown recipient on March 1, 1849, in *From the Other Shore*. Translated by Moura Budberg. George Weidenfeld and Nicolson Limited, 1956.

Hoffman, Daniel. From *Form and Fable in American Fiction*. Oxford University Press, 1961. Copyright © 1961 by Daniel G. Hoffman. Reprinted by permission of the author.

Houston, John Porter. From *Victor Hugo*. Twayne, 1974. Copyright 1974 by Twayne Publishers. All rights reserved. Reprinted with the permission of Twayne Publishers, a division of G. K. Hall & Co., Boston.

Howard, William Guild. From an introduction to *Mozart auf der Reise nach Prag*. By Eduard Morike, edited by William Guild Howard. D. C. Heath & Co., Publishers, 1904.

Howells, W. D. From *Heroines of Fiction, Vol. I*. Harper & Brothers Publishers, 1901.

Howells, W. D. From an introduction to *The Swiss Family Robinson; or, The Adventures of a Shipwrecked Family on an Uninhabited Isle Near New Guinea*. By David Wyss, translated by Mrs. Henry H. B. Paull. Harper & Brothers, 1909.

Hugo, Victor. From a preface to *Les Miserables, Vol. I*. By Victor Hugo, translated by Norman Denny. The Folio Press, 1976. © copyright The Folio Society Limited 1976. Reprinted by permission.

Irvine, Lyn Ll. From *Ten Letter-Writers*. Hogarth Press, 1932.

Irvine, William. From *Walter Bagehot*. Longmans, Green & Co., 1939.

James, Henry. From "Gustave Flaubert," in *Madame Bovary*. By Gustave Flaubert, translated by W. Blaydes. P. F. Collier & Son, 1902.

Kaul, A. N. From *The American Vision: Actual and Ideal Society in Nineteenth-Century Fiction*. Yale University Press, 1963. Copyright © 1963 by Yale University. All rights reserved. Reprinted by permission.

Kazin, Alfred. From *On Native Grounds: An Interpretation of Modern American Prose Literature*. Reynal & Hitchcock, 1942. Copyright 1942, 1970, by Alfred Kazin. All rights reserved. Reprinted by permission of Harcourt Brace Jovanovich, Inc.

Klibbe, Lawrence H. From *Fernán Caballero*. Twayne, 1973. Copyright © 1973 by Twayne Publishers. All rights reserved. Reprinted with the permission of Twayne Publishers, a division of G. K. Hall & Co., Boston.

Lavrin, Janko. From *An Introduction to the Russian Novel*. Whittlesey House, 1947.

Lerner, Max. From *Ideas Are Weapons: The History and Uses of Ideas*. The Viking Press, 1939. Copyright © 1939, renewed 1966, by Max Lerner. Reprinted by permission of the author.

Lewis, R.W.B. From *The American Adam: Innocence, Tragedy and Tradition in the Nineteenth Century*. University of Chicago Press, 1955. © The University of Chicago, 1955. Copyright under the International Copyright Union, 1955. Renewed 1983 by R.W.B. Lewis. Reprinted by permission of The University of Chicago Press.

Lindsay, Martin. From *German Men of Letters: Twelve Literary Essays, Vol. V*. Edited by Alex Natan. Wolff, 1969. © 1969 Oswald Wolff (Publishers) Limited, London. Reprinted by permission.

Lovett, Robert Morss. From "Harold Frederic," in *The Damnation of Theron Ware*. By Harold Frederic. Albert & Charles Boni, 1924.

Lynd, Robert. From *Books and Writers*. J. M. Dent & Sons Ltd., 1952.

Macy, John. From *The Spirit of American Literature*. Doubleday, Page & Company, 1913.

Male, Roy R. From *Hawthorne's Tragic Vision*. University of Texas Press, 1957. © 1957 by the University of Texas Press. Reprinted by permission of the author.

Martin, Terence. From *Nathaniel Hawthorne*. Revised edition. Twayne, 1983. Copyright 1983 by Twayne Publishers. All rights reserved. Reprinted with the permission of Twayne Publishers, a division of G. K. Hall & Co., Boston.

Marzials, Frank T. From *Life of Victor Hugo*. Walter Scott, 1888.

Masaryk, Thomas Garrigue. From *The Spirit of Russia: Studies in History, Literature and Philosophy, Vol. I*. Translated by Eden Paul and Cedar Paul. The Macmillan Company, 1919.

Masefield, Muriel. From *Women Novelists From Fanny Burney to George Eliot*. I. Nicholson and Watson Limited, 1934.

Matthiessen, F. O. From *American Renaissance: Art and Expression in the Age of Emerson and Whitman*. Oxford University Press, New York, 1941.

Maurois, André. From an introduction to *Les Miserables: A Novel*. By Victor Hugo, translated by Lascelles Wraxall. The Heritage Press, 1960. Reprinted by permission of the author and the author's agents, Scott Meredith Literary Agency, Inc., 845 Third Avenue, New York, NY 10022.

Mazade, Charles de. From an extract, translated by J.D.M. Ford, in *Main Currents of Spanish Literature*. By J.D.M. Ford. Henry Holt and Company, 1919.

Michaud, Régis. From *The American Novel To-Day: A Social and Psychological Study*. Little, Brown and Company, 1928.

Mickel, Emanuel J., Jr. From *Eugène Fromentin*. Twayne, 1981. Copyright © 1981 by Twayne Publishers. All rights reserved. Reprinted with the permission of Twayne Publishers, a division of G. K. Hall & Co., Boston.

Mirsky, D. S. From *A History of Russian Literature from Its Beginnings to 1900*. Edited by Francis J. Whitfield. Vintage Books, 1958. Copyright © 1958 by Alfred A. Knopf, Inc. Reprinted by permission of the publisher.

Monsman, Gerald. From *Confessions of a Prosaic Dreamer: Charles Lamb's Art of Autobiography*. Duke University Press, 1984. Copyright © 1984 by Duke University Press, Durham, NC. Reprinted by permission of the Publisher.

More, Paul Elmer. From *Shelburne Essays, second series*. G. P. Putnam's Sons, 1905.

Morgan, Forrest. From a preface to *The Works of Walter Bagehot, Vol. 1*. By Walter Bagehot, edited by Forrest Morgan. The Travelers Insurance Company, 1889.

Murphy, Robert Cushman. From an introduction to *The Swiss Family Robinson*. By Johann Wyss. The Heritage Press, 1963.

Myer, Valerie Grosvenor. From an introduction to *The Semi-Attached Couple*. By Emily Eden. The Dial Press, 1979. Copyright © 1979 by Valerie Grosvenor Myer. All rights reserved. Reprinted by permission of Doubleday & Company, Inc.

Nietzsche, Friedrich. From a letter to Malwida von Meysenbug on August 27, 1872, in *Selected Letters of Friedrich Nietzsche*. By Friedrich Nietzsche, edited and translated by Christopher Middleton. University of Chicago Press, 1969. © 1969 by The University of Chicago. All rights reserved. Reprinted by permission of The University of Chicago Press.

Nodier, Charles. From an introduction to *The Swiss Family Robinson; or, Adventures of a Shipwrecked Family on a Desolate Island*. By Johann Wyss, translated by W. H. Davenport Adams. T. Nelson and Sons, 1871.

O'Donnell, Thomas F. and Hoyt C. Franchere. From *Harold Frederic*. Twayne, 1961. Copyright © 1961 by Twayne Publishers. All rights reserved. Reprinted with the permission of Twayne Publishers, a division of G. K. Hall & Co., Boston.

Parrington, Vernon Louis. From *Main Currents in American Thought: The Beginnings of Critical Realism in America, 1860-1920, Vol. III*. Harcourt Brace Jovanovich, 1930. Copyright 1930 by Harcourt Brace Jovanovich, Inc. Renewed 1958 by Vernon L. Parrington, Jr., Louise P. Tucker, and Elizabeth P. Thomas. Reprinted by permission of Harcourt Brace Jovanovich, Inc.

Peyre, Henri. From *Literature and Sincerity*. Yale University Press, 1963. Copyright © 1963 by Yale University. All rights reserved. Reprinted by permission.

Prince Kropotkin. From *Ideals and Realities in Russian Literature*. McClure, Phillips & Co., 1905.

Quinn, Arthur Hobson. From *American Fiction: An Historical and Critical Survey*. D. Appleton-Century Company, Incorporated, 1936. © 1936, renewed 1963. All rights reserved. Excerpted by permission of Prentice-Hall, Inc., Englewood Cliffs, NJ 07632.

Raleigh, Walter. From *On Writing and Writers*. Edited by George Gordon. Edward Arnold & Co., 1926.

Read, Herbert. From *The Sense of Glory: Essays in Criticism*. Harcourt Brace Jovanovich, 1930.

Richard, Jean Pierre. From "Love and Memory in 'Madame Bovary'," translated by Paul de Man, in *"Madame Bovary" by Gustave Flaubert: Backgrounds and Sources, Essays in Criticism*. Edited and translated by Paul de Man. Norton, 1965. Copyright © 1965 by W. W. Norton & Company, Inc. Reprinted by permission of W. W. Norton & Company, Inc.

Rousset, Jean. From "'Madame Bovary': Flaubert's Anti-Novel," translated by Paul de Man, in *"Madame Bovary" by Gustave Flaubert: Backgrounds and Sources, Essays in Criticism*. Edited and translated by Paul de Man. Norton, 1965. Copyright © 1965 by W. W. Norton & Company, Inc. Reprinted by permission of W. W. Norton & Company, Inc.

Rzhevsky, Nicholas. From _Russian Literature and Ideology: Herzen, Dostoevsky, Leontiev, Tolstoy, Fadeyev_. University of Illinois Press, 1983. © 1983 by the Board of Trustees of the University of Illinois. Reprinted by permission of the publisher and the author.

Sagarin, Edward. From _Raskolnikov and Others: Literary Images of Crime, Punishment, Redemption, and Atonement_. St. Martin's Press, 1981. Copyright © 1981 by St. Martin's Press, Inc. All rights reserved. Used with permission of the publisher.

St. John-Stevas, Norman. From _Walter Bagehot_. Longmans, Green & Co., 1963. © Norman St. John-Stevas, 1963. Reprinted by permission of Profile Books Limited.

Saintsbury, George. From his _A History of English Criticism_. W. Blackwood and Sons, 1911.

Saintsbury, George. From _A History of English Prose Rhythm_. Macmillan and Co., Limited, 1912.

Saintsbury, George. From _A History of the French Novel (to the Close of the 19th Century): From 1800 to 1900, Vol. II_. Macmillan and Co., Limited, 1917.

Sampson, R. V. From _The Discovery of Peace_. Pantheon Books, 1973. Copyright © 1973 by R. V. Sampson. All rights reserved. Reprinted by permission of Pantheon Books, a Division of Random House, Inc.

Sand, George. From a letter to Gustave Flaubert on January 12, 1876, in _The George Sand—Gustave Flaubert Letters_. By George Sand and Gustave Flaubert, translated by Aimee L. McKenzie. Boni and Liveright, 1921. Copyright, 1921, by Boni & Liveright, Inc. Renewed 1949 by Aimee L. McKenzie. Reprinted by permission.

Sartre, Jean-Paul. From _Search for a Method_. Translated by Hazel E. Barnes. Knopf, 1963. Copyright © 1963 by Alfred A. Knopf, Inc. All rights reserved. Reprinted by permission of the publisher.

Saurat, Denis. From an introduction to _Les Misérables, Vol. 1_. By Victor Hugo, translated by Charles E. Wilbour. Everyman's Library, Dent, 1958. © Introduction, J. M. Dent & Sons Ltd., 1958. All rights reserved. Reprinted by permission.

Shelley, Percy Bysshe. From a preface to _Adonais: An Elegy on the Death of John Keats_. N.p., 1821.

Sisson, C. H. From _The Case of Walter Bagehot_. Faber and Faber, 1972. © 1972 by C. H. Sisson. Reprinted by permission of Faber and Faber Ltd.

Slessarev, Helga. From _Eduard Mörike_. Twayne, 1970. Copyright 1970 by Twayne Publishers. All rights reserved. Reprinted with the permission of Twayne Publishers, a division of G. K. Hall & Co., Boston.

Starrett, Vincent. From _Books Alive: A Profane Chronicle of Literary Endeavor and Literary Misdemeanor_. Random House, 1940.

Stern, J. P. From _Idylls & Realities: Studies in Nineteenth-Century German Literature_. Methuen, 1971. © 1971 J. P. Stern. Reprinted by permission of Methuen & Co. Ltd.

Stewart, Randall. From _American Literature & Christian Doctrine_. Louisiana State University Press, 1958. Copyright 1958 Louisiana State University Press. Reprinted by permission of the Literary Estate of Randall Stewart.

Strachey, G. L. From _Landmarks in French Literature_. H. Holt and Company, 1912.

Thibaudet, Albert. From _French Literature from 1795 to Our Era_. Translated by Charles Lam Markmann. Funk & Wagnalls, 1968. Translation copyright © 1967 by Harper & Row, Publishers, Inc. All rights reserved. Reprinted by permission of the publisher.

Thibaudet, Albert. From "'Madame Bovary'," in _"Madame Bovary" by Gustave Flaubert: Backgrounds and Sources, Essays in Criticism_. Edited and translated by Paul de Man. Norton, 1965. Copyright © 1965 by W. W. Norton & Company, Inc. Reprinted by permission of W. W. Norton & Company, Inc.

Thompson, Denys. From "Our Debt to Lamb," in _Determinations: Critical Essays_. Edited by F. R. Leavis. Chatto & Windus, 1934.

Tillotson, Geoffrey. From "The Historical Importance of Certain 'Essays of Elia'," in _Some British Romantics: A Collection of Essays_. James V. Logan, John E. Jordan, Northrop Frye, eds. Ohio State University Press, 1966. Copyright © 1966 by the Ohio State University Press. All rights reserved. Reprinted by permission.

Tillyard, E.M.W. From an introduction to _Lamb's Criticism: A Selection from the Literary Criticism of Charles Lamb_. By Charles Lamb, edited by E.M.W. Tillyard. Cambridge University Press, 1923.

ISBN 0-8103-5810-7